The Making of Sociology

A Study of Sociological Theory

VOLUME TWO

The Making of Sociology

A Study of Sociological Theory

Ronald Fletcher

VOLUME TWO

Developments

NELSON

THOMAS NELSON AND SONS LTD
36 Park Street London W1Y 4DE
PO Box 18123 Nairobi Kenya

Thomas Nelson (Australia) Ltd
597 Little Collins Street Melbourne 3000
Thomas Nelson and Sons (Canada) Ltd
81 Curlew Drive Don Mills Ontario
Thomas Nelson (Nigeria) Ltd
PO Box 336 Apapa Lagos
Thomas Nelson and Sons (South Africa) (Proprietary) Ltd
51 Commissioner Street Johannesburg

Copyright © Ronald Fletcher 1971
First published in Great Britain 1971 by Michael Joseph Ltd
Published in Nelson's University Paperbacks 1972

ISBN 0 17 712077 0
Printed in Great Britain by A.Wheaton and Co., Exeter

To Roma, Paul and Adrian
with love

'Sociology is not, then, an auxiliary of any other science; it is itself a distinct and autonomous science, and the feeling of the specificity of social reality is indeed so necessary to the sociologist that only distinctly sociological training can prepare him to grasp social facts intelligently.

... the time has come for sociology to spurn popular success, so to speak, and to assume the exacting character befitting every science. It will then gain in dignity and authority what it will perhaps lose in popularity .... The time when it will be able to play this role successfully is still far off. However, we must begin work now, in order to put it in condition to fill this role some day.'

EMILE DURKHEIM (1895)

Contents

3   THE PSYCHOLOGICAL ASPECTS OF SOCIETY

Introduction

Diagrams—continued

Acknowledgements

My thanks are due to the following publishers for permission to use material from books in which they own the copyright:

Routledge and Kegan Paul, for quotations from *Community and Association* by F. Tönnies, *Suicide* by E. Durkheim, *Primitive Classification* by E. Durkheim (Ed. R. Needham), and *Structure and Function in Primitive Society* by A. R. Radcliffe-Brown.

Macmillan & Co. Ltd., for quotations from *The History of Human Marriage* and *The Origin and Development of the Moral Ideas* by E. Westermarck.

The Macmillan Company, New York, for quotations from *A Natural Science of Society* by A. R. Radcliffe-Brown, and *The Division of Labour in Society* by E. Durkheim.

The University of Chicago Press, for quotations from *George Herbert Mead on Social Psychology* (Ed. A. Strauss).

Allen & Unwin for quotations from *The Elementary Forms of the Religious Life* by E. Durkheim.

Wm. Hodges Ltd. for quotations from *Theory of Social and Economic Organization* by M. Weber.

Methuen & Co. for a diagram from *An Introduction to Social Psychology* by W. McDougall.

The Free Press of Glencoe for quotations from *The Methodology of the Social Sciences* by M. Weber.

Schocken Books, New York, for quotations from *Social Organization* and *Human Nature and the Social Order* by C. H. Cooley.

The Hogarth Press, for a diagram from Volume XVIII of the *Standard Edition of the Complete Psychological Works of Sigmund Freud*, revised and edited by James Strachey.

Pall Mall Press, for quotations from *Vilfredo Pareto: Sociological Writings*, introduced by S. E. Finer.

The University of North Carolina Press, for quotations from *A Scientific Theory of Culture* by B. Malinowski.

Also to Sir George Catlin for permission to quote from his edition of *The Rules of Sociological Method* by E. Durkheim, and to the executors of the estate of L. T. Hobhouse and Curtis Brown for permission to quote from *Morals and Evolution* and *Development and Purpose* by L. T. Hobhouse.

Preface

In turning to this second volume, I would like it to be borne in mind, again, that this book has been written not only for full-time students but also for all those who are seriously interested in sociology for its own sake: who sense its importance for understanding themselves, their own problems in society, and the large social issues of our time, and who are seeking as full and satisfactory a grasp of its nature and scope as they can get. There are many, I think, who are impatient with trivial introductions on the one hand and labyrinths of incomprehensible terminology on the other. It is with those who are genuinely interested in the subject—students in the best sense of the word—that I want to communicate, and I have therefore made great efforts to be clear. This raises an important point of emphasis.

In this volume we come to more difficult areas of study. Our argument is bound to become more complicated as we move away from common sense assumptions, from earlier kinds of social theories and the first foundation-statements of the subject, to the increasingly detailed and exacting systems of the more recent sociological theorists. This cannot be avoided. Indeed, it *should* not be avoided. An understanding of these systems of ideas (and all are essential for an understanding of the nature of the subject) requires the *study* of them, not an unreflective acceptance of fashionably held opinion—which is almost always wrong. The point I want to stress is this.

Though these later stages of our argument become more *difficult* (in having to be more involved, more variously qualified, etc.) they are still always *clear*. So that if a reader persists, an understanding of these theories and their interconnections can, without doubt, be gained; and—as a result—a full appraisal of all the important dimensions of the subject (which must be a complex subject if it is to do justice to the richness and subtlety of its subject-matter) can, without any doubt, be achieved. Nothing in our ongoing study is needlessly obscure. It is with this, as with the introduction of one eminent poet—which had been much criticized for being 'dark and laboured':—

" . . . it may," he wrote, "perhaps seem dark to rank riders or readers that have no more souls than burbolts; but to your comprehension, and in itself, I know it is not."

Suffolk   RONALD FLETCHER
August 1970

Introduction

Point of Arrival and Departure

In Volume I, we clarified, as well as the range and complexity of the literature would allow, the most important elements which went into the 'Beginnings' and the 'Foundations' of Sociology, and now occupy a firm position from which to move to a critical study of those 'Developments' which were made during the first forty years or so of the present century.

It would not be unduly exact to think of this period of 'Developments' (as I want to discuss them) as lasting up to the second world war; because it was immediately *after* that war (i.e. during the past 25 years) that the systematic reconsideration of the nature of sociological theory became a major preoccupation: a preoccupation which has lasted up to the present day. The present century can therefore be feasibly divided into two periods which are marked off from each other by the 1939–45 war as a kind of watershed. The latter period (the strictly contemporary period) has been dominated by a concern for radical theoretical re-assessment—the concern from which our own study stems. The former period was one during which developments were undertaken of specific elements within the over-all 'conspectus' which we have outlined as the achievement of the nineteenth century. It is the contribution of this first period with which we are now to be concerned.

Our assessment of the work undertaken during these years will be all the clearer if, by way of preparation, we remind ourselves of one or two points, and, in particular, if we stop to provide ourselves with a clear vision of the kind of continuity which was afoot at the turn of the century. This vision, in a very interesting way, must on the one hand include a clear awareness of an area of growing complexity, but, on the other, must focus strong concentration upon a central simplicity. Without either of these elements, our vision would be misleading.

To take complexity first: it would be absurd to think that the achievements of men's thought, as of any other aspect of their activity, enjoyed a nice clean terminus at the end of one century, and a nice clean starting-off at the beginning of another. Strictly speaking, centuries do not end or begin. History does not walk in hundred-year strides. Centuries are marks on the ruler with which we try to measure time manageably. This goes without saying. But it is important, in connection with this, to remind ourselves that the very clarity which we strive to achieve is bound to be faulty in some respects. The nineteenth century did not end with a conspectus, clearly stated as we have stated it; a 'document' of agreements which could be 'circulated',* so to speak, and from which basis of equal understanding every scholar could then make his fresh start. The conspectus was *there* all right; all its components had been outlined clearly in the several contributions of the nineteenth century; but scholars at the turn of the century were differentially aware of this or that part of it, and differentially concerned with this or that aspect of it, as must always be the case in any *contemporary scene* of scholarship. No individual thinker can have a *complete* over-view of the entirety of a field of scholarship: like some omniscient intellectual God looking down from Olympus. Though an over-all conspectus can be distinguished, a subject moves along in a complex, and not always articulated, fashion. We must, then, though jealous of meticulous clarity in stating the nature of sociology, and distinguishing the steps of advancement in its making, take care not to overlook complexities.

To take simplicity next, however, it is in fact the case that when all such complexities have been taken into account; when all the variously paced developments of different dimensions of the subject have been properly disentangled and assessed; there was, indeed, a marked and quite definite 'point of arrival and departure' in the making of sociology during the first five years of the twentieth century. In this case, to take the turn of the century as a point of arrival and departure: a point of arrival—at which the 'Foundations' had been laid; and of departure—from which specific 'Developments' were deliberately undertaken; is as near correct in its exactitude as it needs to be for our purposes. A peculiar concatenation of events makes it almost possible to speak of a particular year—1903— as the year in which this awareness crystallized. This seems absurdly precise—but, in a moment, I will mention the grounds which lead me to make such a claim.

It is enough for now simply to note that, within a situation of scholarship that was more complex than our treatment has been able to indicate, there was, nonetheless, this strong simple central awareness that a significant turning-point in the making of sociology had been reached. All the directions of development which took place during the next forty years can be systematically clarified by understanding both the detailed and the general concerns which were voiced at this point of arrival and departure. These concerns exemplified, yet again, the cumulative continuity of the efforts which went into the making of sociology.

---

* Although, as we shall see, to some extent this was done.

(I) THE COMPLEXITY OF DEVELOPMENTS AT THE END OF THE NINETEENTH CENTURY

The kind of complexity which I have in mind, and which must not be forgotten, can best be clarified by giving a few examples. It will be remembered that though our statement of the 'Foundations' of sociology was of the agreements reached by the end of the nineteenth century, and though far and away the greater part of the work we have considered was produced during that century, we did, nonetheless, include one book by Lester Ward (*Pure Sociology*, 1903) and one by Sumner (*Folkways*, 1906) which were written in the first few years of the twentieth century. This was justified in that these books were undoubtedly the outcome of agreed positions arrived at by the turn of the century, and reflected these positions very clearly. We have also noted from time to time that the 'Early Americans' referred in their work not only to the sociologists who had preceded them, but also to some of the European sociologists who were writing at the same time as they. Some of the work of Georg Simmel had appeared in the American Journal during the last decade of the nineteenth century, and both he and Durkheim had received attention.

We must now note the position of these writers more directly; and the central, but rather paradoxical point is simply this: that they too could be said to be important nineteenth century scholars, but the influence and emphasis of their work was such as to be more relevant to the critical developments of the twentieth century than to the formulation of the nineteenth century 'conspectus' produced by the other thinkers we have considered. In some cases this was to be explained simply in terms of a certain delay in the spread of awareness of their work. The best example of this is the case of Ferdinand Tönnies.* Tönnies published his book *Gemeinschaft und Gesellschaft* (translated as *Community and Association*) in 1887, but this only became widely known after its second edition in 1902. Thereafter, it became (and is still) one of the 'classic' influences in sociology. Georg Simmel* in a rather different way was influential before the end of the nineteenth century but produced the work for which he became chiefly known in sociology proper (he was chiefly a philosopher) after the turn of the century. The more difficult example is that of Emile Durkheim* who was undoubtedly the most dominant influence in French sociology after Comte and Le Play.

The bulk of Durkheim's published work was produced during the last ten years of the nineteenth century. In many ways it was an

---

* The dates of these men were: Tönnies 1855–1936; Simmel 1858–1918; Durkheim 1858–1917.

excellent example of the kind of continuity in the growth of sociology from earlier subjects that we have been at pains to establish. Durkheim moved, himself, from critical studies of thinkers such as Rousseau and Montesquieu to his critical appraisal of the main achievements of Sociology from Comte onwards. All this we shall see later; and in it, he accepted in great part, the 'conspectus' we have outlined (though neglecting certain aspects of it). At the same time, however, even in his acceptance of nineteenth century sociology, Durkheim (though by no means free from ambiguities of his own) was sharply critical of it, and sought to sharpen its methods of study, to question its large-scale generalizations; and, in general, to bring it face to face with the rigorous demands of critical science. This meant that the force of Durkheim's work was undoubtedly aimed at the *critical development* of the nineteenth century 'conspectus', and thus came to be most influential during the first few decades of the twentieth century when these developments were being pursued. It is therefore altogether proper, from our point of view, to place our critical assessment of him in the thick of these developments, in which he was to play such an important part.

There were also, of course, American sociologists working for the furtherance of the subject towards the end of the nineteenth century other than Ward, Sumner and Giddings; and some of these—for example, Albion Small and W. I. Thomas—were especially important in developing sociology as an academic subject to be taught in colleges and universities. Our lack of mention of them does not indicate their lack of importance: only that they were not so central as the three men we have selected for clarifying the *theoretical foundations* of the subject.

What this amounts to, then, is that the last ten years or so of the nineteenth century, and the first ten years or so of the twentieth, witnessed a very considerable increase in the contributions to sociology and in the critical discussion which surrounded them. A growing complexity was afoot, and a new extension of the consideration of the place of the subject within education and research (adversely critical as well as favourably so) was taking place—both in scale and in detail. It is quite impossible for us to take all the 'to's and fro's' of argument in all this into account, but the important thing is that we should be *aware* of it. Our own clarification of the system of analysis which had been successfully founded stands firm, and is altogether valid. But this clarification must not yield to over-simplification. We must remain aware that within and around this 'conspectus', arguments were beginning to seethe with a new degree of complexity.

(II) THE CENTRAL CLARITY OF CONTINUITY: THE SOCIOLOGICAL SOCIETY: 1903

Having noted these elements of complexity, however, it is now much more interesting to turn—positively again—to the abundantly clear evidence for the strong central awareness among so many scholars of the time, that a significant point of arrival and departure had been reached. And it is pleasurable, too, to be able to demonstrate so completely, again, the cumulative continuity in the making of sociology of which so many critics seem totally and disastrously unaware.

Let us note again that the kind of view that so many critics put forward is that sociological thought has consisted of a 'rag-bag' of 'bit-and-piece' contributions, quite disagreed and disconnected with each other, and giving no evidence at all of being a unified, distinctive, and growing 'discipline'. It is, as they say, with the academic profundity of a Kingsley Amis, a 'non-subject'. There were (says this kind of view) a handful of nineteenth century individualists (some of them megalomaniacs!)—each preaching a totally unique and idiosyncratic viewpoint: Comte preaching Positivism; Mill preaching Individualism; Spencer preaching Evolution; Marx preaching Historical Materialism, and . . . but they do not even know the Americans at all! Then (and here we find many contemporary sociologists of this persuasion too), there were one or two English sociologists—Westermarck and Hobhouse, who were still 'Evolutionary' fuddy-duddies; rooted with philosophical laxity in the cloudy enormities of the nineteenth century. Quite separate and distinct was the work of Durkheim: very modern and scientific, and rejecting the 'evolutionists'. Quite separate and distinct again was the development of German sociological theory which focused upon the subjective 'understanding' or 'interpretation' of social action and was rooted in Tönnies (and Dilthey) and developed especially by Max Weber. And so on. . . . The impression given is one of disconnected 'bits' all awaiting a kind of synthesizing Newton to see the golden thread which could be seen to bind them all together; a kind of: 'Twelve characters in search of a Novelist' situation.

We have already seen what a completely nonsensical picture this is of the making of sociology during the nineteenth century, and we can show how absurd a caricature it is of the development of the subject from the turn of the century onwards. There are many points to be made about the various aspects of this 'bridge passage', so to speak, from the nineteenth century 'conspectus' to the twentieth century 'developments', but we can begin by being very exact about the coincidence of certain occurrences which will serve to emphasize the centrality of continuity which I wish to demonstrate.

The year 1903 witnessed a number of things.

In that year Lester Ward published his *Pure Sociology*. This, as we have seen, was itself something of a compendium statement of the nature of sociology at that time, but, for Ward, it was—quite distinctively—the basis for *new beginnings*. Ward undoubtedly thought of the nineteenth century foundations of the subject *not* as a *terminus*, but as a basis upon which new work could be undertaken, and from which new developments could arise. His book was dedicated in this fashion:

'I dedicate this Book
To
THE TWENTIETH CENTURY
On the first day of which
it was begun.'

Grandiose perhaps: but forward-looking without a doubt; a powerful sense of awareness of a point of arrival and departure.

1903 also saw the death of Herbert Spencer, and this, to many scholars, was almost symbolic of the ending of the first long formative period of the making of sociology: the period of the laying of the foundations. There was the sense of the significant *ending* of a period of achievement, just as there was the awareness and hope, as expressed by Ward, of the significant *beginning* of a new period of development. But the *awareness* was not all. There was also, at this juncture of significant events and within this atmosphere of 'deaths and entrances', a collective concern among a growing number of scholars, administrators and others, that the subject should now be considered more deliberately as a part of education—in both teaching and research, and that a systematic and organized public *effort* should be exercised to ensure that the accomplished foundations of the subject were recognized, and that its best directions of development were properly conceived, and made secure. These men were not all *agreed* about every aspect of the new science of sociology, but they *were* agreed about its importance, and the need to subject it to detailed, constructive, critical discussion at the hands of eminent scholars, administrators, and practitioners drawn from all relevant fields.

Already, the academic 'organization' of sociology had been seriously worked upon in the United States, and an American Sociological Society was being formed. Already, too, in France, there had been an organized development of research and teaching on the basis of the ideas of Durkheim and Le Play. Journals, too, had been founded: *L'Année Sociologique* in France and the American Journal of Sociology. Similar developments took place in Italy, Germany,

Belgium, and elsewhere. In 1903, however, a 'provisional committee' of scholars put their heads together in London; printed a paper by Victor Branford *On the Origin and Use of the Word Sociology*; and, together with this, circularized a large number of philosophers, historians, scientists (both 'natural' and 'social'), and men of practical affairs, asking for their views on the idea of founding a Sociological Society. A first conference was attended by about 56 representatives; it was agreed to proceed; and, at a meeting in November, the Sociological Society was formed at the London School of Economics. Its proceedings—the reading and discussing of papers; the holding of occasional conferences, etc.—were open to people from all fields of learning; the most searching criticism was encouraged in the effort to secure the most reliable establishment of the subject; and—both by the visits of eminent scholars, and by an active correspondence—an international scope of work was desired, sought, and achieved.

The reports of all the details of the subsequent meetings of the Society—including, besides the papers presented and the discussions recorded, correspondence from many eminent scholars, and press-notices from, for example, the *Westminster Gazette*, the *Speaker*, the *Daily Chronicle*, *The Times*, *The Academy*, and other journals—contain so much of fascination that it is difficult to know where to start. We can do no more than confine ourselves to the points most relevant to our central purpose.

(a) Continuity: from Old to New

The first striking fact which these proceedings made abundantly clear was the uninterruptedness of the continuity from the work, ideas, and concerns of the men of the nineteenth century to those of the relatively younger men who were in the full course of their careers and anxious to devote themselves in the most effective ways possible to the furtherance of the subject. A few examples will be enough to show how rich and definite a set of connections were brought together in the single focus of this society.

It will be remembered that the work of Francis Galton on the genetic qualities of populations had been centrally taken into account by the early Americans. At the first major meeting of the Sociological Society, Francis Galton himself agreed to forsake his retirement briefly in order to deliver a paper on *Eugenics*. The discussion ranged among men like Karl Pearson, J. M. Robertson, Benjamin Kidd, L. T. Hobhouse, and Dr Maudsley on the one hand to literary men such as H. G. Wells and George Bernard Shaw on the other. On a subject like 'selective breeding', the liveliness of the disagreements can well be imagined, and the contributions still make good

9

reading (especially that of Shaw—who was outrightly in favour of 'selective breeding'!), but, for our purpose, it can be seen that here was a continuity *not* simply of *ideas*, but of *men*. The elder scholars, and the younger who were to influence ideas so greatly during the next forty years, were *actually involved in face-to-face discussion*; were actively continuing, and sharing the same concerns about social theories and social policies.

Similarly, a number of papers were devoted to 'Civics', and the problems, both theoretical and practical, of town-planning. The man most prominent in delivering the papers was Patrick Geddes (who was himself very much rooted in the 'ecological' methods of Le Play), but the significant continuity from old to new may be seen in the fact that his meetings were chaired by Charles Booth, and a contribution to the discussion was made by W. I. Thomas from the newly flourishing sociology department of Chicago University.

The continuity of the theoretical ideas of the nineteenth century was also clearly in evidence. The conceptions of Spencer and Comte were continually referred to. In the case of Comte, for example, much discussion came from Dr Bridges—who had been very active, like John Stuart Mill, Congreve, Lewes, and Harrison in publicizing Comte's ideas in Britain; from S. H. Swinny who also continued to try to give a clear exposition of the systems of Comte and Le Play; and from L. T. Hobhouse who was only just about to begin the major part of his own work—which derived so much from Comte's influence. Shand, who developed Mill's proposed study of 'Ethology' also contributed; so did Graham Wallas who was concerned to incorporate the advances of psychology and sociology in a deepened study of politics.

The continuity from old to new, then, was very plainly, and very fully there—and not in terms of ideas only, but among men actively discussing the furtherance of the subject.

(b) Continuity of 'Conspectus': Branford

A second point which is well worth our while to note is that, although it was true that no detailed statement of the 'conspectus' achieved during the nineteenth century was drawn up—literally, in one document—it was the case, nonetheless, that the initial paper written by Victor Branford *On the Origin and Use of the Word Sociology* (and an accompanying *Note on the History of Sociology*) which was circulated with the initial letter exploring the possible interest in the foundation of the society, came very close to being such a document: though a brief one.* What is of great interest is that it recognized

* This, and all the papers referred to in this introduction, are to be found in *Sociological Papers*, Macmillan, 1904, and 1906.

and incorporated most of the strands in the making of sociology which we ourselves have traced. It touched briefly on the 'roots' of sociological thought in the preceding work of Vico, Hume, Kant, Hegel, Montesquieu, Condorcet, Adam Smith, and others, and then pointed to the systematic, unifying 'foundation statement' of Comte. It then outlined the contributions of Mill and Spencer, and gave quite a detailed picture of the developments during the last ten years of the nineteenth century—mentioning the Americans especially, and men like Simmel, Tönnies, and Durkheim in Europe. In order to indicate briefly the rapid development of specialist work *within* the conspectus of sociology, and the considerable extent of this, Branford* also provided an analysis of sociological literature summarized in the French Journal—*L'Année Sociologique*—for the year 1902: which is reproduced as a matter of interest.

Here again, then, in the introductory document of the society, the clear awareness of the position at which sociology had arrived by the turn of the century was perfectly plain; and, again, in the light of the compendium of work in 1902 reflected in the table overleaf, the idea that sociology is a science newly emergent since the second world war can be seen to be the absurdly comical notion that it really is. Only people grossly ignorant of the developments of the social sciences could possibly entertain such a view.

The nineteenth century 'Conspectus', as we have called it, was—at least to some extent, then—produced and put forward as a conscious basis for new critical discussion at the outset of the twentieth century.

(c) Continuity from Old to New: The International Awareness

The third aspect of the meetings of the sociological society which I want especially to emphasize; indeed to point out sharply and to insist upon; is that they gave indisputable evidence that *there was a wide international awareness* of this point of arrival and departure *among most of the scholars who were going to be influential during the early decades of the twentieth century.*

What I wish especially to demonstrate here, is that it is *quite untrue* that the men who undertook the developments of sociology early in the twentieth century were working in separation from each other; ignorant of one another's ideas: producing, again, a 'rag-bag' of bit-and-piece contributions which bore no relation to each other. On the contrary, most of these men *shared their awareness* of this

---

* It may be noted that Branford, too, was much influenced by Le Play, and was a member of the group—like Geddes—who undertook 'ecological' studies and sought to link sociological theory and social practice. See Appendix: *The Sociographers* in the present volume, p. 832.

ANALYSIS* OF THE SOCIOLOGICAL LITERATURE (IN BOOKS AND IN PERIODICALS) SUMMARIZED IN THE 'ANNEE SOCIOLOGIQUE' FOR 1902

NUMBERS OF PUBLICATIONS IN—

	France	Italy	United States of America	Germany	England	Other Countries	Total
I. GENERAL SOCIOLOGY	26	10	8	6	5	1	
1. Objects and Methods of Sociology	9	5	2	2	—	—	18
2. Social Philosophy—General Theories	7	2	4	2	—	1	16
3. Mentality of Groups	5	2	—	—	—	—	7
4. Civilization in General and Types of Civilization	1	1	1	1	2	—	6
5. Collective Ethology	2	—	—	—	2	—	4
6. The Social Milieu and the Race	2	—	1	1	1	—	5 56
II. RELIGIOUS SOCIOLOGY	29	5	12	75	29	11	
1. General Conceptions Methodology	4	1	1	2	—	—	8
2. Elementary Forms of Religious Life	1	1	5	18	11	5	41
3. Magic	1	—	1	5	—	3	10
4. Beliefs and Practices Concerning the Dead	4	—	1	4	2	1	12
5. Ritual	4	1	2	9	5	1	22
6. Religious Representations	12	1	1	27	8	1	50
7. Religious Society	1	1	1	6	1	—	10
8. General Studies on the Great Religions	2	—	—	4	2	—	8 161
III. JURIDICAL AND MORAL SOCIOLOGY	45	15	5	34	7	10	
1. General Considerations	10	4	—	—	2	—	16
2. Social Organization in General	2	—	1	5	2	—	10
3. Political Organization	5	2	1	1	—	4	13
4. Domestic Organization	11	2	—	14	2	—	29
5. Law of Property	2	1	—	1	—	1	5
6. Law of Contract	4	—	1	—	—	1	6
7. Criminal Law	7	1	—	8	—	4	20
8. Procedure	1	3	—	1	1	—	6
9. Miscellaneous	3	2	—	4	—	—	9 114
IV. CRIMINAL SOCIOLOGY AND MORAL STATISTICS	12	9	1	5	3	5	
1. Statistics of Domestic Life	2	—	—	2	—	—	4
2. General Criminality in the Different Countries	1	2	1	1	—	1	6
3. Factors of General Criminality	4	3	—	1	—	2	10
4. Special Forms of Criminality and Immorality	2	2	—	1	2	1	8
5. Crime-making Milieus. Societies of Malefactors and their Customs	2	2	—	—	—	1	5
6. Functioning of the Repressive System	1	—	—	—	1	—	2 35
V. ECONOMIC SOCIOLOGY	21	4	5	35	5	3	
1. Methodology—General Problems	1	1	1	2	3	—	8
2. Economic Systems	2	—	1	—	1	—	4
3. Regimes of Production	—	2	1	6	—	2	11
4. Forms of Production	1	—	—	7	—	—	8
5. Elements of Distribution	1	—	1	1	—	—	3
6. Economic Classes	2	—	—	2	—	—	4
7. Professional Associations	1	—	—	1	—	1	3
8. Special Economics (Agrarian, Commercial, and Colonial)	4	—	—	8	1	—	13
9. Social Legislation	4	1	—	4	—	—	9
10. Miscellaneous	5	—	1	4	—	—	10 73
VI. SOCIAL MORPHOLOGY	7	1	1	6	2	4	
1. The Geographical Base of Society	1	—	1	—	1	—	3
2. Population in General	3	—	—	3	1	2	9
3. Urban and Rural Groupings	3	1	—	3	—	2	9 21
VII. MISCELLANEOUS	6	4	—	4	1	2	
1. Aesthetic Sociology	2	2	—	2	1	1	8
2. Technology	2	1	—	—	—	1	4
3. Language	1	—	—	1	—	—	2
4. War	1	1	—	1	—	—	3 17
	146	48	30	165	52	36	477

* *Sociological Papers*, 1904, Macmillan, p. 13
N.B. In each horizontal section, the total (excepting the final total is at the *top* of each column.)

particular juncture of sociology and undertook their own work *within a common perspective, and with agreed scientific aims and concerns*, even if they were not agreed on every item of substance and method.

Let us, again, take specific examples.

In these meetings there was a common agreement that Britain was probably the most backward country of all (within Europe and America) in developing sociology as an academic subject. There was, therefore, much discussion about the possibility of introducing the subject into the universities, especially into the University of London, and this was, in fact, made possible under the benefaction of Mr Martin White. First of all, courses of lectures were provided (by Geddes, Haddon, Westermarck, and Hobhouse), and then the first two Chairs in Sociology were founded. The point of significance here is that the men who filled these two Chairs—Edward Westermarck and L. T. Hobhouse—were both active participants in the sociological society. Their work began in the context of these early discussions and developments. But this—and this is the point—was by no means an isolated London, or British, development. At the self-same meetings, and in the correspondence connected with them, eminent scholars from all countries pooled their ideas. We need note only a few examples.

It was not only Victor Branford who wrote on the 'conspectus' of sociology for these earliest meetings, but also Emile Durkheim. Durkheim was, indeed, the most prominent contributor on the nature of Sociology and questions concerning its relations to the other Social Sciences and to Philosophy. Far from being a sociologist quite distinct from developments in Britain; putting forward views totally disconnected with the views put forward there; Durkheim, on the contrary, was actively involved in the discussions which marked the beginnings of 'official' academic sociology in Britain. The work of Hobhouse and Westermarck was not of a different time, or of a totally different persuasion from that of Durkheim. All of them were aware of the same juncture in the subject; were engaged in the same deliberations; and were pursuing their work contemporaneously.

Another scholar who contributed notably by correspondence was Ferdinand Tönnies. Tönnies, like Durkheim, was in agreement with much of the nineteenth century foundations, but critical only of parts of them; but, again, both in his letters to the discussions and in an article for the press, he welcomed the formation of the sociological society as being significant for the juncture at which the subject had arrived. His own work was seen quite clearly within this context.

It has been mentioned, too, that W. I. Thomas of Chicago University contributed to the discussion on the planning of cities; but American interest was also more conspicuously represented by Professor Wenley who was Professor of Philosophy in theUniversity of Michigan. He addressed the society on the topic of *Sociology as an Academic Subject*,* and, with the founding of academic sociology in Britain in mind, he outlined the difficulties which had been experienced in trying to achieve this in the United States. This contribution was not only indicative of the internationally shared concern for the planned development of sociology, but also portrayed clearly some of the problems which were attendant upon the educational 'professionalization' of the subject. To mention but a few points: Professor Wenley described how, firstly, a rapid expansion in the demand for, and the provision of, the subject could easily result in a deterioration of teaching standards. His words have a peculiarly timely ring when we are setting up new universities and rapidly expanding our higher education in Britain.

'It is impossible,' he wrote, 'for any country to staff an enormous number of institutions satisfactorily. Supposing there were to be founded in Great Britain today a dozen new universities,† could they be staffed as satisfactorily as the present ones? No. The result is great inequalities of teaching. We have men who might be called survivals, and we have men who, in the expressive Yankee phrase, have "happened into" subjects without knowing the reason why. This happens in new subjects far more than in old. Because we know little of sociology today, many men can arise and pose as authorities.'

Secondly, he described how, in its early introduction in universities, sociology:

'is too frequently made a mere addendum to other departments. We find it as the latest decoration of the School of Commerce, or as a culture element of the School of Economics. Sometimes it lives a precarious existence on the verge of philosophy, and the verge of philosophy is a misty region. This is an unsatisfactory situation . . . but we must do the best we can with the situation as it stands.'

In this sort of situation, thirdly, he showed how a multiplicity of 'pretenders' to the title of sociologists arose: many of whom were fanatically disagreed with others as to what the nature of the subject really was. 'Some sociologists think that sociology is statistics, or psychology, or a kind of metaphysics. . . .' The difficulties encountered by the subject were therefore, he said: 'intensified, if I may say so, by some of the sociologists themselves'. And, fourthly, he described how the subject tended to become a repository for any kind of

* *Sociological Papers*, Macmillan, 1906, pp. 281–93.
† This was said in January 1906.

literature that was, even faintly, concerned with the 'social': reportage, journalism, even fiction, as well as academic treatises.

'. . . we are continually confronted by sociological literature,' he wrote. 'And the most we can say about much of it is perhaps this, that, like a rolling stone, it gathers no moss, "but think of the excitement it has". I am told there is more nonsense written about sociology than about anything else, except about the subject dignified by the name of pedagogy.'

Wenley made many other points, but these few will have been sufficient to show how topical his comments now appear, and how true it is that there are factors in the 'professionalization' of the subject which are as much likely to retard and to despoil as to advance it.

However, the chief point here is that—whether concerned with the continuity of ideas from the nineteenth century; with the critical appraisal of those ideas; with the furtherance of special fields of study; or with the dilemmas of establishing the subject as an academic discipline—in these meetings at the very beginning of the century, British, French, German and American sociologists were all engaged in discussions about these problems. Westermarck, Hobhouse, Durkheim, Tönnies, Thomas, Wenley, were all engaged on their own work—*but with an awareness of their common concerns.* The subsequent twentieth century 'developments' were themselves, therefore, rooted in a certain measure of common discussion. They were far from being disparate, disconnected, unaware of each other.

It is worth while to emphasise that I have mentioned only a few outstanding examples—of men like Hobhouse, Westermarck, Durkheim, Tönnies, Thomas, who became very important and are not normally thought of as having any connection with each other whatever—but the examples could be greatly multiplied. If I mention Professor Paul Barth (Leipzig), Lévy Bruhl (Paris), Cosentini (Italy), Alfred Fouillée (Institute of France), Professor Gide (Paris), Ingram (Dublin), Kovalevski (Moscow and Paris), Loria (Turin), Stein (Berne), Steinmetz (Leyden), Winiarski (Geneva) as only a *handful* of names represented in *one* discussion, the *range* of the international awareness which then existed can be even more clearly seen.

In addition to this continuity of thought and this wide international community of concern there were a few other characteristics of the meetings of this society which are worthy of note.

(d) Common, Co-operative Interest among Representatives of all Subjects

One of the things which is so impressive when looking back on these meetings at the turn of the century is the rich array of the most

15

eminent men drawn from so many subjects who thought it worth-while to attend. It was not only men likely to be professionally concerned who contributed, but men well-established in other subjects who must have participated purely out of intellectual interest and pleasure. We have already seen that this society for the making of sociology attracted men like H. G. Wells and George Bernard Shaw, but there were men from other academic subjects proper, and from fields of practical governmental activity, all of whom gave evidence of the widest co-operative interest in the subject. A mention of their names and some of their contributions will serve to show the kinds of people (and their subjects) who, at that time, felt that sociology was of interest and importance to them.

The presence of Dr Maudsley, Wilfred Trotter, Mr Shand, and William McDougall, for example, was enough to make it clear that it was still thought possible to discuss psychology and sociology in the closest relations with each other. In all these cases, too, it was, of course, the development of *social* psychology which was the compelling interest.

The attendance of Dr Haddon and R. R. Marett also made it clear that anthropology (i.e. not yet *social* anthropology) and sociology could work in close agreement with each other.

And—in connection with both psychology and anthropology and their relations with sociology—this co-operation was not only evident in the discussion of ideas or methods. It was more interestingly present in the study of particular *subjects*. Thus in the discussion of a paper on *The Origin and Function of Religion* by A. E. Crawley, psychological aspects were raised by Shand and by Professor Starbuck (who was one of the earlier writers on the psychology of religion); anthropological considerations were introduced by R. R. Marett; and sociology was represented by Tönnies among others. In short, it was accepted that in the study of a particular social institution *all* the contributions of psychology, anthropology, and sociology were warranted and co-operatively necessary.

To this same point can be added the acceptance of the relevance of other subjects: history, philosophy, law, politics, and economics, especially; and, also, of the considerations of men of practical administrative experience. The range of other subjects mentioned was represented by such men as J. B. Bury, James Bryce, J. M. Robertson, J. A. Hobson, Graham Wallas, Professor Bosanquet, Muirhead, and many other philosophers. There was one young philosopher, for example, by the name of the Hon. Bertrand Russell. This was a time, then, when men from all subjects—though far from agreeing on every count—found such interest in the making of sociology as to be led to participate in discussions for its furtherance as an academic subject. They felt the subject relevant to their own concerns, and their own disciplines relevant to it. It is marvellous, for example (but, alas, a thing of the past), to read a Professor of Political Economy advocating, in the strongest terms, a detailed re-appraisal of Comte for an understanding of the relations between the social sciences!

The close relation desired, and seen to exist, between theoretical sociology and social practice was also very clearly in evidence. As well as papers on the nature of sociological theory and method, there were descriptive studies (in addition to the studies of 'Civics' already mentioned) of, for example, *Life in an Agricultural Village in England* (by Harold Mann) and *The Problem of the Unemployed* by a gentleman named W. H. Beveridge (this paper was delivered in 1906). Besides academics and writers, the men taking part in the discussions represented, also, for example, a 'Citizens' Association', an 'Arts and Crafts Exhibition Society', a 'Garden City Association', and similar movements, and, in connection with the Beveridge paper, there was detailed discussion of the necessity for quantitative surveys (e.g. of the *numbers* of the unemployed), and of specific administrative matters—such as 'labour exchanges'. Even the study of 'Methods of Investigation' in these meetings had its very practical side. The chief paper on this subject, was given by Mrs Sidney Webb (Chaired by Edward Westermarck!), and, for Mrs Webb, scientific method meant getting down to an accurate study of facts with a vengeance. It is worthwhile to repeat, too, that the people one might properly call the '*sociographers*' (men like Booth, Geddes, Branford) who were, in general, keen to discover facts by the methods of the survey and the 'ecological' study, were, in these early meetings, able to deliberate side by side with those concerned with sociological theory in its widest historical and comparative perspectives (whether these were historians, philosophers, or sociologists proper.)* Social theory and social practice were not by any means divorced. Sociology and Social Administration were not at odds with each other.

It is good, again, to savour this situation in which men who were doomed to be caricatured as 'large-scale evolutionary theorists', completely 'un-empirical' (Westermarck and Hobhouse); men who were to be known as students of 'social facts as metaphysical entities' (Durkheim especially); men who were to be separated from others as exponents of 'subjective understanding' (like Tönnies); men who were doomed to be castigated as narrow 'fact-grubbers' (Booth, Branford, Geddes); men (and a woman) who were doomed to be dubbed the 'social administrators' (Beveridge, Mrs Webb); men who were

* See Appendix, p. 832.

17

doomed to become the fuddy-duddy 'philosophers' among social psychologists (Shand, McDougall, Trotter); were all side by side in a common concern; and all (though having their different dimensions of interest) of a like mind in their concern for the making of sociology; and all able to share a common discourse—not only with each other, but with historians, philosophers, and even the most startlingly eminent writers of their time. Since then, as Keats might put it, they have all 'been sorted to a pip'—and quite erroneously.

Those—obviously—were the days! The days when the nineteenth century 'conspectus' of sociology was followed by these systematic discussions in order to secure the establishment of the subject, and in order to clarify the ways ahead for its best developments. We can dwell on this 'point of arrival and departure' no longer; but I hope we have done so sufficiently to substantiate, with complete clarity, the points we set out at the beginning. It is, I hope, abundantly clear:

(1) That there *was* a distinct 'point of arrival and departure' at the beginning of this century: a distinct recognition of a 'conspectus' achieved, a juncture arrived at, and a time at which systematic deliberation was required for the undertaking of further 'developments',

(2) That this 'bridging continuity' was marked by a considerable growth in the *complexity* of contributions and interests that were coming together,

(3) But that centrally, at the heart of this complexity, and perfectly clear to be seen, was a strong simple focus of persuasion and concern—which manifested itself not only in the culmination of a current of ideas, but, more tellingly, in the close conjunction of certain events, and, most impressively of all, in the voluntary meeting and organized correspondence of a large number of scholars in order to grapple responsibly with the situation which—as they saw so clearly—had been reached.

The final emphasis remains: that our consideration of the several aspects of this 'point of arrival and departure' serves us not only as a 'bridge' between the nineteenth and twentieth centuries—as a way of leaving the 'conspectus' of the foundations of sociology behind, and moving us on to the 'developments' of the twentieth century—but also as a clear *guide* in our approach to these developments. A brief final note can clarify this.

Point of Departure : From Theory to Theories

We have now seen clearly what the chief components of the nineteenth century 'conspectus' of sociology were, and we have seen the nature of these earliest twentieth century discussions. We have seen that men like Hobhouse, Westermarck, Durkheim, Tönnies, Thomas and other American scholars were actively aware of the juncture which had been reached, and of their several positions in understanding it. The simple situation was that—each in his particular way, and each in pursuit of his own interest and persuasion—all these scholars then undertook specific and more searching studies within one dimension or other of the nineteenth century 'conspectus' in order to deepen and to develop sociology more satisfactorily. The several aspects of this shared position give a clear guidance to the understanding of their subsequent developments.

First of all—the fact that all these (and other) scholars pursued *different dimensions* of study in *different fields* (e.g. Durkheim in studying Suicide, Religion, and the Division of Labour in society; Tönnies in studying the transition from a traditional to a complex industrial type of society; Westermarck and Hobhouse in studying the sociology of morality in society) did not mean, at all, that this was a disconnected 'rag-bag' of developments. All this work was undertaken, as we have seen, from a rootedness in a common context; and all these several directions of work *deepened* sociology in those directions and *supplemented* each other. Indeed, as we shall see, they turned out to have very considerable degrees of agreement.

Secondly—these developments were in *no* case *rejections* of the nineteenth century foundations. They were not 'new starts' from a point of no achievement. In *every* case, these developments sprang from a position of *acceptance* of the nineteenth century foundations —but from *criticism* of some aspects of them, and a desire to correct, improve, add, and deepen. They were all movements of development deployed from a common base. This is not, of course, to say they were planned in concert: like some vast military campaign. They were not. Nonetheless, as we have seen, they did spring out of a certain consensus of critical appraisal of what had been previously accomplished, and what now needed to be done.

The third consideration, however, deserves (though in the context of the others) the strongest emphasis of all. It is this: that, underlying these common persuasions about the furtherance of the making of sociology, there was the central agreement, among all these scholars, that the more satisfactory development of the subject required a movement *from THEORY to THEORIES*! That is to say: that the achievement of sociology by the end of the nineteenth century had, indeed, been just that of laying down the firm foundations of an over-all conspectus of analysis (though certainly including certain specific theories.) A clear framework of sociological analysis had been provided within which, and with the aid of which, scientific studies could be pursued. A way of describing, analysing, classifying, comparing social systems and their patterns of change, and certain

19

ways of explaining them—of clarifying 'evolutionary' adjustments among institutions; of subjectively understanding sequences of social action; etc; had been made clear. What was now needed was actually to undertake scientific studies in specific fields in order to sharpen the techniques of the subject, but, more particularly, to prove its worth by providing substantive knowledge in areas where it did not, as yet, exist. Thus Westermarck decided to devote himself to the detailed study of the *'sanctions'* which lay at the heart of social institutions. Hobhouse was concerned to study more closely, and with more exact comparative detail, the centrality of *knowledge* in society; its ramifications in morality and social control; and the relevance of it for understanding the actualities of 'evolution', 'development', and 'progress' in institutions and societies. Durkheim was especially concerned to understand the precise nature of 'associational' facts (and their 'collective' psychological aspects), and the ways in which patterns of *associational* constraint had to be understood in order to 'explain' *apparently* individual behaviour—such as suicide. Tönnies was especially concerned to understand the different kinds of willing, thinking and feeling which people experienced as society ceased to possess a simple, traditional framework; a simple pattern of clearly shared community; and was characterized more and more by a vast complexity of specialized 'associations' of which people were members only in a partial and rather remote sense. Mrs Webb—though fully persuaded about the importance of historical and comparative studies—wanted especially to sharpen very specific methods and techniques of investigation (such as the use of intensive interviews in conjunction with statistical methods, and the accurate use of documentary evidence, etc.) so that contemporaneous facts could be known, on which reliable policy decisions could be taken. Without exception, then, all these scholars responsible for the new developments—and we have mentioned only a prominent few— were agreed in this central persuasion of working *within* the conspectus of sociological analysis, and *using* it, in order to produce specific *theories* in the direction of their own interests and concerns.

In order to give some substantiation of all this, it might be of interest to see how Durkheim himself put the matter in a paper on *Sociology and the Social Sciences** written in collaboration with Fauconnet and printed with the proceedings of the sociological society (its date was 1903).

'During the last twenty years,' he wrote, 'we have witnessed a veritable flood of sociological literature. The production of works upon this subject,

* *Sociological Papers*, Macmillan, 1904, pp. 258–80. See also an Abstract *On the Relation of Sociology to the Social Sciences and to Philosophy*, pp. 197–203.

formerly intermittent and rare, has become continuous; new systems have been built up; they are in course of construction every day. But they are always or almost always systems in which the whole science is brought back, more or less openly, to a single and distinctive problem. To see all these workers searching for the supreme law, for the cause which determines all causes, for the key which opens all locks—one can hardly help thinking of the alchemists of former times in search of the philosopher's stone.

Each sociologist makes it his aim to construct a complete theory of society. Now, systems of this amplitude, whatever their merit, must of necessity suffer the grave inconvenience of being too closely linked to the personality and temperament of their author to be readily detached. Consequently, each thinker being tied to his own doctrine, all division of labour and continuity in research become impossible, and as a result no progress can, in a scientific sense, ensue. In order to master a reality of such large extent and such complexity, it is necessary, and that moreover at each moment of time, that the greatest possible number of workers should participate in the task, and that even successive generations should co-operate. Now, such a co-operation is only possible if the problems are taken out of this indefinite generality for purposes of differentiation and specialisation.'

This did not mean, for Durkheim, an abandonment of the nineteenth century 'conspectus' of the science—only the need for a breaking down of special problems (of the need for pursuing specific theories) *within* it. Thus he wrote:

'The lesson to be learned therefore from the actual condition of sociology is not at all that the Comtist conception was sterile, that the idea of a positive science of societies comparable with biology must be abandoned. *On the contrary, this idea keeps still today all its value, and we must resolutely maintain it.* Only to make it a fruitful one, it must be applied to suitable subject matter . . .'*

And here, Durkheim insisted that a division of labour within sociology was necessary; that, in order to achieve accuracy of knowledge, and to develop the scientific rigour of sociology more satisfactorily; delimited and more specifically defined areas or problems of study should be marked out and pursued. Indeed, in addition, Durkheim thought that the specialist social sciences themselves should be revitalized and re-orientated by the 'sociological idea' (i.e., of the essential *interdependency* of social facts), and that a unity of the social sciences might then be achieved.

'We must,' he wrote, 'implant the sociological idea more deeply in these various techniques, which doubtless are spontaneously raising themselves towards it, but only slowly, in doubt and darkness of mind. Then, indeed,

* *Sociological Papers*, Macmillan, 1904, pp. 258–80.

the Comtist conception will cease to be a vision of the mind, and will become a reality. For the unity of the social kingdom cannot find adequate expression in a few general and philosophical formulae far removed from facts and the detail of investigation. Such a conception can only have as its organ a body of distinct and unified sciences, all animated with a feeling of their solidarity.'*

Indeed, Durkheim went further, and envisaged the re-unification of the social sciences with social philosophy in a truly Comtian way:

'Moreover, one can forsee that these sciences, once organized, will restore to philosophy, with interest, what they have borrowed from it. For, from the relations established among them, common doctrines will emerge, which will prove the soul of the organism thus constituted, and will become the subject-matter of a renewed and rejuvenated social philosophy that is positive and progressive, like those very sciences whose crown it will be.'*

This, again, serves to show the *continuity* of the earliest conceptions of sociology within these deliberations which marked the earliest twentieth century developments. But the essential point here is to note the agreed emphasis upon the need for the depth and vigour of specialist studies within the over-all framework which was commonly accepted.

From THEORY to THEORIES: this was the central slogan which underlay the new point of departure.

It follows from this, that our study (in this third section) of the 'Developments' of sociology, can be a straightforward matter of tracing the specific studies which were undertaken within each of the main dimensions of the nineteenth century 'conspectus'.

Some studies clarified still further the notions of 'evolution', 'development', and 'progress' in the understanding of social change; explored particular dimensions of this (e.g., the central role of knowledge); and emphasized the centrality of *morality* in society which all the nineteenth century theorists had come to stress. Westermarck and Hobhouse were especially important in this, but we shall also include, with them, the work of Tönnies.

The work of Durkheim was important in itself in that he sought to develop a much more rigorous delimitation and definition of 'social facts', and appropriate methods for the 'objective' study of them, so that we shall need to consider his contribution separately.

Connected with this, and with a marked movement towards a desire for theoretically oriented field-work in Anthropology, the 'Structural-Functional' component of sociological analysis received

* *Sociological Papers*, Macmillan, 1904, p. 280.

22

a good deal of attention: such, indeed, as to give rise to a supposed 'school' of 'Functionalism', and this, too, deserves particular clarification.

The component of the 'subjective understanding of social action' as a necessary dimension of explanation also received a new and very powerful impetus from the influential work of Max Weber, so that this also requires a careful assessment.

Then there were quite a number of thinkers—all approaching the subject from different sides—who tried to develop more precise and useful studies of what we have called 'the psychological aspects of society'. The ideas of the early Americans were immediately taken up and followed by Cooley and Mead. In Europe, the massive influence of Freud was felt. Simmel's study of the 'forms' of human association formed an important way of thinking about patterns of 'social' psychology. And Pareto attempted a large-scale analysis of the social system as an entirety in terms, largely, of the 'psychological forces' which moved, warred, changed, and were accommodated, within it. This too, then, formed a major and distinctive area of development.

We can now turn to consider the developments which were made in each of these chief 'components' of sociological analysis, and see how far they were genuine advances—and consequently of value and use; or how far they were the outcome of misunderstandings—and therefore retrogressive. When we have accomplished a critical appraisal of these 'Developments', we shall have provided ourselves with a reliable basis on which we can then come to our assessment of the most recent contributions to sociological theory during the past twenty-five to thirty years.

(1)
Theories of Social Evolution

1
Ferdinand Tönnies:
From Natural, Living Community
to Contrived, Artificial Society

Tönnies can be placed at the very beginning of our study of twentieth century developments (and at the beginning of our consideration of the theories of social evolution especially) for a number of very definite and important reasons. I believe that his work, in many ways, can serve as a strong unifying thread: showing clear ties between elements of sociological theory which have been thought to lack connection; and proving a unity of concern and a similarity of ideas among men who have been thought to be so disparate as to have created quite distinctive and separate 'schools'. Tönnies linked the nineteenth and twentieth centuries very satisfactorily, whilst at the same time sounding a particular note of profound *warning* that it is well worth our while to heed. By way of full preparation, it is important to try to make all these points clear.

(i) A LINK BETWEEN THE NINETEENTH AND TWENTIETH
    CENTURIES

There was, in the first place, a certain peculiarity in both the nature and the timing of Tönnies' work which led him to straddle the two centuries very substantially. His most influential book was his closely argued essay entitled *Gemeinschaft und Gesellschaft* (translated as *Community and Association**). This was first published in 1887. It was only, however, after the second edition in 1902 that it became widely known. From that point on the book was reprinted in a number of editions, and Tönnies was able to add notes and comments, writing his last short preface to the eighth edition in 1935— the year before his death. He also wrote quite a substantial article on the ideas of the book in 1931.

What this amounts to is that the theory put forward by Tönnies— a theory rooted, as we shall see, in so many aspects of nineteenth century sociology—was an important, living, creative idea throughout

* *Community and Association*, Ferdinand Tönnies, Tr. Charles P. Loomis.
Routledge & Kegan Paul Ltd., 1955.

the first few decades of the twentieth century. It was a central idea; a 'seminal' idea; and it grew in the extent and importance of its influence throughout this period. Indeed, it is *still* as important, both theoretically, and as an indicator of practical social problems, as it ever was.

The work of Tönnies carried a central focus of nineteenth century sociology into the heart of twentieth century discussions, where it has remained ever since. It was a living embodiment of the 'point of arrival and departure', the developmental continuity in the making of sociology, which we have so strongly sought to emphasize. And as such, it was a common ingredient, a common concern, a common ferment, in many apparently diverse theoretical persuasions. These, we shall come to. For now it is enough to see that from 1888 to 1936, the work of Tönnies was a living link, connecting a wide range of discussions, past and contemporaneous, about sociological theory.

(II) THE ORIGINAL PROBLEM OF SOCIOLOGY—NOW SHARPLY POSED

One other characteristic of Tönnies' work which made it a strong significant link of continuity was its quite central and dominant concern for that problem which, from the beginning, had been the very 'raison d'être' for the emergence of sociology: namely the disruption of the old traditional order of society and the explosive development of a new commercialism and industrial capitalism. As we have seen, the whole of the making of sociology during the nineteenth century had been rooted in the need to understand this rapid, revolutionary transformation of society and, on the basis of such understanding, to reconstruct a new and appropriate order of social institutions. The knowledge of sociology was sought as a basis for wise political action.

Comte, Mill, Spencer, Marx, Ward, Sumner, Giddings (and many others) had all, in their several ways, provided an analysis of this crucial transformation of society, and had put forward their proposals for dealing with it. All in their various ways had been concerned with 'progress' and had sought a reconstruction of society which preserved and furthered the humane qualities which were in danger of being destroyed; and all had insisted that conscious and deliberate *effort* was necessary.

The great power, the attraction, as well as the theoretical and practical relevance of Tönnies' work, was that it focused attention very sharply upon this central problem.

His book constructed two clear 'types' of society: on the one hand, the living community (the 'Gemeinschaft'), in which all members were bound together in a shared order of natural relationships: of families, kinsmen, and neighbours sharing their intimate work and life within a known and loved territory; and whose rules, values, and social arrangements sprang from these clearly seen and felt natural bonds; and, on the other, a complex network of formally and rationally devised 'associations' (the 'Gesellschaft') of which men were members only in a 'contractual' sense; only in so far as they thought such associations useful to themselves as a *means* for the attainment of certain ends; and in which their relationships rested entirely on means-end assessments, calculations, manipulations, utilizations—not at all upon moral values which they felt as whole men, bound together by deeply accepted traditions. His picture—which we shall come to later—was one in which the living community was continuously over-laid by this increasingly impersonal network of specialized associations; and in which the living values of human individuals and community traditions were lost and destroyed in this spread of formal, rational, contractual interconnections—in which both men and principles became impersonal *abstractions*.

Tönnies did not offer solutions to anything. Indeed, he tried not to *judge* anything. His whole task was simply to construct a 'typology' which would throw light upon the transformation of society from one type (or one condition) to the other; to illuminate fully and clearly the nature of the human processes involved. And because of this, the central preoccupation of sociology came, in his work, to be very sharply posed.

Again, however, this was not just a *retrospective* thing. It was not only that he sharply and succinctly posed the concern which had lain at the heart of sociology during the nineteenth century. The fact was, and is, that this was the concern that has continued to lay at the heart of sociology during the twentieth century. It has remained, and must remain, the crucial concern in our modern and contemporary era. Consequently, Tönnies' sharp polarization of these 'types'—'Community' and 'Society'—had a most telling *prospective* reference, and was to underlay almost all the important developments in sociology from the turn of the century onwards.

The old problem was now posed in terms so sharp as to place it conspicuously in the forefront of subsequent discussions of theory. It is in this sense that Tönnies' work constituted a thread which linked together practically all the sociologists from 1900 to 1940 whose work we shall be discussing. We shall see in a moment, for example, that Tönnies was an 'evolutionist', and that his contribution was similar in many respects to those of Westermarck and Hobhouse (far more similar than is commonly appreciated). Tönnies' 'typology' was also, however, of considerable influence upon Emile

Durkheim, and we shall see that Durkheim's own analysis of the transformation from a simple traditional to a complex industrial society owed as much to Tönnies as it did to Spencer and Comte. Similarly, Tönnies construction of these 'types' of society in terms of *understanding* the kinds of *'willing'* which distinguished the human relationships in them, was an important influence upon Max Weber, and we shall see that Weber's own 'types' were very similar indeed —in substance, as well as in the methods employed in their construction—to those of Tönnies. But also, we shall see that even those sociologists who concerned themselves with developing the study of the 'psychological aspects of society' mirrored Tönnies' ideas very closely. To give one example: the distinction which Cooley was to make between 'primary' and 'secondary' groups; the relative importance of each for the development of values in the individual's character; and the attendant analysis of 'communications' for understanding the problems and the 'malaise' of modern 'mass-society'— was a set of ideas fitting almost exactly with Tönnies' 'typology'. This, too, we shall see in detail later.

The continuity from 'old' to 'new' was therefore manifested very powerfully in Tönnies' concentration upon this one crucial problem which was persistently at the heart of the making of sociology. This concern had been the point of departure at the beginning of the nineteenth century. Now, it formed the central concern, emphasized anew, and with equal strength, at the beginning of the twentieth.

(III) TÖNNIES AND THE ENGLISH SOCIOLOGICAL SOCIETY

We have already seen that Tönnies was one of those continental scholars (as was Durkheim) who took the trouble to communicate with the newly formed Sociological Society in London, and who strongly supported it. It is worthwhile to mention this again, here, simply to emphasize that there was an actual degree of inter-communication and shared thinking and argument between many of the scholars we are now noting; but also, especially, it is important to realize how many-sided a collection of scholars this was. Two points are particularly noteworthy. The first—that the *'sociographers'* (like Booth, Geddes, etc.) were among the members. And second, that Westermarck and Hobhouse—who were to be designated grand-manner 'evolutionists'—were also involved in these discussions simultaneously with Tönnies and Durkheim. There were not the same distinctions between these men *then* as have subsequently come to be drawn. Tönnies, apart from his own central study, also attached much importance to 'sociography' as a part of sociology, though this is not a point we need to emphasize here. More important, however, is that Tönnies was, in fact, an 'evolutionist', just as much as Wester-marck and Hobhouse, and it is this on which something more must be said.

(IV) EVOLUTIONARY SOCIOLOGY

No word has received more invective in recent times, in sociology, than the word 'Evolution'. To listen to some contemporary teachers and students, one could not help but believe that 'evolutionary' sociology was a completely distinctive 'school' of sociology, and that it had been dead and buried for so long a time as scarcely even to merit a nod of derision. For some, it is no more than a taken for granted shrug of the shoulders. Here I want only to point out that *all* the twentieth century sociologists we shall be discussing were evolutionary sociologists. Durkheim was. Weber was. Even those who came to be called 'Functionalists' (Malinowski and Radcliffe-Brown) were. Certainly Tönnies was; as were Westermarck and Hobhouse. None of these men ever denied evolutionary sociology. The kind of distinction one has to make among these scholars is not at all with regard to whether or not they accepted an evolutionary perspective of the nature and change of societies, and of social institutions—they *all* unquestionably *did* accept this—but with regard to the particular dimension and method of sociological analysis which they thought it most important to emphasize. This we shall come to as we study each in turn; but this point at least may be made here: that some of these men—like Durkheim, Weber, and the 'Functionalists'—are better considered under a title *other* than that of 'Social Evolution', *not* because they rejected this, nor even because they did not make important contributions to it (in fact, they did!), but only because their *distinctive* contribution lay in the direction of some *other* emphasis, which may, indeed, have been rooted in criticism of some *aspect* of evolutionary sociology. By contrast, some—like Westermarck and Hobhouse—*are* best considered under the heading of 'Social Evolution' because they quite deliberately tried to extend, develop, make more rich and precise, certain elements of evolutionary theory. It is this kind of distinction which guides our own treatment.

However, the altogether unwarranted error that can still follow such a procedure, is that some theorists can come to be totally segregated from others as being, or not being, 'evolutionists' (as though this itself was a sharp, significant, and definitive division); and it is for this reason that I have chosen to place Tönnies first in our consideration of the developments of theories of social evolution. In this way, I hope to show that there is *not* the sharp distinction

31

between these several bodies of work that is commonly supposed; but, on the contrary, that apparently distinct (i.e. fashionably separated) scholars have, in fact, contributed very similar bodies of analysis and knowledge to commonly conceived problems. Though Tönnies' central method was the construction of a 'typology' for purposes of analytical understanding, and, as such, this was a method for understanding fluctuating tendencies of change in all societies; even so, he postulated definite and substantive evolutionary changes as large in their historical scope as anything proposed by Comte, Spencer and Marx in the nineteenth century, or Westermarck and Hobhouse in the twentieth. Furthermore, he grounded his analysis in philosophy, in philosophical psychology, in the analysis of the individual's will and character, even more than they did. This is not, by any means, or in any sense, to denigrate his work; only to say that to set men like Tönnies, or even Durkheim, on one side as being scholars of sharp, analytical, scientific exactitude, and to set men like Westermarck and Hobhouse on the other side, by contrast, as being rather fluffy philosophers, is simply ludicrous, and reveals an insufficient knowledge and understanding of the work of all of them. Actually, in many respects, Westermarck and Hobhouse were very much more empirical in their scientific conceptions and methods than was Tönnies.

But again—in trying to redress balances and correct perspectives I do not want to appear to be driving new kinds of juxtaposition. My aim is essentially to see *all* these men as possessing similar orientations and common concerns, and I think this may best be achieved by placing Tönnies in this unusual place as a companion to Westermarck and Hobhouse. My reasons will, I hope, become the more clear as we explore their ideas more deeply.

Meanwhile, *some* of these reasons, and *some* of the grounds on which the continuity I have tried to emphasize rests, may be seen by pointing to a few of the many rich connections which Tönnies' work had with the ideas and insistences of other scholars. Here, these will not be defended: only indicated.

(V) SOME IMPORTANT ELEMENTS AND CONTINUITIES IN TÖNNIES' WORK

(a) Psychology, Choice, Will and Character: John Stuart Mill

One quite basic aspect of Tönnies' treatment of the nature of society, of social relationships, and, within this context, of the individual person, which it is well worth our while to note: is that it is one of the best examples in the literature (and there are very few) of a treatment which escapes the kinds of errors against which John Stuart Mill warned. Tönnies dealt quite forthrightly with the *social* aspects and relationships of men. He accepted fully the existence of *'social systems'*, as entire interdependencies of rules, values, procedures, structures of organization, and the like. At the same time he never made the mistake of 'reifying' these societal elements; of attributing to them an 'objective' existence as 'entities' independent of men. He saw them—and this was analysed and expressed with a marvellous lucidity—essentially as the embodiment of human wills in inter-relationships. The idea of 'society' as a 'super-organic' kind of actuality, but still an actuality of the interrelated wills of men, received an excellent and persuasive account at his hands. But—and this is the essential point—Tönnies rested his entire analysis on a very firm conception of the *concrete individual person*: not just as an item in a population; not just as a 'personality' which was the outcome of environmental 'conditioning'; not just as an organism 'driven' by impulses; not, indeed, just as an object of any kind, but as a con-scious, deliberating, willing, evaluating, *person* who—in the context of all the psychological and social factors he encountered—was engaged in the government of his own nature and conduct, and there-fore consciously involved in the shaping of his own character. In short, whilst elaborating a quite complex *psychological* analysis of both individual and associational elements of experience and behaviour, Tönnies did not neglect the fact that man is essentially a *choosing, deliberating* person, and that these elements of *will* and *character* had therefore to be fully taken into account in any under-standing of man and his social relationships which could be counted satisfactory.

Tönnies was not, therefore, in any sense whatever, guilty of empirical naïvety. The nature of his analysis was such as fully to appreciate all the distinctive aspects of the human *person*, as well as all the objective psychological and societal elements in any human situation. As part of this point, however, it is necessary to note that the psychological analysis Tönnies offered would be much criticized by almost all modern psychologists. Tönnies was still of a generation well-grounded in the philosophers; and his analysis borrowed points from men like Hobbes (in his discussion of 'power'); Spinoza (in his discussion of the passions and the will); Plato, Goethe—and many others who would now be fairly definitely ruled out of the courts of psychology. Tönnies' method, in psychology, was still one of a very careful introspection and analysis of experience coupled with a close observation of social relationships and an analysis of their impli-cations of *meaning, motivation, intention*, etc. There was nothing of the nature of experiment as such. Our essential point here, however, is only that—though attempting an elaborate *psychological* account of human motivation, deliberation, will and character formation—this was never such as to ignore the elements of choice, self-government, conscious purposive direction, and the like, which Mill (and, of course, the early Americans) had insisted upon as being so important.

Voluntary (teleological) as well as 'conditioned' (genetically caused) elements of action were fully taken into account.

(b) An Elaborate Psychology, and a Close Relation Between Psychology and Sociology

A second point of interest is that, basing his analysis upon his direct recognition of the nature of the human person, and the *will* of the human person, Tönnies did in fact take it for granted that a detailed psychology of human nature was necessary for any understanding of 'society'. He did not so much think that psychology and sociology were closely related, as that they were all of a piece. He did not even think fit to consider them separately. And this—important in itself— is even more important than it seems. For it is not commonly understood that Tönnies did not only *interpret* the human will according to certain 'types' or categories; he also, in fact, undertook a very detailed psychological analysis of this in almost exactly the same terms as other social psychologists both before and after him. His terms would have been quite happily accepted by Adam Smith, Darwin, Ward, William James and McDougall; but, what I most wish to emphasize, is that his terms were also entirely similar to those employed by Westermarck* (especially) and Hobhouse. Tönnies saw the nature of man as being that of one animal species among others (incidentally, he shared the basic analysis of Aristotle here†). In this sense his picture of human nature was set completely within the context of nature and of evolution; and his psychological analysis was in terms of basic *instincts*; the formation of *habits* which followed upon their activation; the establishment of *sentiments* attendant upon the objects of these habitual attachments; and the growth (in part deliberate) of constellations of motive, evaluation, judgment, and elements of desire, aspiration, endeavour and will, within this entire context of natural and social experience and behaviour. Reason and will were seen as growing out of impulse, emotion, habit, sentiment, as individuals grew from infancy to the maturity of adult character among their fellows.

If we reject the psychology of a Westermarck—in accounting for 'custom' and 'sanctions' in terms of instinct, habit, sentiment, and

---

* Westermarck, as a matter of interest, *did* derive his ideas from Adam Smith (i.e. in his *Theory of Moral Sentiments*) and from Darwin.

† I have in mind the distinction of forms and levels of life into vegetative, animal, and mental.

the emergence of general, impartial, disinterested rules and values of social conduct: then we must reject Tönnies too: for it is well-nigh the same account. If we think that any psychology resting upon 'instinct theory' is dead—then Tönnies is dead. If we think that the analysis of 'social facts' cannot be approached from the study of the 'wills' of concrete individual persons—then we must reject Tönnies.

I will not elaborate this point further; but only say how absurd a situation can arise when theorists are categorically distinguished from each other without care. Tönnies was not *only* a theorist who sought *subjectively to understand* two distinct types of society; he employed an entire psychological analysis to substantiate the kind of subjective understanding which he proposed; and *his* analysis, as we shall see, was significantly in accord with that of Westermarck, Hobhouse, and others. Indeed, it might be said that Tönnies was more satisfactory than Max Weber in this: that Weber tended to explore subjective understanding in terms of *meaning*—only indicating where the boundaries of psychological analysis proper might lie; whereas Tönnies did, in fact, undertake a psychological analysis to support the 'types' of willing in society which he interpreted.

The similarity between Tönnies and the other twentieth century 'evolutionists' will be made clear in what follows.

(c) *The Parallel, and the Continuity of Ward's, Sumner's and Giddings' analysis*

Another striking continuity in the statement and influence of Tönnies' work during the first four decades of the twentieth century was that of supporting entirely, and of reinforcing, the kind of analysis put forward by the early Americans in particular. This need not be elaborated. We have seen how Ward described the long period of the 'genetic' laying down of the established order of traditional societies, and then the growth of attempts to accomplish the conscious direction of society, and the attendant emergence of specialist associations as knowledge increased. We have seen how Sumner painted the same picture: of a development from Folkways and Mores to specialized Institutions and formal Law; and, even among these, how he distinguished between 'crescive' and 'enacted' institutions. And we saw how Giddings supplemented this same kind of picture with his 'types' of social action: impulsive, traditional, and then (with the proliferation of special associations) the rational. The typology which Tönnies constructed—providing an analysis of the development from Gemeinschaft to Gesellschaft; from living traditional community to the complex society of formal and specialized associations; was exactly the same. This, then, is a point of development, too, to be noted. And it is especially important because

35

of a considerable qualification which Tönnies made: which led him, really, to be more Sumnerian than Sumner. But this I will leave for now.

(d) The Considerable Affinity with Marx

A similarly clear continuity—though, again, by no means an entire agreement—was Tönnies' considerable sympathy with the analysis of Marx. Tönnies was, throughout his work, influenced by Marx, but, even so, his ideas developed concurrently with those of Marx; it was not simply a straightforward agreement with, and acceptance of, finished ideas. Tönnies, for example, emphasized the characteristics of mercantile *trade*; of commerce; of the 'middle-man' kind of activity of the merchant; as being the major factor leading to the disruption of traditional agrarian communities and the gradual creation of a shallow, calculating, contractual society in which abstract (ex-human) ghosts danced to the tune of profits. He did not agree with the technological emphasis of Marx's theory (i.e. that changes in the means of production were the basic levers of social changes). Nonetheless, he did agree very much with Marx that the 'Gesellschaft' society dehumanized men, and abstracted everything and everybody into a bloodless dance of categories—i.e. *commodities*. Nothing was valued in and for itself any more: by whole men in a community of persons. Everything, men included, were simply commodities: to be calculated for profitable purchase and sale. Everything had its price. There is no doubt, too, that Tönnies regarded the contractual, highly commercialized society as being 'immoral', as did Marx; but unlike Marx, he proposed no solution, and, it seems, was very sceptical about the possibility of one. At any rate, scientific understanding was his objective—not political resolution. But the similarity with Marx was very clear.

(e) A Continuity of Methods: the Construction of Typologies

Tönnies also exemplified a certain continuity of *methods* in sociology, and one or two points deserve special notice in this connection. It goes almost without saying that he fully accepted the importance of the historical and comparative methods in sociology, as well as all those other elements of method—observation, analysis, description, classification, etc.—which the major nineteenth century scholars had clarified in their attempt to achieve such scientific exactitude as was possible. There were, however, two particular aspects of Tönnies' conceptions of method which are worth special mention.

The first of these is very simple: but its very clarity is important, and, at the very end of our study, we shall find it of use in being clear about the several elements of sociology and their relations to each other. It is simply this: that Tönnies saw not the slightest difficulty in embracing, within the total work of sociology, the most descriptive factual study and the most abstract theoretical deliberations. His position was that sociology comprised three clear levels of work: the first was that of pure theory (the construction of clear models, the clarification of concepts, for theoretical analysis and the actual conceptualization of theories); the second was that of the application of theoretical constructs in detailed empirical studies and in the study of specific problems; and the third was that of 'sociography': namely the collecting of descriptive facts by various survey methods—perhaps for 'ad hoc' purposes (e.g. because such knowledge was *needed* in connection with some social policy); or perhaps in relation to some theory. Thus, some people may wish simply to discover how many families in a particular city are living below the 'poverty line'. To be able to provide such knowledge accurately and reliably is a legitimate part of sociology. It will readily be seen—simple though this conception is—that it gives a completely clear framework for sociological investigations at all levels; and without insisting that there need *always* be a *necessary* connection between them. This, in itself, is a very liberating thing: making for a perfectly acceptable division of labour within the subject—and in accordance with the interests, choices, preferences of the individual: another simple ingredient for satisfying and satisfactory scientific work which is much under-estimated (i.e. that individuals should work in accordance with their interests, and at the level for which they feel most fitted, and which they most enjoy). But this point is one which we shall elaborate in our conclusions.

The second emphasis—and a much more specific one—in the work of Tönnies, was his concentration on one particular method:* that of the clear construction of 'models' or 'types' in order to facilitate the analysis, interpretation, and understanding of actual social relationships. It will be remembered that Comte advocated the method of constructing 'rational fictions' to analyse clearly certain sequences of social development; and constructed his three 'types' of society—The Theological, Metaphysical and Positive—as three institutional systems for relating feeling, thought, and action; and that Spencer, too, constructed his two 'types'—the Military and the Industrial types of society—to supplement the understanding of social change which was indicated by his analysis in terms of levels of

---

* That is to say: Tönnies' best known and most influential work made use of this particular method. In other studies—of trade unions, strikes, the social and economic conditions of seamen, aspects of criminality, and suicide, conducted in Hamburg and Schleswig-Holstein—he did, of course, utilize 'sociographic' methods.

'social aggregation'. Giddings, too, constructed his 'types' of social action to add dimensions of interpretation to the other components of analysis (structural-functional analysis, etc.) It was this method especially which Tönnies employed, and, as we have mentioned earlier, the 'types' which he constructed exerted a considerable influence upon both Durkheim and Weber and the 'models' which they, in turn, and in relation to their own methodologies, put forward. In exemplifying the use of this method in particular, then, Tönnies not only made a contribution which was worthwhile in its own right, but also, again, served as a distinct and influential link of continuity between the uses of the method by the earlier nineteenth century, and by the most important twentieth century, thinkers. It is worthwhile to note, in passing, that Tönnies was, in fact, quite directly and considerably influenced by Spencer in all this.

We have already mentioned Tönnies' philosophical psychology and his basic assumption that a satisfactory sociology must necessarily incorporate psychological analysis, and this aspect of his method need not be repeated. But it is of interest just to mention that, on the basis of this theoretical position, he took part in the production of a series of books (during the first decade of the twentieth century) which emphasized it.* It was the people who were involved in this enterprise which makes it a point of interest. The editor of the series was Martin Buber—subsequently well-known for his concern for man the *person* amid all the impersonal complexities of modern society; and two of the authors other than Tönnies were Werner Sombart (whom we noted in connection with Marx) and Georg Simmel. Here too, then, continuities between 'then' and 'now' were highly significant and very firm.

(VI) ONE CONTINUITY: BUT WITH A MAJOR WARNING

There was one other striking continuity which I have left as our last preliminary point, because in it Tönnies sounded a very sombre note of doubt and warning; and it is worth our while to take this very seriously. It is in this that I said earlier that Tönnies became more Sumnerian than Sumner, and this now needs some clarification.

The particular continuity was this. Practically all the theorists we have mentioned so far—from Kant, through Comte, Spencer, Marx, to Ward and Giddings—had maintained that the large-scale transformation of traditional societies (with all their geographical, historical, regional, cultural diversities) by the rapid development of

* The book which Tönnies wrote for this series was his essay on *Custom* (*An Essay on Social Codes.*) Tr. A. Farrell Borenstein, The Free Press of Glencoe Inc., 1961.

science and industrial technology would gradually sweep throughout the entire world, embracing all societies in the grasp of its influence, and would ultimately culminate in a global unity of mankind. With this 'prognosis' (and with a good deal of the 'diagnosis' on which it rested) Tönnies agreed. There was thus, in his work, a reiteration, a reinforcement, of this perspective of sociological analysis: that not only was the contemporary world caught up in a vast, disrupting transformation, with science and industrial technology at its heart, but also that this entailed a bringing of all traditional communities into a vast global interdependency with each other. A new 'universalism' was afoot. Science would be shared. Industrial technology, commercial interconnections, urban characteristics, would be shared. Common problems of political interdependency would have to be encountered and resolved. The continuity of this perspective was therefore plain; but Tönnies put it forward with a distinct and important difference: and this difference constituted a tremendous warning.

It was this.

Though none of the earlier thinkers had thought that this global interdependency of human societies would be achieved without difficulties, complexities, and effort, they did, nonetheless, assume (and this was true even of Herbert (Laissez-Faire) Spencer) that it was desirable. 'The Unity of Mankind' was not a phrase of sociological analysis only, but had a great ethical ring about it. The prevailing 'ethos' of all these theories was the ethos of 'progress'. Traditional societies, the 'ancien régime', were being disrupted; the task of social reconstruction was one of grave difficulty; but science could provide the knowledge, and the means for both natural and social control; and responsible effort could accomplish this great end. Science, in general, was the servant of control and progress. A science of society, in particular, could be the servant of social control and social progress.

The complexion of Tönnies' assessment was, however, decidedly different. It would be wrong to say that Tönnies, in the last resort, was opposed to the possibility of 'progress' in these vast social changes. Like Sumner, having made very firm and deep qualifications, he saw the *possibility* of progress and certainly advocated judicious efforts towards its achievement; but the significance is that one has to say: 'in the last resort'. It would be wrong, too, to give the impression that Tönnies was cynical. He was decidedly not this. Let us put it simply like this: that certain elements of his analysis made it impossible for him to be sanguine. The full force of his idea we shall come to in a moment, but here the most telling of his persuasions can be put briefly.

On the one hand, as a matter of social and psychological *fact*, Tönnies believed that the qualities of life, mind, morality, and behaviour brought about by the hyper-rational calculation (and market-manipulation) of the special, contractual, relationships of mercantile trade and industrial capitalism were very much an *impoverishment, diminution,* and *worsening* of the living qualities of whole men fulfilling their clear tasks in traditional communities. The new commercial-industrial-urban type of society ultimately forced all men to think, and calculate, and act, in terms of 'means-end' utility. Things, qualities, persons, were not valued for themselves, but as 'commodities'. And even working people themselves (whose labour *was* a commodity to the merchants and employers) came to think of *themselves* as commodities, and learned to buy and sell their labour contractually. In short *all* the members of the 'Bourgeois' society (literally, for Tönnies, the society dominated by the qualities of mind of the 'trader', the 'middle-man', the 'commercial bargainer') were infected with the 'Bourgeois' mentality; and all qualities suffered. But for Tönnies, it was *exactly* this 'Bourgeois' mentality which possessed the inherent logic of 'universalism'.

Traditional communities were particular, unique, clearly bounded, idiosyncratic, specific in their beliefs, prejudices, rituals, and the like. They wished to maintain their living differences. Their qualities depended upon *avoiding* universalism. Their members performed distinct functions in society—shepherd, smith, carpenter, scholar, priest, judge—but their qualities of craftsmanship were part and parcel of this clear distinctness. On the contrary, all the tendencies of 'trade and industrial capitalism' and the ever-increasing size and competitiveness of 'the market' (which was international, and ultimately global in its scale) were such as to rub out all these distinctions and reduce 'human labour' to an abstraction—a commodity the same the world over whose 'price' would be bargained for by 'associations' of workmen and opposed 'associations' of employers. The 'unity of mankind' was therefore likely to be a unity not of *men*—but of abstractions of the market-situation.

To put this in another way, the forces making for the global interdependency of human societies, in Tönnies' estimation, were all the forces which were such as to diminish and despoil the essentially personal qualities of life, mind, skill, and active enjoyment, which men found as members of intimate traditional communities.

On the other hand, and *this* was the reinforcing dimension of warning in Tönnies' analysis, *science* (which others had held up as the possible basis of salvation; of feasible social reconstruction) *was, in fact, one other leveller among all these others*. Science itself was essentially *analytical*. It reduced actualities to *abstractions* in its

methods. It was peculiarly appropriate to the analysis of the impersonal articulation of social systems, and market situations. Science
was quite foreign to the direct unity and idiosyncrasy of personal
and traditional will as expressed in particular communities. Science
was, in fact, an analysis of living fact into soulless categories; it was
not at all a direct and deliberate statement of will, judgment, purpose,
intent, desire, value. Science *alone*, then, could not help. Indeed, it
might well be one of the arch-enemies! Men might well be gulled
into placing their hope in it—only to find that it was one of the
destroyers: a 'Bourgeois' tool to handle 'Bourgeois' abstractions.

Now, clearly, I have stated this very boldly, and I will not here
qualify it. Nor will I yet introduce Tönnies' own qualifications. I
think it is a good thing, for the moment, just to dwell on this point:
to savour it to the full.

It seems to me that, properly understood, Tönnies—while reinforcing a generalization which had come to the fore and been
continued in sociology—gave voice to a tremendous doubt and
warning: one that remains acute and of the most critical importance
in our own day.

What if it should be the case that the very factors which are
driving mankind towards a global unity are, at one and the same
time, the factors which are most stripping him of his essential
humanity? What if the creation of the 'unity of mankind' is the
creation of a vast, highly articulated, massively organized prison
within which men—stripped of all individual fulfilment—are doomed
to work their impersonal treadmills . . . to keep the system going?
What if the ethical aim of 'progress' turns out to be a dry sterile dust;
and that men have destroyed their nature in seeking it? And what if
the science of society—the hope men set their hearts upon—turns
out to be one major weapon in the armoury of destruction?

There is a further question—just to link this point with the dangers
we mentioned earlier (and provisionally) of the 'professionalization'
of sociology. Tönnies made much of the fact that the experts in the
new 'associational' world of specialization pursued their own calculated self-interest in terms of a purely rational appraisal of means-
end utility, and, whilst maintaining a certain manner of politeness,
were committed to no morality which stood in the way of their own
calculated interest, and so pursued their manipulations without
qualms. But what if this same attitude of uncommitted rationality
were to obtain among 'professional' scientists, and 'professional'
social scientists? What then?

These are very grave issues indeed—and they were raised by the
stark clarity of analysis provided by Tönnies' two 'types'—'Gemeinschaft' and 'Gesellschaft'. We must now look fully at these ideas.

41

'Gemeinschaft' and 'Gesellschaft'

These two terms seem unnecessarily obscure and mystifying simply because they are German, but if we take them to mean 'Community' and 'Society' as indicating qualitatively different kinds of human relationships, we can readily see how they spring from distinctions we make in our common experience. Interestingly enough, Tönnies began his attempt to clarify the difference between them by referring to the distinctions made in common sense and the common use of language. Thus, we commonly speak of 'belonging' to our 'community', in the sense of living in a familiar context of family, kinship, neighbourhood relationships within which we are persons well known among other persons, sharing known expectations among them, and being related to them as whole persons, all our many-sided characteristics being taken into account. We speak of 'society', by contrast, as being some set of formal, public regulations, relationships, and requirements which exist as a larger network of rules going beyond our community, and with which we do not feel, at all, the same sense of familiarity. We speak easily of 'community-life', but would find it odd to speak of 'society-life'. When a young person is leaving home, we may try to warn him about 'society' in which he will feel a stranger, and may warn him against 'bad society'—whereas it would seem odd to warn him against 'community' or 'bad community'. We speak of a religious 'community' but a 'society' for the prevention of cruelty to animals. We speak of the 'community' of property between husband and wife in the family, not the 'society' of property. Many other examples come readily to mind.

The fact is, Tönnies argued, that, in all our common thinking about the ways in which we are related to each other, there is this one fundamental distinction. On one hand we think of ourselves (and others) as members of a *natural order of relationships*—as members of a family, relatives among kinsfolk, neighbours in a particular area, citizens in a certain defined community. On the other, we think of ourselves (and others) as sometimes, and for some particular purposes, having to associate formally with others—not as whole persons, but partially and with a certain distance between us—in order to accomplish a certain end (which may be chosen, or may be forced upon us). And this kind of formal 'association' rests not at all upon any feeling of familiarity, as being members of the same group, but upon a purely rational purpose; a rational calculation. Thus I may to to the seaside for my holiday because all the family want to go, and because it is a common enjoyment and expectation among all the people in our part of the world (and has been for generations) that you go to the seaside for your summer holiday. On the other hand, I may put on a clean suit and shirt and go, as on a special occasion, to sign a contract in a solicitor's office, simply because that is the only and the proper way in which I can complete the purchase of a house. In one case I am a full-blooded member of my family and local group, acting through my shared values and enjoyments. In the other case, the fact that I am a person has not much to do with it. I have, rationally, for a certain limited purpose, to associate with a solicitor, so I obliterate myself in a clean suit, wrap all my idiosyncrasies up in a clean shirt, and—all impersonal—sign the paper. In the first case, I act as a member of a 'community'; my relationships with people are a matter of our all being members of the same 'community'. In the second case, I 'associate' with the solicitor (as, indeed, with the person who is selling me the house) impersonally, for a specific purpose only; and the formal procedure of the transaction is a requirement of 'society'.

The distinction is *there* in our common experience, Tönnies pointed out. Social relationships are relationships among and between the *wills* of human beings (their desires, intentions, purposes, voluntary actions); and 'community' relationships seem to involve quite a different kind of *willing* than do the formal, specialized 'associations' in 'society'. We feel very differently about them. They seem to have different sources in our nature. And certainly one kind seems to spring quite directly from all our personal qualities of living and feeling, from ourselves and our lives as natural beings; whereas the other seems to be the outcome only of a *rational* consideration of a particular end that has to be attained, and a certain means that has, therefore, to be employed. It is all the difference between the many-dimensioned fullness of personal living, and the narrow means-end calculation of specifically orientated pure reason; between a situation in which things are fully valued for themselves and for their living qualities among persons, and one in which things are valued only narrowly as *means* to achieve *ends*. The first seems *natural*, an outcome of *organic life*; the second seems rationally *contrived* and *artificial*—in the strict sense of being an 'artifact' which has been rationally devised and constructed. The distinction is *there* in our experience, Tönnies claimed, and, furthermore, much of the 'malaise' of social life (especially of modern social changes), much of what constitutes the 'social problem', seems to stem from the ways in which the artificial qualities of 'society' spread over, constrain, impoverish and choke, the living spontaneity and enjoyment of 'community'. It seemed to him worthwhile, therefore, to clarify these two principles of 'willing' on which these two kinds of social relationship rested, so that the analysis of the nature of the social 'malaise' could be made as clear as possible. This was the task that Tönnies set himself.

43

It is important to remember that, in doing this, Tönnies was quite definitely *not* writing an essay on *ethics*, *nor* advocating a course of *political action*, and, in his last preface, a year before his death, he reiterated this very plainly. He was concerned with one exercise only: to construct clear models of the two distinct kinds of social relationship, resting on the two distinct kinds of 'willing' which seemed to exist in human experience, for the purpose of achieving the clearest possible analysis of the problems which concerned him. That was all.

Besides this consideration of common experience and common sense, however, there was one other important source of the two 'types' elucidated by Tönnies which, by introductory mention, can help to make their nature clear. Tönnies was very well-grounded not only in philosophy, but also in jurisprudence, and he drew considerably upon those who had put forward theories of law in society, and of the philosophy of law. In particular, he was much influenced by the work of Sir Henry Maine. In his book on *Ancient Law*, Maine had written:*

'The movement of the progressive societies has been uniform in one respect. Through all its course it has been distinguished by the gradual dissolution of family dependency and the growth of individual obligation in its place. The Individual is steadily substituted for the Family, as the unit of which civil laws take account. The advance has been accomplished at varying rates of celerity, and there are societies not absolutely stationary in which the collapse of the ancient organization can only be perceived by careful study of the phenomena they present. But, whatever its pace, the change has not been subject to reaction or recoil, and apparent retardations will be found to have been occasioned through the absorption of archaic ideas and customs from some entirely foreign source. Nor is it difficult to see what is the tie between man and man which replaces by degrees those forms of reciprocity in rights and duties which have their origin in the Family. It is *Contract*.

'Starting, as from one terminus of history, from a condition of society in which all the relations of Persons are summed up in the relations of *Family*, we seem to have steadily moved towards a phase of social order in which all these relations arise from the free agreement of *Individuals*. In Western Europe the progress achieved in this direction has been considerable. Thus the status of the Slave has disappeared—it has been superseded by the contractual relation of the servant to his master. The status of the Female under Tutelage, if the tutelage be understood of persons other than her husband, has also ceased to exist; from her coming of age to her marriage all the relations she may form are relations of contract. So too the status of the Son under Power has no true place in the law of modern European societies. If any civil obligation binds together the Parent and the child of full age, it is one to which only contract gives its legal validity.

* *Ancient Law*, Routledge, 1913, Ch. V, pp. 139–41.

44

The apparent exceptions are exceptions of that stamp which illustrate the rule. The child before years of discretion, the orphan under guardianship. the adjudged lunatic, have all their capacities and incapacities regulated by the Law of Persons. But why? The reason is differently expressed in the conventional language of different systems, but in substance it is stated to the same effect by all. The great majority of Jurists are constant to the principle that the classes of persons just mentioned are subject to extrinsic control on the single ground that they do not possess the faculty of forming a judgment on their own interests; in other words, that they are wanting in the first essential of an engagement by Contract.

'The word Status may be usefully employed to construct a formula expressing the law of progress thus indicated, which, whatever be its value, seems to me to be sufficiently ascertained. All the forms of Status taken notice of in the Law of Persons were derived from, and to some extent are still coloured by, the powers and privileges anciently residing in the Family. If then we employ Status, agreeably with the usage of the best writers, to signify these personal conditions only, and avoid applying the term to such conditions as are the immediate or remote result of agreement, we may say that the movement of the progressive societies has hitherto been a movement *from Status to Contract.*'

This distinction, so clearly drawn, between 'Status' and 'Contract' almost exactly reflected the distinction between the qualitatively different kinds of 'willing' which Tönnies wanted to make clear, so that his typology was constructed very firmly on it. Again, we can see the twentieth century continuation of a large nineteenth century generalization. It remains only to be said that, in constructing his 'types', Tönnies was entirely similar to Comte and others in maintaining that such 'types' were *'fictions necessary for scientific analysis'*; exaggerated *'models'* which made hypothetical understanding clear; and that their focus (as 'models' in sociology) was distinctively upon the *social* aspects of man's nature. His own 'fictions', said Tönnies, were not concerned with human beings as *biological* units, but were focused upon their *relationships and associations*—(1) as growing organically out of their many-sided nature as persons; and (2) in sharp contrast, as 'mechanical' constructions or 'artifacts' of rational calculation. The clear comprehension of these two types, he maintained, made possible the incisive analysis of some of '. . . the most important problems of growth and decay of human culture.' For, he wrote, the very *existence* of culture:

'. . . is change, and, as such, development and dissolution of existing phenomena or forms. All change can be comprehended only from the continuous sequence and interrelation of fluctuating concepts.'*

* *Community and Association,* p. 266. It is very clearly apparent here how fully Tönnies shared the persuasion of the nineteenth century scholars that society was *essentially historical,* and how his own procedure of analysis and explanation was related to this recognition.

The best way of clarifying Tönnies' two types—'Gemeinschaft' and 'Gesellschaft'—is to take each in turn: attempting, first, a straightforward description of their general characteristics; second, an outline of the kinds of will—the 'Natural Will' and the 'Rational Will'—which underlay them; and then, third, an indication of some of the more important characteristics of law and social control which distinguished them.

Gemeinschaft : The Relationships of Natural Community

(1) GENERAL CHARACTERISTICS

The relationships between the wills of men in 'community' were typified, Tönnies argued, by the intimate relationships in and among *family* groups. The relationships between mother and child husband and wife, brothers and sisters, were all rooted in natural instinct and attendant emotion; and the psychic bonds between such members of a family were continuously and mutually affirmed and re-affirmed by use, wont, and habituation. These relationships were not without conflict, but the very fullness of shared conflict and resolution; of shared problems; of shared efforts and gratifications; of shared sorrows and joys; of the most intimate nature and among total persons; was such as to bind the members of a family into a close community of wills. A unity of experience was found in the care of parenthood, the passing on of skills and values, and the continuity of generations. And in the common concerns for work, sustenance, the protection of property, the secure provision and perpetuation of a home, there developed (though, again, not without conflict), a shared *enjoyment*. In all the patterns of conflict and co-operation a certain working-balance of authority, obedience, and consensus of accepted ways of getting along, came to be established; and authority itself rested upon the naturally rooted factors of age, strength, and wisdom. But such 'naturally rooted' relationships were not *confined* to family groups, though their qualities of an intimate belonging to deeply shared practical traditions could be *typified* by them.

Families were never isolated, but *related* through patterns of marriage in wider networks of *kindred*, and among kinsfolk the same intimate bonds of shared life, shared problems, shared work and experiences, came to be deeply established. Such kinship relationships could assume large and quite complex proportions—manifesting themselves in the organization of clans, tribes, and even unions of tribes. All such relationships were rooted in the natural bond of blood. But even kin-groups were not isolated.

Families and kin-groups shared their life together as co-operative workers, and as friends and *neighbours*, in a common *territory*. They produced and apportioned among themselves the same livelihood. They mixed their labour with the same resources of nature. They worked the same land. They defended the same boundaries. The same ground held the graves of their dead. Their shared world of nature became peopled with their own ghosts; was given colour and rich meaning by their own myths and legends. Nature itself was deepened by their beliefs, their rituals, their traditions. Kinship, neighbourhood, friendship, comradeship, and a cumulatively shared history bound men together in a culture embracing both time and space. And the size of human habitation was enlarged. Men lived not only in homes, but in villages, appropriately placed within their territories.

Within this shared life men also came to adopt clear tasks; to learn and practice clear skills; to fulfil clear functions. And such 'crafts' had the nature of 'callings'. They were important parts of the total social life, which men fulfilled with due concern for their qualities. Since tasks and responsibilities have their inequalities: inequalities of status also arose among men, and judicial, priestly, and political functions also became necessary; but these tended not to go beyond the bounds of the recognition of the wholeness of the community, and the reciprocal concern of all its members. Again, as in families, a working-balance of known authority was worked out.

In the context of all these shared activities—continued over generations—common traditions, common values and ideals, a common understanding, a certain 'concord' of understanding developed, and were manifested in quite a basic way in a common language. Such a 'mother-tongue', said Tönnies, was never 'invented' by anyone; it was never an 'artifact' consciously and deliberately created by someone in a 'society': it *was*, in *fact*, the *actuality* of the 'common understanding', of the 'concord', of the 'common sentiments and common will' which had grown and taken shape in that community.

In these ways, then—rooted in natural relationships, and in the necessary organic growth of social arrangements—a community possessing a common pattern of 'willing'; a natural set of relationships among wills; developed. From *instinct* and emotion, through *habit*, and through the formation of shared *sentiments*, there developed a common body of *custom* which richly enshrined the communal experience, the culture of the people, and within which men felt a 'concord' of understanding, and a 'natural basis of will' for all their many activities.

This, of course, involved a deep sense of property: of commitment to home and hearth, to fields and house and farm and village; a deep sense of the qualities of social arts and crafts; and a deep sense of religion too, as a bond of commitment which bound a man—as a total person—to a sacredness of values and traditions which, though giving him a treasured basis for his own life, went far beyond him as an individual. Such a community could extend beyond purely rural and village boundaries to the town as an organic growth for trading; and in the town the same focus upon art, religion, and clear cultural values was manifested in the 'guild'—as a moral, educational, and cultural association; by no means simply an economic one.

In all this, as Tönnies described it, things, activities, persons, ideals, were valued *for themselves*, for *persons*, and for the enrichment of *natural relationships*, which were not invented, or devised, or contrived, but *found* in the nature of things; possessing therefore a given justification: a natural and customary rightness. And in this entire 'community', men's relationships and activities thus stemmed directly and concretely from 'custom' and 'natural will'.

(2) NATURAL WILL

Tönnies then went on to characterize the distinctive nature of this 'natural will', and his starting-point was very similar to that of John Stuart Mill. He discounted all ideas of 'psychological forces' in abstraction—whether biologically or socially rooted. He dispensed with any conception of men being 'determined' (like objects) whether physically, biologically, psychologically or sociologically. And he rejected all notion of 'institutions' as objective 'entities', independent of men, and, in some peculiar way, living a life of 'aggregations' in some queer sociological realm. Tönnies regarded human beings as, essentially, *persons* who, in all their experience and activity, their feeling and thinking, came to live and act in accordance with their *wills*. A man was not just a shadow-show of psychological categories: but felt, lived, thought and acted on the basis of a unitary *will*. And again, like Mill, Tönnies did not think of anything mysterious or metaphysical here. He did not think of the 'will' as some kind of given (and unchanging) entity implanted in human nature, which, in some abstract sense, was 'free'. He thought of a man's will as a certain unitary formulation and organization of a multiplicity of feelings, instincts, desires, thought, and growing knowledge, into certain established dispositions of judgment and character: from which basis his *subsequent* thoughts, intentions, actions would stem in a directed fashion. And, exactly like Mill, Tönnies saw that the 'willing' of human beings was among the 'causes' of human action; an understanding of men's 'wills' was essential for an understanding of the *directional tendencies* towards certain actions.

Given this, Tönnies then distinguished the kind of concrete willing which stemmed from a man's many-sided dispositions as a natural person and a member of a community of natural relationships, as we have described it above (including the thinking which was involved in this), from the kind of willing which stemmed *purely from thinking*, and had reference *solely* to the construction of *artificial* action (i.e. in the strict sense of consciously creating a technical—whether mechanical or social—*artifice*) as a means *calculated* to attain a certain end. The former, he termed, '*natural will*', the latter—'*rational* will', and it was the former which *typically* formed the basis of men's actions and relationships within a 'community'.

'Natural will' was a concrete unity of dispositions which stemmed from the experience of the *past*. It came to be formulated within the growing pattern of instinct, habit, sentiment, and custom, and took shape in the closest relationship with a person's ongoing *activities* among others in the community. It had its roots innately in the very nature of the unitary 'organism' (Tönnies sometimes referred to the 'natural will' as the 'psychical equivalent of the body'), and it grew and developed—not deterministically; but as a continuing process of 'self-generation'—within the context of the individual's social experience as he grew from birth to maturity. There was a certain *sequence* of the components which went into its formulation. Natural instinct initially involved an awakening of impulses and appetites, and a pleasure in, and liking for, the objects which satisfied these impulses. And these 'instinctual' components were themselves not isolated and arbitrary but possessed a unity within the development of the whole individual. There was an overall 'will to life', a 'will to survival', and, within this, a will towards the activities which sustained life (nourishment, protection, etc.) and towards those which reproduced it (sexuality and procreation). In relation to all these, there were also the pleasurable activities of the *senses*. Dispositions of behaviour then came to be patterned by 'habit' in relation to social and practical experience, and it deserves much emphasis here that Tönnies did *not* regard 'habit' as necessarily 'non-rational', 'irrational', or such as to block other activities of mind by its 'blind' responses. On the contrary, he thought that the formation of habit was a selective, necessary, convenient, and liberating element in the growth of the human will. It formed a basis of taken-for-granted workable responses which left the mind free to devote itself to matters beyond it. Habit, said Tönnies, was 'an essential and substantial element' of a person's mind, and, far from being a dead thing, was a 'principle of ability' and of 'active will'.

Both in, and beyond, habit, however, were the processes of

49

learning, which essentially laid down *memory*; and this memory itself was an active and centrally important element in the formation of the will. In discussing this, Tönnies gave quite an elaborate account of the nature of 'feelings', the development of 'preferences', the establishment of 'sentiments', the experience and appreciation of certain *qualities* of life and action (for example 'passion' for life in relation to 'liking'; 'courage' in relation to the perseverance of sustained 'habit'; and 'genius' in relation to the conscious creativity following deliberately upon 'memory'; and the like); and in all this he emphasized the concrete, positive, *living unity* of the will, and described 'thinking' as being *part and parcel of this creativity of living*: not as an analytical, abstracting, activity, but as a kind of creative furtherance of feeling: conceiving idealities for aspiration, qualities for judgment, ideals for morality.

Developed within the context of the community of natural relationships, this meant that 'natural will' possessed always a concrete personal nature; was rooted in past actual experiences of activities and important values; gave rise to 'conscience' as a basis of positive values, qualities and ideals; and included a commitment to concrete elements and processes of *imagination*, *art*, and *work* in relation to quite clearly seen personal and social objectives.

The natural relationships of 'Community' (Gemeinschaft), thus rested upon this concrete kind of 'natural will'. The actions, intentions, aspirations of men, as persons, stemmed from dispositions rooted in all aspects of their own nature, and in the natural order of relationships within which they had grown to maturity.

(3) SOCIAL ORGANIZATION AND THE NATURE OF LAW

These qualities of 'community' life and 'natural will' were also characterized, however, by equally distinctive forms of social organization and law. The system of *law* in such a community was one: 'in which human beings are related to each other as natural members of a whole', and again, for Tönnies, it was typified by 'Family Law'. It paid special attention to *persons* possessing *statuses* as members of *families* and *community groups*; to the *property* of such families, which focused centrally upon property in *land*; and was embodied distinctively therefore as a system of *family law*. Even the pattern of control over human beings with regard to the fulfilment of their functions and duties in such a system, was governed according to the statuses of persons as members of groups: as, for example, in the control of the father over his children, or of the master of a house over his servants. The fulfilling of functions was therefore essentially a matter of appropriate *service* within a system of statuses, so that, again, it was a *concrete* matter of the performance by a *person* of the task appropriate to his *status*.

'All law of the nature of Gemeinschaft,' Tönnies wrote, 'is a product of the human mind. It is a system of thoughts, rules and maxims and as such is comparable to an organ or product which has been created through corresponding activity. . . . Thus it is an end in itself, although necessarily related to the whole to which it belongs, from which it derives, and in which it embodies itself. This presupposes a solidarity of mankind and, furthermore, a protoplasm or essence of law as the original and necessary product of their collective living and thinking. . . .'*

Tönnies undertook an elaborate discussion of the nature of 'common law' and 'natural law' in relation to this—into which it is impossible for us to go fully; but it is enough for us to note that he sharply distinguished this kind of body of concrete law from the extended 'civil law of *contracts*' which was characteristic of 'Gesellschaft' relationships—and which we shall come to later.

The other essential component in Tönnies' analysis here was his description of those elements of *social organization* in which a 'common will' of a community came to be established, and was thus appropriately regulated by such a body of concrete custom and law which always went back to an 'original unity of natural wills' related by 'concord' and 'understanding'.

The substance of this common or collective 'will' was most clearly manifested in the folkways and mores of a people which centred upon their *homes*, their *land*, and their *territory*. This body of custom was an embodiment of the manifold traditions of the community which had been created over many generations. The entirety of the community could properly be called a *Commonwealth* to which all contributed and in which all shared; and *persons*, in *assemblies*, could properly regard their commonwealth as a *social body*; a social entity; which they wished to serve and protect and to which they felt allegiance. Within this commonwealth, distinct 'estates'—the nobility and the commoners, for example—also felt, both within and between themselves, a community of experience, and were closely related to each other in an order of precedence and attendant functions. This kind of *community* organization could extend as far as a *feudal* system and the kind of entire *civic* state as exemplified by the Greek 'Polis'; but this, according to Tönnies was the limit of the 'size' of the social entity within which 'community' could be deeply established and felt. Beyond this, larger and more formal elements of social organization tended to destroy and obliterate the intimacy of the regional bonds.

* *Community and Association*, p. 229.

And finally, the unity of the *common* will and the *common* law in such a 'natural community' of 'natural wills' was emphasized by the authority of *religion*. Religion was the reinforcing base of all morality. Tönnies' conception of the intimacy of the relation between Religion and the life of the 'community' is well worth quoting. He wrote:

'Religion *is* family life *itself*, for the care and assistance given by father or mother is the origin of all divine and godlike guidance and remains its innermost truth. . . .

Religion itself is, then, part of morality made real and necessary by tradition and age, and the individual human being is born into and brought up with it as he is brought up with the dialect, the way of living, the manners of dress and food of his native land, faith of the fathers, belief and custom, hereditary sentiment and duty.

Everywhere religion, even in the state of highest development, retains its hold and influence over the mind, heart, and conscience of men by hallowing the events of family life: marriage, birth, veneration of the elders, death. And in the same way religion hallows the commonwealth, increases and strengthens the might of the law. The law as the will of the elders and ancestors possesses its own dignity and importance; as the will of the Gods it becomes still more powerful and infallible.'*

This, then, was Tönnies' one '*type*'; that of the '*Community of natural relationships*', linking men in definite fashion as whole persons with natural wills (stemming from instinct, habit, and sentiment as well as thought); having its body of concrete law rooted in common and deeply shared custom; and having its own appropriate elements of social organization and social control. This was 'Gemeinschaft': the living, natural, social order.

Gesellschaft : The Relationships of Artificially Contrived Associations

The other way in which human wills were linked together in social relationships was described in Tönnies' second '*type*': '*Gesellschaft*'; and, obviously, its characteristics were the very opposite of those attributed to the 'Community relationships' we have just outlined. It must be noted, again, that Tönnies purposely drew a very *sharp* contrast between his 'types' so that the nature of *actual* social fluctuations and transformations could be the more clearly analysed. But we will leave any qualifications until we have done our best by way of straightforward exposition.

* *Op. cit.*, p. 254.

(1) GENERAL CHARACTERISTICS

In a Gesellschaft-type relationship, men were bound together by one thing only: a specific and carefully delineated *contract* to attain a mutually rationally calculated *'association'* entered into for a clearly defined *purpose*. There was no assumption of any *preceding unity* among the men who entered into the association. There was no assumption as to whether they were, or were not, members of any *'natural order'* or *'group'*. They were regarded entirely as autonomous individuals, free and responsible, and bound only to the extent, and in the ways, of the specific terms of their 'contract'. No 'union', no 'concord', no 'common will' or 'understanding' was expected of them beyond the specific undertakings of the contract.

In such relationships, men were bound only in relation to their agreed 'transactions'. The 'exchange' of obligations specified in the contract was the total obligation of the relationship 'willed' between them. There was, then, no *value* of objects or activities *for their own sakes*, or with regard to any community of culture or tradition going beyond the transaction. Things had value only in terms of specific calculations for the transaction; they were of value only with strict regard to the attainment of the end contracted for. Things possessed value, then, if they were possessed exclusively by some and desired by others, and a 'trading' transaction was a purchase from some and a sale to others in order to secure a 'profit'. Things were of value only in relation to calculations of *'profit'*.

In associations formed by contract, it was also the case that men, though working for the 'contracted association' were only doing so with regard to their own particular interest. No unity, or common value, could be expected going beyond this personal interest. Claims to 'property' in such relationships were defined strictly in terms of contract: they were situations of defined 'debt' and 'credit'. And therefore the power to effect contractual transactions resided chiefly in *money*, and the possession of, or the claim to, money; and the 'value' of the objects manipulated in transactions was translated into 'price'. This entailed a movement away from the uniqueness of things, people, and services in human relationships, and a movement towards a calculated 'abstraction' of them for the purposes of clear and binding transactions. Instead of thinking in terms of a particular carpenter, or blacksmith, or farm-worker, the tendency was for competitive transactions to result in a 'price of labour' of particular kinds.

Furthermore, such contractual associations and transactions knew no 'communal' bounds. The very mental orientation of the merchant, for example, was to be a 'man of the world', well-travelled, with wide sources of information and channels of communication, so that he could best see what was in cheap supply in this part of the world, and in great demand in that. His 'interest' was supreme over any tie pertaining to his 'membership of a community'. 'Natural relationships'; 'natural will'; were subordinate to his contractual undertaking and interests. Tönnies was of the opinion, with Aristotle and Marx, that the 'trader's' use of money to manipulate the exchange of commodities to beget a greater amount of money, was 'unproductive'.* Economists, of course, would disagree with this, and with good justification (i.e. in that the entrepreneurial function does lead to an allocation of factors of production to meet effective demand, and therefore is as 'productive' in the market situation as any other element of production). Even so, Tönnies' point is not affected: that the ground of 'willing', and the supreme valuation of the 'self-interest', underlying the *contract* is sharply in contrast with the 'natural will' of 'Gemeinschaft-relationships' and such as to cut across them, change them, and disrupt them.

One other aspect of this same point is that there was literally no limit (i.e. of social boundary) to the possible 'extent of the market' in such abstract, contractual, transactional associations. Whereas 'communities' were well-defined, unique, specific; and contained the inherent 'logic' of wanting to *conserve* their own loved traditions, to *defend* their own established boundaries (in every sense: geographical, cultural, etc.); these mercantile, contractual relationships which had to follow interest in terms of abstract calculations of quantities, prices, etc. contained an inherent 'logic' of *'universality'*. Their dimensions were global and all-embracing. The 'extent of the market' knew no bounds other than those of the competitive possibilities of factors of production and consumer's demand. The 'global' extent of 'Gesellschaft' was thus, quite strictly, the making of the entire world into a 'market' of calculated associations; a market which transcended and cut across all 'Gemeinschaft' unities within it.

Specific 'associations' of this contractual kind rested only on the *convention* of the rules and regulations pertaining to the upholding of contracts made; which was something very much more partial and limited (as a commitment), than the folkways, mores, customs and traditions of community relationships. All such specially contrived associations approximated to the contractual relationship of the 'merchant'; so that men, in such relationships of 'wills', possessed attitudes of mind approximating to those of 'trade'. They calculatedly manipulated each other in terms of their interests. They followed their own interest, and supported others only in so far as this furthered their own interest. If anything should conflict with their own interest,

* 'Unnatural' in the earlier 'community' sense.

then this interest came first, for there were no more binding moral obligations beyond it. A contract was a contract! This was the understanding assumed (as the 'convention') to be the very basis of contractual relationships.

There is no doubt whatever that Tönnies thought that these contractual and calculating relationships necessitated, encouraged, and extended 'immoral' qualities. They flatly cut across and denied the Gemeinschaft feelings of 'conscience'; of direct commitment to concrete, traditionally 'proven', values, qualities, and ideals. The *conventional* life of *society* (i.e. as distinguished from the concretely committed 'natural' life of 'community') went on within an accepted and mannered surface of *politeness*. There was a veil of 'civilized manners', beneath which all the members of 'society' knew very well that they were all consciously, and even ruthlessly, pursuing their own interests; trying to manipulate each other, to outwit each other, in such contractual ways as to maximize their own profit. It was a 'painted veil' beneath which sharp practice flourished as the rule. In all such formal, contractual, and polite relationships of 'society', people had one hard core of intent only: to get their own pound of flesh. The one motive was self-interest, and the one purpose was the maximization of profit in a specific direction. The aim was to deploy as little as possible of one's own wealth to get as much as possible of the wealth of others. Under the polite, urbane,* civilized 'skin' of 'society', the relation of all to all, said Tönnies, was one of continuous potential hostility or war. Polite society:

'. . . consists of an exchange of words and courtesies in which everyone seems to be present for the good of everyone else and everyone seems to consider everyone else as his equal, whereas in reality everyone is thinking of himself and trying to bring to the fore his importance and advantages in competition with the others. For everything pleasant which someone does for someone else, he expects, even demands, at least an equivalent. He weighs exactly his services, flatteries, presents, and so on, to determine whether they will bring about the desired result. Formless contracts are made continuously, as it were, and constantly many are pushed aside in the race by the few fortunate and powerful ones.'†

The attitudes of mind in such 'society' were therefore those of deception, of scheming, of calculatedly measuring and using others in order to further and secure ends of your own. And in all this— things, work, art, loyalties, people, far from being valued for them-

---

* Notice the significance of this word: the smooth, sophisticated, self-assured, experienced way of the city-dweller, the man of the world which cannot be trusted.

† *Op. cit.,* p. 89.

selves, were 'weighed up', calculated, costed, and manipulated as 'means' to your own end.

The spread of such contractual relationships was the spread of a new kind of power. The maximization of 'profit' and '*wealth*' led to a furtherance of power in effecting subsequent contracts; so that the accumulation of '*capital*' became the great repository of power. The contractual associations of 'capitalists' became the dominant ways in which men and their resources came to be bound together in 'society'. Men—in all their trades—became 'prices' of 'labour'. Relations between 'capital' and 'labour' were thus abstract relations of power between men within a vast network of contracts. And the relations of power were relations of calculated 'exploitation'. (The close similarity between Tönnies and Marx can be plainly seen here.) Furthermore, men themselves, in order to be effective in any kinds of negotiation with those who held power over them, had to learn to operate within the same 'abstract' framework. They themselves, therefore, had to bargain for the improvement of their 'price' (their 'wages' in the market-situation). They, too, came to have the clearly formulated objective of maximizing their 'price' in the mesh of contractual relationships. They, too, in short, fell a prey to the new 'nexus' of relationships, the new qualities of mind, of 'Gesellschaft'. *Bourgeois society* thus became all-embracing; every human relationship was infected; the formal, calculating, scheming, manipulating 'ethos' of the 'contractual relationship' percolated down into men's very souls: making a self-centred, self-interested manipulator of everyman.

It will be perfectly clear, in all this, how Tönnies saw 'Bourgeois Society' as being set sharply over against 'Traditional Community'. *Society* (resting on rational contractual calculation) was clearly distinguished from *Community* (resting on natural relations among natural groupings); but it was further characterized as *Bourgeois* Society simply because the entire complex of contractual relationships in it was *typified* by (approximated to) the relationships of *commerce*, of *trade*, of the *merchant*. The contract of the trader came to be the archetype of *all* the contractual associations of men in such a society. And it can clearly be seen, with this, how true it was that Tönnies posed the old problem of the disruption and despoliation of the traditional agrarian régime of the past by the massive revolution of commerce, manufacturing industry, and urbanization, in new, sharp, living, and telling terms. As one reads Tönnies' exposition of 'Gesellschaft-type' relationships, one's blood runs cold with the stark realization of the menace of the new contract-minded Leviathan that strides rampant through, and over, all the communities of the world as the twentieth century advances.

Here, indeed, was a new and powerful focus upon the distinctive problem of the modern world: the problem which increases in its menace as the global tentacles of industrial technology spread out, and which we must learn to deal with quickly. And Tönnies further elaborated the characteristics of his 'Gesellschaft' type in his discussion of the nature of 'Rational Will', and (parallel with his description of 'Gemeinschaft') his account of the attendant forms of law and social organization.

(2) RATIONAL WILL

Whereas, in 'natural will', the will of a person—rooted in instinct, habit, sentiment, custom—*included* thinking; in 'rational will', Tönnies argued, thinking *dominated*, or *encompassed*, the will. *Feeling* was now entirely subordinated to *reason*.

Rational will (as a sharply distinguished 'type' of willing) was not rooted in the *past*, finding its grounds and justifications of action in already established sentiments and customs, but, exactly on the contrary, was based upon a consciously calculated foresight of the *future*, and thus rested upon *purpose*.* It did not spring concretely from a context of *established activities;* on the contrary it *imagined* a future end, and *action* was its calculated *realization*. Rational will was characterized therefore by clear and critical conceptualization, by careful abstract analysis, by deliberation and discrimination, by critical judgment, by clear intention, by measured calculation and planning, and—crucially therefore—by a concentration upon 'means-end' sequences of purposeful action.

Tönnies thought that there was something 'unnatural' about 'rational will' even in the sense that, of its very nature, it seemed to have (critically) to disengage itself from both 'natural' impulse and appetite (seeking to govern them), and from 'naturally accepted' custom and tradition (seeking critically to assess, judge, and manipulate them). This, obviously, was a questionable point about which much could be argued; but there were many more apparent ways in which Tönnies thought that 'rational will' entailed characteristics and attitudes which conflicted with the qualities and relationships of 'natural will'.

It was of the very nature of rational calculation of self-advantage, for example, that men should continuously seek to *control* both nature

* To use the language of the early Americans, it was 'teleological' in its emphasis rather than 'genetic' (stemming from 'efficient causes'). It will be noted how Tönnies dealt with the same distinctions as the Americans—e.g. the increasing dominance of the growth of 'purposeful associations' out of earlier social orders of 'tradition' ('genetically' established over very long periods)—but with a decidedly different 'flavour'.

and other men in so far as it was conducive to their purposes. It necessarily, in short, entailed the struggle for *power* among men; and a struggle in which there was no real arbiter of value other than that of *success* in attaining interests. Tönnies agreed with Hobbes that there existed:

'. . . a general inclination of all mankind, a perpetual and restless desire of power after power, that ceaseth only in death. And the cause of this is not always that a man hopes for a more intensive delight than he has already attained to, or that he cannot be content with a moderate power, but that he cannot preserve the power and means to live well, which he hath present, without the acquisition of more.'*

Since *money* was the *effective* source of power in contractual relations, this struggle for power was, to a very large degree, a perpetual struggle for money, wealth, capital. But also—running through it all, parallel with self-interest—was a characteristic 'measuring-up' of men against each other: an insatiable competition of self-love; of vanity. Again, Tönnies quoted the comment of Hobbes that:

'. . . joy consisteth in comparing himself with other men,' and 'can relish nothing but what is eminent . . .'

Tönnies went further than this, pointing to the fact that *ambition* came to be one of the most powerful of hungers in the 'contractual' type of society, and that this, together with vanity, dominated even those activities commonly thought to be 'self-less' and beyond the passions and bargaining of the market-place: as, for example, in scholarship: in the quest for knowledge. He did not think this was a *necessary* accompaniment to the 'life of the mind', but that in 'Gesellschaft' it could easily be infected by, and become a part of, ambition and the lust for power. In this point we can see clearly Tönnies' analytical criticism even of science, and the uneasiness to which it gave rise.

These attitudes of mind attendant upon contractual calculation tended, therefore, to be supremely 'egotistical' and 'individualistic', having reference *not* to common habit, sentiment, and custom, but only specific interest, and, as such, tended, again, always to have the 'ethos' of hostility: a continual readiness for sharp conflict. And again, they led to trickery, deception, intrigue, and any kind of open or veiled ('behind the scenes') manipulation in order to attain the ends desired.

* *Leviathan.*

One other important distinction which Tönnies emphasized rested upon his differentiation between an 'organ' and a 'tool' in man's activities. An organ was part of a living totality, which sustained and supported it, and within which living whole it found a clear function and meaning in creative activity. 'Natural will' had its living place in the 'natural relationships of community' in this way. It stemmed from, and was part of, a 'psychologically real existence'. A tool however, is an extraneous, specially devised and constructed artifice, the nature of which is determined by the particular job to be done. It is a mechanical means to a calculated end. 'Rational will' was concomitant with the calculated device of special contractual institutional 'artifices'; with the construction of the bits and pieces of a 'technology' of 'society'. The special distinguishing feature, therefore, was that 'Rational will' was particularly and sharply concerned with the elaborate *'apparatus'* of society in connection with calculated ends; and this, again, gave it a dominating concern with the *formal*, the *abstract*, the *artificial*; whereas 'Natural will' was rooted in the unique embodiments of the living community.

Tönnies also argued, in constructing this typology, that it was therefore of the nature of 'Rational will' to carry with it *constraint upon* freedom. The social artifice that some men created would be likely to interfere with the interests of others; to obstruct their pursuit of those interests; and therefore it would engender other artifices which sought to protect these other interests. A vast and intricate labyrinth of contractual relationships was therefore almost an inbuilt logic of the extension of 'Rational will'.

In all these associational forms of the contractual society, the attitudes of mind which men adopted to their tasks were not those of the 'calling'—the fulfilling of a function with the highest qualities of excellence as accepted in the community; but those of *'business'*. Men approached their jobs not as something worthwhile in themselves, but *instrumentally*. Their knowledge, judgment, action had to be appropriate and correct as *instrumental means* to attain the contracted end. Again, men's attitudes towards other men were dominated by being instrumental means within an entire instrumental apparatus. A man was a tool among tools in a larger machine. And again, Tönnies made it especially clear that *science* was among the supreme components of this abstract, efficient, precise, means-end calculating apparatus of 'Gesellschaft'. Science (and its attendant kind of technology) was the supreme creation of the 'Rational will'. 'Natural will' was characterized by the spirit of creative *art*: the flowering of concrete, unique creativity in a community of persons. 'Rational will' was of the essence of the abstract, the analytical, the logical, the calculating—the epitome of which was *science*.

59

A final, and very important distinction was that which Tönnies made concerning the nature of morality. We saw earlier that he 'typified' morality in 'Gemeinschaft' as being essentially a concomitant of the qualities, values, idealities which had come to be firmly established as being of supreme worth in the traditions of the community; and which were sanctified and glorified by religion. Moral feelings were related to the aspirations towards these standards, and related to the extent to which a person genuinely obeyed them, or approximated to them, or fell far short of them. Thus 'shame', for example, was a central element of 'conscience'; and shame was experienced as an outcome of fear and awe in relation to authoritative standards, and a sense of degradation at having failed them.

For the 'rational will' in the 'contractual society' even morality came to be a matter of shrewdness, pretence, and calculation. 'Shame', for example, or any such moral *feeling* was a stupid sentiment which obstructed the clear-sighted pursuit of your end, or interest. In relation to the polite expectation of society; the conventions; it might be *useful* to *appear* to be morally genuine; to *appear* to abide by certain qualities and standards; but, always, it was absurd to allow any such sentiments to be more than skin-deep. The final arbiter was—self-interest: and all moral notions were subordinate to this, and should be calculated accordingly. *Feelings* were neither here nor there; commitment to *qualities* was neither here nor there; rational will sought specified ends and calculated means accordingly. What mattered was that the calculations were correct, and the end successfully attained.*

The force of our earlier statement—that Tönnies thought that the qualities of mind engendered by the purely 'contractual' type of relationships were 'immoral'—can be seen in all this. Tricks, lies, deceit, intrigue, sharp-practice . . . all were assumed to be going on in a society of such relationships. The entire façade of pretence in such a society was permitted, indeed assumed, said Tönnies: '. . . because in trade it does not count as deception'.

(3) SOCIAL ORGANIZATION AND THE NATURE OF LAW

We have seen how Tönnies described the context of 'Natural will' as being typified by the relationships of *family* groups, and of all those attendant 'natural groupings' of kindred, class, tribes, and interdependent neighbours occupying a territory; and also how he described the distinctive law of such communities as being typified by

* In all this there is an uncannily accurate flavour of the expedient teaching of the sophists of classical Greece, against which Socrates, Plato and Aristotle were so powerfully opposed.

'*family law*' with a central focus upon '*property*'. Relationships stemming from 'Rational will'; *contractual* relationships; went beyond these forms of social organization and law, and cut across them.

The body of law which distinguished these relationships was clearly the 'law of contracts' (what we now term 'civil law'); and the basis of efficacy of such contracts was now not so much 'property' as 'wealth'. Property in the older sense of the possession of a landed estate had considerably yielded (with regard to the growth of 'contractual transactions') to 'wealth' in the sense of the possession of 'money'. Obligations in contracts were very largely 'money' obligations; money-claims were the most abstract, exact, effective statements of contractual commitments.

Such contractual law came greatly to supersede and supplant earlier law in defining human relationships. So that even the relationships of men in their work and employment were now not a matter of men possessing a *status* and performing a *service*, but autonomous individuals who entered into a *contract* of employment in terms of work to be done for a *wage*. Again, men became contractual parts of the entire apparatus of the contractual fabric of society—a depersonalized, artificial, mechanical fabric; which 'equalized' men by abstracting them as items in generalized contracts.

This law also led to the creation of 'legal persons and institutions'. In the 'community', persons and assemblies formed 'unions'. In the 'contractual-type' of society—'*Associations*' were deliberately formed. Such unity as existed among men was an outcome of the contractual inception of their relationships—and to a large extent limited to the purposes of that contract. Such an 'association' could be a created legal entity which could be answerable to the courts and could act through the courts. By and large, associations which were definite legal entities of this kind were those whose basis was wealth; those which had to meet and to make claims upon wealth. The *typical* organizational form of the 'Gesellschaft' relationship was therefore the 'Joint Stock Company', and, of course, its typical place was the complex commercial city.

Distinguishing this kind of law from the customary and common law which held among the natural groupings of a community and a 'commonwealth', and doing so in such a way as to show its *independence* of community groupings, Tönnies wrote:

'The general civil law of contracts is the corollary of general contractual trade and grows with it until it finds its most adequate expression in a codified commercial and maritime law, the national character of which is obviously not more than an accidental and provisional aspect of it.'*

* *Community and Association*, p. 236.

It will be noticed that even the close association between the growth of such law and the rise of the modern nation state—in conflict with the earlier solidarity of Christendom in Europe—was stated as being of little significance by Tönnies. Indeed, his emphasis was almost that it was the rise of contractual, mercantile law which produced modern nations rather than vice versa.

Tönnies undoubtedly also saw this spread of contractual relationships and the increasing dominance of the law of contract as a *disintegration* of community relationships; but he also pointed to the way in which the concept of 'Natural Law'—rooted in the elucidation of the universal elements in custom and the 'jus gentium', but coming to take the form of the philosophical idea of justice—was of importance as a vehicle whereby an overall order of codification and planned legislation might be (and was being) re-introduced in larger societies. This was one way in which a new kind of blend between 'community' and 'society' relationships might be achieved—but we will look at Tönnies' limited comments on this later.

The final 'organizational form' which he emphasized as being distinctively attendant upon 'contractual relationships' and 'rational will' was the special association of the *State*. Whereas the commonwealth of a community consisted of all the natural groups within it, bound by custom and tradition into a whole 'union'; in 'contractual societies', the State was one special association among others; conceived in terms of 'contract';* its 'constitution' being framed within the general rule of contractual law in the society. In this sense, the law was 'above' the State; the constitution of the State was itself part of that law. It was the rule of contractual law which was the predominant feature. If the State failed to fulfil certain desired ends satisfactorily, it could be re-devised (by constitutional reforms) like any other institutional artifice; like any other piece of the associational apparatus. One other element of this point was that whereas 'religion' was the reinforcing agency in uniting wills in the 'community', the only basis of agreement among the members of the contractual society and the State was that achieved in *public opinion*. The agencies which made for the formation of a widely shared public opinion were therefore crucial for the unity and the authority of the modern State, and chiefly, Tönnies held, they rested upon *written communications widely distributed*. In short, the *Press* was the most important instrument of public opinion, and this, like all the other elements of 'rational will', contained the inherent logic of universality. The Press knew no 'community' boundaries. Its universality paralleled the universality of the 'extent of the market'.

* We may recall the 'social contract' theories which accompanied the emergence of the modern nation states.

'It can be conceived as its ultimate aim,' Tönnies wrote, 'to abolish the multiplicity of states and substitute for it a single world republic, coextensive with the world market, which would be ruled by thinkers, scholars, and writers and could dispense with means of coercion other than those of a psychological nature . . . The existence of natural states (communities) is but a temporary limitation of the boundaryless Gesellschaft.'*

This, then, was Tönnies' second 'type' of relationship between human wills: the purely rational, purposeful, contractual *association*; brought into being for a limited end, and deploying carefully calculated means; dominated purely by 'rational will'; and resulting in a boundaryless fabric of formal, contractual commitments, with the State as the one special association among others, resting upon the ever-variable consensus and differences of thought arrived at by public opinion; a 'society' of calculated manipulation of man by man within the complex, artificial legalistic apparatus of his own devising.

And these, then, were the two sharply distinguished 'types' which Tönnies constructed for the interpretive understanding of 'some of the most important problems of growth and decay of human culture'. We have devoted a good deal of time and care in our effort to present a satisfactory clarification of them, but it is still necessary, for a pletely fair understanding of Tönnies' treatment, to make a few brief comments on the way in which he regarded the relations between them, and the way in which he thought of his typology as a 'theory'.

Some Further Comments on the Nature of 'Gemeinschaft' and 'Gesellschaft' and the Relations Between Them

(a) Conceptual 'Types': Not Social Actualities

The first point of which one has to remind oneself over and over again in reading Tönnies is that in this work of analysis he was distinctly *not* describing social or historical actualities. Many times, one feels that his account of 'natural will', or 'rational will', or any other element of his 'types', are greatly exaggerated, and suffer from this. But, of course, this was exactly the point of Tönnies' method; the central aim of his exercise. These two types *are* exaggerated; they *are extreme forms* of the two principles of 'willing' which we can distinguish in our experience, together with an analysis of their appropriate forms of law, social organization, etc. Tönnies did *not*

* *Op. cit.*, pp. 256–7.

wish to say that any particular society, or any particular epoch of civilization, was *entirely* of a *gemeinschaft* or a *gesellschaft* nature. He did *not* wish to claim that 'natural will' existed entirely separately from 'rational will' in such and such a society or epoch, (or, indeed, in any individual). On the contrary, he thought that *all* human societies would *always* be some *blend* of 'community' and 'society' tendencies, since the two fundamental ways of 'willing' were always active in human nature. The whole point was, however, that if two completely clear conceptual types ('models') were drawn up, with all the logical and organizational and regulatory entailments in them laid bare, then the *analysis* and *interpretation* of any *actual* social situation or social-historical change could be much more satisfactorily undertaken.

This, we must be completely clear about, as Tönnies himself always was. The *materials* from which he constructed his 'types' were drawn from actual societies, but the 'types' themselves were '*conceptual constructions*' in the light of which we could analyse and interpret social actualities.*

It may be of help to present the two 'models' in sharp summary contrast by collecting into one scheme, the several summary statements which Tönnies himself provided (see table opposite).

(b) Interpretive Understanding : The Central Method of Sociology

It will have been seen that Tönnies did not concern himself with a discussion of all the elaborate components of a scientific sociology—such as those which formed so large a part of the earlier nineteenth century scholars who had laid the foundations of the science. He accepted the greater part of this, and simply did not bother to discuss it further. However, the entire emphasis of his work was to the effect that *interpretive understanding* was the crucially distinguishing, and the only satisfactory, method of sociology.

Certainly psychological facts about human nature were important: facts about the bio-psychological endowment of man, and the detailed nature and sequences of his patterns of learning. Certainly 'sociographic' and statistical facts about man's social conditions were important. Certainly historical knowledge about the nature and changes of human institutions in societies at all times was important. Certainly the organizational analysis of social forms—families, kinship systems, clan and tribal organization, the structure of feudal relationships and of civic nations, commercial cities, empires, modern nation states, together with the constitutions of their forms of government

---

* We shall come to a full appraisal of the fundamental significance—for sociological *theory*—of such 'types' in our discussion of Max Weber, pp. 381-458.

GEMEINSCHAFT AND GESELLSCHAFT: SUMMARY SCHEME

(1) GEMEINSCHAFT (NATURAL RELATIONS IN COMMUNITY)

General Characteristics	The Social Will: Concord, Folkways, Religion	Occupation and Intellectual Life	Transition (Epochs)
Natural Will	1. Family life = concord. Man participates in this with all his sentiments. Its real controlling agent is the people (Volk.)	(A)1. Home (or household) economy, based upon liking or preference, viz. the joy and delight of creating and conserving. Understanding develops the norms for such an economy.	1. Family and Kin, Clan and Tribe.
Self	2. Rural village life = folkways and mores. Into this man enters with all his mind and heart. Its real controlling agent is the commonwealth.	2. Agriculture, based upon habits, i.e. regularly repeated tasks. Co-operation is guided by custom.	2. Cultivation of soil. Neighbours and Village.
Possession			
Land	3. Town-life = religion. In this the human being takes part with his entire conscience. Its real controlling agent is the church.	3. Art, based upon memories, i.e. of instruction, of rules followed, and of ideas conceived in one's own mind. Belief in the work and the task unites the artistic wills.	3. Town and Civic Nation.
Family Law			(THE AGRARIAN COMMUNITY)

(2) GESELLSCHAFT (RATIONALLY CONTRACTED ASSOCIATIONS)

General Characteristics	The Social Will: Convention, Legislation, Public Opinion	Occupation and Intellectual Life	Transition (Epochs)
Rational Will	1. City life = convention. This is determined by man's intentions. Its real controlling agent is Gesellschaft per se.	(B)1. Trade based upon deliberation; namely attention, comparison, calculation are the basis of all business. Commerce is the deliberate action per se. Contracts are the custom and creed of business.	4. Commercial City
Person	2. National life = legislation. This is determined by man's calculations. Its real controlling agent is the state.	2. Industry based upon decisions; namely, of intelligent productive use of capital and sale of labour. Regulations rule the factory.	5. The Modern Nation and the 'State'.
Wealth			
Money	3. Cosmopolitan life = public opinion. This is evolved by man's consciousness. Its real controlling agent is the republic of scholars.	3. Science, based upon concepts, as is self-evident. Its truth and opinions then pass into literature and the press and thus become part of public opinion.	6. ? Some global administrative unity?
Law of Contracts			(URBANIZATION)

... all these components of knowledge were important. *But*, crucially, men in their social relationships were different from other kinds of 'subject matter' in that their relationships were associations of '*wills*'; they were *meaningful* in terms of feelings, commitments, values, standards, ideals, persuasions, intentions, ends, means, calculations, and the like.

Systems of human relationships (the subject-matter of sociology) *could not*, therefore, be *explained* in terms of the kinds of generalization (whether contemporaneous or historical) which could be made of other objective facts: about mountains, climates, rivers, plants, animal species, etc. They could *only* be explained in terms of *meaningful understanding*; in terms of an *interpretation* of relationships and actions which was understandable, and therefore provided an adequate basis of *explanation*. This, it will be seen, rested crucially on the recognition of men as *persons*, whose actions and relationships involved and were mediated by their *wills*. It was essentially the same persuasion as that of John Stuart Mill, and of the Americans' insistence upon the necessity of a 'teleological' component. It reinforced all the emphasis that had been placed, by earlier thinkers, on the difference between human *action* and the *events* of nature. And—what cannot be too much emphasized—it *ruled out*, as an *impossibility*, any 'explanation' of systems of human relationships in terms, whatever they might be, which did not *include* these dimensions of interpretive understanding, and which failed to recognize these distinctive qualities of men and their relationships.

Without being ostensibly methodological, therefore, Tönnies, in his concentration upon producing his 'typology' for the interpretive understanding of the actual problems which disturbed him, was overwhelmingly clear and persuasive in the method of sociology which he put forward, and, indeed, embodied. This is why, in outlining Tönnies' contribution, it has seemed justifiable to explore the dimensions of his 'types' in so much more detail than we devoted to the 'types' put forward by men like Comte and Spencer. Tönnies' 'typological method' was not another methodological argument, but an actual *development* of this method; an actual *demonstration* of its value by the undertaking of a specific, incisive study. It furthered sociological analysis by showing convincingly the *deepening* interpretation of social processes which it made possible; and, indeed, there is scarcely any change which is now taking place among the communities of the world that cannot be profoundly illuminated by the analysis which Tönnies provided.

This was a *development* of sociology. It was *not* another large scheme of scientific components; *not* another version of the nineteenth century 'conspectus'; but a typological analysis, worked out in thorough detail, which could be perennially useful, and which permitted such subsequent amendment or elaboration as any other investigator might find, after careful study, to be necessary. It was a *specific theory* within the agreed conspectus. The pudding was *proved* richly in this one particular eating.

(c) *A Theory ABOUT Historical and Evolutionary Change : Not a Descriptive Generalization of it*

A third point to be emphasized is that Tönnies' theory was a development of 'Evolutionary' sociology in a number of ways; indeed, it was a development of historical sociology. The particular point worth making here is that his theory was *not* just another descriptive generalization about the sequences of institutional change which *had* occurred among societies in history; nor was it just another setting out of the kinds of causal factors that should be taken into account in tracing the changes of social evolution. On the contrary, it was a *specific theory*, stemming from the construction of models which *drew upon* historical data, but which were in large part *deduced*, analytically, from principles of 'willing', and which yielded clear hypotheses of understanding which could guide the interpretation of actual historical changes. It was a theory *about* history and social evolution which stemmed *not* from generalizations drawn from the past, but from the analytical need to understand certain problems of the present. Thus, Tönnies wrote:

'In contradistinction to all historical theory deducing its findings from the past, we take as our actual, even necessary, starting point that moment in history when the present spectator enjoys the inestimable advantage of observing the occurring events in the light of his own experience, and perceives, although chained to the rocks of time, the approach of Oceanus' daughters.'*

And again:

'The concepts and findings which have been presented in this book will help us to understand the tendencies and struggles which have come down from earlier centuries to the present period and will reach out into the future.'†

This was a theory *about* social evolution, then, which, far from being simply a dead generalization about the past, was *continuously aware* of those problems which were *perennially* at the heart of the fluctuations of social change.

---

* *Op. cit.*, p. 275.   † *Op. cit.*, p. 274.

(d) But Still : A Theory of Social Evolution

Having said this, however, it is still true, nonetheless, that Tönnies' analysis yielded a theory of social evolution which was as large in its historical coverage as any of those offered by Comte, Spencer, Marx, Ward, Sumner, or Giddings. He presented a cogent and persuasive analysis of the ways in which traditional communities (of varying sizes and compositions—from families, clans and tribes to civic nations) were gradually changed and superseded as the contractual relationships which grew with trading contact between them developed. His generalization was as large as the movement towards the global society ordained by the 'unsociable-sociability' of mankind put forward by Kant: but, of course, it was worked out in much more considerable detail. And, in many respects, his generalization was fully in accord with (parallel to) the generalizations offered by all these earlier people. From the Theological to the Positive type of society in the ideas of Comte; from the Militant to the Industrial type in the ideas of Spencer; from Folkways and Mores to formal associations and formal law in the ideas of Sumner; were very much the same as from Gemeinschaft to Gesellschaft in the ideas of Tönnies.

It must be noted (and reference may be made to our earlier 'summary scheme') that Tönnies was very definite about this. Though regarding all societies and epochs as experiencing some 'blend' of the two types; and all social changes as manifesting some 'fluctuations' between them; he was, nonetheless, quite definite in his view that a decided long-term trend of development was discernible in history.

'Two periods,' he wrote, 'stand thus contrasted with each other in the history of the great systems of culture: a period of Gesellschaft follows a period of Gemeinschaft.'*

He followed this with a description of the transition from traditional Agrarian Communities to increasingly urbanized States and to the development of some global administrative consensus which he saw as a necessary outcome of 'Gesellschaft'. It is also most important to see here that Tönnies did not only propose this as a descriptive historical generalization. He argued that there was an insistent *logic* of such developments. That the development of mercantile trade; the growing dominance of contractual relationships was *necessarily* accompanied by closely related changes in forms of social organization and the law. That this *necessarily* upset, weakened, disrupted, cut across, the values and traditions of established communities.

* *Op. cit.*, p. 270.

And, further, that 'Gesellschaft' itself was driven by a logic of competition to a necessary situation in which State legislation had to attempt central administrative order, and even some unified modicum of a sense of 'Gemeinschaft' in the new complex societies. Some ultimate degree of 'collective' administration was thus logically and organizationally inherent in 'Gesellschaft'—and this, of course, was in conflict with its own ethos of completely unfettered freedom to form contracts. Tönnies also wrote of this historical transition, then, as a movement from a simple family communism, through a 'village-town individualism' resting on this, to an 'independent, universal, urban individualism', and, as a necessary outcome of the unrestrained competition in this, to a 'socialism' of both *state* and *international* type. Here was a large-scale theory of social evolution and social development indeed!

It goes without saying, too, that this was an analytical generalization which has become ever more telling, urgent, and useful as the traditional communities of the world are, at an increasingly rapid rate, being swept along in the common tide of industrial and commercial change. Here, undoubtedly, then, was a development of evolutionary theory in the grand manner, as well as in the more limited methodological sense.

(e) A Typology Applicable at Many Levels

It is also important to note that, besides being a set of concepts of considerable and quite central interest, and besides yielding an evolutionary theory of very large extent, Tönnies' 'typology' was applicable, as a useful interpretive set of concepts, at many levels and with regard to many social situations, both large and small. Without enquiring in any detail as to how justified all these points were, we might simply note that Tönnies himself discussed the relevance of the 'gemeinschaft-gesellschaft' distinction to all the following kinds of human difference.

He considered the different nature of the *sexes* and the different nature of their contribution to social life—arguing that, by and large, feeling and 'natural will' were the more dominant features of woman's nature, and 'rational will' the most dominant in man's. He discussed the nature and role of the *artist* in society, arguing that, by and large, the artist was chiefly dominated by 'gemeinschaft' (and even feminine) qualities; seeking always the making of something which synthesized, in harmonious concrete form, feeling and reason, natural and rational will. In a way, art brought science into relation again with unifying philosophy, and, Tönnies wrote:

'. . . when science becomes philosophy, the human being regains, through

69

the highest and purest knowledge, the joy of contemplation and love which had been destroyed through reflection and ambition.'

Artistic 'genius' was the creative *unifier* of all the dimensions of human nature. Tönnies also discussed the relations between '*youth and age*' in society, arguing that 'gemeinschaft' qualities belonged to the pristine experience of the young, and the rational, calculating qualities of 'gesellschaft', to the old. Similarly, he compared kinds of *social groups* and *social classes*. Thus, he thought that the common people in a community were more governed by 'natural will' with its roots in instinct, habit, and sentiment, and that the 'educated classes' (what we would now call the 'professional élites') were, by contrast, chiefly dominated by abstract knowledge, and the scheming, calculating, manipulating ways of 'Gesellschaft'. In the same way, he discussed morality in society; the relation between the economic 'market' and other institutions in society, and the like.

We have said enough, however, to show that the 'typology' of Tönnies was (and is) applicable to many specific relationships, groupings, classes, and even sequences of individual growth *within* society, as well as to societies as entire 'systems of culture', and to large sequences of historical change. Growing from childhood to adulthood; experiencing the conflicts between generations, between the professionals and the ordinary people; experiencing the appeal of art, as distinct from the analytical dryness of science . . . in all these, and many other ranges of experience, Tönnies demonstrated the worthwhileness of his distinction. Supremely, then, his 'typology' was of many-sided *use*.

(f) The Centrality of VALUES—of MORALITY—in Society

When we were seeking to clarify the chief concerns and persuasions; the common concepts and convictions; of the scholars of the nineteenth century, it will be remembered that I insistently stressed the one (though not the only) fact that centrally and powerfully emerged—that, for all these men, *values* constituted the core of all those *institutional activities* which formed the bed-rock of society. All of them dwelt emphatically upon man's *practical activities*, his purposeful *action*, and (in relation to, and in the context of, all this) the emergence of s*tandards*, *qualities*, *criteria of judgment* which were *proven* in the actualities of experience, and which thus came to *regulate* all these manifold activities in a certain societal order. We saw that even Marx in his supposed 'materialism' had this basic persuasion; and that the Americans, especially, quite directly recognized this in their picture of folkways and mores which gradually yielded to a more purposive devising of special associations resting on a more reflective deliberation about criteria of judgment. I now want to return to this point, and again to emphasize as weightily as I can, the plain continuity of it throughout the making of sociology, and—here—from the work of the nineteenth to that of the twentieth century.

In the early emergence of the social sciences, men—like John Stuart Mill—referred to them as the '*Moral* Sciences'. In this was the plain recognition of the fact that these sciences were concerned with a central qualitative distinction: that they were dealing with a subject-matter—men in their many social relationships—which was characterized by the possession of will; the capacities of purpose, reason, choice, deliberation; and with *connections of relationships* (interconnections of institutions) which were relationships of 'wills', and which, at their core, rested upon regulatory *values*. Man's distinctive characteristics could be best summarized in that he was a *moral* being; and human society could be best distinguished from all other 'orders' in nature in that it was a *moral* order. All social institutions were forms of *regulation*: they prohibited this, they sanctioned that. At their very heart, therefore, lay established *values*. Moral values were at the very heart of society.

It will be perfectly plain that what I am now wanting to emphasize is that the conception of Tönnies was exactly and most deeply and richly rooted in this tradition, and was a most powerful restatement and reinforcement of it. We have seen how he completely encompassed the insistence upon the 'will' which Mill had emphasized, and, in the most interesting way, had interpreted all the massive material, technological, contractual, exploiting, alienating, changes of Bourgeois society which Marx had attacked, whilst never leaving the level of men's wills and the meaningful logic and contradictions of their relationships. And it is plain beyond doubt that Tönnies' analysis rested absolutely centrally upon his conception of man as an 'evaluating' person; whose 'will' rested upon appraisals of value of certain kinds; and that his two 'types'—Gemeinschaft and Gesellschaft—constituted a sharp juxtaposition of two fundamentally different *kinds* of value, which lay at the heart of two fundamentally different sets of institutional structures. Two kinds of 'morality' lay at the heart of the two different sets of social relationships; and one was incompatible with the other. The radical change from one to the other was therefore at one and the same time *both* a *social and* a *moral* malaise. The two were inseparably connected.

I do not think that this point needs further elaboration here; the forcefulness of Tönnies' argument is self-sufficient. All I would like to note, however, and with the utmost firmness, is that, just as in the earlier theories, so in Tönnies' work too, a theory of society, a theory

D

71

of social evolution, was, at its very centre, a theory about the nature and change of the *moral values* which lay at the heart of the social order; which interpenetrated the entire system of social institutions.

I do not want to labour this point here, but, in my opinion, Tönnies' analysis also contained—with a definite implicit logic—a theory of 'progress'. But this we can leave for the moment, as we can come to it briefly in mentioning one or two final points of criticism and assessment.

Points of Criticism and Assessment

No more need be said about the ways in which Tönnies' work constituted a *development* in the making of sociology. His work was rooted in the context of earlier nineteenth century achievements. His 'typology' was fully in the spirit of moving 'from Theory to Theories'. It was, indeed, one detailed study within the 'evolutionary' dimension of the nineteenth century 'conspectus', and it proved the worth of sociological analysis in throwing light upon a wide range of social relationships and social systems with the aid of a concisely constructed set of 'models'. In the most telling and incisive way, Tönnies demonstrated the close relationship between a meticulous concern for clear theory, a detailed interpretive understanding of social facts, and the most pressing practical social problems. Theoretical construction and interpretation of the most specific facts were seen to be two sides of the same coin. Without the one—there could not be the other. And this is a point on which all those who attack sociological theory for its *distance* from social facts and problems should dwell. *Without the theory, the facts cannot be interpreted or explained.* Only those with the most primitive conception of science, or, indeed, with no conception at all, could fail to see this.

In this final section of critical assessment I would like to dwell on two matters especially: one concerning Tönnies' *difference* from earlier theorists, and his stark posing of the *warning* which we mentioned earlier; the other concerning certain criticisms of his emphasis in the construction of his two 'types' which, it seems to me, can easily lead to error, and which can lead us on to see clearly the worthwhile corrective (on this particular point) of the later contributions of Westermarck and Hobhouse.

(1) A Warning : The Grave Dangers of Reason and Science
There is one major distinction which marked Tönnies' perspective of social development off from all the others of the nineteenth century (excepting perhaps that of Sumner) which, to my mind, deserves

great emphasis. It is plain enough that Tönnies shared the prevailing concern of all sociologists from Comte onwards with the problems rooted in the disruption of traditional, agrarian societies by the massive spread of commerce and industrial capitalism. It is also plain that Tönnies, like all these men, saw this modern transformation of society as one of deep cleavages of interest and bitter conflicts until some kind of 'modus vivendi' had been worked out on a global scale. There is no doubt, too, that some of these nineteenth century scholars were sceptical of any solution, and, indeed, feared some of the solutions which were being proposed and pursued. Sumner clearly feared a rash and hasty imposition of administrative 'reforms'; deeply convinced that they might well be destructive of such wisdom in the folkways and custom as might remain. Spencer obviously feared and detested 'collectivism' as being retrogressive; a 'going back' on social evolution which could well bring in a new era of despotism. It would be quite mistaken, therefore, to mark Tönnies off from the others in any total, or even in too marked a way.

Even so, it seems to me that Tönnies did face this vast perspective of modern change in a way that sounded a deeper tone of considered scepticism, of considered pessimism. Though by no means wholly negative in his attitudes or proposals, he saw real difficulties with a very realistic, with a really judicious, eye; and, in particular, he saw that some of the 'tools' of the social processes making for world unity were, at one and the same time, weapons which threatened to 'dehumanize' man in society, and to impose a new, abstract, administrative Leviathan which would hold people throughout the world calculatedly in thrall. Properly understood, this seems to me to have been a new turning point, a new development in interpreting the perspective which sociology had produced; a new and more mature realization not only that an understanding of modern problems may not mean, necessarily, a power to resolve them, but—more especially —that the achievement of scientific exactitude, the possession of scientific knowledge, was by no means the end of the matter. Indeed Tönnies' analysis made clear the complex realization not only that science could be used *against*, as well as *for*, any humane and reasonably based re-organization of society, but also, more deeply, that the very science to which men looked for their desired knowledge of society might well be a central factor in diminishing the very nature of man and society which they wanted it to serve.

As to his scepticism about the possible intractability of the difficulties, Tönnies' reasoning was this. On the one hand, he believed that the spread of 'Gesellschaft' would be disruptive of the earlier 'Gemeinschaft' culture of communities, and that this process would be so riven by cleavages of class-interest and class-struggle, by the bitter

73

conflict of factions, that any deeply shared culture was in danger of being wholly destroyed.

'The entire culture,' he wrote, 'has been transformed into a civilization of state and Gesellschaft, and this transformation means the doom of culture itself if none of its scattered seeds remain alive and again bring forth the essence and idea of Gemeinschaft, thus secretly fostering a new culture amidst the decaying one.'*

On the other hand, the entirely competitive drives and interests of 'Gesellschaft', completely unrestrained over a long period of development, could not remain so. The state—one association among the rest—had, increasingly, to constitute administrative procedures whereby claims and counter-claims could be dealt with. So a certain 'Gesellschaft' *order* (almost a contradiction in terms) had to be increasingly imposed upon 'Gesellschaft' relationships. Two elements were involved here. First, an attempt might be made to produce a new entirety of culture: re-cultivating elements of 'Gemeinschaft' within the new State-order of 'Gesellschaft'. This would perhaps stem from the realization that, as mentioned above, all cohesive elements of culture were fast being destroyed, and the realization that some such ground of common values was necessary in the 'union' of the State. Also, there would be the inherent necessity we have mentioned, within the mature development of complex 'Gesellschaft' relationships, to accomplish some central legislative order. But—and this was Tönnies' central point here—this involved major contradictions.

Whether a 'Gesellschaft-dominated' legislature could calculatedly engender and nourish a new groundwork of 'Gemeinschaft' appropriate to its own nature was at least dubious. More important, however, was that the central legislative order to which the complexity of 'contractual' relationships necessarily led was itself a massive constraint upon these self-same relationships. It was 'Gesellschaft' being compelled to create for itself a strait-jacket unsuited to its nature, and within which it was bound to chafe. In an extreme sense, it was a matter of 'Gesellschaft' destroying itself (which was very redolent of Spencer's idea). Tönnies therefore felt that, come what may, this necessary movement towards a national and global administrative order would be an uneasy and tenuous business. Its necessity was clear, but the conflicts heaving within it were also clear. The process of some such administrative accommodation was afoot— but it would be a seething, restless process, and Tönnies was tentative in his pronouncements about it.

* *Op. cit.*, p. 270.

He wrote on the two elements of contradiction we have mentioned as follows. On the question of a possible re-creation of 'Gemeinschaft' culture:

'In the end the state will probably realize that no increase in knowledge and culture alone will make people kinder, less egotistic, and more content, and that dead folkways, mores, and religions cannot be revived by coercion and teaching. The state will then arrive at the conclusion that in order to create moral forces and moral beings it must prepare the ground and fulfill the necessary conditions, or at least it must eliminate counteracting forces. The state, as the reason of Gesellschaft, should decide to destroy Gesellschaft or at least to reform or renew it. The success of such attempts is highly improbable.'*

And on the self-destroying tendency inherent in 'Gesellschaft':

'A socialism of state and international type is inherent in the concept of Gesellschaft, although in the beginning it exists only as an actual interrelation between all capitalistic powers and the state, which maintains and promotes order in the social organization. Gradually attempts are made to impose a uniform regulation on the social organization and labour itself through the mechanism of the state, but success in this would necessarily dissolve the entire Gesellschaft and its civilization.'†

Again, then, its success was dubious. It will readily be seen that Tönnies was undoubtedly seeing deeply into one of the greatest problems of our time here—and all the complex varieties of 'collectivism' which have arisen and are being tried and destroyed continuously since his time‡ : of fascism, national socialism, communism, the welfare state, etc; are examples of the contradictory forces which he has so realistically envisaged. They are also problems we have not resolved.

Besides this clear vision of the degree of intractability of the problems themselves, however, the other serious warning that Tönnies' analysis made clear was with regard to the qualities of science. Though, again, the nineteenth century scholars had been by no means naive in their conceptions of science, it tended to be the case that they saw science as the new method of achieving exactitude of knowledge and the best possible basis for prediction and judgment. From Comte's statement of 'positivism' onwards, science and especially in its application to the study of man and society, had come to be looked upon as the servant of humane social re-construction.

---

* *Op. cit.*, p. 269.   † *Op. cit.*, p. 274.
‡ Let us remember that he died as recently as 1936, and think of all the phenomena of 'totalitarianism' which have troubled the world since then.

Tönnies did not disagree with much of this. Like all the others, he was insistent upon the development of as exact a science of sociology as was possible. Yet his analysis resulted in a grave warning in two ways.

His first emphasis was exactly a look at the other side of the coin that the emergence of a science of society had been distinctive of the modern social transformation in which industrialism was supplanting and disrupting the earlier traditional order, All others had seen this distinctive connection, but Tönnies in particular saw that social science (as science in general) was especially the tool of the new kind of 'contractual' relationships. It was associated with, indeed it was an integral part of, the spread and proliferation of 'Gesellschaft'. It was itself part of the new 'ethos' which was abstract, generalizing, calculating, precise, analysing every qualitative fact of nature, human nature, and human society into conceptual categories. The zealous support of the spread of social science might well itself be a mistake: the humanitarians of the nineteenth century might be hugging a viper to their breasts; they might be setting up a God who would not save, but malignantly destroy the very human qualities they wished to sustain and advance. Science was *part* of 'Gesellschaft' and had the same de-humanizing qualities.

The second emphasis, which was chiefly an implication of his entire analysis, was that the successful achievement of exact scientific knowledge decided nothing whatever as to the ends for which it might be used. Sociology might be successfully established. It might yield knowledge of a measurable degree of exactitude. *But*, this knowledge could be just as well put to use by those who wished to perpetuate the unlimited contractual freedoms of 'Gesellschaft', as by those who wished to reconstruct society as a whole. The *attainment* of a science of society was thus no end in itself; it secured no direction of effort and policy in itself.

These large degrees of doubt about the self-sufficiency of a science of society to meet the major human problems from which it had emerged constituted a new 'tone' in sociological thought, and, it seems to me, were very salutary.

The same kind of growing fear that the science which man had created was a kind of inhuman Frankenstein that might destroy him was voiced by many people during the first few decades of the twentieth century. The optimistic growth of science during the nineteenth century could be understood; but now science had come to have a dominating vogue; and perceptive men feared it. From Wordsworth to D. H. Lawrence it had been feared in literature, and perhaps Lawrence's 'Women in Love' was a kind of literary culmination of this deep-rooted fear that the highly articulated organization of industrial and scientific man would destroy all the instinctual and spiritual richness of the 'personable' man and of his living experience of nature. One of the best statements of this fear of science is to be found in George Gissing's book: 'The Private Papers of Henry Ryecroft'. Here, I will quote only a little, but enough to lend force and colour to the tone of warning which I have in mind.* Gissing wrote:

'I hate and fear "science" because of my conviction that, for long to come if not for ever, it will be the remorseless enemy of mankind. I see it destroying all simplicity and gentleness of life, all the beauty of the world; I see it restoring barbarism under a mask of civilization; I see it darkening men's minds and hardening their hearts; I see it bringing a time of vast conflicts, which will pale into insignificance "the thousand wars of old", and, as likely as not, will whelm all the laborious advances of mankind in blood-drenched chaos.

For myself, I can hold apart, and see as little as possible of the thing I deem accursed. But I think of some who are dear to me, whose life will be lived in the hard and fierce new age. The roaring "Jubilee" of last summer was for me an occasion of sadness; it meant that so much was over and gone—so much of good and noble, the like of which the world will not see again, and that a new time of which only the perils are clearly visible, is rushing upon us. Oh, the generous hopes and aspirations of forty years ago! Science, then, was seen as the deliverer; only a few could prophesy its tyranny, could foresee that it would revive old evils and trample on the promises of its beginning.'

This was a new warning of which to take heed. For our own purposes, I would like only to note a few points with which I want to connect it in our argument. First: let us note that this raises very tellingly the question as to how far social science—and sociology in particular (since we are here chiefly concerned with it)—can be allowed to develop independently of moral and social philosophy. Secondly, but as part of this same point, it raises and intensifies the difficulties which could foreseeably arise with the development of *professional* sociology and sociologists. For they, too, are part and parcel of Gesellschaft! They too, must be expected to be moved by career motives, contractual-motives, profit-motives. They too are part of the larger, abstract, 'market-situation'. They too can be employed for specific contractual purposes within it; and why should we suppose that the *humane ends* of sociology, as had been conceived and assumed by the nineteenth century sociologists (who were *not* professionals), should have any claim upon *them*? Why should we assume that

* It is interesting to notice that this book, too, was published in 1903 (Constable). See pp. 245–6 in the 1928 Reprint.

there are values outside science which have a greater claim on sociologists than those of science itself, or those of self-interest?

These are great and grave problems; much is attendant upon them; and we must come back to them later; but here it is enough to *realize* them with the forcefulness with which Tönnies' analysis raised and emphasized them.

Having said all this, and given this warning note its full weight, it is necessary to say that Tönnies did not confine himself to this scepticism and degree of pessimism, but did at least indicate the positive way in which these problems should be approached. And it was in these suggestions that it can be seen that, although he was 'more Sumnerian than Sumner' in his scepticism about legislative possibilities, ultimately, so to speak, his final position was not different from Sumner's final position, and was, in fact, in agreement with most of the earlier theorists from Comte to Giddings. And it was in this position that it can be plainly seen that he possessed certain criteria of 'progress' within all these sequences of evolution and development.

For ultimately, Tönnies maintained that reason, and the 'rational will' was not *entirely*, or not *necessarily*, confined to analytical, means-end, contractual relationships, but that it could operate in the service of the feelings, and, with imagination and art, and with a carefully constructed rational ethic, try to create a new order of society in which the qualities of 'Gemeinschaft' and 'Gesellschaft' could be satisfactorily blended. Furthermore, though undoubtedly *difficult*, Tönnies thought that such a social reconstruction was *possible*, and that the effort should be made. In the book 'Gemeinschaft and Gesellschaft' itself, having described the destructive and purely rational 'individualism' of Gesellschaft, he wrote:

'However, the possibility of overcoming this individualism and arriving at a reconstruction of Gemeinschaft exists . . . Growing group consciousness, like that of the isolated thinker, can develop and rise to a moral-humane consciousness.'

And, in an additional note in 1912, in which he drew attention to the rise of 'Co-operatives', he wrote:

'It is evident that, under a form adapted to conditions of Gesellschaft, there has been revived a principle of Gemeinschaft economy which is capable of further significant development. This antipodal (as it is called by Staudinger) movement is also important for the pure theory of social organization. It may become the focus for a resuscitation of family life and other forms of Gemeinschaft through better understanding of their significance and their essential qualities. The moral necessity for such resuscitation has, since this book was written, been recognized more and more by all those who have proved themselves capable of judging the tendencies of modern Gesellschaft clearly and without bias.'*

And similarly in a note of 1922:

'The cry for "Gemeinschaft" has become more and more vocal, very often with explicit (or, as in the case of British Guild socialism, tacit) reference to this book. This cry deserves the more credit, the less it voices a Messianic hope in the "spirit" alone. For the spirit as a separate entity is real only in "ghost" magic. To attain reality, it must incarnate itself in a living principle capable of development. Such principle is found in the idea of co-operative production, if and when it is able to protect itself against relapsing into mere business.'†

It was in his later essay on *Custom*, however that Tönnies stated most clearly this more positive (though still by no means unguardedly optimistic) view.

'The spirit of Gesellschaft remains the same: it cannot jump over its own shadow,' he wrote. 'But in its forward movement lies the possibility of surmounting it. This lies in the reorganization of the economic foundations. If the natural interchange of production and consumption were to replace the predominance of the movable capital of trade and commerce, then, too, life would again become more stable, more quiet and more healthy. Consciously-nurtured custom and the fostering of art would again be possible.

Even religion would find new life as a *Weltanschauung* in the spirit of truth; or better, the idea of religion would be re-awakened in the struggle for the spirit of truth and reverence. A society that unanimously pursues such a course, and with a clear and strong consciousness, would manifest an abandonment of the whims of fashion and an ability to produce a rational will. The growth of its rationality is that which in general distinguishes it. It is that which lies in the developmental lines of custom and civilization, and as such in its ennoblement and refinement.

There developmental lines have been repeatedly stressed: emancipation from superstition, spiritism and magic, the joy in intellectual pursuit, which itself can become an appreciation of art, and a striving for artistic naiveté and creativity. The present contains such elements and moments, although only in the form of a few scattered grains of seed. It can rather be said that the future *ought to be* developed in such a direction than that it *will* be.'‡

Within the modern State, he argued, people will come to desire a common cultural unity, *not* simply an administrative expediency.

* *Op. cit.*, p. 227.   † *Op. cit.*, p. 228.
‡ *Custom: An Essay on Social Codes*, Free Press, 1961, pp. 136–7.

'A people which is in the process of becoming spiritually more mature and stronger will again want to be its own master. It wants to recognize its own identity in the state, and to form itself into the state. It wants to again be self-ruling in the smaller groups.

To the extent that a people succeed in this, a kind of renaissance of custom is possible. This will hold so long as society and the spirit of the time do not oppose it, so long as the freedom acquired and maintained by the ruling classes for their own purposes is not used in society and state to suppress the freedom of the people.'*

The 'rational will' was still dominantly that concerning itself with means-end calculations and expediency. But, Tönnies wrote:

'. . . this association is not necessary and essential. Scientific thought can also be united with natural will and with the taste which is at its core. It will be inclined toward that, the more profoundly it grasps the facts of organic life and creativity; in other words, the more it grasps the work-shop of moral and artistic genius. Thus, too, will the freest thinking recognize, acknowledge and favour in myriad ways the morality of custom. Thus it will be said: Rather an imperfect custom than no custom at all!'†

Furthermore:

'The thinking person must recognize the unconscious creativity in the human, social and individual spirit, and must find rationality not only in what is rational in *its* form. He will then do justice to habit and custom and to the extremely important function which they eternally fulfill in an individual and a social sense.'‡

Tönnies' firm statement concerning the necessity of a rational ethic, developed from a considered criticism of custom, came as the conclusion of the same essay. Nothing could be clearer than this:

'The morality of custom has long since become inadequate. It must be purified in the fire of criticism and it needs—however much of it may prove to be pure gold—supplementation. A new lawbook of morality which does not hold itself bound to custom has thus become necessary. The more liberated we become *from* custom and become free *within* custom, the more we will need a conscious ethic—that is, the recognition of that which makes man human and the self-affirmation of reason. And reason, precisely through this, must cease being merely a scientific, analytical power. Rather it must develop into the joyous creation of *Gemeinschaft*. It is chiefly by this means that reason will prove to be the "height of human potential"; or, rather, it will only then become it.'§

* *Custom*, pp. 141–2.   † *Ibid.*, p. 145.   ‡ *Ibid.*, p. 143.
§ *Ibid.*, p. 146.

Here then, undoubtedly, was a *development* of nineteenth century sociology which, after contributing much, and after deepening an appreciation of the intractability of the problem that remained, nonetheless returned to the same fundamental persuasion as that which had dominated the nineteenth century 'conspectus': that of utilizing the science of society to reconstruct the modern social order in such a way as to make use of the new technology and the new complexity of contractual relationshops whilst sustaining and furthering all the concrete excellences and values which earlier traditional communities had achieved. It was an analysis of evolution and development which provided a basis for possible progress.

(II) A CRITICISM OF TÖNNIES' 'TYPES'

A final consideration can move from one or two criticisms of Tönnies' 'typology' to an introduction to the work of Westermarck and Hobhouse which followed, and which achieved developments of evolutionary theory of a different kind—though still with the crucial concentration upon the centrality of *morality*, or *values*, in society.

The criticisms I would like to introduce of Tönnies' 'types' can be stated briefly, and are not far-reaching, but I think they serve to point to the importance of the theorists who followed. It would be beside the point to criticize Tönnies' 'types' as such—since he constructed them as 'extremes' of systems resting upon 'natural will' and 'rational will' for the sake of interpreting the problems which concerned him. However, it seems to me that one or two aspects of his treatment could easily lead to certain one-sided emphases, if not to possibilities of error. I do not think his analysis of the sharp conflicts between elements of Gemeinschaft and the contractual relationships of mercantile and industrial capitalism should be diminished in any way. These are sharp and real; and Tönnies' analysis is persuasive. Still: I feel that his typology gives a certain balance of judgment that is in many ways questionable.

The following criticisms, it seems to me, are worth voicing. One is that the way in which Tönnies drew his types as sharp extremes led him to provide a picture of 'Gemeinschaft' which was decidedly glorified. All the points he made about the living nature of such traditional communities are true enough. Yet we know that such communities have manifested patterns of limitation, constraint, poverty, harshness of life, insensitivity and brutality of human relationships, deplorable material and moral conditions, and kinds of tyrannical authority far worse than those found in many modern conditions of 'Gesellschaft'. A second criticism which follows is, of course, that Tönnies' extreme contrast of 'types' tended very much to emphasize the destructive and dehumanizing aspects of

81

'Gesellschaft', and gave little consideration at all to the ways in which they have possibly liberated and improved human relationships. The consequence is that Tönnies' picture is one of a general *deterioration* of relationships, standards, values, and morality, as Gemeinschaft gives way to Gesellschaft. Now this, as a total generalization, is very questionable.

A third criticism is that, in emphasizing his 'extreme' type of Gesellschaft, it will have been noticed that Tönnies concentrated almost entirely on contractual relationships in *trade*. Now in such special 'contractual' associations, certainly 'profit' is the end, and intermediary means are calculated to attain it. *Rational* action is certainly of a means-end nature here. However, *not all* specially devised associations are of this commercial kind, and—and this is the crucial point—in *other* kinds of special association the *end* (though no doubt entailing calculations of cost, etc.) may well be such as specifically to secure or protect humane standards. Here, I am wanting only to make the limited point that *rational will*, even in specially contracted relationships, need not be only expedient with regard to profit or self-interest as an end. Rational, contractual associations can have 'other-regarding' ends and concrete human values in mind as well as customs stemming from 'natural will'.

Closely related to this, but not confined to it, a final criticism is that—in juxtaposing his two extreme forms of 'willing'—Tönnies focused attention upon only *one aspect* of *rationality*, which could easily lead to a false estimation of the part which reason plays, and can play, in personal and social life. As we have seen, Tönnies portrayed the 'rational will' as being such that all elements of instinct, emotion, habit, sentiment, custom and tradition were subordinated to it; and, especially, that they were subordinated to its essentially calculating, expedient, scheming concerns simply to achieve specific contractual interests. Now it must be emphasized again that there is no objection whatever to the *type* which Tönnies draws; and it has been clear that, with the help of it, he was able to throw much light on certain aspects of changing human relationships. It *could*, however, if accepted without reflection, and without a proper appreciation of what Tönnies was doing, give the impression that *reason* and *rational will* were related to elements of feeling and custom *only* in this one way. But this, of course, would be quite false, and a very one-sided picture. In fact, reason and rational will may quite well operate reflectively and actively *in the service of feeling*, and creatively and constructively in devising social relationships in which they may best be fulfilled.*

* As, indeed, Tönnies himself recognized in his discussion of the part played by reason in 'natural will'.

These criticisms, then, are *not* criticisms of the extreme 'types' which Tönnies drew, or of his methodological correctness (and his right) to draw them for his own analytical purposes. They are only criticisms of some aspects of these types, and the strong impressions to which they give rise, which, if accepted unreflectively, could be quite misleading and lead to basic errors. And it is a good thing to end our account of Tönnies' contribution with these critical points because it was in the work of Westermarck and Hobhouse that this other, and more positive, role of reason in relation to instinct, habit, sentiment, custom—and, indeed, to morality generally —was stressed. The work of Westermarck and Hobhouse was therefore *complementary* to that of Tönnies in a very necessary and important way. They had exactly the same problems at heart as he; they concerned themselves with the same kind of *development* of sociology by undertaking more searching studies within the nineteenth century conspectus and within its 'evolutionary perspective' in particular; they were centrally concerned with the same issue of morality in society, indeed, with almost exactly the same conceptual components of morality; but they dealt with the role of reason and knowledge in all this in a different way.

Seeing this clear connection, we can now consider the developments in the making of sociology for which they, in their turn, were responsible.

2
Edward Westermarck:
The Sociology of Morals: 'Sanctions' at the Heart of Social Institutions

It will already have become clear that there is no such thing as *the* theory of social evolution. 'Evolution' is a general notion of the interconnected change and development of material things, organic species, and societies: seeing them always within the context of their environments, and assuming a shape and nature in accommodating themselves to their many environmental factors. It is a theoretical perspective for the analysis, description and explanation of those 'patterns' of change and persistence, of those changing and persisting 'forms' of phenomena, which we find in the world. Within it, there-fore, there is room for many emphases and many special directions of study. This is especially relevant to our consideration of Wester-marck. Nowadays, if he is ever considered at all, he tends to be simply bracketed with the 'large-scale evolutionists' of the nine-teenth century, and left there. Yet, strictly speaking, Westermarck did not seek to offer a theory of *social* evolution; an all-embracing theory about the massive changes of human civilizations; as, say, Spencer or Marx had done. His emphasis was much more specific.

Strictly speaking, the focus of Westermarck's work was upon this: the attempt to show that the *biological* (and especially the *Darwinian*) theory of evolution provided the grounds for clarifying the *causes* of the emergence (and necessity) of social institutions in human communities. And, by *social institutions*, Westermarck meant, quite directly, those regular and established human relationships which were *sanctioned* in any society. For him, the analysis of the insti-tutions of the social system was the analysis of *sanctions*, and it can be seen immediately how his analysis reinforced all the tendencies in sociological theory we have continuously stressed so far which saw *morality* not as one aspect or sector of society, but as lying at the heart of *all* the institutions of society; as being the very bed-rock of the entire social order.

Many points lay in this central emphasis, and we can make them clear in such a way (again) as to demonstrate the strong, deep-rooted, and many-sided continuity in the making of the subject.

84

(1) WESTERMARCK AND SOCIOLOGY IN BRITAIN

We noted earlier that, like Tönnies (but, of course, even more directly in that he addressed and chaired several of the meetings) Westermarck was among the early supporters of the English Sociological Society founded in 1903–1904. More important was the fact that he was one of the two men appointed to the first Chairs of Sociology in the University of London following upon the active desire to found the subject 'officially' which was voiced in those early meetings. Westermarck's home was in Helsingfors, in Finland, and on one or two occasions he had visited England to study at the British Museum and at Oxford. In 1903 he had met Victor Branford and so became involved in the founding of the society in London. In 1907 he was appointed to a Chair in London, and from that time on he held both this appointment and the Chair of Moral Philosophy at Helsingfors, dividing each year between the two universities (his London Chair was at the London School of Economics), and spending summer months in Morocco where he undertook field investigations.

Westermarck, then, was one of the founders of 'official' academic sociology in Britain, and it is of interest at once to see that this was no relatively 'parochial' concern of the L.S.E., or London, or even Britain. The first Chairs of Sociology in Britain were rooted in discussions which were fully international in their scholarly scope, their concern, and their membership; and one of the first two professors in the subject was a Scandinavian.

More needs to be said about this to see Westermarck in true perspective: as a scholar at the forefront of a growing subject, rather than as an 'echo' of nineteenth century 'things past'. Far from being a nineteenth century figure, Westermarck's work was chiefly produced between the turn of the century and his death in September 1939 (on the brink of the Second World War.) He was a contemporary not only of Tönnies, Hobhouse, Haddon, Frazer, but also of Durkheim and Malinowski. Like Durkheim and Freud, he searched the writings of Spencer and Gillen on the Australian aboriginal peoples, and puzzled over the significance for religion and society of 'totemism'. Some of his books—like 'Early Beliefs and their Social Influence', 'Pagan Survivals in Mohammedan Civilization', etc.—were coming out in the nineteen-thirties, and, on subjects like religion, and the attempted distinctions between religion and magic, they took the views of Durkheim and his 'school' as thoroughly into account as they did the ideas of Tylor, Frazer, Marett, and others. They also took into account Malinowski's 'Argonauts of the Western Pacific' when Malinowski was already himself a professor. We have already noted that he chaired a meeting for Beatrice Webb; and during the nineteen-twenties, he produced abbreviated versions of his work on the 'Origin and Development of the Moral Ideas' for the Rationalist Press Association. He was, in short, a *modern*, indeed almost a *contemporary* scholar; involving himself in contemporary research and topical disputations. He died when those of us who are between 45 and 50 were watching the sand-bags being filled on the beaches of sea-side resorts in the late summer of 1939, and wondering (little knowing) what was actually afoot. Westermarck, like Tönnies, is of our own time. We are speaking of the 'history' of the subject here only in terms of what was happening in our own youth.

Two other points might be noted briefly here. The first: that the beginning of British sociology was marked by this central interest in the sociology of morals, and by this persuasion—reiterated by all before, and echoed by all at the time (Ward, Sumner, Tönnies, Durkheim, etc.)—that *values* lay at the very heart of the structure of society. To this, we shall return. The second point is of more particular interest with regard to Westermarck, and is that Westermarck himself was one of the earliest pioneers of *field-work*, of personal *field-investigation*, in sociology. Though undertaking wide and detailed comparative studies of a documentary nature, he also saw the necessity and value of first-hand empirical investigation—and this he undertook in Morocco. It is worth mentioning, too, that he initially hoped to undertake *comparative* field studies—but found that the limitations of time, and the difficulties of studying even *one* society in detail in this manner, were such as to make this impossible.

Westermarck, then, was modern not only in his context of associates and influences, but also in his insistence upon the importance of field-work as well as the most searching library-research. Westermarck was a modern empiricist. He wanted to observe and to study social facts as actual, living phenomena; and he wanted, as a sociologist, to do this *himself*; in the flesh, so to speak—and not only through volumes in libraries. In this he was entirely in agreement with all the leading scholars from 1900 onwards; agreeing with the need for an extension of empirical studies in relation to specific theories; and, indeed, he was far more of an empiricist in *practice* than most others—than Durkheim, for example, who talked about this, but himself continued to use, chiefly, secondary sources. Thus Durkheim's book on 'The Elementary Forms of the Religious Life' was entirely book-work: based on secondary sources; whereas Westermarck did at least *observe* social facts in Morocco in living detail.*

* Westermarck was sufficiently 'modern', for example, to have taken Bertrand

British sociology, from its 'official' beginning then, had this emphasis not only upon the centrality of *values* in society, but also upon *empirical* study. It was not only Booth and Rowntree and the Webbs (who looked at budgets and drainage systems in the back-streets of Britain and thought, chiefly, of administrative problems), but also Westermarck who was exploring a *theory* about the causal factors in the *sanctioned relationships* of society, who insisted upon empiricism. *All* were equally concerned with the study of social *facts*.

(II) WESTERMARCK AND ELEMENTS OF CONTINUITY

Undoubtedly, then, Westermarck was a modern scholar in the best sense of that word, engaged in the earliest founding of academic sociology in Britain; but it is also important to see that here again, in his qualities of mind, in the influences which impressed him and which he drew together, and in the substantial contribution of his work, he provided an example of the constructive continuity in the making of the subject.

Like the scholars of the nineteenth century, Westermarck was a man of extraordinarily wide and detailed erudition. He was well informed about most of the major contributions that had been made in founding the human sciences. He was well aware of, and acknowledged his debt to, such earlier thinkers as Mill, Spencer, Darwin, Adam Smith, and also, as we have seen, to the more important anthropologists of his own time: Tylor, Frazer, Marett, Haddon, Malinowski, etc. His own work was a deliberate attempt at the *development*, the filling out, of some of these earlier ideas; the undertaking of elaborate studies to test them; and, especially, the attempt to achieve an exhaustive classification and comparative study of *social institutions* in order to establish the causes of their emergence and persistence, and in such a way as to demonstrate the correctness and worth of the new sociological perspectives and methods.

He agreed completely with Comte and Mill that biological and psychological facts lay at the roots of sociological phenomena, and that these had fully to be taken into account for any satisfactory understanding of the origins and nature of social institutions, and

Russell to task for his *insufficiency* of comparative study. In *The Future of Marriage in Western Civilization* (1936), he criticized some of Russell's claims about 'free love' (made in *Marriage and Morals*), and wrote: 'This allegation is apparently based (like some other statements made by him with reference to "matrimonial societies") upon the customs of one small matrilineal people, the Trobriand Islanders in Melanesia.' In this comment Westermarck also points out the *narrowness* of the range of some comparative study stemming from the new anthropology.

especially of their wide degree of universality and persistence despite the many elaborate changes which had attended them throughout history. But he also believed, further, that it was the theory of evolution offered and developed by Darwin, in particular, which provided a firm ground for understanding the basic biological and psychological endowment of human nature. According to Westermarck, the biological theory of evolution (including the knowledge it provided of the basic human endowment of sensation, perception, instinct, emotion and the like), provided the firm foundation for the observational and experimental science of psychology which both Mill and Comte had advocated. The theory of evolution provided the basis for many of those fundamental 'laws of life and mind' to which Comte and Mill had referred. It made possible a systematic and testable exploration of certain general propositions about human psychology and of the social institutions which always appeared to develop in societies on the basis of them. In this, Westermarck drew very considerably from (and followed very closely) the ideas of Adam Smith in his book on the *Theory of Moral Sentiments*, as well as from the work of Darwin. Adam Smith's study had been another early exploration of the ways in which the basic psychological endowment of human nature appeared to lead necessarily to certain rules and institutions in society, and to the insistence upon certain moral qualities, and qualities of character, among its members. Westermarck believed that the new theory of evolution reinforced this kind of theory, and now offered firm ground for the kind of hypotheses that Comte and Mill had thought necessary in explaining *how* social factors operated upon the basic psychological endowment of man to produce social institutions and the changes which took place in them. Perhaps it is also worth noting that Westermarck not only drew upon Smith, Darwin, and Mill; he was also a personal friend of Shand—who had developed the theory of the 'sentiments' with John Stuart Mill's 'ethology' (the science of character) centrally in mind—and he also took these ideas fully into account.

It goes without saying that the 'evolutionary' analysis of Herbert Spencer had also exerted a tremendous influence upon Westermarck, but here we will only note again that Westermarck himself did not put forward a total schema of social evolution (i.e. of the evolutionary changes of various kinds of societies); he stressed instead the way in which the Darwinian theory of *biological* evolution was of central importance *within* sociology for giving a causal account of the necessary emergence of social institutions. Westermarck's 'evolutionary' theory in sociology was very specific and limited to this; though, as we shall see later, he had a certain developmental theory too. At any rate, here was a clear continuity of the centrality of the notion of evolution in sociological theory, and a specific development of it.

The most important point for understanding the direction and the central concern of Westermarck's work, however, is the fact that he was, prior to and during his work as a sociologist, a moral philosopher. But, exactly like Sumner, he was, as such, extremely impatient with the orthodox methods of philosophical ethics. Ethics, Westermarck thought, was bedevilled by too predominant a concern with 'ratiocination' in abstraction from any serious study of the *facts* of morality. It was essential, he felt, before one could reflect adequately (with both clarity and *sufficiency*), about the nature of moral judgments, that one should have a wide-ranging *knowledge* of what such moral judgments were actually like in human societies. His own primary concern, in turning to sociology, was therefore to collect and establish a broad and detailed body of knowledge about the *facts* of moral behaviour, the actual nature of moral judgments, the actual roots and components of moral experience, and the functions which they fulfilled in society. Philosophers, he said, ought not to 'waste their ingenuity in sophisma about the sovereignty of law and its independence of the realm of justice', but could more profitably 'study the moral consciousness as a fact'. They might then, he maintained, be in a better position both to understand, and to serve humanity.

The comparative study of morals in society was therefore his central concern, but it is clear from all this that his approach was different from all earlier studies (other, perhaps, than that of Sumner) in that it incorporated biology, psychology and sociology as well as philosophical ethics. Continuity and development were, again, clearly in evidence. The great similarity of his conclusions with those of men like Ward, Sumner and Tönnies—and with those of men to whom we shall come later—like Durkheim and Pareto—will be seen when we turn to outline his ideas in some detail.

(III) WESTERMARCK AND THE CENTRALITY OF MORALITY: A CLEAR SIMILARITY WITH TÖNNIES

One such similarity can, however, be pointed out at once because it is so striking, and constitutes such a strong continuity (running through Ward, Sumner, Tönnies and on into men like Pareto), that it deserves very considerable emphasis.

We have indicated with sufficient clarity the centrality of morality in society (the fact that values actually *constituted* the core of the institutions of society as 'sanctions'), which formed the focus of

Westermarck's theoretical orientation, and how this was the continuity of a central persuasion among the writers before him; but now the degree of this continuity can be stressed much more firmly. And in doing this we shall be able to see a link of complete agreement between Tönnies and Westermarck in their developments of evolutionary theory. For it turns out to be the case that both these men were not only agreed about the centrality of moral values in the nature of institutions, but also about the particular biological and psychological components which went into the formation of them.

We have seen that Tönnies emphasized natural *instinct*, the formation of *habit*, and the establishing of *sentiments*, in the gradual establishing of *custom* in communities. Resting his arguments on the theories of Adam Smith and supporting them by the new ideas of Darwin, Westermarck put forward exactly the same kind of analysis. We shall come to a clear picture of his 'model' in a moment, but here it is enough to see that exactly the same components and concepts were involved.

But here we can introduce one of the points of criticism with which we ended our discussion of Tönnies. There, we noted that Tönnies' account of the 'rational will' was such as to give the impression of a rather one-sided relation between *reason* and 'feeling'. One difference of Westermarck lay here: that he introduced reason as something which operated in such a way as to qualify and change feeling (and moral judgments) in certain ways which he termed 'enlightened'. Actually, he himself was by no means free from ambiguity here, and we shall see that this was an issue of argument which passed on into the work of Hobhouse before it came to be clarified satisfactorily.

Here again, however, was a clear continuity of themes and of an agreement upon the elements which had to be taken into account in any satisfactory analysis of them. Perhaps this particular continuity can be best emphasized by drawing attention to the very close agreement between Sumner, Tönnies and Westermarck on all this. We shall argue right at the end of our study that the position which these men adopted, and its strong continuity—from Adam Smith to Westermarck and beyond—has existed because it is *true*; and that it must be incorporated, as a permanent element, in sociological analysis.

(IV) WESTERMARCK'S CONCEPTION OF SOCIOLOGICAL METHODS
   AND OF THE 'CAUSES' OF SOCIAL INSTITUTIONS

Some care must be taken to be clear in our assessment of Westermarck's conception of sociology and its methods for a number of reasons. First of all, methodology was not Westermarck's strong point; neither was it a pre-occupation which appealed to him. Like Tönnies, he was anxious to be about the study of his own theoretical and empirical interests, and his methodological comments were relatively brief, and given in the context of, or by way of preface to, his substantive studies. Perhaps because of this, however, Westermarck has sometimes been thought of as having no systematic empiricism at all—of being a cloudy conjecturalist, or an old-time speculative philosopher, so to speak; and sometimes as being so unorganized in his empirical collection of facts as to have no systematic theory whatever. It is necessary, therefore, to look at his actual statements about method, in order to show that any extreme judgments of this kind are unwarranted. But there is a more particular reason for doing this: which is that Westermarck is (it seems to me) often quite basically misunderstood with regard to what he was trying to claim as an account of the 'causes' of 'sanctions' at the heart of 'institutions'. This too can be clarified by examining carefully what he had to say about his assumptions concerning his methods of study.

It is almost enough to say that Westermarck wanted so much to get on with studying the *facts*, that he thought it a fairly straightforward matter simply to indicate the sources of his information and the methods he had it in mind to pursue in order to establish testable knowledge about them. His proposals were very simple and clear.

'It is in the firm conviction' (he wrote, at the beginning of the book on the history of human marriage) 'that the history of human civilization should be made an object of as scientific a treatment as the history of organic nature, that I write this book. Like the phenomena of physical and psychical life, those of social life should be classified into certain groups, and each group investigated with regard to its origin and development. Only when treated in this way can history lay claim to the rank and honour of a science in the highest sense of the term, as forming an important part of sociology, the youngest of the principal branches of learning.

Descriptive historiography has no higher object than that of offering materials to this science. It can, however, but very inadequately, fulfil this task. The written evidences of history do not reach far into antiquity. They give us information about times when the scale of civilization was already comparatively high, but scarcely anything more. As to the origin and early development of social institutions, they leave us entirely in the dark. The sociologist cannot rest content with this, but the information which historical documents are unable to afford him may be, to a great extent, obtained from ethnography.'*

* *The History of Human Marriage*, Macmillan, 1891, p. 1.

In short, Westermarck proposed the classification and the comparative and historical study of institutions, as laid down by Comte, Mill, Spencer, and the early Americans before him, though, it must be said, without anything approaching the analytical care which they had shown. One important difference must be noted very particularly, and it is here that Westermarck's chief deficiency lay, though, taking his work as a whole into account, it seems to me not very serious. The actual method of classification and comparison he followed was that proposed by Tylor, the anthropologist, and was a rough and ready 'statistical' method of investigating the development of institutions. Tylor had maintained that causal relations among social facts could be discovered by way of tabulation and classification. As Westermarck put it:

'The particular rules of the different peoples are to be scheduled out into tables, so as to indicate the adhesions or relations of co-existence of each custom, showing which peoples have the same custom and what other customs accompany it or lie apart from it. If then, starting with any two customs, the number of their adhesions is found to be much greater than the number of times they would co-exist, according to the ordinary law of chance-distribution—which number is calculated from the total number of peoples classified and the number of occurrences of each custom —we may infer that there is some causal connection between the two customs.'*

This was practically the same method as that used by Hobhouse, Wheeler and Ginsberg in their study of *The Material Culture and the Social Institutions of the Simpler Peoples*. They, however, confined this method to uncovering the correlations between institutions in one range of societies only: the non-literate, 'primitive' societies. Westermarck applied it, quite literally, to *all* kinds of society; to all those societies which had emerged in the development of human civilization about which knowledge could be gleaned. Obviously, a comparative study of this kind was likely to be of the greatest worth; was likely to produce a large body of empirical knowledge (as Mill would put it: a large number of *empirical generalizations*) concerning the social regularities of mankind. However, the deficiency to be noted is that Tylor and Westermarck grouped and compared institutions which had been isolated by this act of selection from the 'whole societies' (the 'social systems') of which they were a part. Westermarck was far from being ignorant of the fact that institutions could only thoroughly be understood within the context of the social systems within which they existed, but nonetheless, he did not take this fact centrally into account in his comparative

* *Op. cit.*, pp. 4–5.

studies. This was rather strange in view of his knowledge of the methods proposed by Mill and Spencer in particular, and shows, I think, that Westermarck was as much influenced by particular anthropologists as by earlier sociological writers. However, this deficiency in his *conception* and use of the comparative method did not stand seriously in the way of what he himself was trying to do.

Having pointed out the inadequacy of historical data for understanding the origin, early nature, and development of social institutions, Westermarck then asked—how far it was possible, from ethnographical facts, to acquire reliable information concerning the early history of mankind. He proposed two immediate methods of dealing with this question.

Firstly, he claimed, we should try to establish the *causes* of these social phenomena. Then from the wide prevalence of the causes, we might well be able to infer the wide prevalence of the institutions themselves. 'The former must be assumed to have operated . . .' unless '. . . checked by other causes.'

The causes on which social phenomena are dependent fall within the domain of different sciences, biology, psychology, or sociology. The reader will find that I put particular stress upon the psychological* causes, which have often been deplorably overlooked or only imperfectly touched upon, and more especially do I believe that the mere instincts* have played a very important part in the origin of social institutions and rules.'

It is perfectly clear from this, that Westermarck saw social institutions as being rooted in man's basic endowment of *instincts*. Social institutions were social arrangements, procedures, regulations, made necessary by the existence of the instincts.

Westermarck's second important point of method here was simply that we should collect and collate as many facts as possible.

'If historical researches based on ethnography,' he wrote, 'are to be crowned with success, the first condition is that there shall be a rich material. It is only by comparing a large number of facts that we may hope to find the cause or causes on which a social phenomenon is dependent.'†

It was particularly important to have a rich assemblage of material

---

* *Op. cit.*, p. 5. It should be noted here that Westermarck was quite deliberately emphasizing the significance of *psychology* for sociology and, more particularly (and as a part of the biological theory of evolution), that he quite deliberately emphasized the importance of '*instinct*' as being at the roots of social institutions.
† *Ibid.*, p. 4.

also, Westermarck argued, because of the unreliability of many of the available sources of knowledge.

'What is wanting in quality must be made up for in quantity, and he who does not give himself the trouble to read through a voluminous literature of ethnography should never enter into speculations on the origin and early development of human civilization.'*

Two or three other subsidiary points of methodology were also stated.

We could not attempt an *exact* study of the earlier stages of human development, Westermarck thought, excepting by the use of guide-lines suggested by at least *some* previous knowledge of them. Fortunately, he said, some knowledge was already established about them which could be considered to be above the level of mere hypothesis, and he quoted the statement of Sir John Lubbock with approval:

'. . . that man was at first a mere savage and that the course of history, has on the whole, been a progress towards civilization, though at some times, and at some times for centuries, some races have been stationary or even have retrograded.'†

Westermarck recognized quite plainly, however, that all *contemporary* primitive societies were likely to differ considerably in their conditions from the primitive tribes which (*chronologically*) had first emerged in the history of man, and that our knowledge of contemporary primitive peoples had to be used with this qualification in mind. The development of human society was one which, over a very long period of time, had moved from simple groups who were descendants of some ape-like ancestor, and who must have struggled with extraordinarily primitive conditions, to the complex civilizations of which historical records now provide us with knowledge. In our method then, this over-all pattern of gradual, cumulative change; this perspective of social development; could be assumed as a perspective for guidance.

We could also assume, Westermarck maintained, that all the basic physical and mental qualities that man now has, and has in common with those animal species nearest to him in the evolutionary scale, must have come into existence as an outcome of biological adaptation in the earliest stages of human civilization. That is: that the basic physical and psychological endowment of the human species was the same in the earliest historical times as it is now.

* *Op. cit.*, p. 5.   † *Op. cit.*, p. 4.

The changes brought about in man between then and now were likely to be changes due predominantly to the changed *social* conditions of man, not to any *genetic* difference in his nature.

A third point of warning in the matter of method which Westermarck made (and this was made in consciousness of the work of other anthropologists, such as Maclennan) was that:

'We must be extremely careful not to regard as rudiments, customs which may be more satisfactorily explained otherwise.'

Westermarck made this particular point because he believed that many errors had been made by earlier students of anthropology and history by regarding institutions that existed among the *present-day* simpler societies as being conjectural evidence of *earlier* stages of social development. Such conjectures, he thought, should be regarded with great care. Like Radcliffe-Brown a little later, Westermarck disapproved of '*conjectural history*'.

A fourth subsidiary point of Westermarck's method, of great interest nowadays, is that he was strongly in favour of carrying the comparative method for elucidating the *causes* of social institutions beyond the study of man alone to the study of other animal species. In a word, Westermarck was much in favour of what we have come to call 'comparative psychology', and what has come more recently to be called 'Comparative Ethology'.* He wrote in his introduction to the study of human marriage:

'The expression, "human marriage", will probably be regarded by most people as an improper tautology, but, as we shall see, marriage in the natural history sense of the term, does not belong exclusively to our own species. No more fundamental difference between man and other animals should be implied in sociological than in biological and psychological terminology. Arbitrary classifications do science much injury.'†

Having outlined all these points of method, Westermarck then concluded:

'It is only by strictly keeping to these principles that we may hope to derive information touching the early history of man. In doing so, the student will be on his guard against rash conclusions. Considering that he has to make out the primary sources of social phenomena before writing their history, he will avoid assuming a custom to be primitive only because at the first glance it appears so. He will avoid making rules of exceptions and constructing the history of human development on the immediate ground of isolated facts. It is true that the critical sociologist, on account of the deficiency of our knowledge, very often has to be content with hypotheses and doubtful presumptions. At any rate, the

---

* The comparative study of animal behaviour.   †*Op. cit.*, p. 6.

interests of science are better looked to if we readily acknowledge our ignorance than if we pass off vague guesses as established truths.'*

The scientific temper and care of Westermarck's work is clearly beyond doubt, and many of his points which we have only briefly touched upon deserve careful emphasis when one considers that, for some reason, only certain recent anthropologists—such as Malinowski and Radcliffe-Brown—have been selected as being 'modern' in their scientific approaches.†

Westermarck's method, then, was:

(1) The classification of those social institutions in all societies which were distinguished by the existence of *sanctions:* which therefore involved moral ideas, moral values, and attendant procedures and rules;

(2) a detailed comparative study of their nature at the level of actual social behaviour and social function;

(3) an exploration of the biological and psychological facts in which they were rooted, and which appeared, universally, to attend them; and (in possession of this collection of social facts, and the hypothetical causes of them);

(4) an elucidation of the changes and developments of these 'sanctions' which had taken place in the history of all known societies.

In addition, Westermarck devoted a good deal of attention to making meticulously clear the sources of his knowledge, and considering with much care the degree of reliability of these sources. He was, in fact, rigorously and critically empirical in method.

The documentary material upon which he drew consisted of:

'The records of moral maxims and sentiments found in proverbs, literary and philosophical works, and religious codes.'‡

And, furthermore:

'The sources, which, from an evolutionary point of view, are of the most comprehensive importance for our study, are tribal and national customs and laws.'‡

---

* *Op. cit.*, p. 6.

† Again, it is well worth emphasis that Westermarck took much of the work of Malinowski quite fully into account. Malinowski was not noticeably more *recent* or more *modern* than Westermarck; he was only, as we shall see later, more *conspicuous*, and chiefly because of his teaching of a relatively simple 'functionalism': in short, for *seeming* to commit what we called earlier the 'error of Social Anthropology'. Actually, as we shall see, Malinowski was, himself, not anywhere near being as prone to this error as some of those who were infected by him, and who adopted 'functionalism' almost as a fashion.

‡ *The Origin and Development of the Moral Ideas*, Macmillan, 1912, Vol. 1, p. 158.

Also, however, Westermarck realized, indeed insisted upon, the value of *actual field work* in addition to the searching scrutiny of documentary evidence, and, as we have already seen, he undertook field work of this kind in Morocco. Westermarck was thus one of the pioneers in undertaking field work in relation to comparative and theoretical sociology (as distinct from what Tönnies called 'sociography') and those who continually maintain that, in the past making of sociology, the construction of large-scale theories has taken place at a curious distance from the detailed study of facts, will see that this is quite demonstrably wrong. The work of Westermarck is an example of scholarly study in which, at one and the same time, theories were being formulated to explain a wide, systematic survey of concrete facts, and the investigation of facts was being undertaken in the light of testable assumptions—both at the level of documentary evidence and at the level of face-to-face observation in the field. Indeed, one of the characteristics common to all theorists we are considering in this section on the 'Developments' of sociology (Tönnies, Hobhouse, Durkheim, Weber, etc.) is the very close relationship between theory-construction and investigation of facts in the studies they pursued. *All* these men insisted that theories should be constructed in order to produce definitive studies of a specified range of social facts. They moved from the 'theory' (the over-all 'conspectus') of the nineteenth century to the 'theories' of the twentieth in order to deepen and demonstrate the worth of their subject.

The one thing that this outline of Westermarck's methods has perhaps not yet made as clear as is desirable is what exactly he had in mind when speaking of the 'causes' of social institutions. In fact, when speaking of both the 'origins' and 'causes' of sanctioned relationships, he had in mind *not* some original, chronological early events, but rather *the basic psychological propensities* (the instincts, emotions, habits, and sentiments) which were explicable in terms of biological evolution and the attendant elements of social experience and response to which they gave rise, which seemed, universally, to make these institutions *necessary*. To use the earlier language of John Stuart Mill, Westermarck was really seeking to uncover the *functional requisites* of human society: the psychological and social conditions which made certain sets of 'sanctioned relationships' indispensable. This, however, will become more satisfactorily clear as we turn to Westermarck's actual theories.

The best way of outlining these is to consider them in the order in which he himself undertook them: first of all, concerning ourselves with the 'sanctions' in society relating to the regulation of sexuality and procreation in particular—the institutions comprising 'marriage and the family'; and secondly, considering Westermarck's extension of this same theoretical approach to the explanation of the origin and development of *all* the moral ideas in human society.

The Theory of Human Marriage

Westermarck's analysis of the 'causes' of marriage as a universal institution in human society; his account of the 'history of human marriage'; was a very specific forerunner (almost a pilot study—though that is rather too simple a term for what was, in fact, a very extensive investigation) of his total theory of the 'causes' of 'sanctions' in society. It will therefore be enough if we give a brief summary account of it simply to help us to move to a full understanding of the larger study, and, particularly, to Westermarck's fundamental theoretical position.

First of all, Westermarck accepted and adopted Darwin's theory of evolution (with its stress upon natural selection as the factor chiefly determining the *survival* of species) as a substantiation, or supporting explanation, of his view that the family, as a universal group in human society, was a primal fundamental form of social organization based upon the *instinctual* endowment of man; that it was rooted in certain universal factors—biological and psychological—which man inherited.

In the case of the human species, the number of offspring produced in any one birth was small. Also the length of time during which the human offspring was utterly dependent upon its parents, was more prolonged than in any other species. The biological conditions ensuring the survival of both individual and race must therefore have included prolonged parental protection. Natural selection was responsible for establishing these necessary biological conditions, by equipping mankind with an appropriate instinctual endowment whereby the male was led to stay with the female (or females), and their young, and to protect them. These basic biological conditions, the close bonds initiated by the activation of the instincts, established the *habit* whereby male and female came to live together and rear their offspring together. Let us notice, by the way, that Westermarck did *not* confine his analysis purely to the *enumeration* of a *set of instincts* (one common criticism of any account of instinct which is now as dead as the theory of instincts itself was once thought to be). He described, going beyond this, how instinctual impulses, dispositions and communications, led to the establishment of *habits* and the formation of *sentiments* in human experience. These relationships, established upon the basis of instinct, habit, sentiment, then came—with the extension to others attendant upon sympathy—to be *approved* among all the people of the community. They now possessed the general, obligatory qualities of the *sanction* of custom and law. Marriage was an integral part of these relationships between the sexes, carrying the obligations of desired and approved bonds and duties between parents and children in the family. Marriage was the *institutionalized* procedure, whereby the family was founded in society; whereby the appropriate 'sanctions'—the set of rights, duties, obligations regulating sex and parenthood—were entered into and sustained. 'Marriage', Westermarck said, 'is rooted in the family rather than the family in marriage.'

Because of this firm foundation, this deep-rootedness, of some form of the family and marriage in the fundamental instinctual nature of man, Westermarck was convinced that the family and marriage would always exist as a group of primary importance in society despite far-reaching changes in other social institutions.* There is nowadays little doubt that this view of Westermarck's is sound and is largely supported by current psychology and by those sociological studies that have been undertaken since Westermarck's time. And it is important to see that this theory of the nature of the human family and the institution of marriage rests upon facts and hypotheses drawn from all three levels of biology, psychology and comparative sociology. This seems to be a good and valid example of the kind of position and method which Comte and Mill sought to achieve—in which the empirical generalizations concerning the regularities of social institutions (whether of persistence or change) could be shown to be validly grounded in the fundamental 'laws of life and mind' (of biology and psychology). Or, as Mill put it, if the social *'requisite'* resting upon certain biological and psychological facts of human nature is found, by the comparative study of all known societies, to be dealt with by a certain distinctive kind of social institution (such as those of family, marriage, and kinship), then: '. . . the consilience of the two processes raises the evidence to proof, and the generalizations to the rank of scientific truths.'

During the course of his study of marriage and the family, Westermarck made many important points and discussed many interesting questions since his object was to explore fully all the *moral feelings* or the *sanctions* relating to the regulation of sex and parenthood, but it is not, of course, to our purpose to give a detailed account of these.

* Not, however, without detailed qualification. After his careful discussion in *The Future of Marriage in Western Civilization*, his last words were: 'But although such assumptions possess a very considerable degree of certainty so far as the near future is concerned, they cannot lay claim to everlasting infallibility . . . If there will be a time when conjugal and parental sentiments have vanished, I think that nothing in the world can save marriage and the family from destruction.'

He offered, for example, an account of the 'incest taboo' which is a universal fact of social regulation and kinship organization, and, as such, requires explanation and understanding. He also eliminated completely, and with firm evidence, the view that mankind was, in its primal condition, promiscuous, and that the family and marriage were somehow subsequently *devised* by human reason and social regulation. He showed quite definitely that we never have any knowledge of human groups in which some form of marriage and the family does not exist, and that where such instances appear to exist, they are of the nature of negligible exceptions. He also showed that those animal species closest to man in the evolutionary scale also live in simple family groupings, so that the family, and even a rudimentary kind of 'marriage'—i.e. an instinctively 'ritualized'* and sustained mating relationship—can be taken as a fundamental form of *social* organization rooted firmly in the instincts and the needs of the species.†

Another point of interest is that Westermarck paid much attention to the role of the *father* in the family. For some curious reason, many people have nowadays come to believe that the biology of parenthood is confined to mothers. Parental instincts, it seems, are feelings which smoulder only within the female breast, and though many people can clearly see that it is a biological fact of human nature that *mothers* are led to care for their children, they cannot believe that *fathers* have this same kind of natural propensity. It is worthwhile to note that our modern views are the *exception* in human history! Westermarck presented much evidence to show that they were rather absurd, and that the father, as well as the mother, has always been of importance within the structure and functions of the family unit, and, indeed, has always wanted to be so, from the earliest times.

'I do not, of course, deny,' he wrote, 'that the tie which bound the children to the mother was much more intimate and more lasting than that which bound them to the father, but it seems to me that the only result to which a critical investigation of facts can lead us is that in all probability there has been *no* stage of human development when marriage has *not* existed, and that the father has *always* been, as a rule, the protector of his family,'‡

---

* If this language seems strange, compare with the findings of contemporary 'Comparative Ethology', which seem to support Westermarck fully in this.
† It is also worth pointing out that there is no necessary distinction, or dichotomy, or juxtaposition, between the 'psychological' (including the 'instinctual') and the 'social'. In fact, the bio-psychological endowment of most species is such as to *include* social dispositions and social patterns of behaviour. The *social* is in many respects *natural*!
‡ *History of Human Marriage*, p. 50.

In this way, then, Westermarck sought to demonstrate that the universality of 'sanctions' pertaining to sexual conduct and parenthood; the universality of marriage and the family in human society, were rooted in universal features of *instinct* and *emotion* established in the nature of the human species by the process of biological evolution, and by the universal (and attendant) processes of *habit* and *sentiment* formation and the gradual emergence of *custom*. This account is better illustrated, however, in Westermarck's general theory of the 'moral ideas'.

The Origin and Development of the Moral Ideas

Here, we will confine ourselves to a straightforward account of Westermarck's theory, but it is necessary, in view of certain criticisms of his work, to comment separately (and later) on his notions of ethical 'subjectivism' and ethical 'relativity'. For the present it is best to see quite directly what Westermarck claimed (*a*) about the 'origins' and (*b*) about the 'development' of moral ideas, and it is here that we shall come to see more fully and accurately what he meant by clarifying the 'causes' of 'sanctions' and 'institutions'.

(*a*) *The* Origin *of the Moral Ideas*
In this much larger study, Westermarck extended to *all* moral ideas, to *all* institutions sanctioned in society, the theory and the methods that he had successfully applied in his study of the family and marriage (i.e. the study of the moral ideas, the 'sanctions', pertaining especially to sex). However, he was careful to begin by pointing out that the study of sanctioned relationships in human society must be *circumscribed*, must be limited, in some way, for in many human societies even the slightest kind of behaviour may be governed by sanctions; may be intricately regulated on the basis of custom, or 'immemorial usage'. In such societies, things must be done *now* in certain ways simply because *they have always been done* in that way. He gave one or two examples.

'Among the Wanika, if a man dares to improve the style of his hut, to make a larger doorway than is customary; if he should wear a finer or different style of dress to that of his fellows, he is instantly fined.'*

Similarly if, during the performance of a ceremony:

'. . . the ancestors of an Australian native were in the habit of painting a white line across the forehead, their descendants must do the same.'*

* *The Origin and Development of the Moral Ideas*, Vol. 1, p. 327.

101

Amongst the simpler societies communities had customs and fixed rules for every possible circumstance, no matter how slight. In view of this, he argued:

'It is necessary that we should restrict outselves to the more important modes of conduct with which the moral consciousness of mankind is concerned. These modes of conduct may be conveniently divided, into six groups. The first group includes such acts, forebearances, and omissions as directly concern the interests of other men, their life or bodily integrity, their freedom, honour, property and so forth. The second includes such acts, forebearances and omissions as chiefly concern a man's own welfare, such as suicide, temperance, asceticism. The third group, which partly coincides with, but partly differs from, both the first and the second, refers to the sexual relations of men. The fourth includes their conduct towards the lower animals. The fifth their conduct towards dead persons. The sixth their conduct towards beings, real or imaginary, that they regard as supernatural. We shall examine each of these groups separately in the above order, and not being content with a mere description of facts, we shall try to discover the principle which lies at the bottom of the moral judgment in each particular case.'*

Again, it is clear from this that Westermarck was not undertaking a comparative study only to establish empirical generalizations. He was attempting also, given these empirical regularities, to uncover causal explanations by deductions and hypotheses drawn from his knowledge of human psychology, which, in its turn was rooted in biological evolution.

'We shall,' he said, 'proceed to discuss in detail and from an evolutionary point of view the various elements of which the subjects of moral judgments consist.'†

In *all* human relationships then (as in the case of the family and marriage) Westermarck based his account of moral impulses, judgments and rules primarily upon those basic instincts and emotions which, according to the theory of evolution, were established by heredity. It was on this basis that Westermarck developed further the arguments of Adam Smith who, in *The Theory of Moral Sentiments*, had rested his own analysis upon the central importance (for morality) of human *sympathy*, and upon the feelings of *approval* or *disapproval* of particular acts experienced in terms of this sympathy. Westermarck also agreed with, and utilized, Smith's emphasis upon the basic importance of the emotions of *gratitude* and *resentment*. These emotions, he now argued, possessed biological

* *The Origin and Development of the Moral Ideas*, Vol. 1, p. 328.
† *Ibid.*, p. 216.

survival value for the species. They were not in themselves moral, however, They *became* moral when, after society had come gradually to recognize and sanction the modes of behaviour to which they referred, they acquired the qualities of *generality, disinterestedness* and *impartiality*.

They became general and impartial since, when sanctioned by society, they applied to *all* members of the community. They were no longer confined only to the self-centred interests of particular individuals. They became disinterested in that men in society were now able to sympathize with other men imaginatively, as it were; at a distance; in relation to their known or appreciated situation, and not only in relation to people of their own immediate acquaintance with whom they were personally involved. In short, these feelings and judgments became part of the custom of the people. The 'sanctions' became *institutionalized*.

No matter how complex and sophisticated in a large civilization these customary moral rules might become, Westermarck maintained that they continued to be upheld only by the fundamental fact that, if broken, they aroused strong disapproval. The force which sustained moral rules, sanctioned institutions, in *all* communities—simple or complex—stemmed in the last analysis from those emotions of gratitude and resentment, approval and disapproval, and sympathy, which were clustered about certain sets of habits and sentiments, and which were themselves, in turn, rooted in fundamental instinct.

The moral ideas which lay at the heart of all human institutions, 'originated' and regulated certain modes of behaviour. Ultimately, they rested upon the fundamental instinctual dispositions of man, his attendant emotions of approval and disapproval, gratitude and resentment, and his capacity for sympathy. The important point to emphasize very strongly here was that the emergence and formulation of *moral* ideas (of *sanctions*) in human society was *actually the process of institutionalization*. The sanctions, the moral ideas, *were* the institutions. This is a point I very much want us to hold firmly in mind—remembering all that we have said before about the ways in which all the earlier theorists (in one way or another) spoke about the folkways and mores, the institutions, the established relations of men to each other in their practical activities, as stemming from the co-operation and conflict of men as they sought their natural interest, their 'natural will' and the like, in working upon nature. This essential point—that man is essentially and distinctively a *moral* being; a being in whose nature *will* and *character* are distinctive; and that the human *social* order is essentially and distinctively a *moral* order—will, I think, come to be seen as one

103

WESTERMARCK'S SYSTEM OF ANALYSIS

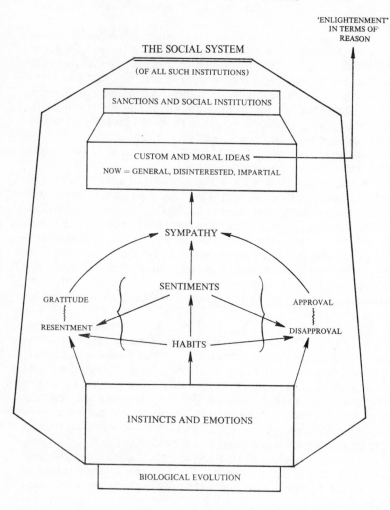

'ENLIGHTENMENT'
IN TERMS OF
REASON

THE SOCIAL SYSTEM

(OF ALL SUCH INSTITUTIONS)

SANCTIONS AND SOCIAL INSTITUTIONS

CUSTOM AND MORAL IDEAS

NOW = GENERAL, DISINTERESTED, IMPARTIAL

SYMPATHY

SENTIMENTS

GRATITUDE

RESENTMENT

APPROVAL

DISAPPROVAL

HABITS

INSTINCTS AND EMOTIONS

BIOLOGICAL EVOLUTION

of the most important central points of our study. But here, I want only to recall the insistences of earlier theorists, to note Westermarck's reinforcement of this point of view, and to insist again that *institutionalization* (*the establishment of a societal order; the creation of social systems*) *is actually and essentially a* MORAL *process.*

Westermarck's analysis might be made more clear by the simple diagrammatic representation opposite.

(b) *The* Development *of the Moral Ideas*

So much for the basis of the *origin* of moral ideas: the psychological endowment of man, and the sequence of action, habit, sentiment, sanctions, which were the 'causes' giving rise to moral rules and institutions. Westermarck's further theory as to the *development* of moral ideas was entirely a matter of his views concerning the place of reason in morality; the function of reason in reflecting upon these customarily given moral judgments, and the ways in which, by such reflection, it could affect and change them. Westermarck argued that reflection could change (and had changed) our moral feelings and judgments in a number of ways.

Firstly, our emotions of approval or disapproval were sometimes altered as our knowledge of a certain situation increased. When we came to know more about the set of circumstances in which a certain action had been performed, and also about the detailed influences at work upon the character of the agent who had performed it, our judgment of the 'rights or wrongs' of the action was sometimes changed. A good example of what Westermarck had in mind is our whole change of attitude towards pathological criminals in our own day. Some people who were thought morally blameworthy a few decades ago are now known to be suffering from certain kinds of mental illness. Whilst still disapproving of the *acts* they commit, we no longer, to the same extent, have the same feelings of disapproval towards the criminals themselves. Similarly, quite apart from extreme pathological conditions, even when we know that a person is normally in full command of his actions, we are nonetheless inclined to a more lenient view of a wrong action he has committed if we gain a deeper understanding of particularly harrowing circumstances which were provoking him at the time. In these ways, Westermarck argued, reflection could modify our feelings, change our jugments, and, let us note, 'enlighten' our moral ideas.

Our feelings of approval and disapproval could also change when, on reflection, we came to realize that we held these particular feelings simply because of the social context within which we ourselves had been born and brought up. We might well come to see that some of our feelings and personal judgments of others were due to attitudes which we held simply because of the society, the social group, or the social class of which we had always been members. Reflection upon this could bring about an increasing understanding of the points of view of others; an increasing tolerance of *their* subjectively held convictions; and if this growing tolerance was a mutual or reciprocal thing, our moral ideas and judgments could change considerably. *Irrelevant* factors and differences could come to be stripped away from our judgments, leaving a core of principles about which we might more easily reach agreement with others; which could be rationally upheld.

Some of the value judgments which people held in different societies or in different groups clearly rested, also, upon the religious beliefs, doctrines, or 'superstitions' of these societies. A growth and change of knowledge and following reflection could obviously change these. Our judgments concerning the rightness or wrongness of human sacrifice, of witchcraft, of homosexuality, for example, have demonstrably changed as our knowledge has grown beyond that of the religious beliefs on the basis of which these judgments of value seem first to have been formed. Nowadays, instead of burning people at the stake we send them to hospital; and, in the case of homosexuality, have no difficulty in accepting people as our friends in spite of their different feelings, different tastes, and different points of view.

Westermarck also pointed out that certain customs which were held *generally* in a society sometimes had their origin, not in *all* the people of the community, but in the powerful influences of some particular privileged class, or group. The fact that most people conformed with these rules and judgments in a society, and even accepted them, might stem *not* from considered *moral* grounds at all, but purely from social emulation. And again, an extension of knowledge and reflection could lead people to probe more deeply below this level of conventional acceptance. They might seek some more fundamental basis of moral rules; again—rules more rationally defensible; whereupon those which were rooted in privilege, possessing no grounds of justification beyond this, could be rejected.

After his very wide and painstaking comparative study, Westermarck claimed that there had, in fact, been a progressive 'enlightenment' in these kinds of directions in human society. Without claiming any historical *inevitability* (let it be noted) about this, his opinion was that such 'enlightenment' would be likely to increase as knowledge and reason increased. The extension of knowledge and considered reflection would be likely to establish a more reliable basis for a responsible direction of social processes.

This, then, was Westermarck's theory of the 'origins' and the kinds of 'development' of the moral ideas which were the institutionalized sanctions of society. It will be seen that, in slightly different terms, this was a theory of the origin and development of *society itself*: a theory which saw the growth of a systematic order of social institutions rooted in certain constellations of psychological impulse and emotion established by heredity, and, as an ongoing development, sequences of change brought about by knowledge and reflection. Though more detailed in its account of the connectedness between biological evolution, inherited psychological conditions, and the processes of 'institutionalization'; and though bringing theories such as those of Darwin and Adam Smith together in a new way; it can be seen to be fully in accord with the theories of social evolution which had preceded it and which had emphasized the centrality of knowledge and purpose for the 'development' of social orders which had slowly taken shape in terms of earlier 'genetic' causes. Westermarck's theory was clearly a development of certain specific dimensions within this entire perspective of social evolution, whilst being of quite basic and general importance for it; and its extremely close similarity to the analysis provided by Sumner and Tönnies especially scarcely needs pointing out.

We must now, however, dwell a little more on Westermarck's conception of the place of reason in relation to the feelings, and on the implications of this for what has come to be called 'relativity in ethics', because this is an aspect of his work for which he has been much criticized, and which was clarified with greater philosophical accuracy by L. T. Hobhouse.

Ethical Subjectivism and Ethical Relativity

It goes without saying that we would fully expect any wide comparative study of human societies to reveal quite a considerable *diversity* of social institutions. Our common-sense tells us that human communities encounter different geographical conditions the world over, and develop their own historical traditions in relation to them. Differences are to be expected. At the same time, if, as Westermarck claimed (and as our common-sense also suggests to us) moral ideas are rooted in the basic instinctual and emotional characteristics of human nature, then we would also expect to find a basic similarity, a certain universality, of moral concerns and 'sanctions' underlying these circumstantial diversities. We would expect to find a basic *similarity* as well as circumstantial differences in all human societies. And, in fact, Westermarck's study did show this, and did bear out these expectations. This is a point worth emphasis, since—nowadays

—any mention of comparative study seems to give people the idea that wide *diversities* of behaviour will be the rule. This current view rests on recent anthropological monographs describing the relatively strange life of specific 'non-literate' societies. Westermarck's study, better based in its comparative range, showed *both* similarities *and* differences in a more reliable way. It was in his discussion of these similarities and differences, however, that he seemed to present a certain ambiguity with regard to his conception of the relation between reason and feeling, and it is worthwhile to try to clarify this—if only to show that, in the last analysis (as with Sumner and Tönnies), despite his lack of philosophical accuracy, he *did* conclude that reason could serve the feelings, and could reform institutions, in a 'progressive' way.

Westermarck thought that the *differences* of the moral ideas in various societies could be attributed to three main causes.

(I) ENVIRONMENTAL CONDITIONS

When the effects of the different environmental conditions which men had to confront were sufficiently understood, what appeared to be the *same* action was, in fact, seen to have a different character in different situations. In contemporary Britain, for example, infanticide (a parent's killing of his own child) was regarded as an immoral and illegal act and there was a quite general and strong disapproval and condemnation of it. In an Eskimo tribe, however, when the people were confronted by an extremely harsh winter and it became clear that all the members of the tribe could not possibly survive on the limited food supply, it may well become necessary to kill one's own children. There was indeed, among such tribes, sometimes an 'order of priority' as far as killing was concerned. First, perhaps, the dependent aged would be killed (indeed, they may feel it incumbent upon themselves to commit suicide). Secondly, the dependent children would be killed—leaving alive only those adult members of the community who could fend for themselves, and who, if they survived, could have other children and ensure the continuity of the tribe. Even in more complex and 'civilized' societies (as, for example, among the peasantry of traditional China) many people had to endure harsh conditions of poverty, and in such a situation, the action of killing one's child could be felt less blameworthy; an action more easy to understand, perhaps even to sympathize with; than if it were committed by a person enjoying secure conditions of life in a modern industrial society.

(II) KNOWLEDGE OF THE CONSEQUENCES OF ACTIONS

Some differences in the moral ideas in different societies could also be explained in terms of *differences in the knowledge of consequences of certain actions* due to differences in the religious and magical beliefs already mentioned. If the people of a community believed that the sacrifice of human beings in the spring would ensure the fertility of the land during the coming year, then human sacrifice would seem a sensible and necessary, if not a noble, action. And, indeed, in some societies of antiquity people volunteered to sacrifice themselves in this way for the welfare of their community as a whole. In a society possessing scientific knowledge of the causes of the fertility of land, however, in which it was known that there was no connection between human sacrifice and the fertility of soil, human sacrifice would seem stupid and wrong, and if so, would be regarded with strong disapproval.

(III) DEGREES OF 'ALTRUISM'

Some differences in moral ideas and rules could also be accounted for, Westermarck thought, in terms of *the differing degrees of altruism* experienced by individuals and communities. Both individuals and societies had differing conceptions of the range of people to whom their moral rules applied. Individuals might readily recognize duties to members of their own families, but still feel that other people's families were none of their concern. Similarly, the people of a community might feel bound by certain moral precepts in their conduct towards members of their own 'nation' or 'race', but not to the members of *other* nations whom they regarded as being 'inferior' to themselves—to the point, indeed, of thinking that they were not human beings, of the same nature as themselves.

But it was not only, according to Westermarck, that people could have a different *conception* of the range within which their moral rules ought to apply; they might also possess different emotional capacities for sympathetic feeling and, therefore, differing degrees of sensitivity to certain actions in terms of their feelings of 'gratitude and resentment', 'approval and disapproval', and the like. Differing capacities of sensitivity, emotion, sympathy, could result in quite different persuasions concerning the range of one's moral commitments. In this sense, one man could be extremely sensitive to his moral duty to all men throughout the world, whilst another could be 'blind' to his moral duty to a family in the next street. Moral 'duty' was a concomitant of emotional and sympathetic capacity.

None of these differences, of course, need seriously disturb the idea of the universality of moral judgments of the kind that most moral philosophers have insisted upon, since philosophers have never wished to deny the *diversity* of morals, they have only claimed that, following reflection upon them, certain presupposed standards and ideals concerning 'the good life' or 'right action' can be uncovered and clarified. But it was in connection with the *third* set of differences above—correlated differences in emotional dispositions and persuasions about the range of people to whom one's moral rules apply—that Westermarck claimed that there must be a 'relativity' in ethics. This relativity was rooted in the inescapable *subjectivity* of moral emotions and moral judgment. The presumed *objectivity* of moral judgments, Westermarck argued, was a 'chimera'. There could be no moral 'truth' in the sense in which this term is generally understood (as, for example, in science). Having considered the ways in which he thought that moral judgments or 'the moral law' came to 'appear' objective, and having, he thought, rebutted them, he concluded that ethics, if it was to be used as the name for a science, 'can only be to study the moral consciousness as a fact'.

Now it is in connection with this point that Westermarck's ambiguity became evident, and one or two criticisms are necessary concerning his position.

Firstly, it was a curious position for Westermarck to have adopted since, in many other ways, he maintained quite definitely, and believed he had demonstrated, that reason and reflection could effectively *change* and *amend* our subjective feelings. Why then, should he have regarded the emotional dispositions and the extent of sympathy which people possessed as being somehow unalterable; making for unalterable differences in morality? Why should these elements of human experience too not be changed at least to some extent, by conscious awareness, rational reflection, and a consideration of their consequences for the making of judgments?

Secondly, as Morris Ginsberg has pointed out,* with regard to this point in particular Westermarck seemed to erect a false dichotomy, too hard and fast a distinction, between *feeling* on the one hand, and *reason* and *reflection* on the other. Surely it is the case that feeling and reflection are all of a piece in human experience. It is because of disquiet, doubt, and dissatisfaction in our feelings that reflection comes into play. Reason exercises itself in order to uncover and understand the grounds for this disquiet, and to resolve the questions to which it gives rise. If this is so, then reflection is not only a *cognitive* and *logical* matter, but is itself a process of exploration and clarification stemming from, and being pursued

* *The Life and Work of Edward Westermarck.* (In: *Reason and Unreason in Society*)

within the context of our feelings.* This seems, then, an unwarranted dichotomy in Westermarck's analysis, and one which, from different points of view, has been much discussed in philosophy.

Third, however, and this is the most important point for the moment, it is clear that this view placed Westermarck in a position of inconsistency. On the one hand, he wished to claim that ethics were 'relative' to subjective feeling; that there were no objective criteria on which impartial judgment could be exercised between various moral views. On the other hand, when speaking of the development of moral ideas, having clarified the nature of their 'origins', he wished to clarify not only the *changes* which had taken place in them (which would be warranted), but also the *progress* and the *enlightenment* of such changes. But how, if we have no standards for adjudicating between different ethical views 'relative' to the emotional capacities of those who hold them, can we speak of progress and enlightenment at all? Clearly, if we speak of *progress* we must have some standard or criterion in mind (*a*) which is thought to be *demonstrably* good (i.e. on some grounds other than the assertion of one emotional disposition among others), and (*b*) against which the varieties of ethical rules in human societies can be judged. It seems very curious that Westermarck should fall into such a simple inconsistency. But in order to see that he did, in fact, hold this inconsistency, and that it is not one of our own interpretation, we may glance at the following quotations.

Having described his position of 'ethical subjectivism', he went on to try and defend it and, indeed, to maintain that it was an ethically superior position to adopt.

'Could it be brought home to people,' he wrote, 'that there is no absolute† standard in morality, they would perhaps be somewhat more tolerant in their judgments and more apt to listen to the voice of reason. If the right has an objective existence, the moral consciousness has certainly been playing a blind man's buff ever since it was born and will continue to do so until the extinction of the human race, but who does admit this? The

* This was a dichotomy similar to that erected by Tönnies. Tönnies, however, could be understood in that he was quite legitimately exaggerating *types* of willing; the danger lay in our misunderstanding of the exaggerations he drew. Westermarck, as we said earlier, remedied such a danger by emphasizing the more *positive* role of reason in relation to the feelings; and yet he involved himself in ambiguity in another way.

† *Origin and Development*, Vol. 1, p. 20. It may be noted how frequently the terms 'relative' and 'absolute' are used, without examination, as the only exclusive opposites in moral and ethical discussion. They are *not*, of course, exclusive opposites. It is possible to maintain certain elements of 'relativity' in moral judgments and to reject the existence of 'absolute' standards whilst still maintaining that the criteria of ethics are not 'arbitrary' but can be rationally clarified.

popular mind is always inclined to believe that it possesses the knowledge of what is right and wrong and to regard public opinion as the reliable guide of conduct. We have indeed no reason to regret that there are men who rebel against the established rules of morality. It is more deplorable that the rebels are so few and that, consequently, the old rules change so slowly. Far above the vulgar idea that the right is a settled something to which everybody has to adjust his opinions, rises the conviction that it has its existence in each individual mind, capable of any expansion, proclaiming its own right to exist and, if need be, venturing to make a stand against the whole world. Such a conviction makes for progress.'

This passage is utterly *riddled* with inconsistencies; but the logical absurdity of Westermarck's position is made starkly clear in the word 'progress' with which he ends it. How could he possibly believe that his own ethical proposals were 'better' or more 'progressive' than the other ethical opinions to which he referred, if all moral persuasions are subjectively adequate for every person and every society in accordance with the feelings and conceptions they happen to possess? If he wished to maintain a position of subjectivism and relativity in ethics, then in his comparative study of morals he could well have spoken of *similarity*, or *diversity*, or *change*, in systems of morals; which would have been quite consistent and correct. But to use the term progress must imply, whether he himself clearly saw it or not, that reflection could uncover or clarify some *criterion* of judgment in the light of which progress or retrogression could be assessed. And that he did believe in the idea of progress may be seen in another quotation when he was writing about the effect of reflection upon moral judgments.

'The influence of intellectual considerations upon moral judgments,' he wrote, 'is certainly immense. We shall find that the evolution of the moral consciousness to a large extent consists in its development from the unreflecting to the reflecting, from the unenlightened to the enlightened.'

Clearly this implied not only a *factual* change and evolution of moral ideas in society; not only a movement from 'unreflecting' to more carefully 'reflecting' points of view concerning morality; but also a movement from the 'unenlightened' to the 'enlightened'. Westermarck was undoubtedly claiming that some moral points of view were more enlightened than others, and that this constituted progress.

The fourth point of criticism following very closely upon this is simply that, in his own way, Westermarck fell into the same difficulty of method from which Comte, Spencer and Marx had not sufficiently disentangled themselves. That is, his study of the *facts* of social change and development became thoroughly mixed up with his *ethical* assumptions and considerations as to whether these factual changes also constituted a moral advance. For a satisfactory enquiry into this question, it is clear that a study of facts is, in itself, not sufficient. To put it more bluntly: scientific sociology itself cannot answer it. A philosophical clarification of the ethical standards employed in assessing the progress or retrogression of social changes, giving the grounds on which they are adopted, must also be taken into account. It was this, as we shall see, which was a point of method much more correctly handled in the work of Hobhouse.

This criticism does not, however, invalidate in any way the comparative study of the moral facts in various societies that Westermarck achieved. It is a criticism only of Westermarck's views on the relationship between ethics on the one hand, and the comparative study (the sociology) of morals on the other. It is also worth mentioning, though this can by no means be taken as a philosophical defence of Westermarck's position on these points, that his ultimate position was such as almost to ignore all this ambiguity. And—though, no doubt, this is a terrible thing to say academically—I am not at all sure that it mattered. I sometimes think that Westermarck's position was, in all the force of his substantive study, quite plain—and that the sophisticated philosophical holes one can pick in him are of little consequence. He himself rode to the finish, so to speak, with very clear and forthright pronouncements. Here, for example, are some of his concluding statements on the extension of altruism, the moral emotions, and the range of people to whom moral rules were held to apply. Having stressed the fact that differences are still felt between a member of a person's own community and a member of a strange society, Westermarck wrote:

'But although the difference between a fellow countryman and a foreigner has not ceased to affect the moral feelings of men even in the midst of modern civilization, its influence has certainly been decreasing. The doctrine has been set forth, and has been gradually gaining ground, that our duties towards our fellow men are universal duties, not restricted by the limits of country or race. Those who recognize the emotional origin of the rules of duty find no difficulty in explaining all these facts. The expansion of the commandments relating to neighbours coincides with the expansion of the altruistic sentiment.'*

And again:

'Besides the extension of duties towards neighbours so as to embrace

* *Origin and Development*, Vol. II, p. 743.

wider and wider circles of men, there is another point in which the moral ideas of mankind have undergone an important change on the upward path from savagery and barbarism to civilization. They have become more enlightened. Though moral ideas are based upon emotions, though all moral concepts are essentially generalizations of tendencies in certain phenomena to call forth moral approval or disapproval, the influence of intellectual considerations upon moral judgments is naturally very great. All higher emotions are determined by cognitions—sensations or ideas; they therefore vary according as the cognitions vary, and the nature of a cognition may very largely depend upon reflection or insight . . . The change of cognitions, or ideas, has thus produced a change of emotions. The evolution of the moral consciousness partly consists in its development from the unreflecting to the reflecting stage, from the unenlightened to the enlightened.'*

There is no lack of clarity here as to what Westermarck thought about the way in which reason could change the moral emotions, and there was no doubt whatever about his view of what would be likely to happen to the extension of altruism in the future.

'There can be no doubt,' he wrote, 'that changes also will take place in the future, and that similar causes will produce similar effects. We have every reason to believe that the altruistic sentiment will continue to expand, and that those moral commandments which are based on it will undergo a corresponding expansion; that the influence of reflection upon moral judgments will steadily increase; that the influence of sentimental antipathies and likings will diminish; and that in its relation to morality religion will be increasingly restricted to emphasizing ordinary moral rules, and less preoccupied with inculcating special duties to the deity.'†

It is perhaps worthwhile to note, too, how similar this view was to that of Comte who also argued for the extension of altruism and thought that this was correlated with the diminution of the 'theological' elements in religion. The position of Westermarck was therefore very clear in spite of his philosophical muddles.

One or two additional considerations may just be mentioned.

Comte, Mill, Spencer, Marx and others believed that it would be possible, if we had a sufficient explanation of the nature of man and the nature of social institutions, to state predictions on which we could base the making of reliable social policies. In 'seeing', we should be able to 'foresee'. It is interesting to note that such predictions did emerge from Westermarck's work, and in connection with every institution that he studied, although he himself did not stop to elaborate them.

* *Origin and Development*, Vol. II, p. 744.   † *Ibid.*, p. 746.

To give a small example—on the basis of his drawing together of biological, psychological and sociological knowledge, Westermarck predicted that the family and marriage in human society would not disappear despite the many and rapid changes of other aspects of modern society.* Furthermore, he gave very clear pronouncements about the nature of the problems involved in the family as a social group and the functions which were fulfilled by it. These pronouncements are borne out in studies of present-day society just as much as they were borne out in all the study of the simpler societies and societies of the past that Westermarck undertook. This kind of predictive value of Westermarck's work could be demonstrated in every field he mentioned. For example, his writing about the law and the punishment of criminal offences has a quite up-to-date bearing on our modern discussions of crime and punishment: the various theories of punishment—retributive, reformative, deterrent; and of the concept of responsibility. Indeed, his treatment of these matters seems to me far superior to many of the new essays on the subject now being published. The same is true of every institution to which he turned his attention.

My point in mentioning this, is simply to show that Westermarck not only accepted and developed some of the methods and theoretical perspectives which had been outlined by earlier sociologists, but also, in his work, actually *demonstrated* how these methods could be *used* in studying a new wealth of empirical data which he himself collected, and was able to produce generalizations on the basis of which qualified predictions can still be made.

It may be worthwhile, also, to reiterate our earlier point that *some* of the present-day influences of social anthropology on comparisons of human behaviour and morals are very questionable when compared with the work of Westermarck, in that they stem from a range of comparison which is dangerously narrow. Without by any means wishing to criticize modern anthropological monographs on all counts, it is surely the case that a study of two or three isolated primitive communities, selected as being illustrative of wide differences, can give a completely erroneous impression of an infinitely malleable diversity of human behaviour throughout the world.† In fact, in the wider context of the careful comparative study that Westermarck undertook, which was inclusive of major historical trends and areas of civilization, human behaviour was shown to have very extensive *similarities* throughout the world, not by any means differences only.

* Though, as we have seen, these kind of prediction were very carefully qualified. See: *The Future of Marriage in Western Civilization*, pp. 264–5.
† See footnote, pp. 86–7.

There is a tendency for anthropology, since it offers colourful accounts of simple communities which have a pattern of life markedly different from our own, to give a false impression of the diversity of behaviour in all societies. The fact is that many social developments in the world have been brought about by the extensive ongoing influences of major historical civilizations: of Egypt, China, India, and of European civilization—spreading into, and being developed, in America. These historical civilizations have very marked similarities, as well as differences, and the tendency to discuss human behaviour in terms of two or three rather remote and simple communities in the Pacific Islands or in Africa, can easily become something of an absurdity if it leaves out of account any historical awareness of these much more vast areas of interconnected social growth and development. Westermarck's comparative study of the 'sanctions' of social behaviour is very much more sound and worthwhile than many of the criticisms stemming from recent and influential anthropological monographs might lead us to think.* Indeed, in very recent years, there is a tendency for social anthropologists to return, to some extent, to the wider comparative perspective of the kind that Westermarck employed and, indeed, even to the concept of evolution in discussing this—though, of course, they do not necessarily agree with his conclusions. Good examples are Margaret Mead's recent study of 'Continuities in Cultural Evolution' and von Fürer-Haimendorff's 'Merit and Morals'.

Some Criticisms

It is worth our while, finally, just to enumerate the main kinds of criticism which have been made of Westermarck's position.

First of all, it is a valid criticism that Westermarck's particular method of classification and comparative study is not as adequate as it might be, in the sense that it ignores the earlier attempts to conduct such studies within the framework of a careful classification of *'types of society'*, and, connected with this, in that it does not sufficiently take into account the interrelations of institutions within the total social systems of which they are a part. Indeed, Westermarck's 'delimitation' of those 'sanctions' which he considered 'most important' was rather arbitrarily selective. Even so, his work does not seem to have suffered unduly when his *particular objectives* are borne in mind. Though it is true that Westermarck did draw social

* Indeed, Radcliffe-Brown's writings on 'sanctions' and the essential nature of 'institutions' adopt a position indistinguishable from Westermarck's. See our later section on Radcliffe-Brown, and especially pp. 738–48.

institutions from their wider context, he was, nonetheless, well aware of their functional setting within societies, and, given the mass of comparative details which he succeeded in bringing together (and, again, bearing his objective of clarifying the socio-psychological roots of 'sanctions' in mind), the merits of his work far outweigh this particular inadequacy of his methodological approach.

Secondly, the centrality of the concept of 'evolution' in Westermarck's work has been much criticized, as it has in the work of Spencer and others. One point, however, should be made very clear. Westermarck did *not* try to trace particular universal stages of social evolution and he quite definitely *rejected* the idea of a unilinear sequence of social evolution. Westermarck, as we have seen, used the idea of evolution purely in its *biological* sense. He simply *accepted* the Darwinian theory of evolution claiming that it provided a basis for understanding and explaining certain fundamental aspects of human psychology, on the basis of which further hypotheses could be formulated about the *social* and *moral* regularities of human behaviour, and their patterns of development as knowledge grew. In this, it seems to me that he was surely correct, and contemporary studies in comparative psychology support him.

It is true that he used the word evolution to speak of the growth and change of societies from a condition of simplicity to a condition of complexity (accepting the picture provided by earlier theorists); from a condition of 'unenlightened, unreflective' acceptance of custom, to a condition of 'reflective and criticial' assessment of it; towards a more sophisticated clarification of moral ideas. Certainly, he outlined general tendencies of this kind. But, in the main, Westermarck's 'evolutionary' theory was only an employment of the *biological theory of evolution proper* to form a basis for his wider comparative sociological studies, and to lend systematic support to them.

In so far as he explained the nature and emergence of institutions by taking into account the instinctive and emotional dispositions of man, Westermarck was also criticized by some followers of Durkheim, who claimed that social facts could not be explained in terms of 'individual psychology'. In the same vein, he might also be criticized by followers of Karl Popper—who would be inclined to speak of this kind of explanation of social institutions as a reduction to 'psychologism'.

Here again, however, I think that Westermarck's position (with regard to his combination of psychology and sociology) was largely sound as Mill's position in method was sound, and that Durkheim's approach has been not so much overstressed in recent sociology, as, in some respects, positively misunderstood. I hope to show later that

Durkheim's position was not in any sense opposed to, or in conflict with, that put forward by Mill and Westermarck. Durkheim sometimes gave a false impression of his position by arguing too forcibly against what he considered to be an *improper* and *inadequate* kind of psychological explanation; but, when the different approaches between himself and Mill and Westermarck are carefully examined, the differences are seen to be slight. At any rate, I shall argue that the position adopted by Mill and Westermarck is valid. This can better be left until we consider the work of Durkheim, but, even here, it is right that we should see clearly that Westermarck, in taking basic psychological features of human nature into account, was by no means *reducing* sociology to psychology. Westermarck did *not* hold that the *instincts* themselves were *moral*. He did *not* maintain that the emotions of gratitude and resentment, approval and disapproval, or even the quality of sympathy were in themselves *moral*, or that they themselves (as innate psychological elements) comprised *moral ideas*. Not at all. What he argued was that these psychological facts gave rise to *habitual* relationships and to the formation of *sentiments* which took shape in the associational activities of the community, and that distinctively *moral* ideas ('*sanctions*') became established in the process of *institutionalization*; in the slow establishment of custom. Westermarck insisted on the *societal* context of the creation of moral ideas, and, in doing so, wrote in a way which, even without further reflection, reads almost like Durkheim himself. Let us take one example. Having explained that the feelings of approval, disapproval, retribution, etc., which came to be central in *moral* emotions and *moral* judgments belonged to a wider class of emotions, Westermarck deliberately raised the question as to how we are to explain how they came to be differentiated from them.

'To this question,' he wrote, in summarizing his argument, 'the following answer was given: Society is the birthplace of the moral consciousness.* The first moral judgments expressed not the private emotions of isolated individuals but emotions which were felt by the community at large. Public indignation is the prototype of moral disapproval and public approval the prototype of moral approbation. And these public emotions are characterized by generality, individual disinterestedness, and apparent impartiality.'

There is surely no doubt as to the *societal* emphasis in this conception. Later, arguing the other way round, so to speak, we shall see, similarly, that, contrary to many present-day notions, Durkheim was not only prepared to entertain psychological dimensions in socio-

* *Origin and Development*, Vol. II, p. 740. This could well be a statement from Durkheim's own lips!

logical explanations, but *insisted* on them—so long, that is, as they were properly conceived.

Westermarck has also been scathingly criticized by some—for example by C. Wright Mills,* who seems to have been as tempestuous in his early as in his later writing—because of his supposedly 'limited' empirical work, and the fact that he drew most of his data from documentary sources. This criticism, of course, is beside the point, and of no consequence whatever. Westermarck, in fact, had the merit not only of seeing the necessity and importance of first hand field investigation, but, also, of actually undertaking it. Indeed, when beginning his field work in Morocco, he had it in mind to undertake similar studies on a comparative scale; to study the moral rules, the 'sanctioned' institutions, in several societies; so that this field work could supplement his documentary studies. He found, however, as many other social investigators have found, that to study *one* society at first hand and in sufficient detail was a task which required all his available time and effort. Consequently, documentary evidence for comparative purposes was not only desirable, but clearly necessary.

Having insisted, however, that Westermarck was, in fact, one of the pioneers of field work in sociology, let us also immediately insist upon the simple point that there is nothing 'non-empirical' about documentary evidence; and scientific sociology would be lost without it. Indeed, the criticism of scholars like Westermarck by recent American sociologists on the grounds that he was not sufficiently 'empirical' really calls for the most sardonic comment on several counts. Talcott Parsons, for example, insists that he is undertaking an 'empirical' study when he critically examines the *ideas* of Marshall, Durkheim, Weber and Pareto in 'The Structure of Social Action'; when, that is, he is undertaking *textual criticism*.† There are, however, more social facts in one chapter of Westermarck than in the whole of Parsons' book. In another direction, the idea that 'empiricism' is simply a matter of walking out into the street and observing what is *there*, under one's nose, through one's own eye-balls; or even undertaking intensive interviews; is itself incredibly naive, and anyone who believes in this narrow conception of empiricism, at least as far as sociology is concerned, cannot have begun to understand the difficulties in the way of the science and a consideration of its most appropriate methods.

* See H. B. Barnes: *An Introduction to the History of Sociological Thought*, University of Chicago Press, 1958, Ch. XXXIII, p. 634.
† It is worthwhile to glance at Parsons' comments in this book to note his peculiar insistence (almost a compulsive insistence) that his study is of an *empirical* nature.

Westermarck's ethical 'subjectivism' and 'relativism' has also been subjected to much criticism, but this has been on philosophical grounds and we have already said enough about it.

A further criticism of Westermarck which we have had in mind throughout, is that he did seem sometimes to speak as though to uncover the *origins* of social institutions were the same thing as to uncover their *causes*; and it might be said that there are causes of social institutions *other* than their origins. Again, it is Karl Popper who has most rigorously attacked this idea that we can satisfactorily explain social institutions by uncovering their origins* (though not only with reference to Westermarck). Having mentioned this criticism, however, it is clear that it reveals a misunderstanding of what Westermarck was attempting to do. We can say, first of all, that there is nothing *erroneous* about seeking a knowledge of the origins of institutions even in a historical (chronological) sense. It is true that to uncover these origins would not be to offer a *complete* causal explanation of them; many *more* causes being involved in the historical change and development of them; but, of course, Westermarck was himself well aware of this, and his causal explanation of the *development* of moral ideas and sanctions did take into account factors other than their origins.

The second and more important point, however, which it is important to make completely clear, is that in speaking of the *causes* and *origins* of institutions, Westermarck was *not* simply thinking in *chronological* terms. He was, more properly understood, following the method proposed by Mill. He was utilizing the basic knowledge of biology and psychology in order to understand the reasons why institutions of particular kinds existed in all societies. He was clarifying the '*requisites*' of social order, and the ways in which 'sanctioned' relationships and procedures were established to meet them. Elucidating the biological factors which led to certain kinds of groupings and certain kinds of behaviour, enabled him to give reasons why institutions of these particular kinds existed. This explanation of the existence of social regularities, with the aid of a knowledge of psychology; this hypothetical explanation of how social regularities stemmed from the psychological nature of man; was not the same thing as to speak of the 'origins' of institutions in a purely chronological or historical way. It was an uncovering of the factors in which institutions 'originated' at *any* time and in *any* society. Westermarck's conception here was correct. Elsewhere, we have considered Popper's idea of 'psychologism' and shown that he is quite wrong in maintaining that people who utilize psychology in sociological explanation are trying, as he puts it, to '*reduce*' social

* See Appendix IV in Vol. I of *The Making of Sociology*.

explanation to 'psychological terms'.* No question of reductionism is involved. And Comte's discussion of the 'hierarchy of sciences'—each with its appropriate methods and techniques for the study of its own 'level' of facts—should have made this perfectly clear. It is simply a matter of what is a sufficient and correct method of explanation. It is enough, however, simply to note that by 'origins', Westermarck did not mean the earliest historical circumstances, but, rather differently, the basic psychological factors; the universal 'causes' in this sense; in which institutions were rooted.

A final criticism which has validity, is that Westermarck discussed the *development* of moral ideas almost exclusively in terms of the operation of reason upon feeling; or the operation of reason in reflecting upon the moral ideas of customary usage. The criticism of this position is that there may well be, in the complex historical changes of societies, factors *other* than the operation of reason which bring about changes in moral ideas. This is a fair point, though we must note that, like Comte, Mill, Ward and others, Westermarck really considered this in relation to the central factor of the growth of knowledge; and this, as we have seen in these other authors, was capable of taking other dimensions of technical and social change into account.

Actually, for anyone who has read with any thoroughness at all, the massive array of detailed evidence which Westermarck brought together in support of his theory—on large-scale institutions such as slavery, property, industry, religion, as well as on 'sanctions' governing such items of behaviour as diet, suicide, leisure, attitudes towards the lower animals, and many others besides—such criticisms will appear trivial indeed. As Westermarck himself said when considering certain objections to his study:

'I think I may confidently ask, with reference to its fundamental thesis, whether any other theory of the moral consciousness has ever been subjected to an equally comprehensive test.'†

These criticisms of Westermarck can be seen then, not to possess considerable weight. In spite of them, his work can be seen to constitute a justification and a supplementation of the methods already put forward by the nineteenth century sociologists. It was a contribution to the development of the science of sociology in that it undertook a concrete empirical study of a certain range of social facts in an attempt to establish a theory about them, and demonstrated that the perspectives and methods of explanation put forward by earlier thinkers, could really produce a substantial and important

* Appendix (iv), Vol. I. † *Origin and Development*, Vol. II, p. 742.

extension in our knowledge of man and society. Westermarck was a scholar who contributed to the making of sociology not by elaborating new methodological rules, but by undertaking detailed empirical studies (both in field-research and in comparative documentary studies) of actual institutions, and demonstrating the superiority of sociological methods over those philosophical, conjectural, and historical methods that had been pursued before his time.

*   *   *

Here, then, was one more substantial development of evolutionary theory in sociology; strikingly similar to that of Tönnies in its analysis of instinct, habit, sentiment, in the development of the 'sanctioned relationships' of custom; but yet distinctively different in that—as distinct from Tönnies' strictly *typological* interpretation, Westermarck produced a detailed linking of biological evolution with the understanding of human society, and—supporting his analysis by wide-ranging comparative, empirical studies—a detailed theory of the socio-psychological requisites and processes in relation to which the institutions of society took shape. Strictly speaking, Westermarck produced *a systematic analysis of the universal socio-psychological requisites which underlay the order of human societies.* Biological evolution was the theory which gave him the grounding for this. And, having systematically outlined the emergence of the sanctioned social order, he was able at least to take his analysis further, and show how knowledge and reason could effect (and had effected) a *development* of this order. Westermarck's was therefore a considerable and distinctive achievement in the furtherance of the subject.

3
L. T. Hobhouse:
Evolution, Development and Purpose

The system of sociological analysis elaborated by Hobhouse was
thoroughly, though critically, rooted in almost all the contributions
of the nineteenth century—and was fully comparable in scale, in
detail, in richness of treatment, with any one of them. It is not too
much to say that in his development of the central notion of 'evolution' in relation to the making of a satisfactory science of man and
society, Hobhouse was probably the last scholar to accomplish an
entire 'system' of sociology with success.* He was undoubtedly a
sociologist in 'the grand manner'; a 'system-builder' of the largest
scale; but since—in prevailing fashions of thought—to say this is
almost synonymous with saying that a man's work is fit only for the
wastepaper basket, certain important points must immediately be
noted.

The first of these is that throughout his work, Hobhouse was
emphatically an *empiricist*: not in a narrow (epistemological†)
sense, but in insisting always that scientific theories—sociological
theories no less than others—should be essentially explanations of
distinctive ranges of *facts*; and that they should always be con-
constructed, and tested, in clear relation to these facts. Hobhouse's
sociology was always *empirical, comparative, historical* sociology. It
was *never* purely speculative in the sense of constructing theories
without detailed reference to facts. It was *never* 'philosophical' in any
cloudy, metaphysical, 'normative', non-empirical sense. And this
requires solid emphasis since, as in the case of Westermarck,
Hobhouse has often been *contrasted* with social investigators such
as Booth, Rowntree, and the like, as being 'philosophical' and of the
'grand manner', whilst the latter have been lauded as examining
facts, and as being '*empirical*'. To make this kind of contrast is a
complete misrepresentation of Hobhouse. His 'system' was based
upon, and substantiated by, empirical—and even experimental—
knowledge.

* With the exception of the very recent 'systems-analysis' of Talcott Parsons;
but this is a very different matter—really a 'categoreal scheme'—and we shall
come to it in Volume III, in our consideration of strictly contemporary sociology.
† I.e. in the sense of advocating and pursuing a 'factual' orientation totally
lacking in theoretical direction.

It is also quite mistaken to think that because Hobhouse's comparative studies were of a wide range, incorporating very considerable historical detail, and because he spent much time and care clarifying the philosophical issues connected with some of the distinctions which have to be made in sociology (e.g., between concepts such as 'evolution', 'development', 'progress', etc.), his work was in any sense whatever vague, irrelevant to the perspectives of modern times, and without concern for social and political *practice*. In fact, Hobhouse was totally within the tradition—very firmly established from Comte onwards—of desiring to construct a reliable sociology because of *need*; because of the massive task of the *conscious* re-construction and direction of society which man had to assume with the emergence and implications of science and industrialization. For Hobhouse, the effort towards a satisfactory sociology was a central and necessary part of man's awareness of his new *self-responsibility* for the understanding and direction of society. His focus was sharply upon the contemporary human predicament, and his feelings were deeply engaged in the *application* of the new science to accomplish conditions of social order which would maximize individual welfare and fulfilment. Much of his writing (and activity—on Wages Boards, etc.) was quite directly aimed at social and political practice; and, indeed, in some of his books on immediate political matters—such as *The Labour Movement*, and *Liberalism*—there was a sharper and more telling statement of some of his intellectual positions than in some of his more academic essays—such as, for example, *The Rational Good* and *The Elements of Social Justice*.

This *practice*, this humane *engagement*, also deserves very powerful emphasis. Because the system of knowledge a man produces is large in scope, philosophically exact in its care, and wide-ranging in its erudition, it does *not* mean that he is *not* committed to social purpose, social practice, and social action. One does not have to wait for Herbert Marcuse for an advocacy of the 'engagement' and 'commitment' of knowledge to humane action in society. Every sociologist from Comte had pressed this conviction passionately; it was part of their reason for *wanting* sociology. Hobhouse was no exception.

It must also be emphasized that Hobhouse's 'system' was far from being just another summary compendium; a bringing together of many components which were already seen to be related to each other. It was very far from being a 'book-work' synthesis. It was, in fact, a very substantial *development* in the clarification of certain ambiguities; and it involved, too, many independent studies of a quite original kind in comparative psychology and comparative sociology. Indeed—rather like the initial work, the 'founding statement', of Comte—the synthesis achieved by Hobhouse was remarkable for the number of important contributions which it managed successfully to weave into a single, coherent, systematic statement. Comte's system had brought together the many contributions in various branches of philosophy and the embryonic social sciences as they had developed before his time. Hobhouse, similarly, brought together almost all the main contributions to sociology proper which we have so far mentioned. He did this, however, by way of *critical assessment*—not just by a process of lumping components together. Also, he was very much aware of the philosophical trends of his own time, and of the advancing contributions of psychology in particular, and these, too, were developed and taken fully into account. Hobhouse was, both by intellect and by self-imposed training, very well-equipped to undertake such a task of systematic study, and was sensitive to all those influences of his own time which were leading towards the kind of critical synthesis which he achieved.

We are here faced, then, by a 'development' of evolutionary theory in sociology which was of an altogether larger scope than the kind we have examined in Tönnies and Westermarck; yet all the chief emphases in their work—of the centrality of reason and knowledge, and of morality, in society—were central also in Hobhouse; and—a fact of which we must continuously remind ourselves—Hobhouse, Westermarck, Tönnies were all men of the same period, aware of the same ongoing efforts towards the advancement of the subject, and all concerned to improve the clarity of concepts and methods within it, and to enrich and improve it by establishing more exact theories about specific ranges of facts. The same continuity from the nineteenth century 'conspectus' to twentieth century theories, the same creative development from common roots, were therefore strikingly evident in Hobhouse's work.

The full scale of Hobhouse's achievement can only be appreciated if we take care to note the major contributions and influences which he drew together.

(I) THE INFLUENCE OF COMTE

First of all, the influence of Comte himself was quite central. Hobhouse forthrightly acknowledged his indebtedness to Comte and consciously attempted a filling out of Comte's scheme; but this influence had many sides and was not adopted without qualification.

With regard to the theory of knowledge of 'positivism', for example, Hobhouse qualified Comte in important, though not in radically critical, ways. It will be remembered that Comte argued that the knowledge of positive science was, at bottom, only a knowledge of man's *experience* of the world, and was therefore always 'relative' to man's nature and situation, but, even so, not '*arbitrary*' in that certain criteria of accurate knowledge could be observed. Hobhouse took this further. He was critical of the picture that it gave—that knowledge was only a kind of 'human perceptual curtain' beyond which 'genuine reality' must remain forever undiscoverable. He did not probe in metaphysical terms *beyond* human perception,* but simply argued that our careful study of the world could produce knowledge of 'what the existent *is*', not only of how it *appeared* to us. Indeed, he thought it metaphysical in itself to suppose that there *was* a 'world in itself' (Kant's 'noumena') *beyond* our perceptual and rational knowledge, and that the human mind possessed intrinsic 'categories' which *created* a world of experience different from the objective elements of the world on which they acted. He really, therefore, simply pressed Comte further and argued that, as far as we could possibly be aware, we could be confident that our knowledge, if pursued carefully, could be of the *actual nature of the world*—though we could never assume that it was, or ever could be, complete.† The 'object of knowledge', Hobhouse wrote:

'... is a world of reality, consisting partly of mental phenomena, partly of an order external to the knowing subject. Of this order it is acquainted with but a fraction, though many of its principles claim validity over the whole sphere of existence. But the order, so far as it is known, has an "absolute" reality, i.e. one that is not dependent for its existence on the fact that it is known, not coloured in its nature by the activities employed in cognition ... We do not know the whole, but we know in part, and what we do know we can trust. It is reality, not seen through a glass darkly, nor—still worse—projected on some distorted plane of our own vision, but so far as it goes, and however limited it may be, true, genuine reality seen face to face: and thus limited as is the kingdom we have as yet won for ourselves, and slow as are the steps of progress, each addition to knowledge is in sober truth one step further to the goal of all effort, the right understanding of the whole of things as they are in their inmost nature.'‡

Hobhouse also insisted that *all* avenues of human enquiry, taken with the same care, could be pursued to give us the richest and most reliable account of the actual nature of the world that it was possible for us to get. Art, speculative philosophy, the symbolism of religious

* I.e. he did not wish to argue that 'genuine reality' was in all respects *other than* that discovered through human perception.
† It may be noted that, on these philosophical issues, a treatment which was as important as any we are considering here, was that of Bradley—in *Appearance and Reality:* a book which deserves the most careful study, but which is beyond the scope of our discussion here.
‡ *The Theory of Knowledge*, Methuen, 1896, pp. 622–3.

myth, and not only science, could, properly understood, be exhaustively explored in this same 'positive', empirical spirit, and with the same confidence that it was the most reliable knowledge of the world which we could possibly attain.

'In science and in common sense,' he wrote, 'we are in contact with reality. In some dimmer, less articulate fashion we learn truth also through feeling and imagination. The best and soundest view we can give of things is by synthesis of all methods. The system of philosophy to which our theory would serve as an introduction would be a correlation of the results of science, physical and social, in which an attempt to understand what poetry and human nature mean would not be left out. The great permanent laws of nature, the broad outlines of biological and historical development, and the analysis of the moral consciousness would all enter into its scope. And finally, in summing up its results, what is already reduced to systematic order, i.e. to science, our philosophy would take as true and finally true, but not as the whole of truth. It would recognise an ore of truth in the presentiment which we cannot prove, and would be trying always to extract the metal from the ore. It would be conscious of limitation, but within its own limits would be confident of truth. This is no new view—it is as old, we might say, as philosophy itself; but as new difficulties arise it requires constantly to be restated, and the form in which it can be put forward has to be conceived anew.'*

This, then, was a more positive extension of Comte's own 'positivism', and it may be remembered that Hobhouse was, in fact, in close touch with the English positivist movement and with men—such as Bridges—who were doing their best to support the dissemination of the ideas of Comte in England.

Comte's emphasis upon the central importance of *mind* in the development of society—of the growth of knowledge and the growing powers of mind to control the conditions of its destiny—was also firmly accepted and adopted by Hobhouse and given an equally central place in his own system. Again, however, this point was *developed* extensively by Hobhouse. On the one hand, he undertook detailed studies in psychology (and in biology) in order to clarify by very firm empirical criteria, distinctive 'levels of mental development' among all animal species (including man) in the evolutionary scale. Also, he carried out Comte's suggested programme (which Comte had, to a certain extent, accomplished himself) of undertaking a comparative study of the major *institutions* of society on the guiding hypothesis that they would be significantly correlated with the central growth of knowledge and the attendant powers of control of the human mind. This therefore led to a systematic picture of the

* *The Theory of Knowledge*, p. 621.

'development' of mind through all animal species and all known patterns of historical change in human societies.

In all this, Hobhouse's perspective and conclusion was entirely at one with that of Comte: namely the clear picture that out of a long past of struggles and cumulative developments which had *not* been deliberately purposive, had emerged the conscious knowledge of man which *was* deliberately purposive. And with this knowledge; with this consciousness; with the complex social transformations which accompanied them; had arisen the inescapable *self-responsibility* of man for the future direction of society. In short, sociology still stood with Hobhouse where it had stood with Comte, as a science necessarily entailed in man's distinctively modern predicament. The making of sociology was the intellectual part of making modern society. This perspective ran right through the whole of Hobhouse's system, and he was perfectly explicit about it. Thus, at the close of an essay on Comte's method in the *Law of the Three Stages*, he wrote:

'That we are creatures of a development which has been unconscious, and stand at the point at which it begins to understand itself and so to become self-directing is the central conception of Comte's sociology which the criticism of method only serves to confirm and extend.'*

It goes without saying, of course, that this perspective was common to almost all the other scholars we have mentioned: from Mill right through to Ward, Sumner and Giddings, and—in their different terms—to Tönnies and Westermarck. Here then, was the re-statement and development of a firm, continuing theme of central importance in the making of the subject.

(II) THE INFLUENCE OF SPENCER AND THE BIOLOGICAL THEORIES OF EVOLUTION

Just as directly, Hobhouse also acknowledged the influence upon him of Herbert Spencer. Though taking issue with him on certain ambiguities about the relation between philosophical ethics and the factual study of morals in the evolution of society, he quite deliberately commended and praised his work. Like Spencer, he was persuaded of the necessity of the evolutionary perspective for tracing and understanding the development of life, mind, and human society. It was a perspective which was, he believed, true. And he also strongly approved of Spencer's attempted synthesis of science and philosophy.

* *Sociology and Philosophy*, London School of Economics (Bell & Sons, Ltd.), 1966.

'Doubtless metaphysical analysis and scientific specialism', he wrote, 'has each its sphere, but they cannot maintain an attitude of mutual indifference to the end. Neither is all-embracing, and a true philosophy, a really concrete interpretation of our experience as a whole, must aim rather at a synthesis in which the analysis of first principles figures as the key stone of the arch of science. In this respect, Mr Spencer, whatever the defects of his method, seems to me to have been justly inspired.'*

Hobhouse also, of course, like Westermarck, made use of the Darwinian theory of evolution, and had the advantage of being acquainted with all the biological work that had been undertaken since that of Darwin. He was, for example, well aware of the work of Jennings on the behaviour of the lower organisms, and many other works in comparative biology (on which we shall amplify a little in a moment). All this material helped him in building up a detailed evolutionary account of the development of biological species, of levels of mental activity in these species, and of the development of mind in human society. Here then was a continuity and development of the concept of evolution from its early roots in Spencer and Darwin, and incorporating the much extended work undertaken since they first emphasized its importance.

Perhaps, again, it is worth while to repeat the point here, that it was the kind of emphasis put forward by Comte and Lester Ward which Hobhouse particularly adopted as the central feature of evolution: the emphasis upon the increasingly *conscious* powers of the human mind in society to achieve a growing degree of self-direction and purpose in social development. The similarity of viewpoint between Hobhouse and Lester Ward especially was very striking, and Hobhouse was thoroughly aware of this.†

(III) COMPARATIVE PSYCHOLOGY AND SOCIAL PSYCHOLOGY

A third major part of Hobhouse's system in which continuities were strongly marked, and which he developed very considerably indeed, was the entire area of psychology and social psychology. I do not think it can be claimed that Hobhouse made a contribution of very considerable substance to social psychology proper, unless one counts as such a detailed account of the psychological *basis* of society; an account of the massive body of inherited impulse, emotion and instinctual response which was established by biological evolution, and in which social responses and social relationships were rooted. Such an account—very similar (as can be seen) to that of Wester-

---

* *Development and Purpose*, Macmillan, 1913, p. xviii (Introduction).
† See *Mind in Evolution*, Macmillan, 1915, Preface, p. vi.

marck—he certainly did provide. Indeed, it can be argued that his account was as successful as, and preferable in some respects, to that put forward a little later by McDougall;* but much the same could be said of Ward—who preceded them both. Hobhouse's real—and very substantial—contribution here was his active, indeed pioneering, development of Comparative Psychology in which he undertook some of the earliest experimental studies.

For his study of *Mind in Evolution*, it is not well-known that Hobhouse was sufficiently fortunate to have the collection of animals at the Belle Vue Gardens in Manchester placed at his disposal, and that here he carried out experimental studies on quite a wide range of species. This really was *comparative* psychology, and, bearing in mind the present-day emphasis upon 'experimental' psychology it is well worth while to read the investigations in this book and to remember that they were undertaken towards the end of the *nineteenth* century, and published in 1901. But it is also—bearing in mind the clear historical perspective we are trying to achieve—a salutary thing to note the other scholars and range of work which Hobhouse took into account: especially in the period between 1901 and 1915 —the date of the second edition.

Even in this book strictly on Comparative Psychology, Hobhouse drew upon the influences of Comte, Mill and Spencer. Quite specifically, however, he acknowledged the work of Lester Ward (his *Outlines of Sociology*, 1898) and emphasized the similarity to his own of Ward's general view of evolution. One other central influence was that of Lloyd Morgan who was himself a pioneer in comparative animal studies. But even Lloyd Morgan is not known nowadays. The names that indicate the relative modernity of Hobhouse's references are, more probably, those of Fabre, Jennings, Thorndike (E. L.), Ebbinghaus, Wundt, Lankester (Sir Ray), Sherrington, McDougall, and Yerkes (R.M.) These names, of course, are now 'dated', but only very recently so, and some of them still figure quite firmly in the bibliographies of contemporary studies of comparative animal behaviour. Hobhouse was taking their studies into account, in close relation to his own, from the very beginning of this century. Later, too, he took into account the work of W. Kohler and also of J. B. Watson. His work was not only original, therefore, but also as well-informed by other studies in the same field as was possible at the time.

It is also worth while to note, in connection with this point, that Hobhouse was still, like all his predecessors, firmly convinced of the close relations between biology, psychology, and sociology. There was never any doubt in his mind—both in terms of the *facts* of human

* *An Introduction to Social Psychology*, Methuen, 1908.

social experience and behaviour, and in terms of the construction of satisfactory theoretical *explanations* of these facts—that all these sciences should be seen as being indispensably connected with each other. This again, then, was another example of firm continuity of conception. The biological, psychological, and social sciences were seen in the closest co-operative relations with each other.

(IV) THE INFLUENCE OF JOHN STUART MILL

We might also note briefly that Hobhouse's thought—in sociology and psychology, and in moral philosophy and his conception of the relations between philosophy and the sciences of society—was strongly and sympathetically rooted in the ideas of John Stuart Mill. The roots in Mill's considerations of the *methods* of sociology will be clear enough, but it is especially the case that Mill's essays on social and political philosophy had a great influence on him. He stood firm by Mill's viewpoints on *Individualism* and *Liberty*; and a modified 'utilitarianism' formed one of the most substantial elements in his philosophical account of the criteria of the 'good life' and of the 'principles of social justice' in the light of which he measured the degrees of progress attained in particular sequences of social development. It is at this point, perhaps, that it is best to introduce this matter of Hobhouse's bringing together of ethics and sociology—for this can be very easily misunderstood, and it is important to see that Hobhouse accomplished a very necessary, and correct, clarification here.

(V) EVOLUTION, DEVELOPMENT, AND PROGRESS: ETHICS AND THE SOCIOLOGY OF MORALS

In dealing with the earlier makers of sociology, we have noticed one particular and crucial problem among all of them—namely, that of insufficiently clearing up the ambiguity attending the philosophical clarification of standards of ethical judgment on the one hand, and the sociological study of the *facts* of developing institutions and moral ideas on the other. All the earlier sociologists, as we have seen, were, in some way or other, directly or indirectly, concerned with the idea of 'progress'. Whether, without searching question, they assumed progress to be concomitant with social development; whether, again without much question, they assumed that men's practical activities were characterized by a strain to 'improvement'; whether they thought that the reflections of reason brought 'enlightenment'; or whether they saw 'progress' as the manipulation of society for the attainment of certain ends; the problem was the same.

There was an unresolved confusion between theories about social facts, and the evaluation of them in the light of ethical assumptions. The problem was that of achieving methodological correctness in pursuing, at one and the same time, a philosophical elucidation of ethical standards and a sociological study of moral systems. It is on this major point particularly that Hobhouse made a clear advance upon his predecessors.

In the context of the fashionable thought of the moment, to introduce a sociologist by referring to his discussion of *philosophical ethics* as being an important part of his work seems puzzling and outmoded, if not completely inexcusable. Sociology, it is thought, has long outgrown the swaddling clothes of moral philosophy. We shall have to come back to this question as to how far philosophy can ever be regarded as a set of garments which a 'science' can shed as it grows from 'infancy' towards 'maturity'. For now, it is enough to state quite starkly that to think that any condition or sequence of social facts can be *evaluated* as being '*better*' or '*worse*' than others, without reference to any criteria of judgment which have been philosophically clarified independently, is to be quite basically mistaken. Facts are facts; the study of facts is the study of facts; explanatory theories about facts may explain facts; but there is nothing in all this to warrant an ethical *evaluation* of these facts. It is possible to *assert* that certain criteria (ethical standards) are the ones to be accepted, but this, of course, leaves the field completely open to innumerable assertions—all of which, *at that level of competitive assertion*—provide no grounds of adjudication between them at all. Such a situation is a battle-ground of unexamined assumptions. In short, it is exactly the situation which obtained before Socrates stopped dead in his tracks (so to speak) and realized that philosophical ethics was necessary. To follow the 'image' for a moment longer, one might say that to assert implicit evaluations of social facts as a sociologist, without seeing the necessity of a philosophical clarification of the ethical presuppositions which are, in fact, being employed in such assertions, is to adopt the position of pre-Socratic thick-headedness. It is to wallow around, no doubt with an appearance of sophistication, as Thrasymachus and Polymarchus did, banging their heads against each other. But this, entertaining though it may be for those who like a circus, is no substitute for good method.

It might be said that sociologists need not (*as* sociologists) evaluate social facts at all; and this is a possibility. Here, however, we need only note that if sociologists *do* wish so to confine themselves, they must cease, altogether, to speak about the 'progress', 'advancement', 'improvement', 'reform', or 'enlightenment' of social institutions, and even of practical activities; and it is very doubtful whether they can even speak of a 'drive towards progress' as a factual human impulse which is different from any other; or whether they can even speak of 'development' in so far as this implies some sort of 'advancement' or 'improvement' of the human condition. And, to bring the point to much current discussion, there are no grounds whatever why 'social and economic growth' should be considered a *good* thing; and no grounds for *deploring* an 'increasing gap between the advanced and the under-developed nations'. Indeed, what does 'under-developed' mean? And if, for example, the 'primitive' tribes of Brazil, or the Eskimos of the Canadian Barrens are exterminated (quite literally) by the interests, perhaps even by the governments, of modern technological societies—what is the problem? It is only an example of social change; of the *facts*. There is nothing in sociology as such (on this conception) to lead one to think that it is 'retrogressive', or to be designated 'worse' if a small society is disrupted and destroyed and disappears. Is there? To survive or not to survive. It is only a matter of facts.

We cannot stop to argue this issue here, but it is enough simply to say that Hobhouse achieved a far greater clarity of method in relation to it than any of his predecessors, and this, in itself, was a very considerable achievement.

Whether one agrees with his specific ethical theory or his specific ethical criteria is, in a way, beside the point. What is of central importance is the correctness of his procedure. Hobhouse thoroughly accepted, indeed insisted upon, the scientific requirements of sociology proper and saw that it was necessary to undertake a comparative study of moral and institutional facts themselves which was as free from evaluative assumptions as possible; which was independent altogether of criteria of an ethical nature. But he also saw quite clearly that it was necessary to undertake a philosophical enquiry in order to clarify those criteria of moral judgment, those standards, in the light of which he was going to exercise an ethical judgment upon sociological fact. Having done *both* of these things, he could then apply his ethical standards to the facts, and judge, accordingly, whether the *facts* of social development could be shown to have been attended by moral *progress*—in the light of these established criteria. In this, Hobhouse made a distinctive contribution of clarification and adopted a position which is, surely, still perfectly correct. It is the position which social scientists can, with reliability, both now and in the future, continue to adopt.

As with scientific knowledge and philosophical deliberation themselves, of course, such judgments could never claim to be 'final'. They would simply be the clearest, most reasonable, most reliably based judgments that carefully clarified procedure could provide: but *that*

133

would be a *lot*! Hobhouse did conduct *both* a sociological *and* an ethical enquiry, and these we shall consider later, but here it is the clarity of his procedure and method alone which it is important to note.

(VI) OTHER PHILOSOPHICAL INFLUENCES: NEO-HEGELIAN IDEALISM

With philosophical issues in mind, it is also necessary to note that Hobhouse was sensitively aware of other philosophical movements in his time which had a direct bearing on social theory. Whilst he was at Oxford, the ideas of Mill and Comte were under attack and he had felt disposed to defend them. But he was also led—by its marked influence—to come to terms with a newly developed 'Idealism' which stemmed from a reconsideration of Hegel's philosophy and was led chiefly by T. H. Green. Here, again, we can see the continuity of early elements of philosophical thought about the nature of man and society right into the making of modern sociology. In itself, however, philosophical 'Idealism' was not accepted by Hobhouse. It was the core idea of 'development' in terms of the 'realization' (in the actuality of the world and society) of mind and spirit which he thought worth while; which he thought possessed something of truth; and which could be utilized within the context of 'evolution'. His own position was a philosophical union of this element of the idealistic school of philosophy, and the positivism of Comte. About the 'Idealists', he wrote:

'Many of their contentions were empirically sound even if they could not carry the whole weight of the metaphysical structure placed on them. Green's permanent self-consciousness, for example, if it is not a spiritual principle, eternal or timeless, is an empirical fact within the world of time.'

'It seemed to me', he continued, 'that, details apart, the Hegelian conception of development possessed a certain rough empirical value . . . Further, if this conception was interpreted in terms of experience, it indicated a point of union where one would not expect to find it, between the idealistic and the positivist philosophy. This higher self-consciousness would be the humanity of positivism regulating its own life and controlling its own development.'*

In short, the development of mind in nature and in the history of society was an *actuality*, and could be studied *empirically*, and was a *fact* to be taken into account in any empirical explanation of man and society *whatever* its 'ultimate' philosophical grounds might turn out

---

* *Development and Purpose*, p. xix.

to be. The Hegelian notion of 'development'—the 'realization', the 'actualization' of what was 'potential'; the 'making real' of what was an 'idea'—was a core of truth concerning the actual course of the evolution of species of life in nature, and the actual course of the creativity of mankind in the history of societies, even if one discarded (or was obliged for philosophical reasons to ignore) the 'Idealist' metaphysic on which this picture rested.

In Hobhouse's study of mind in nature and society, then, the idea of 'development' was couched within that of 'evolution', and both together yielded an account of the emergence of 'purpose'. Within a wider 'evolution', mind 'developed', and men in the cumulative achievements of society came to be increasingly aware of all the many dimensions of their nature: all the many elements of nature and society of the past which had made them what they were; and, with this deepening consciousness, they could act with 'purpose' in such ways as to enrich still further, and more fully, the many dimensions of their natures.

Though a philosophical influence, then, stemming from Hegel, this was an important strand woven into Hobhouse's empirical sociology.

(VII) HOBHOUSE'S AWARENESS OF THE MAKING OF SOCIOLOGY

Enough has been said to show that Hobhouse was well-grounded in the work of his nineteenth-century predecessors, and that he was well aware of developments of thought in his own time—developments in the related fields of psychology and philosophy. It is especially interesting to take note, further, of the extent to which Hobhouse was aware of the ongoing efforts to establish and improve sociology as a science, and the extent to which he worked consciously and deliberately within this context. It must not be forgotten that Hobhouse was, with Westermarck, one of the first professors of sociology in England; that, again with Westermarck, he was one of the participants in the founding of the Sociological Society in London; and that, as a very active 'academic' he had a very considerable influence not only in laying down the first pattern of the degree in sociology at the London School of Economics but also in introducing the subject into many related courses: of politics, social administration, and the like. Hobhouse, from 1907 to his death in 1929 was probably the most dominant influence on the making of sociology in Britain: and this active academic creativity was based upon his successful incorporation of most of the earlier major contributions into his system of sociology which could now be *taught*.

In this central activity of laying down the foundations of the sub-

135

F

ject as a university degree course, it is very important to see that Hobhouse, and 'British Sociology' were not at all isolated, or insular, or rooted in English nineteenth-century figures alone, at the expense of being aware of international developments of the time. We have seen that the English Sociological Society was not so much 'English' as an English 'venue' for a wide international focusing of discussion, and we have already seen quite clearly that Tönnies, Durkheim, Thomas and many other prominent continental and American scholars were involved in these discussions in which Hobhouse and Westermarck were at the centre, and came increasingly to be at the centre as, jointly, they became responsible for the academic founding of the subject in the country. We have also emphasized Hobhouse's strong affinity with Lester Ward, and the firm link of conscious influence here. But we must now take this indication of influences a little further.

The many essays and articles which Hobhouse produced—even up to 1920—show quite plainly that he was very fully acquainted with all that was afoot in American Sociology. He was familiar, not only with Ward, but also with Giddings, Albion Small, Ross, Ellwood, and with all those who were attempting the writing of satisfactory text-books of sociology in America and who were continuously working away at the clarification of the place of psychology in sociological explanation, and similar basic matters which the nineteenth-century writers had introduced. He was also aware of Veblen's work, and, a little later, of that of Sorokin. As to the developments in continental Europe, a few examples will be sufficient. He was familiar here not only with the nineteenth-century scholars we have mentioned—including Gumplowicz (whom we have not)—but also with all those who were developing the subject in his own time. He was well aware of Durkheim's work, and his distinctive position in sociology. He also saw the importance of Simmel. And he was aware of Max Weber's work on religion, and was as 'up-to-date' in the controversy about his essay on 'The Protestant Ethic and the Spirit of Capitalism' as to have taken Tawney's 'Religion and the Rise of Capitalism' into account. And it goes without saying that he was in touch with the developments of the subject in Britain, and in developments very closely related to it—such as those of Graham Wallas in taking the subject into 'Politics', and of McDougall in trying to debunk the sterility of much early psychology and press forward with the introduction of *social* psychology and the study of human motivation, emotion, habit, sentiment, and the like.

When all these influences of *concurrent* work, as well as the major influences of nineteenth-century work, are reviewed, it becomes abundantly clear that Hobhouse was trying, in his 'synthesis', to incorporate all the most worthwhile developments in the making of sociology that had taken place from the beginnings of the subject onwards. And he was doing this with a certain eye on the *teaching* of the subject in the universities. Consequently, his work has very considerable value. There is one sense in which he brought to a head, brought to a fairly satisfactory conclusion, the many elements in sociology which sought for an over-all perspective of evolution and development within which the nature, persistence and changes of the many actual societies in the world, and the 'types' of society, could be studied and understood. His over-all 'schema' still holds good. In this same sense his work can be said to give a very clear picture of the perspective for judgment which we need in grappling with the contemporary human situation. Here, too, his work, in a sense, fills in and rounds out those directions of need and enquiry which had stemmed from Comte. However, there is another sense in which his work might be said to have a *prospective* reference: in that it is *exactly* the problems of social 'development'—the satisfactory analysis of 'development' in order to understand it and to deal satisfactorily with it—which are now coming to press with increasing insistence and urgency throughout the world. In this, Hobhouse's analysis may still have guidance to offer.

Certainly, far from trying to promote an insular view of 'British Evolutionism' (whatever that might mean), Hobhouse produced his own work in the development of sociology within the context of an awareness of the widest influences of those scholars in America and Europe who were also committed to this task. Sociology has, in fact, always been international.

(VIII) HOBHOUSE'S 'QUALIFICATIONS' FOR HIS TASK

A word or two is worthwhile, finally, on the ways in which Hobhouse was equipped, and indeed, deliberately equipped himself, for the wide range of differing investigations which his synthesis demanded of him. Primarily, Hobhouse was a philosopher. His earlier writings were concerned with the theory of knowledge, although he was— even then—already anticipating this large-scale study of the evolution of mind and already feeling the necessity of attempting a synthesis between philosophy and the sciences, and of undertaking a large scale study of the development of human society, within which the growth of human mentality and human knowledge had taken place.*

He was therefore well-equipped to undertake the several kinds of methodological and philosophical clarification which he thought

* Again—a perspective exactly like that of Comte.

137

necessary. Initially, however, he had also been a student of ancient history, and this gave him a very good grounding for the wide and very exacting comparative and historical study of social institutions which he undertook. None of this, however (it might be said), qualified him for work in comparative biology and psychology. But here, what is of great interest is that Hobhouse himself saw this lack in his training and therefore spent some time in a laboratory in Oxford working on the physiology of the brain, in order to equip himself, as satisfactorily as was possible, for experimental work in these fields.

It is clear then, without elaborating upon these matters further, that it was not only the case that Hobhouse was sensitive to a wide number of influences and contributions which he was able to synthesize in his work, but also that, in his pattern of study and training, he was remarkably well equipped to handle all the various kinds of material which he drew together. If, to this, is added the practical concerns and activities which Hobhouse showed, and in which he was engaged—such as journalistic writing on pressing social problems, and taking a part in wages discussions; and if, too, we bear in mind his involvement in the detailed work of founding and administering the earliest academic courses in the subject—then his stature as a scholar and as a person becomes very apparent.

Let us now turn to the particular development of evolutionary theory which Hobhouse accomplished.

In order to give as clear and comprehensive an account of Hobhouse's system of thought as is possible, I think it may be helpful, again, to make use of a preliminary diagrammatic 'scheme' (opposite). It will be clearly seen from this that Hobhouse provided an account of the nature and development of man and society within the entire context of the emergence and evolution of life in the world; and that this was an account in which (in accordance with all the earlier theories) the growth and change of social institutions was seen as being essentially correlated with man's *activities* in nature, and with his increasing *knowledge* and *control* over his physical and social environment. I shall deal with each element of the accompanying diagram in turn, but I would like the reader to think, beforehand, about the interconnection between all these elements as they are depicted in the diagram, and then to refer back to the diagram from time to time as the argument proceeds. I think that, in this way, the entire and coherent scheme of the basic elements of Hobhouse's system—each in itself quite complex—can be made clear.

THE SYSTEM OF L. T. HOBHOUSE

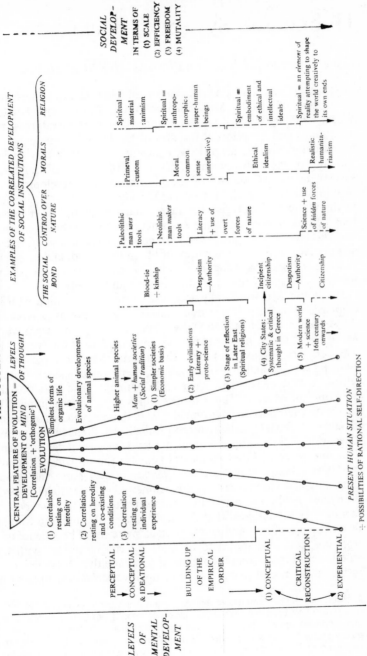

Hobhouse's System of Sociology

(1) *The Essential Basis and Perspective of Evolution*

The central and fundamental feature of Hobhouse's system was (as in that of Comte, Mill, Spencer, Marx, Darwin and Huxley, Ward, Giddings, and all the major nineteenth century thinkers) the acceptance and adoption of the idea of 'evolution' as the only one which could provide an orderly, coherent, and satisfactory understanding of the development of all forms of life, of all biological species, in the world, and of the life and mental development of man in society. That all the forms of life, and all the forms of society in the world had emerged and taken shape gradually, over a very long period, in relation to the characteristics of their environments, was, Hobhouse thought, *true*. This new nineteenth and twentieth century perspective on the nature of life in the world, and on man's place in nature, was therefore the *correct* and *necessary* perspective for any satisfactory understanding of man and society.

Hobhouse also specifically accepted *Darwinian* evolution with its emphasis upon natural selection; but as a *basis*—not as a *terminus*. As we shall see, he qualified Darwin in certain very important ways. More particularly, however, he was concerned to show (what—he was convinced—was true) that, throughout the whole pattern of evolving species, and evolving societies, there was one single feature which became increasingly clear and dominant—and that was the development of *mind*. Those species which were better equipped to survive in their natural environment, were those which became more capable of flexible, adaptive, controlled and directed responses. They were those equipped with higher levels of *mental* development. The emergence of levels of mental activity; the growth of 'mind'; was thus demonstrably *the central feature of evolution*. And it was this which led Hobhouse to speak distinctively of '*ORTHOGENIC*' *evolution*: evolution markedly characterized by this *one central feature*.* He maintained that the development of mind, the coming into existence of new and more intricate 'patterns' of experience and response, could be shown to be quite directly correlated with the emergence of more complex organic species, and that this culminated in the emergence of man, and the cumulative *social* development of

---

* Hobhouse did not emphasize this as being a *new* view of evolution; he knew well that it had been the central persuasion of many from Comte to Ward. He laid emphasis upon it because it was *true*; and because it formed the central guiding thread of his whole system. It should be noted very clearly, too, that this was *not* a 'unilinear' theory of evolution. The two are not necessarily connected.

man, who was not only better fitted to survive in relation to other animal species simply because his qualities of mind were so superior, but who also came, through knowledge and technology, to *impose* the desires of his own mind upon the rest of nature and so came to be, with increasing consciousness, a central *influence upon* evolution.

Having spoken of the way in which the human mind, coming to critical and self-conscious awareness, became increasingly capable of controlling and directing its own development; and having discussed this in relation to the union between 'idealism' and 'positivism'; Hobhouse wrote:

'But further, if this was the true empirical account of Evolution, our interpretation of that process would be fundamentally changed. The factor of consciousness . . . would influence the course of development. If my view was right it would turn out even to be the *central* point in development. To the fully conscious mind in man everything would lead up, and from it, once formed, all future movement would be derived. This was indeed to assume that along with knowledge there would go control, but in the first place it could, I thought, be shown that control extends in a kind of geometrical ratio with each new turn in the development of consciousness, and in the second place, as the full meaning of the self-conscious mind worked itself out it was seen to imply a grip on those underlying conditions of life which, as long as they remain obscure, thwart human effort and distract man from that social collaboration which is necessary to the greatest efforts.'*

And, even in this basic statement of the nature of 'evolution', Hobhouse was already probing towards a clear and correct conception of the relationship between this and the notion of 'progress'. He argued:

'By emphasizing consciousness and its control moreover, several difficulties as to the relations of evolution and progress could be met. To begin with, it was possible to conceive of evolution in general as a blind and even brutal process, dependent on the anarchical struggle for existence, but to maintain that in the course of this struggle there had arisen among other species one which owed its survival to a *mind*. How this had happened was not for the moment the point. It *had* happened, and there *was* a being with a mind, looking before and after, also looking around him upon his fellows and on the whole, working with as well as against them. Something of this mind moreover existed in lower species, and it was important to notice that even there, in proportion as mind began to exert itself, *it tended to supersede the struggle for existence.* It was possible to display one particular line of evolution, for which I afterwards found Mr Sutherland's expression "orthogenic evolution" as a series of advances in the

* *Development and Purpose*, p. xx.

development of mind involving a parallel curtailment of the sphere of natural selection. The conclusion was clear that *natural selection* was *not* the *cause* of *progress*. How mind came into being, how it grew, what were the conditions of its further development, I did not at first enquire. I saw no light upon the question, and I thought that the empirical account leading up as it did to the control of life as a whole by consciousness was the most important or at least the first thing to prove.'*

Two points are strikingly clear in this passage and must be seized upon and emphasized as being extremely important. The first is that there was here a very clear qualification of the all-sufficiency for the explanation of the *entire* process of evolution of Darwin's principle of 'natural selection' and 'fitness to survive'. Even the *actuality* of the process of evolution, beyond a certain point (e.g., beyond the point of the emergence of a conscious, deliberate, willing, controlling *mind*) could not be explained in terms of the operation of genetic transmission and 'natural selection' alone. The 'teleological' powers of mind were a *fact* in the *actuality* of evolution. But also, 'natural selection' could not possibly be, in any ultimate sense, a bed-rock criterion for measuring 'progress',—and certainly not a bed-rock *ethical* criterion! Hobhouse's qualification really did, without any question, clarify the relations between the notions of 'evolution' and 'progress', and pointed very firmly to the only direction in which any satisfactory clarification of the concept of 'progress' could be pursued: namely within the context of the 'teleological' powers of mind. It made it equally clear that Darwinian evolution alone was *not*, and could not be, sufficient for an account of 'progress'. And the second point of great interest is that Hobhouse's conception here was *exactly* that of Lester Ward; even to the use of the self-same language. Thus Hobhouse made the clear distinction between the 'teleological' and the 'mechanistic' or 'genetic', and was completely clear as to the distinction between what constituted a 'causal' account in each. This was a *complete* agreement with Ward, and, of course, going beyond him, with all those (from Mill to Tönnies) who had insisted that a causal explanation of many aspects of *man* and *society* had to include an understanding of the choices, deliberations, and purposeful actions which men *willed*, as well as a 'genetic' account of other conditions and factors, and of the 'unintended consequences' of men's social actions. This was therefore a clear acceptance and continuity of this dimension of psychological and sociological explanation; and it is most important to see that the recognition of this point was not, in any sense, a *going beyond* the methods of science. On the contrary, it was an insistence that the very *facts* of

* *Development and Purpose*, pp. xx–xxi.

142

the evolution of life and human society could not possibly be understood or explained without it.

Here then, was an extremely important point. It is equally important to stress that it would be a complete misunderstanding of Hobhouse's position, to believe that he thought the progress of mind in the evolutionary scheme of things and the continued advancement of the human mind and its influence in the world, to be purely automatic, inevitable, and ensured. On the contrary, though Hobhouse believed that mankind had now achieved the conditions for future self-control and self-directed advance, he believed that the accomplishment of this was by no means inevitable, but a matter first of conscious recognition, and then of responsible effort on the part of man. In the introduction to *Development and Purpose*, he wrote as follows:

'I was never one of those who think that the general fact of progress may be readily assumed, or that mankind constantly advances to higher things by an automatic law which can be left to itself. On the contrary, I believed that there was no upward tendency in things as such, that apart from the operations of the human mind, the struggle for existence ruled, that the sun of its favour shone impartially on the just and the unjust, and the east wind of its implacable severity nipped the buds of loveliest promise as readily as the garden weeds. Not only so, but until the mind should come into its kingdom man himself was subject to the same rule. The struggle for existence was not the cause of mind, but mind had to undergo the struggle for existence. Each animal species that relied on a dawning intelligence for its living had to maintain itself against others that might be harder of shell or stouter of limb. Each race of man that made some advance in ideas, in industry or the social arts had to fight for its place.'

'There was no *a priori* reason to suppose that it *would* survive. Its mental development would be on the whole an advantage, but it would only be one advantage among many possibilities, and a higher birth-rate, a tougher hide, stouter muscles, or greater powers of resistance to some microbe might easily turn the scale of any conflict in favour of a rival race of lower mental endowment. It was therefore clearly possible, and the historical record showed that it was the fact,* that the higher type may often be beaten by the lower, and beaten to extinction so far as its achievements in civilization are concerned. Only if mind should once reach the point at which it could control all the conditions of its life, could this danger be permanently averted. Now it seemed to me that it is precisely on this line that modern civilization has made its chief advance, that through science it is beginning to control the physical conditions of life, and that on the side of ethics and religion it is forming those ideas of the unity of the race,

* It may be noted perfectly clearly here that Hobhouse was well aware that the facts of history did not reveal any 'unilinear' evolution of either species or societies.

and of the subordination of law, morals and social constitutions generally to the needs of human development which are the conditions of the control that is required. It seemed of secondary importance that there should have been little or no progress in other respects, provided that this essential condition of future advance had been realised.

The first object then, as it seemed to me, was to show that mental evolution had in point of fact consisted in a development of consciousness from stage to stage in the manner supposed.'*

Here then was the clear basis for Hobhouse's entire system: the truth of the evolutionary perspective and the particular emphasis upon the development of *mind* as the central feature within this perspective. This statement of mind in evolution brought together in clear, summary form all the persuasions and contributions of the earlier thinkers from Comte to Ward and Tönnies. It was the statement of a clear basic perspective: accomplished and acceptable.

(2) *The Growth of Mind in Evolution : Levels of Mental Development*

Hobhouse's first task was therefore to trace and to demonstrate this central aspect of life in evolution: the growth of mind; and this necessitated the clear analysis of such 'levels' of mental development as could be distinguished—among all animal species, and among the variety of societies which had come into being in the history of mankind—as ways in which mind had become more effective in coming to terms with its environmental conditions and exercising control over them. The central problem here was to find some clear basis for the *distinction* and *measurement* of levels of mental development in all the forms of life and society.

(i) THE IDEA OF 'CORRELATION': THE 'CORRELATING' ACTIVITY OF MIND IN BEHAVIOUR

Hobhouse adopted this position: that mental activity—from the level of the simplest living organism to that manifested in the most complex human society—was always concerned with *correlating* various aspects of experience and behaviour, of *bringing things into relation with each other*, in such ways as to secure that kind of response to the environment, that kind of adaptation to, or manipulation or control of, the environment, which would be satisfactory in terms of the particular need, function, or purpose of the

* *Development and Purpose*, pp. xxi–xxiii.

organism, the conscious individual, or the group. These words indicate very clearly that mental activity could sometimes be of a very limited, almost automatic physiological reaction, not entailing consciousness, but also, at the other extreme, of fully conscious and intelligently planned purpose. But at *all* levels, mental activity was a *correlating* activity, and, once this was accepted as a basis for conceptualization, different *kinds* of correlation could be clearly distinguished. Hobhouse wrote:

'I came to take the correlation which is effected in consciousness between different portions of our experience or between different acts and purposes as the basis of a classification. The starting point of this conception is exceedingly simple. If we utter a simple sentence we bring different words, and the words stand for ideas or elements of ideas, into relation. If we execute a purpose we bring a series of acts into relation with one another. It is by correlation that the mind introduces order and establishes its control. There is, however, in organic life a certain degree of correlation apparently independent of consciousness. Thus the several organs of the body act on the whole in concert, or, to take an instance of another kind, the successive operations of an instinct, e.g. the spinning of a spider's web, are nicely correlated with one another, though we cannot assume that this adjustment is effected by intelligence. The term correlation therefore serves, first, as a *summum genus* under which all kinds of vital activity, conscious or unconscious, might be subsumed, and secondly, as a standard by which they might be compared, certain assignable differences in the method and scope of correlation yielding the required differences of type which are successively evolved. There was here a standard measure for the evolution of mind, and to carry it right through that evolution has been the principal task.'*

(II) 'KINDS' OF CORRELATION: A SYSTEMATIC CLASSIFICATION OF 'LEVELS' OF MENTAL ACTIVITY

On this basis, Hobhouse then worked out—resting his work very thoroughly upon the empirical data of biology and comparative psychology, as well as upon his own comparative experimental investigations—a very detailed classification of the 'types of correlation' to be found among all animal species, including man; a precise classification of all the 'levels of mental development' which could be distinguished when the knowledge of biology and psychology was taken into account. It would be going too far out of our way to undertake a full exposition of this classification here, but, for the sake of completeness, a broad outline must be attempted—enough, at any rate, to make clear its place in Hobhouse's entire system.

* *Development and Purpose*, p. xxiii.

(a) Correlation Resting Solely upon Heredity

Amongst the very simplest forms of organic life (the unicellular and simplest multicellular animals) there existed a correlation between elements of behaviour and specific environmental conditions which was established completely by heredity, which was more or less invariable whatever the environmental circumstances might be, but which served, by and large, to ensure the survival of the organism. If, however, environmental circumstances changed considerably, then the inflexibility of such responses rendered them mal-adaptive. These responses correlating organic processes with environmental conditions, were purely an outcome of the simple physiological functioning of the organism, the operation of certain automatic 'mechanisms' as simple, for example, as reflex action. Indeed, 'reflex action' was the highest form of correlation resting purely upon heredity that Hobhouse specified: a uniform response to a certain kind of external stimulus in addition to the 'structural activity' of the internal processes of the organism. This most simple level of mental development was termed by Hobhouse *correlation resting on heredity*.

(b) Correlation Resting on Heredity and Adjustment to Co-Existing Conditions

Among the more complex organisms in the evolutionary scale, however, certain patterns of behaviour and response could be distinguished which were still established by heredity, but which permitted, and even provided, kinds of modification and flexibility in relation to variations that could occur in the co-existing environmental conditions. These were still quite stereo-typed responses; still established by heredity in the physiological processes of the organism; but they were capable of degrees of adaptation if the external circumstances changed. The organism was not only equipped with behavioural responses which were well-adapted to the *normal* ecology of the animal, but also equipped with a certain capacity for flexibility and adjustment of responses, some capacity for learning (of a kind), which enabled it to come to terms with changed and *abnormal* conditions. The likelihood of survival was therefore increased.

Hobhouse clarified a range of behavioural patterns of response—equilibration, sensory-motor action, instinct, etc.—which made possible a modifiability of behaviour, and simple kinds of 'learning'; but, at this level, he had in mind only the most limited kinds of learning (or established adjustments) which gave no evidence whatever of being *consciously directed* by the individual; only those kinds of adaptation which seemed to be spontaneous reactions of organic processes (simple modifications of sensory-motor action and instinct), and which, even though *adaptations*, still seemed to be 'type-responses' of the species, having only a limited range of variability.

(c) Correlation Based on Individual Experience

Finally, Hobhouse distinguished the level of mental development at which the correlation of elements of experience, behaviour and circumstance rested upon the *experience of the individual* and upon the experience of circumstances *peculiar to the individual*. These were responses going beyond those laid down purely by heredity, and beyond those simpler learned reactions which were more or less 'type-responses' common to the whole species. These were sequences of behaviour peculiar to the individual itself; adopted and pursued in relation to its own particular circumstances. Even at this level, many of the responses could be largely of the nature of physiological and mental habituation, but—increasingly in proportion with the complexity of the organism—conscious memory, interest, desire, and conscious purpose, entered into experience. Furthermore, these elements of experience now came to be co-ordinated, in patterns of learning, in a composed and articulate way. With the focal awareness of the continuity of the self, this, at the higher levels, thus gave rise to an articulate co-ordination of *knowledge*, not only, now, as a bit-and-piece ingenuity with regard to particular actual responses and particular momentary interests, but also with reference to behaviour organized as a whole—with reference to the individual's own awareness of self, of his total situation, of the conditions of his well being, and, in relation to these, of planned purpose.

Even at this level of conscious individual learning; of conscious purpose and the deliberate establishing of well-adjusted behavioural skills; Hobhouse thought it necessary and important, however, to make a further distinction. There was, he thought, a crucial difference between *perceptual* and *conceptual* (or *ideational*) knowledge which reflected significantly different levels of mental development. It was this which largely distinguished man from the animal species nearest to him in the evolutionary scale, but it was a distinction which was still significant when applied to human experience itself. The distinction can best be stated, perhaps, as that between establishing effective judgment and skills in practical experience on the one hand, and that of establishing an articulate system of explicit knowledge of those concepts and principles which are *implicit* in these judgments and skills, on the other. It is indicated in what people commonly call the distinction between theory and practice.

147

To take an example: a batsman (in cricket) may sense very well, and know very well in terms of his well-practised judgment and skills, exactly how to perform a certain stroke, given the approach of the ball and the nature of the wicket, to send the ball speedily to the boundary. He may know, with a very clear eye and a very fine touch, how to execute an off drive, a leg glance, and so on; but this may be purely at the *perceptual* level of experience and practical ability. His co-ordination of experience and behaviour for the practice of his art will not be in terms of concepts and propositions as it would have to be, for example, if he were trying to teach others. If, instead of merely playing the game himself, he had to act as a tutor to other people, he would have to work out in his mind, a *conceptual* body of knowledge, an explicit statement of those principles which were implicit in his practice, which he could then expound verbally, as well as demonstrate practically, to his pupils. This systematic knowledge—in terms of concepts, ideas, propositions— could clearly be the ground for transmitting the excellences of his skill to others and could be, therefore, a ground for further clear analysis and improvement.

In this entire discussion of 'correlation based on individual experience', Hobhouse outlined a variety of mental processes (enduring organic effects, acclimatization, selective modifications, assimilation, etc.), but he especially distinguished the *perceptual* articulation of experience and behaviour as a 'co-ordination of *concrete elements*' (emphasizing the experimental 'feel' of judgment in practical skills); and the *conceptual* systematization of knowledge as a 'correlation of *universals*': as a critical process of analysis and synthesis whereby all that was involved in the *perceptual* co-ordination of experience was made explicitly clear and brought into clear consciousness as a system of ideas and propositions. He wrote:

'The data of perception are resolved into distinct elements of character recognized as qualifying experience (analysis), and such elements can be combined to form new wholes without any reference to the order in which they are perceived (synthesis). Hence are formed *thought constructions* or *concepts* which take us altogether beyond the world of perception.'*

In this passage, Hobhouse's notion of the *creative* contribution of conceptual knowledge is made perfectly clear. Once a critical conceptual *analysis* of the elements of perceptual experience were made clear, they were loosened, as it were, even freed, from their specific context in experience, and could be combined, in new

* *Development and Purpose*, p. 81.

148

processes of *synthesis*, in quite new ways—thus paving the way for an *extension* of experience and an *advancement* of both knowledge and control.

This level, of course, was *distinctively* the level of human thought and experience or, at least, of *much* human thought and experience, and Hobhouse considered certain features characteristic of this stage to be of the very greatest importance. Strictly speaking, all these points indicated the crucial importance of *society* for the emergence of levels of mental development beyond a certain stage; but it is best to take each point separately.

'In the first place,' Hobhouse wrote, 'this stage of mental development *goes beyond the consideration of the individual alone*. It is conceivable that the process of analysis and synthesis might arise in the mind of the isolated individual, but as we know it, it is *the product of communication between mind and mind*, resting on and in turn facilitating the development of *language*.'*

The communication *between* mind and mind, *between* individuals, by means of *language* was held to be characteristic of this stage. And even this, clearly, was a *social* condition.

When discussing 'the common elements which we find in experience and which serve as a basis of interconnection between its parts', when we are pursuing the clarification of conceptual knowledge, Hobhouse stressed two things: (1) Resemblance, and (2) the continuity of existence of the individual.

The *resemblances* between features of perceptual experience might at first, be loose and vague, and the advance of exact thought consisted in clarifying these similarities and differences, analysing them into elements of exact resemblance and definite difference: arriving, that is to say, at precise concepts about which verifiable, or falsifiable, propositions could be made. This enabled us to undertake a classification of all the features of our experience, by reference to which we could then judge new individual cases, and on the basis of which we could generalize and form reliable rules of action.

The second basis of interconnection between features of experience equally definite and essential for knowledge, was the continuity of the individual.

'Here again the concept is a basis of correlation between an indefinitely great number of concrete elements of experience, and when it is brought to bear upon action serves to correlate the act of the moment with permanent interests and general principles. By its means the individual

* *Development and Purpose*, p. 82.

149

consciousness grasps the continuity running through its experience and projects it into the future. It becomes conscious of self—for the self . . . is the element of continuity running through the acts of consciousness— and at the same time and by the same methods aware of other persons and of the social groupings which they form. It can focus its own experience in generalizations, and learn and teach others by communication.'*

And it was this emergence of the consciousness of the *'self'* and its continuity in the context of *communication* with *others*, which led Hobhouse to stress the importance of *society* in the mental development of mankind.

'*Henceforth*', he wrote, '*a social tradition comes into play*, the past history of society acquires a significance, and action may be guided by a conception of the social future. Lastly, on the practical side these larger interests appeal to the self as a whole and often conflict with the solicitation of some more special and immediate end. In that case they prevail only when they can obtain a response from some dominating central impulse of the self wherein the desires are either harmonized or controlled. This central impulse is what we call the *Will*, and it is influenced by the relatively persistent feeling-tone of the self as desire is influenced by the temporary feeling attending its realization . . .'†

The important features characteristic of the stage of *conceptual thought* and the process of *explicit reasoning* were, then, (*a*) the knowledge of self, and of other beings as persons, (*b*) the formation of a social tradition, including the essential elements of communication and language, and (*c*) that organization of impulse within the individual's experience of 'self' which we call the 'will'.‡

'Any one of these,' Hobhouse insisted, 'involves the rest and is distinctive of the human as opposed to the animal grade of development.'

Again, it will be readily seen how this position took accurately and sufficiently into account, all that had been insisted upon about the emergence of the 'self' amid the communications of society by men like Ward and Giddings; about man being 'social' before he was 'human'; and about the nature of the human will and its importance stressed by thinkers from John Stuart Mill to Tönnies. But perhaps the chief point which Hobhouse emphasized in this connection, was

---

* *Development and Purpose*, p. 83.   † *Ibid.*, pp. 83–4.
‡ The elements of this position may be compared with the ideas of McDougall, Cooley, Mead, etc., in Ch. 3.

that this level of correlation went beyond the development of the individual as such, and was the product of *social* processes. And here we can see the great similarity between Hobhouse's conception and Ward's idea of the 'genetic' building up of the order of human society in the early periods of historical development—out of which a new *conscious purpose* of re-creating society was to grow.

'The building up of the conceptual order is a long and gradual process,' wrote Hobhouse. 'It is essentially an achievement . . . of the minds of men in continuous interaction throughout the generations.

The forces to be considered are now *social* rather than *psychological*, or, more accurately, are matter of *social* rather than *individual* psychology. We have to do not with the emergence of any new faculty, not with any essential change in the structure of the brain or in the sum of hereditary dispositions or capacities, but rather with *the social product* to which the individual mind contributes its mite, which is gradually built up by millions of individual workmen in the course of ages and which undergoes profound modifications within the limits of recorded history. This branch of our inquiry, that is to say, is concerned with . . . the Order formed by the operation of mind on mind, incorporated in a social tradition handed on by language and by social institutions of many kinds, and shaping the ideas and the practice of each new generation that grows up under its shadow. The enquiry into the growth of this tradition is rather *sociological* than *psychological*. It is an enquiry into institutions, into creeds, into social relations, rather than an enquiry into the consciousness of individual human beings.'*

It is abundantly clear, here, that Hobhouse was insisting that the processes of *society* were creative of the qualities of *individuality*; that it was necessary to see *psychological* processes within a *sociological* perspective in order fully to comprehend them; that the study of *social* facts and processes was necessary for the understanding of the nature of the *individual*. And this was not only an echo of Comte and others, but (and this deserves special note and emphasis) a statement strikingly in keeping with that of Emile Durkheim. This, however, we shall see more clearly later.

But to return to our exposition: this point—that all the modes of 'correlation' in the mental development of man, up to and including this 'correlation of universals', took place within this complex building up and conditioning of particular social traditions—is of the utmost importance for a clear understanding of the final stage of intelligent understanding and control which Hobhouse described. Let us simply note, however, before moving on to this that the 'correlation of universals' can be summarized as the conscious

* *Development and Purpose*, p. 84.

clarification, the making explicit, of the common elements, the universals, which ran through, or were implicit in, the *perceptual* order—which itself, however, arose within an established *social* order.

'It arises,' wrote Hobhouse, 'as these universals, which previously operate unconsciously, emerge into explicit objects of consciousness, and are thus capable of correlation. With their aid it arranges masses of experience in ordered groupings and forms general rules for the guidance of action.'

'But still, upon this plane,' he concluded, 'however far-reaching the order may be, the methods of correlation are determined by massive forces reaching far into the background of social tradition and racial heredity. The characteristic work of the stage now described is a Correlation of Universals based on the conditions of racial and social development which are not yet (themselves) brought into consciousness.'*

Finally, Hobhouse maintained, the forces of biological and social heredity; all the complex interacting influences of the social tradition which had hitherto continually conditioned the growth of conceptual thought; themselves came to be brought, by critical analysis into human consciousness. At this stage, there took place what he called the '*Correlation of Governing Principles.*' That is to say: men became aware that their own systematic thought had, in fact, itself been influenced and shaped by these forces. This consciousness came about as the inadequacies and inconsistencies of the previous stage of development gradually made themselves apparent. Attempts to remove these insufficiencies were then made by what Hobhouse called a process of *critical reconstruction*. Those forces which had hitherto *operated on* human consciousness, were now clarified by analysis and *brought before* human consciousness. Men now became aware of the conditions which lay at the roots of their own mental development, and now sought to establish systematic knowledge of the previous modes of correlation (conditions and 'levels' of mental development) themselves.

'. . . the factor in question is nothing less than the correlating activity itself, the structure of mind, the entirety of the data and the processes by which and out of which the mind evolves its percepts, its thought and its purposes. The nature, the growth, the potentialities of mind itself form the keystone of the complete synthesis at which reconstruction aims.

The distinguishing feature of this stage is the explicit recognition of the conditions operating on or in the mind itself, the entrance among the data to be correlated of the correlating processes or activities. It is a self-conscious correlation, a correlation of methods and results, or, briefly, of ultimate principles. If we conceive this critical movement carried through

* *Development and Purpose*, p. 85.

it would analyse our mental world down to its elements, and our purposes to the ultimate sources of their value, and it would bring them together into a working whole of rational comprehension and purposive activity. It would correlate the system of racial experience with the ultimate ends of racial development. It would thus cover the entire sphere of human life, bringing its past and future within the compass of a single synthesis. . . . The development of mind would come within the knowledge of mind, and, it may be inferred, in some degree within the control of mind.'*

Man had arrived at a situation in which, through his thinking about the world and society, he was confronted with the necessary task of analysing the nature and conditions of his own mind which was, itself, doing the thinking. And this brought with it a responsibility for control which was quite unprecedented. The agreement with Comte in all this, of course, is well-nigh complete, and is very striking.

In this very brief description of the classification of 'Kinds of Correlation', of 'levels of mental development', which Hobhouse put forward, we have a clear outline of his main thesis: that the development of mind turns out to be not a side-line but the main and central fact of the evolutionary process. Though maintaining that there is nothing inevitable about the future of human development, Hobhouse traced the stages of social development which *have* occurred in human history and showed that the conditions do, in fact, now exist for the achievement of this last stage of mental development: in which man can consciously investigate, and know, the manifold conditions of his own development; can assess his own potentialities and values; can to a very considerable extent exercise control over his environmental and social conditions; and can thus establish the means for carrying out a responsible self-direction of his life.

One point it is most important to remember, in considering this classification of levels of mental development, is that, for Hobhouse, the higher levels (e.g. intelligent conceptual thought) do not *supplant* or completely *supersede* the lower levels (e.g. physiological need and instinct), but include or subsume them in a higher mode of correlation. For example, Instinct includes the earlier elements of Structural Activity, Reflex Action, Equilibration, and Sensori-motor Action, but is itself a higher and more plastic mode of correlated action than any one of these separate features. Similarly, the higher modes of human correlation, which we might simply call those of 'intelligent control' do not *supersede* the instincts in man but arise *within the sphere of instinct*. No matter how intricate and compli-

* *Development and Purpose*, pp. 86–7.

153

cated intelligent control becomes, it always rests upon the massive modes of 'correlation' established by heredity. But though the hereditary basis of any new generation of human beings is essentially the same as that of previous generations, it is always variously influenced by the characteristics of the particular social traditions of the time.

'When we come to human society,' Hobhouse continues, 'we find the basis for a social organization of life already laid in the animal nature of man. Like others of the higher animals, man is a gregarious beast. His interests lie in his relations to his fellows, in his love for his wife and children, in his companionship, possibly in his rivalry and striving with his fellow-men. His loves and hates, his joys and sorrows, his pride, his wrath, his gentleness, his boldness, his timidity—all these permanent qualities, which run through humanity and vary only in degree, belong to his inherited structure. Broadly speaking, they are of the nature of instincts, but instincts which have become highly plastic in their mode of operation, and which need the stimulus of experience to call them forth and give them definite shape.

The mechanical methods of reaction which are so prominent low down the animal scale fill quite a minor place in human life. The ordinary operations of the body, indeed, go upon their way mechanically enough. In walking or in running, in saving ourselves from a fall, in coughing, in sneezing, or swallowing, we re-act as mechanically as do the lower animals; but in the distinctly human modes of behaviour, the place taken by the inherited structure is very different. Hunger and thirst no doubt are of the nature of instincts, but the methods of satisfying hunger and thirst are acquired by experience or by teaching. Love and the whole family life have an instinctive basis, that is to say, they rest upon tendencies inherited with the brain and nerve structure; but everything that has to do with the satisfaction of these impulses is determined by the experience of the individual, the laws and customs of the society in which he lives, the woman whom he meets, the accidents of their intercourse, and so forth. Instinct, already plastic and modifiable in the higher animals, becomes in man a basis of character which determines how he will take his experience, but without experience is a mere blank form upon which nothing is yet written.'*

In this way, Hobhouse provided an account of the biological and

* *Morals in Evolution*, Chapman and Hall, 1951, p. 10. The controversy has long raged, and still rages (see *Man and Aggression*, ed. Ashley Montague), as to whether man's experience and behaviour has 'instinctive' components or is 'learned'. It can clearly be seen in Hobhouse's treatment that this controversy need not rage at all. There is no 'black and white' issue here. Certainly man's nature includes inherited instinctual components, but this is not in any sense whatever to exclude modifiability, learning, intelligence, or the influence of social factors. *All* of these are involved, and this has been clear from the writings of Darwin onwards.

psychological basis of social life which can be seen to be in accordance with the accounts of all his predecessors, Comte, Mill, Spencer, Ward, Sumner etc. and also with those of his contemporaries—such as Tönnies and Westermarck. This systematic picture of levels of mental development enabled Hobhouse to place man and society with complete intelligibility and validity within the evolutionary scheme of all animal species, and to see the complete continuity between animal and human life, but also to see the crucial *distinctions* between them. It enabled him to see the place of all the simpler physiological and psychological mechanisms of experience and behaviour—such as instinctual experience and behaviour (which were in many respects common with other animal species)—within the life of man in society, but at the same time, as we have seen, to give full weight both to the part played by cumulatively changing social institutions and cultural traditions in shaping the nature of man, and to the fact that, within this context, men could come to a fully conscious rationality in deliberately planning their actions. Within this scheme of analysis Hobhouse could see man clearly—*both* as an organism in his environment *and* as a conscious actor pursuing deliberate ends within his social situation; it was not one thing *or* the other—but *both* in proper relationship and in proper perspective. There was no sharp dichotomy whatever between the one and the other, nor had there ever been from Comte onwards, and this will be a point worth recalling later.

The full weight of some of Hobhouse's distinctions—such, for example as that between the 'conceptual' and 'experiential' phases of the critical reconstruction of the empirical order of society (see the earlier diagram), as conceptual knowledge increasingly explored 'perceptual experience'—cannot yet be properly shown. For this, we need to look in more detail at other components of his system; but at the end of our exposition these things will be drawn together.

For the present, it is necessary to consider in more detail the crucial significance which Hobhouse attached—for the understanding of the levels of development of mind in man—to the development of *society*. So far, Hobhouse had provided a classification of the levels of mental development in evolution in accordance with the 'correlating' activities of mind, and chiefly with reference to the entire range of biological species. He also, however, as we have seen, thought that *some* levels of mental development were not only biologically based, nor only a matter of individual effort and achievement, but were attendant upon certain cumulative achievements of *society*; and his next task was to distinguish the criteria of these *social* levels of mind in action.

(3) *SOCIAL Evolution : Levels of Mental Development in SOCIETY*

No more need be said about the 'levels of mental development' which Hobhouse distinguished in the whole range of biological species. It is perfectly clear how the classification of species commonly accepted in biology—ranging from the simplest unicellular organisms through all the more complex multicellular creatures to the higher vertebrate mammals and man—could be arranged in accordance with his criteria of measurement; and how, from simple to complex, the increasing flexibility and adaptability of behaviour to environmental conditions could be demonstrated. The increasing effectiveness of 'mind' in the scale of emergent biological species is clear enough, can be taken for granted, and requires no further comment.

There was a marked difference of *kind* however, with the emergence of *man* in nature. Man was one animal species among others, and we have seen that Hobhouse fully recognized this, and gave full weight to the bio-psychological endowment—of certain determinate features of anatomical structure, physiological function, sensation, impulse, emotion, maturation, behaviour, etc.—which was established by heredity, and which formed a given and perennial basis for his social life. But two points of difference were very strongly emphasised here.

The first was that the capacity of the human mind—whether at its perceptual or conceptual levels—was such that men were no longer confined to *adapting* themselves to their environment, or even to the constraints of their own nature! A new creativity was possible, and was distinctively characteristic of man. In the light of past experience and the accumulation of knowledge and skills, men could now deliberately *transform* their environment in accordance with their known needs and purposes. The human mind was *purposive* and *creative*.

The second was that this cumulative knowledge, control, and power of creativity was essentially a concomitant of the interaction and intercommunication of men with each other in *society*. The development of the human mind was not one of individuals in isolation; not one of the accumulation of individual experiences and skills; but essentially of the shared growth of *communal traditions*. The sharing of need and activity; the shared experience of co-operation and conflict; the communication through language; the settlement of certain ways of doing things *within the community*; was the very contextual condition for the growth of the human mind to new and unforeseen levels going far beyond that of other animal species.

In this we can see the fullest accord with the fundamental positions held by the nineteenth century founders: from Comte and Marx right up to the distinction made by Ward between the 'genetic' and the 'teleological'.

Up to this point, the entire emergence of life in the world, and all its forms—the evolution of species and their mental equipment—could be explained in terms of biological adaptation alone; in terms of genetic transmission, genetic mutation, and natural selection. *From* this point, however, it was no longer possible either to measure or to explain new emergent levels of the human mind in terms of biological adaptation alone. Now, the purposive powers of mind and the quite central and fundamental fact of the cumulative *social tradition* had to be taken into account. Men of new generations, born within the traditions (the historical continuity) of their own societies, did not come to possess different 'levels of mentality', giving them new degrees of 'control' over their environment, because they were *biologically* or *psychologically* different from their forebears in any hereditary sense, but because, in their training and education they acquired the accumulated stock of knowledge, skills, rules, procedures, values, which earlier generations had contributed. *Societies* were *new* systems of organisation,* new co-ordinations or 'correlations' of accumulated *social* facts, which were themselves bearers of knowledge, beliefs, attitudes of mind, accomplishments of art, value-laden symbols of language and other kinds of expression and communication; and which could be continually improved and enriched as generation followed generation.

There entered into the development of mind, then, procedures of transmission of a distinctively new kind—*social* procedures of continuity—which were quite distinct from the *biological* mechanisms of transmission. There was now a *social heritage* in addition to a *biological heritage*; a process of '*social* evolution' built upon the basis of '*biological* evolution'—not *supplanting* it but *supplementing* it. And this 'social heritage' meant that the qualities and activities of the human mind among men in society were no longer confined to a negative process of adaptation. The accumulation of knowledge; the continuous pursuit of skills, ideas, and ideals; the creation of an actual fabric of 'culture' and 'social organization' made possible a setting up of aims, goals, principles of conduct and endeavour, which could be fully and positively purposeful; and in the light of these ends the elements of the environment could be creatively transformed. Mind, now creative and purposeful, could even become a new directing and controlling factor in evolution itself.

One very important emphasis which can be seen with quite

* 'Super-organic' systems in Spencer's terms.

luminous clarity in all this is that—like Comte, Mill, Marx, and others—Hobhouse was portraying the way in which the *social* was *essentially* the *historical*. *Social* processes, *societies*, as distinct from other facts in nature, were persisting and *cumulative* processes in time, and man (even man the individual) could not be understood excepting within this context. Even what appeared to be 'simpler' and 'static' patterns of culture were, in fact, cumulative traditions which had taken shape among a people as an outcome of their efforts in coming to terms with their environment during an immemorial period. But in 'literate' societies, of course, the historical sequences of culture, tradition, and institutionalization, could readily be traced.

It was clear then that, with the distinctive emergence of human society, some study of *social* traditions, of the transmission from generation to generation of a *social* heritage, was necessary in order to trace and to measure any *subsequent* advance in 'levels of mental development' in the world. Some way of distinguishing levels of mental development in human *societies* had to be provided and the criteria of such distinctions—though new forms of 'correlating activity'—would have to refer to social *institutions*, and were, clearly, different from those applicable in biology.

Levels of Mental Development in Society

Undertaking a wide-ranging comparative and historical study of those societies of which we possess some degree of testable knowledge, Hobhouse then proceeded to classify societies according to the distinctive levels of mental development which were manifested in their institutions. These distinctions were still based upon the same principle of measurement. They were new kinds of 'correlation' of mind and action in relation to ends pursued—though new correlations established in terms of essentially *social* patterns of knowledge, thought, and skill. And they were still indications of new kinds and degrees of *control* over both nature and society.

Perhaps it is necessary simply to point out here that—in 'classifying' societies of the past and present in accordance with these distinguishing levels of mental development—Hobhouse was in no sense whatever trying to provide a picture of a necessary historical sequence of the development of mind in society. Over and over again, he made it perfectly clear that he quite definitely rejected any necessitarian account of the 'inevitability' of sequences in history; that he actively disagreed with, and indeed could disprove, any theory of a 'unilinear' direction and trend of social evolution; that he saw nothing inevitable about a historical movement from 'lower' to 'higher' qualities of mind or morality; and that he was far from accepting the view that societies now were 'better' in all respects than societies in times past. All he was concerned to do was to carry out to completion his task of distinguishing those levels of mental development which *had*, in *fact*, emerged in the world, and, in so far as these were *social* levels, to classify societies in accordance with them. Such a classification certainly *had* its historical dimensions, necessarily! But it involved no assumptions of 'inevitability'. And—this is the chief point—it was, from the point of view of sociology, a *scheme for contemporary analysis*. It made possible generalizations about the state of knowledge in a society and the connected condition, and nature, of all its social institutions. It aimed, in short, at being a *classificatory scheme*—and contemporary societies (as well as societies of the past) could be grouped, compared, and studied within it. It provided a scheme for comparative study *as such*—whether the societies compared were of the past or of the present.

Hobhouse concluded that at least five distinct levels of mental development could be clarified in human history, and it will be worthwhile to give a brief outline of each of these.

(I) THE SIMPLER, PRE-LITERATE SOCIETIES

In the first place, Hobhouse grouped together all those societies which were crucially distinguished by the absence of literacy. Such societies were relatively small, possessed relatively simple techniques in all their tasks and activities and had no written records of their past; of their accumulated traditions of knowledge, beliefs, values, and skills. The social tradition in its entirety was transmitted from the elders to the young by oral, artistic, ritual, and practical means in an essentially 'face-to-face' situation. They were societies dominated by 'primary group' relationships.

Not all pre-literate societies possessed the same level of mental development, the same level of accomplished knowledge, however, and since the differences between them were not evidenced in written form, some other criterion of measurement had to be looked for. Hobhouse found this in the kind of knowledge which their degree of *control* over their environment, as revealed in their *technology*, implied. The skills and techniques employed in earning their livelihood, in building their dwellings, in curing their diseases, in ritually emphasizing certain beliefs, all rested upon certain suppositions of knowledge, so that these techniques of control provided a satisfactory basis for a kind of sub-classification *among* the pre-literate societies. Basically, this classification was three-fold—distinguishing simpler communities in accordance with whether their livelihood depended upon simple hunting and food-gathering, the practice of settled agriculture, or the development of a pastoral economy. But the full classification is represented in the following diagram.*

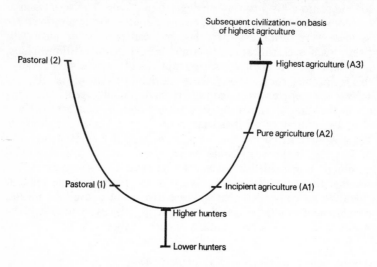

(a) The Hunters and Gatherers

The Lower Hunters were those small groups who lived almost entirely by the simple gathering of fruits and nuts, the collecting of shell-fish, and the catching of reptiles, insects and vermin; who had no permanent dwellings, but constructed wind-breaks, lived in caves, or put up very ephemeral huts of boughs and leaves; who possessed no 'secondary arts' such as spinning and weaving, pottery, metal-work, and practised crafts only at a very low level of skill— such as the making of very poor canoes; and who had no domestic animals except the dog and a few other small pets.

The Higher Hunters were characterized by the possession of those arts and crafts which the Lower Hunters lacked. These groups lived more by *organized* hunting, by the organized *chase*, than by the simple collection of food. They constructed substantial houses, even if they were temporary—for example, of hide and skin. They practised spinning, weaving, pottery, and were capable of considerable skill in all their crafts; and they had domesticated certain animals—especially the horse.

A third kind of group was also distinguished—*the Dependent*

* Taken (and slightly adapted) from *The Material Culture and Social Institutions of the Simpler Peoples*, by Hobhouse, Wheeler and Ginsberg.

Hunters—though they were rather a special case. These were hill and jungle tribes who lived on the outskirts of more established villages and settlements and whose mode of earning a livelihood was related to, and dependent upon, the economy of the more settled group. They collected jungle products such as wood, dyes, silk-cocoons, and traded them with the settled community. They also performed certain services, such as protecting crops and acting as beaters on large-scale hunting expeditions. Sometimes, too, they became entertainers, and were sometimes employed in criminal activities. They represented, in short, a mode of life which was itself undeveloped; having this kind of 'symbiotic' relationship with more developed groups.

These three kinds of community were the simplest of all in terms of knowledge and related techniques. Beyond this level, human ingenuity seemed to have developed two major lines of technical advance: the one developing the techniques of settled agriculture; the other resting its mode of life on the keeping of herds of animals; but it is very important to see that Hobhouse *in no sense* thought of a 'pastoral *stage*' or an 'agricultural *stage*' as following each other in a certain order. He did no more than *classify* those societies which demonstrated skills and knowledge in these various ways. And, again, certain *grades* of knowledge and technique were distinguishable in each direction.

(b) The Agriculturalists

Incipient Agriculture (A1) was a category which Hobhouse used to designate those societies in which the food supply was still predominantly derived from hunting and gathering, but in which there was some definite evidence of the clearing, digging, and planting of the land. Women did field work, and the 'digging-stick' was used as an implement—indeed, it was the chief implement used. These societies were still nomadic as the hunters and gatherers were. There was very little domestication of animals—perhaps poultry and the keeping of pigs. There was no use and knowledge of metal. And no specialized trade was carried on: only some barter in kind.

Pure Agriculture (A2) was the grade marking those societies in which agriculture had become the *chief* basis of subsistence. Secondary arts were also practised—spinning, weaving, pottery, etc.— but still not as specialisms. Substantial, settled dwellings of timber were constructed. There was a more extensive domestication of animals, but, even so, there was no keeping of herds of larger animals (cattle), and animals were still not *used* in agricultural work. And again, trade was limited to simple barter.

Highest Agriculture (A3) was the condition of societies which

161

practised a full 'mixed agriculture'. Animals were now put to use in agriculture; they were kept in flocks and herds, and used in transport. They were also a part of the pattern of cultivation. There was a manuring of the land, irrigation of the land, some rotation of crops—all of which were clear evidence of some knowledge concerning the using up, and the resuscitation, of certain qualities of the soil. In cultivation, too, there was now the use of the plough. There was a fully developed system of mixed agriculture, and, on this basis, new specialized industries emerged: metal-work, woodwork, and the making of textiles. Also, with this, there was regular and specialized trade which went far beyond simple barter.

(c) The Pastoralists

The pastoral kind of economy was regarded by Hobhouse as a development beyond the level of hunting and gathering which was an *alternative* to agriculture, and here he distinguished two grades.

Pastoral (1) was the grade of those societies which gained their livelihood from the keeping of herds of animals but in which there was little or no attendant agriculture of other kinds, and in which there was no evidence of the development of other, secondary, arts and industries. They were marked purely by the herd as their fundamental mode of subsistence.

Pastoral (2) was the higher grade in which, in addition to the keeping of large herds, other kinds of agriculture were also developed, or were practised by a neighbouring or subjected people, and made use of. There was, in short, a qualification of the purely pastoral economy by other agricultural methods. In these societies, too, the secondary arts and specialized industries were well-developed; there was a knowledge and use of metals; trade was well-developed and extensive; and there was also a development of organized warfare.

The first pastoral grade carried a level of material culture equivalent to that of 'Incipient Agriculture', and the second pastoral grade, a level of culture equivalent to that of the 'Highest Agriculture'. Indeed, at this highest level, the 'agricultural' and the 'pastoral' societies approximated very closely to each other, but could still be distinguished in accordance with whether the mode of life was chiefly determined by the necessary movements of large flocks and herds, or by the sedentary requirements of a settled, mixed agriculture.

It will be readily seen, in this analysis, how the technical accomplishments of these pre-literate peoples were clearly indicative of different levels of knowledge, and Hobhouse made much of the fact that—in the absence of literal records—these criteria of material culture and techniques had the supreme advantage of being *observable.* They were clearly evident, and they were the clear embodiments of differing grades of knowledge. They indicated, in short, 'levels of mental development' and attendant levels of 'control over the environment' among the pre-literate societies. There was one other extremely interesting point which emerged from Hobhouse's classification, and that was that all *subsequent* advances in the levels of mental development in society rested upon the condition of 'Highest Agriculture' rather than the highest Pastoral grade. A pastoral economy seemed capable of yielding and sustaining only a certain level and complexity of social life. Only on the basis of a settled, mixed agricultural economy could settled industries, settled trade, settled urbanization develop. This, it seemed, was the basis for subsequent social growth and technical advance. This was a point of much interest, and was borne out, or reinforced by the next category which Hobhouse felt to be distinguishable.*

(II) LITERACY AND PROTO-SCIENCE: THE EARLY AGRICULTURAL CIVILIZATIONS

The next level of mental development which was clearly marked in human society, Hobhouse thought, and a level of tremendous significance, was that of the emergence of *literacy*—and, with it, for they were all significantly associated, *numeracy*; the development of a systematic 'rule-of-thumb' *science* ('proto-science'); and an extension of planned technical control over the forces and resources of the environment. Again, we must deal with a large and interesting subject all too briefly.

It is worth noting that all the characteristics of the higher 'Pre-Literate Societies' which Hobhouse described were the characteristics accomplished by societies in the 'Neolithic' period of pre-history. This next development of the human mind took place in the earliest agricultural civilizations as neolithic groups of this kind extended their settlements, and were amalgamated with each other, in particularly fertile spots in the world—in fertile river valleys, or on river deltas in a maritime situation. This was a long and gradual establishment of a new, larger-scale civilization, and came into being roughly between 3,000 and 2,000 B.C., and on the basic accomplish-

* This, it will be realized, is an extremely brief account of Hobhouse's classification, with an eye, really, on an exposition of his entire system. But his study of these 'levels' of social development were of the greatest interest. Here, Hobhouse, was simply *classifying.* But it is interesting to read archaeological, anthropological and historical accounts of the remote past to see what a close conjunction there is between Hobhouse's classification and these studies. One or two books by V. Gordon Childe are excellent examples of this: e.g. *What Happened in History*, and *Man Makes Himself.*

ments (the sowing of grain, etc.) of the neolithic peoples during the previous thousand years. By long processes of drainage and irrigation, successive generations of people managed to cultivate exceptionally fertile areas which had been, for example, areas of swamp, frequently flooded.

The yield of crops, of barley for example, in this situation was something like 86 times the sowing. There was, then, a very large agricultural surplus. The accumulation of 'capital' became a possibility, and, with it, economic and social developments in all directions.* The large surpluses of grain made trade possible; but trade, in these areas, was also both *required* and *facilitated*. It was needed because of the lack of certain materials—timber, stone, metal, etc.; and it was made easy by the accessibility of neighbouring societies by means of the waterways of river and sea. Specialized manufactures, specialized trade, were established, and large urban settlements—centres of trade, government, and administration, grew to new proportions of both size and complexity.

The *city* was established; walled off from the surrounding environment; and within its walls was an *artificially transformed* nature; a nature selectively re-created by human culture: with carefully planned and maintained canals and dykes, tilled fields, guarded pastures and flocks, cultivated gardens, and large, settled households. '*Civil*ized' life was begun. At the heart of these cities were the 'city-temples' or 'temple-households', each of which—dedicated to some deity—was, literally, a large-scale household incorporating an extensive division of labour. It was not too much to say that the neolithic division of labour had been brought indoors! Besides the priests—who were the clerks and administrators—there were bakers, brewers, spinners, weavers, smiths, and other craftsmen and artisans; and, beyond the household, were the agricultural labourers, merchants, etc. Such a complexity of urban life also carried with it a clear centralization of political authority, organized administration of the law, military power, religious sanction, and economic management—in short, a necessary system of *public administration*.

For all the complexity of this work—the cutting and maintenance of canals, the regulation of river traffic, the management of all the work of the temples, the levying of taxes, etc.—the priests and clerks were accountable to the City Governor. Communications and commands had to be given at a distance; clear accounts had to be kept; disputes had to be resolved by procedures which were not arbitrary. Pure word of mouth, pure uniform ritual, was now no longer enough. New techniques of calculation, communication, and

---

* The importance of the accumulation of 'capital' for subsequent social development—stressed by Comte and Marx—was clearly borne out here.

record-keeping were essential, and the development of these marked a new level of human mental development which had the most far-reaching importance for the subsequent developments of civilization.

The keeping of records and the issuing of commands and instructions at a distance necessitated some sort of intelligible *written* symbols, and led to the invention of writing. From *pictograms*, more simplified *ideograms* were developed which came to have phonetic attachments, and these led to stylized letters. Some kind of *numerical* notation was as necessary as a written script. There was therefore a concern for numbers, and methods of computation and calculation, and the development of arithmetic and geometry. The same concern stemmed from other practical tasks such as those requiring 'standards' of weights and measurements, including recorded divisions of *time* in relation to sowing, harvesting, etc., and this led to a preoccupation with the working out of a reliable calendar, not to mention the development of sundials and clocks!

All this, in short, led to the development of *literacy*, a rough systematic *science*, and a connected, applied *technology*. *Always*, however—and hence Hobhouse's term 'proto-science'—this 'scientific knowledge' was, though systematic, related to *practical* tasks: of building temples, calculating numbers of bricks, working out the cycle of cultivation of the year, knowing the heavens for the navigation of ships, and the like. It did not entail a level of philosophical criticism going beyond this. And this 'level' of literacy and proto-science was typical of all the agricultural civilizations of antiquity: the Sumerian cities and Babylonia, Egypt, Ancient China, etc. It was on the basis of these great accomplishments that new refinements of civilization were to grow.

Hobhouse's emphasis upon 'Literacy and Proto-Science' as a distinct point of demarcation in human mental development is clear enough, but it is worth while to note and accentuate some points. First let us reiterate that this was a *social* point of demarcation, and it is worth emphasis that an element such as *literacy* and a *language which can be written*, which we all take so much for granted simply as a feature of our *humanity*, was, in fact, a long cumulative *social* development which was rooted in quite distinctive necessities accompanying certain conditions of social growth. A *written language* is not simply a putting into 'literal' form of a kind of *verbal* (oral) articulation which was already there. It involved a new creation of literal and numeral symbols and ways of arranging and compounding them, and ways of incorporating them into *speech*; so that something much more complicated was involved. It signified, in fact, *new* kinds of mental (social) process, and it was, indeed, the distinctive and highly significant point of demarcation that Hobhouse claimed.

165

Other things may be noted. This development of literacy also marked the first *institutionalized* education. The 'Temple-Schools' now had to instruct those who were going to become priests, clerks, and administrators in the new 'symbols' on which the entirety of this recorded administration rested. This was almost entirely a matter of rote-learning; but still, it was a new necessity.

One of the most important things, however, was this. Literacy brought into societies the new element—of vast importance—of a *known historical perspective*. It is hardly too much to say that *literacy created history*. With written, accurate, dated records of their past, the people of a society now had a new sequence of time in terms of which to understand and reckon their destiny. It was no longer a matter of an 'immemorial custom', from a distant past whose dimensions were unknown, and whose eternal elements and values were embodied in myth and ritual. It was now a matter of firm, temporally exact record. Of course, traditional religion still loomed large in these societies; very large; but still—the significant difference was born. Now—with literacy—societies could be aware of known stretches of their past; of their immediate situation in the present; and of their projected possibilities for the immediate future. A historical consciousness of a new kind was possible. Reason, calculation, judgment, purpose were now given firmer materials on which to work.

(III) REFLECTION IN THE LATER EAST: THE SPIRITUAL RELIGIONS

The new range of control over the natural environment brought about by literacy and the systematic knowledge of 'proto-science' is quite evident and can quite readily be seen, but the next level of mental development which Hobhouse distinguished reflected a new *kind* and *dimension* of control—and was really a development in man's mind which sought control over *himself*, over his own inner character and outward conduct, and over the nature of his own society. Curiously, too, the evidence of this new development seemed to occur, in various societies, during the same period—from the eighth to the fifth centuries B.C.

By and large the early large-scale societies of antiquity of the kind we have just described were 'traditional' societies. Established traditions of government, law, military power, religion, even occupational groupings passed on from generation to generation through long, relatively little-changing millennia. In relation to certain determinate elements of social change, however, critical assessments of the beliefs and sanctions which had long been accepted came to be made.

In China, for example, the traditional religion of antiquity came to be in danger of disruption as the empire became restless with new modes of economic change and attendant political conflict. Confucius, seeking to re-establish traditional order, reflected upon the ancient books of traditional Chinese religion and provided a re-considered teaching of the life of the good and 'superior' man in society, stating certain luminously clear principles of belief and morality which were relevant to individual and state alike. In India the archaic nature of Hinduism, priest-ridden and caste-ridden, encountered the criticism of Jainism and Buddhism, and, by the leaders of these 'new' religions, new spiritual rules for guidance in life and for the achievement of salvation were set against the heavy burden of traditional Brahminic doctrine and ritual. The religion of ancient Persia was criticized and re-vitalized by the newly founded religion of Zoroastrianism. Judaism, from among its cleavages, and in its particular political situations, gave rise to Christ and Christianity. The 'traditional' religions were critically assessed by these new moralists, these 'founders' of new religions which were more sensitive to individually felt needs, and such as to provide clear principles for spiritual aspiration and moral guidance.

These new religious movements, according to Hobhouse, were distinguished by a new mental awareness: that the qualities and ends of human belief, and moral and political endeavour, were not something simply laid down in immemorial tradition; in routine, stereotyped dogma; but were open to personal question, honest reflection, and individual effort. But—also—they gave rise to a new kind of knowledge and a new kind of creative impetus in society. They gave a new kind of knowledge—in that they provided new statements of ideality; new statements of reflective thought about beliefs and moral experiences; which were clear and useful for guidance and practical personal conduct. And they produced a new kind of impetus—in that (a) they introduced new dimensions of social control. Men could now direct their minds and skills not only to changing their *physical* environment, but also to creating improved organization within their *societies*, aiming at new idealities. And (b) they inspired in men a new kind of moral and spiritual endeavour actively and purposefully to pursue—in social, political, and personal action—a mode of life which was commonly thought to be 'better'. It was a new dimension of 'idealism', of committed 'spirituality'; a qualitatively new level of mental development and moral endeavour within society; a development, too, which, like the cumulative achievement of the earlier civilizations, was pregnant with many subsequent developments to come.

(IV) CRITICAL AND SYSTEMATIC THOUGHT IN GREECE

The next level of mental development distinguished by Hobhouse was that marked by the intellectual achievements of the 'classical' Greeks in the City States. Here, it was not only that men came to be *aware* of new ideals, of new moral principles, of new knowledge gained by the criticism of past traditions. Greek thinking went far beyond this. Whereas other peoples clarified new ideals (in the 'spiritual' religions), produced new elements of knowledge (in 'proto-science'), the Greek philosophers probed analytically and critically into fundamental questions as to the *nature* of their new ideals, and their new concepts, and, indeed, as to the nature and validity of the very procedures of thought, information, and conceptualization, whereby men arrived at these concepts and ideals.

It was not only, for the Greeks, that men knew how to build houses or pyramids by conceiving 'angles' and the 'calculation of the length of sides in triangles', and the 'areas of rectangles', but, much more fundamentally: what is the nature of these ideal forms which lie at the heart of mathematical formulations and formulae? What *is* a circle? What is its relation to the actualities of 'round' objects in nature? And what is its relation to the human mind which can somehow apprehend both the ideal form and the sensible object, and reason about both?—and which, indeed, finds its calculations about the ideality relevant to its manipulation of the actual object?

Similarly, for the Greeks, it was not only that we should seek 'truth' and 'justice' in morality—but that we should delve to the bottom of such questions as: what *is* ethical truth? Why does it seem to make *claims* upon us? What *is* justice? What *is* righteousness? When we see that differing societies appear to have such varying customs and beliefs pertaining to righteousness—can there be said to be any such thing? Or is it simply a matter of 'convention'?—and *relative* from society to society? If it is *not*: what are the criteria of ethical truth whereby we can adjudicate between such customs?

In short—the Greeks manifested a new level of analytical and critical thinking in that they not only produced descriptive masses of facts, or even systematic bodies of facts, which would be *useful* for navigating ships, growing crops, building temples and the like, but produced in addition, fundamental *theories* about matter, about human nature, about human society, about human ideals and moral principles, about the very foundations of thought and being itself; indeed, about the very nature of the universe and the possible nature of God—and of qualities such as truth, beauty and the like. And they produced theories in *general* terms. It was not now, like Herodotus: '. . . the Egyptians do this, the Persians that, the Spartans this, the Athenians that . . .'—but: what is the nature of man *as such*?

This new development laid the basis for a critical philosophy and science as profound as any of which we have yet become aware, and of the most basic importance for all subsequent explorations of our knowledge of the world. Whether about the nature, foundations and varieties of political constitutions and the ethical principles on which they should rest; whether about mathematical forms and procedures of inference; whether about the analysis of poetry and rhetoric or of other forms of art; whether about the nature of human character and the principles of education . . . in every conceivable direction, the Greeks laid the foundations for all the most fundamental analysis and critical examination of human experience. Though it was to be lost for a while with the overthrow of classical civilization, it was to re-emerge, and—fused with new elements—to form the firm basis for all the secure developments of human thought and knowledge. The level of general thought in Greece was, indeed, the highly significant advance which Hobhouse took it to be.

(v) SCIENCE IN THE MODERN WORLD

The final 'level of mental development' which Hobhouse thought it possible to distinguish in society was the level of modern 'empirical' science, as it was developed—first in the natural, and then in the human and social sciences—from Renaissance Europe to the present day. This, of course, built upon a gradual, and then a sharp criticism of the 'theological' mode of thinking of medieval Europe, and of the 'metaphysical' or 'speculative' tone and nature of much classical thinking. It culminated philosophically in the kind of sharp 'critical' thinking which came with Hume and Kant, and its position was distinguished by two major characteristics. First, it insisted, in all its construction of 'theories', upon crucial conditions of test. It *always* subjected its propositions to the test of logical scrutiny and factual verification. And secondly, it became the most effective and reliable basis for utilitarian action in the entire world of practical affairs. Whether in the breeding of animals, the excavation of collieries, the building of bridges, the application of steam-power to railways and ships, the curing of diseases, the attempts to ameliorate poverty, crime, or aggression in society—it was always the assembled knowledge, the tested theories of science (as exact as was possible at the time) to which people came to turn for guidance. This acquisition and application of the methods of empirical science;

169

this fusion of the most acute speculative thought with the most exact procedures of testing; gave man, again, of course (for better, for worse) far greater kinds and degrees of control over nature and society than did earlier kinds and levels of knowledge.

These, then, were the 'levels of mental development' which Hobhouse distinguished as the outcome of the cumulative achievements of *society*, and which rested upon, but went far beyond, the levels of mind and control over the environment established by the purely *biological* processes of evolution. The centrality of 'mind' in evolution was thus demonstrated by carrying this analysis of the 'correlating activities' of mind through all organic species and through all known levels of knowledge in society. It will be quite obvious in this, that Hobhouse not only *agreed* with Comte that the one feature of clear cumulative advance in the history of man and society which could be demonstrably observed and measured was the advancement of knowledge; but that also he did, in fact, *accomplish* such a demonstrable measurement. It can readily be seen, too, how Hobhouse saw this development of knowledge as being closely attendant upon man's 'practical activities'—as emphasized by all the earlier thinkers from Comte and Marx to Ward, Sumner and Giddings—in his insistence upon its close relation to the degree of *control* which it enabled man to exercise over his destiny: a control which was, at once, material, technical, organizational, and moral. There was here, then, a very considerable consolidation and a much more detailed and improved demonstration of earlier points of view.

This demonstration of the advancement of mind and knowledge in life and society was, however, for Hobhouse, as it had been in the proposals of Comte and Mill, only the *beginning*. The establishment of these levels of mind and knowledge clearly gave a firm basis for the *classification of societies*. The level of mental development as manifested in the stock of knowledge possessed by societies, and in the kinds of control exercised in all directions of social action on the basis of this knowledge, was at least one completely clear criterion, one completely clear 'yard-stick' of measurement, by which they could be classified. It would then be possible to study comparatively all the societies so brought together in this classificatory scheme, in order to see whether, at each level of knowledge, there did exist an appropriate 'consensus' of all other social institutions. It would be possible, in short, to establish 'empirical generalizations' about the interdependencies of social institutions at each level of knowledge, and see whether, in fact, a demonstrable 'social evolution' (in the sense of a full concomitant development of all the institutions of society—the family and kinship systems;

the economic institutions of the division of labour, property, etc.; political institutions; religion; education; military institutions; social class; and the like) *was* closely attendant upon this advancement of mind and knowledge. Furthermore, this seemed, as a hypothesis, to be very feasible; for one would fully expect any improved knowledge which men possessed to affect all their modes of life and action—their technology, their organization of work, their administration of law and government, their religious beliefs and aspirations, their methods of education and instruction, their methods of warfare, etc. This central 'yard-stick' of knowledge could serve, then, as a clear classificatory principle, and a hypothetical guide, in undertaking a systematic comparative and historical sociology.

This, plainly, was a very comprehensive bringing together, in the form (now) of actual, substantive studies, of many of the theoretical positions put forward earlier. It was a *development* of the most concrete and detailed kind: an actual undertaking of the wide and systematic empirical studies which had been proposed and conducted (as by Comte) in outline. And Hobhouse did, in fact, carry out this detailed comparative study of social institutions—drawing upon anthropological reports on the simple societies, and on an extremely wide range of documentation (legal codes, religious doctrines, political papers, etc.) in his study of historical societies. It is, of course, quite beyond the bounds of possibility, to give a satisfactory picture of such extensive studies within the compass of a brief statement—but it is possible to indicate *some* of the main directions of his work, and *some* of his findings in such a way as to indicate the nature of his entire system.

(4) *The Comparative Study of Societies and Social Institutions*

The outline of Hobhouse's comparative studies is now clear enough. Having established his clear criteria of 'levels of mental development', he classified societies accordingly, and went on to see whether, or how far, the other institutions of society were correlated with these levels.* One or two important points need to be noted, however, before we look at Hobhouse's findings on particular institutions.

We must note, first of all, that this was *not*, in any sense, a direct

---

* It will be noted that this was quite a different notion of 'correlation' than that employed centrally in exploring the activities of mind. This was now purely a matter of tracing the *interconnections* between the level of knowledge and the other institutions of society.

causal hypothesis. It was not a statement that the 'changed stock of knowledge' was the one, *single* factor that *caused* changes in all other institutions. Hobhouse was not advancing a 'mono-causal' theory here. It was simply a luminously clear *method* for classification and comparison, by means of which to *investigate systematically*, such interdependencies as there might be between the levels of knowledge and the patterned forms of the other major institutions of society. Detailed questions of 'cause' and 'effect' were left quite open. The attempt was simply that of *systematic study*: in order to *discover* such patterns of social institutionalization, social change, and social development as actually existed in societies possessing measurable levels of knowledge. It was a classificatory, analytical and descriptive attempt to *establish empirical generalizations.**

At the same time, as we shall see, and again without enunciating 'cause and effect' *laws*, the picture so provided was one which allowed Hobhouse to assess in a very clear and useful way the institutional conditions and trends in the contemporary human situation, and to present a clear perspective for reliable and responsible *judgment* and *action* within this situation. 'To *see* in order to *foresee*' was a desire underlying all the work of Hobhouse, as it had been that of Comte.

A second point is of very considerable importance. When discussing Westermarck (and, at the same time, referring to Tylor), we were critical of any mode of attempting a classification and 'correlation' of social institutions which neglected to take into account the 'setting' of specific institutions within the society as a whole of which they formed 'parts'. In short, we raised the persuasion, adopted by all the earlier thinkers, that a society was a 'system' of institutional elements, and that it constituted a certain structural-functional entirety (though by no means an entirely harmonious unity), within which its particular parts could be understood. And we agreed with these thinkers that no single institution could be fully (or satisfactorily) known and understood if it was considered only, and altogether, outside of this context. It is important here to see that Hobhouse did not fall into this error. Though classifying societies in accordance with the criterion of the level of their knowledge, and though investigating the 'correlation' of other institutions about this criterion, he was nonetheless, quite thoroughly aware

* It may be noted that Popper's exclusive emphasis upon the 'hypothetico-deductive' method as being the supreme method of science is rather too extreme a point of view. Sometimes suppositions are not clear-cut cause-effect hypotheses, but established points which can be seized upon to direct further studies; but the further studies can be genuinely exploratory: they do not know what they will find. In this sense one can properly speak of inductive procedures, if not inductive logic.

that he was comparing *societies*. He was quite clear that a society *was* a system of interrelated parts: and it is therefore worth while to see (*a*) the way in which he thought of the 'functional interdependency' of institutions in a total society, but also (*b*) the qualifications which he found it necessary to make to this conception. This is important because it is one other clear example of the way in which those scholars responsible for the foundation and development of sociology insisted upon 'structural-functional' analysis as a necessary component of sociological analysis, but, at the same time, did not accept at all the ideas that societies were completely unique and autonomous, or that all the internal aspects of them were 'integrated' in something called 'functional unity' or 'functional harmony'. 'Structural-functional' analysis was by no means synonymous, in their minds, with the acceptance of these other propositions.

The Nature of Society

As to the interrelationships between the elements of social structure in a whole society, Hobhouse was quite clear. In his book *Social Development*, he wrote:

'. . . every community that endures is a structure in which the parts, upon the whole, work together. Farmer, tailor, shoemaker, lawyer and doctor perform their several functions, not thinking of very much beyond them, and in the broad result the community gets itself fed and kept in passable health and peace. The community, then, is a structure which in general maintains itself, and that not like a stock or a stone without the necessity of internal activity, but like an organism by the continuous output of energy and regular interchanges between its parts . . . These facts have suggested the famous organic analogy.'

Having discussed the term 'organic', he went on:

'The organic whole is the system formed by several such parts in permanent relation, and it is one in which each part is determined—in a degree at least sufficient for the maintenance of the system—by the requirements of the whole, while the whole is determined in respect of some of its features by the requirements of each part.'

Hobhouse took great care to point out all the ways in which the analogy between a living organism and a society broke down—as Spencer had clearly done before him. Even so, he then concluded:

'. . . Behind this far-reaching difference, there is still the true analogy that, by whatever method the result is reached, in the end we have *a whole of*

173

parts conditioned by mutual requirements. From this relation arise the fundamental features of organic life found alike in physical organisms and in societies.'*

There is no doubt whatever, then, that Hobhouse regarded societies as 'social systems' and saw the necessity of studying institutions within this context. At the same time, he took great pains to make it clear that he had no naïve idea of 'functional harmony' in mind, and that, like earlier thinkers, he saw the institutional fabric of society as something coming into being as a result of conflict as well as co-operation. But in addition, he emphasized points of difficulty which stood in the way of achieving an accurate comparative study of total societies and their institutions in this way.

Some Difficulties in the way of Studying Societies as wholes

First of all the documentary evidence which existed, especially on the simpler societies, was very variable in quality and perspective. Frequently, all that was available was a set of 'snapshots' of the social life of a people, indeed of *aspects* of their social life, taken at different periods and in quite an unconnected way. Such evidence was by no means systematic, nor did it possess historical continuity. Secondly, documentary reports referred to aspects of social life in quite different ways: sometimes speaking, for example, of small local groups of aboriginal peoples as 'tribes', and sometimes using the term 'tribe' to refer to the people inhabiting an entire region of a continent (e.g. as in the case of the Australian aborigines). Sometimes, too, they referred simply to some such vague entity as the 'Australian native'. These, however, were relatively minor points about the insufficiencies of available data (though important, for all that!) There were more fundamental problems.

Hobhouse maintained that sometimes it proved exceedingly difficult to be clear and certain about the *unit of study*, when studying unfamiliar societies. Analytically, it is easy enough to distinguish between 'family', 'clan', 'tribe', 'kingdom'. But in the actuality of investigation, he held, there seems sometimes only to be a very loose central unity connecting a people, and for all evident and practical purposes, groups seem to function as separate clans and tribes. Though 'institutions' should therefore properly be studied within their 'societal context', it was sometimes not easy to see what that context was. Sometimes trees could be seen more clearly than the wood!

The same kind of problem loomed large when one came to consider the *defining boundaries* of a society. Societies, in fact, very

* *Social Development.*

frequently interpenetrated each other in many ways. The extent and the degree of 'culture contact' was very difficult to ascertain; but it was very common and almost always existed among human groups. To take particular examples: are particular forms of property, of the law, of the family, of ecclesiastical organization, of social stratification, etc., in modern Britain, France, Germany, Italy, to be understood in terms of their 'functional setting' within each of these 'autonomous social systems'? Or are they to be understood, in great part, as institutions which were (and are still to some extent) common elements of an all-embracing 'culture-area' which was (and is) wider than specific political boundaries? Can one ever speak altogether of 'indigenous developments'? Or are there always some kinds and degrees of cultural 'diffusion'?

Well: we need not deal with these questions here.* It is enough simply to establish our point, and to make clear the position of Hobhouse, that he *was* quite clear about the necessity of thinking in terms of the total context of a society, when trying clearly to delineate and compare particular institutions, *but*, at the same time, qualified this position both in rejecting any assumption of 'functional harmony' in societies, and in raising these qualifications about studying them as well-defined, autonomous 'systems'. The interesting thing about Hobhouse's care on this matter is that it demonstrated quite plainly the *complementarity* of comparative studies and studies of functional interconnection, and this might be best emphasized by looking at the statement of Professor Morris Ginsberg, a student and colleague of Hobhouse, who has put the issue very clearly. In *Sociology*, he wrote:

'If anything is well established, it is that all parts of social life are intimately related and interwoven. If society is not an organism, it certainly has something organic in its nature, in the sense that its parts function together and that changes at any one point have repercussions that affect the whole. It is, therefore, of the greatest importance that societies should be studied as wholes, and that the nature of the interactions between its various elements should be understood.'†

Similarly, in a paper on *The Problems and Methods of Sociology* after having outlined some of the chief elements of social structure, he wrote:

* It is of interest to note that Hobhouse's discussion and conclusions on these matters were almost exactly the same as those of Malinowski (*A Scientific Theory of Culture*) and Radcliffe-Brown (*A Natural Science of Society* and *Structure and Function in Primitive Society*).
† *Sociology*, Home University Library, 1949, p. 13.

'The study of functional interconnection is . . . a necessary complement to the detailed study of specific associations and institutions.'

Furthermore:

'. . . in the study of the more advanced societies, at least, the functional and the comparative methods are complementary. For it is only by means of comparative study that we may hope to be able to distinguish between mere concomitance and functional interconnection.'*

Nothing could be clearer than this.

There was, however, one other element of Hobhouse's treatment in establishing his framework for a systematic comparative sociology which specifically rested upon his awareness of the necessity to study societies as wholes. This was his introduction of a *second* principle of classification, and it is most important that we should note it. We may remember that Spencer had thought it necessary to use *two* principles of classification: the strictly empirical one of the 'degree of social composition, or aggregation' which societies actually possessed, and the analytical one of the construction of 'types'—the Militant, Industrial, and Ethical types—for purposes of additional interpretation. Hobhouse found a similar procedure necessary to make his own emphases clear. In addition to the 'level of mental development' which societies possessed, he also wished to compare societies as wholes—not just as strings of institutions— and, for this purpose, he took *'the nature of the social bond'*, the active principle which formed the effective basis for the unity of a people within their defined political community, as a second criterion of classification. Societies at different 'levels' of knowledge seemed, as total entities, to be bound together by different principles of allegiance, belonging, or membership; and these might well not be arbitrary, but concomitant with, and attendant upon, other institutional conditions.

Types of Social Bond: Types of Society
Hobhouse distinguished three clear principles of 'social union' within which certain sub-divisions were made. They were:

(1) *The Principle of Kinship: The Blood Tie*
Among all the simple (pre-literate) societies, the principle of belonging to the group was the principle of *blood-membership*. People were *born* into the political community, and the ties which bound them together were the close ties—both limited and extended—of

* *Reason and Unreason in Society*, Longmans Green, 1947, p. 14. This point may be noted later in the methodology of Durkheim who also classified societies and undertook comparative studies to make clear the 'normal' functional interdependency of institutions.

kinship. Families, by particular patterns of intermarriage, had their places in Clan and Tribal forms of organization: among which, of course, there were variations such as clans resting upon the maternal or the paternal principles. In all this, it should be noted that Hobhouse did not ignore the great range of size and complexity that marked the 'pre-literate' societies. He took into account relatively large-scale confederations of tribes, and even the formation of kingdoms in some cases. The central fact, however, was that in all these societies at this 'pre-literate' level, *kinship* was the *authoritative bond* of society, and, at this level, it seemed sufficient.

(2) *The Principle of Force and Authority: Despotism*

The emergence of the distinctive level of 'literacy' clearly seemed, however, to mark a growth in the scale and complexity of human societies in which kinship, *alone*, was no longer sufficient as a basis of social union and authority. Kinship continued to exist as a most important factor in these larger-scale societies, but it was superseded by another over-riding principle: that of centralized despotic power (supported by centralized military force). These larger civilizations were, in fact, 'amalgamations' of earlier kin-groups and village communities: whether by long peaceable union, or by the impositions of conquest; and the complex relationships of society went far beyond the governance and clear delineation of earlier kinship procedures and regulations. *Despotism* formed the new basis of regulation, power, and authority; some form of central rule became a focus for political, legal, ecclesiastical, and military power all combined (as in the Pharaoh of Egypt and the Divine King or Divine Emperor of other societies). Here, Hobhouse defined three sub-categories of 'Despotism':

(*a*) *Personal:* in which the military and bureaucratic hierarchy was focused upon the central figure of one person (in whom 'divinity' resided).

(*b*) *Feudal Monarchy:* which seemed appropriate where power had to be delegated over a wide area, and where the hierarchy of a widely dispersed governing class had to be unified by a central power.

(*c*) *The International Empire:* a form of central power which came into being when an aggregation of kingdoms occurred; when national and local boundaries were over-stepped; but when a central unity and organization had to be sustained. In this kind of despotic authority, varying kinds of relationship between the central power and the regional and local (provincial) 'units' were possible.*

* These categories may be compared with Max Weber's sub-divisions of the 'traditional' type of authority: see p. 448.

(3) *The Principle of Citizenship: The Recognition of Personal Rights and the Effort Towards the Common Good*

With conditions of 'critical knowledge' in society, however, at the levels of critical, analytical thought in ethics and in science, despotic authority seemed to give way to a principle of social union of quite a different kind. Now power and authority, and the claims on which they rested, had to be *justified*, and were exposed to criticism to this end. In the context of such criticism, there came to be a recognition of the rights of persons as members of the community (in which decisions at the centre were going to be binding upon them) to make claims upon society, and, reciprocally, to see their duties in contributing to the commonweal on which rested the good of society as a whole. The principle of the social bond came therefore to be of effective *political citizenship*: the principle that all men, as members of the political community, should be constitutionally recognized as such, and that their rights and duties and procedures of political action should be constitutionally made clear.

This, obviously, was a kind of bond altogether distinguishable from the traditional authority of Kinship, and the sheer power of Despotism, but here again, Hobhouse made two further distinctions:

(a) *'Incipient Citizenship': the City State*

This was the situation among the small City States of 'classical' times, especially in Greece (and Rome) where critical thought and knowledge emerged, and where citizenship replaced both kinship and divine kingship to very considerable degrees, but where this was not entirely so, and where, especially, the free 'citizens' still rested upon a population in bondage. Political citizenship was not extended to *all* the members of society. And, furthermore, all these constitutional advances towards citizenship were swallowed up and largely lost with the spread of the Macedonian and Roman empires, and completely lost with the decline of the Roman Empire, the Dark Ages, and the gradual establishment of Medieval Feudalism.

(b) *Full Citizenship: the Modern Nation State*

Full citizenship, as the basic nature of the social bond in society over-riding all others, was, Hobhouse held, only accomplished in the modern 'nation states' which had developed constitutionally as independent political communities following the disruption of Medieval Christendom. In these nations all traditional kinds of power and authority had given way before the demands that *all* the members of society should possess recognized political citizenship;

and a detailed making of political constitutions had taken place (and was continuing to take place) in order effectively to base the political unity and the political authority of society on that principle. The intricate administrative apparatus of the state, the political machinery, was constructed explicitly to serve this principle, and all earlier kinds of authority were abandoned as being insufficient and unjust.

These, then, were the 'kinds of social bond' in terms of which Hobhouse classified societies as wholes. This was his *secondary* principle of classification, and it is perfectly clear how these categories of 'social union' paralleled his criteria of 'levels of knowledge'. The two together provided Hobhouse with the classificatory scheme within which his comparative study of societies, and their institutions, could be systematically, reliably, and *testably* carried out. And again, before leaving this, it is worth while to emphasize in our attention, how completely this schema and its perspective was in accord with all the great generalizations of the similar frameworks of Comte, Spencer, Marx in his fashion, Ward, and Giddings. Later we will draw all these generalizations together in a simple schematic way to demonstrate their considerable and profound agreement; but here it is enough to see that Comte's 'Three Stages'; Spencer's kinds of 'social aggregation' and distinction between 'Militant, Industrial, and Ethical' types; Marx's distinctions between the kinds of 'productive forces'; and the distinctions made by Ward and Giddings; were all to be seen again in this developed and much more detailed and carefully qualified scheme.

It is only necessary to notice that, having carefully clarified these categories of the 'social bond' for strict purposes of classification (as '*types of society*'), Hobhouse was still at very great pains to make it clear that he did not think that these, in the *actuality* of existing societies, existed in *pure form*, or, in other words, that they were all *mutually exclusive*. The categories, he claimed, were *types* of social bond; they were clearly distinguished *criteria* for classificatory use. He wrote quite distinctly, for example:

'The types of social organization that have been sketched are not mutually exclusive. A despotic oriental monarchy may rule over a hundred thousand village communities, each consisting of a dozen or a score of patriarchal households in which some residual traces of mother-right and totemism may still be found. An independent commune may rest on a clan system founded on mother-right, and such clans may, like the Iroquois, build up a federation resting on assent rather than force, and so correspond rather to a state than to a despotic kingdom. What we have distinguished are (1) *certain principles of organization* which, when they work out unencumbered by other principles, form (2) *distinguishable types of*

179

social structure*—types which we may take as landmarks by reference to which we may place other social forms. These types may co-exist as constituent parts of a larger order, or may be blended with one another in various ways. It follows that we cannot say that one of these forms succeeds another in serial order as we ascend the scale of culture. The history of society, unfortunately, is not so simple. All that we can say with some confidence is that the three principles distinguished and the forms of social union arising out of them *preponderate at successive stages in the order named.* That is to say, that the lowest form of social organization is the group loosely connected with other groups of the same tribe; that at a somewhat higher stage tribal government develops; that above these societies are found organized kingdoms; and that the "state" in the true sense is developed only among peoples of the highest civilization. There is, as it were, a mean point in the scale of social advance belonging to each principle, and though it extends far above and far below we place the principle in the series by referring it to this point.'

It may be noted in this passage, too, that Hobhouse again insisted that he had in mind no 'serial order' of succession of these types in history; no 'inevitable' historical movement from one to the other. They were *distinguishable types of society,* at *distinguishable levels of mental development,* about which generalizations might be made with regard to the interdependencies of social institutions which they embodied. And, given the clear formulation of this classificatory scheme, Hobhouse then proceeded with his detailed comparative studies in order to discover what these institutional correlations might be.

Institutions and their Correlations in the different 'Types' and 'Levels' of Societies

It is completely impossible to give a *summary* account of Hobhouse's comparative study of social institutions in such a way as to be faithful and accurate with regard to all his details and qualifications. I have, in fact, struggled to do this, but found the task beyond me. However, I very much want to make clear the nature of the detailed, systematic body of knowledge which he accomplished, and, especially, to make as clear as possible the perspective for judgment about the *contemporary* human situation which it provided—so there is nothing for it but to offer *some* kind of condensation. In view of the difficulties, it seems to me that only one course is possible.

First: to *indicate* only (*not* to try to describe summarily) the picture which Hobhouse presented of the interdependency of

---

* *Morals in Evolution*, p. 69. Again, it is borne out with complete clarity that the construction of 'types' was *always* a central method in the formulation of systematic comparative studies and the construction of theories. All the major theorists, each in his own way, made use of it.

institutions which were typical of each *kind of society* at each *level of knowledge*; and to do this solely by means of schematic 'tables'. This might serve, at least, as a clear 'skeletal' guide to the very extensive system of knowledge which he provided; and might succeed in pointing out clearly the kind of correlation between institutions which his findings portrayed; without pretending to be anything other than an indicative 'chart' or 'teaching aid' drawn up on a blackboard: all the details of which *could* be filled in were there time for further elaboration. Then, secondly, with this basis, we can go on to outline, in rather more detail, some of the directions of 'social evolution' in *specific social institutions* (as indicated on the right of my original diagram) which he described, and his estimations of the 'net' accomplishments of human society which he took into account in his final judgments as to the facts and possibilities of social development. And in this second task we can note very clearly the qualifications which he made.

First, then—the 'interdependencies' or 'consensus' of institutions typical of each kind of society at each level of knowledge. I have arranged these in such a way as to show a certain 'sequence' of social change in order that it may fit into my first diagram—but we will note important qualifications to this arrangement later.

Now this 'schema' is, I think, clearly indicative of the vast range of empirical knowledge about social institutions and their interconnections which Hobhouse succeeded in bringing together, and of the generalizations about the 'consensus' of institutions in each 'type' and 'level' of society which he succeeded in stating and demonstrating. The significant 'interdependencies' of institutions constituting each 'type' of social system are writ large. Furthermore, the cumulative growth and development of society through the sequence of 'types' and 'levels' seems perfectly plain and convincing. The correlation of social institutions to the centrally clarified development of mind and knowledge in society seems also to be well established. Before coming to any qualifications of all this, let us see, secondly, the kind of picture which Hobhouse drew of the way in which the 'evolution' of certain *particular institutions*, within this entire context was correlated with the central measuring-rod of the 'advancement' of mind in society.

Specific Institutions and their Relationship to the Development of Mind

In his book *Morals in Evolution* particularly, Hobhouse took each social institution in turn—marriage and the family, property, law, the relations between communities, class relations in society, etc.—and sought to clarify, within the large comparative schema which we have indicated, the way in which each had changed in relation to the different levels of knowledge. Here, we will briefly outline his findings on a few of these, simply to see the kind of correlated change which he portrayed. But again, as we consider each of them, it will be worth while to bear in mind the clear similarities and connections between them, and, especially, to begin to pay particular attention to the way in which his studies clarified a *perspective for judgment* about the societies and institutions of the *contemporary* world. It was this—the clear understanding and accurate assessment of the *contemporary* situation—which was foremost in Hobhouse's mind.

Bearing in mind the close and significant connection which he emphasized between knowledge and *control*, we might take first of all the institutions most directly related to the power of *control* over both the physical and the social environment.

(1) *Technology, Science, and the Economic Utilization of the Forces and Resources of Nature*

The development of technology in society, and the attendant economic exploitation of natural resources was, Hobhouse argued, quite clearly correlated with the levels of knowledge in society, and was quite clearly revealed by comparative studies. During the long Palaeolithic period, men were able, because of their limited, rudimentary knowledge, only (at best) to *use* as tools the sticks or stones which they found about them. Their mode of life was still, like that of other animal species, primarily *adaptive*. The Neolithic period was marked by the great advance that men were able not only to *make* tools, but to make tools in order to make tools, and this knowledge and practical skill extended their power over nature enormously. This made possible larger human settlements of men capable of making tools, weapons, and developing the 'secondary arts'. Men were able to *transform* their environment. Even so, it was only with literacy, numeracy, and proto-science that men became capable of a more systematic, regular, and reliably planned exploitation of natural resources. From this point on, men were able—with increasing success—to harness for their use the *overt* forces of nature—such as wind, fire, and water. With varying applications, and varying degrees of skill, this continued until the emergence of science in the modern world. And the distinctive difference and extension of control here, was that men could now both know and make use of the *hidden* forces of nature. The knowledge of gas and electricity, for example, provided greater sources of fuel and greater degrees of power. The knowledge of genetics made possible the deliberate breeding of plants and animals in order to maximize the yields of certain products. The knowledge of radium, of nuclear power, etc., are other obvious examples.

The advancement of k..owledge was therefore correlated in the clearest way possible with the organization of technology in society and the economic organization of methods for the utilization of resources. Also, in the clearest way possible, it was made plain that man in the modern world possessed an infinitely greater degree of control over nature for the satisfaction of his many needs than he had ever possessed before.

(2) *Morality and the Regulation of Society*

The development of knowledge was also clearly correlated, according to Hobhouse, with men's conceptions of morality and the relation of this to the control over the *social* as well as the *physical* environment. In the simpler societies, the regulation of the social order was a matter of the observance of *'primeval custom'*. Immemorial usage carried its own sanctions. Critical, reflective conceptions of morality did not exist. With literacy and proto-science and the large myths of the traditional religions of the early agricultural civilizations, there was a certain clarification of a moral code. This again, however, was not a matter of critical philosophical reflection upon personal rights or duties, but only the statement of a certain set of 'rule of thumb' moral dictates laid down by authority and sanctioned by religion. It was, said Hobhouse, of the nature of an unreflective *'moral common sense'*.

Out of the criticism of these traditional authorities and religions, however, arose the 'spiritual' religions rooted in individual 'founders' which established high-level ideals to which men should spiritually and ethically aspire, and in the light of which they should consider themselves responsible for regulating their personal and social conduct. One important kind of 'idealism' was that of the philosophical ethics of the Greeks—in which the most fundamental quest of critical thought took place for the formulations of righteousness and justice in the individual and society.

This *'ethical idealism'*—whether with or without a context of religious organization—was changed significantly only with the critical thought, the scepticism, the humanitarianism, and the concern for the concrete 'putting of wrongs to right' in the actuality of society, which came into being with the emergence of science, and the temper of critical science and philosophy, in the modern nation states. Men were now no longer satisfied simply to *have* and to *know* sublime ideals, or to *aspire* towards them; they also wished to approximate to them as closely as they could in the day-to-day institutions of political society and personal conduct. 'Idealism' alone was no longer sufficient, and was given an active, practical, political flavour in what Hobhouse called the new period of *'Realistic Humanitarianism'*.

In relation to the regulation of *society*, then, as well as to the control of the *natural* world, the institutions of men came increasingly to rest upon the persuasion that, in the light of knowledge and clarified standards of judgment, they should consciously *act* to *change* and *transform* society in such ways as to approximate as closely as possible to these standards. To *know*, as the Greeks had put it, seemed to be concomitant with the duty to *become*.

(3) Religion

Closely connected with this development of morality was the development of religion in society, and this too seemed to be significantly correlated with the different levels of knowledge. At the limited level of knowledge of the pre-literate societies, with the limited technological control and economic organization, and with the rule of 'primeval custom', the conception of 'the spiritual' was such as to be inseparably connected with—almost *identified* with—the conception of the 'material'. There was barely a distinction. The world was pervaded with an 'occult' power; every *thing* of nature had its spiritual nature. 'Animism' was very prevalent. All the events of nature—malevolent and benevolent (the words are significant)—were interpreted as the willed purposes of gods, spirits or occult forces. Even the realm of the dead, the 'after-life', was conceived in 'quasi-material' terms; a picture closely resembling the living world.

With the systematic knowledge of the large agricultural civilizations, with proto-science and literacy, with intricate myth and doctrine, with new levels of human control and with a clarified 'moral common sense'—the 'spiritual' took the form of 'superhuman beings'. The gods were now in human form—with both the virtues and the vices greatly exaggerated: more than 'life-size'. The conception of the 'spiritual' became 'anthropomorphic'.

This anthropomorphism, though not entirely discarded, was much qualified with the development of the 'spiritual religions' and 'ethical idealism'. Though god, or the 'divine', was still to some extent referred to in 'personal' terms (i.e. as a 'being')—the new emphasis was that such ways of speaking, even of 'knowing', were inescapable because of the limitations of human nature, but that, nonetheless, the 'ineffable' was really beyond all human description. The conception of the spiritual was thus that of the embodiment of the highest ideals; of the sublime; of truth, goodness, and beauty—ideals which man could only dimly apprehend. And in such a conception, the spiritual was equated with *reality*.

184

In the modern world of science and critical philosophy, Hobhouse thought that—though by no means fully worked out—man's conception was becoming at once more limited and more modest, but also more compelling towards activity and towards conscientious effort. In the world as revealed by the intricacies of modern knowledge, men found it impossible to equate the spiritual with the whole of reality. Still experiencing profound 'intimations' of something they could only call the 'spiritual', and of the compelling strength of the values rooted in it, it was, nonetheless, possible for men only to conceive of 'the spiritual' as *one element* of reality (and not necessarily even with nature or history on its side; not even sure of success in the outcome of its destiny) which was in a condition of *struggle* in the totality of things—and was committed to the attempt to shape the world creatively towards its own ends.

Again, then, the development of religion in correlation with that of knowledge, technology, and morality, was such as to give rise to a greater range and degree of critical reflection, and also to confront man in the contemporary world with a greater degree of responsibility for conscious judgment and control.

We might turn now to those other institutions which form part of these developments (e.g. 'property', or 'class relations', as part of technological and economic organization), or those which must in some way be an over-all embodiment of them (e.g. the political institutions of the 'State'), and those which would certainly fall within their conditions and regulations (e.g. the family).

(4) Political Institutions: the Basis of the 'State'

We have already seen the way in which Hobhouse classified the distinctive types of 'social bond', and how these were correlated with the levels of knowledge; and we have seen that this depicted a development from 'Kinship' societies to societies based on 'Despotic Authority' and then to the emergence of political communities based upon 'Citizenship'—in which the making and changing of complex political constitutions took place. We need not reiterate any details of this—but it is worth while to see how Hobhouse himself summarized this direction of social change.

'The nature of social growth', he wrote, 'is best understood by considering the basis of social union, that which tends to hold societies together and also to keep them separate from one another. Certain determinants, such as territorial contiguity or isolation, and community or diversity in ideas, customs and speech are operative at all stages of growth, tending to extend or contract the limits of union as the case may be. But, in addition, there are certain principles which give character to the social structure as a whole, and are distinctive of successive stages of development. The earliest form

185

of social structure is that of the relatively unorganized local group, which takes more distinctly organized shape as a clan, or a community of inter-marrying clans. We may reckon these together as societies based on kinship (including affinity). More extensive societies are formed mainly by conquest, and rest ultimately on force. The principle of force clothes itself in the form of authority, and in greater or less degree reacts on the whole structure of society. It may be simply superimposed on the simpler communal life, or it may reorganize it on a feudal basis. It may divide society into castes or into the familiar ranks of nobles, freemen and serfs or slaves. It is the characteristic social form of the middle civilization. In the higher civilizations it is partially or wholly replaced by the principle of citizenship or mutual obligation as between the community as a whole and its component members. A Society so constituted may be called in the stricter sense a State. It rests on an ethical basis, and is the foundation of ethical development. The State has existed in the form of the City State of antiquity and the Middle Ages, and of the Nation State of modern times. But the Nation State in turn is expanded by the federal principle, and federal states and federal or quasi-federal empires begin to fore-shadow the possibility of a true international Society.'*

The forms of political authority and political organization were therefore also correlated with the levels of knowledge and we see here the clear picture which Hobhouse gave of the development of political society from the earliest bond of 'kinship' to the emergence of the 'modern nation state' and, beyond this, to the various kinds of 'federation' making for a 'global' political interdependency of states in some form of international political organization. It is important to notice in the picture of the *facts*, the central place taken by reflective *ethics*. The development of the *moral* conscious-ness and the *ethical* sophistication of mankind, within the wider context of developing knowledge was an essential component in the development of actual political forms, and the institutional *facts* of the latter could not be understood without it. And again, the picture given of man's situation in the modern world is one of an active engagement in the conscious making and re-making of political society in the light of a refined conception of citizenship, with all the complexities of rights and duties and the best administrative forms for ensuring and sustaining them, that this entails. Increasing power—but increasing responsibility: this is the theme portrayed with a stark clarity.

(5) *Law: Public Justice*
The same correlated development was to be found in the closely connected institutions of *law* in society. In the societies resting on

* *Development and Purpose*, pp. 220–1.

'Kinship', with their limited level of knowledge and the rule of 'primeval custom', the resolution of disputes was largely dealt with by the 'blood-feud': a matter of retributive retaliation between kin-groups governed by custom. Punishment was chiefly 'corrective' and 'repressive' and concerned with offences against the security and sanctity of tribal order and tradition. At the higher economic grades, however, 'restitutive' punishment also emerged.

With the level of literacy and proto-science in the 'Despotic' societies with their complexities of relationships and their much more complex administrative systems, some mode of resolving disputes going beyond 'kinship' custom was necessary. Indeed, in a larger society consisting of an amalgamation of kin-groups, the 'blood-feud' would be positively disruptive. The law of society thus came to be centralized and administered by formal procedure. 'Courts of Justice' were established—central and provincial—with a Chief Justice, a number of judges, and what we would now call 'clerks to the court'. Procedures of bringing charges, defending against charges, determining guilt, recording judgments, and allotting punishments were laid down. The law became *written* law, and gradually the complexities of the law came to be *codified*. At this level, however, though there were more 'rational' court *procedures* there were still very rude methods for determining guilt: trial by *ordeal*, for example.

Later developments were the establishment of greater degrees of the professional 'autonomy' of the law and its administration from political and religious power; the increasing preponderance of 'civil' and 'restitutive' law; and the refinement of court procedures. More careful methods of determining guilt were achieved. Procedures of 'advocacy' for the public prosecution and defence of 'cases' were instituted in order to bring all relevant evidence before the judge (the legal expert) and the jury (the lay members of the court), so ensuring, as far as possible, impartial judgment.

These developments were extended and refined in the modern nation states (and with the development of *international* law and courts of justice), but there were also new elements. These chiefly centred upon new attitudes of mind towards the 'criminal'—which were themselves the outcome of the extension of knowledge (in the human sciences)—and involved new conceptions of degrees of guilt and responsibility, and questions as to how far, and under what circumstances, criminals should perhaps be 'treated' rather than punished.

Law, then, like other institutions was clearly correlated with the levels of knowledge in society, and, again, the picture of modern society was one of an increasing complexity of law—of kinds of dispute brought to the law, of legal procedures, etc., and—again to

187

be emphasized—of the centrality in these intricate developments of *ethical* questions arising from new knowledge. There was a conscious and responsible remaking of law itself.

(6) *Relations between Social Classes*

It is particularly interesting to link Hobhouse's account of 'class relations' in society to his discussion of the development of law, because it indicates very clearly the close interdependency between all these elements of 'institutionalization' (showing that, though dividing our subject into 'parts'—economic, political, religious, legal, etc., we are really talking all the time about the same total 'complex' of social life), but also because it enables us to add another dimension to what Hobhouse said about 'law' and to show his insight into problems which have become more acute and inflammatory since his time.

Hobhouse gave an account of class differentiation in society in relation to the levels of knowledge, technology, the division of labour, the divisions of authority and power in society, which was clearly demonstrated—but unexceptionable. He described the sources of differentiation among the simpler societies—sex, age, etc.—and the growth of royal and noble families and the development of sectional property as the economic complexity of such societies increased. The increasing complexity of class and administrative hierarchies in the large 'Despotic' societies, and in all societies beyond that level, was also quite thoroughly made clear with the aid of detailed legal, governmental, and religious documentation. Also—the major kinds of 'stratification' which have emerged in human society: slavery, serfdom, caste, the 'estates' in feudal society, and 'class' in modern societies (which is *not*, any longer, defined in the law, but rests simply upon differences of property, income, occupation, authority, education, etc., and attendant 'styles of life') were all given clear accounts, and shown to be correlated with levels of knowledge and the other institutions already discussed.

The particular interest of Hobhouse's treatment, however, was, again, his analysis of citizenship and social class in the modern world, and his demonstration of the ways in which the *facts* of stratification in society could only be understood by taking into account a ferment of new ethical conceptions and efforts which aimed at treating men as *individual citizens* of the community in accordance with the principles of social justice. Indeed, in his entire account of 'social class', Hobhouse showed how important a factor was the *social ethic* which was active in society—and not only conservatively *reinforcing* the particular class-system of the time, but sometimes *criticising*, *combating* and *rejecting* it, as among the 'spiritual religions' and 'ethical idealism' in their opposition to 'caste' and slavery, for example.

In *Morals in Evolution*, Hobhouse wrote:

'The primitive group was relatively small and homogeneous. But as society grows divisions come, and a new form of group-morality arises— distinctions of high caste and low caste, bond and free, and the like. In engendering, accentuating and maintaining these distinctions, military conquest, economic inequalities, religious differences, race and colour antipathies, have all played their part, and up to the middle civilization social divisions probably tend to increase rather than diminish. Combated by the teaching of the higher ethical and religious systems, they have been mitigated and in large measure overcome in the modern world. Most tenaciously maintained where the "colour line" is the outward and too visible symbol of deep-seated differences of race, culture, character, and tradition, they are countered even here by the fundamental doctrine of the modern state that equal protection and equal opportunity are the birth-right of all its subjects. Thus, though the colour line is the last ditch of group-morality, here too in the modern period, taken as a whole, Universalism has made great inroads.

With the improvement of communication and the growth of commerce, Humanity is rapidly becoming, physically speaking, a single society— single in the sense that what affects one part tends to affect the whole. This unification intensifies the difficulties of ethics because it brings into closer juxtaposition races and classes who are not prepared by their previous history to live harmoniously together. Hence it is not surprising that law and morals do not show a regular, parallel advance. Nevertheless, the upshot of the evidence here reviewed is that, ethically as well as physically, humanity is becoming one—one, not by the suppression of differences or the mechanical arrangement of lifeless parts, but by a widened consciousness of obligation, a more sensitive response to the claims of justice, a greater forbearance towards differences of type, a more enlightened conception of human purposes.'*

And again, in *Development and Purpose*, emphasizing the changing conceptions of the nature and extent of 'obligations' among men as 'citizens', and the way in which these have affected, and are affecting, class-relations, he wrote:

'In the earliest phases . . . there is a clear line of demarcation between the member of a certain group and the outsider. In the kinship societies there is in general approximate equality between those of the same sex and the same local group or kin, while the "stranger" stands outside the sphere of obligation. In authoritarian societies differences of rank, caste or class

---

* *Morals in Evolution*, pp. 316–17. The similarity of Hobhouse's view to that of Comte, Westermarck, etc., on the extension of enlightened 'altruism' to a 'global' condition, is very strongly marked here.

appear, which reflect the same principle of group-morality, though with various modifications of form and limitations of stringency. But in the higher authoritarian societies the ethical principle of equality makes itself felt, and for some purposes at least all Roman citizens under the empire, or again all Moslems and in a measure all Christians are equal, though they may be subject to autocratic rule. Equality, however, in this stage is generally conditional—either on uniformity of religious belief or on some assignable legal qualification. The fuller elaboration of the principle of equality as dependent on the conception of personality is naturally the work of the state, and is carried through in proportion to the thoroughness with which the principle of citizenship is applied. In the modern state the class barrier has disappeared, and the sex barrier is disintegrated. There remains the colour line, of which it is not possible to speak with precision in general terms. In some cases it has been surmounted, in others not. It may be said upon the whole to remain in the modern world the only serious exception to the general rule of fundamental equality of rights and obligations. Lastly, in so far as obligations attach to personality they transcend natural and political boundaries, and this is recognized, both in the higher forms of authoritarian society and of the state, in the growth of international law. The principle that personal rights persist even in a state of war and after conquest is fairly well established.

The further development of the same conception which attaches definite rights and duties to the state as such and also to nationality as such is, on the other hand, struggling for existence. It is neither a mere ideal nor an admitted principle, but an operative influence contending with immense forces of collective egoism and passion. On the issue of the contest may be said to depend the question whether it is possible to form a true community of the world, and therefore the question whether the work of modern civilization will endure.'*

I have selected these particular quotations because they make clear a number of important points. Firstly, they show the intimate interconnection between the forms of 'social stratification' and the political and legal institutions of society which Hobhouse had in mind, *and*, in addition, the intimate relation between *morality* and them all. Secondly, they show the marked effectiveness of Hobhouse's analysis in that it points with incisive clarity to the fact that *colour* is the last remaining factor, and obstacle, standing in the way of the universalism of the principles of citizenship. Since his time this has become ever more apparent, and an ever more acute issue—and in the 'apartheid' and the bitter street-riots, if not the open civil war of our times, as well as in the growth of 'Race Relations' as a specialism within sociology. But Hobhouse's analysis of stratification was already perfectly clear about this matter. Thirdly, these passages make it clear, too, and this we shall emphasize again in our conclusions, that these movements of social change in

* *Development and Purpose*, pp. 222–3.

the contemporary world are by no means to be thought inevitable, nor is it at all to be assumed that they must have, and will have, a successful outcome. They are changes bristling with questions and with sources of conflict and disagreement, and the furtherance of human civilization beyond this point now hangs in the balance. What is *essential* is that we should have a sound perspective for judgment, effort, and action. On our knowledge, judgment, effort, action, all will depend. Again, then, we can see as plainly in Hobhouse's work as in that of all his predecessors, that sociology is a *needed* science.

(7) *Property and 'Contract'*

One of the most central factors in the division of society into classes is, of course, the emergence of great distinctions of property. 'Property' is one of the most significant institutions of *power* in society, and Hobhouse showed how this, too, was closely correlated with knowledge, technology, political and legal regulation, and, indeed, with all other social institutions.

At the lowest level of knowledge, in the pre-literate societies, whilst there was always 'private property' in the form of personal possession of clothes, tools, weapons, and the like, property was chiefly property in land, and was 'communal property'—in that the territory of the tribe was apportioned to clans and families within the over-all regulation of tribal custom. At the higher economic levels, however, 'sectional' property, and also the letting and leasing of 'individual' property was found. This new complexity of property continued and was extended in the large, agricultural civilizations in which trading became important, and the arrangements between merchants and the owners of capital (e.g. in Babylon especially) approximated quite closely to a simple 'company' organization. With feudal society and the growth of the town, again concomitant with the great extension of international trading, a much more complex commercial capitalism developed, followed by industrial capitalism, and this was accompanied by the complex development of the several kinds of 'company organization' (from 'chartered companies' for trading to the giant modern 'joint-stock companies with limited liability'), the vastly increased size of capital-accumulation and methods of concentrating capital for various kinds of investment, and the intricate division of labour—from the 'Craft Guilds' and 'Guilds Merchant' of the medieval town to the detailed and highly specialized industrial relations between the employers and employees of modern firms.

All this showed the increasing dominance of 'contract' in all economic and property relations in modern society, and showed, too, a clear movement firstly towards an ever-extending 'freedom of contract' and 'freedom of competitive enterprise' and secondly, qualifying this, towards a new kind of social regulation of this freedom. Again, it was in his picture of this significant problem of achieving some new kind of social regulation of property, whilst retaining freedom within it—the problem central to modern society— that Hobhouse was most interesting. It is worth while to see how he himself put these matters.

In *Development and Purpose*, he wrote:

'The right of property is recognized in early society in the sense in which other rights are recognized. But the most important property, the land, is more often common to the group. If it is subdivided, ownership is hardly distinct from occupation, and when separate property arises it is still rather to the kindred than to the individual that the land belongs. So far private property as a basis of personal enterprise and accumulation hardly exists. With the growth of authoritarian society a feudal tenure of land is generally found in which property is associated with office, rank and status, and is neither in the absolute ownership of the individual nor, therefore, the subject of unfettered bequest or free exchange. With the rise of industry and commerce, capital on the large scale becomes as important as land, and the tenure of property becomes individualistic, only to give rise, as the economic problem unrolls itself, to new forms of social control. In this case, again, we are at the beginning rather than the end of a stage, and have to recognize a problem rather than a solution. But it would seem clear that the condition of any solution is not to ignore the personal right to acquire, hold and exchange, which has been gradually won, but rather to define more accurately the conditions within which these rights are contributory to the general welfare.

The case of contract is closely analogous. Here again early custom reveals contract in our sense as something imperfectly understood. It is not consent but some ceremonial form that is binding, and in the archaic structure of society contract could at best have no important place. The feudal régime admits of contract within limits, but these limits mark out the main lines of life for all classes. Unfettered contract is the ideal of a commercial society which has thrown off feudal bonds, but, like unrestricted individualism in property, is soon seen to necessitate a new form of social control.'*

And in *Morals in Evolution*:

'. . . Land has long ceased to be the only important means of production, From the beginnings of pasture, and with the application of animal power in agriculture and transport, stock became an important factor in wealth. The rise of industry, commerce, and the consequent formation of

* *Development and Purpose*, pp. 224–5.

towns established classes of artisans and merchants, who gradually abandoned the cultivation of land and lived by manufacture and exchange. Capital lent itself more readily to absolute ownership, exchange, and free bequest than land, and capital, which becomes more and more a mere paper lien on the industry of others, occupies the larger share in the economic life of the advanced community. It is in the accumulation and use of capital that absolute ownership displays its full power, and that the contrasts of gigantic accumulation and utter destitution are most dramatically displayed. Speaking very roughly, we may say that humanity has hitherto known three stages of economic development. In the first, the fruits of the earth are open to all to gather. There is general poverty, but also general opportunity. In the second, labour, like all social life, is more organized, men have their status of master or slave, lord or vassal, superior or dependent. There is discipline but not freedom. In the third, while the individual is free to make his own career within the limits of the social order, it falls out through the working of competition and the cumulative factor of inheritance, that there are those who have a lien on the fruits of earth in the industry of others, and those—and they are the majority—who have none. The man of property and the man of none are the contrasted figures of modern civilization, and their reconciliation a problem which becomes more urgent as industrialism advances.'*

It is worth while to note, too, that in the development of the social forms of property, ethical conceptions and activities again had their important part to play. With sharp distinctions of wealth and poverty in 'despotic' and 'feudal' societies, *charity* became more emphasized. This itself, however, came to be ethically criticized within the context of the attempt to reconstruct society in such a way as to eliminate unjustified distinctions and move towards a more just distribution of the wealth created by the community. Charity gave way, therefore, to a detailed working out of the rights and duties of social justice: to what we would now call the making of the 'Welfare State'.

'With the development of property,' Hobhouse wrote, 'the ethics of benevolence is closely correlated. Here we have first the simple hospitality of early communism, with as much care for the helpless as the general conditions of life allow. Then we have charity as a duty of the superior, a duty which is also a moral luxury and a means of other-worldly advancement. This gives way to a criticism of benevolence in the interests of individual character, and this criticism, taken in conjunction with the hard facts of economics, is seen to necessitate the establishment of the definite right to the primal needs of a civic life on the basis of a system of mutual obligations as between the individual and the community.'†

In the modern world, then, property, too, was an institution caught up in a rapid process of change, and which had to be respons-

* *Morals in Evolution*, p. 332.　　　　† *Development and Purpose*, p. 225.

ibly reconsidered and reconstructed in the light of new conflicts of interest and a new social ethic.

(8) *The Family and Marriage*

Hobhouse's account of the family in society was very detailed, and is difficult to condense, but here again, he demonstrated a correlation between the nature and quality of the relationships between husbands and wives, parents and children, in the family, and the level of knowledge and wider patterns of authority in society.

In the pre-literate societies family and kinship ties were of basic importance; the relationships between families in wide kinship systems were very closely interwoven and complicated; and the family and kin groups were 'multi-functional' in that almost all other social activities were part and parcel of them. Property, procedures of government and justice, the division of labour, etc; were all aspects of the kinship network of family, clan and tribe. The 'matriarchal' principle of kinship organization predominated among the Hunters and Gatherers, and was replaced by the 'patriarchal' principle almost entirely among pastoral societies and in half the societies which rested on settled agriculture.* There appeared to be a movement towards the predominance of 'patriarchal' organization with the growing scale and complexity of society.

Marriage in these societies took various forms: marriage by the arrangement of elders, by the consent of bride and groom, by the exchange of gifts between them, by the 'purchase' or the 'giving of some consideration' for the bride, and by rather more dramatic methods—such as capture and abduction or permitted elopement. Far and away the most common method was that of giving some consideration for the bride: the 'bride-price'—whether by the provision of some agreed quantity of wealth in kind or the performance of services to the wife's kinsfolk. Furthermore there was a marked increase in the incidence of this mode of marriage in the higher economic grades.

As to the number of partners involved in marriage, Polygyny was by far the most common arrangement and, here again, there was an increase in the incidence of it among the higher grades. Divorce was common among these simpler societies; in scarcely any case was marriage indissoluble; and divorce seemed to rest upon the consent of the partners, involving some arrangement as to the repayment of the bride-price. There was evidence of concern for the stability of the

---

* It must be emphasized that these are very simplified statements, condensed from very complicated studies. They ought, strictly speaking, only to be taken as indications of Hobhouse's findings, though they are, in fact, his general conclusions.

family, however, in the growth of public justice, among the higher economic grades. There seemed to be a clear growth of public punishment for marital and family misdemeanours—such as adultery; a clear decline in certain practices—such as wife-lending; and a clear development of the condemnation of pre-marital sexual relations: of unchastity.

In general the status of women in the simpler societies was low; they did the harder work in society, were often subject to the chastisement of men, and had little or no part to play in the responsible and authoritative roles in the social order. Furthermore, with the advance in knowledge and technical control in the higher grades, the predominance of the status of men increased. The superior status of men and the inferior status of women seemed to become more definitely and formally institutionalized.

This tendency was continued in the 'Despotic' societies at the level of literacy. In all such societies the low and subjected status of women was reinforced and might even be said to have been conserved by religious doctrines. Women were depicted as the source of 'evil' and had to remain institutionally subordinated to men. The same situation continued—with variations—up to the medieval world. Only in the modern world, with the growing repugnance felt for the exploitation of women and children in various fields of labour, were both given a much improved status—both within and beyond the family—and the nature and the functions of the family came to be increasingly supervised by the State, and aided by its provisions.

Again, the development of the family in society showed this culmination in the deliberate provision of a new kind of 'state' which gave the conditions of security and social justice, and sought to uphold, effectively, the improved quality of relationships which a refined ethics desired.

Hobhouse wrote:

'In the history of the family the power of the husband and father has effects which in their way resemble those of the element of force in the social structure. The earlier history of the family—meaning by the term the union of husband, wife and children—is not easily grasped owing to the diversity of types with which anthropology presents us. But alike of the system of mother-right, of polyandry and of the many forms of union in which divorce is so easy that the name of marriage is barely applicable, it would seem true to say generally that they represent the family (in our sense) in an incomplete form. From this point of view the patriarchate is a step in advance. It represents (like the military state as compared with a congeries of ill-disciplined tribes) a closer, more compact, more efficient form of organization. This advance, however, is balanced by the lowered status and unprotected condition of the wife and children, the former of whom probably experiences an actual loss of status in the decay of mother-right. It is accordingly an ethical advance when the rights of wife and children are brought under the full protection of the state. Society in this stage stands in direct relation to the members of the family as individuals, and from this basis it is advancing in our own time to the position of 'over-parent', in which it supervises and at need supplements the functions hitherto left to parental care. This position, it may freely be allowed, raises problems of the relation of parental to communal responsibility which are not yet solved, but it has already developed far enough to enable us to conceive the family as a unit organism contributory to and dependent on the larger organism of the social life. From this point of view then we may distinguish four stages—the incomplete natural family, the Patriarchate, the Individualist family, and the Social family.'*

In all this, of course, the status of women in society was quite central, and on this Hobhouse wrote as follows:

'With the development of the family the whole position of woman is inti-mately bound up. Broadly the development here is a particular case of the generalization of rights. The superior rights generally claimed by the male are a case of group-morality, and the growing recognition of the equality of status due to woman a simple application of the general ideal of universalism. Historically the case is complicated by the many factors affecting marriage and the family life. Comparing the patriarchate with earlier forms of society, we receive on the whole the impression that women lost rather than gained status, and there are a few cases in early society when they appear to have an equal or even a superior position to men. Nevertheless, guided by the general and omitting the exceptional, we may regard the position of women in the earlier societies as varying from one of inferior rights to one little distinguished from a servile status. This status is qualified by the social respect which they have enjoyed uniformly in mediaeval and modern Europe, by the ethics of chivalry and the code of the "gentleman". A higher stage was reached for a time in Roman law, and has been regained in modern Europe, where it is being rapidly developed to the point of according the woman, married or unmarried, full equality of status, civil, social and political, with the man.'†

The correlation between the family and all the other institutions—property, law, religion, morality, etc.—of political society as a whole was thus made perfectly clear.

In drawing this outline of Hobhouse's account of particular in-stitutions to a close, it is worth while to see how, in his analysis, so many of the institutional changes of the contemporary world seem to be understandable in terms of what he called this 'double movement' —towards freedom of the individual on the one hand, and a necessary qualification of this by the working out of a new system of collective

* *Development and Purpose*, pp. 223–4.   † *Ibid.*, p. 224.

regulation on the other. There is a sense in which this point serves as a summary of the broad pattern of change in modern society which is at the root of the changes of all the particular institutions taken separately.

On this 'double movement', Hobhouse wrote as follows:

'On the one hand, in the more advanced societies there is a breakdown of older social structures limiting the actions of the individuals, and so a fuller recognition of personal right. On the other hand there is a process of reconstruction, in which the community as a whole exerts powers and undertakes functions previously left to the individual, the family or some other body. This is a fuller recognition of a common collective responsibility. These two elements, personal right and common responsibility for mutual aid, are the two pivotal points of social ethics, and with regard to their relations generally we may say that in the kinship society the individual has little scope for development apart from the common life; in the authoritarian society his life is usually determined in its main outlines by his status, nor has he any standing ground save that of force for resistance to law and constituted authority. The same is at bottom true of the ancient state, where the subjection of the individual to the common weal is an undisputed axiom. In the modern world there first appeared the conception that the right of the individual as such might limit the law, and this is not merely a conception but a regulative principle in much modern legislation. But it is a principle which has in turn to be checked by the complementary truth that the rights which the individual can claim must be constituent conditions of a self-consistent social order, and to base liberty on law and the common life on liberty is the specific problem of contemporary statesmanship.'*

Points of Emphasis and Qualifications

We have now seen, in so far as it is possible within the scope of a brief treatment, how Hobhouse compared societies and their 'inter-dependencies' of institutions in such a way as (a) to show the kind of institutional 'consensus' which, empirically, was found to be 'typical' of (b) the distinctive 'levels of knowledge' (or of 'mental development') and (c) the nature of the political bond possessed by them.† We have seen how, (d) with the use of this classificatory framework, he *established* a systematic body of *knowledge* which could be *tested* by any equally rigorous comparative study, and which provided a basis of generalization for the further analytical understanding of the inter-linking of institutions in each 'type'. And we have seen

---

* *Development and Purpose*, pp. 225–6.
† It will be seen how reminiscent this is—though so much more elaborately and empirically done—of the main 'schemes' for the comparative study of societies, put forward by Montesquieu, Condorcet, and the great figures like Comte, who succeeded them.

how this (*e*) provided a clear perspective for an understanding of the institutional changes experienced in contemporary societies.

A system of comparative sociology—drawing upon the proposals of the earlier scholars, from Comte to Ward—had not only been set up, but *developed* and *carried out in detail* in such a way as substantially to advance our *knowledge* of societies and social processes, past and present. On the basis of the 'evolutionary perspective' and the perspective provided by the evolution and advancement of the powers of *mind* in particular, a systematic empirical sociology—comparative and historical—had been provided, which advanced our *intellectual understanding* of the nature of human society, and also provided knowledge which was *needed* and *useful* for forming those judgments on which action could most reliably be based in the contemporary world.

This brief account, however, by no means satisfactorily presses home the detailed worth and the many dimensions of Hobhouse's achievement; neither does it sufficiently bring out the forcefulness and significance of his qualifications. Nor is this the end of the story. Very important considerations remain. It is necessary, and it will be very worth while for our later discussion of the positions adopted in contemporary sociology, to state—though very briefly—a few points of special emphasis which are very important at this stage. These will 'hammer home' some of the very important aspects of Hobhouse's system; high-light, as luminously as possible, the important qualifications which he made; and lead us on to an understanding of the further elements of his system of analysis.

(I) CORRELATION AMONG INSTITUTIONS IN SOCIAL EVOLUTION ESTABLISHED, AND COMPARATIVE SOCIOLOGY VINDICATED

The first point which deserves much emphasis is that Hobhouse did, in fact, find (*a*) a close correlation between social institutions and the 'measuring-stick' of the levels of knowledge in societies, and (*b*) also among institutions in each kind of society. His comparative studies were a successful carrying out of the kind of systematic sociology proposed by Comte and others, and constituted a vindication of such methods. To classify societies, to arrange knowledge of them within such a classificatory scheme, did in fact lead to a body of knowledge which revealed a significant patterning of institutions in societies as wholes and a significant pattern of the cumulative development of institutions. The notion of 'evolution' was also vindicated in that it provided a satisfactory perspective for the emergence and advancement of the powers of *mind* in both nature and society (history), and, furthermore, this was *not* an 'evolution' of '*adaptation*' to environmental circumstances, but, in addition to this, the *demonstration* of an awakening and increasingly articulate, conscious, deliberate and effective *purpose* of mind in the qualification and direction of evolution. Particular aspects of this will be emphasized in a moment—but this first point is of the utmost importance: that Hobhouse provided a sophisticated picture of the growing purpose of mind in nature and society which was *substantiated* by comparative evidence; which was *true*; and which still *holds good*. His achievement, coupled with that of all those from Comte to Lester Ward, was by no means transient, and is one we must still take with full seriousness.

At this point, let us note just two brief statements in which Hobhouse spoke of his conclusions—though we shall add more definitive dimensions later.

In his conclusions in *Morals in Evolution*, having studied the interconnections between social institutions, and between them and the centrality of knowledge and morality, he wrote:

'In Social Evolution as a whole there is, in fact, a correlation, however rough and irregular in detail . . .

Among many simpler societies we see (1) the fundamental institutions of the family and government still very incomplete. We trace (2) the growing consolidation of the little community on the basis of kinship, then (3) the extension and improved organization of society on the principle of Authority and (4) finally, the advance towards a harmony between liberty and authority in the state. In the first two stages we have the morality of custom gradually passing into that of impartial law. In the third we have the reign of law and in its higher phases the ethics of the world-religions. The fourth is associated with humanitarian ideas. At the same time social growth does not always go with ethical progress. Social changes are in large measure unconscious, uncontrolled by any intelligent direction, and the more completely so the further we go back into the beginnings of history. Hence they do not run precisely parallel with the growth of mind, but at times impede, at other times, again, forward it. But as the higher phases are reached the two processes fuse into one. For the state rests on a measure of Right in the relations of men, and is so constituted as to be modifiable by the deliberate act of the community. In the method in which changes are effected, indeed, we find a definite evolution from the unconscious and unnoted changes of custom, through the deliberate changes introduced on occasion by the fiat of authority to the organic legislation of the modern world in which at its best there is an effort to determine social progress in accordance with a rational ideal. When this stage is reached social and ethical evolution become one. This union becomes realized in proportion as the mind attains that control over its own growth which it already possesses over the processes of nature.'*

* *Morals in Evolution*, pp. 632–3.

H

Also:

'Amid all the variety of social institutions and the ebb and flow of historical change, it is possible in the end to detect a double movement marking the transition from the lower to the higher levels of civilized law and custom. On the one hand, the social order is strengthened and extended. The blood feud yields to the reign of law, personal chieftainship to a regular government and an organized police. At the same time the social organization grows in extent. Instead of small primitive groups we have nation-states or continental empires, great areas enjoying internal peace and owning a common law. On this side the individual human being becomes more and more subject to social constraint, and, as we have frequently seen, the changes making for the tightening of the social fabric may diminish the rights which the individual or large classes of individuals can claim, so that fewer rights may be enjoyed, though, with the improvement of public order, those which remain are more secure. In this relation liberty and order become opposed. But the opposition is not essential. From the first the individual relies on social forces to maintain him in his rights, and in the higher form of social organization we have seen order and liberty drawing together again, the underlying truth that unites them being simply that the best ordered community is that which gives most scope to its component members to make the best of themselves, while the "best" in human nature is that which contributes to the harmony and onward movement of society.

Thus the modern state comes to rest more and more on the rights and duties, the obligations and responsibilities that we include under the ethical and legal conception of personality. The responsible human being, man or woman, is the centre of modern ethics as of modern law, free so far as law and custom are concerned to make his own life, bound by no restrictions of status nor even of nationality or race, answerable for his acts and for those of no other, at liberty to make the best or the worst of himself, to accept or decline relations with others. On the other hand, as this free individual breaks the shell of the older groupings, he comes into direct relations with the state as a whole which succeeds to many of the rights and duties of the older groups. The social nature of man is not diminished either on the side of its needs or its duties by the fuller recognition of personal rights. The difference is that, so far as rights and duties are conceived as attaching to human beings as such, they become universalized, and are therefore the care of society as a whole rather than of any partial group organization. The typical instance of this change is the rise of public courts enforcing a law which is equally binding on all members of society.

But, lastly, the universalism which the idea of personality holds within it cannot be satisfied with the limits of the nation-state. In proportion as obligations are determined by human nature as such they overstep national and racial as well as family and class limitations, and apply to humanity as a whole. Hence, as has been seen in analysing the idea of internationalism, the double meaning of "humanity" as an expression for a certain quality that is in each man, and as an expression for the whole race of men, is not a mere ambiguity. The two meanings are intimately related, for "humanity" as a whole is the society to which, by virtue of the "humanity" within each of us, we really belong, and these two meanings are the poles between which modern ethical conceptions move.

It is easy to recognize that it is the same principle which is seen from two different sides, and that the conscious efforts to better the life of humanity in which the whole tendency of modern thought is summed up, can work through no other channel than the humanity which is alive in every man and woman.'*

The pattern of the actual nature and course of Social Evolution was thus given a clear statement.

(II) EVOLUTIONARY AND COMPARATIVE SOCIOLOGY VINDICATED IN TERMS OF *NEED* AND *UTILITY* FOR THE FULLER UNDERSTANDING OF SPECIFIC CONTEMPORARY PROBLEMS IN SOCIETY

A second aspect of this same point also deserves strong emphasis in view of much present-day misunderstanding of what is entailed in an 'evolutionary' perspective. There are those who think that 'evolutionary', or 'grand manner' sociology is of little *use* because comparative studies of class, property, the family, religion, crime, law and punishment, etc.; in societies of antiquity, in City States, in Feudal Society, and the like, throw no light whatever upon these institutions in, say, modern Britain. Now this is a great blindness. Hobhouse vindicated sociology—in its full scale as a scientific study of all known forms of society—exactly in this further way: that he showed how *much* light could be thrown on all the specific concerns of modern society—on the changing nature of family relations, on new conceptions of crime and its treatment, on the changing nature of property, on the crucial focus upon 'colour' or 'race' as the most unresolved feature of social differentiation, on the detailed problems of modern government and administration—by these large-scale evolutionary perspectives. Indeed, he showed that such specific modern concerns could *only* be understood within such perspectives. Modern class and citizenship *cannot* be understood, excepting in relation to all the earlier kinds of bondage out of which it has emerged. Modern forms of property and 'contract' *cannot* be understood excepting in the context of the earlier forms of property and property-relations out of which they have grown. People who distinguish sociology in the 'grand manner' from 'empirical' sociology, and think that the nature of institutions can only be known by the

* *Morals in Evolution*, pp. 356–8, p. 364.

latter, i.e. by conducting interviews (doing surveys) of a 'sample' of people in the streets, are vastly mistaken. The nature of changing institutions *at the present time* can only be known within the context of wide comparative and historical studies, and Hobhouse demonstrated this in very considerable detail.

Again, this was a vindication of the conception of sociology put forward by Comte, Mill, Marx, Spencer, Ward, and many others: that a thoroughgoing science of all known societies was *needed* for the basis it could provide for the very specific *pragmatic* tasks facing mankind in the contemporary world.

(III) SOCIOLOGICAL KNOWLEDGE NOT FOR 'PREDICTIONS' OF THE FUTURE IN A 'DETERMINISTIC' SENSE, BUT AS A BASIS FOR DELIBERATION, JUDGMENT, AND ACTION

A third aspect of Hobhouse's 'evolutionary' system was that—like Mill and Ward and Tönnies especially—he emphasized the recognition of *will* in human nature. In his portrayal of the increasingly self-conscious powers of mind, and the responsibility which this entailed for the deliberate re-making of society, he was quite plainly opposed to any conception of the 'inevitability' of social evolution, or of sociological and psychological generalizations as 'laws' of a mechanistic or deterministic kind. Sociological knowledge was of the interdependencies of social institutions and processes of the past and of the present, but this gave men a basis for the critical assessment of their own condition and situation: a basis for judgment, and a basis for planned action which could alter their situation towards the ends which they desired. Far from being 'deterministic', therefore, for Hobhouse, the knowledge of sociology was the basis for creative activity in the shaping and re-shaping of society. It was not a 'scientistic' prison of determinate 'laws', but a basis for the achievement of greater social freedom.

(IV) THE PRESENT POSITION OF SOCIAL EVOLUTION: NOT THE *END*, BUT THE BASIS FOR A QUALITATIVELY NEW *BEGINNING* ABOUT WHICH *DOUBTS* MUST BE ENTERTAINED

It is also important to notice that, in clarifying the contemporary situation—as the culmination of the evolution of institutions which *had* in fact occurred in the past—Hobhouse by no means thought that modern society was *better* in every respect than societies of the past; that the tendencies now shown to be afoot would *continue* or would culminate in *success*; or that society had in any sense arrived, finally, at its destination. On the contrary, he thought that the present culminations of social tendencies confronted men now with the most difficult, urgent, and responsible tasks of self-direction that they had ever experienced in the entirety of history; and he was well aware that man's efforts in this contemporary situation could founder, just as efforts to sustain and further the achievements of civilization had met with failure and disaster in times past. There was nothing consoling in Hobhouse's picture. There was nothing to show that 'history' or anything else by way of the forces of destiny was 'on man's side'. On the contrary, Hobhouse's picture clarified all the enormous problems which modern man faced in his task of conscious self-direction, all the elements of his insecurity, and emphasized chiefly the need to *recognize* this juncture in human history, and the need for the most diligent and committed effort.

These points were all stressed, and stressed time and time again, in the qualifications which Hobhouse made to his statements about the institutional correlations which he had established. Among the important qualifications were these:

(v) COMPARATIVE SOCIOLOGY SHOWS A SEQUENCE OF SOCIAL EVOLUTION—BUT NO *NECESSARY* HISTORICAL SEQUENCE

One quite central and important qualification which Hobhouse made was such as to defend the whole conception of comparative sociology within the evolutionary perspective from a simple mis-understanding which, alas, seems to dog the minds of critics peren-nially. It was simply this: that though the *classification of societies* essentially took into account *historical societies* (societies of the *past*, as well as historical societies of the *present*); though it certainly regarded societies as essentially *historical* kinds of phenomena— cumulative, temporal processes, persisting and changing; and though it certainly did reveal a cumulative pattern of growth and develop-ment in those societies which had, in fact, experienced changes into all these types during their history—*even so*: it did not, at all, assume, or insist upon the idea that there was a *uniform* and *necessary sequence* of change through these 'types', which all societies are bound to experience in their history.

The classificatory scheme was a classificatory scheme: no more. It sought systematic knowledge about all societies by arranging descriptive and analytical studies within a framework of 'types' as best it could. As such, *all* societies: pre-literate societies of the present, pre-literate societies of the past; feudal societies of the present, feudal societies of the past; despotic societies of the present, despotic societies of the past; as well as *all contemporary* societies—whatever their level of knowledge and development; could be arranged within this scheme. Generalized knowledge of each level and type was thus possible. But it was *not at all* assumed that all societies necessarily experienced a uniform transition from one type to others; let alone to *all* others.

Some societies *remained* pre-literate; some *remained* traditional agricultural societies with a central despotic authority for thousands of years; others experienced extensive and rapid changes; some were destroyed. There was no certain way ahead for the industrialized nation states of modern times. No specific, deterministic, sequence of historical change was either assumed or proposed.

Hobhouse was thoroughly aware of the vast and complicated details of historical change: no one could be more aware. He was fully aware of the circumstantial diversities of societies. His one central persuasion was that *essentially in relation to the development of mind, knowledge, power of control, and purpose* all these diverse societies, with all their institutions, were drawn increasingly together in a *global* interdependency, into a global awareness of the natural and social situation of mankind as a whole, and that this brought with it a new conscious responsibility for the re-shaping of human society in accordance with clarified ethical ends. Whether this was so could be discovered by *classifying* societies in accordance with their level of knowledge and the nature and extent of their political authority, and establishing knowledge of the institutional developments 'correlated' with these criteria.

Hobhouse's comparative sociology was a quest for generalizations about the institutions of 'types' of societies resting on these criteria. That is all. This can be substantiated more fully when we have looked at other, closely related, qualifications.

(VI) COMPARATIVE SOCIOLOGY ESTABLISHES CORRELATIONS— BUT NO *NECESSARY* CORRELATIONS, AND, ESPECIALLY, NO NECESSARY *UNILINEAR* CORRELATIONS OF EITHER FACTUAL DEVELOPMENT OR MORAL BETTERMENT

Another qualification on which Hobhouse went to great pains to insist was that—although he claimed to have established certain correlations among institutions in the several types of society—*all* the items of social life, or elements of social structure, were not connected in any necessary way in over-all sequences from type to type, nor were they all attended by moral betterment in similar, connected degrees. A similar condition of society, or of a specific institution could be reached by different historical paths. Unity and harmony among some groupings in society were directly correlated with sharp enmity and conflict between them and others. Certain sequences of change seemed sometimes (if not always) to entail gains in some institutions and losses in others. The degree of connectedness between societies was very different in different periods, and the degree of *pervasiveness* of standards of cultural achievement also differed: so that though the 'peaks' of achievement in one society seemed very considerable, they may have existed in a prevailing condition (i.e. among the greater part of society) of ignorance, poverty, and barbarism; whereas at other periods the levels of institutional achievement might have been widely shared by the entire population of the community.

Any criticism of Hobhouse's evolutionary picture, then, as that of an effete 'liberal minded philosopher writing for the *Manchester Guardian*' and seeing the entirety of human history as an ever onward and upward movement towards sweetness and light is the absurd, uninformed, superficial and unworthy point of view which it seems. Hobhouse qualified himself time and time again with regard to the diversity of historical detail, and it is time to substantiate this defence of his position by a number of examples.

Even on that kind of development in society—of knowledge and the attendant control over physical conditions—which he thought most clearly demonstrable, and in which he thought that the direction of human evolution was quite markedly clear, he wrote:

'Yet even on this side it is not a straightforward continuous movement. The material culture of classical antiquity was in large measure destroyed in the fall of the Roman Empire, and it was not till the later Middle Ages that all the lost ground was made good. Nor is it probable that this is the only break which a full investigation would disclose. If we speak, then, of a tendency or a progress towards the growth of knowledge and the increased command of nature, we must not think of this as an automatic process, as a "law" of progress which must inevitably effect itself. It is something dependent on further concurrent conditions which may work against it and arrest it. It does not, so to say, represent a straight line to which the movement of humanity is confined and along which it is always marching. All we can say is that, with whatever halts and back turnings, it is a direction in which humanity, or a large part of it, has actually moved a very considerable distance, and is at present moving with greatly increased velocity.'*

Similarly on the possibility of a continuous, unilinear sequence of development (and moral betterment) in *any* social institution, he wrote:

* *Development and Purpose*, p. 207.

'It is rarely, if ever, that we can say of *any* institution or *any* order of ideas or of activity that its growth can be traced as a continuous process from its first beginnings to its present form. Normally we find a series of actions and reactions, and must be more than content if we can find in the upshot some definite result indicating a net movement in some distinct direction. Take, for example, the position of women. We conceive of the equality of the sexes and the freedom of women as one of the distinctive ideas of modern times, and it is not uncommon to hear the position of women spoken of as one of the tests of general civilization. If this were so, and if progress were continuous and were something that affected the life of society all round, the inference would be that the study of history would reveal a continuous advance in the position of women from slavery to equality. *This view will not stand the most cursory examination of the data.* Among the historical peoples the position of women has more than once been far higher in many important respects than it was in the times of our fathers, and among savages it is by no means uniformly low. It is, in fact, affected by other causes than the general level of culture, and at certain stages the advance of culture has probably affected it injuriously. Take, again, political freedom. It is an ideal towards which the modern world is still striving. It was in large measure realized by Greece and Rome and the mediaeval city. True, if we look deeper we find that freedom for us has a fuller meaning and a larger scope. It is not to be denied that there are essential differences between a modern and an ancient democracy. But in the interval between them it would be true to say that there were periods when the idea of political freedom was dead. By no stretch of imagination could we represent the measure of political freedom to which the modern world has attained as something towards which the art of government has moved by successive steps all pointing in the same direction. The most that we can say in these and countless similar cases is that, when we consider the life of humanity as a whole and compare our own civilization with the whole series of earlier forms, together with their survivals at the present day, there appears, when all actions and reactions are set against one another, a certain net movement.'[*]

Again—nothing could be clearer than the following on the *lack* of necessary connectedness between some institutional developments and ethical progress.

'In general the ethical factor is only one of the influences shaping the life of man, and the social structure at any time is the result of the interplay of countless individual forces moved by their own impulses, seeking their own ends, good or bad, social or anti-social. Shaped by these forces, the social structure grows, stagnates or decays. But even when it grows it is by no means to be assumed that it necessarily advances on ethical lines. On the contrary, the mere increment of strength may itself induce elements of discord, and, in fact, of sheer iniquity in the recognized code from which a simpler life is relatively free.'[†]

[*] *Development and Purpose*, pp. 207–8.   [†] *Ibid.*, p. 220.

And on the fact that any such 'net result' of social evolution involved a complex picture of conflict and co-operation, of progress and decay, of gain and loss, Hobhouse wrote quite clearly:

'A net result is arrived at in many cases by very devious paths, and of this we can now in a general way appreciate the reason. True social co-operation as here understood involves a reconciliation or synthesis of conditions which in all but their most refined form are opposed to one another. The strength of the blood tie that gives vigour to a barbaric clan, that vitalizes the tenderness of natural affection within its limits, maintains a personal and a common pride which is also the source of its warlike prowess. To hate the enemies of the clan is at this stage simply the other side of love for the clan itself. The spontaneous growth of each group means war between the groups. If a higher power imposes peace upon them, there is gain in industry and the ways of peace at the cost perhaps of the vital energy which could only flourish in independence. History is full of such exchanges, in which loss and gain seem almost evenly balanced. To take a single instance. The free Roman Republic had become a corrupt and turbulent oligarchy, wholly incapable of administering the vast dominions it had conquered. The new empire was efficient, and it was equalitarian in tendency. It gave a great part of the world peace and civilized law, and by degrees equality in citizenship. There was great gain here to counterbalance the loss of Roman freedom, and yet we may think that the loss of freedom meant ultimately the loss of life. It is perhaps superfluous to multiply examples. Throughout history an advance in one direction is affected at the cost of loss in another. In particular the growth of Authority, valuable for order, stability, industrial progress and some forms of intellectual development, is often correlated with the most serious ethical retrogression.'*

Lastly, on the multiplicity of developments in many and diverse societies which were only gradually drawn together as knowledge and intercommunication expanded, he held that:

'. . . when we seek to conceive social development as a process going forward in time, we must revert to what was said at the outset of the manifold centres from which the movement proceeds. There are and have been a great number of societies, and their development is in large measure independent and of very unequal rapidity. It is only by a gradual process that civilization becomes a single stream. We see the process of unification going on rapidly in our own time. In earlier periods interconnection was less constant and less vital, and so, instead of one evolution of culture, there were many evolutions, and certain societies reached a high pitch in one direction or another, even like the Greeks in almost all known directions, which pitch they were unable to maintain. This fact alone destroys

* *Development and Purpose*, pp. 226–7.

any attempt to conceive social evolution as from the first a unitary process. Its beginning is with many separate strands, which are but gradually woven together, and this weaving is itself an important part of progress. Or we may think of development as a line along which many societies make independent advances, reaching a certain point and then resting or perhaps turning back. Yet over long periods the result is an advance in the general level, because with the rise of intercommunication one advance on the average helps another, and the highest point of one date becomes the mean point of another.'*

These few examples are enough to demonstrate our point as to Hobhouse's care in qualifying the nature and extent of the 'institutional correlations' which he established; but they could, in fact, be multiplied many times over. There is one other point which is worth mentioning separately in all this.

(VII) SOCIETIES ARE 'SYSTEMS' OF INTERCONNECTED INSTITUTIONS —BUT TAKE SHAPE IN DEALING WITH CONFLICT AS WELL AS CO-OPERATION; CONTINUOUS TENDENCIES TO CHANGE AS WELL AS TO PERSISTENCE; AND THE DIVERSE CHALLENGES OF OTHER SOCIETIES AS WELL AS NEEDS FOR ADJUSTMENT WITHIN THEMSELVES

Implicit in all that we have seen of Hobhouse's system is this further point deserving emphasis: that he *did* regard societies as *wholes*; as 'interdependent sets of institutions'; but, even so, that he was well aware of their conflict, their lack of harmony, their susceptibility to influence from outside, their complex changes, as well as the continual interweaving and interconnection of all the institutions within them. In short, he adopted a 'structural-functional' conception of entire societies—but by no means a conception which failed to recognize conflict and change. The evidence of this is already plain in the illustrations quoted above.

In all these ways then, it can be shown that Hobhouse achieved the classified body of knowledge at which he aimed, but qualified this with the most astringent care and realism.

It might be asked, however: if Hobhouse found it necessary and correct to qualify his findings in all these ways, did his large-scale scheme of comparative sociology arrive at any conclusion whatever that was worthwhile, clear, and useful? The answer is: yes!—and it was this.

* *Development and Purpose*, p. 228-9.

(5) The 'net result' of social evolution: The development of mind from 'genetic' processes to conscious 'teleology': The purpose of mind guided by knowledge and morality in the contemporary world.

The central conclusion emerging from Hobhouse's massive comparative study was indicated by this term—the *'net result'* of social evolution—which we have already noticed in one or two of his statements, but which was, in fact, his continual theme in bringing to a conclusion his study of each institution. What Hobhouse meant was that—despite all the historical diversities and complexities to which he had drawn attention—it was nonetheless possible, with the aid of this comparative 'scheme' of knowledge, to arrive at a clear assessment of the *'net result'* of social evolution *as it now existed* in all the societies of the contemporary world. It was possible (to use the headings of my early diagram), to provide a clear assessment of the *present human situation* (within the context of the developments of the past) and to assess the possibilities of a *rational self-direction* on the part of mankind in dealing with it. And Hobhouse maintained very strongly: (*a*) that it was this critical assessment of the 'net result' of social evolution in our own time which was our most important task, and (*b*) that some extremely important things about this 'net result' had been laid bare.

'For our purpose,' he wrote, '—which is that of appreciating the *actual result of social evolution up to the present time*—it is the *net movement* which is of primary importance.'

And there was no doubt, according to Hobhouse, that this 'net result' of social evolution was completely and demonstrably clear, and constituted a distinctive juncture in the history of man in society. Despite all the intricacies of past developments there was no denying that man had arrived at a situation of knowledge, power of control, and inter-communication throughout the world, at which it was both possible and necessary to *know* all the conditions which had attended the growing power of mind hitherto; all the conditions which had gone into the making of the institutional fabric of society; and to *re-construct* and *direct* the future development of society—consciously, deliberately, responsibly—in the light of this knowledge: part of which was a refined, and critically clarified rational ethic.

The situation was that the manifold *problems* of the contemporary world could be deeply analysed and *understood* within this perspective of knowledge (as the many-sided outcome of the increasing *inter-dependency* of the many societies of the world at all levels of develop-

209

ment; the increasing *rapidity of institutional change* within and among them; and the increasing *thoroughness* of the spread of new knowledge and the struggle for the conditions of justice and welfare through all layers and all sectors of the populations of modern states), and, furthermore, that mankind actually possessed the *wherewithal* of knowledge and control to *deal* with these problems by positive political reconstruction—if only he would consciously assume responsibility for the task, and commit himself to it.

There were a number of extremely important elements and dimensions in this position which we must make unmistakably clear.

The first is that this 'net result' fully bore out Hobhouse's contention that the development of *mind* and *knowledge* was the central factor for throwing a perspective of understanding over the whole changing mass of institutions in the making of human societies in the world. This was not a 'mono-causal' theory, but it seized upon the central human capacity and activity which—amid all the multiple and unforeseen events of human societies—gradually came to be the dominating, articulating, directing activity drawing all societies together, critically judging the condition of them, and then consciously moving towards the 'progressive' remaking of them.

'Looking now over social development as a whole,' Hobhouse wrote, 'we can see a much closer correspondence in the net movement than in the stages that make up that movement in each case. The movement of thought is reflected in the control of physical nature, where the advance is from the empirical handling of surface effects to the apprehension and control of deeper and larger forces. And we now see that in social organization on its many sides, though the way is crooked, the final tendency is to realize that free co-operation of humanity which is the condition of a harmonious development. *This correspondence is no mere parallelism.* It is rather the effect of an interaction, and is at every turn part cause and part effect of the then stage of the development of mind. Were society, as some have suggested, really of "spiritual" character through and through there would be no such interaction. There would be steady growth alone. The parallelism on all sides would be complete. But in tracing the history of mind we are dealing with one cause only—a cause that acts in a *milieu* of complex forces, but, acting steadily, if our account is correct, gets the upper hand among them little by little.'*

It hardly needs pointing out how fully this was a validation and development of the main supposition of the nineteenth century writers—from Comte, through Marx and others, to Ward and Giddings—of the centrality of the distinctive creativity of the human mind in working inventively in relation to its manifold practical activities, and then moving gradually, and with conflict, out of the

* *Development and Purpose*, pp. 227–8.

210

tangled interdependencies and divisions of the 'unforeseen consequences' which shaped societies, to the conscious achievement of a humane society within which the many interests of men could be pursued and fulfilled with due and continuous regard to the dignity and equal citizenship of all men as individual persons.

But this is the second dimension of Hobhouse's picture of the 'net result' of social evolution; namely his complete and clear agreement with Ward especially (though we have seen that others adopted this position too) that man and society were characterized distinctively by their *purposive* or *teleological* qualities, and that the historical evolution of society was one in which mankind had moved *out* of a predominantly 'genetic' situation (in which the making of society was a complex result of unforeseen consequences; of hidden and unknown interdependencies) to a situation which was increasingly 'teleological'—in that, with a fuller knowledge and understanding of both nature and society, he could act more deliberately in the more complete and unencumbered pursuit of his purposes.

Hobhouse gave, in fact, a very detailed analysis of this. Having established the 'levels of knowledge' and the correlated 'interdependencies of institutions', he made very clear indeed this overall movement of the capacity and efficacy of man's mind in action from earlier conditions dominated by 'genetic causation' to a condition of increasingly conscious purpose.

Throughout the earlier epochs of civilization when the great systems of social institutions were taking shape—in kinship societies, agricultural despotism, city states, empires, and feudal societies—Hobhouse traced what he called the *'building of the Empirical Order'* of society. Without a *conscious* 'over-view', without conscious intent, the many activities of men had assumed a definite shape of interdependent institutions in relation to the necessitous stress of problems, vicissitudes, and social conflicts and resolutions. Mind was at work, but in a tangled, disconnected, partial way, and the 'empirical order' of societal achievement assumed a shape which was not consciously directed. Gradually, however, men came to be conscious of insufficiencies, evils, irrationalities, in the given 'traditional' order of society which they found about them. Authority and power were questioned; social divisions were criticized; the 'sanctity' of tradition itself came to be doubted. With the 'spiritual religions', 'ethical idealism', the critical general thought of the City States, and, crucially, with the development of critical philosophy and science in the post-Renaissance world—there came to be a period of *'critical reconstruction'*. The 'empirical order' of society which had been laid down without over-all conscious design became increasingly exposed to the critical judgment made possible by new, more reliable knowledge, and by a hard-won freedom from the domination of 'authority'. This period, and process, of critical reconstruction itself could be seen to have two fairly distinguishable phases. During its early part, it was predominantly a matter of *conceptual* reconstruction'. Men critically appraised the *concepts*, *doctrines*, *principles* of the empirical order, and clarified new concepts which seemed more defensible. New standards of knowledge and ideals of purposive conduct were set up. Then, following this in the world of modern science, this developed into a more active, pragmatic process of *experiential* reconstruction'. Men now possessed not just conceptual clarity—but *empirical substantiation*. Concepts and theories were now *subjected to tests* within experience. Men were no longer content only to criticize the empirical order *conceptually*; they wanted now to *change* it. They wanted to *reconstruct* the institutions of society in accordance with their new concepts.

This picture has a completely telling relevance to our contemporary predicament when Hobhouse's conclusions about the entire range of social institutions is borne in mind. Scientific knowledge, harnessed to technology, had enormously increased man's power of control over the physical environment and now made possible a great increase in material welfare. Economic organization had developed in the form of competitive large-scale enterprises based upon contract and harnessing vast concentrations of capital and property. But the degree of freedom of 'competition' and private contract and property had now to meet increasing criticism with regard to the distribution of wealth and the maintenance of certain minimal standards of welfare below which no members of the community should be allowed to fall. The intricacies of contractual industrial capitalism had to be qualified with reference to the 'common good'. The political bond of society was everywhere coming to be that of an insistence upon citizenship, and the fullest and most responsible participation of all in the taking of those decisions which were taken at the centre but were binding on all. Political constitutions had to be constructed to give effective administrative and procedural form to the complex web of rights and duties which this conception entailed. The divisions of 'class' in society were being radically questioned and changed. The old kinds of bondage were gone, and the new kinds of difference of wealth and status had to be qualified in the light of the conception of citizenship. Even in the family, the new freedom coupled with the emancipation of women was now being qualified by the achievement of a form of the family aided in all its functions by new provisions of the state. In all this, religion could no longer exert an all-embracing and dogmatic authority. Even the conception of the spiritual was of a limited and undogmatic kind, entailing a commitment to a struggle to shape events in the light of certain values. And in morality, the situation was one in which to set up clear ethical standards was no longer in itself enough, but had now to be informed by the prevailing 'ethos' of 'realistic humanitarianism'.

In short, all the institutional developments in the contemporary world were in a condition of critical change. Problems abounded, but these were themselves actual elements of the new juncture of knowledge, criticism, and power of control itself, and man did in fact possess the wherewithal to solve them. A new responsibility for deliberate judgment and purposive action was sharply posed. The modern world was distinguished by a ferment of change—but the ferment was itself of a complex, moral nature.

And this was a third extremely important aspect of the picture of modern times which Hobhouse was at pains to paint clearly. His essential vision was that the *factual* changes of social institutions in the modern world *were* part and parcel of the *intellectual* and *ethical* changes. This point needs to be established very clearly. It was *not* the case, according to Hobhouse's analysis, that *factual* changes took place in society which were independent of questions about ethical standards, but which, if we wished, we could *evaluate* in the light of these standards. On the contrary, with the growth of increasingly exact knowledge, reflection, and effective control over nature and society; with the growth of an increasingly self-conscious knowledge on the part of man—not only of the world, but of the nature and situation of his own mind and his own society within the world; with, in short, the increasing degree to which the *teleological* qualities of man's thought and behaviour emerged from the conditions of earlier *'genetic'* determination, and superseded them; so the *facts* of social change were increasingly identifiable with man's *conscious knowledge*, his *deliberate use* of this, and the *ethical principles* which were the basis of the formulation of his *purposes*. *Teleological* action in society *entailed* all these dimensions. Furthermore, this was not simply a matter (from the point of view of sociological analysis) of looking at this whole modern scene with objective detachment, and interpreting this or that 'principle' or 'moral motive', this or that 'element of knowledge', this or that 'fact of institutional change', as though they were all separate factors which could be linked. They were *in complex fact—all of a piece*. The changing institutions were patterns of knowledge and purpose. The ethical principles were part of the changing condition of knowledge and organizational control. And in the entire complex situation, all the intense arguments which were afoot were also all of a piece. In their intense struggles between free economic competitiveness and the economic intervention of the state for the establishment of services for public welfare, and similar problems, men were *at one and the same time*, struggling to make institutional forms in the light of knowledge, conflicts of interest, and ethical persuasion. The *actuality of society*, the *actual nature of social organization*, the *facts of society—were, in fact*, the composite embodiment of all these elements of *value, purpose, knowledge*, and forceful *deliberate action*.

Hobhouse has often been accused of confusing *ethics* and *scientific sociology* in his system, but this is not the case. We shall see, in a moment, how he approached the problem of judging the net *development* of social evolution, and how this was related, in his thinking, to his system of philosophical *ethics*, but here it is enough to see clearly his central contention—that, from its emergence; human society has always been characterized by the two elements of genetic and teleological causation; that the teleological element has progressively grown more dominant with the development of mind and knowledge; and that, as a necessary entailment of this, in the culminating social changes in the contemporary world, there has come to be an intimate interdependency between conscious knowledge, consideration of ethical principle, deliberate technical and social control, and actual organizational change. The teleological reconstruction of society; the 'experiential reconstruction' of the 'empirical order' in the light of 'realistic humanitarianism'; *means* the close conjunction of all these elements. *Social* development and the embodiment of *ethical* concerns are therefore inextricably part of the actuality of society in the contemporary world.

With regard to this movement from 'genetic' to 'teleological' and this interdependency of social and ethical development in the modern situation, Hobhouse wrote, for example:

'Thus, looking through social development as a whole, we observe first the development of an organ of social control and the increasing efficacy of ideas in the organization of life; secondly, the equalization of rights and duties, and the consequent destruction of many of the barriers that divide mankind; lastly, the development of the principles of personality on the one side, and of collective responsibility on the other. But these are the general conditions of social co-operation, the essence of which lies in the reconciliation of free growth, whether in the individual personality or in the family or in any form of collective life, with organized and disciplined effort for the advancement of the race. Thus, taking each side of law, custom and government in turn, we find that the net movement is to contribute the appropriate condition to the realization of the ethical ideal.'*

Other points of the very greatest importance for the nature of sociological analysis are implicit in this position adopted by Hobhouse, but there is one special point we must take care to note conspicuously before leaving this straightforward statement. This is the point we have been at pains to indicate very strongly throughout our study—namely that, in all these nineteenth and early twentieth century thinkers, there is a central emphasis that *morality* is at the heart of society; at the *core* of all social institutions. In the work of Hobhouse, as we have seen, this point received a new, reinforced, and developed importance. For in his system it was not only made plain that, even in the earlier epochs of the laying down of society, morality was at the core of all institutions, but also that, as the *teleological* dimensions of man's activity came ever more conspicuously to the fore in the world of modern science, the ferment of interrelated change in all social institutions was not only intimately and profoundly, but also consciously and deliberately focused upon *ethical* issues. One can put the matter quite starkly: as knowledge, criticism, and the responsibility for deliberate control have increased in modern society, so the factual changes in social institutions have come to be centrally worked out in relation to ethical principles and concerns. The re-making of modern society is the conscious shaping of social institutions to approximate as closely as possible to clarified ethical standards.

This is a most important point, and, again, brings to a head the persuasion of all those from Comte to the twentieth century.

These considerations of the emphases and the qualifications which Hobhouse very deliberately made bring us to the end of our outline of his comparative study of societies and social institutions; and the picture of 'social evolution' which it provided (including the 'net result' as it now exists in our own world) is reasonably clear. They also, however, lead us to understand Hobhouse's concern to go beyond this analysis of 'types' of society and 'correlations' of institutions, to come to terms, as clearly and as explicitly as possible, with those difficult questions of the assessment of 'social development' and 'net development', and of ethical evaluations. His study of those problems led to additional elements in his system.

(6) *Social Development and Social Progress*

Hobhouse was not content, as we have seen, simply to produce a

* *Development and Purpose*, p. 226.

215

body of testable, descriptive, classified knowledge. By disposition and personal commitment he wished to do more: to assess and evaluate the contemporary situation of mankind in order to contribute as clear as possible a perspective for immediate judgment and action. Now it is possible for a social 'scientist' with contemporary professional perspectives (i.e. end-of-nose limitations of vision) to say: 'Well, that may be all well and good for Hobhouse; but for our part, we are not interested in his dispositions and personal commitments, we are interested only in knowledge. Questions of assessing and evaluating "net-developments" of social changes are not for us.' But this is far from being the end of the story, and we come here to some very difficult epistemological questions as to what must be involved in sociological 'knowledge'.

In the first place, it is commonly thought that 'evaluating'—in the social sciences—is entirely (or very largely) an 'ethical' matter. When people speak of keeping 'value-judgments' separate from 'scientific method', they are referring usually to 'moral' judgments. In this sense, almost every social science begins with a warning that it is 'positive'—not 'normative'. It is concerned with what *is*, not with what ought *to be*. But this, of course, is only a superficial consideration of what is a very much more complicated problem. The fact is that this question as to how far 'knowledge' is a set of propositions which derive from 'evaluative assumptions' leading to selectivity in our procedures of study, is a question going far beyond 'ethical' matters alone. It is a fundamental issue in the theory of knowledge as such. For specific 'theories' in science can rest just as much upon implicit evaluative assumptions of 'perceptual' and 'conceptual' (for example) kinds, as upon 'ethical' kinds. And Hobhouse's much more fundamental starting point in raising these issues was that even in our attempt to establish *knowledge* in sociology we meet inescapable philosophical questions as to what our criteria of measurement, of judgment, and of 'appropriateness of evidence', are to be for the various kinds of testable proposition which we seek to make.*

Thus, for example, without by any means pursuing this question to its philosophical depths, it seems possible to put forward scientific theories of the temporal persistence, difference, cumulative processes, etc; of societies (which, we must remember are essentially historical phenomena) in terms of *change, growth, evolution, development*, without involving ourselves in any kind of 'evaluation', Social 'change' can be explored in terms of institutions simply becoming *different* from what they were before'. Social 'growth' can be explored in terms of straightforward increase in the size of societies.

* This was exactly the central problem explored by Max Weber—as we shall see later.

Social 'evolution' can be explored in terms of emerging 'patterns of institutions' which are the outcome of 'inherited traditions' and changes of 'adjustment' or 'adaptation' to 'environmental conditions'. Social 'development' can be explored in terms of changes in artefacts or institutions which are not *arbitrarily* different from what they were before, but emerge out of previous *cumulative changes* in a certain direction (in the performance of a certain function) and advance these changes further in the improved fulfilment of that function.

The idea of '*progress*', it might be argued, clearly *does* involve ethical evaluation, but since we are concerned only with scientific knowledge and not ethical evaluation—we can simply rule the idea of progress out of our vocabulary; out of our usage.

All this *seems* plausible, until we look into these matters more carefully, and here we might concentrate on the concept of 'development' by way of example. It is clear that the term 'development' can be used neutrally in speaking of a sequence of events, simply to indicate that 'one thing led to another'. We can speak of the 'development' of the events of the 'French Revolution' purely as a sequential connectedness of actions. But, also, it is equally clear that very often we have to use the term 'development' in such a way as necessarily to include the *evaluation* of advancement. Thus, we would say that wheeled vehicles were a development of rough wooden sledges; that power-driven wheeled vehicles were a development of (let us say) horse drawn wheeled vehicles; that air-borne power-driven vehicles were a development of power-driven vehicles on land and water; and so on. Here our conception; quite properly, accurately, and testably; is that the one kind of vehicle grew out of the cumulative achievement of the past, and went beyond it; was an *advancement* upon it; in that it achieved a much more efficient fulfilment of its functions: in this case to convey people and things over distances easily, speedily, comfortably, safely, and so on. What is clear here is that the idea of *progress* is *implicit* in this *factual* idea of *development*; and, furthermore, that the idea of progress is *not* only an ethical one. It is also important to see that even in purely *technical* terms, the estimation of *advancement* includes a reference to a *function* or *end*. *Without* some kind of conception of the end which an artefact serves, or the function which it fulfils, it would be impossible to *estimate* or to *evaluate* the directions of *development*. There must therefore be some kind of firm criteria, some kind of scale of measurement in mind, when speaking purely of technical development. Judgment in relation to ends, as well as 'scientific' knowledge for the creation of the 'means', is implicit in it.*

* It is worthwhile to note that the very *perception* of what constitutes a technical

Even in technical matters proper—the harnessing of nuclear power the skilled methods of accomplishing the transplanting of organs, etc;—it is obvious that *ethical* matters are very difficult to exclude from conceptions of development, but we will not stick too closely to these issues. What is more interesting is that we can (and do) speak, quite correctly, about the 'development' of social institutions in exactly the same way. We can speak, as Hobhouse did, of the *development* of the institutions of 'public justice'—demonstrating the growth of sophisticated procedures of advocacy for bringing all relevant evidence before an expert judge and a lay jury, out of earlier and simpler court procedures possessing less rational methods for the determination of guilt and punishment, and out of the earlier 'blood-feud' in the simpler societies. And in this, we can show the emergence of each new procedure out of earlier cumulative achievements, and can show that they are an *advance* with reference to the end, or function, they fulfil: in this case, the statement and resolution of disputes, or the trying of people who are charged with 'crimes' against society. Now in a sense this is just as '*technical*' a matter as the development of wheeled vehicles: it is the improvement of an artifice to accomplish an end; but, at the same time, it is clear that the *end* here, in terms of which the technical efficiency has to be judged is in large part an '*ethical*' end: it is the approximation to the ideal of justice, including such notions as truth and objectivity in evidence, equality before the law, impartiality, etc.

The ethical ends of men are among, and, indeed, are part and parcel of, all the other ends of men in society in the light of which institutions are made, criticized, and re-shaped in history. In short, the 'technical' notion of 'development' in social institutions entails judgment, at least in part, of 'ethical' ends and principles.

Thus, the idea of *progress* cannot in any naïve way be thought of as a conception sharply cut off from the concept of *development*: the one implicitly containing ethical elements, the other not. The concepts are more intimately interconnected than this. Similar considerations (though not the same in each case) apply to the other concepts of *change, growth,* and *evolution*.

In this quite immediate sense, then, the establishing of certain kinds of knowledge in sociology necessitates a clarification of the grounds for certain kinds of judgment and estimation which go beyond the ordinary level of 'hypothesis and experimentation' in science. Hobhouse himself wrote:

'Up to this point our method is purely empirical. We have simply to

development requires this *judgmental* awareness of *ends* and appropriateness of *functions*.

analyse and compare the operations and achievements of mind in successive phases, to show how one phase may be conceived as issuing from another, and to indicate the nature of the changes successively introduced. But particularly as we reach the higher phases we shall see that another set of questions underlies our whole enquiry. When for example we deal with the emergence of rational method, as in science and philosophy, we shall have to take account of the claim of such a method to yield *truth*. This claim is an integral part of this particular phase of development, and we shall not be able to understand that phase or place it in due relation to others without enquiring into the nature of rational method and thus opening up the question of *the validity of thought*. Similarly on the ethical side we shall come upon theories of conduct or of human well-being which we shall not be able to interpret without opening questions as to the *meaning of such terms as good and bad, right or wrong.*

It is true that we might keep to a purely historical method by merely recounting the opinions which men have held or the methods which they have in fact pursued. But it is clear that our conception of a given intellectual movement will differ radically according as we hold that it is a movement towards truth or towards error, or again towards a goal of real value or to one of no greater account than any other. Thus if our object be not merely to record the successive phases in the movement of mind but to appreciate the direction and magnitude of that movement, it is clear that we have to go outside the purely historical method of treatment; we must apply a philosophical theory of the basis of rational belief and action in order that we may take stock of the position at which we have arrived.

If, for example, we can satisfy ourselves that we have some knowledge of reality, grounded, let us say, on the methods of science, then we shall be able to treat the historic development of science as a movement towards the knowledge of reality. If, on the other hand, we take the view that scientific method suffers from incurable defects or limitations which preclude it from ever supplying a genuine interpretation of the reality of things, then clearly we shall put quite a different valuation upon its growth, and our whole estimate of modern civilization will be vitally changed. Thus *from the study of historical facts we are led on to a study of values, of the ultimate grounds of belief, the meaning of rationality, the possible scope of knowledge,* the considerations which reasonably determine action. We have not only to distinguish successive phases of development, but we have to estimate the direction of development as a whole, and *for this purpose we must make use of valuations which open up all the ultimate questions of meaning and validity.'*

It is worthwhile to notice, too, that Hobhouse thought that exactly the same problem was implicit in speaking of the 'evolution' of mind in nature and society; and this passage serves to illustrate again how far he was from glibly assuming an 'ever upward' sequence of progress which terminated in our own modern society—which was 'best'. One object of our enquiry, he wrote:

* *Development and Purpose,* pp. 14–15.

'. . . is to measure the growth of mind from the lowest to the highest phase of development. But how are we to know which is highest? The term itself implies a valuation, and unless we have a reasoned standard of value we have no scientific means of determining the *terminus ad quem* of our narrative. We certainly cannot take our own civilization as the highest product of the social mind without any dubiety or any reasons given. It does not, to say the least, stand so high in its achievement above some earlier civilizations which arose and flourished and passed away. Human development, it is well to recognize from the outset, does not proceed continuously in a straight line. If we make the civilization of our own day the terminal point of our narrative we have still to ask whether this point is the "highest" yet reached or whether it marks a decline from some earlier stage, and this is a question which can only be determined by the aid of a standard upon which the "higher" and the "lower" are clearly marked. If in the end we come to the conclusion—as for reasons which will be given, I believe we may—that our own civilization does upon the whole represent a certain net advance on the previous efforts of humanity, this conclusion must be based upon a clear-sighted comparison of the historical facts with an agreed standard of values.'*

This element in Hobhouse's concern about the concepts of 'development' and 'progress' is clear enough. There was, however, another: and this was his conviction that the teaching of the philosophical 'Idealists'—from Hegel to T. H. Green—possessed an important kernel of truth. They, it will be remembered, thought of the actualities of nature and history as the gradual *actualization* of an initial *idea*; the *realization* of the *potentialities* of spirit; and they believed that individual human beings came to their own realization of the qualities of spirit, realising their own fulfilment, in so far as they experienced the objective embodiments of these qualities (greater than they) which had taken shape, as an outcome of the many-sided quests and conflicts of history, in the *institutions of society*: in the 'totality of the state' in their own time.

Hobhouse was very wary of the metaphysical grounds of this 'Idealism'; he was sceptical to a degree it is difficult to be sure of about its large claims as a position in philosophy; but, this aside, he thought that this conception pointed to a valid dimension in human history, and provided a valid dimension for sociology in the interpretation of this history. 'Idealism' and 'Materialism' aside, it *was* the case, Hobhouse maintained, that human nature, with its emergence among other animal species, was distinctive in its 'teleological' dimensions: its capacity of developing knowledge, understanding, control, and ever more clarified purpose; and that the creative activities of men in the evolution of society had, in fact, been an *actualization* of their *potentialities*. What was undeniably true (despite

* *Development and Purpose*, pp. 15–16.

the tangled details of history) was that man *now*, in the modern world, had inherited a 'net result' of all earlier developments of social institutions, which placed him in the position not only of knowing about nature and society in a simple objective sense, but of knowing about *himself*—of establishing a full understanding of how he himself, his own mind which was contemplating this entire situation, had come to be what it was—and of having the knowledge not only of how responsibly to reconstruct the 'empirical order' of society, but the consciousness of being centrally responsible for the future direction of the evolution of life in the world. This was by no means a claim of arrogance—but only a recognition of the dominance which the development of man had come to assume in affecting the life and future conditions of all other species in the world. In a completely empirical and realistic sense, then, the net outcome of '*social evolution*' (clarified by comparative studies) had been also a '*development*' in this further sense of constituting an extensive degree of *realization* (in institutional forms which made a freedom and richness of personal life possible) of the *potentialities* of human nature; and provided the basis for the conscious and responsible pursuit of this realization even further.

This notion of development, then, was the idea of a process whereby qualities which were initially *potential* came to be *actualized* within the context of life and the struggle with certain conditions. As far as man and history was concerned, it was a conception of the potentialities of the human spirit: '. . . subject to conditions and achieving its full growth only by mastering them.'

Exercised by these considerations, and clearly needing criteria for the judgment of social *development* in addition to his classified knowledge of '*social evolution*', Hobhouse clarified certain distinguishable aspects of 'development',

One condition in human society which was necessary for the increased realization of human potentialities was a growth in *scale*. Among larger populations in larger societies the institutional fabric for a richer fulfilment of human needs and qualities was possible. Size alone, however, was clearly not enough. A second condition which was necessary—together with a growth in size—was a growth in *efficiency*. Only with a more efficient deployment of these greater resources—a better allocation of means to ends desired—could a society cater to best effect for a richer fulfilment of the lives of all its members. Again, however, scale and efficiency were not in themselves enough, for a large and efficient society might well be tyrannical, and repressive with regard to a large proportion of its members. A third necessary condition was that of *freedom*. Only if all the citizens of a society were able to state their claims frankly, to resolve them by open discourse, to pursue their many interests freely, could it be at all ensured that the potentialities of all were being realized as fully as possible. But again—completely unrestricted freedom; competition with no regard whatever to the conditions and claims of others—could well lead to such a tangle of conflict and inefficiency as to ruin any basis for a maximal fulfilment of the potentialities of all. Only if —as well as freedom—there was the all-pervading 'ethos', and constitutional requirement, of *'mutuality'*: of sensitivity and concern among all for the consideration of the claims of others, could the best social context for the secure pursuit of desired diversity be provided.

Societies could be judged and assessed with regard to the *facts* of social development, then, in accordance with the presence or absence in them of these four criteria: *scale, efficiency, freedom*, and *mutuality*. Applying these criteria to the picture of social 'evolution' which his comparative schema had provided, Hobhouse argued that the institutional changes of the modern world (which were the 'net outcome' of this evolution) did, indeed, give evidence of development in these terms, and, especially, were demonstrably a basis for the conscious direction of such development in future.

In addition to these concepts, however, Hobhouse also undertook a detailed enquiry into moral philosophy, in order to establish the *ethical* criteria in the light of which we had to judge institutions. This was a complex study, and one into which it is impossible to go in sufficient detail. One or two points, however, are perhaps enough for our own particular purposes. The account of the 'good life' and of the attendant (i.e. implied and interrelated) 'principles of right action' which Hobhouse put forward was of the kind offered by Plato and Bishop Butler: that of a satisfying fulfilment of human desires, the pursuit of the highest standards of excellence in this, and the *qualification* of the specific desires by *reason*—not in a repressive sense, but in the regulatory sense of achieving a certain balance and appropriateness of the gratification of the appetites in the light of an over-all conception of functional harmony which reason was able to clarify. It was a picture of 'the rational good', but it is perhaps also worth saying that it borrowed much of the feeling (though not by any means all of the philosophy) of *'Utilitarianism'* in emphasizing *'happiness'* as the outcome of the good life for individuals and society.

A few points need special emphasis. Firstly, Hobhouse deliberately connected in his ethics the ideas of the *right* and the *good:* two elements which have been radically separated by many modern philosophers. Like Plato, he looked at what constituted the good life for the individual, and then considered what principles of right action between individuals in the community this implied. And this, of course, led him to outline principles of *social* justice and a model of the good society. In all this he was essentially sound, and Hobhouse's *Elements of Social Justice* is still one of the most useful essays for seeing how the 'right' and the 'good' are essentially interrelated, and how they can lead to a detailed working out not only of such large principles as 'equality', 'liberty', 'impartiality' and the like, but also the very detailed application of these to such specific matters as the payment of wages, relations between the sexes, social class and privilege in education, etc.

The second point, however, which is exceedingly important, and which we intimated earlier when commenting on the ideas of Tönnies, is that Hobhouse showed quite fully that although *reason* refers to elements of experience and knowledge which go beyond *feeling* as such (instinct, emotion, sentiment, etc.) it is not by any means necessarily *in conflict* with feeling. A few points are involved here. Firstly: reason is, in part, an extension of what is already embryonic within feeling itself. Reason grows out of feeling. Thus feeling can entail a sense of the sublimity of an ideal—and reason is employed in the elucidation of it: thus adding further dimensions of enhancement to feeling. Also, feeling can deeply sense an *in*justice, but is not clear what justice is—but reason can elucidate what is presupposed in this moral feeling. Feeling, too, can be a sense of being 'arrested' by a compelling beauty in the world—a sense which is beyond its understanding: but reason can elucidate some dimensions, at least, of what is involved. It is worth pointing out that *reason* is not only the kind of mental process embodied in, say, Hegel's 'Logic' or Kant's 'Critique of Pure Reason', but also the kind embodied in Wordsworth's 'Prelude'. Reason can be, and very often is, *in the service of feeling*, providing important dimensions of understanding of what are, at first, only profound 'intimations' of feeling. Secondly, though reason gives grounds for the qualification of feeling (the regulation of it), it can do so still in the service of feeling, in the sense of regulating the feelings and desires *in relation to each other*, and in relation to *an over-all ideal of character*, which might well be unattainable if the feelings were ungoverned. Plato, for example, portrays colourfully the *tyranny* of the passions if they are allowed completely free rein; and the government of reason which he recommends is such that each desire, each 'part of the soul', should enjoy its proper satisfaction within the whole. But the third thing is that reason, as such, cannot be said, in itself, to exercise the qualifying control over feeling which its knowledge and judgment suggests is best. Such control is accomplished by what we refer to as 'the *will*', and it is enough to note that this is some compounding of deliberate choice

223

and intention which includes *both* reason *and* attendant feeling. Into the intricacies of this we need not go—but it is important that we should note it in relation to Tönnies' distinction (on which he hangs so much) between the 'natural' and the 'rational' will. What we are now saying is that though this distinction can be considered valid for Tönnies' purposes—it is not the whole of the story. Reason and will can deliberately pursue and serve the satisfaction and harmony of natural instinct, emotion, and sentiment, not necessarily be sharply distinguished from them, nor in conflict with them. In the same way—rationally contracted relationships in society can have the service of 'natural feelings' as their end.

However, the central point to be made here is that Hobhouse clarified a set of *ethical* criteria in the light of which institutions and societies could be *morally* judged, and his procedure and effort in this was a considerable advance on those who had preceded him, and who had tended always to get their ethical judgments and their factual hypotheses mixed up. Hobhouse was perfectly clear in his own conception, and in his proposals of method, here. But now we come to a point on which much care is needed.

Hobhouse's position was this. Having seen the necessity of estimating the 'net outcome' of the evolution of social institutions, he had considered (*a*) criteria for a *factual* estimation of social development: the factors which, in *fact*, societies needed to have for the maximal realization of human potentialities, and (*b*) criteria for an *ethical* estimation of social progress: the ethical principles with which the institutions of a society should be in accord in order to be approved of as a close approximation to a 'just' society. Now— when he applied these criteria to the correlated facts of social *evolution* (the evolution of mind in nature and society) which his comparative studies had made clear—two things were apparent, and their conjunction was significant. First: the criteria for judging the *facts* of social development and the criteria for judging societies *ethically—coincided* with each other. The criteria of the good life, and of the institutional embodiments of the principles of social justice which made the good life possible for all the members of a society coincided with a society in which scale, efficiency, freedom and mutuality were present. In short, this direction of social development could be ethically approved; and to pursue the furtherance of these conditions of social development was ethically right. And secondly, the 'net outcome' of social evolution (the estimation of the changing nature of social institutions in the modern world in which social evolution had resulted) was seen, in fact, to be in accordance with these criteria of factual development and moral progress.

The 'net outcome' of social evolution, the conditions of social development which could lead to the increased realization of human potentialities, and the criteria of moral progress were all coincident in the contemporary world. And this was no accident, according to Hobhouse, but a thorough-going corroboration of the fact that the human mind in society had attained this new condition of knowledge and control, and this new basis for embarking upon the fully conscious and responsible direction of its own destiny. The 'teleological' capacities of human nature had now come to a basis of conditions—increasingly spread throughout the world, and increasingly spread throughout all the strata of all societies (no longer confined to a few)—on which its powers of purposive control could not only be firmly established: but were so prominent, and so filled with both promise and danger, that they had to be confronted, and, if possible, assumed in such a way as to lead to responsible purpose.

There was here, it will readily be seen, an almost unbelievably massive scheme of thought and knowledge which pictured the responsiblity for control with which man was now faced in the modern world as the culmination of all the long processes of natural evolution and social evolution in the world; which threw a perspective of interpretation over the entirety of this; but which also meticulously pointed out the significance of this for every specific area of institutional change in modern society. This was a scheme of knowledge, a scheme of judgment, and a scheme for positive social and political action.

I am hesitant to try to introduce even larger dimensions into the already large canvas of Hobhouse's system, especially things which seem out of tune with our own (immediate) time, but this must be done if only because the truth of these matters *is* so large as, ultimately, to go beyond us, and it is—from the point of view of the making of sociology—important to see that sociology has not shirked a recognition of these dimensions; but also because it is necessary to see the most intimate link between Hobhouse's highly complex and developed system of evolutionary sociology and the central persuasions which had moved Comte in his very first statement of the subject. For the vision of Hobhouse, like that of Comte, was not only of a contemporary world vexed by rapid and radical changes, a world straddling perhaps the biggest watershed in history—between traditional agrarian society on the one side, and all the complex changes and problems of scientific industrialized society on the other; a world of explosive revolution and simultaneous promise; but also a world in which generations of men were rootless and lost in their religious, moral, and intellectual searchings. In the vortex of modern social forces—when the expansion of no one generation was like that of the last, when all doctrines were vulnerable to a thousand questions—men had no firm ground of belief and commitment on which to stand. Men felt stripped of significance in a spiritual vacuum. And just as Comte had felt that sociology could not only provide a basis for the reconstruction of society but also the perspective for a new, humanist religion, so, too, Hobhouse thought that a new clarification for a firm human stance and effort could be provided.

He was *very* far from proposing a '*positive religion*' with all its ritual trappings such as Comte had so indefatigably worked out, but, still, the central notions of a new basis for religious and moral feeling resting on a considered ground of intellectual belief, and the significance of the achievement of a new science of man and society for the task of responsible reconstruction with which man was faced, were there—and were very forcefully and movingly expressed, Here, we may note one or two examples.

In '*Morals in Evolution*', having described the modern world as a stage at which: ' . . . social and ethical evolution become one . . . ' and having argued that: 'This union becomes realized in proportion as the mind attains that control over its own growth which it already possessed over the processes of nature,' Hobhouse went on to say:

'Here, as Comte first made plain, lies the true significance of the history of science. Through science mind dominates nature; first physical nature, then organic nature, lastly the conditions—physical, psychological, social—of its own life and growth. This movement goes on at an ever accelerating rate, and as it proceeds the conditions of a rational guidance of social life are one by one being satisfied. At the basis of these stands the mastery of external natural conditions, in which regard the last hundred and fifty years have witnessed a complete revolution, and so far there is every indication that the changes of the coming century will be not less, but even more sweeping. Next come the laws of life, the conditions of health, the causes of disease, the factors of physical evolution. The scientific treatment of these subjects can scarcely be said to be more than seventy years old, and it may be maintained without exaggeration that, little as we know even now, the sum of what we have learnt in that time as to the true causation of disease, as to the nature of heredity and the modifiability of organisms, far outweighs all that had been learnt in the previous two thousand years. There follow the laws of mental growth, and here our own time has witnessed the emergence of psychology as a science, and education as a true art aiming at educing from the mind what is in it, aiding natural development, and stimulating or correcting it at need, as the physician follows the efforts of the body towards the restoration of the balance of health—the whole a conception still in merest infancy, but already promising a vigorous life. Here, then, we have the conditions forming for development of body and mind and their maintenance in health. To these have to be added the scientific adjustment of the relations of man to man—sociology. Here, again, we have a science in its infancy, but the mere attempt to deal with public questions in the spirit of science implies an advance ethical as well as intellectual. At any rate it is on the possibility of controlling social forces by the aid of social science as perfectly as natural forces are controlled at present by the aid of physical science, that the permanent progress of humanity must depend.'*

Hobhouse did not, by any means, believe that man's efforts would necessarily be successful, but he was sure that, fraught though they were with difficulties, they were of a nature more worthy than those of earlier civilizations in that they were seeking to develop the conditions for the fulfilment of human life quite literally throughout the world and through all strata of all societies for all men—whereas the peaks of culture in earlier times had been very limited 'islands in a sea of barbarism'. He wrote, for example:

'That modern civilization may share the fate of earlier periods of culture is, of course, possible. The reasons for hoping for a better event have been implied in discussing the potentialities of that which we take to be the highest stage of mental development. Modern civilization stands above that of Greece or Rome not because it has realized greater happiness for the world or a more beautiful order of life or greater works of genius. These things none can measure. Happiness is naught until it is complete, and only full development of Mind could render it secure. If the world process were to be arrested here, it might plausibly be contended that in the actual fruition the life of Athens was something finer and more worth having than the life of England or France. The modern world stands higher because it is further on the road to the goal, though it may be that its portion of the road lies through less smiling country, and it is further on the road because its Thought has advanced a clear stage in the control of the conditions of life and in the conception of its own aim and end. For the same reason it is gradually subduing both the barbarian without the gate and the Philistine within.'†

Whatever the difficulties which confront it:

'. . . the future development of society,' he wrote, 'will follow a very different course from its past history, in that it is destined to fall within the scope of an organizing intelligence, and thereby to be removed from the play of blind force to the sphere of rational order. Such a change must be gradual and attended with many setbacks. The very ideas which are to direct it are yet in their infancy. Yet the social self-consciousness which gives them birth, arrived at as it is by a blending of the moral, the scientific and the religious spirit, is for us the culminating fact of ethical evolution. But such an end can only be a beginning. Mind grasps the conditions of its development that it may master and make use of them in

---

* *Morals in Evolution*, pp. 633–4.   † *Development and Purpose*, p. 230.

its further growth. Of the nature of that growth, whither it tends and what new shapes it will evolve, we as yet know little. It is enough for the moment to reach the idea of a self-conscious evolution of humanity, and to find therein a meaning and an element of purpose for the historical process which has led up to it. It is, at any rate, something to learn—as, if our present conclusion is sound, we do learn—that this slowly wrought out dominance of mind in things is the central·fact of evolution. For if this is true it is the germ of a religion and an ethics which are as far removed from materialism as from the optimistic teleology of the metaphysician, or the half naive creeds of the churches. It gives a meaning to human effort, as neither the pawn of an overruling Providence nor the sport of blind force. It is a message of hope to the world, of suffering lessened and strife assuaged, not by fleeing from reason to the bosom of faith, but by the increasing rational control of things . . .'*

On the 'religious' basis for human life which this perspective presents it is worthwhile to note the emphasis which Hobhouse laid upon the fact that man did not create the conditions for his own advancement himself, but *discovered* them as the outcome of the processes of the world which had taken shape before him. In short, the world of reality (of both nature and history) which was *larger* than man, had produced the basis for man's mental and spiritual growth, and man *discovered* his own stature in pursuing his understanding of it. In this sense, Hobhouse went so far as to suggest that the fulfilment of the human spirit may be in relation to a larger spiritual reality which is in some way implicit in the processes of the world. It is a position very close indeed to 'Idealism'; and I think it is right that we should take note of it, bearing in mind especially the tremendous link between this developed concluding statement of Hobhouse and the foundation statement of Comte.

'Humanity,' Hobhouse wrote, 'in the sense which the best Positive writers have given to that word, Humanity as the spirit of harmony and expanding life, shaping the best actions of the best men and women, is the highest incarnation known to us of the divine. If, indeed, we come to the conclusion that God is, and are asked what He is, we may reply that God is that of which the highest known embodiment is the distinctive spirit of Humanity. And of this account of the relation of the empirical to the central mind there is in the empirical account itself more than a hint.

For at each stage we have shown that the conditions of a higher stage are already present. It is not the mere empirical mind itself that works out its own progress. It is the empirical mind operating upon other conditions of progress that are already laid down. *The human mind is a germ for whose maturity provision is already made.* Furthermore, at the highest known phase of development we say that the mind comes to realize itself,

* *Morals in Evolution*, p. 637.

that is, to realize what are the fundamentals of its structure as it has been all along. In this new consciousness it discovers a unity underlying the differences and divergences of life and a plan containing the possibilities of a future self-realization. *It does not invent this unity and this plan. It discovers them.* It finds that they are already there, and have been among the conditions operating to determine its growth from the earliest stages. Its own purposeful activity is merely the continued operation of these conditions completed by the unifying link of the consciousness of their significance. Hence, if the mind does not directly through the religious consciousness become aware of its relation to a greater Spirit, it does have to recognize the existence of conditions appropriate to the operation of such a Spirit, and to admit in its own history a process in which such conditions are working out their natural results.'

The conclusion of such a perspective of thought, Hobhouse said:

'. . . by no means answers all the questions that men ask of experience. But, if it is sound, it does settle the fundamental questions—whether the life of man is full of hopeful purpose or void of meaning, whether he can recognize in the constitution of things something that meets his hopes and answers to his aspirations, whether he can make for himself a religion without self-deceit, whether he can finally improve the conditions of his race by effort or is doomed always to fall back from every apparently forward step, whether he can trust to his reason or must admit the ultimate futility of thought, whether the spirit of human love is justified of her children or blood and iron must continue to rule the world. To all these questions the conclusion here reached supplies a definite and a positive answer. It is, however, maintained here, not as something which is to satisfy all emotional cravings or end all intellectual doubts, not because it is artistically complete or even because it is proved with demonstrative certainty, but merely on the humble and prosaic ground that, on a complete and impartial review of a vast mass of evidence, it is shown to be probably true.'*

It will be clearly seen that this is a very qualified agnostic and sceptical position, resting firmly upon a 'Comte-like' humanist stance and upon scientific knowledge and rational judgment, and yet entertaining the possibility that a larger spiritual perspective might lie beyond. This we will not comment on—having seen the link with Comte which it was important for us to see. It is a position which most contemporary sociologists would either treat with scorn, or ignore, but perhaps, when all is well considered, it may be a position to which men may return.

The final point to note, is that after this entire system of analysis of the evolution and development of all types of societies, Hobhouse portrayed this culminating stage of modern society not as the end—

* *Development and Purpose*, pp. 371–2.

but as the *beginning*: the beginning of man's conscious and responsible control over his own destiny.

Here then, in the work of Hobhouse, was another contribution which concentrated upon the development of the *evolutionary* perspectives of sociology. The richness of the many aspects of his treatment; the careful and detailed carrying out of his classification and comparative study of societies; the great care exercised in elucidating exactly his conception of evolution, development, and ethical progress; his care to show the detailed relevance of comparative sociology to the understanding of specific contemporary problems; his clear distinction between the 'genetic' and 'teleological' elements in human society and his portrayal of the growing dominance of the latter in modern times and the significance of this for the explanation of contemporary social institutions; all these show clear elements of advance on his nineteenth century predecessors whilst, at the same time, they draw these earlier contributions together in an entire scheme of analysis.

It is plain, too, that Hobhouse was in complete agreement with Tönnies and Westermarck in certain respects: especially in the picture they presented of an increasing *rationality* of modern society. He agreed very considerably, even, with the harsh judgment which Tönnies formed on many of the 'contractual complexities' of a modern society dominated by 'bourgeois' values, aspirations, and unremitting competitiveness. Yet, at the same time, there was the marked difference that he emphasized greatly the extent to which the 'rational will' could, in approaching social organization with conscious purpose, act in such a way as to preserve and further elements of feeling, sentiment, and humane principle, not only in such a way as to destroy them. In Tönnies there was a great warning against the dehumanizing danger of too 'rational' a society; in Hobhouse there was also a great warning—but of a different kind. In his case it was the encouraging teaching that all the institutional dilemmas of our age were, properly understood, the concomitants of a great promise; but—and this was the warning—that this promise would only be accomplished if men clearly recognized and clearly committed themselves to the task of deliberate social reconstruction that lay before them. Without this, a great disaster, a grave failure, a catastrophe of retrogression might lie ahead.

4
Theories of Social Evolution: Summary Comments

Our studies of Tönnies, Westermarck, and Hobhouse have shown beyond all doubt that very considerable developments in the making of sociology had been accomplished by the beginning of the second world war on the basis of the idea of 'evolution' as a true perspective for the study of human societies. Without needing to comment on every relevant detail, it has become clear how these men—and perhaps Tönnies and Hobhouse especially—drew together practically all the chief elements of sociology which had been clarified by the end of the nineteenth century, and utilized them in achieving more accurately qualified and more mature systems of analysis, and in providing a deeper understanding of the nature of society, and especially of the institutional changes which wracked the modern world: which underlay the modern 'malaise'. A decided maturing of sociology couched within this perspective of 'evolution' had taken place.

Like the nineteenth century scholars, these men regarded societies as 'social systems': total political communities consisting of certain 'interdependencies of institutions'. Like them, they conceived of these 'systems' in 'structural-functional' terms, but also, like them, they did not think that this implied any conception of 'functional harmony' or of a 'static' picture of society which did not include, or permit, conflict and change. On the contrary, both the 'genetic' shaping of societies (the interdependency of institutions brought about by 'hidden consequences') and the 'teleological' shaping of societies (the conscious reshaping of societies according to deliberate purpose) were seen as the necessary outcome of *both* conflict *and* co-operation; and the structural-functional analysis of societies was especially used to explore and explain patterns of social *change*. Like the nineteenth century thinkers, too, they were completely agreed that *societies* were *essentially* historical processes (i.e. distinguished from other 'phenomena' in nature, by the fact that they were cumulative, developing processes in time); and they employed historical methods in their studies. For the purpose of achieving testable generalizations (i.e., to achieve *knowledge*) they saw also the necessity for classification and comparative studies—and they under-

231

took such studies in great detail and with meticulous care. They saw also, with complete methodological clarity, that such studies entailed the construction of 'types' or 'models' and that these were never 'exhaustive collections of empirical detail', so to speak, but were built carefully for particular hypothetical purposes. They were completely clear, too, about the necessary relations between biology, psychology, social psychology, and sociology, and readily drew together the relevant and interrelated aspects of them all, as and when necessary. Furthermore, they were also—in their many emphases upon reason, purpose, and willing in social relationships—never naively 'scientistic' in their conceptions of either psychological or sociological elements in the entirety of the human situation. No naive 'determinism'—which so often passes for an accurate picture of science—was to be found among them, though they were insistent upon meticulous exactitude (at this particular level of science) when 'genetic' or 'mechanistic' causation was relevant. Like all the nineteenth century 'founders', they also especially focused their attention upon the vast social changes and dilemmas of the contemporary world.

All these elements (and others) were fused in their attempts not only to accomplish advances in methodology, but to deepen sociology by providing *specific theories* which could be seen to deepen our knowledge of society and could be seen to be directly relevant to the problems of our time, and useful in trying to deal with them. One of the striking differences between the work of these men, and that of most of the nineteenth century founders is that much less time was devoted to a discussion of purely *theoretical* and *methodological* issues. In men like Comte, Spencer, Ward, there was much on the nature of science and its application to the study of man and society. In Mill—it was *all* theory and method (and properly so—for him.) But in Tönnies, Westermarck and Hobhouse, though very considerable points concerning theory and method were made, it was always in the context of their working study of facts. The truth is that they took the achievement, the foundation, of what we have called the 'nineteenth century conspectus' for granted, and were chiefly concerned to *use* it, and to improve upon it, as and when necessary, in their studies. They busied themselves with *doing* sociology rather than continuing a methodological argumentation for its own sake.

In the detailed but specific theories which they provided and the systematic bodies of descriptive knowledge which they achieved, the *developments* which they accomplished within the context of the nineteenth century conspectus were very real. We might comment, in a very summary way, on some of these.

In the first place, large-scale comparative studies of societies, and of the structural-functional interdependencies of institutions which were appropriate to differing types of society, were, in fact, actually carried out. In the case of Westermarck and Hobhouse the most wide and exacting researches were carried out, and a tremendous and carefully classified, compilation of empirical knowledge was achieved. In the case of Tönnies, the same exactitude was focused upon the detailed construction of his two 'types' for the analysis of that pattern of change in human societies which he thought to be of central importance. These writers did not simply methodologically *advocate* the advisability, or correctness of 'classification' and 'comparative studies'—they *undertook* them: and with clear and substantial results.

Secondly, the perspective of *evolution* within which sociology saw its true place, the conception of *evolution* which sociology thought fit and necessary to use in the study of societies, was made unmistakably clear, and was purged of any mistaken notions which critics might have thought that it had. It was made perfectly clear that—though recognizing the true and proper context of biological evolution, and the place of the emergence of man within the evolution of other animal species—the conception of evolution used by sociology was distinctly *not* confined to the conception used by biology. Biological evolution was confined to explaining the diversification of species in terms of genetic inheritance and *adaptation* to the forces of *natural selection* in the environment. It was at the level of '*adaptation*', and confined to '*genetic*' explanation (in Ward's and Hobhouse's sense). Social evolution, however, though seeing the roots of human nature and society in such processes of biological adaptation, *went beyond this* in recognizing the *additional* element of *teleology*, of the capacity of conscious purpose in mind, and the fact that mind, with cumulative knowledge, could progressively *transform* the nature of its environment, and, ultimately, find itself in a position of being able to dominate even biological evolution itself to a very considerable extent. This made the additional criteria of development, of *progress*, of technical *knowledge* and *ethical principle*, essential for any satisfactory analysis of the *transformation* of society and nature of which man had proved capable. As we have seen—all these new and necessary qualifications were in fact clarified by these writers, and it is interesting to see that all three were totally in agreement on this point. Tönnies quite emphatically insisted upon the recognition of *will*, and the difference which this made to an adequate 'scientific explanation' of man. Westermarck, despite his inconsistencies, was insistent upon the operation of reason in bringing about 'enlightenment' and enlightened change in the moral ideas at the heart of social sanctions. And the significance of Hobhouse for all this is plain.

All other possible misconceptions—of 'unilinear' evolution, of the 'inevitability' of evolution, of the essential 'progressiveness' (in ethical terms) of evolution, and other such notions—were thoroughly and completely knocked on the head—at least, for all those who chose to *read*. Those who have not seen the fundamental significance of these clear qualifications and additions to the biological theory of evolution, cannot possibly have understood the developed theories of social evolution at all—and, of course, we have seen that these developments were really only a stronger and more detailed elaboration of the distinctions which were already there in the nineteenth century.

A third contribution which stands out as being clearly evident, is the fact that these men accomplished a very much more detailed and better documented analysis of the institutional 'juncture' and the institutional changes of the contemporary world than had been accomplished earlier. Again this was not, as a contribution, a total *innovation*, but a *development*, a deepening in detail, of the kind of analysis of the transformation of modern society—with all the dimensions of threat and promise—which had been indicated so forcefully by Comte, Mill, Marx, and Spencer. Hobhouse and Tönnies in particular each provided a very telling *diagnosis* of the changing nature of modern society; they each—without in the slightest degree being superficially 'historicist' in their arguments—offered a certain *prognosis* of the course and consequences of these institutional changes *if* such and such attitudes and actions *were*, or *were not*, adopted. And in all this they undoubtedly provided the kind of insight into the nature of modern dilemmas, and the kind of basis of knowledge for action in trying to deal with them, that Comte had hoped, from the beginning, that sociology would provide.

There is the further point that I wish, over and over again, to emphasize, that these men, in their various ways, made clearer even than it had been made clear in the nineteenth century (and it had been made very clear even then) that *morality was an all-pervading element in the institutionalization of human relationships*. Morality was not one *aspect* of society, but some regulating principle at the core of every social institution, and entailed in the interlinking relationships between institutions in society as a whole. Tönnies' concentration upon 'natural' and 'rational' kinds of willing; upon 'community' and 'contractual' types of relationships showed the intimate place of morality in the changing nature of modern institutions. Westermarck demonstrated very thoroughly that 'sanctions' lay at the heart of (*were*, indeed, the core of) institutionalization, and showed the universality of kinds of 'moral ideas' (with all their psychological dimensions) which underlay these. And the treatment of Hobhouse was especially illuminating, for he showed not only that morality was (as Sumner and Westermarck had shown) involved in the very emergence of 'custom' in the early 'empirical order' of societies, but, more particularly, that the growth of knowledge and powers of purposive control in society entailed an increasingly conscious awareness that the deliberate reconstruction of institutions was *essentially* a matter of re-shaping them in accordance with ethical principles which had been well-considered and clarified. In short, morality was not only at the heart of the institutions of human society—but came increasingly to be the *central* concern in the conscious reconstruction of society in the modern world. Furthermore, this was not just a basis for *applied* sociology; it was a necessary ingredient for the understanding of the *facts* of modern society. For the detailed struggles to re-shape or to retain institutions in the modern world were, in *fact*, only comprehensible in terms of this ethical and ideological factor. This, then, was another point which received clear and reinforced emphasis from the developments which these men achieved.

Many other, more detailed, points could obviously be made, but what these various contributions amount to is this. During the first few decades of this century, by the beginning of the last war, the development of the theories of social evolution (one basic aspect of the nineteenth century conspectus of the nature of sociology) had accomplished a demonstrably firm perspective for the comparative study of societies of all types. Within this clear perspective, societies of all types—pre-literate (of various kinds and levels), oriental despotisms, city states, empires, feudal societies, modern nation states and their varying kinds of federations—could be reliably studied in such ways as to yield generalizations of a testable kind. Within this established framework of empirical knowledge, a firm and reliable perspective for knowledge and judgment of *contemporary society* had also been accomplished—and this not in any abstract way, but in a detailed way which gave a specific analysis of changes in specific institutions (family, class, race, etc.). Also, this systematic study had yielded a very clear analysis of *morality* in society, and especially in modern society, in such a way as to provide a clear *ethical position* for judgment. This is not to say, of course, that this ethical position was such as, necessarily, to be totally accepted; but it was extremely well worked out—and required that any *other* ethical position (or any *denial* of an ethical position) preferred in its place, should *demonstrate* the superior grounds on which it *was* preferred.

This position provided also, then, a firm basis for arriving at the most reliable judgments for social action, but, even so (as we have seen) it was far from being naively optimistic or 'historicist' in any sense of predicting necessary developments or necessary success. Indeed, on the contrary, it was extremely realistic in a very well-balanced way. Tönnies presented a specific theory *within* the evolutionary perspective which was of the greatest *diagnostic* value, and was such as to raise a warning of the gravest kind about the kind of human condition into which our 'contractual' kind of society was leading us. This warning was, and is, of the utmost seriousness, and may yet prove beyond our power of control. And yet Tönnies did not only present a black picture; but suggested ways in which the danger might be dealt with. Hobhouse, seeing rationality and feeling as having rather different relations with each other, and emphasizing the importance and the possibility of the conscious reconstruction of society, nonetheless saw all the dimensions of inhumanity about which Tönnies wrote, and was extremely cautious in his statements of what might be hoped for. Both were agreed in their realism, though rather in a Sumner/Ward way: Tönnies, like Sumner, seeing starkly the difficulties of reform and suggesting the possibility with much qualification; Hobhouse, like Ward, emphasizing the positive significance of the increasing powers of mind to know, to act purposively, and to control—but nonetheless pointing to the difficulties in the way.

But surely no approach to the difficulties of modern society could be wiser than that which these men advanced? They illuminated the crucial distinguishing characteristics of our time; put their finger upon the central malaise of the vast changes we are experiencing; and proposed an approach of knowledge and judgment which was as sane as any that one can find. And this accomplishment of a 'perspective' on the problems of modern society was a full, detailed, and realistic culmination of almost all the proposals and contributions which had been made by earlier thinkers like Condorcet and Kant, and all the men of the nineteenth century—Comte, Mill, Spencer, Marx, Ward, Sumner, Giddings. It was a development in which all the many elements of these contributions were digested and reworked in the most admirable and detailed way

Since the war, these theories of social evolution have been neglected—though the work of Tönnies has continued to be in the forefront of attention. In the main this has been through sheer fashion and ignorance. By some the concept of evolution has been despised as being completely outmoded. By others, men like Westermarck and Hobhouse have been regarded as 'grand-manner' philosophers whose place was more properly the nineteenth century, or as 'collectors of historical data' possessing no theoretical direction other than that of ethical bias. By and large, however, no-one now reads these writers. Like many of the nineteenth century writers, the most attention they receive is an insufficient chapter in a text-book. On the other hand—and on the only worthwhile hand!—in their pursuit of more specific theories about more delimited aspects of society, it was to be expected that many scholars would leave aside their concern for the correctness or otherwise of this larger context and move towards more specialized topics of research. And this has happened, and can be, to quite an extent defended. But some final considerations need strong emphasis.

It must be remembered that the clarification of this perspective of *evolution* constitutes a firm perspective which has taken a century and more to build. It cannot be laid aside just by whim. It may, of course—by those concerned chiefly with Ph.D.'s and promotions— but not by those concerned with the true dimensions of their subject. It must be borne in mind, too, that the perspective of evolution is a necessary, justified, and true perspective; validated by all the evidence. The entire perspectives of the world's knowledge have been gradually re-formed about the nineteenth-century concept of evolution, and its new orientation towards 'Man's place in Nature'; and this is a new perspective the truth of which cannot be denied. A third corollary of this is that the illumination thrown by this perspective on the nature and dilemmas of our own time is *needed*: both in order to give men a clear basis for reliable judgment—to *see* things in proper perspective; and to give them a basis of intellectual *meaning*. I know that I am much out of tune with professional 'academics' in saying this; but I still believe it to be true that many people (perhaps more than we think) need a satisfactory 'philosophy of life' within which to couch their specific purposes clearly, before they can live with full meaning and satisfaction, and, in a time in which settled doctrines of all kinds have been shattered, it seems to me that any satisfactory philosophy or ideology for our times must, at least, contain within it this correct evolutionary perspective. In short, I think the perspective which these men achieved can provide men with a systematic position of meaning for their personal lives, in addition to giving them a firm basis of knowledge and judgment about the world and society. (Strictly speaking, of course, for any thinking person, these are all part of the same thing.)

This is to say no more, of course, than Comte himself when he argued that sociology was *needed* for the achievement of a satisfactory relation between *feeling*, *thinking*, and *acting* in the society of our times; that to 'know ourselves' we had to 'know history'; and that to shape our own personal destiny we had to participate in the satisfactory re-ordering of society. It is no more than Hobhouse's own insistence that the realization or fulfilment of one's '*self*', entails (properly understood) the effort to improve the lot of all men:

237

to try to achieve, everywhere, the conditions, at least, whereby *all* men may find their 'self-realization'. 'Self' and 'Society'—whether in fact or in aspiration—cannot be separated.

It is worth bearing in mind, too, that this evolutionary perspective has never really (except in certain 'pockets' of academic professionals) been out-moded. We shall see, later, that ever since the last war (and we are, of course, only talking of the past 25 years!), developments of evolutionary sociology have been pursued; and recently even Talcott Parsons—who began his first large book with the unqualified statement that Herbert Spencer was dead—has discovered that he is still alive and kicking, and that the evolutionary perspective is still necessary and useful in sociology. A lot of disciples can now be expected, therefore, to swallow the last fashion, and flock back.

The development of evolutionary sociology was therefore of much value, and well worth our consideration. Later, I shall want to return to this whole question—on which we have again touched briefly in this section—as to how far sociology, in having to take issue with existing doctrines which contain theories of society, is itself inescapably involved in some kind of ideological commitment. For the moment—without wanting to go anywhere near the extremes of Comte's 'positive religion', it does seem to me to be the case that in its clarification of the modern predicaments of social change, sociology must, as Hobhouse maintained, be so committed. We can do no better than close with a moderately stated but very appropriate statement of the matter, by Morris Ginsberg, which seems to draw together admirably the emphases of both Tönnies and Hobhouse.

'The history of humanity is the story of an increasing conflict between the rational and irrational elements in human nature. Factors making for unity and co-operation are blended with others making for rivalry and exclusiveness, fears and jealousies. As the scale of operation expands, the conflict is embittered by the growing complexity of life, and the multiplication of opportunities for discord. The notion that this vast process can, and ought, to be consciously controlled or directed, has emerged in theory. But the conception of a self-directed humanity is new, and as yet vague in the extreme. To work out its full theoretical implications, and, with the aid of other sciences, to inquire into the possibilities of its realization, may be said to be the ultimate object of sociology.'*

* *Sociology*, pp. 243–4.

(2)
The Objective Study of Social Facts and the Subjective Understanding of Social Action

An Introductory Note

We come now to two of the most influential developments in the making of sociology during these first few decades of the twentieth century: the contributions of Emile Durkheim and Max Weber. Before coming to grips with each of them, however, it is worthwhile to pause and throw a certain net of perspective over the course of our discussion, because these two men mark a significant point in the development of the subject. The elements of sociological theory which they developed were very distinctively different from each other in quite fundamental ways. Yet, at the same time, though exploring conceptual positions which seemed to be at opposite extremes, the theoretical emphases of the two men were strikingly the same. In what follows, we must clearly examine the contribution of each man separately—but in this introductory note I want to suggest that it will be very worthwhile to consider them in the closest relation to each other. The points I have in mind are these, and I will enumerate them simply in order to make as clear as possible the perspective of judgment which I think important.

The first point is that in the work of both these men we are faced with something different from that of the twentieth century theorists we have considered so far. This difference must not be exaggerated or distorted for there were many similarities and continuities in their work of all the chief components of sociological analysis established by the earlier thinkers; but still—a certain difference was there, and we must try to be clear about it.

Durkheim and Weber did not differ from Tönnies, Westermarck, Hobhouse, and others who developed the evolutionary aspects of sociology in that they rejected these aspects. On the contrary, both of them *accepted* the evolutionary perspective for sociological studies, and, indeed, made detailed contributions to the clarification and elaboration of it in their work. They did not differ from these other theorists in rejecting the '*conspectus*' of nineteenth century sociology. In fact they accepted all the major components of it. They did not differ in being more *original*—in the strict sense of being *innovators* in sociological theory. They were not. Each of them concentrated upon a searching and rigorous development of one component of analysis which was already there.

The existence of 'associational facts' as a distinctive level of phenomena, and their importance in the engendering of distinctively 'human' qualities in individuals—which Durkheim was especially concerned to emphasize—had been stressed by everyone from Comte

241

onwards. And the importance of the 'subjective understanding of social action', and the construction of 'types' of social action—on which Weber especially concentrated—had, as we have clearly seen, already been stated with much clarity by the early Americans in particular. The work of these two men really did consist in *developing* dimensions, or components, of the subject which had already been substantially introduced. They did not differ about the generally agreed tendency to move from 'theor*y*' to 'theor*ies*'. In fact they accepted this, stressed it, and worked very powerfully to support it. They did not differ—at least in all important respects—in their view about the 'malaise' of the rapid transition from traditional to modern industrial societies which was the core-concern of all the early sociologists; and in their persuasion that a science of sociology was necessary for reliable judgment on the many problems connected with it, and the formulation of reliable policies to deal with them. In all these matters, they agreed with the other theorists, and, in many respects, the details of their actual work were all of a piece with that of the earlier scholars. Indeed this is much more so than is commonly realized.

The distinctive difference of these two men—that which gives them a special significance in the development of sociology—lay chiefly in two factors.

The one—which was true of both of them, and is perhaps of the greatest importance—was that they were great *liberators* in sociology. Though they accepted the nineteenth century 'conspectus'; its achievement, its value, its importance, as a basic framework for the subject; they were not *content* with it, they criticized some elements of it *radically*, and—most of all—they did not want to be *bound* by it. In seeking to move from the general 'theory' of this conspectus to specific theories about particular facts and problems, they both insisted upon the necessity of producing *definitive* studies which were vulnerable to *test*. General statements of analysis, method, and theory were no longer enough. Definitive theories about concrete facts and problems, clearly defined, were now required. And—each in his own way—both Durkheim and Weber argued in their theoretical systems for the freedom of the investigator to pursue those studies which interested him. Both regarded clear concepts, rules, and procedures of theory, as *tools* for *application* in the *production of definitive studies*. In the writings of these two men, the discussion of sociological theory was such as to result in sharply clarified methods which could be *used* in specific investigations. This must not be exaggerated. Every theorist, from Comte on, of course, had expounded his theoretical conceptions for *use* in sociological investigation. But it remains true that—without at all rejecting the earlier foundations of the subject—the theories of these two men had a certain cutting edge of clear application which was more marked than in the earlier writers, and carried what can only be called an *enthusiasm for specialization.* * They wanted liberty for the sociologist to study what was of importance and interest to *him*: though, of course, to do so with the greatest accuracy of which he was capable. Another way of putting this was that these two men especially paved the way for a genuine professional development of the subject—whilst still remaining rooted in all that was important of the early 'foundation-statement' of the subject.

The second point is that—each in his own way—both of these men actually were *specialists* themselves in a very important sense. Instead of dwelling upon *all* the components in the *entire* conspectus of the subject, each concentrated on studying to the deepest and most rigorous extent of which he was capable, that *one* component which seemed most important to him. Each concentrated upon that *dimension of social reality* which, in his view, had not been sufficiently emphasized, clarified, and explored; and upon developing those kinds of theory and method which were most *appropriate* to the study of this dimension. Durkheim concentrated entirely on *objective* methods of studying those phenomenal attributes of 'social facts' which were externally observable, as if they were '*things*'. His rules of method were directed to achieving accuracy particularly in this. Weber concentrated wholly upon the 'subjective understanding' (in terms of 'meaning') of the sequences of 'social action' in which men deployed determinate means in the pursuit of certain ends; and his theoretical principles and methods aimed at accomplishing an accuracy of 'causal explanation' in this particular sense,

This had two interesting consequences. First: because each man concentrated on elaborating methods for exploring one dimension—his resulting proposals were very precise indeed. Their very *delimitation* led them to astringency and discipline. Secondly, however, and this is our important consideration here—because each man explored what might be called 'opposite' extremes, their resulting contributions to theory were *complementary* to each other in the most useful way, and this is why I think it is particularly fitting to study them together in this one section. Both taken together moved towards a system of sociological analysis which was richer and more satisfactory than either could possibly be in itself.

This is the kind of perspective that I would like to emphasize, and which it will be worthwhile to hold in mind as we explore these two very different contributions.

On the one hand we need to be completely clear about the con-

* Durkheim especially made almost an *ethic* of specialization. See his *Division of Labour in Society*.

tinuity and similarity of both of them with the ideas of all the other theorists we have considered so far. On the other, we must clarify as sharply as possible the separate contribution of each man—the study of '*objective facts*' as understood by Durkheim, of '*subjective understanding*' as understood by Weber; and so reveal the *differences* of their emphasis by contrast with the earlier thinkers. But also, after having done this, we need especially to see clearly the *complementary* nature of the two contributions; the way in which they fit satisfactorily and usefully together. If this perspective is borne in mind throughout, the ultimate connections to be made will be seen the more clearly.

Perhaps this perspective can be put more sharply like this.

So far we have clarified the 'beginnings' and the 'foundations' of sociology, and, in some of the early twentieth century theorists, have seen how the whole of the evolutionary perspective of sociology in particular was deepened, extended, and studied in more detail. Now we come to other developments which were different in that they sharply emphasized *special dimensions* of the subject; aiming at definitive studies of these dimensions, and the clarification of very precise methods appropriate to the study of them. Each important dimension of sociological analysis was now coming to be developed in turn, separately, and to a certain extreme. But after such developments, all these components could then be drawn together to provide a *complete* system of analysis. The 'objective' and the 'subjective' dimensions of social actuality and of sociological explanation as explored by Durkheim and Weber were especially important. In dealing with them, we are beginning the process of tracing the very recent development of each special aspect of sociological analysis, which has subsequently gone into the making of that complete system of analysis which we now possess. We are beginning, now, to examine the making of strictly *contemporary* sociology.

1

The Objective Study of Social Facts: Emile Durkheim

With only a little exaggeration, Emile Durkheim might be said to be one of the 'Gods' of contemporary sociology. In his work—a remarkably consistent body of work in its entirety—we come to what is commonly regarded as one of the most important contributions to the making of sociology since its earliest formulations. Together, chiefly, with Max Weber* (and the coupling of the two has, as we have said—and as we shall see, its good justification) Durkheim is generally thought to have been specially responsible for the rigorous defining of 'modern sociology' as we now know it. His contribution is thought to be quite distinctive (indeed, sharply distinctive) from the work of the nineteenth century 'founders' and from that of the 'evolutionists' of the twentieth century which we have just considered. He is thought to have been logically more exact and demanding than they; in scientific method more accurate and astringent; in specific studies more rigorously empirical; in theoretical perspective more properly limited in scope (i.e. in the sense of scientific precision: as being correctly 'delimited' by the accurate definition of subject-matter); in the statement of theories more free from the error of ethical evaluation; and, in general, much less rooted in any remaining cloudiness of speculative philosophy and metaphysics. He was one of the modern scholars, it is thought, who accomplished the final liberation of sociology from the cradle of social philosophy out of which it had not yet successfully scrambled by the end of the nineteenth century.

Durkheim, in short, is fashionable in sociology. Whether this large claim for his importance is sound is a question we must try to answer very carefully. In my opinion most of these claims are unfounded. They involve misconceptions of Durkheim's positions which are very fundamental; and assume a sharp distinction between his and earlier theoretical positions which is not borne out in a detailed study of his work. Indeed, it is arguable that the very efforts which Durkheim made towards his own notion of what constituted scientific exactitude in the study of society can be shown to

* Though Pareto, too, was a very eminent figure.

245

be largely responsible for many of the conceptual dilemmas—indeed, errors—which have beset sociology during the past thirty years. If his efforts on behalf of sociology had certain merits, it can be argued, too, that it was in connection with his over-zealous pressing of certain points to extremes that at least *some* of the modern obscurantism set in to the subject. Yet it remains true that the contribution he made was undoubtedly of importance. He was responsible for *much*—both good and bad; and our problem will be that of disentangling the one from the other as accurately as possible.

It may be worthwhile to point out that this 'mixed' estimation of the qualities of Durkheim's work is far from being a matter of personal bias. It is, indeed, amusing, as well as instructive, to see that even those who wish to extol Durkheim's value, including his translators, are driven to qualify their judgments not only slightly—but radically. Thus Professor George Catlin whilst claiming that Durkheim's book on *The Rules of Sociological Method* is not only 'a landmark in the history of the social sciences' but also 'a beacon burning as a guide to travelling students', has, nonetheless, also to say that it is so 'no less by the warnings which the weaknesses of this magistral statement should signal to the student than by the soundness of its general design'. He has, in addition, to say that the position that Durkheim adopted in it resulted in 'a *deplorable* effort' to interpret social phenomena in terms of a collective consciousness. In assessing Durkheim's study of religion, he states, too, that his principles of explanation and his notion of 'social facts': 'have an unsatisfactory complexity and a vasty air to them'; that they are 'no less superstitious than the beliefs which he flatters himself that he explains'; and that, here again, 'Durkheim's failings establish a series of warnings for students which they neglect to study at their peril'.*

This, it will be agreed, is a most odd mixture of judgments to come from a *supporter*, and, of course, I am not saying here that they are correct ones, though it makes one wonder what an *adverse* criticism would look like! It is almost as though, in worshipping their God, some have felt compelled to excuse the discomfort they have felt in noticing that his feet have a disquieting appearance of clay. Many similar judgments could be quoted from those who have been concerned to *advance* Durkheim's arguments, and here I mention them simply to show that we shall not be alone if we arrive at a mixed conclusion!

---

* It is almost as though, in Sociology, you can't *lose*! You are a great instructor whether you arrive at great truths or commit great errors! In either case, students will benefit much from studying your greatness!

Durkheim was certainly the most influential sociologist in France after Comte and Le Play, and, like Westermarck and Hobhouse in England, was particularly important in being at the centre of the development of sociology as a subject in the universities—in the organization of both teaching and research. He held a Chair of Sociology (which was created for him) at the University of Bordeaux for five years from 1887, before moving to Paris and the Sorbonne. He founded the journal *L'Année Sociologique* in 1897 and edited it until 1912, and this was tantamount to founding and leading the major school of French sociology: a school which has not only exercised very considerable influence in sociology in general, but continues to do so in social anthropology in particular.* He was born (in Alsace) in 1858 and died just before the end of the first world war—in 1917. He was therefore of almost exactly the same period as the other men we have considered—Tönnies, Westermarck, Hobhouse; was concerned in exactly the same way to improve the rigour and exactitude of sociology as a subject; to establish it in the teeth of much opposition; to demonstrate its worth and utility as a necessary basis for coming to terms with the problems of modern society; and he was, as can be seen, almost a contemporary of our own. All these men were producing important work and exercising important influences up to between fifty and thirty years ago.

The fact is that the contribution of Durkheim was so many-sided, so filled with doubtful points and arguments as well as with propositions of great worth, that it is an extremely difficult task to arrive at a just assessment of it. Yet, obviously, this is what we must try to do. It would be worthless to rest content with yet another oversimplified caricature of his position; and it would be a disservice to his ideas, and to the subject, to let them pass without the best critical examination of which we are capable.

It would, I think, be unnecessarily burdensome even to indicate, in an introductory manner, the apparent deficiencies of Durkheim's treatment. It would not make for clarity. The best procedure is to begin at once by examining the various and quite specific ways in which his work gave evidence of the kind of detailed continuity in the making of the subject which we are seeking to establish in this study, and to indicate what I take to be current misunderstandings, and misconceived judgments of his position in each of these. In the dis-

* See especially the series of books and translations produced under the influence of Professor E. E. Evans-Pritchard by past and present members of the Department of Social Anthropology in the University of Oxford. One example we shall particularly have in mind is *Primitive Classification* by Durkheim and Marcel Mauss, translated by R. Needham, Cohen and West, 1963.

cussion of them we can at least begin to make clear the merits and deficiencies of the positions which he adopted. Then we can plunge fully into a thorough analysis of his entire system; and it will be in the pros and cons of this argument that our considered assessment can take shape.

One important consideration, however—by way of a point of departure—should preface this.

We can, provisionally, take Durkheim's entire contribution to the 'development' of sociology to be distinctive at least in *this* one sense: that whereas the thinkers we have considered so far in this volume on twentieth century influences, attempted a more satisfactory development of *evolutionary sociology itself* (though in some respects critical of it); Durkheim—though accepting, indeed insisting upon, the evolutionary perspective—concentrated upon a *precisely defined delimitation of specific sociological studies within* this perspective, and upon a clear statement of *the rules of scientific method* for accomplishing this. In a very direct sense, then, Durkheim wished to *go beyond* the 'conspectus' which had been clearly formulated on the basis of 'evolution', and to move towards the more detailed accomplishment of *specific, definitive theories* about *precisely defined social facts* within it. His was an attempt to move—almost through impatience, though not only that—from *theory* to *theories* in exactly the way we have spoken of it as the central concern which informed all these developments of the early twentieth century. It is undoubtedly the case that his critique of the nineteenth century 'conspectus' was more sharply, vigorously, even polemically, carried out than anything in the writings of the other men we have considered; and there is no doubt that his polemic was worthwhile; had much right on its side; and has, in fact, accomplished a sharpening of sociological method since his time. We shall see later the very doubtful dimensions to which this polemic led, but, for now, this is enough.

Durkheim's 'development' of sociology certainly involved an attack upon the evolutionary perspective *with a difference*—with a hot, provocative difference—yet it was a critical attack which basically *accepted* this perspective. It was very far from being a *rejection* of it. And it is here, at once, that the misunderstandings of Durkheim's position begin to raise their head.

Some of the more important of these can serve us as an introduction, leading us into a fuller engagement with his ideas; and we shall then become progressively entangled with these as we go on. Not all the points here, however, will be raised for purposes of adverse criticism; it will be as well to enumerate quite fully all the points which seem most serviceable in providing a comprehensive introduction.

The Continuities in Durkheim's Work and some Misunderstandings of them

In view of the widespread misconception that the statement of distinctive viewpoints in sociology is evidence of the fact that the subject is a 'rag-bag' of disparate and opposed theoretical positions, and that the subject has had no coherent development as a unitary discipline, the first few points may be used to demonstrate completely the place of Durkheim in the ongoing argument of sociology and the clear continuity of his work with that of the earlier sociologists—out of which it grew most consistently. Durkheim was, indeed, a living example of this close continuity. No writer could have been more so.

(I) DURKHEIM AND THE BRITISH SOCIOLOGICAL SOCIETY

The first point to be emphasized is that, as we have seen earlier, Durkheim was very far from being a scholar isolated from those we have already mentioned. On the contrary, his work was not only already known to some of the early Americans, and to Tönnies, Westermarck and Hobhouse, but he actually contributed papers and correspondence to the early meetings of the British Sociological Society in London to which these other men also contributed. Durkheim was already known internationally as a scholar at the turn of the century, and, what is of chief importance, was a member of this large group of sociologists (and others) who were agreed in their desire and efforts to further the subject, and who were reasonably agreed about the necessity of proving its worth by the undertaking of more specific rigorous studies. Durkheim was one scholar among others of a like mind; all of whom had common roots and common interests. His theoretical position came to differ from theirs in some respects, but *only* in some respects. In others, as we shall see, he was remarkably similar, and the influences out of which his system grew by critical study were the same. It will be worthwhile, as we go on, to point out some of these fundamental similarities and agreements, as well as his distinctive points of difference, because some of them—in the context of fashionable assessments—will seem surprising. It may astonish some, for example, to learn that Durkheim's position was in very close agreement with that of Westermarck as to the place of sentiment and sanctions in the institutions of society—which were held to constitute a *moral* reality; but such was indeed the case—and very clearly so. In being distinctive in certain ways, then, Durkheim's work did not *contradict* all that was being accomplished at the hands of other scholars in his time; in many ways it coincided with, and reinforced it.

249

(II) DURKHEIM—LIKE TÖNNIES—A LINK BETWEEN THE NINETEENTH AND TWENTIETH CENTURIES

A second-point which is important for our assessment of the continuity of Durkheim's work and influence in the making of sociology is that, like Tönnies, he had accomplished much by the end of the nineteenth century, but did not have his full impact upon the subject until his books appeared in translation. His work was known by the turn of the century, but to nothing like the extent it became known after the 1930's. Just to point this perspective very sharply: it may be of interest to note that it was only by about 1950 (barely twenty years ago) that courses in the theories and methods of sociology at the London School of Economics began to include the study of men like Durkheim and Weber. Beyond this relatively small group in one British university—few in Britain had even heard of Durkheim, and Weber was known almost entirely in relation to his essay on the *Protestant Ethic and Capitalism*. It can be seen therefore, very markedly, that we are now thinking of *very recent* developments in the subject.*

Durkheim had produced three of his most important books during the last decade of the nineteenth century: *The Division of Labour in Society* in 1893; *The Rules of Sociological Method* in 1895; and *Suicide* in 1897. These were translated, respectively, in 1933, 1938, and 1950—and (it may be noted) by American scholars.† *The Elementary Forms of the Religious Life* was, in fact, produced in the twentieth century (1912), and translated in 1915, and Durkheim's later work on *Moral Education*—a subject which increasingly concerned him—was only published posthumously, and translated very recently indeed. As was the case with Tönnies, then, the major impact of Durkheim's ideas has been a twentieth century impact— indeed, a very recent impact, and this is why we are dealing with him in this place. But he was, in fact, one of the major thinkers straddling

---

* It may be of interest simply to note that when, in 1951, I went to the L.S.E. as a post-graduate student, the group of graduates there was seething with discontent because their courses did not contain an adequate treatment of relatively recent European and American scholars (Parsons and Shils, for example, quite apart from Weber and Durkheim, were beginning to be known). Most of those students are now Professors of Sociology. The wide difference in the number and range of courses in sociological theory which have taken place between then and now can well be imagined. We are talking now, therefore, of the developments of a living generation—developments which are still active in the problematical making of the subject today. For the academic wars are far from being over!

† A tremendous debt is owed to American scholars for this sheer task of translation; of making so many important continental books readily available for study.

the two centuries—his roots very firmly embedded in the nineteenth century thinkers, but his own critical ideas very much the seeds of ferment and growth among scholars of the twentieth.

(III) THE CONTINUITY OF INFLUENCES IN DURKHEIM'S SOCIOLOGY

Durkheim's roots were to be found in the work of all the major European thinkers of the nineteenth century to whom we have referred. His debt to Comte was enormous. He knew Comte's work intimately, and many of his central ideas were really critical developments of those of Comte. His insistence that 'society'—the interdependent network of institutionalized conduct—was a recognizable *level* of facts in its own right ('sui generis') and therefore required methods of study distinct from those of the biological and psychological dimensions which were part and parcel of it, was a direct agreement with Comte. His emphasis that we could better explain the nature of individuals in terms of society, rather than society in terms of individuals, and that 'all psychology is *social* psychology' (though this is not a strictly accurate way of putting it), was drawn from Comte. And, indeed, many of his more specific ideas—such as the centrality of the division of labour for an understanding of the 'social solidarity' and the 'moral' order of a society, and the probability that the nature and functions of institutions would be better understood by studying both their 'normal' and their 'pathological' forms— were ideas taken from Comte and made the focus of elaborate studies. Similarly, his knowledge of John Stuart Mill's 'Logic', and especially Book VI, was very detailed, though this did not prevent him from falling into some of the errors against which Mill had warned. Durkheim took all Mill's 'experimental methods' very seriously, but did not sufficiently see that Mill's chief concern was to *reject* them in relation to the 'Compound-Chemical' method of conceiving society—which was exactly the method which Durkheim himself deliberately adopted. Spencer, too, was studied in the greatest detail by Durkheim, and, again, many of his ideas—on social evolution, the classification of societies, the division of labour, the social functions of religion, etc.—were rooted in Spencer's treatment of these subjects. Durkheim mentioned Marx—but to a very limited extent; but it is clear that he knew Tönnies' *Gemeinschaft und Gesellschaft* very well indeed, and must have been much influenced by this in writing his own book on the *Division of Labour*. The parallel between Tönnies' 'typological' analysis of the movement from 'community resting upon natural will' to 'society contrived by rational will' and Durkheim's analysis of the movement from 'mechanical' to 'organic' solidarity is very close, despite the apparent contradictoriness of the terms used.

Durkheim's own work then, grew quite directly out of a full critical engagement with the ideas of his predecessors, and the full continuity of his contribution is completely clear and demonstrable. It is here, however, that one has to begin to take issue with Durkheim, because though his knowledge of these men sometimes seemed very full, and there is no doubt that he acknowledged the originality and continued authority of them in many places, yet at other times it led to peculiarly cavalier judgments, to say the least, and was very selective. Thus, for example, he could write: '. . . in the *entire work* of Spencer the problem of methodology occupies *no* place'; and the only book he thought fit to mention (and that to rule out of consideration) in this connection, was *The Study of Sociology*. Spencer's discussion of how properly to conceptualize the nature of society and its institutions, of how to classify them and establish empirical knowledge about them, in his section on 'The Inductions of Sociology' in the *Principles*, let alone all he had to say on the nature of science and its application to the study of society in *First Principles* and elsewhere, was simply not mentioned. Yet, elsewhere, Durkheim employed Spencer's notions considerably—even to a full insistence upon certain detailed biological analogies. Similarly, Durkheim conceded that Mill had dealt with the question of methodology at length, but, he added, had only 'refined with his dialectics what Comte had already expounded, without adding anything original'; and Comte's own contribution was, he asserted, confined to 'a chapter in the *Cours de Philosophie Positive*'. To regard this as the extent of Comte's thought on methodological matters, and to regard Mill as a mere annotation of Comte, is, of course, an absurd over-simplification. And to characterize the work of these men as resulting only in '*vague generalities* on the nature of societies', and to say that they were '*content*' to make only a '*superficial enquiry*' into the proper methods of sociology, as Durkheim did in fact do, was to hold up and publicize a completely unwarranted caricature.

The 'voluminous sociology' of Spencer, Durkheim maintained, 'has scarcely any other purpose than to show how the law of universal evolution applies to human societies. Certainly no special and complex methods are required for the treatment of these philosophical questions'.

Now as to the truth of these (and many similar) judgments, one can do no more than ask readers to examine what Spencer had to say about specific social institutions—from the last section of Volume 1 onwards in the *Principles*, and what Comte had to say about them in *Social Statics* and *Social Dynamics* in the *Positive Polity*—and consider whether these are 'vague generalities' or a treatment of 'philosophical questions' only.* But the more important point is this: that when he was wanting to make a point forcefully and emphatically (rather in the manner of a public orator), Durkheim was often prone to a sheer dogmatic assertiveness which at once carried the appearance of a justifiable casting away of certain past positions on the basis of firm derogatory judgments; and of an admirable terseness, incisiveness, and scientific economy and exactitude of statement. Now when terse, incisive, scientific economy and exactitude of statement is correct and well-founded—it is to be welcomed; but when it is, in fact, an assertion of glib, partial and ill-considered judgment, in order to get somewhere quickly, it is important that it should be seen to be such.

It is from statements of the above kind that certain misconceptions have been sown. For example, the above statement certainly seems to suggest that the application of the evolutionary perspective to the study of societies is a 'philosophical' question only; that it is a matter of 'vague generalities'; and that it must be left behind in the more astringent quest for specific, complex scientific studies. It seems to suggest that evolutionary sociology has had its day; that it was an early, and fairly superficial, preoccupation of the nineteenth century thinkers, when the subject was struggling from its swaddling clothes; that it was not seriously in keeping with incisive scientific studies; and that acute, empirically-oriented, intellectually tough-muscled modern scientists should now eschew it in order to get on with their man-sized jobs. And this is exactly the absurd kind of 'ethos' that this kind of judgment has carried with it into contemporary sociological deliberations.

And the interesting fact is that this impression completely belies Durkheim's own position; for, as we shall see, he was not only completely committed to evolutionary sociology in his rules of method, but also one of his chief criticisms of the nineteenth century 'founders' was *not* that they had *adopted* the evolutionary perspective but, on the contrary, that they had not treated it *thoroughly enough* in their methodology. Durkheim insisted on treating the reality of social evolution *more thoroughly* than they: in order demonstrably to *test*, not only to *illustrate* hypotheses.

What I am trying to say, then, is that Durkheim's 'pat' judgments, and superficial way of expressing didactic estimations of the work of the men from whom he drew his ideas, were not only unfortunate in

* Compare, for example, Spencer's account of 'Ecclesiastical Institutions' with Durkheim's study of Religion; or Spencer's and Durkheim's account of the Division of Labour; or their discussion of the problems of classifying societies; etc.

that they were frequently partial, one-sided, and in many ways untrue, but also in that they had the effect of falsifying Durkheim's own position, or of confusing the estimation of his position, in the minds of his readers.

Very many examples of this cavalier treatment or the peculiar neglect of treatment of the position of others could be given, and, simply to buttress the point, I will briefly mention just two more. In his section on the 'Observation of Social Facts' (in the *Rules*) Durkheim castigated Comte and Spencer for defining social facts in terms of 'subjective preconceptions' (which, he claimed, was a '*lay* notion'*) and, thereafter, studying them as 'concepts' rather than as objective actualities. In the definition which Spencer gave of society, Durkheim claimed, 'the thing itself disappears, giving way to the preconception he has of it. He postulates as a self-evident proposition that 'a society is formed only when, in addition to juxtaposition, there is co-operation . . .'. Then, on the basis of this 'subjectivism' (Durkheim argued) Spencer classified societies into two types—the 'Military' and the 'Industrial'—according to the *kind* of co-operation to be found in them. This distinction, he maintained was 'the *germinal idea*' of Spencer's sociology, and—because it was a *conceptual* distinction only—

'. . . here again a certain conception of social reality is substituted for reality itself. What is thus defined is clearly not society but Spencer's idea of it. And he has no scruples in proceeding thus, because for him, also, society is and can be only the embodiment of an idea, namely, this very idea of co-operation by which he defines it.

'Thus, although he claims to proceed empirically, the facts accumulated in his sociology seem to function principally as arguments, since they are employed to illustrate analyses of concepts rather than to describe and explain things. Actually, all the essential points of his doctrines are capable of direct deduction from his definition of society† and the different forms of co-operation. For, if our only choice is between a tyrannically imposed co-operation and a free and spontaneous one, the latter is only too evidently the ideal toward which humanity does and ought to tend.'

The superficiality of this presentation of Spencer's work is beyond belief. Durkheim—who knew Spencer's work well—made no effort whatever to point out that this was only *one* of Spencer's methods of classifying societies; that the *other*—namely the kind of social *aggre-*

* We may note the beginnings of the scientific 'professional' in sociology.
† *The Rules of Sociological Method*, The Free Press, 1962, p. 21. Readers might consider how far Durkheim's supposed charge was as much true of himself as of Spencer. His entire system was, in a sense, a set of corollaries of his central conviction that '*social solidarity*' was a *healthy* and, as such, a *good* thing in society; but we shall come to this later.

gation or *composition* (which Durkheim himself used)—was one permitting the arrangement of societies according to some *objective* criterion and that the 'Militant-Industrial' distinction was, expressly, an *additional* 'typology' for the further interpretation of the major pattern of change which such societies seemed to undergo. None of this was mentioned at all, quite apart from the spurious selectivity in presenting this mention of 'co-operation' as the sole, and 'subjective', element in Spencer's definition. An equally superficial picture was given of Comte's treatment.

A final puzzling example is in connection with Tönnies. There is no doubt whatever that Durkheim knew Tönnies' work well. He reviewed the 1887 edition of *Gemeinschaft und Gesellschaft* in 1889*, though critically, and there is no doubt that the typology of Tönnies was actively in his mind in considering the crucial differences between the 'traditional community' with its simple solidarity and authority, and the modern 'contractual society' with all its complexities and dilemmas. This was four years before he produced his own book on *The Division of Labour in Society* which put forward a typology corresponding very closely indeed to that of Tönnies, and yet, in this latter book, there was utter and complete silence about Tönnies.

The fact is that Durkheim's references to the work of others—whether predecessors or contemporaries—were of very uneven quality, very selective, very partial, and all oriented to the furtherance of the specific argument upon which he was intent. (The impression continually given was that definitive scientific sociology began with the French school of *L'Année Sociologique*.) But the impression must not be left that this was entirely so. Nor must it be thought that to be caustic about Durkheim's argumentative preparation for laying emphasis upon a particular methodological position is the same thing as to *decry* that position. On the contrary, this is just where the difficulty of judging Durkheim's contribution lies. In many places his care to acknowledge the authority of his predecessors—Comte, Spencer, and even Tylor (with whom he disagreed a good deal)—was very fastidious; and frequently the incisive efforts in which his questionable preambles resulted—such as his attempt to state clear rules of method for sociological studies—were important and worthwhile.

However, it is important to see that the critical judgments which Durkheim delivered with such didactic firmness were highly questionable, and often gave a faulty appearance of his own actual position. The truth is that Durkheim was a very difficult mixture of rigour, and laxity; of energetic argument and bad logic; of astringent definition and metaphysical blindness; of scientific delimitation in 'moral-

* *Revue Philosophique* XXVII (p. 416).

ity' and sheer assertiveness in 'ethics'—and the dimensions of this mixture will be seen to be more complex as we proceed. Of the continuity of his work, however, with that of the men we have considered earlier, there is no doubt.

(IV) THE CONTINUITY FROM SOCIAL PHILOSOPHY TO SCIENCE, AND FROM THE SPECIAL SOCIAL SCIENCES TO SOCIOLOGY

One or two other important aspects of this continuity also deserve brief mention before we leave the matter. It is worthwhile to mention that Durkheim's intellectual roots went back far beyond the ideas of the nineteenth century sociologists themselves. Like them, he was well aware that the roots of sociology were themselves embedded in earlier important contributions of philosophy and in many contributions of classical scholarship. In his earliest work, he discussed the work of men like Rousseau and Montesquieu, and—like many French thinkers—retained many of the persuasions of Montesquieu especially. In his conception of the role of the statesman, or the legislator in society, the cast of Montesquieu's mind was very apparent. But there is a further point. Like Comte, Durkheim believed that sociology was not simply another *special* science, but a science of society which brought with it a certain unifying perspective among all the so-called 'special' social sciences. This we need not dwell on here, excepting to point out one thing—namely that Durkheim, again like Comte, thought much of the ideas of Adam Smith in this connection, and especially valued his emphasis upon the 'division of labour'. There were, therefore, these additional elements of continuity in Durkheim. On the one hand he saw, very fully, the movement from the 'roots of sociological thought' to 'sociology as a science' as we have tried to portray them in this study. His work was, in fact, an important part of furthering this movement. And, on the other, his emphasis was always that of linking the social sciences together, and seeing their relations with each other as clearly, correctly, and intimately as was possible.

(V) A FUNDAMENTAL AGREEMENT WITH ALMOST ALL THE MAJOR COMPONENTS OF THE NINETEENTH CENTURY 'CONSPECTUS'

In establishing the continuity of Durkheim's work, it is important, too, to see that he was agreed with almost all the main elements in the nineteenth century 'conspectus' of sociology. Though this need only be briefly indicated here in preliminary fashion, it will serve to make more clear, especially, the one or two points on which he differed.

Durkheim was completely agreed with the basic persuasion that the point of departure for sociology as a science was a recognition of the existence of 'social systems'. Societies were 'systems' of institutions, each of which could only be understood in terms of their interdependency. He also agreed that such systems could be best analysed and described by employing a 'Structural-Functional' analysis. He was fully persuaded, too, that societies were essentially historical processes; that social institutions were essentially historical kinds of 'facts'; and that historical and evolutionary methods should therefore be applied in the study of them. That is to say, for him, structural-functional, historical, and evolutionary methods were all of a piece. He completely accepted the necessity of classificatory and comparative methods of study in all this: both for systematically arranging subject-matter, and for testing generalizations and theories. He also—rather like Spencer—came to employ two methods of classification; but these we can come to later.* In the study of social change, by using structural-functional concepts, he also clearly adopted an 'equilibrium-disequilibrium' method of analysis. And there is no doubt, too, that he desired the establishment of sociology as an exact science (in so far as this was possible) for the direct purpose of practical need. Like everyone from Comte onwards, sociology was conceived by Durkheim as a subject necessary for providing the grounds for effective engagement with the problems of modern society. Durkheim was as pragmatically oriented as anyone.

In all this, however, it is necessary to note, finally, two very important differences, and perhaps a third which we shall want to qualify later. All these points are closely connected.

The most important is Durkheim's complete rejection of any 'teleological' element in human society and in the explanation of it. This is an absolutely fundamental point; an astonishing one; a dogmatic one; to my mind, an insupportable one—but almost everything in Durkheim's system (his conception of 'social facts', his conception of 'causality', his conception of 'science', etc;) hung upon it; and, even though one may flatly disagree with it, it must be conceded that some of Durkheim's essential contributions came from his insistent following through of all its implications. It will be remembered that almost all the men we have considered so far—though convinced that human society was *more* than a sum of the intentions and purposes of individuals and groups; that it included 'genetic' factors of causation; that it took shape according to 'un-

* One—in the *Rules of Sociological Method*—according to the 'degree of social composition' of societies (Spencer's 'degree of aggregation'), and the other—in the *Division of Labour*—specially concerned with exploring the change from 'mechanical' to 'organic' solidarity in society.

257

foreseen consequences' and institutional adjustments that were 'hidden'—nonetheless believed that the essential characteristic that distinguished man from other species was his capacity to learn, to establish knowledge, to act purposively, to direct his activities to the accomplishment of ends, and, with increasing knowledge, to exercise a growing degree of control over nature and society. All of them, in one way or another, thought that institutional patterns arose gradually (over-all) as men (with their limited purposes) pursued their 'practical activities'; and that, gradually, with knowledge and technical skill, man's 'teleological' direction of his destiny became increasingly dominant over the 'genetic' forces which had constrained him in earlier natural and social conditions.

All this, Durkheim rejected—again in the dogmatic name of science—without ever thinking it necessary to give his detailed grounds for doing so; and so successful has his faulty 'scientism' been, that, to this day, the term 'teleological' has a bad smell in sociology: as being a term redolent of metaphysics and theology. Indeed, more often than not, it is rejected, without any thought, as being quite incompatible with 'science'. We shall come back to this in a moment —thundering!

The second important difference—really a corollary of this rejection of 'teleology'—is that Durkheim's conception of societies as 'social systems', of social institutions as 'social facts' which were more than individuals and their purposes, etc, though having a continuity with the similar ideas of his predecessors, was qualitatively of a very different emphasis. Thus, though all the men we have considered—Comte, Mill, Spencer, Marx, Ward, Sumner, Giddings, Tönnies, Westermarck, Hobhouse—were agreed that social systems were more than the sum of individuals, they nonetheless thought of 'institutions' and the 'consensus' that existed among them as the detailed, continuing outcome of men and groups in processes of purposeful *action*; and they all warned, specifically, of the error and danger of attributing (conceptually) a 'misplaced concreteness' to them; of treating them as though they were in some sense '*societal entities*' which exercised cause and effect relations upon each other without the mediation of *men* in active association with each other. This, however, is exactly what Durkheim did claim. He was so anxious to demonstrate that sociology had a subject-matter of its own—at a level quite distinct from the facts of biology and psychology—that, quite deliberately, he went to the extreme of maintaining that 'social facts' existed as 'things' in their own right; that they were inter-linked by cause and effect relations in the 'social system' as an entirety; and that they, and changes in them, could only be explained in terms of other 'social facts'—and not at all in terms of the conscious action of the individual members of society. In this sense, Durkheim advanced a conception of the 'social organism', consisting of its interdependent set of societal *entities*, which had a degree of 'realism' going far beyond the kind of 'super-organic' conception (to use Spencer's term) which the other thinkers had held. Here, we will not critically assess Durkheim's position—but only take note of it.

The third difference, again, is a corollary of these two points, and is that whereas all the other thinkers were insistent upon the closest interdependence between biology, psychology, and sociology—both in that biological, psychological, and sociological facts were all involved in the total actuality of human society, *and* in that the findings of these sciences were all therefore necessary for a full knowledge of this actuality—Durkheim *appeared* to insist upon their separateness. We shall soon see that the word *appeared* is the most important word here. But it *is* the case that Durkheim insisted that *associational* facts existed at a level of their own; possessing attributes that were distinct from those of the biological attributes of organisms and the psychological attributes of individuals; and that therefore they should be *explained* by reference to other facts at their own appropriate level, and not *derivatively* from the levels of biology and psychology below them.

There certainly was, therefore, a detailed continuity in the work of Durkheim from that of his predecessors, but there was an insistence upon certain points which made his position appear sharply different and startling. We shall criticize these differences, and the grounds for them, a little later. For the moment, however, let us continue to note the points of continuity in Durkheim's ideas—though now we can come to some central and specific notions, and clarify some of the misconceptions which have come to gather about them.

(VI) THE CENTRAL CONTINUITY OF 'EVOLUTION': DURKHEIM'S CRITICISMS AND INSISTENCES

It has undoubtedly come to be thought by many that Durkheim deliberately opposed the 'evolutionists'; rejected their largeness of conception and methodology; and provided, instead, a much more sharp and astringent methodology for the study of delimited social facts which broke away from this evolutionary largeness and rendered it unnecessary. Now this assessment of Durkheim's position is utterly mistaken, and it is time to say, quite specifically, how and why.

It is true that Durkheim criticized the 'evolutionists'—but he did not reject the essential idea of evolution. It is true that he outlined a clear set of rules of method which sought to insist upon a new astringency of definition, delimitation, and accuracy of study—but he did not exclude evolutionary rules from this methodology. Quite on the contrary: Durkheim, throughout his entire work, never questioned the indispensability of the evolutionary perspective for sociology. He took it completely for granted. His concern was chiefly that *premature* generalizations based upon it should not be taken to be *demonstrated theories*, and that the necessary, evolutionary dimensions of sociological studies should be *thoroughly* and *rigorously* carried out. To this end, his *Rules of Sociological Method* actually included (and insisted upon) specific rules for the classification of 'social species' (kinds of societies); the further classification of particular 'social facts' (institutions) within this scheme; and—for a full understanding of any one of these 'social facts'—the tracing of its development throughout all social species. It was a rigorous insistence upon a necessary evolutionary dimension of analysis and explanation. We shall come to these rules in detail in a moment, but it may be noted that Durkheim insisted on them because he decidedly believed that human societies had grown and developed by a definite process of 'segmentation' and 'aggregation'; and he sought to be very much more precise, and definite, about the patterns and sequences of this 'social composition' than anyone had been before him.

Here we will just note a few of Durkheim's statements to substantiate our point. In the *Rules*, for example, he characterized his method as:

'. . . a method which makes social evolution depend on objective conditions defined in space . . .'

Social phenomena, he claimed, could only be studied accurately, and could only be distinguished as being normal or pathological, if they were studied within a classification of 'social species'.

'We know', he wrote, 'that societies are composed of various parts in combination . . . all societies are born of other societies without a break in continuity . . . The constituent parts of every society are societies more simple than itself. If, then, we understand the most simple society that has ever existed, to make our classification we should have only to follow the way these simple societies form compounds and how these compound societies combine again to form more complex wholes.'*

Durkheim did, in fact, classify societies on this basis and, in considering the 'normal' nature of institutions as being that found on the average within each type, he argued:

* *Rules*, pp. 80–1.

'It is the functions of the *average* organism that the physiologist studies; and the sociologist does the same.'*

Furthermore, he held that human society was of such a nature as to permit a clear classification into average 'types' of this kind.

'Social life', he wrote, 'is an uninterrupted series of transformations, parallel to other transformations in the conditions of collective existence; and we have at our disposal data concerning not only the transformations of recent epochs but many of those through which extinct peoples have passed. In spite of its gaps, the history of humanity is clear and complete in a different way from that of animal species.'†

It is worthwhile to note, too, that, having classified 'social species' according to his criterion of 'social composition', Durkheim deliberately spoke of societies passing 'from *lower* to *higher* types'. But, even when discussing the study of *specific social facts within* these types, Durkheim was just as insistent upon the necessity of being precise about the process of social evolution. Any particular social fact, he wrote:

'. . . can be called normal for a given social species only in relation to a *given phase of its development*; consequently it is not enough to observe the form it takes in the *generality* of societies belonging to this species; we must also take special care to consider them *at the corresponding phase of their evolution.*'‡

Even then, Durkheim went on, it was not enough to know the nature of a social fact in any *one* type of society; it was also essential to trace its development from its 'genesis' and 'sources' through all earlier 'types'. Here the 'comparative method' was essential—but, let us note very clearly—this was *not* simply a matter of comparing the nature of an institution in all the societies *of one type*; but also of comparing the institution in its development throughout *all* types. It was in this connection that Durkheim was impatient with any evolutionary 'theory' which simply *illustrated* a generalization by *selecting* evidence. 'To illustrate the idea,' he claimed, 'is not to demonstrate it.'

'It is necessary to compare not isolated variations but a series of systematically arranged variations of wide range, in which the individual items tie up with one another in as continuous a gradation as possible. For the variations of a phenomenon permit inductive generalizations only if they reveal clearly the manner in which they develop under given circumstances.

* *Rules*, p. 56.   † *Ibid.*, pp. 134–5.   ‡ *Ibid.*, p. 57.

261

There must be between them the same sequence as between the different stages of a given natural evolution; and, in addition, the evolutionary trend that they establish ought to be sufficiently extended as to lend some certainty to its direction.'*

Now this is very definite indeed, but let us glance at the definitive rule (in Durkheim's 'manual', so to speak) in which all these considerations resulted.

'*To explain a social institution belonging to a given species, one will compare its different forms, not only among peoples of that species but in all preceding species as well.* For example, in the matter of domestic organization the most rudimentary type that has ever existed will first be established, in order that the manner in which it grew progressively more complex may then be followed, step by step. This method, which may be called "genetic", would give at once the analysis and the synthesis of the phenomenon. For, on the one hand, it would show us the separate elements composing it, by the very fact that it would allow us to see the processes of accretion or action. At the same time, thanks to this wide field of comparison, we should be in a much better position to determine the conditions on which depend their formation. *Consequently, one cannot explain a social fact of any complexity except by following its complete development through all social species.*'†

It will be seen in all this that, for Durkheim, comparative sociology and evolutionary sociology were essentially one. They were, in fact, *sociology*—as it had always been conceived. Durkheim's plea was only for greater thoroughness, precision, diligence, accuracy.

'Comparative sociology', he wrote, 'is not a particular branch of sociology; it *is* sociology itself, in so far as it ceases to be purely descriptive and aspires to *account* for facts.'‡

With this, of course, all his predecessors would have agreed. All the comments mentioned here are drawn from Durkheim's argument in the *Rules of Sociological Method*, but many equally telling examples could be drawn from each of his major studies. Simply to demonstrate our point beyond all doubt, let us glance in the briefest way possible, at two instances in his study of *The Division of Labour*. When discussing the question as to how to determine whether a particular *moral* fact was *normal* in a certain *type* of society, Durkheim wrote:

'It must not be forgotten that the normal type is not some stable thing whose traits can be fixed at an indivisible instant. On the contrary, it

---

* *Rules*, p. 135. † *Ibid.*, pp. 138–9. ‡ *Ibid.*, p. 139.

evolves, as do societies themselves and all organisms. We are, it is true, disposed to believe that it blends with the average type of the species during maturity, for it is only at that time that the organism is truly itself, for it is then all it can be. But ... there is a normal type in infancy, another in the prime of life, another in old age, with societies as with individual organisms.

'Consequently, to know if a moral fact is normal for a society, we must take into account the age of the society and determine the normal type which serves as landmark. Thus, during the infancy of our European societies, certain restrictive rules of liberty of thought which have disappeared in a more advanced age were normal. To be sure, one cannot be specific about what moment of evolution either a society or an organism has reached. To number the years would not be enough; one may be older or younger than one's age. Only according to certain characteristics of the structure and functions is it possible scientifically to distinguish old age from infancy, or maturity, and these have not yet been determined with sufficient precision. However, besides being the only method of procedure, we shall find nothing insoluble about the problem. Certain of these objective signs are already known (for example, for a society, regular lowering of the birth-rate may be used as proof that the limits of maturity have been reached or passed); on the other hand, if the number of years is not always a satisfactory criterion, it may, however, be usefully employed provided it be used with reserve and precaution. Ultimately, the progress of science will make this determination more exact.'*

It will be readily understood that here we are not necessarily *upholding* Durkheim's every particular persuasion about evolution (some of the points in the above passage are, of course, very questionable); we are only seeking to establish what his point of view actually *was*. He was equally definite when arguing that the solidarity of society was first of a 'mechanical' nature resting upon repressive authority and then of an 'organic' nature resting upon an increasingly complicated differentiation of occupations (division of labour).

'If, then,' he wrote, 'social evolution rests upon the action of these same determinate causes—and we shall later see that *this hypothesis is the only one conceivable*—we may be permitted to predict that this double movement will continue in the same path, and that a day will come when our whole social and political organization will have a base exclusively, or almost exclusively, occupational.'†

This, it can be seen, was not only very definite in its acceptance of the actuality of social evolution, but also went so far as to suggest that its course might be *predicted*.

* *The Division of Labour in Society*, The Free Press, 1960, p. 433.
† *Ibid.*, p. 190.

There is absolutely no doubt, then, that Durkheim fully accepted, and was fully committed to the perspective of evolution as an essential framework for comparative (scientific, explanatory) sociology; so that his work was fully in the tradition which we have been able to trace clearly so far. His criticisms of the evolutionary 'conspectus', and the kinds of generalizations which it had so far produced, (not, as we have seen, always reliable and just criticisms) were: (*a*) that they were *premature*—and required, before any reliable theory could be produced, a much more rigorous study of the many social *facts* they sought to explain, and (*b*) that they proceeded by *illustration* of *generalizations*, whereas it was imperative that they should be sharpened and made more thorough, so that—more properly, in scientific terms—they should proceed by way of *demonstrating* accurately delimited *theories*. Here it becomes clear how it is the case that though one can be impatient of the insufficiencies of many of Durkheim's cavalier judgments one can nonetheless very much approve of the objective which he was striving to achieve.

(VII) THE CENTRALITY OF MORALITY IN SOCIETY: THE CONTINUITY, IN DURKHEIM, OF THE IDEA THAT MORALITY WAS AT THE HEART OF THE PROCESS OF ALL INSTITUTIONALIZATION

Running through the entire work of Durkheim, we find perhaps the most forceful statement we have yet encountered (and many, before, have been very forceful) of the fact—a central theme, explicit or implicit, in all the men we have studied so far—that the network of social institutions in any society rested essentially upon a core of *moral* sanctions; that morality, far from being *one aspect* of society, interpenetrated the whole. Durkheim was especially powerful in his insistence upon this as a fundamental fact. Throughout his work he spoke of *society* as a *moral reality*, and—whether writing of religion, of the division of labour, of domestic institutions, or even of social 'currents' of crime or suicide and the conditions of group membership with which they seemed always to be correlated—he conceived the associational emergence of a collective 'constraint' upon conduct (as an institutionalized 'regulation') as an element of 'collective *conscience*'. This must be insisted upon very clearly, and very strongly. Durkheim did not *only* think that, as an outcome of human association, a 'collective *consciousness*' was created (though he *did* think this), but *also* that such collective ways of perceiving, thinking, feeling, acting, included elements of *constraint*, of *obligatoriness*, and that they therefore constituted a collective *moral* consciousness. And this emergence of a collective *conscience* in relation to specific areas of associational behaviour (marriage, the family, property, occupations, laws, political constitutions, education, religion, etc.) was, in fact, the process of *institutionalization*.

Now this is a most important point, and let us again, stop to be meticulously clear about it. Durkheim was not at all claiming that 'moral ideals'—in any 'Idealist' sense—were the basic elements in the light of which men purposively created their institutions. On the contrary he flatly rejected 'Idealism'—whether ethical, or of any other nature; and he flatly rejected 'teleological' explanation. Neither was Durkheim at all setting 'moral' elements up as against 'material' or 'organizational' elements in the actual nature of human social life. He readily admitted the natural (material) context of human life, and readily saw that human associations took shape in relation to the many pressing (necessitous) aspects of it. All he was insisting upon was that the *creative process of human association*—which gave rise to definite institutionalized patterns of conduct—was this *collective emergence* of ways of perceiving, feeling, thinking, acting, which had not existed in individuals *before* the process of *association*, but which, as a continuing result of it, carried elements of *externality, constraint*, and *obligation*. The process of *institutionalization* among men in communities, *was*, in fact, this associational creation of elements of *collective conscience* regulating specific areas of conduct. It was neither 'material', nor 'idealist', nor 'purposely invented' by individual minds; it was *the human associational process in its own right*.

Now certain points will immediately be seen. The first—which we will come to emphasize centrally and strongly as the essential point which Durkheim struggled militantly to make—was that, in his conviction, *human association was a psychologically creative process at its own level, and of its own unique kind*. Human *society* was a creative process *productive of collective, cumulative, cultural, institutional* qualities and patterns of experience and behaviour within which *individual minds and personalities* came to take their own shape. Association was *creative* in ways other than those of prior *individual intent*. Many, many things hang on this point—but we must be content just to note it—though with all the strength we can—at this stage.

The second is that it will immediately be seen how closely agreed were the positions of Durkheim and Westermarck—up to a certain point. Both of them emphasized collective *sentiments* with their attendant emotions of *approval* and *disapproval* as being at the root of *custom*—with its generality, disinterestedness, and impartiality (i.e. as being a set of *collective* rules general *throughout* a society)—and forming the *sanctions* which were the core of social *institutions*.

The similarity between the analysis of the two men was overwhelmingly powerful*; both of them sought to emphasize the same kind of point; and both of them, even, emphasized the 'relativity' of systems of morals and beliefs to specific social systems. This similarity (as an aspect of the continuity and unity on the making of sociology) is worth dwelling on further, before we come to the difference—which is, though only *apparent*, not *real*, nonetheless very significant.

It is most interesting to see that Durkheim's point of departure in sociology was almost exactly that of Westermarck—namely a vast impatience with philosophical ethics. It will be remembered that Westermarck looked upon ethics as being far too 'ratiocinative'; taking no care at all to inform itself, empirically, about those detailed and diverse *facts* of morality in the variety of societies in the world about which it exercised its reflection. Durkheim's impatience was exactly the same.

'There is not a single system of ethics', he wrote, 'which has not developed from an initial idea in which its entire development was contained implicitly.'

And again:

'. . . all the problems ordinarily raised in ethics refer not to things but to *ideas*. Moralists think it necessary to determine with precision the *essence* of the *ideas* of law and ethics, and not the *nature* of ethics and law . . . It is only the super-structure of ethics, viz., its prolongations and echoes in the individual consciousness, that becomes the basis of ethical systems . . .'†

Having deplored such methods of reflective and deductive ethics, Durkheim went on to insist that since any general 'law' of ethics could only be of value if it had taken into account the diversity of moral facts:

'. . . these must first be studied if we wish to arrive at a law. Before discovering a summarizing formula, the facts must be analysed, their qualities described, their functions determined, their causes sought out; and only by comparing the results of all these special studies shall we be able to extract the common characteristics of all moral rules, the constitutive properties of the law of ethics. When we are not even definite about the nature of particular duties and particular rights, how can we understand the nature of their principle?'‡

* Indeed, we shall see that this was a central, striking and impressive agreement among *all* the writers we are here considering.
† *Rules*, pp. 22–3.
‡ *Division of Labour*, pp. 418–19.

And he then went on to sweep aside

'. . . the antithesis between science and ethics with which the mystics of all times have wished to cloud human reason . . .'

—and to set himself the task of establishing the *science of ethics*. In his preface to the *Division of Labour*, for example, his objective was stated in the first sentence with a stark clarity.

'This book', he wrote, 'is pre-eminently an attempt to treat the facts of the moral life according to the method of the positive sciences,'*

And at the end of the same book he claimed: 'Our first duty is to make a moral code for ourselves'. This, however, could no longer possibly be done by the moral philosopher 'in the silence of his study', but could only be accomplished by a full sociological study of '*the complete system of social relations, since the moral law penetrates all*'.

Now without at all wishing to diminish the importance emphasized by both Westermarck and Durkheim of a study of the actual moral systems of the world, it is clear that in their over-zealous attack on philosophical ethics, they very much mistook its nature, and themselves completely confused it with the 'sociology of morals'. Neither of these men possessed the clarity of thought about the relations between moral philosophy and the sociology of morals which, as we have seen, was to be found in the system of Hobhouse. This was, in fact, a glaring example of Durkheim's faulty logic, to which we will come back later. Our point here, however, is simply to point to the very great similarity of all these thinkers. Westermarck in concentrating upon the scientific study of 'social institutions' found that he was led to concentrate on 'sanctions', and produced a study on *The Origin and Development of the Moral Ideas* which lay at the heart of institutions. Durkheim, too, produced an entire body of work on the nature of society and its institutions which was, really, a *sociology of morals*—or, putting it more significantly—which was an entire analysis of *institutions* in terms of the elements of 'collective conscience' which lay at the heart of each. And this similarity was very much more profound than we have so far been able to convey. Perhaps the best brief indication possible is a mention of Durkheim's analysis of 'social solidarity'† in his study of the division of labour.

'*Social solidarity*', Durkheim claimed, in seeking to analyse its nature exactly, '*is a completely moral phenomenon*.' Since it did not lend itself to easy measurement, we should seek a reliable 'external

* Preface to First Edition.
† See Ch. 1 and 2 of the *Division of Labour*.

index' which we could observe. 'This visible symbol', he went on, 'is the law'.

'The more solidary the members of a society are, the more they sustain diverse relations, one with another, or with the group taken collectively, for, if their meetings were rare, they would depend upon one another only at rare intervals, and then tenuously. Moreover, the number of these relations is necessarily proportional to that of the juridical rules which determine them. Indeed, social life, especially where it exists durably, tends inevitably to assume a definite form and to organize itself, and law is nothing else than this very organization in so far as it has greater stability and precision. The general life of society cannot extend its sway without juridical life extending its sway at the same time and in direct relation. We can thus be certain of finding reflected in *law* all the essential varieties of social solidarity.'*

Juridical rules were the best indicator of institutionalized relationships in society; the Law (and Custom) in society was the best indicator of the network of established institutions. But then, Durkheim argued, it was necessary to determine the most exact way of observing these juridical rules in such a way as to have some measure of degree of seriousness with which they were taken in society (quite apart from their exactitude as legal rules). His conclusion was that the best criterion was that of the *sanctions* concomitant with the rules.

'Every precept of law', he wrote, 'can be defined as a rule of sanctioned conduct. It is evident that sanctions change with the gravity attributed to precepts, the place they hold in the public conscience, the role they play in society. *It is right, then, to classify juridical rules according to the different sanctions which are attached to them.*'†

The question then arose, however, as to what the sources of these '*sanctions*' were (indeed, *what* exactly they were!); why the sanctions attached to different rules of conduct varied (but with regularity and persistence in a society) in intensity; and why the breaking of these rules was regarded, with indignation, as being 'criminal'? Durkheim's answer to this was that:

'. . . the only common characteristic of all crimes is that they consist . . . in acts universally *disapproved of* by members of each society.'

And, further, this disapproval stemmed from the fact:

* *Division of Labour*, pp. 64–5.   † *Ibid.*, pp. 68–9.

'. . . that crime shocks *sentiments* which, for a given social system, are found in all healthy consciences.'

We will let the word 'healthy' pass for the moment, only noting that Durkheim added that these 'collective sentiments'—'are common to the average mass of individuals of the same society'; and are 'strongly engraven in all consciences'. In short they were general and compelling throughout the particular society. The maintenance of the rules rested upon shared *sentiments* which the members of the society felt it necessary to uphold, and by the fact that the breaking of them caused *offence* to these sentiments and called forth strong feelings of *disapproval*. Durkheim was very definite and deliberate about this.

'We must not say', he argued, 'that an action shocks the common conscience because it is criminal, but rather that it is criminal because it shocks the common conscience. We do not reprove it because it is a crime, but it is a crime because we reprove it.'*

The centrality in Durkheim's analysis of established collective *sentiments* carrying collective feelings of approval and disapproval and attendant, graded sanctions is plain beyond doubt, and this was further emphasized by Durkheim's connected account of crime, and punishment for crime. The fine attempt to *grade* punishment according to the severity of the crime committed would be inexplicable, he argued, 'if we did not believe that the culpable ought to suffer because he has done evil, and in the same degree'. Punishment, in short, has always been, and remains, an act of vengeance and expiation. 'What we avenge, what the criminal expiates, is *the outrage to morality*.' Collective vengeance, Durkheim argued, 'remains the soul of penalty . . . Punishment consists in a passionate reaction of graded intensity'.

The great similarity between Durkheim's analysis (of sentiments, feelings of approval and disapproval, sanctions at the heart of social institutions, and their 'rules' in custom and law) with that of Westermarck—and, indeed, of Tönnies and many others among the earlier writers, is perfectly clear, and is very substantial indeed. We are led to the question: what, then, was the *difference* between them? And this leads to another very distinctive aspect of Durkheim's position about which, it seems to me, there has been much misunderstanding.

(VIII) PSYCHOLOGY AND SOCIOLOGY: CONTINUITY AND
　　DIFFERENCE

We have seen the centrality of the place given to the collective *sentiments* in the process of institutionalization by Durkheim, and

* *Division of Labour*, p. 81.

the similarity of this with the ideas of others. But now—given the important place which they occupy—what further explanation did he give of these sentiments? The answer is: that he gave none.*

'As for the intrinsic nature of these sentiments,' he wrote, 'it is impossible to specify them. They have the most diverse objects and cannot be encompassed in a simple formula . . . By this alone can we recognize it: a sentiment, whatever its origin and end, is found in all consciences with a certain degree of force and precision, and every act which violates it is a crime.'

And again, having maintained that crime shocks 'sentiments which, for a given social system are found in all healthy consciences', he went on to state: 'It is not possible otherwise to determine the nature of these sentiments . . .'.

What this amounts to—quite directly and quite simply—is that Durkheim *took his analysis no further than this recognition of a level of collective sentiments.* (Sometimes he referred to these as 'collective representations' and sometimes as the 'collective conscience'.) And he did this not as an accidental oversight or omission, but quite deliberately. Westermarck, however, like Tönnies and others, tried to 'explain' these social sentiments in terms of the psychological components—of instinct, emotion, habit—which, in communal association, gave rise to them; and, indeed, they also showed how these psychological components were rooted in the attributes of man as a biological organism. Some of these men, too, like Tönnies and Mill, thought of these collective sentiments as being aspects of *human wills in association* with each other within the context of natural and social conditions.

Durkheim's system of sociological analysis and explanation started with the recognition of collective sentiments at the associational level; was concerned to know and to explain these collective facts at this level; and never went beyond it. Sociology, for him, was concerned with a study of '*social* facts' only: with facts of a distinctive, collective level. All the other thinkers—though certainly recognizing a distinctive *associational* level of experience, behaviour, institutionalization, culture, which certainly required study at its own level—nonetheless thought that the processes of institutionalization; the ways in which sentiments, sanctions, rules, emerged; could be illuminated by a study of their *psychological* dimensions. And this, as we have seen, in two ways: first, in the study of those elements of experience—instinct, emotion, habit, etc.—which were involved in the formation of sentiment; and second in the study of

* It is in connection with an account of such 'sentiments' that Pareto was of importance, and we shall see how he, too, adopted a position which was much in agreement with the ideas of the earlier writers.

the wills, characters, rational and moral (and other) principles, and the consciously directed and purposive *action* of men in the pursuit of their ends.

Now many important points are involved in this difference; misunderstandings have clustered thickly about many of them; so that we must disentangle them clearly and carefully.

We must be clear, first of all, about Durkheim's own position, and there are several distinct points here. First: Durkheim's '*social facts*' *were* of a *psychological* nature. This requires very definite emphasis, because there are those who think that, in his emphasis upon *social facts*, Durkheim was insisting upon the existence of certain kinds of facts which were *not of a psychological nature at all*.

This, as we have been able to see quite clearly already, is quite emphatically not true. Social facts were collective ways of acting which could be distinguished by clear observational criteria (like juridical rules, graded sanctions, etc.); but which were essentially of the nature of collective *sentiments*—constellations of elements of perception, conception, feeling, judgment, obligation, condemnation, and the like.* They were psychological facts *of a collective kind*. Secondly: Durkheim, of course, never for a moment wished to deny this. His chief insistence was that *human association* was itself a psychologically creative process at a level *other* than that of the biological organism and *other* than that of such psychological components as existed in individual 'minds' (whatever they might be) *prior* to the experience of association. *Association* was a psychologically *fertile* process: it took place in *collective conditions* which went beyond individuals; it was itself a context of *involvement in relationships* which went beyond the intention of individuals; and it engendered elements and qualities of experience—language, loyalty,

---

* It is most important to see that Durkheim's 'social facts' were of a *sociopsychological* nature, exercising inner *moral* constraint, even though he sought marks of 'externality' for the clearest possible basis of observation. Durkheim himself expressed this very clearly in *The Elementary Forms of the Religious Life*. He wrote (see footnote, pp. 208–9):

'Since we have made constraint the *outward* sign by which social facts can be the most easily recognized and distinguished from the facts of individual psychology, it has been assumed that according to our opinion, physical constraint is the essential thing for social life. As a matter of fact, we have never considered it more than the material and apparent expression of an interior and profound fact which is wholly ideal: this is *moral authority*. The problem of sociology—if we can speak of *a* sociological problem—consists in seeking, among the different forms of external constraint, the different sorts of moral authority corresponding to them and in discovering the causes which have determined these latter.'

It is also perfectly clear from this statement how far it was the case that—for Durkheim—the study of *institutions* was the study of *morality in society*. Here, he almost *equates* sociology with this.

criteria of beauty, conflict, indignation, expectations of conduct, and a thousand and one other experiences—which simply did not exist before. In short: *much of the psychological experience distinctive of human beings was associational in origin.* This psychological experience could only be explained, therefore, *in terms of association*; and in terms of the collective conditions in which it took place. The nature of the conditions and processes of *association* had to be understood in order to explain the psychological elements to which they gave rise; it could not be the other way round. The third corollary of this, according to Durkheim, was that it was therefore a definite error to think that the explanation of facts at the *associational* level could or should be *reduced* to the propositions of biology or psychology. Sociology was therefore quite distinct from psychology and biology; its distinctive level of facts (associational facts) could not be satisfactorily explained by any 'reduction' to the lower-level propositions of either of them. Perhaps we should add the fourth point that Durkheim's attack upon 'reductionist' psychology took the specific form of an attack upon 'Individual Psychology'. Since associational processes provided the very context within which individuals gained their experience and assumed their own individuality—it was a flat error to think that *social* (associational) facts could be explained by the individual experiences which were, in fact, their consequence. On the contrary, the study of associational facts and of collective conditions was much more likely to provide an explanation of the experience and conduct of individuals!

Durkheim was indefatigable in his pressing home of this argument. No error, he thought, was so difficult to overcome as this. It was perhaps the greatest intellectual illusion of all: to think that—because the minds of individuals were equipped with the perceptions, conceptions, expectations, motives which were operative in their society— the nature of *society* could be simply explained in terms of their conscious intentions as individuals. On the contrary, Durkheim insisted, man would only truly and realistically come to know himself, and to have such control over his society and his conditions of life as he desired, if he overcame this illusion and saw plainly that it was the *collective life of society*; the interconnected complex of many *associations*; which had been creative of the nature of his own experience. Like control over *nature*, so control over *society*, Durkheim maintained, could only be effectively achieved if man first tempered his egotism and realized that the *facts of society* had a nature going beyond himself, and had to be known objectively before they could be manipulated. In this intellectual illusion, Durkheim believed, lay great practical peril as well as sheer scientific and philosophical error.

272

In this, again, can be seen the profound—indeed tenacious—continuity in the work of Durkheim of that of Comte, and all others of this sociological persuasion. Ultimately, he argued passionately in his preface to the *Rules of Sociological Method*,* everything rests on, and grows out of this fundamental principle of the objective reality of social facts:

'And we are certain that, in attributing to it such dominating importance, we are remaining true to sociological tradition; for it is upon this principle fundamentally that all sociology has been built. .. The history of sociology is but a long endeavour to give this principle precision, to deepen it, and to develop all the consequences it implies.

In spite of the great advances which have been made in this direction, numerous survivals of the anthropocentric bias still remain and here, as elsewhere, bar the way to science. It displeases man to renounce the unlimited power over the social order he has so long attributed to himself; and on the other hand, it seems to him that, if collective forces really exist, he is necessarily obliged to submit to them without being able to modify them. This makes him inclined to deny their existence. In vain have repeated experiences taught him that this omnipotence, the illusion of which he complacently entertains, has always been a cause of weakness in him; that his power over things really began only when he recognized that they have a nature of their own, and resigned himself to learning this nature from them. Rejected by all other sciences, this deplorable prejudice stubbornly maintains itself in sociology. Nothing is more urgent than to liberate our science from it, and this is the principal purpose of our efforts.'†

Durkheim's position, then, was abundantly plain, and it was surely much to be supported and commended. But now, let us turn to other sides of the matter and try to disentangle certain elements—both on the side of Durkheim and those who oppose him—which have become hopelessly muddled. It may be that this can lead us to fresh and clear conclusions.

The next important step is to be exactly clear about Durkheim's complete position with regard to psychology, because his very militant argument against *reductionism* to 'individual' psychology has led many to think that he was outrightly *opposed to psychology altogether*, and that he believed it could contribute nothing to the understanding of man in society. But such a view is totally mistaken. It is true that Durkheim was ambiguous about this, but some of his statements were completely clear and cannot be misinterpreted, and I want to make a number of points which end in the judgment that, far from denying the value of psychology for sociology, Durkheim's position—especially when it is carefully seen in relation to the

* 2nd edition.   † *Rules*, pp. lvii–lviii.

273

position of others—was such as to give *social* psychology the central and important place within sociology that it should have.

To put this even more radically: I want to argue that Durkheim substantiated the intimate relationship—indeed the inseparable relationship—between sociology and social psychology that had been made clear long ago by Mill especially (even though the two men seem at first glance to be at opposite poles), more trenchantly than had been accomplished before; and also—more radically still—that Durkheim substantiated the viewpoint (seen before in Marx, for example) that no science of (human) psychology was *possible* outside the sociological perspective.* This, again, was the original emphasis of Comte—but Durkheim, in his several works, literally made this viewpoint *live*.

One (but a minor) point always to be borne in mind is that Durkheim was attacking the sufficiency for explanation of psychology during the last decade of the nineteenth century when—apart from the Americans, whose work he did not seem to know†—psychology, especially in the context of sociology, had not got very far, and was still chiefly characterized by the fairly superficial 'associationism'; the introspective study of conscious states of mind. There seems little doubt that he would have considered more seriously the schools of psychology which grew during the early decades of the twentieth century and which did, in fact, concentrate upon motivation, emotion, the formation of 'sentiments', and the like.‡ However, this is only a point to have in the background; it does not at all affect the fundamental principles of Durkheim's position.

Bearing it in mind, however, the much more important point is that Durkheim—having made his position about the nature of social facts and the error of reductionism clear—went out of his way to say that psychological knowledge could not only *facilitate* the explanation of human nature and behaviour, but that it was *indispensable*, and, indeed, that the training of the psychologist was of the greatest use to the sociologist *so long as he was careful to go beyond it*, and see the essential level and perspective of *social* facts. When discussing his rules for the explanation of social facts, Durkheim wrote quite plainly:

'We do not mean to say, of course, that the study of psychological facts is not indispensable to the sociologist. If collective life is not derived from individual life, the two are nevertheless closely related; if the latter cannot

* What we called, in Vol. I, the 'error of psychology'.
† Though he knew something of William James.
‡ Especially the viewpoints of Cooley, Freud, Pareto, etc., whom we shall consider in our next section.

explain the former, it can at least facilitate its explanation. First, as we have shown, it is indisputable that social facts are produced by action on psychological factors. In addition, this very action is similar to that which takes place in each individual consciousness and by which are transformed the primary elements (sensations, reflexes, instincts) of which it is originally constituted. Not without reason has it been said that the self is itself a society, by the same right as the organism, although in another way; and long ago psychologists showed the great importance of the factor of association in the explanation of mental activity.

Psychological training, more than biological training, constitutes, then, a valuable lesson for the sociologist; but it will not be useful to him except on condition that he emancipates himself from it after having received profit from its lessons, and then goes beyond it by special sociological training. He must abandon psychology as the centre of his operations, as the point of departure for his excursions into the sociological world to which they must always return. He must establish himself in the very heart of social facts, in order to observe them directly, while asking the science of the individual mind for a general preparation only and, when needed, for useful suggestions.'*

Now there undoubtedly seems to be some contradiction or ambiguity between this statement (and the position we have outlined above) and, for example, with Durkheim's flat statement in the *Rules*, that:

'. . . there is between psychology and sociology the same break in continuity as between biology and the physiochemical sciences. Consequently, every time that a social phenomenon is directly explained by a psychological phenomenon, we may be sure that the explanation is false.'†

But, though by no means wishing to claim that he was free from ambiguity, it remains true that, properly understood, Durkheim's case stands firm, and perhaps the clue lies in the word '*directly* explained by a psychological phenomenon' in the above passage. At any rate, it is very clear that Durkheim did not discard psychology altogether, nor deny its value; his chief insistence was upon the fact that *society* (association) was a creative source of the psychological experiences of man at a new level—beyond the purely biological and individual. What this amounts to is that Durkheim was insisting upon the necessity of an *associational* (social) psychology, and an attempt must be made to see his point—and one or two important dimensions of it—very clearly.

In the *Division of Labour* Durkheim struggled to make his point clear by contrasting the nature of man—in the context of his continuous, cumulative history, and that of animals—in the context of

* *Rules*, pp. 111–12.   † *Ibid.*, p. 104.

their natural environments. In the case of animal species, the situation remains always one of a limited range of biological and determinate psychological responses (which Durkheim characterized as 'instinct') to a normal set of natural environmental conditions. In the case of man, however, the many cumulative aspects of society *transform* the environment and are superimposed, so to speak, upon the purely organic attributes of human nature.

'The organism', wrote Durkheim, 'is spiritualized.

The individual is transformed in accordance with this change in dependence. Since this activity which calls forth the special action of social causes cannot be fixed in the organism a new life, also *sui generis*, is superimposed upon that of the body. Freer, more complex, more independent of the organs which support it, its distinguishing characteristics become ever more apparent as it progresses and becomes solid. From this description we can recognize the essential traits of psychic life. To be sure, it would be exaggerating to say that psychic life begins only with societies, but certainly it becomes extensive only as societies develop.

That is why, as has often been remarked, the progress of conscience is in inverse ratio to that of instinct. Whatever may be said of them, it is not the first which breaks up the second. Instinct, the product of the accumulated experience of generations, has a much greater resistive force to dissolution simply because it becomes conscious. Truly, conscience only invades the ground which instinct has ceased to occupy, or where instinct cannot be established. Conscience does not make instinct recede; it only fills the space instinct leaves free. Moreover, if instinct regresses rather than extends as general life extends, the greater importance of the social factor is the cause of this. Hence, the great difference which separates man from animals, that is, the greater development of his psychic life, comes from his greater sociability.

If man is a reasonable animal, that is because he is a sociable animal, or at least infinitely more sociable than other animals.'*

The development of the distinctive psychic life of human beings lay, then, in their *sociability* and in the cumulative transformations of the social facts which resulted. But it is interesting to note here the juxtaposition which Durkheim raised between 'instinct' and 'conscience' (or the 'collective sentiments' which result from association). It is important to notice that Durkheim did *not* claim that there were no instinctual elements in human nature; only that they were progressively overlaid by the cumulative growth of society. This is especially worth bearing in mind with reference to Freud's position—which we will come to a little later—that 'civilization' is founded upon 'the suppression of the instincts'. Freud's position was, really, that it was the energy of the instincts which was creatively channelled

---

* *Division of Labour*, p. 346.

into the making and sustaining of society—by the operation of a variety of 'mental mechanisms'—but at a cost: of conflict and anxiety; but we must leave this for now, whilst only noting the interesting connections, here, that can be made between Durkheim and Freud.

Durkheim then pressed his argument further—to claim, in even more detail, that the very *kind of individuality* which human beings had experienced and could experience, was closely concomitant with the detailed qualities of the *social milieu* in which they lived. In short, *varieties of individuality* were correlated with the *various conditions of societies*. We cannot follow these arguments too far here, but it is enough to note that Durkheim focused his discussion on the statement that man depended upon only *three* kinds of milieu: the organism, the external (natural) world, and society. The human organism and the natural world have not changed notably since the emergence of man in the world, and therefore: 'there is only society which has changed enough to be able to explain the parallel changes in individual nature'.

And it is at this point, after this kind of argument, that Durkheim came to this conclusion:

'It is not, then, audacious to affirm that, from now on, whatever progress is made in psycho-physiology will never represent more than a fraction of psychology, since the major part of psychic phenomena does not come from organic causes. This is what spiritualist philosophers have learned, and the great service that they have rendered science has been to combat the doctrines which reduce psychic life merely to an efflorescence of physical life. They have very justly felt that the first, in its highest manifestations, is much too free and complex to be merely a prolongation of the second. Because it is partly independent of the organism, however, it does not follow that it depends upon no natural cause, and that it must be put outside nature. But all these facts whose explanation we cannot find in the constitution of tissues derive from properties of the social milieu. This hypothesis assumes, at least, very great probability from what has preceded. But the social realm is not less natural than the organic realm. Consequently, because there is a vast region of conscience whose genesis is unintelligible through psycho-physiology alone, we must not conclude that it has been formed of itself and that it is, accordingly, refractory to scientific investigation, but only that it derives from some other positive science which can be called socio-psychology, The phenomena which would constitute its matter are, in effect, of a mixed nature. They have the same essential characters as other psychic facts, but they arise from social causes.'*

* *Division of Labour*, pp. 348–9. Again this points clearly to the 'error' of a psychology which seeks to explain human experience and behaviour without reference to all the many qualities and conditions of its *societal* context.

This, it seems to me, besides being a remarkably clear summary statement of his position, makes it clear in the most demonstrable way, that Durkheim was not seeking to abandon psychology *as such*, but was trying his best to insist upon the necessity for a *new perspective* for psychology. He was not rejecting psychology in sociology—he was rejecting an insufficient and narrowly conceived 'individual' psychology (as being sufficient for the explanation of societal facts) and insisting upon the necessity and correctness of a new *associational psychology*. There is not a shadow of a doubt about this. Far from rejecting psychology, Durkheim was emphasizing the *central place* of *social psychology*. His very conception of *sociology*—properly understood—was that it was of a *socio-psychological* nature; a study of *socio-psychological* facts.

Furthermore, he was completely correct, it seems to me, in illuminating what we have called, earlier, '*the error of psychology*'. He was surely right in this insistence that since so much of the totality of human experience and conduct is attendant upon the complex context of associational life, no psychology which ignores this context, and concentrates only upon the neuro-physiological facts (and closely attendant experiential and behavioural responses) of the human organism, can be more than a fractional subject. With the proper qualifications which I hope we have made clear, the Comte-like dictum—that 'all human psychology is social psychology'—is true: and Durkheim pressed this home in his system more vividly and convincingly than almost any other writer.

Having made this clear, let us now move back to the supposed '*difference*' between the approaches of Westermarck, Tönnies, and earlier writers, and that of Durkheim, because this, I believe, can now be satisfactorily resolved—at least to the last ditch of one point which must remain, I think, a disagreement. We have now sufficiently seen the *significance* of this apparent difference; this apparent obtuseness and resistance of Durkheim in wishing to go no further than the recognition of 'collective sentiments'; and we have seen that this was because of his intense desire to argue the case for the *associational* perspective for psychology. Having seen his qualifications, however, that a psychology which bears this perspective in mind may *facilitate* explanation, and that it is *indisputable* that social facts exercise their influence upon psychological factors, we can now see quite plainly that the apparent difference was, in fact, *apparent* and not *real*. To be complete, let us deal separately with two sets of considerations: first, the kind of analysis in terms of instinct, habit, emotion, etc.; of Westermarck, Tönnies, etc., and second, the kind of analysis which emphasized *character* and *will* rather than any simple notion of mechanistic causation: as found in Tönnies and, especially, Mill.

It can now readily be seen that there is quite literally no conflict whatever between the Westermarck-type analysis and that of Durkheim. For let us note (*a*) that Westermarck (and Tönnies and others like them) was not at all seeking to *reduce* the explanation of collective sentiments, sanctions, and institutions to lower-order components of human psychology. On the contrary, he was concerned to analyse the *associational* processes whereby the psychological elements of instinct, emotion, habit, and sympathy came to be *collectively transformed* to the new associational level of *custom, sanctions*, and *institutions*. Westermarck's analysis was a detailed study of the psychological elements (and their biological roots) which were involved in the process of institutionalization. It was, then, *supplementary* to the kind of study of social facts at their own level, which Durkheim chiefly wished to undertake; and, as we have seen, it was certainly very much in keeping with Durkheim's own account of the nature of sentiments, sanctions, and institutions. In this sense, then, the close relationship between biology, psychology and sociology which had long been accepted in sociology, and which Tönnies and Westermarck perpetuated, could continue still; and Durkheim's position was not in opposition to it. But let us note also (*b*) that Westermarck, Tönnies, and the earlier writers of a similar persuasion were never seeking to reduce the explanation of associational facts to something called '*individual*' psychology.* They simply did not do this. They analysed in general terms the psychological elements of human nature which—*in the associational relationships of the community*—were compounded and translated into institutional forms, and patterns of willing. This, it seems to me, was one other fault in Durkheim's argumentation: namely, the very frequent tendency to *identify* psychology with *individual* psychology. But, of course, this is not a necessary identification at all—and certainly these men were not guilty of it; they were sociologists completely in their perspectives. In this direction, then, we can see, again, clear continuity—and *real* continuity—where there was apparent conflict.

The second consideration is more difficult, but I think, permits of the same kind of resolution—expecting for the one 'last-ditch' disagreement. It is really the question as to the differences which are involved in thinking of 'social facts' as Durkheim described them as 'collective sentiments' brought about by some sort of socio-psychological compounding, or as patterns of '*wills* of individuals in relation with each other'. Tönnies reviewed Durkheim's *Division of Labour* as Durkheim had reviewed his own book, and argued that what Durkheim had called a 'social fact' he had called the 'social will'. But there are important issues here, and the best way of clarify-

* The same, of course, is true of Hobhouse.

ing them is to compare Durkheim and John Stuart Mill who seem, on the face of it, to stand at completely opposite poles.

It will be remembered that Mill argued a number of things very clearly in his system. First: that an experimental science of psychology was necessary. Second: that 'empirical generalizations' about the interconnections between societal facts (social institutions) could be stated clearly. Third: that it was a mistake, however, to regard these societal facts as *things* or *entities* which had cause and effect relations between themselves. Fourth: that therefore any *explanation* of the interdependent changes among *institutions* could only be achieved by taking into account the 'settled character dispositions' of the *people* of the society and their pattern of reaction to the particular institutional change. Fifthly, however: these 'settled dispositions of character and personality' were themselves a result of the influences of the 'societal facts' upon 'psychological endowment'; and therefore a special study of this 'middle range' (to provide the 'axiomata media') of social psychology was necessary. Taken together, the psychology, the social psychology, and the sociology, could provide an adequate framework for all the kinds of explanations sought in a 'general science of society'. There was the one final point, however, that the human *will*, and dispositions of *character*, were not *caused* in a purely mechanistic sense, but, though certainly among the causes of experience and behaviour, were the exercise of deliberate choice (though choice constrained by (*a*) existing character-traits; (*b*) the adherence—sometimes, and to varying degrees—to rational principle; and (*c*) particular existing circumstances).

At first glance it looks as though Mill was distinctly opposed to the kind of position Durkheim proposed (and, indeed, he was in certain matters). It seems, on a surface view, that he accepted psychological explanations whereas Durkheim did not; that he required explanation in terms of the individual members of society whereas Durkheim denounced it; and that he rejected the sufficiency of explaining 'societal facts' in terms of each other, whereas Durkheim insisted upon it. Now all I want to do in this connection is to move the point of agreement as far as it will go; and I am well aware that it cannot go the whole way.

But there are these very important things to be said. On the one hand, Durkheim clearly maintained that psychology could *facilitate* social explanation, and would therefore have no difficulty in, or objection to, conceding some of Mill's emphasis upon psychology *if the associational perspective was borne in mind.* And, on the other hand, Mill certainly *did* bear the associational perspective in mind. Certain points need clarifying here. The first was that Mill certainly did not maintain that societal facts could be directly explained by simple reference to the findings of experimental psychology. On the contrary, he insisted that societal facts exerted a great determining influence upon psychological endowment. Secondly, therefore, Mill did not *reduce* the explanation of social facts to propositions of psychology. This is a false and naïve way of presenting his position. Mill only insisted that the changes in institutional structure in a society required, for a full explanation, the consideration of the 'settled dispositions of character'—the social ideals, the moral convictions, the socially engendered habits of perceiving, feeling, thinking, acting, etc.—of the members of the society. But as soon as one stops to think critically about this—it is perfectly plain that this is essentially incorporated in what Durkheim referred to as 'social facts'. They were, in fact, the 'collective sentiments'; the elements of the 'collective conscience'. The simple truth is that Durkheim incorporated in his notion of (socio-psychological) social facts the *two* levels which Mill distinguished in his own system;* namely the generalizations about the structural-organization of institutions as such, and the socio-psychological actualities of the 'collective sentiments' engendered within the context of them. Properly assessed, therefore, there was no impossible cleavage of opinion here—even when the difference seems at first sight diametrically opposed. To this extent at least—and it is a very substantial extent—there was no basic conceptual disagreement which could not, with a little critical consideration, be resolved.

We must now, however, recognize the 'last-ditch' source of disagreement (though we shall see there are others to come), which is crucially entailed in the concept of the *will*. We have seen a very commonly agreed distinction among all the writers other than Durkheim between *action* (as behaviour consciously directed to the attainment of an end) among men, and *events* (physically connected phenomena) in nature. *Action* was held to entail 'teleological' components—and therefore required them in explanation. *Events* did not. The emphasis upon *choosing* and *willing* in Mill, and in Tönnies (to take these as examples) was a deliberate recognition of the fact that though men are certainly played upon by natural and social causal factors, there is nonetheless this distinctive difference in human beings that—*to some extent*—they are capable of learning, knowing, controlling, manipulating, planning, (etc.) their conduct. Therefore the entire pattern of social and psychological explanation had to contain provision for this element of deliberation and purpose. To some extent, and, as knowledge grew, to a growing extent, men could control their behaviour, and even aspects of their institutions, in the light of purpose.

* See Diagrams, *The Making of Sociology*. Vol. I, p. 235.

To some extent, therefore, individuals must be held—by the exercise of their own will, alone or in combination with the wills of others—to be capable of changing society by conscious purpose, and responsibly.

Now on this one point Durkheim, by his theoretical position, was opposed. In *fact* he was continuously ambiguous and inconsistent in his treatment of it—and terminated his work, as we shall see (and worthily), with a tremendous plea that men should act teleologically—in accordance with *his* point of view! But, in the strict terms of his sociological system, he could be none other than in disagreement. When we come to consider Durkheim's conception of 'social facts', we can return to this question. For now, we can simply note it.

However, our discussion in this section has covered much useful ground, and made clear both Durkheim's own position with regard to psychology, and the relations between this and the apparently differing positions of the earlier writers. Again, we have been able to trace and demonstrate a very clear and powerful strand of continuity, where, in general, there has been thought to be flat disagreement.

The one central fact which has come undeniably and demonstrably through our many-dimensioned discussion, and which must be given the very strongest emphasis, is that to think of Durkheim's 'autonomous sociology'—the science especially concerned to study 'social facts' at their own level—as one which has nothing to do with psychology, which rejects psychological dimensions completely as forming part of its subject-matter, and which discards psychology totally as a source of possible and helpful explanation, is utterly to misconceive his position. *Just as Durkheim took evolution seriously, so he took social psychology seriously.* It was a falsely conceived 'reductionism' of sociological explanation to the terms of a falsely conceived 'individual' psychology, and the taken-for-granted assumption of the *sufficiency* of this, that he attacked root and branch. And though he over-reached himself in pressing his argument to extremes which are unacceptable, in his main emphasis he was surely correct.

(IX) THE NATURE OF SCIENCE AND ITS APPLICATION TO THE STUDY OF SOCIETY: CONTINUITY AND DIFFERENCE

In all that has been said, it has been obvious that Durkheim was committed to the most rigorous pursuit of the scientific method in his work. Just as much as all his predecessors, he wished to clarify the nature of science and to make the way in which its methods should be properly applied to the study of human society clear beyond all doubt. He wished also to *prove* the superiority of these methods in the study of society over all previous (and other) methods of conjectural and speculative philosophy. Furthermore, in his insistence upon the *demonstration* of *theories* as against the *selective illustration* of *descriptive generalizations* (and all that this implied for precision of observation, definition, classification, comparative study, etc. in seeking to pose clear conditions of *testability*); and upon the recognition of distinctive 'levels' of facts for which distinctive concepts and methods were necessary, and his denunciation of 'reductionism'; he was completely in accordance with the principles of science enunciated by Comte—even to his agreement with the 'hierarchy of sciences'.

This is so clear as to require no further demonstration. However, even in this, Durkheim presented a very mixed position—of clarity and rigour in certain directions, and insufficiencies in others. As usual, some of these insufficiencies were closely connected with his pressing of certain arguments to extremes; but there was also a peculiarly didactic simple-mindedness, a dogmatic blindness, in his conception of some aspects of science. These matters, again, need comment, because of the reputation which has accrued about Durkheim's name; the attachment of some to the limited conceptions which he proposed; and the fashionable rejection of many of the earlier dimensions of sociology which has been attendant upon this. The ramifications of this are very extensive indeed in modern sociology—but, to mention one example, the entire development of modern social anthropology has been based upon a very extensive adoption of Durkheim's ideas of the analysis of social systems in terms of the functional interdependence of 'social facts' and the establishing of non-teleological connections among them, and this, itself, has become a very influential position in general sociology as against which many earlier positions have been rejected. Durkheim's conception of *science*, and the *science of society*, has come to be regarded as a great step forward in clarity; the accomplishment of a really precise and exact statement; whereas the earlier conceptions embracing 'teleological' dimensions have come to be set aside as containing earlier elements of misconception, muddle, and confusion. The truth, however, is the reverse. Of all the men we have considered so far, Durkheim had the most simple-minded notion of inductive science. His clarity was the clarity of intellectual myopia. Your vision can seem very sharp if you are only seeing part of the landscape—and if your eyes are such as to shut out all the rest. But even this is not quite correct: because Durkheim's seemed, in places, and in some respects, to be a *deliberate* myopia. He *deliberately* shut out all the rest—but only by dogmatism: not by giving *grounds* for doing so. By contrast, the other men we have studied—from

Comte, Mill, and Marx (even) to Ward, Giddings, and up to Hobhouse—had a very much more considerable grasp of the nature of science, and, especially, the philosophical problems in the way of applying it satisfactorily to the study of man.

We are compelled, then, to consider an about-turn of reputations here; a reversing of very fundamental positions which have come to be almost entrenched; but, even so—and here the difficulty of judging Durkheim raises its head again—it is important to emphasize that this adverse criticism of his position must not be taken as a denial of its value. For still—peculiarly enough—Durkheim's myopia did result in a sharpening of methods for the study of what it was that he sharply saw; despite his errors in neglecting other factors. And, in a preliminary and summary way, this really indicates the estimation we shall finally form of Durkheim's contribution to the making of sociology: namely, that, despite many errors against which we must take care to be on our guard, his conceptions and arguments produced far and away the clearest rules for the *objective* study of the *phenomenal* aspects of *social facts*. This was by no means his *only* contribution, but it was his central one.

Let us, then, attack Durkheim again in order to clarify what was of dubious value and what was worth while in him.

Science, according to Durkheim, was the observational study of 'things' which arrived at an accurate description of them, a classification of them, and explanations of the ways in which they were connected in spatial and temporal relations—explanations which could always be tested by reference to the 'things' themselves. These 'things' possessed objective attributes which existed independently of the subjective suppositions of the observer, and therefore the scientist had to go outside of his own mind, and critically beyond his own preconceptions, to *discover* them. Furthermore, he had to go critically beyond the ordinary notions and assumptions of common sense, because these were frequently ill-founded and even distorting. Each science therefore dealt with a particular order of 'things', or 'perceptual facts', in nature. The attributes of the 'things' or 'facts' were given in 'sensation' and 'perception'—the basis on which all scientific knowledge rested. And finally, such descriptions, classifications, and explanations of 'things' provided as accurate a basis as it was possible to achieve for prediction and reliable practical action.

Now this, it will be seen, did not go, in any way, beyond the earlier conceptions of the nature of science we have considered. But some of Durkheim's emphases must be noted. Firstly, he tied science very rigorously to the *objects of sensation*. We cannot go too much into epistemology and the philosophy of science here, but it is perhaps enough to note that whereas Comte, Spencer—and Kant before both of them—had at least been aware that 'reality' might go beyond what science could 'know' about it; that—even in sensation and perception—the human mind contributed dimensions of its own to the nature of the 'things' perceived; and that even speculative philosophy and theology (at the extreme) could be sources of *hypotheses* about perceptual reality; Durkheim was much more dogmatic in claiming that the objective attributes of things were *reality*. Knowledge was of *them* and their qualities; no more. Durkheim varied his emphasis upon this throughout his work, but this— *and especially in sociology* (as we shall see)— was his basic position. Secondly, though the propositions of science were always to be subjected to tests, for Durkheim they were always arrived at *inductively*. The course of science was—quite literally—firstly, and with painstaking care, to *describe* what the 'things' of its subject-matter were, to observe and record their qualities; second to *classify* them in accordance with the observable varieties among them; third, to investigate the *causes* of their nature and their varieties (by, let us note, 'methodical inductions'); and then, fourthly, to compare all these results in order to arrive at a statement of general 'laws': i.e. statements of *constant concomitance* which existed among them. This, it will be seen, was a very simple notion of *induction* as the procedure of science, and did not entertain to anywhere near the same extent as Comte and Mill had done, the role of *hypothesis* in science.

Even so, the extreme limitations of Durkheim's conception of science are not so apparent in this general statement about scientific method as such, as they are—immediately—as soon as we come to consider his application of them to the study of man and society. And here, the deficiencies of some of his emphases, and of the elements of omission from some of his concepts (as, for example, the denial of teleological elements in human association, and the diminutive role attached to hypothetical 'hunch' in orientating scientific studies) must enter into our discussion and become very plain.

For Durkheim went on to insist that sociology, as a science—like each other specific science—was concerned with a specific order of 'things'. *Social facts* were 'things', and, if it was to be scientific, sociology should confine itself to establishing accurate knowledge of these 'things' and their qualities *as sensation revealed them*. These 'things' should be described, classified, arranged according to their variations, and the investigation into their causes and the statement of general 'laws' about them should be undertaken *inductively*. The 'things' were the social '*reality*'; they existed beyond individuals— 'in their own right'; and to think of people acting purposively within

285

the context of them, and to introduce 'teleological' elements into the explanation of them, was an error. Furthermore these 'things' (the special order of 'social facts') were 'compounded' out of the associational activities of individuals, and existed as a *social reality* independent of individuals (independent of their 'individual manifestations'). Causal relations existed among them at their own level, and these should be established inductively.

Now later, we shall examine Durkheim's rules for the study of social facts, and sift out in them what seems valid and invalid in his conceptions and arguments. And we might say, here, that a better case can be made for *some* aspects of *some* of the points made in this summary way above, than might be thought. However, our concern here is only to establish Durkheim's conception of science as applied in sociology to the study of the distinctive 'things' which constitute its subject-matter, and I would like to buttress certain specific points in turn.

Firstly, Durkheim's complete (and very Comte-like) acceptance of the application of 'positive' science to the study of society was stated quite directly in his preface to the first edition of the *Rules*.

'Our principal objective,' he wrote, 'is to extend scientific rationalism to human behavior. It can be shown that behaviour of the past, when analysed, can be reduced to relationships of cause and effect. These relationships can then be transformed, by an equally logical operation, into rules of action for the future .What critics have called our "positivism" is only one certain aspect of this rationalism . . . Correctly understood, facts are as basic in science as in practical life: in science because there is nothing to be gained by looking behind them to speculate on their reason for being, and in practical life, since their very usefulness is their only justification.'*

The insistence that science should not seek to go beyond the regularities of facts which it is studying—to some more 'ultimate' reality; the connections made between knowledge and prediction, between scientific knowledge and guidance for practice; are clearly the same here in Durkheim as in Comte and all his predecessors. The qualification was made in a footnote that this scientific 'rationalism' was not to be confused with the 'positive metaphysics' of Comte and Spencer, but, as we have seen, they had no positive *metaphysics*; on the contrary, it was Durkheim who pressed this. And we can begin to see this more clearly if we look at Durkheim's misconceptions of other kinds of social (philosophical) thought and social science.

We noted earlier that Durkheim castigated Ethics for not concern-

* *Rules*, pp. xxxiv–xl.

ing itself with the objective study of the nature and functions of morals in the actual social systems of the world, and it is obviously true that the more knowledge of this kind that ethics had at its disposal, the more satisfactory its reflections would be likely to be. At the same time Ethics is *not* the same thing as the *sociology of morals* (or a *science* of morals, even), and Durkheim did, in fact, completely confuse the two. Thus, he argued:

'. . . that there is not a single system of ethics which has not developed from an initial idea in which its entire development was contained *implicitly* . . .'

—that ethics reflected upon 'fundamental ethical concepts', and that:

'. . . it is always with *ideas* that his (i.e. the moral philosopher's) reflection is concerned.'

Moralists, he claimed:

'. . . think it necessary to determine with precision the *essence* of the *ideas* of law and ethics, and not the *nature* of ethics and law.'

—and all this was put forward as a *denunciation*. But Durkheim completely failed to see that *this was, in fact, what ethics properly was, and all it sought to do*!

When he complained:

'Ethical theory is limited merely to a few discussions on the idea of duty, the good and right. And even these abstract speculations do not constitute a science, strictly speaking, since their object is the determination not of that which is, in fact,* the supreme rule of morality but of what it ought to be.'*

* Actually there is a very important ambiguity here that would need a lot of attention to clarify fully. Moral philosophy has been busy with it from Socrates on. Durkheim's supposition is that *facts* can be *observed* by the *senses* whereas *idealities* are, in some way, less firm constructions of reflective reason. But this is completely questionable. Our senses may give only certain 'data'—but the *facts implied* by these data may need deductive inference for their discovery. Thus moral experience of rules in society may give us '*factual*' experiences of guilt, injustice, the compulsive sense of obligation, but the *actual* source of these experiences (in terms of which, alone, they may be explicable) may well be a *principle* or an *ideal* which is *implicit* in social behaviour, but not *explicitly* clear. Reflection may be necessary to discover explicitly what the nature of this ideality *is*. It can be seen, therefore, that (*a*) *facts* may not be totally knowable by the senses, (*b*) idealities may be facts—actually operative in experience, though not explicitly clear, (*c*) that philosophical reflection may be necessary for the 'observation' of some facts, and that (*d*) science may be as dependent upon philosophy as philosophy is upon science. The philosophical naivety of Durkheim's 'scientism' is therefore clearly apparent. He clearly took it for granted that to say that a subject was not a *science* was to condemn it; which is, of course, nonsense.

287

—he did not see that this was no criticism whatever, because this was exactly what ethics *was*; it did not seek or pretend to be a *science*. Ethics—from Plato to Kant—had been *exactly* this: to deliberate very searchingly on the central concepts of moral experience—such as, for example, the notion of 'justice', of 'obligation', of 'duty', of the 'good', of the 'right'—in order *exactly* to make fully *explicit* what the *implicit* presuppositions of them were. Ethics was deeply concerned to *elucidate* all the implications of these compelling conceptions which were certainly ideas (but by no means clear ones) at the heart of our distinctively *moral* experience. In this sense, philosophical ethics was chiefly concerned with clarifying the *normative* aspects of our experience; it was not a *scientific* study of social facts at all! Consequently, when Durkheim went on to complain, with a mounting intensity of derogation, that moral philosophers:

'. . . have not yet arrived at the very simple truth that, as our ideas (*representations*) of physical things are derived from these things themselves and express them more or less exactly, so our idea of ethics must be derived from the observable manifestation of the rules that are functioning under our eyes, rules that reproduce them in systematic form. Consequently, these rules, and not our superficial idea of them, are actually the subject matter of science, just as actual physical bodies, and not the layman's idea of them, constitute the subject matter of physics.'*

—he was simply clambering ever more frantically up a gum tree. It simply was not the business of moral philosophers to study the rules of morality in societies *scientifically*. Durkheim could well have argued that ethics was not sufficiently informed about the *facts* of morality in human societies, and that it would benefit greatly from a more rigorous development of a sociology of morals. Instead, however, (or, perhaps, in addition) he argued, much more radically, that ethics was superficial and ill-founded, and that it should be *replaced* by the sociology of morals; by a *science* of morality. But this is a complete misconception. No matter how extensive a sociology of morals is, it can never possibly *replace* philosophical reflection upon the nature and standards of ethical evaluation, and how far, and in what ways, these are to be held compelling in clarifying how we *ought* to behave. The two kinds of intellectual enquiry ask questions of a different kind and of a different level. Both are reciprocally helpful, but one can never replace the other. And Durkheim moved into many inconsistencies because of this 'category' mistake, and his extreme desire not just to prove the worth of socio-

* *Rules*, p. 23.

logy in its relation to other disciplines so much as to obliterate the other disciplines altogether.

Exactly the same error underlay his denunciation of other social sciences—especially of economics (in connection with which, curiously enough, his criticism was *least* appropriate, as Mill had made very clear already in Book VI of the Logic), and we can note certain very peculiar points in the argument he used here.

The definition of economics which he took as the point of departure for his attack was that of John Stuart Mill, which emphasized, as its subject matter—'those social facts the goal of which, principally or exclusively, is the acquisition of wealth'. Actually, Mill went into much more detail than this in defending economics as a special social science, pointing out how the phenomena of 'exchange' in market situations and the significance of 'price' for the adjustment of demand and supply in such situations, could be 'isolated' from other organizational facts, and constituted a clear subject-matter for scientific analysis.* However, it was the common definition of the processes involved in 'the production and distribution of wealth' which Durkheim emphasized. He then argued that the first task of such a science should be to make clear the criteria by which such 'facts', thus defined as 'things', could be distinguished for 'observation'.

But, he went on:

'When a science is in its infancy, we do not have the right to affirm the existence of such facts, to say nothing of asserting the possibility of their identification. Indeed, in every branch of research, it is possible to establish that facts have a meaning, and what the meaning is, only when the explanation of the facts is sufficiently advanced. There is no problem more complex or less likely to be solved on the first attempt. Nothing, then assures us in advance of the existence of a sphere of social activity wherein the desire for wealth really plays such a preponderant role. Consequently, the subject matter of economics, so defined, comprises not the *realities* given to immediate observation but merely *conjectures* that are the product of pure intellect.'†

We may note the oddness of Durkheim's argument here—because he not only revealed very clearly his naïve *inductivism*, and his naïve notion of *facts*: i.e. that they are 'things' revealed by 'sensation'; but also employed a peculiar kind of special pleading. What I have in mind is that—in attacking economics—he was dogmatically insistent

* i.e. Whether it is governments, or private individuals, or corporate groups (companies), or religious bodies, or groups of people even in pre-literate non-monetary societies, who are involved in situations of *exchange*—the procedures of *exchange* are common to all of them, and possess factors (e.g. of scarcity) which can be clearly isolated for analysis.
† *Rules*, p. 24.

that there was 'no right to affirm the existence of' its distinctive facts whilst the science was in its infancy. In sociology, however, he rested the whole case for the necessity of the science on the existence of 'social facts' of a distinctive level; and he argued very passionately about the nature of these facts and their independence of 'individual manifestations' even before (in his view) the science had properly begun! However, the much more important point is to make clear the naive 'observationalism' and 'inductivism' which Durkheim's argument revealed.

It was quite specious for Durkheim even to argue, as he did (above) that the economist's initial definitions were not based upon observation, but were 'conjectures' of 'pure intellect'. The procedures of production and exchange and bargaining over prices are observable to any housewife. The *selective definition* of problems in terms of *conceptually significant* elements of human behaviour and *conjectural suppositions* about their interrelationships was flatly attacked by Durkheim.

'In order to construct economic theory,' he wrote, 'the economist is content to meditate and to focus his attention on his own idea of value, that is, as *an object capable of being exchanged*; he finds therein the idea of utility, scarcity, etc; and with these products of this analysis he constructs his definition.'*

But it was wrong to introduce such a theory of value in market exchange at the outset; before the *facts* had been properly *observed*.

'When the economist,' he went on, 'undertakes the study of what he calls "production", he thinks he can straightway enumerate and review the principal agents of that process . . . If, from the beginning of his research and in a few words, he proceeds to this classification, it is because he has obtained it by a simple, logical analysis. He starts from the idea of production; in analysing, it, he finds that it implies logically the ideas of natural forces, of work, and of tools or capital, and he likewise treats in their turn these derivative ideas.'†

The idea that science might proceed by the detailed clarification of a *conjectural hypothesis* which was itself rooted in a compelling *conceptual interpretation* of *observed facts* (and that the *conceptual* interpretation might well itself be a significant factor in determining the *perception, designation,* and *observation* of the facts) was quite foreign to Durkheim's conception, and this is even more clearly borne out by his alternative proposals. For what, according to him, should the economists study of 'value' be? 'Value', he insisted (and

* *Rules*, p. 25.   † *Ibid*., pp. 24–5.

let us notice the sheer 'observationalism' here—i.e. that a fact is a 'thing' with properties, which can only be perceived in sensation), should be studied like any other *'fact of reality'*. The economist should:

'. . . indicate, first of all, by what characteristics one might recognize the *thing* so designated, then classify its varieties, investigate by methodical inductions what the causes of its variations are, and finally compare these various results in order to abstract a general formula.'*

The formula, the statement of 'laws', would be *abstracted* from the systematic classification of the totality of described 'facts'. This was, beyond all doubt, a sheer inductivism. Durkheim's conclusion, that economics, because its system of analysis was rooted in concepts rather than 'things', was—exactly like Ethics—a *normative* study; a study of what market-systems *ought* to be; was completely misguided. Furthermore, this *equating* of the 'things' of nature with the institutionalized patterns of conduct of men in society, revealed a dogmatic and ill-considered metaphysic and a lack of readiness to consider whether the subject-matter of the human sciences was not, in significant ways, different from that of the natural sciences. It revealed a flat, dogmatic assumption that the *facts* of *all* science were of the nature of *perceived things*; that the *reality* of things consisted of the 'objective† properties' of them which the *senses* conveyed; and that *all* sciences—whatever their specific set of facts—pursued the same methods, of the same order. Thus when he claimed that:

'. . . this *logical necessity* (i.e. of the "laws" of the conceptual models of the economists) resembles in no way the necessity that *the true laws of nature* present.'

—he was claiming, quite dogmatically, that the only true scientific laws were those of the natural sciences; the statements of regularities between 'things' perceived by the senses; and that all other subjects, to be scientific, must produce 'laws' of the same kind. A 'natural law', Durkheim stated, was—'an inductively determined way of behaviour in nature'.

Now it is most important to note very strongly, in arguing like this, that we are *not* maintaining, as against Durkheim, that all inductive procedures in science and social science are without value; or that procedures of careful description, classification, and the establishing of empirical generalizations, are not a correct and useful part of science. In all our argument throughout this study so far,

* *Rules*, p. 25.   † i.e. 'phenomenal' properties.

we have seen that all these components of scientific method are to be defended. What we are arguing against is Durkheim's dogmatic insistence on *confining* the conception of science to these procedures, and, especially, to a conception of *facts* which confines them to '*things*' and their qualities as perceived by the senses. And that this narrowness in Durkheim was, in fact, what we conceive it to be, can be demonstrated clearly in his statements about the nature of '*social facts*' as the subject-matter for sociology.

Having denied economics the right to designate certain categories of 'things' whilst the science was in its infancy, Durkheim went on to claim, without any vestige of doubt, the existence of a certain category of 'things' for sociology.

'Social phenomena,' he wrote, 'are things and ought to be treated as things.'

Furthermore, he went on magisterially:

'To demonstrate this proposition, it is unnecessary to philosophize on their nature and to discuss the analogies they present with the phenomena of lower realms of existence. It is sufficient to note that they are the unique data of the sociologist. All that is given, all that is subject to observation, has thereby the character of a thing. To treat phenomena as things is to treat them as data, and these constitute the point of departure of science. Now, social phenomena present this character incontestably. What is given is not the idea that men form of value, for that is inaccessible, but only the values established in the course of economic relations; not conceptions of the moral ideal, but the totality of rules which actually determine conduct; not the idea of utility or wealth, but all the details of economic organization. Even assuming the possibility that social life is merely the development of certain ideas, these ideas are nevertheless not immediately given. They cannot be perceived or known directly, but only through the phenomenal reality expressing them.'*

We must not leave this kind of dogmatic assertion without noting the unconsidered assumptions in it. Let us note that Durkheim simply *asserted* that when we *observe* society—what is *given* is not the *ideas* men have of value, moral ideals, and the like, but only the *values*, and *rules* established in social relations. *The ideas are not given*; only *phenomenal reality*. But it does not need more than a moment's reflection to see that these assertions are, at the very least, highly questionable. When Durkheim says 'What is *given*', he means given *by (or to) the senses*—which, we may note, is given the status not just of *phenomena* (as Comte, for example, would have it), but of pheno-

* *Rules*, p. 27.

menal *reality*. But whether we *sense* the institutionalized behaviour of men as a set of raw data through nose, eye, ear, mouth, and—occasionally—touch, is, of course, highly debateable. And once we question *that*, and think it at least *possible* that we might *perceive* and *observe* patterned behaviour of men in terms of concepts and *ideas* that, in part at least, we share with them, then it is also possible that the *ideas* of value and morality which men have are as much *hard data* as the colours and shapes which are entering through our eye-balls. And it can even be supposed further than it *might* be the case that certain phenomenal facts can only be correctly *observed* in the light of the interpretation of these ideas.

Now it is not necessary to say that this *is* so, but only to suggest that it *might* be so (as we have done) to reveal Durkheim's epistemology as the metaphysical dogma that it is. For we are then led to ask: what *grounds* did he give for his assertion; and the answer is that he gave none. Before saying a little more about this, let us note again—quite definitely—Durkheim's insistence on his position. When considering the definition of 'social facts', he wrote:

'In order to be objective, the definition must obviously deal with phenomena not as ideas but in terms of their inherent properties. It must characterize them by elements essential to their nature, not by their conformity to an intellectual ideal. Now, at the very beginning of research, when the facts have not yet been analysed, the only ascertainable characteristics are those external enough to be immediately perceived.'*

And by *perceived*, he meant:

'Since objects are perceived *only through sense perception,*† we can conclude: Science, to be objective, ought to start, not with concepts formed independent of them, but with these same perceptions. It ought to borrow the materials for its initial definitions directly from perceptual data. And, as a matter of fact, one need only reflect on the real nature of scientific work to understand that it cannot proceed otherwise. It needs concepts that adequately express things as they actually are, and not as everyday life finds it useful to conceive them. Now those concepts formulated without the discipline of science do not fulfil this condition. Science, then, has to create new concepts; it must dismiss all lay notions and the terms expressing them, and return to sense perception, the primary and necessary substance underlying all concepts. From sensation all general ideas flow, whether they be true or false, scientific or impressionistic.'‡

Durkheim's position was therefore very clear and forthright. But to return to the question of *grounds*, the nearest we can come to this is to point to three things. First, Durkheim was impatient

* *Rules*, p. 35. † My italics. ‡ *Rules*, pp. 43–4.

with the power of common-sense notions in thought about the nature of society, and wanted to shatter the impregnable obstacle that they presented to any critical thought which suggested that the causes of social facts might be unusual and unfamiliar. Secondly, he was impatient with 'teleology', and especially with the assumption that the regularities of social behaviour could be explained in terms of individual purpose. And thirdly, he was impatient of large-scale generalizations in sociology and wanted to *delimit* its theories to such facts as were in some definite way *observable*; theories, in short, which could clearly show that they were *testable*.

All these, it almost goes without saying, were 'impatiences' which can well be understood and sympathized with, but Durkheim over-reached himself in doing battle with them. Thus, instead of insisting that it was necessary to be critically reflective of common-sense assumptions about society, he argued bluntly that they were *opposed* to the truth, and, in general, false. Besides arguing that a science of society must go beyond common-sense notions, he also exhorted the reader to bear in mind: 'that the ways of thinking to which he is most inclined are *adverse*, rather than favourable, to the scientific study of social phenemena . . .' The sociologist, he wrote:

'. . . ought to repudiate resolutely the use of concepts originating outside of science for totally unscientific needs. He must emancipate himself from the *fallacious* ideas that dominate the mind of the layman; he must throw off, once and for all, the yoke of these empirical categories, which from long continued habit have become tyrannical. At the very least, if at times he is obliged to resort to them, he ought to do so fully conscious of their *trifling* value, so that he will not assign to them a role out of proportion to their real importance.'*

With regard to common-sense 'sentiments' about the nature of society, he also argued:

'Sentiments pertaining to social things enjoy no privilege not possessed by other sentiments, for their origin is the same. They, too, have been formed in the course of history; they are a product of human experience, which is, however, confused and unorganized. They are not due to some transcendental insight into reality but result from all sorts of impressions and emotions accumulated according to circumstances, without order and without methodical interpretation.'†

Durkheim, in statements like these, did not simply argue that common-sense concepts, sentiments and generalizations should be carefully *questioned*; that they were *prone* to error, and probably

* *Rules*, p. 32. † *Ibid.*, p. 33.

inexact and not, in their existing form, appropriate for scientific use; he went much further and *repudiated* them as being devoid of value.* But our chief point here is that he did not think it necessary to *demonstrate* this; he simply *assumed* and *asserted* it.

Similarly, he did not argue, that since 'teleological' explanations could easily be mistaken, great care should be taken about them, and care taken to study in detail the objective conditions of social life, and the 'genetic' interconnections between social facts which might well go beyond conscious intention and purpose (as others had argued before him). He claimed, on the contrary that *all* 'teleological' explanation should be *excluded*, and that 'social facts' should be treated as 'things' not possessing 'teleological' dimensions. Thus, when discussing the explanation of social facts, and introducing the notion of 'needs', Durkheim immediately thought it necessary to point out:

'The fact that we allow a place for human needs in sociological explanations does not mean that *we even partially revert to teleology*. These needs can influence social evolution only on condition that they themselves, and the changes they undergo, can be explained solely by causes that are deterministic and not at all purposive.'†

The word teleological had become a dirty word! Later, we shall see why Durkheim attacked 'teleological explanation' so strongly, but here it is only necessary to see that he went much too far in his attack; and equated *all* scientific explanation with *deterministic* explanation at the most limited level of *causal regularities* between *perceived objects*—without giving anything approaching sufficient grounds. As to the third question of impatience with large-scale generalizations which could not (as he claimed) be *tested*, this was in itself no ground for claiming that the *only* criteria of testability were to be framed in terms of sense-perception, and 'objectivity' in this sense.‡

Now all this amounts to the fact that the work of Durkheim showed the same continuity in the concern for applying the methods of science to the study of society that had characterized all the earlier contributors to the making of sociology; that the same methods of observation, description, classification, empirical generalization,

---

* There is some considerable inconsistency even here, for elsewhere he claimed that the collective sentiments in society—in the varieties of religious beliefs and rituals, for example—were always *true*; and that they would not continue to exist in society if it were otherwise.
† *Rules*, p. 93.
‡ Max Weber, as we shall see, proposed a similarly exacting 'delimitation' of scientific studies, but on the basis of a '*subjective* understanding' of social '*action*'.

L

attempted explanation, and prediction, were there; but that—in pressing his arguments to unwarranted extremes—there were certainly differences in his treatment which were in marked disagreement with what had been generally maintained before, and these differences were deficiencies for which no good grounds were given—even though they brought with them a sharpening of methods in certain directions.

Some additional elements of this insufficiency in Durkheim's work must be remarked quite carefully if we are to be able to judge it correctly in the context of the work of others, and trace certain developments in the making of the subject from his time onwards. The following are quite clear aspects and characteristics of Durkheim's work which deserve particular attention. Here we will note them and treat them sufficiently for the emphasis we wish to place upon them, but, as with all these points, we shall uncover other (mixed!) dimensions of them when we come to Durkheim's specific rules and theories.

(a) *Durkheim's 'data' for the study of 'social facts' were drawn from DOCUMENTARY sources and were SELECTIVE. He was little different in this from his predecessors.*

This point is necessary not so much to take issue with a grave deficiency in Durkheim, as to emphasize a certain judgment about the nature of his work which will enable us to place and assess it properly, in relation to that of his predecessors, and in the making of the subject as a whole. It is commonly thought—because he insisted upon the definitive study of specific social facts, and upon scientific rigour in procedure—that the 'facts' which Durkheim used in his own studies, the 'data' about which he formulated his own theories, were firmer, more accurately observed, in some way more *concrete*, more *reputable* (scientifically speaking) in being empirically based and *objective*, than those used by his predecessors and others. With one exception (and an important exception)—this was not so. Durkheim's sources were in every way the same documentary sources as those used by others.* They consisted of legal codes, books of law, documents (books) of religious doctrine, the writings of historians, the reports of other social scientists, publicly provided statistics and government reports, and the like.

Thus, in *The Division of Labour* in addition to his continuous critical use of the familiar writings of Comte, Spencer, Mill, and

* See Evans-Pritchard: 'It is a fact, which none can deny, that the theoretical capital on which anthropologists today live is mainly the writings of people whose research was entirely literary.' This is with special reference to Durkheim and the French school. See: Introduction to 'Death and The Right Hand', Robert Hertz, 1960.

others, he critically used also the writings of men like Wundt, Weismann, Lombroso, Dumont, Topinard, Galton, Romanes, Perrier (not to mention Plato, Aristotle and Plutarch) on such matters as physiological psychology, genetics, heredity, population, criminality, race, and aspects of the relations between animal and human behaviour; and these are only a few names *representative* of the kind of work which he drew together. His study of ancient society was extensive, and he relied on Tacitus, for example, in discussing the structure of the German tribes, and Fustel de Coulanges for his account of the City States, but he also drew upon the studies of 'tribes' and 'confederations of tribes' provided by men like Morgan and Robertson Smith. His chief 'sources', however, were the legal codes of the ancient world as recorded in Rome, Greece, and—for the Hebrews—in the Bible (Durkheim referred, for example, to Exodus, Leviticus, Deuteronomy, etc.).

The fact is that *The Division of Labour in Society* is an analytical essay, constructing two 'types' of social solidarity, and drawing upon documentary sources substantially to do so. It is—with regard to the 'data' employed, the 'social facts' actually 'observed'—no different from the work of others. It is, indeed, exactly of the nature of Tönnies' essay on *Gemeinschaft und Gesellschaft*. This, let it be clear, is not to *denigrate* Durkheim's essay; it is only to say that the subject-matter employed is just the same.

Similarly, Durkheim's study of religion—*The Elementary Forms of the Religious Life*—was no more a face-to-face (in the sense of field-work) empirical study of social facts as 'things' than any of the studies we have so far considered. It focused chiefly upon the accounts provided by others of the tribal organization and religious practices of the Australian aborigines—particularly that provided by Spencer and Gillen; but this kind of work was incorporated into comparative and theoretical studies just as much by other scholars—like Hobhouse, for example; and even by Freud. Durkheim's scholarship was certainly admirable in its extent; he critically appraised all the leading theories of religion, and collated a vast amount of work; but all it is important to see is that his 'facts', his 'sources' were no different from those used by others. And, indeed, Durkheim's use of these facts could be said to be *more* selective, rather than less, than the use made of them by others (like Hobhouse) in their systematic comparative schemes. Certainly Westermarck was very much more empirical in the sense of seeking to observe social facts in the actuality of field studies than Durkheim ever was.

It is worthwhile to make the point, too, that Durkheim's studies were of the same *scale* as those of the other sociologists. It is sometimes thought that *they* produced vast theories in 'the grand manner' about the entire evolution of human society, whereas Durkheim produced definitive studies of specific social facts. We shall see that there is some truth in this, but not much. For Durkheim's 'specific social facts' were such as to entail grand manner theories about the entire nature and development of human society. Thus, *The Division of Labour* is an entire theory about the evolution of human society. The study of religion is such as to reinforce this same large theory— and to propose an entire sociology of knowledge and 'ideology' into the bargain. And even the study of 'Suicide'—than which nothing could seem more specific—was, really, a study attendant upon the others. The truth is that *all* Durkheim's studies were several facets illuminating one entire, large-scale theory of the nature and evolution of human society, and the stature of these studies was of the same order as the others we have considered. Durkheim certainly attacked the 'grand manner theorists', but his own manner shared an affinity with theirs. He was, so to speak, one king attacking others—not a proletarian brandishing a hay-fork.

However, I want to make the emphasis of this point *absolutely* clear. It is *not* to derogate the value of Durkheim's documentary sources, *nor* (at this stage) to criticize his theoretical treatment of them, *nor* to derogate the studies themselves. It is certainly *not* to derogate documentary sources as such, and to claim that empiricism in the form of a notebook and pencil in the streets is *superior* to the systematic, comparative studies which documentary sources permit. It is *certainly* not that! It is *only* to make it clear that Durkheim's 'raw-material' for his studies was the *same* as that of the other scholars we have considered. The talk of 'scientific study' of 'social facts as *things*' has led some to think that the facts collated to form the subject-matter of Durkheim's studies were sharply distinct from the facts collected by other scholars. But this is decidedly not so. Such a sharp distinction is a myth. Durkheim's work in the making of sociology was largely of the same nature as the work of others; it was part of the ongoing argument of the formation and development of the subject; his was not—on all counts—the completely distinctive *innovation*, or *new point of departure*, it has often been thought to be.

Here, however, we must mention the very important exception in which Durkheim was able to do much to justify the forcefulness of his theoretical position—whether or not it suffered from unwarranted extremes. This was his study of 'Suicide'. We shall come to the details of this later, but here it is enough to say that in *this* study, it can justifiably be claimed that Durkheim handled 'data' in his study of 'social facts' in a distinctive and impressive way; and in such a way as to demonstrate the validity of some of his concepts and rules. In this study, Durkheim did not only draw upon documentary sources. Indeed, even though he did draw upon publicly provided statistics, he did not simply take them in their existing form, but manipulated them and re-presented them in such a way as to move towards a really definitive study. This was truly an important contribution to the sharpening and development of sociological study: utilizing quantitative facts and the establishing of correlations between them in order to substantiate a qualitative theory about human behaviour in the context of specifiable social conditions. Here *facts* were certainly used in a much more specific way, in a definitive theoretical study, than had ever been the case before. Again, then, we have to conclude that, with all his continuity, Durkheim had a *difference*: and this difference contained real *worth*, whatever the errors into which (in its extremes) it might have fallen. We will come back to this mixture, even more deeply, later.

(b) *Durkeim's dogmatic 'Scientism' and prodigious scholarship clothed inaccuracies and logical errors against which we should be on our guard.*

This point, again, is not to decry Durkheim—though it is a matter of adverse comment—but to try to place him properly within a perspective of judgment. Because of Durkheim's incisive and dogmatic manner (as of a man very sure of himself), and his insistent proposals for scientific rigour and accuracy, the judgment has gained wide currency that the positions he proposed were correct, and that his logic and method were professionally impeccable, whereas those of the other men we have considered were imprecise and woolly—in fact 'philosophical'. One can only say of this judgment that it is in large part wrong. Indeed, it is a great pity that Durkheim himself did not possess the philosophical clarity of some of his predecessors and contemporaries; for it was he who was philosophically woolly—not they. One must never judge a man from his manner. A Hyde-Park orator may not *sound* woolly—with his polished, didactic manner (any more than a Member of Parliament in the Commons), even though his cerebral cortex is positively *made* of the stuff. The fact is that Durkheim's assertiveness provided a quick bridge to a good many chasms which were left yawning; so that many who have been borne quickly across them think they are closed.

We have said enough, for now, on some aspects of this. We have seen that—in the full spate of committed argument—many critical judgments were made of the positions of earlier sociologists which were insufficiently considered, to say the least. We have seen also that certain dimensions of social actuality and sociological explanation—e.g. the 'teleological' element—were ruled out of existence, without it being thought at all necessary to advance good grounds for this. We have seen, and shall see again, the almost unbelievable logical errors which Durkheim made in his assertions about 'ethics' and sociology. These need not be repeated now—but still it must be noted how pervasive the view has become that Durkheim was *correct* in all these matters. There are many contemporary sociologists who sneer at the work of the nineteenth-century scholars, and men like Westermarck and Hobhouse; who smile condescendingly at the outmoded error of 'teleological' explanation; because Durkheim, they think, demolished all that. And there are those who think that, with Durkheim, moral philosophy was put in its grave.

It is worthwhile, then, to say again, that such judgments are wrong—as well as being dangerous.

The further point which must be insisted on here is that a thing is not made any the more *scientific* or *accurate* only by being *called* so; but very frequently Durkheim *asserted* that certain elements of his thought were scientifically valid and accurate, and acceptable as such, when they were *not*.

Thus, to take one example, having dispensed with 'ethics' as such, but desiring to claim that sociology as a *science* could provide knowledge and guidance as to what social facts *ought* to be, Durkheim then asserted that social institutions which were found to be *normal* in society (i.e. found on the average in societies of that type) could be said to be *healthy* for society, whereas those which were *abnormal* (i.e. *not* found on the average in societies of that type) could be said to represent a condition of *morbidity* (were *pathological*). Health was good and desirable; disease was bad and to be avoided; and therefore this provided a scientific way of establishing a body of normative guidance—for the statesmen as well as the sociologist. It may be pointed out, too, that Durkheim inserted this decisive point in his argument in *one short paragraph*. Having, in short, demolished centuries of moral philosophy with a quite spurious logic, he set up his *own* ethic by sheer assertion in eight lines. And yet Durkheim then bowled along* with his 'scientific' argument as though all were nicely settled, firmly established, scientifically cut and dried—*precise* and *accurate*. To read Durkheim in some passages is enough to send one up through the ceiling in a puff of smoke! And yet there are those who—though it is beyond all belief!—read on through such stuff and *fail to* notice what is going on. There are those who cannot see this peculiar brand of French metaphysics when it hits them in both eyes like a sledgehammer! And *these* are the people who talk about the

---

* One is reminded of Elgar's comment to a friend when they were just about to listen to a Beecham performance on the radio (at Beecham's tempo) of one of his symphonies: "Ah well! . . . Here we damned well go!"

woolliness of Anglo-Saxon philosophy! There are times when one could positively embrace Henry Sidgwick!

Many such examples could be given, but again, in order to show that this is not just a personal bias, let us note the judgments of others. The most telling—and astonishing—is that of Rodney Needham who translated the essay by Durkheim and Mauss on 'Primitive Classification'. In his introduction, Needham claims that the argument of the two authors was 'clear, concise, and amply documented; but . . .'—and here our 'mixture' raises its head—'. . . in logic and method is open to serious criticism.' He gives, and substantiates, a great many examples of what we have called science and accuracy 'by assertion', and here it is enough only to mention a few of these to demonstrate this point. This essay was one in which Durkheim and his colleague wished to establish that the basic 'categories' of the human mind—of space, time, and other fundamental cosmological notions—were not innate in a Kantian sense, but were engendered (as 'collective representations') by social grouping. Stating their objective as being the demonstration of the fact 'that a classification of groups is prior to one by reference to nature', Needham shows that when describing the system of classification among the Omaha: 'even though they lack any *evidence* of changing modes of classification among the Omaha themselves, they *assume* that which they intend to establish.' And again, when they describe the congruence in another tribe between moieties, clans, and sub-clans and certain classificatory categories, Needham claims that the two authors:

'then assert that this is based on an evolutionary social progression in which moieties are the "oldest" social groupings and the clans the "more recent". Here again, they merely assume a course of development of which they have given no empirical proof, but which it is to the advantage of their thesis to suppose.'*

Needham goes on:

'This tendency to argument by *petitio principii* is more seriously expressed elsewhere in the essay, beginning with the very first example of classification which Durkheim and Mauss consider. They take a four-section scheme of social classification, by which all the members of a society are comprehensively and integrally categorized, and then abruptly assert that the congruent classification of non-social things 'reproduces'' the classification of people. This single word, that is, immediately assumes that which is to be proved by the subsequent argument, viz. the primacy of society in classification. Again, they claim that the astral mythology of certain

* *Primitive Classification*, Cohen & West, 1963, p. xiv.

301

Australian tribes is "moulded" by the totemic organization, when all that they have really shown is that stars are so part of a general classification that they may stand in definite relationships to social divisions. In these examples they do not merely assert an evolutionary development in social organization, from the simple to the complex, which makes their argument more plausible, but they expressly presuppose the very thesis of the argument itself.'*

Many other insufficiencies and inaccuracies are quoted, and then Needham, incorporating the criticism of Evans-Pritchard, comes to the most serious conclusion that the procedure of the two writers cannot really be said to be scientific at all, in the crucial sense of *testing* their theory.

'It is perhaps their most serious methodological failing,' he writes, 'that Durkheim and Mauss do not subject their thesis to test by concomitant variation. That is, they do not expressly look for societies with identical organization but different forms of classification, or for societies with different organization but similar classifications. Not only this, but when their own evidence presents them with such cases they do not recognize what consequences these must have for their argument. It is not simply that they ignore negative instances, the charge which Evans-Pritchard has laid against the *Année Sociologique* school in general, but that when they do identify such instances they try to explain them away by what he has justly described as Durkheim's irritating manoeuvre, when a fact contradicts his thesis, of asserting that its character and meaning have altered, that it is a secondary development and atypical, although there is no evidence whatsoever that such changes have actually taken place.'†

The criticisms go further. It is found that in a number of cases the authors: 'do not supply any evidence at all for statements which they make, or the evidence is contrary to their argument'. With regard to their claim that the 'emotional value' of ideas is the dominant characteristic in classification, Needham writes:

'This is a profoundly important assertion about a fundamental feature of all human thought, and few propositions could be of more consequence; yet it has to be realized that this factor of emotion is abruptly and gratuitously introduced in this sense only at the end of the paper, and that nowhere in the course of their argument do the authors report the slightest empirical evidence, from any society of any form, which might justify their statement.'‡

Even this is not the end.

'Yet,' Needham continues, 'all such particular objections of logic and

* * *

* *Primitive Classification*, pp. xiv–xv. † *Ibid.*, pp. xvi–xvii.
‡ *Ibid.*, p. xxii.

method fade in significance before two criticisms which apply generally to the entire argument. One is that there is no logical necessity to postulate a causal connexion between society and symbolic classification, and in the absence of factual indications to this effect there are no grounds for attempting to do so . . . If we allow ourselves to be guided by the facts themselves, we have to conclude that there are no empirical grounds for a causal explanation. In no single case is there any compulsion to believe that the society is the cause or even the model of the classification; and it is only the strength of their preoccupation with cause that leads Durkheim and Mauss to cast their argument and present the facts as though this were the case.'*

We see again the prevalent tendency in all Durkheim's work for his desire to present a forceful argument to run away with him to the extent of *asserting* his 'scientific' grounds and procedures rather than thinking it necessary to *produce* them. Needham also found it necessary to comment on:

'. . . the surprising extent to which Durkheim and Mauss lapse from the conventional requirements of scholarly publication. Disregarding recognizable abbreviations of titles, and the simple omission of author's name, initials, or place of publication, there are no fewer than sixty-nine bibliographical errors, many of which definitely mislead a student seeking the sources of information used in the essay. To be particular, these comprise five instances in which the name of the author is misrendered (including one extreme case in which an article is attributed to a quite different person than the actual writer); twelve in which the title is substantially inaccurate; fifteen in which the year is incorrect; and thirty-seven wrong page-references. There are also more than a dozen mis-spellings of names of persons, places and things in the text. More seriously, there are a number of places at which Durkheim and Mauss misrender their sources, and at one point they cite a non-existent publication.'†

This is, as Needham puts it, a 'rather dejecting catalogue'; but all this is enough to demonstrate our point that—for someone who insisted on *scientific* procedure and *accuracy* of method, as Durkheim continually did—this is not a very prepossessing record. Other judgments of the same kind could be introduced—and always (as, indeed, is the case with Needham) from scholars who are fully alive to the value and influence of Durkheim's work *despite* these errors, not, by any means, by opponents; but our point is sufficiently made.

We must not conclude, then, that Durkheim was more scientific and exact than his predecessors (and those contemporaries who followed more carefully in their tradition) simply because he *said* so. In fact, in many respects, he most emphatically was *not*.

* *Primitive Classification*, pp. xxiv–xxv.   † *Ibid.*, pp. xlvi–xlvii.

In some respects he was far less exact, and less logically consistent than they. To accept the view that Durkheim stood out with sharp distinction from all the others who were involved in the making of sociology, as one who, at last, produced the definitive basis for sociology as a science, is therefore to make a false judgment. And to discard many elements of the careful thought of others as being outmoded because of this new basis is to set aside and cease to consider profound and essential dimensions of the subject.

(c) *Durkheim's inconsistencies in dealing with elements of 'Ethics' and 'Teleology' were very considerable—and intruded upon his 'scientific' conceptions and methods.*

We have seen already that Durkheim's rejection of philosophical ethics and of the necessity to recognize a 'teleological' element in human association and any satisfactory explanation of it was based on logical confusion and never supported by adequate grounds. We have also—though briefly—seen that he asserted his own ethic, his own normative dimensions, under the guise of concepts supposedly scientific. It is necessary now to note further that Durkheim was continuously inconsistent in these respects—and to such an extent as to belie the conceptual grounds of his own system of explanation. Here again we will do no more than note a few examples—but, nonetheless, examples which will indicate the very considerable importance of this point.

When ruling 'teleological' elements of *fact* and *explanation* out of his own method of explaining social facts, Durkheim wrote:

'Where purpose reigns, there reigns also a more or less wide contingency; for there are no ends, and even fewer means, which necessarily control all men, even when it is assumed that they are placed in the same circumstances. Given the same environment, each individual adapts himself to it according to his own disposition and in his own way, which he prefers to all other ways . . . If historic development took place in terms of ends clearly or obscurely felt, social facts should present the most infinite diversity; and all comparison should be almost impossible.

But when one comes in contact with social phenomena, one is, on the contrary, surprised by the astonishing regularity with which they occur under the same circumstances. Even the most minute and the most trivial practices recur with the most astonishing uniformity. A certain nuptial ceremony, purely symbolical in appearance, such as the carrying-off of the betrothed, is found to be exactly the same wherever a certain family type exists; and again this family type itself is linked to a whole social organization . . . This wide diffusion of collective forms would be inexplicable if purpose or final causes had the predominant place in sociology that is attributed to them,'*

* *Rules*, pp. 94–5.

On this basis, Durkheim then insisted that social facts should be explained in terms of *efficient* causes and their *functions*, not in terms of purposes at all. And this, he argued: 'precisely because social phenomena do not generally exist for the useful results they produce'.

When we come to consider Durkheim's account of 'Crime' as a social fact, however, we find—astonishingly—that its existence is explained in terms of the *purpose* which it fulfils within the wider *purposes* of society, which includes the flexible *purposes* of individuals, and is part of that flexibility of society and the tempering of its moral authority which is necessary to ensure *progress*. And crime is found to be *useful* in the securing of these conditions for 'normal evolution'. Crime in society, wrote Durkheim:

'. . . is necessary; it is bound up with the fundamental conditions of all social life, and by that very fact it is useful, because these conditions of which it is a part are themselves indispensable to the normal evolution of morality and law.'*

Let us note that this social fact is said to be *useful* because (among other attendant facts) it results in conditions indispensable to the 'normal evolution of morality and law'. Its utility is related, if not to a 'final end' at least to an implicit purposive trend in society. And if this is thought to be interpreting Durkheim harshly, let us see how his argument continued. With regard to this 'normal evolution', he argued:

'. . . *in order that* these transformations may be possible, the collective sentiments at the basis of morality *must not be hostile to change*, and consequently *must have but moderate energy*. If they were too strong, they would no longer be plastic. Every pattern is an obstacle to new patterns, to the extent that the first pattern is inflexible. The better a structure is articulated, the more it offers a healthy resistance to all modification; and this is equally true of functional, as of anatomical, organization. If there were no crimes, this condition could not have been fulfilled; for such a hypothesis presupposes that collective sentiments have arrived at a degree of intensity unexampled in history. *Nothing is good indefinitely and to an unlimited extent.* The authority which the moral conscience enjoys *must not be excessive*; otherwise no one would dare criticize it, and it would too easily congeal into an immutable form. To make progress, *individual originality must be able to express itself*. In order that the originality of the idealist whose dreams transcend his century may find expression, it is necessary that the originality of the criminal, who is below the level of his time, shall also be possible. One does not occur without the other.'*

* *Rules*, p. 70. † *Ibid.*, pp. 70–1. My italics.

In this passage it is perfectly clear that Durkheim was, incredible though it seems, doing no more than postulating the conditions of individual, institutional and ideological *flexibility* which society *must* have *in order* that its transformations, its 'normal evolution' may be possible. And even the expression of individual originality must be catered for—'to make progress'! It can be seen here, too, how Durkheim vacillated in his arguments. When 'purpose' is to be eliminated from society and any explanation of it, then the *uniformity* of society is emphasized in the most meticulous details of social behaviour, but when crime has to be explained as fulfilling a useful function in society, then all the institutions of society *must* be *flexible*; *must* only have *moderate energy*; and even individual originality comes into its own again!

The simple truth is that 'purpose' was shown out of one door and brought back through another—but now with a 'scientific' hood over its head and the label of 'function' across its chest. But this is not *science*. It is an obscurantist pretence of spurious exactitude. And it is this which has introduced into the endless and worthless debates of the past 25 years all the wrangles about 'functions' and their hidden 'teleological' elements, and the like. It is Durkheim's inconsistencies, and many people's acceptance of them at their 'scientific' face value, which lies at the heart of all this.

The best example, however—because it is an example central to his whole work—of the complete and utter tangle of inconsistency into which Durkheim's dogmatism on ethics and teleology drove him, is to be found in his discussion of the *Division of Labour* and the nature of 'social solidarity'. Our illustrations of his inconsistencies here must be impossibly limited—because strictly speaking, Durkheim's *entire work* was the study of 'social solidarity'. Indeed, his entire work would not be falsely characterized if we were to call it the statement of an 'ethic of social solidarity'. Almost every page that he wrote referred to this central issue—and therefore we can do no more than *indicate* by our small points a really vast and intricate tangle: but a tangle about which we must become clear, if we are to become clear in our assessments of what has gone into the making of sociology.

We can begin by noting that Durkheim's focus of concern was exactly that of all the earlier sociologists from Comte onwards: it was the concern with the fact that the vast, complex, highly specialized, rapidly changing processes of industrial capitalism had disrupted and made completely outmoded the old orders of traditional societies, without assuming a satisfactory order of its own. Mankind was adrift, dragged along, so to speak, behind a Juggernaut which he could not control, and Durkheim, like all his predecessors, was centrally concerned with the task of social reconstruction. And for the making of modern society, the making of sociology was necessary. Durkheim's central aim was to provide an understanding of society on the basis of which a new 'social solidarity' could be achieved which was appropriate to the new complexity of economic and social conditions. He was deeply concerned, deeply distressed, about the unrest, the instability, the insecurity, the lack of firm beliefs, the lack of a settled morality, the 'anomie'—or general 'normlessness' which attended the lack of fit between many institutions in this modern situation; and he wished to resolve these problems.

Now all this was completely within the tradition we have traced so clearly among the earlier writers, and was completely justifiable, and, indeed, laudable in terms of intellectual appraisal and humane commitment. But let us see the strange tangle of concepts into which Durkheim's system landed him in trying to come to terms with these problems in strict accordance with his own dogmas.

We may note also, secondly, that Durkheim argued, in dispensing with ethics, that social facts were to be considered 'normal', 'healthy', and 'good', if they were found on the average in societies of the same type and at the same phase of evolution, and 'pathological', 'morbid', and 'bad', if they were abnormal in this sense. The role of the statesman was not to strive for political reform in the light of ethical ideals, but to seek to keep society in a condition of 'normal health'. We have seen, too, that, according to Durkheim, 'social facts' existed in their own right, adjusted themselves to each other in accordance with the conditions within which society as a whole was placed, and that it was an error and futile to seek to understand and explain these processes of social facts in terms of purpose.

But now let us look at the curious position in which Durkheim's conception placed him.

In the *Division of Labour* he argued that, in the evolution of societies, a very simple division of labour in society, concomitant with a social solidarity resting chiefly upon a strong traditional authority (resting upon repressive law), gave way to a much more highly differentiated division of labour in which the social solidarity was a concomitant of the division of labour *itself* (resting upon restitutive law)—which was the real basis of the moral bond in society. Let us note that, strictly speaking, this was a two-fold *typology* (like that of Tönnies): a construction of a 'mechanical' type and an 'organic' type of social differentiation and social solidarity in the light of which specific changes could be interpreted; but Durkheim did give much comparative illustration of these kinds of division of labour among his various kinds of 'social species', and we must remember than any conception of the '*normal*' division of labour in a society was, according to him, that which was found on the average in that social species and at that particular phase of evolution. 'Social solidarity' and its appropriate division of labour at a particular level of social evolution was therefore 'normal', 'healthy', and 'good'.

But let us note, now, a rather odd reinterpretation of the term 'normal' which is made the basis of analysing 'pathological' conditions of the division of labour at the end of Durkheim's study. Strictly speaking, Durkheim's position is that the normality and health of a social fact is established solely by its being found on the average in all societies of its type and at that particular stage of evolution. If he has shown that, in many societies, different kinds of division of labour are concomitant with different kinds of social solidarity—all well and good. But if he then finds, on comparing all societies at the phase of evolution of industrial capitalism, that the division of labour exhibits an extraordinary degree of specialization which is concomitant with a highly mobile, flexible change among many institutions which leaves them disconnected and ill-fitting, and both they and the individuals among them insecure, restless, anxious, pulled by hectic motives of material gain, status-emulation, and the like—then his conclusion should be that *this* is the '*normal*' condition of the division of labour, and that social *instability* (*not* now social *solidarity*) is found 'on the average' in societies of this type and at this phase of evolution. As the 'normal' condition of this 'social fact' in this type of society, it should be held (by both sociologist and statesman) that 'instability' is the 'healthy' condition of this society—'good' and 'desirable'; and the statesman's task should be to keep it in this condition of 'normal health'. But is this what Durkheim thought?

Well—he certainly did recognize that this was the 'normal' condition of societies characterized by industrial capitalism.

'*There*', he wrote, and this must be noted very carefully, '*the state of crisis and anomie is constant and, so to speak, normal.*'

But did Durkheim then accept that this was a condition of *health*—good, and desirable—for modern society? Curiously—no! Indeed, he was anguished about this '*normal social fact*' which he had discovered in his comparative study of modern industrial societies. Furthermore, he was not just disturbed about this social fact as a thing in its own right, but for the consequences for its 'individual manifestations'. He wrote, for example, about the social 'anomie' which he had discovered to be 'normal':

'From top to bottom of the ladder, greed is aroused without knowing where to find ultimate foothold. Nothing can calm it, since its goal is far beyond all it can attain. Reality seems valueless by comparison with the dreams of fevered imaginations; reality is therefore abandoned, but so too is possibility abandoned when it in turn becomes reality. A thirst arises for novelties, unfamiliar pleasures, nameless sensations, all of which lose their savour once known. Henceforth one has no strength to endure the least reverse. The whole fever subsides and the sterility of all the tumult is apparent, and it is seen that all these new sensations in their infinite quantity cannot form a solid foundation of happiness to support one during days of trial. The wise man, knowing how to enjoy achieved results without having constantly to replace them with others, finds in them an attachment to life in the hour of difficulty. But the man who has always pinned all his hopes on the future and lived with his eyes fixed upon it, has nothing in the past as a comfort against the present's afflictions, for the past was nothing to him but a series of hastily experienced stages. What blinded him to himself was his expectation always to find further on the happiness he had so far missed. Now he is stopped in his tracks; from now on nothing remains behind or ahead of him to fix his gaze upon. Weariness alone, moreover, is enough to bring disillusionment, for he cannot in the end escape the futility of an endless pursuit.'*

This is hardly the recognition of a 'healthy' state of affairs; even though it was a 'normal' social fact. But then we notice Durkheim's change of argument. Instead of adhering to the concept of the 'normal' we have noted so far, he then changed to the argument that since the division of labour had 'produced' social solidarity in all the societies studied so far, that should be taken as its 'normal function'. We can then say that it is pathological in a society if it produces something else. This, it can be seen, is a complete inconsistency, for it is specifying as *abnormal* in one type of society a social fact which is found to be *normal* in that type of society, simply on the assertion that its nature in all *other* types of society establishes its *normal function*.

But let us note further that to assert that it is the *normal function* established in societies which have emerged so far which is *healthy, good, desirable*; and that any new *normal* social fact, in new social conditions, must be considered *abnormal, pathological*, and to be *avoided* in terms of this assertion; and that the object of the statesman should be to avoid the new 'pathological' condition and preserve this earlier 'normal, healthy' function; is to construct a vast intellectual, ethical, ideological, and political apparatus of conservatism! And a conservatism which walks in the mummer's robes of science!

* *Suicide*, Routledge and Kegan Paul, 1952, p. 256.

It must be insisted, too, before proceeding with this, that this inconsistency in the use of the term 'normal' is a very grave methodological flaw which Durkheim introduced into his comments and studies on many social facts and is a source of the gravest errors. It was also prominent in his study of religion especially. But we must return to our demonstration of these very important critical points.

'Though *normally* the division of labour *produces* social solidarity,' Durkheim wrote, 'it sometimes happens that it has different, and even contrary results. It is important to find out what makes it deviate from its *natural* course . . . The study of these devious forms will permit us to determine the conditions of existence of the normal state better. When we know the circumstances in which the division of labour ceases to bring forth solidarity, we shall better understand what is necessary for it to have that effect.'*

It is worth noting, as a quite important additional point here, Durkheim's introduction of the word 'natural'. In many places, he spoke of a social fact being *'denatured'* if the function which it appeared to have in certain societies became transformed in later and more complex changes; but this is a very odd notion if social facts and their functions are *differently* normal in *different* 'social species'. The word 'natural' seems arbitrary here, to say the least; simply being used to lend strength to *particular* social facts as the argument requires. Elsewhere, incidentally, Durkheim used similar terms which carried a moral connotation. Thus he not only spoke of the 'denaturing' of social facts, but also the 'debasement' of human nature. Ethical as well as intellectual presuppositions of *judgment* were written into these supposedly scientific classifications of facts.

It was also part and parcel of Durkheim's account of the evolution of the division of labour that the strength of the early kind of 'collective conscience' (connected with strong traditional authority) became enfeebled, as a more complex and rational moral consensus came with greater differentiation in society. This, too, therefore was 'normal'. It could not therefore be used to explain the supposed 'abnormality' of the 'normality' of 'anomie'! Durkheim wrote:

'But since we have shown that the enfeeblement of the collective conscience is a normal phenomenon, we cannot consider it as the cause of the abnormal phenomena that we are studying. If, in certain cases, organic solidarity is not all it should be, it is certainly not because mechanical solidarity has lost ground, but because all the conditions for the existence of organic solidarity have not been realized.'†

* *Division of Labour*, p. 353.   † *Ibid.*, pp. 364–5.

In short, Durkheim explained the 'abnormality' of the actual 'normality' of the relations between the complex division of labour and social instability by the simple expedient of asserting that, in modern industrial-capitalist societies, the course towards a new social solidarity was not yet completed. The 'conditions of equilibrium' had not yet been arrived at. The many conflicting interests in society had 'not yet had the time to be equilibrated'. Analytically, Durkheim had no doubt that the disequilibrium-equilibrium processes were at work. Why? Because 'social facts' as 'things' in 'social systems' *did* establish new equilibrium situations; and since the 'normal function' of the division of labour in society *was* to 'produce social solidarity'—social solidarity it *would* produce: given time for equilibration*—and this, despite the finding that all the *facts* demonstrated that *anomie* was *normal* in these societies.

However, we must now come to see—bearing in mind all we have said about 'teleology' and ethics—that, despite his analytical system, Durkheim was by no means confident that 'social facts' *would* move on towards a successful equilibrium; not—that is—without a good deal of *purpose, ethical direction*, and strenuous *effort*. And we must note again some of his very considerable inconsistencies and sheer assertive assumptions in both ethical and theoretical matters.

Commenting again on the 'unstable equilibrium' of the 'anomic state' of industrial society, Durkheim wrote in his preface to the second edition of *The Division of Labour*:

'That such anarchy is an unhealthy phenomenon is quite evident, since it runs counter to the aim of society, which is to suppress, or at least to moderate, war among men, subordinating the law of the strongest to a higher law.'†

We now find not only that the 'normal' condition of the division of labour in these societies is *unhealthy*, but also that society has *'an aim'*. But that is not all. Society is not only surprisingly 'teleological', but also surprisingly ethical, for it turns out that it has *duties* as well as *aims*. Attacking the defence of the freedom of economic enterprise and its social corollaries, Durkheim went on:

'To justify this chaotic state, we vainly praise its encouragement of individual liberty. Nothing is falser than this antagonism too often presented between legal authority and individual liberty. Quite on the contrary, liberty (we mean genuine liberty, which it is *society's duty* to have respected) is itself the produce of regulation.'‡

* It will be seen here, at least a little, how Durkheim far out-Spencer'd Herbert Spencer in dogmatizing on the mechanisms of adjustment that super-organic entities got up to!
† *Division of Labour*, p. 3.   ‡ *Ibid.*, p. 3.

Again, we must make it clear that we are not considering the truth or falsity of any argument about the relations between liberty and authority here—we are only demonstrating Durkheim's *inconsistency*.

The simple truth is that Durkheim believed that 'society' had *failed* to accommodate all its institutions to the new economic conditions and relationships, and his entire effort of argument was to the end that something purposive and effective should be done about it —in order to remedy and correct the existing social chaos. In the 'organic' type of division of labour, it was the industrial 'corporation' that was the basis of the moral consensus and solidarity of social life. It was needed—with the rise of great industry and the large-scale contractual relations of commerce—not because of its economic functions:

'. . . but because of the *moral influence* it can have. What we especially see in the occupational group is a *moral power* capable of containing individual egos, of maintaining a spirited sentiment of common solidarity in the consciousness of all the workers, of preventing the law of the strongest from being brutally applied to industrial and commercial relations.'*

But, though these industrial corporations were '*needed*', 'society'— the interdependent set of 'social facts' as 'things' with their functional adjustments—had somehow failed to develop them. Indeed, it had 'discarded' them. The old corporation, Durkheim wrote:

'. . . had to be transformed to continue to fill its role in the new conditions of economic life. Unfortunately, it had not enough suppleness to be reformed in time; that is why it was discarded. Because it did not know how to assimilate itself to the new life which was evolving, it was divorced from that life, and, in this way, it became what it was upon the eve of the Revolution, a sort of dead substance, a strange body which could maintain itself in the social organism only through inertia. It is then not surprising that a moment came when it was violently expelled. But to destroy it was not a means of giving satisfaction to the needs it had not satisfied. And that is the reason the question still remains with us, and has become still more acute after a century of groping and fruitless experience.'†

'Society' had failed. It was necessary, then, that men should act *purposefully* to *reconstitute* industrial corporations in order to re-suscitate the moral life and the social solidarity of society, and, in fact, Durkheim laid down proposals for this task for the guidance of statesmen.

---

* *Division of Labour*, p. 10.   † *Ibid.*, p. 23.

'The absence of all corporative institution', he 'wrote, 'creates, in the organization of a people like ours, a void whose importance it is difficult to exaggerate. It is a whole system of organs necessary in the normal functioning of the common life which is wanting. Such a constitutive lack is evidently not a local evil, limited to a region of society; it is a malady *totius substantiae*, affecting all the organism. Consequently, the attempt to put an end to it cannot fail to produce the most far-reaching consequences. It is the general health of the social body which is here at stake.'*

We need not note here the detailed nature of the 'corporation' which Durkheim prescribed; it is enough, at this stage, simply to note that this was a programme of purposive reform, and, furthermore, that it had powerful ethical motives at its root. Indeed, it was not enough for Durkheim that such a programme should be attempted in a piecemeal way. '*Justice*,' he wrote, '*must prevail*' throughout the entire network of contractual relationships.

'For the obligatory force of a contract to be complete,' he wrote, 'it is not sufficient that it be the object of an expressed assent. It is still necessary for it to be *just*, and it is not just by virtue of mere verbal consent.'

And again:

'It is not enough that there be rules; they must be *just* . . .' and for this, there must be 'absolute equality in the external conditions of the conflict'.

Now this is surely ethical declamation indeed.

'The ideal of human fraternity', Durkheim stated, 'can be realized only in proportion to the progress of the division of labor. We must choose: either to renounce our dream, if we refuse further to circumscribe our activity, or else to push forward its accomplishment under the conditions we have just set forth.'†

And it is surely as 'teleological' as any position in the literature of sociology. But let us note also some very strange quirks of dogmatism in Durkheim's assertions about ethics. It is curious to find, for example, that he could only regard as a 'moral' action, one which *would* contribute to social solidarity! Any action which disturbed it could not be called such.

'It is, indeed, impossible', he wrote, 'to regard some practices as moral

* *Division of Labour*, p. 29.　　　† *Ibid.*, p. 406.

313

which would be subversive of the societies observing them, for it is a fundamental duty everywhere to assure the existence of the fatherland.'*

This sounds remarkably like Hegel peering across the French frontier! And it gives good ground for our earlier suggestion that Durkheim's work was really, at bottom, an ethic of social solidarity. It was the social condition against which all other things were judged. But Durkheim also even made it a matter of absolute principle to defend the relativity of ethics to the death.

'Moral rules,' he wrote, 'are moral only in relation to certain experimental conditions; and, consequently, the nature of moral phenomena cannot be understood if the conditions on which they are dependent are not determined. Possibly, there is an eternal law of morality, written by some transcendental power, or perhaps immanent in the nature of things, and perhaps historical morality is only a series of successive approximations; but this is a metaphysical hypothesis that we do not have to discuss. But, in any case, this morality is relative to a certain state of humanity, and as long as this state is not realized, not only will it not be obligatory for healthy consciences, but it will even be our duty to fight against it.'†

Another ethical duty for the sociologist!

Given the urgent need for the reconstitution of the industrial corporation: 'How ... important it is', said Durkheim, 'to put ourselves at once to work establishing the moral forces which alone can determine its realization!' And he concluded:

'The task of the most advanced societies is, then, a work of justice. That they, in fact, feel the necessity of orienting themselves in this direction is what we have already shown and what every-day experience proves to us. Just as the ideal of lower societies was to create or maintain as intense a common life as possible, in which the individual was absorbed, so our ideal is to make social relations always more equitable, so as to assure the free development of all our socially useful forces.'‡

This, surely, might well have been Hobhouse speaking—but without such a broken, tangled trail of bad logic behind him!

Many other such examples could be given; one which is particularly interesting and important being Durkheim's very over-simplified treatment of education (especially moral education) and its place in society; but we have seen enough for the establishment of our point: that Durkheim's inconsistencies connected with his rejection of teleological dimensions and his confusions about ethics were very grave indeed, and such as to throw confusion and ambiguity into his

* *Division of Labour*, p. 423.   † *Ibid.*, pp. 423–4.   ‡ *Ibid.*, p. 387.

very apparatus of concepts and scientific explanation. In many areas of his work, then, Durkheim's 'science' was there only in *name*, rather than *fact*.

(*d*) *Durkheim's extreme reification of Society as an Organism.* It has been a long-standing criticism of the earlier sociologists that— by the false use of what was an analogy only—they conceived of 'society' as an actual organic entity, over and above the heads of all the individual members of it; a 'super-organic' entity whose parts blended, were differentiated, were integrated, were adjusted, etc. at their own level, in relation to environmental conditions; almost like a great leviathan that had a life of its own. We have seen, however, that this criticism is almost entirely unfounded with regard to all the men we have studied so far. It is true that, in their own (but very similar) ways, all these men used the *analogy* between a society and an organism—but, and even with the extreme of Spencer, they were quite well aware of what they were doing. We say *almost* entirely un-founded, because it is plausible to say that Spencer, particularly, did take the analogy to extremes which were perhaps unnecessary, and which gave a false impression to careless readers.* But this slight exception aside—and it was not seriously damaging even to him— we have seen that this criticism was quite unfounded. The nineteenth-century founders of the subject used the analogy to try to make clear what they meant by the interdependency of institutions in the organizational structure of society as a whole; what they had in mind when speaking of the kind of 'consensus' which they thought existed among social institutions in any total society; and they certainly wished to emphasize the ways in which—out of the conflict-ing and co-operating activities of men in the pursuit of their many interests—consequences were brought about in the interconnected changes in institutions which were unforeseen by individuals and groups. They wished, very much, to insist upon this *institutional level* of organization within which the associational activities of men were ordered, regulated, patterned, constrained. But they were very careful to guard against the error of *reification*. They warned against con-ceiving 'institutions' as 'entities' which were actively involved in cause-and-effect relations among each other at a level *independent* of the members of society. Social forms—clear certainly; permitting of description and analysis as forms of organization—were, nonethe-less, not *entities* having a nature and life of their own, independent of the *activities of people*. About this—and perhaps Mill was the best and most articulate example—all these earlier thinkers were quite clear.

* Who are always the majority, and easily selective according to false fashions.

The fact is—and curiously, again, despite all his supposed accuracy of conceptualization—it was in the work of Durkheim that this error was substantially committed. It is in relation to *his* work especially that the criticism has validity. And again, the extent to which Durkheim committed this error must be made clear, *not* for the sake of demolishing or discarding all his conceptions concerning the nature of society, but for the sake of disentangling the elements of real worth which they contain. And for this, we must look more closely at his conception of 'social facts' as 'things'.

We have already seen that Durkheim's insistence was that *association* in human experience and behaviour was not *sterile* (simply being an additive sum of previously existing individual consciousnesses) but *creative*. *Association* (and all the qualities which came into being with it) was not something concocted by individual intention—and from individual minds which previously possessed all the qualities to be found in association; it was *always a primal fact of human nature*. Human nature was cradled in *association*; there is no evidence that it was ever otherwise; and individuality itself took shape within this context of collective qualities of feeling, thinking, acting, speaking, etc; which were *essentially* and *naturally* associational. Durkheim was concerned therefore to put this order of assumptions right, to establish that individuals could only be understood within their associational milieu, and to demonstrate beyond all doubt that it was an *error* to think that this milieu itself could be explained in terms of the pre-associational qualities of individual minds. He wished to make clear the *associational level* which was operative in creating the essential and distinguishing features of human nature.

Much of his argument—to which we shall return more positively later—accomplished this successfully, and in a very telling manner, but in his zeal to establish his particular perspective for explanation, he went to conceptual extremes which seem unwarranted. And it is useful, perhaps quite crucial, to point out that when speaking of 'social facts', Durkheim never really distinguished any varieties of these. It is clear, for example, that—let us say—the books, documents, and codes of law are one important set of facts in any legal system; the actual organization of procedure in the courts, the structure of administration within the entire profession of the law, including its relation to the government and other sources of authority in society, comprise another; and there are also all the collective 'sentiments' which the members of society feel in relation to (and in the context of) this associational structure of the law. Now these differing kinds of 'social facts' are clearly '*observed*' in quite different ways: in one case the observer is reading documents; in another watching sequences of behaviour and ritualized procedures; in the third, somehow trying to uncover the constellations of symbols, feeling, thinking, meaning, etc, which hold force in people's minds. But Durkheim did not differentiate at all: he simply spoke of 'social facts' as having a real objective existence (to be treated as 'things'); and within this large category he included the entire range of 'associational' phenomena—from political and legal structures to rates of suicide. The point I am really trying to get at here is that when Durkheim spoke of treating social facts as 'things' he always had in mind 'socio-psychological entities' (collective representations, collective consciousnesses); he wished above all to show that these could not be explained in terms of any preceding individualism—that they were something more than, and other than, individuals; and it was in over-reaching his argument in this direction that his error lay.

Two points were very striking in his discussion about the nature of social facts; both of which possessed truth and value up to a point, but were false when taken to extremes. The first was his argument that what emerged in the processes of association were facts of a new order which only resided in that order, and not in the individual units as they were when they originally combined. In this, it seems to me that Durkheim committed completely the error of the 'chemical compound' method as criticized by Mill. But this error was reinforced by his second point that these new facts, at this new associational level, existed independent of their individual manifestations. There is something of importance to be said for both these points, but in the way that Durkheim proposed them and used them, they are false.

On the first of these points, Durkheim argued as follows:

'What is so readily judged inadmissible in the matter of social facts is freely admitted in the other realms of nature. Whenever certain elements combine and thereby produce, by the fact of their combination, new phenomena, it is plain that these new phenomena reside not in the original elements but in the totality formed by their union. The living cell contains nothing but mineral particles, as society contains nothing but individuals. Yet it is patently impossible for the phenomena characteristic of life to reside in the atoms of hydrogen, oxygen, carbon, and nitrogen . . . Life could not be thus separated into discrete parts; it is a unit, and consequently its substratum can be only the living substance in its totality and not the element parts of which it is composed. The inanimate particles of the cell do not assimilate food, reproduce, and, in a word, live; only the cell itself as a unit can achieve these functions.

What we say of life could be repeated for all possible compounds. The hardness of bronze is not in the copper, the tin, or the lead, which are its ingredients and which are soft and malleable bodies; it is in their mixture. The fluidity of water and its nutritional and other properties are not to be found in the two gases of which it is composed but in the complex substance which they form by their association.

Let us apply this principle to sociology. If, as we may say, this synthesis constituting every society yields new phenomena, differing from those which take place in individual consciousnesses, we must, indeed, admit that these facts reside exclusively in the very society itself which produces them, and not in its parts, i.e. its members. They are, then, in this sense, external to individual consciousnesses, considered as such, just as the distinctive characteristics of life are external to the mineral substances composing the living being. These new phenomena cannot be reduced to their elements without contradiction in terms, since, by definition, they presuppose something different from the properties of these elements. Thus we have a new justification for the separation which we have established between psychology, which is properly the science of the mind of the individual, and sociology.'*

Now this is as clear a statement of what Mill castigated as the 'chemical-compound' conception of social facts as any in the sociological literature. It could not have been set up more succinctly as a target for Mill's attack if Durkheim had never read Mill (which he had!). Let us note a number of points about it. Firstly, let us note clearly the dichotomy that Durkheim drew between psychology and sociology: it was the sharp distinction that psychology dealt with *the mind of the individual*, whilst sociology dealt with the *socio-psychological facts of human association*. Durkheim was very emphatic about this:

'Social facts do not differ from psychological facts in quality only: *they have a different substratum*; they evolve in a different milieu; and they depend on different conditions. This does not mean that they are not also mental after a fashion, since they all consist of ways of thinking or behaving. But the states of the collective consciousness are different in nature from the states of the individual consciousness; they are "representations" of another type. The mentality of groups is not the same as that of individuals; it has its own laws. The two sciences are thus as clearly distinct as two sciences can be, whatever relationships there may otherwise be between them.'†

But we must note again (a) that social facts were held to be of a psychological nature—but of human beings *in association*, not in *isolation*, and (b) that this distinction between the two sciences is only one in terms of Durkheim's own assertion—and, furthermore, is obviously an insupportable one. For, on the one hand, if individuals come to have their qualities and attributes in the context of association, the psychologist (even if studying the individual mind) must

* *Rules*, pp. xlvii, xlv, xlix. † *Ibid.*, p. xlix.

take account of these socio-psychological processes. He must be a social-psychologist in order to be a good student of individuals. But also, on the other hand, why should he *not* be? Why should psychology—by definition—be said to be confined to the study of the individual mind? There is no reason at all other than Durkheim's assertion, and, as we have seen especially in Mill, formulations of psychology, sociology, and social psychology had been produced which avoided this sharp and unrealistic dichotomy.

But three other points are more important.

The first is that Durkheim quite clearly took the processes of *'association'* to be qualitatively *the same* at the chemical, bio-chemical, and human psycho-social levels—which was exactly what Mill argued should not be done without critical thought. To say that 'compounds' of chemical elements manifest, in their 'compound-totality' qualities (kinds of facts) which the elements themselves do not possess, is not, in itself, a substantiation of the proposition that human individuals are compounded into qualitatively new kinds of facts in society. Men in association are qualitatively different from chemical elements in a kind of synthesis. The second point, following upon this, is that though it is undoubtedly true that human beings experience elements of 'group consciousness'—ideals, motives, linguistic expressions, and a thousand and one other impressions, conceptions, and modes of behaviour which are engendered in them as an outcome of association; it by no means follows that these socio-psychological facts have a realm of existence *independent of them*. It is true that the creative processes of association produce qualities of group (collective) consciousness within which individualities are different (to some extent) from what they were before; but, even so, they are still individualities, and remain the ground of existence of the collective *socio-psychological* phenomena. It is of significance to notice that Durkheim said that the 'new phenomena reside not in the *original* elements but in the totality formed by their union'; but, of course, in the case of human beings in the process of association, though the *individualities* remain, they are not the *original* individualities (as an element of carbon might be), but individualities which are now *transformed* (to some extent.) But they remain individualities for all that, and—what is the important point—they themselves, as transformed individualities, are the only actual grounds of existence of the new *socio-psychological* facts. There is none other! And this leads to the third point—which incorporates both our earlier indication that Durkheim failed to differentiate between kinds of social facts, and our much earlier criticism that he left completely out of account any 'teleological' components. It is this: that though, in the process of association, there is a creation of a new objective apparatus of social

319

organization and ordered social life—libraries, languages, law-courts, political constitutions, roads, vehicles, schools, etc.—(a) these are not *socio-psychological facts* which have an existence independent of the activities of individuals, and (b) their continued use (and even change) in social life cannot be understood excepting in relation to the *purposive activities* of individualities: *changed* individualities though these may well be (i.e. continuously changing—to some extent—in the context of continuous association).

It is one thing to say that association is creative of many aspects and qualities of individualities in relation to the group conditions in which they are placed, but quite another to argue that the qualitatively new facts resulting from association exist *objectively*—at the level of the *totality* of the new social *synthesis*—and *independently* of all the individualities who are members of the collectivity. It may be thought that Durkheim could not possibly be asserting the position we are attributing to him; but here we come to his second point about which he was equally emphatic.

'The social fact', he wrote, 'is a thing distinct from its individual manifestations.'

Certain social ways of acting and thinking, he argued:

'. . . acquire, by reason of their repetition, a certain rigidity which on its own account crystallizes them, so to speak, and isolates them from the particular events which reflect them. They thus acquire a body, a tangible form, and constitute a reality in their own right, quite distinct from the individual facts which produce it . . . they are given permanent expression in a formula which is repeated from mouth to mouth, transmitted by education, and fixed even in writing. Such is the origin and nature of legal and moral rules, popular aphorisms and proverbs, articles of faith wherein religious or political groups condense their beliefs, standards of taste established by literary schools, etc.'*

And these social facts could be quite *dissociated* from the form, or nature, in which they were embodied in the minds of individuals.

'It is the *collective aspects* of the beliefs, tendencies, and practices of a group', Durkheim insisted, 'that characterize truly social phenomena. As for the forms that the collective states assume when *refracted in the individual*, these are things of another sort.'*

Social facts could thus be disentangled from the socio-psychological impressions of them which existed in individualities. And— and here comes the extreme emphasis of Durkheim—they should be

* *Rules*, p. 7.

kept quite separate as distinct subject-matters, and only the former was the concern of sociology.

With regard to the 'individual manifestations' of social facts; social facts 'as refracted in individuals', Durkheim argued:

'... these are indeed, to a certain extent, social, since they partly reproduce a social model. Each of them also depends, and to a large extent, on the organopsychological constitution of the individual and on the particular circumstances in which he is placed. Thus they are not sociological phenomena in the strict sense of the word. They belong to two realms at once; one could call them sociopsychological. They interest the sociologist without constituting the immediate subject-matter of sociology.'*

Now let us stop to notice here (a) that 'social facts' were now lifted, by Durkheim, to the position of an existence independent of all the socio-psychological aspects of individuals as they had been affected by the processes of association, and (b) the study and explanation of them was to take place without reference to these socio-psychological aspects of individuals. They existed in some realm of reality in their own right, and they were to be explained solely in terms of each other and such processes of interdependence as existed among them.

There is no doubt, then, that when Durkheim spoke of *society*—as a system of interdependent *social facts* which were *things* possessing *functional relations* with each other, changing, differentiating, integrating in relation to the *total environmental conditions* of the *whole*; and in accordance with an *equilibrium-disequilibrium* process of *adaptation*—he really meant what he said. He really did have in mind a new substantive kind of reality: a super-organic *being* of a qualitatively distinct kind of *associational* facts in conditions of *interdependency*. It was in ill-considered French metaphysics, borne along by the euphoria of its own incisive assertiveness that it was *science*, that the mystique of one particular brand of 'functionalism' was born.†

I think this entire point has probably, by now, been sufficiently made, but it is most important to see exactly how Durkheim went on to speak of society *as a whole*, and also with what piety—almost devotion—he regarded it. He did not—like Comte in his own extreme extravaganzas—light so many candles for the worship of 'The Great Being' in the ornate cathedral of a new religion—but he certainly knelt at the same shrine.

---

* *Rules*, pp. 8–9.
† I.e. the 'brand' marketed, a little later, by Radcliffe-Brown especially: see pp. 710–49. Malinowski's version of 'functionalism' was free from these errors.

The constraint of social facts, he wrote:

'. . . is due simply tö the fact that the individual finds himself in the presence of a force which is *superior* to him and before which he bows; but this force is an *entirely* natural one. It is not derived from a conventional arrangement which human will has added bodily to natural reality; it issues from innermost reality; it is the necessary product of given causes. Also, recourse to artifice is unnecessary *to get the individual to submit to them of his entire free will*; it is sufficient to make him become aware of his state of natural dependence and *inferiority*, whether he forms a tangible and symbolic representation of it through religion or whether he arrives at an adequate and definite notion of it through science. Since the *superiority* of society to him is not simply physical but intellectual and moral, it has nothing to fear from a critical examination. By making man understand by how much the social being is richer, more complex, and more permanent than the individual being, reflection can only reveal to him the intelligible reasons for the *subordination* demanded of him and for the sentiments of attachment and respect which habit has fixed in his heart.'*

Again, one sees Hegel peering across from Prussia. And what are we to make of this, written at the conclusion of Durkheim's study of religion:

'Society is not at all the illogical or a-logical, incoherent and fantastic being which it has too often been considered. Quite on the contrary, the collective consciousness is the highest form of the psychic life, since it is the consciousness of the consciousnesses. Being placed outside of and above individual and local contingencies, it sees things only in their permanent and essential aspects, which it crystallizes into communicable ideas. At the same time that it sees from above, it sees farther; at every moment of time, it embraces all known reality; that is why it alone can furnish the mind with the moulds which are applicable to the totality of things and which make it possible to think of them. It does not create these moulds artificially; it finds them within itself; it does nothing but become conscious of them. They translate the ways of being which are found in all the stages of reality but which appear in their full clarity only at the summit, because the extreme complexity of the psychic life which passes there necessitates a greater development of consciousness . . . If society is something universal in relation to the individual, it is none the less an individuality itself, which has its own personal physiognomy and its idiosyncrasies; it is a particular subject and consequently particularizes whatever it thinks of.'†

It seems that we owe 'society' a lot!—and that the approach for the sociologist in studying it should be, most properly, on his knees!

* *Rules*, p. 123.
† *The Elementary Forms of the Religious Life*, Allen & Unwin, 1954, p. 444.

We shall see later that Durkheim's readiness to think of society *as a whole* was often such as to lead him to attach less weight than he should to elements of sheer conflict in society—sheer cleavage—and that, here again, he was led too easily to think of *social solidarity* and *equilibrium* as the *normal, healthy* state of the social organism to which all political policies should aspire. Again one can see the emphasis upon 'harmony', 'functional integration', 'functional unity', 'conservatism' which later were targets for the attack upon 'Functionalism'.

One thing only remains here: that is to show that—if Durkheim critized Spencer in many ways—he made use of biological analogies, illustrating societal processes by reference to organic processes, just as much as he. I will give only one or two brief examples—but they could be multiplied many times. When discussing the economic aspects of society and the contractual law pertaining to it, for example, Durkheim referred to them as 'the visceral life of the social organism', and commented that Spencer compared them 'as we have done, to the visceral life of the individual organism'; and then, having criticized aspects of Spencer, he wrote:

'The great social sympathetic must, then, comprise, besides a system of roads for transmission, organs truly regulative which, charged to combine the intestinal acts as the cerebral ganglion combines the external acts, would have the power either to stop the excitations, or to amplify them, or to moderate them according to need.'*

That could easily have been drawn from *First Principles*. Again, when turning to discuss administrative law, Durkheim wrote:

'If we again borrow biological terminology which, though metaphorical, is none the less useful, we may say that these rules determine the way in which the cerebro-spinal system of the social organism functions. This system, in current parlance, is designated by the name, State.'†

And when discussing the relations between restitutive law and repressive law for the purposes of measuring degrees of social solidarity, he argued:

'This law definitely plays a role in society analogous to that played by the nervous system in the organism. The latter has as its task, in effect, the regulation of the different functions of the body in such a way as to make them harmonize. It thus very naturally expresses the state of concentration at which the organism has arrived, in accordance with the division of physiological labour. Thus, on different levels of the animal scale, we can

* *Division of Labour*, p. 218. † *Ibid.*, p. 219.

measure the degree of this concentration according to the development of the nervous system. Which is to say that we can equally measure the degree of concentration at which a society has arrived in accordance with the division of social labor according to the development of co-operative law with restitutive sanctions. We can foresee the great services that this criterion will render us.'*

I will not press this point with further illustrations, but it is worth saying that I have by no means selected the most detailed and lengthy examples of Durkheim's use of this 'organic' analogy. However, the chief point in all this is that in Durkheim, more than in other writers, this analogy was used to buttress a conception of society as a *social organism* which was far more extreme than any we have yet encountered. Again—in pursuing points of real worth, Durkheim exaggerated to the point of considerable error.

There are several other aspects of Durkheim's work which are open to criticisms just as serious as those we have outlined. His statements concerning the relations between sociology and the 'special social sciences' were ambiguous, and need a good deal of criticism before they can be properly appraised. Having eliminated psychology from sociological explanation, he nonetheless continuously drew upon psychological assumptions to support certain social regularities or differences which he uncovered: as, for example, in discussing the differences between the sexes in relation to marriage, divorce, widowhood and suicide. Psychology crept in implicitly. Also, having discarded teleological explanation, he went on to speak of the *functions* of social facts in terms of fulfilling the *needs* of society in ways which were far from clear—and which, again, were to become part of the construction of some versions of 'Functionalism'. There are, then, many other things to be said of an adverse nature if our critical appraisal of Durkheim's system were to be complete. We have, however, said enough to see what a difficult mixture Durkheim was: having a highly significant continuity from the earlier writers, but also differences from them; differences which had understandable and laudable objectives. but which, taken to extremes, led to very dubious and even false positions. It is time now, bearing all these critical qualifications in mind, to come to a positive outline of Durkheim's ideas, in such a way as to state clearly the worthwhile contribution to the making of sociology which he made. It might well have been thought, in moving through all these criticisms, that a writer who had so many faults could not have contributed much. It may also have been thought that these criticisms have arisen from a thoroughly antagonistic approach to Durkheim (on my part), and a

* *Division of Labour*, p. 128.

desire to belittle his contribution. Neither supposition is true. Our criticism of Durkheim has been undertaken firstly to see him thoroughly and correctly in the context of the continuity of the argument which has gone into the making of the subject (so that he is not seen as a starkly different and 'modern'—whatever that means—figure); to see him among his predecessors and contemporaries; and secondly to strip his work of all the errors it contains so that (a) they are not taken to be virtues, and (b) what is of real value in it can be seen with complete clarity. And all this has been done, of course, *not* because Durkheim's work has been thought of little consequence, but, on the contrary, because what comes out of it—when all the fog of inconsistency has been removed—is so important.

We cannot escape critical comments in what follows: they remain necessary here and there; but—having moved through such a tangle of criticisms in our approach—we can now attempt a straight-forward, clean-cut statement.

Durkheim's System of Sociology

(1) *The Existence of a Distinctive Level of Associational Facts : The Creativity of Society*

A new science was to be considered necessary, said Durkheim, only if a distinctive range or level of facts was recognized for the explanation of which the existing sciences were insufficient. Is it the case that a distinctive level of 'associational facts' exists? If so—sociology is necessary. If not—it is not.

Durkheim's answer was: emphatically yes! Social facts do exist; many intellectual misconceptions have rested on a failure to recognize this; and therefore their nature must be made clear beyond all doubt. There is, he argued, a deep-rooted illusion in the minds of individuals resulting from their sense of *familarity* with the general facts of their society. Because they act with familarity among the associational forms they find about them; because their own minds share and comprehend the sentiments and meanings of all the elements of associational life about them; they take it quite for granted (a) that they *know* what these associational forms are, and (b) that these associational forms were simply *created by individuals*—since human individuals are of such a basic nature as to possess all these qualities of sentiment, morality, reason, etc, beforehand—quite apart from society. Both these basic assumptions are, however, illusory. People in a society are demonstrably ignorant about all but a little of the social forms (and facts) among which they live. They are so used to talking about 'the government', 'the law', 'the Roman Catholic Church', 'right and wrong', 'the coal industry', 'the educational system', and so on, that they *think* they know something about them. In fact, however, as Durkheim put it (using Bacon's terminology) these words are 'idols' in their minds, sets of assumptions or 'preconceptions', behind which is a great obscurity. Thus if people were asked to sit down and write an essay on what they *demonstrably knew* about any one of these elements of the society in which they lived, their information would not cover many pieces of paper! It is clear on even a moment's reflection that every associational actuality in our society has factual characteristics that go far beyond the personal knowledge of any one of us. Even the most obvious social facts, then, are *other* than, and *more* than individuals, and have an existence which goes beyond individual knowledge. They cannot be *known* by a process of individual *introspection*. If we desire knowledge of them, we must go *outside* our own minds and *observe* their objective characteristics.

The second assumption also, however, that the associational fabric —including all its collective sentiments—of society is to be explained purely in terms of individual *intentions*, and in terms of some psychological nature of individuals which existed *before* society and which exists *independent* of society, is equally untrue and untenable. A moment's thought makes it clear that—even on a very limited level of scrutiny—the very mental conceptions and sentiments by which people perceive, interpret, and understand the associational fabric of their society, exist in their individual minds as an outcome of the long influences upon them of this complex associational fabric itself. The very language in terms of which people express their conceptions of their society is itself a 'social fact' which goes beyond individuals, which was not 'invented' by any one set of individuals, and which certainly could not be said to exist as an attribute of 'original human nature' before association of any kind had been experienced.

It is apparent, then, that 'associational facts' of the most large-scale and intricate nature—varying from constitutional forms of government, to a language, to a commonly shared sentiment (let us say about the 'Royal Family' or the 'Presidency'), etc;—do exist as something more than and other than individuals; and that—certainly—neither biology nor psychology are sufficient for their explanation. But Durkheim wished to press this point completely home, because he felt this intellectual illusion to be so deep-rooted, and believed that much antagonism and opposition to sociology stemmed from it.

The fundamental insistence which he wanted to press home was (*a*) that *association* is the basic, perennial, universal, *natural* condition of human life; and that human individuality always arises within this context, (*b*) that *individuality* did not (either chronologically—in evolution and history, or analytically—in any human society) *precede* association, (*c*) that *individual* human nature could not therefore be separated from the *associational context* in such a way as to *account* for it, (*d*) that *human association was a socio-psychologically creative process* (not at all a *sterile* matter of a simple addition of individual units which made no difference to them), and that (*e*) these processes required to be studied at their own level—by careful observation, description, analysis, classification, comparison, etc.—if *knowledge* about them was to be reliably established.

This, it can be seen, was a re-statement of the fundamental persuasion of all Durkheim's predecessors which, for them too, formed the point of departure for sociology as a science. It was the insistence that the *distinctive* qualities of *human* nature (as different from the nature of other animal species) lay in the *associational life* of men and in all the ramifications of the complex developments of *society*. Man was *social* before he was *human*—with all the qualities of language, culture, morality which we now attribute to him. At the hands of Durkheim, however, this very fundamental statement received a new vitality; a new forcefulness.

This essential *creativity* of associational processes; this conception of *society* as a new level (in nature) of socio-psychological creativity within which individuality comes to possess new dimensions; is at the very heart of Durkheim's teaching. There are those who think, he claimed, that this way of thinking of the nature of individuality as being *attendant upon* association is such as to strip individuality of its basic significance; such, almost, as to *deny* this significance. But— bearing in mind all the errors to which he was prone in seeking too extremely to emphasize this—let us note his comment on this: seeing meanwhile, his conception of *society* as a fund of creative forces.

'Attributing to society,' he wrote, 'this preponderating role in the genesis of our nature is not *denying* this creation; for society has a creative power which no other observable being can equal. In fact, all creation, if not a mystical operation which escapes science and knowledge, is the product of a synthesis. Now if the synthesis of particular conceptions which take place in each individual consciousness are already and of themselves productive of novelties, how much more efficacious these vast syntheses of complete consciousnesses which make society must be! *A society is the most powerful combination of physical and moral forces of which nature offers us an example*. Nowhere else is an equal richness of different materials, carried to such a degree of concentration, to be found. Then it is not surprising that a higher life disengages itself which, by reacting upon

327

M

the elements of which it is the product, raises them to a higher plane of existence and transforms them.

Thus sociology appears destined to open a new way to the science of man. Up to the present, thinkers were placed before this double alternative: either explain the superior and specific faculties of men by connecting them to the inferior forms of his being, the reason to the senses, or the mind to matter, which is equivalent to denying their uniqueness; or else attach them to some super-experimental reality which was postulated, but whose existence could be established by no observation. What put them in this difficulty was the fact that *the individual passed as being the finis naturae—the ultimate creation of nature*; it seemed that there was nothing beyond him, or at least nothing that science could touch. But from the moment when it is recognized that above the individual there is society, and that this is not a nominal being created by reason, but a system of active forces, a new manner of explaining men becomes possible. To conserve his distinctive traits it is no longer necessary to put them outside experience. At least, before going to this last extremity, it would be well to see if that which surpasses the individual, though it is within him, does not come from this super-individual reality which we experience in society. To be sure, it cannot be said at present to what point these explanations may be able to reach, and whether or not they are of a nature to resolve all the problems. But it is equally impossible to make in advance a limit beyond which they cannot go. What must be done is to try the hypothesis and submit it as methodically as possible to the control of facts.'*

It can readily be seen that this recognition of the distinctive level of *associational processes*, and of the *creativity of society* as a new level in nature of socio-psychological interaction and creation, can be accepted without at all accepting the *reification* of a social organism, completely independent of 'individual manifestations', to which Durkheim—in his extremities of argument was led.

'Social facts' do exist, then, Durkheim insisted, and, furthermore, they can be seen to possess *at least* a number of characteristics. (*a*) They are *external* to the individuals in society (they do not exist in their minds). (*b*) They are *constraining* upon individuals, in that individuals *find* them objectively there, and are compelled to come to terms with them. (*c*) They are *diffused*—and in the most established cases *general*—throughout the society, and (*d*) they have a nature *going beyond their individual manifestations*.

Now some immediate qualifications to these points are necessary.

We say that social facts have *at least* these distinguishing characteristics, because Durkheim claimed, obviously, that they had *more* qualitative and quantitative characteristics than these. But these were *minimal* characteristics by means of which these *socio-*

* *The Elementary Forms*, pp. 446–7.

psychological facts could be distinguished from *other* human facts of a biological or psychological nature.

Secondly, the fact that social facts *constrain* individuals does not mean that their constraint is necessarily *felt*, nor that they cannot be changed. Education and habit can accustom people to the coercive requirements of society to a point where they are as familiar as breathing. Even so, at any time, the *breaking* of them can be seen to call forth the coercive sanctions which are *there*, and on which they rest. Thus people find it familiar and graceful to use soup-spoons; but if—at college high table—or even at a private table in a restaurant—you lift up the plate and drink the soup directly out of it (which, actually, is a very pleasant thing to do!), you will undoubtedly become aware of a certain force of disapproval and constraint in the atmosphere about you. Even in the simple matter of wielding a special tool at meal-time—the constraint is there! Similarly, as Durkheim argued, social facts may be changed: but *try* and change them, by deliberate effort, and the *resistance* which you encounter is, at least, sufficient to demonstrate that the constraining fact is *there*.

Thirdly, Durkheim specially pointed out that not *all* social facts were *general* throughout a society. Some *were*: like laws, governmental regulations, and the like. But social facts were continuously coming into being, becoming more crystallized, going out of being, as collective conditions—in localities and regions, as well as in society as a whole—changed.

'There is thus,' Durkheim wrote, 'a whole series of degrees without a break in continuity between the facts of the most articulated structure and those free currents of social life which are not yet definitely molded. The differences between them are, therefore, only differences in the degree of consolidation they present.'*

And finally, it will be noticed that we formulated the last characteristic—(*d*)—in a more moderate phrase than Durkheim's own, in order especially to show that—his extremes aside—there is good reason for it. Durkheim's own statement was that social facts 'exist in their own right, independent of their individual manifestation', and we have seen that this can lead to a peculiar metaphysic. What he meant, however, was this.

If we consider any regularity of social behaviour—say the institution of marriage—it is clear that we could observe all the 'individual manifestations' of this. We could travel north, south, east and west at Easter-time in Great Britain and see the white veils blowing, the bridesmaids delicately holding their little bouquets, and the vast

* *Rules*, p. 12.

trails of confetti from church to household and even making a mess of the station platforms (and being pecked at in perplexed fashion by the pigeons.) We could even interview the brides and grooms who were doing this kind of thing in Gloucester, New Cross, Birmingham, York and Walthamstow, and discover what they thought about what they were up to. The question is, however: would this observation of all these 'individual manifestations' of marriage give us a full and reliable knowledge of the nature of the institution of marriage in British society? And the answer, clearly, is that it would not. Anybody who has spoken to brides and grooms (and anybody else for that matter) in Gloucester, New Cross, Birmingham, York and Walthamstow, will know very well that they are very vague indeed as to what they are up to: they have varying conceptions from that of a spiritual union between themselves and God to that of a binge before bed-time. It is quite obvious that to know *fully* and *reliably* the nature of the institution of marriage we would have to go to that which lay *behind* all these individual manifestations; that general, constraining set of facts in accordance with which each couple (and their families) were obliged to act in the way in which they were acting. We would have to go to the *law* pertaining to marriage, the regulations and provisions and sanctions it comprised, and also the similar and additional requirements, where appropriate, of the religion or denomination within which the marriage was being solemnized. The 'social fact' of marriage clearly possesses characteristics which *go beyond* the individual manifestations of it, and it is this basic requirement of the law which accounts for the individual manifestations—not they which account for it!

To say, then, as Durkheim did, that social facts existed *independently* of their individual manifestations was to take the matter further than he needed; it is enough to insist that they have important characteristics *going beyond* their individual manifestations, and that a full knowledge could not be achieved by looking at the individual manifestations alone. There is therefore a very important truth in Durkheim's point, even when his extreme statement of it is qualified.

Social facts did exist, then, and a new science was necessary for the study of them. Durkheim concluded as follows:

'We thus arrive at the point where we can formulate and delimit in a precise way the domain of sociology. It comprises only a limited group of phenomena. A social fact is to be recognized by the power of external coercion which it exercises or is capable of exercising over individuals, and the presence of this power may be recognized in its turn either by the existence of some specific sanction or by the resistance offered against every individual effort that tends to violate it. One can, however, define it also by its diffusion within the group, provided that, in conformity with our previous remarks, one takes care to add as a second and essential characteristic that its own existence is independent of the individual forms it assumes in its diffusion.'*

Durkheim also defined 'social facts' elsewhere, but this statement indicates very plainly their characteristics.

(2) *A Definition of Sociology : The Scientific Study of 'Social Facts'*

The distinguishing of this level of 'social facts' thus enabled Durkheim to give a very clear definition of sociology. It was, quite simply, the new science which had to be created to study this distinctive set of facts. But Durkheim's specific words are of interest here. Having spoken of the creativity of associational processes, and of 'social facts' as being the outcome of *joint activity*, he wrote:

'Since this joint activity takes place outside each one of us (for a plurality of consciousnesses enters into it), its necessary effect is to fix, to *institute* outside us, certain ways of acting and certain judgments which do not depend on each particular will taken separately. It has been pointed out that the word "institution" well expresses this special mode of reality, provided that the ordinary significance of it be slightly extended. One can, indeed. without distorting the meaning of this expression, designate as "institutions" all the beliefs and all the modes of conduct instituted by the collectivity. Sociology can then be defined as *the science of institutions, of their genesis and of their functioning*.'†

This is as clear a definition of sociology as one can find; perfectly satisfactory, without ambiguity, and completely in keeping with all the definitions we have noted earlier. There are only two things we might note about it which are important: one is implicit in all we have seen of Durkheim's conception; the other an additional point which deserves emphasis.

The first is simply that in this scientific study of *institutions*, their *genesis* and *functioning*, it was implied, for Durkheim, that these institutions were part of *social systems*, and could only be studied within this context of society as a whole. This, we have sufficiently seen, and it is worth noting again the fact that the study of the *origins* of institutions was as important for Durkheim as for others. We shall see again, in a moment, Durkheim's strong agreement with the position of Westermarck here.

* *Rules*, p. 10.   † *Ibid.*, p. lvi.

The second point—of much importance—is that in seeking to define a *specific set of social facts*, and to define sociology itself very clearly in relation to them—Durkheim was quite deliberately seeking to *delimit* the subject-matter of sociology; to *delimit* its scope as a science. One of his discontents with the sociology of the earlier nineteenth century writers was that it was too all-embracing: seeming to include *everything* pertaining to human nature—biological and psychological elements as well as those of a strictly *societal* nature. It seemed a compendious study of the entire nature of man in the world. No science could achieve exactitude, Durkheim thought, whilst trying to cover such a large canvas. It was necessary to *delimit*—correctly and accurately—the scope of a science to those *distinguishable* facts which, *alone*, were its own special province. Once this was done, then exacting efforts could be made to encompass this specific range of facts adequately within its studies.

One important contribution of Durkheim, therefore, was to *delimit* the subject-matter and the definition of sociology; and, again, it can be seen that this was a very worthwhile thing quite apart from any errors he may have made in being *too* extreme in his attempt to isolate social facts from qualities which might be extraneous to them.

(3) *The Rules of Sociological Method : Procedures For the Definitive Study and Explanation of Social Facts*

Having defined the nature of social facts—or at least the distinguishing characteristics of them—and having defined sociology as the scientific study of them, Durkheim then turned quite directly to the task of providing a set of rules whereby this scientific task could be carried out and accomplished. And this was another very important contribution—for it had not been done before. There are many criticisms which can be levelled at the conceptions contained in these rules, but the fact remains that having read them, a student is equipped with a clear set of procedures with which he can set out on a sociological study. They are clear, direct proposals and guide-lines of procedure for the scientific work of sociology; and nothing like them—at least in such a succinct form—was to be found in the work of the earlier sociologists. Again, in giving an outline statement of these rules we will keep ourselves as free from obscuring criticisms as possible, though, occasionally, it will be necessary to raise them.

(I) RULES FOR OBSERVING SOCIAL FACTS

There were, strictly speaking, six rules which Durkheim proposed for the initial and basic task of *observing* social facts reliably. In science, everything depends upon accurate observation of the facts about which theories are being presented. Agreed rules for observation are therefore of fundamental importance, and, for Durkheim these were all corollaries of the *essential* rule: that sociologists should *consider social facts as things*. Now we have criticized strongly the extreme view that social facts can be held to *be* things, in some sense *existing in their own right* and *independent* of their individual manifestations in society, but now we can emphasize—such criticisms aside—the important degrees of truth in Durkheim's insistence. The first rule can be stated—using Durkheim's more moderate phraseology—in this way:

(*a*) *Social Facts should always be treated AS IF they are Things*
What Durkheim was seeking to emphasize here was that no *knowledge* of all the many-dimensioned nature of associational facts could possibly be obtained if investigators simply practised *introspection* or *personal conjecture* of any sort; as if the social facts were already familiar in their minds and simply needed reflective clarification. It was *essential* to recognize that social facts had characteristics which were *objectively there*, *outside* our minds, and to go *out of ourselves* to observe them. To adopt the *attitude of mind* towards the study of social facts that we employ in the study of things—recognizing that they possess attributes which we can only *know* about if we undertake a careful, painstaking *observation* of them—was absolutely necessary.

In his preface to the second edition of his *Rules* Durkheim did, in fact, phrase his notion of treating social facts as things in a much more qualified and acceptable way. Instead of asserting bluntly that social facts *were* things (without qualification or differentiation), he claimed instead that they were *to be TREATED as things*—which is very different. And he made this further statement, which puts the matter very clearly indeed:

'We assert not that social facts are *material things* but that they are things *by the same right* as material things, although they differ from them in type. What precisely, is a "thing"? A thing differs from an idea in the same way as that which we know from without differs from that which we know from within. Things include all objects of knowledge that cannot be conceived by purely mental activity, those that require for their conception data from outside the mind, from observations and experiments, those which are built up from the more external and immediately accessible characteristics to the less visible and more profound. To *treat* the facts of a certain order *as* things is *not*, then, *to place them in a certain category of reality but to assume a certain mental attitude toward them* on the

333

principle that when approaching their study we are absolutely ignorant of their nature, and that their characteristic properties, like the unknown causes on which they depend, cannot be discovered by even the most careful introspection.'*

Now this is so clear as to require no further comment, and if Durkheim had been always as carefully qualified as this a good many difficulties in understanding his conceptions would have been avoided. One other passage, I think, deserves inclusion here because of its clarification of this same point

'Our principle, then, implies no metaphysical conception, no speculation about the fundamental nature of beings. What it demands is that the sociologist put himself in the same state of mind as the physicist, chemist, or physiologist when he probes into a still unexplored region of the scientific domain. When he penetrates the social world, he must be aware that he is penetrating the unknown; he must feel himself in the presence of facts whose laws are as unsuspected as were those of life before the era of biology—he must be prepared for discoveries which will surprise and disturb him. Sociology is far from having arrived at this degree of intellectual maturity.'†

The remaining rules follow as clear corollaries.

(b) *The Voluntary Nature of a Social Fact should never be assumed beforehand*
By this rule, Durkheim again wanted to ensure safety for the full observation of the objective attributes of social facts against the error of thinking that their characteristics could be exhaustively and accurately known by reliance upon the views of the participants that they were *voluntary*; or that they could be sufficiently known in terms of individual *purposes* alone. To be fair to Durkheim he did *not* assert here that social facts were *not* voluntary, or that they did not contain voluntary elements. His emphasis was that for correct and exhaustive *observation*, we should not assume their voluntary nature *beforehand*.

(c) *All pre-conceptions should be eradicated*
Knowing that our common-sense familiarity with social facts creates 'idols'‡ or 'preconceptions' in our minds about them; and that these are an outcome of limited impressions, orientations of practical use, and may therefore be distorting; Durkheim argued that we should

* *Rules*, p. xliii.   † *Ibid.*, pp. xlv–xlvi.
‡ Durkheim followed the arguments of Francis Bacon—in his 'Novum Organum' —here, and it is interesting to wonder how much his 'inductive' notions of science might well have sprung from this same influence.

always be critical of them when coming to the task of scientific observation. Whether preconceptions can be (or ought to be) *completely eradicated*, is beside the point here. Durkheim is undoubtedly right that they should be critically appraised very exactingly.

(*d*) *Observation should seek always those external distinguishing characteristics about which there can be no doubt: which can be objectively perceived by others*

Again, no matter how *subjectively* convinced an investigator might feel that a social fact was such-and-such; he should seek always such *external* attributes which could be the ground of common and testable observation.

(*e*) *Observation of Social Facts should go beyond that of their Individual Manifestations*

This point we have covered. The individual manifestations of social facts, clearly, must themselves be observed, but observation should also go beyond them to the more general, constraining set of facts on which they rest.

(*f*) *The Observation and Study of Social Facts should be DEFINITIVE as far as possible*

All the rules mentioned so far provided clear methods for the observation and description of any particular social facts in which an investigator might be interested. In this final rule, however, Durkheim insisted upon the clear definition of the *range*, or *area*, of observation; or a certain *completeness of coverage* of any particular study. His full rule was that:

'The subject-matter of every sociological study should comprise a group of phenomena defined in advance by certain common external characteristics, and all phenomena so defined should be included within this group'

Now this rule was one of the most important of all. It is clear that the following of it would mean that sociology would become as scientific as it could possibly be in the sense that every study it produced would be as *definitive* a study as was possible of that particular group of social facts with which it tried to deal. Any such study would be directly vulnerable to test by all other equally qualified investigators. We must note that the *definition* of the social facts dealt with should be entirely in terms of the characteristics of social facts as Durkheim had mentioned them: externality, generality, and constraint. The whole objective was to define social facts in

335

such a way as to permit testing by others and to exclude any imponderable elements of subjectivity. The insistence that *all* social facts covered by the definition should be included in the study would clearly make it as *definitive* as possible so that (given subsequent testing by other investigators) *knowledge* about this group of social facts could be progressive and ever more exact. This was a ground for cumulative scientific knowledge indeed.

Durkheim's clarity about this cannot be too much praised.

'Every scientific investigation,' he wrote, 'is directed towards a limited class of phenomena, included in the same definition. The first step of the sociologist, then, ought to be to define the things he treats, in order that his subject matter may be known. This is the first and most indispensable condition of all proofs and verifications. A theory can be checked only if we know how to recognize the facts of which it is intended to give an account.'*

So much, then, for careful observation and description, and the clear statement of definitive studies.

(II) RULES FOR DISTINGUISHING BETWEEN 'NORMAL' AND 'PATHOLOGICAL' SOCIAL FACTS

Knowing how to observe and describe social facts clearly, we should then seek, Durkheim argued, to establish their 'normal' and 'pathological' condition in particular types of society. We have already seen that Durkheim was in great confusion in specifying his rules for this particular purpose. He thought it necessary to clarify such rules when facing the question as to whether the social scientist could make a contribution to the knowledge not only of what society *is*, but also what it *ought* to be. And his effort was to show that sociology as a science could make such a contribution.

Having emphasized, like Comte, that 'to see is to foresee'; that science was a basis for prediction and guidance in practical action; that 'by revealing the causes of phenomena, science furnishes the means of producing them'; he went on to discard the reliability of the 'master-concepts' which ethics and ideologies of various kinds had erected as goals or ends in the light of which actual social facts could be judged and towards the attainment of which they should be manipulated. We must, he argued, see, a 'master-concept' which is in keeping with the objective methods of science. Almost unbelievably, he wrote as follows:

'It is possible for us to vindicate the legitimate rights of reason in the solution of the problem just stated, without reverting to ideology. Briefly,

* *Rules*, p. 34.

for societies as for individuals, health is good and desirable; disease, on the contrary, is bad and to be avoided. If, then, we can find an objective criterion, inherent in the facts themselves, which enables us to distinguish scientifically between health and morbidity in the various orders of social phenomena, science will be in a position to throw light on practical problems and still remain faithful to its own method.'*

Durkheim never thought for a moment that it was necessary to justify this evaluation, and yet it is clear that he was not only raising the pursuit of 'health' and the avoidance of 'disease' in society to the rank of a central ethic, but also that he was assuming—again with no grounds whatever—an implicit analogy between health and disease in an organism, and health and disease in a *society*. He *assumed* conditions of health and illness in societies, and then *sought* objective criteria for them. In fact, however, he was doing the reverse. He was investing the *regularity of occurrence* of facts in society with the additional connotations of the word 'health' and social *irregularities* with those of the word 'illness'.

Durkheim followed this analogy through very consistently. Thus, in finding that rates of crime are regularly found in society, he argued strongly:

'Let us make no mistake. To classify crime among the phenomena of normal sociology is not to say merely that it is an inevitable, although regrettable phenomenon, due to the incorrigible wickedness of men; it is to affirm that it is a factor in public health, an integral part of all healthy societies. This result is, at first glance, surprising enough to have puzzled even ourselves for a long time.'†

Even Durkheim and his colleagues, it seems, could be puzzled; but it never occurred to them that they were using words mistakenly —pressing an analogy falsely. For why should the question of the *healthiness* of crime arise at all? Why should it *not* simply be said that crime is *normally* found in societies—related to this and that condition? Why should we ask whether society is *healthier* with so much crime or so much more or less?

Similarly, Durkheim carried the analogy completely into his conception of the role of the statesman or legislator. Political leaders should not seek to change society in accordance with ethical ideals. It may be discouraging for men to feel that their 'ideals' in society are not going to be attained, but, he went on, political activity:

'. . . is no longer a matter of pursuing desperately an objective that retreats as one advances, but of working with steady perseverance to maintain *the*

* *Rules*, p. 49. † *Ibid.*, p. 67.

normal state, of re-establishing it if it is threatened, and of rediscovering its conditions if they have changed. The duty of the statesman is no longer to push society toward an ideal that seems attractive to him, but his role is that of the physician: he prevents the outbreak of illnesses by good hygiene, and he seeks to cure them when they have appeared.'*

This, it can be seen, raises some very curious situations and we might glance at a few examples. If, to think of crime, the *normal* rate of murders in societies of the same type as his own should give, say, 500 murders a year—and the *actual* number in his own society is only 400: then his society is unhealthy; it is suffering some morbid, pathological condition; so that the statesman must bring conditions back to the normal level of hygiene at which there will be 500 murders. If the normal death-rate from small-pox in agrarian societies is such and such, then the statesman must exterminate (or otherwise inhibit) those few who are pressing the reform of inoculation and creating an abnormal, morbid increase in the population. The same goes for 'normal' rates of unemployment, and the like. On the other hand, as we saw earlier, the 'normal' condition of 'anomie' in industrial societies must be combated because the division of labour in these societies is not performing the function which it 'normally' fulfills in *other* types of society. The absurd confusions are endless. But, quite apart from all this, it is plain that this entire conception of the 'normal health' and 'abnormal illness' of societies and the role of the physician-statesman being that of preserving the one and avoiding the other, is no more than a vast and unsupported analogy—containing both scientific and ethical confusions.

However, even in these rules, something emerged which was of value.

The objective criteria as to whether social facts were 'normal' in a society (quite apart from their 'health' or otherwise) all focused upon the central fact as to whether they were found on the average in all the societies of the same type and at the same stage of evolution. Strictly speaking—this was a *statistical norm,* and it was established, clearly, by classificatory and comparative studies. Durkheim's rule was:

(*a*) *A social fact is normal, in relation to a given social type at a given phase of its development, when it is present in the average society of that species at the corresponding phase of its evolution.*
This *regularly found* concomitance of social facts in societies of particular types, however, was, in itself, a firm indication that there existed some pattern of functional interdependency among them which was

* *Rules,* p. 75.

significantly related to the material and social conditions which were peculiar to those societies. We should therefore look further at this regular concomitance and see whether it was bound up with these conditions. This, clearly, would be investigated by a structural-functional and historical analysis. Durkheim's rule was:

(b) *One can verify the results of the preceding method by showing that the generality of the phenomenon is bound up with the general conditions of collective life of the social type considered.*

This entire analysis could be given stronger force, also, if the '*abnormal*' occurrence of social facts (i.e. in types of society where one would not expect them to be) were also investigated in relation to the '*normal*' functional interdependencies established above. The study of the abnormal—important in itself—could also throw light upon the normal, and vice versa. Durkheim's third rule, then, was:

(c) *This verification is necessary when the fact in question occurs in a social species which has not yet reached the full course of its evolution.*

Now when divorced from all questions of health and disease, these rules can be seen to be very specific statements of the procedures which all the earlier sociologists had thought necessary and adopted. They required (a) the establishing of systematic knowledge—by description, classification and comparison—of the 'consensus' of institutions which was found in each type of society, and (b) the structural-functional and historical analysis of these types of 'consensus' in order to understand more fully the interdependent factors involved in the social-historical processes of order and change. The significant connections between the comparative and functional methods which were clearly pointed out in the methods of Hobhouse were clearly reinforced here.

The important thing is, then, that Durkheim's rules were perfectly valid for establishing the 'normal' incidence of social facts within their 'typical' contexts, and for establishing the deeper functional understanding of their interdependencies within these 'types', even when his errors of analogy—with their ethical and political implications were discarded. However, it should be noticed that though—in Durkheim—these rules were stated in half a page, they really point to the entire vastness of comparative studies with which we have seen the other sociologists grappling.

There is also this final point. Though it seems to me we must reject Durkheim's notion of the statesman as physician in the ill-thought-out way in which he presented it, it is still the case that there is, again, a core of wisdom at the heart of his extremes. For though sociology can never, of itself, be in a position of prescribing what '*ought to be*' in society, it is certainly the case that a knowledge of the detailed nature of a society, and the interconnections between all its elements, is an essential ingredient in the formulation of wise political policy. This is really the spirit and conviction of Montesquieu—which, of course, has permeated the making of sociology from his time onwards. Putting this point bluntly: this degree of conservatism at least in the role of statesmanship does seem perfectly valid: that the moral and political aims striven for in a society are only likely to be satisfactorily achieved if the policy proposals and plans for them are rooted in as profound an understanding as is possible of the many-dimensioned nature of that society *as it is*. Such a position need not, and does not, exclude idealistic reform, it only urges *care* in conceiving and undertaking it.

At any rate, errors aside, we can see that Durkheim's rules provided not only for the initial observation, description, and clear definition of social facts, but also for the systematic comparison and functional analysis of them in order to establish their 'normal' nature within the institutional 'consensus' of particular types of society.

(III) RULES FOR CLASSIFYING SOCIETIES: THE CONSTRUCTION OF 'TYPES' OR 'SPECIES'

It followed obviously from the kind of comparison needed to establish the 'normal' nature and function of social facts within each distinguishable 'consensus', that—as in the work of all the other sociologists—some classificatory scheme or framework was necessary; and this meant the definition of certain 'types' of society in accordance with the one or more criteria which were thought to be most significant.

In Durkheim's case, he spoke of these 'types' as 'Social Species', and defined them—as Spencer had on one of his criteria—in terms of their degrees of composition.

'We know,' he wrote, 'that societies are composed of various parts in combination . . . the constituent parts of every society are societies more simple than itself . . . Since the nature of the aggregate depends necessarily on *the nature and number of the component elements and their mode of combination*, these characteristics are evidently what we must take as our basis; and we shall see that it is on them that the general facts of social life depend.'*

It should be noted too that Durkheim added one further qualification. In addition to the mere *existence* of many 'segments' in any one

* *Rules*, pp. 80–1.

'amalgamation' (e.g. of tribes, let us say, in a confederation or an empire) it was important also to know to what extent they had coalesced—how far they had become interrelated in a qualitatively new kind of societal unity. Durkheim's full rule, then, was that we should classify societies:

'. . . *according to the degree of organization they present, taking as a basis the perfectly simple society of one segment. Within these types we shall distinguish different varieties according to whether a complete coalescence of the initial segments does or does not appear.'*

This, Durkheim called 'social morphology' : that part of sociology concerned with the 'constitution and classification of social types'.

It is necessary only to say that, having clarified this basis for classification, Durkheim did not himself attempt such a classification. The task, he claimed was too big for him. He did suggest the form which a classification on his basis would take, and distinguished between (1) a hypothetical 'horde' which was (most probably, according to him) the simplest of all human groupings, (2) the aggregation of these into 'simple polysegmental' societies consisting of clans† within the tribe, (3) the aggregation of tribes themselves into confederations to form 'polysegmental societies simply compounded', and then (4) the aggregation of these unions of tribes to form larger societal forms (like the City-States) which were 'polysegmental societies doubly compounded'; but this is as far as he went. It will be readily seen that his method was completely the same as that of the other earlier and contemporary sociologists, but that he did not carry this task of classification as far as they did. These, after all, were *rules*—not the fulfilled employment of them—but still, it is again important to notice that the full employment of them would result in as large and complex a classificatory and comparative schema as that of Hobhouse or of anyone before him.

A final point worthy of note here, too, though it was not outlined in Durkheim's rules, was that—like others before him, he found it necessary to specify *and* employ *two* rather different kinds of classification. The one above was a large framework for descriptive, comparative and analytical study which we have seen before in Spencer, Hobhouse, and others. But, in addition to this, Durkheim found it necessary to construct a *marked typology*—consisting of two extreme, polarized '*models*'—for the purpose of interpreting the most significant pattern of change which societies had experienced as they moved

---

* *Rules*, p. 86.
† It is worth noting that Durkheim regarded the 'clan' as the primal horde—but with a new name. See 'Rules', p. 84.

from the simple to the complex in this schema of 'social aggregation'. Thus, his study of the Division of Labour in society was a large-scale theory (and interpretation) of social change, for which he constructed a clear, and two-fold typology—of a 'mechanical' type of solidarity in the simplest societies and an 'organic' type of solidarity in those possessing a complex differentiation of occupations. This was a typology exactly like that of Tönnies (Gemeinschaft and Gesellschaft) and that of Spencer (Militant and Industrial)—not to mention those constructed by the other writers. Again, then, a very striking similarity and continuity in the conception of what was necessary in a science of society can be seen between the work of the earlier sociologists and that of Durkheim.

So far, then, Durkheim's rules provided clear guidance for the observation, description, definition, classification and comparison of social facts, and, following an additional structural-functional and historical analysis, a study of their 'normal' nature and functions in specified types of society.

Following this, however, what rules could be laid down for achieving a satisfactory *explanation* of them?

(IV) RULES FOR THE EXPLANATION OF SOCIAL FACTS

It was in his arguments for his own conception of the *explanation* of social facts that all Durkheim's ambiguities and confusions crowded thickly upon one another: the reification of social facts, the exclusion of all teleological considerations, the replacing of notions like 'purpose' and 'use', by 'cause' and 'function', and the like; and I cannot myself see that these rules present any real clarity at all. The dangers of *mis*conception seem to far outweigh any clarity of conception one can find in them. Still—our effort must be to disentangle any element that is worthwhile in Durkheim, and certain things, at least, can be said despite all our criticisms.

In trying to outline a clear set of rules for *explanation*, Durkheim was first concerned to eliminate all those kinds of explanation which he thought to be misconceived.

He first attacked the idea that it was a satisfactory (sufficient) explanation of a social fact to describe its *uses* in society *now;* and, a corollary of this, that it was a correct explanation of that fact to say that it had been *purposely* brought into being to *fulfil* these present *uses*. Now in this, Durkheim was clearly correct, and he made one or two points of considerable importance here. He showed clearly that it was an error to suppose an identity between the *structure* (or form) of a social fact and its *function* in the social order. An element of social structure (the form of a law, a custom, a procedure) can remain the same, or be little changed, though its function may change considerably. While remaining the same, it can come to serve different ends. And Durkheim gave various examples of this: as, for example, that of a law pertaining to marriage which remained essentially the same in the modern French code as it had been in the old Roman Law—but which *then* safeguarded the property rights of a man over children born to his legitimate wife, whereas now it protected the rights of children. It followed, clearly, that the *causes* of the social fact must have been *other* than the needs it now served, and that this present *end* could not have been foreseen as a *purpose* among the people in earlier social conditions.

All this can be conceded, and it can be agreed that Durkheim was performing a service in warning against kinds of social explanation which many accepted without reflection and which were too facile and, indeed, false. We can go further and agree with Durkheim fully that to adopt a teleological approach to explanation in the sense of claiming that all the institutional developments of human societies can be explained in terms of some implicit purpose in history which has culminated in the *final ends* which they are now seen to fulfil is an obvious error—a vast and misconceived over-simplification. Thus to 'explain' the many differentiations in the division of labour in past societies in terms of the ultimate 'happiness' which it might bring about in a later society, is obviously over-simplified and worthless. And we can agree further with Durkheim, therefore, that the correct explanations of the emergence and development of social facts require that we examine much more closely the complex and constraining natural and social conditions which men in society, in their own day and age, confronted and had to come to terms with.

With all this we can agree, and we can therefore say that this preamble of Durkheim's—of a 'warning' nature—to the problems of explanation was worthwhile. But when his first rule comes to be framed in these terms:

(a)* '*When the explanation of a social phenomenon is undertaken, we must seek separately the EFFICIENT CAUSE which produces it and the FUNCTION it fulfils . . .*'

—we are compelled to take issue with him *with regard to the extreme way in which he conceived these causes and functions*, because, once again, in eliminating *some* erroneous notions of *utility* and *teleology* he went much too far in excluding them all. This led to his conception of an *efficient cause* in the essentially 'natural science' sense: of a regularity of interconnection between 'things' or 'events' in nature—

* The further elaborations of this rule follow on p. 347.

excluding any notion of *purposive action* or *willing* of men in the context of their institutions altogether: thus eliminating completely that distinguishing kind of causality (resting on apprehension of ends, deployment of means, choice, calculation, purposive pursuit of interests, etc.) on which everyone from Comte and Mill to Ward, Sumner, Giddings, Tönnies, and Hobhouse had insisted. And, of course, it implied his conception of social facts as things 'existing in their own right' *independent* of feeling, thinking, acting individuals. Social facts, he claimed: 'can be explained solely by causes that are *deterministic* and not *at all* purposive.'

Durkheim was very deliberate about this. In the wording of this rule, he also deliberately used the term 'function' in *preference* to 'end' or 'purpose'—'*precisely because social phenomena do not generally exist for the useful results they produce*'. But here again, this was going much too far, and gave rise to much ambiguity.

Following upon the above very definite assertion, Durkheim *seemed* to be making a very clear distinction between 'function' and 'use'. He spoke of the uncovering of the function of a social fact in several ways. One was that of determining whether there was '*a correspondence between the fact under consideration and* THE GENERAL NEEDS OF THE SOCIAL ORGANISM, *and in what this correspondence consists*', and this should be without regard to whether or not such 'correspondence' had been intentional. Another was his statement that the *function* of a social fact (far from being an 'end' which—foreseen—was the 'purposive' cause of that fact) '*served to maintain the pre-existent cause from which it was derived*'. Now quite apart from the fact that we are now faced with the task of determining something called '*the general needs of the social organism*' before we can clarify the function of any specific social fact, we are clearly speaking of a *function* in terms of the satisfaction of *needs* of some sort—and this is not at all distinguishable from speaking of its *use*. And, indeed, inconsistent though it seems, Durkheim—despite the statement which we noted a short time ago that social facts do *not* exist for the useful results they produce—now claimed:

'. . . if the usefulness of a fact is not the cause of its existence, it is generally necessary that it be useful in order that it may maintain itself. For the fact that it is not useful suffices to make it harmful, since in that case it costs effort without bringing in any returns.'*

It turns out that 'functions' are 'useful' after all. And this is even more emphatically clear in the argument as Durkheim continued it—and here, too, we see the looming significance in his analysis of the

* *Rules*, p. 97.

social organism 'as a whole'—as a *system* which is always moving—though through disequilibrating conditions—to an *equilibrium* of order and solidarity.

'If,' he went on, 'the majority of social phenomena had this parasitic character, the budget of the organism would have a deficit and social life would be impossible. Consequently, to have a satisfactory understanding of the latter, it is necessary to show how the phenomena comprising it combine in such a way as to put society in harmony with itself and with the environment external to it. No doubt, the current formula, which defines social life as a correspondence between the internal and the external milieu, is only an approximation; however, it is in general true. Consequently, to explain a social fact it is not enough to show the cause on which it depends; we must also, at least in most cases, show its function in the establishment of social order.'*

And its *functions* are its contributions of *utility* in establishing social order; in satisfying the *general needs* of the social organism *as a whole*.

Now the earlier sociologists, as we have seen, were quite agreed that there were strains to consistency in those interdependencies of institutions in society which were, to some extent, unforeseen consequences of the activities of men, and they were certainly ready to *analyse* the changing patterns of institutions in equilibrium-disequilibrium terms—but they did not think of a *societal entity*, a 'super-organism' of interdependent social facts, which proceeded on its equilibrium-disequilibrium journey *independent* of the purposeful activities of men. Their structural-functional analysis was not related to the *general needs* of the objectively existing social organism as a whole, but to all the manifold activities of men which were continuously taking place within (but also changing—and sometimes consciously!) these institutional forms.

When Durkheim came to give his reasons for excluding the purposive activities of men as 'causal' dimensions in the emergence and development of social facts, they proved to be mixed up with his antagonistic attitude to 'individual' psychology and to teleology in any form.

'At the same time that it is teleological,' he wrote, 'the method of explanation generally followed by sociologists is essentially psychological. These two tendencies are interconnected with one another. In fact, if society is only a system of means instituted by men to attain certain ends, these ends can only be individual, for only individuals could have existed before society. From the individual, then, have emanated the needs and desires

* *Rules*, p. 97.

determining the formation of societies; and, if it is from him that all comes, it is necessarily by him that all must be explained.'*

But what an absurd and over-simplified juxtaposition this was. It is clear that if one is discussing the purposive (teleological) activities of men in society one is not at all necessarily doing so in terms of some 'basic' psychology which leaves out of account all social influences, conditions and constraints. One may well be doing so in terms of *associational elements of human psychology*. Also, one may be doing so not *solely* in terms of psychology at all, but also in terms of *meaning*: in terms of ends, means, calculations, aims, choices, deliberations; and all this, of course had already been very thoroughly discussed by men from Mill to the early Americans and Tönnies. But thirdly, one is not necessarily assuming *at all*, that individuals with *this* associational psychology, and *these* meaningful purposes existed with these qualities *before society*, and that the entirety of society is being explained in these terms.

This sort of argument is just an absurdity. In discarding a kind of large-scale metaphysical notion of 'teleology' as an explanation in terms of 'final ends' (I suppose an Aristotelian—and then a theological—kind), Durkheim also thought fit to discard all elements of human purposiveness whatsoever as constituting grounds of 'causality' in social affairs. But his grounds for doing this were quite specious. And again, here, we must see the metaphysical *entity* of society as Durkheim conceived it.

'Society,' he insisted, 'is not a mere sum of individuals. Rather, the system formed by their association represents a *specific reality* which has its *own characteristics*. Of course, nothing collective can be produced if individual consciousnesses are not assumed; but this necessary condition is by itself insufficient. These consciousnesses must be combined in a certain way; social life results from this combination and is, consequently, explained by it. Individual minds, forming groups by mingling and fusing, give birth to a being, psychological if you will, but *constituting a psychic individuality of a new sort*. It is, then, in the nature of this *collective individuality*, not in that of the associated units, that we must seek the *immediate and determining causes* of the facts appearing therein.'†

The peculiarities of Durkheim's arguments on this matter could be pursued at much greater length, but it is enough to see that in insisting upon the uncovering of *efficient causes* and *functions* as the only satisfactory explanation of social facts, he was, in fact, asserting this peculiarly extreme metaphysical dogma for which he gave no good grounds. Society was a *natural entity*, a *system of social facts*

* *Rules*, pp. 97–8.   † *Ibid.*, pp. 103–4.

at their own level, and an explanation of any of these facts and their relationships was a *deterministic* explanation in terms of cause-and-effect connections between a certain species of 'things'. On the basis of this conception he fully and deliberately excluded all 'purpose' in 'individual consciousnesses' and all 'uses' which individuals could apprehend as 'purposes' from being possible sources of 'explanation' —replacing them completely by *'efficient causes'* among the inter-connections of social facts themselves, and 'functions' in terms of their fulfilment of *societal* needs. It can be seen that the first was arbitrary, and the second a source of much ensuing confusion—since it muddled 'purpose' and 'function', 'use' and 'end' and 'need', in a fog of thorough-going ambiguity. The two distinct rules which were the outcome of this discussion were:

(b) *The determining cause of a social fact should be sought among the social facts preceding it and NOT among the states of the individual consciousness,*

and

(c) *The function of a social fact ought always to be sought in its relation to some SOCIAL end.*

The ambiguity—even in the one rule (b)—can be seen when remembering that Durkheim did not differentiate with any clarity at all between *kinds* of social fact. What is certain (viz. our example of the 'collective sentiments' on which 'crime' was supposed to rest) is that —*among* social facts—were those 'collective representations', elements of 'collective conscience', 'collective sentiments', which were the very bed-rock of the *sanctions* which formed the heart of *institutionalization.* These, he argued, were 'engraven' in the conscience of individuals. If, then, we are not permitted to consider 'the states of the individual consciousness' among the members of a society at any given time—how are we to take into account these social facts of such evident importance? This is not only ambiguity; it is surely sheer mystification. The kind of differentiation made by Mill surely possesses an infinitely greater degree of clarity, analytical accuracy, and good sense.

However, even here, let us note one virtue of Durkheim's rules: namely, that—for the explanation of any social fact they do specify that *two* things, at least are essential: (*a*) a *historical* account—of how a social fact has come to be what it is in terms of antecedent social facts, and (*b*) a *functional* account—of how the social fact is related to the others in society, in a certain pattern of interconnection. These two emphases again we can accept, despite the clouds of disagreement through which we come to them. And this emphasis

347

upon the historical account of social facts leads us to Durkheim's final rule of explanation (i.e. final at least at *this* point; he had other observations to make, as we shall see, when considering sociological *proofs*).

For if social facts can only be explained in terms of the social facts which preceded them, and can never be 'reduced' to any preceding psychological or biological factors, we are involved here in an almost 'infinite regress' of social facts. Only *almost* infinite though! Because the backward tracing of the development of social facts must have a finite terminus in *some* social fact which was original—in the sense that it could be reduced to nothing further. And Durkheim did meet the logic of this situation. Even the *original* causes of a social fact, he argued, resided *not* in any straightforward biological or psychological conditions, but in certain *collective conditions* of the *social milieu*. His rule was:

(*d*) *The first origins of all social processes of any importance should be sought in the* INTERNAL CONSTITUTION *of the* SOCIAL GROUP.

There are two elements in any social milieu: material and immaterial conditions and artefacts (e.g. codes of law, works of literature, etc.—as well as natural resources, buildings, tools, weapons, etc.) on the one hand, and the human milieu (the people of the group in their collective conditions) on the other. Clearly, Durkheim argued, only the latter can be the source of the creative energy that leads to institutionalization and the development of society. The sociologist must therefore seek some characteristics of this human–social milieu which—without reduction to psychological and biological factors—can be shown to be responsible for the *causation* and the development of social facts. There were, he claimed, *two* such characteristics. These were firstly—the sheer *number* of units in the group (the sheer size of population in the society), and secondly—the degree of '*dynamic density*' of all these units in their interaction in the group as a whole. The growth in the size of a population, together with an increase in its 'dynamic density' (or 'moral intensity') as the greater number of people are brought together in a shared interdependency of effort in meeting the conditions of their collective existence: these are two major factors, at least, which underlie the emergence of 'collective sentiments', 'sanctions', 'institutions' and the detailed developments of social facts. It is important, too, to notice that Durkheim stressed the importance of these factors for special groups *within* a society (e.g. familial, professional groups, etc.) as well as for a society as a *total* population. Always, he insisted, the concentration of the sociologist should be upon the *milieus* of groups—whether small or large; it was in the qualities and conditions of these *group milieus* that the *causes* of thè *origins* and *developments* of social facts were to be found.

Now here again—all our disagreements aside—it is clear that Durkheim clearly contributed a very firm and important, indeed a *crucial* emphasis. For—whether men act purposively or not—it is certainly within the *collective* conditions of their life (which bring definite constraints, influences, possibilities of opportunity, necessity, to bear upon them) that *associational* sanctions, procedures, sentiments, arise. And in this, again, Durkheim emphasized an essential aspect of the sociological perspective more vividly than almost anyone else. All errors aside, he directed clear attention to the *objective conditions of collective existence* as the *milieu* within which distinctively *associational* facts arose, And very important matters were attendant upon this emphasis, because in considering it, Durkheim was especially clear as to what, fully, he took a *causal* relation to be. A causal account of a social fact was not either a historical account *or* a functional account; but *essentially required both*. A historical account could trace the actual sequential nature of a social fact, but comparative and functional analysis could clarify its place within the conditions of the social milieu. *General, causal* relationships between social facts could thus be established—not simply historical chronologies, or functional analyses, but the *explanation* of their *actual* (and *universal*—in societies of specific types) *interdependencies within specified social milieus*.

'This conception of the social milieu,' Durkheim argued, 'as the determining factor of collective evolution, is of the highest importance. If we reject it, sociology cannot establish any relations of causality.'*

It is most important, too, to notice very strongly here what Durkheim meant by 'origins'—because this, both in him and in others, has so often been misunderstood. And again it is very interesting to see that Durkheim's position here was exactly that of Westermarck. In insisting upon the necessity (for a full and satisfactory explanation of a social fact) of an accurate analysis of its 'origins'—Durkheim very specifically did *not* mean an attempt to uncover the very first instance of it (chronologically speaking) in history. He meant quite clearly the necessity of clarifying those fundamental social causes (conditions of the social milieu) which (wherever and whenever they were found) accounted for its emergence. And it was *in this sense only*, that he sought the 'origins' of social facts in the simplest available forms of human society. This is a very important point, and I would like to substantiate it very forcibly by a brief

* *Rules*, p. 117.

glance at Durkheim's argument in approaching his study of the nature of religion.

'Why,' he wrote, 'give primitive religions a sort of prerogative? Why choose them in preference to all others as the subject of our study?—It is merely for reasons of method.

In the first place, we cannot arrive at an understanding of the most recent religions except by following the manner in which they have been progressively composed in history. In fact, *historical analysis is the only means of explanation* which it is possible to apply to them. It alone enables us to resolve an institution into its constituent elements, for it shows them to us as they are born in time, one after another. On the other hand, *by placing every one of them in the condition where it was born*, it puts into our hands the only means we have of determining *the causes* which gave rise to it. Every time that we undertake to explain something human, taken at a given moment in history—be it a religious belief, a moral precept, a legal principle, an aesthetic style or an economic system—it is necessary to commence by going back to its most primitive and simple form, to try to account for the characteristics by which it was marked at that time, and then to show how it developed and became complicated little by little, and how it became that which it is at the moment in question.'*

But, Durkheim argued strongly, to seek to clarify the *origins* of religion is not at all (in his method) simply to discover its *first instance*.

'The study we are undertaking,' he went on, 'is therefore a way of taking up again, *but under new conditions*, the old problem of the origin of religion . . . If by origin we are to understand the *very first beginning*, the question has nothing scientific about it, and should be resolutely discarded. There was no given moment when religion began to exist, and there is consequently no need of finding a means of transporting ourselves thither in thought. Like every human institution, religion did not commence anywhere. Therefore, all speculations of this sort are justly discredited; they can only consist in subjective and arbitrary constructions which are subject to no sort of control. But the problem which we raise is quite another one. What we want to do is to find a means of discerning the *ever-present causes* upon which the most *essential forms* of religious thought and practice depend. Now for the reasons which were just set forth, these causes are proportionately more easily observable as the societies where they are observed are less complicated. That is why we try to get as near as possible to the *origins*.'†

And he further emphasized this in a footnote:†

'It is seen that we give a wholly relative sense to this word "origins", just

* *The Elementary Forms*, p. 3.   † *Ibid.*, p. 8.

as to the word "primitive". By it we do not mean an absolute beginning, but the most simple social condition that is actually known or that beyond which we cannot go at present. When we speak of the origins or of the commencement of a social fact, it is in this sense that our statements should be understood.'

This, it will be seen was exactly the position of Westermarck in seeking the 'origins' and the 'development' of *sanctions* (as *institutionalized* relationships) and the moral ideas which lay at the heart of them. It was an attempt, in exactly the same way, to get at the conditions of *causality* of human institutions. The similarity and continuity in these apparently widely separated developments in the making of sociology are very striking.

These, then, were Durkheim's rules for explaining the origins and changing nature of social facts once they had been observed, described, compared, and arranged by classification for further analysis. The next question, however, was how to *test* such explanations? How to establish sociological proofs? These final rules were perhaps the most interesting and distinctive that Durkheim proposed, and they contained one or two further dimensions of 'explanation'.

(v) Rules for TESTING Sociological Explanations : for Establishing Sociological PROOFS.

Durkheim's rigorous effort to establish sociology as an independent *science*, dealing with a distinctive range of facts, was perhaps nowhere more evident than in this insistence upon the *testability* of theories. All his rules were directed to clear *definition*, to the laying out of clear, delimited, *definitive* studies which offered specific theories of specific facts, and—finally—he insisted that the crucial culmination of scientific work was its deliberate concentration upon *testing* these theories as carefully as possible. Of course, all the earlier theorists had been concerned with this problem, but it is fair to claim that Durkheim adopted a more rigorous position with regard to it than they.

His fundamental standpoint was stark and simple: the *only* exact method of testing theories (explanations) was that of the *crucial experiment*. In sociology this seemed impossible, and the only alternative was therefore that of *indirect experiment: the comparative method*. 'Social Facts', as Durkheim had described and defined them, could not be artificially manipulated, or even produced, to accord with anything like controlled experimental conditions; it was only possible to 'bring them together in the way that they have spontaneously been produced' and compare and contrast them in some carefully controlled way; within the framework of some carefully constructed procedure.

It is worthwhile to note one point immediately: and that is that 'the Comparative Method' has been variously conceived in sociology. Here—two such conceptions can be clearly distinguished. In the work of Comte, Mill, Spencer, Hobhouse (and others), and even in some part of the work of Durkheim itself, the Comparative Method was advocated and employed in a predominantly exploratory and inductive sense. Categories of 'types' of society, social species, levels of development, were set up, and descriptive knowledge about many societies was manageably brought together and arranged within these frameworks to establish or to demonstrate certain regularities of institutional 'consensus'. We have seen that this was by no means entirely 'inductive'—but it was certainly a schematic method for systematic descriptive and analytical study. A second conception of the 'Comparative Method' was, however, quite sharply distinguished from this—and this was the strict conception of it as the only alternative to the experimental method possessed by sociology. The first was (though not entirely) a schematic method of study; the second was the *strictest possible method of testing*. And it is important to see that, though Durkheim advocated both—it was the second on which he placed by far the greatest emphasis, with regard, that is, to the *scientific exactitude and accuracy* of sociology. Indeed Durkheim and Weber—each in his own way—were distinctive especially for their emphasis upon this astringency. Theories should be definitive; and they should be *tested*; and the Comparative Method should be construed to meet as satisfactorily as possible the discipline of experiment.

John Stuart Mill, chiefly, had discussed the difficulties of experimentation, and Durkheim showed himself well aware of Mill's ideas.* Like Mill, he rejected the methods of 'agreement', 'difference', 'residues', and the like, and for the same reasons—that societies, in all their complexities, could not be found which could be analysed and matched to meet all the demands of such methods. Here, however, it is enough simply to state Durkheim's positive conclusions.

His first insistence was that the comparative method was to be employed to test explanations of *causal* connections between social facts, and that it must proceed on the assumption that *a given effect has always a single corresponding cause*. In societies, the actual entanglements of cause and effect were exceedingly complex, but still—this should lead only to a realistic recognition of complexity, *not* any rejection of this assumption of the cause—effect relation.

* It is important to notice the continuity in the making of the subject even here. Durkheim's 'Rules' were arrived at by way of a critical assessment of Mill's proposals of method—as well as those of Comte, Spencer, and others.

In this, Durkheim again asserted that social phenomena differed from other phenomena *only* in their 'greater complexity', and therefore thought of the 'causal relation' in terms of ordinary 'efficient causation', and this, as we have seen, was a very insufficient position, hiding hosts of problems. However, his insistence upon his own extreme did in fact produce a very valuable method—one which Mill had mentioned, but which Durkheim raised to the method 'par excellence' of comparative sociology.

The Comparative Method, he argued, should be rigorously based upon the method of 'concomitant variations' or 'correlation'. Constant concomitance between social facts, he insisted, was *a law in itself*. If comparative studies demonstrated that two social facts (and variations in them) were constantly concomitant with each other—then this was a proof that some definite relationship existed between them. To establish such correlations was, in itself, to establish *regularities*, or *laws*, which could then be further and more fully investigated. And this method had, Durkheim claimed, certain great advantages.

Firstly, such concomitance between specified facts could be established, even though it may not have been possible to exclude all other variables. The method did not require that variables be 'isolated' in any rigorous experimental sense. It was, therefore, a *manageable* method. But the constant 'parallelism' between two facts, if established in a 'sufficient number and variety of cases', was 'proof that a relationship existed between them'. And this meant, secondly, that a deeper analysis of the 'cause-effect' actualities which underlay this correlation could be fruitfully pursued. The 'constant concomitance'—though a 'law'*—was not necessarily observed as a *causal* relation. Indeed, it may not *be* a direct causal relation. It may be that some other (third) factor, or condition, was causing concomitant effects in both. The point was, however, that such details could be deeply investigated once the constant concomitance was established. Durkheim himself gave the example of the fact that the tendency to suicide varied directly with education, but suggested that this connection might well require a *causal* explanation in terms of a third condition—the weakening of religious traditionalism. He formulated this part of his rule in this way. Once the constant concomitance between two facts has been established:

'We shall first investigate, by the aid of deduction, how one of the two terms has produced the other; then we shall try to verify the result of this deduction with the aid of experiments, i.e. new comparisons. If the

---

* We may remember Comte's notion of a 'law' simply as a 'regularity of connection' between phenomena.

deduction is possible and if the verification succeeds, we can regard the proof as complete. If, on the contrary, we are aware of no direct bond between these facts, especially if the hypothesis of such a bond contradicts laws already demonstrated, we shall begin to look for a third phenomenon on which the other two depend equally or which have served as an intermediary between them.'*

This was perfectly clear. The third advantage of this method was, Durkheim claimed, its simplicity, or—perhaps better—its scientific economy. One of the disadvantages of the comparative schemes of the earlier sociologists, was, quite literally, the hugeness of the compendiums of knowledge which they assembled and seemed to require. With the method of concomitant variations, Durkheim argued:

'In order to obtain results, a few facts suffice. As soon as one has proved that, in a certain number of cases, two phenomena vary with one another, one is certain of being in the presence of a law. Having no need to be numerous, the documents can be selected and, further, studied more closely by the sociologist.

Not only will he thus limit more intelligently the extent of his comparisons, but he will conduct them with a more critical spirit; for, by the very fact that he will confine himself to a restricted order of facts, he will be able to check them with more care.'†

Again, this was meticulously clear, It is very important, however, to bear strongly in mind that though Durkheim was writing in simple terms here about *definitive*—and therefore critically delimited— studies, the *scale* of such studies was, nonetheless, very considerable. It is worthwhile to recall his earlier rule that once a social fact has been defined, *all* facts falling within this definition should be brought into the particular study. This is especially important here because, having set out this account of the comparative method, resting essentially upon 'concomitant variations', Durkheim then went on to argue that such studies should cover the investigation of the 'forms' which these concomitant social facts assumed in *all social species*: so that, in fact, he was back to a picture of very substantial and wide-ranging studies indeed. His final element of this account of the method of establishing proofs was:

'One cannot explain a social fact of any complexity except by following its complete development through all social species.'

If one thinks, for example, of tracing the relationship between

* *Rules*, p. 132.   † *Ibid.*, pp. 133–4.

354

the tendency to suicide, education, and the state of religious tradition-alism (to take the example mentioned by Durkheim) *in all social species*—it will be readily seen that, this is not a light, or a limited, task! Though, therefore, Durkheim's account of the comparative method was unquestionably clear and astringent, it did not, indeed it could not, escape the largeness of scale which any worthwhile and sufficient sociological theory must encompass. Durkheim's rules for establishing proofs can be summarized as follows:

(1) Crucial experiment is the method of testing theories.
(2) The Comparative Method is the only (and the closest) alternative to experiment which sociology possesses.
(3) The most stringent formulation of the Comparative Method is to base it upon the method of 'Concomitant Variations'.
(4) To establish constant concomitance is itself to establish 'laws' —to establish demonstrable 'regularities of connection'.
(5) The causal relations underlying this concomitance can then be investigated further—by deductive inference, more refined hypotheses, and further comparisons.
(6) For a full explanation of such a 'concomitance', and for a full test of such an explanation, the social facts in question should be studied in all social species.

It will be seen that one further merit of this comparative method (and one which Durkheim exploited a great deal in his own particular studies), was that it could accomplish much by the process of *elimination*. Without itself having arrived at a conclusive *causal* analysis, it could—with the establishment of 'concomitance'—at least *eliminate* all those existing hypotheses which failed to take this accurately into account. It was, indeed, a method of *testing* existing theories, even whilst yet pursuing a positive *causal* explanation itself. And this was a very telling point in its favour.

Before going further it is worthwhile to note this one very straight-forward, but extremely important point: that Durkheim had produced a set of 'rules of sociological method' which gave clear guidance to any student who chose to read them. These rules—in reasonably short compass—defined the subject-matter of sociology; defined the nature of the distinctive 'social facts' with which it dealt; made clear the attitudes of mind which should be adopted in the empirical observation, description and classification of them; set out what was required, *at the very least*, for a satisfactory explanation of them, and, finally, gave an account of that conception of the comparative method—the alternative to experimentation—by which such explanations (such theories) could be tested. Though it could be argued, as we have argued, that there were many insufficiencies and ambiguities in Durkheim's conceptions—this straightforward fact remained: that a meticulously clear procedure had been laid down for the production of carefully outlined *definitive* studies which would be open to test in quite determinate ways. This was, then, a very considerable achievement, and a most important contribution to the making of the subject. Whatever dimensions might be *lacking* in Durkheim's conception of causal relations between the 'facts' of human society, the establishing of 'laws' of constant concomitance between the objectively perceived attributes of social 'facts' and the attempt to look further into the causal relations among the specific 'nexus' of elements thus revealed, could only be of positive value in the advancement of knowledge.

The major contributions of Durkheim can now be very clearly seen, but, before stating our summary conclusions about these, it is worthwhile to glance—though briefly—at the studies of specific social facts which he himself undertook, because this will not only indicate the degree of utility of his rules when actually applied, but will also reveal quite fundamentally—by making clear the subject-matter on which Durkheim concentrated—the complete continuity of his work with that of his predecessors.

(4) *The Application of the Rules : Durkheim's Study of Particular Aspects of Social Solidarity*

It is impossible, clearly, to undertake a thorough critique of each of Durkheim's major studies, but something can be gained from limited comments about them. In the first place, it is a considerable point in Durkheim's favour that he did not *only* attempt a clarification of sociological theory and method, or only produce a number of empirical studies. He did both. His theoretical conception and his rules were formulated in the actual efforts to produce accurate and reliable explanations of problems which were of concern to him. In short, Durkheim's work was marked by a great consistency of effort to clarify sociological method and to demonstrate its usefulness in application. *And*—and this is supremely important—this effort was undertaken *not* for the sake of establishing a 'professional expertise' alone, but because of his concern for real human problems which disturbed him greatly, and his commitment to the task of not only *understanding* them, of *knowing* about them, but also of *solving* them by political and social action. And it is when we come to ask what these problems were that we see Durkheim's complete agreement with the concerns which had wracked the minds of his predecessors from Comte onwards.

Not much can be attempted by way of substantive analysis of each of these studies, but we will have an eye to two things chiefly: firstly Durkheim's consistency in the application of his rules, and the extent to which they were proved useful, and secondly, the basic nature of the social problem which formed their subject-matter—because this was the feature which unified his entire work, and also linked him closely and vividly with the other founders of sociology. At first glance, Durkheim's particular studies seem to cover a wide and unconnected range of topics—*The Division of Labour in Society*, *Suicide*, and *The Elementary Forms of the Religious Life*—but, in fact, they were all aspects of *one* concern: a concern to understand the conditions which produced *social solidarity* (settled community) in society; and how to overcome those conditions in modern industrial society which seemed—tragically—to be destroying it. It will be seen at once that this was the central 'malaise' of modern industrial society which had wracked the minds of all those committed to the making of sociology from Comte onwards—which had been the central theme in Mill, Marx, Spencer, the Americans, in the nineteenth century, and was still the central theme in all the developments of the twentieth —in Tönnies and Hobhouse, for example. And Durkheim was forthrightly clear in his own position that the making of sociology as a science was necessary *because* the understanding of society was necessary for its satisfactory reconstruction. It was the task of re-making society which necessitated the making of sociology—this was the order of things in his mind. Though clearly distinguishing the role of the sociologist from that of the statesman, it was the *practical utility* of the results of sociology to which Durkheim attributed ultimate importance.

'Our constant preoccupation,' he wrote at the end of the *Rules*, 'has been to orient it so that it might have practical results.'*

And, in *The Division of Labour:*

'. . . we should judge our researches to have no worth at all if they were to have only speculative interest. If we separate carefully the theoretical from the practical problems, it is not to the neglect of the latter; but, on the contrary, to be in a better position to solve them.'†

Let us glance briefly at each of the three studies mentioned to see the nature and dimensions of the 'malaise' of modern society as Durkheim saw it.

(I) THE DIVISION OF LABOUR IN SOCIETY

On the face of it, this would seem to be a limited study of the econo-

* *Rules*, p. 143.　　　　　† *Division of Labour*, p. 33.

357

mic aspects of society, and, in a sense that will become clear, this was its central concentration. The entire emphasis of Durkheim, however, was to insist that the division of labour in society was the most basic and all-pervading *moral* fact of society and that it was the rapidly changing nature of the division of labour which was leading to the disruption of social solidarity in the modern industrial world and the moral 'malaise'—the directionlessness of beliefs, ideals, values, rules for the ordering of aspiration and conduct—which men experienced in it. It is as good an indication as any to say that Durkheim's account of the changing division of labour was exactly of the kind put forward by Tönnies: that of a change from stable traditional community to a condition of complex, contractual associations—marked by a growing fever of restlessness, discontent, bewilderment, dissatisfaction, and—above all—a sense of isolation in the individual from the social complexity, within which he was compelled to live. Like Tönnies—Durkheim, too, constructed two 'types'—in his case the 'Mechanical' and the 'Organic' types of social solidarity—in order clearly to analyse the nature of this transition; and, like Tönnies, too, his study culminated in proposals for solving the malaise—though he was a good deal more positive in this than Tönnies was prepared to be. But this first point is—really— that Durkheim's study, though *apparently* focused upon changes in the *economic* structure of society, was, in fact, a large-scale study of the entire moral, legal and political dilemmas experienced by society as simple, traditional, agrarian societies gave way increasingly to the conditions of industrial capitalism. It was, in short, the same kind of full-scale analysis of the dilemmas of industrial capitalism as that offered by Comte, Marx, and Tönnies—to mention only a few. The problem was the same!

Consistently with his rules, Durkheim looked for the causes of the growth of the structural and functional complexity of society *not* in individual psychology *nor* in individual *purposes* (e.g. the further- ance of happiness). He saw men as being *constrained* towards greater complexities of social organization by collective conditions arising in the social *milieu*. Two factors, at least, he thought, producing such conditions, were clear. Firstly, the sheer growth in the numerical size of a population, and secondly, the concomitant growth in the *dyna- mic density* or *moral intensity* experienced by such populations as they had to make greater demands upon each other in meeting their needs by working together in exploiting the same natural resources. The more complex division of labour in society was an outcome of this increased dynamic density.

Clearly, however, this division of labour—in relating men to each other and to their social tasks—was therefore the most important basis of social solidarity and morality in society. It was in this network of reciprocal, co-operative. interdependent relationships that men encountered their most urgent obligations and duties, and in relation to their most urgent needs. And, indeed, Durkheim sought to show in his comparative studies, that the 'normal' function of the division of labour (again consistently with his rules—'found on the average in each social species') was, in fact, to produce and preserve social solidarity. In modern industrial societies, however, the division of labour which was 'normal' to the new market situation of manufacture and commerce was 'pathological'* in society at large, in that it produced there—not solidarity and moral order—but, on the contrary, a condition of 'anomie'—of 'normlessness', a condition in which the thinking, feeling, and acting of men in their personal life and social relations was characterized by *disorder* and, indeed, by moral anarchy.† How could this be explained?

'This work had its origins,' wrote Durkheim, 'in the question of the relations of the individual to social solidarity. Why does the individual, while becoming more autonomous, depend more upon society? . . . these two movements, contradictory as they appear, develop in parallel fashion. This is the problem we are raising. It appeared to us that what resolves this apparent antinomy is a transformation of social solidarity due to the steadily growing development of the division of labour.'‡

In order to analyse this transformation of the division of labour and the nature of social solidarity, Durkheim constructed his two 'types'. Having, as he thought, established that the function of the division of labour was to unite the specialization of tasks in society in an over-all social solidarity; and having insisted that this was essentially a basic *moral* order pervading society; Durkheim then sought the *external characteristics* (consistent with his rules) whereby the nature of the morality existing among the people might be measured. To put this slightly differently—he looked for some *observable index* of the nature and intensity of the *collective moral sentiments* which operated in a society. This 'visible symbol', he argued, was *the law* in society, and, going a little farther than this, it was the *sanctions* manifested in the law which were a clear index of the intensity with which certain moral precepts were held in the 'sentiments' of the community. He then argued that two 'great classes' of sanctions could be distinguished among juridical rules— 'repressive' and 'restitutive' sanctions: the first characterizing penal

* We have already noted Durkheim's inconsistency on this point.
† The great similarity with Comte's analysis can be seen clearly here.
‡ *Division of Labour*, p. 37.

N

law, the second characterizing other elements of the law—such as civil, commercial, procedural, administrative and constitutional law; and his two 'types' of social solidarity were constructed on this basis.

In relatively simple societies—possessing a relatively simple division of labour, with simple techniques traditionally regulated and repeated from generation to generation; with only a moderate 'dynamic density' among the population; with a wide-spread familiarity of awareness and a sense of 'likeness' or similarity among its members; and with—predominantly—a body of regulatory law which was 'repressive'—there was what Durkheim called a 'Mechanical Solidarity'. People, though performing special tasks, did so within a simple framework of rules, traditions, and expectations and were not too much dependent on each other. The values and rules of society could be upheld by a simple 'repressive' law which visited the indignation of society upon the offender—punishing him, seeking an 'expiation' of his guilt in so doing, and, above all, reinforcing the traditional morality of the people as a whole. Such a society could become quite large—even embracing the earlier civilizations and the 'City States' of antiquity, and the 'ancien régime' of Christendom. The crucial element to which Durkheim pointed was that— in all such societies—the 'industrial corporation' (or the occupational group) was not only an economic enterprise; a narrow contractual relationship of an economic nature only. It was in the fullest sense a *social* group—providing many social and communal supports, functions, festivities (even)—and being also a basis of *moral* and even of *religious* life. The 'industrial' (or economic) life of the people still found a fully ordered place within the intimate context of the wider fabric of values and other social institutions. There was a clear, supported, and continuously reinforced consensus of traditional values and practices linking man's economic life meaningfully and richly with the entirety of society.

At the other extreme there was the sharply distinguished 'type' of the very large and complex society of the nation based upon modern industrial capitalism; and this was characterized by curious—but clearly related—paradoxes. First of all a greatly increased population brought with it a greatly intensified *dynamic density* among its members; a greatly increased *moral intensity* of reciprocal demands, contracts, needs, obligation, duties. Secondly, this brought into being a division of labour of a much more highly specialized kind which brought with it curiously conflicting tendencies : indeed *paradoxical socio-psychological* conditions. On the one hand, the extreme specialization bound men together in bonds of close dependence upon each other which were—*objectively*—quite inescapable. Men could not now manage *at all* to sustain their mode of life alone—to make their own spectacles, motor-cars, fountain pens, shoes, suits of clothes, etc. They were inextricably bound up into the complex fabric of economic organization. They were objectively constrained by these general, external 'social facts' (which were themselves rooted in inescapable 'collective conditions'). At the self-same time, individuals were *subjectively* denuded of many dimensions not only of social and moral, but also of *economic* life. They were themselves, now, simply units of labour, factors of production. Work itself was not a creative activity—embodying personal skill in creating a whole object for clearly seen use; it was a specialized, automatic 'bit' of a process of production. Even the work-relations of men (their group-relationships at work) were no longer of a full social nature—but narrowed down to the sheer economic compulsion of wage-earning. And the complex, contractual structure of economic enterprise was oriented entirely to contractual interest—so that no over-all unity of belief or morality; of social or personal discipline; unified this complexity. There was, in fact, a condition of 'anomie'—of 'normlessness' —in which men—compulsorily constrained by the objective pressures of specialization, were subjectively adrift: unrelated to each other in any satisfying way, and possessing no framework for a meaningful life—whether as citizen or as person. This complexity was both marked, and, if anything, furthered, by the growing predominance of 'restitutive law'—whose 'rationale' was simply to make restitution for injuries done; to ensure 'the return of things as they were'; but this reinforced little more than the propriety of contract itself. This second 'type' was that which Durkheim called 'Organic Solidarity'—to indicate the intricate nature of interdependence within it.

One of his crucial points was that, in the movement from the 'Mechanical' to the 'Organic' type of solidarity, the division of labour itself became the principal ground of social solidarity. His argument was that social change had proceeded so rapidly that there had not been time for a thorough 'adjustment' of social institutions to take place, and his ultimate proposal was that such an 'adjustment' should be assisted by political policy by deliberately bringing about an appropriate 'reconstitution' of the 'industrial corporation'.

Many of Durkheim's comments—by way of diagnosis and prognosis of this vast economic and social 'malaise'—are of the greatest interest and relevance to the problems now besetting our societies— of struggles within Trades Unionism, between Unions and Employers, and between both of these and Government, in relation to some new structure of industrial organization and industrial relations—and the 'Division of Labour' is a powerful and important book which still has to be taken into account in all our thinking about these problems.

Durkheim argued, for example, that 'provincialism' was dead—and that nothing could now be effective which did not recognize the largeness of scale and the centralization of society. Similarly no 'political' solution—whether 'regional' or 'central' could put these matters right. They were beyond the range of ordinary political policies. They required a thorough re-organization from top to bottom of industry itself. Especially, they required the actual re-creation, the resuscitation, of the entire *industrial corporation* itself —for, Durkheim argued, this had come to be too much split up into senseless and expedient 'specialisms'; and this should give its attention again (as in all previous societies) to social, moral, communal aspects of the provisions for life of its members—and not to economic matters alone. Similarly, Durkheim had much to say about the kinds of orientation to values that would best give the individual a stable and meaningful basis for life within these modern conditions and his chief suggestion was that of making a virtue out of *specialization*. The days were gone when men could think of a full, rounded education and life encompassing all. Their emphasis should now be upon performing one task with satisfactory skill in contributing to the complex division of labour as a whole. In such an orientation could lie a satisfactory 'ethic', and, perhaps, a satisfactory personal and social ideology for life within these new industrial conditions. 'The categorical imperative of the moral conscience,' Durkheim argued, 'is assuming the following form: *make yourself usefully fulfill a determinate function.*'

Certain aspects of Durkheim's proposals in all this—both with regard to society and the individual—seem so important as to deserve a rather more elaborate statement. It is important to see that in his proposals for the reconstitution of the 'industrial corporation' he saw this as a kind of 'filling in' of the gap between individual and state with elements of socio-economic organization which would effectively focus men's allegiance and many-sided social life and effort; and as the provision of an actual set of social conditions which would themselves engender new moral sentiments and new juridical rules—rather than any simple legislative provision of 'laws' themselves, which, for Durkheim, was putting the cart before the horse. The nation, he wrote:

'... can be maintained only if, between the State and the individual, there is intercalated a whole series of secondary groups near enough to the individuals to attract them strongly in their sphere of action and drag them, in this way, into the general torrent of social life. Occupational groups are suited to fill this role, and that is their destiny.'*

And again:

'The only way to resolve this antinomy is to set up a cluster of collective forces outside the State, though subject to its action, whose regulative influence can be exerted with greater variety. Not only will our reconstituted corporations satisfy this condition, but it is hard to see what other groups could do so. For they are close enough to the facts, directly and constantly in contact with them, to detect all their nuances, and they should be sufficiently autonomous to be able to respect their diversity. To them, therefore, falls the duty of presiding over companies of insurance, benevolent aid and pensions, the need of which are felt by so many good minds but which we rightly hesitate to place in the hands of the State, already so powerful and awkward; theirs it should likewise be to preside over the disputes constantly arising between the branches of the same occupation, to fix conditions—but in different ways according to the different sorts of enterprise—with which contracts must agree in order to be valid, in the name of the common interest to prevent the strong from unduly exploiting the weak, etc. As labour is divided, law and morality assume a different form in each special function, though still resting everywhere on the same general principles. Besides the rights and duties common to all men, there are others depending on qualities peculiar to each occupation, the number of which increases in importance as occupational activity increasingly develops and diversifies. For each of these special disciplines an equally special organ is needed, to apply and maintain it. Of whom could it consist if not of the workers engaged in the same function?

This restoration, the need of which is universally felt, unfortunately has to contend with the bad name left in history by the corporations of the ancient regime. Yet is there not more proof of their indispensability in the fact that they have lasted not merely since the Middle Ages but since Greco-Roman antiquity, than of their uselessness in the fact of their recent abrogation? If occupational activity has been corporatively organized, except for a single century, wherever it has developed to any extent, is it not most probable that such organization is necessary, and that if it was no longer equal to its role a hundred years ago, the remedy was to restore and improve, not radically to suppress it?'†

Because of the supreme importance of getting this aspect of Durkheim's position clear, I cannot forebear the inclusion of the following meticulously clear passage in his book on *Suicide* which not only states the matter clearly but also indicates the sweep of historical comparison that Durkheim took into account in his studies.

Our historical development, he wrote, has:

* *Division of Labour*, p. 28.   † *Suicide*, pp. 380–1.

'. . . swept cleanly away all the older social forms of organization. One after another, they have disappeared either through the slow usury of time or through great disturbances, but without being replaced. Society was originally organized on the family basis; it was formed by the union of a number of smaller societies, clans, all of whose members were or considered themselves kin. This organization seems to have remained long in a pure state. The family quite soon ceases to be a political division and becomes the centre of private life. Territorial groupings then succeeds the old family grouping. Individuals, occupying the same area gradually, but independently of consanguinity, contract common ideas and customs which are not to the same extent those of their neighbours who live farther away. Thus, little aggregations come to exist with no other material foundation than neighbourhood and its resultant relations, each one, however, with its own distinct physiognomy; we have the village, or better, the city-state and its dependent territory. Of course, they ao not usually shut themselves off in savage isolation. They become confederated, combine under various forms and thus develop more complex societies which they enter however without sacrificing their personalities. They remain the elemental segments of which the whole society is merely an enlarged reproduction. But bit by bit, as these confederations become tighter, the territorial surroundings blend with one another and .ose their former moral individuality. From one city or district to another, the differences decrease. The great change brought about by the French Revolution was precisely to carry this levelling to a point hitherto unknown. Not that it improvised this change; the latter had long since been prepared by the progressive centralization to which the ancient regime had advanced. But the legal suppression of the former provinces and the creation of new, purely artificial and nominal divisions definitely made it permanent. Since then the development of means of communication, by mixing the populations, has almost eliminated the last traces of the old dispensation. And since what remained of occupational organization was violently destroyed at the same time, all secondary organs of social life were done away with.

Only one collective form survived the tempest: the State. By the nature of things this therefore tended to absorb all forms of activity which had a social character, and was henceforth confronted by nothing but an unstable flux of individuals. But then, by this very fact, it was compelled to assume functions for which it was unfitted and which it has not been able to discharge satisfactorily. It has often been said that the State is as intrusive as it is impotent. It makes a sickly attempt to extend itself over all sorts of things which do not belong to it, or which it grasps only by doing them violence. Thence the expenditure of energy with which the State is reproached and which is truly out of proportion with the results obtained. On the other hand, individuals are no longer subject to any other collective control but the State's, since it is the sole organized collectivity. Individuals are made aware of society and of the dependence upon it only through the State. But since this is far from them, it can exert only a distant, discontinuous influence over them; which is why this feeling has neither the necessary constancy nor strength. For most of their lives nothing about them draws them out of themselves and imposes restraint on them. Thus they inevitably lapse into egoism or anarchy. Man cannot become attached to higher aims and submit to a rule if he sees nothing above him to which he belongs. To free him from all social pressure is to abandon him to himself and demoralize him. These are really the two characteristics of our moral situation. While the State becomes inflated and hypertrophied in order to obtain a firm enough grip upon individuals, but without succeeding, the latter, without mutual relationships, tumble over one another like so many liquid molecules, encountering no central energy to retain, fix and organize them.

To remedy this evil, the restitution to local groups of something of their old autonomy is periodically suggested. This is called decentralization. But the only really useful decentralization is one which would simultaneously produce a greater concentration of social energies. Without loosening the bonds uniting each part of society with the State, moral powers must be created with an influence, which the State cannot have, over the multitude of individuals. Today neither the commune, the department nor the province has enough ascendancy over us to exert this influence; we see in them only conventional labels without meaning. Of course, other things being equal, people usually prefer to live where they were born and have been reared. But local patriotisms no longer exist nor can they exist. The general life of the country, permanently unified, rebels at all dispersion of this sort. We may regret the past—but in vain. It is impossible to artificially resuscitate a particularist spirit which no longer has any foundation. Henceforth it will be possible to lighten somewhat the functioning of the machinery of government by various ingenious combinations; but the moral stability of society can never be affected in this way. By so doing the burden of over-loaded ministries can be reduced or a little more scope given to the activity of regional authorities; but not in this way will so many moral environments be constructed from the different regions. For in addition to the fact that administrative measures would be inadequate to achieve such a result, the result itself is neither possible nor desirable.

The only decentralization which would make possible the multiplication of the centres of communal life without weakening national unity is what might be called *occupational decentralization*. For, as each of these centres would be only the focus of a special, limited activity, they would be inseparable from one another and the individual could thus form attachments there without becoming less solidary with the whole. Social life can be divided, while retaining its unity, only if each of these divisions represents a function. This has been understood by the ever growing number of authors and statesmen, who wish to make the occupational group the base of our political organization, that is, divide the electoral college, not by sections of territory but by corporations. But first the corporation must be organized. It must be more than an assemblage of individuals who meet on election day without any common bond. It can fulfil its destined role only if, in place of being a creature of convention, it becomes a definite institution, a collective personality, with its customs

365

and traditions, its rights and duties, its unity. The great difficulty is not to decree that the representatives shall be selected by occupation and what each occupation's share shall be, but to make each corporation become a moral individuality. Otherwise, only another external and artificial sub-division will be added to the existing ones which we wish to supplant.'*

And in all this, Durkheim not only portayed the clear position of the individual, but also tried to emphasize that—if such a reconstitution were possible, and could be achieved—the complex, specialized society did in fact provide the basis for the richest fulfilment and freedom of the individual, and, indeed, that there was a definite illusion in looking back to the traditional society with its 'mechanical solidarity' as being something happier or superior.

Emphasizing that man was a moral being only because he lived in society, and that, as society advanced in size, growth, and com-plexity of specialization, the division of labour *itself* became the essential condition for social solidarity and the foundation for the moral order, he then went on to argue that:

'. . . in more advanced societies, man's nature is, in large part, to be an organ of society, and his proper duty, consequently, is to play his role as an organ.'

But his essential point was that *being a free discriminating individual person*, as we now think of it, is *only possible within such a condition of society*. In the 'mechanical' society, the obligation on a man (and the overwhelming constraining pressure) is to 'resemble his compan-ions'—in short, to conform with others. Only in the highly specialized society is the individual 'autonomous' to any degree. Durkheim put the matter like this:

'To be a person is to be an autonomous source of action. Man acquires this quality only in so far as there is something in him which is his alone and which individualizes him, as he is something more than a simple incarnation of the generic type of his race and his group. . . .' The develop-ment *from* the 'Mechanical' *to* the 'Organic' type of solidarity: '. . . at the same time that it necessitates a very great specialization, partially lifts the individual conscience from the organic environment which supports it, as from the social environment which envelopes it, and, accordingly, because of this double emancipation, the individual becomes more of an independent factor in his own conduct. The division of labour itself contributes to this enfranchisement, for individual natures, while specializ-ing, become more complex, and by that are in part freed from collective action and hereditary influences which can only enforce themselves upon simple, general things.

* *Suicide*, pp. 388–91.

It is, accordingly, a real illusion which makes us believe that personality was so much more complete when the division of labour had penetrated less.'*

Though we have not been able to emphasize this sufficiently, it will be seen from this kind of treatment, that Durkheim's entire analysis of the transformation of human society from the simple traditional to the modern industrial type was *also* an analysis of the kind of *individuality* which was possible in each. It was, in short, a demonstration that even the understanding of the nature of 'individual personality' in society required an analysis in terms of 'collective conditions' and 'social facts'.

This brief and all too inadequate sketch of Durkheim's study of the Division of Labour does not, of course, entail an agreement with every aspect of it, and our earlier criticisms indicate that there are many elements of it that, in a full critique, we would have to reject. But here I have tried only to point to the kinds of important perspective that it presented—chiefly to demonstrate its clear continuity with the views of the earlier thinkers. And there are two final points which I would like especially to stress because they will show a much greater degree of agreement and affinity between Durkheim, the earlier thinkers, and Hobhouse in particular, than is commonly thought to exist.

The first is that Durkheim, like many of the others we have mentioned, not only emphasized—but stated quite directly—that his study of the changing nature of social facts as traditional societies yielded to modern industrial societies was essentially a study of *morals*. His entire emphasis was that *moral* sentiments and *moral* sanctions pervaded the whole structure of institutions in society; that *morality* lay at the heart of *institutionalization*. 'The moral law', he wrote, 'interpenetrates all: the complete system of social relations.' This vision was essentially the same as that we have laboured to uncover in so many of the major sociologists.

But this agreement went still further. We were at pains to make clear how, in the conception of Hobhouse, there was an essential relationship between the growth in 'teleology', conscious knowledge, and conscious control in society and the extent to which ethical issues entered directly into the actual shaping of social institutions. *Normative* conceptions of social *justice* entered into the *actual* (positive) nature of institutional reality. Now Hobhouse has been much criticized for mixing these *ethical* and *factual* dimensions together (though, as we have seen, he was perfectly clear about these matters), but it seems not to be realized that Durkheim took *exactly*

* *Division of Labour*, pp. 403–4.

the same position—and with decided inconsistency in his own case, since he had so utterly rejected 'teleological' notions.

The 'organic' division of labour, Durkheim argued, brought into being an entire system of rights and duties. The condition of 'anomie' required the reconstruction of the 'industrial corporation' to bring about an adequate 'fit' between the several levels and elements of society. But, he insisted, it was not enough that there should be a new structure of rules and relationships: these should also be seen to be *just*. Durkheim was quite definite about this.

'It is not enough that there be rules; they *must be just*.... If we remember that the collective conscience is becoming more and more a cult of the individual, we shall see that what characterizes the morality of organized societies, compared to that of "mechanical" societies, is that there is *something more human*, therefore *more rational*, about them. It does not direct our activities to ends which do not immediately concern us; it does not make us servants of ideal powers of a nature other than our own, which follow their directions without occupying themselves with the interests of men. It only asks that we be thoughtful of our fellows and that we be just, that we fulfil our duty, that we work at the function we can best execute, and receive the just reward for our services. The rules which constitute it do not have a constraining force which snuffs out free thought; but, because they are rather made for us and, in a certain sense, by us, we are free. We wish to understand them; we do not fear to change them. We must, however, guard against finding such an ideal inadequate on the pretext that it is too earthly and too much to our liking. An ideal is not more elevated because more transcendent, but because it leads us to vaster perspectives. What is important is not that it tower high above us, until it becomes a stranger to our lives, but that it open to our activity a large enough field. This is far from being on the verge of realization. We know only too well what a laborious work it is to erect this society where each individual will have the place he merits, will be rewarded as he deserves, where everybody, accordingly, will spontaneously work for the good of all and of each.'*

This is, it will be agreed, the 'realistic humanitarianism' of Hobhouse, and it is interesting to note that Durkheim emphasized in this the fact that there was 'something *more human*' and 'more rational'. It may come as a shock to some to realize that Durkheim, as well as the British sociologists, was 'guilty' of proposing a 'rational ethic'—but, without any question whatever, he was!†

This is how Durkheim summarized his own conclusion.

* *Division of Labour*, pp. 407–8.
† Indeed, Durkheim's entire concentration was upon the 'sociology of morals' in almost exactly the same way as that of Westermarck and Hobhouse. The extent to which this was so can be seen not only in all the works to which we have referred, but also—very explicitly stated—in *Sociology and Philosophy*, Cohen & West, 1953. See especially, pp. 71–2.

'Morality—and by that must be understood, not only moral doctrines, but customs—is going through a real crisis. What precedes can help us to understand the nature and causes of this sick condition. Profound changes have been produced in the structure of our societies in a very short time; they have been freed from the segmental type with a rapidity and in proportions such as have never before been seen in history. Accordingly, the morality which corresponds to this social type has regressed, but without another developing quickly enough to fill the ground that the first left vacant in our consciences. Our faith has been troubled; tradition has lost its sway; individual judgment has been freed from collective judgment. But, on the other hand, the functions which have been disrupted in the course of the upheaval have not had the time to adjust themselves to one another; the new life which has emerged so suddenly has not been able to be completely organized, and above all, it has not been organized in a way to satisfy the need for justice which has grown more ardent in our hearts. If this be so, the remedy for the evil is not to seek to resuscitate traditions and practices which, no longer responding to present conditions of society, can only live an artificial, false existence. What we must do to relieve this anomie is to discover the means for making the organs which are still wasting themselves in discordant movements harmoniously concur by introducing into their relations more justice by more and more extenuating the external inequalities which are the source of the evil. Our illness is not, then, as has often been believed, of an intellectual sort; it has more profound causes. We shall not suffer because we no longer know on what theoretical notion to base the morality we have been practising, but because, in certain of its parts, this morality is irremediably shattered, and that which is necessary to us is only in process of formation. Our anxiety does not arise because the criticism of scholars has broken down the traditional explanation we use to give to our duties; consequently, it is not a new philosophical system which will relieve the situation. Because certain of our duties are no longer founded in the reality of things, a breakdown has resulted which will be repaired only in so far as a new discipline is established and consolidated. *In short, our first duty is to make a moral code for ourselves.* Such a work cannot be improvised in the silence of the study; it can arise only through itself, little by little, under the pressure of internal causes which make it necessary. But the service that thought can and must render *is in fixing the goal that we must attain.'*

The clarification of a satisfactory ethic and the sociological study of the actual institutional complexities of modern society should go hand in hand—and both were involved in a full understanding of the dilemmas of modern society and in any sound approach to its reconstruction. Here again was the central theme of the making of a new society which had been the mainspring of concern for the making of sociology from Comte onwards.

* *Division of Labour*, pp. 408–9.

(II) SUICIDE

Durkheim's study of suicide seems rather an odd departure after such a large-scale study of the division of labour and its implications for morality and the moral 'malaise' of modern society, but it was, in fact, a development of the study of 'anomie'—a deeper study of the relationships between conditions of group membership and social and individual stability. And in this study more than in any other, Durkheim most consistently applied his rules and most successfully demonstrated their utility. There were, however, a number of other points which were of importance.

In his 'Rules' Durkheim had argued strongly that it was not sufficient to turn to individual psychology for an adequate explanation of social facts, and in the study of suicide he took an extreme example to prove his point. Of all kinds of action that a man can commit it would surely seem to be the case that that of taking his own life was supremely an individual one. When a man puts a gun to his temple and pulls the trigger one would surely suppose that he is acting from purely individual motives which he alone has experienced, and that his act can therefore only be explained in individual terms. Durkheim maintained, however, that even in this highly individualistic sphere, it was still demonstrable that the incidence of suicide in society was a 'social fact', not just an individual one, and that it could only be explained by considering the conditions, characteristics, and constraining pressures of the social milieu of the society within which it took place. And it was in showing this that Durkheim most radically proved the importance of his new conceptual point of departure.

Two aspects of this were especially important. One was the demonstration of Durkheim's insistence upon the fact that *associational conditions* were psychologically creative. In this study, for example, clearly the individual had *private* experiences which constrained him to take his life. These certainly *were* individual experiences. But Durkheim showed that they *were* what they *were* in the individual because of associational conditions in the particular groups of which he was a member, and that these—by comparative studies—could be proved to be *general*, and constantly concomitant with the *rate* of suicide. And the second aspect of this which was a central emphasis in the whole of Durkheim's work was the attempt to show that man the individual was not a being of infinite capacity for moral freedom or for the dominance of social authority—but that his stability was a matter of social *limits*. 'In the order of existence, no good is measureless', was his dictum. Things are good for man— to a *limiting condition*. Things are bad for man—to a *limiting condi-*

tion. And it was part of the business of sociology and 'associational psychology' to establish what these limiting conditions of human health and stability were.

Very briefly, we may note the consistency of Durkheim in this study.

First of all, he applied his comparative method as a procedure of test to all the existing theories of suicide: those which explained it in terms of psychological motives, climatic conditions, racial characteristics, alcoholism, psycho-pathological states, etc. All these he was able to eliminate by demonstrating that there was no concomitant variation between any of them and the rate of suicide.

Then he eliminated the various moral preconceptions which exist in our notions of suicide, and *defined* it in such a way as to avoid these. Suicide, he claimed: *'is applied to all cases of death resulting directly or indirectly from a positive or negative act of the victim himself which he knows will produce this result'.*

Then, following upon this definition, he classified this defined 'social fact' into three types which enabled him to bring 'all known phenomena, so defined,' into the range of his study. In short, he so outlined his investigation as to be *definitive,* and therefore open to test. Statistical evidence showed that the *rates* of suicide remained constant in each society, but differed from each to each, and, furthermore, that the rates fluctuated in a constant manner in relation to certain social conditions. These, Durkheim explored within the framework of his three 'types.'

First of all he described ALTRUISTIC SUICIDE. This was a type of suicide brought about in conditions where there was a preponderant power and constraint of the group over the individual; in those societies and social groups where the value of the group, and of loyalty to the group, was enforced upon the individual and when the value of the individual's own life to himself was minimized. Even in Western societies, for example, suicide was higher among the members of armies than among the civilian population, and—within armies—was higher among officers than amongst men. In Japan—it was an honourable act of the warrior to commit suicide in the context of military behaviour rather than bring disgrace upon his society. In India—widows were under constraints to burn themselves upon the funeral pyres of their husbands rather than remain alive in a diminished human and social condition. In such societies there was an *over-weighted discipline*; the individual was *subordinated* to severe group-pressures in many respects.

Secondly, and at the other extreme, Durkheim described EGOISTIC SUICIDE. This took place in those groups and societies where considerable emphasis was placed upon individual *autonomy*; upon self-responsibility; where too little support was provided for the individual within the group-conditions; indeed where individuals were *required* to be self-sufficient and independent. The examples Durkheim gave were of certain marital and family conditions, and certain conditions of religious membership.

Single people, for example, were found to commit suicide more frequently than married people; married people with one child more frequently than married people with two children, etc. The size of family group with its demands and constraints seemed actually to minimize the risk of suicide in the individual, whereas when individuals were exposed to isolation—whether single, widowed or divorced—the risk of suicide was higher. Similarly Jews committed suicide less frequently than Catholics, and Catholics less frequently than Protestants, and it is important for an understanding of Durkheim's point of view that the kind of individual responsibility with which a person was confronted in his experience was not a matter of his own choice but was a requirement, an expectation, imposed upon him by the religious sect, church, or movement of which he was a member. Thus the Roman Catholic church enjoined its members to accept the authority, organization, and rituals of the church and its priesthood. In the Protestant sects, however, the reverse was the case. Here, the requirement was that the individual should work out his own salvation with God. He was, to rather misuse Rousseau's expression, 'forced to be free'. He could not be a Protestant without accepting this responsibility; it was a requirement of his God that it should be so. In short, these varying conditions of group integration were laid down by the groups and were not a matter of individual creation or individual choice.

The third type of suicide which Durkheim described was what he called ANOMIC SUICIDE,* and this took place within conditions of suddenly imposed reorientation; or, better, within suddenly imposed conditions of unfamiliarity which made a new orientation of values, aims, and conduct imperative. Durkheim found a constant concomitance between rates of suicide and any rapid fluctuation of circumstances. It might be thought, for example, that if there was a sudden fluctuation in economic circumstances, a sudden loss of wealth, or employment, or a sudden economic depression—the increased rate of suicide would be easily explicable because the individual concerned would have lost everything that he possessed. The validity of Durkheim's emphasis is demonstrated, however,

---

* Actually, Durkheim also mentioned a *fourth* type of suicide—'*Fatalistic Suicide*' which was the polar opposite of the Anomic type, just as Egoistic Suicide was the opposite of the Altruistic type; but he did not discuss this in any detail.

when one discovers that the rate of suicide was equally correlated with sudden *improvements* in economic circumstances. It seemed to be the sudden unfamiliarity, the sudden lack of orientation, the sudden absence of a supporting context of values and expectations, which lay at the heart of the instability here.

In comparative studies of this kind (and he re-worked the statistical material available to him in very original ways), Durkheim was able to move towards a 'law' of constant concomitance which was demonstrably found in all these varieties of group conditions—in religious, domestic, and political groups. His law was, that:

'Suicide varies inversely with the degree of integration of the social groups of which the individual forms a part.'

And his conclusion was that the rate of suicide in society could only be explained sociologically; that: 'at any given moment, the moral constitution of society establishes the contingency of voluntary deaths'. When it is considered that Durkheim was able to eliminate all the existing theories concerning the incidence of suicide, and to achieve the formulation of a 'law' of constant concomitance which rested upon a definitive study of carefully defined comparative data—and which was thus exposed to test—it can be seen that this study was, indeed, a very considerable vindication of his rules.

To show the close relation of this study with that of the *Division of Labour*, we might note the following passage—which makes this very clear. Commenting on the rapid growth of suicide in modern industrial societies, he wrote:

'We may believe that this aggravation springs not from the intrinsic nature of progress but from the special conditions under which it occurs in our day, and nothing assures us that these conditions are normal. For we must not be dazzled by the brilliant development of sciences, the arts and industry of which we are the witnesses; this development is altogether certainly taking place in the midst of a morbid effervescence, the grievous repercussions of which each one of us feels. It is then very possible and even probable that the rising tide of suicide originates in a pathological state just now accompanying the march of civilization without being its necessary condition.

The rapidity of the growth of suicides really permits no other hypothesis. Actually, in less than fifty years, they have tripled, quadrupled, and even quintupled, depending on the country. On the other hand, we know their connection with the most ineradicable element in the constitution of societies, since they express the mood of societies, and since the mood of peoples, like that of individuals, reflects the state of the most fundamental part of the organism. Our social organization, then, must have changed profoundly in the course of this century, to have been able to cause such a growth in the suicide-rate. So grave and rapid an alteration as this must be morbid; for a society cannot change its structure so suddenly. Only by a succession of slow, almost imperceptible modifications does it achieve different characteristics. The possible changes, even then, are limited. Once a social type is fixed it is no longer infinitely plastic; a limit is soon reached which cannot be passed. Thus the changes presupposed by the statistics of contemporary suicides cannot be normal. Without even knowing exactly of what they consist, we may begin by affirming that they result not from a regular evolution but from a morbid disturbance which, while able to uproot the institutions of the past, has put nothing in their place; for the work of centuries cannot be remade in a few years. But if the cause is so abnormal, the effect must be so, as well. Thus, what the rising flood of voluntary deaths denotes is not the increasing brilliancy of our civilization but a state of crisis and perturbation not to be prolonged with impunity.'*

(III) RELIGION

To comment in any detail on Durkheim's study of religion in society would not add greatly to the outline of his system of sociological analysis that we now have. It will readily be seen that Durkheim's concern about religion lay in the fact that it was one of the main agencies of solidarity and morality in society, and was therefore part of the central problem of social solidarity which he wished to explore, but it is enough to say that he applied his rules with a similar measure of consistency in this, as in his other studies—though not by any means with the consistency that he accomplished in his work on suicide—and that it formed a consistent part of his entire contribution to sociological theory as we have already outlined it. As in all his studies, there were many elements of great interest quite apart from his central concern. Thus, he had much to say of importance for the sociology of knowledge (on the social formation of the categories of perception, conception, etc.), and much on the relations between religion and science—but these would take us too far away from our basic task of clarifying his contribution to sociological theory.†

(5) *Conclusions*

We are now in a position, then, to arrive at our peculiarly 'mixed'

* *Suicide*, pp. 368–9.
† This decision *not* to include a summary account of Durkheim's 'Elementary Forms of the Religious Life' is in no sense a reflection on its quality in relation to the other studies—though it is far less consistent than 'Suicide'. It is *simply* that—since this study is a long one—I have not wanted to make it any longer than is necessary for the thorough clarification and assessment of Durkheim's distinctive approach to sociological theory.

conclusions about the merits of Durkheim's system of sociological analysis; the worth of his contribution to the making of sociology.

(I) ASSERTIONS, AMBIGUITIES, INCONSISTENCIES, ERRORS

On the one hand, we have seen—as a matter of negative, or adverse assessment—that Durkheim's over-all position was riddled with unsupported assertions, unresolved and even harmful ambiguities, and—worst of all—entailed a complete blindness to all that was needed in sociology in the direction of understanding the willed, purposeful, actions of men. We have seen, too, that in many parts of his work, and especially in his final diagnosis, and proposals for purposive action, he was quite inconsistent in this—introducing, and insisting upon, conscious purposive action in re-making society on as large a scale as any of his predecessors. But all this has been said plainly enough and need not be repeated. Perhaps we should only note that this must lead us quite definitely, to reject the sufficiency for a complete system of sociological analysis of Durkheim's supposed 'objectivity'. That is to say: 'social facts' are not *only* such as to possess the 'objective' attributes of 'things';* they require *more* than an 'objective' study of the attributes given through 'sensations' to the investigator. And we must come back to this.

(II) DURKHEIM'S ACCEPTANCE OF THE NINETEENTH CENTURY 'CONSPECTUS', AND MANY ELEMENTS OF IT. HIS DISTINCTIVE EMPHASIS IN SEEKING THE DEVELOPMENT OF THE SUBJECT

Again we may note without repeating in any detail the fact that Durkheim accepted the 'conspectus' of the subject which had been established by the end of the nineteenth century, and did *not* reject it but worked *within* it in trying to further the making of a clearly defined, disciplined, and accurate science. He accepted the evolutionary perspective, the recognition of the distinctive existence of 'social systems' as the point of departure for sociology, the necessity of a structural-functional analysis of such systems; the necessity of a detailed historical account of their transformations; and all the detailed methods of observation, description, generalization, classification, comparison, and the like, including the emphasis upon attaining 'positive' knowledge (i.e. knowledge testable in experience). His major, most glaring fault was his flat rejection of all that was entailed (in perception of 'fact' and in consideration of appropriate method) in a recognition of 'teleological' elements of society, and the over-simplified notions of reified institutions, socio-psychological

---

* I.e. *phenomenal* attributes.

375

actualities as 'things', and causal relations between such 'things' which led to a one-sided and insufficient conception of the nature of 'empirical science' in sociology. But on all other counts, the continuity of his contribution—its rootedness in the established 'conspectus'—was plain to be seen.

Durkheim's distinctive emphasis was decidedly that of moving from 'theory to theor*ies*'; of insisting essentially and tirelessly on the necessity of producing *specific, delimited, definitive, testable* theories about *objectively recognizable* and *measurable* social facts— if the subject was genuinely and demonstrably to accomplish the nature and status of a *science*. In using all the other components of the subject—classification, comparison, structural-functional analysis, etc.—his entire emphasis was that of fastening on the *objective* aspects of associational facts: of seeking always the *external, observable* indices—or recognizable attributes—of social facts, and producing rules of method which could accomplish testable theories about these. Durkheim's was therefore a contribution to the making of sociology *heavily concentrated on the development of one element in the earlier 'conspectus'*—the accurate study of what was *objectively to be perceived* of the nature of those 'associational facts' which were the distinctive subject-matter of sociology.

(III) THE WORTH OF DURKHEIM'S 'OBJECTIVE STUDY OF SOCIAL FACTS'

Despite all his errors and ambiguities, then, we can see that in deliberately pursuing his own extreme conceptions to their greatest extent, Durkheim did undoubtedly contribute elements of the most essential worth to the making of sociology. Though there are dimensions of society *other* than those 'objective' aspects of social facts on which Durkheim concentrated, nonetheless he did see these dimensions of his own vision very clearly and fully indeed, and consequently his rules for studying *these aspects* of society are of great value, even if we need other methods *in addition*. To regard social facts *as things* is an error, but to adopt the attitude of mind towards them which studies them *as if* they were things—to scrutinize preconceptions, to realize the insufficiency of the 'idols' of our familiar common-sense notions, to realize that one has to go *out* to investigate their nature, etc.—all this is important and salutary. To think one can explain social facts entirely—and prove these explanations—in terms of 'efficient causation' of the same order as that of the natural sciences, is an error: but to establish relationships of constant concomitance which are objectively demonstrable—and whose causal intricacies can then be analysed in depth further—is a method of the most basic importance in establishing sociological knowledge.

Durkheim, in short, established methods which were productive of testable knowledge about the objective aspects of social facts, and which were, as such, a decided advance in certain ways upon his predecessors, even though he left other dimensions of society unseen and untouched.

We can go further than this, and say that—whatever dimensions of *subjective meaning* and *purpose* the facts of society may entail or contain—it is true, nonetheless, that they do also possess the many objective attributes on which Durkheim insisted. And two points of importance can be distinguished here.

(IV) SOCIAL FACTS DO POSSESS THE OBJECTIVE ATTRIBUTES INSISTED UPON BY DURKHEIM

First of all—and quite directly—there are, clearly, objective (phenomenal) aspects of social facts about which knowledge can only be established by the use of the methods which Durkheim proposed. There are detailed elements of social organization (the family, kinship, occupational groups, etc.), detailed structures of social relationships (the legal system, the political constitution, etc.), detailed elements of culture (tools, buildings, and artefacts of many kinds), and detailed conditions of social life (size, density and distribution of population, etc.)—all of which are objectively *there*, and require objective study. The historical and structural-functional studies, the classificatory and comparative studies, outlined by Durkheim could certainly produce testable knowledge of these aspects of society—whatever else might be required. Indeed, demonstrable knowledge could not be achieved without them. In clarifying methods which were applicable to all these aspects of the subject-matter of sociology, Durkheim clearly made a contribution of the greatest value.

(V) THE 'SOCIO-PSYCHOLOGICAL' ASPECTS OF 'ASSOCIATIONAL FACTS'

Secondly, however, and this is more important, Durkheim did succeed—in his discussion of the nature of social facts—in clarifying and emphasizing more powerfully, more graphically (almost) than anyone else, *the psychological creativity of social processes*. In this sense, far from dispensing with psychology, he demonstrated more clearly than others the central reality of *socio-psychological processes* and the central place in a science of society of *associational* (*social*) *psychology*. We have seen that even this was carried to a point of

377

error by Durkheim—to the length of insisting that these 'collective representations' came to have an existence (and cause-and-effect interdependencies with each other) quite independent of individuals —but, given the great difficulty of making his point clear, such an error of over-emphasis can be readily understood. It is, in fact, one of the most difficult points to demonstrate to people whose minds have been rendered obtuse by common sense and professional notions alike of something they call 'individual psychology', and one can readily sympathize with Durkheim's over-statement in trying to make his persuasion clear. But there is no doubt that he succeeded.* *Associational processes* are *psychologically creative* and engender collective elements of human experience and behaviour (which go into the very creation of individuals) which cannot be said to have existed in individual minds *before* the association took place. Language, symbols, constraining obligations, external pressures to conformity, ideals, sentiments, currents of feeling stemming from collective conditions . . . and a thousand and one other elements of human experience *are* the outcome of *social processes*. In this sense, too, then, it can be said that Durkheim was correct and successful in pointing to 'associational psychological facts' which objectively exist in society and which can only be *known* by the use of such objective methods of study as he proposed.

Durkheim's very telling, and emphatically worthwhile contribution was that he saw the dimensions of the socio-psychological actuality of human beings in society more richly than most; succeeded in conveying this vision very clearly; and produced a body of clear rules for objective study whereby the objective aspects of this actuality could be testably known. His major deficiencies lay in the fact that—with a peculiar and mistaken metaphysical assertiveness— he refused to entertain the 'teleological' activities of men and the necessary 'teleological' dimensions of sociological explanation; and, as we have seen, endless ambiguities filled his pages as a result of this. But it is exactly in this realm of subjectively understanding the meaningful conduct of men in the pursuit of ends, that Max Weber came to offer his own conception of sociological analysis—and so, in complementary fashion, supplied the dimensions which Durkheim lacked. But there is this one last point which deserves the fullest emphasis before we turn to Max Weber.

(VI) THE LIBERATIVE INFLUENCE OF DURKHEIM'S METHODOLOGY

Durkheim was of the greatest importance in the making of sociology

* Later, we shall see that Cooley was successful in conveying this point—though in a different, and perhaps better way. See pp. 482–511.

in that he was *liberative*. The establishment of the over-all 'conspectus' of sociology by the great nineteenth century founders had been of the most fundamental importance. But it *was* established. It was no longer necessary for every scholar and every student to try to encompass the entire 'universe of discourse' of the subject. It was important to move *from theory to theories*! And in his clear insistence upon the *definition* of social facts, the *delimitation* of investigations, the carrying out of *definitive* studies, and the detailed *testing* of the specific theories advanced—and also in the manageability of the range of studies brought about by the method of concomitant variation in his account of the comparative method—Durkheim paved the way for specialist studies which could, by their very delimitation, be more accurate. The making of sociology had now reached the stage where—*within* the context of the initially founded conspectus of the subject—detailed specific studies could be undertaken and made vulnerable to criticism and test. Knowledge on special aspects and problems of society could now be demonstrably advanced. Sociology had now the basis for becoming professionally mature in the best sense.

(VII) THE MAKING OF SOCIOLOGY FOR THE MAKING OF SOCIETY

We have also seen, too, that—whether with consistency or not—Durkheim shared the essential vision of all his predecessors and contemporaries of the disruptive 'malaise' which accompanied the rapid transition from traditional to modern industrial societies. Like them he saw the making of sociology as a necessary task in the making of a new society, and we have seen that he was as fully committed in terms of human concern and moral conviction and endeavour as any other thinker we have considered. Indeed it was quite forthrightly Durkheim's position that the effort towards truth and utility in *science* was one part, and one of the highest parts, of *moral* commitment and endeavour.* Those who take for granted the 'relativity of ethics' should think on these things! But—quite apart from seeing the nature of Durkheim's vision of the modern social transformation itself—there is one point which is supremely important here. And that is that Durkheim's driving effort for the professional accuracy and liberation of sociology was not for the self-assured complacency, or even benefit, of the *professionals themselves*! On the contrary—professional commitment to scholarly accuracy was in order to ensure the benefit of men in society. Society was in the throes of a great transformation—in many ways an

---

* A view very similar to that held by Sir Karl Popper.

agonizing and tragic transformation—and those who engaged in the making of sociology, who professionally committed themselves to sociological studies—were playing their own part, among and together with all others, in grappling with this transformation, and seeking to resolve its many dilemmas.

Exactly the same kind of liberation of the sociologist; of vocational commitment to the professional accuracy of the subject; and all this because of a powerful commitment to the effort of understanding and resolving the pressing dangers towards inhumanity in the largeness of scale of modern society; characterized the work and influence of Max Weber—to whose own distinctive contribution we can now turn.

2
The Subjective Understanding of Social Action: Max Weber

Like Emile Durkheim, Max Weber is now taken to be one of the chief founders of distinctively modern (contemporary) sociology, and there is no doubt whatever that this judgment is wholly justified. In his work we come to a detailed and definitive working out of *one* of the essential components of the nineteenth century 'conspectus': a precise and elaborate development of the methods appropriate to the 'subjective understanding of social action' in terms of human *purpose* and *will*; that dimension of both social actuality and theory, in short, which was explicitly lacking in Durkheim, explicitly denied by him, and which is, therefore, clearly complementary to the kind of analysis which he constructed. A few preliminary points will help us to move towards a clear sight of the context of Weber's work, and then to a clear assessment of it.

Preliminary Points

In the first place, it is a decided advantage to come to our study of Weber after a detailed examination of Durkheim's arguments about the 'objectivity' of social facts and sociological methods, for, in one sense, Weber was such a flat, stark contradiction to Durkheim, that his position becomes clear by sheer contrast. We shall have to be careful concerning this supposed 'opposition' of objectivity and subjectivity in the systems of these two thinkers—because they are certainly *not* opposed in some senses; but it is enough, for now, simply to note that whereas Durkheim outrightly denied a place to *the understanding of the purposive actions of individuals* in his scheme for the causal explanation of the nature and transformations of society, Weber not only insisted upon its inclusion, but—much more radically—insisted that it was *the distinguishing feature* of sociology, as a science of society, that it could, and should, provide causal explanations in these terms. Weber's contribution to sociological theory was therefore a filling in of that dimension which Durkheim left wholly untouched; which, indeed, he rejected. Important points follow immediately upon this.

First of all, it will be seen that Max Weber—who was born in 1864 and died in 1920—was a contemporary of Durkheim, and, indeed, of all the people we are considering in this section (Tönnies, Westermarck, Hobhouse, etc.); and, exactly like them, was concerned to *develop* that dimension of the nineteenth century approaches to sociological theory which he thought most essential and promising for the furtherance of the science. Like them, he 'straddled' the nineteenth and twentieth centuries, and his work was chiefly important and influential in the twentieth century developments of the subject. It may be noted, in fact, that Weber's work on sociology proper was chiefly produced in the present century (after about 1904), and was thus a little later than that of Durkheim. At the same time, it must be made clear that Durkheim and Weber developed their distinctive contributions, their explorations of their different 'dimensions', parallel to, and independent of, each other. There was no dialogue, or argument, between them as persons; though each took into account the kinds of emphasis the other insisted upon because they were ongoing components of the subject exposed to continuous debate. It is important to note this, because our own methods of dealing with the two contributions in close relationship might easily suggest a relationship between the two men themselves, which did not, in fact, exist. But the essential thing is that Weber was of the same generation of men devoted to the making of sociology as Durkheim, Tönnies, Hobhouse, etc., and that, like them, he was concerned to develop *one dimension* of the subject especially in seeking to further the accuracy of the science.

The second immediate point which must be noted (and which will be substantiated later) is that whereas Durkheim forthrightly rejected the distinctive features of explanation emphasized by Weber, the converse was not true of Weber. That is to say: Weber did *not* reject conceptual approaches to sociology other than his own. On the contrary, he took great care to emphasize that he was devoting himself to the elaboration of that element of sociological analysis and theory which seemed of crucial importance, and was of greater interest, to *him*; and that it went without saying that there were approaches *other* than his that were clearly worthwhile. Several aspects of this point are of importance. The first is that Weber was even more of a *liberator* in the making of sociology than Durkheim. He too wished, in some way, to achieve—within the compendious scheme of the subject as laid down during the nineteenth century— some *delimitation*, some sharper *definition* of the *distinctive* nature and boundaries of the subject, so that testable, definitive studies could be undertaken and accuracy could be achieved. His aim was the same as Durkheim's: to clarify the nature and *limits* of sociology as a distinctive science. Like all the theorists we are now considering, too, he wished to move (as part of this concern for accuracy of definition and study) *from theory to theories*. His clarification of the distinctive explanatory methods of the subject was—entirely and supremely—for *use*. Weber made great efforts towards clarifying the science, the profession, the vocation (even) of sociology—*not* however, for the sake of the profession itself—but for the sake of accurate engagement in the study and explanation of those concrete issues of cultural significance which seemed important to the investigator in his own time; in the clutch of his own historical circumstances. But in all this—and this is the central point here— Weber was much more of a liberator than most, in that he *expressly denied the sufficiency for* ALL *purposes* (*for the investigation of* ALL *problems*) *of any* ONE *conceptual schema in sociology*. We shall see more of his arguments on this theme, but it is enough here to see that though he pursued his own conceptual apparatus to the greatest degree of accuracy possible, he did not deny the utility of others. His theoretical proposals were 'open-ended'—not as a matter of loose relativity of any sort—but in the most accurately justified way. He very definitely was *not* seeking to set up one 'school' of sociological theory which rendered all others unnecessary. This is why, as we shall see, it is perfectly correct to speak of these various contributions for the analysis of various dimensions of social actuality as being *complementary* to each other—in sociological analysis as a whole—without in any necessary sense being tightly integrated with each other.

Weber's own work was, then, *deliberately selective*; a *deliberate concentration*; but—though a concentration on that feature which he thought *crucially distinctive* of sociology—it was *an addition* to other approaches, not at all a total *replacement* of them.

We must also note immediately the importance of the point on which Weber's position was in flat disagreement with that of Durkheim, because it indicated very clearly the particular and substantial nature of Weber's contribution. The disagreement was, of course, on the recognition of what others had called the 'teleological' dimensions of the relationships of men in society. Durkheim had distinguished 'associational' facts from all others; had emphasized their 'objective' attributes—externality, constraint, generality, etc.; and had argued that causal relationships among them were of the same nature as the causal relations existing among *any* species of 'fact' in nature, and that to entertain notions of 'teleological' explanations of them was an error. Weber, though not denying that associational facts possessed objective attributes, insisted, on the contrary, that men and their relationships in social institutions— *were* distinctively different from all other facts of nature in a *qualitative* sense, in that men oriented their actions to each other in terms of *meaning*. They actively sought to achieve certain *ends* of

383

which they were (often) consciously aware. They employed certain *means* (and discarded others) in striving to attain these ends. They exercised choice; they deliberated; they calculated; they took decisions; and they then acted in relation to other men to accomplish their purposes. They exercised *will* in disciplining their thought and emotions, in channelling their energies and resources, in the conscious pursuit of clearly foreseen objectives. The *action* and *social action* of men could *not* satisfactorily be 'observed' and 'explained' in the ordinary sense applicable to objects or 'things'. On the contrary, the very observation of *action* (*always* selective), implied, and rested upon, some *interpretation* of it in terms of its *meaning* for the actors themselves. These elements of meaning, motive, choice, deliberate effort, were at least *among* the causes of sequences of human action, and had to enter into any adequate *causal* account. The *causes* of sequences of human action in society included causes *different* in kind from those which were operative in sequences of events among connected *things*. Furthermore, in such a process of interpretation, the investigator was, in some sense or other, in a position of having to *impute* meanings and motives to the actors in the situation, and this made necessary a kind of approach to scientific understanding which was very different from that of the other (natural) sciences.

Weber's importance lies in the fact that he successfully accomplished the clarification of a methodology for this kind of 'interpretive' sociology, and we shall examine his system fully a little later; but what is of preliminary importance here is that we should be clear about the degree of this achievement. It has often been claimed that Weber was the 'founder' of 'interpretive' sociology; that the subjective understanding of social *action*, as a component of sociological analysis was an innovation of his. Now we have seen quite clearly that this is simply not true (and, indeed, Weber himself did not claim it). We have seen that, in all the thought which went into the making of sociology from that of Comte onwards, there was always a recognition of the distinct element of *action* (as distinct from *events*) in society; of a 'teleological', purposive element in the practical activities of men; and a recognition of the fact that the methods of sociology had to incorporate elements *different* from those of the natural sciences. In Mill especially, in the early Americans, and in Tönnies (to mention only the most striking examples) there had been this clear recognition of elements of *will*, *character*, and *deliberate action* in human society, which was something at a level different from that of psychological and social fact; something which involved *considered principle* and *choice*. We have seen, too, that Mill attempted to accommodate these elements by incorporating 'choices' into

384

'causes'; and—more impressively—that the early Americans*
(Giddings especially) had actually constructed 'types' of social
action (impulsive, traditional, and rational); and that Tönnies had
constructed much more specific and highly elaborate 'types' for the
analysis of a particular problem—the transition from a community
resting upon natural will to a society of complex associations
artificially contrived by rational will. There is no doubt whatever,
then, that Weber was no innovator here. Furthermore, Weber
himself drew on other theorists whom we have not mentioned—
such as Dilthey and Rickert (as well as Tönnies)—and clearly thought
of his own work as being a development of theirs, and, indeed, as
being only a painstaking task of making *explicit* what, in fact, everybody did *implicitly* when undertaking explanations of social
problems.

The importance of Weber, then, was not in being *new*, in recognizing and exploring these dimensions of society and method, but in
*clarifying a set of concepts and methods whereby the study of these
dimensions could be* SATISFACTORILY *incorporated into sociological
analysis, and whereby they could be successfully carried out.* Putting
this in another way: Weber brought to a definitive conclusion (in so
far as he thought it *should* be a *conclusion*) the development of a
methodology for this distinctive component of sociological analysis
which had been *recognized* from the earliest formulations of the
subject; which had been much thought about; but which had not—
until his own efforts—been satisfactorily worked out. Just as Durkheim brought to a definitive stage the study of the *objective attributes*
of associational facts, so Weber brought to a definitive stage the
methods for accomplishing a causal account of social *action* in terms
of *subjective understanding.* This was therefore a *culminating* development of the greatest importance.

There is a further important point concerning the advantages of
studying Weber after Durkheim. Durkheim, as we saw, was difficult
to study clearly because there was such a task of disentangling
ambiguities whilst assessing his points accurately (and justly) and
gradually sifting out what was worthwhile in his system. Weber too
is difficult to encompass with justice in any summary critique—but
with him it is very different. Weber was remarkably consistent and
clear in his theoretical scheme: so with this we should have no
difficulty. The only difficulty here is that of summary treatment—

---

* I do not know enough about this, but the similarity between Weber's and
Giddings' 'typologies' seems too close to be accidental. Weber visited the United
States in 1904—and its seems plausible to suspect that he noted these American
views at that time. The great 'types' of social action may well have gone from
America to Germany, rather than vice versa.

because Weber's own writing on his concepts and methods was so disciplined, so tightly argued in a propositional, programmatic way, that it is hard to summarize without losing something essential. The much greater difficulty in presenting an account of Weber's work is that of doing justice to all the substantive studies which he undertook. The fact is that the range of Weber's knowledge and of his many-sided comments on various aspects of society is so enormous and so rich that no summary account of his contribution to the theoretical making of the subject can possibly be adequate as an indicator to all the dimensions of his contributions as a whole. On this one has, at the outset—in terms of sufficiency of teaching— simply to admit defeat. No summary can possibly do!

Here, then, we shall concentrate only on his contribution to sociological theory, and on this we can be clear: but two points are worth making at the outset. Firstly—some *apparent* ambiguities in Weber's theoretical discussion are not, it seems to me, *real*. They stem really from the fact that Weber did not work out to their conclusions every relationship between elements *attendant upon* his system. He only made them clear as far as seemed necessary for his argument. For example he accepted the worth of 'generic' as well as 'genetic' propositions in sociological explanations of 'typical' as well as 'ideal-typical' categories; of 'average-types' as well as 'ideal-types'; and confusion has stemmed from the fact that he never worked out to a *systematic conclusiveness*, the relation between them. The reason he did not do so was not at all because of a theoretical 'blind-spot', but because, quite deliberately, he thought it absurb to try. He thought it a theoretical absurdity to try to encompass *all* these relations in one complete conceptual schema. Talcott Parsons is one who has walked into the kind of theoretical maze which Weber consciously eschewed, and seems never likely to come out. But these points we shall be able to clarify. Secondly—because of its very clarity; its distinctiveness—Weber's approach to theory has often been emphasized out of its context. It has been too much *isolated* from other elements which he recognized. It has thus come to be presented as a distinctive, separate 'school'. Because of this, I want especially to put Weber back *into a context*. I want to insist that Weber's *chosen concentration* within sociological theory was seen *by him* as being one crucial dimension within others—such as structural-functional analysis; the analysis of evolution and development; the study of socio-psychological facts as Durkheim saw them, and the like—and that it was never his intention to deny these. In short, I want to establish the fact that Weber accepted the 'conspectus' of sociology which was outlined earlier, and worked *within* it: sharpening that one component which he himself thought to be crucial and most in need of attention and development. This can be achieved by noting Weber's own statements as we proceed, and the continuities of his work from a critical recognition—and sometimes adoption—of earlier positions.

Weber, then, was exactly like Durkheim in seeking to accomplish a sharp delineation of sociology; to make clear beyond doubt its crucial distinguishing features; and to elaborate a conceptual schema which would prove useful in producing testable theories and accurate knowledge. He differed from Durkheim chiefly in having a diametrically opposite conception of what the crucially distinguishing features of sociology were, and in being—in ways which we shall see—even *more* delimited in his conception of sociological theories.

We can now try to grasp this distinctive view-point of Weber's as clearly as possible, and this can best be approached by a brief glance at certain biographical facts which seem to illuminate certain qualities of his mind and character and certain directions of his thought, and by an examination of some definite continuities of his thought with that of earlier scholars. This will provide us with a reliable picture of the context within which his own position was clearly constructed.

Biographical Facts

We have already noted the dates of Weber's life, and that he was a contemporary of certain other important thinkers. The relevance of this fact is given much greater weight when Weber's family life is borne in mind. His biographers tell us that the family context within which he grew up (his family moved to Berlin when he was five years old) was one of continual stimulation: of an intellectual kind, and of concern for practical political affairs. His father was very active in the law and in politics, and Weber met many eminent men of affairs and scholars* in his home. The point of the greatest importance which arises from this in relation to the characteristic qualities of Weber's work is that he was always a scholar oriented towards political action. Though his intellectual range was enormously wide, though his sheer intellectual curiosity roamed in every conceivable direction, Weber's central focus was always upon a commitment to as full and accurate a grasp as he could accomplish of what was of concrete political and cultural significance in his own time—and to the *use* of knowledge for engagement in responsible action. Weber was a morally committed man in a very decided and distinctive way:

* Such as Dilthey and Mommsen.

he scorned the idea that a commitment to scientific accuracy entailed any kind of looseness or simple-minded relativism in the consideration of ethical judgments; and—and this is the essential thing—his approach to the quest for sociological knowledge was always emphatically diagnostic. It was to *diagnose* in order to *judge* and to *act*. This, as we shall see, was, and always remained, a central principle of Weber's approach to 'theorizing'.

Another central element of this kind was that Weber grew to maturity within a classical, humanist (in the broadest sense) and liberal tradition; within the deep influence of the ideas of the Enlightenment: within which the wholeness of the individual—the rounded, many-dimensioned nature of the individual—indeed the dignity of the individual's responsible stance in nature and society—was much emphasized. This, too, remained at the heart of Weber's conceptions—scientific and ethical alike, and in all directions of his thought. His clear conception of the *limits* of science (including sociology) sprang from his vision of all the many dimensions of nature, and of the nature of the human individual. His insistence upon the elements of meaning, will, deliberate action, etc., in sociological explanation stemmed from his clear and strong persuasion of these distinctive attributes of human mind and character. His fear of the bureaucratic nature of modern society, and his attack upon it, stemmed from his sympathy with the whole individual and his fear that the humane qualities of life might be lost. And, indeed, his dislike of the sheer efficiency of the specialization of the modern industrialized society stemmed from his hatred of any diminution of the stature and dignity of the human person. Whereas Durkheim advocated an ethic of specialization, Weber stood for an ethic of the whole individual person—and abhorred anything which eroded this. Even, for example, his attitude to Freudian psycho-analysis (whatever we may think of it on other grounds) was one of disgust and antipathy in that it seemed to transfer the responsibility of a person in confronting his own problems to a clinician; and, in so doing, robbed the individual of the dignity even of his own tragedy. His attitudes to suicide reflected the same conception of the dignity of the individual *character*—in being free to take his own decisive steps of destiny: even, under certain circumstances, to that of his own destruction.

Weber's vision of nature and human nature was too full for him to accept the sufficiency of science alone; and to conceive of a man as a creature entirely compounded of psychological 'factors' and social 'roles'; and this influenced his approach to sociological theory quite fundamentally. Weber was a man and a scholar whose nature went far beyond that of the present conception of the narrow 'professional social scientist' who prides himself on his lack of ideological and moral commitments.

The same element was connected with Weber's response to one other profound influence upon him—namely that of the ideas of Marx. But this was of a complicated nature. It is sometimes thought that Weber's entire work was a kind of commentary on Marx, and that his work on the part played by the Protestant Ethic in the development of industrial capitalism was simply a qualification of Marx (though some speak of it as a flat refutation). But the truth is that though Weber was ready to entertain (indeed he expressly advocated) 'one-sided' theories, which emphasized specific hypotheses to extremes; and was ready to consider Marxism among such theories; he definitely rejected it; and it is quite impossible to think of his elaborate conceptual system as just some kind of qualification of Marx. But one interesting point is that Weber was—together with Sombart and Jaffé—involved in the editorship of the *Archiv fur Sozialwissenschaft und Sozialpolitik*—and in this there was much discussion of the ideas of Marx. But the point of importance here is that in this journal (and in much of his writing apart from this) Weber was really writing as an *economist*. And it is worthwhile to remember—when we come to consider Weber's central method of the construction of 'ideal types'—that, to a considerable extent, he had in mind the kinds of analytical 'models' carefully constructed within economic analysis. But here again, his vision of the many-dimensioned nature of man the individual prevented him from accepting the sufficiency of any such specialist science alone. The fact is that Weber's vision of the actuality of the world, and of man within it, was such as to go far beyond the range of the efficacy of science; and this led him always to see the *limits* of science, as well as, within these limits, the accuracy of which it was capable.

There is one other point of a biographical nature which deserves emphasis. We have mentioned many other sources of the subjective understanding of the purposive actions of men in society (Mill, Ward, Giddings, etc.), but Weber himself worked out his own position within the context of an ongoing debate among German scholars. In the discussion which attended the whole question of the emergence of science out of the earlier context of speculative philosophy, a marked distinction came to be drawn in German thought between the science of *nature* (of all the inanimate and organic objects and processes of which it consisted) and the sciences of *Spirit* (or mind). This was a sharp distinction between the *natural sciences* which could establish laws about phenomena and their interconnections and those studies which sought to establish knowledge about matters involving human mind, will, choice, freedom, purpose, etc. It was held by some that these latter studies could not possibly be sciences in the former sense. Scientific exactitude was impossible here. Weber responded to this debate, and resolved this question in a very particular—and not a simple 'either-or'—way. On the one hand he rejected the distinction—and argued that the *only* demonstrable knowledge was the *causal* knowledge of science, and that this was as essential in establishing knowledge about man in society as about the facts of nature. But, on the other hand, he upheld the distinction in agreeing that the concepts and methods of the sciences of man—which involved imputations and interpretations of *meaning*—had to be qualitatively different from those of other sciences. Even so—these had still to be *scientific* methods which exposed theories to test—and they had to accomplish the rigorous demands of science. Weber, in short, adopted a position exactly in agreement with the earliest statement of Comte—that only science was productive of testable knowledge, but that the methods of each science had to differ in so far as they had to be worked out appropriately to the qualitatively different kinds and levels of facts and problems they were concerned to study. But, in Weber's case, this position was rooted in the discussions of men like Rickert, Jaspers, Simmel, and Tönnies. Many aspects of his own arguments therefore carry the implications of this particular biographical and 'national' context—but, clearly, it was the same problem which had been worked out in a similar way elsewhere.

These biographical facts had a considerable bearing on the basic stand-points and 'slants' of Weber's ideas, and were all-pervasive in his work. Bearing them in mind, we can now—in tracing some of the chief continuities of his work with that of others—construct a clear picture of the context of basic elements within which his own distinctive contribution to theory was couched.

Basic Continuities and Positions adopted

In this section I want scrupulously to demonstrate the similarities and differences between many of the basic stand-points adopted by Weber and those of the other theorists we have considered. In all this, *emphases* have often been taken to be *dichotomies*; *qualifications* have been taken to be *rejections*; and it is most important that we should see clearly Weber's position on these major components of sociology *other* than his own distinctive development, if we are soundly and properly to be able to assess the worth even of that.

(I) ON SCIENCE AND KNOWLEDGE

(a) *Weber's Acceptance of Positive Science*

In the first place, Weber agreed completely with the epistemological position of Hume, Kant and Comte. He rejected completely any quest (in science) for knowledge of 'ultimate' or 'final' causes, or, indeed, of any kind of supposed reality which 'transcended' our empirical experience in, and of the world. Science did not, could not, and did not claim, to go beyond the systematic analysis and ordering of experience and the establishing of causal relations between those elements of it which we clarified in our investigation of problems. Indeed, Weber was very definite and emphatic in this— insisting that science, as such, was not only unable to provide knowledge of 'ultimates' of this kind, but also that it could do nothing to provide or substantiate ethical standards, and that no larger 'meaning' of the world or of life as a whole could be simply derived from it. Empirical science was concerned to provide testable theories about specific problems which were clearly formulated about experience. That was all.

'. . . it can never be the task of an empirical science,' he wrote, 'to provide binding norms and ideals from which directives for immediate practical activity can be derived . . .

The fate of an epoch which has eaten of the tree of knowledge is that it must know that we cannot learn the *meaning* of the world from the results of its analysis, be it ever so perfect; it must rather be in a position to create this meaning itself. It must recognize that general views of life and the universe can never be the products of increasing empirical knowledge, and that the highest ideals, which move us most forcefully, are always formed only in the struggle with other ideals which are just as sacred to others as ours are to us.'*

The tone of this immediately shows, however, that Weber was very far from claiming that responsibility for accurate criteria of judgment in matters going *beyond* science should be abandoned; or, indeed, that the great influence of these 'extra-scientific' beliefs, ideals, values, *upon* science should be ignored. On the contrary, he argued for the greatest responsibility and clarity of mind about these matters, and some immediate qualifications must be indicated. First: he made it perfectly clear that he did *not* think that because metaphysical speculations about the 'meaning' of the world went beyond empirical science, they performed no 'useful cognitive task'.

* *The Methodology of the Social Sciences*, Free Press, 1949, pp. 52, 57.

391

o

Secondly, he made it completely clear that this position did not imply at all any acceptance of a loose 'relativity of ethics'. 'An attitude of moral indifference,' he wrote, 'has no connection with scientific objectivity.' And thirdly, he by no means implied that the practice of empirical science necessitated an absence of commitment to practical and cultural issues. On the contrary, Weber expected that problems of science—especially social science—would arise *exactly because* of practical, cultural, and ideological commitments. The entire emphasis of his argument was to *liberate* men in approaching empirical science in the pursuit of accurate explanations of their problems. His emphasis was only to *clarify the boundaries* for accuracy of conception and accuracy of work.

(b) The 'Delimitation' of Science

Weber's emphasis upon the *limits* of science went beyond this relatively simple statement of the claims of 'positive science', however. We said earlier that he was even more emphatic about the delimitations of science than Durkheim, and here we can see, at least to a greater extent, in what respects this was so.

In the most direct sense, Weber saw that the world of actuality—as well as that of human society—with all its vastness, its intricacies and complexities, its continuities and its changes, was always so rich in its detail as to elude the net of any scientific theory. At best, human science could be but a limited glance (as accurate as could be, no doubt) at one aspect of this complex actuality. Furthermore, science was necessarily *selective*. Its particular concepts were constructed to enquire into specific problems, and its observations were confined only to those phenomena which were 'relevant'. Yet science knew that, beyond these relevancies, these self-same phenomena included endless other dimensions. Science was always, and must always be, limited in this large sense. But there were two even more specific limits within this already clear limitation.

The first was that science was only *accurate* in proportion to its *artificial delimitation* of definition of subject-matter and method. Measurable, testable accuracy was, in short, a function of *deliberate delimitation*. And the second, very closely related to this, was that science could never move to a situation of *progressively complete* knowledge, because these delimited conceptualizations of scientists were not, and would never be, uniform parts of an agreed and entire conceptual framework—on the contrary they were continuously changing as scientists of new generations, in new situations, encountered and conceived new problems. Science, in short, must be a never-ending kaleidoscope of differently posed views of different problems.

392

The idea that *reality existed in its totality* and that science was an increasingly specialized method of studying all its aspects, so that, in the long run, human knowledge of this reality would be complete was, said Weber, not true.

No such completion was possible.

Science, on the contrary, was an ever-changing set of concepts and techniques whereby changing men in the changing scene of the world investigated their changing problems. To expect, or to hope for, some grand comprehensive schema of concepts within which all aspects of actuality could—with a kind of conceptual consensus of agreement—be 'completely visioned', so to speak, was an unrealistic dream, and should be abandoned.

It will readily be seen in this position, that, though expressed in a different way, Weber also agreed with Comte's conception of the limits of positive science to a degree far more profound than has properly been realized. And the recognition of this agreement seems to me to bear home as forcibly as anything possibly could the kind of position which both men wished to make clear—namely the awful position of contemporary man in this full realization of the implications of his knowledge, the responsibility for the making of his own world, but—at the same time—the endless vista of a lack of any finality that lies before him. It can be seen, more clearly what Weber meant in describing his position as one of considered pessimism, of tragedy, and one of a morality of responsibility rather than of an espousal of an 'inspirational' morality. It can at least be seen, too, why Comte believed that men could not well confront this contemporary situation without a new religion. I hope I do not seem to be pressing this too far in pointing to the suggestion that it might be no accident that these two men suffered intense mental derangement—were, at particular points of their lives, insane. The vision which both had of man's contemporary—and inescapable—predicament, was one of a stark and profound realization of tragic dimensions indeed, and one of a full realization of the overwhelming effort of mind, character, and responsible action which it required. But we might come back to such considerations later.

The point which I chiefly wish to stress here is that Weber clearly agreed with Comte's position that positive science was not only limited, but also (*a*) that it was never *final*, and (*b*) that it was always *relative* (relative to the developments in knowledge itself, the changing condition of man's situation, the changing problems which oppressed and interested him, etc.). Though claiming, then, that positive science alone was productive of testable knowledge, Weber was very exacting in his delineation of its proper, and its theoretically necessary, *limits*.

(c) Relative—but not Arbitrary

The immediate qualification has to be made, however, that—though conceiving of the 'relative' delimitations of science in these ways— Weber was far from accepting an easy-going 'relativity' of knowledge. Science was delimited conceptually relative to the problems formulated and the interests and values from which the problems were seen, but—once problems *were* formulated—it insisted upon the utmost rigour in pursuing all the enquiries relevant to the problem and to the testing of the explanation offered. Science—though relative in some senses, was not *loosely* so, and, to use Comte's terms again, though relative it was by no means *arbitrary*. It may be noted that Weber was as insistent upon this in all other kinds of rational discourse, as well as that of science. The simple-minded juxta-positions between 'absolute' standards and the 'relativity' of ethics which pass for philosophical discussion at the present time seem the tissue-paper thin inanities which they *are* when compared with the treatment of men like these. But here we must stay close to 'relativity' in scientific knowledge proper. Weber was very clear. Having discussed the matter of 'relativity' (in terms of cultural attachment to values, etc.), he wrote:

'It has been and remains true that a systematically correct scientific proof in the social sciences, if it is to achieve its purpose, must be acknowledged as correct even by a Chinese—or—more precisely stated—it must constantly *strive* to attain this goal, which perhaps may not be completely attainable due to faulty data. Furthermore, the successful *logical* analysis of the content of an ideal and its ultimate axioms and the discovery of the consequences which arise from pursuing it, logically and practically, must also be valid for the Chinese. At the same time, our Chinese can lack a "sense" for our ethical imperative and he can and certainly often will deny the ideal itself and the concrete value-judgements derived from it. Neither of these two latter attitudes can affect the scientific value of the analysis in any way.'*

We shall see later how Weber clarified methods for the scientific testing of theories with this desirable degree of rigour, but it is at least clear that there was no abandonment of the exactitude of logical inference and experimental testing here.

(d) Sciences distinguished by their problems

One final point of a general nature is that Weber—like many before him—thought that though scientific method was always charac-terized by the one central factor: of rendering theories vulnerable to crucial conditions of test—its concepts, techniques, and kinds of

* *Op. cit.*, pp. 58–9.

explanation differed in accordance with the nature of the facts and problems studied. This we have already mentioned, but it may be noted further here that, for Weber, the emphasis in this was upon the nature of the *problems*. And in his position on this Weber, though substantially agreeing with others, nonetheless entered a difference of emphasis which again indicated his own very specific view of the free activity of science in being a formulation of problems in relation to the validity of which facts were seen, rather than in being in some sense *obliged* to study certain pressing *objectivities* of *facts themselves*. Weber wrote:

'It is not the "actual" interconnections of "things" but the *conceptual* interconnections of *problems* which define the scope of the various sciences. A new "science" emerges where new problems are pursued by new methods and truths are thereby discovered which open up significant new points of view.'*

Again, the difference between Durkheim and Weber is indicated quite strongly in this statement, and the greater degree of 'liberation' of Weber in his conception of the delimitations of science can readily be seen.

On all these general points concerning the nature, limitations, and claims of science to establish knowledge; the rejection of metaphysics; and the distinctiveness of the sciences in relation to their own level of facts and problems studied; it is clear that Weber was considerably in agreement with positions already laid down.

(II) ON THE SCIENTIFIC STUDY OF MAN AND SOCIETY

(a) *Only Science can provide testable knowledge of causal relations in Society*

It goes without saying that Weber agreed with his predecessors that only by the application of the methods of empirical science could knowledge be established about the nature of man and society. The only point we need to emphasize here is that Weber definitely conceived of such a science as a science of *causal relations* and its role as that of providing *causal explanations of unique social facts*. For him, the only genuine science was a science of causal relations, and in ways that we shall come to shortly, he held that the establishing of '*laws*'; the statement of *empirical regularities*; was not the end of a science of society, but rather the *means* whereby specific explanations could be achieved of concrete, individual social phenomena. Sociology was a generalizing science only to achieve *specific explanations*.

* *Op. cit.*, p. 68.

Thus, to give an example, Weber studied comparatively certain common economic elements and their relation to certain kinds of religious ethic *not* simply to establish *generalizations* for their own sake, but in order to achieve an accurate causal explanation of the *unique* development of industrial capitalism in Western Europe. The full significance of this for Weber's methodology will be seen later, but here it is enough to note that he was fully agreed as to the necessity of a science of society, and that he conceived of this as the uncovering of relations of *causality*.

(b) Societies as Systems of Social Institutions

Weber also completely agreed as to the existence of societies as entire systems of interconnected institutions and groups. He agreed that 'associational' systems formed a distinctive level of phenomena —a distinctive *'configuration'* other than those of a purely inanimate, biological, or psychological nature—the explanation of which required a distinctive science. His system of concepts was elaborated to take into account all the observable elements of social order: corporate groups of all kinds—territorial, political, religious, industrial, familial, etc.; their structures of organization and administration; the patterns and principles of power and authority in them; various systems of social relationships within and among them; kinds of order, and conflict, and processes of selection of personnel; and patterns of interconnection among them in certain social 'types'—e.g. 'Feudalism'. Weber also agreed that, unquestionably, observable empirical regularities among all these elements of 'cultural' and 'social' systems could be traced. All this we shall elaborate further in a moment. The important emphasis we have immediately to note, however, is that although Weber readily agreed that such systems and configurations were 'objectively there', he decidedly opposed any 'reification', or 'hypostatization', or false 'objectification' of them as *entities*, because, in his view, such relationships only 'existed' in the sense that the subjective meanings and motives shared by all the members of society were such as to sustain the *probabilities* of these continuities of behaviour. But this again, we can leave for now. It is enough here to see that he agreed with his predecessors as to the existence of a distinctive level of configurational fact—and, an additional point, that any explanations of this could not be 'reduced' to terms of biology or psychology.

(c) The Teleological Dimensions of Man and Society: the Distinguishing Feature of Sociology

Without dwelling upon this too much here—since we must examine it soon as the very central element in his entire system—we must note at this point the fact that Weber was also agreed with many of those before him who had emphasized the 'teleological' characteristics of the human mind and of human action as being that qualitative distinction which differentiated the subject-matter and the methods of sociology from those of the 'natural' sciences. There is one point of distinction which is important to make at this stage: a distinction between two notions of the term 'teleological'. Of course, Weber—as all the earlier writers we have mentioned—completely rejected one notion of 'teleological explanation': that is the idea of explanation in terms of 'final ends'. The earlier metaphysical notion that there existed ultimate ideal forms to whose nature all the actual objects or individuals in the material world were striving to approximate (or which they were striving to become), was completely rejected. It was only in the second sense that this principle was held: namely that men apprehended *ends* which they wished to attain; that they undertook sequences of action calculated to achieve these ends; and that therefore the understanding of this means-end activity and endeavour in terms of *meaning* was a necessary element in the *causal* account of such action; indeed, that such action could not even be '*observed*' correctly (i.e. *as* action, as distinct from a mere connection of events) in the absence of some *imputation* of meaning. This was, strictly speaking, still an analysis of *efficient* causation, but it necessitated the recognition of a *purposive* pursuit of *ends* foreseen.

This, and only this, was the important dimension on which Weber, among others, insisted, but it was a dimension which transformed the conception of appropriate scientific method. A few other points can be noted in this place.

The first is that the insistence upon this dimension as the distinguishing feature of sociology meant a discarding of any false conception of the all-sufficiency of 'objective' methods resting upon the dogma that social actualities possessed only the observable attributes of 'things'. It did not mean that such objective attributes did not exist and should not be studied: only that to *confine* attention to them was not sufficient.

Secondly, his own conception of this point led Weber to make even more telling comments on the 'selectivity' and 'delimitation' of science. In the most general sense, Weber maintained that there was no complete array of objectively given 'facts' in nature or society which the scientist simply observed, but, on the contrary, that, out of the infinitude of the dimensions of actuality, 'facts' were those elements selectively looked for by the 'presuppositions' of the theory (implicit or explicit) being employed. In short, that even the business of science itself was an ordering of elements of experience in the light of subjectively held values, presuppositions, or sharply defined concepts.

'. . . an *exhaustive* causal investigation,' he wrote, 'of any concrete phenomena in its full reality is not only practically impossible—it is simply
nonsense. We select only these causes to which are imputed in the individual
case, the "essential" feature of an event.'

And, again:

'The *objective* validity of all empirical knowledge rests exclusively upon
the ordering of the given reality according to categories which are *subjective*
in a specific sense, namely, in that they present the *presuppositions* of our
knowledge and are based on the presupposition of the *value* of those
truths which empirical knowledge alone is able to give us.'*
'. . . without the investigator's evaluative ideas,' he insisted, 'there would
be no principle of selection of subject-matter and no meaningful knowledge of the concrete reality.'

All empirical science was therefore a delimitation resting upon
subjectively held presuppositions, but, in sociology, the imputations
of *meaning* involved in the sequences of social action of men rested
on presuppositions of *understanding* of quite a different kind. The
dimensions of *subjective meaning*—both in the actors themselves in
their actual situation, *and* in the activity of the scientist in imputing
meaning to them on presuppositions of his own—were very complex
indeed. Here, we need only note that this was the methodological
problem to which Weber devoted his attention.

A third point deserving mention here is that Weber also agreed
very substantially with earlier thinkers (from Comte to Ward and
Hobhouse) about the directions of human, social *development* in the
world. We will deal with this in noting Weber's views on evolution,
but we might simply mention here that he agreed that the development of man was out of an early situation dominated by instinct and
feeling *towards* a situation in which knowledge, rationality and
conscious purpose became increasingly predominant. To use Ward's
language, 'genetic' processes of development gave way gradually to
'teleological' processes. This was, quite definitely, Weber's view.

This mention of the 'teleological' distinctiveness of sociology here,
however, is really only for purposes of systematically indicating the
continuities of Weber's thought; and we must come back to it in
real detail later. Having mentioned it in its place, however, we can
come back to the other (immediately) more interesting elements of
his position which are not commonly thought of in connection with
him.

* *Op. cit.*, p. 110.

(d) Structural-Functional Analysis

One extremely important point is that Weber quite explicitly accepted a structural-functional analysis of the institutionalized order of society as an indispensable part of sociological analysis. In this, clearly, he was in agreement with all the other theorists we have mentioned, and it is obviously quite false to think of his own system of analysis as rejecting or excluding this. Also—like all others—he did not think of this mode of analysis as 'static' in any sense or as implying a harmonious adjustment of all the elements of order and organization in society. On the contrary, he thought of social processes as being essentially 'genetic', historical, developing processes, and he was quite explicit in thinking that problems of power and conflict were endemic in society. Nonetheless, he thought structural-functional analysis a necessary component of sociology. The only thing is that he did not think it all-sufficient in itself, and, indeed, he thought of it really as a clarification of social relationships *preliminary* to his own distinctive task of achieving the subjective understanding of social action. It is important to demonstrate that this was, in fact, Weber's own view, and two or three of his statements are quite conclusive.

In his attempt to clarify what he regarded as the fundamental concepts of sociology, Weber went out of his way to point out and agree that there were certain social regularities—other than the subjective interpretation of social action which he was selecting for distinctive emphasis—which it was important to take into account. Among these were structural-functional interconnections, and Weber wrote quite clearly as follows:

'It is the method of the so-called "organic" school of sociology to attempt to understand social interaction by using as a point of departure the "whole" within which the individual acts. His action and behaviour are then interpreted somewhat in the way that a physiologist would treat the role of an organ of the body in the "economy" of the organism, that is from the point of view of the survival of the latter. How far in other disciplines this type of functional analysis of the relation of "parts" to a "whole" can be regarded as definitive, cannot be discussed here; but it is well known that the bio-chemical and bio-physical modes of analysis of the organism are on principle opposed to stopping there.

For purposes of sociological analysis two things can be said. First this functional frame of reference is convenient for purposes of practical illustration and for provisional orientation. In these respects it is not only useful but indispensable. But at the same time if its cognitive value is overestimated and its concepts illegitimately "reified," it can be highly dangerous. Secondly, in certain circumstances this is the only available way of determining just what processes of social action it is important to understand in order to explain a given phenomenon. But this is only the

399

beginning of sociological analysis as here understood. In the case of social collectivities, precisely as distinguished from organisms, we are in a position to go beyond merely demonstrating functional relationships and uniformities. We can accomplish something which is never attainable in the natural sciences, namely the subjective understanding of the action of the component individuals.'*

This is an admirably clear statement and made it perfectly plain that Weber thought of the subjective understanding of sequences of social action as being a *further* step of analysis which could be undertaken effectively only within the indispensable context of a preliminary structural-functional analysis. Nothing could be plainer.

In his discussion of the relevance of animal studies to the study of man and society, Weber also pointed to the use made of the method of 'functional analysis' as being really the only method available. It was possible to describe and analyse the division of functions among the various groups in societies of termites, for example, but it was a limited kind of analysis and did not itself provide an *explanation*. Indeed, Weber thought that it was a relatively *easy* matter to clarify the ways in which the various parts of the 'society' functioned with reference to survival in the typical environment—but, again, this did not constitute an *explanation*. For explanation, it was necessary to go *beyond* such a functional analysis, and Weber doubted how far this was possible in animal studies. In the study of man in society, however, the subjective understanding of social action *did* provide a method for going beyond functional analysis to explanation, but the former was still a useful and necessary part of analysis.

It is worthwhile to enter the point here—as we did when discussing Tönnies—that this emphasis might well be true. It might well be the case that it is in this dimension of the subjective understanding of social action as Weber described it that the most essential and powerful tool of sociological explanation lies. But this we shall return to in our concluding discussion.

One other statement of Weber's is worth noting on this point. In commenting variably on the work of Othmar Spann, he wrote in this way:

'He is undoubtedly correct in doing something to which, however, no one seriously objects, namely, emphasizing the sociological significance of the functional point of view for preliminary orientation to problems. This is what he calls the "universalistic method". We certainly need to know what kind of action is functionally necessary for "survival", but further and above all for the maintenance of a cultural type and the continuity of the corresponding modes of social action, before it is possible even to inquire

* *The Theory of Social and Economic Organization*, Free Press, 1947, pp. 102–3.

400

how this action has come about and what motives determine it. It is necessary to know what a "king", an "official", an "entrepreneur", a "procurer", or a "magician" does; that is, what kind of typical action, which justifies classifying an individual in one of these categories, is important and relevant for an analysis, before it is possible to undertake the analysis itself. But it is only this analysis itself which can achieve the sociological understanding of the actions of typically differentiated human (and only human) individuals, and which hence constitutes the specific function of sociology.'*

Again, nothing could more definitely prove Weber's acceptance of the 'functional' point of view, and the way in which he thought of the subjective understanding of social action as being couched within it, but going beyond it.

In this again, then, Weber was in agreement with the earlier and contemporary scholars we have studied.

(e) The Relevance of Animal Studies

Since we have already mentioned the question of animal studies, and since the reconsideration of animal studies in relation to the study of man is now receiving a new vogue (at its best level—justified; at its worst—positively dangerous), it is worthwhile simply to note that Weber did pay careful and serious attention to it. We will say all we want to about it, however, in the section on 'evolution'; but is worth emphasis that Weber—like many of his predecessors and some of his contemporaries—took this subject seriously.

(f) Psychology and Sociology: the nature of 'socio-psychological' facts

Weber also considered the part to be played by psychology in sociological explanation, and his position on this compared with those of the other men we have studied was rather complicated in being partly in agreement, and partly not. What is certain is that he agreed with all in insisting that sociological explanation could not be reduced to psychological terms and any kind of compounding of them. Perhaps two points were uppermost in his mind in taking this position. One was that complex patterns of *associational* relationships were of a new *configurational* order, the characteristics of which could not possibly be explained by, or deduced from, the elements which were compounded in them. A plant or an animal consisted of chemical elements, but the analysis of the nature of the chemical elements themselves could not provide a satisfactory description, analysis, or explanation of the new *configuration* of them in the form of the plant or animal. The qualitatively new configuration had

* *Theory of Social and Economic Organization*, pp. 106–7.

attributes of its own which required analysis at its own level, and which, indeed, was necessary to explain the behaviour of the components within it. The same was true of society and its sub-groups and classes, and its individual members. Indeed, Weber argued exactly in this way about 'social psychology'—emphasizing that the discussion of psychological processes could often be seen to presuppose a previous analysis of their social context.

'The procedure,' he wrote, 'does not begin with the analysis of psychological qualities, moving then to the analysis of social institutions, but that, on the contrary, insight into the psychological preconditions and consequences of institutions presupposes a precise knowledge of the latter and the scientific analysis of their structure.'*

However, Weber by no means rejected the possible value of social psychology—which he thought had still to be created. It was psychological *reductionism* which he repudiated.

'In concrete cases, psychological analysis can contribute an extremely valuable deepening of the knowledge of the historical cultural *conditioning* and cultural *significance* of institutions . . . Through social-psychological research, with the knowledge of individual institutions as a point of departure, we will learn increasingly how to understand institutions in a psychological way. We will not however deduce the institutions from psychological laws or explain them by elementary psychological phenomena.'†

The second point, however, was more radical and definite and was simply that psychological knowledge, as such, contributed no more than any other science to the subjective understanding of social action *in terms of meaning*. The rational employment of certain means to attain certain ends in prescribed conditions was what it was —whatever the psychological states of individuals, or whatever the psychological 'ethos' of groups in collective conditions. In this sense, again, and quite distinctly, sociological explanation was something *more* than the knowledge that psychology could provide. Weber did not deny *all use* to psychological knowledge, but only insisted that sociological explanation was something more. In some cases of social action, he argued:

'. . . it is legitimate to assert that in so far as the action was rigorously rational it could not have taken any other course because for technical reasons, given their clearly defined ends, no other means were available to the actors. This very case demonstrates how erroneous it is to regard

* *The Methodology of the Social Sciences*, p. 88. † *Ibid.*, pp. 88–9.

any kind of "psychology" as the ultimate foundation of the sociological interpretation of action. The results of a type of psychological investigation which employs the methods of the natural sciences in any one of various possible ways may naturally, like the results of any other science, have, in specific contexts, outstanding significance for sociological problems; indeed this has often happened. But this use of the results of psychology is something quite different from the investigation of human behaviour in terms of its subjective meaning. Hence sociology has no closer logical relationship on a general analytical level to this type of psychology than to any other science. The source of error lies in the concept of the "psychic". It is held that everything which is not physical is *ipso facto* psychic, but that the *meaning* of a train of mathematical reasoning which a person carries out is not in the relevant sense "psychic". Similarly the rational deliberation of an actor as to whether the results of a given proposed course of action will or will not promote certain specific interests, and the corresponding decision, do not become one bit more understandable by taking "psychological" considerations into account. But it is precisely on the basis of such rational assumptions that most of the laws of sociology, including those of economics, are built up. On the other hand, in explaining the irrationalities of action sociologically, that form of psychology which employs the method of subjective understanding undoubtedly can make decisively important contributions. But this does not alter the fundamental methodological situation.'*

Weber was clearly in agreement with his predecessors on the fundamental aspects of this, but went perhaps further than they did on this latter point.

It is important to notice here, too, Weber's position with regard to the kinds of socio-psychological facts—'collective consciousnesses' or 'collective representations' engendered by association within the constraints of collective conditions—which Durkheim thought so important. Here again, Weber was quite clear. He argued that a clear methodological distinction was to be drawn between social action which was meaningfully oriented, or even between a meaningful social relationship, on the one hand, and purely *reactive* behaviour on the other—when many people in a crowd, or group, or encountering the common influences of press publicity or advertising, were *affected* in the same way by these collective conditions. The latter did not need subjective understanding in terms of *meaning* for their *causal* explanations; the former did. Weber himself thought the *meaningful interpretation* of social action the distinctive problem of sociology, and wished to concentrate upon this, but—again—he made it perfectly clear that this did not mean that he rejected the importance of studying the '*reactive*' kinds of social facts. He said,

* *Theory of Social and Economic Organization*, pp. 108–9.

403

indeed, that—in the empirical situation—the line between them was very hard to draw.

'Mere "influence" and meaningful orientation cannot therefore always be clearly differentiated on the empirical level. But conceptually it is essential to distinguish them, even though merely 'reactive' imitation may well have a degree of sociological importance at least equal to that of the type which can be called social action in the strict sense. Sociology, it goes without saying, is by no means confined to the study of "social action"; this is only, at least for the kind of sociology being developed here, its central subject matter, that which may be said to be decisive for its status as a science. But this does not imply any judgement on the comparative importance of this and other factors.'*

Again—very clear. Weber distinctly accepted the existence of the socio-psychological facts of the kind which Durkheim emphasized; he only wished, himself, to concentrate upon the study of social action. It is surely perfectly clear that Weber was selectively concentrating upon the one particular dimension of sociological explanation which he thought to be its crucially distinguishing feature. But this did not mean *at all* a lack of agreement about the existence and usefulness of other components.

(g) *Historical, Evolutionary and Developmental Studies*
Weber was also basically in agreement with the other theorists we have considered in all that he thought about the historical and developmental aspects of society, and in holding a similar evolutionary perspective, but, here again, he made his qualifications very clear.

As to history, there was no doubt whatever of Weber's agreement that social processes were *essentially* historical and *developmental* processes. For him, history was a study of the specific concrete facts of social development, and it was also possible to trace and establish regularities among the facts which the knowledge of history provided. He was quite clear, too, that certain long-term evolutionary trends could be assumed—trends of exactly the same nature as we have seen articulated by other scholars. With all this Weber agreed. He only made the same kinds of qualifications as they did together with others attendant upon his own distinctive approach. A number of his more important positions can quickly be made clear.

Like all others, he made it plain that he did *not* maintain the existence of a single, unitary, unilinear trend of social evolution which was true of all societies and *inevitable*. Similarly, he rejected the ideas that the *facts* of evolutionary developments (*a*) removed the necessity for causal explanations of specific patterns of social action, (i.e. that

* *Theory of Social and Economic Organization*, pp. 114–15.

the establishing of evolutionary 'laws' was in itself sufficient), and (b) carried with them any kind of *ethical* demonstration.

As to moral stand-points and human responsibility to work them out and to work out their implications for the methods of social science, Weber wrote:

'Only an optimistic syncretism, such as is, at times, the product of evolutionary-historical relativism, can theoretically delude itself about the profound seriousness of this situation or practically shirk its consequences. It can, to be sure, be just as obligatory subjectively for the practical politician, in the individual case, to mediate between antagonistic points of view as to take sides with one of them. But this has nothing whatsoever to do with scientific "objectivity". *Scientifically the "middle course" is not truer even by a hair's breadth*, than the most extreme party ideals of the right or left. Nowhere are the interests of science more poorly served in the long run than in those situations where one refuses to see uncomfortable facts and the realities of life in all their starkness . . . The capacity to distinguish between empirical knowledge and value-judgements, and the fulfillment of the scientific duty to see the factual truth as well as the practical duty to stand up for our own ideals constitute the programme to which we wish to adhere with ever-increasing firmness.'*

There was to be no loose reliance on the acceptance of 'evolutionary trends' or historical 'inevitabilities' for either moral or methodological stand-points as far as Weber was concerned.

It is important too to see exactly what Weber meant by the insufficiency of evolutionary laws for the explanation of specific instances of social action. Though accepting that evolutionary trends could be traced, Weber thought that the concept of evolution had been a danger in throwing a kind of blanket of all-embracing assumptions over science—leading to the persuasion that all that had to be done was to trace the regularities of evolutionary patterns (or sequences) and to state them as 'laws'. This *was* science. The full established knowledge of the actual universal process of evolution. But Weber was especially concerned to insist that this was a misconception. No doubt such empirical generalizations could be traced, and no doubt they were of use, but they were *not* explanations of *specific instances*. In his discussion of this, Weber attacked not only the misconception of the nature of science which could attend this 'evolutionary totality', but also the 'abstract theory' which came to be developed with it—for this, too, he felt, contained a definite and dangerous error of conception. It is very important to see exactly what Weber said on this not only for its own sake—but in order to see clearly a basis of criticism of much of the 'abstract theory' in contemporary sociology.

* *Methodology of the Social Sciences*, pp. 57–8.

405

On the influence of the biological notion of evolution, Weber wrote:

'When modern biology subsumed those aspects of reality which interest us *historically*, i.e. in all their concreteness, under a universally valid evolutionary principle, which at least had the appearance—but not the actuality —of embracing everything essential about the subject in a scheme of universally valid laws, this seemed to be the final twilight of all evaluative standpoints in all the sciences. For since the so-called historical event was a segment of the totality of reality, since the principle of causality which was the presupposition of all scientific work, seemed to require the analysis of all events into generally valid "laws", and in view of the overwhelming success of the natural sciences which took this idea seriously, it appeared as if there was in general no conceivable meaning of scientific work other than the discovery of the *laws* of events. Only those aspects of phenomena which were involved in the "laws" could be essential from the scientific point of view, and concrete "individual" events could be considered only as "types", i.e. as representative illustrations of laws. An interest in such events in themselves did not seem to be a "scientific" interest.'*

'Abstract theory' in social science became captivated by this idea that science aimed at the establishing of a total system of 'laws' in terms of which 'specific instances' could be 'deduced', and *thus* explained, and Weber was opposed to this with equal force.

'In order to arrive at these laws—for they are certain that science should be directed towards these as its highest goal—they take it to be a fact that we always have a direct awareness of the structure of human actions in all their reality. Hence—so they think—science can make human behaviour directly intelligible with axiomatic evidentness and accordingly reveal its laws. The only exact form of knowledge—the formulation of immediately and intuitively *evident* laws—is however at the same time the only one which offers access to events which have not been directly observed. Hence, the construction of a system of abstract and therefore purely formal propositions analogous to those of the exact natural sciences, is the only means of analyzing and intellectually mastering the complexity of social life . . . Empirical *validity* for the propositions of abstract theory is now claimed in the sense of the *deducibility* of reality from "laws" . . .
This claim fails to observe that in order to be able to reach this result even in the simplest case, the totality of the existing historical reality including every one of its causal relationships must be assumed as "given" and presupposed as known. But if *this* type of knowledge were accessible to the finite mind of man, abstract theory would have no cognitive value whatsoever.'†

We shall see other dimensions of this point in a moment when considering Weber's conception of the relation between 'generic'

* *Methodology of the Social Sciences*, p. 86.   † *Ibid.*, pp. 87–8.

and 'genetic' elements of explanation, but it is enough to note here that he regarded such 'laws' as *means* to the formulation of *causal* explanations of specific instances—*not* as an *end* of science in themselves.

This leads us to perhaps the chief emphasis in Weber's attitude to history and evolution. The whole force of his concern was to show that science was for the testable explanation of the *specific instance*. All the various components of analysis in a science were to be regarded as *tools* whereby the scientist was able to formulate that *artificially delimited conceptual type* which best enabled him to get at the most accurate causal explanation possible of the *specific problem* about the *specific object of knowledge* which troubled him. In this sense—the creation of concepts in science, and the causal explanations both sought and achieved, were never-ending. There could be no final, or complete, conceptual rubric of a science—unless it was a prison: a cage of specific evaluations and hypotheses. Whilst ever men conceived changing problems—so they would construct new conceptual 'types' or 'models' or hypotheses'. Weber's position, then, was this.

Whatever the complex actualities of history and evolution might be, the 'object of knowledge' within them was *selectively defined* by the theoretical questions which the sociologists asked. 'Facts' were defined by 'problems'. The directions of knowledge, the formulations of theory, were thus a function of the sociologist's *present* evaluations of what problems were now *significant to him*. They were therefore inexhaustible in their variety, and the scientific attitude should be such as to see that this remained so.

In short, historical 'data' and evolutionary trends and 'laws' were the *servants* to the clear formulation and the effective testing of specific causal explanations. They were not some kind of massed body of objectively given fact which imposed an obliged direction of knowledge upon the scientists. Whilst this was clearly recognized, the conceptual 'types' or 'models' for specific explanations could obviously deal with historical, developmental or evolutionary problems—as with any other kind of clearly formulated problem; but *care* should always be taken to see that the 'type' was a 'theoretical construct' and that it was not 'reified' into some falsely dominating 'objectivity'. Again, we must see how explicit Weber was about this.

Having rejected the notion and possibility of history as a 'presuppositionless' copy of 'objective' facts, Weber clarified the use of 'ideal-type' constructs in order to ask *theoretical questions* about history; as a way of moving as accurately as possible to the causal analysis of some specific problem of social interconnections.

407

'The ideal-type,' he wrote, 'is an attempt to analyse historically unique configurations or their individual components by means of genetic concepts.

It is a conceptual construct which is neither historical reality nor even the "true" reality. It is even less fitted to serve as a schema under which a real situation or action is to be subsumed as one *instance*. It has the significance of a purely ideal *limiting* concept with which the real situation or action is *compared* and surveyed for the explication of certain of its significant components. Such concepts are constructs in terms of which we formulate relationships by the application of the category of objective possibility. By means of this category, the adequacy of our imagination, oriented and disciplined by reality, is *judged* . . .

. . . there is only one criterion, namely, that of success in revealing concrete cultural phenomena in their interdependence, their causal conditions and their *significance*. The construction of abstract ideal-types recommends itself not as an end but as a *means*.'*

The danger always, he insisted, was that of confusing theoretical *type* with objective *reality*.

'Nothing is more dangerous than the *confusion* of theory and history stemming from naturalistic prejudices. This confusion expresses itself firstly in the belief that the "true" content and the essence of historical reality is portrayed in such theoretical constructs or secondly, in the use of these constructs as a procrustean bed into which history is to be forced or thirdly, in the hypostatization of such "ideas" as real "forces" and as a "true" reality which operates behind the passage of events and which works itself out in history.'†

Weber was quite clear, too, on the use—if the dangers are guarded against—of 'ideal-type' constructions of 'developmental sequences'.

'*Developmental* sequences too can be constructed into ideal types and these constructs can have quite considerable heuristic value. But this quite particularly gives rise to the danger that the ideal type and reality will be confused with one another. One can, for example, construct a pure ideal picture of the shift, conditioned by certain specific factors from a handicraft to a capitalistic economic organization. Whether the empirical-historical course of development was actually identical with the constructed one, can be investigated only by using this construct as a heuristic device for the comparison of the ideal type and the "facts". If the ideal type were "correctly" constructed and the actual course of events did *not* correspond to that predicted by the ideal type, the hypothesis that medieval society was *not* in certain respects a *strictly* "handicraft" type of society would be proved. And if the ideal type were constructed in a heuristically "*ideal*" way—whether and in what way this could occur in our example

* *Methodology of the Social Sciences*, pp. 93–4. † *Ibid.*, p. 94.

will be entirely disregarded here—it will guide the investigation into a path leading to a more precise understanding of the non-handicraft components of medieval society in their peculiar characteristics and their historical significance. *If* it leads to this result, it fulfils its logical purpose, even though, in doing so, it demonstrates its divergence from reality. It was—in this case—the test of an hypothesis. This procedure gives rise to no methodological doubts so long as we clearly keep in mind that ideal-typical developmental *constructs* and *history* are to be sharply distinguished from each other, and that the construct here is no more than the means for explicitly and validly imputing an historical event to its real causes . . .'*

Having noted these qualifications, it is only necessary to see that Weber did in fact, in his own work, take these historical, evolutionary, and developmental problems very seriously. He did not only *methodologically provide* for them, but also took them fully into account in his own particular studies and causal explanations. Here it is worthwhile to note the long-term evolutionary perspective which he quite clearly accepted (but did not much dwell upon), and more specific developmental accounts of particular social institutions.

It is in this long-term perspective that we come back to considerations which stemmed from Weber's discussion of animal studies. He did in fact think that any 'subjective understanding' of animal social behaviour akin to that possible in the study of man was only plausible 'within narrow limits', and that the relevance of animal and human studies for each other was very strictly limited. Again, however, he was far from discarding the subject altogether, and came to this conclusion:

'. . . in the field of animal psychology, human analogies are and must be continually employed. The most that can be hoped for is, then, that these biological analogies may some day be useful in suggesting significant problems. For instance they may throw a light on the question of the relative role in the early stages of human social differentiation of mechanical and instinctive factors, as compared with that of the factors which are accessible to subjective interpretation generally, and more particularly to the role of consciously rational action. It is necessary for the sociologist to be thoroughly aware of the fact that in the early stages even of human development, the first set of factors is completely predominant. Even in the later stages he must take account of their continual interaction with the others in a role which is often of decisive importance. This is particularly true of all "traditional" action and of many aspects of charisma. In the latter field of phenomena lie the seeds of certain types of psychic "contagion" and it is thus the bearer of many dynamic tendencies of social processes. These types of action are very closely related to phenomena which are understandable either only in biological terms or are

* *Methodology of the Social Sciences*, pp. 101–2.

subject to interpretation in terms of subjective motives only in fragments and with an almost imperceptible transition to the biological. But all these facts do not discharge sociology from the obligation, in full awareness of the narrow limits to which it is confined, to accomplish what it alone can do.'*

A number of quite basic points are contained in this statement. First—for our immediate concern—it is quite clear that Weber saw human social evolution as a very long-term process which moved from an early condition in which instinctive factors were predominant to a later condition in which rational purpose had conspicuously increased. This, obviously, was the position held by all the other writers. Secondly, it is equally clear that Weber thought that these factors were *still operative* in society even when rational purpose *had* increased. In short, he agreed with others that the analysis of instinct, impulse, emotion, and of unforeseen consequences—as well as the subjective understanding of action in terms of *meaning*—continued to form a necessary part of sociological explanation. Thirdly—a very important point—he clearly thought that such factors were very relevant to the explanation of socio-psychological 'contagion', the formation of sentiments, and—in short—all those socio-psychological processes attendant upon association which Durkheim emphasized. But fourthly, we can see quite plainly that Weber then thought of interpretation in terms of *meaning* as an *additional* component of sociological analysis, and that which, to him, seemed its *distinguishing* characteristic. All these points are of the greatest interest—but we can especially note (*a*) the long-term evolutionary perspective of human development which Weber clearly assumed, and (*b*) the evidence—again—that he saw *all* these dimensions of analysis as being important, but was only concerned (himself) especially to develop one.

As to specific examples of evolutionary and developmental studies in his own work—they are so numerous that any selection is almost arbitrary. The best thing is simply to recommend, especially, the reading of his book on 'General Economic History'. In that book—resting on his last course of lectures—Weber gave detailed accounts (to give only a few examples) of the evolution of the family, the evolution of the clan, and the evolution of the House Community; of the development of kinds of property, economic unit, and industrial organization; of the whole evolution of modern industrial capitalism and its specific institutions; and even of the evolution of the 'Capitalist Spirit'. History, evolution, development were therefore writ large in his work—*but*: with the methodological qualifications on which he

* *Theory of Social and Economic Organization*, p. 106.

insisted. It is worth emphasis, too, that Weber's central preoccupation —like that of all the men we have considered, from Comte on—was that of the development of modern industrial capitalism and its conflicting—indeed its paradoxical—problems. This transition from 'traditional' to 'modern industrial' society was itself a specific development of which he sought an accurate causal explanation.

There can surely be no doubt whatever, then, of Weber's agreement with the other writers about the importance of these components within sociological analysis as a whole.

(h) Observation, Classification, the Comparative Method, and other general methods of Sociology

It is worthwhile simply to note, as a corollary of these foregoing points, that Weber also agreed in general with all the other elements of sociological method which had been previously insisted upon. He agreed that there should be accuracy of observation and description, careful classification where necessary, precise historical studies, and the rigorous employment of the comparative method for testing explanatory theories. In this latter emphasis he was as emphatic as Durkheim—i.e. in regarding the comparative method as the alternative to crucial experiment. We have seen, too, that he readily saw the worthwhileness of the application of these methods in problem-areas which he himself was not specially concerned to explore.

His only central qualification to all this was that he himself wished especially to work out a way of applying these methods to the *subjective understanding of social action in particular*. It was the sharpening of *this* particular approach to causal explanation, which he considered distinctive to the subject, upon which he wished to concentrate.

Here again, however, it was his emphasis upon the causal explanation of the *specific instance* which makes it necessary to look a little further at his conception of the relation between *generic* regularities ('laws') and *genetic* explanations (of concrete instances).

(i) 'Laws' and Explanations: Average-Types and Ideal-Types: Generic Regularities and Genetic Causes

This question can appear quite complicated, but in this place it is necessary only to make one or two essential points quite clear. It is necessary to see exactly what Weber meant by the distinction, and then—chiefly—to see that his methodological concentration on the causal explanation of the specific instance, and his insistence on the insufficiency of generic regularities for this purpose—did not at all mean the *rejection* of the noting and tracing of these generic regularities. In short, he did not *object* to the tracing of 'laws' of empirical

411

regularities, he wished only to see them in their correct place in the process of *explanation*.

It is best to begin with Weber's conception of the causal explanation of the specific instance—and then see, in relation to this, the relevance of 'laws'.

His central and basic insistence—on which all else rested—was that, *in the cultural sciences*, all *knowledge* of social actuality was essentially (whether this was only *implicitly*, or fully *explicitly* realized) knowledge *from particular points of view*. In seeking explanations of the concrete actuality of culture and society, men were *inescapably* themselves social and cultural beings. The *problems* which they posed, the *questions* to which they sought answers, were rooted in issues which were of *cultural significance to them*. Weber was very definite and insistent about this, and about the fact that we needed to understand the *unique, particular* configurations of social actuality in which our problems lay.

'The type of social science in which we are interested,' he wrote, 'is an *empirical science* of concrete *reality*. Our aim is the understanding of the characteristic uniqueness of the reality in which we move. We wish to understand on the one hand the relationships and the cultural significance of individual events in their contemporary manifestations and on the other the causes of their being historically *so* and not *otherwise*.'*

And again:

'. . . nothing should be more sharply emphasized than the proposition that the knowledge of the *cultural significance* of *concrete historical events and patterns* is exclusively and solely the final end which, among other means, concept-construction and the criticism of constructs also seek to serve.'†

The sociologist's task was essentially that of being able to formulate a method whereby he could achieve an accurate causal explanation of the *specific social actuality*, the *particular social-historical configuration* which constituted the 'object of knowledge' *defined by his problem*; and this problem was rooted in what, in terms of *his* evaluations, was of cultural significance *for him*. For this purpose, then, the sociologist had to mobilize all the *general* knowledge which was *relevant*, in the construction of an 'ideal-type' conceptualization whereby he could explore, very sharply, the *actual causes* of *this one situation*. The 'ideal-type' was 'ideal' in the sense of being a sharp, artificially clear, rationally delimited 'model' which embodied the investigator's existing hypothetical persuasions; and which—by its

* *Methodology of the Social Sciences*, p. 72.   † *Ibid.*, p. 111.

very clarity of being a 'limiting' case—enabled him to *test* these persuasions and, perhaps, to see the necessity of exploring *other* hypotheses—by a careful comparison with the *actuality* it was constructed to explain. The comparative studies related to it were essentially focused *not* upon the establishing of *generalizations* for their own sake, but for the adequate explanation of this one concrete instance.

Weber, of course, thought that such 'ideal-types' should be constructed in terms of 'subjective understanding', but this we shall come to later—excepting to note this one very important point in passing: that his classification of the *subjective* elements involved in the definition of problems was entirely in the service of the most accurate *objectivity* in the causal explanation of the problem. But this we must leave for now. The essential point here is only to see clearly the relationship in Weber's mind between this attempt to achieve explanation of the concrete instance and the availability for use of 'laws' about general empirical regularities—and especially to see his agreement with other writers on this. Weber's emphasis was the more forceful because he felt that the conception of science as being *only* concerned with elucidation of general laws had somehow had the influence of making an interest in *specific instances* almost scientifically *improper*. And he wished strongly to redress this balance.

He made the matter more clear by emphasizing the distinction between 'ideal-typical' and 'average-typical' concepts; between the 'genetic' and the 'generic'. And this distinction enables us to make certain clear points.

The first of these is that Weber very definitely *did* think that *empirical regularities* could be perceived and traced in all the institutions of human societies, and that these could be stated as *generic* regularities (of form, quantitative fact, etc.), or as '*laws*'. He thought, quite emphatically, that 'typical' regularities could be distinguished in the sense of the 'average', uniformly found, incidence of phenomena. And he thought that statistical regularities could also, without doubt, be established. He also believed that the tracing of such empirical regularities was of great importance as part of sociological science: that it was important in focusing attention upon problems, and of great use as generally available knowledge to bring to bear upon (and to explore further) specific 'ideal-type' analyses when pursuing comparative studies. Weber was completely in agreement with all the other writers, then, in desiring such a body of 'average-typical' knowledge; such a systematic awareness of empirical regularities. (As Mill would put it: he saw the utility for explanation of empirical generalizations.) The burden of Weber's argument here is that such *generic* statements, the analysis of such 'laws' and 'factors'

413

are not in themselves enough, and, especially, that the *explanation* of any *specific instance*—as defined by a new problem—constitutes an *additional* task and a *distinct* and additional conceptual method. In short, the analysis of 'laws' and 'factors' becomes *useful* for specific explanation, but is selectively drawn upon in the light of the 'ideal-type construct' which has been hypothetically set up for the explanation of the specific instance as a concrete configuration having specific, actual, socio-historical causes. Let us note a few of Weber's statements in this.

Here, for example, we see that empirical regularities can point the way to 'types' of social action requiring explanation:

'It is possible in the field of social action to observe certain empirical uniformities. Certain types, that is, of action which correspond to a typically appropriate subjective meaning attributable to the same actors, are found to be wide-spread, being frequently repeated by the same individual or simultaneously performed by many different ones. Sociological investigation is concerned with these typical modes of action.'*

Theoretical analysis of any such types in concrete historical situations can only, Weber claimed, be undertaken by constructing 'ideal-types', *but*, he pointed out, *other* knowledge was also useful.

'It goes without saying that *in addition* it is convenient for the sociologist from time to time to employ average types of an empirical statistical character.'

The determination of 'laws' and 'factors', he wrote was of great value, and, indeed, 'indispensable' as a heuristic means, but this could only be:

'. . . the first of the many operations which would lead us to the desired type of knowledge. The analysis of the historically given individual configuration of those "factors" and their *significant* concrete interaction, conditioned by their historical context and especially the *rendering intelligible* of the basis and type of this significance would be the next task to be achieved. This task must be achieved, it is true, by the utilization of the preliminary analysis but it is nonetheless an entirely new and *distinct* task.'†

This additional task was that of the explanation of specific instances. Perhaps Weber's essential point here can best be seen in his dictum that concrete reality cannot be *deduced* from 'laws' and 'factors'. Concrete reality assumes *specific configurations*, and in the

* *Theory of Social and Economic Organization*, pp. 120–1.
† *Methodology of the Social Sciences*, pp. 75–6.

causal explanation of any such specific configuration, 'laws' and 'factors' form only a groundwork of preparatory (and abstract) knowledge, and must be *made use of* in a *specific explanatory formulation*. Such a specific causal explanation, Weber termed a 'genetic' explanation by contrast with a 'generic' law—but these terms are of no particular significance. It is the clarity of the distinction that matters.

A second aspect of Weber's emphasis, however, must be noted—which is one of qualification. Though agreeing with the value of 'laws' and the analysis of 'factors' and all such generalizations as to the *common* elements of human societies, Weber's entire persuasion was that these generalities were in themselves only of a very limited nature, and of only moderate value *excepting in relation* to 'ideal-typical' analysis. He felt on the one hand that the richness of cultural detail in human societies was such that statements of regularities of social forms, etc. were bound to be rather abstracted from their concrete content—to an extent that one had to be very careful in the weight one attributed to them. Also—at a last logical ditch—even these were 'categories' rooted in the culturally significant values of the investigator, and so might well be attendant upon 'ideal-type' notions which were *implicit*. But, above all, they were not in themselves *explanatory*. It is almost true to say that in Weber's scheme of analysis, the elements of 'laws' and general statements about 'factors' are the most *trivial* components—*in a methodological sense*; and there is, indeed a marked similarity between his and Popper's formulations of the scientific procedure of seeking causal explanations.

We have, however, said enough to be clear about the essential point here: that Weber sharply distinguished causal explanation in science from the more general establishing of laws—but that, though having a qualified view about the importance of the latter, he nonetheless agreed that they were indispensable in terms of *use*, and *availability* for use, in relation to specific explanations. And in all this we can see strong degrees of agreement with the earlier thinkers. We have seen, from Comte's notion of the construction of 'rational fictions' onwards, the *manipulation* and *interpretation* of empirical generalizations by the method of constructing 'types' and 'models' of various kinds, and for various uses. Weber's difference was in clarifying this dimension of sociological method more sharply, and —his chief distinction—in actually working out a method for the construction and employment of such 'ideal types' in sociological research.

(j) The Malaise of the Modern World: Weber's Perspective
We must come, when considering Weber's system, to his detailed

415

analysis of the 'rational-legal' and 'bureaucratic' order of modern industrial society, and the kinds of dilemma and danger that this entailed for mankind, but here—by way of tracing continuities in the making of the subject—it is worthwhile to note that he was completely in agreement with all the major sociologists before him and in his time, in his assessment of the malaise accompanying the transition from the decline and destruction of the 'ancien régime' of the past, to the industrial, urban, and other contractual complexities of the present. And, like all the others, he had his own very powerful analysis of the *paradoxical* nature of this malaise. At this point, his position, and his agreement with others, can best be clarified briefly by concentrating upon his emphasis upon the increasing *rationality* of modern society as it moved beyond the conditions of industrial capitalism in seeking to deal with the problems to which this new system of social relationships had given rise. There were many dimensions in Weber's emphasis upon increasing rationality—but here we can simply note that this was completely in agreement with Comte's movement towards 'positivism'; Spencer's movement towards an 'industrial' and then 'ethical' type of society; all the early Americans' conceptions of a movement towards rational re-construction in society; Tönnies' movement towards a domination of contractual associations contrived by the rational will; Hobhouse's movement towards a more rational and ethical kind of 'realistic humanitarianism' in grappling with modern complexities; and Durkheim's similar notion of an increasingly rational and ethical effort to reconstitute industrial society in such ways as to alleviate the directionless malaise of 'anomie'. Weber emphasized all these same aspects: the change from the traditional authority of the community to the rational authority based upon the rule of law; the movement from the claims of an 'inspirational' ethic to the claims of a morality of 'responsibility'; the movement from relatively simple and clear relationships resting upon accepted sentiments and beliefs among people who felt themselves to 'belong' to a community to a complexity of contractual relationships aiming at the fulfilment of rationally calculated ends of self-interest—all comprising a massive and highly articulated bureaucratic machine in which 'officials' fulfilled 'roles', and within which the individual as a whole person was lost sight of. His fear was the same fear of dehumanization and the destruction of all those qualities and freedoms which—for him— were of supreme value.

Just as Durkheim emphasized a *paradox* in the development of the 'organic' division of labour—in that men became *objectively* more interdependent but *subjectively* more estranged; so Weber emphasized a paradox in the development of the 'rational-legal bureaucracy' of the modern state. On the one hand this bureaucratic kind of administrative order had come into being to clarify new relationships, to provide procedures for resolving complex claims and counter-claims, to solve problems of power and its arbitrary abuse: in short, in the service of technical competence and justice; and in this sense it was the most *efficient* apparatus of social organization human society had ever accomplished. Yet, on the other hand, its very legalistic articulation and its largeness of scale made it—literally —a routinized machine which threatened the very qualities of individual, personal humanity it was supposed to serve. Weber's perspective was, in short, one other version of the 'Frankenstein Problem' which had been in the forefront of the minds of all the other thinkers—the fear that, in the vast modern transformation of human society—the machine that men were making to serve their needs might turn out, instead, to be one which destroyed them. This vast evolution of industrial capitalism in the west—its causes, and the concrete course of its development: this was the social phenomenon '*of cultural significance*' to Weber in his sociological work. This was the unique social development that he passionately wanted to understand; and he sought the understanding so that political *judgment* could be wisely made and practical *action* could be effectively taken.

Once again—quite centrally in Weber's work, and in agreement with all his predecessors—we see that the concern for the making of sociology was an integral part of the concern for the particular malaise of the modern social transformation, and for the re-making of society in such a way as to preserve and further the welfare and dignity of human individuals and to overcome all these real and grave dangers which threatened this. The making of sociology was for the making of society.

The upshot of all these points of continuity in the several aspects of Weber's position is that—beyond any doubt whatever—Weber was not setting up a 'school' of sociology to discountenance all others; he was *adding* and *developing* that dimension of methodology which he thought to be crucial. Weber *accepted* the socio-psychological dimensions of men in societies, the structural-functional method of analysis, the importance of historical, developmental and evolutionary sequences of change, the establishing of general 'laws' and the analysis of 'factors', the importance of the comparative method, and the like. He *accepted* the 'conspectus' of the subject, with all its components, as it had been outlined. But this was the *context* within which he wished to develop—selectively—that one component of analysis and explanation which he thought crucial—the *subjective understanding* of social *action* in terms of *meaning*. We must now try to clarify this distinctive methodology which he presented.

Weber's System of Sociological Analysis

The Subjective Understanding of Social Action in terms of Meaning for the Causal Explanation of Specific Social Configurations

Like Durkheim, Weber was intent upon furthering the accuracy and efficacy of sociology, and to this end he sought to *delimit* its proper work by a precise definition of its *distinguishing features* as a science,* and then a concentration upon the formulation of a methodology strictly appropriate to this. We can now try to trace the outline of his system as clearly as possible, beginning with his ideas as to what constituted the *distinctive* nature of the subject.

(1) *The Distinguishing Characteristics of Sociology*

For Weber, the distinguishing features of sociology lay crucially in what all the earlier writers had referred to as the 'teleological' dimensions of its subject-matter: the fact that men in society were, at least in part, *purposive* in their activities. They exercised knowledge, choice, rational calculation, and deliberate *will* in seeking *ends* of many kinds. Sociology was not confronted with a subject-matter which was only perceptible by the *senses*. The attributes of its subject-matter were not simply external sensory qualities about which an objective knowledge of 'regularities of interconnection' could be achieved. Sociology was not faced only with 'events' of interconnected 'phenomena'. Certainly such attributes existed, and sociology had to take them into account, but the *distinctive* fact was that its subject-matter (men and women in their systems of relationships) consisted in large part of associational *actions* which could be *understood* in terms of *meaning*. There was this kind of *internal* dimension of *understanding* and *interpretation* which was altogether different from (*a*) the subject-matter, and (*b*) the problem of accomplishing scientific knowledge, in all other (natural) sciences. At this point, we can note this only as a *fact of our experience, a fact* of empirical *recognition* or *awareness*. But it at once raised the point that—in the case of *this* subject-matter of men and women in their 'configurations' of interrelationships—an adequate *causal* explanation would have to include (in *addition* to other things) an accurate understanding of those states of mind, ends

* Actually, Weber writes about the distinguishing features of '*the cultural sciences*', and we will come back to this by way of criticism.

desired, motives, calculations, and employment of means, in terms of which these actions were directed and sustained. Since the subject-matter *contained* these dimensions of actuality, no causal account (no scientific explanation) could possibly be sufficient unless it included a demonstrably satisfactory account of them.

This was the distinguishing feature of sociology (of sciences of 'cultural' phenomena). Its efficacy as a science depended, therefore, upon its success in constructing a methodology effective for this distinctive problem of explanation. This—quite directly—was the task which Weber set himself: to clarify such a methodology.

'Sociology,' he wrote, 'is a science which attempts the interpretive under-standing of social action in order thereby to arrive at a causal explanation of its course and effects.'*

A number of very important points are embedded, as implicit assumptions, in this starting-point of Weber's, and it is worth our while to make them all deliberately clear.

(a) *Subjective Understanding as a* Causal *Explanation*
The first thing about which we must be meticulously clear is that Weber was not insisting upon the subjective understanding of the *meaningful* dimensions of human behaviour as something other than, or different from, or supplementary to a causal account. He was insisting upon its central necessity *as a* *causal* account in the study of this distinctive subject-matter of the social action of human beings. The ends to which men felt themselves obliged, and to which they aspired; the ways in which they purposively calculated their means; the motives to action which they conceived in their situations *were actually causes* of the courses of action which they pursued. Any account which purported to be a causal explanation—whilst remaining at the conceptual level of the natural sciences and not taking these elements of meaning into account—was *bound* to be insufficient, and was most probably (depending upon the range of its claims) false! Weber's insistence was, then, very basic indeed. It was that the kind of interpretive account which he proposed *was* a causal account, and, further, that it was *only* by the inclusion of this approach that a sufficient causal account could *possibly* be attained. This was putting Mill's point† that choices, deliberations, dispositions of character in relation to principle, etc. should be thought of as being among the

---

* *Theory of Social and Economic Organization*, p. 88.
† It was, of course, a point which went back as far as Vico, and, implicitly, had been present as a distinction even in the earliest formulations of philosophy and the sciences.

causes of man's behaviour in society with a new degree of power. It was making it the central distinction for the considerations of adequate theory in the new science.

(b) Men in Society—a Qualitatively Distinctive Subject-Matter

Enough has been said on what Weber thought about this, but one point deserves the strongest emphasis here. So far, we have only pointed to the *empirical recognition* of this distinctive nature of men in society as a subject-matter, and gone on to say that *with this recognition* comes the methodological problem of constructing an *appropriate* science. But it is important simply to note the tremendous importance of (*a*) this first condition of empirical awareness: of sensitivity to the richness and the qualitatively distinct levels of the actualities of nature and society, and (*b*) the *order* of this step: i.e. *from* sensitive awareness and imaginative insight *to* sophisticated concern for appropriate methodology and theory. For the simple, but absolutely fundamental point is that men have frequently moved in the reverse order. Having a desire to be *scientific*, and having a preconceived notion of what the categories and procedures of science *are*, they then proceed to an *imposition* of this conceptual mould upon the actualities they purport to study. With a *paucity* of sensitive awareness of the rich complexity of actuality, they then *reduce* the nature of fact to the categories they employ, and will entertain no other. This conception of science is that of a blind man's prison!

In the work of Weber, it was man as a whole—man as a feeling, thinking, willing, acting, and *responsible* being—who was seen and known in the actuality of sociology's subject-matter—and the science was formulated to be *adequate* in the exploration and explanation of these distinctive facts. It seems to me that all those from Comte and Mill to Weber who have taken this standpoint have been right, and that the other position is an error in science—and an error which carries the grave danger of purveying and popularizing a deficient conception of man, and one which could be seriously erosive of the dimensions of human responsibility.

There is only the particular point to reiterate and make clear here, that Weber was *not* saying that we can have no 'phenomenal' knowledge of men in their social situations. For example we could see all the children in a school class-room sitting in desks; we could see their size, their age, their clothes, the colour of their hair, their postures. We could see a man on a platform before them making chalk-marks on a blackboard. We might see his cheeks grow red; the chalk leave his hand and break to pieces on the head of a child who was moving more than others and making noises, and whose lips were more extended horizontally and curved upwards at the corners than those of the other children. We could observe this and much else besides *phenomenally*. But once we started speaking of the man being a *teacher*, and writing an *arithmetical sum* on the board in order to *explain a calculation*, and of the children as being *attentive* and trying to *learn*. And once we explained the man's red cheeks and the behaviour of the chalk in flying through the air and exploding on the boy's forehead in terms of the teacher becoming *angry* and *losing his temper*, and *hurling* his chalk at Billy who was being deliberately restless and noisy—and who was *grinning*. . . . As soon as we spoke like this, we would be *interpreting* what we saw *phenomenally* in terms of a *subjective understanding* of the *actions* which took place in this *social situation*. And our understanding of the meaningfulness of the situation would be necessary for a *causal* account of what we saw phenomenally. Indeed, it will readily be seen that, in fact, we only *perceive* elements of a human social situation in terms of our implicit interpretive assumptions. Thus, if Billy had been *smiling*, the chalk might not have exploded on his brow; but because he was *grinning*—it did!

It is worth saying too, that the situation would not be crucially different if we were seeing Napoleon, in the parliament at Paris, ordering an intransigent aristocrat off to be executed; or, let us say, Stalin deciding that a certain man should be eliminated from the party committee in Leningrad. 'Great' sequences of social action are not crucially (in terms of theory) distinct from 'small'—we *explain* them by *imputing* meanings in terms of our own *hypothesis* in the context of our own *understanding*; and it is especially interesting to note that even our *perception* of the elements of the situation rests really upon *implicit theory*. It would hardly be too much to say that *perception IS implicit theory*.

There is, then, no lack of clarity at all in recognizing the truth of Weber's point that the *subject-matter* of sociology contains these subjective dimensions of meaning which are actually operative as *causes* of social action.

(c) The Scientific Study of Man in Society—a Distinctive Dimension of Explanation

Enough has been said too on the fact that in order to investigate and explain the distinctive characteristics of the *subject-matter* of sociology, the *science itself* has to have a distinctive dimension of methodology—different from that of the natural sciences. A causal account in terms of the subjective understanding of meaning, is very different from the normal 'phenomenal' explanations of science; and this is clear. However, there are a few elements of this which can be usefully clarified here.

421

Perhaps the central point is that, in sociology, there is a far deeper dimension of *engagement* of the investigator with the investigated. This does not mean, at all, a greater degree of *commitment* in any ethical sense. Purely in a methodological and theoretical sense, the sociologist is not only engaged in an accurate perception of *phenomenal actuality*—as the scientist who is studying, say, static electricity, or osmosis, or the reflection and refraction of light. He himself is a person who knows what it is to have a goal of endeavour, to seek an end, to deliberate about means, to make decisions, to order action in relation to his expectations of the conduct of others. His *understanding* of the social action of *others*, in short, rests upon his *own* awareness of what is involved in social action *himself*. To put this in another way, the additional and distinctive dimension of scientific analysis and explanation which the sociologist employs is essentially rooted in the fact that he is of the same nature as his subject-matter: he is *engaged* in the *interpretation* of his subject-matter in the sense that he is inescapably a *participant* in what constitutes this subject-matter—and his theorizing stems from his direct experience of what meaningfully oriented social action *is*. This enagagement of the investigator with the investigated; this engagement of the scientist in the very nature of his distinctive subject-matter; is, qualitatively, totally different from the situation among the natural sciences.

Sociology, in this sense—or, to put it more broadly, the *cultural sciences*—are *richer* in their subject-matter than the natural sciences can possibly be. Their 'facts' have dimensions *other* than the phenomenal, which the natural sciences simply do not possess.

This intimate engagement with the subjective dimensions of human action, however, makes a few other distinctions necessary.

One most crucial distinction is that between at least two kinds of 'subjective understanding'; (*a*) in terms of 'empathy', and (*b*) in terms of 'rational meaning'. It is obviously of help in explaining the social actions of individuals or groups if we can appreciate their states of mind; if we can 'feel our way into their feelings'; if we can 'put ourselves into their shoes'. Thus—observing the situation in the school classroom which we took as an example—we may *feel* the continuous irritation and then the sudden explosion of anger experienced by the teaʳher at the boy's rudeness; and this will certainly help us to 'understand' and 'explain' the course of action which followed. On the other hand, we can also understand the action of throwing the chalk in terms of a clear means-end action. The teacher, provoked beyond control, wished to bring a halt to the child's behaviour, to make his indignation known forcibly to the boy and to the rest of the class, and to vent his indignation upon him; to punish him. This kind of understanding (though closely related to the states

of mind which gave rise to it) is logically independent of the appreciation of the states of mind themselves. The end in mind, the particular
means employed, the calculations which went into the choice of
these means rather than the *others* objectively possible in the actual
conditions of the situation—all these could be analysed and interpreted in terms of *rational meaning* quite *apart from* (though usually
in addition to) any 'empathic' appreciation of states of mind and
feeling. We will come to Weber's detailed discussion of this later,
but it is at once clear here that the observer can give *a rational account*
of the means-end elements in any sequence of action without claiming
pure rationality on the part of the actors in the situation. Thus we
can give a completely clear, rational explanation of the teacher's
action even whilst fully appreciating the hot explosion of feeling
which, momentarily, led him to act in *this* way rather than a number
of other ways open to him. This is a very important point because
Weber made the analysis of the means-end sequence of social action
the clearest case of subjective understanding in terms of *meaning*;
that case which permitted a meticulously clear analysis of the *validity*
of action in relation to the *values* and *ends* empirically held by the
actors, or hypothetically *imputed* to them. But here it is only necessary
to note the distinction.

The final point is worth noting again here, that any *psychological
knowledge* about the factors which have gone into the emergence of
the states of mind in a situation (whether of individuals, or groups, or
'collective conditions'), can *help* in explanation, but can never *replace*
either the empathic or (and this especially) the rational understanding
of the means-end sequence of action in terms of its *meaning*. The
analysis and explanation, in terms of *meaning* is on quite a different
and distinct level from that of the psychological 'factors' which are
involved in producing the state of mind. It is important to see, then,
and Weber made it completely clear, that the insistence that there
are 'subjective dimensions' to the relationships and actions of men
in society does *not* mean *only* that there are *psychological* dimensions
which can be satisfactorily explained by analysing psychological
factors. Certainly there *are* such dimensions, and psychology and
social psychology can contribute to our knowledge of them; but—
in addition—there is a subjective orientation of action in terms of
meaning which is of a different order; and sociology is concerned
with this interpretation of *meaning* in a way which goes beyond
psychology.

We can be very definite here and say that Weber showed that
though the contribution of psychology is of value and importance,
the distinctive causal analysis of sociology is *other than* psychology,
additional to psychology, and, in large measure *free from* (in the

sense of being *independent of*) psychology. Now it is important to notice that this is not a statement *antagonistic* to psychology. We have in many places insisted upon the essential worth of psychology and social psychology for certain elements and levels in any satisfactory science of man in society. This statement of Weber's is only to insist upon a level of causal explanation in sociology which goes *beyond* the contribution of psychology.

(*d*) *Sociology a Science Richer in Subject-Matter and Methods— but therefore less exact*

Weber was also perfectly clear about the price which sociology had to pay for the greater richness of its subject-matter and its more intimate methodological engagement with it. This was—quite simply —that it could neither hope nor expect to attain the same degree of measurable exactitude in its studies as could the natural sciences. This did not, however, mean that sociology was not scientific. It meant only that the nature of its subject-matter and the methods necessary to take this nature sufficiently into account only permitted certain kinds and degrees of exactitude; and that it was positively *un*scientific to look for more. However, sociology was certainly scientific in its methods in seeking such accuracy as it was possible to attain. This, again, can be seen to be the point made at the outset by Comte.

(*e*) *Values and Problems in Scientific Sociology*

One other very important feature which distinguished sociology as a science was the place of values and evaluations in the perception, formulation and study of *problems*. For Weber this was a fundamental distinction which had the most important implications for methodology, and in considering this, we can see again the sharp distinction which he drew between generalizations about 'factors' and 'laws' and causal explanations of specific instances. It was here, wrote Weber, that:

'. . . we arrive at the decisive feature of the method of the cultural sciences. We have designated as "cultural sciences" those disciplines which analyze the phenomena of life in terms of their cultural significance. The *significance* of a configuration of cultural phenomena and the basis of this significance cannot however be derived and rendered intelligible by a system of analytical laws, however perfect it may be, since the significance of cultural events presupposes a *value-orientation* towards these events. The concept of culture is a *value-concept*. Empirical reality becomes "culture" to us because and insofar as we relate it to value ideas. It includes those segments and only those segments of reality which have become significant to us because of this value-relevance. Only a small portion of existing concrete reality is colored by our value-conditioned interest and it alone is significant to us. It is significant because it reveals relationships which are important to us due to their connection with our values. Only because and to the extent that this is the case is it worthwhile for us to know it in its individual features. We cannot discover, however, what is meaningful to us by means of a "presuppositionless" investigation of empirical data. Rather perception of its meaningfulness to us is the presupposition of its becoming an *object* of investigation.'*

Weber was concerned again to make it clear that the analysis of the *generic* features involved in a cultural configuration were still of importance, but was only a *preliminary* task. The distinctive task was the analysis of the *cultural significance* of the *concrete historical fact*. But the chief point is clearly seen in the above passage: namely that what constituted a *problem* for sociology was inescapably rooted in *evaluations* of what was of cultural significance to the investigator. The problem, and what was required in a causal explanation, were therefore quite different from the problems and methods of the natural sciences. But Weber's connected points were that the evaluations of the investigator were the determining selectivity in accordance with which the problem was perceived, and that it was these, therefore, which *defined the object of knowledge*, and decided which elements of social actuality were to be concentrated upon as being *relevant* to this object, and which aspects of social action were to be considered *valid* in relation to it. In short, the *objective validity* of aspects of social action selectively emphasized by the investigator could only be defined in terms of *value-relevance*; in terms of the *meaning imputed* to the actors by the investigator. There was no such thing as an *objectivity of phenomenal facts* for sociology—which was *given* in a *presuppositionless* way. For sociology, the very 'object of knowledge' of which an explanation was sought, and the objective validity (in relation to this) of *certain* elements of social action rather than *others* were defined by the cultural evaluations of the scientist, and the *meanings* which he imputed to the participants in that configuration of social action which he was concerned to understand. It will be clearly seen what Weber meant by claiming that sociology was a science (and a skill) of *imputation*.

However, the central point we must be clear about is simply that—for Weber—the scientific problems and methods of sociology were distinctive in that they were defined by cultural evaluations. It was therefore of the utmost importance in sociology that the evaluations defining and delimiting an investigation should be made explicitly clear.

* *Methodology of the Social Sciences*, p. 76.

425

The one other question of 'values' which Weber was careful to distinguish from all this, was that of *ethical* evaluation. We have already seen that he definitely rejected any loose notion of ethical relativity and argued that men should stand by their considered ethical principles in judgment and action as much as they should stand by their considered philosophical and scientific principles in intellectual work, and, furthermore, that the same effort should be devoted to making such implicit values explicitly clear. However, this question of the ethical evaluation of the rights or wrongs of a particular configuration of social action was logically quite distinct from the 'evaluations' of cultural significance which defined an object of knowledge and the imputations of meaning which were specified in seeking a causal explanation of it. The place of values in *theory and method* was quite distinct from the matter of *ethical judgment,* and Weber—like others—insisted that the two should be kept quite separate in investigation.

This entire difficulty of disentangling the part of values in sociological theory and method, however, was part and parcel of its distinctive nature as a science, and indicated very clearly its difference from the natural sciences.

These, then, were the more important ideas which Weber put forward in seeking to *delimit* sociology and to *define* it strictly in accordance with its distinguishing characteristics. The problem to which he then devoted himself was that of clarifying the distinctive concepts, methods, and procedures of constructing theories, which sociology had to employ in its distinctive task. And the word 'clarifying' is significant; for Weber did not claim originality in his methodological achievements: he claimed only to be making completely *explicit* those conceptual assumptions and presuppositions which were *implicit* in what all students of the cultural and historical sciences actually *did*. This is worth bearing in mind—for nothing astonishes common sense and common practice more than an explicit statement of what its own assumptions imply.

(2) *The Distinctive Methods of Sociology*

(a) *No 'Presuppositionless' Knowledge: The Subjective Understanding and Explanation of Social Action from One Interpretive Point of View*

We may state Weber's first basic position in moving towards a distinctive methodology as a summary of his preliminary points. His insistence was that there was no such thing as (a) *an objectively* given body of *'presuppositionless'* knowledge, or (b) a *totality* of objective 'fact' which science was progressively illuminating to an *ultimate completion.* On the contrary (thinking now only of sociology) *knowledge* was always only of those aspects of social actuality which were relevant to the *problem defined*; and this principle of selectivity was rooted in some (implicit or explicit, direct or indirect) evaluation of cultural significance. *Objective* knowledge was relative to *subjective definition*; but, even so, once the subjective definition was clear, what was relevant for explanation had an *objective validity*; certain elements of actuality were eliminated as being objectively irrelevant to the problem, whilst others were selected as being probably relevant.

'All knowledge of cultural reality . . . is always knowledge from *particular points of view.*'

General empirical regularities may be established of a certain order of knowledge, but these were not sufficient in themselves but *of service* in the *imputation* of meaning to the particular instances of which concrete causal explanations were sought. Because of the nature of men in society, such causal explanations distinctively included meaning in the sense of purposes and the deliberate pursuit of ends by the employment of means.

'From our viewpoint, "purpose" is the conception of an *effect* which becomes a *cause* of an action. Since we take into account every cause which produces or can produce a significant effect, we also consider this one. Its specific significance consists only in the fact that we not only *observe* human conduct but can and desire to understand it.'*

Scientific knowledge in sociology was therefore a never-ending matter of producing specific explanations of specific problems which were of significance to specific investigators. The crucial matter was to produce the best conceptual *tools* possible as the *means* to achieve accurate explanations. Weber was thus explicitly opposed to the idea of any effort to achieve a total system of concepts which would be sufficient for the posing of all problems at all times; and his emphasis even in methodology was upon providing the *means* whereby men could achieve accurate *knowledge* about the problems which were *important to them*. Methodology and theory were *never* for their own sake! Weber's position was more or less summarized in these words:

'In other words, the choice of the object of investigation and the extent or depth to which this investigation attempts to penetrate into the infinite causal web, are determined by the evaluative ideas which dominate the investigator and his age. In the *method* of investigation, the guiding "point

---

* *Methodology of the Social Sciences*, p. 83.

of view" is of great importance for the *construction* of the conceptual scheme which will be used in the investigation. In the mode of their *use*, however, the investigator is obviously bound by the norms of our thought just as much here as elsewhere. For scientific truth is precisely what is *valid* for all who *seek* the truth.'*

The construction of a conceptual scheme sufficient for investigating and testing the causal interpretation of a cultural configuration derived from 'one point of view': this was the central task of sociological method; and it was this which led Weber to insist upon the centrality of the 'Ideal Type'.

(b) The Ideal Type

This concept was so central for Weber that it is best to begin by looking at what is perhaps the best and clearest of his own statements about it. This was written in his essay on ' "*Objectivity*" *in Social Science*', and had particularly in mind, by way of illustration, the economic model of a society organized on the 'principles of an exchange economy, free competition and rigorously rational conduct' —but it is an extremely clear statement about the nature of the 'Ideal Type' in general.

'This conceptual pattern brings together certain relationships and events of historical life into a complex, which is conceived as an internally consistent system. Substantively, this construct in itself is like a *utopia* which has been arrived at by the analytical accentuation of certain elements of reality. Its relationship to empirical data consists solely in the fact that where relationships of the type referred to by the abstract construct are discovered or suspected to exist in reality to some extent, we can make the *characteristic* features of this relationship pragmatically *clear* and *understandable* by reference to an *ideal-type*. This procedure can be indispensable for heuristic as well as expository purposes. The ideal typical concept will help to develop our skill in imputation in *research*: it *is* no "hypothesis" but it offers guidance to the construction of hypotheses. It is not a *description* of reality but it aims to give unambiguous means of expression to such a description. It is thus the "idea" of a *historically* given society, which is developed for us by quite the same logical principles as are used in constructing the idea of the medieval "city economy" as a "genetic" concept. When we do this, we construct the concept "city economy" not as an average of the economic structures actually existing in all the cities observed but as in *ideal-type*. An ideal type is formed by the one-sided *accentuation* of one or more points of view and by the synthesis of a great many diffuse, discrete, more or less present and occasionally absent *concrete individual* phenomena, which are arranged according to those one-sidedly emphasized viewpoints into a unified *analytical* construct. In

* *Methodology of the Social Sciences*, p. 84.

its conceptual purity, this mental construct cannot be found empirically anywhere in reality. It is a *utopia*. Historical research faces the task of determining in each individual case, the extent to which this ideal-construct approximates to or diverges from reality, to what extent for example, the economic structure of a certain city is to be classified as a "city-economy". When carefully applied, those concepts are particularly useful in research and exposition.'*

Practically all the important characteristics of the 'Ideal Type' as a device for research can be found in this statement and it is worth-while to list them very specifically.

(1) The 'Ideal Type' is a clearly constructed ideal model of the specific set of social relationships (the system of social action, the social configuration) of which an understanding and causal explanation is sought.

(2) It is *not* a *description* of those factors or laws which are thought to be found '*on the average*' in that *kind* of configuration—though such factors and laws may be drawn upon.

(3) It is an ideality of rational construction *imputing* certain *meanings* in terms of values held, ends sought, calculations made, and means employed, in which the imputed meanings of actions are interpreted as having causal validity in terms of value-relevance. It is a clear rational construction of the nature, essentially, of an exercise in imputation of meanings for causal understanding.

(4) It is *not* ideal in the sense of *ethically* good or right.

(5) It is *not* rational in the sense of assuming pure rationality among men and women in the specific configuration of actions and relationships. The investigator knows well enough that non-rational and irrational elements are powerfully present in much human behaviour.

(6) It is ideal and rational only in the sense of being a conceptual and logical ideality imputing a pure rationality of means-end actions simply *as a limiting case*. As an artificially contrived *limiting case*, it can be compared very clearly with the *actuality* of the social configuration it seeks to explain. By such comparison, those elements of actuality which are at variance with the model will be clearly revealed —so that dimensions of non-rationality, and other conditions may be uncovered; new directions of investigation may be shown to be necessary; and new imputations of causality may come to be more reliably made.

(7) It is essentially a 'one-sided' model: deliberately emphasizing those imputations thought to be worth postulating and testing. In this sense it is purposely selective, and of the nature of experiment.

* *Methodology of the Social Sciences*, p. 90.

(8) Its nature is not, therefore, to be an *exhaustive* description or account of an entire social configuration. Many 'ideal-types' can be constructed about any specific social configuration, each selectively emphasizing one 'point of view' and submitting its particular imputations to test. The *adequacy* of an ideal-type is measured purely in so far that it gives a correct explanation of the specific social configuration which it is examining.

(9) It is not a basis of comparative experiment for the purpose of setting up '*general laws*'. On the contrary, it is a limiting case for the explanation of a specific configuration. Comparative tests are always such as to throw light upon the *specific configuration* and check the adequacy of the specific ideal-type. Thus Weber, in his very wide studies in the sociology of religion, examined the relationship between the religious ethics in various societies and elements of economic development there. But this was *not* to establish general laws about the relationships between 'religious ethics' and 'economic development'; it was essentially to check the sufficiency and validity of his ideal type of the relationship between the protestant (Calvinist) ethic and the emergence of industrial capitalism which was unique to Western Europe. This emphasis upon the comparative method as a test of the ideal type as a *limiting case* for the explanation of the specific concrete social configuration is very important in that it is a clear difference *both* from the large-scale 'inductive' notion of the comparative method for establishing empirical generalizations, *and* from the notion of the comparative method as an alternative to experiment—but still for the sake of establishing causal laws (as in Durkheim).

(10) The Ideal-Type is also selective in that—given its imputations of meaning and its knowledge of conditions—it gives a clear picture of those courses of social action which are valid (in terms of value-relevance) and *objectively possible*, and those which are not. Its range of hypothetical suppositions can thus be objectively defined; and each direction of supposition can be clearly delineated and tested against the social actuality. *Elimination* is therefore possible and the progressive approximation to the most satisfactory causal explanation.

Another excellent brief statement was given by Weber in the *Theory of Social and Economic Organization*, and is especially useful in emphasizing its nature as a *limiting* and *artificially defined* case (as is the 'vacuum' given as illustration:)

'. . . Sociological analysis both abstracts from reality and at the same time helps us to understand it, in that it shows with what degree of approximation a concrete historical phenomenon can be subsumed under one or more of these concepts. For example, the same historical phenomenon may be in one aspect "feudal", in another "patrimonial", in another "bureaucratic", and in still another "charismatic". In order to give a precise meaning to these terms, it is necessary for the sociologist to formulate pure ideal types of the corresponding forms of action which in each case involve the highest possible degree of logical integration by virtue of their complete adequacy on the level of meaning. But precisely because this is true, it is probably seldom if ever that a real phenomenon can be found which corresponds exactly to one of these ideally constructed pure types. The case is similar to a physical reaction which has been calculated on the assumption of an absolute vacuum. Theoretical analysis in the field of sociology is possible only in terms of such pure types.'*

These are the more important characteristics of the Ideal Type as Weber described it, and it will readily be seen that the entire emphasis was upon its nature as a *tool* of research. But there were other aspects of the 'Ideal Type' which we should stress separately.

(c) *The Ideal-Type and Common Sense*

If Weber's conception seems at all abstract or extreme, it is worthwhile to note and think about his insistence that he was only clarifying what, in fact, people *did* in their ordinary discourse. And as soon as we stop to reflect, it is clear that all our discussion of social forms and social problems *implies* selectively defined 'ideal types' as Weber described them. We are not commonly aware of this because, as a rule, we do not make our assumptions explicit, and, in fact, we do tend always to make the error of 'reification' which he warned against. Thus, when in our arguments, we distinguish a 'communist' from a 'democratic' society; or 'The Roman Catholic Church' from 'The Baptists'; or 'The Pope' from 'The President of the Methodist Conference'; or 'Pakistanis' from 'Irish' immigrants; or the B.B.C. from I.T.V.; it is quite plain that we do not, and cannot have in mind all the exhaustive details of each vast social reality to which these names refer. We have in mind only those selected attributes which—to *us*— are the features of cultural significance. We have an implicit 'model' in mind which is really a selective picture built up of the features which *we think* are distinctive and important for the problems which worry us. A little thought, then, shows that ordinary human conversation and argument necessarily employs 'ideal-types'—*implicitly*. Weber's proposal was only that such models should be made *explicit*, and—in rigorous scientific enquiry—fitted for logical exactitude and accurate test.

* *Theory of Social and Economic Organization*, p. 110.

(d) The Ideal-Type in History, the other Social Sciences, and Science in General

Exactly the same point can be made with regard to studies other than sociology. Indeed, as Weber clarified his conception of the 'Ideal Type' in his many-sided discussions it became clear that this was far from being a kind of conceptual construction used only in sociology, but was, on the contrary, a central tool in the pursuit of systematic knowledge in all subjects. It was, in fact, a concept at the very heart of the idea of accurate, empirical knowledge—which must always be, by its very nature, selective.

Weber pointed out that in all the studies of history (as a subject), no matter how limited in scope, 'ideal types' were used *implicitly*. As soon as historians tried, even in the slightest way, to uncover, or point out, the cultural significance of the 'items' they were studying; to clarify their cultural context; to 'characterize' them; they were seen to be making use of 'ideal types'. Such notions as 'Feudalism', 'Mercantilism', the 'City State', 'Medievalism', or even 'the Manor', 'the City', or such a term as 'conventional' . . . all these indicated the operative use of selectively constructed 'models' which were *ordering* knowledge, even though they might never be made explicit. Weber gave an extremely clear example of this in the apparently simple and taken for granted notion of 'Christianity'.

'Those elements of the spiritual life of the individuals living in a certain epoch of the Middle Ages, for example, which we may designate as the "Christianity" of those individuals, would, if they could be completely portrayed, naturally constitute a chaos of infinitely differentiated and highly contradictory complexes of ideas and feelings. This is true despite the fact that the medieval church was certainly able to bring about a unity of belief and conduct to a particularly high degree. If we raise the question as to what in this chaos was the "Christianity" of the Middle Ages (which we must nonetheless use as a stable concept) and wherein lay those "Christian" elements which we find in the institutions of the Middle Ages, we see that here too in every individual case, we are applying a purely analytical construct created by ourselves. It is a combination of articles of faith, norms from church law and custom, maxims of conduct, and countless concrete interrelationships which we have fused into an "idea". It is a synthesis which we could not succeed in attaining with consistency without the application of ideal-type concepts.'*

A little reflection demonstrates that such 'models' lie at the heart of all the studies of man and society, but in some they are more sophisticatedly used—as a tool of analysis consciously employed—than in others. In History, they tend to a large degree to be implicit. In Economics, however, the clarification of 'ideal-types' resting on

* *Methodology of the Social Sciences*, p. 96.

the imputation of specific meanings and motivations in systems of market exchange, and the tracing of the probable courses of action and their effects which stem from them is the method which actually *constitutes* economic analysis. Conceptions such as 'the Pure, Self-Adjusting Market Economy', or 'Monopoly' or 'Monopsony' or 'Oligopoly', or the 'Macro-Economic' models based, let us say, on Keynesian conceptions of the relevant variables, as distinct from 'Micro-Economic' models—are all carefully constructed ideal-types for the interpretation and explanation of specific configurations of 'exchange'. They are, exactly as Weber portrays them, extreme limiting cases, based upon a rational interpretation of means-end sequences of action and relationships, and their *adequacy*, as models, is discovered by comparing them, scrupulously, with *social actuality*. In other social sciences too—Political Science, Jurisprudence, and the like—typologies are operative: of 'types' of political constitution, of 'types' of law, custom, convention, etc.; though in no case has such analysis reached the sophistication with which it is employed in Economics.

It is quite clear, too, that in psychological and biological science the ordering of empirical knowledge rests essentially upon the construction of 'types' based upon selectively emphasized attributes. Thus 'types' of personality, and 'types' of animal species are constructed, and the whole ordering of knowledge tends to be focused upon these theoretical emphases. The same, obviously, is true of all the physical sciences: the 'models' of the genetic composition of chromosomes; the varying concepts of the 'atom' in physics; etc.

The construction of ideal-types turns out, then, to be a central conception and necessary procedure in all empirical knowledge. The only thing we must crucially bear in mind here, is that Weber distinguishes the 'types' constructed in the 'cultural' as against the 'natural' sciences in that they are essentially based upon *evaluative* conceptions and consist of an imputation of *meanings* which can be *subjectively understood* as well as phenomenally observed. We should also note Weber's emphasis on the distinction between constructing types for the explanation of specific instances and for establishing generic laws. His distinction holds good; but later we will think again about this. For now, we have at least seen clearly that Weber was not—in his 'Ideal Type'—proposing a methodological oddity, difficult to comprehend, but, on the contrary, clarifying a tool of research, a method of accurate study, which was of central importance in the pursuit of all empirical knowledge.

(e) Imaginative Experiment
Much is usually said to the effect that Weber proposed a method of

'imaginative experiment', and to an extent this is true, but one or two clear qualifications need to be made to this. Strictly speaking, Weber's emphasis in this was strongly on the fact that sociological explanation was an exercise in *imputation*. It was an imaginative and rational task of *understanding*, and required the *imputation* of meanings from the point of view which the scientist thought significant. He *used* his existing knowledge of comparative and historical facts, and of empirical regularities, in making specific *imputations* and clarifying a causal explanation in terms of them. In all this, certainly the construction of the 'Ideal Type' was a matter of 'imaginative' or 'mental' experiment. However, Weber in *no* sense meant that such a mental conjecturing was enough! His emphasis here should undoubtedly be placed on the word *experiment*, rather than '*mental*'. For the only point in the mental (imaginative) imputation and causal account was that it could be *tested* against the actuality it sought to explain, and that it should demonstrably *achieve* an accurate understanding and explanation. And perhaps the most important point here is that Weber actually spoke of the 'imaginary experiment' as being something of a last resort; something which must certainly be tried—but only when all more direct methods of testing a theory by comparative studies are not available. Weber was definite about this.

'. . . Verification of subjective interpretation by comparison with the concrete course of events is, as in the case of all hypotheses, indispensable. Unfortunately this type of verification is feasible with relative accuracy only in the few very special cases susceptible of psychological experimentation. The approach to a satisfactory degree of accuracy is exceedingly various, even in the limited number of cases of mass phenomena which can be statistically described and unambiguously interpreted. For the rest there remains only the possibility of comparing the largest possible number of historical or contemporary processes which, while otherwise similar, differ in the one decisive point of their relation to the particular motive or factor the role of which is being investigated. This is a fundamental task of comparative sociology. Often, unfortunately, there is available only the dangerous and uncertain procedure of the 'imaginary experiment' which consists in thinking away certain elements of a chain of motivation and working out the course of action which would then probably ensue, thus arriving at a causal judgment.'*

To think of Weber's method as one of imaginative or mental experiment is therefore correct whilst we realize that he was insisting that it was essentially an exercise of imputation and rational construction, but whilst we also realize that it also involved rigorous testing and a detailed 'saturation' in all the dimensions of the actuality

* *Theory of Social and Economic Organization*, p. 97.

which was being studied. That is to say—it entailed the fullest empirical acquaintance with the subject-matter that was possible whilst seeking a sufficient explanation of it. Weber was very far from proposing any kind of 'mental experiment' in a vacuum, so to speak. All the time it was the correct understanding of the specific configuration of facts which should be the focal concern of the sociologist. His theoretical constructs should always have this definite end.

(f) The Comparative Method: Similarities and Differences

We have already mentioned this point, but it is so central as to deserve separate clarification. Earlier, we distinguished (though not too sharply) between the Comparative Method as employed in the context of large-scale classification (for systematically exploring empirical regularities) and the Comparative Method conceived strictly as the alternative to the experimental method. In terms of this we grouped Durkheim and Weber together as being chiefly representative of the latter emphasis, as against (say) Spencer, Hobhouse, etc., who represented the former. But now it is clear that a distinction of some importance arose between Durkheim and Weber. Both were equally emphatic in their desire for accurate delimitation and rigour of testing; but it seems correct to say that Durkheim's emphasis was that of establishing universal causal laws about the concomitant variations (the constant interconnections) of certain clearly defined social facts, whereas Weber saw empirical and comparative tests crucially as ways of sharply testing the adequacy of his 'model' for the concrete causal explanation of a specific configuration of social action. This is clearly a distinction of importance, and it is also clear that these two conceptions are not mutually exclusive. The positions of Durkheim and Weber present some distinct conceptual and theoretical disagreements, but, with careful qualifications, neither of their points of view need be ruled out.

(g) The Ideal-Type for USE: Other Deliberately Stated Limitations

A final additional point will allow mention of a number of limitations attending the conception of the 'Ideal Type' which Weber quite deliberately made clear. The chief point is to emphasize strongly, again, that Weber's 'Ideal-Type' analysis was deliberately *not* a comprehensive schema for arranging a vast amount of comparative knowledge about societies, and it deliberately disclaimed a 'totality' of any such knowledge or of a system of analysis to provide it. Such a totality of facts and analysis was impossible, and theoretically in error. 'Ideal-Type' analysis was for *use*. It was a method of constructing and testing specific causal theories which *utilized* a knowledge of empirical regularities but went beyond them in explaining—by selective imputation—specific problems of significance to the scientists. It was delimited purely to be as useful as possible for this purpose, and the extremity of Weber's deliberate delimination needs to be seen exactly here.

It is necessary, for example, to be quite clear that, for Weber, the 'Ideal-Type' was delimited *subjectively* as well as *objectively*. It selected not only from the infinite complexity of objective actualities, but also in its imputations of comprehensible motives, states of mind, and meanings. That is to say, because Weber sought subjectively to *understand* social action, and, by the imputation of meanings, causally to explain sequences of action and their effects, it did *not* mean that he thought the sociologist could achieve a *full* empathic and rational awareness of the subjective experience of all the actors in the situation. The scientist was deliberately *one-sided* and *selective* in his imputations of meaning, too. Weber wrote as follows:

'The theoretical concepts of sociology are ideal types not only from the objective point of view, but also in their application to subjective processes. In the great majority of cases actual action goes on in a state of inarticulate half-consciousness or actual unconsciousness of its subjective meaning. The actor is more likely to "be aware" of it in a vague sense than he is to "know" what he is doing or be explicitly self-conscious about it. In most cases his action is governed by impulse or habit. Only occasionally and, in the uniform action of large numbers often only in the case of a few individuals, is the subjective meaning of the action, whether rational or irrational, brought clearly into consciousness. The ideal type of meaningful action where the meaning is fully conscious and explicit is a marginal case. Every sociological or historical investigation, in applying its analysis to the empirical facts, must take this fact into account. But the difficulty need not prevent the sociologist from systematizing his concepts by the classification of possible types of subjective meaning. That is, he may reason as if action actually proceeded on the basis of clearly self-conscious meaning. The resulting deviation from the concrete facts must continually be kept in mind whenever it is a question of this level of concreteness, and must be carefully studied with reference both to degree and kind.'*

Clearly many 'Ideal-Types' were possible in approaching the study of *one* social configuration, and this Weber not only admitted, but methodologically insisted upon, and it is of fundamental importance for the understanding of his position to see the complete *lack of finality* of sociological theories (or knowledge) which he not only recognized, but *stipulated* as being theoretically correct.

Let us see, first, that he was strongly critical of the conception of a

* *Theory of Social and Economic Organization*, pp. 111–12.

'complete' or 'deductive' science—in any field, and decidedly opposed to any idea, in sociology in particular, of constructing a vast system of concepts which could create this 'totality'. He attacked:

'. . . the opinion that it is the end and the goal of every science to order its data into a system of concepts, the content of which is to be acquired and slowly perfected through the observation of empirical regularities, the construction of hypotheses, and their verification, until finally a "completed" and *hence* deductive science emerges. For this goal, the historical-inductive work of the present day is a preliminary task necessitated by the imperfections of our discipline. Nothing can be more suspect, from this point of view, than the construction and application of clear-cut concepts since this seems to be an over-hasty anticipation of the remote future.'*

This is very plain, and elsewhere Weber was similarly critical of 'abstract theory', but the strength of his emphasis in this matter is best seen in his insistence that the development of science necessarily entails the transience or transitory nature of 'Ideal-Types'. On the one hand he argued that in the beginnings of a science an 'Ideal-Type' provided the basis for a guarded exploration of what seems a boundary-less complexity of facts: 'It serves as a harbour until one has learned to navigate safely in the vast sea of empirical facts'. But, on the other, even though such 'models' may remain useful for limited purposes, they become superseded as knowledge grows. The particular reference in the following passage is to Constant's theory of the ancient state—but its point is quite general.

The coming of age of science in fact always implies the transcendance of the ideal-type, insofar as it was thought of as possessing empirical validity or as a class *concept*. However, it is still legitimate today to use the brilliant Constant hypothesis to demonstrate certain aspects and historically unique features of ancient political life, as long as one carefully bears in mind its ideal-typical character. Moreover, there are sciences to which eternal youth is granted, and the historical disciplines are among them—all those to which the eternally onward flowing stream of culture perpetually brings new problems. At the very heart of their task lies not only the transiency of *all* ideal types *but* also at the same time the inevitability of *new* ones.'†

'Ideal-Types' are *used* to produce the knowledge which men find significant in their own time, but they are continuously replaced by others. The following statement gives Weber's conclusions very clearly.

* *Methodology of the Social Sciences*, p. 106.   † *Ibid.*, p. 104.

437

'The intellectual apparatus which the past has developed through the analysis, or more truthfully, the analytical rearrangement of the immediately given reality, and through the latter's integration by concepts which correspond to the state of its knowledge and the focus of its interest, is in constant tension with the new knowledge which we can and *desire* to wrest from reality. The progress of cultural science occurs through this conflict. Its result is the perpetual reconstruction of those concepts through which we seek to comprehend reality. The history of the social sciences is and remains a continuous process passing from the attempt to order reality analytically through the construction of concepts—the dissolution of the analytical constructs so constructed through the expansion and shift of the scientific horizon—and the reformulation anew of concepts on the foundations thus transformed.'*

The movement of science is, indeed, a continuous movement, and so it must remain.

'In the cultural sciences concept-construction depends on the setting of the problem, and the latter varies with the content of culture itself. The relationship between concept and reality in the cultural sciences involves the transitoriness of all such syntheses. The great attempts at theory-construction in our science were always useful for revealing the limits of the significance of those points of view which provided their foundations.'

It is quite clear that with Weber—as with Durkheim (but even more so)—we come to a *development* of certain dimensions within the nineteenth-century 'conspectus' which constituted the winning of a certain freedom from it. We must still be very careful in this estimation; for Weber, like Durkheim, did in fact accept the necessity, the correctness, the value, of many aspects of the foundations of the subject, and himself emphasized their continuity. But it is clear that his formulations were such as to free individual researches from some constraints of what could be the too compendious grasp of the earlier foundations. Even so, this was still the *development* of the movement from theor*y* to theor*ies within* the conspectus embracing all the dimensions of the subject; it was the *selective development* of that dimension of the subject of crucial significance for Weber; *not* by any means a rejection of all the rest. And it is worthwhile, in concluding this section, to see that, following all these considerations of the *limits* of the distinctive methods of sociology, and all the qualifications required because of the *evaluative* roots of theory in sociology and the subjective understanding of *meaning* which it involves, Weber was still completely agreed with all his predecessors that *science* was the *only* procedure whereby *testable* knowledge of man in society could be produced. He wrote:

* *Methodology of the Social Sciences*, p. 105.

438

'Those for whom scientific truth is of no value will seek in vain for some other truth to take the place of science in just those respects in which it is unique, namely, in the provision of concepts and judgments which are neither empirical reality nor reproductions of it but which facilitate its analytical ordering in a valid manner. In the empirical social sciences, as we have seen, the possibility of meaningful knowledge of what is essential for us in the infinite richness of events is bound up with the unremitting application of viewpoints of a specifically particularized character, which, in the last analysis, are oriented on the basis of evaluative ideas. These evaluative ideas are for their part empirically discoverable and analysable as elements of meaningful human conduct, but their validity can *not* be deduced from empirical data as such. The "objectivity" of the social sciences depends rather on the fact that the empirical data are always related to those evaluative ideas which alone make them worth knowing and the significance of the empirical data is derived from these evaluative ideas. But these data can never become the foundation for the empirically impossible proof of the validity of the evaluative ideas.'*

These, then, were Weber's ideas on the distinctive *methods* of sociology which were related to the distinctive characteristics of its *subject-matter*, and the distinctive *position of the investigator* in relation to this subject-matter, and I hope that two things especially have become clear in this discussion: (*a*) Weber's *consistency*, and (*b*) the *uniqueness* of his contribution to the making of the subject. We have seen that almost all the scholars before him had recognized the importance of these 'teleological' dimensions of sociology, but none had worked out their methodological implications to the extent that he did.

(3) *Conceptual Elements of Sociological Analysis: for the Construction of Ideal-Types*

Following this clarification of the distinctive nature and methods of sociology as a science, Weber then went on to provide a set of 'fundamental' working concepts by means of which the interpretive understanding he had in mind could be carried out. This was not, obviously, an attempt to set up an entire schema of concepts of the sort he had theoretically denounced, but one simply to clarify the basic concepts relating to the major elements of any social order in terms of which 'Ideal Types' could be constructed. It is impossible to summarize this entire set of concepts, but we must look at certain of the basic definitions which exemplify his central approach to the 'subjective understanding of social action', and then see, at least, how these enabled him to elaborate his conceptual analysis of all other social forms.

* *Methodology of the Social Sciences*, pp. 110–11.

439

(a) Action and Social Action

Consistently following his aim of *delimiting* sociology so that its scope was defined *precisely*, Weber began by clearly distinguishing between 'events' of sheer 'interconnection' in society, and both *action* and *social action*. Mere 'events of interconnection' in society were those which were not at all meaningfully oriented. The example Weber gave was that of a collision between two cyclists. *Action*, as distinct from mere events, was a subjectively understandable orientation of behaviour—a sequence of behaviour which was meaningfully oriented in terms of ends, means employed, motives, and the like. An example of this which Weber used was that of carrying an umbrella and putting it up when it rained. Now *actions* could produce *events of interconnection* among men in society *without constituting social action*. Thus all the individuals in a market-place might put up their umbrellas when it rained. This would be *similarity* of action, and it might even be (to press this example to extremes) that a statistical regularity of injury to eyes caused by umbrellas on rainy days could be established. This would be an event of interconnectedness of items of human action, but it would not be social action for Weber. According to him the *distinctive* task of sociology had nothing to do with *events* or *actions* in these foregoing senses—because other sciences could deal with all phenomena falling under these heads.

Sociology's *crucially* distinguishing task was the causal explanation of *social* action. And action was *social*, wrote Weber:

'. . . in so far as, by virtue of the subjective meaning attached to it by the acting individual (or individuals), it takes account of the behaviour of others and is thereby oriented in its course.'*

Thus if—*after* the collision of the cyclists, the two cyclists began to fight, each angered by the carelessness of the other; or if they got up, shook hands, and went off in agreement to the police station to sort out their mutual 'damages'; or if, after the putting up of umbrellas in the market-place and the injuries to eyes, some people blamed others and sent off claims to their insurance companies; *all* such conduct which was meaningfully oriented to others would be *social* action, and the *causes* of the course and the effects of such action could not be known without a subjective understanding of the motives, the ends sought, the means employed, of the participants.

Let us quickly notice one or two points. Weber did not say that the *only* causes of *social* action were those uncovered by subjective understanding. Thus the cyclists' collision and the proximity to each other of the people with umbrellas would be *causes* giving rise to sequences of social action, and many such *conditions* of the actors in

* *Theory of Social and Economic Organization*, p. 88.

440

a following situation may have causal significance. Weber was only insisting that *some* of the *causes* of *social* action lay in the realm of the meaningful experience of the actors, and that it was the *distinctive* task of sociology to provide an explanation in terms of *these* dimensions.

The dimension of sociology which Weber wanted to develop was thus this scientific explanation of social action—so defined.

There are one or two further points.

Social action, clearly, was not necessarily *positive* action. It could also involve passive quiescence and quite a deliberate decision *not* to act, or, through indecision, a *failure* to act. But all this entered into the understanding and explanation of the situation, too.

Also—just as *similar* action could be brought about by a simultaneous action of many individuals (as with the putting up of umbrellas), but was not oriented towards others—so many individuals might act similarly because they had responded in a similar way to some particular conditions, or had been influenced in the same way by some particular experience. For example ten million male commuters might slam the door irascibly when they get home because they have all been exasperated by driving through congested traffic. Three million girls might see Marilyn Monroe putting on tights rather than stockings in a film and go out and buy tights the next morning. Or—to use Durkheim's kind of example—a statistically calculable number of people might commit suicide because they are constrained by similar conditions. Now all these kinds of actions may *give rise* to social action, but, as such, they are not themselves social action but what Weber called 'reactive behaviour'. And again, Weber did not deny the *relevance* of such behaviour for the initiation of, or influence upon, sequences of social action; he simply *distinguished* it, and argued (*a*) that it did not require explanation in terms of socially oriented *meaning*, and (*b*) that any *social* action which resulted from it *would* require a causal explanation in terms of meaning, of a kind going beyond explanations in terms of purely 'reactive factors'.

Weber was perfectly clear in this. He was well aware that the borderline between 'reactive behaviour' and 'socially and meaningfully oriented action' was 'often hardly possible to discriminate', but it was essential, he argued, to get the *logical* distinction clear.

Sociology, then, was distinctively concerned to explain *social* action; *not* 'events of mere interconnection', *not* action without social orientation, and *not* reactive behaviour as such. The delimitation of subject-matter was perfectly clear.

(b) Subjective Understanding of Social Action in Individual Terms
One other important theoretical stipulation of Weber's needs state-

ment here, and that is his insistence that any causal account of social action in terms of the subjective understanding of meaning can be expressed in terms none other than those understandable to the individual. The important point is to note that this was not the assertion of a metaphysical 'individualism' on the part of Weber, or a kind of individualistic 'reductionism', but only a logical and methodological point of fact. Weber was well aware, as we have seen, that men were influenced by the cultural ethics of their own society and their own time, and that many interconnections of a 'reactive' nature occurred as a matter of socio-psychological fact among them. He was also aware of the complexities of social *organization* and of the rules and procedures of *institutions* as such. His only point—apart from strongly resisting the perpetual danger of *reification* in all this— was that it is in fact the case that a *meaningful* interpretation of social action—in terms of motives, ends, means, etc—was only such as to be comprehended by individuals. Certainly men pursued their social action within the context of vast and complex collective conditions, but there was no kind of *collective rationality*, no set of *collective motives*, no sort of *collective state of mind*, impulse or emotion which permitted a subjective interpretation of a level of meaning only understandable *by that collectivity*, and *not* understandable by individuals. No matter how complex the conditions within which social action was set, meaning was only expressible in terms of meaning for individuals.

(c) *The understanding of Social Action: The Rational Clarity of the Means-End Type*

We have already noted that Weber distinguished between 'empathic' understanding, and understanding in terms of rational meaning. It is important to be clear that he concentrated upon that kind of social action which deployed *means* in the pursuit of an end, simply because it could be interpreted by a kind of *understanding* independent of 'empathic' elements, and because it was the most amenable to clear empirical testing. Weber wrote:

'For the verifiable accuracy of interpretation of the meaning of a phenomenon, it is a great help to be able to put one's self imaginatively in the place of the actor and thus sympathetically to participate in his experiences, but this is not an essential condition of meaningful interpretation . . . we also understand what a person is doing when he tries to achieve certain ends by choosing appropriate means on the basis of the facts of the situation as experience has accustomed us to interpret them. Such an interpretation of this type of rationally purposeful action possesses, for the understanding of the choice of means, the highest degree of verifiable certainty.'*

* *Theory of Social and Economic Organization*, pp. 90–1.

442

And, he went on:

'The construction of a purely rational course of action in such cases serves the sociologist as a type ("ideal type") which has the merit of clear under-standability and lack of ambiguity. By comparison with this it is possible to understand the ways in which actual action is influenced by irrational factors of all sorts, such as affects and errors, in that they account for the deviation from the line of conduct which would be expected on the hypothesis that the action were purely rational.

Only in this respect and for these reasons of methodological con-venience, is the method of sociology 'rationalistic.'*

This, then, was made meticulously clear: that the imputation of 'rationality' in the construction of an 'Ideal Type' was purely a methodological device, and the *means-end* kind of social action was especially used both because it was such a common kind of human action and, particularly, because it yielded the greatest degree of accuracy.

Weber then went on to specify what, in his view, were the more important types of social action which could be used in the con-struction of 'models'.

(d) Types of Social Action
Weber distinguished four types of social action on the basis of their 'modes of orientation,' and we can best note these in the order of their relative simplicity.

Affective Social Action
Some sequences of social action stemmed quite directly from the states of feeling, impulse, emotion of the actor. Such action was oriented to others in terms of such personal feelings; it sprang spontaneously and powerfully from them, and could be subjectively understood in these terms.

Traditional Social Action
A second type of social action was that which also stemmed from feeling, but, in this case, from *settled* feeling which had been moulded by long habit and was regulated by the deep-rooted acceptance of tradition.

Social Action employing Rational Means in the service of an Accepted End
A third kind of social action could be distinguished in which there was much rational calculation of the means to be employed, and a

* *Theory of Social and Economic Organization*, p. 92.

443

rational direction of means, but in which all this was undertaken in the service of some ultimate end to which the actor was completely and unquestioningly committed. What Weber had chiefly in mind here was the case in which there was complete devotion to some religious or ethical or aesthetic end, some supreme value worthwhile for its own sake, and in relation to which all the means of endeavour were calculatedly oriented. Nothing mattered but the service of the ideality; not even issues of personal success or failure in other dimensions of life.

Social Action Rational Throughout: In the calculation of both Ends and Means

The fourth kind of social action was that in which there was a rational deliberation even about the choice among a number of alternative ends, as well as a calculated assessment of means to be employed. Indeed, in this case, the calculation of means had a bearing on the consideration of ends, and vice versa, so that this kind of social action was rational throughout.

Weber did not claim, at all, that this was an exhaustive classification of the ways in which social action could be oriented, nor did he claim that any particular (empirical) sequence of social action would be *entirely* of one type and could be understood in terms of it. They were 'limiting types', but particular 'types' for the understanding of particular social situations might well require the combining of several of them. It is a useful exercise, however, to consider whether one can find any actual sequence of social actions which could *not* be analysed in terms of one or other or a blend of these four types. In these kinds of definitions of types for purposes of analysis, Weber's analytical clarity, economy, and ability was remarkable.

So far, then, Weber had distinguished the nature of social actions and classified four types which could be subjectively understood in terms of their specific kind of orientation. On this basis he then went on to provide a set of concepts for the subjective understanding of social action within all the chief elements of social order (social structure.)

(e) *Concepts for the Analysis of Social Relationships and the Institutional Order of Society*

It is here that it becomes impossible to summarize Weber's conceptual system in any satisfactory way. We can do no more than glance at the elements of social order with which he dealt, and some particular dimensions of them, in order to see the scope of his analysis, and, especially, its consistency.

First of all, he defined 'social relationships' as being certain patterns of behaviour among a plurality of actors in which all were oriented towards each other in the expectation of the *probability* that certain social action would take place. In short, all the relationships of men in society—of a temporary, small-scale nature and of a complex, large-scale, abiding nature, and of a disruptive conflictful nature—were consistently defined in terms of *expected probabilities* of social action. Here again, then, there was no 'reification' of social forms.

Following this, Weber then distinguished certain empirically found regularities of modes of orientation of social action—usage, fashion, convention, custom, law, and the like; and these were discussed in relation to their appropriate kinds of 'sanction'. Then he analysed the concept of 'legitimate order' among systems of social relationships, and classified certain 'types' of 'legitimate order' and their bases in society. Within this context, he then provided an analysis of 'conflict' and 'types' of conflict. This dimension of Weber's analysis deserves emphasis for two reasons. First, in that it demonstrates again the inclusion of the analysis of *conflict* as well as *co-operation* in the sociologist's discussion of social order. This was a dimension never left out of sight. But second, in that Weber offered in his discussion of 'conflict' an excellent outline analysis of social 'selection'. Conflicts of certain kinds in relation to which social selection of various kinds were continuously taking place were endemic to society.

Weber then went on to analyse types of 'solidary social relationships', and this was very much modelled on Tönnies' distinction between the 'natural order of community' and the 'complex, contractual order of a highly rational society'—again the complex 'system of market exchange of modern industrial capitalism' which, according to Weber, as to all his predecessors, dominated modern western societies.

Distinctions were then drawn between 'Open' and 'Closed' relationships, and, within them, modes of 'Representation and Responsibility', and this led Weber to his definitions of 'Types of Corporate Groups' and his analysis of the larger-scale patterns of power and authority in society.

A 'Corporate Group' was a social relationship in which admission to membership was limited by a set of rules and whose order was enforced by a 'Leader' and an 'administrative staff'. Weber specified types of corporate groups, types of order and organization within them, types of imperative authority, and then concentrated his attention especially on political and religious groups. Political groups particularly formed the focus of his concern since they exercised power and authority within the territory of their jurisdiction and had the monopoly of the legitimate use of force. It will be seen in all this

445

that *power* was probably the central preoccupation in the sociology of Max Weber: *power* and the legitimation of authority to exercise control over it. 'The concept of power,' he wrote, 'is highly comprehensive from the point of view of sociology.' The problems of power, conflicts of power, the exercise of power, were ubiquitous in all social relationships. Transformations of society were transformations of power, and some of Weber's most important work concentrated upon this theme.

This has been no more than a brief indication of the range of concepts which Weber provided—but it will have been sufficient for our purpose of showing how—from his starting point of 'social action' and its several 'types'—he was able to define a set of concepts which were a basis for analysing every element of social structure—from social relationships of a limited and temporary kind to the largest-scale corporate groups such as the 'State' and its legal and administrative apparatus of legitimation and enforcement. All components of society could be analysed (by the method of subjective understanding) in these terms—and it is perhaps necessary to mention that Weber went on to discuss all the major institutions of society: economic organization, property, the division of labour, class relations and social status, the state, types of religious organizations, etc. In short he provided a full apparatus for analysing the institutional order of society as thoroughly as his predecessors had done—but *all consistent with his definitions in terms of meaningfully oriented social action*. And it may have been this kind of definition which led Weber to be tentative about social order, power, authority, and its possible disruption. For if order rests upon meaningful expectations of probabilities of action—it can fall as legitimacy and the firmness of these probabilities falls.

This, then, was Weber's system of concepts: but in leaving it we must reiterate his emphasis—that these concepts of analysis were not in themselves enough. They were to be *used* by the sociologist in the construction of 'Ideal Types' for the explanation of specific concrete problems. And even the construction of 'Ideal Types' was not for its own sake—but for *use* in arriving at accurate explanations. The skill of sociology was—given the preliminary preparation of such concepts—a skill of imputation and rigorous comparative study to achieve a satisfactory causal explanation of specific instances.

Example: Types of Imperative Authority

It is usual to illustrate Weber's methodology by pointing especially to his study of western industrial capitalism and of the Protestant Ethic in relation to this, and to the wide comparative studies of religion which were all related to it, and there is no doubt whatever about the importance of this. There are one or two reasons why I shall not do this. The first—and most obvious—is that so much has been written about it that of all Weber's work it is the most familiar. But secondly —it seems to me that Weber's methodology is so clear and distinctive in itself as not to need detailed illustration, and that it might therefore be best just to concentrate a little upon that particular 'typology' which led him to a clear analytical statement about his fears concerning the development of modern industrial society.

Weber's construction of the three 'Types of Imperative Authority' was, and remains, one of the most telling contributions to the understanding of the forms of power and authority in society, and is one of the best and clearest examples in his work of the construction of 'Ideal Types'.

We may begin by remarking that, on the face of it, it would seem absurd to think that all the patterns of imperative authority in human societies (which, at first glance, would seem to be very varied and complicated) could be usefully ordered and clarified by the construction of only *three* types. Yet this is what Weber proposed, and, in examining these types, the question as to the degree of illumination of his 'types' might be borne in mind. We might note only the one further point in beginning, that Weber's *evaluative concern*, rooted in what was of *cultural significance* for him in his time, and which formed the starting-point of his typology was his concern about the same transformation of modern society from an earlier 'traditional' condition to a complex condition of highly industrialized production and market exchange dominated by rational calculation and contract which had been the concern of all the other sociologists from Comte to Tönnies, Hobhouse and Durkheim.

Weber constructed his types of authority on the basis of his definition of the corporate group—which, as we remember, was a set of social relationships within which order was enforced by a 'Leader' and an 'administrative staff', employing a set of rules which included limitations of membership. Types of imperative authority existed within such corporate groups, and Weber distinguished two types which were appropriate to a settled 'routine' order, and a third which explicitly challenged this.

Traditional Authority
The traditional system of order and type of authority was regarded, by the members who lived within it and upheld it, as having always existed, and having always been binding upon them and their ancestors. The traditional, habitual way of things carried its own

447

authority. There was no such thing as 'innovation' in the form of new conscious legislation. If change had to occur it was justified in terms of 'legal fictions'. In the beginning things had been so, they had fallen out of use, but now, since they were necessary again, they were revived.

Such a system of authority had two chief elements. First, its body of rules was a body of concrete rules, the legitimacy of which rested simply on the fact that they had always been so. This was the authority of 'immemorial usage', or 'immemorial custom', and the distinctive characteristic of these rules was that no question arose about their *consistency*. No *rational* justification was thought of, let alone sought or desired. But secondly, the Leader and the administrative staff formed a hierarchical system of *statuses* of *persons* who were legitimately empowered to exercise authority. Several distinctive points were specified here.

First, these persons were *incumbents* of concrete statuses—they were not functionaries occupying tightly defined roles. Secondly, their powers were not *precisely* defined so that they possessed a certain sphere of 'free grace'. And thirdly, authority resided in those incumbents of statuses above one's own when their superiority of status was evident. In short, whilst the incumbent of a status did nothing to disrupt or betray or oppose the traditional authority of the group and of those above him, loyalty was owed to him as a *person* not because he fulfilled a 'role'.

Such a system of statuses made for a 'total' status in which all the many duties of an incumbency were 'integrated' in the person. The property of such a person was closely related to his personal authority and power. His 'group' and 'personal' property and power were not distinct. At the lower levels of such a hierarchy, the lower order was literally an *'unfree'* order. Power from above was a power over property and persons. Group status was fused with personal status; there was no distinction between a 'public' and a 'private' sphere. And this 'personal' integration meant also an integration of family and kinship relationships in the order of public statuses. It was a legitimized order of hereditary power and privilege.

Weber distinguished two sub-divisions of such a 'traditional' type of authority*:—(1) 'Primary Patriarchalism' or 'Gerontocracy'— which existed in localized groups, of which people thought of themselves as 'members', and (2) 'Patrimonialism'—which existed when authority had to be extended beyond the local community, as, for example, in the development of 'feudal' authority. In this large-scale centralization of authority, people were 'subjects' of the 'Leader' in

* Weber's 'types of authority' for various 'routine' orders of society may be compared with Hobhouse's ideas concerning different 'types' of 'social bond' (p. 177).

the corporate group, and seeds of conflict were sown. The area of organization and the scale and scope for authority were increased, but, just because of this, a potential and actual source of conflict was engendered between the Leader and his administrative staff. There was a certain distance between them, but also the Leader had to grant his followers *benefices* or 'bundles of rights' on a personal basis, and grant *'fiefs'* as the basis for the reciprocal obligation, the act of homage, on the part of the follower. The structure of authority now entailed a clear *class*-structure; and this was a foundation of continual authority in one sense, but a source of the possible disruption of it in another.

Rational-Legal Authority

The rational-legal type of authority rested upon a number of features which were all interdependent, but focused upon the acceptance of the 'rule of law' itself.

The central characteristic of this order was the existence of a body of 'abstract' or 'generalized' rules which had been intentionally established—and therefore possessed a rational justification. This body of law was logically consistent and was applied to particular cases by the administrative staff, and again in accordance with defined and regulated procedures. There was the further acceptance of the fact that new legal rules could be established by the agreed procedures of the governing group, and that—introduced by such procedures— they could claim the obedience of the members of the corporate group. These abstract rules covered all specific 'cases' of defined conduct within the range of jurisdiction of the governing body— with the State this was usually a defined territory, and, indeed, the rules included a definition of its range of jurisdiction. The allegiance of members of the corporate group—their specific kind and degree of obedience and obligation—was not to *persons* who were the *incumbents* of *statuses* seen to be 'above' them in the hierarchy of authority, but to the impersonal order of the law, or of the accepted rational-legal procedures, itself. Important points were implicit in this for the nature and functions of the 'Leader' and the 'administrative staff'.

In the rational-legal order all persons exercising authority did so by virtue of the legitimacy of the impersonal order; their kinds and degrees of authority were clearly defined by the rules. They were *not* incumbents of statuses, but 'officials' who occupied 'offices' or who performed clearly defined 'roles'. The persons who obeyed the official, did not obey him as a person; they obeyed the law within which he was serving in a defined capacity. Similarly, the official himself was not obliged to the corporate group totally, as a whole person, but only to the defined extent of his 'public office'. The 'official role' was thus clearly distinguished from the person's private life. His 'property' and range of 'power and privilege' was clearly distinguished between those for which he was publicly responsible—according to the terms of his 'office'—and those pertaining to his private affairs. All the duties of his 'office' were distinguished from his life and relationships as a private person. The 'office' in short was both clearly defined and distinguished from the 'person'. There was, then, no 'sphere of free grace of the incumbent of a concrete status' in which public authority and personal privilege could be fused.

In this type of authority, the entire order of the administrative staff—including the 'Leader'—was essentially of a 'bureaucratic' nature. The 'rule of the office' prevailed. Each official, at his level, performed a sharply defined role with specified grades of duty, responsibility, and scales of remuneration. The entire order received 'salaries' in the form of clearly prescribed money payments. The hierarchical definition of levels was such that each official was subordinate to the one above, and responsible to the one below, and this supervisory control—crucially—included a specified degree of power in appointing, dismissing, promoting or demoting the personnel in lower offices.* Fitness for 'office' and recruitment to 'office' was based also on clearly demonstrated technical competence in the relevant field of knowledge and skill—and selection was therefore competitive and followed appropriate training and formal examinations.

Weber's 'paradox' and his fears can now clearly be seen. In terms of developmental tendencies it is clear that the societies of Western Europe (i.e. in *his* time; in *our* time it is also the larger societies throughout the world) could be seen as moving from the 'Traditional' to the 'Rational-Legal' type. By means of this typology this massive and complex transformation could be interpreted and understood. But it was clear that, on the one hand, the rational-legal type of order was capable of supreme efficiency in all its activities. The technical exploitation of resources, the large-scale and detailed proliferations of variety and specialization in the system of market-exchange, and the sheer efficiency of all means-end relationships and actions in the administration of public affairs . . . all these could be supremely

* There is an extremely interesting parallel here with Spencer's typology—the 'Militant' and 'Industrial' Types. It will be remembered that Spencer typified the Militant order as one with a clearly defined rigidity of grades in which 'all were despots to those below and slaves to those above'—and he feared the bureaucratic developments in the 'Industrial' society because liberal freedoms were in danger of being eroded, and something like a recrudescence of the 'Militant' type was afoot. Weber's fear was the same, but his new bureaucratic order had its new, complex apparatus of control.

efficient. Furthermore, many of the ramifications of bureaucracy—rationally defined and guarded by prescribed and enforced procedures—were such as to obviate many elements of *injustice* in the earlier traditional order. The rational-legal order—in the concrete developments of modern societies—had come into being as a more *just* as well as a more *efficient* order. And Weber was in no doubt about this. He regarded the rational-legal bureaucratic order as the most efficient order which had ever been devised and developed in the history of human society, and he saw modern industrial societies as being completely dependent upon it. But the paradox was, that Weber feared that such enormous bureaucratic hierarchies with their impersonal formalism would be destructive of personal liberties and, indeed, of the recognition of the 'whole man' as a person.* The most efficient order of society and authority carried also the danger of becoming depersonalized and inhuman. We shall return to Weber's 'paradox' in a moment.

These were the two types of authority which Weber constructed pertaining to the routine order of corporate groups. His third type was drawn up as always constituting a radical challenge to any such established order.

Charismatic Authority

Weber's third type of authority was held to reside in the direct appeal to others (and the claims upon them) of the qualities possessed by particular persons. This was why it was termed 'Charismatic'—possessing 'charisma': a 'gift of grace'.

Sometimes an individual possessed qualities—whether held to be superhuman, or even supernatural and of some compelling spiritual significance—which set him apart from other men as a leader. His influence was not of rational persuasion (alone) or buttressed by traditional attitudes, but was a direct personal appeal. These qualities need not only be those we are accustomed to set up as those of 'great men'—such as those of a Christ, a Gandhi, a Napoleon; but were often other indications of the possession of 'powers' which were impressive—the falling into 'maniacal passions' or into states of 'trance', and the like. Weber took *any* such distinguishing quality which led to devotion to a person as a leader as the basis for this type of authority.

* We shall come back to this—but it is of the greatest interest and significance to see that this has been the predominating theme in *literature* as well as sociology and social philosophy over the past 200 years—i.e. during the period characterized by this transformation. It is too long a task even to indicate this theme in poetry—from Wordsworth to now, and in the novel throughout the nineteenth century to now—but an excellent example of its centrality can be seen in the novels of D. H. Lawrence—and especially his *Women in Love*.

This type of authority did not find its place in 'routine' orders of society—whether traditional or rational-legal. Its claim was quite apart from such routine authority, and was thus sharply opposed to it. This was not simply because in any deliberate and considered way it *sought* to be of a conflictful nature; but because its claim was so compelling, total, and of such a nature as to cut across the requirements of routine order and authority, and, indeed, to offer *emancipation* from them. The bearer of this type of authority was always an *individual* leader, a person with a total, living influence, and the relationship of his followers to him was not at all that of being the incumbent of a status or that of fulfilling an official role, but one of totally committed *discipleship*. The leader did not 'represent' or 'express' the will of his followers; their obligations to him were not the requirements of 'offices' or 'statuses'. Their duty was to do what he demanded of them; their duties were what he asserted them to be. His special qualities flowed out into his followers in their close relations with him and as he placed tasks and duties of a non-routine nature upon them. The leader actively introduced a new code of conduct, a new way of life, and brought, himself, his own authority for it.

Weber especially insisted that this type of authority was derisive of routine economic considerations. It did not deny elements of property or reward, but it despised routine economic activity for security, and also any exploitation of 'charismatic' qualities themselves in the pursuit of wealth. The devotion to the *qualities* themselves, to the *leader* himself, this was supreme.

All these attributes were such as to make this type of authority essentially a *revolutionary* force; expressly in conflict with the routine order—whether rational-legal or any form of the traditional. And Weber particularly noted that in periods which were 'stereotyped' by tradition, charisma was the *greatest* revolutionary force to arise. This, of course, is an extremely important point for the explanation of social change in traditional societies before the full onset of the modern transformation to the industrialized rational-legal type of order began.

It is also necessary to note, finally, that the Charismatic Leader was by no means conceived by Weber as being always a kind of remote figure surrounded by his disciples in a wilderness. He saw Napoleon as such a figure imposing himself in the intricate context of political power as well as—say—a Christ in the desert.

But, of course, whatever the claims and expectations, a Charismatic Leader always dies, and those who, in discipleship, still need to sustain themselves within his influence, are driven to seek some way of doing so. And Weber went on to describe the process of 'routinization' of charisma. This was a detailed analysis, but all we need note is that the forms of organization which were necessary to secure some effective continuity of the personal charisma of the leader were such as to produce, again, patterns of 'traditional' or 'rational-legal' authority. For example, some actual *successor* to the leader had to be discovered, and some procedure for selecting such a successor and for continuing the succession thereafter. Also, some kind of 'sacramental' procedure for carrying the charisma of the original leader *through* this procedure of succession; for embodying it, or communicating it, *within* such procedure, had to be achieved. The 'movement' of the followers had now, too, to become organized on an ongoing day-to-day basis. An order of division of labour and functions had to be devised and one, now, which had to make continuing *economic* provisions and provide for the continued life of families. In short, Charismatic Leaders with their immediate followers gave way, with the passage of time, to new *routine* orders possessing the varying characteristics of traditional or rational-legal types of authority.

It can be readily seen how far-reaching, wide-ranging and *useful* Weber's construction of these three 'types' of imperative authority was. We began by remarking that it seemed absurd to think that all the complexities of 'authority' in human society could be usefully 'understood' by the construction of only *three* pure types. But we can now see the admirable degree of success of Weber's typology. A clear appreciation of these three types gives us conceptual tools whereby any *actual* order of authority or any *actual* process of transformation of authority can be interpreted and understood, so that—given a study of the conditions of the specific instance—an accurate causal explanation may be more readily arrived at. This analysis of two types of 'routine' authority, and one type of 'rebellious' authority which itself comes to follow a certain pattern of 'routinization' offers a remarkably wide scope and is extremely clear.

A few other points are worth making. It will be seen quite plainly how Weber's typology was rooted in the transformations of power and authority which were of *cultural significance* in his time. But, of course, these transformations were those of distinctive importance in the entire epoch since about the time of the French Revolution, and remain so to this day. So that Weber's general analysis accords well with those others we have considered from Comte to Weber himself, and still throws light—for us—on our own time. The tremendous transformations of traditional societies such as Russia, China, India into 'rational-legal' orders, with the significant 'charismatic' leaders and their followings which have become routinized within these new patterns all permit of analysis in Weber's terms. The significance of Gandhi in India, of Lenin and Stalin in the Soviet

Union, of Mao Tse Tung (living?—or dead?—that is the question) in China, are too obvious—with reference to this analysis—to need more than mention. But one might think, for example, of the entire order of the Roman Catholic Church (and other elements of Christianity) in our time. Are we not witnessing a rather uneasy, fraught, and very complicated process whereby a system of authority predominantly of the 'traditional' type (following its earlier routinization of an original Charisma) is being constrained to accommodate itself to the predominantly rational-legal order of modern society? As soon as Weber's types are in mind, they immediately sharpen ways of thinking about these transformations of authority which are still of the greatest cultural significance to us, and with which they deal.

But we must also note that these types were excellent examples in Weber's work of the 'Ideal Type' constructions which he proposed. They were framed, with complete consistency, in terms of his emphasis on the subjective understanding of meaningfully oriented social action; and of his 'types' of social action—affective, traditional, rational in the service of a given end, and rational in means and ends throughout. They employed all his array of basic concepts—from 'social relationships' through 'types of legitimate order', 'solidary relationships', and the like, to the types of 'corporate groups'. They also drew into their construction, selectively, a very wide range of comparative and historical knowledge (whose richness, alas, it is impossible to indicate) and thus illustrated well Weber's *use* of the *generic* in constructing the specific 'Ideal Type'. And Weber was careful to emphasize, again consistently with his notions, that any *actual* system of authority was not likely to be *entirely* of the nature of *one* of his types, but some blend of all of them.* They incorporated, too, all those components which Weber readily agreed as being important from the wider 'conspectus' of the subject: 'structural-functional analysis', the interdependency of institutions and groups; the essentially historical and developmental nature of 'social configurations', and the like.

In short, Weber's 'types of imperative authority' provide an excellent, consistent, and successful example of the kind of methodology he proposed, and—without wishing in the slightest degree to diminish the importance of his work on the study of Protestantism in relation to industrial capitalism—it seems to me that these 'types' provide a more immediately clear illustration of his methods—show-

* Many have criticized the attributes of Weber's 'pure types'—but in a section on 'Combination of the Different Types of Authority' he made it quite clear that the 'types' were combined in actual instances. He showed, for example, how the 'rational-legal' type became partly 'traditional'; how 'traditional' types, as well as the bureaucratic 'rational-legal' types, frequently had 'charismatic' leaders; etc.

ing how every component of his conceptual proposals entered into the construction of them. They have also the advantage of being directly relevant to matters of the highest *cultural significance* for us: the problems of power and its containment as modern society moves on with its ever-increasing vastness of scale—and, concomitant with this, its paradox of great potential benefit for mankind, and great potential danger.

Weber's Perspective on the Modern World

We have already seen that Weber's concern about the transformations of the modern world—from the predominantly traditional to the highly formalized bureaucracy of the industrialized 'rational-legal' type of order—was very similar indeed to that of all the other thinkers we have considered. All the great 'syntheses' of the major sociologists from Comte onwards were remarkably similar, even though couched in differing concepts and having differences of emphasis here and there; and they were certainly rooted in the same persuasion as to the *cultural significance* of the rapid process of social change that was taking place. The parallels between Comte's concern for the development of the industrialized 'positive' order of society; Spencer's concern for the movement from Militant to Industrial and then a possible 'Militant retrogression' in this; Marx's concern for the collectivist development of industrial capitalism; the concern of Ward, Sumner, Giddings and Hobhouse for the increasingly rational direction of modern industrial society; the concern of Tönnies for the transition from community to contractual society; the concern of Durkheim for the 'anomie' of the modern industrial order; and then the concern of Weber for the development of rational-legal bureaucracy in modern industrial society are quite striking in their clarity. And we have seen the 'paradoxical' dilemma in all of them. All thought that the modern order had much to offer mankind; that it was bound up with the effort towards progress and justice; but all saw, also, that it contained great threats to the very qualities of human dignity which lay at the heart of this promise. Sociology—for them all—was part of the great task of understanding this process of change in order to judge and act within it—and in such ways as to prevent or ameliorate the dangers, and to further the securing of a society which actively embodied the humane values and qualities to which they all subscribed. This consensus was completely plain.

Here, we may note a little more fully some further elements of Weber's point of view, just to substantiate the ways in which he shared this perspective. It is clear, for example, that Weber thought the apparatus of rational-legal bureaucracy *inevitable* in modern industrial society, and, curously enough, that it was the capitalist who most succeeded in resisting it. He wrote:

'Bureaucratic administration means fundamentally the exercise of control on the basis of knowledge. This is the feature of it which makes it specifically rational. This consists on the one hand in technical knowledge which, by itself, is sufficient to ensure it a position of extraordinary power. But in addition to this, bureaucratic organizations, or the holders of power who make use of them, have the tendency to increase their power still further by the knowledge growing out of experience in the service . . .

'Bureaucracy is superior in knowledge, including both technical knowledge of the concrete fact within its own sphere of interest, which is usually confined to the interests of a private business—a capitalistic enterprise. The capitalistic entrepreneur is, in our society, the only type who has been able to maintain at least relative immunity from subjection to the control of rational bureaucratic knowledge. All the rest of the population have tended to be organized in large-scale corporate groups which are inevitably subject to bureaucratic control. This is as inevitable as the dominance of precision machinery in the mass production of goods.'*

There was no half-measure in that kind of statement. But Weber then went on to specify some of the consequences and tendencies of bureaucratic control. There was first, he argued, a tendency to the '*levelling*' of social classes in order to achieve the broadest basis possible of the training of available abilities and the recruitment of those capable of competence. Secondly there was a tendency to *plutocracy*—the accumulation of effective power in the hands of the rich, concomitant with the increasing length of education and training. And thirdly, pervading all this was the tendency to a spirit of impersonal 'formalism', and Weber argued that even the legislative measures of reform achieved for humane ends were infected by this 'formalism'. In general, then, the growth of the vast machine of administrative bureaucracy was such as to possess a colourless personality, and a domination of formal categories in which concrete personal individuality might be lost. The great similarity between this picture and that drawn by Tönnies is very clear.

Two other points are worth mention.

One is that Weber also argued that the construction of 'Ideal-Types' had a great *pragmatic* value, in that, in providing accurate understanding, they also gave a sharp delineation of possible courses of positive action and social policy. The tools of sociological analysis were contributions of importance in this practical selection of alternative sequences of action, too, though, of course, they could never provide the grounds for the judgments of ethical value as

* *Theory of Social and Economic Organization*, pp. 339–40.

such. But this was an important point—that, though not directly aiming at administrative action—sociological analysis had a function of clarification even there.

The second point is that—though not in his sociological analysis proper—Weber made an important distinction between 'inspirational ethics' and 'ethics of responsibility'. The first was of the kind in which a person's code of conduct was clearly laid out, and which he followed as a matter of total obedience, whatever the circumstances, because of a complete dedication to the belief (whether derived from a religious idea, or leader, or not) which stipulated such conduct. The 'ethics of responsibility', however, required continued vigilance and *effort* in deliberating about ends, and about means, in seeking knowledge for judgment, in taking decisions, and in taking specific action—crucially, *political* action. For Weber no stipulated spiritual position, no clarified dogma, and—similarly—no body of scientific knowledge, indeed no clarification of the ethical implications of certain evelutions either, could possibly solve the problems of moral decision. Man was never, and would never be, in a position of simple acquiescence in certainties of any kind. He was essentially a *person* within a context of changing cultural conditions and his crucially distinctive nature was that by conscious deliberate action he could affect these conditions. He could not avoid a position of responsibility for them—though he could *evade* it. All one can say here was that, for Weber, there was no such evasion, and, indeed, he would have despised it.

Weber's position was that a person should be as fully committed to rigour in clarifying his principles of evaluation as he should be to rigour in the logic of his pursuit of scientific knowledge. With both in mind, he should then apply himself with equal rigour to an estimation of the actual conditions of the specific problems which confronted and concerned him, and then to deliberation, decision, and action. This was his 'credo'—if that is not too strong a way of putting it—of a man as a politically responsible member of his society.

Again, it will be seen that in this kind of considered relationship between knowledge, moral responsibility, and action, Weber was very much of the same mind as the other serious scholars before him, and of his own time, who had committed themselves to the making of sociology.

Weber's contribution to the subject was, then, quite distinctive, and the 'liberating' nature of his influence must be perfectly clear. If we have spent rather less time on him than upon other authors it is far from being an indication of his being of less importance than they. On the contrary, it is because his contribution was so consistent and clear, that we have been able to characterize its distinctive nature relatively briefly. There are criticisms one can make of Weber, but they would be insignificant beside the great achievement of his work, and they would not advance our estimation of his contribution beyond that which we now have. The one dimension of criticism which would seem worth pursuing to me is the whole question of the distinction which he drew between the establishment of 'generic laws', 'empirical regularities', and the analysis of 'factors' on the one hand, and the construction of 'Ideal-Types' for the causal explanation of specific concrete social configurations on the other. To my mind—though one can accept a very great deal of what he maintained—ambiguities remain here. His distinction can be accepted in large part; the *use* of laws which he proposed in the construction of 'types' for specific investigation and explanation is quite clear; his astringency in his conception of scientific method is strongly in keeping with much that is now held—by men like Popper—in the philosophy of science; and yet some ambiguity seems to remain. It seems to me that *in some way or other*, when Weber was constructing his conceptual types (as, for example, the types of authority we have discussed) he was employing *generalizations at the level of meaning—but in relation to the regularly found forms of social organization* which were more of the nature of 'laws' (though, of course, not laws of 'phenomenal interconnection') than he supposed. In short, it seems to me that Weber in some sense was both *implying* generalizations ('laws' of a kind, if you like) in his construction of 'types', and, in his explanatory understanding of specific situations, *producing* generalizations. The relation between the establishing of 'generic laws' and the construction of specific 'types' might be much closer than Weber's sharp distinction* implied. In this *kind* of sense, I think it is understandable that Talcott Parsons felt that a more comprehensive *system* stemming from Weber's concepts could be worked out; and one can sympathize to some extent with his efforts to accomplish this. However, here it seems to me that Parsons followed a doubtful course—indeed, took a wrong turning—and has ended with exactly the attempted statement of a total, all-embracing system of concepts within which postulates about social actuality can be *deduced*, which Weber not only rejected and abhorred, but the validity of which he thought he had theoretically *disproved*.

---

* Actually, Weber's distinction was not always *that* sharp; and in many places he discusses the issue in quite a complex manner; but he did not, or so it seems to me, leave it completely clear. The same kind of consideration could be given to the relation between 'average-types' and 'Ideal-Types'.

All this, however, we shall come back to in our final consideration of present-day positions in sociology. Here it is enough simply to suggest that there do *seem* (to me) to be some ambiguities in Weber which still deserve much serious critical study; but to pursue criticism here would not really take us further in our appreciation of Weber's actual contribution.

We must now leave him, then, and move to a few comments about the complementarity of his work and the work of Durkheim.

A Concluding Note

Without in any sense derogating the work of the other writers who were engaged in the development of sociology during the period we are discussing (we have, on the contrary, seen how valuable their contribution was) it is perfectly clear how distinctive was the method-ological concentration of Durkheim and Weber. In a much more exacting way than all others, they analysed what (in their view) necessarily went into the statement and testing of a definitive *theory* in sociology, and in both cases their work resulted in a set of precise prescriptions, precise concepts and rules, whereby definitive studies could best be carried out. It is justifiable, then, to claim that the work of these two men in particular, was of the most outstanding distinction and value for the making of contemporary sociological analysis, and it is worthwhile to make quite clear a number of sum-mary conclusions before leaving them.

We must be meticulously clear, first of all, about all aspects of the distinction between the 'objective' study of 'social facts' and the 'subjective understanding' of 'social action'.

In one sense Durkheim's and Weber's distinctions were poles apart, and—each in the exploration of his own extreme—presented completely antithetical methodological positions. And the position our analysis has arrived at is this. First—Durkheim was wrong in confining the subject-matter and the conceptualization and methods of sociology to those 'associational facts' which could be 'objectively' (i.e. phenomenally) perceived, and in denying altogether the inclusion of conscious, voluntary, purposive, 'teleological' action on the part of men in society. We have seen that his position on this was narrow, and a matter of assertion and much ambiguity of argument—indeed, also, a good deal of sheer inconsistency.

Weber, on the other hand was right in insisting that—*in addition to* the distinctive nature of the socio-psychological associational con-figurations of the kind emphasized by Durkheim—*the distinctive*

459

feature which marked off sociology (the cultural sciences) from the natural sciences was the existence among men in society of *action* directed by *meaning*, and the necessity, therefore, in any satisfactory explanation of this, for a subjective understanding of this meaning. Weber was the more consistent, correct, and the more comprehensive of the two—being ready to *include* all that Durkheim insisted upon—but also going beyond this in ways that we have seen to be clearly, validly, and consistently worked out. It is worthwhile to note, incidentally, that we have had to spend more time on Durkheim than on Weber *not* in proportion to his importance (both are important), but in terms of his own ambiguity and inconsistency. The relative brevity of our treatment of Weber is really a mark of the great consistency of his position.

The sum of this first point, then, is that Durkheim and Weber did represent the working out of two distinctive extremes. Durkheim's was the more limited—but he did work out his analysis of both social actuality and method to the fullest extreme. Weber's was the most comprehensive—but he deliberately set aside the kinds of dimensions which Durkheim dealt with, and focused his own attentions completely on the dimensions of 'subjective understanding'. In their work, then, we have sets of concepts and rules which deal with the 'objective' and the 'subjective' dimensions of human social actuality.

The second point we must immediately and emphatically make clear, however, is that though Weber was properly insisting upon the recognition of the *subjective dimension* of meaning in social actuality and in sociological explanation—he was, of course, doing this in the service of sufficient and accurate *objectivity* in sociological studies. In short, *both* the 'objective' *phenomena* (as defined by Durkheim) and the 'subjective' dimensions of *meaning* (as defined by Weber) were conceived to be features of the *actuality* of society; and both Weber and Durkheim were equally pursuing 'objectivity' in the sense of the tested sufficiency of their theories. It would be a complete mistake to think that Weber's methodology was *subjective*, in any less exacting sense than that of Durkheim, simply because he insisted upon the subjective dimensions of human actuality. This is an obvious, and perfectly plain point, but there is sometimes much confusion about it.

The third point—perhaps of the greatest importance for us—is that the two positions of Durkheim and Weber: thoroughly worked out and antithetical in the sense we have mentioned—are clearly *complementary* in the most useful way. And in this sense—from our own judiciously 'eclectic' point of view—they can be brought together in the most constructive way to provide a system of sociological analysis which is very much richer and more satisfactory than either would be—if taken in isolation from the other. Thus, whatever the errors in Durkheim's over-all position, his rules of method, if followed with rigour and care, *can* provide testable knowledge of those attributes of associational facts which are 'objectively' observable. His structural-functional, historical, and comparative methods tracing the regularities and *concomitant variations* which exist among social facts *can* produce testable knowledge *at that level*, and *can* lead to the better directed quest for more refined hypotheses. All the objectively observable attributes of the structural behaviour and organization of any society (of *institutionalized* conduct)—whether quantitative or qualitative; organizational or socio-psychological—can be observed, described, analysed, classified, compared, and to some extent explained, by Durkheim's rules of method. And all of this Weber could accept. But then—*in addition to this*; within the context of it, and going beyond it; the entire conceptual apparatus of Weber's 'subjective understanding of social action', and his 'Ideal-Typical' explanation of specific social configurations can be employed to probe more sufficiently into these other dimensions of meaning, deliberation, choice, will, directed action. *All* these dimensions can be satisfactorily explored without conflict, by bringing Durkheim's and Weber's contributions together to form one system of sociological analysis. And let us note that all this is accomplished by doing little more than just bringing them together, and taking account of both their emphases in any particular study we might undertake. There is no need to undertake any elaborate task of 'theoretical integration'—whatever that might be.

Exploring their distinctive dimensions to extremes, Durkheim and Weber therefore led to a position in which we can draw these extremes satisfactorily together. The making of sociology was now being accomplished in ways which were resulting in a very clear, comprehensive, and *usable*, system of analysis.

A number of other points serve to emphasize and reinforce all this. It has become obvious that Durkheim and Weber were not complete *innovators*, striking completely new trails. They worked within the context of the 'conspectus' of the earlier theorists—with much of which they agreed—and developed to a logical extreme two distinctive strands in the ongoing work of these theorists. Durkheim developed the methods of science, as he conceived them, to study the *creative processes of association* which he took to be the distinctive feature of *human society* as a subject-matter: and formed a kind of culminating extreme of this 'strand' of thought. Weber elaborated the methods of science necessary for the sufficient study of the *meaning* in human social action which he took to be the distinctive feature of human society as a subject-matter: and formed a culmination of all those puzzled dilemmas as to how to incorporate the facts of 'choice', 'will', 'character', etc. into sociological explanations which had been raised, but not resolved, by many theorists from Comte and Mill to Ward, Giddings, Tönnies and others. The contributions of Durkheim and Weber were developments of 'strands' within the over-all conspectus of the subject and the continuous critical elucidations of all the components of it. And in this sense, it was not only Durkheim and Weber who could be brought together within an improved system of analysis; it was really the system of analysis which was implicit in the critical work of *all* these contributors which was gradually being made more explicit, with increasing clarity. Thus the perspective of 'evolution', the 'structural-functional' element of analysis, the differing aspects of the 'comparative method' as an alternative to experiment; all these and many other components besides were accepted and woven carefully into the statements of these new positions. There was a real, constructive, and quite evident creative growth of the subject.

And in all this some central points of *similarity* both between Durkheim and Weber and their predecessors, and between Durkheim and Weber themselves (as well as differences) are worth noting. Quite apart from concepts such as 'evolution', 'development', and the like, it has become completely clear that both Durkheim and Weber were in the fullest accord with all the theorists from Comte onwards about the vast transformation and 'malaise' of the modern commercial and industrial world and the process of disruptive growth from earlier traditional types of society. Both firmly agreed that this was in some central way a *moral* malaise. Both deliberately adopted a responsible *ethical* stand in their discussion of the re-making of modern institutions and both also made the increase and extension of *rationality* a feature of central significance in the development of modern institutionalization. Their emphasis upon morality in institutionalization, and upon reason in the turmoil of modern social change especially, was completely in keeping with the emphasis placed upon these elements by their predecessors and by their contemporaries (such as Tönnies and Hobhouse).

As for important similarities between themselves, we have seen that though following different persuasions as to what the *distinctive* features of sociology was, they were both insistent upon the same kinds of criteria for *accuracy*. In moving 'from *theory* to *theories*', their insistence was emphatically upon strictness of *delimitation*. The achievement of measurable degrees of accuracy was commensurate with clear, deliberately delimited, definitions—both of the subject-matter being studied, and in the statements of the theories being advanced (or attempted) about it. Both wished to move towards the producing of *definitive, testable theories,* rather than the enunciations of a 'conspectus' of analysis; and Weber especially, of course, was quite emphatically opposed to the notion that causal explanations of specific facts could *ever,* in *any* sense, be *'deduced'* from a comprehensive general theory. The two theorists were therefore agreed in important essentials, though having a qualitatively different objective at the end of their road.

And this leads to a final conclusion of importance. It is abundantly clear in all this how and why these two men came to be thought of as 'liberators' in the making of sociology. Though they worked critically and constructively within the context of sociological thought as it had developed, and did nothing to disrupt, destroy, or overthrow the chief accepted positions within this, nonetheless all their emphasis was upon sharpening the methods of sociological analysis for *use* in producing definitive studies of specific, defined areas. Their emphasis was *not* upon just *having* a system of sociological analysis; upon just *possessing* an apparatus of concepts and rules for the correct construction and testing of theories—but upon *using* these for the production of new, demonstrable knowledge. And this is the spirit—for better, for worse (and we must come to criticize this later)—that has come to dominate contemporary sociology.

There is this one emphasis, however, upon which both men were clearly agreed. Both were quite adamant about the aim of scientific accuracy, as such, in sociological study; and both agreed that personal ethical persuasions should not be allowed to cloud or bias scientific investigation. Both wished to insist upon the highest *professional* standards in scientific sociology and were 'liberative' in this as in their general insistence upon standards of exact scholarship. But here is the point. . . . *Neither* of them equated the scientific or the professional attitude with that of human or cultural *detachment.* Durkheim, as we have seen, was passionately concerned for the reconstruction of the economic, social, and moral order of modern society. Weber maintained that the *problems* of the sociologist were essentially rooted in *values,* and that his very awareness of what constituted a problem for him was a matter of *'cultural significance'.* On the same ground, he argued that the problems of the sociologist were bound to change from age to age, from cultural situation to situation. In short, both men, though seeing science clearly, did not take it to be the whole of man's preoccupation and endeavour. Though desiring professional standards for the pursuit of their subject, they did not think professional concern their central preoccupation. Science was for man. Professions were for society. They were, like all their predecessors, *engaged* men; men committed to accuracy in science—but *because* they were also committed to

463

larger values, and larger human ends. In this, too, Durkheim and Weber were of the sociological tradition.

Taken together, then, the work of these two men constitutes one of the most important and substantial contributions to the making of sociology. Indeed, it is not too much to say that they have brought the subject to where it now is—though crowned with an array of fireworks from the United States which we shall come to consider in our final section.* But there is one gap in the work of both—though not one which calls any blameworthy criticism down upon them— which leads us on to one further 'development' of the first few decades of the twentieth century: this is the dimension of the psychological aspects of associational processes.

Durkheim was of importance in directing attention to the fact that human *association* was—in many respects—psychologically *creative*, in personal as well as 'collective' terms; but he did not himself pursue this further, simply because he wished to concentrate upon the distinctive level of 'associational facts' themselves. Weber, too, recognized that these socio-psychological processes were of importance and could aid sociological explanation. He did not *reject* them, or the place of their explanation in sociology; he was only concerned, himself, to concentrate upon the methodology necessary for the incorporation of the dimensions of *meaning* in human social action, and this, as he correctly insisted, was logically quite distinct from these socio-psychological processes. The study of the *psychological* aspects of *associations* was therefore neglected by Durkheim and Weber. It had, however, formed an important part in the conception of a 'science of society' from Comte and Mill onwards, and had begun to receive a quite systematic treatment at the hands of the early Americans—Ward and Giddings—in particular. This component too came to be developed in several quite distinctive ways after the turn of the century.

* See *The Making of Sociology*, Vol. 3: *Reassessments: Consolidation and Advance?*

(3)
The Psychological Aspects of Society

Introduction

We come now to the third major 'development' in the making of sociology during the first few decades of the twentieth century: the more careful analysis of the *psychological aspects* of all these collective, regulated, institutionalized patterns of behaviour and action which comprised 'society'; and of the very creation and nature of the individual 'self' within this context. There is little doubt that, for many, this is the most intriguing dimension of sociology. One of the reasons why people are both attracted to and repelled by the subject is that it inescapably raises questions of the most profound kind about what is commonly taken for granted—the 'given' nature of the human personality. The 'human soul'—so long taken to be a definite and unique entity; so long assumed to possess a fundamental and eternal reality in the changing, mortal flux of things—came, at last, to be placed under the microscope of scientific analysis. Sociology came to probe into the deepest, most sensitive, most highly valued of personal feelings. This—it still does, and must do.

(I) AN AGREED COMPONENT OF THE NINETEENTH CENTURY 'CONSPECTUS'

From the earliest foundation of the subject, we have seen that some position had to be adopted about the place of psychology in sociological explanation. There was never any doubt that some relationship of the most intimate kind existed between psychology and sociology, and that it was necessary to work it out. Indeed, all the great theorists had something definite to say about it. Comte believed that there was an inseparable relation between the two (and between them and biology) but was quite decided that—apart from the limited generalizations that biology could provide—'all human psychology was social psychology'. Human nature was essentially, distinctively, of a social nature. It came to be what it was within the context of the cumulative cultural history of society. Only with a knowledge of society (coupled with moral philosophy) could one move towards an understanding of 'man the individual'. Marx, too, was equally definite. No 'science of psychology' was possible which failed to see that man's nature was a creation of his historical activity. Man was 'social before he was human', and it was in creating his own social fabric that his own nature was shaped.

Mill had a very clear conception of the place of an experimental psychology, a social psychology, and generalizations about social institutions and their changes, within a 'general science of society'. He was quite clear that the institutional forms of society had a

467

formative influence upon the basic psychological endowment of men in such ways as to give rise to established dispositions of character, attitudes, sentiments, beliefs, values and the like, among the members of society—and that a knowledge of these social-psychological processes was necessary as the 'axiomata media' without which social explanation must always be insufficient. Spencer stated clear correlations between 'types of social order' and 'types of personality and character'. And all these notions were taken over and developed considerably by the early Americans.

In Ward and Giddings in particular, the effort was made to elaborate a clear *analysis* of the collective 'psychological forces' that accompanied the patterned *activities* of society, and of the psychological aspects (*a*) of the various kinds of action involved in being 'members 'or 'functionaries' of institutions, and (*b*) of 'socialization': the way in which the child became a social *person* by experiencing its social environment (of groups, institutions, values, etc.) in a certain *sequence* from birth to adulthood.

Already, then, in the 'conspectus' accomplished by the end of the nineteenth century, this 'psychological dimension' of society was recognized and stated with great clarity as a necessary part of a satisfactory sociology.

(II) AGREEMENT AND REINFORCEMENT AMONG ALL THE TWENTIETH CENTURY WRITERS SO FAR CONSIDERED

We have now also seen, in addition, that all the major developments of the early twentieth century were such as to show agreement about this importance of a knowledge of the psychological dimensions of society, and to reinforce the persuasions of the earlier writers. Indeed, we have seen that very substantial points of agreement became clear among all these twentieth century writers, even though they seem, at first glance, to have adopted such widely differing conceptual and theoretical approaches. It is worthwhile to note some of these points of agreement very clearly, because they are much more substantial than is commonly supposed, and, as we shall see, very considerably in agreement with those thinkers to whom we must now turn—Cooley, Mead, Freud, Pareto, and others—who focused their attention almost entirely upon these psychological matters.* Here we can enumerate them quite briefly, but their full relevance will be seen as we come to discuss the work of these psychologically orientated authors.

* Pareto, of course, was rather different from the others here—offering a general system of sociology within which his social-psychological theories played a big part.

(a) *A complete agreement about the necessity of the component of*
   social psychology

It is interesting and important to see, first, that all the writers we
have considered—Tönnies, Westermarck, Hobhouse, Durkheim,
Weber—were in fact agreed upon the importance of the dimension
of psychology, even though they themselves were especially concerned
to develop other aspects of sociology: social evolution, typologies of
social change, the analysis of institutions, the objective study of
social facts, the subjective understanding of social action, etc.
Tönnies, Westermarck and Hobhouse did, of course, substantially
incorporate psychological knowledge—quite deliberately—into their
systems. Durkheim deliberately kept himself at the level of 'associational' facts, but recognized the indispensability of psychology even
though he himself wished to pursue it no further; and, indeed, his
whole system rested on the recognition of 'associational' psychological facts. And Weber too—though having his own methodological
preoccupations—readily emphasized the importance of psychological
knowledge for some purposes. The agreement—at this general level—
was therefore complete.

(b) *The psychological creativity of society; the psychological aspects*
   of 'association'; 'collective' psychological facts; the SOCIAL
   perspective of psychology

We can, however, go a good deal further than this. We have seen that
there was a full agreement among all these thinkers of the main
persuasion of Durkheim's position: that human *'association'* was not
sterile (resulting only in an *addition* of psychological elements and
experiences already existing in individuals), but was *psychologically
creative*. Though they did not follow Durkheim to the point of
'reifying' such 'associational facts', they certainly agreed that
collective conditions and associational relationships, needs, problems,
and conflicts, engendered psychological experiences (which gave rise
to sentiments, values, customs, moral values, sanctions, etc.) which
could not be said to exist in individual human nature before association took place. Tönnies described the qualitatively different kinds of
psychological experience and kinds of willing engendered by relationships of natural community on the one hand and a fabric of contractual relationships on the other. Westermarck analysed the associational processes by which instinct and emotion came to develop into
the form of sentiment, custom, sanction, moral idea and institution.
Durkheim's work clearly needs no reiteration here. But even Weber,
too, though believing that it was the understanding and explanation
of meaningful action which formed the distinctive problem of
sociology, readily agreed that collective conditions produced collec-

tive psychological states which undoubtedly accounted for the existence of certain motives in certain situations.

And in all this, there was the further fundamental point that all these authors saw the psychological experiences of individual men as coming to be what they were within the context of changing *cultural*, *historical* systems of ideas, values, and institutions. Even those—like Westermarck and Hobhouse—who gave a more deliberate place than others to the basic biological and psychological endowment of man (though Tönnies was not greatly different), still emphasized the cumulative traditions of culture and history, and still saw the individual person as coming to the fulfilment of adult personality and character within the social framework of his time. None of these people were *deterministic* in this; they gave a place to choice, will, deliberate action; but they certainly saw the growth of individual personality as taking place within the specific conditions and the ethos of a society and its particular institutions.

In short, they all adopted the 'associational perspective' for human psychology. They were of the same *kind* of persuasion as Comte and Marx. But the detailed implications of this persuasion, we can come to later.

(c) *A specific pattern of agreement: from instincts, sentiments, values, institutions, and traditional developments, to rational action**

One other point of the very greatest interest and importance has emerged from our discussion of twentieth century developments so far: a point which will be quite unexpected to many. The fact is that all the theorists we have considered were agreed about a certain pattern and sequence of the psychological elements and processes involved in institutionalization and the directions of social develop-

---

* This wide agreement is of very considerable importance and quite contrary to what current academic fashion supposes. Perhaps I could draw attention to an earlier book which I wrote in order to demonstrate the extent of this agreement and the strength of its case in *psychology proper*, but centrally *for sociological theory*. This is *Instinct in Man* (1957), which is now available in paperback form in Britain: Allen & Unwin (Unwin University Books) and in the USA: Schocken Books. The reasons for my efforts to re-establish the theories concerning the place of instinct in human experience and behaviour have never, I am sure, been properly understood, and their relevance to sociological theory has not been properly seen. These theories are, however, vitally relevant—and this will be plainly seen in this section as we see agreement reiterated time after time in the supposedly *dissimilar* work of McDougall, Cooley, Mead, Freud, Pareto, Simmel—and as we link to this the equally obvious agreement among all the other theorists: Tönnies, Westermarck, Hobhouse, Durkheim, Malinowski and Radcliffe-Brown. My argument in this earlier book is therefore relevant *throughout* the continuing argument here. Having said this, however, I shall only refer to it again at strictly appropriate points.

ment—and, again, without being 'deterministic'* and 'reductionist' in any doctrinaire sense.

We have seen that all these theorists agreed (*a*) that man, as a species, possessed a genetically established endowment of *instinctual needs, impulses, tendencies, and attendant emotions,* (*b*) that these, however, were not as stereo-typed as those in other animal species; they were more *malleable within a context of learning and control*; and—especially—that man was capable of *purposeful thought, action, and organization* in his practical and social *activities,* (*c*) that these impulses, emotions, and purposeful activities had certain essential *social* connotations (both conflictful and co-operative), (*d*) that the complexities and necessities of social experience led to the establishment of firmly felt *'sentiments',* (*e*) that such sentiments carried with them specific evaluations, feelings of approval and disapproval, and that they were, in fact, established constellations of *moral* judgments and *sanctions,* (*f*) that these sentiments, moral judgments, and sanctions were at the heart of *institutions,* and, indeed, that the formation of them was the socio-psychological concomitant (part of the actuality) of the very process of *institutionalization,* (*g*) that these processes, in interconnection, gave rise to settled *social traditions,* and that (*h*) with certain kinds of change an increase of rational analysis, knowledge, purpose, and control could take place and that man was then faced with the conscious, responsible direction of his society.

This pattern of instinct and emotion, sentiment, custom, morality, and institutionalization, was clearly adopted not only by Westermarck and Hobhouse—but also very firmly by Tönnies, and Durkheim. Perhaps the crucial idea in all this was the centrality of the emergence and establishment of *sentiments* in the process of institutionalization; the idea that 'sentiments' were the socio-psychological actuality concomitant with definite forms of institutional regulation.

But there was also an agreement about the *sequence* and *direction* of social development. The earlier growth of established social traditions, though always containing a purposive and reasoning element in activities, was thought to have taken place as a kind of circumstantial adjustment: an accommodation of instinct, emotion, sentiment-formation, and institutionalization to specific environmental conditions, taking an over-all shape in terms of unforeseen consequences. But with the long accumulation of knowledge, and the extended control it made possible, the element of rational and pur-

---

* In all this, of course, it is Durkheim who is most guilty of driving his concepts and methods to the extremes of metaphysical assertion.

posive direction—of conscious institutional 'reform'* and therefore of responsibility—increased. And again, this was not only the view of Westermarck and Hobhouse, but also that of Tönnies, Durkheim and Weber.

Weber was very specific about the directions of social evolution: from a condition approximating to 'instinct' to a condition of rationality and responsibility. And even Durkheim—in all that he argued about the conscious, deliberate re-organization of modern industrial society in the light of clarified moral aims—was clearly agreed.

One or two very significant aspects of this agreement within developing sociology need to be underlined for important emphasis.

Firstly, it is very commonly thought that only one or two psychologists in particular were responsible for insisting upon 'instinct theory' as a basis for social psychology early in the twentieth century, and, furthermore that they were quickly outmoded. William McDougall, especially, was set up as the 'bête noire' in this connection. It is therefore particularly salutary—by way of correction—to see that there was a firm agreement about this among *all* these major sociologists—including the supposedly 'ultra-modern' Durkheim and Weber. We shall see, in a moment, how much more thorough-going this agreement was than we have yet indicated—that it was even more marked among the 'social psychology' writers proper. But what we are saying in a limited way here is that the strong and central focus upon 'sentiments' and their roots in 'instinct' which was at the heart of the several systems of social psychology was already (and simultaneously) accepted in quite a thorough-going manner by the other major sociologists.

Secondly, it is worthwhile again to notice and to stress (*a*) the great continuity which was apparent—in these areas of psychological discussions—from the nineteenth century sociologists, especially men like Ward and Giddings, to all these men of the twentieth century, and (*b*) the considerable and continuing *international* consensus—and, indeed, the *growth* of international communication. Here—despite apparently different approaches to theory—we have found American, British, French and German thinkers in very substantial agreement. And communication between them was increasing all the time. Thus—quite apart from the inter-communication we noted in the meetings of the British Sociological Society from 1903 onwards—during these early decades we find men like

---

* i.e. in the strict sense of the deliberate 're-formation' and 're-construction' of institutions.

472

Albion Small* and W. I. Thomas in America very much aware of what was happening in Britain and on the continent of Europe. Thomas, especially, was passionate in his teaching that psychology and sociology could only be correctly conceived and taught in the closest conjunction with each other. But also—just as Hobhouse acknowledged the influence of Lester Ward, so Charles Ellwood—who was one of the leading figures of 'psychological sociology' in the United States—acknowledged and very much based himself upon the influence of Hobhouse: after studying with him in England (and with Marett at Oxford) during 1914–15. Indeed, he firmly accepted the historical and evolutionary perspectives of Hobhouse. Similarly, C. H. Cooley knew and drew upon the comparative studies of Tylor, Frazer, Westermarck. The interdependencies of influences and agreements were very considerable indeed—and were increasing.

There was, then, a very wide international consensus in these basic matters concerning the psychological aspects of society during the period we are discussing, and this must be borne in mind when thinking of the supposed 'clashes' between 'instinct theory' and 'behaviourism' which are commonly thought to have characterized this period, and which have, in fact, tended to throw psychology on to false tracks. We shall see in a moment that such 'clashes' were neither true nor necessary when all the points of view (not simply one or two extremes) are considered.

This, indeed, is a third point worth much emphasis: that, among all these thinkers, a *social perspective for psychology* was agreed upon—not only in general terms, but also in some substantial detail. The kind of perspective most vividly taught by Durkheim—that the recognition of the fact that 'association' was a psychologically creative process was absolutely necessary for a sufficient psychology of man—was shared, quite clearly seen, and already worked out in some detail by these thinkers; and the pity is that, to quite a considerable extent, it has been lost sight of.

These, then, are preliminary considerations within which we can set our exposition of those writers who were especially concerned to develop the study of the psychological aspects of society; the psychological aspects of all the processes of 'association' and the growth of the 'self' within them. Clearly it is out of the question to attempt a full account of each man's work (since each one is so considerable), and, furthermore, each writer's work is of such different scope and quality. Cooley and Mead for example, still wrote within the broad context of literature and philosophy and were of a manageable scope (though Mead, especially, rigorously pursued many subtleties

* See, for example, Small's paper on *Points of Agreement among Sociologists, American Journal of Sociology*.

of analysis and covered a far larger scope than appears on the surface), whereas Pareto offered a very comprehensive system of sociological analysis of which his psychological ideas formed only a part—if a very central part. Freud was, very decidedly, further away from a sociological perspective than the other writers—though it was still definitely and significantly there. And Simmel was also chiefly a philosopher, and, though offering the outline of a sociological analysis of the 'forms' of human interaction which was loaded with psychological insights and propositions, he did not present a *system* of analysis—as, say, Pareto did. The thinkers we shall try to bring together here, then, were a very varied group. It is impossible to give them all a meticulously exhaustive, or even to be confident of giving them a proportionately balanced, treatment. It will be enough for our own purposes, however, if we focus our attention on a few clear aims.

Firstly, by bringing these scholars together, we shall be able to see how the making of sociology was developed *in this particular direction*. This is our primary aim.

Secondly, we shall be able to clarify that *social* perspective for a satisfactory human psychology which these men demonstrated (this is not too strong a word) in their work. In this we shall be clarifying a perspective which is of abiding value, and which may make us a little clearer about what we called earlier '*the error of psychology*': i.e. of thinking that a satisfactory experimental science of experience and behaviour can be set up without reference to it.

And thirdly, we shall be able to see even more clearly the centrality of the notion of the formation of 'sentiments' for understanding the psychological dimensions of 'institutionalization' and the growth of the individual 'self' alike.

There is one final point of a preliminary nature which must be mentioned, but which will chiefly be left until the end of the section, and that is that although we shall be concentrating entirely on what these men had to say about the *psychological aspects* of society, it must be borne in mind that all of them shared many of the wider perspectives of theory of the scholars we have already discussed. Almost all accepted the evolutionary perspective; almost all held the same conceptions about the nature of science and its application to the study of man and society; and almost all agreed with other dimensions of sociological analysis—the 'organic' nature of the social system, the structural-functional analysis of it, and so on. They were all men of wide culture, well-grounded in philosophy, and having given their minds to the philosophy of the social sciences generally. It was only that they *chose* to preoccupy themselves with that dimension of enquiry which interested *them* most; which *they* found most important; and it is this on which we shall concentrate. The introductory comment of Cooley (in his book *Social Organization*) will do for them all. Having specified his own objectives of study, Cooley made it quite clear that he was not in any sense, by this selectivity, deprecating *other* approaches. He wrote:

'Our task as students of society is a large one, and each of us, I suppose, may undertake any part of it to which he feels at all competent.'

1
William McDougall*: Instinct, Sentiment, The Self, and Voluntary Action

In this particular section (on the development of theories about the psychological aspects of society) I do not wish to dwell to any great extent on British contributions, and consequently shall not deal with McDougall's work in any length. I introduce him only to defend him in many ways, and to show that—far from being a doctrinaire 'instinctivist', who thought that all the complexities of human behaviour could be explained by the simple enumeration of a set of instincts—and far from being a lone psychologist adopting an extreme and dogmatic position—he was, quite on the contrary, a psychologist fully in the ongoing stream of sociological thinking that we have described, and with all the virtues of this broad position which most earlier psychologists lacked and many subsequent psychologists have—disastrously—lost.

Many aspects of McDougall's work have been quite forgotten and ignored, and the present-day critical verdict upon him is one of the worst outcomes of polemics and fashion.

It is forgotten that McDougall, just as strongly as Durkheim, strove to forge a new approach to scientific psychology in the teeth of the earlier, sterile 'associationism'.† It is forgotten that he adopted the biological basis of psychology, and the evolutionary perspective of both, as the much firmer and more promising basis than that of earlier philosophy. It is forgotten that he was one of the founders of experimental psychology in Britain and that he wrote books on *Physiological Psychology* and *Psychology: the Science of Behaviour* as well as his notorious book: *An Introduction to Social Psychology*. All this, and much more is forgotten; but for us, it was his approach to the psychological aspects of society, of 'association', which is of greatest interest—and here, equally, much has been forgotten or ignored.

Here, we will note only essential points—and those briefly.

---

* See *Instinct in Man*, R. Fletcher, Ch. 11, pp. 47–57.
† i.e. *NOT* 'associationism' in the *social* sense; but the *philosophical* approach to psychology as the introspective analysis of conscious states of mind.

476

It is, of course, perfectly true that McDougall held—like all the other thinkers we have considered—that man, like all other animal species, did not come experientially and behaviourally 'naked' into the world, but possessed a genetically established endowment of instinctual tendencies (some quite specific, some more general) which were closely concomitant with the anatomical structure and physiological functions of his organism. And this position was carefully stated, together with all the evidence for it. It is true, too, that McDougall offered a 'list' (a classification) of these instinctual tendencies, specifying them as the 'springs' of much human behaviour, and as providing some of the universal and ineradicable ends of human behaviour.

But—let us then immediately notice one or two other facts.

(1) This particular part of McDougall's system of social psychology took up just the first *third* of his book. (2) *Nowhere* did he claim that all the complexities of human behaviour (individual or social) could be sufficiently explained by postulating a number of instincts. (3) This statement was in no sense thought to be an exhaustive account of the human mind, but was offered as an exposition of those mental characteristics of man '. . . *of Primary Importance for His Life in Society*'. But other points are even more striking, and we may as well continue to enumerate them one by one.

(4) The second third of his book was especially devoted to an analysis of how instinct and emotion in the complexities of 'associational' life gave rise to the formation of '*sentiments*'. (5) This account not only referred to 'sentiments' as important *social* facts, but also as important elements in the growth of the *self*, and *self-consciousness* in the individual; in the psychic organization of impulse, emotion, cognition, evaluation, purpose, and control in the *individual personality*. (6) McDougall also distinctively treated the 'sentiments' (in both society and individuals) as being the bearers (the actual constellations) of *moral values* and moral *judgments* in the social order. And (7)—like Tönnies, Weber, and others—he saw the growth of rational will, deliberate choice, conscious action, and purpose from these roots—and, again, in both individual and associational conduct. The whole emphasis of his psychology was to give the fullest recognition to the element of 'purpose' in action, and in human action in particular, and to present an account of human, social behaviour which fully and correctly incorporated this 'teleological' dimension. He was therefore fully in accord with all those who had emphasized choice, will and '*action*' (as distinct from mechanistically 'caused' behaviour) from Mill to Weber. There was nothing 'deterministic' or 'reductionist', in any naïve sense, in him.

But let us go further.

(8) The last third of McDougall's book was devoted to the manifestation of these 'primary tendencies' of the human mind in particular social institutions; and it will be enough to note the other authors to whom he referred in this. Who were they? On the family—he referred to Malthus (on population), Buckle, Helen Bosanquet, Frederic Le Play (and other members of his 'school'), and many students of societies of the ancient world—such as Dill, de Lapouge, Fustel de Coulanges, who wrote on Greece and Rome. And (let us notice) he referred—like Durkheim and Freud (and others we have mentioned) to Spencer and Gillen's studies of *The Northern Tribes of Central Australia*. He referred also —in his discussion of religion, play, etc.—to men like Frazer, Robertson Smith, Tarde, Giddings, and Westermarck.

It would be going much too far to suggest that McDougall offered anything approaching a really systematic comparative study of institutionalized behaviour—but, even so, given the scope of his enquiry, he went far in this direction, and the names mentioned above are evidence of the extent to which he tried to make use of comparative history and sociology.

To suggest that McDougall simply 'enumerated a set of instincts' is really, therefore, an absurd—and monstrous caricature. On the contrary, there was here the development of an approach to the study of the psychological aspects of society which was fully in accordance with the new directions of thinking, and we shall see in a moment how similar it was to the positions of other thinkers who are now more in the fashion.

I do not think it worthwhile to dwell on McDougall further, but we might note one or two brief statements of his simply to substantiate some of the points we have made, and, more particularly, to see (later) his similarity with men like Cooley and Mead (as well as Durkheim). First, let us notice how strongly he emphasized that the experience and behaviour of individuals was *not* simply an outcome of 'instincts' but was 'moulded' by society; and how strongly he insisted that the very growth of the 'self' was essentially a *social* process.

'If we would understand the life of societies,' he wrote, 'we must first learn to understand the way in which individuals become moulded by the society into which they are born and in which they grow up, how by this moulding they become fitted to play their part in it as social beings—how, in short, they become capable of moral conduct. Moral conduct is essentially social conduct, and there could be no serious objection to the use of the two expressions as synonymous; but it is more in conformity with common usage to restrict the term "moral" to the higher forms of social conduct of which man alone is capable.

478

While the lower forms of social conduct are the direct issue of the prompting of instinct—as when the animal-mother suffers privation, wounds, or death in the defence of her young under the impulse of the maternal instinct—the higher forms of social conduct, which alone are usually regarded as moral, involve the voluntary control and regulation of the instinctive impulses. Now, volition or voluntary control proceeds from the idea of the self and from the sentiment, or organized system of emotions and impulses, centred about that idea. Hence the study of the development of self-consciousness and of the self-regarding sentiment is an important part of the preparation for the understanding of social pheno-mena. And these two things, the idea of the self and the self-regarding sentiment, develop in such intimate relations with each other that they must be studied together. This development is, as we shall see, essentially a social process, one which is dependent throughout upon the complex interactions between the individual and the organized society to which he belongs.'*

And again, emphasizing the intimate relation between 'self' and 'society', he wrote:

'It is only when we trace the growth of self-consciousness that we can understand how it comes to play its part in determining conduct of the kind that alone renders possible the complex life of highly organized societies. For we find that the idea of the self and the self-regarding senti-ment are essentially social products; that their development is effected by constant interplay between personalities, between the self and society; that, for this reason, the complex conception of self thus attained implies constant reference to others and to society in general, and is, in fact, not merely a conception of self, but always of one's self in relation to other selves. This social genesis of the idea of self lies at the root of morality, and it was largely because this social origin and character of the idea of self was ignored by so many of the older moralists that they were driven to postulate a special moral faculty, the conscience or moral instinct.'†

We shall see this notion of the elements of 'conscience' in the growth of the 'self' in others—especially Freud, but McDougall was quite clear about the essential 'associational' root of this. We might also note, further, how—like Durkheim and Westermarck—he saw the 'sentiments' as the socio-psychological constellations of 'morality' in society.

'It is notorious,' he wrote, 'that the sentiments determine our moral judgments. . . .'

But men do not create such sentiments as individuals.

* *An Introduction to Social Psychology*, Methuen, 1908, pp. 150–1 in 1948 Reprint (29th Edition).
† *Ibid.*, pp. 155–6. This could easily be a passage from Cooley or Mead.

'No man,' he went on, 'could acquire by means of his own unaided reflections and unguided emotions any considerable array of moral sentiments; still less could he acquire in that way any consistent and lofty system of them. In the first place, the intellectual process of discriminating and naming the abstract qualities of character and conduct is quite beyond the unaided power of the individual; in this process he finds indispensable aid in the language that he absorbs from his fellows. But he is helped not by language only; every civilized society has a more or less highly developed moral tradition, consisting of a system of traditional abstract sentiments. This moral tradition has been slowly formed and . . . handed on from generation to generation. . . . And every great and organized department of human activity, each profession and calling of a civilized society, has its own specialized form of the moral tradition, which in some respects may sink below, in other respects may rise above, the moral level of the unspecialized or general tradition.'*

Again, we see the 'sentiments' and the 'moral evaluations' conceived as being at the very heart of social institutions.

Finally, without at all attempting further elaboration, we might note McDougall's complex conception of the psychic organization of the individual personality by considering the diagram opposite.† Here it can be plainly seen how McDougall thought of the impulsive, emotional, cognitive elements of the individual's experience coming to be 'organized' in the form of 'sentiments' (all within the central consciousness of the 'self'), within the context of his *social* experience from infancy to adulthood. There was clearly much more here than any simple 'list of instincts'.

It is worthwhile to point out, too, that McDougall's position itself was not individually arrived at. Quite apart from his roots (with reference to 'instinct and emotion') in several writers from Darwin onwards, he drew his central concepts of the 'sentiment' ('an organized system of emotional tendencies centred about some object') from the work of A. F. Shand (*The Foundations of Character*) and Shand was quite deliberately doing his best to develop the science of 'Ethology' ('Characterology') that John Stuart Mill had proposed in Book VI of his *Logic*. This central development of social psychology in Britain therefore had certain of its roots in John Stuart Mill, just as its main features were couched within the contemporary, ongoing tendencies of the making of sociology.

But we must now turn to two American sociologists who were of quite central importance in developing the study of these psychological dimensions, and who have come to be particularly influential at the present time— C. H. Cooley and G. H. Mead.

* *Introduction to Social Psychology*, pp. 188–9.   † *Ibid.*, p. 441.

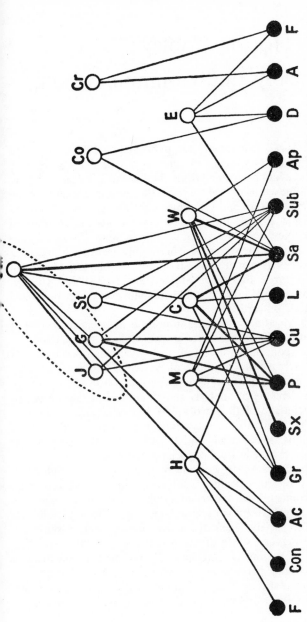

Diagram to illustrate the structure of the character of John Doe, a man who loves his mother, child, and wife (M, C, W), hates his enemy (E), and is proud of his home (H); who dislikes Cowardice and Cruelty (Co, Cr), admires Strength (St) and Justice (J), lovingly admires Generosity (G); who has strong self-respect, has incorporated his sentiments for Justice and Generosity within his self-regarding sentiment, and has extended it to include also his home (H) and his child (C).

The hollow circles of the three higher levels represent the cognitive dispositions corresponding to the objects indicated by the letters attached to them. These are not to be thought of as simple structures, but rather as highly complex and connected in multitudinous fashion with one another; each one stands for a system of knowledge and belief about the corresponding object. The filled circles of the lowest level stand for the conative-emotional cores of the several instinctive dispositions. The lines connecting them with the circles of the upper levels represent their functional connexions with the cognitive dispositions or systems, the strength or intimacy of each connexion being indicated by the thickness of each line. Any one sentiment is represented by one cognitive disposition or system, together with the conative-emotional dispositions with which it is connected in the way indicated by the lines of the diagram; thus John Doe's sentiment for his child consists of the system of which C is the centre, and of which the dispositions Gr, P, L, Sa are the principal conative roots. The key to the conative-emotional dispositions runs as follows: F = food-seeking, Con = construction, Ac = acquisition, Gr = gregariousness, Sx = Sex, P = parental or protective tendency, Cu = curiosity, L = laughter, Sa = self-assertion, Sub = submission or self-abasement, Ap = appeal, D = disgust, A = anger, F = fear.

481

2

Charles Horton Cooley:
Self, Society, and Communications

McDougall's *Social Psychology* was published in 1908 and within forty years (by 1948—roughly the end of the period we are now discussing) there had been 29 editions. This alone is indicative of the scope of its influence. But—before this—the accomplishments of the 'early Americans', Ward and Giddings, were being rapidly followed by developments at the hands of two other American scholars in particular—Cooley and Mead (though there were others of considerable stature). All these men were of roughly the same 'generation' of social theorists as Tönnies, Westermarck, Hobhouse, Durkheim and Weber. Their dates were: McDougall, 1871–1938; Cooley, 1864–1929; Mead, 1863–1931; but their main work was published from about 1902 onwards.

Cooley and Mead are especially important as being indicative of the most distinctive contribution to the making of sociology in America—this concentration upon the psychological aspects of society. They were a clear continuity of Ward and Giddings; working within the same perspective of assumptions, and using and developing the same elements of analysis and thought. But there was this further characteristic of their work. To a considerable extent, the assumption that man's attitudes, sentiments, etc. were a 'reflection' of social conditions, social need, and the like; that the 'personality' was in some sense a 'reflection' of society; had remained an assumption. It remained a rather vague conception and was well-nigh unexplored to any rigorous degree. Cooley and Mead were especially concerned to remedy this, and to undertake a systematic analysis of the detailed 'mechanisms'—or processes—whereby the 'self' *did* come to '*reflect*' society. Their distinctive development, in short, lay in their more detailed study of the actual nature of the 'self' and 'society', and of the intricate, reciprocal relations between them in the formation and persistence of experiential, behavioural, and institutional regularities. They did much to fill in the gap which Durkheim and Weber left empty, and which others left insufficiently explored.

It was in 1902 that Cooley published *Human Nature and the Social*

Order,* and this was followed in 1909 by *Social Organization* and in 1918 by *Social Process*. His chief ideas were put forward and systematically developed in these three books, and few books in all sociology can be so easy and pleasant to read. They are written in a clear, graceful, engaging style—and this was no accident. For Cooley, like all his predecessors of the nineteenth century, and his contemporaries of the twentieth, was a man of wide culture and scholarship—drawing as much upon literature and philosophy as he did upon the human sciences. He drew upon Goethe and Nietzsche as readily as upon Darwin and Thorndike (E. L.); upon Shakespeare, Robert Louis Stevenson, Charles Lamb, Montaigne, Milton, St Paul and Thomas à Kempis as well as upon William James, Herbert Spencer,† Tylor, Tarde, and other social scientists. And, as an American intellectual, his roots were very satisfyingly in the thought of men like Emerson, Thoreau, and Walt Whitman—all of whom had grappled in their own way with the question of solitude and society in their efforts to plumb the depths of the human 'self'.‡

With this same breadth of mind, learning, and judgment, Cooley also shared the perspectives adopted by the other scholars we have talked about. He fully accepted the perspective of evolution—biological and social alike—with all the kinds of implication which had been made clear from Darwin to Ward. He accepted—with proper qualification—the notion of the 'organic' nature of society; the close interdependence of its institutions; the analysis of it in terms of social 'structure', 'function', and kinds of 'groups'. And he accepted the conception of societies as being essentially historical and developmental processes. All this we can take for granted as his background of assumptions. But his own selected concern was this exploration of the *socio-psychological* dimensions of the 'conspectus' of sociology. For him, these were of central and basic importance.

Indeed, the best starting point for understanding Cooley's ideas is his initial rejection of the very distinction between 'individual' and

* In the second edition of 1922, Cooley acknowledged McDougall's book on *Social Psychology* as a 'standard work' on instinct, emotion, sentiment-formation, etc.

† Cooley was critical of Spencer—but readily acknowledged his debt to him. In a footnote in his second edition of *Human Nature and Social Order*, he wrote: 'Having ventured to find fault with Spencer, I may be allowed to add that I have perhaps learned as much from him as from any other writer. If only his system did not appear at first quite so complete and final, one might more easily remain loyal to it in spite of its deficiencies.'

‡ There is an excellent unpublished American thesis on this topic. See: *Society Versus Solitude: Studies in Emerson, Thoreau, Hawthorne and Whitman*, Robert Paul Cobb, 1955 (Dissertation in partial fulfilment of Ph.D. in the University of Michigan).

'society'; and this point, too, serves at once to demonstrate his close agreement with Durkheim. Indeed, one might say that Cooley expressed Durkheim's central persuasion in a more satisfactory way. But Cooley had his own particular set of concepts.

The rejection of the distinction between Individual and Society

His quite basic starting point was to demolish the distinction between 'individual' and 'society'. The common sense assumption that the human individual was an 'entity', an independent 'mind', separate from society (which was simply a set of organizations which individuals deliberately made) was, quite literally, he insisted, an optical illusion. We *saw* 'individuals' walking about as organisms—inside their skins; contained within their suits of clothes, so to speak—and we *assumed* that they were separate, autonomous, psychological entities. Similarly, we thought of 'society' as a network of regulations, procedures, organizations quite independent of the mentality of individuals. But this common sense dichotomy, Cooley argued, was false. Only a little reflection, he argued:

'. . . assures us that the individual has his being only as part of a whole. What does not come by heredity comes by communication and intercourse; and the more closely we look the more apparent it is that separateness is an illusion of the eye and community the inner truth.'*

Now this is not, at first glance, an easy conception, and we must look more closely at it. Cooley was not in any sense wishing to *deny* the existence of unique individual 'self-hood' or the regularities of 'society'. Perhaps the clearest way of stating his position is this.

We commonly think of 'mind' in individual terms; as an *individual* endowment; whereas a moment's thought shows that the *locus* of mind obviously and always lies far *beyond* the individual—it is always and essentially a social-mental complex of many individuals in communication and association with each other. All that emerges in human consciousness other than that biologically and genetically given, is awakened, informed, created in the process of communication with others. We only distinguish 'individual minds' from the 'social forms' of intercommunication in terms of the viewpoint we adopt. In *fact*; in *actuality*; there exists an entire network of social-mental experience within which individuals find themselves to be parts.

* *Social Organization*, Schocken Books, 1962, p. 9. See also the views of Giddings —*The Making of Sociology*, Vol. 1, p. 552. Cooley's discussion was a development of exactly the same idea.

If we think for a moment of the 'boundaries' of our own individual mind, it is quite obvious that this is far more than is contained within our skin. The things we see, smell, hear, touch; the words, gestures, conversations of others in the context of which we find meaning; our moral values and problems; elements of aesthetic taste; the symbols of ritual and belief . . . all these innermost elements of our 'mind' take shape in relation to experiences which are borne in upon us from outside. We cannot define the *boundary* of an individual *self* by throwing a kind of sheath about his skin. A human mind is not like that. It is *not* limited to the boundaries of the body. A *person* cannot be so defined. The dimensions of his mind are spread along all the avenues of his perception and social awareness. One cannot draw a precise boundary about a 'mind'. Mind goes beyond individual selves, and embraces them.

A very important corollary of Cooley's point here was that the *forms* of mind in '*self*' and '*society*' were *not* 'separate-but-parallel', so to speak, but were literally aspects of the *same* social-mental process. In the process of communication, the regularities of senti-ment, attitude, judgment, consciousness of character which emerged, were *simultaneously* individual and social. For Cooley (as with Durkheim's 'social facts'), these associational psychological forms, these collective psychological facts, *were* the *data*, *were* the basic *subject-matter*, of sociology. They *were* the binding facts which we called *institutions*; they *were* the constellations of sentiment and attitude which formed what we called *personality*. Cooley wrote:

'I conclude, therefore, that the imaginations which people have of one another are the *solid facts* of society, and that to observe and interpret these must be a chief aim of sociology.'

With him as with Durkheim: 'collective psychology *is* sociology'. Cooley was very concerned to break through common sense to make his point of view clear, and we must note some of his own statements about it, if only to help us in our exposition of what is, for many, a very difficulty conception to grasp.

'If we accept the evolutionary point of view,' he wrote, 'we are led to see the relation between society and the individual as an organic relation. That is, we see that the individual is not separable from the human whole, but a living member of it, deriving his life from the whole through social and hereditary transmission as truly as if men were literally one body. He cannot cut himself off; the strands of heredity and education are woven into all his being. And, on the other hand, the social whole is in some degree dependent upon each individual, because each contributes something to the common life that no one else can contribute.'*

* *Human Nature and the Social Order*, Schocken Books, 1964, p. 35.

And again:

'A separate individual is an abstraction unknown to experience, and so likewise is society when regarded as something apart from individuals. The real thing is Human Life, which may be considered either in an individual aspect or in a social, that is to say a general, aspect; but is always, as a matter of fact, both individual and general. In other words, 'society' and 'individuals' do not denote separable phenomena . . .

Just as there is no society or group that is not a collective view of persons, so there is no individual who may not be regarded as a particular view of social groups. He has no separate existence; through both the hereditary and the social factors in his life a man is bound into the whole of which he is a member, and to consider him apart from it is quite as artificial as to consider society apart from individuals.'*

These were statements in *Human Nature and the Social Order*. In *Social Organization*, he was equally definite.

'Social consciousness, or awareness of society, is inseparable from self-consciousness, because we can hardly think of ourselves excepting with reference to a social group of some sort, or of the group except with reference to ourselves. The two things go together, and what we are really aware of is a more or less complex personal or social whole, of which now the particular, now the general, aspect is emphasized . . .

Self and society are twin-born, we know one as immediately as we know the other, and the notion of a separate and independent ego is an illusion . .

Self and society go together, as phases of a common whole. I am aware of the social groups in which I live as immediately and authentically as I am aware of myself . . .

This differentiated unity of mental or social life, present in the simplest intercourse but capable of infinite growth and adaptation, is what I mean by social organization. It would be useless, I think, to attempt a more elaborate definition. We have only to open our eyes to *see* organization; and if we cannot do that no definition will help us.'†

This initial point was, then, very clear and definite, but we must now clarify certain important aspects of it, and consider the more specific notions in terms of which Cooley went about his analysis of this 'social-mental complex'.

The following are the distinctive points quite essential to Cooley's conception.

(I) THE SOCIAL-MENTAL COMPLEX: NOT OF 'CEREBRAL'
AGREEMENT, BUT BEHAVIOURAL AND EXPERIENTIAL

It is most important, first, to see that Cooley's entire emphasis was

* *Human Nature and the Social Order*, pp. 36–8.
† *Social Organization*, pp. 4, 5, 8–9.

upon *communication* as an *active process* of interdependent *behaviour and experience,* not as a kind of intellectual conversation. The interrelatedness of minds in social communication was not a matter of what we might call 'cerebral' agreement, but an order of consciousness, feeling, judging, thinking which arose in the close interdependencies of *behaviour.* It is in this connection that Cooley's position can be called *'behavioural'* and that Mead's position (which was a more detailed elaboration of this) came to be called 'behaviouristic' (by himself, as well as others), and it can be seen at once that this was a completely different 'behaviourism' from that of Watson. A very important distinction lies here—and we must come back to it when discussing Mead. But here we can simply note the definiteness of Cooley's emphasis.

'The unity of the social mind consists not in *agreement* but in *organization,* in the fact of reciprocal influence or causation among its parts, by virtue of which everything that takes place in it is connected with everything else, and so is an outcome of the whole. It is the expression of a vital co-operation . . . everything that I say or think is influenced by what others have said or thought, and, in one way or another, sends out an influence of its own in turn.'*

(II) THE ACCEPTANCE OF INSTINCT, SENTIMENT-FORMATION, REASON, WITHIN THE SHAPING OF 'HUMAN NATURE IN SOCIETY'

Secondly, we must note that Cooley's 'behavioural' emphasis did not lead at all to the rejection of the part played by instinct and the formation of sentiments in the shaping of human nature within the process of communication. He quite definitely accepted and used these elements (we shall see later the importance he attached to the 'sentiments'), and, like McDougall, he saw *reason* as an attribute of human nature which could govern and direct instinctual energies—not as something which denied, or could obliterate, their very existence. Having claimed that the instinctual tendencies of man were to a degree malleable, he went on to say that: 'they must be guided, developed, co-ordinated, organized . . . and this is the part of reason'. Then, in his discussion of 'reason and instinct' he made one or two points which, as we shall see, were very much in agreement with the position adopted by Pareto: namely, that even the *reasoning* activities of man had something of an instinctive nature; were rooted in the other instinctual tendencies.

* *Social Organization,* p. 4.

R

487

'Reason,' Cooley wrote, 'does not supplant instinct, any more than the captain supplants the private soldiers; it is a principle of higher organization, controlling and transforming instinctive energies. Indeed, reason is itself an instinctive disposition, in a large use of the term, a disposition to compare, combine, and organize the activities of the mind.* Animals have it in some measure and it is unique in man only by the degree of its development . . .'

One other point deserves mention here. Cooley believed that 'human nature' was 'plastic' and could change with differing social conditions, even though the basic biological endowment of man remained unchanged, but he was impressed (as Westermarck was) with the *universal* characteristics of it. And it is interesting to notice that he attributed these universal elements of human experience and behaviour not *only* to common instincts and emotions, but also to the fact that 'human nature' took shape within 'primary groups' (of family, play group, neighbourhood) which were much the same the world over—even when couched within larger social structures (civilizations, even) which were different. In this sense, 'human nature' could mean, he suggested:

'. . . a social nature developed in man by simple forms of intimate association or "primary groups", especially the family and neighbourhood, which are found everywhere and everywhere work upon the individual in somewhat the same way. This nature consists chiefly of certain primary social sentiments and attitudes, such as consciousness of one's self in relation to others, love of approbation, resentment of censure, emulation, and a sense of social right and wrong formed by the standards of a group. This seems to me to correspond very closely to what is meant by "human nature" in ordinary speech. We mean something much more definite than hereditary disposition, which most of us know nothing about, and yet something fundamental and wide-spread if not universal in the life of man, found in ancient history and in the accounts of remote nations, as well as now and here. Thus, when we read that Joseph's brethren hated him and could not speak peaceably to him because they saw that their father loved him more than all the rest; we say, "Of course, that is human nature". This social nature is much more alterable than heredity, and if it is "pretty much the same the world over", as we commonly say, this is because the intimate groups in which it is formed are somewhat similar. If these are essentially changed, human nature will change with them.'†

What this amounted to was that the *sentiments* of mankind, as well as their instinctual tendencies, shared much similarity and agree-

---

* *Human Nature and the Social Order*, p. 30. This statement, especially, is almost exactly Pareto's conception of what he called one of the 'residues' of the human mind. See p. 599.
† *Ibid*, pp. 32–3.

ment, and chiefly because they took shape within universally similar *primary groups*. There was here, then, a very close link between instinct and emotion, communication, sentiment-formation, and the nature of primary groups; and this was, in fact, quite a basic part of Cooley's theory.

(III) SOCIAL COMMUNICATION ESSENTIAL FOR THE CONSCIOUSNESS OF 'SELF'.

A third quite essential part of Cooley's conception was that social communication (being involved in inter-communication with others) was the indispensable condition for the emergence of the consciousness of 'Self' in the individual. Biological heredity produced all the anatomical and physiological features of the organism with its experiential and behavioural tendencies and potentialities—but the consciousness of 'Self' in the individual was essentially dependent on the creation of meanings, values, judgments in social intercourse with others. The individual came to form a consciousness of 'himself' as he encountered the judgments of others about him, and as he made connected judgments about others. This we shall come to when considering the experience within primary groups and Cooley's notion of the 'looking-glass self'—but here we must only note that *society* (social communication) was regarded as the necessary context for the *origin* of the 'self'. He wrote in the following way:

'By communication is meant the mechanism through which human relations exist and develop—all the symbols of mind, together with the means of conveying them through space and preserving them in time . . . All these taken together, in the intricacy of their actual combination, make up an organic whole corresponding to the organic whole of human thought; and everything in the way of mental growth has an external existence therein. The more closely we consider this mechanism the more intimate will appear its relation to the inner life of mankind, and nothing will more help us to understand the latter than such consideration . . . Without communication the mind does not develop a true human nature, but remains in an abnormal and nondescript state neither human nor properly brutal.'*

Again we can see that 'communication' is the central idea both for his vision of individual and social actuality, and for his method of analysis.

(IV) THE CREATIVITY OF SOCIETY

The point which immediately follows upon this makes abundantly clear Cooley's fundamental agreement with Durkheim's point of

* *Human Nature and the Social Order*, p. xxviii.

view. Durkheim insisted that the collective conditions of association were not *sterile*, but psychologically *creative*: engendering in the consciousness of individuals kinds of experience which they did not previously have. Cooley was quite plainly of the same view, and it is important to see how close this degree of agreement was.

'Most people not only think of individuals and society as more or less separate and antithetical, but they look upon the former as antecedent to the latter. That persons make society would be generally admitted as a matter of course; but that society makes persons would strike many as a startling notion, though I know of no good reason for looking upon the distributive aspect of life as more primary or causative than the collective aspect. The reason for the common impression appears to be that we think most naturally and easily of the individual phase of life, simply because it is a tangible one, the phase under which men appear to the senses, while the actuality of groups, of nations, of mankind at large, is realized only by the active and instructed imagination. We ordinarily regard society, so far as we conceive it at all, in a vaguely material aspect, as an aggregate of physical bodies, not as the vital whole which it is; and so, of course, we do not see that it may be as original or causative as anything else. Indeed, many look upon "society" and other general terms as somewhat mystical, and are inclined to doubt whether there is any reality back of them.

This naïve individualism of thought—which, however, does not truly see the individual any more than it does society—is reinforced by traditions in which all of us are brought up, and is hard to shake off . . .

Individuality is neither prior in time nor lower in moral rank than sociality; but the two have always existed side by side as complementary aspects of the same thing . . .'*

Associational processes gave rise to psychological facts *within* individuals which could not be otherwise explained. The necessity of the *social* perspective for any satisfactory human psychology was therefore perfectly plain. To leave out of view the *creativity of social processes* was to leave out of psychology the causative basis of *distinctively human experiences*. And this is why any psychology which deliberately leaves this dimension out of its conceptual apparatus, or out of its 'universe of discourse', thinking that it can be an 'experimental psychology' if unencumbered by it, is decidedly an *error of psychology*.† Cooley, even more, perhaps, than Durkheim, made this indisputably clear.

It is most important to see that all these writers we are now considering did in fact accept this persuasion about the *creativity of*

* *Human Nature and the Social Order*, pp. 42–3, 45.
† See all that we said in *The Making of Sociology*, Vol. 1, by Marx, pp. 395–9, Ward, pp. 492–3. Giddings, pp. 552–5, etc.

association, and were therefore quite definitely filling in this one dimension of the wider system of sociology that was in the making.

(V) INDIVIDUAL AND SOCIAL 'FORMS' DISTINGUISHABLE NONETHELESS: DEPENDING UPON THE SPECIFIC VIEWPOINT OR INTEREST OF ENQUIRY

It is also important to be clearer than we have been about Cooley's claim that 'unique individuals' and 'forms' of social 'organization' or 'grouping' were legitimately distinguishable (from the point of view of theory and method) to the investigator, even though the socio-psychological actuality was inclusive of them all. The best thing here is to give one or two of his own illustrations.

'When we speak of society,' he wrote, 'or use any other collective term, we fix our minds upon some general view of the people concerned, while when we speak of individuals we disregard the general aspect and think of them as if they were separate. Thus "the Cabinet" may consist of President Lincoln, Secretary Stanton, Secretary Seward, and so on; but when I say "the Cabinet" I do not suggest the same idea as when I enumerate these gentlemen separately. Society, or any complex group, may, to ordinary observation, be a very different thing from all of its members viewed one by one—as a man who beheld General Grant's army from Missionary Ridge would have seen something other than he would by approaching every soldier in it. In the same way a picture is made up of so many square inches of painted canvas; but if you should look at these one at a time, covering the others, until you had seen them all, you would still not have seen the picture. There may, in all such cases, be a system or organization in the whole that is not apparent in the parts. *In this sense, and in no other*, is there a difference between society and the individuals of which it is composed; a difference not residing in the facts themselves but existing to the observer on account of the limits of his perception. A *complete* view of society would also be a complete view of all the individuals, and vice versa; there would be no difference between them.'*

It is perfectly clear from this statement how it is possible to observe the over-all and detailed 'form' of a large social organization, and analyse it without a necessary focus upon the individuals within it, just as it is to examine the individuals independently of the organizational form; and how either or both can be done whilst still having clearly in mind the socio-psychological actuality which is inclusive of them all. There is not the slightest lack of clarity in Cooley's position.

* *Human Nature and the Social Order*, pp. 37–8.

(VI) THE COMMONLY SUPPOSED OPPOSITION BETWEEN 'SOCIETY' AND 'INDIVIDUAL' IS FALSE

There is one relatively small point that is still worth making—that, as a result of this conception, Cooley was able to claim that the very common tendency to explain conflicts, dissatisfactions, or frustrations among people in terms of an over-all conflict between 'society' and 'the individual' was far too over-simplified, and, in fact, false. 'Society' and 'Individual' were *not* definable separate entities, and could not therefore be juxtaposed in such a 'polarized' way. They were both, on the contrary, parts of a common socio-psychological nature. Certainly conflict, dissatisfaction, etc., were experienced by individuals, but any satisfactory analysis of this had to be posed in far more subtle and intricate terms.

'. . . the antithesis, society versus the individual,' Cooley wrote, 'is false and hollow whenever used as a general or philosophical statement of human relations. Whatever idea may be in the minds of those who set these words and their derivatives over against each other, the notion conveyed is that of two separable entities or forces; and certainly such a notion is untrue to fact.'*

In order to be perfectly clear about Cooley's position on some of these quite vital questions, we can do no better than look at one of his own summary statements in which he himself set these matters out in the form of question and answer.

'1. Is not society, after all, made up of individuals, and of nothing else?
I should say, Yes. It is plain, every-day humanity, not a mysterious something else.
2. Is society anything more than the sum of the individuals?
In a sense, Yes. There is an organization, a life-process, in any social whole that you cannot see in the individuals separately. To study them one by one and attempt to understand society by putting them together will lead you astray. It is "individualism" in a bad sense of the word. Whole sciences, like political economy; great institutions, like the church, have gone wrong at this point. You must see your groups, your social processes, as the living wholes that they are.
3. Is the individual a product of society?
Yes, in the sense that everything human about him has a history in the social past. If we consider the two sources from which he draws his life, heredity and communication, we see that what he gets through the germ-plasm has a social history in that it has had to adapt itself to past society in order to survive: the traits we are born with are such as have undergone a social test in the lives of our ancestors. And what he gets from com-

* *Human Nature and the Social Order*, p. 42.

munication—language, education, and the like—comes directly from society. Even physical influences, like food and climate, rarely reach us except as modified and adapted by social conditions.

4. Can we separate the individual from society?

Only in an external sense. If you go off alone into the wilderness you take with you a mind formed in society, and you continue social intercourse in your memory and imagination, or by the aid of books. This, and this only, keeps humanity alive in you, and just in so far as you lose the power of intercourse your mind decays. Long solitude . . . often produces imbecility.

At times in the history of Christianity, and of other religions also, hermits have gone to dwell in desert places, but they have usually kept up some communication with one another and with the world outside . . . We may suspect that St Simeon Stylites, who dwelt for years on top of a pillar, was not unaware that his austerity was visible to others.

5. Is the individual in any sense free, or is he a mere piece of society?

Yes, he is free, as I conceive the matter, but it is an organic freedom, which he works out in co-operation with others, not a freedom to do things independently of society. It is team-work. He has freedom to function in his own way . . . but, in one way or another, he has to play the game as life brings him into it.

The evolutionary point of view encourages us to believe that life is a creative process, that we are really building up something new and worth while, and that the human will is a part of the creative energy that does this. Every individual has his unique share in the work, which no one but himself can discern and perform. Although his life flows into him from the hereditary and social past, his being as a whole is new, a fresh organization of life. Never any one before had the same powers and opportunities that you have, and you are free to use them in your own way.

It is, after all, only common sense to say that we exercise our freedom through co-operation with others. If you join a social group—let us say a dramatic club—you expect that it will increase your freedom, give your individual powers new stimulus and opportunity for expression. And why should not the same principle apply to society at large? It is through a social development that mankind has emerged from animal bondage into that organic freedom, wonderful though far from complete, that we now enjoy.'*

This is a clear and excellent statement. It makes completely clear Cooley's conception of the 'uniqueness' of individuals in the living moment of social actuality, and it also gives a very clear picture of his evolutionary perspective and his positive approach to deliberate social re-creation which was fully in accord with almost all the makers of sociology from Comte to Hobhouse, Durkheim and Weber.

In all this, however, it has become clear that certain basic conceptions—like those of 'sentiment-formation', 'communications', 'prim-

---

* *Human Nature and the Social Order,* pp. 48–50.

ary groups', etc.—were at the heart of his analysis, and we must look briefly at each of these and see the ultimate analysis of the nature and dilemmas of modern industrial society which he drew from them.

Self and Society : The 'Looking-Glass Self'

Cooley's grounds for rejecting any sharp distinction between individual 'self' and 'society' can best be seen in his conception of the way in which the consciousness of 'self' —the very emergence of the awareness of 'self' in the individual—took place; the way, in short, in which the 'self' was *created*. And his fundamental insistence was that the consciousness of 'self' was not a basic, given, element of the human being—present from birth—but that it emerged during the early years of the child's life* as an aspect, a reflection, of *social consciousness*. This he described vividly in his conception of the 'Looking Glass Self'.

Cooley's teaching was this. Though much may be said to be inherited by the human organism—developing physiological processes, modes of sensation (of internal conditions and external stimuli), instinctive impulses, needs, propensities, and the like, which give rise to a stream of impressions from the beginning—there is no initial distinction in the child's mind between 'self' and outer world or 'self' and society. This is an organization of the mind; an ordering of cognition, feeling, impulse, sentiment, and evaluation; which comes into existence as the child grows. And this growth essentially takes place in the context of *other* human beings.

A child comes to the experience of the entire world through its gradual awareness of those other people—its mother, father, brother, sister, and (later) people in the neighbourhood—in relation to whom its pressing needs, fears, pleasures, joys (initially of an inchoate nature) are experienced, and by whom they are satisfied and frustrated. There is an intimate dependence upon these other people (not initially discerned as clearly delineated 'individuals') in terms of total, face to face, involvement. A complex web of communications (beginning long before the meaningful employment of language) is experienced—of movement, of gesture, of gentle touch, of pain, of sound and tone of voice, of facial expression—and gradually, within this complex interchange, the child becomes *socially conscious*. A certain conscious *ordering* of the world is brought into being in his psychic awareness; the constraining environment of this influence of others brings a *focusing* of attention; and this *is* social consciousness, consciousness of an external world, and consciousness of 'self', *all*

* This may be compared later both with Mead, and, more interestingly, with Freud's account of the early processes of 'perceptual consciousness' and the differentiation of the 'ego' and then the 'super-ego'.

simultaneously. Social consciousness is thus as immediate as self-consciousness. It is *the same thing.* There is thus no sense or correctness in seeking to explain one or the other in terms of the *derivation* of one from the other. They are *all of a piece.* The human, personally experienced mind *is social.* It emerges *in association*; and association is its essential condition. And Cooley's particular point here is that the 'self' is a 'looking-glass self' in the sense that it assumes a shape (or nature) within the consciousness of the individual as the individual becomes aware of the judgments and evaluations which others make of him, and in terms of which he learns to make judgments and evaluations of *them.* It is an evaluative, judgmental process emerging in communication.

It will be readily seen, then, that Cooley was not at pains to deny the existence of 'society', or of the 'self' as a 'differentiated centre of psychic life, having a world of his own into which no other individual can fully enter . . . ' (as he put it); he was only at pains to show that the emergence of distinctively human, personal 'selves' or 'minds' was *essentially social.* There was no such thing as 'individual personality' independent of 'society', just as there was no such thing as 'society' independent of this complex web of growing, changing inter-personal communications.

It will be seen, too, that two factors: (1) the earliest groups—the small and intimate groups—of which the child is a member, and (2) the nature of communications, were of the most basic importance in Cooley's system of analysis. Before moving on to consider these, let us only note that so far we have not spoken of the *social tradition* of established language, symbols, customs, values, ideals, which pervade the existing group-communications within which the child is born; but this, clearly, is of crucial significance for the growth of the 'self', and we shall come to it when discussing communications and community.

Primary Groups

Cooley's analysis led him to place the greatest emphasis upon the importance of primary group relationships (and conditions) for the understanding of the growth of the 'self', and this importance was many-sided.

In the first place, he himself made his observations about three particular kinds of group: (*a*) the family, (*b*) play-groups of children, and (*c*) the neighbourhood (community) group of elders. It was within these immediate, small, intimate groups; within the context of their values and traditions; that the child's earliest experiences took place. Cooley distinguished these 'primary' groups from the larger 'secondary' groups in society in terms of the following characteristics.

Primary groups were (1) essentially *small* groups. They were therefore characterized by (2) direct 'face-to-face' relationships. They were also (3) groups of an *unspecialized* nature. People were members of them as *total persons*; seeking the satisfaction of all their many needs and aspirations in their interdependent relations with others. All dimensions of their nature; all the subtleties of their moods, wants, experiences; sought expression, consideration, satisfaction within these groups. It was also the case therefore, (4) that relationships in these groups were very intense, intimate, and demanding. People made intimate demands upon each other, as total persons, about all aspects of their natures, all the time. Furthermore, these groups were also (5) relatively *permanent* and to a considerable extent *involuntary*. Membership of a family and a neighbourhood community (one might even say 'territorial' community) was—at least until the strictly modern, industrial era—relatively long abiding. Entry into these groups (as a child) was not *chosen*, but a very extensive degree of formative experience was unavoidable.

These characteristics obviously made for full and intense relationships and experience—'for better, for worse'. They could be richly fulfilling and chokingly frustrating. They could give the deepest love and joy and security, and make possible the most inescapable tyranny. They were marked by ambivalence of feeling. Whatever else they may be—pleasing or unpleasing—they were bound to be total and intense: and especially for the child during its growth to 'self-hood'.

Secondary groups were all those larger associations in a society which were formally organized, impersonal, of which membership was only partial—for some specific purpose only, and in which the degree of participation or involvement could be voluntarily controlled (at least to some extent). One was a 'member' at a distance, so to speak, and without any total involvement as a person. Cooley wrote, for example:

'An institution is a mature, specialized and comparatively rigid part of the social structure. It is made up of persons, but not of whole persons; each one enters into it with a trained and specialized part of himself. . . .
A man is no man at all if he is merely a piece of an institution; he must stand also for human nature, for the instinctive, the plastic and the ideal.'*

Cooley believed that it was the small, total, intense, demanding intimacy of 'primary groups' which made them so important a *ground*

* *Social Organization*, p. 319.

496

of communications for the growth of the 'self'. In these groups, the child did not 'learn' about human qualities in any abstract sense; these qualities were vividly *embodied* for him in total persons who mattered to him supremely because the satisfaction and fulfilment of his entire nature seemed dependent on them. Judgments, evaluations of character were deeply felt; basic sentiments were deeply grounded in his individual nature. The recognition of 'others' and 'self' were vitally important. The interpretation of the qualities of others and the estimation of his own; the understanding of the 'roles' of members of the group and the formulation of reliable 'expectations' about them and about those who fulfilled them; all these were of the most concrete importance. It will already be clearly seen that for Cooley—as for all the earlier writers we have considered—the emergence of *regularities of association* among inter-communicating people, was essentially one of *evaluation*, of the establishing of *values*; but before we come to this, we must note some other extremely important aspects of 'primary groups'.

Cooley's insistence was that it was this context of primary group experience which was 'the nursery of human nature' as we know it, and some of his specific points deserve very particular emphasis.

Firstly, these primary groups were *primary* in very significant ways.

(1) They were more universal and abiding groups (existing in all societies) than were other more artificially* contrived and complex associations. Complex institutions in large civilizations came into being, changed, and went out of being—but families and neighbourhood groupings always remained.

(2) These primary groups seemed therefore to be more deeply-rooted 'natural' groupings than more complex institutions, and gave rise to what were felt to be the most fundamental 'natural' human relationships. We may remember Tönnies especially on this point, and see that Cooley reinforced his conception.

(3) These groups were 'primary' in the further sense, therefore, that —in all societies—they gave the individual his 'earliest and completest experience of social unity'. And, since they did not change to the same extent as more elaborate social relations, they formed, said Cooley: ' . . . a comparatively permanent source out of which the latter are ever springing'. 'These groups', he argued, 'are springs of life, not only for the individual but for social institutions.'

(4) Furthermore, it was the kind of social bonds, values, loyalties, duties, qualities of character (good or bad, likeable or hateful) which arose among people universally in these universal groups which we

* In the *best* sense of this word: i.e. the making of forms of government, law, etc., as various kinds of 'artifice' to meet variable social needs and problems.

497

came to call 'human nature'. The distinctive qualities of humanity were aspects not only of such genetic endowment as men might inherit—but the common sentiments engendered in these primary group relations. This, again, was a very important point, and Cooley expressed it very clearly as follows:

'By human nature, we may understand those sentiments and impulses that are human in being superior to those of lower animals, and also in the sense that they belong to mankind at large, and not to any particular race or time. It means, particularly, sympathy and the innumerable sentiments into which sympathy enters, such as love, resentment, ambition, vanity, hero-worship, and the feeling of social right and wrong.

Human nature in this sense is justly regarded as a comparatively permanent element in society. Always and everywhere men seek honour and dread ridicule, defer to public opinion, cherish their goods and their children, and admire courage, generosity, and success.* It is always safe to assume that people are and have been human. . . .

The view here maintained is that human nature is not something existing separately in the individual, but a *group-nature or primary phase of society*, a relatively simple and general condition of the social mind. It is something more, on the one hand, than the mere instinct that is born in us—though that enters into it—and something less, on the other, than the more elaborate development of ideas and sentiments that makes up institutions. It is the nature which is developed and expressed in those simple, face-to-face groups that are somewhat alike in all societies; groups of the family, the playground, and the neighbourhood. In the essential similarity of these is to be found the basis, in experience, for similar ideas and sentiments in the human mind. In these, everywhere, human nature comes into existence. Man does not have it at birth; he cannot acquire it except through fellowship, and it decays in isolation.'†

Again, we see in such a statement the fallacy of separating the 'natural' from the 'social'.

(5) Finally, Cooley emphasised not only that primary groups were essential for the growth of the 'self' and the distinctive sentiments of common 'human nature', but that they were *enough*. Having developed the point that 'elaborate' aspects of society were transient, whilst 'human nature seemed relatively stable and universal', he argued:

* Cooley did not only *assert* this, but referred to comparative and historical examples of several kinds. One such example was his reference to Spencer and Gillen in their study of Australian tribes. He commented (p. 29):
'They are generous to one another, emulous of virtue as they understand it, kind to their children and to the aged, and by no means harsh to women. Their faces as shown in the photographs are wholly human and many of them attractive.'
† *Social Organization*, pp. 28, 29–30.

'... the family and neighbourhood life is essential to its genesis *and nothing more is.*'*

Primary (Group) Ideals

From all that has been said, it will be clear that the crucial significance of primary groups for Cooley was that—within their demanding, reciprocal relationships—the fundamental values and ideals which disinguished human nature were discovered and laid down as basic elements of the social tradition.†

'Where do we get our notions of love, freedom, justice and the like,' he wrote, 'which we are ever applying to social institutions? Not from abstract philosophy, surely, but from the actual life of simple and widespread forms of society, like the family or the play-group. . . .

A congenial family life is the immemorial type of moral unity, and source of many of the terms—such as brotherhood, kindness, and the like—which describe it. . . .

The ideal of moral unity I take to be the mother, as it were, of all social ideals.'‡

Cooley's whole point was that here, in the close reciprocity of primary group relationships, such basic ideals were deeply and sharply *realized*. Here the value of impartiality of judgment as distinct from unconsidered or impulsive or deliberate bias; honesty as against deceit; magnanimity as against small-minded meanness; etc., were vividly appreciated in the context of deeply felt attachments, loyalties and conflicts. The qualities of human character, mind, judgment were first—and in the most telling and impressive way—realized here.

We may note that this is an account of what has since come to be called 'socialization'—the way in which the 'self' internalizes the values, goals, and appropriate symbols of the social tradition; but let us note too that nothing was said or implied by Cooley about 'determinism'. The 'self' was not an automatic imbiber of the social tradition. Thought, judgment, deliberation, choice, action were going on. The 'self' was not a kind of 'flotsam and jetsam' floating at the mercy of social tides—but an active personal focus of psychic energies. The 'reflection' by the 'self' of 'society' was not at all a matter of 'determined' automatic adjustment.

Cooley believed, further, that all the larger systems of ideals in society—of religious, political, philosophical systems, etc.,—were based upon, and were extensions of the ideals realised in communities of primary groups. Primary groups and primary ideals remained

---

* *Social Organization*, p. 31.   † Compare Sumner and the *Folkways*.
‡ *Social Organization*, pp. 32, 34, 35.

the touchstone of important moral values no matter how complex human society became. Again we can see this strong insistence that *morality* lay at the heart of human social institutions. Indeed, with the growing complexity of society and interdependence of societies, Cooley thought that men must become committed to a working out of a world-wide order of morality elaborated from these primary ideals. And, as we shall see, he believed that the development of modern 'mass-communications' could be an effective vehicle for this, even though at present it creates vast problems. Man's failure in this task so far, he thought, could be readily understood in terms of its magnitude.

'The creation of a moral order on an ever-growing scale,' he wrote, 'is the great historical task of mankind. . . .*
Society, as a moral organism, is a progressive creation, tentatively wrought out through experiment, struggle, and survival. Not only individuals but ideas, institutions, nations and races do their work upon it and perish. Its ideals, though simple in spirit, are achieved through endless elaboration of means.'†

It was not the case, Cooley thought, that the improvement of modern society called for any essential change in human nature, but for . . . 'a larger and higher application of its familiar impulses'.

Sentiment

Cooley's central element of analysis—quite clearly—was the nature of '*communications*', but before concentrating upon this, it is important to see (with reference to earlier writers and those we are considering in this section) the centrality of the place of 'sentiment-formation' in his system. It was just as central for him as for Tönnies, Westermarck, Hobhouse, Durkheim, McDougall (as we have seen) and for Mead, Freud, and Pareto (especially) to whom we shall come shortly.

'By sentiment,' wrote Cooley, 'I mean socialized feeling, feeling which has been raised by thought and intercourse out of its merely instinctive state and become properly human. It implies imagination, and the medium in which it chiefly lives is sympathetic contact with the minds of others. Thus love is a sentiment, while lust is not; resentment is, but not rage; the fear of disgrace or ridicule, but not animal terror, and so on. Sentiment is the *chief motive-power of life*, and as a rule lies deeper in our minds and

* *Social Organization*, p. 53.
† *Ibid.*, p. 56. The agreement of this whole position with the earlier writers—from Comte and Mill to Ward, Sumner, Giddings, Westermarck, Hobhouse, etc., is remarkably clear.

is less subject to essential change than thought, from which, however, it is not to be too sharply separated.'*

This was a very plain and strong statement, and we might note a few quite fundamental points: (1) That it was the *sentiments*—formed by the socializing processes of communication upon instinct (and other inherited elements) which were the distinctively *human* qualities. (2) That their very emergence implied capacities such as imagination, thought, sympathy, and the power of qualified control and discipline. (3) That the sentiments were the *chief motive-power* of human life (setting the chief directions of human action and judgment), and (4) that they were more deeply established (as abiding constellations of cognition and feeling) than were orientations of *thought* as such, though (5) they were not to be separated too sharply or completely from the activity of thinking.† There is the final point which is not in this particular statement of Cooley's, but derives from his statements (elsewhere) about the universality of both instinctive needs and dispositions and of primary group experience—(6) that there is a certain universality of the basic sentiments in human 'nature' on which a universality of primary moral ideals rests.

These are all extremely important points—both for social-psychological analysis as such, and for such basic issues as the 'relativity of ethics', etc.,—but we must leave this matter of the 'sentiments' now, though we shall come back to them later to see how Cooley refers to them in analysing the 'malaise' of modern society with its maladjustment of communication. But for the basic analysis of this 'malaise' we must first look at Cooley's central notion of 'communications'.

Communications

'Self' and 'society' alike arose, for Cooley as aspects of the process of human *association*. For him, as for Durkheim, *association was not sterile*, but psychologically creative. But the heart of the whole socio-psychological process was therefore *communications*. Out of communications the 'self' arose. Out of communication the *community* of *persons* arose. Communications was the key to the analysis and understanding of 'human nature and the social order'.

'By communication,' Cooley wrote, 'is here meant the mechanism through which human relations exist and develop—all the symbols of the mind, together with the means of conveying them through space and preserving them in time. It includes the expression of the face, attitude and gesture, the tones of the voice, words, writing, printing, railways, telegraphs, telephones, and whatever else may be the latest achievement in the conquest

* *Social Organization*, p. 177.
† Again, see the close agreement with Pareto.

of space and time. All these taken together, in the intricacy of their actual combination, make up an organic whole corresponding to the organic whole of human thought; and everything in the way of mental growth has an external existence therein. The more closely we consider this mechanism the more intimate will appear its relation to the inner life of mankind, and nothing will more help us to understand the latter than such consideration.'

It will be seen in this statement, as we would expect, that Cooley included every nuance of the symbolic intercourse between minds—from facial expressions and tones of voice to the most massive organization of press and transport—in his notion of communications. This was the entire fabric of the social mental complex of created human civilization. Here we need only note that for the child, he especially emphasized *pre-verbal* communication: ' . . . the expression of the face—especially of the mobile portions about the eyes and the mouth—the pitch, inflection, and emotional tones of the voice and the 'gestures' of the head and limbs . . .'. No brief mention of his discussion of such modes of communication can give a sufficient indication of the subtlety and sensitivity of Cooley's analysis. But it is with *speech* and *language* that he began to introduce the entirety of the social tradition, and described the way in which the cumulative traditions of the past were psychologically *creative* for the new-born child.

'A word,' he wrote, 'is a vehicle, a boat floating down from the past, laden with the thought of men we never saw; and in coming to understand it we enter not only into the minds of our contemporaries, but into the general mind of humanity continuous through time. The popular notion of learning to speak is that the child first has the idea and then gets from others a sound to use in communicating it; but a closer study that shows this is hardly true even of the simplest ideas, and is nearly the reverse of truth as regards developed thought. In that the word usually goes before, leading and kindling the idea—we should not have the latter if we did not have the word first. "This way," says the word, "is an interesting thought: come and find it." And so we are led on to rediscover old knowledge. Such words for instance, as *good, right, truth, love, home, justice, beauty, freedom*; are powerful makers of what they stand for.'†

From this kind of position—so excellently expressed—Cooley went on to analyse the whole cumulative fabric of knowledge and communications in society: writing, the cumulative storing and expansion of knowledge, the cumulative growth of sentiment in art,‡

---

* *Social Organization*, p. 61.   † *Ibid.*, p. 69.
‡ *Ibid.*, p. 78: 'Sentiment is cumulative in human history in the same manner as thought, though less definitely and surely. . . . So, Greek sculpture, from the time of the humanists . . . through Goethe to the present day, has been a channel by which Greek sentiment has flowed into modern life.'

the development of new techniques of communication—the printing press, etc; and r ɔwadays he would, of course, have added the enormous and rapid advances in sound and television broadcasting, satellite communication, computerization, and the like. But in all this, his *essential* point was that the very nature of the 'self' and 'society' and the actuality of *community* that existed was a function of the nature of communications—and particularly the link between primary group communication (and the values, sentiments, etc, it engendered) and the formal fabric of relationships in the wider organization of society. Let us see once again, how Cooley regarded communications as the all embracing fabric of human socio-mental activity, and especially now to see how this led him to his analysis of the 'malaise' of modern society.

'If we take a larger view,' he wrote, 'and consider the life of a social group, we see that communication, including its organization into literature, art, and institutions, is truly the outside or visible structure of thought, as much cause as effect of the inside or conscious life of men. All is one growth: the symbols, the traditions, the institutions are projected from the mind, to be sure, but in the very instant of their projection, and thereafter, they react upon it, and in a sense control it, stimulating, developing, and fixing certain thoughts at the expense of others to which no awakening suggestion comes. By the aid of this structure the individual is a member not only of a family, a class, and a state, but of a larger whole reaching back to prehistoric men whose thought has gone to build it up. In this whole he lives as in an element, drawing from it the materials of his growth and adding to it whatever constructive thought he may express.

. . . the system of communication is a tool, a progressive invention, whose improvements react upon mankind and alter the life of every individual and institution. A study of these improvements is one of the best ways by which to approach an understanding of the mental and social changes that are bound up with them. . . .

And when we come to the modern era, especially, we can understand nothing rightly unless we perceive the manner in which the revolution in communication has made a new world for us.'*

It was the 'revolution in communication' which led Cooley to a perspective on the analysis of modern society which fitted exactly with that of the other writers we have mentioned.

Mass-communications and Malaise: Formalism and Disorganization

Cooley's analysis of the nature and problems of modern industrial society was focused upon two fundamental factors: both of which were attendant upon the same process of rapid change which had

* *Social Organization*, pp. 64–5.

been the concern of all the writers we have considered—the change from simple traditional community to complex industrial society. These factors were: (1) the growing predominance of large 'secondary group' organizations over primary groups; and, indeed, the unsettling of the latter, and (2) specific changes in the nature and effects of communications.

The mechanization of transport and communications—in printing (and *cheap* printing and the inundation of books, papers, magazines), photography, the postal system, etc;—had led, said Cooley, chiefly to a new degree of *swiftness* and *diffusion* of information. This, he felt, certainly produced a more informed public, but, necessarily, only *superficially* (indeed, only *apparently*) informed. The newspaper—copious, focusing a good deal on appeals to personality and superficial emotion, necessarily limiting its language, vocabulary, pace and detail of thought to the commonplace, stood for 'diffusion as opposed to distinction'.

'It is beyond doubt that the constant and varied stimulus of a confused time makes sustained attention difficult. Certainly our popular literature is written for those who run as they read, and carries the principle of economy of attention beyond anything previously imagined. ... Generally speaking, mind is spread out very thin over our civilization; a good sort of mind, no doubt, but quite thin.'*

Such *mass*-communications had a cheapening effect. Furthermore, the swiftness of communication—the continual plying of the mind (day after day) with superficial and undigested information—gave rise to a *strain* of superficiality: a perpetual fever of restlessness and discontent, since nothing was ever thought through, or felt and judged profoundly. There was a perpetual titillation of the superficial which possessed no true grounds for contentment; which was not rooted in satisfying values. Modern man, said Cooley, had an 'impatient, touch-and-go habit of mind as regards both thought and feeling' and had his attention provoked to so much that he was 'driven to versatility and short cuts at some expense to truth and depth'. And this seemed to produce a continuous mental preoccupation which was, at the least, a perpetual discontent, and, at worst, a strain which might well be connected with drug-taking, suicide, and other pathological behaviour.

It is very important here to note two things (1) that Cooley was far from being *reactionary* about modern communications, as we shall see later, and (2) more important here, that the significance of this 'revolution in communications' was its effect in relation to

* *Social Organization*, p. 100.

primary group experience and values. On the one hand there might well be a gap between the values and expectations established in primary groups and the complex conduct, information, and values required in large-scale organization; but also, this web of swiftly diffused, superficial communications might *affect* the quality of communications within primary groups and neighbourhood communities. The effect of this up-to-the-minute rapidity of communications in a technologically changing society was such as to keep alive a continuous expectation of *change*. To stand on important values against change came to be thought almost disreputable.

'In our commercial and industrial life the somewhat feverish progress has generated a habit, a whole system of habits, based on the expectation of change. Enterprise and adaptability are cultivated at the expense of whatever conflicts with them; each one, feeling that the procession is moving on and that he must keep up with it, hurries along at the expense, perhaps, of health, culture and sanity.'*

Clearly, Cooley's perspective was exactly that of Tönnies and Durkheim—the 'natural' and simple interdependent relationships and values of 'traditional' community were being over-layed, transformed, disrupted by the calculated, contractual relationships of a complex, formally organized society. And this strong agreement was even more marked in his further analysis of 'Formalism' and 'Disorganization'.

What he meant by 'Formalism' was the condition when the *form* of some institution existed impersonally—like a derelict piece of machinery—when, in fact, it lacked all inner life; when it had no living job to do. And he thought that this was a danger in modern society because of its largeness of scale, its rapidity of change, its quick readiness to 'adaptation', and an 'excess of mechanism'. This proneness to rapid 'organization' carried with it a domination of routine device, routine procedures; a 'rationalization' of organization which was at a distance from living personal involvement; and Cooley decidedly thought that it was cheapening, and, indeed, born of a necessity to be cheap, to make the best use of resources, to be efficient.

'Underlying all formalism, indeed, is the fact that it is psychically cheap; it substitutes the outer for the inner as more tangible, more capable of being held before the mind without fresh expense of thought and feeling, more easily extended, therefore, and impressed upon the multitude. Thus in our own architecture or literature we have innumerable cheap, unfelt repetitions of forms that were significant and beautiful in their time and place.'†

* *Social Organization*, p. 329.   † *Ibid.*, p. 343.

And Cooley felt this carried real dangers.

'The effect of formalism upon personality,' he wrote, 'is *to starve its higher life* and leave it the prey of apathy, self-complacency, sensuality and the lower nature in general. A formalized religion and a formalized freedom are, notoriously, the congenial dwelling-place of depravity and oppression.'*

This pressure towards routine formalism pervaded all large modern institutions—even, for example, education. 'Mass' courses, with routine syllabuses, were worked out to deal with large masses of pupils. 'Even universities', he wrote, 'have much of this sort of cant', and this in spite of the fact that: 'the one essential thing in real teaching is a personal expression between teacher and pupil'. And again he pointed to the stereotyping of language brought about by the production of a cheap press for mass-consumption and hasty reading. Newspapers have, he argued, to give 'a maximum of commonplace information for a minimum of attention . . . '.

This lack of fit between persons in their primary group living, on the one hand, and the largeness of formal organization in which they were involved on the other, led to an unfortunate degree of 'disorganization'. There came to be a *gap* of communications. There was no living link between individuals, primary groups, and the larger organizations of society necessary for the existence of a living sense of community. There was a gap of values; a lack of orientation; a malaise of feeling. There was, in short, Durkheim's 'anomie'. But let us see exactly how close Cooley's and Durkheim's conclusions were. First of all, in portraying the nature of this 'malaise', and the way in which the extent of it was a consequence of communications, Cooley wrote in this way:

'. . . Everyone asks "Why must I bear this?" and the pain of trying to see why is often worse than the evil itself. There is commonly no obvious reason, and the answer is often a sense of rebellion and a bitterness out of which comes, perhaps, recklessness, divorce, or suicide.

Why am I poor while others are rich? Why do I have to do work I do not like? Why should I be honest when others are unscrupulous? Why should I wear myself out bearing and rearing children? Why should I be faithful to my husband or wife when we are not happy together, and another would please me better? Why should I believe in a good God when all I know is a bad world? Why should I live when I wish to die? Never, probably, were so many asking such questions as this and finding no clear answer. There have been other times of analogous confusion, but it could never have penetrated so deeply into the masses as it does in these days of universal stir and communication.'†

* *Social Organization*, p. 343.   † *Ibid.* p. 353.

But—then—this is the way in which Cooley conceived of the basic changes in the nature of *work* and work-relationships.

'I need not point out in detail how the old legal and ethical relations—the whole social structure indeed—of industry have mostly broken down; how the craftsman has lost control of his tools and is struggling to regain it through associations; how vast and novel forms of combination have appeared; how men of all classes are demoralized by the lack of standards of economic justice; these are familiar matters which I mention only to show their relation to the principle under discussion.

In general, modern industry, progressing chiefly in a mechanical sense, has attained a marvellous organization in that sense; while the social and moral side of it remains in confusion. . . .'*

And having emphasized the *progress* in mechanization, organization, and material productivity as such, Cooley went on to give this almost Durkheimian picture of the 'paradox' of the 'organic' division of labour.

'Although the individual,' he wrote, 'in a merely mechanical sense, is part of a wider whole than ever before, he has often lost that conscious membership in the whole upon which his human breadth depends: unless the larger life is a moral life, he gains nothing in this regard, and may lose. When children saw the grain growing in the field, watched the reaping and threshing and grinding of it, and then helped their mother to make it into bread, their minds had a vital membership in the economic process; but now that this process, by its very enlargement, has become invisible, most persons have lost the sense of it. And this is a type of modern industry at large: the workman, the man of business, the farmer and the lawyer are contributors to the whole, but being morally isolated by the very magnitude of the system, the whole does not commonly live in their thought.'†

And it is at this point that we can re-introduce Cooley's idea of the maladjustment of 'sentiments' in this large-scale context of modern society. Pulled by the constraints of values pertaining to large-scale formal organization, which are foreign to the primary group sentiments which are still firmly established within their natures, men can find themselves in a situation of misery—and, indeed, a moral and personal deterioration that they do not really want.

'Our life,' Cooley wrote, 'is full of a confusion which often leaves the individual conscious only of his separateness, engaged in a struggle which, so far as he sees, has no more relation to justice and the common

* *Social Organization*, p. 384.   † *Ibid.*, p. 385.

good than a dog-fight. Whether he win or lose makes, in this case, little difference as to the effect upon his general view of life: he infers that the world is a place where one must either eat or be eaten; the idea of the brotherhood of man appears to be an enervating sentimentalism, and the true philosophy that of the struggle for existence, which he understands in a brutal sense opposite to the real teaching of science. Nothing could be more uncongenial to the we-feeling than this view, which unfortunate experience has prepared many to embrace, taking from life, as it does, its breadth and hopefulness, the joy and inspiration of working in a vast and friendly whole.

Probably most of us are under the sway of both of these tendencies. We feel the new idealism, the sweep and exhilaration of democracy, but we practise, nevertheless, a thrifty exploitation of all the private advantages we can decently lay our hands on; nor have we the moral vigour to work out any reconciliation of these principles. Experience shows, I think, that until a higher sentiment, like brotherly kindness, attains some definite organization and programme, so that men are held up to it, it is remarkably ineffective in checking selfish activities. People drift on and on in lower courses, which at bottom they despise and dislike, simply because they lack energy and initiative to get out of them. How true it is that many of us would like to be *made* to be better than we are. I have seen promising idealists grow narrow, greedy and sensual—and of course unhappy— and they prospered in the world; for no reason, apparently, but lack of definite stimulation to a higher life. There is firm ground for the opinion that human nature is prepared for a higher organization than we have worked out.'*

With his analysis of primary and secondary groups and of communication, Cooley arrived at the same picture of modern society, and the same perspective of judgment as the other writers we have studied. His proposed remedy was also very similar to theirs.

The making of a humane society: a morality resting upon realistic knowledge

Like them, Cooley insisted that man must now be responsible for the re-construction of his own society, for the direction of his own life, and he believed that this could be accomplished by simplifying social institutions to bring them more in accord with primary group values and sentiments. A morality and a programme of social reform and appropriate education was necessary—but now, this should not rest only upon moral philosophy but also upon a thorough-going knowledge of social processes. Several points are worth emphasizing in all this in order to show his essential agreements with other writers.

* *Social Organization*, pp. 193–4.

First, it is important to see that his assessment of modern industrialization and of its new techniques of communication was far from being pessimistic, though what we have said may have given this impression. Cooley certainly thought that modern society was racked by problems—but these, he believed, were not by any means a matter of deterioration as such—but unforeseen problems attendant upon improvements. His discussion of the family, religion, social class, and economic institutions was marked by this very sane balance of judgment. He wrote like this, for example:

'Our material betterment is a great thing, and our comparative freedom a greater, but these rather increase than diminish the need of a higher discipline in the mind that is to use them profitably: the more opportunities the more problems. Social betterment is like the advance of science in that each achievement opens up new requirements. . . .'*

But if the new techniques of mechanization and industrialization could be brought to *serve* individuals in society in accordance with their primary ideals, the present malaise of human life could be overcome. In all this he was completely akin to Tönnies, Hobhouse, Durkheim and Weber—the last with his 'ethic of responsibility'.

A second point worth noting here is that Cooley believed *both* that the basic primary human 'sentiments' and 'ideals' remained (and *would* remain) constant, *and* that modern institutions could be *simplified* and rationally ordered in accordance with them. Indeed, his view was that we required a vast task of *simplification* in society. The creeds of the future, though realistically based, he argued, were 'likely to be simple', and:

'In all institutions there is nowadays a tendency to exchange formulas for principles, as being more flexible and so more enduring. The nearer you can get to universal human nature without abandoning concreteness the better. . . .

It is indeed a general truth that *sentiment is nearer to the core of life than definable thought*. As the rim of a wheel whirls about its centre, *so ideas and institutions whirl about the pivotal sentiments of human nature*.'†

And again:

The '. . . tendency involved in the rise of public will is that toward a greater simplicity and flexibility of structure in every province of life: principles are taking the place of formulas. . . .

. . . in the early growth of every institution the truth that it embodies is not perceived or expressed in simplicity, but obscurely incarnated in custom and formula. The perception of principles does not do away with

* *Social Organization*, p. 380.   † *Ibid.*, pp. 378–9.

the mechanism, but tends to make it simple, flexible, human, definitely serving a conscious purpose and quick to stand or fall according to its success. Under the old system everything is preserved, because men do not know just where the virtue resides; under the new the essential is kept and the rest thrown away. . . .

The modern world, then, in spite of its complexity, may become fundamentally simpler, more consistent and reasonable. . . .

The guiding force back of public will, now as ever, is of course human nature itself in its more enduring characteristics, those which find expression in primary groups and are little affected by institutional changes. This nature, familiar yet inscrutable, is apparently in a position to work itself out more adequately than at any time in the past.'*

But he insisted upon *realism* in these efforts and held exactly the same view as Durkheim that though an accordance of institutions with basic 'sentiments' and 'ideals' was desirable, nonetheless there should be an acceptance of *specialization* in society.

'A likeness of spirit and principle is essential to moral unity, but as regards details differentiation is and should be the rule. The work of the world is mostly of a special character, and it is quite as important that a man should mind his own business—that is, his own particular kind of general service—as that he should have public spirit. . . .

It is not indolence and routine, altogether, but also an inevitable conflict of claims, that makes men slow to exert their minds upon general questions, and underlies the political maxim that you cannot arouse public opinion, upon more than one matter at a time. It is better that the public, like the general-in-chief of an army, should be relieved of details and free to concentrate its thought on essential choices.'†

Finally, in all these proposals, Cooley showed himself much in agreement with many of the other basic teachings of earlier and contemporary sociologists. He agreed that the social development of the past had been to a large extent a matter of 'blind' genetic changes and unforeseen consequences, and that now man could not avoid responsibility for the conscious making of society. He believed that there had been, and was, a hopeful 'advance in the larger self-knowledge of mankind'. He believed that the secularization of the modern world did not endanger a firm basis for morality, and even for the continuity of a 'religious sentiment'.

'The most notable reaction of democracy upon religious sentiment is no doubt a tendency to secularize it, to fix it upon human life rather than upon a vague other world. So soon as men come to feel that society is not a machine, controlled chiefly by the powers of darkness, but an expression

* *Social Organization*, pp. 416–17.   † *Ibid.*, p. 128.

of human nature, capable of reflecting whatever good human nature can rise to; so soon, that is, as there comes to be a public will, the religious spirit is drawn into social idealism. Why dream of a world to come when there is hopeful activity in this?

. . . An ideal democracy is in its nature religious, and its true sovereign may be said to be the higher nature (or God) which it aspires to incarnate in human institutions.'*

And all these positions, as we have clearly seen, were those at the core of sociology from Comte to Ward, Hobhouse, Durkheim and Weber. Cooley, like all those before him, believed that the making of sociology was a necessary part of the political and educational task of making a humane society out of the many difficulties of industrial and urban change.

This development of the study of the 'psychological aspects of society', then, though at first glance of a smaller scale than the other sociological systems we have considered, fitted perfectly well within them, and, indeed, came to the same conclusions as they did—the same broad perspectives of judgment—in addition to making the specific contribution of analysing the relations between 'self' and 'society'.

* *Social Organization*, p. 205.

3
George Herbert Mead:
A Social Behaviourism

Mead was a contemporary of Cooley—born a year before him and dying two years after him—but his ideas and his work developed in a slow, considered, measured way, so that his contribution not only *seemed* to be, but actually was (in many respects) a critical, constructive development of that of Cooley. The excellence and significance of Mead's work tends, indeed, to be hidden by its very unpretentiousness; its quietness and brevity of statement. He claimed no originality. He wrote no large book—only a number of papers sprinkled among several journals. And yet—though small and succinct in bulk of expression—his over-all perspective of ideas was as large and inclusive in scope as those of all the sociologists we have considered; the continuity of all major strands of the nineteenth century 'conspectus' of sociology was plain to be seen in him; and, more important, his own emphases marked quite a distinctive contribution which linked the study of the 'psychological aspects of society' with the (apparently) larger-scale components of sociological analysis (social evolution, 'social facts', 'social action', structural-functional analysis etc;) in ways which were clearer, more telling, and more reliably based than have been accomplished, perhaps, by any other scholar.

Like Cooley—whose work he much admired—Mead was concerned to explore more satisfactorily the relationships between 'self' and 'society' and the 'socio-psychological' nature of 'mind'. Like him, his chief insistence was that the 'self' emerged within a context of 'association' and 'communication', and could not come into existence otherwise. But his own analysis of this process was highly distinctive and important in several ways. We will look briefly, first of all, at his continuities and agreements with other writers, since these are important for an appreciation of his entire position, and then concentrate upon his additions to the kind of social-psychological analysis outlined by Cooley.

Preliminary Points

(I) MEAD—A PHILOSOPHER

The first important quality of Mead's work was its clear philosophical competence—not only in terms of technical, logical precision, but also in terms of careful profundity. Mead was, in fact, a member of the department of philosophy—under the headship of John Dewey—at Chicago University (from 1894 until his death in 1931), but it was not the mere fact of being a philosopher that mattered so much as his range of awareness of the philosophical approaches of the time to the same kinds of problems that were being discussed by social scientists. In discussing evolution and social evolution he was well acquainted, for example, with the new ideas of Bergson (in his 'Creative Evolution'.) And—especially—in discussing the whole field of communication, including language, gesture, 'symbols', etc; he was very deeply acquainted with the ideas of A. N. Whitehead*: a philosopher now much in the shadows, but probably the greatest philosopher of our time. It is not well known (I think) that Whitehead wrote an excellent essay on 'Symbolism' which was very much in keeping with all this exploratory work on the relations between 'self' and 'society'.† But to put this point more broadly: Mead's engagement with these new problems in social science moved from the context of his firm grasp of philosophical problems proper—of epistemology, ethics, etc.—and also from his awareness of contemporary trends of philosophical thought. He shared the large perspective of thought of the other scholars we have discussed.

(II) THE CONTINUITY FROM COMTE AND MILL

Part of this large perspective was his clear knowledge of the important contributions in sociological thought proper from the first foundation statement of Comte. And this was of importance not only in itself (as signifying his sheer coverage of knowledge), but specifically because he saw the developments of Cooley's ideas and his own as straightforward continuities of Comte's own insights. In short, he saw quite clearly the great significance of Comte's emphasis upon the recognition of the 'social system' as the distinctively human level of mental creativity, and couched his own (and Cooley's) 'advancements' within this identical perspective; as parts of it. There was here, again, a quite conscious and deliberate 'development' of one dimension of the recognized and accepted 'conspectus' of the subject. And it was plain too, though we need not make much of this, that Mead was aware of Mill's logical critique of Comte, and, indeed, of other nineteenth century contributions.

* It is of interest to note that Radcliffe-Brown was also much influenced by Whitehead, though not, as it seems to me, to such significant effect as was the case in Mead.
† *Symbolism: Its Meaning and Effect*, Cambridge University Press, 1928. (These were the Barbour-Page Lectures at the University of Virginia, 1927).

Mead was in agreement with, and sympathetic to many aspects of Comte's systematic statement on the nature and elements of sociology, but here we will note only that agreement which was quite central for his own concern about the 'self' and 'society'. About Comte, he wrote:

'What was of importance was his emphasis on the dependence of the individual on society, his sense of the organic character of society as responsible for the nature of the individual. This is what Comte put into a scientific form . . .

. . . you must understand an individual in a society. Instead of thinking of society made up of different entities, Comte thought of it in terms of a union of all which was an expression of a certain social nature which determined the character of the individual. There are two characteristics of Comte: first, his recognition that society as such is a subject for study; and second, his conviction that we must advance from the study of society to the individual rather than from the individual to society.'*

Mead's continuity within the larger perspective of the making of sociology was completely clear. One other important dimension of this continuity was also, however, his acceptance of the 'evolutionary perspective' on a very basic and profound level.

(III) MEAD'S ACCEPTANCE OF THE 'EVOLUTIONARY PERSPECTIVE' FOR SOCIOLOGY AND SOCIAL PSYCHOLOGY

Several aspects of this were of quite basic significance both for appreciating Mead's position as such, and also for our understanding of the relationship between his thought and that of the earlier (and contemporary) writers.

First of all, whilst accepting Darwinian evolution in biology, Mead clearly went far beyond this in thinking of evolution as a concept and theory relating in the most fundamental way to the emergence, perpetuation, reproduction and dissolution of 'forms' in the world. In this his position was that of Herbert Spencer, but also it was rooted in many traditions of philosophy—both ancient and modern. In particular, Bergson and Whitehead were among the moderns. And there is a very important sense in which Whitehead represented a culmination in philosophy of that 'theory of forms' first clearly stated by Plato. But it was a Platonism vitalized by men like Hegel and Spinoza and Bergson and the whole changing fabric of ideas in physical and biological science during the nineteenth and twentieth centuries—the new perspective of conceiving 'reality' as essentially a

---

* *Movements of Thought in the Nineteenth Century.* See: *George Herbert Mead On Social Psychology*, University of Chicago Press, 1964, p. 292. Pt. VIII, Ch. 9, *Auguste Comte.*

continuous 'process' (hence the title of Whitehead's chief book). Mead's statement, though brief and simple, had very many dimensions.

The universe we know, he wrote, is:

'. . . more than particles. It is a world of forms. Now, the question is: Where do these forms come from? . . . What is the origin of these forms of things? . . .

Now the movement to which I am referring, under the term "theory of evolution", is one which undertakes to explain how the forms of things may arise . . .

We are concerned with a theory which involves a *process* as its fundamental fact, and then with this process as appearing in different *forms* . . .

The important thing about the doctrine of evolution is the recognition that the process takes now one form and now another, according to the conditions under which it is going on. That is the essential thing. One must be able to distinguish the process from the structure of the particular form, to regard the latter as being simply the organ within which a certain function takes place. If the conditions call for a certain type of organ, that organ must arise if the form is to survive. If conditions call for an organ of another sort, that other sort of organ must arise. That is what is involved in the evolutionary doctrine. The acceptance of the Darwinian hypothesis is simply the acceptance of Darwin's view that selection under the struggle for existence would pick out the organ which is necessary for survival. The heart of the problem of evolution is the recognition that the process will determine the form according to the conditions. If you look at the life-process as something which is essential in all forms, you can see that the outer structure which it takes on will depend upon the conditions under which this life-process runs on.'*

These short statements are taken from Mead's essay entitled 'Evolution Becomes a General Idea',* and are very clear indeed; but we must note also that Mead believed, like Spencer and others, that the evolutionary process at the level of *man*—involved the changing forms of *societies*. It was *social* evolution. Mead was quite plain about this:

'One more word about evolution. We have a statement of the human animal as having reached a situation in which he gets control over his environment. Now, it is not the human animal as an individual that reaches any such climax as that; it is society. This point is cogently insisted upon by Hegel, the last of the Romantic idealists. The human animal as an individual could never have attained control over the environment. It is a control which has arisen through social organization. The very speech he uses, the very mechanism of thought which is given, are social products.

* *Movements of Thought in the Nineteenth Century*. Ed. M. H. Moore, University of Chicago Press, 1936, pp. 153–168. See: *On Social Psychology*, pp. 15–16.

515

His own self is attained only through his taking the attitude of the social group to which he belongs. He must become socialized to become himself.'*

This, of course, is identical with the views of all the nineteenth century 'evolutionists' we have considered, and with those of Tönnies, Westermarck, Hobhouse, Durkheim and Weber. It is just as complete and all-embracing a perspective of 'evolution' as that of Spencer. But two other aspects of 'evolution' emphasized by Mead were important.

One was his clear insistence that *mind* was an aspect of *social* (not only biological) *evolution* in man. In this, his treatment was exactly that of Hobhouse, Ward and others.

'. . . Evolution,' he wrote, 'also takes place in human society, but here it takes place not through physiological plasticity, not through the development of peculiar physiological functions on the part of the separate individuals. It takes place through the development of what has been referred to on the logical side as a universe of discourse. That is, it takes place through communication and participation on the part of the different individuals in common activities. It takes place through the development of significant symbols . . .

What I want to make evident is that the development, the evolution, of mind as well as of institutions is a social evolution . . . Society in its organization is a form . . . that has developed; and it has many forms developing within it.'†

It was a matter of 'mind in evolution'—but with distinctively *social* processes—as everyone from Comte to Hobhouse had insisted.‡

Finally, we might note that Mead also agreed with the dimension of *progress* within the concept of evolution, as emphasized especially by Ward, Sumner, Giddings—but also, again, by almost all the men we have considered. We will mention the matter of 'ideals' later, but Mead's notion of 'progress' in social evolution and development was essentially the earlier notion of the improvement in technical and social skills in practical activities to further man's practical advantage, and took the form of an increasing differentiation of structure and function in society which made possible greater (in the

* *Movements of Thought in the Nineteenth Century*, pp. 17–18.
† *On Social Psychology*, pp. 36, 40–1.
‡ Again, it is a strange thing that a man like Hobhouse should be 'branded' as an 'evolutionist' and others like Mead should not—when they held identical views. This is one more example of a widespread agreement among scholars about the correctness of the 'evolutionary perspective' even though each of them selected a different emphasis of work within it.

sense of many-dimensioned) individual fulfilment. Mead wrote in this way:

'Ultimately and fundamentally societies develop in complexity of organization only by means of the progressive achievement of greater and greater degrees of functional, behaviouristic differentiation among the individuals who constitute them . . .

The human social ideal—the ideal or ultimate goal of human social progress—is the attainment of a universal human society in which all human individuals would possess a perfected social intelligence, such that all social meanings would each be similarly reflected in their respective individual consciousness . . .

The interlocking interdependence of human individuals upon one another within the given organized social life-process in which they are all involved is becoming more and more intricate and closely knit and highly organized as human social evolution proceeds on its course. The wide difference, for example, between the feudal civilization of medieval times, with its relatively loose and disintegrated social organization, and the national civilization of modern times, with its relatively tight and integrated social organization (together with its trend of development toward some form of international civilization), exhibits the constant evolution of human social organization in the direction of greater and greater relational unity and complexity, also more and more closely knit interlocking and integrated unification of all the social relations of interdependence which constitute it and which hold among the individuals involved in it.'*

The movement towards a global human society as envisaged by Kant, Comte, Spencer is so plainly evident in Mead's statement as to need no comment. Mead's continuity within the 'evolutionary perspective' is therefore clear beyond doubt.

(IV) CONTINUITY OF 'IDEALS'

We can also briefly note, simply to complete the last point, that Mead was in agreement about the 'ideals' to be attained in this gradually controlled pattern of social evolution, as well as about the 'factual' processes of change which were involved. There was continuity here, too. The achievement of a social order which would make possible the maximal fulfilment of individual lives in responsible, reciprocal relations with each other (what Hobhouse had depicted in terms of scale, efficiency, freedom and mutuality) was, he thought, a laudable 'ideal'.

'One can say that the attainment of that functional differentiation and social participation in the full degree is a sort of ideal which lies before the

* *Mind, Self and Society*, see: *On Social Psychology*, pp. 270–1.

human community. The present stage of it is presented in the ideal of democracy . . .'*

Democracy as it then existed, however, Mead thought very limited, and he wished to see it developed in terms of participation and the extension of shared communication so that all could be in the fullest, responsible and reciprocal relations with each other.

'As democracy now exists, there is not this development of communication so that individuals can put themselves into the attitudes of those whom they affect . . . The ideal of human society cannot exist as long as it is impossible for individuals to enter into the attitudes of those whom they are affecting in the performance of their own peculiar functions.'†

There was agreement about moral ideals, then, as well as perspectives of sociological analysis.

(V) UNIVERSAL BIO-PHYSIOLOGICAL ENDOWMENT; STRUCTURAL-FUNCTIONAL ANALYSIS; CONFLICT AND CO-OPERATION

A few other elements were also *assumed* rather than treated in Mead's analysis—but these, too, were sufficiently important to note.

Like McDougall and Cooley, like Westermarck and Hobhouse, Mead also believed that man—universally—possessed certain basic needs and impulses which carried with them certain social problems or situations (what Mill had called 'functional requisites'). These were, Mead wrote:

'. . . fundamental socio-physiological impulses or behaviour tendencies which are common to all human individuals, which lead those individuals collectively to enter or form themselves into organized societies or social communities, and which constitute the ultimate basis of those societies or social communities . . .'‡

Furthermore, Mead—exactly like McDougall—not only accepted the existence of such inherited bio-physiological needs, motives, and sources of human behaviour, but also specified them and insisted upon their essentially *social* nature. Here we see very definitely the rejection of the idea that the 'natural' and the 'social' can be clearly separated, and also the clear postulation of basic 'functional requisites' of human society—rooted in instinct. Mead wrote as follows in a footnote to his point that the physiological organism was an essential basis for the emergence of the 'self'—but not, of itself, sufficient.

* *On Social Psychology*, p. 280.　　　† *Ibid.*, p. 282.　　　‡ *Ibid.*, p. 264.

'(a) All social interrelations and interactions are rooted in a certain common socio-physiological endowment of every individual involved in them. These physiological bases of social behaviour—which have their ultimate seat or locus in the lower part of the individual's central nervous system—are the bases of such behaviour, precisely because they in themselves are also social; that is, because they consist in drives or instincts or behaviour tendencies, on the part of the given individual, which he cannot carry out or give overt expression and satisfaction to without the cooperative aid of one or more other individuals. The physiological processes of behaviour of which they are the mechanisms are processes which necessarily involve more than one individual, processes in which other individuals besides the given individual are perforce implicated. Examples of the fundamental social relations to which these physiological bases of social behaviour give rise are those between the sexes (expressing the reproductive instinct), between parent and child (expressing the parental instinct), and between neighbours (expressing the gregarious instinct). These relatively simple and rudimentary physiological mechanisms or tendencies of individual human behaviour, besides constituting the physiological bases of all human social behaviour, are also the fundamental biological materials of human nature; so that when we refer to human nature, we are referring to something which is essentially social.

(b) Sexually and parentally, as well as in its attacks and defences, the activities of the physiological organism are social in that the acts begun within the organism require their completion in the actions of others . . . But while the pattern of the individual act can be said to be in these cases social, it is only so insofar as the organism seeks for the stimuli in the attitudes and characters of other forms for the completion of its own responses, and by its behaviour tends to maintain the other as a part of its own environment. The actual behaviour of the other or the others is not initiated in the individual form as a part of its own pattern of behaviour.'*

This, unquestionably, is plain McDougall; agreed with, too, by Cooley; so that Mead's position on this was clear beyond doubt. But on the self-same basis he accepted the functional interconnectedness of the forms of social relationship which grew from these roots.

The institutions, the regularities of procedure, which developed about these basic 'behaviour tendencies' were functionally interconnected in their operation and could be sensibly described and analysed in this way. But, at the same time, Mead was quite explicit in his teaching that such functional interconnection did *not* simply consist of harmonious tendencies. It was *not* a matter of functional *harmony*; nor a functional *integration* of well-adjusted dispositions or 'mechanisms'.

'It is true,' he wrote, 'that the fundamental impulses or behaviour ten-

* *Mind, Self and Society*, see: *On Social Psychology*, pp. 203–4.

dencies . . . which are hostile or which make for hostility and antagonism among the individuals motivated by them . . . are "anti-social" insofar as they would, by themselves, be destructive of all human social organization or could not, alone, constitute the basis of any organized human society; yet in the broadest and strictest non-ethical sense, they are obviously no less social than are the former class of such impulses of behaviour tendencies. They are equally common to, or universal among, all human individuals, and, if anything, are more easily and immediately aroused by the appropriate social stimuli; and as combined or fused with, and in a sense controlled by, the former impulses or behaviour tendencies, they are just as basic to all human social organization as are the former and play a hardly less necessary and significant part in that social organization itself and in the determination of its general character.'*

Mead went on to give examples of how 'hostile' impulses and attitudes among 'sub-groups' within a society or between societies as wholes were accommodated by law and institutional regulations in such ways as to both *contain* conflict and to *provide* for it in the entire relational framework of the social order. In short the recognition of common human impulses and of a structural-functional analysis of social institutions did not at all lead him into any postulate of some kind of 'functional harmony' which would make the explanation of change difficult. Like all the earlier writers, he saw both *conflict* and *co-operation* in society, and the order of institutions as coming into being to grapple with both. Here again, then, there was continuity of conception.

(VI) A CRITICAL CONTINUITY OF COOLEY

Finally, we can note Mead's own direct acknowledgement of the fact that he was continuing to develop—though critically—the concepts of Cooley. Having made certain criticisms of Cooley's ideas (which we shall come to in a moment) as points which his own treatment tried to rectify, he nonetheless ended his appreciation of Cooley's contribution in this way:

'But I am unwilling to conclude a discussion of Cooley's social psychology upon a note of criticism. His successful establishment of the self and the others upon the same plane of reality in experience, and his impressive study of society as the outgrowth of the association and co-operation of the primary group in its face-to-face organization, are positive accomplishments for which we are profoundly indebted to his insight and constructive thought.'†

* *On Social Psychology*, p. 265.
† 'Cooley's Contribution to American Social Thought', *American Journal of Sociology*, XXXV, No. 5, pp. 693–706.

The work of Cooley and Mead on the 'psychological aspects of society' can thus quite properly be regarded as *one* body of analysis.*

Mead's Analysis of 'Self' and 'Society'

(I) BASIC AGREEMENT WITH COOLEY

Mead began his own analysis from a fundamental acceptance of the correctness of Cooley's conception of the relation between 'self' and 'society'. He agreed with the demolition of the distinction between them. He regarded them as aspects of the same socio-psychological process; and he agreed that the processes of 'association' and 'communication' were an essential creative context for the emergence of the 'self'. He agreed that it was a mistake to think of the 'locus' of 'mind' as being within the individual. He agreed also that it was the processes of experience and behaviour in primary groups which were of crucial importance for the establishment of the nature of the 'self', and, like Cooley, he analysed especially the behaviour of the child in the family, play-groups, and neighbourhood groups, and it was the mental and behavioural processes of *play* which he thought particularly revealing.

Mead wrote quite unmistakably about these matters.

'Our contention,' he wrote, 'is that mind can never find expression, and could never have come into existence at all, except in terms of a social environment; that an organized set or pattern of social relations and interactions (especially those of communication by means of gestures functioning as significant symbols and thus creating a universe of discourse) is necessarily presupposed by it and involved in its nature. And this entirely social theory or interpretation of mind—this contention that mind develops and has its being only in and by virtue of the social process of experience and activity, which it hence presupposes, and that in no other way can it develop and have its being—must be clearly distinguished from the partially (but only partially) social view of mind.'†

It is worthwhile to note, too, his very clear and definite statement *rejecting* any notion of the individual mind as a 'given entity' independent of social relations, and *rejecting* any notion that a 'mind' was bounded by a 'skin'. Whether one agrees with his position or not, nothing could be more clear and definite than Mead's statement of it.

---

* The ideas of W. I. Thomas, Park, Burgess, Faris, and other sociologists of the time were of a very similar nature. It is not possible to look at more than the central, representative figures in these movements of thought, but this is enough to indicate the very close relationship between psychology and sociology in the making of sociology in America.

† *On Social Psychology*, pp. 242–3.

'In defending a social theory of mind we are defending a functional, as opposed to any form of substantive or entitive, view as to its nature. And in particular, we are opposing all intracranial or intra-epidermal views as to its character and locus. For it follows from our social theory of mind that the field of mind must be co-extensive with, and include all the components of, the field of the social process of experience and behaviour, that is, the matrix of social relations and interactions among individuals, which is presupposed by it and out of which it arises or comes into being. If mind is socially constituted, then the field or locus of any given individual mind must extend as far as the social activity or apparatus of social relations which constitutes it extends; and hence that field cannot be bounded by the skin of the individual organism to which it belongs.'*

The advantage of the 'social theory of mind', Mead argued, was that it did make possible a detailed and explanatory account of the origin and development of mind—which no other theory had been able to provide.†

Again, Mead wrote:

'The self, as that which can be an object to itself, is essentially a social structure, and it arises in social experience. After a self has arisen, it in a certain sense provides for itself its social experiences, and so we can conceive of an absolutely solitary self. But it is impossible to conceive of a self arising outside of social experience.'‡

Mead went on to analyse the way in which any individual developed different 'selves' in relation to different people and different social situations, so that a 'total self' contained within it a multiplicity of all these 'partial selves' that had been engendered by different circumstances, but then he still argued that the total 'self' was, in a thorough-going way, a 'reflection' of all its social situations.

'The unity and structure of the complete self reflects the unity and structure of the social process as a whole; and each of the elementary selves of which it is composed reflects the unity and structure of one of the various aspects of that process in which the individual is implicated. In other words, the various elementary selves which constitute, or are organized into, a complete self answering to the various aspects of the structure of

---

* *On Social Psychology*, p. 243.

† Whether the human 'self' ('mind', 'psyche', 'soul') is an entity at a level deeper than that of the flux of temporal biological and social events and relationships (together with the ideas and idealities which arise within them) is, of course, one of the most fundamental questions in the world. One should accept no position at all on this question, no matter how plausible, without the most searching thought. But, whatever else may lie in this issue, the position of Cooley and Mead certainly allows the explanation of much.

‡ *On Social Psychology*, p. 204.

the social process as a whole; the structure of the complete self is thus a reflection of the complete social process. The organization and unification of a social group is identical with the organization and unification of any one of the selves arising within the social process in which that group is engaged or which it is carrying on.'*

It is quite plain from all this, then, that there was a firm bed-rock of agreement between Cooley and Mead; but it was the *difference* which Mead felt between them which—though seeming very slight— led to very distinctive advances.

(II) DIFFERENCES: THE 'SELF' AS AN 'OBJECT' IN INDIVIDUAL CONSCIOUSNESS. THE 'I' AND THE 'ME'. THE 'GENERALIZED OTHER'.

Mead attached the same importance as Cooley to 'sentiment' and 'attitude' formation, but one criticism he had was that Cooley—in his discussion of 'communications' and the social-mental complex of which the emergence of the 'self' was a part—tended to focus chiefly (and too much) on 'subjective' aspects of inter-change; on the subjective 'imaginations', or 'looking-glass images' which individuals came to have of each other. It was not at all that Mead wished to deny such subjective dimensions, but that he felt the growth of awareness of 'the self' included an 'objective' element which had its roots in more 'objective' elements in the actuality of social behaviour than Cooley had properly emphasized.

First, let us think only of the growth of the 'self' as such in Mead's terms.

His basic insistence was that the growth of the 'self' in the processes of association—indeed, the very recognition (in the individual's consciousness) of an 'order' of the external world and society, and a

---

* *On Social Psychology*, p. 208. The extremely interesting corollary of this point was that it provided a clear analytical basis for a possible *social* explanation of mental disorders. Mead wrote (p. 209):

'The phenomenon of *dissociation of personality* is caused by a breaking up of the complete, unitary self into the component selves of which it is composed, and which respectively correspond to different aspects of the social process in which the person is involved, and within which his complete or unitary self has arisen; these aspects being the different social groups to which he belongs within that process.'

This is an extremely important point which psychiatry and psycho-analysis should fully consider, and we shall be reminded of it when we come to consider Freud. The entire question of the aetiology of mental disorders rests very much on whether one adopts this 'social theory of mind' or one which sees 'mind' as chiefly a matter of bio-physiological processes. Of course, aspects of the two might well be combined.

continued 'order' of the 'self'—required the recognition within the individual of the 'self' as an 'object'. And when one says 'required', Mead's meaning was that *without this* 'self-consciousness' would simply not exist. At least part of the awareness of 'self' was the consciousness of the 'self' as an order of experience and action within the order of nature and society.

'The individual enters *as such* into his own experience,' Mead wrote, 'as an object, not as a subject; and he can enter as an object only on the basis of social relations and interactions, only by means of his experiential trans- actions with other individuals in an organized social environment. It is true that certain contents of experience . . . are accessible only to the given individual organism and not to any others; and that these private or "subjective", as opposed to public or "objective", contents of experience are usually regarded as being peculiarly and intimately connected with the individual's self, or as being in a special sense self-experiences. But . . . existence of private or "subjective" contents of experience does not alter the fact that self-consciousness involves the individual's becoming an object to himself by taking the attitudes of other individuals toward himself within an organized setting of social relationships, and that unless the individual had thus become an object to himself he would not be self- conscious or have a self at all . . .
In order to become aware of himself *as such* he must . . . become an object to himself, or enter his own experience as an object, and only by social means—only by taking the attitudes of others toward himself—is he able to become an object to himself.'*

In the above passage the word 'transactions' may be noted, because Mead, as we shall see, laid specific and fundamental emphasis upon *actions* in human communication. But here, for a while we must still concentrate on the 'self' alone. Mead's next suggestion, following upon his insistence upon the recognition of the self as an 'object', was the conceptual distinction (within the self) of the 'I' and the 'Me', and this is extremely interesting as it has very significant parallels with Freud's thinking.

Mead argued that the becoming aware of the 'self' as an object involved a certain differentiation *within* the 'self'. It involved, on the one hand the laying down of 'memories', of stored 'records' of the judgments, expectations, evaluations of others within particular social situations. This 'deposit' of memories—which was really an 'objective' picture of the qualities of the 'self' formulated by the reflection of 'others'—was the 'Me' of which the immediate self- consciousness of the individual (the 'I') was aware, and which formed a basic 'datum' (so to speak) in its assumptions, calculations, actions,

* *On Social Psychology*, p. 244.

just as did its pictures of the world and of society. The 'I' was the immediately conscious awareness of the 'self' in its moment-by-moment action, judgment and calculation; the 'Me' were those qualities of the 'self' which had been established as a set of actual qualities, and which were objective facts continuously borne in upon the judgments of the 'I'.

The 'I' and the 'Me', Mead insisted, were different 'phases' of the self. The 'Me' was the basic 'structure' of the self, which was conventional, and which 'answered to the organized attitudes of others . . .' the 'I' was the active, calculating consciousness of the momentary situation, and responsible for 'novelty' in the continuous change in the total 'self'.

'Social control,' Mead wrote, 'is the expression of the "me" against the expression of the "I". It sets the limits, it gives the determination that enables the "I", so to speak, to use the "me" as the means of carrying out . . . the undertaking that all are interested in . . .'*

Mead was especially concerned to emphasize that he did not regard this distinction between the 'I' and the 'Me' as *purely* a conceptual device; he believed the distinction actually existed within the essential nature of the human 'self'.

'The separation of the "I" and the "me" is not fictitious. They are not identical, for, as I have said, the "I" is something that is never entirely calculable. The "me" does call for a certain sort of an "I" insofar as we meet the obligations that are given in conduct itself, but the "I" is always something different from that the situation itself calls for. So there is always that distinction, if you like, between the "I" and the "me". The "I" both calls out the "me" and responds to it. Taken together they constitute a personality as it appears in social experience. The self is essentially a social process going on with these two distinguishable phases. If it did not have these two phases, there could not be conscious responsibility and there would be nothing novel in experience.'†

This last passage is of very great importance in making plain two things. First—of the most vital importance—Mead did *not* regard the 'self' (including the 'I' and the 'Me') as being *determined* by society, even though he maintained a 'social theory of mind'. Human 'selves', in association, in communication, were part of a psychologically *creative* process. Certainly, each 'self' assumed its shape by becoming aware of the judgments of others ('reflecting', 'incorporating' society)—but all this in an on-going creative process within which the 'I' was always *more* than either the established 'me' *and*

* *On Social Psychology*, pp. 238–9.   † *Ibid.*, p. 233.

the new situation, and capable of *novelty*; of creative change. 'Selves' made them-'selves' within their constraining social contexts; and, as with any other art, the master was one who could make what he most desired out of the limited materials he found at his disposal.

The second point of equal importance was that Mead clearly recognized in this 'making of the self' the dimension of *responsibility*. Human persons *were* responsible in their making of themselves; in their control of social conduct; in their conduct towards others, and their considered response to the conduct of others. And individuals could not possibly *be* responsible in these ways unless there existed in them *both* a knowledge of the qualities of themselves as 'objects' *and* the conscious ability to govern and change these qualities in the context of new situations.

We shall stress the full implications of these points later, but we can see now that there was no naïve 'determinism' here. We shall come later, too, to Mead's notion of the 'Generalized Other'—but we can note now that, for him, the 'Me' in the 'self', and especially with the growth of the self in creative experience, did not remain a kind of bundle of primitive deposits of the judgments of others, but could become a clear apprehension of *all* the others involved in any *total institutional situation* within which the individual had to act. It could become an articulate and 'abstract' content of 'Me'—a 'Generalized Other' with which the 'I' was, so to speak, in continuous creative dialogue as situation followed situation in experience.

However, having distinguished this 'objective' element in the 'self'; having seen its indispensability for the growth of responsible self-control, social action, and innovation; Mead went on to make other connected and implied points.

(III) THE 'SELF': THE IMPORTANCE OF ATTENTION AND COGNITION

The crucial distinction of Mead's conception was his emphasis upon social *action*; the *behavioural* elements involved in communications; and we shall only properly understand his conception of symbols, language and gesture when we come to that; but—meanwhile—we must note one other point which he made in following up this matter of 'objectivity' in the 'self'.

This was not, strictly speaking, a marked *difference* between himself and Cooley and McDougall, but, even so, it was a consistent emphasis clearly made in his own conceptualization.

The distinctive elements in the psychological processes involved in the emergence of the 'self', he argued, were *not* feeling states (impulse or emotion) as such, *nor* the 'association of states of mind' (or of sensations) as the earlier philosophical notions had it. These were no doubt involved, but the *crucial* elements were (*a*) selective attention, and therefore, essentially, (*b*) *cognition*. Mead was quite definite on these points.

'The psychology of *attention* ousted the psychology of *association*,' he wrote. And:
'The essence of the self . . . is cognitive.'

No understanding of 'associationism' as such could explain *which* elements out of the entire field of conscious awareness, of stimulation, were *selected*, and why. Whereas the very business of *communications*—by gesture, language, or other form of symbolization—was to *call attention* to some aspects of experience rather than others, and to *recognize*, and *securely* and *repeatedly* recognize, certain elements of experience as being significantly differentiated from all the rest.

'Man,' Mead wrote, 'is distinguished by that power of analysis of the field of stimulation which enables him to pick one stimulus rather than another and so to hold on to the response that belongs to that stimulus, picking it out from the others, and recombining it with others. Man can combine not only the responses already there . . . but . . . can get into his activities and break them up, giving attention to specific elements, holding the responses that answer to these particular stimuli, and then combining them to build up another act. That is what we mean by learning or by teaching a person to do a thing. You indicate to him certain specific phases or characters of the object which call out certain sorts of responses . .
One can say to a person, "Look at this, just see this thing"; and he can fasten his attention on the specific object. He can direct attention and so isolate the particular response that answers to it. That is the way in which we break up our complex activities and thereby make learning possible. What takes place is an analysis of the process by giving attention to the specific stimuli that call out a particular act, and this analysis makes possible a reconstruction of the act. An animal makes combinations, as we say, only by trial and error, and the combination that is successful simply maintains itself.
The gesture as worked out in the conduct of the human group serves definitely to indicate just these elements and thus to bring them within the field of voluntary attention.'*

Elsewhere, he distinguished between the learning ability of animals and man by this capacity for the use of symbols:

'It is that, I think, which characterizes our human intelligence to a peculiar degree. We have a set of symbols by means of which we indicate certain

* *On Social Psychology*, pp. 172–3.

527

characters, and in indicating those characters hold them apart from their immediate environment, and keep simply one relationship clear . . . The ability to isolate these important characters in their relationship to the object and to the response which belongs to the object is, I think, what we generally mean when we speak of a human being thinking a thing out, or having a mind. Such ability makes the world-wide difference between the conditioning of reflexes in the case of the white rat and the human process of thinking by means of symbols.

What is there in conduct that makes this level of experience possible, this selection of certain characters with their relationship to other characters and to the responses which these call out? My own answer, it is clear, is in terms of such a set of symbols as arise in our social conduct, in the conversation of gestures—in terms of language. When we get into conduct these symbols, which indicate certain characters and their relationship to things and to responses, they enable us to pick out these characters and hold them insofar as they determine our conduct . . .

These symbols, instead of being a mere conditioning of reflexes, are ways of picking out the stimuli so that the various responses can organize themselves into a form of action.'*

It will immediately be seen that this was exactly Hobhouse's account of the essentially '*correlating*' activity of mind, and the distinction between differing *levels of correlation*: here, especially, the crucial distinction between the '*conceptual*' and '*ideational*' level of the human mind and the '*perceptual*' levels of other animal (and some human) intelligence. And Mead went on to discuss the *guiding* of attention and cognition in communications by *attitudes*. The processes of association and communication within which the 'self' took shape were essentially such a selective '*mapping out*' of behaviour and experience. The social context of attitudes, in this selective sense, '*determined the environment*' of the 'self'.

'Our world is definitely mapped out for us by the responses which are going to take place.'

And the various 'symbols' in the many-dimensioned language of communications lay at the heart of this cognitive process.

'The essence of the self, as we have said, is *cognitive*. It lies in the internalized conversation of gestures which constitutes thinking or in terms of which thought or reflection proceeds. And hence the origin and foundations of the self, like those of thinking, are *social*.'†

Now all this, as we noted earlier, was not really different from the other writers. Certainly McDougall made cognition a central aspect of sentiment and attitude formation (in relation to instinct

* *On Social Psychology*, pp. 183–4. † *Ibid.*, p. 228.

and emotion), and Cooley, too, recognized it in all his discussion of communications. But the significance of this emphasis for Mead himself can be seen fully as we come to his essential emphasis upon social '*Behaviourism*'—and this is the most important aspect of his work.

(IV) SOCIAL BEHAVIOURISM: MIND AND COMMUNICATION IN RELATION TO 'ACTION'. THE 'ACT', THE 'ROLE'. AN ACCEPTABLE BEHAVIOURISM

In this section we must move very carefully, for very important distinctions lay in this aspect of Mead's ideas; distinctions which linked the study of the 'psychological aspects of society' with the larger analysis of social institutions in the most decisive, correct, and reliable way. I shall claim, in this discussion, that Mead successfully outlined the only justifiable form of 'Behaviourism' that has ever been stated, and, furthermore, that it is, in fact, a *necessary* behaviourism which makes completely valid the linking of psychology and sociology in social psychology. We must move very deliberately, step by step.

Let us note again, first of all, Mead's dissatisfaction with what he called Cooley's 'subjectivism'.

'For a social psychology like Cooley's,' he wrote, 'all social interactions depend upon the imaginations of the individuals involved, and take place in terms of their direct conscious influences upon one another in the processes of social experience. Cooley's social psychology . . . is hence inevitably introspective . . . society really has no existence except in the individual's mind, and the concept of the self as in any sense intrinsically social is a product of imagination. Even for Cooley the self presupposes experience, and experience is a process within which selves arise; but since that process is for him primarily internal and individual rather than external and social, he is committed in his psychology to a subjectivistic and idealistic, rather than an objectivistic and naturalistic, metaphysical position.'*

We have seen how Mead then went on to emphasize the 'objective' element in the 'self' and the primacy of *cognition* and *attention* in the process of its emergence. What now was that element in human association and communication which provided this more 'objective' point of reference? It was, Mead insisted, the *act*. Like many of the earlier sociologists it was the *activities* of men in society on which he placed crucial emphasis. In this, Mead regarded all the symbols of

* *On Social Psychology*, p. 244.

529

human communication with the same *pragmatism* as they. Let us see carefully the steps in his argument.

'Our primary adjustment to an environment,' he wrote, 'lies in the act which determines the relation between the individual and the environment. An act is an ongoing event that consists of stimulation and response and the results of the response. Back of these lie the attitudes and impulses of the individual which are responsible for his sensitiveness to the particular stimulus and for the adequacy of the response.'*

In human association *action* was primary; an actual sequence of *behaviour*; and Mead argued that communications were *indications for action*. The *meaning* of symbols in communication lay in the expectation of specific *responses* in *reciprocal conduct*.

'The outstanding characteristic in human communication,' he wrote, 'is that one is making a declaration, pointing out something that is common in meaning to the whole group and to the invididual, so that the individual is taking the attitude of the whole group, so far as there is any definite meaning given. When a man calls out "Fire"! he is not only exciting other people but himself in the same fashion. He knows what he is about . . . The individual is directing other people how to *act*, and he is taking the attitude of the other people whom he is directing.'†

Now the fundamental nature of human communication, Mead insisted, *was itself behavioural*. Basically, it was *gesture* indicative of meaning for expectations of action. Motions of head, hands and body, expressions of face and tones of voice . . . these *were* elements of *behaviour*: analytical, directing *attention*, enforcing *cognition*. But language was also, in itself, an extremely subtle extension of gesture. *Words*, said Mead, '. . . are gestures by means of which we indicate things . . .' Words were 'vocal gestures', and a language embodied the entire cumulative body of knowledge and meaning of a people which provided the social context for the emergence of the 'self' and accomplished 'the organization of *the act* in terms of attitudes'. Language, said Mead, is that part of social behaviour which gives us 'control over the organization of the act'. Let us see exactly how Mead saw this context for the emergence of the self as being not only one of association and communication, but essentially as one of *action*.

'The essential condition for the appearance of what has been conceived of as mind is that the individual in acting with reference to the environment should, as part of that action, be acting with reference to himself, so that

* *On Social Psychology*, p. 92.   † *Ibid.*, p. 38.

his action would include himself as an object. This does not mean that the individual should simply act with reference to parts of his organism, even when that action is social, but it does mean that the whole action toward the object upon which attention is centred includes as a part of this action a reaction toward the individual himself. If this is attained, the self as an object becomes a part of the acting individual, that is, the individual has attained what is called self-consciousness—a self-consciousness that accompanies his conduct . . .'*

But it is important now, before going further, to be perfectly clear about the term 'Behaviourism'. There are two conceptions of behaviourism in general usage—one very extreme, the other relatively unexceptionable.

The extreme view was that put forward initially by J. B. Watson which asserted, completely and dogmatically, that psychology could be concerned *only* with the study of *behaviour* and its physical attributes, since these were all that could be *observed*. Science was concerned only with what was *observable*, and therefore it was 'mediaeval occultism' to maintain that men *thought, felt*, or had *experiences*. The subject-matter of psychology was *behaviour*, and it could only be explained in terms of basic elements of behaviour—'reflexes'—and the ways in which they were 'conditioned'.

The second, unexceptionable view was simply that all psychological hypotheses (even about elements of *experience*) should be submitted to test, and since physiological process and sequences of behaviour were alone accessible to observation, hypotheses should be framed as far as possible in these terms. Thus, even Freud, for example, was continuously trying to make his theories about the nature of the 'psyche' and 'mental mechanisms' approximate to parallel theories at the level of biology and neuro-physiology.

The first of these conceptions is completely superficial and bankrupt; the second may be entertained to a point; but we need not go into the pro's and cons of the arguments on these matters because the important thing is to see that Mead presented a third kind of behaviourism that was quite different, that is not commonly distinguished from the others, and that completely escaped the absurdities of Watson's position in particular.

Mead himself quite flatly rejected Watson's conception as being untenable, and showed that no sequence of *behaviour*, as such, could possibly be explained on Watson's premises. To explain conscious *action* as such took us completely beyond any 'direct observation' of physiological mechanisms; and, indeed, beyond direct observation

* *The Philosophy of the Act*, see: *On Social Psychology*, p. 95.

531

altogether. Watson's position, he argued, led to 'obvious absurdities'.

Mead's 'Behaviourism' did not at all deny, or refuse (or fail) to analyse the *experiences* of mind (of impulse, emotion, attention, cognition, meaning, thought, etc.) in the 'self'—on the contrary it very fully acknowledged them. What it did was to *understand* this experience, and this growth of the 'self', as being derived from *communication in the context of action.* And this included the entirety of the objectively given fabric of language and symbols in society; and, indeed—and this is the crucial point—it took full cognizance of the *existence* of a *system of social action* within which any human being came to be the person he was. In this way social psychology was fully linked with sociological analysis: sharing the same framework of reference, and working from the same observable institutional pattern of conduct in society. Mead's statement about this was of the utmost importance. Rejecting both Watson's extremes on the one hand, and purely subjective introspection on the other, Mead wrote:

'We want to approach language, not from the standpoint of inner meanings to be expressed, but in its larger context of co-operation in the group taking place by means of signals and gestures. Meaning appears within that process. Our behaviourism is a social behaviourism.'

And then, in this statement, Mead made perfectly clear his full conception of the 'social context' for the understanding of the psychological aspects of society and the individual 'self'.

'We are not,' he wrote, 'in social psychology, building up the behaviour of the social group in terms of the behaviour of the separate individuals composing it; rather, we are starting out with a given social whole of complex group activity, into which we analyse (as elements) the behaviour of each of the separate individuals composing it. We attempt, that is, to explain the conduct of the individual in terms of the organized conduct of the social group, rather than to account for the organized conduct of the social group in terms of the conduct of the separate individuals belonging to it. For social psychology, the whole (society) is prior to the part (the individual), not the part to the whole; and the part is explained in terms of the whole, not the whole in terms of the part or parts. The social act is not explained by building it up out of stimulus plus response; it must be taken as a dynamic whole—as something going on—no part of which can be considered or understood by itself—a complex organic process implied by each individual stimulus and response involved in it.

In social psychology we get at the social process from the inside as well as from the outside. Social psychology is behaviouristic in the sense of starting off with an observable activity—the dynamic, ongoing social process and the social acts which are its component elements—to be studied and analysed scientifically. But it is not behaviouristic in the sense of ignoring the inner experience of the individual—the inner phase of that process or activity. On the contrary, it is particularly concerned with the rise of such experience within the process as a whole. It simply works from the outside to the inside instead of from the inside to the outside, so to speak, in its endeavour to determine how such experience does arise within the process. *The act*, then, and not the tract, is the fundamental datum in both social and individual psychology when behaviouristically conceived, and it has both an inner and an outer phase, an internal and an external aspect.'*

This is a remarkable and a remarkably clear statement, and one aspect of it to which I would like to draw attention very strongly is its very close approximation to Weber's conception of the distinctive subject-matter of sociology: namely *social action*. This is even more marked if one considers Mead's own supplementary definition of a 'social act' in his article on *The Genesis of the Self and Social Control*. There he wrote:

'I wish to restrict the social act to the class of acts which involve the co-operation of more than one individual, and whose object as defined by the act . . . is a social object. I mean by a social object one that answers to all the parts of the complex act, though these parts are found in the conduct of different individuals. The objective of the acts is then found in the life-process of the group, not in those of the separate individuals alone.'†

I want in a moment to consider the significance of Mead's ideas for the important linking up of the ideas of others, but before that, to complete our picture of his analysis, we should mention the *sequence* of the growth of the 'self' during childhood, since this clarifies his conceptions further, and also will be seen to be of interest in relation to Freud.

This *sequence* can best be brought out in the clear distinction Mead brought out between 'play' and 'games' in the child's experience, and it was in this that his concept of the 'generalized other' was made most clear.

In the early *play* experience of the child, when the awareness of the judgments of others were becoming established in the child's consciousness (memories were being laid down), but before the 'reflexive' unity of the 'self' has emerged, the child will assume— one after the other—a multiplicity of roles; addressing himself as one or the other; *being* one after the other as response follows upon

* *Mind, Self and Society*, see: *On Social Psychology*, pp. 120, 121.
† *Ibid.*, p. 121 (Footnote).

response. He is a kind of 'theatre' of roles; he carries on a multiple conversation in fancy within himself between one role and another. At a later stage, however, the child plays *games*. Here, the game has definite rules, a definite order, in which the acts of all who play affects the behaviour of the others. In this situation the child has *actually* to fulfil *one role*, and in his awareness of himself and the situation, he has to have a consciousness of the *others* in their own situation with regard to him.* By the 'generalized other'—Mead simply meant this systematic awareness of the whole formal *order* comprising all the 'others' in a total game (or, later, institutional) situation.

The 'self' grew then in this gradual way from an experience of the many 'acts' and 'roles' found in the environment of social relationships, to a reflective order of these in the 'self'—but an order which still held the possibility of the creative change of the 'me' by the 'I' throughout experience.

There is one final point in all this which deserves emphasis: the focus upon the '*act*' or the '*role*' as the basic element of association and communication about which gestures, language, evaluations arose, and about which sentiments and attitudes were found. The introduction of the concept of 'role' into sociological analysis has been attributed to many people. Some credit Linton, some Kardiner, some others with the novelty; but it is evident that it existed quite clearly in the analysis of Giddings in particular and was certainly very fully emphasized in this 'behavioural' analysis of Mead's. '*Role-analysis*', the analysis of patterns of '*action*', for the understanding and explanation of the psychological aspects of 'self' and 'society' was clearly founded.

In this way, then, Mead amended Cooley (and McDougall) by his addition of this system of 'Social Behaviourism', but, as we have seen, this was not at all a behaviourism which abandoned all study of subjective experiences. On the contrary, it was one which secured a more systematic analysis of such experience (individual-social) by relating it to the relevant context of social action and the communications arising within it.

(v) THE SIGNIFICANCE OF MEAD IN RELATION TO OTHER WRITERS AND OTHER ELEMENTS OF SOCIOLOGY

The advance which Mead accomplished in fully linking this sociopsychological analysis with the systematic study of social action is

---

* 'The game has a logic', wrote Mead, 'so that such an organization of the self is rendered possible'.

now quite plain—as is the clear development of this 'dimension' of the nineteenth century' 'conspectus': from Ward and Giddings to Cooley, and from Cooley to Mead. But what is so important—indeed, exciting—here, is to see the way in which this development was so linked with the other 'dimensions' (the other 'building blocks') of sociology as to fill out, consistently and very satisfactorily, the entire system of sociological analysis. There are several aspects of this, each of which deserves to be noted separately.

First of all, Mead (with the basis of Cooley) developed a detailed psychological analysis of 'self-and-social' processes which was firmly grounded (and in the most *living* way *inter-meshed*, so to speak) in the context of the *practical activities* of men in their associations and communications which had been the basis of the analysis of the origin, interconnectedness and development of institutionalization among all the earlier writers. Though very specific in its concentration upon the socially engendered experience and 'selves' of *individuals*, it could thus be firmly and reliably placed within, and was plainly relevant to, the large-scale analysis of Comte, Spencer, Marx and others. The psychological link with these larger theories of society at the institutional level had been forged. The psychological dimensions of these patterns of institutional order and change could now be systematically explored. The conceptual and analytical framework for what Mill had envisaged as the 'middle-principles' of social psychology and the psychology of personality and *character* (his 'Ethology') had now been clearly constructed. All the dimensions of man in society—from the person to the most vast pattern of institutional order and change—were now encompassed within the same network of concepts, the same conspectus of analysis. This was a far more tremendous achievement and advance than Mead's quiet statement claimed, and than—in general—was noticed.

But second: there were many specific corollaries of this which were of the greatest importance. Here, we can mention the most immediately prominent. First—Cooley and Mead together had provided that very *social context* for the making of a satisfactory human psychology which Marx (most dogmatically), but all others too, had moaned the lack of. They had, in short, circumvented what we called the *'error of psychology'*; and had not only clearly seen the necessity of, but had actually constructed a psychology of 'human nature' which could satisfactorily and richly take into account and explore all the *distinctive* dimensions and qualities of man which were inseparable from social behaviour and experience. Second: their system completely avoided any naïve 'determinism' such as any simple application of 'natural science' concepts to the study of man might be guilty of. There was no 'automatic' internalization of separately existing 'social roles' in any simple-minded way. Individual 'selves' were active, creative persons in continuous social communication with others, and the 'I' was perpetually creative, judging, calculating, ingenious in meeting new situations calling for appropriately new action. In short, Cooley and Mead fully took into account those elements of choice, deliberation, purpose—the distinctive 'teleological' characteristics of human beings—in their psychology, and, as another aspect of this, this position therefore fitted with thorough agreement into the theories concerning the active innovations in social change which Comte, Mill, Spencer, Marx, Ward, Sumner, Giddings, and the twentieth century writers had all (in one way or another) put forward. It also perfectly well accommodated, indeed specifically included, an understanding of sources of *willed conflict* in social processes, as well as desired co-operation: again providing for the understanding of many kinds of disruption and change as well as order. And the third point very much worth noting in this is that Mead's conception of the *behavioural* context of human experience (for individual and groups in social communication) was essentially one of *action* (as the earlier writers had distinguished it) *not* one of determined *events* (common with the events of nature). But this deserves more attention in a moment in relation to Weber in particular. One other—fourth—point which should be noted here, however, is that Mead's analysis of the *acts* and *roles* in patterned and institutionalized behaviour, together with the analysis of gesture, language, and symbol in the social communication essentially connected with them, and the analysis of the experience of individual *persons* in these terms, provided a completely clear way in which even the largest entirety of institutional 'structures' (a system of government, a religious system, an educational system, the organization of a large industry or a particular 'firm', etc.) could be analytically 'broken down' into the limited, specific elements of behaviour which entered into the personal experience of, and were undertaken by, *individuals*. A conceptual framework for the completely clear and manageable analysis of *society* in terms which could also bring us to the closest understanding of *individuals* had been provided. Again—a tremendous achievement. It was perfectly clear in this how the analysis of '*roles*' could be the effective link between the analysis of organizational structures in society on the one hand and of the nature and context of the experience and behaviour of individuals on the other.

A third major point is that—though being as specific as anyone could possibly be in their concentration upon their own chosen 'dimension'—Cooley and Mead clearly showed the relevance of their socio-psychological analysis to the understanding and explanation of the *development* and *evolution* of *mind in society*. With no obscurity whatever, they showed that 'mind' was *not* something that could be understood in individual terms, but was concomitant with association and communication, and therefore cumulatively changed with changing environmental and social conditions. In short, this socio-psychological analysis fitted completely with the large-scale theories of social evolution and the evolution of mind offered by all the theorists in their own way—from Comte to Hobhouse. There was *not* the dichotomy between large perspectives of social-mental evolution and small-scale studies of individual 'selves' which is frequently supposed. This dichotomy *never existed*. But the linking up of these several positions is even more interesting when we consider particular theorists. Let us again be rather tenaciously methodical in order to make clear many connections.

First—we have seen a completely clear and close link between McDougall on the one hand, and Cooley and Mead on the other, who are commonly thought of as being quite separate, and, indeed, between British and American social psychology. Because 'Behaviourism' was thought of very narrowly in Watsonian terms, and was largely an attack on 'instinct theory', and because McDougall was wrongly thought to be only an 'instinct theorist'—McDougall and American psychology came to be thought of as being very separate and distinct. We have seen, however, that this was a fallacy—and that McDougall, Cooley and Mead fit with each other very well, and in ways of very basic and important agreement. But this is even more fully seen when we consider the wider *context* of agreement—on instinct, sentiment formation, attitude formation, levels of mental correlation in relation to action, etc.,—within which their own work developed. For their selected 'dimension' was, as we have seen, a clearly delineated part of sociology at the end of the nineteenth century (in Ward and Giddings especially) and a continuing, fundamental part of all the systems of sociology we have considered in the early twentieth century. Tönnies, Westermarck, Hobhouse, Durkheim, and Weber alike all accepted the importance of sentiment formation in collective conditions of institutionalization and action. There was, then, a deep and detailed pattern of agreement here.

Second (we will dwell on the universal importance attached to 'sentiment-formation' no more at this point) we have seen the very strong agreement between Mead and Hobhouse in (*a*) thinking of the nature of mind as a 'correlating' activity in sequences of action and control, and (*b*) distinguishing 'levels' of mental development in both 'self' and 'society' in terms of instinctual dispositions, perceptual order, and conceptual and ideational order (which is the distinctive

537

level of the 'human mind' and gives an articulate, abstract, and increasingly effective—in terms of control—order of *cognition* and *attention* for social-individual learning and purpose). Of course, Hobhouse himself had some of his roots in Ward, just as Cooley had his references to McDougall and Westermarck, so that any supposed gulf between British 'evolutionary sociology' and a more restricted American social psychology of individuals within smaller and contemporary groups had also absolutely no foundation. Hobhouse and Mead spoke the same language.

Third, it is perfectly clear how well the analysis of Cooley and Mead fitted within the conceptual system of Durkheim. Durkheim had insisted upon the *associational perspective* for psychology; the primacy of collective conditions of association for the understanding of the individual; and he himself had concentrated upon the study of 'social facts' at the level (chiefly) of institutional regularity. But Cooley and Mead—accepting the same perspective (though *not* Durkheim's 'deterministic' assumptions)—provided an analysis whereby the nature of 'social-mental complexes' and the emergence of individual 'selves' within them, could be fully explored. This was indeed a filling in of that important additional 'dimension' which Durkheim had left alone. Perhaps, too, it is worth recalling here that Mead's brief indication of the ways in which 'dissociation of personality' might be explicable in some kind of disruption of essentially *associational* processes (or some kind of insufficient personal development or working out of them), was clearly a very close link with Durkheim's own approach to the possible understanding of psychopathology and social pathology in his study of 'Suicide'.

The fourth—equally important and perhaps more interesting link is that very considerable one between all the positions we have mentioned and that of Weber. We saw earlier, a certain distance—noted and clearly seen by Weber, but left alone and unresolved—between Durkheim's treatment of socio-psychological 'facts' arising from collective conditions of association, and Weber's own clear concentration upon the understanding of social *action* as he defined it. And we saw, too, a clear conceptual gap between a kind of 'deterministic' psychological explanation of the existing pattern of motives, impulses, sentiments in individuals and 'corporate groups', and—quite different from this—the understanding and explanation of their purposeful *action* in terms of *meaning*. Now without in any way wishing to deny, or even to diminish, this conceptual distinction between the two levels—which is valid and extremely important, it has, nonetheless, become completely clear that the analysis of Mead, in particular, was such as to *link* these levels very effectively. In short, Mead did provide a valid way, and a conceptually clear way, with very distinct and definite elements of empirical reference (institutional complexes of behaviour, acts, roles, and the attendant symbols of communication), of analysing *action* in Weber's sense of *meaning*, and, at the same time, of explaining the socio-psychological *facts* (their nature, content, and sequential development) which existed within the individual 'selves' in intercommunication.

In short, the analysis of institutionalization in large societies; of small and large patterns of historical change; of large sequences of social evolution and dissolution; of 'development, evolution, and progress' in mind, social organization, and social control; of socio-psychological facts arising from collective conditions of association; and of sequences of social action meaningfully and purposefully pursued . . . the analysis of all these were now linked together with each other, and with the understanding of individual 'selves' by the work of Cooley and Mead. This one 'development' of this one 'dimension' of the 'psychological aspects of society' accomplished a tremendous inter-linking contribution in the making of sociology which has not, even yet, been fully and sufficiently realized.

Even so, Cooley and Mead were not alone in devoting themselves to this dimension, and we must look briefly at three other important scholars. But before this, one final point deserves special emphasis.

(VI) THE AVOIDANCE OF 'DETERMINISM'. AN 'OPEN-ENDED' CONCEPTION OF SCIENCE

Some of these points have arisen in our discussion earlier, but it is worthwhile to repeat them with a particular emphasis.

First of all it is important to note again that Mead satisfactorily incorporated in his analysis all those insistences on the 'teleological' qualities and capacities of the human mind and 'self' which had been made by so many writers from Mill to Ward, Hobhouse, and Weber. This meant that he was completely free from the kind of 'natural science' determinism that bedevilled some of Durkheim's extremes, and completely free from any error—as Comte would have put it—of confusing what were distinctive 'levels' of subject-matter and the distinctive kinds of concepts, propositions, methods and explanations which were appropriate to them. Mead was fully able to explore the dimensions of human psychology at the biophysiological, the experiential, the behavioural, the 'personal', and the 'social' levels alike, and at the levels of both causal connection (among neuro-physiological and environmental *'events'*) and understood purpose (among meaningful *actions*). All kinds of interconnection—from Mill's 'choices', Tönnies' kinds of 'willing', Durkheim's 'collective constraints', to Weber's rationally calculated 'means-end' relationships—could be validly explored within his conceptual framework.

The second important point—not necessarily a corollary of this, but certainly closely connected in Mead's teaching—was that he was very well aware that he was putting forward a *system of analysis* resting upon implicit and explicit hypotheses, and that no *finality* with regard to *the statement of specific theories* was entailed. In fact, Mead explicitly taught that such finality was impossible, and held what we have called here an 'open-ended' conception of science. In this he was in clear agreement with Comte, but also very similar indeed to Weber's complete rejection of the possibility of some complete *deductive scheme* of social science. For him, as for Weber, social science studied *specific problems*, and it was not the business of science to seek to foresee, let alone decide, what the concerns and problems of future scientists would be. Certainly it was absurd to think that science could be 'strait-jacketed' by some exhaustive conceptual scheme, which meant, really, seeing the universe through one special (selective) pair of spectacles.

Indeed, Mead went further and even denied any kind of determination of the direction of scientific enquiry by something called 'objective fact'. This was most apparent in his discussion of the 'objective truths' about the *past*.

'The long and short of it,' he wrote, 'is that the only reality of the past open to our reflective research is the implication of the present, that the only reason for research into the past is the present problem of understanding a problematic world, and the only test of the truth of what we have discovered is our ability to so state the past that we can continue the conduct whose inhibition has set the problem to us.'*

As Karl Popper would now put it, we perceive a problem when our expectations are not borne out in experience; we seek a satisfactory explanation of the problem; and our science—with the central proviso that it should make its hypotheses vulnerable to falsification by specified conditions of test—should then be free to range where it will in what seems to be the best and most appropriate investigations. And as Weber would have put it, the sociologist finds his problems in issues which he feels to be of fundamental cultural significance. Sociologists in different times and different situations will perceive different problems. Science insists upon methods of precision and objective test, but beyond that its concern should be that men should have the most excellent tools for undertaking such tasks of investigation—not that of seeking to provide a 'scheme of

* *The Philosophy of the Act: History and the Experimental Method*, see *On Social Psychology*, p. 324.

categories' that is likely to be sufficient (for the exploration and statement of problems) for all time.

When criticizing Bergson's notion of science, and his question as to whether science could achieve a statement about the *end* of the creative process of the world, Mead stated his position again very clearly:

'What Bergson overlooks in his treatment of science is that science does not undertake to make such a statement. It is continually presenting hypotheses of the world as it is, but science is a research affair and goes forward on the basis of the fact not only that the world will be intelligent but that it will always be different from any statement that science can give of it. That is, we are looking for an opportunity to restate any statement which we can give of the world. That is the implication of our research science . . . It means that we are always restating our restatement of the world. The same is true of our own ends and process in life . . . Life is a happening; things take place; the novel arises; and our intelligence shows itself in solving problems. But the solution of problems is by means of a definite conceptual procedure . . . Our life is an adventure. And . . . we show our intelligence by giving as elaborate a statement of the world as we can.'*

And, of course, the same insistence upon the insufficiency of any statement of a scientific theory for all future contingencies; indeed, its essential *limitation* in its *accuracy* in its selected field; was also evident in Mead's emphasis that *creativity, novelty,* within the context of regularity, was of the very nature of the 'social-mental-complex', the 'socio-psychological' actuality, within which 'selves' in inter-communication were involved. Mead, then, was as clear and reliable in his conception of the proper scope and claims of sociology as a science, as he was in his detailed account of his 'Social Behaviourism' as a development of social psychology.

The American contribution at the hands of Cooley and Mead, and the other social psychologists of their time, was very considerable indeed, but we must now consider other systems of thought in Europe which seemed at first glance, very different, but which were, in fact, very closely related. The most outstanding and influential system was that of Freud.

* *Henri Bergson: see On Social Psychology*, p. 312.

4
Sigmund Freud*: Anxiety, Adjustment, Rational Control

It may seem strange to some that we should include an outline and consideration of Freud's ideas in a study of the making of sociology. Surely, it may be thought, Freud was entirely a psychologist—and a clinical psychologist at that—and cannot be said by any stretch of the imagination to have put forward *sociological* theories. This is true to a very considerable extent, and yet there are firm reasons why the contribution of Freud should not, and must not, be by-passed and ignored.

In this place my chief aim, obviously, is to see his work in relation to that of men like McDougall, Cooley and Mead (and even Tönnies, Westermarck, Hobhouse and Durkheim) in making a contribution of the greatest importance to the study of the 'psychological aspects of society'. In this, too, I shall try to make clear the *similarity* of Freud's analysis to the ideas of these men we have considered. One of the great obstacles to seeing the fundamental agreements, and mutual reinforcements, between the distinctive bodies of work produced by independent (i.e. originally-minded) scholars, is the fact that they tend to be dubbed by labels which stem from some of their central emphases and which tend thereafter (disastrously) to *differentiate* them. Once a band-waggon with a distinctive label is constructed, hundreds of professionals (in search of something firm) jump on to it, and thereafter defend its separateness to the death. The academic world is full of disciples. Thus McDougall was dubbed an 'Instinct Theorist'; Freud was labelled in terms of 'Sex' and 'Psycho-Analysis'; and though these terms do refer to decided emphases in their work, it is quite a mistake to think that their entire schemes of concepts were fundamentally different from, or in disagreement with, each other. Indeed, McDougall himself pointed this out—with some bitterness—before he died. The same is true with

* 1856–1939. Freud's work was becoming widely known at the turn of the century (*The Interpretation of Dreams*, 1900). The first International Congress of Psychoanalysis was held in 1908. The International Psychoanalytic Association was founded in 1910. His writings became increasingly influential from 1900 to his death in 1939. His work therefore falls fully in our period and was strictly contemporary with that of McDougall, Cooley, and Mead.

regard to Cooley and Mead. What I wish especially to do is to show that—despite an array of apparently different concepts—Freud's analysis of the growth of the 'self' in 'society' was, in all important essentials, such as to support and enrich the kind of analysis which McDougall, Cooley and Mead were achieving.

A second important point follows upon our mention of 'self' and 'society'. Freud has been thought by some to concentrate almost wholly upon these sources of individual anxiety which stem from *within the organism*; perhaps exclusively the tyrannical pressures of the sexual instinct and its development within the personality; so that he has seemed to have a predominantly neuro-physiological orientation and a clinical concern. And it is certainly true that he tried always to relate his theories about human 'experience' to the theories of biology and physiology. Similarly, he has been thought to have focused his attention entirely upon the nature and development of the *individual personality*. And for these kinds of reason, he has not been thought of as a *social* psychologist to any marked extent. However, I want to argue here that Freud—though certainly focusing upon the individual personality—was as much a *social* psychologist as Cooley and Mead in his account of the growth of the 'self' and the 'content' of the self's experiences and conflicts; and, indeed, that his analysis vividly emphasized, as theirs did, the crucial importance of *primary groups*. In this, I think it also important to argue strongly that Freud offered a theory of *social learning* which —couched (as with Cooley and Mead) within a context of primary group communication and symbolization—explored in a much richer detail the 'mental mechanisms' which were involved in these patterns of emotional and cognitive attachment, adjustment and attitude formation, etc.; as the 'self' grew to maturity. And it follows, too, that I believe Freud to have given an account of 'sentiment-formation' stemming from 'instinct-experience' and instinctual vicissitudes which was in no basic way different from that of the other writers, but only such as to enrich and reinforce them.

The third point is, of course, that, like all the men we have studied, Freud was of much wider and deeper intellectual scope than the more specific areas on which his chosen work concentrated. His life will be reasonably well known—his linking of work on neuro-physiology by men like Charcot (under whom he worked in Paris) with the 'psycho-analytical' methods of treatment of Breuer in Austria, etc. But, even within his own writing, and even beyond his papers on 'meta-psychology' which went (deliberately) beyond immediate clinical investigations and findings, he thought much, and had much to say, about the wider 'psychological aspects of society'. His *Civilization and its Discontents* suggested other, and perhaps more deeply rooted, dimensions of man's malaise in modern society —going beneath and beyond the 'alienation', the 'anomie', which sociologists discussed, to a perhaps more fundamental and inescapable 'suppression of instinctual energies' and the insoluble tragedies which this entailed. His *Future of an Illusion* discussed the religious dilemmas of a world which (as Weber put it in stressing his 'ethics of responsibility') had 'tasted the fruit of the tree of knowledge'. These, surely, were essays on 'the psychological aspects of society' with a vengeance! But also, beyond this, Freud had his deeper roots in studies of classical literature and philosophy—which is why he could write essays of this kind, encompassing his scientific studies within a wider humanistic scope. And such knowledge was by no means of a 'general' nature. He had, to give one example, translated one volume of John Stuart Mill's *Collected Works*, as well as having a continual interest in philosophy and the history of culture. There is also the further point that he was at least aware of *some* wider comparative studies within the social sciences. We have seen how influential Spencer and Gillen's studies of Australian tribes had been; that Durkheim, Hobhouse, McDougall, and others made quite special reference to them. Freud was no exception. Just as Durkheim had gone to them in considering the *social* functions of religion, so Freud thought them highly significant as social evidence (embodiments) of the *psychological* processes of the human mind (the 'oedipus complex', etc.) he had sought to uncover. Freud, then, was a *social* psychologist more than has been commonly supposed.

A fourth point of importance for us is that since his time, Freud's theories have certainly been made much use of within the context of sociological analysis, so that—for any understanding of the making of sociology—we need to take them into account: to see what they were, and why they came to be thought so relevant to the tasks of sociology. For our own purposes, however, I would like to make one particular emphasis here. Among all the uses of Freud in sociology, one has come to be quite centrally conspicuous: that of Talcott Parsons. Parsons has incorporated Freud's conceptual scheme into his own in order to explore and explain (within the wider context of the analysis of institutions) the ways in which the 'roles', 'values', 'cultural symbols', etc., of the social order come to be 'internalized' by the individual personality. The similarity between this conception and that of Cooley and Mead is quite apparent; as is the obvious point that in this way Parsons has tried to fill in what we have tended to call the 'psychological dimensions' which Durkheim and Weber indicated but left void. All this, we shall come to in our final section; but here it is quite plain that we must have an understanding of

Freud if, later, we are to see clearly how (and with what value) he has been used in contemporary analysis.

Freud, then, for many reasons, was of importance within the same context as McDougall, Cooley and Mead in developing the study of the 'psychological aspects of society'. In his case, however, his theories were advanced in such a wide-ranging number of papers and essays, and changed (cumulatively) so much as his clinical studies and reflections proceeded, that I think there is nothing for it but to attempt a 'schematic' exposition of his system of ideas with the aid of a number of diagrams. This seems the only way in which it is possible to be comprehensive, clear, and brief.

Freud's System of Analysis*

(I) INSTINCTS AND THEIR VICISSITUDES: ANXIETY

'Man,' said Adam Smith, 'is an anxious animal.' Adam Ferguson had the same view: '. . . we mistake human nature, if we wish for . . . a scene of repose.' These simple, direct statements might well have been specially devised to indicate the fundamental persuasion on which Freud's entire account of the human personality—in the world, and in society—was erected. And the elements involved in his conception of this basic starting-point are indicated in Diagram (1) on the next page.

The situation, or dilemma, of the human person, according to Freud, was one of perpetual anxiety—well or ill contained—as the individual, from before birth to death, accommodated (adjusted himself to) three inescapable demands. These three compulsive demands could be comprehended in terms of the 'instincts' and the unavoidable 'vicissitudes' which they encountered, and with which they had to come to terms.

First of all, the 'psychic *experience*' of the individual was, during the early period of physical formation (in the womb); of birth; and of utter dependence upon its mother (after birth); almost entirely an *internal* world of psychic stimulation. From the shaping, growing, inter-active operations of physiological processes, an inner-excitation of energies would arise. The growth of the central nervous system was concomitant with an ordered containment of such physio-psychological excitations, and Freud even regarded the growth of the skin as a kind of 'boundary-sheath' which 'bounded' stimuli and protected, or shielded, the processes of the organism from the kind

* See *Instinct in Man*, R. Fletcher, Ch. VI. *Instincts in Psycho-Analysis*, pp. 168–258.

of formless, chaotic (unselective) bombardment of stimuli which would otherwise (later) be borne in from the external world. During the intra-uterine stage, the child was literally shielded within the mother's body; within the womb, was literally part of a larger whole which was sustaining and protective. But with birth was the traumatic experience of separation. The child now began to experience, as a separate being, the psychological correlates of physiological demands of a necessitous kind—to breathe, to eat, to evacuate waste materials; to move—which could only operate satisfactorily by means of adequate responses to the *external world.*

1
INSTINCTS AND THEIR VICISSITUDES:
ANXIETY

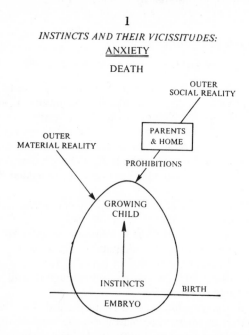

Now, a development of the necessitous ordering of physiological process, peripheral sensory perception and behavioural response, began—which was to be unending throughout life. The separate, vulnerable organism was alive in a world which would never cease to be insistently demanding.

The first inescapable, demanding element of the individual's experience—which could never be eradicated—consisted of the compulsive excitations and drives of the 'instincts'. Here, we need note only one or two of the ways in which Freud characterized the 'instinctual' elements of the human mind. He certainly did believe that specific instincts existed in human nature; that there was a genetically inherited 'order' of human impulses and attendant elements of emotion and that each of these could be distinguished by (1) its '*impetus*'—the specific demand of energy within the organism which it represented (the specific 'drive'), (2) its '*aim*'—to seek the quiescence (satisfaction) of the excitation at its physiological source, (3) its '*object*'—that specific object in relation to which it could achieve this aim, and (4) its '*source*'—the physiological process which produced the stimulus and excitation. However, very important aspects of Freud's teaching were (*a*) that in the human individual these instinctual elements were not inherited (nor did they immediately occur in individual experience) in '*ready-made form*', so to speak, but developed during the relatively long period of growth from birth to maturation, and (*b*) they were (as part of the same point) not equipped with 'automatic' behaviour-mechanisms (as was the case among some other animal species). These facts led Freud further to emphasize other connected points of importance. The lack of automatic responses meant that effective adjustments to external stimuli and situations had to be *learned*. The long period of maturation meant two things: (*a*) that the individual had to *contain* instinctual excitations pressing from within until appropriate responses were possible and had been learned, and (*b*) that this *containment* made probable, and in fact led, to various kinds of 'substituting' of certain 'objects' for what was the 'real' object of the instinct's satisfaction. And finally (for our purposes), these several factors of lack of automatism, long maturation, and delay, were concomitant with the fact that the 'inner psychic life' of the individual, and especially during the earliest years, was suffused with a 'generalized' instinctual energy (not clearly differentiated according to its many specific sources)—which Freud called the 'libido', or referred to as the 'Id' (simply meaning 'It'): i.e. the compulsive insistence of instinctual energy stemming from the inner physiological sources of the body which—for the emerging, conscious 'self'—was an ineradicable, 'objective' factor; something which *had* to be taken into account.

But these instinctual needs of the individual demanded gratification in an external world, a world of *outer, material reality*, which not only carried the promise of satisfaction, but also the constraints of frustration, and the sheer dangers of impoverishment, injury and destruction. The child, driven by the objective force from within of the instinctual desires, was also confronted with this second objective factor in his experience. He could only find the gratification which his instinctual needs demanded if he *learned* about the objective facts, qualities, characteristics, of this external world, so that he could behave appropriately, judiciously, effectively, in relation to them. External reality, with all the changeability and unpredictability of its circumstances, provided one set of vicissitudes.

This, however, was complicated by a third objective element—equally insistent and ineradicable in the early years of the child's life and experience—the *outer social reality* of the family-group within which the child was born; the world, crucially, of the *parents* and the *home*. In experiencing the insistent demands of instinctual energy, the child had to come to terms not only with the *facts* of the material world, but also the *facts* of his home, its conditions, but, especially, the *personal qualities* of his parents in their relationship with him. And the essential characteristic of the insistences of this social reality was that they consisted not only of *facts* but also of *values*. That is to say that even some of the responses which were *possible* in relation to the external *material world* were condemned and *prohibited* by the parents in the *social world*. Here was a new set of vicissitudes.

Four other things need, perhaps, to be stressed before leaving this picture of Freud's fundamental starting point.

The first—very difficult to convey—is that Freud conceived the 'psychic' life of the child—thronged with these unknown and unfamiliar forces, pressures, dangers, rules; and before any kind of coherence was discovered in them or imposed upon them—to be one of a degree of vivid, tearing anxiety such as we tend to have forgotten in our adult life, when, in such deep and many-sided ways, we have 'grown used' to the world. The child's experience was bound to be one of some degree of *anxiety*; and ranged through fears and terrors, glooms of emptiness and despair, excitements and quiescent satisfactions, joys of attachment and agonies of felt separation, which were of a kind of pristine, inchoate *feeling* and of an intensity difficult to describe.

And this leads to another of Freud's emphases—that it was a mistake to think of the adjustments of the child's mind to natural and social reality in terms of our adult 'rational' procedures of language, analysis, and thought. The 'psychic' experience of the child was a life of symbolic-gratifications, of 'fantasy-symbolization' which ordinary language could not come near, but which operated according to certain 'mental mechanisms' which we shall come to later. And this richness of 'psychic' experience, in the sense of the many-sided elaboration of 'fantasy-formation', was especially enhanced by the long period of maturation, of dependence upon parents and home, and of (natural and social) delay in having to come to terms with reality. *Anxiety*, then, was attended by a vividly felt mental life of symbolization and fantasy, which underlay the later, more rational procedures of 'objective' knowledge and conscious, adult control.

The third emphasis was that this entire experience of the instincts and their vicissitudes was, for the growing 'self', *essentially* one of *ambivalence* in relation to the 'objects' of the natural and the social world. For the child, it was *not* that objects in nature could *either* be hated *or* loved: but that they offered *both* the promise of gratification *and* danger. It was *not* that his parents could *either* be loved *or* hated, but that they offered *both* fulfilment *and* frustration. The fact was that human beings were in a situation of ambivalence. In 'nature' they found all they could know of fulfilment, and yet also all their circumstances of limitation, frustration, and destruction. In the immediate attachment to their parents they found love and the conditions of their fulfilment, and hate and resentment in the conditions of their limitation and dependence. Love and hate were for the self-same 'realities'. The dimensions of anxiety were therefore peculiarly deepened.

And the fourth emphasis was that all this, entirely, was in the context of a world which—no matter what solidity it seemed ultimately (in adulthood) to have—was transient, fleeting, perishable; ultimately ending, for the individual, in death. The vividly felt agony within which the world took form as the 'self' grew, was an entirety of experience which would be dissipated when, ultimately, death came. The 'objects' to which we became attached by love, perished.

The human situation, then, was one of anxiety: one which could never be resolved—only contained.

(II) LEVELS OF MENTAL ACTIVITY AND PRINCIPLES OF MENTAL FUNCTIONING

Within this many-dimensioned predicament of anxiety, the early growth of the child, the early 'formation' of the individual mind, was characterized, Freud maintained, by certain distinguishable 'levels' of mental activity and 'principles' of mental functioning. These are depicted in Diagram (2), and they can best be understood if we begin with the same notion of the child having a beginning of experience within the womb, experiencing the 'traumatic' separation of birth, and, in its very earliest years, having to come to terms with the constraining facts of the immediate material and social environment.

In all this, as we have seen, Freud maintained that the child's world of '*inner psychic reality*' was continuously and persistently invaded, disrupted, broken in upon, by the many stimuli from the

549

world of *'external reality'*. These stemmed from unavoidable, necessitous, constraining facts, and therefore the mental and behavioural processes of the child had to make some appropriate adjustments to them. 'Inner psychic reality' had to be modified in such ways as to recognize, know, and deal with 'external reality'. And in this process of adjustment and modification (learning!), two characteristics of human mental life came into operation.

2
LEVELS OF MENTAL ACTIVITY AND PRINCIPLES OF MENTAL FUNCTIONING

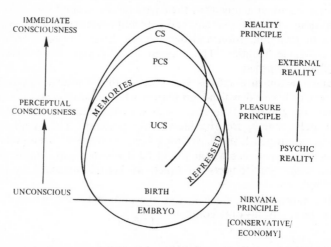

First of all, there was a necessary movement from unconsciousness to consciousness, and this was such as to lead to certain *levels* in the human mind. In the earliest processes of creation within the womb, as the anatomical structure and physiological processes took embryonic form, the inner experiences of excitations would gradually come into being as the basis of the mind. Probably even the simplest responses to the immediate environment of the intra-uterine conditions would come into being. But here, there was only a condition of inner 'feeling'; possibly a kind of 'quiescence' of mental experience; and no conscious awareness of 'self' or of the 'world'. With birth, however, and separateness, and in the new fact that pressing instinctual demands needed outside objects, and that this world of external objects could bring pain and deprivation, there was a new orientation of the child's mind to the *peripheral sensory organs*. The external senses—of taste, smell, touch, hearing and sight—came to have the new significance of accommodating the 'psychic life' of the child to the objective necessities of the world. The process of *perceptual consciousness*' was now progressively extended. Coupled with a growth of conscious awareness, the characteristics of the external world as purveyed by the senses were 'imposed upon' the inner psychic life of the child. Perceiving and learning about the external world was a change in the orientation of the mind, a new level of mental operation, a change and a 'stage' in the formation of the mind, and part and parcel (not just 'connected with') of *becoming conscious*. But Freud's careful emphasis (at this point) was that this was *not* full consciousness, *nor* consciousness of 'self': it was a gradually extending process of perceptual consciousness, of sensory stimulation and awareness involving a growing 'direction' of attention to *outer* objects; the gradual exploration and discovery of a world *outside* and separate from the 'psychic reality', which, so far, had been *all*. And the significant point about 'perceptual consciousness' was that it involved the laying down of *'memories'* in the mind. This led Freud to make the distinction between the 'levels' of *immediate consciousness* and the *memories* resulting from *perceptual consciousness*. As this process continued there came to be a 'store' of memories in the mind of which, at any given time, the individual was *not* conscious, but which he could recall to consciousness if, for any reason, he wished to do so. But, these memories aside, there was always an *immediate, acutely aware consciousness* of the living moment within which the individual was actively perceiving, feeling, calculating, judging.* The human mind, in its growth to awareness, thus manifested these three *levels* of activity: an immediate conscious activity of the moment; a realm of memories which came to be established through the activity (and orientation towards) perceptual consciousness; and a deeper level of unconscious mental activity, deriving from the inner physiological processes of the body and the earliest processes of the very formation of the organism. These 'levels', Freud termed the Conscious, the Pre-conscious, and the Unconscious (in the diagram: Cs, Pcs, and Ucs—abbreviations which Freud himself used).†

But this movement from unconscious to conscious mental activity through the reorientation of perceptual consciousness—involving,

---

* We can begin to see the close similarity with Mead's concepts of the 'I' and the 'Me'.

† Bearing in mind the dangers of 'reification'—it is to be noted that Freud *insisted* that these, and other concepts he proposed, *were only concepts* enabling him to grasp the complexities of psychic reality. He did *not* claim that there were three sharply distinct *levels* in the mind (like distinct *layers*) only that these three levels of mental *activity* were conceptually distinguishable. In any one mind, of course, they were all inter-active in many and complex ways.

T

as it did, a modification of 'inner psychic reality' by 'external reality' —was also accompanied, Freud argued, by certain 'principles' of mental functioning. The psychic energies of the mind, flowing from physiological sources, qualified by sensory perception, memory, and central-nervous control, operated in accordance with a certain 'economy'. This fund, and flow, and stimulated psychic energy— having definite sources—tended always to assume a *pattern of adjustment*. There was a certain economical *patterning* of dispositions within it. And once a certain, satisfactory *pattern of adjustment*— concomitant with a certain *psychic-constellation of feeling*—had been established, the organism and the mind was loth to leave it. The pattern tended to *abide*; the mind tended to *cling* to it; as a founded basis on which reality could be adequately confronted. The individual was only moved from such an adopted 'constellation of feeling' *with reluctance*; indeed, with *resistance*. The 'economy' of neuro-physiological/mental functioning was, in short, a *'conservative'* economy.*

In accordance with this tendency, Freud distinguished three 'principles' which stemmed from it; or, better, were manifestations of it which emerged at different junctures. First, stemming from the very earliest 'trauma' and adjustment experienced by the mind, was the 'Nirvana Principle'. This was the desire of the mind, fundamentally, to remain 'quiescent', 'untroubled', 'unstimulated'. Secondly, with the adjustment to the objects of perceptual consciousness which was *necessary* to secure the gratification of the instincts, the mind operated in accordance with the 'Pleasure Principle' (itself a corollary of the 'Nirvana Principle'), seeking those constellations of action and adjustment which would achieve a satisfaction of feeling; a gratification of impulse; and again, therefore, an appropriate 'quiescence' of stimulation. But thirdly, the mind had increasingly to recognize the compelling facts of external reality, and modify those constellations resting on the pleasure principle which were out of keeping with it. Full, conscious rationality was thus a becoming fully aware of the external situation of action, and the ways in which the inner orientations and desires of the mind were to be governed accordingly. But Freud's insistence, again, was *not* that there were three sharply distinct and different principles, but that each of them stemmed from the 'conservative' tendencies of the mind during certain phases of development, and that all of them *continued* to operate. They thus had continuous influence upon each other, and Freud maintained that even in the fullest recognition of the 'reality principle' the experience and

* Soon, we shall see the close similarity between Freud's account of mental functioning and that of Pareto.

behaviour of the mind was still influenced in part by the 'pleasure' and 'nirvana' tendencies.*

One other point must be made in relation to the conjunction of these 'levels' and 'principles' of mental functioning. It is perfectly clear how the growth from the unconscious to the conscious and the movement from the operation of the 'nirvana principle' to the 'reality principle' were closely linked in Freud's account. But in the close relationship between them, one quite basic 'mental mechanism' was revealed: '*repression*'. When, in encountering 'reality'—through perceptual consciousness, or through such sensation mixed with fantasy—the mind confronted some element of reality which threatened it (i.e. threatened its security, the objects of its love and attachment, etc.) beyond the bounds of toleration, it was possible for it to 'avoid' the threat by driving it into the 'unconscious'. A kind of 'dissociation' of consciousness from it was accomplished. We shall come back to a discussion of such 'mental mechanisms' in dealing with conditions of stress later, but '*repression*' was one of basic importance in Freud's system. Repression was not in itself an abnormal mechanism of the mind; it was an accommodation to severe distress; but it laid down hidden bases of conflict within the complex life of the 'psyche', and, if too severe, could lead to 'pathological' adjustments to stress which took the form of kinds of 'dissociation of personality' which the individual found it impossible, consciously, either to know or to govern. Here it is at least clear how this mechanism was related to Freud's conceptions of 'levels' and 'principles' of mental functioning.

(III) ELEMENTS OF PERSONALITY

Bearing in mind the same growth from embryonic development, through birth, into the early years of childhood; from inner psychic reality to external reality; from unconsciousness to consciousness; and through the operation of the several 'principles' of mental functioning as the mind gradually came to terms with the outer *material* and the outer *social* world; we now come to other developments of the mind which were taking place *simultaneously*. In addition to the changing sequence of *levels* and *principles* of mental functioning, but occurring in close concomitance with them (indeed,

---

* In one of his arguments, Freud linked these notions to his conception of the '*death instinct*' (as against all the positive '*life instincts*'); arguing that this mental disposition towards the obliteration and extinction of stimulation was a deep-rooted accompaniment of the life of the mind. This is a highly dubious conception, and, elsewhere (*Instinct in Man*) I have tried to show that Freud's arguments for it are not satisfactory. I shall therefore ignore it here. Still, it is not a closed question, and should be borne in mind.

as *part* of these same activities) there was also a process of *differentiation of elements of personality*. Here, we come to Freud's account of the actual growth of the 'self'; *both* in relation to the consciousness of the separateness of the 'self' in the material world, *and* the *internalization* of the *values* of loved (or influential) persons in the social world. And here we come very clearly to one other analysis of what Mead called the 'I' and the 'Me'.

3

ELEMENTS OF PERSONALITY

[*DIFFERENTIATION AND CONFLICT*]

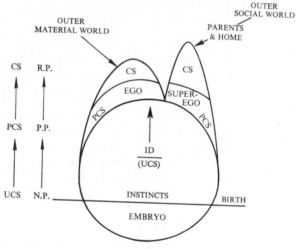

In the activity of perceptual consciousness, the individual came gradually (as part of such perceptual awareness) to be aware of the *separateness* between him-'self' as an organism and all those 'objects' in the external world in relation to which he had to act. Previously, the child had had no conscious distinction (in his 'inner psychic world') between parts of his own body or objects external to it. There came to be, then, a consciousness of 'self' quite literally in close accordance with the awareness of the periphery of the body. There came to be a consciousness of 'self'—of a unified 'entity'—at the same time as memories of the 'preconscious' were laid down, and as the acuteness of immediate consciousness at the level of the 'reality principle' emerged. But this included also an awareness of the *objective demands of the instincts* which were just as compulsive a

554

factor which the 'self' had to take into account as was the totality of the 'external world'. There was, said Freud, a consciousness (a differentiation) within the 'self' of 'I' and 'It'—the consciously active *Ego* and the organically rooted '*Id*' (which was a short-hand term for all the instinctive needs). It will be readily seen that there is nothing more metaphysical in Freud (in speaking about Ego and Id) than in Mead (in speaking about 'I' and 'Me'). It is only that he chose to use Latin terms! And it will also be seen, with this introduction of the 'Ego', how the link between 'levels' and 'principles' of mental functioning became more close in Freud's system. For the 'Ego'—arising in the activities of perceptual consciousness—and being consciously aware of the 'self's' (the body's) boundary and separateness—was a new organization of the mind to defend the 'psyche' against the external world in accordance with the nirvana, pleasure, and reality principles. The 'Ego' (the 'I') had the task of seeking to gratify the demands of the 'Id' by seeking to establish reliable knowledge of the objects of the external world, to avoid their dangers, and to establish effective modes of behaviour in relation to them. The 'Ego' was therefore essentially *expedient*: a kind of 'Scout, and Spy, to range abroad' (as Hobbes described the 'thoughts' in relation to the 'desires'.)

However, this differentiation between the 'I' and the 'It' was not the only one which took place in the growth and formation of the 'self'. The 'self' also took shape *in society*; in relation to the external *social world*; and this affected the consciousness of 'self' in very profound ways. The early 'psychic world' of the child was such as to include the 'objects' to which, in its need, it was attached by love: its parents. Gradually, however, with the growing consciousness of the external world, and in accordance with the reality principle, the child became aware not only of his distinct separateness from the objects of the material world, but also of his separateness from those he loved. The very foundations of the security and emotional reality of his world became vulnerable, separate, perishable (as well as being the objects of ambivalent feeling). The loss of loved objects, the loss of love, the vulnerability of what had been firmly founded bonds and attachments of love, became apparent. With this juncture, the child could not tolerate the abandonment of the loved-objects in separation, and so he incorporated them and their values into himself; into his own mind. Here the ambivalence of feeling had important consequences. On the one hand the child loved his parents; on the other hand he hated them and resented their prohibitions. The 'introjection' of the parent-figures within the psychic-reality of the 'self' contained both of these ingredients. The resentment and hate took the form of demanding moral rules (and attendant inhibitions), or the regulatory aspects of 'conscience'—now felt *within* the mind, rather than coming from outside it. The love took the form of an 'idealization' of the loved objects and the establishment within the mind of 'ego-ideals'. In short, related elements of prohibition (and inhibition) and aspiration were established, as 'conscience' in the child's mind, and, as a concomitant of these ambivalent components, was the experience of 'guilt'—'guilt' stemming from the element of 'hatred', and from the 'self''s knowledge of (sometimes) not obeying the prohibitions and of falling short of the ideals of aspiration.

This further 'differentiation' of the 'Ego', Freud described as the establishment of a 'Super-Ego' within the personality: a part of the 'Ego' which had been incorporated from outside; which thus had an 'objective' reality—as being something going beyond the 'self' (having roots outside the 'self'); and which possessed *authority* over the 'Ego'—regulating it, constraining it, judging it. The 'Ego' thus had the task of acting in relation to the necessities of the external world in order to serve two 'masters'—the instinctual strivings (the Id) on the one hand, which pressed for gratification, and the moral regulations (the Super-Ego) on the other, which insisted on bringing certain standards to bear upon the Ego's intentions and behaviour. Again, however, we must remind ourselves that though Freud thought that these were *differentiations* which were distinguishable within the totality of the 'self', and thus gave rise to *conflictful* experience within the self, he thought of them as all linked with each other in the unity of the 'self' as a whole. There could thus be 'communication' between Ego, Super-Ego, and Id, especially in the symbolic activity at the level of the 'Id' and in the unconscious. There, deeply, a creative intercourse of mental activity took place—whether of imposed conflict, or of a movement towards adjustment and harmony.

But one thing above all needs emphasis here. Almost always, in interpretations of Freud, it is the *harshness* of the Super-Ego which is stressed; the tyrannical authority of the internalized prohibitions of the 'father'; and the savage excesses of *guilt*. But this is very one-sided. Freud quite definitely insisted that there was also an incorporation of elements of the *loved ideal*; that the Ego was therefore given ideal qualities for aspiration and fulfilment. When he spoke of the 'Super-Ego' and the 'Ego-Ideal', he quite definitely meant that—with *both* its prohibitory rules *and* its standards of ideality—a moral element had been planted in the Ego which served as an 'ideal guide' as to the way in which it should seek to conduct its task. The *rational calculation* of the Ego in terms of the ordering of perceptual and conceptual knowledge, and of purposeful action in the world, had thus certain idealities of standards of judgment for its guidance. This analysis of Freud therefore quite clearly provided for the understanding of *conflict* in the personality, but it also provided for the understanding of the struggle towards the resolution of it. This is not commonly taken into account, and very rarely emphasized—but it is most important.

Again, before leaving this point, we might simply note how close this analysis is to the 'internalization of the values encountered in primary group relationships' described by Cooley and Mead, and of the attendant formation of 'sentiments' and 'attitudes'.

(IV) THE IMPORTANCE OF THE SEXUAL INSTINCT

It was, of course, the development of the sexual instinct in particular which was thought by Freud to be of absolutely central significance in this process of the formation of the 'self'. This is *possibly* (I am

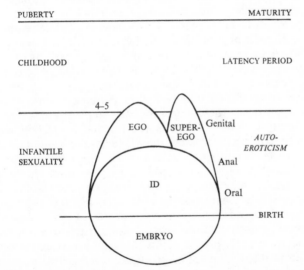

4

IMPORTANCE OF SEXUAL INSTINCT

not really confident of this) the best known element of Freud's theory, and we will therefore deal with it fairly briefly, but in such a way as to emphasize specific points.

Perhaps the most solid thing to stress at the outset is that when Freud spoke of the centrality of the development of the sexual instinct he *explicitly* insisted that he did not mean 'sex' in the straightforward sense of adult copulation. What he had in mind was that it was by the bonds of *love*, of *affection*, of tender *emotional attachments* that the self chiefly developed in its formation and that it was savage disruptions or deprivations of *these* bonds in particular which gave rise to the gravest and most severe personality conflicts.

In *An Autobiographical Study*, Freud wrote quite clearly:

'The nature of my extension of the concept of sexuality . . . is of a two-fold kind. (1) Sexuality is divorced from its too close connection with the genitals, and is regarded as a more comprehensive bodily function having pleasure as its goal and only secondarily coming to serve the ends of reproduction. (2) The sexual impulses are regarded as including all those merely affectionate and friendly impulses to which usage applies the exceedingly ambiguous word "Love".'

This was called, deliberately, the development of the *sexual* instinct because Freud did believe that it was in the closest connection with a sequence of development of the erotogenic zones of the body, as the sexual instinct came to adult maturity, that the growth of these bonds of love took place. Putting it differently, he believed that certain crucial 'constellations' of feeling were marked by the sensitization of certain zones and the control of the behaviour connected with their physiological functions, and that the development of the whole personality could be profoundly affected by the child's experiences at these 'stages'. Indeed, he maintained that certain quite specific 'character-qualities' and 'character-types' were attendant upon the 'fixation' of the individual to the constellation of feeling related to any one of these zones. His basic emphasis, then, was upon constellations of *love* which developed in close connection with the eroticization of specific zones in the whole development of sexuality.

Again, Freud's conception of the development of sexuality must be considered in close, simultaneous relationship with the other sequences of the mind's development which we have clarified so far. And the next important emphasis of his analysis (in connection with these sequences) was upon *infantile* sexuality. Freud believed that the child's growth towards consciousness, towards the reality principle, from 'inner psychic reality' to an awareness of the external world, from the dominance of gratificatory instinctual pressures to the consciousness of 'self' and the inward awareness of moral regulation, was marked, during the first five years of life, by three crucial stages. The first insistent, necessitous, vitally compelling need of the child after birth was for *sustenance*, and this took the form of suckling and involved a dominant orientation in the child's 'psychic life' about the erotogenic zone of the mouth and lips. This was the first crucial link and orientation of the 'psyche' towards the 'external world'. This was the first crucial focus of attachment, of gratification and fulfilment or of frustration and deprivation. But this, after a time, had to be terminated by 'weaning', and the child's growth to consciousness was crucially focused about this particular separation from an object of instinctual attachment. The second such focus was upon the erotogenic zone of the anal region connected with the physiological function of the evacuation of waste material, and the necessary behavioural control of 'toilet training'. And the third crucial stage—at about the age of five years—was the eroticization of the genital organs proper. Two points must be emphasized very strongly here.

First, during this period of 'infantile sexuality' it must be remembered that, according to Freud, the child was only gradually emerging from the world of 'inner psychic reality' as the activities of perceptual consciousness gradually proceeded, and nothing of this experience was of the nature of conscious, rational, ordered perception or conception as known in adulthood. The child's experience was still very much in the realm of the unconscious and perceptual consciousness; of internal excitation gradually qualified by external sensation; of internal feeling dominantly oriented by compelling need towards appropriate external perception. And in this condition, Freud argued, the child's *erotic* experience in *infantile sexuality* was one of *auto-eroticism*. That is to say, the child did not yet distinguish the objects *outside* him from the *parts of his own body* towards which his instinctual excitations were oriented and in relation to which they found their gratification. The child found his erotic gratification in the manipulation of parts of his own body; still dominantly within his own 'inner' world.

But the second point is that the 'genital' stage of erotic experience, according to Freud, was coincident with the stage of the emergence to consciousness of the 'Ego' (the consciousness of 'self'). The awareness of the separateness of the parent-figures, and the psychic adjustment which had to be made to this situation, was coincident with the emergence of the full erotic significance (though still not with ordered rational consciousness) of the genitals. This marked, therefore, a very important juncture. The stage of 'auto-eroticism' was at an end. The consciousness of 'Ego' had emerged. And the incorporation of 'conscience' (of prohibitions and ideals), of the 'Super-Ego', had taken place. And with this conjunction of the 'mature' awareness of the external relevance of genital eroticism with the incorporation of 'morality', there was a temporary 'de-sensitization' of the genitals, and a period followed (of childhood) during which the development of sexuality was more or less 'latent'.

The final 'maturity' of the development of the sexual instinct came with puberty, the full development of all the secondary sexual characteristics, and the full consciousness of and motivation towards adult sexual relations. But at this stage, Freud thought, there was (a) still an incorporation of the earlier elements of eroticism (of oral and anal regions) into the pattern of adult sexuality, and (b) a re-awakening of those 'constellations' of psychic adjustment which had been established at those junctures of infantile experience earlier; and, indeed, an emergence—as adult character-traits—of the dispositions which were laid down in any early 'fixation' at the point of such a 'constellation'.

Freud's account of sexual development has, of course, raised much anger and resentment, and much ill-informed abuse, but it has also been criticized in the light of comparative studies of sexual behaviour in different societies. Here, however, we are only concerned to outline Freud's theory to see its place within his entire conceptual scheme, and, especially, to see its relation to the other theories of the 'self' and 'society'. And this, I think, is sufficiently clear. We might note, however, that comparative cultural studies have not so far been decisive on this issue. Some 'schools' (e.g. the 'Basic-Personality' school) have used corollaries of Freud's theory to clarify the 'basic personality' produced by the child-rearing practices in various cultures. Some have rejected elements of Freud's account on the grounds that the finding of pre-puberal sexual activities in some societies throws doubt on the existence of a 'latency period', and on the universality of some of the complexes— the 'Oedipus Complex', for example—which Freud described in exploring the internalization of parent-figures, values, and 'taboos'. I do not myself believe that any such studies can be said to have seriously 'disproved' Freud's account, though it has to be admitted that such a theory as his is notoriously difficult to submit to crucial conditions of test.

(V) THE FORMATION OF PRIMARY GROUPS

Diagram (5) is Freud's own diagram and serves to make it very clear that his 'theorizing' led him to think beyond individual personality alone to the questions of group membership and the formation of groups. Even as far as we have gone it has been clear beyond doubt that Freud did *not* rest his theory of the growth of the human 'personality' purely on biological, or organic, or neuro-physiological grounds. He insisted on these—certainly. But his entire analysis showed the essential nature of the 'self' as taking shape within the *family*, and in the closest relationship with the *parents*. Freud emphasized the vital significance of *primary group relationships* and *primary group ideals* (and values) in exactly the same way as Cooley and Mead, though using different concepts. And we can now see, further, that (although he himself did not pursue it in any detail) he conceived this kind of analysis as being valid beyond the boundaries

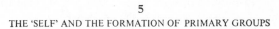

5
THE 'SELF' AND THE FORMATION OF PRIMARY GROUPS

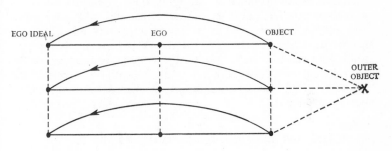

(This is Freud's own diagram: see *Group Psychology and the Analysis of the Ego*, Hogarth Press, 1949, p. 80.)

of the family to other primary groups and, indeed, to the wider structure of society itself. Even in his discussion of the formation of the 'Ego-Ideal' within the family, Freud always clearly had in mind the fact that the values of the parents would to some considerable degree reflect the cultural values of the wider society of which they were members (i.e. of which the particular family was a part); and he also stated in various places in his work that the 'stories' and literature which children would hear and read, and the values of other impressive people who carried authority in their neighbourhood—such as school-teachers—would be such as probably to reinforce those they first experienced in relation to their parents.

In one essay, however, Freud did discuss, quite directly the relationships between 'group psychology' and the 'analysis of the Ego', and, significantly, he confined his attention to those groups, small or large, which did at least possess a clearly perceived central leader: such as the army—with a general, or the church—with a religious leader, or any smaller 'primary' group like a school class—

with its teacher. In all such groups, Freud argued, the solidarity of group feeling, the strength of the social bond among its members, rested crucially upon the identification which the individual members made with each other in relation to their shared idealization of the leader. As in the diagram, a close primary group bond would exist when the 'ego-ideals' of the individual members, which, in each case, had been formed by the 'introjection' of the values of their own parents (the love-objects), were nonetheless also modelled on the same 'outer object'—i.e. the same, shared leader.

We need make no more of this point, since Freud did not carry his analysis very far; but it serves to demonstrate—what we need to see—that his analysis of the 'self' was intimately related to his analysis of 'society': especially the nature of primary groups, or groups with clear symbolic 'heads' of leadership. In these terms, the establishment of a close 'community' identification in terms of the 'communication' and 'internalization' of shared values could be plainly understood.

(VI) MENTAL MECHANISMS OF ADJUSTMENT TO STRESS

Before we think a little further about the extension of Freud's analysis to the wider study of the 'psychological aspects of society', however, it is necessary to clarify in greater detail his treatment of 'mental mechanisms', for this was one of the most interesting aspects of his theory.

We have seen earlier—in McDougall, Cooley and Mead; in Tönnies, Westermarck, Hobhouse, Durkheim; and—earlier still—in Ward, Sumner, and Giddings; that many theorists had argued that the ways in which human individuals became members of the community and living bearers of the social tradition, was not by any straightforward 'learning'—in rational terms, but by the formation of 'sentiments' and 'attitudes' which involved a certain ordering of feeling (instinct, emotion, interest) about 'objects' of cognition, or even about 'symbols' in the cultural order. One of the most considerable contributions of Freud was that he really offered (*a*) an original 'learning theory' in terms of which this 'socialization' of the individual could be understood, and also (*b*) a detailed account of the 'mental mechanisms' involved. The 'learning-theory' we have already outlined: it was an account of the emergence of the 'self'—including 'Ego' and 'Super-Ego'—as the individual was constrained to come to terms with the external material and social world, in the service of the driving instinctual demands of the organism; and it entailed a detailed analysis of the instincts and their vicissitudes, the 'levels' and 'principles' of mental functioning, the 'elements of the personality', the development of the sexual instinct in particular, and the taking place of all this within the most immediate and important persons and relationships in the family and primary groups. But we now come to the 'mental mechanisms' which Freud described as

6
MENTAL MECHANISMS OF ADJUSTMENT TO STRESS

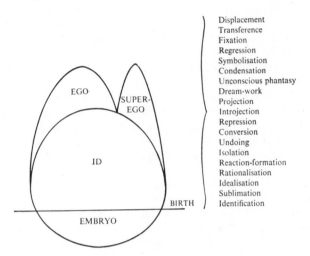

Displacement
Transference
Fixation
Regression
Symbolisation
Condensation
Unconscious phantasy
Dream-work
Projection
Introjection
Repression
Conversion
Undoing
Isolation
Reaction-formation
Rationalisation
Idealisation
Sublimation
Identification

being operative in this entire human situation in which the individual was continuously exposed to conditions of stress.

And the important point to bear in mind is that, according to Freud, these 'mechanisms' were *not* mental operations which individuals *learned*, but *unlearned* responses by which the mind operated as some adjustment to the instinctual demands and the constraints of material and social reality were sought. They were 'mechanisms' by which the mind dealt with its problems of stress; by means of which habitual responses, attitudes, attachments, sentiments, ideals, came to be formed within the context of social conditions; but they were not themselves consciously learned. They were mental processes active among individuals in society, but not deliberately learned or devised by them. Their importance is thus patently clear. A knowledge of such 'mechanisms' would enable us to analyse and understand the psychological aspects of certain sequences of social behaviour, and possibly to explain the kinds of 'non-rational' or 'irrational' social action which Weber referred to in the sense of being 'deviations' from the pure, rational 'means-end' set of relationships.

We must also bear in mind, however, that for Freud, the 'mental mechanisms' were not *themselves explanations*. The *explanation* of them, of their existence and their operation, lay in the fundamental conditions of anxiety and stress which we have outlined. The 'mechanisms' were purely descriptive concepts of those mental processes which Freud found, and distinguished, and I particularly want to outline them clearly not only for their own sake (worthwhile in itself) but also so that we can see their great similarity to (as well as their superiority to) those outlined and used by Pareto.

First of all, we can briefly define those 'mechanisms' which seemed to stem directly from the striving for gratification (including 'substitute gratification') of the instincts.

Displacement was the way in which the energy of one instinct could readily 'switch' from the path of discharge of one instinct to that of another. This meant that there was a great fluidity or flexibility of human instinctual desires. If an obstacle was encountered to the gratification of one instinct, its energy could readily be diverted to another 'object'.*

Transference was a similar mental process, but one which involved the organization of the 'Ego' more. It was the way in which the out-flowing of love (or hatred) towards an object (person) could be transferred to another object. Freud felt that some capacity for displacement and transference was necessary for mental resilience and mental health. *Rigidity* was the more productive of conflict and suffering,† and this leads directly to other, connected mechanisms.

Fixation was a rigid inability to give up an object in relation to which an earlier gratification had been achieved: 'a close attachment of an instinct to its object'. Fixations were thought by Freud, to be highly significant with regard to (*a*) symptom-formation in neurotic illness, and (*b*) the laying down of definite character-traits. This significance was especially revealed by:

Regression—which was the tendency, in the face of severe conflict and anxiety, to fly back to an earlier, satisfactory 'constellation' of feeling and adjustment—i.e. to such a point of 'fixation' as mentioned above.

---

* We must note that Freud termed this out-flowing of instinctual feeling, or libido, or energy to a specific object, a process of 'cathexis'. This is of little importance here, but Parsons later used this terminology a good deal, and we must be prepared for it.

† We must remember that Freud was a *clinical* psycho-analyst, pre-occupied chiefly with diagnosis and cure (or alleviation).

Symbolization was a mental process, operative at the unconscious level, by which one object came to represent one or more other objects, and could thus serve as a 'symbol' towards which several instinctual tendencies through displacement, could be directed in seeking gratification.

Condensation was a process whereby one such symbol or idea could 'subsume' or 'sum up' several such ideas, and thus attract to it the energies previously directed to these several ideas separately.

Unconscious Fantasy was the complex proliferation of all these mechanisms, weaving fantasies within 'inner psychic reality' seeking the gratification of instinctual excitations and, in general, dominated by the desire for 'wish-fulfilment'.

Dream-Work was again, that kind of mental fantasy which proliferated in sleep when, for a time, the Ego had relaxed its control over the instincts. And again, all the other mechanisms were at play in seeking a satisfying fulfilment of feeling. Normally, however, according to Freud, the Ego still retained some control, some 'censorial supervision', so that an individual could be driven into wakefulness by too extreme a 'fantasy'.

Apart from these 'mechanisms' involved in the sheer striving of the instincts, others were chiefly operative as 'mechanisms of defence'—serving to protect the Ego in its continual task of adjustment. These mechanisms, strictly speaking, were operations of the mind in dealing with stimuli or situations which were literally unavoidable, though intolerable.

Projection was a way in which the mind dealt with *inner* stimuli or ideas, which could not be avoided (as could *outer* stimuli) by withdrawal, or escape, or by some effective outward action. That which was disturbing *within* was projected *outwards*, and then seen to pertain to things or people in the environment. The disquieting 'faults' could then be blamed on others, or on external situations, and the 'Ego' felt more capable of dealing with them if they were part of 'outer reality'.

Introjection—almost conversely—was the way in which the Ego incorporated into its own nature, those loved object-choices which, through the constraints of external reality, had to be abandoned. When gratification in connection with a certain 'object' (i.e. or person) proved impossible, the Ego set the object up as part of itself and in this way, attracted the 'outward flow of instinctual energy' to itself. In this way, especially, Freud thought of the 'character' of the 'Ego' as consisting—to an important extent—of 'id-abandoned object-choices', and it is plain, therefore, that this was one 'mental mechanism' which could be of considerable importance for the understanding and explanation of the 'socialization' of the 'self', and, indeed, of important dimensions of 'education'.* Chiefly, of course, Freud had in mind here the setting up of the 'Ego-Ideal' or 'Super-Ego', as the outcome of the introjection of the earliest object-choices: the parents; but, as we have said earlier, other impressive 'objects' in the environment (other impressive persons) could be chosen and idealized by love in the same way.

Repression was the mechanism whereby the Ego rejected and kept from consciousness any *idea* or *affect* against which it must protect itself in the face of the demands of the external world and the Super-Ego. Freud said in his earlier work that the Ego must keep certain instinctual manifestations from consciousness in view of (*a*) the strength of the instincts, and (*b*) its own weakness in the dangerous context of the outer world. Later, he stressed more and more that the chief cause of repression was the Super-Ego and the harsh criticism which it continually directed towards the Ego. These two sources of repression were brought together, however, by Freud's generalization that repression occurred when 'the element of avoiding "pain" (increase of tension and mental conflict) . . .' had 'acquired more strength than the pleasure of gratification'. Freud thought there were two aspects of repression. Firstly, the *idea*, or 'instinct-presentation', of an underlying instinctual impulse could be repressed. This might only constitute a partial or inadequate repression, as, driven into the unconscious, the instinctual tendency— employing the various mechanisms we have mentioned—would seek gratification by attaching itself to other (perhaps remotely-associated) ideas which would be continually striving to penetrate into consciousness. Secondly, the repression could be a repression of *affect*, and though it is difficult to follow Freud's suggestions as to the fate of the repressed affect, it seems that he held this repression to be the chief cause of anxiety. One of the outcomes of repression, and the consequent conflict and anxiety in the personality was:

Conversion: the mechanism whereby the 'psychic content' of the repression was converted into physical or bodily manifestations. This mechanism was typical of hysteria, and, much more than the

* This, of course, has been at the heart of much educational theory, and concern for the attachment (in the individual) to worthy 'ideals' as guidance for 'the good life', from the earliest times. Thus Plato insisted that young children should be surrounded by objects and influences which were graceful and beautiful; and almost all educationalists and moralists have emphasized the importance of *example*—knowing that the implanting in the 'self' of loved 'models' is of central importance. One of the most deeply moving of philosophers on this matter was Spinoza. '. . . the whole of happiness or unhappiness', he wrote, 'is dependent on this alone: on the quality of the object to which we are bound by love.'

other mechanisms we have mentioned, was strictly *pathological*, and is therefore of only minor interest to us here. A mechanism by means of which the Ego attempted to achieve something even more radical than repression was:

Undoing: which consisted of the unconscious attempt to eliminate from the mind completely a past experience which has been intolerably 'painful' to the Ego; to 'blot it out of existence'. A similar mechanism was that of:

Isolation: whereby the memories of past conflict-experiences were deprived of their 'affective' (painful) aspects; leaving in the memory only ideas stripped of their emotional significance.

Reaction-Formation was the mechanism whereby the Ego attempted to *reverse* emotional attitudes and tendencies which persisted in the unconscious. To give an example, a persisting infantile attitude of hatred and hostility towards a parent (say the father) may manifest itself as an excessive anxiety about him or an attitude of excessive devotion. Reaction-formations, however, were only 'appearances', and the actual impulses persisted beneath these surface attitudes. A reaction-formation, might be regarded as a process of conveniently 'camouflaging' the true underlying motives.

*Rationalization** was the outcome of the Ego's need to harmonize or integrate its activities on both the unconscious and conscious levels. In view of all that has been said with regard to the extraordinary ramifications of the unconscious mental processes, it is clear that the Ego could not be aware of all the motives, with their manifold connections, which had provoked it to undertake certain activities; and indeed, many of these motives would have been repressed into the unconscious because of their incompatibility with the claims of the outside world and the Super-Ego. At the unconscious level of the Ego, then, the promptings to activity were nonrational and amoral. At the conscious level of activity, however, the Ego employed a body of ordered knowledge about the world and about its own place in the world, and insisted upon rational consistency in establishing and practising this knowledge. Much of the activity of the Ego prompted by motives at the level of the unconscious would therefore conflict with the rational consistency demanded on the level of its conscious activity. Its actual behaviour would not always permit of an easy and evident rational explanation. Rationalization was the name given to that process whereby the Ego *smoothed over*, or *evaded* the irrationality and inconsistency of its *actual* motivation and behaviour (stemming from impulses and

---

* Here again we must note here a great similarity with Pareto which we shall explore shortly. See also Cooley's point (p. 487) that even aspects of human 'thinking' and 'reasoning' have 'instinctive' roots.

ideas at the level of the unconscious) by arriving at, or constructing, a tolerably coherent explanation to satisfy its conscious rational tendencies and to fit in with its conscious moral properties. We might say, that Rationalization was the way in which the Ego explained and justified its own motives and activities satisfactorily to itself.

Finally, we can turn to three further mechanisms which are, perhaps, the most important for our purposes: Idealization, Sublimation, and Identification.

As far as one can gather from Freud's writing,* *idealisation* stemmed fundamentally from primary narcissism.† From the beginning, there was a core of self-love in the individual, from which centre, love later flowed out towards object-choices. In Freud's terms:

'Thus we form a conception of an original libidinal cathexis of the Ego, part of which cathexis is later yielded up to objects, but which fundamentally persists and is related to the object-cathexes much as the body of a protoplasmic animalcule is related to the pseudopodia which it puts out.'

When love flowed out towards an object in an 'object-cathexis', the primary narcissism was to some extent impoverished, but an element of this narcissism was now transferred to the object and took the form of 'over-estimation' of the qualities of character of the object. It is this over-estimation of the object which was given the name 'Idealization'.‡

'. . . marked sexual over-estimation . . . is doubtless derived from the original narcissism of the child, now transferred to the sexual object. This sexual over-estimation is the origin of the peculiar state of being in love, a state suggestive of a neurotic compulsion, which is thus traceable to an impoverishment of the Ego in respect of libido in favour of the love-object.'§

'Idealization is a process that concerns the *object*; by it that object, without any alteration in its nature, is aggrandized and exalted in the mind . . . For example, the sexual over-estimation of an object is an idealization of it.'||

* 'On Narcissism: an Introduction', Collected Papers, 1914, Vol. iv, III.
† 'Self-Love' rooted in the 'inner psychic reality' and the 'auto-eroticism' of the earliest experience.
‡ It will be seen how these 'mental mechanisms' were held to be inter-connected in their operation. 'Idealization' was a process which preceded, and in part (therefore) explained, the subsequent setting up within the 'self' of the 'Ego Ideal'. There is thus an element of 'narcissism' even in our moral striving.
§ 'On Narcissism: an Introduction', Collected Papers, 1914, vol. iv, III, p. 45.
|| *Ibid.*, p. 51.

Idealization was also involved, however, in the process of introjection and the formation of the Ego-Ideal or Super-Ego. As the individual grew, his primary narcissism suffered a good many blows from the admonitions and corrections of others. We have seen how the earlier object-choices of the child, including these moral precepts and this 'over-estimation', were introjected and incorporated as part of the Ego. The child, therefore, now loved himself, Freud argued, not 'as he actually is' but as 'what he ought to be'.

'To this ideal Ego,' Freud says,* 'is now directed the self-love which the real Ego enjoyed in childhood. The narcissism seems to be now displaced on to this new ideal Ego, which, like the infantile Ego, deems itself the possessor of all perfections. As always where the libido is concerned, here again man has shown himself incapable of giving up a gratification he has once enjoyed. He is not willing to forgo his narcissistic perfection in his childhood; and if, as he develops, he is disturbed by the admonitions of others and his own critical judgment is awakened, he seeks to recover the early perfection, thus wrested from him, in the new form of an Ego-Ideal. That which he projects ahead of him as his ideal is merely his substitute for the lost narcissism of his childhood—the time when he was his own ideal.'

Freud distinguished clearly between Idealization and Sublimation. Sublimation was a process that concerned the *instinct*, whereas, in the way we have outlined, Idealization was a process that concerned the *object*. The formation of the Ego-Ideal should not therefore be confounded, Freud emphasized, with Sublimation. The setting up of the Ego-Ideal *required* sublimation, but could not *enforce* it, and much conflict resulted from the incompatibility between the Ego-Ideal on the one hand and the capacity for sublimation on the other.

Sublimation was defined:

'. . . as a process that concerns the object-libido and consists in the instinct's directing itself towards an aim other than, and remote from, that of sexual gratification; in this process the accent falls upon the deflection from the sexual aim.'†

The sexual instinct was held to be extremely important in human life because of its 'capacity for sublimation'. The end achieved by the mechanism of sublimation, then, was that of deflecting an instinct from its appropriate aim, and it was often described as a process of 'de-sexualization' or 'aim-inhibition'. When frustration resulted from the fact that the discharge of an instinct was prevented by some obstacle, this tension was reduced by the process of sublimation, whereby the instinctual tendency achieved gratification in connection with another, and perhaps remote, aim.

* 'On Narcissism: an Introduction', Collected Papers, 1914, vol. iv, III, p. 51.
† *Ibid.*, p. 51.

Identification was mentioned as a distinguishable mechanism by Freud, but it seems to overlap considerably with what we have described as Idealization and Introjection. Whilst stating that Identification was, 'the earliest expression of an emotional tie with another person', and illustrating it as the boy's special interest in his father (his wish to be like his father) as distinct from the 'true object-cathexis' which was developed towards his mother, Freud said, 'We may say simply that he takes his father as his ideal'. In view of what has been said earlier as to the origin of idealization (the over-estimation resulting from the narcissistic component in the object-choice) Freud now seemed to be holding that, in this process of Identification, there was a more simple and direct setting up of an ideal. Similarly, Freud spoke of Identification, in another sense, in precisely the same way as he spoke of the 'introjection into the Ego of object-choices'. And, thirdly, he suggested that identification could be established when a common quality was perceived to be shared by the individual and some other person or persons. In this latter sense, children would identify themselves with each other in respect of their common position with regard to the parents; and members of an adult group would identify themselves with each other in respect of their common relation to the leader of the group.

'What we have learned from these three sources may be summarized as follows,' Freud wrote. 'First, identification is the original form of emotional tie with an object; secondly, in a regressive way it becomes a substitute for a libidinal object tie, as it were by means of the introjection of the object into the Ego; and thirdly, it may arise with every new perception of a common quality shared with some other person who is not an object of the sexual instinct. The more important this common quality is, the more successul may this partial identification become, and it may thus represent the beginning of a new tie.'

It is clear from this, that Identification cannot be strictly separated from other mechanisms we have described. Essentially, however, according to Freud, Identification was the name given to that process whereby a person attempted to mould his own Ego, 'after the fashion of one that has been taken as a "model".'

It will readily be seen that this account of the 'mental mechanisms' operative in the human mind went very far beyond the contributions of the other 'social psychologists' we have considered, and a number of points are very important here.

First, this substantially supports the suggestion we made earlier that Freud contributed an original and detailed 'Learning Theory'

---

* Chapter VII on 'Identification' in *Group Psychology and the Analysis of the Ego*, 1921.

which had clear and immediate relevance to the understanding of the formation of the 'self' in 'society' and, indeed, to the study of all dimensions of the 'psychological aspects of society'. This was a 'learning theory' going far beyond the 'stimulus-response' type, and all notions of 'conditioning' and 'reinforcement'—which were (and remain!) so hopelessly remote from many of the qualitatively distinctive attributes of human experience and conduct. This 'learning theory' took all dimensions of the human 'psyche' into account in a full 'genetic' analysis, (i.e. from the very conception of the organism, through its embryonic formation, from birth into infancy, and through childhood and adolescence into adulthood). It included neuro-physiological processes; instinctual energies and their somatic and chemical sources; internal and external sensory stimuli; the over-all 'schema' of bodily, physiological, and psychic 'economy' and 'balance'; the emergence of consciousness and the laying down of memories; the emergence of the 'self' and the moral regulations and aspirations of 'conscience'; the elements of conflict and striving in the personality and an analysis of 'normal' and 'pathological' adjustments; but also, finally, this detailed clarification of the many 'mental mechanisms' operative in the mind throughout this complex process of accommodation to the external material and social environment.* It included a detailed account of all those attributes and qualities of human 'learning' and 'thinking' and 'behavioura adjustment' which *were not themselves deliberately learned*, and which went beyond (lay beneath) the more formal, articulate, logically ordered discourse of science, philosophy, and the most exact kind of epistemological, ethical, and political processes of thought and judgment. This was a very considerable and wide-ranging achievement. But there were other very important aspects.

At the same time, this learning theory encompassed *both* the understanding of those mental processes involved in the formation and maturation of the organism and the 'self' *and* the grounds for analysing the many-sided mental processes accompanying the ongoing social relationships and behaviour of adults in all the complexities of society. It offered, in short, an analysis of the 'socio-psychological' complexes of mental intercourse in society within which 'selves' took shape, in the same kind of way as that indicated by Cooley and

---

* Though it is not to our purpose here, it may be noted how all the dimensions of psychological research that have been of significance in the development of psychology can find a place within this conceptual scheme of Freud's: the study of embryology, of neuro-physiology, of 'sensation', of 'memory' and 'selective memory' (Gestalt psychology and Bartlett's *Remembering*), Head's and Bartlett's rather neglected concept of the 'schema', etc. . . . also how the *relations* between biology, physiology, psychology, social psychology, and sociology permit of great clarification.

Mead. Furthermore, Freud obviously in large part *supported* and *enriched* the analysis of 'sentiment-formation' (the attachment of the 'self' by a focusing of emotions about a cognitive 'object'), the 'internalization' of 'primary group ideals', the 'socialization' of the 'self' within the 'values' embodied in 'institutions', and the like which McDougall, Cooley and Mead had provided; but also *went beyond it*, and *added* to it, in providing new dimensions of analysis in linking the processes of the organism with those of 'mind' in 'society', and, especially, providing an account of this rich array of 'mental mechanisms' which supplemented their account of 'communications'—gesture, symbolization, language, etc. The exploration of the 'social-mental complex' of society and individual 'selves' was both deepened and made more comprehensively systematic by Freud's contribution.

Freud's system of analysis, then—on the face of it so different with its emphasis upon sexuality, and its apparently unique concepts —can be seen to 'fit', with no difficulty at all, into the conceptual systems of McDougall, Cooley and Mead. All of these contributions taken together constituted a very considerable development indeed of the study of the 'psychological aspects of society', and we might end this brief exposition of Freud by indicating how a simple extension of his concepts could lead to a very systematic and comprehensive 'social psychology'.

(VII) FREUD AND THE 'PSYCHOLOGICAL ASPECTS OF SOCIETY'

In Diagram (7) we have done no more than suggest a setting out of Freud's ideas within a simple systematic scheme to embrace the whole of a society. We have used the term 'primary impulses' to indicate the 'instinctual' impulses which have their source in the neuro-physiological sources of the organism, and the 'secondary impulses' to indicate those motivations which have been established in the growing 'self' by the qualifying influences of regulations and values. And we have indicated both the *sequences* of the development of the 'self' as Freud conceived them (of infantile sexuality to the age of 5, of 'latency' from then to puberty, and—after adolescence— of full adult participation in the complex roles of society) and the relevant groupings connected with each 'stage'. We have also suggested the *extension* of Freud's notion of the introjection of loved-objects and their values in primary groups in *two* ways: (1) his *own* way—of insisting that the family is a part of a wider society, and therefore the *introjection* of the *parent-figure* will be also (in some way and to some extent) an introjection of wider social traditions, and (2) in showing that, in the process from infancy through adolescence to adulthood, the individual 'self' will accommodate itself to a wide multiplicity of 'roles' and 'values' and 'cultural symbols' as it encounters each institutional element of the social system—since each institution, too, is yet another organization of rules and procedures imposing certain *constraints* related to the *fulfilment* of certain social tasks and objectives (the performance of certain functions).

The diagram scarcely needs comment, but in it, it can be seen clearly how all the 'psychological' aspects of society can be mapped out, and how, within this pattern, the development and experience of the individual can be analysed.

(1) During the first 5 years or so, the individual (with his own genetic endowment, and experiencing the demands of the 'primary impulses') moves from 'inner psychic reality' to a consciousness of

7

THE PSYCHOLOGICAL ASPECTS OF SOCIETY

'self' and of the external material and social world within the family, and in close relation to the parents and the home. At the end of this period the consciousness of 'self' has emerged and the first 'ego ideals' (the Super-Ego) have been established.

(2) During the latency period, the child experiences the 'primary impulses' but also, now, the qualifying 'secondary impulses' which tend to be reinforced in the wider primary groups in the locality and neighbourhood. In play-groups, school-groups, and possibly 'religious groups' (in conjunction with parents) this widening of social experience and reinforcement of values takes place. Throughout this process of 'accommodation' to the social world, all the various 'mental mechanisms' are operative in this 'social learning'.

(3) During adolescence, adult maturity is achieved and the individual then has, in part, to take an important stand and important decisions—deliberately abandoning much of the past of childhood and neighbourhood, of attachment and dependence, and adopting roles in the complex network of social institutions: occupation, property ownership, political responsibility, military service, training for qualifications, social class constraints and differentiations, marriage and the founding of his own family, and the like. The 'mental mechanisms' are still operative, but also, now, conscious formal reason, the articulate arrangement of knowledge, the formation of deliberate judgment and the undertaking of responsible, purposive action come more dominantly to the fore. And in this entire process from infancy within the home to adult responsibility in society, the establishing of sentiments and the formation of attitudes goes on—and all these are closely related to the institutional fabric of society and the sequences of social action which take place within it.

In this way, the 'psychological aspects of society' can be systematically explored with the use of Freud's system of concepts. But before leaving this—let us note that McDougall's, Cooley's, and Mead's concepts could be fitted *exactly* into this same 'schema'. The sequences of experience, the order of groups (from primary to secondary), the internalization of values, the sequential order of motivation, the close relation between 'self' and 'society' through the 'primary group and its values', the growth of the 'self' through 'communication' and 'symbolization', the order and importance of the development of sentiments and attitudes (instinct, values and sentiments, attitudes) . . . all these had the same agreed significance in their respective systems of analysis, and all could—with complete agreement—be fitted together, with mutual deepening and enrichment, into this same diagrammatic scheme.

Only one further comment needs to be made about Freud.

(VIII) DETERMINISM AND AMBIGUITY

In all the other 'socio-psychological' theories we have discussed, there has been an emphasis upon purpose, choice, deliberation, action. As well as the more 'deterministic' relations of cause and effect between psychological factors, there was some substantial recognition (within the theories) of what the earlier writers called the distinctive 'teleological' qualities of the human mind. Freud was peculiarly ambiguous in several ways on this issue, and we must look, at least briefly, at his position simply to see how it fits with that of the other writers. On the one hand, he gave just as firm an emphasis upon the 'purposive' elements in the human mind as McDougall* or anyone else before him. His entire conception of the insistent 'driving' of the instincts, and their 'craving' for quiescence with gratification, emphasized important 'aim-orientated' elements of the psyche with all that is entailed for 'selective' perception, the defence-mechanisms of the mind, the emergence of the 'Ego' in confronting the external world, etc. Yet, at the same time, Freud insisted upon a '*thorough-going determinism*' in all his scientific analysis; declaring that science could do no other than work on the assumption of objective cause-effect connections among the various elements of its subject-matter. In this sense, then, his recognition of the 'aim-orientated' appetites of the mind did *not* entail any lack of 'determinism'. Freud's analysis of all the vicissitudes of the organism and the 'self' proceeded on the most rigorous assumption of determinism.

In his clinical conception of 'psycho-analytic' treatment, however, and the entailed conceptions of what constituted mental 'health', or even the desired 'maturity' of the personality, Freud did not seem able to avoid ambiguity. For 'psycho-analysis' rested on the conviction that the analyst could *not impose* a 'cure' upon the personality of the patient. The patient, through the self-discovering process of talking over his problems with the analyst, had—it was held—to get back to those points of 'fixation' in which his symptoms were rooted, and to the conscious and deliberate re-experience of those severe conflicts which had forcefully imposed the pathological adjustment. Only by finding his own way to the acceptance of the reality underlying these conflicts, and coming to his own conscious accommodation to them, could he 'cure' or 'alleviate' his pathological condition. Now this clearly entailed to *some* degree the assumption of rational *responsibility* within the 'self' for the resolution of its own problems. Furthermore it entailed two other things: (*a*) the distinction between a *true* and *realistic* recognition of the actuality of a situation together with a *positive* mode of accommodating it; and a *false*, or

* What McDougall insisted upon as 'Hormic' psychology.

selectively distorted view of it together with a *defensive avoidance* of coming to terms with it; and (*b*) an assumption that there was a *mature* and *healthy* type of personality, capable of the former kinds of recognition and response, and an *immature, ill-adjusted*, and pathological type of personality, capable chiefly of the latter. It is interesting to note, also, that this implied a distinction between rational, logical, empirically correct criteria of *truth* and that kind of adjustment by means of the 'mental mechanisms'. These distinctions are exceedingly important. But, for our own purposes at the moment, it is plain that there was much more than a simple, 'natural science' kind of 'determinism' here. There was a 'teleological' effort to overcome (deliberately, consciously, as a matter of choice), unfortunate constellations of adjustment in the personality (rooted in the past) and the assumption of criteria of truth by which it could find (though not necessarily) success.

Clearly, Freud was aware of how many of the elements going into the formation of a 'self' were not of the individual's choosing, and not within the range of his responsibility; and, in pathological cases, he was deeply aware of the limitations of reason and 'ideals' alone in overcoming the massively established constellations and forces of feeling in the psyche. No doubt this emphasis upon extensive degrees of necessitous determinism was warranted. Even so, it remains true that he was ambiguous here; that his clinical position (as well as statements in his writings: e.g. in 'The Future of an Illusion') certainly entailed conceptions of purposeful effort, rational action, and deliberate choice; and that there was therefore something of self-awareness and responsible effort in the very making of the 'self'.

Freud's conception can be said, then, even in this, to fit satisfactorily with the theories of the other writers, even though his 'agreement' here rests on ambiguity rather than clear theoretical pronouncement, and it has to be recognized that he himself was strongly committed to the assumption of determinism (rather like Durkheim) in his scientific work.

We are now in a position to see how far these various components which had been clarified in the developing study of the 'psychological aspects of society' were similar to those which formed the foundations of the one other large-scale system of sociological analysis produced during the early decades of the twentieth century: that of Vilfredo Pareto.

5
Vilfredo Pareto:*
The Social System: An Equilibrium of Psychological Forces

Pareto was a social theorist of great stature. He was of the same generation as those other scholars we have considered who made marked contributions to the 'development' of sociology during the early part of the twentieth century, but he was one among them who attempted—and, indeed, succeeded in formulating—an entire system of sociological analysis. The system he produced was as impressive in its scale, detail, and apparent analytical comprehensiveness as any of the systems of the nineteenth century, and as those of Hobhouse, Durkheim, Weber and others in the twentieth.† In this, he was different from the other theorists we have brought together in this (psychological) section. He was a sociological theorist in the fullest sense; working on a much larger scale of the analysis and comparative study of social systems than were they. Strictly speaking, his system of analysis deserves as full a critical study as we have devoted to any of the other great figures in the making of sociology. There are certain considered reasons, however, why it seems fit to discuss his work only to a relatively limited extent, and in this place (i.e. this section) in particular.

There are four limited reasons—all weighty and of importance, but not by any means of themselves decisive. The first is that many of the components of sociological analysis on which Pareto laid much emphasis—the structural-functional interdependency of institutions in society as a whole; the necessity of studying concrete sequences of social action; the rejection of 'mono-causal' theories of social order and social change and the recognition of 'multi-causality'; the use of 'equilibrium-disequilibrium' analysis; and many others besides—have already been dealt with fairly considerably and made sufficiently clear. The general agreement about them among all the major theorists has been sufficiently established, and Pareto

---

* 1848–1923.
† Though, as we shall see, much more open to criticism and much less satisfactory than they.

was no exception. Pareto certainly deserves credit in the same way as Durkheim, Weber and others (these elements were developed in his work from 1896—in the *Course of Political Economy* to 1916—in the *Treatise on General Sociology*) for developing the use of such components in the study of societies, but we should not benefit much by considering them in extensive detail here (though we shall certainly not ignore them). Secondly, though, as we shall see, he wrote in a systematic way about the socio-psychological elements of the social system, his categories were by no means clear, or clearly used, and there was a decided limitation to the extent to which he was prepared to explore relevant and important dimensions of his categories. Putting this in another way, and taking one example, he was too readily satisfied—on discovering empirical regularities of human psychological disposition—to suppose that they were rooted in fundamental 'instinct', without even taking care to establish criteria for supposing that this was so; and then all too ready to impute ineradicable and compulsive forces to them which simply had to be accepted as perennial and universal 'data' of society. Consequently— though full of the many and (to a point) profound insights of a brilliant and original mind—his analysis, in certain respects, did not leave the level of 'common sense' observation and comment. It is in this sense, for example, that Freud can be said (in my judgment) to be so much superior in his account of the 'mental mechanisms' operative in human experience and behaviour. Pareto simply *described* certain 'mechanisms'; whereas Freud gave a detailed account of the elements and stresses of the psyche in terms of which the nature and operation of the 'mechanisms' could be understood and explained. Even so—this is not said with the intention of derogating Pareto's contribution in this direction too much; only to indicate the kind of insufficiency and limitation I have in mind. Actually, Pareto and Freud can very usefully be considered as being complementary to each other.

The third reason is similar—but with regard to *social* facts. We shall see that Pareto did refer to 'composite facts' or 'composite phenomena' at the associational level—elements of 'social structure' and their inter-connections; but, again, his account of them was deficient in terms of organizational and group structure. But the fourth, and most important consideration, is that Pareto's rather 'cavalier' manner of assuming that his conceptual distinctions were all right, though arbitrary, if he could put them to demonstrable use in subsequent scientific analysis, sometimes led him to propound very fundamental cleavages, of dubious correctness, on which entire edifices of theory thereafter rested. To pull such a 'catagoreal' foundation away—meant the toppling down of all the ingenious and elaborate structures built above it. And this, as I shall try to show, was true to the most serious degree with regard to his basic distinction between 'logical' and 'non-logical' action. In short, I think his entire system of analysis was seriously vitiated by this erroneous foundation.

All these reasons, then, have inclined me not to attempt a full critique of Pareto here. However, in themselves they would not be enough. For we examined Durkheim with much care, even though claiming that his work contained a great deal of serious ambiguity and error; and Pareto's system certainly contains much that is of permanent worth (as is the case with Durkheim) even when his 'deficiencies' are laid bare. It is therefore another consideration, in addition to these, which has weighed chiefly with me.

When Pareto's system is analysed in detail, it becomes quite clear that—though the structural patterning of social facts and social relationships formed a part of it—it was, very substantially, indeed essentially, an analysis of the equilibrium of social relationships in terms of basic, universal, enduring *psychological forces*. Far more than any of the other great 'system-builders', Pareto's systematic analysis of society and social change was not only one of 'collective socio-psychological conditions' (as Durkheim's could be said to be), but also rested upon the stipulation of basic psychological propensities of the human mind which *underlay* all the varieties of social and cultural organization in all societies. Perhaps more like Lester Ward than any other of the earlier writers, Pareto definitely conceived of these basic (instinctual) propensities as massive and unchanging psychological *forces*; as active *powers* or *drives* which forms of social organization always had to provide for and take into account. His account of much of this was therefore strikingly similar to those of McDougall, Freud, Cooley and Mead (especially the first two) in dwelling on these instinctual propensities, the all-important '*sentiments*' to which they gave rise in collective, associational conditions, and the 'mental mechanisms' in social action which stemmed from their dominating influence. It seems undoubtedly the case, then, that Pareto's *chief* contribution lay in providing, specifically and exactingly, a systematic account of the '*psychological aspects of society*', and that it is therefore in this place in particular that our consideration of his work best fits into our task of tracing the making of sociology. In this place, especially, we shall be able to see the close similarities between his conceptions and conclusions and those of the other writers in this section, and here, too, we shall best be able to see the way in which (like these others) he developed those 'socio-psychological' dimensions of the analysis of society which the earlier sociologists had left relatively untouched. Having said all this, we

579

shall, nonetheless, in our discussion, at least *indicate* all the main components of his system—though we shall do this fleetingly.*

There are other points about Pareto that should perhaps be mentioned by way of introduction. He is an extremely difficult writer to assess because of his personal idiosyncracies. For part of his life, Pareto enjoyed independent means, and he was, to a great extreme, the independent, uncommitted, self-indulgent scholar. He was urbane, a man of the world, revelling in his self-conscious brilliance, deriding the serious-sounding statesmen of his day (until after the first world war) with sarcasm, satire, and often contempt, and despising anything approaching a moralistic attitude. He was a kind of modern mixture of Byron and Machiavelli with the wide and worldly scholarship of a Montesquieu thrown in. A brilliant mixture! But this makes him difficult to judge. Sometimes his cynicism was refreshing and enjoyable in its zest and in its very effective pricking of pompous political bubbles. When people hotly 'explained' the atrocities of some German troops in the 1914–18 war in terms of a 'peculiar German barbarity', for example, Pareto wrote:

'Such things are of very common occurrence whenever human animals take turns in tearing each other to pieces. At all times and among all peoples this has been so. Everywhere and everlastingly human beings brutally ill-treat, slaughter and destroy their kind. When they cannot behave thus to men of their own race, they mete out this treatment to men of what they call "inferior" races. When they cannot vent their ferocity in foreign wars, they commit ghastly cruelties in civil wars. One notes with a certain wry amusement that it was General Sherman, a fellow countryman, no less, of Woodrow Wilson's, who recommended that the civilian populations of enemy countries should be treated with extreme brutality.'†

Much was written in this vein, and the cynicism seems to have an even more tragic point, and truth, in our own day. In a similar spirit—refreshingly forthright, whether one agrees with his judgment or not—he denounced particular writers. Having pointed out the weakness of an argument of Rousseau's, for example, Pareto then exploded: 'So he goes prating on! . . .' but—'Be it remembered that there are still many, many people who admire such meaningless drivel.' Much of this can be enjoyed and (sometimes) approved; but, frequently, the tone of uncommitted, dilettante cynicism palls, and

* There are several excellent essays on Pareto's sociology, as for example: *The Sociology of Pareto*, in *Reason and Unreason in Society*, Morris Ginsberg; and *Vilfredo Pareto*, Ch. 2. *Main Currents in Sociological Thought*, Vol. II, Raymond Aron. But the best study, together with a selection of Pareto's writings, is: *Vilfredo Pareto:* Sociological Writings, Selected and introduced by S. E. Finer, Pall Mall Press, 1966. Most of my references are to this selection.

† *Facts and Theories*, 1920. See: *Vilfredo Pareto: Sociological Writings*, p. 294.

it is easy to feel irritation, and outright impatience with many of his cavalier judgments. In the same way, his comments on human psychology and reformist political effort (of which we will give examples later) were frequently filled with acute observation and penetrating insight, but sometimes they not only seemed, but were, meretricious, shallow, and uttered with a kind of spurious, theatrical, indeed arrogant 'bravura' which is difficult to stomach. For example, he satirized those who sought (and fought for) *liberty* in society, only to inflict new tyrannies on others in the name of *liberty*. Such satire was, and is, frequently deserved. But his cleverness ran to the point of seeming, smartly, to pour scorn on all efforts to accomplish a maximization of liberty in society at all. And one cannot help but feel impatience with a brilliant dilettantism of 'culture' which had no way of dealing with a rather different, and brutish fascism just round the corner. In quite validly satirizing the idea of a 'war crimes' trial (to mention another example) by the victors in a war, Pareto commented that theories connected with this could not be taken seriously. 'The only appropriate answer to them', he wrote, 'is a mocking smile.' But sometimes one feels that the entire attitude of Pareto was characterized by 'the mocking smile'. One can readily see and admire his brilliance, but sometimes one sickens, and, as with Byron, one sometimes wishes that it was he, and not Shelley, who got drowned in the boat!

However, these comments are made only to indicate that—in Pareto—we come to a very different kettle of fish (as a person!) than we have encountered before. We shall focus our attention on his *ideas*; but it is only fair to remark that one cannot be at all sure that one's judgment is reliable on a writer who so frequently jars on one's sympathies. At the end of our study we shall come back to this by way of a comment on the relation between ethics and social science.

The Context and Continuity of Pareto's Work

Pareto's chief book on sociological theory was his *Treatise on General Sociology* which was written during the five years from 1907 to 1912, and published in 1916, but some of the more important ideas in it— the basic importance of the 'sentiments', the perennial existence in human societies of 'social heterogeneity', élites, and a process of interaction and 'circulation' of élites, etc.—had already been stated in earlier books and were a considered development of them.*

* *Cours d'Economie Politique*, 1896; *Les Systèmes Socialistes*, 1902, and *Manuel d'Economie Politique*, 1909. For a detailed analysis of the development of ideas in these books, and then on into the *Treatise*, see S. E. Finer: *Vilfredo Pareto: Selective Writings*.

Pareto's mature 'system' was thus a well-worked out set of components which had received much reflection over a long period of time; and it is worth remembering, too, that he came to this preoccupation with the theoretical improvement of social science relatively late in his life.

Two things of importance, especially, may be noted about these books with regard to the context and continuity of Pareto's work.

The first thing was that they revealed a clear continuity and acceptance of certain central ideas of the 'nineteenth century conspectus' as well as a decided critical attack upon some of them. Perhaps the most conspicuous and important element of agreement was Pareto's acceptance of the analysis of the social system in terms of interdependent elements of 'social structure' and their 'functioning'—on a parallel with the analysis of the anatomical structure and the physiological processes of the organism—and, particularly (in relation to this) his acceptance of the *fact* of social evolution. Here, although he spoke much of 'Social Darwinism' and of Marxism, the dominant influence was unquestionably Herbert Spencer. Though critical of some aspects of Spencer, he adopted the conception and analysis of 'Social Evolution'* in terms of the development of societies from a simple, undifferentiated condition (of relative homogeneity) to a condition of complex differentiation of structure and function in a process of increasing 'heterogeneity', but with also an increasingly close interdependency of parts. It is arguable, too, that his analysis of social order, conflict and change in terms of sociopsychological processes and the cycles of 'types' of society — especially from the 'militant' to the 'industrial'—and the significantly changing character of each (in terms of emphases upon different psychological qualities and the selection of types of character) was derived very much from Spencer. Altogether, Spencer was very much alive in Pareto's pages. There are many places, too, in Pareto where he quite specifically agreed that human nature became 'milder', more other-regarding—in short, more *altruistic*—as a concomitant of social evolution; and in this was in agreement with Comte's picture of the evolution towards a 'positive, industrial' type of society, and with Spencer's suggestion of the 'ethical' society emerging from the 'industrial'. But here, Pareto tended to look 'behind' these altruistic tendencies for disguised self-interest, and, on occasion, poured scorn on them. As, for example, his acknowledgement of a growth of 'pity' for criminals, but his cynical rider to this, that it showed also a 'decrease in pity for their victims'. Similarly, whilst noting the undeniable rise of socialist movements among the masses, and sympathy for them on the part of intellectual leaders (again, out of pity for

* See, also, Radcliffe-Brown, p. 713 and p. 732.

them in their conditions), Pareto was caustic and cautious about the blend of *self*-interest as well as disinterested devotion to the cause of others. He wrote, for example:

'It may well be . . . that many who derive personal advantage from engaging in practical socialism genuinely believe that they are implementing theoretical socialism for the good of all, or at least for the greatest number.'

This kind of statement carried a kind of caustic undertone of suspicion (suspecting the worst!), as though he could hardly bring himself to believe that it might be true. But the upshot of this is that—though showing agreement with many of the generalizations of the earlier writers—his agreements were always surrounded by a bristling set of critically sensitive antennae (so to speak), always on the ready for acute attack.

It is clear from all this that Pareto's system took shape within the context of the central ideas of the earlier sociologists, and that a continuity of critical development was there. Knowing 'Positivism'—with its 'Humanitarianism'; knowing Spencer . . . he drew from these bodies of work—recognizing their value here and there—but also subjecting them to the most remorseless criticism. He approved of Marxism—to give a good example—for bringing into the foreground of attention the activities of 'spoliation' which went on in societies with the domination of élite groups; but, at the same time, he poured scorn on Marxism as one kind of sociological theory which rested on 'sentiment' rather than the 'logic-experimental method', and saw all available historical 'evidence' through distorting, manipulating spectacles—bending everything to the emotionally rooted hypothesis which rested, really, on a profound wish-fulfilment.

Though accepting central elements of the 'evolutionary' perspective from these earlier theories, however, Pareto's central preoccupation and emphasis was upon analysing the *equilibrium-disequilibrium adjustments of social systems* in terms of certain *cyclical fluctuations*; so that it is fair to say that the overall weight of his theoretical approach was towards the provision of an apparatus of concepts for the *accurate analysis of social systems*, rather than a focus upon the understanding of the long-term pattern of social evolution for its own sake. And this leads us to the second important consideration.

One other highly significant fact for appreciating the *context* of Pareto's sociology was that he was an economist. He was one of the most influential economic theorists of his time—moving away from the earlier 'cost-of-production' theories of value and elaborating the

---

* *The Treatise on General Sociology*, see *Sociological Writings*, p. 232.

U

analysis of systems of market-exchange in terms of 'equilibrium' models. His discussions of economic analysis (and his dissatisfactions with certain aspects of it for certain purposes) and its relation to sociological analysis were very clear and judicious. He did not seek to load economic analysis with qualitative institutional imponderables which were not relevant to its chief task. Neither did he *avoid* such qualitative components in sociological analysis. He did not seek to 'stream-line' the sociological analysis of social systems in such a way as to 'ape' the elegance and mathematical accuracy of economics—only to have falsified the different nature of its subject-matter and its appropriate concepts and methods. Pareto's thinking on the relation between the two sciences was as clear, reliable, and constructive as any that has been undertaken. However, our own concern here is only to point to the quite clear context for Pareto's conception of sociology. Accepting the evolutionary views, and the conceptions of 'society' of some of the earlier sociologists proper; he also thought of sociology as the scientific analysis of social systems (total societies) in the same way that he thought of economics as the scientific analysis of market systems; and his 'analysis' was one of a clear delineation of the major components of the system and then the tracing and understanding of various 'equilibrium situations' in accordance with changing conditions within the system. The implications of this aspect of Pareto's thought—of this 'parallel' between the analysis of market-situations and societal-situations in terms of the equilibrium conditions among the components of specified 'models'—probably deserve much more exploration, and could conceivably lead to a closer relationship between the two sciences. It is highly significant that it was the work of Pareto, more than that of any other theorist, which persuaded Parsons* (and some of his teachers and colleagues) to explore the development of 'systems analysis' for the furtherance of the making of sociology. And it is also highly significant that Parsons himself was an economist. This entire development we shall come to in Volume 3 as the largest single development in the most recent discussions of sociological theory.

It remains only to say that Pareto's work did not have a wide influence until after its English translation by Andrew Bongiorno and Arthur Livingston in 1935 (*The Mind and Society*), but, almost immediately, it then made a considerable, if not an entirely favourable, impact. In 1936, a study—*Pareto*—was published by Borkenau. In the same year Morris Ginsberg offered a critical assessment of Pareto's sociology, based on the new translation. And—most significantly—a group of American social scientists* founded a seminar, at Harvard, to study Pareto, and by 1937, Talcott Parsons'

* Including Henderson, Homans, Talcott Parsons, and Schumpeter.

own detailed study appeared in his very influential book: *The Structure of Social Action*. Pareto's influence in the making of sociology was therefore amost entirely felt in the first few decades of the present century—and especially as recently as the thirties, though like Durkheim, Tönnies and the other important writers, he 'bridged' the two centuries, and had his roots fully in the critical assessments of the nineteenth century theories. We can now turn to an outline of his 'system', emphasizing chiefly the 'socio-psychological' elements of it.

Pareto's System of Sociology

(I) SOCIOLOGY: THE SCIENTIFIC ANALYSIS OF THE CONDITIONS OF EQUILIBRIUM OF SOCIAL SYSTEMS

Following from what we have said, Pareto's concentration was very plain, and can be taken as the starting-point—indeed, the basis—of his whole system. Though accepting the evolutionary perspective, and other important elements of the 'nineteenth century conspectus', his own preoccupation for the *development* of sociology was *the analysis of the equilibrium conditions of social systems*. In the *Treatise*, for example, having agreed that the study of the 'origins' of human 'sentiments', 'residues', etc., was important for some purposes, Pareto set it aside as being of little concern:

'. . . because "origins" are of little or no significance in respect to our enquiry into *the conditions of social equilibrium. This* enquiry is our main purpose . . .'*

But several other important aspects of this emphasis can quickly be noted. First, it involved a structural-functional assumption about the interaction and interdependence of the components in the 'social system'. Second, it clearly entailed continuous interaction among a multiplicity of components, and therefore rejected the possibility of an all-sufficient 'mono-causal' hypothesis for the explanation of all societies in all historical situations. Thirdly, it was a clear extension of the 'equilibrium-disequilibrium' analysis of social change introduced and employed by several of the earlier writers, as well as the extension of the 'equilibrium' analysis which was being developed for economics. But other points deserve, perhaps, special emphasis.

A fourth emphasis was that though he did think of societies as being in a condition of 'equilibration' with their external (physical) environments, as Spencer had done, he explicitly weighted these

* *The Treatise, Sociological Writings*, p. 218.

kinds of environmental factors more lightly than others. Conditions of soil, climate, etc., were, he maintained, of *relatively* minor importance; as were certain characteristics of population—such as those of 'race'. It was the *internal* components of the social system which were of the greatest importance.

A fifth point was that though he spoke of the 'structure' and 'physiology' of social systems and approved of this 'organic analogy' when thinking of social evolution, he explicitly rejected the 'organic' conception of a society as a basis for his 'equilibrium' analysis. Instead, he deliberately adopted a 'mechanical model'—not, however, in terms of a more rigid determinism but, on the contrary, in terms of greater *flexibility*. This kind of model, he argued, could better entertain the continuous action and interaction of a large number of elements within a system.

A sixth point of emphasis here (relevant to our earlier discussion of 'statics' and 'dynamics' in sociology) was that he also insisted upon a model of *'dynamic'* equilibrium. In short, he agreed emphatically with earlier writers that societies were *essentially historical* phenomena; that they were interdependencies of institutional parts moving along in a cumulative process of development; and that they should always be conceived as such. A dynamic model was essential, he argued:

'. . . society in its entirety being borne along by a general movement which slowly modifies it'.

Finally, with regard to the 'structural components' of the social system, we must note what was an *emphasis* but also a questionable *limitation* of Pareto's treatment: namely, that whilst he recognized that the social system had many such components, he chose to focus his attention upon only *two*: (1) the basic *psychological propensities* of human nature, and (2) the ways in which these were distributed among *élites*. The extreme limitation of this selection can be seen in the fact that *neither*, strictly speaking, were components of social organization. Élites might well be seen as the leaders of specific groups, movements, classes, or associations, and therefore studied from a 'structural' point of view; but Pareto was centrally concerned with the distribution of psychological qualities among them. On the side of the analysis of the 'structural components' of the social system, let alone of their interdependent 'functioning', it can be seen how limited, indeed unsatisfactory, Pareto's system was. But we shall see how he thought of the 'psychological propensities' as being part of the structure of 'composite social phenomena'.

With these attendant emphases, then, the distinctive task of sociology as a science, for Pareto, was *the analysis of the conditions of equilibrium of social systems.*

(II) MIND AND ACTION IN SOCIETY: THE DISTINCTION BETWEEN LOGICAL AND NON-LOGICAL ACTION

Since his entire analysis of 'society' and its 'equilibrium' was based upon his persuasion about the universal persistence of certain distinctive qualities of the human mind, Pareto's first step was to make what he considered a distinction of the most fundamental importance. It was the distinction between 'logical' and 'non-logical' action, and it was important because each required a different kind of analysis and understanding and employed distinctive methods of theorizing, and also because one was far more preponderant in social action than the other.

'Logical Action', as Pareto defined it, was almost exactly what Weber called pure 'rational action' (in the calculation of the means-end relationship) with the addition of the fact that it rested upon knowledge which was *objectively true.* Logical behaviour, wrote Pareto, consists of:

'. . . those actions which are logically linked to an end, not only in respect to the persons performing them, but also to those other people who have more extensive knowledge: that is to say, behaviour which is subjectively and objectively logical. . . .'*

The objective knowledge on which such action could reliably rest could only be provided by the use of the 'logico-experimental' method—which removed the examination of a 'theory' from the influence of bias and sentiment and ascertained (*a*) its objective logical consistency (i.e. its *validity* in terms of sequences of *inference*) and (*b*) its accordance with objective facts (i.e. its *truth* in terms of verification by experimental test).

But action resting on such exact knowledge; and purely logical in its accuracy of means-end estimations, judgments, and successful conclusions of action (i.e. actually attaining the ends intended); was, Pareto held, very rare in human affairs. Only a very limited sector of action in society at all approximated to it, and this was related to specific kinds of human propensities and specific fields of action. It was rooted in those instincts and '*interests*' which sought relatively straightforward *material gratification*, and about which, therefore, accurate 'logico-experimental' knowledge could be established; and it formed, therefore, chiefly *economic* action.†

* *The Treatise, Sociological Writings,* p. 34.
† The relevance of this to economics as the analysis of systems of market-exchange; of production to meet patterns of consumption (consumers' outlay); and its openness to quantification and mathematical calculation, is plain.

'Non-Logical Action' consisted of all other kinds of human action which were rooted in attachment to sentiment or subjective desire, sometimes without a definite orientation to ends, sometimes orientated to ends which were vague, diffuse, unattainable, and impossible to estimate in terms of logic or experimental test, and which, in fact, failed to attain either the end, or the achievement (or continuity) of the 'psychic state' which they sought.

It is important to see that Pareto *claimed* that such action was *non*-logical—not *il*-logical; and it is important, too, to see that he was not *belittling its importance* in claiming that it was non-logical. On the contrary, he argued, non-logical attachments of this kind were the very basis of the life of societies; they were the chief springs of aspiration and of conflict; and far and away the greater part of the entirety of action in society stemmed from them.

The theories which men held about non-logical action were supremely important for their *utility*, not their *truth*, and it was his growing consciousness of the significance of this point which was, in fact, the reason why Pareto insisted upon this distinction. He was very definite about this. Having considered certain 'theories of society'—such as religious theories, or 'Marxism'—Pareto wrote:

'. . . we realized that from the logico-experimental viewpoint they were absolutely lacking in precision and devoid of any strict accord with the facts. On the other hand, we could not deny their great importance in history and in determining the social equilibrium. This realization gave strength to an idea which had already come to mind and which will acquire greater and greater importance as our enquiry develops, namely, that there is a clear distinction between the experimental "truth" of certain theories and their social "utility"—these being two things which are not only quite different from one another but may be, and often are, in direct contradiction. The separation of experimental "truth" from social "utility" is as important as the distinction between logical and non-logical behaviour.'*

It is clear, in this statement, that Pareto thought of theories which supported 'non-logical' action in society as being of great importance among the determinants of 'social equilibrium' *irrespective of their truth*. They possessed *power* as ideologies. Even so, Pareto emphasized one other point. Whereas, in 'logical actions', it was the 'logico-experimental method' which tested and demonstrated their truth; in 'non-logical' actions, it was *not* the theory which was the ground for the actions, though this *seemed* to be so. Men held theories as to why they held such-and-such sentiments and performed such-and-such actions, but the *explanation* was *not* in the theories (as they

* *The Treatise, Sociological Writings*, pp. 215–16.

thought), but in the persisting instinctual propensities which underlay their feelings, thinking, and behaviour. In this case the theories
masked (or were variable manifestations of) the underlying propensities; and this is why Pareto came to call them '*derivations*'. There
were '*residues*' in the human mind—basic, perennial, universal—
stemming from its instinctual attributes; and 'theories' were *derived*
from them. *Thinking* was certainly involved in these theories; in these
reasons for action; but it was, said Pareto, of a *pseudo-logical* nature,
and its propositions had no testable basis in fact.*

This was an absolutely fundamental distinction for Pareto, for his
entire analysis of social systems rested upon the basic importance of
the nature, persistence and power of these 'non-logical' components
of mind and action.

'The principle of my sociology,' he stated,† 'rests precisely upon separating
logical from non-logical actions and in showing that in most men the
second category is far larger than the former.'

And again:

'Reason is of little importance in shaping social phenomena. The operative
forces are different ones; this is what I want to prove in my sociology.'†

(III) ELEMENTS OF THE SOCIAL SYSTEM

We now come to Pareto's treatment of the 'psychological aspects of
society'—which are of particular interest to us here; but we will deal
with them in such a way as to see their place in the entirety of his
system, and again, it might be useful to refer to the accompanying
diagram (overleaf) as an initial indication and guide.

(*a*) *Composite Social Facts: actions, correlated 'psychic states',
    and 'explanations'*
The first thing which is of much importance in considering the nature
and sufficiency of Pareto's method, is that although his express
intention was to study the elements of mind involved in the 'non-
logical action' which was so powerfully predominant in society, in

---

* It will be seen here that it is questionable how far Pareto was correct in claiming
that 'non-logical action' was not *il*-logical. It would seem that he was really
saying that '*sentiments*' were 'non-logical' but that the theories derived from
them were, strictly speaking, *il*-logical in that they were '*pseudo*-logical'. There
is a more basic point, however. In arguing that only 'logico-experimental'
knowledge of material 'fact' was 'logical' and 'true', Pareto may have been
unwittingly espousing not so much a '*materialistic*' *metaphysic* as a '*scientistic*'
epistemology. We shall come back to this.
† See *Sociological Writings*, S. E. Finer, p. 20.

PARETO'S SYSTEM OF ANALYSIS

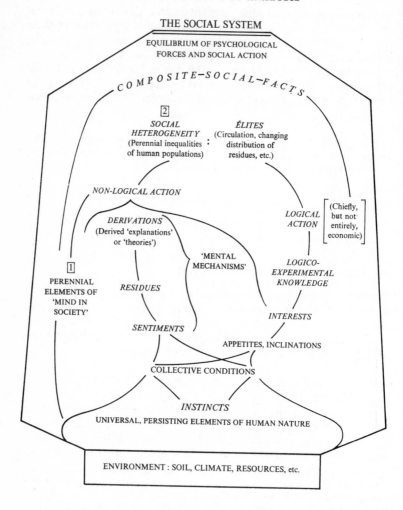

THE SOCIAL SYSTEM

EQUILIBRIUM OF PSYCHOLOGICAL
FORCES AND SOCIAL ACTION

COMPOSITE–SOCIAL–FACTS

2

*SOCIAL
HETEROGENEITY*
(Perennial inequalities
of human populations)

ÉLITES
(Circulation, changing
distribution of
residues, etc.)

NON-LOGICAL ACTION

DERIVATIONS
(Derived 'explanations'
or 'theories')

'MENTAL
MECHANISMS'

*LOGICAL
ACTION*

[(Chiefly,
but not
entirely,
economic)]

1

PERENNIAL
ELEMENTS OF
'MIND IN
SOCIETY'

RESIDUES

*LOGICO-
EXPERIMENTAL
KNOWLEDGE*

SENTIMENTS

INTERESTS

APPETITES, INCLINATIONS

COLLECTIVE CONDITIONS

INSTINCTS
UNIVERSAL, PERSISTING ELEMENTS OF HUMAN NATURE

ENVIRONMENT : SOIL, CLIMATE, RESOURCES, etc.

fact his analysis began with, and never left, the level of *social thought* and *social action*. Very much like Durkheim, his preoccupation was with the analysis of *associational facts* at their *own level*. This was nowhere shown more conspicuously (though we shall see it again in other connections) than in his starting point, and in his opening procedures; and these may be characterized in this way: that he began at the level of '*composite social facts*' and broke them down, by analysis, into their several components. The entirety of 'composite social phenomena' in society formed the distinctive field of 'facts' with which he was concerned. It was never a matter of the *reverse* order: of seeking meticulously to study 'lower-level components' and thereafter 'compounding' them into 'composite social facts'. This was decidedly Pareto's method—which had its logical virtues, but also involved him in ambiguities.

Pareto began his own 'theory' of the social equilibrium by analysing the 'theories' which he found in society. Distinguishing between 'logico-experimental' theories and those which underlay 'non-logical' action, and maintaining (*a*) that these latter were the predominating focuses of those powerful motivations which were active in social equilibrium, and (*b*) that it was their *use* not their *truth* which mattered, Pareto then concentrated upon the analysis of these 'non-logical' theories. An initial analysis, he argued, showed that such theories consisted of two components: (1) a 'constant, instinctive, non-logical element', and (2) a 'deductive element, the purpose of which was to explain, justify and demonstrate the constant element'. This provisional distinction, he claimed, had been arrived at *inductively*,* but it provided the core-elements of a theory of the operation of 'mind in society', which he then proceeded to develop.

Here, we are concerned only to note quite clearly that Pareto *began* with the observation of *composite social facts* which were established modes of action in society together with mental 'explanations' which made sense of them to the actors. Society consisted of a large, complex network of such composite social facts. Each of these could be analysed into the *actions* themselves and the *theories* which men held to explain them. The theories could then be further analysed into the instinctive, non-logical component on the one hand, and the explanatory component on the other. Pareto's analysis, from this starting point was simply a detailed study of each of these two components.

To be as simple as possible, Pareto's point of departure was this. Some social action which men undertook was clearly purposeful in

---

* We will not bother to stop and argue about this, but it will be seen how tenuous and assertive Pareto's 'starting-point' was. It was a hypothetical assertion claiming to be an empirical generalization arrived at 'inductively'.

terms of interests and the pursuit of calculable ends and rested upon testable knowledge. Such 'logical' action could be clearly understood in terms of meaning and rational calculation. It was important, but it occupied only a small part of the action in society, and we could therefore set it aside as permitting of clear explanation. The greater part of human social action, however, was 'non-logical'; resting on some sort of basic instinctual propensity and some attachment of feeling, and including some sort of supporting 'explanation' which was not of a 'testable' kind at all. The fundamental questions for the understanding of the equilibrium conditions of social systems were therefore these: (1) what were the constant, instinctually rooted elements of the human mind which formed the core of such non-logical actions? And (2) what were the characteristics of the 'explaining' or 'theorizing' aspects of the human mind which served to bolster the underlying 'core' but without making (or even wishing to make) reference to logico-experimental conditions of test?

It will be seen that this was no more and no less than an investigation of the basic attributes of the human mind and the 'mechanisms' which characterized its operation in coming to terms with the world and society. How, then, did Pareto distinguish these components into which his analysis had 'broken down' composite social facts?

(b) Analysis of components: residues, derivations, derivates

We can take Pareto's analysis a little further by introducing the terms which he deliberately used.

Those given, instinctually rooted propensities of the mind which were found to be constant in non-logical action, he termed the '*residues*'. The elements of theoretical explanation which supported the residues, and which were also common characteristics of the mind—though resulting in variable 'explanations' in varying social and historical circumstances, he termed the '*derivations*'. And the actual *composite phenomena* of 'action + feeling + specific-theory' in which these were manifested in any particular society, he termed the '*derivates*'.

Bearing in mind what we said earlier about Pareto's procedure, we can think of these terms in the reverse order. Only the *derivates* (the composite social facts) were really *observable* in society. Only concrete sequences of men acting and thinking were *observable*. The 'residues' and 'derivations' were the components into which the observed totalities and regularities of social action could be analysed. But such analysis *was* justified, he held, not only by conceptual distinction alone, but also by the results of very wide comparative studies. And these enable us to see more clearly what Pareto meant by 'residues'—because the propensities of mind which he had in mind here were much more than a straightforward list of 'instincts' such as other psychologists had put forward. It is best to take a specific example.

Wide comparative studies showed, he claimed, that very many groups and societies held that certain *days* were of evil omen. Catholics, for example, regarded Friday as a day of evil omen; the 'explanation' given for this being that that was the day of the Crucifixion. Now this *might* only mean that the Crucifixion *had* taken place on a Friday, and had been remembered as such. But Pareto went on to show that many peoples had the common and *constant* propensity of believing that particular *days* were of evil omen, but had a multiplicity of reasons for thinking so. There was a *common, constant* element—which therefore seemed a basic, universal characteristic of the human mind, and a variable element—the many theoretical explanations of its existence. The *explaining* was also itself a common propensity, but the *specific explanations* varied. It seemed therefore that the 'explanations' *had* to be produced in some form—but were *derived* from the residue, since the residue itself was constant throughout.

It will readily be seen in this example that the 'residues', for Pareto, were not just inherited neuro-physiological impulses with their correlated cognitive and behavioural elements (as with McDougall, for example), but basic *constants* in the manifestations of the human mind in all societies; basic mental *dispositions* which were always found in societies—even though their theoretical and institutional 'dress' (so to speak) was different. And we shall see in detail, in a moment, what, according to him, the residues were. But here we need only note that they were distinguished, by Pareto, solely on the ground that they were constant, common features of the human mind found at the heart of institutions in all societies. The residues were *observationally evident* in all known societies, at the level of *social facts*. Their constancy, their universality, therefore required explanation, but, as far as sociology was concerned, they could be taken as *given;* they were found to be fundamental components—no doubt rooted in the biological and psychological nature of man—which always characterized the operation of 'mind in society'. A knowledge of them was thus quite basic to sociological analysis.

(c) Instincts, Sentiments, Interests: the Psychological Foundation

This postulation of basic 'residues' really, in one sense, amounted to the specifying of a determinate *'psychological basis of society'*; and this, indeed, was Pareto's meaning. But it was in his attempts to be both clear and deliberately (methodologically) vague about the

593

psychological roots of the 'residues' that much ambiguity was let loose in his system; and yet we must see that the very ambiguities had their virtues. Pareto's looseness in these particular matters can be defended on certain understandable grounds—though I do not think they can ultimately be upheld. But what is certain is that in his treatment of the psychological dimensions of the residues, his conceptions and conclusions proved to be in quite basic agreement with the ideas of all the other writers we have considered.

The most important range of Pareto's discussion for our purposes was that in which he emphasized the *instincts* and the formation of *sentiments* as being the basic psychological sub-stratum (so to speak) in which the residues were rooted. Several very important points need to be noted in this connection.

The Basis of Instinct
First: Pareto quite definitely supposed and postulated a realm of *instinct* in man; the existence of instinctual attributes, capacities, propensities of the human mind which were genetically given, ineradicable, and universal. Second, he *supposed* this level of instinctual experience, with discernible attributes, *because* of the universality of the residues (not vice versa!): a universality which could not be explained in terms of the 'rational theories' which *apparently* accounted for them—since *these* were the most *variable* elements! Third, he recognised, nonetheless, (a) the experiential and behavioural imprecision of human instinct—as compared with instinct in other animal species,* and (b) that it could not be assumed that the examination of the instinctual elements manifested in the 'residues' would constitute an *exhaustive* account of instinct. There might well be, he argued, instinctual qualities of feeling, perception, thinking which were *not* reflected in specific residues, and which went beyond them. Some might be manifested in straightforward appetites and interests; but even this might not be exhaustive. Certain other points of importance were closely attendant upon these considerations. The fourth point was that though the 'residues' were rooted in instincts, they were not to be *identified* with them. Instinctual experience no doubt had dimensions going beyond specific 'residues', but also 'residues' consisted of *more* than their instinctual components. The fifth point was that Pareto insisted that the 'residues'—in so far as it was possible for us to observe and know them—were always manifestations of

* This did not mean that Pareto thought human instinct *different* from animal instinct in all respects. In fact, he compared them very frequently in discussing various propensities, dispositions, impulses, emotions, etc. We are referring here only to the degree of *plasticity* of instinctual experience and behaviour in man.

594

instinctual experience within *collective (associational) conditions*. In this, again, he was insistent that sociology was concerned, essentially, with *social* facts. There existed (in human societies) only human experience and behaviour as manifested in *composite social phenomena*. Only *social* patterns of experience and behaviour were *observable*. The 'components' were elements of *conceptual analysis*—which should be pressed as far as seemed necessary and sufficient, but which must always be seen to be what it was, and no more. Such an analysis did not 'reify' components (among which were 'instincts') any more than a reverse method might 'reify' a total 'society' by extrapolation from composite social facts. The final, sixth point here, then, was that any *reductionist* psychology—which sought to lay bare 'instincts' as the *original* components of composite social facts, was not the concern of sociology. Pareto was very clear here: he did not reject the worthwhileness of any such investigation of 'origins'. He simply insisted (*a*) that the observable field of facts which concerned sociology were 'composite social facts', and (*b*) that for the understanding of the equilibrium conditions of social systems the basic, constant, universal 'residues' should be analysed as far as seemed necessary—but could not be 'atomized' into 'original' components. Social facts were always psychological patterns *within collective conditions*, and should be seen to be such. This was Pareto's way of insisting upon what, elsewhere, we have called the essential *'associational context'* for any satisfactory human psychology.

It will be quite clear in all this that Pareto had important, and to some extent justifiable grounds, for his view about the relation between the 'instincts' and the 'residues', but that, by the very difficulty of both the *human (social) actuality* and the *conceptual distinctions*, some ambiguity was unavoidable. Consequently he sometimes referred to 'residues' as instincts, though sometimes distinguishing them carefully.

'Residues,' he wrote in The Treatise, 'correspond to certain human instincts; they are therefore usually deficient in precision and strict delimitation. . . .'

But:

'We must guard against confusing residues with the sentiments or instincts to which they correspond. . . .'

Despite this warning, however, ambiguity of language abounded in Pareto. The last comment, however, shows that the same ambiguity attended his discussion of the relations between the *sentiments* and the residues, but before turning briefly to this question, we might

595

note one final point about Pareto's conception of the 'instinctual' attributes of man. Because of his concentration upon those instinctual propensities manifested in 'residues',* he regarded as being 'instinctive' certain propensities of the human mind which went beyond the 'inherited impulses' of some psychologists. Thus, even certain propensities in *combining things* in perception and feeling—in short, kinds of *'thinking'*—were, in his view, basic, universal attributes of the human mind which seemed to be *'given'* in the human species, and did not seem to be 'rationally learned' in any sense. In all this it is clear that Pareto's ideas could not only agree in accommodating certain of Freud's dimensions of 'instinctual experience', but also in accepting some of Cooley's suggestions that even certain propensities of *perceiving* and *thinking* were instinctive. These points —raised here only to indicate agreement among ideas—are well worth consideration in their own right; since much recent discussion has tended to separate 'instinct' and 'learning' in the most limited and spurious way.†

Sentiment

It is also of central importance for us to notice that the great importance which Pareto attached to the 'residues' for the understanding of the conditions of social equilibrium and disequilibrium, was a very strong agreement with the emphasis of practically all the other writers on the importance of the *sentiments* in society. For Pareto thought of the residues as being essentially rooted in *sentiments* as well as in the *instincts*; and, indeed, he thought of instincts, sentiments, and residues as having the closest relationships with each other. Again, therefore, the same ambiguity was strongly marked.

The 'sentiments' arose, Pareto thought, from the operation of the 'instincts' within the natural and social conditions (and cumulative traditions) of the life of a people.

'These sentiments originate in man's nature combined with his life-circumstances. . . .'‡

They formed, he held, the 'hard-core' of the residues. They were also patterns of feeling about standards of value, and in this Pareto clearly agreed with other writers that *morality* lay at the heart of social institutions.

* The focus of concern of sociology, he argued, is: '. . . our enquiry into the conditions of social equilibrium. This enquiry is our main purpose, and therefore the instincts and sentiments which correspond to 'residues' assume paramount importance'.
† Excepting among some of the 'Comparative Ethologists'.
‡ *Manual of Political Economy*, See *Sociological Writings*, p. 43.

'Human beings . . . have certain sentiments which, in particular given circumstances, serve as the norm of their behaviour. These sentiments affect various classes of human activity, amongst which are . . . religion, morality, law and custom. . . .'*

And in many places Pareto tended to state that the residues in 'composite social phenomena' almost *corresponded* with sentiments. Thus, he wrote in the 'Treatise' that the residual element was 'the expression of certain sentiments'. The residue was ' . . . a psychic state—which can be termed a principle, or a sentiment, or what you will . . . ' and since it was : ' . . . clearly that to which the human being is most strongly attached . . . ' it was 'the element of the greatest importance for our investigation of the social equilibrium'.

As with so many theorists, with Pareto too—the *sentiments* formed the socio-psychological core of social institutions; of the very process of *institutionalization*. All this is reasonably clear, but in order to indicate the kind of difficulty and ambiguity which attended Pareto's very efforts to become clear, we can do no better than quote one very relevant passage.

'To clarify the terms we are using, it should be noted that, since sentiments are manifested by residues, it will often be the case that—for the sake of brevity—we shall refer simply to "residues", designating thereby also the sentiments they manifest. When we say that residues are among the elements which determine the social equilibrium, this statement must be translated and understood as meaning that "the sentiments manifested by residues are among the elements which have a relationship of reciprocal determination with the social equilibrium". Yet this statement also is elliptical and needs to be translated in its turn. We must beware of attributing an objective existence to residues or even to sentiments. What we observe in reality are human beings whose psychic state is revealed by what we call sentiments. Our proposition must therefore be translated in the following terms: "The psychic states revealed by the sentiments expressed in residues are among the elements which have a relationship of reciprocal determination with the social equilibrium." But even this is not enough if we want to express ourselves with the utmost precision. What are these "psychic states"? They are abstractions. What underlies them? So we must say: "The actions of human beings are among the elements which have a relationship of reciprocal determination with the social equilibrium. Among such actions are certain manifestations which we term 'residues' and which are closely correlated with other actions, so that if we know the residues, we may in certain circumstances know the actions. Hence we shall say that residues are among the elements which have a relationship of reciprocal determination with the social equilibrium.'

* *Manual of Political Economy*, See *Sociological Writings*, p. 149.

Derivations also manifest sentiments. They directly express the sentiments corresponding to the residues from which they originate; indirectly they express sentiments through the residues which serve for purposes of derivation. But to speak of derivations in place of the residues they express, as is customary in ordinary language, could lead to serious errors; therefore we shall refrain from doing so in all cases where any doubt about the meaning of a statement is possible.'*

It will be seen in this passage that even *derivations* as sell as the residues in which they are rooted were held to 'express sentiments'. The looseness of Pareto's language is therefore quite apparent—but also apparent is the central importance of the sentiments as the very core of his analysis of residues and derivations alike. To emphasize the great underlying importance of the instincts and sentiments, we might note one more brief statement. The residues, Pareto wrote:

'. . . are the manifestation of sentiments and instincts, in the same way as the movement of mercury in the thermometer is the manifestation of a change in the temperature. Only in an elliptical way, to shorten the argument, do we say that the residues—together with the appetites, interests, etc.—play the principal role in determining the social equilibrium, just as we say that water boils at 100°C. The complete proposition would be: 'The sentiments or instincts which correspond to the residues, together with those which correspond to appetites, instincts, interests, etc.; play the principal role in determining the social equilibrium. Water boils when its calorific condition reaches a temperature which is indicated by 100 degrees on the scale of the Centigrade thermometer.'†

It is quite plain that the changing intensity of residues and derivations were really held to be the *socially observable indicators* of the underlying conditions of instincts and sentiments, and that it was the *latter* (the instincts and sentiments themselves) which were the psychological forces which moved—like the hidden currents of fire within a volcano between equilibrium and disequilibrium conditions. To call them the 'prime movers' of all the complexities of action in human society would not be far removed from Pareto's meaning.

Interests
There is the final point that the instinctual dispositions of human nature were such as to give rise not only to sentiment-formation and appropriate 'theoretical justifications', but also to direct appetites and clearly related *interests*. These were the other powerful sources of motivation in the psychological basis of society, but, as we have seen, Pareto thought that these could chiefly and satis-

* *The Treatise, Sociological Writings*, pp. 218–19.   † *Ibid.*, p. 217.

598

factorily be incorporated in an analysis of 'logical action', and so we can leave them out of our consideration here.

We have seen sufficiently clearly for our purposes, the way in which Pareto thought of the instincts, sentiments and interests as forming—in the closest interrelationship with each other—the central core of the residues and derivations on the one hand, and the rationally calculated action on the other. We must now look more closely at his description and analysis of the 'residues' and 'derivations' themselves.

(d) The Residues

Pareto described six distinguishable kinds of residue; six basic classes among those propensities of the human mind which persisted in all kinds of society; and each of these was then more elaborately analysed into 'sub-classes'. The ambiguity of Pareto's terms will be clearly seen as we proceed.

The first, and perhaps the most important of all the 'residues', was the '*Instinct of Combination*'. This was the universal, distinctively human tendency to *see relations between things*; to associate like with like; to distinguish objects according to relevant similarities or differences; to establish links between things (between elements of experience) which were sensed to be significant. Clearly this 'instinctive tendency' or 'disposition' of the mind underlay all systematic perception and knowledge; it underlay all 'discovery' of the connections between things in the world; but, Pareto argued, it was by no means necessarily *rational* in the sense of carefully controlled logical thought and observation. The human mind moved through its experience with a many-sided and never-failing ingenuity in linking things together in all kinds of non-rational and irrational ways. Things may be grouped together as 'generic forms' through the possession of some attribute. 'Magical associations' were formed between events and following occurrences—as, for example, when good things were associated with fortunate events, or malevolent things with terrifying events; and between names and the things they designated: so that to *name* a thing could be held to exercise some active power over it. But this *urge to combine* went beyond establishing specific (bit-and-piece) links between things, specific regularities, to a desire to bring some order to bear within and among these regularities. Thus the human mind had a tendency to *combine the residues themselves*: to produce a *synthesis* of them; to create a *systematic whole* of experience. And this was often coupled with the urge to seek *logical* explanations. The two were not necessarily connected. In art, the creative unity of sentiments and symbols might not include logical explana-

599

tions. But in the creation of a philosophical system, obviously logical considerations would be involved.

Intriguing questions arise from Pareto's point of view. Earlier—in connection with theorists like Hegel and Marx—we mentioned the tendency which is often apparent for men of this stature to wish to work their systems out to some kind of *entirety* and *conclusion*. It is an entailment of Pareto's view that the completeness and conclusiveness of 'systems' of thought might well be more a product of a prevailing and powerful instinctual disposition of the mind than of an orderly universe. Man is a 'theorizing animal' according to this view, and creates 'systems' out of inner disposition perhaps as strongly as out of any constraining order of 'objective facts'. Man imposes his 'theoretical systems' upon the world. These are intriguing notions; as is also the possibility that the urge to the systematic completion of a *scientific* theory might well lie in an *artistic* disposition. However, we need only note, here, that, for Pareto, the instinct of combinations was a distinctive disposition of the human mind which underlay the most 'non-rational' association of sentimental attachments to the most extensive speculation which men might undertake in seeking systematic coherence in their experience of the world.

The second—and similarly important—residue, was the *'Persistence of Aggregates'*. When combinations had come to be established in the human mind, there was a strong tendency towards a *conservative attachment* to them; to abide by them; to be reluctant to change them. And this was concomitant with several characteristics of human association, residence, and communal experience. There was, for example, a strong tendency for bonds of attachment to spring up between individuals in the same families, groups, social classes and neighbourhood communities; and also between these people and the *places* (the territory, etc.) in relation to which they shared the basic conditions of their community life. The 'combinations' established did in fact take the form of deep-rooted sentiments, and these came even to be 'personified' and given 'objective reality' by certain kinds of symbolization. Such sentiments could come to have the binding force of a 'religious' dedication; indeed, such a process might well *be* the *institutionalization* of *religion* in society.* And Pareto discussed, for example, the way in which the persistence of relations between the dead and the living; between the 'ancestors' and the living members of a community; could come to cement the bonds of these communal sentiments.

There was, then, a disposition of the human mind not only to *establish* combinations, but, once they were established, to *retain*

---

* Note the great similarity to Durkheim here.

them. The human mind had strong dispositions which were both *speculative*, and *conservative*.

The third basic disposition of the mind was that of enhancing, strengthening, reinforcing such sentiments by repeated *acts* of certain kinds: the '*manifestation of sentiments by activity*'. When men are attached to sentiments, they have a strong disposition to *enact* them in positive ways: as, for example, in dances, celebrations, rituals, ceremonies. And Pareto argued that such *enactments* (involving specified modes of activity and participation in them) *both (a)* reinforced the sentiment in those who already held it, *and (b)* could serve to instil it in those who did not.

A fourth set of dispositions were all aspects of man's essentially *social* nature: the '*residues of sociality*'. The human mind, Pareto argued, was naturally disposed to association in many, if conflicting, ways. There were straightforward desires to associate with others in order to share enjoyed activities or seek particular advantages. There were shared experiences of happiness and hardship, of kindness and cruelty; of connected feelings of pity for those who suffered hardship and cruelty; of repugnance and disapproval against those who caused it; and of a desire to impose a uniformity—even equality—of procedure on all men in society to eliminate such injustices.* There was a desire to be like others in society, but also a resentment against those who strained to be different; and therefore roots of both self-discipline and the insistence of imposed discipline in society. Sentiments were also formed about the classes and ranks in society—of superiority and inferiority, of authority and obedience, of power and dominance and submission and respect. And there was also a need for the approval of others which, however, was also paralleled by the disposition of some to escape society and to seek a life of solitude, of withdrawal from society, of simple asceticism. Again, the similarity with Freud is very clear here: the idea that, given frustration, the instinctual dispositions could even seem to turn about upon themselves; to be hidden; to seek apparently strange forms of 'substitute' gratification. And Pareto was very plain—throughout his discussion of the 'residues'—in his teaching that no one composite social *act* could be identified directly with one residue.

'All social phenomena,' he wrote, 'are complex, mingling many residues . . .'

The fifth class of residues—those dispositions upholding and furthering the '*Integrity of the Individual and his Appurtenances*'— was thought by Pareto to be complementary to the residues of

* The similarity with Adam Smith and Westermarck especially is very clear.

sociality, but I would like to place a particular emphasis upon these. The residues themselves were clear enough. There were basic dispositions in the individual, Pareto held, to secure and increase his own property—his own foundation for life; to establish securely his own personality—with all its dispositions, sentiments, needs, ideals; to secure and perpetuate—and if possible improve—his position in the hierarchy of status in society; and to act in such ways in society as to maintain that 'status quo' which was most in accord with all these dimensions of his personal life. These 'individually' orientated sentiments would themselves support kinds of motivation and social action which would have important consequences for the equilibrium or disequilibrium of the social order: making for its conservation or its change.

The vitally important point here, however—on which we shall later hinge a fundamental criticism—is this. One might well ask: on what grounds should Pareto consider social action stemming from *these* dispositions *non-logical*?* Surely, we might think, the individual in pursuing the security and furtherance of his own person, his own property, his own class-and-status position, and the kind of changes in (or defences of) the social order which will best ensure these things, is pursuing his *interests*, in a *calculated* way, and acting deliberately to attain determinate *ends*. How does this differ from 'logical action'?

And, strangely enough, Pareto himself fully acknowledged the substantial ground for such a question. He wrote:

'That sum of sentiments called "interests" is of the same nature as the sentiments to which the residues of the present class correspond. Sentiments of "interests" therefore ought strictly to be included in this classification, but they are of such great intrinsic importance for the social equilibrium that it is better to consider them separately from residues.'†

For the moment we will not pursue the criticism to which this point gives rise, but it will be seen at once that though Pareto's distinction may be understood, in that he wanted to distinguish the 'logical' and 'non-logical' kinds of action which were rooted in the same 'individually orientated sentiments', even so this acknowledgement of their fundamental similarity in this case of the 'integrity of the individual', opens the door to the question as to why there should be *any* crucial distinction at all between actions oriented to the attainment of ends—whether stemming from residues or interests, whether economic or political, or, indeed, with regard to the retention or change of any institutional aspect whatever of the social system. Is there any ground at all for such a crucial distinction?

* Later, we shall pose the same question about *all* the residues.
† *The Treatise, Sociological Writings*, p. 234.

We shall come back to this point.

The sixth, and final residue distinguished by Pareto was the '*sex residue*', and we need say little about this. Pareto was not concerned about the nature and strength of the sexual appetite as such—though he did believe that it possessed 'tremendous strength', and was such as to make seem 'ridiculous . . . those pygmies of our day who imagine they can repress it'. He was centrally concerned to see how sexuality entered into common forms of social action and 'theory': as, for example, in religion and in political and legal forms of regulation. Very much like Freud, he was aware of the many ways in which sexuality, in conditions of regulation, took other "disguised' forms of behaviour and thought.

To summarize: a comparative study of composite social facts and their attendant 'theories' revealed the existence, claimed Pareto, of six common, basic, persisting dispositions of the human mind. Always, in society, men in their feeling, thinking and acting (1) established regularities of combinations between elements of their experience (2) tended to conserve them, once established, (3) reinforced, enhanced, and perpetuated such sentiments by social 'enactments' of various kinds, (4) were led into both order and conflict by their various (though essential) dispositions of sociality, which were (5) complemented by their pursuit of individual security of personality, property, and social position, and (6) were driven—both directly and indirectly—by their powerful appetite of sexuality.

These comprised the constant, common psychological basis of human action in societies.

(e) Derivations

The 'explanations' or 'theories' which attended the residues were, according to Pareto, of four chief kinds—though each, again, had its several sub-classes.

The first kind of 'explanation' was no more and no less than sheer *assertion*. Sometimes the ground for acceptance of a 'residue' was a straightforward assertion of *supposed* (not necessarily *true*) *fact*. (For example: women are weaker than men; or—black men are inferior to white; or—Jews are of higher intelligence than other races.) Sometimes, it could be a sheer assertion of the *sentiment* itself. (For example: 'It is right to love your neighbour as yourself.') And sometimes it was an assertion of some mixture of *both* supposed fact *and* sentiment. But in all cases the sheer assertion was taken to be the satisfactory justification (and explanation) of the relevant set of residues.

The second kind of 'explanation' was, in one of several ways, a clear indication of *authority*. Sometimes, a particular individual was indicated as a satisfactory authority. If this lay in a field of his special competence—as, say, in claiming that Sir Bernard Lovell held a certain view about the solar system—this had a certain rationale; but sometimes, Pareto argued, the authority had no clear 'logical' relevance at all, as, for example, if Sir Bernard Lovell was named—let us say, in a television programme—as supporting a particular theological doctrine or a view about sexual morality. Sometimes the authority referred to was that of 'tradition'—some pronouncement, or document, or ritual, of 'custom' or 'sanctioned usage'. And sometimes, it was of a religious nature—referring to the authority of 'God' or 'the gods' or of some 'divine representative'.

The third kind of 'explanation' was that of claiming (and supposedly showing to the hearer's satisfaction) that the 'residue' was *in accordance with the wider sentiments or principles of others*. In the same way, the denunciation of certain sentiments of others could be achieved by claiming that they were absurdly *out of keeping* with the wider sentiments and principles of others. This, of course, speaks for itself.

The fourth and final kind of 'explanation' was that of '*verbal proofs*'. These were, strictly speaking, *pseudo-rational* explanations which gave the appearance of being thoughtful, analytical, deliberately reasoned, but which were, in fact, couched in terms which had no determinate meaning, in propositions which could in no way be subjected to test. They were, said Pareto, 'logical sophistries'.

It will be clearly seen, particularly in the second, third and fourth of the 'derivations' that Pareto fully acknowledged that 'conceptualization' and 'thought' of a kind went into the support and justification of the residues and the sentiments and instinctual dispositions which they contained, but it was thought *not* of a logico-experimental kind aiming deliberately at demonstrable knowledge, but of a rhetorical kind, aiming at bolstering, justification, persuasion and manipulation.

Pareto's distinction can be seen very clearly in the following quotations concerning the *use* to which an understanding of 'non-logical action' in society could be put by the self-conscious manipulators of government.

'The art of government,' he wrote, 'lies in finding ways to take advantage of . . . sentiments, not in wasting one's energies in futile efforts to destroy them—the sole effect of which, frequently, is simply to strengthen them. The man who can escape the blind domination of his own sentiments is in a position to make use of the sentiments of other people for his own ends . . .'*

* *The Treatise, Sociological Writings*, pp. 244–5.

And:

'Legislation can be made to work in practice only by influencing interests and sentiments; and it must be stressed that the derivations which will have to be used for this purpose differ entirely from the logico-experimental reasonings employed in determining what legislative measure is best adapted to a given end.'*

Three things are worth noting very briefly in these statements. First, we can plainly see the 'flavour' of dilettantism and the Machiavellian slant of Pareto's own position. Secondly, however, we see, too, that *some* men can evidently 'escape the blind domination' of their own sentiments. And thirdly—very important—they can influence interests and sentiments to manipulate a population towards their own ends of power. *But*—if these things are possible—*then* (a) logico-experimental knowledge and 'logical action' can be utilized as the basis for manipulating political power—even if this gives knowledge of how to use other kinds of 'derivations' *and* (b) there is therefore no reason why those in government *need* be Machiavellian. They can just as plausibly try to *educate* the population to free them from the blind dominance of sentiments so that they, too, may learn to participate in a mode of democratic government which makes more use of 'logical' than of 'non-logical' action. It can be seen that there are quite fundamental criticisms of Pareto's entire position here. However, we must first see how he completed his 'system' for the analysis of society.

So far, we have seen the place of the instincts, the sentiments, the residues to which they gave rise in collective conditions, and the derivations which arose to explain and justify them to men in particular social systems, in forming the perennial elements of the human 'mind in society'. We have seen, too, how all these, strictly speaking were described by Pareto as 'mental mechanisms' (to use Freud's term) in terms of which the psychological forces among human beings in association were accommodated to each other in equilibrium-disequilibrium conditions of the entire social order. This was Pareto's basic picture of the psychological aspects of society.

But within this context, Pareto also built another element of analysis to interpret, or 'explain', the ways in which the 'disequilibrium-equilibrium' tendencies in society took place, and to offer, in short, a theory of both the *structural order* of society and of its patterned sequence of *change*.

(f) Social Heterogeneity : Élites

The single, powerful emphasis; the one starkly clear focus of attention; which Pareto selected and developed for the analysis of 'the

* *The Treatise, Sociological Writings*, pp. 244–5.

conditions of social equilibrium' rested upon the simple fact that men were always *unequal* in their physical, intellectual, and moral qualities. In every activity which men undertook—in any craft or occupation, in any profession, in commercial enterprise and the management of business, in politics, in education—those who were associated in that activity possessed different capacities and levels of ability and skill, and could be graded—according to any simple convention of measurement—into a 'scale' of relative superiority and inferiority. There was, in short, always a 'hierarchy' in the organization of any human activity, and those who were at the head possessed distinctive degrees of power and influence over the nature, range, and quality of social affairs. All the many activities in society were always marked by their appropriate *élites*.

Now Pareto quite deliberately decided *not* to pursue detailed studies of all the organized activities in society as such. He was crucially concerned to understand *the conditions of equilibrium and disequilibrium in society*, and, he argued, it was the nature and change of *élites* that could be taken to be the central and crucial issue for this purpose. This was, then, a strong, deliberate selection of what he took to be the vital factor in social order and social change.

But Pareto made one or two further points of qualification. First, he claimed, the many *élites* in society could never be sharply and accurately distinguished at any particular moment of time. All social activity was a process—and a cumulative but fluctuating process—and the *élites* in all organized activities were continuously changing by recruitment, promotion, replacement, and displacement. Besides identifying social élites as accurately as possible, it was therefore also necessary to focus attention upon their *changing nature*. But secondly, Pareto simplified his position further by claiming that among *all* the élites of a society, *one* was of dominant importance (again—with special reference to social equilibrium)—and this was the *governing* élite: that élite responsible for the manipulation of power, and the taking and implementing of decisions which were binding throughout society. But this too was continuously changing as certain personnel displaced others.

In order to analyse the conditions of equilibrium of a total society, Pareto therefore proposed a division of its entire population in this two-fold way. First: we should distinguish clearly—in *all* the activities of society—between the élite-groups and the larger non-élite. These could be regarded as the two significantly different 'classes' in society. Then, secondly: we should make a distinction among the élites themselves—distinguishing between the *governing* (political) élite on the one hand, and all the other specific élites, who could be grouped together as the *non-governing* (non-political) élite, on the other.

There were, then, two outstanding components in Pareto's system of sociological analysis : (1) his schematic analysis of 'élites' and (2) his analysis of the psychological forces of society (instincts, sentiments, residues and derivations, taking the form of specific composite social facts). The link between the two was Pareto's persuasion (hypothesis) that (*a*) the specific *structuring* of the residues and derivations in the specific *equilibrium* (or disequilibrium!) of all the composite social phenomena at any time, depended crucially upon the nature and change of the élites, (*b*) that the character and qualities of the élites was crucially a matter of the distribution of a certain dominating pattern of residues and derivations among them, and (*c*) that the *changing* equilibrium-disequilibrium condition of society was centrally a matter of a *circulation* among the élites coupled with a *changing distribution of residues* within and among them in accordance with changing situations. This conceptual apparatus thus permitted a systematic analysis of the equilibrium conditions of social systems in terms of those components which, according to the focus of his own hypothesis, Pareto considered to be the most important; and though it was *limited* (eschewing the detailed study of many aspects of social organization), we have seen that it was *deliberately* so. The 'apparatus' was consciously and selectively delimited in relation to Pareto's strong hypothetical persuasion.

(g) Cycles of Interaction

Having clarified the components of his system, Pareto then offered a very detailed analysis of the *interactions* between them in such a way as to provide explanations of the changing conditions of social equilibrium.* In this it is interesting to see that (like others) he conceived of 'ideal types' or 'models'.

It would be possible, Pareto said, to construct two extreme 'types' of social system: one in which *sentiments* were solely operative (without any reasoning), and one in which logico-experimental reasoning was solely operative. This, it will be seen, would be very similar to Tönnies' 'natural community' and 'contractual society' typology (which, indeed, itself rested upon Tönnies' distinction between the two kinds of 'willing' in the human mind). In fact, however, a human society (as distinct from animal societies) was always somewhere between the two 'poles'; sentiment and reasoning being always in varying ways and to various extents combined. Pareto wrote:

* Let us note that there was no question here of 'order' and 'change' or any (misconceived) 'statics' and 'dynamics'. For Pareto social systems were *always*, *essentially*, *processes*—and 'order' and 'change' were aspects of the process; the social process was *always* in some condition of equilibrium or disequilibrium, and it was the task of sociology to be able to analyse and explain this condition.

607

'Human society lies between the two types . . . As well as by environment, its form is determined by sentiments, by interests, by logico-experimental reasonings which serve to satisfy sentiments and interests, and by subordinate derivations which express and sometimes strengthen sentiments and interests, and are in certain cases effective as methods of propaganda. Logico-experimental reasonings have value and importance when the end is assumed and when appropriate means are sought for to achieve this end. Hence we find them employed with great success in the arts and crafts, in agriculture, industry and commerce. Thus it has been possible to create, not only many technical sciences, but also a general science of interests—economics—which presumes that such reasonings are exclusively employed in certain branches of human activity. They are also of great value in warfare and have given rise to such sciences as strategy. They could possibly be highly relevant to the science of government, but— either because the objective is not determined, or, if known, it is considered undesirable to reveal it—they have so far been employed in this field more as an art by particular rulers than as elements in the creation of an abstract science. For these and other reasons, logico-experimental reasonings have in general played little part in the ordering of society. Scientific theories are still lacking in this field; in all that concerns it men are moved much more by sentiments than by reasoning. Some of them know how to profit from this circumstance to satisfy their own interests; as opportunity occurs, and according to the requirements of this or that situation, they employ reasonings which are empirical and to some extent logico-experimental.'*

The four clear components in all the activities which had to assume *some* sort of equilibrium in *any* social system were: (1) residues, (2) interests, (3) derivations, and (4) social heterogeneity—élites and their circulation, and Pareto went on to analyse the '*cycles of interaction*' that took place between them. He did this quite systematically, exploring for example:

The nature, extent, and importance of the ways in which:

(*a*) 1 acts upon 2, 3, and 4,
(*b*) 2 acts upon 1, 3, and 4,
(*c*) 3 acts upon 1, 2, and 4,
(*d*) 4 acts upon 1, 2, and 3,

and in this way estimating the part played by each in sequences of social change. Briefly, he believed that (1) *residues* were of very great importance in providing the very basis of the system of social institutions; and, furthermore, that they were of crucial importance in securing social *continuity* since they varied only very slowly in

* *The Treatise, Sociological Writings*, p. 256.

608

(historical) time, and maintained a very powerful hold over the minds of men and their 'traditions'. Here, again, we see Pareto's agreement with all those who had emphasized the central power of the *sentiments* in institutionalization; and we can see, too, what a solid *consensus* of agreement among all theorists this was. (2) *Interests* were also of great and perennial importance, and Pareto credited Marx with having recognized this—though he thought Marx had distorted their degree of importance by over-emphasizing them to the exclusion of all else. Again, we can see here Pareto's clear agreement with all those who had emphasized in their systems of analysis the purposeful practical activities of men in seeking practical advantages. (3) Derivations were, Pareto claimed of the least importance, since they were, strictly speaking, the servants of the much stronger residues (sentiments) and interests in which they were rooted. The power of social 'theories' to influence the actualities of social feeling and behaviour was, he thought, very limited, and, indeed, illusory. (4) Élites and the circulations within and among them, Pareto also thought of crucial importance, but we must look more closely at what he had to say about the process of 'circulation'. What we should emphasize here is that though Pareto discussed these *'cycles of interaction'* between the four chief 'components' schematically in the way we have indicated, he nonetheless insisted that *always* the *concrete equilibrium* which existed in a particular society was a product of *all* these components in complex inter-connection. The analysis of interactions with the concept of a *theoretical equilibrium* was, and could only hope to be, an *approximation* to a full picture and a complete knowledge.

(h) The Circulation of Élites: The Distribution of Residues

Some of the 'cycles' of interaction which Pareto described were of particular importance for illustrating what he had in mind as the 'circulation' of élites coupled with a changing distribution of residues in society. And we should note here that, for Pareto, it was the relative distribution, among élites, of the first *two* kinds of residues which was of determining significance: that is—the disposition towards 'combinations' (the connecting, speculating, dispositions) and the disposition towards the 'persistence of aggregates' (the conservative dispositions to retain connections and sentiments which have already been established.)

One of the clearest 'cycles' Pareto outlined was what he called the 'military-industrial' cycle. This, in fact, was very similar to Spencer's typology of 'Militant' and 'Industrial' social orders, and was almost a utilization of these on the part of Pareto to fit his own conception of the analysis of changing 'equilibria'. In the 'military society'—

pursuing conquest successfully, and establishing the security, power, prestige, and possessions which resulted from war—the governing élite possessed a dominating concentration of the '*conservative*' residues. The extension, and the stability of social equilibrium, of a military society intensified such 'conservative' dispositions; insisted upon the upholding of established sentiments in society at large, and recruited élite members with these qualities into the *governing* élite. Following upon the conclusion of war, however, and with the settled conditions of peace and peaceful activities there was a change towards the increasing importance of the 'combining, speculative' residues. Among the non-governing élites new directions of activities would open up and be extended. The governing élite itself would be influenced by these new interests, but, chiefly, the growing forceful-ness of the new dispositions and activities would force changes in the governing élite. Personnel would infiltrate and be recruited to power who possessed a predominance of the 'speculative' residues. The composition and the qualities of the governing élite would be changed. But this would itself *weaken* the '*conservative*' capacities to sustain stability of government and power. And therefore, after a time, an *unstable* equilibrium would result; disequilibrium conditions would exist; and therefore—perhaps even by revolution—the 'speculative' governing élite would be displaced by a new 'conservative' élite which would re-introduce a powerful basis of order and stability. A new equilibrium would be established.

A second kind of 'cycle' which Pareto outlined was predominantly in the field of *economic* action. It was too simple, he held, to lump all those who were influential in property-ownership and economic enterprise as 'capitalists'. Among the economic 'élites', too, it was possible to distinguish those who possessed predominantly the 'speculative', from those who possessed predominantly the 'con-servative' residues. The former could be called the 'speculators'—making and exploring ever new connections in enterprise; the latter could be called the 'rentiers'—who were much more cautious and much more concerned to defend the resources of wealth already securely established.* The one group was always pressing for change; the other always cautiously restraining it—not *denying* it, but wanting to move in a slow, sure, well-considered way.

'The different proportions in which speculators and rentiers are combined,' Pareto wrote, 'amid the governing class correspond to different types of

---

* Pareto was careful to make it clear that he did *not* identify 'speculators' with political 'progressives', or 'rentiers' with political 'conservatives'. The 'speculator' and the 'rentier' were two 'types' which would be combined, or be in conflict, differently in different situations.

civilization; these proportions are among the chief characteristics which have to be considered in social heterogeneity.'*

In this way, then, Pareto saw the *governing élite* in a society changing its composition, qualities and character in accordance with changed situations, by a process of *cycles of circulation* between the non-élite population, the non-governing élites, and the governing élite alike; this circulation consisting chiefly of an appropriate redistribution of the 'combining-speculative' and the 'persistence-of-aggregate' residues.

'By the circulation of élites,' he wrote, 'the governing élite is in a state of continuous and slow transformation. It flows like a river, and what it is today is different from what it was yesterday. Every so often, there are sudden and violent disturbances. The river floods and breaks its banks. Then, afterwards, the new governing élite resumes again the slow process of self-transformation. The river returns to its bed and once more flows freely on.'†

This, then, was Pareto's system of sociological analysis. This was his conception of the nature and change of social systems. Throughout, we have been able clearly to see the absolutely fundamental place given to the psychological aspects of society and the changing distribution of them, mediated (so to speak) by the changing composition of élites. Our central concern has been to clarify this one other 'development' in the study of the psychological aspects of society, and we can now briefly assess Pareto's treatment, and suggest certain criticisms in coming to a conclusion.

Criticisms and Conclusions

(i)   THE PSYCHOLOGICAL ASPECTS OF SOCIETY

We have seen that, after Ward, Pareto offered an account of society (a system of sociological analysis) which, more fully than almost any other dwelt upon the psychological elements which formed the basis of society, and, indeed, upon the powerful psychological *forces* which were held together in the formation of sentiments and the more complex conditions of social equilibrium. A number of points deserve to be noted very clearly.

First of all, Pareto did undoubtedly lay emphasis upon the fact that the human mind possessed discernible qualities, tendencies, capacities, powers which were of a resistant, abiding nature—not

---

* *The Treatise, Sociological Writings*, p. 265.   † *Ibid.*, p. 250.

alterable in radical ways by the changing culture of societies, not easily obliterated by the changing dress of history—and that these qualities were, without any doubt, powerful compulsive *forces* which we had to take into account as such, and which were harnessed by no means easily and comfortably within the constraining fabric of social institutions. It has become unfashionable to speak of psychological *forces*, but Pareto would (if we were among those who held this view) regard us with his mocking smile, and ask us to think again about the seething cauldron on which we were looking with such professional, conceptual nicety. Pareto was cynical—but he had a healthy respect for the *powers* of the human mind. In this he was even more forceful than Ward, though he would have agreed with his recognition of, and respect for '*socio-psychological forces*'. He would have agreed with McDougall with the emphasis placed upon the *instinctual* dispositions of man (though he would have thought McDougall rather narrow and limited in his treatment); and—perhaps especially—he would have agreed with the kind of picture of the compelling *forces* of the mind conveyed by Freud. It may be that in our contemporary awareness of the diversity of cultural forms, we tend altogether to under-estimate not only the basic, common, qualities of the human mind with which all societies have to deal (in their institutional organization), but also the wide-ranging dimensions and powers of the mind which may well go beyond all institutions. Pareto's emphasis, at any rate, was very firm: the psychological aspects of 'society' were the most fundamental facts of all!

Secondly, we have seen that Pareto (though with an apparatus of different concepts) emphasized the same basic ideas concerning 'socio-psychological processes' as all the other twentieth century writers. He fully insisted upon the 'associational context' for any understanding of human psychology. He held the same conception of the 'socio-psychological aspects' of 'institutionalization': the shaping of '*instinctual*' dispositions into '*sentiments*' and the development of conceptual and ideational *thinking* within this context. He placed the fullest emphasis upon the '*sentiments*' as the heart of institutions and the vehicles (so to speak) of *values* in society; and he saw the growth of '*sanctions*' and '*authority*' and '*theories*' (derivations) about such '*sanctions*' in much the same way as other theorists had done. Also—as with Freud—he had detailed many 'mental mechanisms' by which the mind operated in the process of adjustment to social conditions and constraints *in addition to* straightforward 'logico-experimental' reasoning as such. Pareto did not focus his attention upon the relations between the 'self' and 'society' as did McDougall, Cooley, Mead and Freud; his own concern was much more on the psychological aspects of the larger-scale conditions of social equilibrium. Even so the many-sided agreement between his conceptions and those of the other writers is very plain.

There are, however, one or two criticisms of Pareto which seem to be necessary, even on this basic matter of the psychological aspects of society.

First, as we have seen, he deliberately stopped short of analysing all the elements of 'instinct' in man, and all the detailed processes of 'sentiment-formation'. He was content only to *discern* the basic *residues* of the human mind as manifested in the composite social phenomena of many societies, and to *suppose* that they were rooted in instinct and sentiment. Without losing sight of his methodological clarity in this, it is clear, nonetheless, that this left a gap in Pareto's system. His account not only excluded a study of these elements of 'socio-psychological' processes, but, as an important part of this, gave no explanation of the grounds for the tenacity and power and relative unalterability of the 'residues' and their equally dominating power in engendering and influencing the 'derivations'. These, however, were dimensions which McDougall, Cooley, Mead and Freud filled in—so, for our purposes, it might seem that we need not make too much of this point.

It is a point of real substance, however, and must be pressed further to be linked with, and to encompass, one other criticism: namely, that Pareto's deliberate methodological limitation led him into an ambiguity of concepts, terms, and the use of them, which was so loose as to go beyond any clear bounds of control. Sometimes he called a residue an instinct; sometimes he insisted the residues were more than instincts. Sometimes he spoke of the residues as synonymous with 'sentiments'; sometimes he warned against identifying the residues with sentiments. Sometimes he clearly distinguished between 'residues' and 'derivations' on the one hand, and 'interests and logico-experimental reason' on the other; yet in discussing the 'integrity of the individual' he suggested that, in this case, they were both the same. And when it came to the re-distribution of the residues in the circulation of élites, his use of terms went completely beyond the bounds not only of clearly controlled conceptual distinction, but also of any kind of test of application. Without at all derogating the 'components' which Pareto thought to be important, then, it is nonetheless the case that his methodological delimitation left not only a *gap* in his account of socio-psychological processes, but also, and consequently, led to an impossibly loose conceptual ambiguity.

The same point may be made in comparing Pareto with Freud in one important respect. Pareto certainly gave an account of 'mental mechanisms' in his discussion of the residues and derivations which was full of interest, and paralleled Freud's account in certain (and supportive) ways. But because of his lack of a more detailed analysis of the components and processes which gave rise to the residues, and continued to influence the derivations, his account was, strictly speaking, only of a 'literary' or 'common sense' kind throughout. Freud's account, on the other hand, was arrived at and constructed by a meticulous linking of concepts.

All this amounts to this conclusion. On the one hand, Pareto's analysis of the psychological dimensions of society, and of the socio-psychological processes of institutionalization, were such as to show very substantial agreement with the conceptions of the other writers we have considered, and, indeed, to go beyond them in some respects (in the analysis of 'élites', etc.); and certainly to agree in emphasizing their importance, and the importance of developing the study of them. On the other hand, his methodological limitations—though deliberately imposed for understandable reasons—left serious gaps in his analysis, and, worse, involved him in uncontrollable (i.e., logically and scientifically uncontrollable) ambiguities. The categories which Pareto employed were insufficiently exact for the detail which he wanted them to convey. Despite all this, however, we have been able to see—what is of chief importance for our own task of tracing the 'developments' in the making of sociology—how, even in what, at first glance, seemed such a different system of sociological analysis as that of Pareto, there was such close agreement between him and the other writers in their analysis of the psychological dimensions of social processes.

(II) INSUFFICIENCY OF CATEGORIES AT THE LEVEL OF SOCIAL STRUCTURE AND SOCIAL EQUILIBRIUM

Criticisms of the same kind can be levelled at those of Pareto's concepts by which he sought to analyse the conditions of equilibrium among composite social facts. His classification of élites was certainly clear and worthwhile, as was his focus of attention upon them, and, indeed, it could be said that this way of conceiving the 'classes' in society, or the 'hierarchies of status', was much more promising than that of Marx. It was not doctrinaire; not at all one-sided; and permitted an open-ended investigation of the many-sided changes of 'status' and 'class' in society. However, we have seen two things clearly. First—and again for deliberate reasons—that Pareto set aside any detailed study of 'structured' social organizations; and second—even in his study of élites, his concentration was not upon their organizational positions and relationships and changing situations, but upon the 'distribution of residues' among them. This meant that—apart from his one analysis of élites—he provided no picture of the *structure of social institutions* at all. It was entirely a disequilibrium-equilibrium picture of socio-psychological forces. Indeed there was another aspect of his approach to theory which (I think) lends force to this same criticism, and deepens it.

It will be remembered that in choosing a 'model' for the 'equilibrium analysis' most appropriate to the study of social systems, Pareto deliberately selected the 'mechanical' as against the 'organic' model. He was not doctrinaire about this by any means, and quite clear. He had no objection to the 'organic' model for the conceptualization of social evolution: the process of increasing differentiation of structure and function; but he rejected it in favour of the 'mechanical' model for purposes of 'equilibrium analysis'. And this was because he felt the 'organic' model was too de-limited with its definiteness of structural-functional formations, whereas the 'mechanical' model would permit the most fluid analysis of a multiplicity of 'points' within the 'system'. The criticism which seems to me to be quite basic here is this. In adopting this model, and for this reason he gave, Pareto clearly showed an 'atomistic' conception of the elements of the social system. His conception, really, was that of a multiplicity of particular 'composite social phenomena'—consisting of residues and derivations which were themselves borne upon instincts and sentiments, but having no kind of *structural framework*. As we have seen above, only the élites were clearly selected, but these were more or less abstracted from their specific hierarchical organizations and considered chiefly in terms of the particular distribution of residues they possessed.

There was, then, an insufficiency of categories in Pareto's system at this level too, and one cannot help thinking that the 'organic' model was more suitable than Pareto supposed—even for an appropriate 'equilibrium analysis'—since the nature of social systems *is* such as to have organized parts (specific institutions and associational organizations), and is *not* just a vast multiplicity of flexible elements. Spencer's 'structural-functional' equilibria of 'types', for example, were much more clearly delineated on the basis of the 'organic' type of system that was Pareto's analysis in terms of a 'mechanical' system. Here again, however, it seems probable that this was a matter of Pareto the economist—thinking of a 'system of market exchange' (which *was* conceived as a vast multiplicity of decisions of consumers and producers), applying the same conception, erroneously, to sociology—as an analysis of 'societal systems'.

Certainly, for all Pareto's apparent clarity in delimiting the categories of his system, there was a vagueness and insufficiency of his categories at the level of analysing the *structural components of society* as well as at the level of *socio-psychological processes*. But we come now to what I think is the most fundamental criticism of Pareto.

615

W

(III) THE INSUFFICIENCY AND HARM OF PARETO'S BASIC DISTINCTION BETWEEN LOGICAL AND NON-LOGICAL ACTION

The criticism—stated baldly—is this. There is no ground whatever for Pareto's primary distinction between 'logical' and 'non-logical' action. The entire analysis erected on this basis is therefore prone to ambiguity and error in sociological analysis proper, and is also ethically and politically harmful.

Now this is not only a bald, but also a very large statement, and we must consider the grounds for it.

Clearly, first of all, some of Pareto's points can readily be accepted. It is true enough that non-logical attachments to sentiments, asserted 'principles', asserted 'authorities', are at the heart of much social action. It is true enough that 'non-logical' instinctual processes are involved in the formation of 'sentiments', and that these are very powerful focal points of attachment, of values, and of motivation in much social action. It is true that a distinction can be drawn between kinds of 'reasoning' that really seek the justification and promulgation of sentiments, and kinds that seek, in deliberately controlled ways, the establishment of testable knowledge. It is also true that this latter kind of 'reasoning' can be more easily, effectively, and demonstrably carried out in kinds of enquiry and in relation to kinds of action which have very specific and clearly measurable ends. In this sense, it is true that an *economic* action—in, say, combining factors of production to make a commodity to sell at a price to yield a certain margin of profit, may well be more demonstrably 'logical' in its means-end inferences and calculations, and may well rest on more testable knowledge (of material substances, and market situations) than a *political* action—in supporting a particular party because its policies are more *just*, or (to go to extremes) a *religious* action—in resisting, say, a political dictator, because of a commitment to the supreme value of certain spiritual and moral values. It is also true that many social 'theories' are important for their *use* rather than for any known demonstration of their truth. And it could be admitted, further, that Pareto's analysis was certainly of value, as any delimited explanatory scheme might be, in throwing light upon these distinctions.

Yet there is something fundamentally questionable about the way in which Pareto laid this down as an absolutely basic distinction— bringing in its train a number of equally questionable dichotomies. I will try to clarify this matter by beginning with a direct statement, and then, after this, seeking to justify it by introducing Pareto's own inconsistencies.

In the first place, Pareto had no clear grounds for calling his distinction one between *logical* and non-*logical* action. In the second place, he had no clear grounds for attaching the pursuit of *interests* by *means-end* calculations to *logical* action alone, and the support of *residues* by (pseudo-logical) *derivations* to *non-logical* action alone. In the third place, he had no grounds for attaching the 'logico-experimental' method of reasoning to logical action alone, and categorizing all reason stemming from the sentiments (whether in support or in criticism of them) as being the pseudo-reasoning of 'derivations'. And we might say as a fourth point that in all these cases his distinctions were drawn much too sharply: the best example being between so-called 'interests' and so-called 'residues'. Let us look at each of these points in turn.

On the face of it, Pareto's distinction between logical and non-logical action was innocent enough; he was free to define these terms as he wished for his own analytical purposes, and he certainly did not propose them in a dogmatic manner. His '*logical behaviour*' consisted of those actions which were logically linked, both subjectively and objectively, to an end. All other action was termed *non-logical*, since it was rooted in 'sentiments'; (strictly non-logical feelings, values, persuasions, or principles). But as soon as we stop to consider this distinction it clearly does no more than set *scientific knowledge* in sharp contra-distinction to all other kinds of thinking. Only empirical science can 'objectively demonstrate' the *factual* truth of its propositions, so that only calculated means-end action resting on scientific knowledge could possibly be 'logical action' in Pareto's sense. And Pareto would say: 'Yes: this is exactly what I do mean.' But why should that action orientated towards ends which rest on science alone be considered 'logical'? Surely, a very great deal of social action stemming from a 'non-logical' attachment to 'sentiments' also seeks to attain ends set by the sentiments—such as, for example, the attempt (like a Socrates or a Plato) to *make explicit in thought* the *presuppositions* of the human sense of *injustice* and *justice*, and (like a Solon or a Cleisthenes) to construct political constitutions of such a kind as to approximate as closely as possible to the *ideals* which have been logically disentangled and made clear? Such thought and action could not claim to rest upon demonstrable scientific knowledge, but it could surely claim to be as scrupulously careful in its logical inference as the reasoning of science; as insistent upon excluding arbitrariness; and as judiciously related to the attainment of ends—though not phenomenally measurable ends like eating a meal, or making a 10 per cent return on capital, or constructing effective drains in a city. The fact is that the second kind of thought and action would also entail *judgment*—but why should this be thought to be any the less *logical* than 'science'?

617

Now it could be thought that this was just a quibble against Pareto's terminology, and an over-sensitive one at that; for—it might be claimed—Pareto did in fact agree that logical reasons were given in support of the 'sentiments'—his only point was that it was the kind of reasoning which did not permit of factual demonstration. But it is just this which shows quite clearly why this is far from being a linguistic quibble. For implicit in Pareto's distinction was the fact that this latter kind of reasoning, (i.e. of the 'derivations') was 'pseudo-rational'; it was no more than a process of *rationalization*, a kind of fabric of impressive symbols the sole use of which was to *serve, support*, and *defend*, the sentiments. And, indeed, in much of his writing, Pareto enjoyed making a continuous mockery of such 'theories'. But it must be insisted that to term the first kind of knowledge and action 'logical' and the second 'non-logical' (and then 'pseudo-logical') is a fundamental and damaging error. Without denying the existence of *bias* in some arguments rooted in 'sentiments', and without at all wishing to diminish the correctness of maintaining an acute awareness of 'rationalization' and other mental mechanisms, it must nonetheless be insisted that the *reflection, reasoning, judgment*, and *planning* of *considered social action* which men undertake from a consideration of their 'sentiments' can be every bit as 'logical' and 'rational'—and as scrupulously concerned for *exactitude* and *reliability* in logic and reason—as science and scientifically based action. The fact is that although Pareto sneered at 'positivism', 'materialism' and other supposed 'metaphysical' positions, he himself did no more, in this basic distinction, than dogmatically assert a *scientistic epistemology. Knowledge* was only that which could be tested against facts at the level of sensation, and only this was logical. All other processes of reflective inference—in uncovering idealities, in making clear grounds for judicious belief and judgment—were not only *not scientific* (with which, of course, one would agree), but not *logical* with the same degree of accuracy and reliability. This, then, was a quite unwarranted and very insufficiently considered distinction—indeed a false and misguiding distinction—from which to start, and it was then augmented, deepened, and worsened by the additional distinctions in his system. Before moving on to these, however, there is one other point which is worth more than a moment's thought.

Was Pareto right even in assuming that the 'sentiments', and the sense of attachment to them, were entirely 'non-logical' sources of social action? To a degree at least worthy of serious consideration, he was surely wrong. Again, it must not be thought that we are wishing to deny the existence in the human mind of 'non-logical' elements of taste, appetite, attachment. Clearly these exist. However, the 'sentiments' in a society are by no means 'naked' elements of feeling. As the earlier writers—such as Ward, Sumner, Giddings—and as all the twentieth century writers, maintained: the 'sentiments' were constellations of impulse, emotion, cognition, judgment, feelings of approval and disapproval, and—essentially—of *values*. In short they were, at least to an extent deserving of consideration, constellations of many components of feeling, thinking, judging and acting, which involved much *implicit* reasoning: some of which was of a reflective, imaginative, exploratory and creative kind. Other writers (Sumner was an excellent example—though Westermarck, Hobhouse, and others were equally clear) had suggested that the early laying down of a social order in human communities had gradually developed within the context of man's continuing 'practical activities', and that this body of 'folkways' with their attendant 'sentiments' was the outcome of man's early purposive action, discovery of knowledge, and establishing of effective ways of doing things. Out of these 'nuclei' (so to speak) of 'rule-of-thumb' and 'implicit' reasoning—*explicit* reasoning developed: not only in establishing scientific knowledge of fact and pragmatic courses of 'technical action', but also in extending 'mores' from the 'folkways', and clear 'laws', 'institutions' and precepts of 'morality' from the 'mores'. In short, they had portrayed the gradual development of mind, reason, logic, and more effectively directed social action—in *all* the areas of social activity. What this amounts to is that where others had seen what we might call (bearing in mind its many dimensions!) a 'unitary' development of mind and reason in *all* forms of social action, Pareto had insisted *as the very starting point of his entire system* on a starkly distinguished *dichotomy* in the development of mind which was simply without warrant. But we can now turn to see how his additional distinctions were such as to build up the two sides of the dichotomy in even more 'separating', but even less justified (more ambiguous) ways.

The second clear distinction which Pareto made, for example, was one among the 'instinctual' dispositions. Some of these dispositions were *appetites* or *inclinations* which sought clear and direct gratification (fulfilment) in the attainment of certain ends. They thus engendered clear '*interests*', and action in the service of them could be clearly calculated in terms of the means to attain their ends. Others, however, were 'residues'—basic, universal dispositions, tendencies, qualities of the mind—which were just 'psychic states', not seeking clearly determinate ends, and which gave rise, therefore, not to interests, but to 'sentiments' and 'derivations' which were 'logical sophistries' or 'pseudo-scientific theories' giving a supporting, justifying 'explanation' of them. Social action of a clear means-end nature in the pursuit of interests was closely identified with 'logical'

619

action; social action stemming from residues and derivations was closely identified with 'non-logical action'. But again, we must stop to ask why? And a number of points immediately arise.

First: is there really the clear distinction between 'appetites' and 'residues', between 'interests' and 'sentiments and derivations', between action based upon 'means-end calculations' and that based upon 'derivations', as Pareto claimed? And is there any reason why the 'means-end' kind of action should be thought to be more appropriate in relation to 'appetites' than to 'residues'? As soon as we consider these questions, Pareto's ambiguities become over-whelmingly evident, and we need mention only a few of them.

Is sexuality, for example, an 'appetite' or a 'residue'? It is, said Pareto, *both*; but he was chiefly concerned with its existence in the mind as a 'residue' giving rise to all kinds of pseudo-logical 'derivations' to support certain kinds of control, or regulation, in society. Thus 'theories' and institutions upholding abstinence, or insisting on the 'tabooing' of sex outside marriage, were held to be 'derivations' and really 'disguised' the residue of sexuality proper. But where is the clarity in all this? Where is the clarity of the means-end relationship in action, and Pareto's other distinctions? Presumably, if a society legalized prostitution, so that an appetite for intercourse could be gratified at a price calculable in terms of the supply and demand of the market situation: sexuality was an appetite with a means-end sequence of action about which 'logico-experimental knowledge' was appropriate. If, however, a society upheld the institution of mono-gamous marriage (which might be rooted in some earlier sentiment or religious assertion) and supported it as against the introduction of polygyny in terms (say) of the rightness of ensuring personal choice between partners, the equality of status of man and wife within and beyond marriage, equality in the sharing of family property—and other ethical and political judgments; then this would be regarded in terms of 'residues', 'derivations', and 'non-logical action'. But why? The social action in each case is the provision of means to attain ends, and the 'reasoning' in each case permits of an equal clarity of logic. The only supposed distinction is that the lust for intercourse is a clear *appetite* with a clearly connected *interest*, whereas the maintenance of the institution of marriage is a residue, attendant upon sentiments, and bolstered by pseudo-logical justifications. But here we see the curiously definite one-sidedness of Pareto's dichotomy. Two things are plain. First, his distinction involves, at the heart of it, an unsupported *grading* of desires, and a *separation* of them in terms of this grading. Thus an 'appetite' is some drive which stems directly from some organic source; a desire for a relationship of mutually sensitive equality of consideration in marriage (what Marx called a

distinctively *human* need), is not to be considered a direct desire at all
—but a residue disguised in excuses. The two *desires* are given a
'graded separation' from each other. Even if we allowed this (which,
however, we cannot do) the second clear aspect of Pareto's treatment
is that he allowed an *interest* for the attainment of an *end* only to
pertain to the simpler level of the *'appetite'*. But why? Cannot the
more complex *desire*, or *need*, for a certain quality of relationships in
marriage also give rise to an *interest* to attain an *end*? In this case, the
upholding of one institution of marriage as against a proposed
alternative?

It might still be argued by Pareto that the gratification of the
appetite at a price was *measurable*, and therefore 'logico-experimental'
knowledge could be established about it; whereas the satisfactory
end of the institution of marriage could never be tested in this way,
but would necessarily remain at the level, only, of considered judgment. But this exactly emphasizes our point. For, on the one hand,
is it really true that the simpler gratification of an appetite can be
said to be calculated with objective accuracy on the basis of scientific
knowledge, whereas the more complicated situation cannot? Or is it
not the case that they are both *to differing degrees* in the realm of
imponderables. And is it not the case anyway, that legalized prostitution is itself an institution (one could even claim that it was rooted
in earlier sentiments and traditions) and it could easily be, in a differing social situation, in the position (as we have envisaged mono-
gamous marriage) of having to defend itself against proposed
alternatives. But the second, and chief point, is, again, that Pareto
was doing no more than assert a *scientistic epistemology*. Reasoning
could only be said to be reliably *logical* if it was the reasoning of
science, or the completely pragmatic proposals for achieving certain
ends by certain means on the basis of it. But so much of human
action—even when *including* scientific knowledge—has to proceed
by way of carefully clarified principle and considered judgment; yet
the logical inference involved can be equally scrupulous and impeccable.

At the heart of all our argument here, however, is the crucial point
that there is not the clear distinction between 'appetite and interest'
and 'residue and derivation' which Pareto claimed; and that therefore this served even further, and more forcibly, to exaggerate the
false, unwarranted and misleading distinction between 'logical' and
'non-logical' action.

The best example of Pareto's own ambiguity was (as we indicated
earlier) in his treatment of the 'residues' of the 'Integrity of the
Individual and his Appurtenances'. These were the residues which,
together, focused upon the individual's disposition to seek and

establish the security of his own personality, to establish and extend the security of his property, and to secure and further his position in the hierarchy of social status. Now it is perfect¹y plain (*a*) that such propensities were bound to be closely concomitant with, if not inseparable from the appetites, (*b*) that they clearly posited certain ends, certain interests, and certain sequences of calculated action: an undertaking of certain means in order to attain clearly desired ends, and (*c*) that 'logico-experimental' knowledge was distinctly necessary for any action in relation to them.* Pareto himself clearly saw this, and it is worthwhile to repeat his statement.

'That sum of sentiments called "interests" is of the same nature as the sentiments to which the residues of the present class correspond. Sentiments of "interests" therefore ought strictly to be included in this classification, but they are of such great intrinsic importance for the social equilibrium that it is better to consider them separately from residues.'†

Now we can readily see that Pareto wished to describe certain 'sentiments' which accompanied this set of 'residues', but our point is *only* that if there was this almost entire identity between 'appetites and interests' and 'sentiments and residues' as he here acknowledged, the *dichotomy* between (*a*) instincts—appetites—interests—logical action—and logico-experimental knowledge on the one hand, and (*b*) instincts—sentiments—residues—and non-logical action resting on derivations on the other, was *simply not tenable*: so that a total theoretical analysis based upon it could only convey a misleading confusion.

We can bring this criticism to this conclusion: that whilst it was a worthwhile thing to seek to understand the influence of instinct, interest, and sentiment upon social theories; to clarify 'mental mechanisms' in all these activities of mind in society as distinct from deliberate logical reasoning; and to consider the part played in society by various kinds of 'theories' in the equilibrium-disequilibrium conditions of society, quite apart from their 'truth'—it was unwarranted, and, indeed, false, to lay down at the outset a sharp dichotomy between 'logical' and 'non-logical' action which was buttressed by other 'polar' distinctions, and which ran right from

---

* The almost complete ambiguity of Pareto in this particular case can be seen in his definition of 'interests' as 'means to some personal end' or as desires: '. . . prompted by instinct and reason to acquire possession of material goods which are useful, or simply pleasurable, for the purposes of living, and also to seek considerations and honours . . .'. Clearly this embraces everything in the residues connected with the 'Integrity of the Individual', but it is also difficult to see why the 'sentiments' and 'residues' should not be regarded as 'desires' in the same way—and giving rise to the same purposeful actions.
† *The Treatise, Sociological Writings*, p. 234.

top to bottom of Pareto's entire system. Mind in society may well possess all the dimensions to which Pareto drew attention—but they do not take the form of two sharp divisions; of two sharply divided categories and areas of social action.

There is no reason why we should not suppose that mind in society, possessing all these dimensions, is not active and operative in *all* the fields of social activity; deploying itself similarly in all areas of thought, judgment and action—using now scientific knowledge, now philosophical reflection about idealities, now imaginative constructions of social plans, now all of these together in formulating judgments, as and when appropriate: and with regard to *all* social institutions. There was nothing in Pareto's 'dichotomous scheme'— despite his assertions and cavalier judgments—to lead us away from that other view of the growth of mind in society that was commonly held by almost all the other major theorists from Comte to Durkheim and Weber. But this now brings us to the other crucial reason why Pareto's 'dichotomy' and its attendant spilling out of dogmatic assertions cannot be taken lightly, but must be considered a basic, and dangerous error. It concerns Pareto's rejection of the idea of 'progress', his supposedly 'value-free' conception of social science, his position with regard to the direction of development of 'mind in society', and, at the root of all, his complete relativity with regard to ethical standards and political judgments.

(IV) THE INSUFFICIENCY OF PARETO'S ETHICAL RELATIVITY

Pareto's distinction between logical and non-logical action was dangerous and damaging as an influence in social theory as well as being merely unwarranted in theoretical terms alone, because, on the apparent strength of it he assertively and cynically denied any grounds for clarifying ethical standards of progress in society. Now we are not at all saying here that any philosophical case for relativity in ethics is necessarily mistaken and unworthy of examination. We are saying only that Pareto, in fact, made no such case whatever. He simply *asserted* that he did. And his assertion rested upon his basic error of regarding all reasoning other than that of empirical science as being a matter of 'logical sophistry'. And further, it needs to be said that such an assertive discarding of the careful scrutiny of moral experience and the careful reflection upon ethical and political standards is *not* value-free, but is an unwitting (at best) or an outright support (at worst) of a negative irresponsibility in the field of human judgment and, indeed, in serious issues of social theory. It is, in short, a value-commitment even in its decisive rejection of any intention of taking value-judgments seriously.

623

Let us note first that in his comparative studies of societies, Pareto came quite definitely to the conclusion (as had all the other theorists) that modern society was characterized by an increase in 'reason' and in the extension and application of knowledge. He wrote:

'Taking account of modern life as a whole, we may safely conclude that Class I residues and the findings of logico-experimental science have widened the field of their sway. To this fact, indeed, is largely due the great diversity of characteristics in contemporary societies as compared with the societies of ancient Greece and Rome . . . We would not be mistaken, therefore, in ascribing to "reason" an increasingly important role in human activity; indeed, such a view is wholly in accord with the facts . . .'*

There was, then, a marked *direction* in the growth of reason, knowledge, and the extension of conscious and deliberate thought and control in society. Furthermore, Pareto was continually having to remark on the upsurge of movements of political reform. There was the rise of 'socialism' among the masses, supported by intellectual leaders. There was the movement towards increased gentleness and sensitivity in society; the growth of 'pity' as he put it. There was the movement towards the maximization of 'liberty'; and the decided movement towards the extension of 'democracy'. All these, Pareto recognized—as *factual* occurrences. However, his attitude to them was very predominantly one of cynicism. On the one hand he claimed to be 'value-free' as a scientist. But, on the other hand, he scorned such movements, and, in so doing, was clearly himself evaluating them. His cynicism had various grounds—all of which stemmed from his basic theoretical distinction (as various aspects of it). First, these were, he claimed, only parts of recurring 'cycles' of interaction, and would come to show a different face in due course. Second, they only *appeared* to be *logical*. They only *claimed* to be *ethically* motivated. In reality, they—and their 'derivations' (i.e. theories of equality of citizenship, socialism, liberty, democracy, etc.)—*disguised* motives which were fundamentally self-interested and self-regarding. Pareto sometimes remarked—almost with an air of surprise and disbelief—that 'progressive' leaders were probably genuine and sincere in their motives and ideals; but his basic estimation was that, really, they rang hollow, and that underneath the 'sounding brass', so to speak, were the true, underlying, most powerful, motives rooted in appetites and 'sentiments'. But thirdly, and most important, they *could* not be regarded as possessing any 'objective' criteria of a logical and rational nature because they did not refer to the measurable *phenomena* and did not possess the

* *The Treatise, Sociological Writings,* p. 283.

logico-experimental techniques, of *science*; and their 'means-end' proposals for social action (the extension of democracy in a political constitution, for example, to approximate more closely to the ideals of social justice) were not of a determinate, measurable, pragmatic nature. They were therefore 'derivations'—not arbitrary with regard to their *use* within the arena of political power, but arbitrary with regard to 'truth'.

It is, I hope, perfectly clear from this how Pareto's basic distinction led him into a complete 'relativity' with regard to the criteria of logic and judgment in all fields of human discourse and action other than that of science. This was, again, the tyranny of Pareto's 'scientistic epistemology', and it is most important to see that it was a tyranny of *assertion*, for he nowhere *demonstrated* that all fields of logical reflection other than science *were* characterized by a complete lack of criteria; by a complete 'arbitrariness'. Here, we are concerned centrally with Pareto's arbitrariness in the field of *ethical* reflection; in the application of the mind in critically clarifying the presuppositions of *values* in society (rooted in residues and sentiments and derivations) and the taking of judgments, and the making of changed political constitutions on the basis of them; but let us note, that this is a very clear example of the way in which considerations of philosophical ethics are inescapably involved in the reliable 'scientific' understanding of '*institutional facts*' in social systems. And let us think about one or two of Pareto's specific examples.

When discussing 'verbal proofs' as one category of 'derivations', Pareto drew attention to the concept of 'Liberty' and the social action men had undertaken in order to extend, or maximize, it.

'The fate which has befallen the term "liberty",' he wrote, 'is comical enough. In many cases it now signifies precisely the opposite of what it used to mean fifty years ago. But the sentiments it arouses are the same in that the word still has a connotation which is agreeable to those who hear it . . . Half a century ago in England, the name of "Liberal party" was given to the party which sought as much as possible to reduce restrictions which deprived the individual of the power to dispose of his person and his property as he wished. Today the party called "Liberal" is the one which is seeking to increase the number of these restrictions. The Liberal party used to be in favour of reducing taxes: nowadays it is all for increasing them . . . The metaphysicians among them add that thus "the state creates liberty".'*

Pareto gave many such examples of *reversals* in the conception and practical political implementation of 'liberty', and regarded them all as 'logical sophistries' and 'verbal trickeries'. Men used the high-

* *The Treatise, Sociological Writings*, pp. 241–2.

sounding name of 'liberty' (which constantly appealed to the 'senti-ments') in order to accomplish, under its guise, any political arrange-ment which served their interests. Now again no-one would wish to deny that such political chicanery goes on, or, indeed, that human nature is extensively prone to it. Nor would one wish to discount the value of Pareto's frankly stated cynicism in pointing to the interest-laden reality which all too often lies behind the veil of public talk. It is only that Pareto—*because*, no doubt, of his confident cynicism—failed to take his analysis far enough, and failed to consider with sufficient seriousness the possibility of rational criteria even within this vexed field of values in the struggle for power.

Let is consider three points. Firstly—the reversals to which Pareto pointed in the passage above were only *apparent* reversals. In fact, in the whole development of 'liberalism', there has been an increasing awareness of the fact (which was implicit even in its earliest state-ments) that certain measures of governmental regulation—of the law; of supervision of the fluctuations of the economy; of the insistence of certain minimum standards of income (below which no citizen should fall); and of certain patterns of taxation, and therefore certain related regulations of 'maximal levels' of incomes, etc.—are necessary for the maximization of 'liberty': and this, even for the *economic* liberty of the '*free-market*' which Pareto himself upheld, let alone many other much more subtle conditions for liberty such as the equalization of the status of men and women, the extension of educational opportunity, the exclusion of irrelevant and arbitrary elements in the claims to full political citizenship of 'races', and multitudes of other political issues. What this amounts to is that Pareto's discarding of such kinds of social thinking in the struggle for 'liberty' as being *mere* verbal trickeries was atrociously superficial. It was one more case of an economist—who could think with excellent expertise about the mathematically calculable adjustments within models of market exchange—bringing the same narrow accuracies of mind to bear upon socio-philosophical dimensions which he did not have either the patience or the intellectual commitment to plumb. The fact was that the efforts to clarify the ideal of 'liberty'; to clarify its relation to other ideals—such as 'equality'—which in some ways seemed in conflict with it; to work out political constitutions which seemed most to approximate to all these considered and interrelated ideals; and actually to re-construct (reform) existing political con-stitutions so that such ethical advancements could be *achieved* to the greatest degree possible—were long and sustained efforts which could not possibly be formulated intact, with scientific precision, by one philosopher, by one generation, by one age of political struggle. In the historical processes of thought and action the many dimensions of this ethical and political task were uncovered, clarified, explored, critically discussed; and in the creative process of political action—the actual *construction* of working constitutions—certainly particular directions of action had to be modified in the light of practice and experience.

Pareto's cynicism was therefore an all too easy exercise. It was a completely unwarranted throwing aside of profound issues and achievements of social thought and political practice by smart and clever gestures which were superficial even in their appreciation of the actual issues dealt with. It was a dilettante scorning of the continuing contemporary efforts to resolve the dilemmas and improve the nature of modern society. It was an 'about-face' in failing to appreciate and respond to the distinctive dilemma of the modern world in moving away from 'traditional' societies to a conscious reconstruction of institutions—coming to terms with industrialization and science and a new global interdependency, which all the other sociologists had clearly recognized from Comte onwards. It failed to pursue deeply enough the implications of the new powers and possibilities of conscious control and the issues of considered responsibility which they posed.

Similar examples could be given from Pareto's discussion of 'democracy', 'equality', and the like, but this point is sufficiently clear. The second point, however, is equally important. In all this discussion of theories about 'liberty' (or any other ideal), Pareto was quite ready to agree that there might be clear means-end propositions for political action which would bring such issues into the field of 'logico-experimental' knowledge and pragmatic testability—and to these cases he would not have the slightest objection. About this, too, there is no lack of clarity and no need for disagreement. But the very important point is that Pareto did not see or concede *at all* that the 'ideal' of 'liberty' within the larger 'ideal' of 'justice' permitted of rational clarification by a logical process of scrupulous criticism of those ideals presented as residues, sentiments, and derivations; that judgments could be formed about ways of approximating to these ideals; and that this process of reasoning and judgment though *not susceptible* to scientific test, could still clarify criteria of its own which rendered its discourse far from being arbitrary. Part of this criticism is that Pareto did not seem to see or to concede, either, that *political practice* was itself a continuous source of further *judgment* in the light of which both ideals and administrative procedures could be rationally modified, but that such *judgment*—though no doubt pragmatic in certain senses—was by no means such as to permit of precise scientific test. The political judgment, for example, which came to insist upon a separation of the Judiciary from the Legislative and

627

Administrative branches of government, and upon the provisions of court procedures and appeals procedures as ways of approximating as closely as possible to 'justice', could never possibly be a matter of 'scientific test'—but yet its criteria of reasoning, its clarification of ideals and principles, and its exercising of judgments, were all very far from being arbitrary.

And this leads to the third point of great consequence here—that this superficial view of those elements of thought and judgment which were involved in the clarification and pursuit of ideals in social institutions—entailed a very definite conception of the *factual nature* of these institutions. We have seen that all the other sociological theorists saw *values* at the heart of the social institutions which arose from the complex of men's purposeful practical activities. The thinking and feeling and pragmatic judgments of men were at the heart of these institutional regularities—in sentiments and folkways, customs and traditions, and then in increasingly considered, deliberate, articulate thought. The development of mind, of reflection, of knowledge, was an *actual part* of human institutions; of *all* human institutions; and the very directions of change of institutions were closely correlated with these changes in mental development. Now the point of extreme importance is this:—part of the theorist's conception of the actual nature of institutions *is* his conception of the nature of these processes of feeling, thought and judgment which form important elements of them. The other theorists we have considered—from Comte, Mill, and Marx to Hobhouse, Durkheim and Weber—were all clearly persuaded that the *rational* and *moral* developments in man's experience were vitally important in social institutions, but, also (and especially significant) they were all quite decisively persuaded that—with the growth of knowledge, and responsibility for the conscious re-making of institutions—*rational* and *ethical* elements were, increasingly, the most important elements in the institutional change of the modern world. They all, in short, accepted the 'Comtean' perspective of the essential task of modern man as being the conscious, deliberate, responsible re-making of society in accordance with clarified ethical ideals. Rationality and ethical responsibility were crucially in the forefront of the *actuality* of social change.

But we can see that, for Pareto, these 'derivations' had no more validity than the residues and sentiments from which they stemmed. As at other times, cycles of change would occur, replacing old derivations with new. The circulation of élites would go on. One set of 'verbal trickeries' would be replaced by another. Social systems would continue to consist of the same massively rooted residues, dressed up in the logical sophistries of 'derivations' according to the conditions of 'social equilibrium' of the time. Very plainly—his view of the *actual nature* of institutions was radically coloured by his conception of the nature of human thought pertaining to values within them.

In all this it must be insisted that his position *was* a result of insufficient consideration, *not* just a matter of lack of awareness, because, as we showed earlier, Pareto was quite well aware that some men could free themselves from the domination of blind sentiments, and could then manipulate others in terms of their own clearly formulated objectives. But if *this* was possible, a *rational clarification of morality* was possible (a critical assessment of the values of sentiments—in freeing oneself from them); and a *rational plan of political action* in relation to *clearly formulated principles* and *ideals* was possible. Indeed, if such freeing from sentiments and the manipulation of others was possible—ethical questions and political questions became necessary and obligatory. This possibility *posed* ethical problems. And ethically directed political reform and education was just as possible as expedient, self-interested manipulation.

The upshot of all this, is that when one looks a little beneath the surface of Pareto's apparently incisive denunciations, beneath the surface brilliance of his supposedly 'value-free' assertions, it is all too clear that his ethical 'relativity' had no demonstrable basis whatever. It rested, like most of the conclusions of his entire theoretical system on the initial *assertions* accompanying his distinction between the too sharply separated kinds of action and knowledge. In his theoretical system—this distinction was insufficiently considered and led to a dubious view of the actuality of institutions; in his ethical assertions —it became harmful in a variety of ways. We can see again that to be 'value-free' in social science is impossible. The philosophical estimation of values which men hold—whether ill or well considered, whether superficially held aside (or in abeyance) or seriously reflected upon—must necessarily *be a part* of their conception of *social actuality*. To uphold a 'value-free' position in sociology is to uphold a myth for the philosophically blind!

I said earlier that I found great difficulty in being confident in my critical assessment of Pareto because he jarred so much on my own sympathies, and I think it must now be clear how much this is so.

In order to show, however, that this kind of conclusion about the questionable nature of his fundamental distinction and the unfortunate corollary that it carried for his position in ethics is something more than just personal bias, I would like to refer to the judgments of two other present-day sociologists of very considerable eminence whose criticisms of Pareto rest upon lengthy study.

In his book on *Main Currents in Sociological Thought*, Raymond Aron wrote:

629

'I have a final observation to make . . . touching on the theory of the logical and the nonlogical. I have indicated that given Pareto's definition of nonlogical actions, these actions could be divided into several categories . . . Is it a good idea to place in a single category scientific errors, metaphysical superstitions that seem anachronistic today, acts inspired by optimistic or idealistic convictions, ritual behaviour, and magical practices? Do these forms of behaviour truly belong to a single category? Can one argue, as Pareto does, that since none of these acts is determined by reasoning, they are therefore determined by sentiments or states of mind? Does the logical-nonlogical duality give rise to the duality between actions determined by reasoning and actions determined by sentiments or states of mind? Is it not true that this oversimplified antinomy not only is dangerous but distorts reality? Is it so evident that an action governed by propositions that are apparently scientific but later turn out to be erroneous can be explained by a mechanism comparable to the one that accounts for a ritual practice or a revolutionary action?

It is true that one can gradually complicate Pareto's classification, but the duality between logical and nonlogical actions which leads to the antithesis between action-through-reasoning and action-through-sentiment is dangerously schematic and leads Pareto to a dualistic view of human nature in the theory of residues, and then to a dualistic typology of élites, types of élites, and types of regime. These oversimplified images, these stylized antagonisms by their very nature imply a philosophy to which Pareto would not subscribe but which it would be difficult for him to deny completely.'*

This is far from being a caustic criticism; it is very carefully considered in its recognition of the difficulty of judging Pareto completely; but it is completely in accordance with our own conclusion. A second conclusion—also careful, but equally definite—is that of Morris Ginsberg. Pareto, he wrote:

'. . . insists that . . . growth in the power of reason has not affected political and social activities to any great extent, and that in any case there is no ground for the belief in continuous progress. The notion of progress is never mentioned by him without bitter derision. But it will be noticed that, though according to him there can be no reliable criteria of progress, he does not hesitate to speak of decadence which requires criteria of the same kind.

To me it is clear that Pareto has developed no adequate method for estimating the role of reason in law, morals, and politics, and that he vastly under-estimates what has on the whole been achieved in these directions. The growing interconnection between economic and social and political movements which he himself stresses is an important phenomenon and one which may compel humanity to make increasing use of

* Weidenfeld and Nicolson, 1968, Vol. 2, p. 176.

rational agencies. The fact also that the notion of conscious control of social change in its application to humanity as a whole is relatively new must be taken into consideration in estimating future trends.

No one nowadays believes in automatic progress or in indefinite and unlimited perfectibility. What is asserted is that it is theoretically possible to formulate a coherent ideal of human endeavour, and that from a study of the failures as well as the successes of mankind in dealing with its problems, there is ground for the belief that such an ideal permits of realization if men are prepared to work for it. Pareto's denial of human progress rests upon (a) his disbelief in any rational ethics; (b) his view that history so far has disclosed no significant changes but only oscillations. As to (a), I do not find that he provides any reasoned justification for his disbelief. As to (b), it seems to me that he greatly exaggerates the constant elements in human history, and that if there is no law of human progress neither is there any law of cyclical recurrence. From the point of view of policy, in any event, if a choice is to be made between persistent aggregates and combinations, I see no reason for not choosing combinations.'*

These statements, it seems to me, are admirably clear, and the judgments in them fully borne out by a careful study of Pareto.

(v) CONCLUSION

Our conclusion must be that—though impressive in its scope, and filled with insights of many kinds (many of which are worthwhile)— Pareto's was the least satisfactory among the great systems of sociological analysis. In so many ways—though always dealing with important dimensions of social actuality—its categories were insufficient. Three points seem worth special attention in bringing our study of him to a close.

First and foremost, for our own immediate purposes here, we have been able to see clearly the ways in which Pareto's system represented a large-scale attempt to develop the study of the 'psychological aspects of society'. We must conclude that, even here, his own concepts were not such as to mark a really demonstrable advance in the making of sociology. Even so, certain aspects of his system were of importance. Firstly, there is no doubt whatever that his own emphasis upon (a) the *instinctual dispositions* of the human mind; (b) the *sentiments*—as powerful 'core' elements of social institutions, and constellations of values which were of basic importance for the continuity of social order; (c) the extent of their common and persisting existence in all societies at all times; and (d) the influence which they exerted upon

* *Reason and Unreason in Society*, pp. 102–3.

social interests, thinking, and action—was such as to agree with, and lend the fullest support to, all the other theorists who were preoccupied with these questions of social psychology. Secondly, there was much significance in the similarity between Pareto's and Freud's conceptions, and especially the 'coincidence' of their analysis of 'mental mechanisms' by which the mind characteristically operated, but which it could not be said to have 'learned'. The presenting of 'mental mechanisms' by Freud strictly in relation to the individual, and Pareto in relation to social groups, institutions and movements was of great interest; as was, also, the coincidence in the actual 'mechanisms' themselves: 'rationalization', for example. Pareto, like Freud, had the merit of forcing attention upon the socio-psychological reality which may lie *behind* overt, public 'reasonings'; and though in both cases this could be taken too far (i.e. to the point of asserting that socio-psychological reality was *only* what lay *behind*, and *never* what was forthrightly apparent), even so its emphasis was of value. Thirdly, Pareto undoubtedly agreed in emphasizing, too, the 'associational' perspective for human psychology—which we have noted. And fourthly—though he himself lacked the dimensions of analysis of the 'self' and 'society' which Cooley and Mead contributed—Pareto did at least have the virtue of striving to see the psychological dimensions of society in ways which went beyond them, and did seek an adequate analysis of the psychological aspects of complex human association within the constraining conditions of the social system as a whole. In this, Pareto's psychological account of associational conditions came, perhaps, nearer to what Durkheim and Weber had in mind at their own levels of sociological analysis; it fitted better within a framework of analysis of the collective conditions of the social system as a whole (Durkheim) and of large-scale sequences of social action within it (Weber). And it did have the virtue of drawing attention, in yet another way, to the fact that *collective conditions* might well *operate* upon the psychological qualities and dispositions of the mind in society in such ways as to be *psychologically creative* and responsible for certain processes of selection and distribution of qualities which had hitherto been unsuspected. It goes almost without saying, too, that Pareto's emphasis upon the *sentiments* fully accorded with all the theorists we have considered in other sections: Tönnies, Westermarck, Hobhouse, Durkheim and Weber—as well as the 'social-psychologists' proper—McDougall, Cooley, Mead, and Freud. There was much in Pareto to support this very considerable unity of conclusions, and this was all the more impressive since it came from a thinker who was, at first appearance, so distinctively different.

A second point is that Pareto's system did focus strong attention upon one particularly important component of analysis: the study of élites. His own analysis was deficient and dubious in certain respects, but, even so, the study of all the élites within the social system, and of the relation between the governing élite and the rest in particular, was shown to be of the greatest importance, and in this Pareto made a considerable and lasting contribution. It could also be said that his discussion of 'élites' and 'scales' of measurement within each hierarchy opened up a new and useful conceptual scheme for investigating all those aspects of 'status' and social mobility which had tended to be thought of in too 'solid' and doctrinaire a way in terms of social 'class'. Pareto's concept and classification of 'élites' *supplemented* the conception of 'class' such as Marx had put forward, and thus made more satisfactory the analysis of 'stratification' in society.

A third and final point is made with some hesitation, but might be worth a good deal of consideration. It is with regard to Pareto's conception of 'the social system' and the most appropriate 'model' for its analysis. We have said earlier that—if we are to talk in terms of analogies at all—the 'organic' type of 'system' may be preferable to the 'mechanical' system: simply because society does in fact consist of definitely organized and distinguishable parts (or sectors)—a number of industries, the banking system, the educational system, religious organizations, etc.—within which, about which, and between which, human experience and behaviour takes place in a patterned way. Pareto chose the 'mechanical' system for the analysis of a vast multiplicity of composite social facts—deliberately adopting what we called an 'atomistic' position. Now it seems to me that a further point can be made about this. On the face of it, Pareto's system *was* always a system for the analysis of social *action*. Men were pursuing ends in terms of their interests or seeking to uphold their sentiments and derivations. This cannot be denied, and Pareto cannot be held ever to leave this position—for men were still *acting*, even if they were driven by residues and deluded by derivations. Even so, I think it fair to say that a certain peculiarity crept into, and characterized, Pareto's system because of his denigration (and underweighting) of 'derivations', and his insistent emphasis of the determining influence of the *residues* and their *distribution*. My point is this. That although Pareto *seemed* always to be speaking of a system of *social action*, in fact, by (*a*) his adoption of a 'mechanical' model for analysing 'equilibrium-disequilibrium' conditions (*b*) his conception of a given 'fund' of *residues** which (*c*) were *distributed* in certain ways through the media

---

* It might be noted that Pareto never seriously considered the possibility that *all* men in *changed* situations might *think* differently (from a similar equipment of mental dispositions): i.e. that changed associational conditions might engender

of the circulation of élites, and (d) the stripping away of the import-ance (to the point of being negligible) of the thinking and valuing within the social system—which he subsumed under the term 'deriva-tions' . . . his system was in fact substantially a 'mechanistic' model of a distribution and re-distribution of atomistic elements moving between conditions of disequilibrium and equilibrium in accordance with changing conditions. It was, in fact, a vast sociological extra-polation of an economic system of market-exchange; indeed, one might almost say, the model of 'perfect market competition'. But it was also a 'mechanistic model' which very severely restricted the considerations of deliberate *'action'* (as, say, Weber wished to insist on it) and gave almost full rein to the conception of 'elements' assum-ing patterns of equilibrium-adjustment by an almost mechanistic re-distribution.

I do not wish at this stage to over-stress this argument because I am by no means altogether sure of its importance. But I have two clear points in mind in making it—and we shall see their relevance later. One is this. I think that—in abandoning what they have re-jected as the 'organic analogy'—many recent sociologists have, to an extent not altogether noticed, slipped into the employment of a new analogy: the analogy of the *'machine'*. A new *'mechanical analogy'* is being used, much less explicitly, I think, than was ever the case in the use of the 'organic analogy', and this seems to me to eliminate very dangerously all these elements of *social action proper* (including the 'teleological' attributes of the human mind) which so many of the earlier sociologists were so concerned to keep a clear sight of. And secondly—I think it probable that Talcott Parsons and some of his colleagues—who took their 'systems analysis' very much from a consideration of Pareto—have, possibly unwittingly, fallen into this same trap. So that they *speak* in terms of *voluntaristic*, social *action*, but—in fact—are operating in terms of a *mechanistic* model for the analysis of the *equilibrium conditions* of *social systems*. And this may be a fundamental contradiction built into the very heart of their system—just as it was in the system of Pareto.

In our study of Pareto, then, we have tried *primarily* to see his relevance to those other writers who, in the early twentieth century, were developing the study of the 'psychological aspects of society',

appropriately different ways of thinking and acting in the *same* actors; that in *some* situations they might be *conservative*, and in others ready to pursue speculative 'combinations', etc. He *assumed* that there was a *distribution* of residues (in terms of the structured, or graded, inequalities of men in society) and that, in changed situations, a *re-distribution* would occur. Again, deliberate thought, control of judgment and character, seem to be at a minimum, and the *re-distribution* of *elements* to a new *equilibrium* is the picture given.

but, simultaneously, we have tried to achieve a brief outline of his total system, and, in criticizing this, have established certain points which have a vital relevance to our later understanding of the making of sociology in our own day.

6

Georg Simmel*:
Socio-Psychological 'Forms'
of Interaction

There remains one other theorist who made important contributions to the making of sociology during the early part of the twentieth century, and whose work falls most fittingly under this heading of 'the psychological aspects of society'. This was Georg Simmel. Like all the other men we have considered, he developed his work within the general 'conspectus' of ideas which was predominant towards the end of the nineteenth century, but with his own quite distinctive style. This distinctive approach makes it incorrect to say that his work was *wholly* concerned with the psychological dimensions of social relationships; and, even in so far as it was so, it was qualitatively quite different from the schemes of analysis presented by McDougall, Cooley, Mead, Freud and Pareto. The fact is that Simmel was a *philosopher* and an *essayist*, and his work really consisted of probing conceptual analysis—drawing on empirical examples; always illuminating them; to some extent indicating how they could be systematically studied—but never presenting in any completeness *either* a total system of analysis *or* a systematically arranged body of empirical knowledge. The *essayist* is the title which fits Simmel best.

There are some men whose awareness of all the dimensions of actuality is always so sensitive, widely and deeply visioned, and intense, that they are also acutely and continuously aware of the insufficiency of all their conceptual attempts to penetrate it. To them, to attempt a 'comprehensive system' would be a kind of megalomania. All they can do is to engage in very carefully conceived 'forays' into it; to 'invade' actuality, so to speak, in limited, indicative ways; trying to carry a light into it here and there; but knowing very well that a total conquest is impossible; and, indeed, being so concerned that the awareness of the richness of actuality itself should not be *diminished* or *impoverished* among others by their own conceptual efforts, that they incline always to carefully qualified limitation rather than to bold conceptual entirety. Simmel was such a person. He presented no large 'scheme'. All his essays were explorations. And his manner of

* 1858–1918.

work had some of the limitations as well as the important virtues which the essayist (if his experience, insight, thought and comment is worthwhile) is almost bound to have. Sometimes, his carefully limited starting points for his studies tended to be over-simplifications (even occasionally to the point of falsifications) of positions previously held—though this was never a matter of serious distortion, and was valid for his own purposes; but also his selection of empirical illustrations was, if not arbitrary, certainly very variable in a quite unsystematic way. Thus, in discussing the deep-rooted elements of *conflict* as being essential ingredients in all abiding human relationships, he moved from the level of erotic relations between persons to that of the relations between 'prince' and 'nobles' in the 'courts of Central Europe up to the thirteenth century', within the same breath (so to speak) of argument. Always, his empirical illustrations were of such a wide scatter; and, only introduced *as* illustrations, were not scrupulously documented (or even outlined in any real detail), so that he could not be counted a systematic, empirical sociologist at all: not in the same sense, that is, that Hobhouse, Durkheim, Weber, and similar theorists were. At the same time, these well-considered 'limitations' of the essayist produced the most scrupulous analysis of very clearly specified group relationships, and of characteristerics which distinguished *kinds* of groups (such as the mere 'number of members'); and, throughout all his work, there was the feeling of *close personal engagement*. Simmel explored these dimensions of social and personal actuality because they were obviously of importance to *him*: not only as a *scholar*, but also as a *person*—for the sufficient understanding of his own life and nature.

One other aspect of this careful 'limitation' of approach was very important. Like all the major sociologists, one of Simmel's primary concerns was to clarify the distinctive subject-matter of sociology; to make the nature and scope of sociology very clear. In dealing with this problem, his approach was very much like that of Giddings. Sceptical about grandiose definitions; very much aware of the error and dangers of carelessly 'objectifying society'; he thought of human 'association' in a *verbal* way. It was the *activity* of '*sociation*' which was the focus of his attention; and this led him to concentrate, in his analysis, *not* upon the major elements of social organization as such, but upon the detailed *social relationships* which were carried on within them. In this sense, Simmel contributed to the development of one particular dimension of the 'conspectus' of sociology especially. Within the larger analysis of the elements of social structure in society, and the connections between them, he 'built in' the more detailed analysis of the *social relationships* between individuals as members of groups. This, as we have said, was something *more* than a study of the psychological dimensions of human relationships—Simmel believed that the *forms of social relationships* were 'sui generis' (constituting a distinctive *level* of *social* phenomena which could not be *reduced* to the psychological elements which were operative within them)—but, even so, it necessarily included a very close study of psychological, and socio-psychological factors.

Strictly speaking, therefore, Simmel was of crucial significance as a kind of *intermediary* figure. Durkheim and Weber (and others) provided ways of analysing the larger-scale 'social facts' and 'sequences of social action' in the social system. Cooley and Mead (and others) provided ways of analysing the growth of the 'self', and the socio-psychological processes of group-communications, which took place within the larger institutional framework of society. And Simmel offered an analysis which effectively *linked* them both. He operated *strictly* at the level of *associational structures* AND *processes*: but was concerned to analyse the detailed *relationships* of which these consisted; and therefore had also to take into account the *psychological elements* which were involved. It was this important mid-way territory of the nature of societies, of social experience and behaviour, which Simmel illuminated: of specific social relationships within varying kinds of group-membership. And two points deserve special note. First: this furthered the analysis of social *roles* and their attendant socio-psychological processes, which Giddings had outlined, and which Cooley and Mead (Mead especially) were also emphasizing and developing. But second: though, as an 'essayist', Simmel did not offer a comprehensive *system* of sociology, he did indicate quite clearly how the analysis of this complex mid-way territory of social relationships could be undertaken. His contribution was therefore a highly significant one, and has subsequently proved one of the strongest influences giving rise to studies of 'small groups', 'role-analysis', and 'group relations and behaviour' generally.

It was, of course, no accident that the work of Simmel and that of Giddings (among the early Americans) and then of Cooley and Mead, were so similar and so close in their agreement, because—though his writings were then of a limited nature—Simmel had probably been one of the best-known European scholars in America. We noted earlier that some of his work appeared in translation in the American Journal of Sociology during the last decade of the nineteenth century, and some American teachers—Albion Small especially—were very much concerned to promote his influence. Like Tönnies, Durkheim, and others, however, Simmel was one of those scholars who 'bridged' the two centuries, and whose work chiefly became known in the early decades of the twentieth as it became increasingly available in translation.

Simmel, then, added essential elements to the making of the subject. It is possible to clarify quite briefly those aspects of his work which are of particular significance for our purposes, and they can be grouped under three heads. The brevity of our treatment, however, should not be misleading. In his analysis of the socio-psychological *forms* which characterized social relationships of *apparently* different kinds, Simmel added a distinctive and essential component to sociological analysis. And in his analysis of the nature of *conflict* in social relationships, he emphasized elements of social actuality and of social theory which have come to be very much at the heart of present-day controversy (though, I think, misleadingly.) We need to understand Simmel in order properly to understand strictly contemporary issues. We shall see (as with regard to many other theoretical positions adopted), that these vexed questions of the moment are in many respects misguided; and have their roots in a number of basic confusions.

(I) THE DIVISIONS OF SOCIOLOGY: CONTINUITIES AND AGREEMENTS

Like Durkheim, Weber, and others, and for the purpose of achieving accuracy, Simmel was concerned to define sociology in terms of a clear delimitation of its distinctive subject-matter. Here, we need only see how, in moving towards a formulation which allowed him to concentrate on a very specific area, his position was in basic agreement with that of other writers.

Like everyone from Comte onwards, Simmel recognized in *associational* phenomena, a *distinctive* level of 'facts' which required special study—involving particular concepts and modes of observation, description, analysis, classification, etc. which were in certain ways different from those employed in other sciences and certainly could not be *resolved* into, or *reduced* to, them. Human 'sociation' *involved* biological and psychological elements, and had reference to various kinds of *non-human* (e.g. environmental) facts, but it formed a *distinctive order of relationships* in its own right—no component of which could thereafter be understood excepting by reference to its inter-connection with others. For example, the relationships between *two* people were distinctively different from those among a group of *three* (let us say after a third person had joined them): and the set of relationships between the *three* could not be resolved into the components of the *two* and the *one* which had existed *before* the group of three was formed. The relations between the members of *any* group of *three*, have certain determinate attributes—because such a 'triadic' network was a *distinctive kind of associational fact*. Now this, of

639

course, is a very small example of an 'associational order', and Simmel, it goes without saying, conceived of an entire range of such orders in an entire society: from small groups (of friends), to large groups ('aristocracies', and the 'masses'); from relatively informal to highly institutionalized sets of relationships. *Associational* systems, systems of *relationships*; formed the distinctive subject-matter (the distinctive 'level' of facts), of sociology. But this, even so, was not sufficiently clear for accuracy of study—since it comprised such a vast *range* of facts. Furthermore the *content* of many of these sets of social relationships formed the subject-matter of the *special* social sciences: economics, political science, jurisprudence, etc. Simmel therefore divided this entire subject-matter (to some extent shared by the other social sciences) into certain clear sections of study.

'*General Sociology*' included studies of many kinds about the entire, many-sided *content* of all the associational facts of human societies. Many kinds of empirical investigation, establishing generalizations at various levels (individuals, populations, groups, institutions, etc.), were possible. Within this entire range of facts, however, certain recurrent *forms* of human interaction were discernible. *Pure Sociology* was the concentrated study—chiefly analytical, but also having empirical and comparative reference—of these *forms* of social relationship. There then remained *Philosophical Sociology* which was divided into (*a*) 'epistemological' studies: the clarification of concepts, methods of study, etc. and (*b*) 'metaphysical' kinds of study which carried research and conjecture into possible considerations which went beyond the range of immediate knowledge and experience.

This division of the over-all range of tasks in sociology was sufficiently broad to make room for all levels of enquiry, and all ranges of interest, but it was *Pure Sociology* (which we shall come to in a moment) which focused upon what—for Simmel—comprised the *distinctive* subject-matter of sociology: the *forms* of association.

In his entire elaboration of these elements of sociological study, Simmel showed the continuity of much of his thinking—by way of criticism—from earlier positions (e.g. of historical materialism), and had much to say about a 'sociological' orientation to the study of the facts of history which showed him to be completely in sympathy and agreement with evolutionary and developmental accounts. But many other agreements could be traced of the kind that we have so substantially established, among the other writers. The close interdependence of elements of the social system (and the structural-functional mode of analysis); the deliberate emphasis upon the understanding of social *action* within the context of institutionalized relationships and structured groups; the rootedness of the forms of social relationships in basic instinctual 'drives' and ensuing sentiments, and even the establishing on this basis (compare Pareto) of 'residual' dispositions in the experience of men in society; the insistence upon the closest relation between 'structural' and 'sociopsychological' dimensions in the analysis of social relationships; the ways in which 'morality' lay at the heart of regulated social relationships; the emphasis upon careful scientific method—observation, analysis, comparison, etc: all these conceptual elements—common among the other writers—were plainly to be found in Simmel's work. With these agreements in the background, it is of more interest to us to turn to the two specific contributions on which he had much that was quite distinctive to say.

(II) PURE SOCIOLOGY: THE STUDY OF SOCIETAL 'FORMS'

It was in his treatment of 'Pure Sociology' that Simmel introduced a conceptual element into the study of the psychological aspects of social relationships which was quite new—and which, indeed, advanced the study of the *structure* of social relationships as such. So influential was this contribution that, by some, it signified the creation of a new 'school' of sociology—'Formal Sociology'; but Simmel had no such separate 'school' in mind. 'Pure Sociology' was concerned with the recurring 'forms' of association, and the alternative term—'Formal Sociology'—was Simmel's own. But, as we have seen, this was only one (though the central) part of the work of sociology as a whole.

Simmel explained his conviction that the essential 'core' of sociology was the study of associational 'forms' in this way. A wide acquaintance with social facts, with the whole range of institutions in human societies, made it clear, he argued, that—despite their diverse *content*—they were manifested in certain *forms* of relationship (including specific *patterns* of psychological experience) which constantly recurred and which, upon careful reflection, seemed indispensable. Certain *forms* seemed *necessary* in group relations of various kinds. These *forms* could be *abstracted* from their *content* and then carefully categorized and analysed in terms of the group conditions, the patterned relationships, the psychological elements, and even the specific pieces of behaviour (e.g. the nature and significance of the *lie*) and the qualities that came to reside in individuals (e.g. particular attributes of sociability), involved. For example, in all the detailed activities of a society—in industrial firms, in the armed forces, in the church, in the law, in political parties and the procedures of government, and even in the family—it could be seen that particular relationships were organized about the allocation of *authority*.

641

There were—in all these areas of social activity—*hierarchical* relationships: of *authority* and *obedience*; of *dominance* and *submission*; of *super-ordination* and *subordination*. The *content* of these relationships (*a*) in each field of activity—religion, industry, politics, etc. and (*b*) in all such fields of activities in different *societies* or in different *historical epochs*, was clearly qualitatively different. Yet the *form* of the relationship was the same. It should be possible, then, to *abstract* this *form* of human association, and to analyse it in formal terms (having reference, of course, to particular examples as and when necessary) so that a much fuller understanding of it could be achieved for the interpretation of it in *any* field of human relationships thereafter.

Sociology could thus accomplish a distinctive body of analysis and understanding about its distinctive subject-matter—all the discernible *forms* of social relationships—which could then make possible the detailed interpretation and explanation of any specific set of social relationships in any specific area of social activity.

This was an extremely clear formulation, and two points are immediately evident. First, this was a method for the systematic construction of *types* of social behaviour which was very close indeed —though not, of course, the same—as that proposed by Weber (and also by Tönnies, and, as we have seen, others). Weber wished to construct 'ideal types' for the causal explanation of specific, concrete sequences of social action; whereas Simmel proposed a systematic analysis of those discernible 'forms' of social relationships which were commonly found; but it is quite evident that the two kinds of analysis (bearing in mind also Weber's more formal analysis of sociological categories) could fit together very satisfactorily. The 'Simmel-type' analysis would be of the greatest use in the 'Weber-type' construction of 'models' for the subjective understanding of specific social situations. In this consideration we can see clearly how structural analysis, the understanding of action in terms of meaning, and socio-psychological analysis could fit together very well. But the second point is more central for our immediate consideration of the study of the psychological aspects of society.

It will be clearly seen that Simmel here introduced a component for the analysis of the psychological dimensions of social relationships which was *additional* to those put forward by McDougall, Cooley, Mead, Freud, and Pareto, and was such as to *link* their own kinds of socio-psychological analysis more formally with the analysis of elements of social structure. And it was such as to accomplish this whilst abstracting itself from the *apparently* dense complications of *apparently* diverse areas of experience and behaviour. The complexities of experience and behaviour in economic, religious, political, military, educational, family behaviour, etc. were acutely and plausibly pared away from a central analysis of socio-psychological *forms* of relationship which were common to them all. This did not mean at all that there were *no* differences of quality in all these areas of experience; only that, whatever these differences—certain essential forms, common to them all, permitted of clear analysis. And this again meant that the conceptual apparatus for *explanation* in sociology was simplified (and made distinct) from the categories for *description*. Thus, it was still necessary and correct to have concepts of social *structure* and *function*, and of the *structured parts* of a total society—the religious system, the economic system, the political system, etc. for a systematic description and analysis; but the *explanation* of social processes of order and change was *not* simply a *weighting* of one or other of these, but the use of more central concepts which permitted a *general* application among them all. And this was true *both* of social-structural *and* of social-psychological dimensions. In both cases, a simplified central analysis of *forms* had been made possible without at all losing sight of or discountenancing the density and differential qualities of experience and behaviour in each institutional field.

This was, then, a very considerable contribution which linked together many of the components of analysis provided by other writers, and we can see clearly once again how the many-sided development of ideas in the ongoing making of sociology was continuously moving towards an enriched, more comprehensive, and better-clarified system of analysis. All these contributions interlinked with each other in an exciting and satisfactory way.

Simmel, of course, developed his 'Formal Sociology' very extensively. He classified kinds of groups on the basis of their numerical size, and analysed the determinate limitations of size in relation to required group qualities (e.g. the limitations to the size of aristocracies); the relationships between the size of groups and *variations* in certain of their qualities (such as cohesiveness); and the degree of subtlety of communications possible in small groups and large (e.g. the 'masses'). In his account of the growth of custom, law, and morality among groups—especially in his account of the growth of 'morality' in the individual—he gave a picture of the growth of the 'self' which came close (though it was not developed in anywhere near the same detail) to that put forward by Cooley, Mead, and Freud. He gave a detailed analysis of the individual; of relationships between *two* individuals (the Dyad); *three* individuals (the Triad), and individuals in larger groups. And then—of particular interest—he gave a detailed analysis of certain 'forms' of relationship; especially those of 'Superordination and Subordination' which we have mentioned.

643

Strictly speaking this was an analysis of the relationships and procedures of authority and power, of varying aspects of hierarchical gradation, and of kinds of promotion and demotion, of upward and downward mobility. But no brief note of this kind is sufficient to indicate the great richness of Simmel's treatment. Apart from the analysis of such *formal* relationships he also explored the relationships in such groups as 'secret societies', and the mental mechanisms of the individual mind in coming to terms with the complexities of urban life, of life in the metropolis; and there was a continuous originality of observation, comment, and statement in his writing that can only be appreciated by a careful reading of him. Because of the very self-imposed 'limitations' of his deliberate 'essay-style', Simmel's writing is very dense, and no summary indication can possibly do justice to it. But, in addition to his introduction and development of the analysis of 'forms' of social relationships there was one other emphasis in his work that has come to be specially stressed in recent times and of which we must take special note. This was his treatment of 'conflict'.

(III) CONFLICT: AN INGREDIENT IN INTEGRATIVE SOCIAL BONDS

One all-pervading element of human 'sociation', Simmel pointed out, was 'conflict', and—as with other aspects of social relationships—*'forms'* of conflict could be abstracted from their *contents* in various fields of social action, and studied analytically. And such a study, Simmel did, in fact, carry out. His essay was detailed, profound, and indeed—in his discussion of the nature of some irreconcilabilities—deeply moving to those who have known such intractable and final human situations. But here, we will concern ourselves only with his central emphasis.

As we have seen in all the work we have studied from Comte onwards, *all* the major sociological theorists were agreed that the institutions of society came into being in the context of the practical activities of men, and as an outcome of their *conflict and co-operation*. This was a perennial theme: fully agreed upon. And Simmel himself was quite clear and deliberate in disclaiming any *originality*. 'The sociological significance of conflict', he wrote, 'has in principle never been disputed.' No-one had ever thought to dispute it. And it is important to be completely clear about this. The recognition of the importance of conflict in shaping social cohesion, and in making many social institutions necessary, had always been 'writ large' in all the work of the earlier writers.

Simmel's particular *emphasis* which *did* have originality was his claim: (*a*) that conflict was not only a *divisive* influence in society; nor (*b*) did it contribute to the shaping of social order *only* in that it made institutions of control and regulation (and arbitration and conciliation) necessary (though this was true); but also (*c*) that it was actually a contributory factor of a *positive* kind in the establishing and sustaining of social bonds: indeed, that it was an integrative element at the heart of all important, abiding relationships. Conflict, in short, performed a *positive function* in establishing binding relationships. Conflict possessed, Simmel wrote, a 'sociologically positive character'.

Now Simmel did think, obviously, that conflict *was* in some respects divisive, and, indeed, was sometimes irreconcilable, but he distinguished it very definitely from *indifference* or *apathy*, in that strong, positive elements were at its roots. Furthermore, he believed that there were very powerful propensities (rooted in 'instinct') towards a quick readiness for opposition, hostility, aggression, which could rapidly develop into hatred. Within the context of these propensities, and given the constraining conditions of society, and the many, various, and contending interests of classes, groups, and individuals, he insisted that the very nature of the individual personality attained its unity '. . . not exclusively by an exhaustive harmonization—according to logical, objective, religious, or ethical norms—of the contents of his personality . . .' but: '. . . on the contrary, contradiction and conflict not only precede this unity, but *are operative in it at every moment of its existence**'. Conflict was a *continuous aspect* of the maintenance of individual *'unity'*. And similarly, he argued, society, too, only *assumed a form* as a continuing outcome of constraint, limitation, and competition as well as motives making for co-operation, mutuality, and the harmonious pursuit of interests. The *form* of society was always the outcome of a *simultaneity—not* of a negative (on the one hand) and a positive (on the other) set of forces—but of the *two positive* forces of conflictful and harmonious disposition. And Simmel went on to show how—even in very specific and interpersonal relationships, such as marriage, as well as in larger groups and associations—conflictful, de-limiting, and competitive elements were actually *integrative* forces. To try to point Simmel's conception exactly, we might note one special example he gave in connection with the mental mechanisms for living tolerably within urban stress that we mentioned earlier. In such a situation, he argued, feelings of *opposition* and *aversion* to city life were part and parcel of the sustaining of urban relationships as a tolerable pattern.

'Without such aversion,' he wrote, 'we could not imagine what form

* My italics.

645

modern urban life, which every day brings everybody in contact with innumerable others, might possibly take. The whole inner organization of urban interaction is based on an extremely complex hierarchy of sympathies, indifferences, and aversions of both the most short-lived and the most enduring kind. And in this complex, the sphere of indifference is relatively limited. For our psychological activity responds to almost every impression that comes from another person with a certain determinate feeling. The subconscious, fleeting, changeful nature of this feeling only seems to reduce it to indifference. Actually, such indifference would be as unnatural to us as the vague character of innumerable contradictory stimuli would be unbearable. We are protected against both of these typical dangers of the city by antipathy, which is the preparatory phase of concrete antagonism and which engenders the distances and aversions without which we could not lead the urban life at all. The extent and combination of antipathy, the rhythm of its appearance and disappearance, the forms in which it is satisfied, all these, along with the more literally unifying elements, produce the metropolitan form of life in its irresolvable totality; and what at first glance appears in it as dissociation, actually is one of its elementary forms of sociation.'*

Social *order*, then, was always the outcome of *unifying* and *conflictful* forces in combination with each other; the two were inseparable.

We need not attempt to outline all the elements of Simmel's discussion. It is enough for our own purposes to note one or two points clearly.

First: that this was not, strictly speaking, as original a contribution on the part of Simmel as was his emphasis upon the importance of the analysis of societal 'forms'. All the early sociologists emphasized that conflict *and* co-operation were continuous elements in the formation of institutions, and in the crucial emergence of *values* at the heart of institutions (which was another point which Simmel himself made). We have seen that all those who studied the psychological aspects of society also emphasized conflict as well as harmony in the growth of the 'self' in society. Even so, Simmel did provide a more detailed analysis of the integrative role of conflict in *social relationships* which could certainly be said to be a worthwhile additional contribution, and which supported and supplemented the theories of the social psychologists proper. Simmel himself certainly felt that he was only *extending* a dimension of sociological analysis rather than making any *innovation*. And it is important to clarify this matter only to make it perfectly clear that Simmel was *not* setting up a distinctive *kind* of sociology—termed '*Conflict Sociology*', any more than he was setting up a distinctive *school* of '*Formal Sociology*'.

---

* *Conflict and the Web of Group-Affiliations*, Tr. R. Bendix, Free Press, p. 20.

He was contributing simply to the making of *sociology*: and the analysis of *'forms'* of social relationships, and of *'conflict'* within them, were important elements of *sociological analysis* as a whole. The importance of this emphasis will be seen later.

The second point is simply that—for Simmel—part of the recognition of the all-pervading nature of conflict in society was the recognition that conflict fulfilled *positive functions* in sustaining *forms* of social relationships; and, indeed, *forms* of individual personality. Putting this in another way, Simmel studied the nature and interdependency of societal forms in terms of *structural-functional analysis*, and *conflict* was *included* among the factors which performed *positive functions* in achieving and sustaining social 'forms'; though, certainly, it could *sometimes* be divisive and disruptive. The extremely important point here, is that *conflict* was not thought to be some aspect of social relationships that was opposed to some other aspect called *'functional unity'*, or *'integration'*, or *'harmony'*. Dimensions of conflict were *part and parcel* of *all* the dimensions of society which were analysed in 'structural-functional' terms. This, again, is a point of much importance for our later assessment of some of the theoretical claims in sociology.

The work of Simmel, then, was another important contribution to the development of the study of the psychological aspects of society —parallel to all the others we have considered; quite distinctive in its own ways; and yet very substantially reinforcing them.

X

Summary

We are now in a position to summarize the more important elements on which there was agreement among all those theorists who contributed to the development of this one dimension in the making of sociology. This need not be detailed, since the close similarity between the ideas of the various systems is so plainly apparent. Nevertheless, it is worthwhile to make a brief statement of major points established and agreed upon, because so much, in fact, had been basically accomplished during these early decades of the century. A clear appreciation of it is worthwhile for its own sake, but it is also necessary for any sound assessment of later work.

We can start with broad points and perspectives and then move to specific issues.

The Psychological Aspects of Society now thoroughly explored

The first obvious conclusion is that this one important dimension of sociological analysis—so much referred to by the earlier writers*, but left so unexamined—had now been very thoroughly explored. All the theorists we have studied in this section—the bulk of whose work was produced between 1900 and 1940—were convinced that the study of man in society could not possibly be satisfactory without a fuller, systematic knowledge of the psychological factors involved. They concentrated deliberately on the 'development' of these particular aspects of the study of man and, in the total achievement of their work, there was hardly an element of human experience and behaviour which had not been richly and deeply illuminated. Thinking of the making of sociology: before 1900, the study of these areas had been confined to such thinking as the methodological ideas of Mill and the analytical proposals of Ward and Giddings (excellent though these were); but, within the three to four decades of their work, these new writers had constructed an entire conceptual fabric which could usefully be applied at any level: from the inner experiences of the individual, the emergence of the 'self', the relationships and communications of small groups, right up to the experience and behaviour involved in the most complex institutional roles, and the 'forms' of socio-psychological relationship which seemed common to all institutions and societies. A whole new fabric of concepts had

* Though, of course, Ward and Giddings in particular had had much that was worthwhile to say.

been created within the over-all 'apparatus' of sociological analysis: fitting well with all the other components, and making possible the exploration of all these socio-psychological dimensions in much more systematic and satisfactory detail.

We must bear in mind that this 'development' was taking place *simultaneously* with the development in all the other dimensions of the nineteenth century 'conspectus'—the more detailed study of social evolution, the 'typological' studies of social change, the 'objective' study of 'social facts', and the 'subjective understanding' of 'social action'. During this period, the making of sociology was advancing in the development of *all* its components. The construction of these concepts for analysing the psychological dimensions of society was one great achievement among—and parallel to—all the others.

The Social Basis for a satisfactory Human Psychology laid down

The most central and important single principle agreed upon and carried into their work by all these writers was that which all other earlier and contemporary writers had insisted upon: *that the associational context was essential for any satisfactory human psychology.* There was an entire agreement about this. Their work not only rested upon it, but substantially demonstrated its validity, and this is a matter of such vital importance that we must be clear about several specific aspects of it.

(I) THE PSYCHOLOGICAL CREATIVITY OF SOCIETY

First: it is important to see that all these writers agreed with Durkheim's basic contention: that *associational processes* were *psychologically creative.* It was not possible to explain society in terms of separate individuals (as though individuals were definable *entities* independent of society, and society was no more than a *sum* of them, or something consciously created by them) because (*a*) associational processes were essential conditions for the creation of the individual 'self', and accounted for much of the *content* of the 'self's' experience, and (*b*) collective conditions of association engendered elements of experience (conative, affective, cognitive, conceptual, idealistic) which could *not* be said to exist in individuals *prior* to these situations. Society was a *creative* psychological process—not only of cumulative 'collective' traditions, but also, correlated with these, of elements of *personal, private* experience which would not otherwise have had a

649

existence at all. It is most important to notice that *all* these writers were agreed on this quite fundamental matter. Even in the work of Freud—the least 'socially' orientated of them all—the relationships of the family and primary groups, and the constraining regulations and values found within them, were *indispensable* in any analysis of the individual 'self' or 'personality'.

It is true that none of these writers was as dogmatically narrow on this point as Durkheim. They did not deny the possibility of purpose-ful, teleological action *within this context* as Durkheim did (though Freud's determinism, and Pareto's cynicism came very close). All of them, in varying degrees, incorporated consciousness, choice, reason, deliberate action within this complex of socio-psychological crea-tivity, and certainly thought them possible on the basis of it. Even so—all were agreed with Durkheim's basic point of the necessity of recognizing the psychological creativity of 'society'; of recognizing a level of psychological process beyond the boundaries of the separate 'self'.

(II) SELF AND SOCIETY

It followed clearly that a specially important element of this wider persuasion was that—far from it being the case that society could be explained in terms of individual entities—on the contrary: the 'self' was essentially rooted in associational processes; and a knowledge of associational processes was indispensable in providing a satis-factory account of it. The 'self' and 'society' were, in fact, *not* mutu-ally exclusive, totally separable, categories. The study of *socio-psychological processes* was necessary in order to comprehend both.

(III) THE SOCIO-HISTORICAL CONTEXT ESSENTIAL FOR THE UNDERSTANDING OF HUMAN EXPERIENCE AND CONDUCT

Another important element of this conception was that since associ-ational processes were psychologically creative and since the institu-tional developments of society were historically cumulative (including ideas and ideals, aesthetic and religious perceptions, linguistic conceptions, entire systems of myth and doctrine, etc.)—'human nature' itself was to some extent *historically created* (not just materi-ally and biologically created); and, indeed, was continuously *in the making*. The conceptual developments of these theorists provided a *sociological context* for the *psychological study of man* which was now completely in agreement with the persuasions of the earlier theorists, and completely filled out the kind of objection that Marx had put forward in denying the possibility of a *science of psychology* which abstracted man (as one animal among others) from the creative processes of history. This, he had argued, was to slice ninety per cent of the subject matter away—and thus, at the outset, to falsify it!

This, again, is a point of the most fundamental importance, and we might note again, sharply, that to attempt a study of elements of 'human nature'—e.g., of neuro-physiology, sensation, perception, motivation, emotion, learning, etc.—as elements of a basically given *organism*, abstracted from associational processes, and to claim that *this* alone is the scientific study of human psychology is a fundamental fallacy. 'Human psychology', 'human nature' *is* in very large part *associationally* (and *historically*) *created*, and no account of neuro-physiological and bio-psychological components *in themselves*, can *possibly be sufficient*. Even the development of an apparently simple element—like 'perception'—in the unfolding experience of the human individual may be inseparable from associational components—from the introduction of 'conceptual' categories (which are social), for example. Human nature simply is not *a given datum* independent of associational and historical processes, and to regard it as such is a fundamental conceptual error in the formulation of the human sciences.

Again, we have seen that all these theorists were agreed on this point. Even Freud, who solidly believed in a neuro-physiological and instinctual basis of human nature nonetheless could not interpret and explain the vicissitudes of man's experience and behaviour, and all the attendant mechanisms of the human mind, except in terms of the constraining factors of 'civilization'. And even Pareto—who also believed solidly in the existence of constant dispositions of the human mind—nonetheless understood them as 'residues' within 'collective conditions' and 'composite social phenomena'.

This, then, was a working out in detailed conceptual terms of a conviction which had been common to the major sociologists from Comte onwards; and it amounted to a very full confirmation of what they had held to be *the error of psychology* as a science of human experience and behaviour abstracted from its associational and historical context.

(IV) THE AGREED CONTEXT OF 'EVOLUTION' : BIOLOGY, PSYCHOLOGY, SOCIAL PSYCHOLOGY, SOCIOLOGY

Having made this point very emphatically, however, we must note equally emphatically, that all these theorists were also completely agreed in accepting the 'evolutionary perspective' and in seeing the development of human societies within the wider context of the material and biological processes of evolution. All of them saw

651

human social propensities and activities as being rooted in instinctual dispositions which were a part of man's biological endowment; and they all desired the closest relationship of work and knowledge among the several sciences—physical, biological, and social. Their position was not *at all* that *no* useful knowledge of the bio-psychological elements of man's genetic endowment could be provided; only that this in itself was not *definitively human nature*! Their emphasis was only that the recognition of the *creativity of associational processes* as an *additional* area of causal processes was *indispensable*, and that it was a conceptual error to regard associational facts just as a kind of added overlay—which could readily be explained in terms of the lower-order processes. McDougall and Freud especially were very much concerned to have as reliable a basis of neuro-physiological and bio-psychological knowledge as possible; and, indeed, they emphasized its importance. Their position, and the position of the others, was only that this in itself was *not sufficient*, and that—even for the understanding of sentiments and values within the 'self, and of the formation of the individual 'personality' itself—associational processes had to enter.

We have seen that these views and developments were such as to substantiate many of the earlier assumptions of Comte, Marx, and others; but it is also clear that they could all fit well within, and fill out satisfactorily, the schema proposed by John Stuart Mill. Generalizations at the level of (1) experimental psychology and (2) sociology (about the nature and interdependency of *institutions*) could now be linked by (3) these 'middle-principles' of 'associational psychology' which had been so richly developed. The entire scheme of analysis for 'A General Science of Society' was now beginning to look complete.

The social basis for a satisfactory human psychology had been successfully laid down, and the *error of psychology*—independent of this—had been indisputably laid bare.

These were extremely important general principles on which there was completely firm agreement. Within this context, we can now enumerate the other distinctive points on which complete clarity was achieved.

Specific points established and agreed

(I) INSTINCT IN MAN : INDIVIDUAL AND SOCIETY

It is of the very greatest interest to note firstly that there never was any such thing as an 'instinct' school in this study of the psychological aspects of society—separate and distinct from other work—as has been commonly supposed. We have seen that McDougall himself (usually the target for attack) was far from being just an 'instinct' theorist, and emphasized sentiment-formation and the development of the 'self' in society as much as anyone else. But—that aside—the crucial thing to see, and to see quite *incontrovertibly*, is that *all* these theorists rested their entire analyses upon the acceptance of the existence of *instinctual* elements in the human mind. They were *all* agreed that, in man's basic bio-genetic endowment, there were established correlations of anatomical structure, neuro-physiological process, psychological experience, and elements of behaviour, which provided quite basic, perennial elements in individual and society. These included conative, affective, and cognitive elements of experience; but certain other things—all important—may be noted. (1) They were not held to be behaviourally *automatic* or *inflexible*—as was the case in most other species. But, even so, (2) they were powerful, persisting elements of drive and appetite at the core of human motivation which could neither be ignored nor eradicated. And (3) their compulsive nature lay at the heart of the 'vicissitudes' experienced by the self in society, and these vicissitudes could not be explained without reference to them. Furthermore (4) some of these writers were also of the opinion that even broader dispositions of the human mind could properly be said to be of an 'instinctual nature'. Thus, even the propensity to 'link' things in experience; to attach oneself conservatively to 'links' already established, etc;—in short, elements of 'thinking'—were held to be basic attributes of the mind which were not themselves 'learned'. And, going beyond this, there were 'mental mechanisms' too, by which the mind 'functioned' in adjusting itself to its conditions of vicissitude, which could not be said to be 'learned' in any ordinary sense. These, too, were explained in close connection with the instinctual energies, their interplay and the conflicts to which they were vulnerable.

There was basic agreement among McDougall, Cooley, Mead, Freud, Pareto, and Simmel about all this, but we may remember that there was also a similar close arrangement—though not elaborated in such detail—in Tönnies, Westermarck, Hobhouse and Weber. The simple truth is that all these early twentieth century theorists accepted the existence of these bio-psychological roots of human experience and behaviour. They *all* accepted that *instinctual* components were of basic importance in the life of both individuals and society.

All of them, too, adopted this kind of position deliberately: in preference to the early philosophical 'associationism' (i.e. of sensations and conscious states of mind) and maintained it as against any simple minded 'Behaviourism' which sought to explain all the intricacies of human behaviour in terms of 'conditioned reflexes'. Two points deserve special note in these connections. First: that this recognition of instinctual dispositions in the human mind led to the elaboration of richer and more subtle theories of 'learning'—in McDougall, Freud, Cooley and Mead alike—than were possible on the much narrower 'stimulus-response' basis, or the quite unwarranted basis of 'reflexes' and their 'conditioning'. Secondly, that this acceptance of 'instinct theory' was *not in opposition at all to a properly considered behaviourism*. This we shall note separately in a moment; but it is important to see that it was the absurdly narrow 'school' of *Watsonian* 'behaviourism' that was the exception here, and Mead— the social behaviourist and the instinctivist—rejected it completely. But the third point is that the explorations of the processes of 'learning' to which this acceptance of instinct and attendant mental mechanisms led, were such as to emphasize the importance of *associational processes* for the shaping of experience and behaviour in both individuals and society.

(II) THE CENTRAL IMPORTANCE OF THE 'SENTIMENTS' IN INDIVIDUAL AND SOCIETY

These theories of 'learning' especially pointed to and rested upon the very close relationship between impulse (and need), emotion, and cognition in human learning. They introduced and stressed the *affective* element in it. They considered learning essentially as a process of accommodation to *social situations* and the *symbols* in them, as well as to *objects* in the physical world. And this led, as we have seen, to one other central agreement of the greatest importance: the centrality of *sentiment-formation* in the establishment of psychological and behavioural order in both 'self' and 'society'. *Sentiments*—the organization of feeling about particular objects, persons, or symbols—were seen to be elements of the very greatest importance in the structuring of the content and process of the *psychic life of the individual* (giving an established pattern of impulse, emotion, perception, cognition, attachment, evaluation, and attitudes) and also simultaneously, those psychological 'constellations' in society (involving the organization of the same elements) which were the experiential correlates of *institutionalization*. In individuals and in institutions, *sentiments* were the established focal points of psychic order, the constellations of abiding values, those socio-psychological facts *which actually were the heart* of much personal judgment and continuing social traditions. It was the sentiments that were the chief carriers of values; the touchstones of social judgments; bearing the powerful feelings of approval and disapproval in relation to each particular area of social conduct which they served to regulate.

The sentiments were formed in the process of stabilization of the instinctual dispositions about the objects, persons, places, and symbols, in relation to which they found their satisfaction. They were thus *evaluations* in which the full power of these instinctual dispositions were canalized. They were strong in having the support of these powerful dispositions. And the sentiments clearly linked the analysis of the processes whereby the psychic life of individuals (in association) assumed a certain order, with the analysis of the emergence and establishment of *institutional regularities* themselves. Individual 'order'—institutional 'order'—were two aspects of the same socio-psychological process.

It is of the greatest significance that this concept of the *sentiments* as the outcome of *instinctual accommodation* to appropriate 'objects' encountered within *associational conditions* was not only agreed upon so substantially by McDougall, Cooley, Mead, Freud, Pareto and Simmel—all those who especially devoted themselves to this socio-psychological analysis—but also with complete unanimity by Tönnies, Westermarck, Hobhouse, Durkheim and Weber. In all cases the *sentiments* and the *values* they embodied were held to be the powerful core of social institutions. And again we can see the overwhelmingly impressive extent of the agreement that *values* lay at the heart of institutions.

It must be remembered, too—to appreciate this point with the absolutely fundamental significance that it possesses—with what great force all the sociologists held it. Westermarck made the sentiments the core of his 'sanctions'. Durkheim declared that the sentiments were the powerful realities at the heart of the law, Pareto emphasized the instincts-and-sentiments as the massive elements in the persisting 'residues', Cooley saw the 'pivotal sentiments of human nature' at the heart of ideas and institutions . . . Each man not only made this point, but made it the most central point in his treatment of the nature of *institutionalization*.

(III) THE GROWTH OF THE 'SELF' IN SOCIETY

The similarity of conception which all these writers had of the growth of the 'self' in society needs no further comment: it is so plain. What we must note, however, besides the thorough acceptance of the view that associational processes were the essential conditions for the growth of the 'human' self, was the fact that a very detailed array of concepts had been provided by which every aspect of this process could be analysed, and, moreover, these concepts were in very considerable agreement with each other. McDougall's account of the growth of the sentiment of the 'self'; Cooley's account of the 'looking glass self'; Mead's account of the 'I', the 'Me', the 'Generalized Other'; Freud's account of the 'Id, Ego, and Super-Ego', were all remarkably similar; dealing with essentially the same elements of experience. And the same extensive similarities could be traced in the various accounts of all other elements in the emergence of the 'self'—the growth of perceptual consciousness and the 'differentiation' of parts of the 'self', the laying down of memories, the significance of language and other symbols, the 'internalization' of values and ideals, the significance of primary group relations and communications, and so on. A very considerable consensus of analysis was provided in all these apparently diverse contributions, and, again, it is plain that all these conceptions taken together formed a system of analysis far richer than had existed previously and far richer than any *one* of these contributions taken in isolation from the others.

(IV) THE ANALYSIS OF GROUPS AND COMMUNICATIONS

Part of this system was the classification and analysis of different kinds of *groups*, and the nature of *communications* appropriate to each of them—with special reference to the growth of the 'self' and the establishment of sentiments, values, and attendant attitudes. Here again agreements were very extensive, but we might mention a few. There was complete agreement about the crucial significance of primary groups and primary group ideals during the early years of the child's experience. There was agreement about the centrally important place of the nature of *communications* as the *very process* of socio-psychological creativity. And there was agreement about the importance of the nature of the *symbols* (including those of *language*) which were operative in such communications, and the kinds of 'mental mechanisms' which were powerfully operative in the formation of sentiments about them. And there was, with this, the possibility of extending the analysis to the entire system of communications in society (as Cooley did) in relation to the whole network of *primary* and *secondary* groups. Group relations and communications were firmly established as important and indispensable elements of study.

(V) THE ANALYSIS OF 'MENTAL MECHANISMS'

All these scholars, too, were agreed about the insufficiency of any simple notion of cognitive learning—whether conscious or other-

656

wise. With the instincts, their vicissitudes, their processes of accommodation to conditions of stress, the formation of sentiments in mind—they were all aware that mental processes, in being driven to patterns of adjustment, went far beyond simple responses to stimuli, and entailed far more than conscious purpose and reason. In their various ways, they gave their accounts of what Freud termed the 'mental mechanisms'—in terms of which the processes of the mind *operated*, but which were not themselves learned. Here Freud and Pareto were obviously the chief contributors—and the considerable coincidence between their accounts of various 'mechanisms' was of the greatest interest: especially bearing in mind that Freud spoke chiefly in individual and clinical terms, whilst Pareto was describing what he observed in *social* processes of feeling and thinking. But, even here, it is plain that their account had much in common also, with the conceptions of Mead and the other writers. The study of the 'mental mechanisms' operative in the accommodation of individuals and groups to collective conditions; in the adjustment of instinctual dispositions, the formation of sentiments, and the kinds of 'theorizing' which stemmed from them (and were powerfully influenced by them); was established as an important part of socio-psychological investigation and social theory.

(VI) CONSCIOUS REASON AND PURPOSE

Despite this full recognition of all those forces and dispositions of the mind which were of a *non-rational* nature; despite the full recognition of their great power and importance in self and society; despite the full awareness of the complex inter-play among them which lay behind the outer show of *reason*, and inter-mingled with it in such subtle ways of influence as not only to lead sometimes to outright *ir*rationality, but also to a calculated *use* of rationality for the furtherance of their insistent desires and ends; the great virtue of all these writers was that they did not *exclude* from their systems a full consideration of the place of conscious reason, deliberate learning, deliberate judgment, responsible choice, and purposeful action in human experience and behaviour. Pareto was ambiguous in this—but still he recognized the distinction. Freud, too, was ambiguous in his 'determinism' on the one hand, and the assumptions underlying his 'therapy' on the other. Even so, he made the distinction between reasoning which rested on deliberate logic, reference to careful empirical test, and led to considered judgment, and responsible action—and the various patternings of the 'mental mechanisms' as such, and any 'pathological' resolutions which were forcibly established in the 'psyche' in the face of intolerable conditions of stress. 'Knowledge' was distinguished from 'illusion'.* And certainly Freud thought—though without attributing undue degrees of power to rational knowledge, even when it existed—that it was the most desirable situation when full and clear rational knowledge (and self-knowledge) guided all the dimensions of the mind into a satisfactory order.† With the other writers—McDougall, Cooley, Mead, Simmel—the full incorporation of conscious reason, responsible control, and the direction of action by purpose, was quite clear.

In developing their study of all these psychological dimensions of self and society, these authors—whilst elaborating concepts for the fullest understanding of the *non*-rational elements—nonetheless preserved a conceptual framework within which conscious reason, choice, and responsible action could also be incorporated and dealt with. This was a real excellence of judgment, and of both philosophical and scientific accuracy. And again, we can see the continued development of that insistence upon the inclusion of 'choices' and deliberate acts of 'will' within the entire field of socio-psychological 'causation' which had been so clearly stated by Mill and emphasized later by Ward and others, and also, among the early twentieth century writers, by Tönnies, Westermarck, Hobhouse, and Weber. This full exploration of the *non*-rational and the *ir*rational elements in man and society was established without at all jeopardizing, discarding, or losing sight of, the important place of the *rational*. It was a very real advance in making possible an accurate and much more realistic appraisal of *all* the dimensions of 'mind' in society.

(VII) THE SIGNIFICANT LINK OF 'ACTION': A RELIABLE 'SOCIAL BEHAVIOURISM'

This importance still attributed to consciousness, choice, judgment, reason, was nowhere more evident than in the new emphasis (i.e. new in psychological studies) placed upon *action*; but this entailed other important points which deserve our clearest attention. The most significant contribution here was unquestionably that of Mead, and his ideas were of a degree of importance far outstripping their apparent simplicity.

The first point of new and great significance for socio-psycho-

* See especially *The Future of an Illusion*. Very profound *philosophical* issues are, of course, involved here— as to what constitutes 'knowledge', and criteria of the sufficiency and truth of 'knowledge'; and I am not suggesting that these authors solved *these* problems. We are here only noting that their systems were such as to make room for *all* these dimensions in their scientific analysis.
† Freud's position was most *strikingly* similar to that of Plato.

logical analysis (of 'self', 'groups', 'society', alike) was that the *acts* of individuals in association were made the central focus of attention. This had many important aspects. First and foremost, *acts* were now clearly seen to be the complex units of human experience, knowledge, meaning, judgment, and purpose which they *actually were*. Secondly, and a part of this, they were seen to be composite *associational* facts, embodying many reciprocal elements of *communication* involving far more than language (although language was a crucial aspect of them), but yet facts which were units of conduct (behaviour) for *individuals*. *Action* was the concrete embodiment of the very stuff of the socio-psychological process. And thirdly, *acts* were behaviourally the most evident and extremely important elements about which 'symbols', meaning, values, judgments were organized (acts *were* the organized *forms* of these components*); and therefore of great importance in the formation of 'sentiments'.

The second major point was that with this new emphasis a clear behavioural link was formed between the analysis of *experience* on the one hand (the instincts, sentiments, motives, attitudes and reasonings of individuals in association) and of the *structure* of *organized institutions* on the other. Ordered actions were at one and the same time the items in the regulated procedures of institutions *and* the sequences of behaviour of individuals. Psychological experiences and institutional forms were no longer *juxtaposed*, so to speak. A living link of analysis had been forged—which did not so much just bring them into contact as show how interrelated, as parts of the same socio-psychological process, they were. It was as though all the interstices of the entire framework of society could now be seen in their rich, living processes of interconnection. And in this way, again, the expectations of experience, the meaning of 'symbols', could be seen to have a firm rootedness in the *observationally evident* patterns of action which were (*simultaneously*) elements of institutional procedure and individual conduct alike.

The third important point was that this conception forged a most important link between (*a*) the objective 'social facts' of Durkheim, (*b*) the socio-psychological processes—of 'self' and 'society'—emphasized by these writers themselves, and (*c*) the 'subjective understanding of social action' of Weber. The entire socio-psychological and organizational network of human 'selves' and their relationships in society could now be explored by a linked and unified

---

* i.e. '*acts*' were the behaviourally evident 'objective social facts' of Durkheim, and the 'composite social phenomena' of Pareto. They were the associational embodiments of all the elements of experience, value, judgment and purpose which they contained.

scheme of analysis. The cleavage between 'objective social facts' and 'meaningful social action' and the differing ways of approaching the explanation of each was now no longer unbridgeable; no longer necessary. Indeed, it no longer existed in the sense that a new orientation of concepts could interconnect them both.* This was a very considerable achievement of conceptual clarification.

But the fourth aspect of this emphasis upon the *act* (in human communications, socio-psychological processes, the form of institutions, and the growth of the 'self') was of equal if not greater importance. It formulated, for the first time, a satisfactory *Social Behaviourism*. It was satisfactory not only because it was so clear and acceptable, incorporating all the advantages mentioned above, but also, and *primarily*, because it formulated a conceptualization of the behaviour of human persons in association with each other which had firm reference to actual, observable units of *behaviour*, but which also fully encompassed all the elements of *experience*, *meaning* and *subjective judgment* which it was necessary to take into account—and without which *action* (as distinct from *events* of nature) simply could not be either recognized (i.e. distinguished from *events*) or interpreted. This, again, was an achievement of the very greatest importance, and we can see that it was not only an achievement of analytical clearness and completeness as such, but also one of finally putting into clear formulation conceptual distinctions which had been insisted upon and striven after, but not satisfactorily *stated*, by many of the earlier theorists (i.e. in a clear but complex form which could be analytically *used*). It was a *culminating advancement* in one particular line of conceptual development.

This entire question of 'Behaviourism' is so important, and so bedevilled by confusion, that it is worthwhile to make it absolutely clear. I said earlier that Mead's formulation rejected Watson's narrow and unwarranted kind of 'behaviourism', and it is appropriate here to justify this claim. And, in doing so, let us note this. In general, 'Behaviourism' is thought of *only* as Watsonian behaviourism; as being in flat opposition to 'instinct' theory and to the regarding of any element of '*experience*' whatever as a legitimate part of psychology as a *science*. *Experience* cannot be *observed*; therefore it cannot be held to *exist*. *All* sequences of observed human behaviour, no matter how intricate, can only be explained in terms of the conditioning of the basic units of behaviour—the 'reflexes'.

How anyone could ever have subscribed to such nonsense it is well-

* i.e. conceptually and logically the two levels were distinct—but they could now be incorporated in a conceptual analysis of their intermixture in the actuality of human experience, 'selfhood', and action.

nigh impossible to understand,* but nothing could make the difference between a 'neuro-physiologically' orientated and an 'associationally' orientated psychology more clear than Mead's rejection of it. For Mead clearly showed that the human *act* was simply a *qualitatively different behavioural phenomenon* from a composite conditioned set of neuro-physiological units. *No* amount of 'conditioning' of 'reflexes'—with no *experience* whatever intervening—could qualitatively comprise a *meaningful act*, in which values, purposes, and grounds of judgment resided. An *act* was a *behaviourably observable unit*, but the very perceptual distinction of it on the part of the scientist in his field of empirical reference (as being different from regularities of events) required conceptual interpretation. The *social* behaviourism of Mead was therefore of the very greatest importance in that (*a*) it took the conceptually distinct *act* as the unit of behavioural reference as against any organic or biological unit, and this made it possible to incorporate all the other dimensions of *experience*, including *meaning*, and (*b*) it again emphasized the *associational context for any satisfactory human psychology*. The error of psychology again! A psychology which confined itself solely to the biological and neuro-physiological level and entertained no consideration of 'experience' whatever (and therefore no consideration of the psychological creativity of the processes of association) was no psychology at all! It was misconceived at the most fundamental level.

Mead's ideas were of the very greatest significance here—and his '*Social Behaviourism*' was a formulation the importance of which it is difficult to exaggerate. Let us see, however, that he quite positively rejected Watson. Having discussed the elements of symbolism, meaning, value, judgment which were embodied in *acts*, Mead wrote this:

'Such experience . . . plays a part, and a very large part, in our perception, our conduct; and yet it is an experience which can be revealed only by introspection. The behaviourist has to make a detour about this type of experience if he is going to stick to the Watsonian type of behaviouristic psychology.

Such a behaviourist desires to analyse the act, whether individual or social, without any specific reference to consciousness whatever and without any attempt to locate it either within the field of organic behaviour or within the large field of reality in general. He wishes, in short, to deny its existence as such altogether. Watson insists that objectively observable behaviour completely and exclusively constitutes the field of scientific psychology, individual and social. He pushes aside as

---

* Though it is still promulgated with the tenacity of a religion by some psychologists, such as H. J. Eysenck. A religion is about all it can be held to be.

erroneous the idea of "mind" or "consciousness", and attempts to reduce all "mental" phenomena to conditioned reflexes and similar physiological mechanisms—in short, to purely behaviouristic terms. This attempt, of course, is misguided and unsuccessful, for the existence as such of mind or consciousness, in some sense or other, must be admitted— the denial of it leads inevitably to obvious absurdities . . .

Watson apparently assumes that to deny the existence of mind or consciousness as a psychical stuff, substance, or entity is to deny its existence altogether and that a naturalistic or behaviouristic account of it as such is out of the question. But, on the contrary, we may deny its existence as a psychical entity without denying its existence in some other sense at all; and if we then conceive it functionally, and as a natural rather than a transcendental phenomenon, it becomes possible to deal with it in behaviouristic terms . . .

If we are going to use behaviouristic psychology to explain conscious behaviour, we have to be much more thoroughgoing in our statement of *the act* than Watson was. We have to take into account not merely *the complete or social act* but what goes on in the central nervous system *as the beginning of the individual's act and as the organization of the act*. Of course, that takes us beyond the field of our direct observation. It takes us beyond that field because we cannot get at the process itself . . . Present results, however, suggest *the organization of the act in terms of attitudes*.'*

A study of Mead is of the first importance for the clear under-standing of those extremes of behaviourism that had to be rejected, and of that formulation of *Social Behaviourism* which was such a decided and important advance.

(VIII) ROLE ANALYSIS AND SOCIAL PSYCHOLOGY: THE DETAILED EXPLORATION OF INSTITUTIONAL AND INDIVIDUAL FORMS OF BEHAVIOUR

One other achievement of the conceptual schemes formulated by these writers, and especially by this focus upon the *act* in human association, was that—in addition to the analysis of the 'self' in the context of group-relations and communications, and of the growth of sentiments and constellations of attitudes, etc., in society—they opened the way quite clearly to an effective study of the *organized action within institutions*. The procedures of institutions, the formalized 'tasks' of the members who carried them out, were also the sequences of action which, taken together, formed a very large part of the total behaviour of individual persons. This detailed analysis of *roles* was again, therefore, an important link in the study of individuals and of the groups and institutions of the wider social

* From *Mind, Self and Society*, see George Herbert Mead *On Social Psychology*, pp. 124–5.

order of which they were members. And it permitted the thorough analysis of any on-going system of social behaviour in terms of experience, meaning, and action all combined. In this way the study of socio-psychological processes fitted with perfect clarity into the larger analysis of the structure, functions, interconnections, and patterns of change of all the distinguishable elements of social organization.

(IX) LINKS WITH THE ANALYSIS OF THE ENTIRE SOCIAL SYSTEM

It follows from the last point, and, indeed, has been evident throughout, that these new developments in the study of socio-psychological processes gave promise of an extension to the analysis of the social system in its entirety. Focusing primarily upon the growth of the 'self' through communications in primary groups, it was clear that this range of concepts—of institutions, their symbols, their structures of action, the sentiments and attitudes at the core of them, the patterns of communications in the groups within them, and the growth to 'self-hood' of individuals within these groups— could give a system for analysing the psychological dimensions of every element and every level within an entire society. Again, it was clear that the system of sociological analysis envisaged by the earlier writers, was becoming rounded out to completion.

We have seen, too, that some of these writers were already thinking in these large-scale terms. Even McDougall, Cooley, Mead, and Freud, though having their focus chiefly upon the 'self' and the smaller, primary groups, were nonetheless clearly thinking of this within the larger framework of society as a whole; and in his more general essays—such as 'Civilization and its Discontents' and 'The Future of an Illusion'—Freud obviously applied his analysis of the mind in the widest way to considerations of the nature and future of human society. In Pareto and Simmel especially, however, this larger scale of thought was quite deliberate and forthright—though different in each case. In Pareto, for example, there was the attempt to analyse the equilibrium of the entire social system in terms of psychological forces and (especially) the distribution of psychological elements throughout the unequally endowed members of the population. At this large societal level, however, two contributions, in particular, were most important as new components of analysis. Pareto was responsible for one; Simmel for the other.

Pareto had introduced the study of *élites* (and their changing nature and composition) as being of central significance for an understanding of the equilibrium conditions of society; and without necessarily agreeing with his own theory of them, it is clear that this was an important component for any system of analysis; one that was likely to produce useful knowledge—quite apart from providing a new and flexible approach to the study of 'stratification' (the hierarchy of 'statuses') in society. And secondly, Simmel had introduced his analysis of those *'forms'* of socio-psychological relationships which seemed common to all institutions in all societies, and which (since it was possible to abstract them from their particular *contents*) promised a *general* analysis of specific *types* of relationship which could then be applied interpretively to specific instances. This was a rather different 'typological' analysis from the kind put forward by Tönnies and Weber, and was of a more systematic analytical nature than theirs. Even so, a similarity was there; and it was clear how the different conceptions could supplement each other. The chief point, however, is that in Simmel's conception in particular, the study of the psychological aspects of society was lifted to the highest (i.e. most general) level of analysing the distinctive *forms* which characterized all the institutional regularities of society.

The study of the psychological aspects of society had, then, been effectively developed to explore—carefully and systematically—every kind and every level of human association: from the most particular level of the growth of the individual 'self' within the smallest groups of family and neighbourhood, to the most general level of the leading *élites* and the *'forms'* of relationship which characterized all the institutions of society. What had been a gap within the over-all conspectus of sociology was now admirably filled in. The study of socio-psychological processes now fitted very satisfactorily into the larger framework of sociological analysis as a whole, and, indeed, served to link all the other components together in an excellent conceptual clarity.

(X) CONFLICT AN INESCAPABLE AND POSITIVE ASPECT OF SOCIO-PSYCHOLOGICAL FORMS

A final point which needs only a brief note—but is sufficiently important to mention separately and with strong emphasis—is that all these theorists, in their various ways, were agreed that the human situation in the world and in society was inescapably one entailing conflict. 'Man is an anxious animal.' 'Man was not made for repose.' In all cases, the emphasis was not only that human experience had its harmonious *and* discordant sides; that human activities and relationships had their elements of co-operation *and* conflict. It was more, and deeper than this, and had a strong affinity with the earlier persuasions about the 'dialectics' of nature and history and the emergence, evolution, and dissolution of 'forms' in the *interdependencies of process* which was *reality*. The persuasion was that *form* was always a kind of embodiment of equilibrium brought about at the focal point (so to speak) of a multiplicity of conditions and forces. Thus the 'self' was a unity of experience stemming from many sources which were far from being harmoniously related. Similarly, the 'forms' of social relationships, of institutions, came into being in the *simultaneous* conditions of interest, desire, possibility, purpose, co-operative activity *and* of limitation, opposition, competition, thwarting frustration, and conflictful activity. Conflict was a continuous and ubiquitous ingredient in all human experience and activity and in all associational forms. It was, strictly speaking, the 'other side of the coin' of any desire, plan, and action. And consequently it performed *positive functions* in the making and sustaining of individual and social patterns. It was Simmel who most forcibly and succinctly put this point; but, as we have seen, every other writer—in his account of the formation of the 'self' and the 'sentiments' in society—adopted the same position: seeing the assumption of 'form' in the context of multiple and continuing pressures. It is, indeed, clearly arguable, that *values*—which lie at the heart of the 'structuring' of the *self* and of *institutions*—only exist in a condition not only of promise, but of possible loss.

Simmel's view was also, as we have seen, a development of what had been a common persuasion among all the nineteenth-century writers. Again, then, this was a culminating clarification.

In this dimension of the 'conspectus' of sociology, then—the study of the psychological aspects of society—as in all others, we have seen that very considerable developments were made during the early decades of the present century. Working in different countries—Germany, Italy, Austria, Britain, America; orientating their intellectual efforts to different kinds of problems, and within *apparently* different intellectual traditions—Simmel with his philosophical, humanistic essay-probing; Pareto with his 'economist-political-commentator' grand manner as though he was speaking from a balcony in Rome; Freud with his primarily clinical concern; McDougall in his efforts to provide a more valid basis for scientific psychology; Cooley and Mead in their continuing development of the core of American sociological thinking—they nonetheless arrived at systems of ideas which showed a wide, exciting, and impressive range of agreement. Working within the agreed context of the larger perspective of natural and social evolution, all these writers—on the face of things so different—constructed a set of concepts which

665

were not only in agreement on very basic and important matters, but also made possible the detailed study of every socio-psychological dimension of society: from the largest level of institutional forms down to the most specific level of each particular individual.

But I said *apparently* different intellectual traditions. And we have said enough to see that—despite the differing national and professional contexts of their work—the spreading of the thought which was the making of sociology was continuously and increasingly at work. McDougall drew on many sociological writers in his attempted formulations of psychology. Cooley and Mead drew on Westermarck and knew of Simmel and Tönnies as well as other and earlier nineteenth-century writers—both American and European. Freud not only knew Mill and had a wide literary, historical and cultural knowledge, but was also drawn into the consideration of social and anthropological literature. We have seen that Spencer and Gillen on the Australians was of well-nigh common influence among them all. Pareto, too, was widely aware of the literature of the social sciences and the nineteenth century social theories, and, most conspicuously, was rooted in Spencer. The net of ideas was thus being cast over an ever wider community of international scholarship. And we must bear in mind two other things.

First—we have so far, and properly, considered these writers as a distinctive group in relation to their major contribution. But they were, of course, in their own working, not at all distinctively *bounded* as a group in this way. They were all contributing individually to the advancement of the study of man in society, and—the point I wish to emphasize especially here—they were as much in agreement with the sociologists contributing in other areas, as they were among themselves. Thus we have seen how their ideas were also in firm agreement with those of Tönnies, Westermarck, Hobhouse, Durkheim and Weber, and had the great merit of linking these other areas of thinking together. This we shall come back to later—but the tremendous range and detail of the work conducted during these few decades, and the tremendous achievement in the development, interconnection, and advancement of all dimensions of the subject, is already very clear. And the second point is that all this work was coming to a head *on the brink of the second world war*: as short a time ago as that. It had all been *produced* by then, but it was by no means clearly and coherently seen in its interconnections then. But these accomplishments were made, and our awareness and assessment of them brings us right up to the brink of contemporary sociology. We might note again, that the one book towards the end of this period which was probing towards a theoretical unification of at least some of these major contributions was *The Structure of Social Action* by Talcott Parsons—published in 1937. However we may come to assess his ideas later, it is clear that Talcott Parsons was the theorist most conscious of the many-sided theoretical agreements then being reached from many directions, and most pre-occupied with the task of clarifying the theoretical integration which they all seemed to promise. His own efforts provide the most conspicuous 'point of arrival and point of departure' for an understanding of the contemporary theoretical scene. And to this we shall come back later.

There is, however, one central point with which it seems most fitting to conclude this section. All those thinkers we have here considered not only demonstrated the *insufficiency* and *error* of a *science of psychology* which abstracted man from his social and historical context (with their conditions *creative* of distinctively 'human' nature), and not only pointed to the fact that an *associational context of analysis was essential for any satisfactory human psychology*—they also *provided it*. One great accomplishment of these authors was the actual *creation* of a conceptual apparatus for the study of those socio-psychological processes within which every dimension of human experience and behaviour—personal and social —could be understood. The making of sociology was also the making of psychology. This is not, even now, fully understood. It is of the greatest importance, and cannot be emphasized too strongly.

The sociological context is the only context—the indispensable context—for a satisfactory psychology of man.

(4)
Functionalism

Introduction

We come now to a development which has grown into the largest single source of mythology in contemporary sociological theory—'Functionalism'. This is the one remaining 'development' of these early decades of the century which we must take into account: but it was one with a difference . . . or at least an *apparent* difference. And this was where the rub lay. It was the acceptance of the *appearance*, instead of the *reality*, which caused all the trouble. It was a highly conspicuous development; highly colourful: apparently simple, clear, strong in its analytical incisiveness and economy of statement. It seemed highly original—as it was certainly productive of a new kind of systematic knowledge about the social life of 'primitive' societies. It seemed to herald the birth of a new subject: Social Anthropology.

We have said much about 'The Error of Psychology', and now we have arrived at what I called earlier *'The Error of Social Anthropology'*. Then*—in order (provocatively) to draw attention to it— I wrote deliberately in an exaggerated and polemical vein; but now we must consider it in a colder blood: seriously, thoroughly, carefully; because it is an issue of great importance. The task is difficult because of the mythology. To clarify the issue properly means cutting through layer after layer of myth that has been woven round an initially unexceptionable statement. But we will adopt the simplest of all procedures: that of looking at the *actuality* of the development as it took place: at what was *actually* claimed in the statements that came to be known as 'Functionalism', and at the context within which they were made.

Strictly speaking, these 'Structural-Functional' formulations were receiving their clearest culminating statements only just before, and during, the second world war; and some were only published in book-form after the war (e.g. *Structure and Function in Primitive Society* and *A Natural Science of Society*—both by Radcliffe-Brown); so that—like that of Talcott Parsons—this was one theoretical position which carried over with a continued immediacy of controversy, into the post-war and strictly contemporary period. Even so, its main development took place from about 1906 (when Radcliffe-Brown went to the Andaman Islands) and 1914 (when Malinowski went to Melanesia) to about 1942 (when Malinowski died); and it therefore paralleled all the other developments we have

* See Vol. I, p. 596–600.

671

studied—though being marginally later than they, and sufficiently so to be much influenced by some of them. The books and articles which were to exercise such marked influence began to appear in 1922 with Radcliffe-Brown's *The Andaman Islanders* and Malinowski's *Argonauts of the Western Pacific* (though Malinowski had published earlier—in 1913—*The Family Among the Australian Aborigines*) and continued until 1944 with the posthumous publication of Malinowski's *A Scientific Theory of Culture*. *Structure and Function in Primitive Society* by Radcliffe-Brown was published in 1952 (with an excellent new introduction, to which we shall refer) but all other than two of the papers in this collection had been contributed before 1941; and similarly, though *A Natural Science of Society* was not published until 1957,* it was the un-revised (and again posthumously published) record of a now celebrated seminar held in Chicago in 1937. By far the most important contributions to this development—indeed, those which, strictly speaking, *constituted* this development—were, as is already obvious, those of Malinowski and Radcliffe-Brown. We shall consider each of these 'Fathers' of modern Social Anthropology separately, because they differed significantly in certain ways, and there was a decided degree of contentiousness between them; but, first of all, it is necessary to set the scene for our discussion.

Preliminary Considerations

People have come to feel clear about 'Functionalism'—as a distinctive 'school' of theory (and whether adversely critical or not)—as about nothing else in sociology. If anything is thought to be simple and clear, it is this. The most deep-rooted assumptions have come to be embedded as dogmas within their conception of it: for example, that it gives a 'static' analysis of society; that it rests on the assumption of 'functional harmony'; that it cannot give an account of 'conflict' and 'change'; that it is 'a-historical', 'anti-evolutionary'; and the like. The unshakeable solidity of these assumptions has to be *heard* to be *believed*—coming from the mouths of students who are taught by those only acquainted with what is called 'modern' theory. Controversy has raged about it. It has—with certain, supposedly profound amendments—become one of the dominating 'schools' in contemporary theory. Much effort has been invested in the controversy. Other 'schools'—'Conflict Sociology', for example—have arisen out of it. Strong commitments have been staked out in relation to it in many ways. In the same way, controversy has also surrounded—and still surrounds—claims and

* I am not sure whether or not an earlier edition was published in 1948.

counter-claims arising between Sociology and Social Anthropology, and the supposed distinctions and relations between them. The subject seethes with controversy.

Now to suggest—as I want both to suggest and to demonstrate—that all this is plain error; that it is no more than a hot air of misconception; that it is a hectic, coloured, confused smoke that deserves only one thing—to be blown away; is clearly, within this context, to suggest a lot. It is especially so (and may seem, in fact, perverse) when, having done this—having shown that 'Functionalism' does not exist; and that Social Anthropology does not exist either (as a science distinct from Sociology)—I shall want to uphold the contributions of Malinowski and Radcliffe-Brown in certain ways (though not in all), and to show that they were not by any means wholly responsible for the obscuring cloud which followed upon their heels. Indeed, in disclaiming 'Functionalism' and 'Social Anthropology', I shall want to show that I am doing no more than stating clearly, again (i.e. as against the confusion they sought to guard against), their *own* point of view. The fact is that nothing in this presently-compounded myth is simple at all—and a task of dismantling needs to be done. In tracing this particular 'development' of the 'structural-functional' component of the conspectus of sociology, we have, then, at one and the same time, *both* to see its actual nature clearly *and* to discountenance, and see beyond, certain common misconceptions. A tangle faces us, which we have to unravel; but the task will be well worth our while because it will clarify many errors and provide us with an excellent platform of judgment on which we can stand firmly in assessing many of the post-war developments of theory.

Certain basic general points must therefore be made clear at the outset—as serious premises of our discussion; as 'orientations' of our argument—if we are to escape radical misunderstanding. These points will seem dogmatic at first, but they will give us a stark clarity of approach, and later they will be seen to be both necessary and justifiable. We must avoid at all costs yet another over-simplified statement of what 'Functionalism' is supposed to be; we must move as far as possible towards a definitive statement; and these initial points must therefore be taken very seriously, and considered seriously, if we are to achieve a proper critical appreciation of what it was of worth that these authors had to say.

(I) A PROVISIONAL STATEMENT OF 'FUNCTIONALISM'

It is necessary, first of all, to have some brief definition of the theoretical position we are talking about, and this can be stated simply: but we must bear in mind that this is a rather naked, indicative, provisional definition only. It is, however, sufficient.

The 'functionalist' approach to the study of society maintained that society was a *system* of social institutions and attendant patterns of culture. Social institutions were ordered, regulated patterns of social action which were rooted in men's need and interests; which rested upon strongly established sentiments, and—as forms of social regulation—were crucial, organized embodiments of values. Culture was the total material, mental, spiritual apparatus and 'ethos' which was instrumentally related to these institutions. The patterning of 'culture' was concomitant with the pattern of 'institutionalization'. The total 'social structure' of a 'society' (a 'social system') could be systematically analysed in terms of its institutional-cultural 'parts'. However, the *whole* was a *system* of interconnected parts. The parts were *inter-operative*; they worked (functioned) in a process of interdependence with each other. No part could therefore be understood excepting within a knowledge of the whole. The very *nature* of a *part* of a society lay in its functional interconnections with, and contributions to, *other parts* in the entire social system. The study of society had, therefore, to rest upon this primary recognition of the *social system* (of the inter-connectedness of social facts); and could only provide a reliable body of knowledge about its subject-matter if it employed the '*structural-functional*' method of analysis.

This, believe it or not, was the substantive 'core' of 'Functionalism' as a supposedly distinctive theoretical approach. Of course, each theorist explored a little differently what the term 'function' should be taken to mean: one emphasizing 'needs', another emphasizing 'operative interconnection', etc.; but these were, really, quite slight points. There was some analysis of the nature and components of institutions and the ways in which they could be usefully classified. And we have not, in this brief statement, included any statement about the *entailment* of any other propositions—for example, an 'a-historical' approach to sociological analysis, an 'anti-evolutionary' approach, a 'static' mode of analysis, an assumption of the 'functional integration and harmony' of social systems and a lack of theoretical interest in 'conflict' or 'social change' and so on. The reason why we have not done this is, quite simply, that they were *not* entailments. But such details can be examined later when we come to the specific statements of Malinowski and Radcliffe-Brown.

Now this 'core' statement of 'Functionalism' must seem rather sparse. It was sparse. It can be seen quite plainly that it was no more than a statement of *one* of the basic premises of sociology

674

which had been completely accepted from before the time of Comte (in Montesquieu, for example), and which had received a very much richer elaboration at the hands of Comte and many others after him.

As it stands, the statement of 'Functionalism' seems little more than a *recognition*, a *discovery*, of *sociology* and its use for the better study of primitive peoples. And this—as we can now go on to see— is, quite literally, all that it was.

(II) NEGATIVE CRITICISM ADOPTED

Following upon this first point, it will readily be seen that many of our earlier positions of criticism will seem, necessarily, to have a negative and destructive tone. They will seem to be unsympathetic. They will seem to be purely antagonistic to the position of Malinowski and Radcliffe-Brown, and, indeed, to the work of Social Anthropology. All I can say here, is that this apparently negative 'debunking' is necessary and that, at the end of our argument, it will be seen to have been of positive service in defending the position that these writers were *really* advocating, and in discarding misconceptions that they did not hold. For the time being, this can only remain to be seen—but the spirit of this point must be borne in mind in the particular statements of orientation that follow. I am being starkly negative here to be correctly positive in the long run.

(III) 'FUNCTIONALISM' NO MORE RECENT OR 'MODERN' THAN OTHER DEVELOPMENTS

The first of these apparently negative but true points is that those who think that 'Functionalism' was a distinctively recent or 'modern' formulation of theory are obviously mistaken. In so far as 'Functionalism' *was* a development, it was one among all the other developments taking place during the first few decades of the century. It was parallel to them and in no sense whatever more recent or more modern than they. We shall be more radical than this in a moment.

(IV) THE 'FUNCTIONALISTS' NOT DISTINGUISHABLE FROM OTHER SOCIOLOGISTS AND ANTHROPOLOGISTS OF THIS PERIOD

A second salutary point is that the 'Functionalists' were in no theoretical way distinctive from the other sociologists and anthropologists of the period we are considering, and in no sense whatever more 'modern' or more 'advanced' they they. This, it must be understood, is by no means simply a carping claim as to 'who said

675

what first' or 'who was most important'. On the contrary, its full recognition is essential for a correct critical appraisal of these men's work. One or two examples might make the point. Westermarck, for example, is scarcely considered in social anthropology today; his analysis of 'customary usage' and institutions in terms of instinct, sentiments, values and sanctions is thought out-moded beside the 'structural-functional' approach of (say) Radcliffe-Brown. And yet Radcliffe-Brown's entire account of the nature of social institutions stressed exactly the same components. We shall see that—like all the other twentieth century thinkers—Radcliffe-Brown agreed completely about the importance of sentiments and sanctions as the core of institutions. Westermarck and he and Malinowski were contemporaries, and all of them shared many quite fundamental points of view. They were all—and none more strongly than Malinowski and Radcliffe-Brown—rooted in the same tradition and the same influences of Tylor and Frazer, though all were seeking a more incisive and productive mode of analysis than that they had inherited. A second example is that of Durkheim. Radcliffe-Brown was able in his studies of totemism and religion to make positive, correcting, and useful amendments to (not rejections of) Durkheim's theories. But his entire theoretical approach was little more than a complete acceptance of Durkheim's sociology. This can most plainly be seen in 'A Natural Science of Society'—where the entire seminar was based upon a draft statement of Radcliffe-Brown's which was—as he directly acknowledged—drawn from Durkheim and his followers in France. Indeed, in the introduction to *Structure and Function in Primitive Society* (one of Radcliffe-Brown's clearest and most comprehensive statements) he made it perfectly clear that he was adopting, accepting, and putting to use the greater part of the making of sociology from Comte on.

'The theory,' he wrote, 'can be stated by means of the three fundamental and connected concepts of "process", "structure" and "function". It is derived from such earlier writers as Montesquieu, Comte, Spencer, Durkheim and thus belongs to a cultural tradition of two hundred years.'*

There is no lack of clarity in that. And I hope it is becoming plain that this attempt to discount the *distinctiveness* of these writers is in no sense an attempt or a desire to *denigrate* them. On the contrary, it is a desire and attempt to see them plainly as part of the common tradition, and contributing part of the common flow of ideas, in the ongoing making of sociology: *as they saw themselves.*

* Cohen & West, 1952, p. 14.

676

We shall return to this thread later, and pull it together with others, but, for now, it is enough to see that Malinowski and Radcliffe-Brown did *not* produce a sharply distinctive body of ideas. They were working among, and working over, the commonly shared ideas of others, but directing them to a specific purpose: which we shall come to in a moment.

Our argument can best move ahead, now, by distinguishing *two strands* which have tended to become conjoined in the controversy: first, the consideration whether 'Functionalism' is a distinguishable theoretical approach; and second, whether 'Social Anthropology' is a distinguishable subject. We will take each in turn—again sharply and definitely.

(v) 'FUNCTIONALISM' NOT A DISTINGUISHABLE THEORETICAL APPROACH

On the first 'strand' it is quite clear not only that 'Functionalism' was not a distinctive theoretical approach *within sociology*, but, more radically, that it simply did not exist. It was not a distinctively clear theoretical entity at all. In very recent controversy,* which we cannot anticipate too fully as yet, it has been argued that 'Functionalism' was not a distinguishable school within sociology for the simple reason that, strictly speaking, it *was* sociology. All we are saying here is clearly in sympathy with this approach, but we must go further. It is not true even that 'Functionalism' could be, or can be, *identified* with sociology. For, obviously, in its emphasis upon '*structural-functional*' analysis and the recognition of the social *system* it was emphasizing only *one* component, and *one* set of premises, among the many which, in their entirety, comprised sociology.

It is true that in all the many other details and qualifications of their work Malinowski and Radcliffe-Brown embraced all the other dimensions of sociology: but this is only to say that *they* were *sociologists* and accepted all the dimensions of the subject. But it remains the case that 'Structural-Functionalism' as such, simply did not exist as a distinctive theoretical entity. There is the further point, of course, that structural-functional analysis as one component of the larger apparatus of sociology was what it was: *one component of analysis*. It was not in itself—by any stretch of conception— a distinctive, substantive *theory* of some kind; a separate theoretical '*school*'. Nor could it ever be.

The clear correctness of one long-established premise of sociology —that associational facts were interrelated in their nature and operation in total social systems; and the clear necessity and utility

* Kingsley Davis, *The Myth of Functional Analysis as a Special Method in Sociology and Anthropology* (1959).

of one long-established component of sociological analysis—structural-functional analysis; came to be raised into a distinguishable 'theory' and 'school' which was simply false and unwarranted.

And again, we must note that this was the view of the 'Fathers' of the supposed 'Functionalism' themselves—though Malinowski had a greater ambiguity in his statements on this than had Radcliffe-Brown. All aspects of this can be seen amusingly in the opening proviso which Radcliffe-Brown made in his lecture *On Social Structure* to the Royal Anthropological Institute (1940).

'I have been described,' he said, 'on more than one occasion as belonging to something called the "Functional School of Social Anthropology" and even as being its leader, or one of its leaders. This Functional School does not really exist; it is a myth invented by Professor Malinowski. He has explained how, to quote his own words, "the magnificent title of the Functional School of Anthropology has been bestowed by myself, in a way on myself, and to a large extent out of my own sense of irresponsibility". Professor Malinowski's irresponsibility has had unfortunate results, since it has spread over anthropology a dense fog of discussion about "functionalism". . . . The statement that I am a "functionalist" would seem to me to convey no definite meaning.'*

Nothing could be clearer than that.

(VI) SOCIAL ANTHROPOLOGY NOT A DISTINGUISHABLE SUBJECT

On the second 'strand' of our argument we can be equally definite; equally debunking; but, in clarifying this issue, we shall begin to see where—error aside—a real 'development' took place at the hands of these writers. Here, however, let us still be strongly negative.

We have seen that 'Functionalism' did not exist as a distinguishable theoretical position. These writers were really doing no more than discovering, recognizing and clarifying some of the central assumptions of sociology and applying them to the study of the pre-literate societies. There was, then, no new and distinguishable science of Social Anthropology at all. There was only a more rigorous insistence upon the use of sociology—and the extension of this use—in studying this particular range of societies.

Theoretically speaking, neither Malinowski nor Radcliffe-Brown made any original conceptual contributions whatever. They did not, in any sense, create or construct a new social science, and there is nothing in their work to justify such a view. We shall see that all their concepts and perspectives were those of sociology, and had already received a more elaborate treatment at the hands of others than anything they themselves accomplished.

* *Structure and Function in Primitive Society*, p. 188.

Again, let us note the statements of the supposed 'Fathers' of the new science themselves. Malinowski rarely (if ever!) referred to 'Social Anthropology'. He spoke throughout *A Scientific Theory of Culture* (which was his fullest exposition of his 'functional' theory), of *Anthropology* and the sound introduction into it of *sociology*; not at all of 'social anthropology'. Here is one example.

'W. Robertson Smith,' he wrote, 'was perhaps the first clearly to insist on the sociological context in all discussions which refer not merely to organization of groups but also to belief, to ritual, and to myth. He was followed by the leading French sociologist and anthropologist, Emile Durkheim, who developed one of the fullest and most inspiring systems of sociology . . . In many ways, Durkheim can be regarded as representing one of the soundest of those tendencies in modern anthropology which aim, above all, at the full scientific understanding of culture as a specific phenomenon.'*

The same was more exactly true of Radcliffe-Brown, and (as he indicated) even of Frazer. In the introduction to *Structure and Function in Primitive Society*, seeking to define Social Anthropology, he wrote in this way:

'The theoretical study of social institutions in general is usually referred to as sociology, but as this name can be loosely used for many different kinds of writings about society we can speak more specifically of *theoretical* or *comparative sociology*. When Frazer gave his Inaugural Lecture as the first Professor of Social Anthropology in 1908 he defined social anthropology as that branch of sociology that deals with primitive societies.'†

And again:

'Comparative sociology, of which social anthropology is a branch, is here conceived as a theoretical study of which the aim is to provide acceptable generalizations. The theoretical understanding of a particular institution is its interpretation in the light of such generalizations.'‡

And in his previously mentioned lecture *On Social Structure* he wrote this.

'I conceive of social anthropology as the theoretical natural science of human society, that is, the investigation of social phenomena by methods essentially similar to those used in the physical and biological sciences. I

---

* *A Scientific Theory of Culture*, Chapel Hill, University of North Carolina Press, 1944, p. 19.
† *Structure and Function in Primitive Society*, p. 2. ‡ *Ibid.*, p. 3.

am quite willing to call the subject "comparative sociology", if anyone so wishes. It is the subject itself, and not the name, that is important.'*

Clearly, in all this, no distinction whatever was drawn between Sociology and Social Anthropology. Social Anthropology was nothing more or less than a branch of sociology. It was the use of sociology in the systematic investigation of the social systems of pre-literate peoples.

However, the term 'Social Anthropology' obviously arose on the basis of these men's work. Why? It is here that we come to the specific 'development' for which Malinowski and Radcliffe-Brown were chiefly responsible; the particular contribution they made.

(VII) SOCIOLOGY INTRODUCED INTO ANTHROPOLOGY TO PROVIDE A SATISFACTORY BASIS AND DIRECTION OF INVESTIGATION

Anthropology had a clear sequence of development as a subject from about the middle of the nineteenth century. The new developments of geology and biology; the new 'time-scale' of the world and of the emergence of living species, and the new perspective on the relationship between man and other species; brought about a new orientation to 'Man's Place in Nature'. Anthropology—which was conceived as the entire Science of Man—was firstly, and primarily, *physical* anthropology. Its concentration was upon man as a biological species, the distinctions between the races of man and their distribution, Later, this preoccupation was increasingly superseded by *cultural* anthropology. The tracing of the process of civilization by the tracing of cultural artefacts—their diffusion about the world from certain centres (or *a* centre), or the independent invention of them in human settlements everywhere—became the focus of interest. And—at the turn of the century—these 'diffusionist' and 'evolutionary' schools of *cultural* anthropology were the substance of controversy. Tylor and Frazer were working within the context of them.

Two things, however, were becoming increasingly clear as Malinowski and Radcliffe-Brown learned from their late nineteenth-century masters. The first was that these large 'schools' of controversy were of dubious value for any furtherance of knowledge. The main reasons for this were (*a*) that, beyond a point, they appeared not to be testable: they were riddled with historical 'explanations' of a largely 'conjectural' nature, (*b*) they provided no kind of systematic conceptual clarity whereby subsequent studies could be undertaken, knowledge acquired, and theories tested, and

* *Structure and Function in Primitive Society*, p. 189.

(*c*) they contributed little, if anything, to an improved understanding of the pre-literate societies which existed in the world *at the present time*. These vast conjectures about the diffusions or otherwise of 'culture' were not only vague, but they failed to satisfy basic requirements: they seemed not to contribute to an improved knowledge of immediate fact; and they seemed to rest upon a mistaken focus of attention for an understanding and explanation of the creation of culture and civilization in human societies. It was the *societal* processes—so it now seemed—on which attention could be better concentrated.

The second increasing persuasion was that anthropology should get to work on the study of the *existing* 'primitive' societies whilst there was yet time. Colonial problems from the later eighteenth century onwards had increasingly thrown up an awareness of alien cultures, of 'tribal' societies—in the Americas, Australia, New Zealand, Africa; and governments still had to deal with these problems. But also, it was becoming increasingly obvious that the spread of 'western' civilization (whatever one's judgment of it) was of such an extent and rapidity that all the simpler societies, no matter how remote, would soon be encompassed by it, and changed (to some extent) within it. If the simpler societies of the world were to be studied at all—as autonomous communities—it was necessary to study them quickly.

These two considerations taken together—combined also with the clear developments in the making of sociology towards the end of the nineteenth century and from the turn of the century onwards—clearly explain the development *from* physical and cultural anthropology to *social* anthropology. Scholars like Malinowski and Radcliffe-Brown recognized the significance of sociology (*a*) for the tasks of socio-cultural explanation in the most basic and extensive sense (i.e. as being fundamentally correct as against the 'physical' and 'cultural' orientations as such), and (*b*) in the more immediate sense for the acquisition of systematic knowledge about the existing primitive peoples. For them—sociology was an essential corrective within anthropology. The new emphasis upon *social* anthropology *was*, then, *quite literally*, the adoption of sociology in anthropological studies. Social anthropology *was* a branch of sociology: the sociological study of simpler societies.

Before we take our argument on to the next step, let us be as meticulously clear as we can about terminology: to try and eradicate any possible prejudicial feelings (from any direction) which might still misconstrue the point we are making. It should be clear that what we are saying is no kind of stiff-necked claim for the superiority of sociology over social anthropology. Like Radcliffe-Brown, we can agree that words do not matter. It would be a perfectly tenable usage to accept Anthropology as the entire Science of Man, and then, within this totality, to accept specific divisions such as Physical Anthropology, Cultural Anthropology, Social Anthropology (etc.) as those special studies dealing with particular, distinguishable aspects of man. In this sense—Social Anthropology would be the equivalent of Sociology—meaning the study of the *associational* aspects of man. Alternatively, Sociology might be accepted as the total study of the *associational* aspects of man, and Social Anthropology might be retained to refer to that branch of sociology dealing with pre-literate societies. Now many other detailed and weighty issues arise here. For example: the question as to whether a 'Science of Man' itself has legitimate scientific boundaries. Biology, psychology, sociology may well all be definable sciences which properly include dimensions going beyond man himself (but subsuming 'man' as a part of the defined 'universe of discourse'). Also, a second example: the question as to whether sociology can properly be divided into *branches* which deal with *specific kinds of society*, or whether this itself is not an arbitrary drawing of distinctions within it. In short—the question as to the proper distinctions to be drawn between the sciences is extremely complicated, and is not likely to be solved—with any general agreement—quickly; especially since massive problems of established departmental organizations and the interests they engender are bound to militate against any changed conceptual alignment. But it is at least possible to agree that—despite these larger problems—and the unlikelihood of any basic change in terms and titles, there is no conceptual problem whatever concerning Sociology and Social Anthropology. Social Anthropology was, and is, the introduction of sociology into the wider field of anthropology to achieve an improved basis and direction of investigation. No separate science of social anthropology was created, and none exists.

To return to the two-fold need for this change in anthropology— (*a*) as the basis for an improved explanation of socio-cultural processes, and (*b*) as the basis for the systematic acquisition of fresh knowledge—we can now readily understand the direction, emphasis, and insistence of the work and teaching of Malinowski and Radcliffe-Brown. And we can now appreciate the 'development' for which they were responsible.

On the one hand, they had to bring the new sociological perspective into the work of anthropology as a new *theoretical apparatus* which would have a telling, persuasive, powerful impact; which would strongly militate against the existing vaguenesses, and provide a new conceptual scheme for general analysis and explanation.

On the other hand, they had to introduce this conceptual scheme in such a way—with such a delimited simplicity and clarity—as to demonstrate its immediate utility for systematic field research.

They needed a theoretical scheme, and they needed clearly related guide-lines for field-work. And these they provided.

The 'development' which these two men accomplished; their contribution to the making of sociology; was that they appropriately simplified and clarified the established nature of sociological analysis so that it set anthropology on to substantially improved lines, and made possible the systematic field-study of a wide range of primitive societies. Setting academic niceties slightly aside for the moment— they did, in fact, succeed in establishing sociology in the study of the simpler societies, and they did, in this sense (remembering all our qualifications), establish *social* anthropology as a rich, distinctive and effective field of sociological study.

This was a contribution to the making of sociology *not* in the sense of constructing any new and distinctive 'theory' within the conspectus of sociology—but in *applying* this conspectus *effectively* to a particular range of societies, and producing new knowledge about them.

(VIII) THE ERROR OF SOCIAL ANTHROPOLOGY

The *error* of social anthropology—as I have called it—lay in the fact that, for many, the nature of this development inside the ranks of sociologists as well as outside—was not clearly recognized. 'Functionalism' *was* accepted as a separate 'school'—with all the attendant entailments we have mentioned, and more besides. Social Anthropology *was* assumed to be a social science distinct from Sociology. Intellectual *issues* were professionally dreamed up. What were the relations between 'Functionalism' and 'Evolutionism'— and 'Holism' and 'psychologism', and all kinds of other 'isms'; between 'Functional' theory and 'Conflict' theory? What was necessary to make the 'statical' analysis of 'Functionalism' capable of examining problems of social change? What were the relations between 'the anthropological method' and 'sociological methods'? And the like. The 'dense fog'—as Radcliffe-Brown called it— descended, and it grits the eyes of students of sociology and social anthropology to this day.

Later—in our final volume—we shall see how this fog drifted across the Atlantic and was puffed up into denser fumes in the Free World. We shall see how—having felt themselves locked inside a closed 'Functionalism'—scholars produced new conceptual keys to open the doors which had never been closed, and, in the doing of it, gained professional reputations for their 'advancements': so providing generations of students with examination-regurgitations for the next two or three decades. This, however, we must not come to too soon. But two points we might simply note.

First: the deep-rootedness and the extent of this error—and all its attendant errors of supposed 'entailments'—are infinitely more profound than can be indicated in the words of a book. They are deeply entangled in the very organization of departments; in the appointments to university 'Chairs'; in the attitudes of mind of research foundations; all of which militate against movement towards intellectual clarity. Second: the rapid spread of these errors has been closely attendant upon the 'professionalization' of sociology and social anthropology in the universities. It is a function not only of 'organization' and 'interests', as indicated above, but also of sheer numbers and the intellectual superficiality of 'speed', and organized courses of instruction. When fashionable errors are sprinkled into thousands of minds during their three-year rush through 'academia', they are spread the more widely—like a thin, opaque cement that is, really, a disaster of falseness, and which prevents anything else from going in. All Pareto's residues and derivations fly round those errors like witches on broomsticks; or like a horde of something or other let loose from Pandora's box.

All of which, I fear, will suggest that this is a matter about which I feel rather strongly! But still: let the purple passage stand! I ought, really, to paint it a violent red!

There is one final point about this error. Though Malinowski and Radcliffe-Brown were clearly not responsible for those who could not read their painstaking qualifications, it is the case that *some* of the error of social anthropology was rooted in their work. In my judgment it was Radcliffe-Brown who was at fault here. For the moment we might say that he incorporated into social anthropology the one-sided errors of Durkheim, and then, unwittingly (i.e. in the sense that people interpreted one of his points differently from his intention) extended them. But this we shall see in his work.

(IX) AGREEMENT WITH ALL OTHER 'DEVELOPMENTS' OF SOCIOLOGY

When all these qualifications which hinge upon 'Functionalism' and 'Social Anthropology' are taken into account and placed in proper perspective, it is decidedly the case that the kind of development accomplished by Malinowski and Radcliffe-Brown was thoroughly in keeping with the other developments we have discussed—both in the 'tone' and general persuasion of their efforts, and in the detailed agreements which they quite specifically accepted.

By their 'tone' and general persuasion, I mean that—like all the others we have mentioned—they wished to achieve a substantial improvement in sociology by the movement from *theory* to *theories*. They were concerned with conceptual and theoretical clarity as such, but in essential relation to the furtherance of knowledge and the understanding of problems; and, especially, they believed that the accuracy of sociological analysis would be most advanced by the statement and testing of specific theories about specific areas of social fact. Thus Radcliffe-Brown *tested* Durkheim's theories of 'totemism' and 'the functions of religion' by undertaking specific comparative studies of his own; and then, on the basis of these, advancing Durkheim's theories one step further—but still posing these new theories as being vulnerable to *test*. It was the same in his examination of Frazer's study of 'taboos'. Their *way* of advancement was clearly the same.

By the detailed agreements, I mean such facts as these: that they accepted completely the same conception of the scientific method and its application to the study of social systems; the same distinctive focus of attention upon 'social systems' as such; the same conception of the nature of institutions, their functions, their interrelatedness, the basic 'requisites' or 'functional imperatives' in which they were rooted and the 'forms' they adopted in differing social conditions; the same conception of the sequence from instinct, need, and interest to sentiment and value formation in both institutionalization and the 'socialization' of the individual alike; the same conception of the use of classification and the comparative method for studying patterns of persistent order and change—and testing generalizations about them; the same conceptions of social evolution . . . and many other conceptions besides; as those held by all the other twentieth-century sociologists we have considered.

In the fullest sense, they accepted sociology with all its dimensions and simply re-phrased its conceptual apparatus into a form suitable to the field studies of the simpler societies which they wished to undertake. They were involved in the 'development' of the 'structural-functional' component of the 'conspectus' of sociology in particular because it provided the best mode of analysis, the best orientation and pattern for field work, in relation to the societies they wished to study (societies without recorded history, etc.); but in no sense did they construct a new 'theory', a new 'school', or a new 'science'. They were *sociologists* involved in the making of sociology among other sociologists; seeking to clarify and advance its conceptualization and to extend the knowledge of human society which it could produce by applying it effectively to the study of the remaining 'primitive' societies in the world in particular.

685

This ground-clearing discussion of quite basic issues has at least made clear in an *indicative* way the continuity and agreement which existed between the work of Malinowski and Radcliffe-Brown and the other 'developments' of their contemporaries, and also the nature and direction of their real contribution. We must now briefly examine the system of ideas proposed by each of them to see how true this assessment of them is, but also to enrich it with detail.

1
Bronislaw Malinowski: Needs, Institutions, Culture

Malinowski is often presented as a man and teacher who possessed not only great intellectual ability and clarity (so that he was a good and effective teacher), and not only an infectious enthusiasm for his subject, and an absorbed commitment to it (which also made him a good teacher), but also certain idiosyncratic qualities of temperament which made him a colourful—perhaps even flamboyant—personality. All this, of course, we cannot know sufficiently, but often, on the basis of it, Malinowski—when compared with Radcliffe-Brown—is given the appearance of being the more extreme, the less cautious scholar of the two. It was he (this kind of statement goes) who most starkly claimed originality for the 'Functional Theory'; he who was most responsible for claiming the creation of a separate 'Functional School'; he who most forcefully set up 'Functionalism' as a theory in sharp opposition to an outmoded 'Evolutionism'; he who was especially guilty of emphasizing the obscuring concept of 'Culture' . . . and so on. I mention these elements of reputation because—as far as an assessment of his *work* is concerned—they are simply not true. It may be that in his lecture-touches (of provocative statement) Malinowski claimed this or that about the originality or separateness of his 'Functional' method; but a thorough study of his written theoretical statements shows a careful balance and meticulous fair-mindedness of judgment. Even in waging war against 'Diffusionist' theories, for example: after having attacked them, he then carefully agreed about their proper place. It is difficult to find extremity or 'closed-mindedness' in him. As far as sociology is concerned, his position (compared with that of Radcliffe-Brown) was the more reliable, the least narrow, of the two.

In this brief exposition of his own outline of sociological theory and sociological analysis, I want to do no more than to show how completely he was rooted in the nineteenth century 'conspectus' and in agreement with the chief elements of the other twentieth century developments we have considered so far.

(I) AWARENESS OF, AND ROOTEDNESS IN, EARLIER THEORIES

Malinowski's awareness of the earlier contributions to the making of sociology was very wide, and covered certain distinctive areas of

687

work. First, he was well acquainted with the major contributions of the nineteenth century and, especially, their relatedness. He stressed the importance—to mention only a few names—of Spencer, Tylor, Morgan, Sumner; and was directly opposed to viewing these contributions as a number of unconnected bits and pieces. He was well aware of the *continuity* of all these efforts in the cumulatively improved formulation of the subject.

'All these thinkers,' he wrote, 'as well as some of their successors, have been gradually working towards a scientific theory of human behaviour, towards a better understanding of human nature, human society, and human culture.'*

Similarly, he was well aware of all the continued developments which sprang from these roots, and were being undertaken in his own time. He knew, and valued, the work of Westermarck, Hobhouse and Durkheim especially. He was also one of the first theorists to draw the ideas of Freud significantly (though critically) into the analysis of society. But Malinowski's most central link with nineteenth century theory; indeed his quite specific contact with the changing nature of anthropology from the nineteenth into the twentieth century; was the personal influence of Frazer. He had a close knowledge of Frazer's own nineteenth century roots, but also of all the subsequent work which was undertaken under the sway of his influence: of Spencer and Gillen (in Australia), of Haddon, Rivers, Seligman, Myers (especially on their expedition to Torres Straits), and of various scholars in Africa. He knew also of the wider influences of Frazer: the uses made of his work by such a variety of people as Durkheim, Westermarck, Gilbert Murray, Andrew Lang, Marett, and (again) Freud.

There was in Malinowski, then, no narrow notion of his own 'originality'. He saw clearly the contextual perspectives and trends within which his own developments had their place; and his sense of making *explicit* what had already been *implicit*, and of drawing earlier contributions together within a new and more balanced statement (rather than brusquely dispensing with them), can be seen very clearly in his *Biographical Appreciation* of Frazer after Frazer's death in 1941 (and, as it turned out, very shortly before his own.) He wrote this:

'Frazer's theoretical position, his evolutionism, his comparative treatment of cultures, and his explanations by survival are at times not acceptable. Yet . . . Frazer lays down the main principles of the modern scientific

* *Scientific Theory of Culture*, p. 4.

approach in anthropology. He believes in the essential similarity of the human mind and of human nature. He sees clearly that "human nature" has to be assessed primarily in terms of human needs; of those needs which permanently have to be answered if man is to survive, reproduce, live in order and security, and to progress. In his contextual treatment of the material he proves to us also that the primary necessities of mankind are satisfied through inventions, tools, weapons, and other material contrivances which, again, have to be managed by groups who co-operate and work and live in common, and where tradition is handed on from one generation to another. This implies that such characteristics of human groups as law, education, government, and economics are as necessary to man as his food, mating, and safety. His treatment . . . implies the theory of derived needs.

'. . . Frazer is as much the pioneer in modern scientific anthropology as the spokesman of his generation. The ground-work of his approach cannot be rejected. The comparative method is still the main theoretical tool for the formulation of general principles of anthropological science. The assumption of man's primary needs must remain the starting point in our inquiry into cultural phenomena. The evolutionary principle and its capital outfit will never become completely rejected by anthropology or humanism. Frazer's psychological interest appears to us sounder now than it seemed to be a quarter of a century ago.

We are beginning now to see clearly that evolutionism and the historical method, the principle of development and the fact of diffusion, explanations in terms of mental processes and sociological theories, are neither mutually exclusive nor intrinsically hostile, but complementary and inevitably correlated.'*

Malinowski's full consciousness of the context and continuity of his work was therefore clear beyond doubt. The same was plain in many of his specific conceptions.

(II) THEORY, SCIENCE, PRAGMATISM, PURPOSE

In many important ways, Malinowski's conception of science and its implications (past, present, and future) for human action and purpose were in agreement with the earlier and contemporary writers. Here we will note a few.

Like the most contemporary philosopher of science, he was perfectly clear in his statement that there was no such thing as 'theory-free' knowledge—even at the level of supposed description. The simplest 'facts' were, really, *selected* in accordance with some framework of concepts and assumptions. In this sense he thought that all past 'theories' entailed *implicit*, embryonic scientific principles. Modern science was, by critical analysis, able to make these

* *Scientific Theory of Culture*, pp. 211–13.

explicit, and to rid them of imprecisions, irrelevancies, and ambiguities. In this sense, too, he thought that all human *action* (*all* men's *practical activities*, and the invented devices used in them) from the earliest times, *implied* science. And this had certain implications. It meant that men, in their inventions and pragmatic actions, were always establishing knowledge as a basis of expectation and prediction. Knowledge and prediction were two aspects of the same process of practical control through action. But, also, this clearly implied a conception of *ends*, and a calculated use of appropriate *means*. In short, man was essentially and distinctively a *reasoning* and *purposive* being; and his *cultural* achievements had an *instrumental* value for the attainment of ends.

We need not stay to disentangle all the elements of absolutely basic importance in this bundle of agreements—they are so obvious— but let us note that, in the development of them, Malinowski accomplished a perfectly clear statement of the nature of science— both *in* human life, and for the study of it; a perfectly clear conception of social *action* (in relation to which cultural achievements and social institutions could be understood); and a perfectly clear and valid incorporation into sociological analysis of the '*teleological*' aspects of the human mind so much insisted upon by all the earlier and contemporary writers other than the dogmatic, mistaken Durkheim. We might note, in passing, that one of Radcliffe-Brown's faults and deficiencies (when assessed in comparison with Malinowski) was that he accepted Durkheim's dogmatic mistake.* Malinowski certainly did not.

(III) SOCIAL SCIENCE, SOCIAL ENGINEERING, ETHICS

Following upon this clarification of science and its use in practical activity and control, Malinowski went on to clarify the nature of a science of society. This—we shall come to. Here, we might note two attendant points which he made very clearly. The first was his complete agreement with the other sociologists (from Comte onwards) that in the rapid transformation of society in the modern world, social science was a necessary basis for effective 'social engineering'; and, indeed, that social engineering was sadly ineffective—if not absurd—without it.

'In the present crisis of our civilization we have risen to vertiginous heights in the mechanical and chemical sciences, pure and applied, and in materialistic theory and mechanical engineering. But we have neither faith in, nor respect for, the conclusions of humanistic arguments, nor yet in

* And was involved in the same unresolved ambiguities.

the validity of social theories. Today we very much need to establish the balance between the hypertrophied influence of natural science and its applications on the one hand, and the backwardness of social science, with the constant impotence of social engineering, on the other . . .

Social science . . . must develop into the power of mind used for the control of mechanical power.'*

His second, equally important and interesting agreement was that *ethical principles* and moral concern—far from presenting obstacles to the quest for accuracy in social engineering and social science—on the contrary (properly understood), positively *required* and *insisted* upon it. Here, too, Malinowski held a broad position: recognizing all the humanistic aspects of the study of man which went *beyond* science, but clearly seeing that there was no necessary conflict between the two.

(IV) EACH SCIENCE ITS APPROPRIATE METHODS

Exactly in agreement with Comte and others, Malinowski also insisted that each new science needed to work out its own appropriate methods. Indeed, he argued that simply to borrow the methods of older, existing sciences, without criticism, was one of the most dangerous procedures possible. This could lead to a completely insufficient conceptualization of the subject-matter. The first task was sufficiently to define the distinctive subject-matter, and then to work out appropriate methods. On this point, too Malinowski was clearer and more correct than Radcliffe-Brown, who simply thought of a science of society as employing the same logical methods as were applied in the physical and biological sciences—again accepting the influence of Durkheim.

(V) FUNCTIONAL ANALYSIS AND THE COMPARATIVE
      METHOD

Malinowski was also completely agreed about the indispensability of the comparative method in sociology. It was never the case that he thought of the study of primitive societies in terms of the production of isolated descriptive monographs. Always, it was a matter of *generalization*, and the *testing* of generalizations. Only by careful comparative studies was it possible to uncover the essential nature of certain institutional connections, or to understand certain 'typical' organizations, and, above all, to *test* any propositions about them. Structural-functional analysis and comparative study

* *Scientific Theory of Culture*, p. 13.

went hand in hand, together with the careful definition and classification which they implied.

'This whole approach presupposes a really scientific definition of the realities compared. Unless we list, in our exhaustive inventories, really comparable phenomena, and are never duped by surface similarities or fictitious analogies, a great deal of labour may lead to incorrect conclusions . . . The comparative method must remain the basis of any generalization, any theoretical principle, or any universal law applicable to our subject matter.'*

Again, nothing could be clearer.

(VI) FUNCTIONAL ANALYSIS AND SOCIAL EVOLUTION

It is such a common (and frequently dogmatic) assumption that 'Functionalism' was in direct opposition to theories of 'social evolution' in sociology, that we must be emphatically clear in showing that Malinowski himself decidedly did not hold this view. Indeed, his upholding and understanding of some evolutionary viewpoints was very perceptive indeed (compared with all that has come since!) Here, for example, was one of his statements:

'Evolutionism is at present rather unfashionable. Nevertheless, its main assumptions are not only valid, but also they are indispensable to the field-worker as well as to the student of theory . . . Our interest in tracing back any and every manifestation of human life to its simplest forms remains legitimate and indispensable to the full understanding of culture . . . I believe that ultimately we will accept the view that "origins" is nothing else but the essential nature of an institution like marriage or the nation, the family or the state, the religious congregation or the organization of witchcraft.'†

This was not only clear but a clear understanding that Westermarck's (and Durkheim's) approach in seeking 'origins' was really the effort to uncover basic 'causes'.‡ And he went further in insisting that 'the concept of 'stages' remained as valid as that of origins'. 'The general principle of evolutionary analysis', he argued, 'remains.'

After having clarified his system of functional analysis, he said quite explicitly:

'. . . such a scientific approach does not by any means override or deny the

* *Scientific Theory of Culture*, p. 18.   † *Ibid.*, p. 16.

‡ i.e. Westermarck in seeking the 'origins' of the 'sanctions' at the heart of institutions, and Durkheim in seeking the 'essential' functions in the simplest known form of religion.

validity of evolutionary or historical pursuits. It simply supplies them with a scientific basis.'*

A last point of interest here is that—like all the evolutionists (including Radcliffe-Brown)—Malinowski saw the process of social evolution as one of an increasing differentiation of structure and function (i.e. an increasing 'specialization' of institutions.) Having agreed, emphatically, that '. . . Certain forms definitely precede others . ...' he had this to say when discussing occupational and professional associations:

'Here the evolutionary principle cannot be dismissed from the functional theory. For there is no doubt that in the course of human development the needs for economic organization, for education, for magical or legal services, have been increasingly satisfied by specialized systems of activities. Each group of specialists becomes more and more closely organized into a profession. Nevertheless, the subject of discovering the earliest type of occupational groups is fascinating, not only for the student interested in wide schemes of evolution, but also for the field-worker and the comparative student.'†

Malinowski the 'Functionalist' was also Malinowski the 'Evolutionist'—very plainly and forthrightly so.

(VII) SOCIOLOGY AND PSYCHOLOGY

Another extensive area of agreement between Malinowski and the other writers lay in his views on the relations between sociology and psychology. Like Durkheim (and everyone else) he rejected a purely psychological account of all the attributes of institutions and social systems. Indeed, he was critical of Frazer, Westermarck, and Freud for emphasizing psychological elements perhaps too much. Even so, he was completely in agreement with the fusing of psychology and sociology if it could be properly done. He did not elaborate his thinking on this beyond a fairly provisional (and elementary) stage, but it is interesting to see that he saw quite clearly the way in which Freud's ideas could be (and were beginning to be) incorporated into sociological analysis, and how this promised a systematic theory of the 'socialization' of the individual.

'The real contribution of psychoanalysis,' he wrote, 'is its insistence on the formation of mental, that is, also sociological, attitudes during early childhood; within the context of the domestic institution; due to such cultural influences as education, the use of parental authority, and certain primary drives associated with sex, nutrition, and defecation . . .

* *Scientific Theory of Culture*, p. 42.   † *Ibid.*, p. 167.

'Psychoanalysts are bound to search for organic drives as determinants of culture . . .' and '. . . will never be able to disregard the organic relationship of cultural elements embodied in social groupings. This type of psychology deals with such factors as authority or the use of force, the following up of organic desires and their transformation into values, the study of norms as agencies of repression. All this has already led many adherents of Freud towards a more-or-less systematic institutional analysis, within which they have placed mental processes.'*

This, however, did not prevent Malinowski from advocating a 'Behaviourist' approach to the observation of behaviour in field work, nor did it lead him to exclude explanation in terms of conscious thought, meaning, and purpose. His notion of 'Behaviourism' was limited,† but there is no doubt that he would have much agreed with the 'Social Behaviourism' of Mead, had he known it. It will be noted in this connection (in the above quotation) that—exactly like McDougall, Cooley, Mead and Freud—Malinowski thought of 'socialization' as a 'transformation' of desires into 'values' and 'norms'. Also, in the same connection, he included in his analysis of 'culture' a systematic account of the 'symbols' of society. All the elements of the 'socio-psychological' analysis which we considered in the last chapter were therefore completely in keeping with his thought.

Psychology, at any rate, though insufficient in itself, could be, and should be, reliably built into sociological analysis.

(VIII) FUNCTIONAL ANALYSIS: A GUIDE TO FIELD-WORK

All the above points demonstrate quite clearly the very full extent to which Malinowski accepted all the main components of the 'conspectus' of sociology. There was no major departure at all in his position. His concern was chiefly to vitalize anthropology and to reshape it by achieving a formulation of sociology appropriate to its tasks. Before moving on to this formulation, we might note a last clear point: that he attempted this *not* for the sake of 'theory' alone, but also to provide clear guide-lines for productive field-research. Or, perhaps, it would be better put like this: that, for him, considerations of theory and effective field-work were one.

'The functional theory, as here presented,' he wrote, 'claims to be the prerequisite for field-work and for the comparative analysis of phenomena in various cultures. It is capable of yielding a concrete analysis of culture

* *Scientific Theory of Culture*, p. 22. The study he had chiefly in mind here was 'The Individual and His Society', by A. Kardiner and R. Linton.
† i.e. of the 'stimulus-response' type.

into institutions and their aspects. If you imagine a field-worker supplied with such guiding charts, you will see that they might be helpful to him in isolating, as well as relating, the phenomena observed. It is meant primarily to equip the field-worker with a clear perspective and full instructions regarding what to observe and how to record.'*

But again, even in such a direct statement, limited to such a practical point, he took pains to make his qualifications clear.

'Functionalism,' he went on, 'I would like to state emphatically, is neither hostile to the study of distribution, nor to the reconstruction of the past in terms of evolution, history or diffusion.'*

All these qualifications and intentions of Malinowski were, then, perfectly plain, and we can now turn to a brief outline of the clear system of analysis which he presented.

The Functional Analysis of a Cultural System

This account can be brief indeed, because Malinowski's system was so clear. There are only occasional aspects of definition which need particular emphasis, and we will take each item in turn.

(I) CULTURE

Much has been made of Malinowski's concentration upon *culture*, but there was no problem whatever in it, and, as we shall see, he meant nothing by it but the *social system*. His emphasis—like that of Ward—was only that what distinguished man from other animals was his *cumulative creation of a cultural tradition*, a cultural system, an *achievement* of creative activity in relation to nature. Whether we think of a very small simple cultural system of 'primitive' people, or a large, complex civilization, we are confronted, he wrote:—

'... by a vast apparatus, partly material, partly human and partly spiritual, by which man is able to cope with the concrete, specific problems that face him. These problems arise out of the fact that man has a body subject to various organic needs, and that he lives in an environment which is his best friend, in that it provides the raw materials of man's handiwork, and also his dangerous enemy, in that it harbours many hostile forces.'†

(II) NEEDS AND FUNCTIONAL IMPERATIVES

The creation of culture stemmed, he argued, primarily from the activities undertaken to satisfy basic biological needs. Men had to

* *Scientific Theory of Culture*, p. 175. † *Ibid.*, p. 36.

eat, to drink, to find shelter and protection, to reproduce their kind (etc.) if they were to survive. Basic biological needs impelled men to action. Culture was created to meet these *basic imperatives*.

In succeeding in these activities, however, men created a new environment of artifacts. They made tools, weapons, dwelling places, and devised organized methods of winning a livelihood. This cultural equipment of society itself (at once both technical and institutional) had to be replaced and renewed by work upon natural resources, and this involved not simply an acquisition of material substances, but also a retention and transmission of skills. Men were involved in a level of *instrumental needs* (rooted in the activities to satisfy *basic needs*) and culture had therefore to meet *instrumental imperatives*.

In all these co-operative and conflicting activities, however, men also experienced the need for regulation, for generally agreed values, norms, sanctions, and, indeed, for principles and procedures of authority and control. There was a level of *integrative needs*, and the system of culture had to meet *integrative imperatives*.

This—quite obviously—provided a very clear analysis of the entirety of a system of culture in terms of distinguishable levels of *needs* and *functional imperatives*. And such an analysis of the *nature of culture* could provide: '. . . predictive statements as guides for field-research, yardsticks for comparative treatment, common measures in the process of cultural adaptation and change.' In Comte's terms, the 'laws' of 'statics' provided guide-lines to 'dynamics'—the detailed study of particular, actual systems of social order and change. And we may note here that Malinowski quite plainly envisaged studies of 'adaptation and change'—not only of 'persisting order'.

(III) INSTITUTIONS: THE DISTINGUISHABLE ISOLATES IN
     CULTURAL REALITY

The manifold activities of men in meeting these functional imperatives and seeking the satisfaction of needs was also, however, *organized*. In seeking their ends men formed groups and had to organize their activity. The entire cultural activity of a society could therefore be analysed into its distinguishable units of organization. Such a unit, Malinowski termed an *institution*, and it was institutions, he insisted that should be agreed upon (for purposes of systematic, scientific study) as the *definite isolates* of culture. The study of institutions would systematically encompass the entire analysis of culture—as an apparatus which (in any particular society) met the several kinds of functional imperatives and needs.

It is absolutely clear from this that Malinowski's use of the term 'culture' was not in the slightest sense obscure. His analysis of culture was entirely that of an integrative and instrumental apparatus closely linked to a clear institutional framework of organization. It was—in the plainest possible terms—a '*structural-functional* analysis' of a total society.

'Our two types of analysis, functional and institutional,' Malinowski wrote, 'will allow us to define culture more concretely, precisely and exhaustively. Culture is an integral composed of partly autonomous, partly co-ordinated institutions. It is integrated on a series of principles such as the community of blood through procreation; the contiguity in space related to co-operation; the specialization in activities; and last but not least, the use of power in political organization. Each culture owes its completeness and self-sufficiency to the fact that it satisfies the whole range of basic, instrumental and integrative needs.'*

This was a clear analytical scheme: of institutions, and of their functions in meeting basic needs and instrumental and integrative imperatives. And again, we must especially note that Malinowski explicitly expected this scheme to be used in the study of processes of 'time' and 'change', as well as persisting order. There was no 'fallacy of the stationary', as Ward had called it, here.

The rest of Malinowski's system was a detailed elaboration of each part of this scheme, and it is only necessary to indicate the nature of his treatment so that we can see its agreement with the larger-scale systems of ideas we have considered.

(IV) THE ANALYSIS OF INSTITUTIONS

Having linked all groupings of men in society and all items of culture to *institutions*; having argued that a comprehensive knowledge of a total society could best be achieved by a systematic analysis of its institutions; and having pointed out that the study of institutions (analytically and comparatively, in all societies) could be submitted to a 'definite analytic scheme', Malinowski then went on to provide such a scheme.

Any institution (unit of organization) could be analysed, he argued, into six component parts:

(1) *The Charter:* the ostensible purpose, or values, of the institution for the pursuit of which its members had become organized.

* *Scientific Theory of Culture*, p. 40.

(2) *The Personnel:* the group of members—organized in terms of tasks, privileges, rewards, and some principle of authority.

(3) *The Rules or Norms:* the technical, ethical, and legal regulations accepted by, or imposed upon the members in relation to their skills and behaviour in the group.

⎱ (2) and (3) were contingent upon (1)

(4) *The Material Apparatus:* that 'portion' of the total capital of the society used by the particular institution, (wealth, property, instruments, etc.) and the continuing income, profit, or equipment created by it.

(5) *The Activities:* the *actual* behaviour of the members in their institutional tasks—related to the 'ideality' of the 'Rules or Norms', but also, in part, deviating from them.

(6) *The Functions:* the 'integral *results*' of the organized activities—for its own members, for other institutions, and for society at large: in relation to basic, instrumental and integrative needs.

The study of the institutions of any society based upon this analytical scheme could provide a comprehensive, testable body of knowledge. By following it, each single *element of social structure* could be known in detail; and—more than that—the study of *all* such elements and their interconnections could provide a *full* knowledge of every component of the *actuality* of the socio-cultural system. And part of the basic 'sociological assumption', Malinowski held, was that all such institutional elements were essentially inter-related, and each could only be understood within its context. We may note again here—that in maintaining this, he had no simple notion of functional 'integration' or 'harmony' in mind. In our last quotation it will be seen that distinguishable institutions were 'partly autonomous, partly co-ordinated . . .' The only insistence was that in their emergence, their coming to possess a particular form, their inter-operation with each other, their inter-connected results (some seen, some unforeseen)—they were bound to share inter-connected qualities and to experience inter-dependent influences; and, within the same total society, were bound to come within the sway of (and to become, to some extent, adjusted to) wider principles and procedures of regulation, arbitration, and government. These latter were themselves, however, *institutions* of an *integrative* level; so that all institutions formed part of the total interrelated associational fabric. But this was by no means the postulation of some kind of tight interlocking unity which gave no possible room for institutional conflict or change. Malinowski would have regarded such a postulate as an outright absurdity.

To complete this 'scheme' for the study of institutions, he simply listed the major institutions to be found in all societies, and showed their rootedness in basic, instrumental, and integrative needs. The family, marriage, and kinship organization were related to reproduction; institutionalized sex- and age-distinctions were related to physiological differences, and sequences of growth and ageing; occupational and professional institutions were related to instrumental imperatives; political and religious institutions to integrative imperatives; and so on. The kind of analysis is crystal clear, and it is enough to say (a) that a (fairly) comprehensive list of institutions was drawn up, and (b) that the *universality* of both needs and institutions (despite the diversity of institutional *forms*) was made the clear basis for systematic, comparative, *generalizing* study. It is also worth noting that in describing (in terms of levels of 'needs') what he called 'a set of universal problems which are solved by each culture in a somewhat different manner. . . .' Malinowski was providing a basic analysis of those 'functional requisites' which had been seen by Comte, Mill (and following writers) as forming the determinate universal bases of institutional organization.

(v) FUNCTIONAL ANALYSIS: AN ANALYSIS OF PURPOSIVE SOCIAL ACTION

In elaborating his conception of a 'functional' analysis of institutions, Malinowski made other important points quite clear. The varying *'forms'* adopted by institutions in different societies in meeting the same 'functional imperatives' was an outcome of the *activities* of men in coming to terms with their differing geographical and historical (environmental) conditions. Malinowski rejected any kind of 'sociological determinism'—the Durkheimian view that (as he put it) there existed an '. . . objective moral being, which imposes its will upon its members . . .'; a 'collective censorium'. Culture, including institutions, was *instrumental*. Men acted purposively. They sought ends in relation to their needs, and they creatively *changed* the natural world, and their social apparatus, in doing so. And in all this, Malinowski emphasized '. . . one other cardinal constituent of cultural reality . . .'—that, in their institutionalized activities, men lived by 'norms, customs, traditions, rules.' In short, the organization of men's practical activities was *essentially* a matter of *evaluation and regulation*. Again—values were emphasized as comprising the heart of institutionalization.

699

Though insisting upon a close observation of *behaviour* in sociological studies, Malinowski was nonetheless quite definite, therefore, that this must be a study of *purposive action* as distinct from determined behavioural events.

(VI) HUMAN NATURE AND SOCIALIZATION

In his discussion of the psychological basis of the 'primary needs' of human nature—on which so much of his analysis of 'functional imperatives' rested—there were two points of special importance.

First—like all the other writers—he accepted unquestioningly the existence of universal instinctual elements in human nature. These were 'determined biologically, by the physics of the environment and by human anatomy' and were 'invariably incorporated in each type of civilization'. And, specifically, they were primary *impulses* or *drives* 'determined by the physiological state of the organism'. The extremely interesting aspect of Malinowski's treatment here (which was not, however, very extensive) is that it was not only completely in accordance with McDougall's analysis of instinct, but was also formulated in a way completely agreeing with the present-day analysis of the 'Comparative Ethologists'. He set out a 'schema'

PERMANENT VITAL SEQUENCES INCORPORATED IN ALL CULTURES*

(A) Impulse	(B) Act	(C) Satisfaction
Drive to breathe; gasping for air	intake of oxygen	elimination of CO_2 in tissues
hunger	ingestion of food	satiation
thirst	absorption of liquid	quenching
sex appetite	conjugation	detumescence
fatigue	rest	restoration of muscular and nervous energy
restlessness	activity	satisfaction of fatigue
somnolence	sleep	awakening with restored energy
bladder pressure	micturition	removal of tension
colon pressure	defecation	abdominal relaxation
fright	escape from danger	relaxation
pain	avoidance by effective act	return to normal state

* *Scientific Theory of Culture*, p. 77.

indicating his distinction between the *impulse* (resting on specific neuro-physiological conditions; the consummatory *act* which terminated in the attainment of the certain 'object' desired; and the ensuing 'satisfaction' concomitant with neuro-physiological 'quiescence'. This is exactly the 'schema' of a Lorenz, Tinbergen, or W. H. Thorpe.*

One cannot help remarking again on the very curious oddities of academic 'fashion'. McDougall was sneered at and abandoned as an 'instinct theorist' whilst Malinowski was lauded as one of the founding fathers of the new 'functional analysis' of culture in the new science of Social Anthropology. Yet both rested their ideas upon an identical analysis of instinct. (Perhaps Pareto's cynicism has much more to be said for it than one likes to admit!)

But the second point we can notice is that Malinowski thought of 'socialization' as, basically, a *'re-definition of impulses'* within the symbolic and behavioural context of 'traditional activities'. Each impulse, he argued, '. . . is remoulded by tradition.' *Drives* became *motives*: '. . . meaning by this the urge as it actually is found in operation within a given culture.' This, clearly, was exactly the same conception as that of Cooley and Mead, and we shall see in a moment that this agreement went significantly further in Malinowski's emphasis upon the importance (for 'socialization') of the family and primary groups. Again, however, it is worthwhile to note that—even in this basic process of 'socialization'—Malinowski went out of his way to insist that *rules*, *evaluations*, and *norms* were just as indispensable, as elements in the social system, as technical, material provisions. *'Prescribed'* behaviour was important as a cultural imperative; and this entailed, too, the necessity of *education*. As part of the process of socialization: '. . . educational systems, the gradual imparting of skills, knowledge, custom and ethical principles must exist in every culture'.

(VII) LEVELS OF NEEDS AND INSTITUTIONS: A 'CHAINED' SERIES

Malinowski then elaborated his analysis of the levels of basic, instrumental, and integrative needs, their attendant kinds of 'functional imperatives', and the more specific and more general kinds of institutions rooted in them, in such a way as to show that they were linked in a 'chained series'. They were inter-connected in

* See *Instinct in Man*, R. Fletcher, Unwin Books, 1968: p. 115, Thorpe and Lorenz; p. 133, Tinbergen. For list of 'instincts' (primary impulses, general instinctive tendencies, and secondary impulses) to compare with Malinowski's 'schema'—see pp. 309–15.

a *definite* way—instrumental imperatives growing out of activities to satisfy basic needs; integrative imperatives growing out of the complexity of instrumental institutions, etc.; and in a *sequential* way—in that socialization began in the family and neighbourhood groups, and was then extended on that basis, as each new generation in society gradually came to terms with the complex cultural imperatives in all the institutions in which their adult actions had to take place. This pattern of analysis is again so clear that only a few distinctive points need be made.

With regard to the *sequential* functioning of institutions we can simply note Malinowski's extension of the notion of socialization mentioned earlier. Of particular importance is the way in which he regarded the family ('domestic institutions') as being the crucial group for fulfilling the functions of socialization, and—because this was a *universal* fact in *all* human societies—how, yet again, this provided a guide-line for field research. He wrote as follows:

'The family is . . . a reproductive unit. Cultural reproduction, however, includes the training of the young, for which the economic, as well as physical basis, is provided in the organized household. We can, therefore, state that the production, the ontogenetic and cultural development of the young, and their equipment for tribal life with regular status and material outfit is the function of the domestic institution. We could rephrase it even more briefly: the family transforms the raw material of the new organisms into full citizens, tribal or national. Such a definition fits all human societies. It demands, when applied to field-work, an answer in terms of observed fact and provides a comparative basis for any cross-cultural survey.

We see, thus, that although at first sight our definitions may appear "vague, insipid, and useless", in reality they are condensed formulae which contain extensive recipes for the organization of perspective in field-work. And this really is the hallmark of scientific definition. It must principally be a call to a scientifically schematized and oriented observation of empirical fact.'*

(VIII) DERIVED NEEDS: INSTRUMENTAL AND INTEGRATIVE
        IMPERATIVES

Following upon his discussion of the 'basic needs' of human nature, Malinowski then elaborated a little further his analysis of the 'derived' needs (and imperatives) which were attendant upon the creation of culture. Certain preliminary points were made of some importance.

First, he took care to point out that the complexity of the levels

* *Scientific Theory of Culture*, p. 114.

of social need and the institutions involved was such that it would be an error ever to think that any *one* institution could be *identified* with the satisfaction of any *one basic* need. The activity which finally satisfied basic needs was complex activity couched within institutional requirements which had to fulfil instrumental and integrative imperatives too. Every institution had its several (multiple) functional aspects. Even so there was nothing here to prevent clear analysis.

Secondly, in clarifying the nature of derived needs and imperatives, Malinowski stressed, in a way similar to Durkheim, the *creativity* of society. New needs (at the instrumental and integrative levels) were experienced in the context of *associational* activity, which did not exist at the biological level *prior* to association. And these needs and imperatives engendered new levels and qualities of judgment, evaluation, thought, action. In particular, the institutions which came into being to meet them fundamentally involved rules, norms, values, sanctions and principles of authority. The cumulative framework of culture and institutions was therefore *creative* in the two senses: (*a*) that the organization and canalization of human energies and activities greatly increased the power of man's effort and control (i.e. beyond that of the same number of unrelated, unorganized individuals) and (*b*) that it brought with it qualitatively new levels of feeling, evaluation, judgment, and calculated action. At the same time, however, it was also a network of regulated *limitation* of human conduct. The derived imperatives brought greatly increased derived potentialities and powers, but also a more complex network of responsible restraints. It carried both liberation and constraint; both creativity and disciplined control. It certainly comprised a new level of *determinacy* which had to be taken into account in understanding and explaining the patterns and directions of human action. This, clearly, was very similar to Durkheim's view.

And thirdly, on this matter of contraint, Malinowski emphasized that—although they were '*derived*' from the activities serving *basic* needs—these instrumental and integrative imperatives were experienced in society as being just as *necessary*, just as *indispensable*, as the basic needs themselves. The continued satisfaction of the basic needs—at that particular level achieved in the social order—necessitated the continued renewal of the material, technical and organizational fabric of society. Without this, the secure satisfaction of need would be jeopardized; threatened. But also—for individuals—the constraining pressures of established institutional rules and procedures were just as 'objective' a set of demands in their experience as were their felt needs themselves. The maintenance of the social order became part of the 'necessary conditions for survival'.

'. . . derived needs,' Malinowski wrote, 'have the same stringency as biological needs, and this stringency is due to the fact that they are always instrumentally related to the wants of the organism.'*

Having emphasized these characteristics of derived needs and imperatives, he then undertook an analysis of them. This, however, was simple and straightforward, and had no distinction worth our while to note. Here we need only note firstly: that he distinguished *four* major areas of instrumental need (four *instrumental imperatives*); (1) economic, (2) customary and legal (which he termed 'social control'), (3) educational, and (4) political; and commented on the *institutions* which came into being to deal with them; and secondly: emphasized *within* them the *integrative* imperatives and *their* appropriate institutions. We should perhaps note, too, that in this he took into account such elements as language and symbolism as well as the more conspicuous elements of social *organization* such as religion and law.

Malinowski then tried to *summarize* his 'functional analysis' of the social system in as simple and clear a way as possible; and it is worth our while to look at this as it will make quite clear—once and for all—the question as to how far 'functional analysis' can be said to be an *explanation* of society. In the first place, Malinowski offered a summary definition of the emergence and nature of human culture. It was this.

'. . . the origins of culture can be defined as the concurrent integration of several lines of development: the ability to recognize *instrumental objects*, the appreciation of their *technical efficiency*, and their *value*, that is, their place in the *purposive sequence*, the formation of *social bonds*, and the appearance of *symbolism*.'†

Then, he clarified the link which his analysis envisaged between *human action in the context of cultural imperatives* and *human action to satisfy the basic organic needs* in the following diagram—to which he referred as 'The Instrumentally Implemented Vital Sequence'.

DIAGRAM OF INSTRUMENTAL SEQUENCE‡

DRIVE (1) → INSTRUMENTAL PERFORMANCE
  1. Object
  2. Technique
  3. Co-operation or tradition
  4. Context of situation

DRIVE (2) → CONSUMMATION GOAL-RESPONSE ——————→ SATISFACTION

* *Scientific Theory of Culture*, p. 124.   † *Ibid.*, p. 136.   ‡ *Ibid.*, p. 137.

The thing it is most important to note in this summary definition and this diagram is that—for Malinowski—to clarify the nature of (instrumental) institutions; the relations between them (in their 'linked chain'); and the relations between them and the various levels of needs and imperatives; by means of *functional analysis*— was not, in itself, an *explanation*. Or, to put it differently: the postulation of *function, functional interrelatedness,* or *functional inter-operation,* was not *in itself* the sole explanatory factor being proposed.

Functional analysis was what it said it was: a scheme of *analysis* which systematically clarified the nature of the socio-cultural system about which sociology sought to establish testable knowledge. It clarified the nature of the components and of the relationships existing among them within the whole. It thus presented a *schema with* which systematic empirical investigation could be undertaken, and *within* which specific theories could be clearly stated, studied, and tested.

It is true that the functional connections proposed in the schema were postulations of *some* causal connections and *some* conditions of causal connections; but it was emphatically *not* the case that the postulation of function was taken to be a sufficient statement of *cause.* And two points need quite definitive statement here.

The first is: that for Malinowski, his scheme of analysis was entirely a *systematic study of purposive social action.* The causal factors built into his scheme were: (1) insistent, ineradicable, basic needs, (2) powerful, purposeful motives to action for the satisfaction of these needs, (3) conscious, calculated reasoning and deliberate action to attain appropriate ends (4) the co-operative making of a material, technical, institutional, moral order of social organization (5) the recognition of derived—instrumental and integrative— necessities (including co-operation and conflict) within this social order, and (6) the continuous problematical activity—in feeling, thought, knowledge, judgment, action—in improving cultural skills, increasing human welfare, puzzling over the problems of increasing specialization, and wrestling with the more detailed problems of integrative order involved.

Several important points are implicit here. First: this was a schema for the analysis of *social action* (i.e. within the functionally connected framework of institutions). Second: it postulated *psychological* and *socio-psychological needs* and *motives*—in relation to organizational problems—as being initiating and sustaining elements in their action. Third: it saw this action—though within a creative-constraining pattern of institutions—as being in large part *purposive.* Fourth: it saw society as an ongoing process of creativity, change, and attempted progress (not at all 'static' functional unity); and in this had essentially the same perspective as almost all the other writers. But fifth—and of special importance here—it postulated *all these elements* as the substantive causal factors which underlay the 'functionally inter-connected institutions' of the social system. There was no tendency whatsoever in Malinowski to speak of the *functions* of *institutions* (as societal entities) as being determinate *causes* of society. The causal factors were the needs, purposes, evaluations, actions of men—and the functional interconnections between the instrumental elements of culture were subsequent (and then ongoing) entailments of further need and organizational problems. Structural-Functional analysis was a *scheme of analysis*.

No new causal theory in sociology had been set up.

But the second basic point concerning *explanation* is this. Malinowski was quite plain in his teaching that his 'functional analysis' was a scheme for empirical investigation, empirical generalization, and the testing of such generalizations. It was not a *substantive theory* as such. The specific *forms* which particular *institutions* manifested in particular *societies* within particular *life-conditions* would clearly *differ*. Any full causal explanation of any concrete *case* of institutionalization would therefore include not only all the *factors* postulated in the scheme of analysis, but also all the differing empirical peculiarities of that specific social situation. In short, the scheme of categories would be *used* in specific causal explanation—not in any sense *imposed* as some kind of 'blanket-type' *'functional'* explanation.

Structural-Functional analysis—simplified for his purposes by Malinowski—was certainly *not* a new *causal* theory in sociology. It was one *component* of systematic analysis within the over-all 'conspectus'; and—with Malinowski, as with all his predecessors—the other components in the 'conspectus'—elements of psychology, social psychology, purposeful and meaningful social action, etc—were all there.

Only one other point—which we have no more than mentioned—needs a little fuller statement before leaving it here. We noted a moment ago, that Malinowski also—like most of his predecessors and contemporaries—saw society as a continuous process of creativity and re-creativity which included a strain towards progress. It is worthwhile to notice how much it was the case that he not only recognized the rapidity of modern social change, and the dominant spread of 'western' (industrialized) civilization, but also how strongly he adopted the same rational, ethical position towards the *re-making of institutions* in this period of transition as all the other major sociologists from Comte to Hobhouse, Durkheim and

Weber. Much of his writing was concerned with problems of power and freedom in complex modern societies, but an excellent summary statement of some aspects of his ethical approach was given in the final section of his appraisal of Sir James Frazer: in the chapter entitled '*Whither Anthropology?*' In this he briefly considered such issues as the validity of 'war' as a continued institution among modern states; the nature of 'nationality'; the desirability of 'cultural integration' between societies as against 'political control' over them; and several others; but here, I will select only a few statements to illustrate this ethical commitment clearly. But let us note that— for Malinowski too—the making of sociology was for the making of society.

'Such concepts,' he wrote, 'as democracy and freedom, communism and capitalism, the role of competition and of planning, can and must be submitted to a full anthropological analysis, inspired by the evolutionary as well as historical, psychological and sociological approaches. Problems of primitive law and order, of early forms of education and also of primitive types of science, magic, and religion, should be taken up with direct reference to the vital issues of today, and illuminated by the search for a common measure between the earlier and later forms studied, or by reaching out to questions of origins in terms of the fundamental role played by a type of activity, or by an institution in human development.

Anthropology can take up its serious role of *magistra vitae* side by side with history, in the classical sense of that word, and with other branches of humanism . . .

At the present historical moment the phase and development through which we are now going is dominated by diffusion. The Western civilization, like a steam roller, is moving over the face of the world. *The study of this cultural change, going on in Africa and Asia, in Oceania and in the New World, is the principal historical contribution of the ethnographer.* Modern anthropology has already recognized this, and is becoming increasingly aware of its importance.

Culture change also is a practical problem which post-war reconstruction* will have to face, and there is no doubt that after the present catastrophe is over the relations between races will have to be based on certain new principles of common rights, a share in privileges as well as duties, a co-operative collaboration and prosperity in which political, legal, and educational mechanisms will undergo a profound change. The anthropologist believes, on the one hand, in the right of all races, white, brown and black, and in the right of all minorities to equal treatment. He also has the conservative bias which makes him recognize the value of tradition, the value of the diversity of cultures, in their independence as well as in their cross-fertilization. His advice would be that our culture must not be imposed on others by the force of arms, the power of wealth, and

---

* This was written in 1941.

the stringency of law. The missionary spirit in the crudest form will have to be modified, at least. Nationalism, in the sense of a conservative reaction and the recognition of the integral value of its own culture by each nation, is spreading like wildfire all over the world. We, the members of the white race, are primarily responsible for that, and we have been giving our religion, our education, and many other spiritual boons to other races and other peoples, with an implied promise that once they accept our civilization they will become our equals. This promise has not been redeemed.

We are beginning now to see how dangerous it is to speak about the white man's burden, and to make others shoulder it and carry it for us. We give all the promises implied in our concept of human brotherhood and of equality through education, but when it comes to wealth, power, and self-determination we refuse this to other people.

Whether the anthropologist does not come too late into the picture, and whether his advice would still be of much value, even if he were allowed to take part at any conference table of the high and mighty, is one question. That the anthropologist cannot remain silent is another.'*

This was only a part of Malinowski's 'programme' of the practical political implications of the sociological study of the simpler peoples. Many other issues—self-determination of cultural groups; collective security; etc—formed a part of it. 'All this', he wrote, 'may be Utopian and visionary.' For our part, we need only note that it was of 'Utopian and visionary' concern in the same way that almost all the sociologists had been.

(IX) CONCLUSION

It is surely clear from all this that Malinowski was one among the 'makers of sociology', and not in any sense a sharply distinct, purely innovating scholar, who set up a new school or a new science. We need not dwell upon the extent of his originality, but I think it is clear that his analysis of the nature of *institutions* was little different from that offered by Sumner† and Giddings, and we have seen that there was nothing new in structural-functional analysis as such, and that all the other components of sociology had been, and were being, more richly developed elsewhere. Malinowski was not original in any major theoretical sense. His contribution lay in effectively bringing sociology to bear upon certain chosen fields and directions of effort.

First: he was one of the most powerful influences in re-shaping anthropology by effectively introducing sociology into it. Second: he succeeded in presenting a simplified 'schema' of sociological

* *Scientific Theory of Culture*, pp. 217–18.
† See *The Making of Sociology*, Vol. 1, p. 529.

analysis which was directly useful in field-research, for gaining new systematic knowledge about the simpler societies. Third: he himself led the way with such first-hand field-investigations of his own which not only contributed fresh knowledge of importance (and immense interest) in its own right, but stimulated many other similar studies. Fourth: it is probably true that his simplification of structural-functional analysis drew attention to sociology more than did the much more voluminous authors; and that he performed a service in clarifying a *useable* schema of systematic analysis which few had gleaned from other, larger tomes. (An essay of about 140 simple pages is easier to read than the volumes of a Spencer, a Hobhouse, or a Westermarck.) Still—this point is dubious: because it may well have been this over-simplification which gave rise to all the dangers and difficulties of the 'Error of Social Anthropology' which quickly followed after, But fifthly: all this amounts to the fact that Malinowski contributed much to the making of sociology by establishing its effective use and application in the study of an entire 'category' of societies—the existing 'pre-literate' societies— which had not previously been studied in this way. Since his day, and largely as a result of his efforts and influence, a wide body of knowledge about these societies has been produced.

2
A. R. Radcliffe-Brown:
A Natural Science of Society

Like Malinowski, Radcliffe-Brown was clearly an exciting and effective teacher. He held prominent professorial appointments in several parts of the world—in Australia, Africa, the United States, and Great Britain (where he held the Chair of Social Anthropology at Oxford)—and his teaching influence was, quite literally, of an international scale. He therefore made an enormous contribution to the spread and development of the subject which can never properly be estimated by a critique of our own kind—which must rest necessarily upon an analysis of his published ideas; and this is particularly true in this case, as he himself tended not to set too much store by his written pieces. Indeed, the collections of those of his articles and lectures which focused especially upon *theory* were published in book-form chiefly at the instigation of students and colleagues, and when it is borne in mind that these included Professor Evans-Pritchard and scholars of like stature the quality of this teaching experience can only be appraised as having been of the very highest order. Similarly, Radcliffe-Brown was as strongly influential as Malinowski in bringing about the theoretical re-orientation of field-research in anthropology and in undertaking such studies himself: therefore contributing fresh knowledge of the simpler societies and a fresh example of the new, more analytical, and more effective methods of study. All this—and it is a lot—must be fully acknowledged and appreciated at the outset.

There is no doubt whatever that, together with Malinowski, Radcliffe-Brown was the crucial influence in re-shaping anthropology in the light of sociological analysis, and in contributing much to the making of sociology by applying it effectively to the study of the still existing pre-literate societies. There is no doubt, either, that—in many important respects—his theoretical position was considerably in agreement with the ideas of Malinowski and of all the other theorists we have considered. Yet—at the same time—qualifications must be made in two main directions. First: there were differences between himself and Malinowski which (*a*) were not stated without ambiguity, (*b*) had wider implications than just the level of personal disagreement, and on which (*c*) Malinowski was right. This is to put complex matters very simply—but, I think, truly. Second: though Radcliffe-Brown's intellectual roots were many (in Montesquieu, Comte, Spencer and—contemporaneously— A. N. Whitehead; to mention but a few important influences), it was the influence upon him of Durkheim which was dominant; and this led to certain insufficiencies in his conceptual scheme. It is important that we should see the grounds for these qualifications clearly—not only for their own sake—but. chiefly because it is arguable that they contributed substantially to the *error* of conceiving 'Functionalist Social Anthropology' to be a distinctive theoretical 'school' (or position) within Sociology; an error which— in many places in his writing—Radcliffe-Brown was especially concerned to deny. It is even probable that they contributed *more* to this error than did the supposedly brash and 'irresponsible' claims of Malinowski. But these preliminary points mean—crucially—one thing: that Radcliffe-Brown's contribution is very difficult to deal with in a way that can satisfy oneself as to its fair-mindedness. Many of the very points which he put forward which possessed substantial importance were also, nonetheless, insufficiently worked out in some respects; so that one has to disagree with him on *some aspects* of points on which one still wishes to express some substantial agreement. And one has to disagree on some particular conceptions, whilst still wishing to present a positive appreciation of his contribution as a whole. An example lies in our title. One can warmly approve of his emphasis that 'man in society' is as much a part of 'nature' as any other element of the world of which we have experience. There is nothing, surely, 'non-natural' about man and his societies within the entire scheme of things. And one can warmly approve of his effort, therefore, to uphold a science of man and society as being just as valid a 'natural science' as any other. And yet—in his further insistence that sociology should adopt the *same logical methods* as the *other* '*natural*' sciences—one has to remark that he fell into error here in insufficiently recognizing that the distinctive attributes of human social behaviour were such as to require *different* logical methods. So—we are faced with difficulties.

Here, we will consider the chief points of his system of ideas one by one, in order—first of all—to show as clearly as possible the continuities and agreements with the ideas of others in his thought, but also—afterwards—to bring out equally clearly the *differences* which were of so much consequence. But we must bear in mind—as a particular focus of attention throughout—the fact that, though offering a clear outline of 'structural-functional' analysis for field-research in anthropology, Radcliffe-Brown certainly did *not* think of this in abstraction from all the other components of sociological analysis, and did *not* think of it as a clearly distinct 'school'. For

z

him—quite clearly—'Functionalism' did not exist. And for him—quite clearly—no new science of Social Anthropology had been created on the basis of it.

The Acceptance of Sociology: Continuities, Agreements and Disagreements

We noted earlier that Radcliffe-Brown thought of his theoretical notions as belonging to 'a cultural tradition of two hundred years', and we must now see plainly that his position was no more and no less than a full acceptance of the 'conspectus' of sociology as it had already been clearly stated. Like Malinowski, his awareness of the earlier making of sociology was quite extensive, and his own statement of what he took to be (and accepted as) the chief components of it was clear beyond any doubt whatever.* The subject he was concerned to promote and advance was, he said *'theoretical or comparative sociology'*. And it was Social Anthropology: *'that branch of sociology that deals with primitive societies'*—in which his own chief interests lay. What, according to his conception, was the nature of this science?

(I) THE SUBJECT-MATTER: 'FORMS OF SOCIAL LIFE'

First of all: a distinguishable science must have a clear and distinguishable subject-matter. What was that of sociology? What were the *observable phenomena* with which its theories were concerned?

They were, said Radcliffe-Brown, observable *forms of social life*. The complex actions and interractions of men within a territory which constituted their *process* of social life manifested certain *regularities*: ways of burying the dead; of marrying; of teaching the young; of making and exchanging goods; and many more besides. These regular *forms* of social life were the *facts* which theoretical sociology sought to understand and explain.

Sociology was the comparative theoretical study of forms of social life; and social anthropology was that branch of it which studied such forms amongst primitive peoples.

(II) THE SOCIAL SYSTEM: FORMS OF SOCIAL LIFE IN INTERCONNECTION AND INTERDEPENDENCE

Forms of social life, however, were not isolated or arbitrary. The

---

* The best statement is to be found in his own *Introduction* to *Structure and Function in Primitive Society*, Cohen & West, 1952.

central, guiding persuasion of theoretical sociology in approaching the study of these 'forms' was that they were interconnected and interdependent within a *system* of relationships of which each of them was a part. The recognition of the existence of total social systems; and of the '*social system*' as a kind of 'consensus' qualitatively distinct from other kinds—such as physical (mechanical) systems, and biological (organic) systems—was the other basic starting-point of sociology. Part of the assumption was that no one 'part' of a society—though it *could* be distinguished *as* a part for purposes of analysis and description—could be fully understood or explained excepting within this context of the whole. This basic idea, said Radcliffe-Brown, was introduced by Montesquieu and developed by Comte. It was ·a theoretical 'law' of 'social statics': not an empirical generalization alone, but 'a guide to investigation'.

'It gives us reason to think,' he argued, 'that we can advance our understanding of human societies if we investigate systematically the interconnections amongst features of social life.'*

(III) SOCIAL STATICS AND SOCIAL DYNAMICS

It is quite clear from the above point that Radcliffe-Brown also fully and explicitly accepted Comte's distinction between 'statics' and 'dynamics' in any empirical science: and in sociology no less than in any other. 'Statics' was concerned with the analysis and clarification of the *nature* of the *distinctive consensus studied* (in sociology: the nature, and conditions of existence of *social systems*.) 'Dynamics' was concerned to study the actual forms and varieties of this 'consensus' which existed in the world, and the patterns of order and change which they manifested in the *process* of actuality (in sociology: the patterns of order and change in the actual societies of history.) The analytical propositions of 'social statics' thus *guided* the substantive studies of 'social dynamics'.

Within his general acceptance of this division of the work of sociology, Radcliffe-Brown also clearly specified the necessity of some *classification* of social forms, and that this required the construction of '*types*'.

(IV) SOCIAL EVOLUTION

In connection with the classification of 'types' of social forms, and the study of order and change within and among them, Radcliffe-Brown also accepted not only the 'evolutionary perspective' in

* *Structure and Function in Primitive Society*, p. 6.

sociology—but also the specific all-embracing evolutionary theory of Herbert Spencer. Spencer, he thought, offered a satisfactory scheme of analysis for studying the emergence, maintenance, change, and dissolution of 'forms' (whether physical, organic, or social) within the entirety of nature. Furthermore, he accepted Spencer's basic proposition that there had been a process of diversification by which (*a*) 'many *different* forms' of organic or social life had been developed out of a 'very much smaller number of original forms', and (*b*) 'by which more complex forms of structure and organization' had arisen 'from simpler forms'. He did not entertain all of Spencer's 'pseudo-historical speculations', but, he maintained:

'We can give provisional acceptance to Spencer's fundamental theory . . . and that acceptance gives us certain concepts which may be useful as analytical tools.'*

(V) SOCIAL SYSTEMS AS ADAPTATIONAL SYSTEMS

One advantage of the evolutionary perspective, he argued, was that of seeing 'forms' (of both persisting order and change) as embodiments of processes of adaptation to environmental conditions; and this was applicable to 'social systems' as to all other 'forms'. Though not following Spencer with any closeness or detail here, Radcliffe-Brown did, nonetheless, distinguish *three* adaptational aspects of social systems: (1) the *ecological* (survival by accommodation to the outer physical environment), (2) the *institutional* (the internal achievement of an appropriate *order* of social life—regulating co-operation and conflict), and (3) the *cultural* (the socialization of individuals: the imparting of those qualities of mind, character and conduct required by the social order to its individual members). These, however, were only conceptually clarified aspects of what was a *total* adaptational system; and the *stability* and *continuity* of a social system were *aspects of* this adaptation. It is worthwhile to see how closely Radcliffe-Brown thought of this analysis as part of a theory of social evolution.

'The theory of social evolution,' he wrote, 'therefore makes it a part of our scheme of interpretation of social systems to examine any given system as an adaptational system. The stability of the system, and therefore its continuance over a certain period, depends on the effectiveness of the adaptation.'†

* *Structure and Function in Primitive Society*, p. 8.
† *Ibid*, p, 9

(VI) STRUCTURAL-FUNCTIONAL ANALYSIS

The study of order and change as an adaptational process within the perspective of social evolution (within which there was an increasing differentiation of more complex social forms from earlier, simpler ones) could only be accomplished by an analysis of *elements of social structure* and their *functional interconnections*. In short, the analysis of social systems had to take the form of *structural-functional analysis*.

Persons were not related *arbitrarily* in their actions in social life; their relationships followed definite regulated procedures. There existed regular *forms of interrelationship* (in the family, economic activity, religion, government, law), or *social institutions*. These were the units of sociological analysis; and it is most interesting to notice that Radcliffe-Brown defined institutions in terms of 'norms'. Yet again, we see the recognition that it was *values* which lay at the heart of the process of institutionalization. His definition was this:

'An institution is an established norm of conduct recognized as such by a distinguishable social group or class . . . institutions refer to a distinguishable type or class of social relationships and interactions.'*

Such regulated institutions therefore always referred to *groups* (or *classes*) and specified *relationships within* them and also *among* them (within the social system as a whole). Radcliffe-Brown also distinguished *organizations* of *activities* (with internal structures of *roles*) from *institutionalized relationships* (with internal structures of *positions*), but this is of no real consequence here.

The *function* of an institution was the part it played (the contribution it made) to the *process* of the social system as a whole; and in clarifying this, Radcliffe-Brown used the 'organic analogy' in exactly the same way as Spencer had done. In an organism, a *structural organ* (say, the heart) fulfils a *function* by making some essential contribution to the *process* of *the whole* (pumping the blood throughout the body). The continued existence of the whole depends upon the interrelated functioning of all the parts. *Structure, function,* and *process* are then, he argued, essentially related aspects of the *system* as a whole. Continuity and change alike—of social 'forms'—can only be analysed in terms of them.

Now for the moment we will not stop to mention critical differences in all these points; these can come later. But it will be readily agreed that none of these ideas so far outlined on the nature, definition, and elements of sociology were either exceptional or original. They were a simple statement of some of the basic notions made clear

* *Structure and Function in Primitive Society*, p. 10.

by the earliest founders of the subject. Nothing more. But—before coming to criticism—let us go further and specify all the other agreements of this kind which were to be found in 'A Natural Science of Society' as well as in the papers of 'Structure and Function in Primitive Society': simply to make it abundantly clear that Radcliffe-Brown accepted the entire 'conspectus' of sociology.

(VII) SCIENCE AND PHILOSOPHY: THE ABANDONMENT OF METAPHYSICS

His discussion of scientific method and the role of hypothesis in science was, in fact, extremely limited when compared with earlier writers like Comte and Mill, but, at least, his conclusions were similar, and one point especially was well worth the making. His agreed conclusions were that metaphysical speculations (or dogmas) were to be dismissed because they went beyond all bounds of testability, and that scientific methods alone were capable of providing testable generalizations: the only knowledge which could serve as a reliable basis for both prediction and action. His worthwhile point was that science and philosophy could never sensibly be divorced from each other. As one can imagine in someone much influenced by Whitehead: there was nothing of a narrow 'scientism' about his position.

'In so far as the scientist is incapable of philosophical speculation,' he wrote, 'he will make little contribution to the advancement of his science; and in the measure in which the philosopher fails in the logic required in science, his contributions lack significance for the advancement of knowledge.'*

(VIII) THE DIVISION OF THE SCIENCES ON THE BASIS OF THE NATURAL 'SYSTEMS' WHICH THEY STUDY

Within the context of this general agreement about the nature of science, Radcliffe-Brown also accepted the position of Comte and others that each particular science could be defined in terms of the particular 'consensus' of phenomena which it studied. Each was concerned to establish 'laws' about the 'events' and the 'relations between them' which characterized that 'natural system' (that 'conceptually isolated phenomenal reality') which was its defined subject-matter. Each 'natural system' could be divided into its 'units' and the 'relations' between them, and—in the case of the social system—its units were human beings in 'sets of behavioural events' and its relations were 'social' relations.

* *Structure and Function in Primitive Society*, p. 10.

(IX) SOCIOLOGY DISTINCT FROM PSYCHOLOGY

On the basis of this distinction between 'levels' of phenomena, or kinds of 'natural system', Radcliffe-Brown also agreed with many other writers that Sociology was distinct from Psychology. Sociology was to Psychology, he thought, as Physiology was to Chemistry: there was a clear distinction of *level* between them. However, his discussion of this entire question was very slender and insufficient, and we shall criticize it later.

(X) THE COMPARATIVE METHOD ESSENTIAL

Like Malinowski and all other writers, Radcliffe-Brown also insisted that the Comparative Method was crucial to sociology—as the only alternative to artificially controlled experiment. Indeed, his emphasis was almost exactly that of Durkheim and Weber—that the Comparative Method was essential for purposes of *testing* theories—though it was not worked out in anything approaching the same detail.

'Experiment in the laboratory,' he wrote, 'is not essential. What *is* important is comparison of two or more instances of certain things . . . if there is to be a natural science of human societies, its method will be the method of comparing, one with another, social systems of different kinds.'*

And the *advance* in the efficacy and accuracy of sociology, he argued, rested really on the improvement (and discovery) of techniques and procedures by which ever more exact comparisons could be made.

One of the major difficulties lay in the more accurate *definition* of society and the units of societies themselves, but also in the problems of *classification*. It was the problem of constructing clear '*types*' for classification and comparison to which he chiefly drew attention. An accurate 'taxonomy', a reliable 'social morphology', he argued, was an indispensable part of sociological analysis.

(XI) SOCIAL SYSTEMS WITHIN SOCIETY AS A WHOLE

It is also a point worthy of note that Radcliffe-Brown thought of 'social systems' as manifesting a very wide range—from the simplest to the most complex set of relationships—within society as a whole. A 'social system' was any ordered pattern of interaction within which people found 'some convergence of their interests'. Thus—the inter-action of a shop-salesman and a client in the purchase of a hat

* *A Natural Science of Society*, Free Press, 1964, p. 38.

(the ordered interrelationships of two people only)—was a 'social system', just as the enormous pattern of inter-action involved in, say, a national conference of trade unions, or the re-organization of a large industry, or a governmental ministry. A *society* was therefore a totality of many (small, large; simple, complex) 'social systems' within it. Within the total *institutional structure* with all its *functional interconnections* an analysis of all these '*social systems*' was possible. It will be seen in this that, for Radcliffe-Brown as for others, the 'units' of social structure were *regulated acts* resting upon *values*; and human behaviour—from individual conduct to massive organization—could be systematically observed, analysed, studied, in these terms.

(XII) SOCIAL COAPTATION AND SOCIALIZATION

Radcliffe-Brown did not give much attention to the socio-psychological processes whereby human individuals became *social persons*—vested with the ways of feeling, thinking and behaving required of them within the institutional order; but his limited discussion of the whole matter was in agreement with those of others. Whereas *instinct* regulated behaviour among other animal species, the *acquisition of culture* regulated the behaviour of men in social systems. *Coaptation* was the 'standardization of the behaviour of individuals' in society. Culture was thus an aspect of social systems and was imposed by rules and norms. But this imposition was not purely a matter of external compulsion (though this was certainly there), it was also a matter of coming to share a 'common set of ways of *feeling* and ways of *thinking*'. 'Society', he said, 'is fiduciary.' It involved—within the structure of society and within the individual personality alike—*sentiments* and *beliefs*, and Radcliffe-Brown discussed these in terms of meaningful communication within the context of *symbols* of all kinds—of revered things and persons, of language, of gestures, etc.

All this is so much in keeping with conceptions of the other sociologists that no comment is needed; but it is worth emphasizing—in getting our perspectives right—that Radcliffe-Brown's treatment of these theories was very much more limited than theirs. Like Mead, he was one of the few people who seems to have been aware of A. N. Whitehead's essay on *Symbolism*,* but, peculiarly—since his 1937 seminar was held at the University of Chicago—I cannot find that he made any reference to Mead, or to Cooley. His references were continually to Durkheim and those French scholars who

* *Symbolism: Its Meaning and Effect*, A. N. Whitehead (Barbour-Page Lectures, University of Virginia), 1927. C.U.P., 1928.

followed him. This seems to me to have been a peculiarly blinkered focus.

His critical attack in this seminar was reserved for Adler (who had tried to present Psychology as the single, all-embracing science of man) and Sorokin (who was—for Radcliffe-Brown—so patchy in his eclecticism as to have no theoretical direction at all); but how he could have ignored Cooley and Mead in this discussion is, for me, inexplicable.

Still—his general agreement was clear.

(XIII) FUNCTIONAL CONSISTENCY AND STRUCTURAL PRINCIPLES

In his entire treatment, Radcliffe-Brown was concerned to emphasize that though it was possible to distinguish elements of social structure conceptually—for purposes of analysis and description—there was a close inter-operational connection within society as a total process of social life. There was a reciprocal *involvement* of the parts in each other, and thus a *functional consistency* which pervaded them all.* The rules, sentiments, beliefs, usages in a society could not be sharply separated into 'economic, familial, educational, religious, and so on', but possessed an interconnected consistency which to some extent pervaded all these institutional areas.

Now it is important here to notice that Radcliffe-Brown quite explicitly did *not* claim that there existed some sort of total functional *integration* or *harmony* or *unity* in society. This postulate of 'functional consistency' was, in the first place, a *conceptual abstraction*; but it rested on reasonable suppositions and much observation of many societies, and could therefore be held *as a guide for investigation*. But he insisted strongly that the *degree* of such consistency varied, and was no doubt likely to vary, from society to society. But it was an important entailment of the conception of 'social systems' that the nature and degree of the functional consistency that did exist in the institutional framework of society should be a part of any empirical investigation.

* It is of much interest to note that (compare Pareto, p. 586) Radcliffe-Brown argued that the 'organic' analogy was more appropriate than the analogy of a 'mechanical' system for clarifying the nature of 'society': its parts and their functional inter-connections in the entire *process* of the social life of the whole. See: *A Natural Science of Society*, p. 86:
'I would like to suggest that the closest analogies which we shall get in social science are not with the physical sciences but with biology and physiology. To make an analogy between a society and a physiological system is less open to fallacy than to make one between society and a mechanical system.'
This is an emphasis much more important than it seems. See our earlier discussion of Pareto, p. 614, Section (ii).

This, it can be seen, was part of Comte's conception of the 'consensus' of social systems, and also—more apparently—Sumner's conception of the 'strain towards consistency' among the structural elements of a society.

Following upon this emphasis upon 'functional consistency', Radcliffe-Brown then also claimed that there existed certain definable 'structural principles' which were of a more abstract nature than institutions as such, and, again, inter-penetrated them all. The example he gave was 'The Abstract Structural Principle of Justice', and this, he claimed was *characteristic of all social systems*. This was the principle 'of just retribution', 'of an equivalent return: good for good, evil for evil, or, in the last instance, indemnification for injury'. It was a universal principle which entered into relationships in all social systems; and universal experiences such as vengeance, guilt, expiation, social indignation, punishment, could not be understood except in terms of it.

Here, we need not go into this example in any detail, but it is very much worth our while to notice that the nearest Radcliffe-Brown could come (this was how he himself expressed it) to the statement of a universal structural principle was, in fact, the statement of a universal *moral* principle. Again, we see that *values*; some conception of *justice* in the regulation of human activities and relationships; was held to lay at the heart of all institutionalization. And, indeed, the one universal proposition about the attributes of social systems on which Radcliffe-Brown was prepared to stand firm was this.

'I will', he wrote, 'give you one statement I believe: "Every human society has a system of morals." Note that is not a positivist statement; it is not a statement of an observation of several societies. It is a statement I believe true—a natural law—true of all societies that have ever existed, that exist now, that will ever exist. It is a statement which is intended to be true of the whole class of societies. I am suggesting that of such are the fundamental propositions which we want to discover and prove.'*

There is no doubting the definiteness of that statement. In all this, however, Radcliffe-Brown's chief insistence was to *deny* the idea that *institutional parts* could be abstracted from their context in the social system and satisfactorily studied in isolation, and, on the contrary, to *uphold* the idea that the institutions of a total society were *essentially* interrelated within a common *functional consistency* (outside of which they could not fully be known and understood) and that there were certain common *structural principles* which made it incorrect even to 'separate' specific institutions

* *A Natural Science of Society*, p. 72.

(economic, educational, etc.) too far. The *whole society* should be the central focus of sociological analysis, just as it was the recognition of this 'consensus' which was its central 'raison d'être'.

(XIV) ONLY ONE SCIENCE OF SOCIETY: THEORETICAL SOCIOLOGY

Following upon this last emphasis, Radcliffe-Brown also maintained that there could only possibly be *one* theoretical science of society, and that science could *not* be psychology.* It could not be psychology because the *associational* level of human experience and behaviour could not be *reduced* to pre-social psychological elements. And *special* sciences—of economic systems, political systems, religious systems, etc.—were not possible, and not valid, because such *institutional areas* could not soundly be isolated from the total social systems and social processes of which they were parts.

Radcliffe-Brown's discussion of this large theme of the relations between the social sciences was, again, very much more limited— neither as full nor as accurate—as the earlier treatment of men like Comte and Mill, and his rejection of economics as a special social science went farther than it should. Even so, his conclusions were again very much in agreement with all the other positions with which we are familiar.

There is, then, no doubt whatsoever that Radcliffe-Brown was *not* in any sense seeking to create a new 'school' of 'Functionalism' and a new 'science' of 'Social Anthropology'. His concern was to support, clarify, and advance 'theoretical, comparative sociology' and to see it applied effectively to the study of the 'primitive' societies in particular; and we have seen that his 'structural-functional' analysis was only a part of his acceptance of the entire 'conspectus' of sociology.

We must now, however, come to the qualifications which we mentioned earlier.

The Differences and Limitations of Radcliffe-Brown's Position

In his discussion of almost all the points mentioned above—on which, as we have seen, he was in general agreement with others— Radcliffe-Brown adopted certain positions, stipulated certain limitations, made certain assertions, which were sometimes strangely

---

* Here, he was especially rebutting Adler, but, for us, his point has a wider range of agreements.

and unnecessarily deprecatory, sometimes ambiguous, and, in the long run, unfortunately false. We will look at some of the major issues of this kind not only for the sake of critical appraisal alone, but also—perhaps the most important matter—in order to lay bare and eliminate some of the errors which have crowded about 'Functionalism' since his time.

(1) A DEPRECATION OF EARLIER AND OTHER ACHIEVEMENTS

One feature of Radcliffe-Brown's treatment which is difficult to understand was his frequent tendency to belittle—and not even to trouble to elaborate—the conceptual accomplishments of his predecessors. This was strange because, whilst acknowledging them, he did little more than draw their ideas together in a much simplified manner, and—if he had known them thoroughly, which we must suppose he did—he must also have known that their own conceptual and theoretical work was very much more considerable and detailed than his own. And it was harmful because it conveyed the impression —to those who did not know the earlier theorists—that his own simple formulations were *original*: even that they constituted an *advance*. In this sense the much simplified formulation of the 'structural-functional analysis' of social systems came to be adopted as a clear advance upon the much more profound theoretical discussions of which they *were* simplifications; and—thereafter— amendments which had to be made to these simplifications (in order to take other dimensions of social complexity into account) came themselves to be thought 'original'—instead of being not only re-discoveries of America, but also distorted views of the shore! Let us note just a few examples of this.

First: when arguing (in 1937) that a theoretical science of society was *possible*, Radcliffe-Brown nonetheless claimed: '. . . *that such a science does not yet exist in its elementary beginnings*'. He then went on to pronounce that the development of such a science depended upon the improvement of the comparative method and then the undertaking of a 'systematic comparison of societies of diverse types'. This would require, he wrote:

'. . . (a) the continuous improvement of our methods of observing and describing societies; (b) the elaboration and exact definition of the funda- mental concepts required for the description, classification and analysis of social phenomena; and (c) the development of a systematic classification of types of societies.'*

* *A Natural Science of Society*, p. 4.

Now to say that sociology did not exist in its elementary beginnings in 1937 was simply ludicrous. To say that, and then to do no more than offer an over-simplified outline of some of its components was even more so. But the air given in all the later proposals as to the main components of the analysis of social systems was one of originality and advance, whereas, in fact, the discussion of every single element was (as we have seen) very much richer in the earlier theorists than anything which he himself put forward. Radcliffe-Brown's sociology was not in any sense an 'advanced' theoretical apparatus *derived from* the 'tradition of two hundred years'; it was *nothing more than* a simplified regurgitation of some of the elements of that many-dimensioned tradition.

In exactly the same way, when speaking of the concepts required for a science of society, Radcliffe-Brown wrote:

'I am suggesting that we have not yet thought of the important concepts for social science. These are still to be discovered and developed and defined.'*

This, again—after all the conceptual work which, as we have seen, preceded him; which he himself drew upon; and which was very much more thorough than anything he himself produced—was a peculiarly deprecating didacticism amounting almost to arrogance.

Consider, too, his statements about the *classification* of societies. Having seen (as we have), all the thought that had gone into this problem of classification throughout the nineteenth century and during the early decades of the twentieth (even leaving aside Weber, whose work might not have been well known), is there not something positively off-putting about a personal didacticism which can say this:

'I would suggest that an examination of the other sciences immediately suggests that the first step in social science will be to undertake the task of taxonomy and classification, and in the first instance, the classification of social systems themselves. I propose that no scientific study of societies can get very far until we have made some progress towards a classification of social systems into whatever types, groups, or classes suggest themselves as expedient, that is, likely to lead to valid generalizations with respect to all societies.'†

Radcliffe-Brown was well aware that much had been said on these matters; he himself mentioned Comte, Spencer, Durkheim, Steinmetz, and Le Play; but his verdict on them was:

'. . . if we look at what has been done, we can see that we have hardly taken the first steps toward a scientific classification.'‡

* *A Natural Science of Society*, pp. 28–9.   † *Ibid.*, p. 33.   ‡ *Ibid.*, p. 33.

Now nobody would wish to claim too much for the several systems of classification put forward, but very substantial comparative studies had been accomplished on the basis of them, and to shrug them off in this slight way was inexcusable. Especially inexcusable in that Radcliffe-Brown himself offered no proposals which even began to come near the clarity of the classifications he put aside. Indeed, he even misunderstood some of these. Thus he criticized Hobhouse on the basis of his classification of the simpler peoples alone, completely ignoring the more complex classification in *Morals in Evolution* (which was published in 1906). And again, bearing in mind all the thought which had been devoted to the *complexities* in the way of accomplishing clear criteria of classification was it not positively jejune to say:

'I do not want to discuss at this point the classification of societies, but merely to remark that societies are exceedingly complex. There is an enormous number of difficulties in the way of any satisfactory classification. All I want to say at the moment is that we cannot get anywhere particularly until we have established classifications.'*

But did Radcliffe-Brown *ever* provide a better system of classification? To the best of my knowledge, he did not. The nearest he came was to propose a grouping of societies into 'types' in a very inductive way: i.e. when, after having gathered descriptive studies of many of them, you found that they possessed common attributes.† 'It is a matter of empirical determination to discover that they all possess certain abstract characteristics in common', he wrote.† The facile nature of such a statement, after the systems we have examined, requires no comment.

The fault of such a manner of acknowledging earlier theorists, but not elaborating their thought and not urging students to the study of them, but simply moving to a highly simplified statement of some of their notions as constituting an advance upon them, and as a basis for further advance, was that a platform for work and discussion was erected which gave a false picture of the level and detail of accomplishment at which the subject had arrived. It is easy for students to appear original if they are ignorant of all that the past has taught. And one's own personal 'suggestions' and 'proposals' can easily seem original to those who have not read many books in the subject. Such criticism of earlier positions might possibly be justified if real conceptual advancements were proposed in their place, but when this is not so, but the conceptual pronounce-

* *A Natural Science of Society*, p. 34.   † *Ibid.*, p. 73.

ments put forward are more limited and less sufficient than they— then real dangers of scholarship are afoot.

(II) A DEPRECATION OF OTHER ANTHROPOLOGICAL POSITIONS: THE STUDY OF CULTURE

In a similar way, Radcliffe-Brown flatly opposed certain other positions within anthropology, and all I wish to say in drawing attention to this point is that unfortunate and unnecessary ambiguities were created which, in the long run, led to error on his part. We must look at several issues of this kind, but here at the study of *'culture'* in particular. In this, as in a few following points, there were significant differences between Radcliffe-Brown and Malinowski. The issues, however, went beyond their own supposed disagreements, and the ambiguities and insufficiencies were (in my judgment) on Radcliffe-Brown's side.

On this one question, Radcliffe-Brown was quite emphatic. There could, he claimed, be no science of *culture*; and this seemed to set aside the 'Cultural Anthropologists' (among whom some have set Malinowski, and—later—Margaret Mead and Ruth Benedict) from those who focused their analysis upon *social structure*. In many ways, Radcliffe-Brown thought the concept of culture vague: so much so as not to lend itself to the systematic study of societies; and he thought that studies of 'culture contact' (of which he specified Malinowski's proposals for studies in Africa) were misleading in that they lost sight of the actuality of detailed inter-mixings of individuals and groups in sequences of behaviour. No one would wish totally to deny the force of some of his criticisms here. But his chief emphasis was *not at all* that culture did not exist in social systems, only that it could not properly be studied or understood excepting in relation to the *institutional order* of social systems.

Indeed, as we have seen in his treatment of 'coaptation' and socialization he insisted on the concept of *culture* to distinguish the regulating basis of human societies from that of animal societies— which was that of *instinct*. And he was very definite about this.

'Earlier,' he wrote, 'I put a taboo on the word "culture". I wish to revoke that taboo now for two reasons.'*

One was the distinction between animal and human societies mentioned above. The other was because, without it, he could not satisfactorily conceptualize the process of coaptation. We have seen,

---

* *A Natural Science of Society*, p. 90.

too, that this involved a full analysis of sentiments, beliefs, rules, norms, and the symbols of the social order—including, especially, language. Radcliffe-Brown's position, then, turned out to be only this:

'You cannot have a science of culture. You can study culture only as a characteristic of a social system. Therefore, if you are going to have a science, it must be a science of social systems. . . .

Social coaptation *implies* on the one hand a set of relations between persons, that is, social structure. Social coaptation in any society *is* the standardization of the behaviour of the individuals in the society. In animal societies that standardization is by instinct; in human societies we refer to that standardization by the term "culture". Neither social structure nor culture can be scientifically dealt with in isolation from one another.'*

But as soon as we have this kind of qualification, it becomes perfectly clear that there existed no difference between Radcliffe-Brown and Malinowski on this score whatever. For Malinowski quite clearly analysed the total socio-cultural system which constituted a society in terms of its structured institutional order. *Institutions* were the 'isolates' for structural-functional analysis and the many-sided 'culture' of the social order was systematically analysed in close relation to (as part of) these institutions. There was therefore no difference here—at least on this specific point alone. The difference was an *apparent* one.

(III) THE CONCEPT OF FUNCTION

This kind of apparent difference was very real, however, in some of its other implications, and here very important issues were raised. It will be remembered that for Malinowski 'culture' was essentially *instrumental*. Men were (amongst other things) conscious, feeling, thinking, purposive, acting beings. They sought ends, and the collective creation of culture was instrumental in the attainment of them. The *functions* of institutions were not only, therefore, their interacting operations with other institutions in the over-all maintenance of order, but also the serving of differing levels of *needs*: basic, instrumental, and integrative. For Radcliffe-Brown, however, this was not so. The *function* of an element of social structure was only and always the contribution which it made to the activity of the whole.

Now the antagonism between the two men on this issue was quite evident. Malinowski, defending his fuller treatment of the functions of institutions, wrote:

* *A Natural Science of Society*, pp. 106–7.

'Functionalism would not be so functional after all, unless it could define the concept of function not merely by such glib expressions as "the contribution which a partial activity makes to the total activity of which it is a part", but by a much more definite and concrete reference to what actually occurs and what can be observed ... such a definition is provided by showing that human institutions, as well as partial activities within these, are related to primary, that is, biological, or derived, that is, cultural needs.'*

The 'glib expression' which he quoted was, of course, Radcliffe-Brown's; and it is instructive to see the context of the quotation because this reveals the clear dangers of Radcliffe-Brown's position. The quotation was drawn from his paper: *On the Concept of Function in Social Science* (American Anthropologist, 1935.)

'By the definition here offered "function" is the contribution which a partial activity makes to the total activity of which it is a part. The function of a particular social usage is the contribution it makes to the total social life as the functioning of the total social system. Such a view implies that a social system (the total social structure of a society together with the totality of social usages in which that structure appears and on which it depends for its continued existence) has a certain kind of unity, which we may speak of as a functional unity. We may define it as a condition in which all parts of the social system work together with a sufficient degree of harmony or internal consistency, i.e. without producing persistent conflicts which can neither be resolved nor regulated.'†

Now Radcliffe-Brown immediately insisted (and we have noted the same emphasis before) that the 'functional unity' of a social system was a 'guiding hypothesis' only; but it is quite clear from this quotation that this was a conception of a social system with functionally inter-operating parts—and the function of any part was its contribution to the functioning of the whole. This was a very different picture from Malinowski's picture of 'partly autonomous, partly interdependent' institutions which were the regulated activities of purposive men. The 'teleological' aspects of the human mind; of men in their practical activities; had been lost sight of. The *articulated system*, as such, had come into the foreground of the picture. And this was no accident.

(IV) PURPOSE IN SOCIAL ACTION

The fact is that Radcliffe-Brown—as a direct outcome of his acceptance of Durkheim—rejected 'purposive' explanations of social

* *Scientific Theory of Culture*, p. 159.
† *Structure and Function in Primitive Society*, p. 181.

727

action, and was thus involved in both ambiguity and error. His ambiguity was plain—but difficult to understand.

On the one hand, he made the 'units' of the science the observable *actions* of men, and there is no doubt that he regarded 'social systems' as sets of relationships in which men found some convergence of *interests*. Let us look at a particular example which he gave.

'. . . a social system can be said to exist whenever two human beings come together and find some convergence of their interests. For example, I enter a store. I want to get a hat. The clerk wants to get rid of a hat. We enter into a relationship; he shows me a hat; I don't like it; I say I don't want that hat. He says it is a good hat. The system develops as he brings out more hats and I try them on. Finally, I either buy a hat and the system closes or I go off without one and the system is broken.'*

Now if there were no *motives*, no *ends*, no *purposes* in this instance, there would be no *interests* and not the slightest reason why there should be any *beginning*, *sequence*, or *end* of this 'social system' whatever. Indeed (as Weber would have said) it would be impossible to *conceive* and *perceive* this sequence of 'events' as a 'system of social action' *without* the interpretation of *meaning*.

But what did Radcliffe-Brown himself say about the use of the concept of '*interests*'—which he agreed to be indispensable for the definition of distinctively *social* relationships? He wrote as follows.

'*Interest* implies purposive behaviour. I use the term similarly to the use of the concept of *force* in physics. Force and interest are not real entities. *Force* is a logical fiction, a convenient concept by which we can describe a certain type of physical phenomena. *Interest* is a similar logical fiction for describing biological phenomena; it is a short-hand description of a series of acts of behaviour—not itself a real entity, but valuable in describing phenomenal reality.'†

Now this is a most important defect—a clear error—in Radcliffe-Brown's position, and we must see it clearly. Finding that he was *compelled* (by the distinctive attributes of human social relationships and actions) to introduce concepts implying *purpose*, he sought to utilize a terminology that—even so—*reduced* them to the kinds of *events* dealt with by the other natural sciences. This was a complete failure to see the distinctive conceptual levels and what this distinction implied for theory and method. It is unbelievable that he could have accepted the bogus nature of his terminological usage. The 'interest' of the buying and selling of a hat (which *alone* dis-

* *A Natural Science of Society*, p. 59.   † *Ibid.*, pp. 43–4.

tinguished this as a meaningful *social* relationship) was now not an actual empirical component of the situation—but only a 'logical fiction' to enable the investigator to link 'events' in his 'description of phenomenal reality'. Again, let us notice the peculiar blindness that *that alone* can be said to be scientific which deals only with *phenomenal* reality. It is a pity that A. N. Whitehead did not influence Radcliffe-Brown more! Consider the following.

'It does not matter for science where one draws the dividing line between purposive and mechanical behaviour. An amoeba has a positive, purposive interest in food, a negative, purposive interest in danger. We cannot describe those purposive acts in terms of forces, so we describe them in terms of interests. It may be that some day we will have a way of describing an amoeba's behaviour in terms of forces rather than of interests. At present we are unable to describe purposive *human* behaviour except in some such terms as those of interest.'*

We cannot at the moment reduce human beings to the same level of phenomenal reality as amoeba—but, no matter!—one day we will; and then all will be scientifically well, and all manner of thing will be scientifically well. The Godot of science will have turned up at last. Meanwhile . . . we can get on with our 'logical fictions'.

In such a way does mistaken 'scientism' fob off artificiality on unsuspecting anthropologists!

For the moment we will leave this point—only remarking that other substantial borrowings from Durkheim, to which we shall refer later, made it even more clear that this rejection of 'purposive' explanation was Radcliffe-Brown's committed position. For now we can simply note how clearly in error this position was, and how that of Malinowski was much more correct and much more in keeping with the conceptions of the major sociological theorists.

(V) A LIMITED AND INSUFFICIENT CONCEPTION OF SCIENTIFIC METHOD IN SOCIOLOGY

The same error spilled over into (or was part of) Radcliffe-Brown's conception of the scientific method in its application to the study of human society. We have seen that he rejected metaphysics and upheld the methods of science in producing testable knowledge, and also that he was not by any means narrow in his views about the relations between science and philosophy. Even so his conception of science was entirely bounded by the methods employed by the 'natural sciences'; and his idea of rendering sociology 'scientific' was that of subjecting 'social systems' to study by the self-same

* *A Natural Science of Society*, p. 44.

methods as: '. . . those that are applied in the physical and biological sciences'.

The only concepts needed for science, he argued, were two: (1) events, and (2) relations between events; and science established 'natural laws' about them. 'Laws' were statements of regularities of various kinds:* statements about relations of actual connectedness, and statements about logical relations, and perhaps the chief distinction among them was between those which were quantifiable (or statistical) and those which were only statements of *relations*. As we have seen, Radcliffe-Brown saw sciences as being distinguished according to the 'natural systems' which they studied. But—in his entire treatment—there was never any consideration of the fact that human *actions* were a qualitatively different subject-matter from the *events* of nature; that they were *not* just *phenomenal*, and required meaningful interpretation for the very *perception*, let alone the *explanation*, of them; and that the recognition of this required *different* concepts and methods of science. Here again we can see (*a*) that this conception of science lent itself to a 'mechanistic' explanation of 'social systems' without reference to human purposes, and (*b*) that Malinowski's treatment of the question had, again, been much superior, and much more in keeping with the conclusions of most of the major sociologists.

In fact, Durkheim was the one exception to this; and it was the exception of Durkheim which produced the exception of Radcliffe-Brown.†

(VI) THE NARROWNESS OF CONCEPTION OF THE RELATIONS BETWEEN SOCIOLOGY AND PSYCHOLOGY

Radcliffe-Brown's considerations on the relations between Sociology and Psychology—though slight—were by no means all deserving of adverse criticism, and we shall comment on some aspects of them later. Here, however, we will concentrate only upon the limitations of his conception, and these, centrally, rested on the drawing of too sharp a dichotomy between the *individual* (as a psycho-physical entity) and *society* as a set of *social relations*. This, really, was an even sharper distinction than that drawn by Durkheim.

Radcliffe-Brown tried to specify clear relations between general

---

* Radcliffe-Brown's statements about various bases for 'natural laws'—theological, 'positivist', etc.; were very superficial, and that concerning 'positivism' was a sheer misunderstanding.
† It may be noted that Radcliffe-Brown accepted Durkheim's 'basic postulate' that 'social facts' were to be treated (i.e. studied) as if they were 'things'. See *A Natural Science of Society*, Appendix, p. 151.

psychology, sociology, and the mid-way subject of social psychology; and some of his propositions came quite close to those of John Stuart Mill. But the chief point worth emphasis is that after the work of Cooley and Mead in particular, the division of subject-matter which he drew between psychology and sociology was not only unwarranted, but positively stood in the way of the social psychology which their concepts had opened up.

Whatever might be said about 'social psychology', Radcliffe-Brown's first and firm persuasion was that sociology (the study of 'social systems') was quite *distinct* from psychology: '. . . just as distinct as physiology is from chemistry.' He agreed that the two might come together—as in the study of coaptation—the way in which the individual mind grew in society; but his distinction was drawn sharply about the delineation of the *individual* on the one hand and a *social relation* (between two or more individuals) on the other. His statements were startlingly emphatic. The psychologist studied mental relations, 'mind', *within the individual.* The sociologist studied *relations between* individuals. But let us see how strikingly this distinction was conceived.

On the one hand, he wrote:

'No relationship *between two persons* can by my definition be a psychological relation.'*

And, on the other:

'The only psychological relations are those which exist within one mind . . .*
The moment you get outside the skin of that individual, you have no longer psychological, but social relations.'*

But nothing, of course, could be more dogmatic—and a dogma even contrary to Durkheim's whole conception. Chiefly, however, it took no account whatever of the 'social-mental complexes' of Cooley and Mead, and the clear fact that it is a sheer 'phenomenal' illusion to suppose that 'mental' or 'psychological' facts are bounded by the skins of individuals. The whole emphasis upon *communications* as a process of psychological growth for both 'self' and 'society' simultaneously was lost in the severity of Radcliffe-Brown's distinction. Indeed, this bounding of the psychological nature of the individual by his 'skin' could not have been better calculated to set off the difference between him and Cooley and Mead more sharply.

There was also something ambiguous (despite this sharp dis-

---

* *A Natural Science of Society*, p. 47.

tinction) in Radcliffe-Brown's position. For example in his discussion of norms and values in institutions, and in his discussion of 'co-aptation', he had laid great stress upon *sentiments*. When asking how a psychological might be distinguished from a sociological generalization, however, he said:

'. . . if it is a generalization with respect to what binds together human beings—marriage, or rank, or subordination, or superiority—it is a sociological generalization and it is not a psychological one . . .'*

But, of course, all the instances he mentioned here included, and indeed rested upon, *sentiments*. But sentiments were not *social relations*, though they were engendered within them; nor were they bounded by the *skins of individuals* though they were certainly experienced within them. In the sentiments, therefore, was a clear socio-psychological element of both individual and society that cut completely across his definitional boundaries!

This element too, therefore, was insufficient, and Malinowski was much the clearer of the two, but we shall see later that Radcliffe-Brown's treatment of particular empirical studies was such as not to be hindered by the constraints of his conceptual boundaries.

(VII) STATICS, DYNAMICS, AND HISTORY

We now come to one of the most difficult of considerations about Radcliffe-Brown's system, but it is probably the most important—in that, linked with his conception of the 'articulated social system', and his analysis of 'social systems' without full regard to the 'purposive actions' of men in society, it probably contributed more than any other single element to the peculiar characterization of '*Functionalism*' as a '*static*' analysis of society which could not, within itself, give an account of conflict or social change.

In almost all respects Radcliffe-Brown was clear on this issue—but the *effect* of his teaching seems to have been different from his intentions, and his introduction of one particular point seems (or, at least, so it seems to me) to have tipped the scales in favour of this misconception of 'static analysis'.

The chief points can be made briefly.

First: we have seen that Radcliffe-Brown completely accepted the Spencerian conception of social evolution. As part of this, he agreed completely that social systems were essentially *historical processes*. As part of this, he also agreed that *historical explanation* (as to how social systems had come to be what they were) was necessary and

* *A Natural Science of Society*, p. 52.

desirable when it could be reliably obtained. He was as much in favour of the historical as of the comparative method—*when it could be reliably employed*. Furthermore, he agreed that *as* processes in time, social systems *essentially changed*. There was nothing of Ward's 'fallacy of the stationary' here, either. Radcliffe-Brown focused the question here as: 'what is the way in which the social system manages to persist?'—and he distinguished two kinds of change: (1) the continuous changing re-adjustment within the same over-all institutional form of society as it persisted in time, accommodating itself to problems; and (2) major changes to meet large disturbances (internally or externally brought about) which produced a change in '*type*' of the society (e.g. say from tribe to civic nation). He was also clear (however one values the distinction—Malinowski thought it was 'hackneyed', and a 'philosophical red herring'!) in his distinction between 'nomothetic' and 'ideographic' studies: 'ideographic' being studies of particular empirical facts: 'nomothetic' being studies which sought to generalize. Sociology is certainly the latter, and history *might* be said to be the former, but, as Radcliffe-Brown well realized, there were now many historians who would not accept that as a valid distinction between the subjects.

In all these matters, Radcliffe-Brown was quite clear and we can be sure that he nowhere advocated something called a 'static' analysis of society, and nowhere denied either the historical nature of societies or the historical method of studying them. His one objection here—which all anthropologists share—was to the earlier method of *conjectural* history or *pseudo-historical* explanations which rested on no reliable evidence whatever. This he rejected, but, as he said quite clearly:

'This does not in any way imply the rejection of historical explanation but quite the contrary.'*

The one slight ambiguity lay in his discussion of 'Statics' and 'Dynamics' which he accepted (rightly) from Comte. This was by no means altogether unclear, and, in his full treatment of this, he certainly did not misunderstand Comte. Even so, there was a slight emphasis in his treatment to the effect that 'statics' studied the *conditions of existence* of social systems whereas 'dynamics' studied *conditions of change*; indeed, these were the expressions he used. But it was a slightly false emphasis, for Comte really meant that '*statics*' was the *analytical* part of sociology which clarified the nature of its subject-matter, the nature of the distinctive kind of 'consensus' which 'social systems' were; whereas '*dynamics*' was the employment of this analysis in the study of the actual varieties of

* *Structure and Function in Primitive Society*, p. 3.

social system which existed in the world—and which therefore were *essentially* historical kinds of facts. There was nothing in Comte's distinction to suggest that 'statics' was concerned to achieve a kind of 'snapshot' of *society in the moment* (in a condition of *stasis*, so to speak) whilst dynamics then studied it as moving through time. And Radcliffe-Brown did not really think this either— but his brief treatment *suggested* it, and perhaps the terms 'statics' and 'dynamics' themselves were then enough to clinch the error. For there is no doubt that *this* is the conception of statics and dynamics which has come to be prevalent among many: to such an extent that 'Functionalism' has been thought incapable of dealing with change, and has had to be 'amended' in order to 'improve' it as a mode of analysis for this task. The 'fallacy of the stationary' became as solid as a rock.

There was, however, one other notion of Radcliffe-Brown's which I think contributed to this result: this was his attendant distinction between 'synchronic' and 'diachronic' studies (another set of terms to bemuse students). The concepts were introduced to distinguish the studies of the two types of change mentioned above. Synchronic studies were concerned with the ways by which societies accommodated themselves to specific changes without undergoing a change of 'type'. Diachronic studies were concerned with the ways in which societies changed from one 'type' to another. Radcliffe-Brown thought this distinction essential, and thought synchronic studies the more fundamental of the two; and it may well be that it was his pre-occupation with the study of the pre-literate societies which led him to this emphasis. There is little doubt, however, that it was this distinction in conjunction with the slight emphasis in the interpretation of 'statics' and 'dynamics' which led to the 'fallacy of the stationary'.

Radcliffe-Brown plainly accepted that synchronic studies were, strictly speaking, impossible; yet he insisted upon their necessity. And there is something dubious about the entire distinction. He was quite clear that the separation of synchronic from diachronic problems was an 'abstraction', but then—having emphasized that *both* these studies were of kinds of *change*—he argued that, for the purposes of 'synchronic' studies, societies should be regarded as 'static'.

'. . . insofar as we treat a society only synchronically, we consider it as unchanging . . .

In studying a society synchronically one treats it as though it were persisting relatively unchanged.'*

* *A Natural Science of Society*, p. 88.

And yet, at the same time (and having stressed that synchronic investigations studied *one kind of change*—i.e. a changing adjustment of conditions and elements within the same 'type'), he argued that no society was unchanging for long.

'Fundamentally,' he wrote, 'societies do not remain unchanged. Certain societies which are pictured as remaining the same, change apparently, although not as rapidly as other social systems. Australian society does change, although it is very conservative. China, in spite of its alleged conservatism, has been undergoing rapid changes.'*

Nonetheless, Radcliffe-Brown insisted that without this distinction it would be impossible to arrive at generalizations as to how societies persist.

Now many issues are involved here, and it is not a matter we can resolve quickly, but most considerations suggest that the distinction is really of doubtful validity. First: the distinction between 'Statics' and 'Dynamics' seems to be quite sufficient. 'Statics' clarifies the *nature of the distinctive consensus of a social system*—*not* as a *static* phenomenon, but as an essentially historical kind of institutional actuality: a process of creative, ordered activity in time. 'Dynamics' uses this analysis to study actual, concretely existing societies: which *are* historically changing in the ways which Radcliffe-Brown suggests. This distinction therefore seems enough. Second: the two supposed *kinds* of change might well be *falsely* separated. Social changes of both kinds are *ways of persisting*. Why should they be separated? One may grow out of the other. The gradations may sometimes be imperceptible—*seeming* synchronic but *being* diachronic; and how is one to know if one studies a social system for a year, or some similar short period? Third: it is dubious to what extent it is really possible to study a social system *in the moment* without historical knowledge and interpretation. To look at a society through a-historical eye-balls is probably only to see the tip of an iceberg, so to speak; the massive actuality lies beyond immediate vision.

However, this is not an attempt to demolish the distinction, only to raise serious doubts about it. It is clear, on the other hand, that *synchronic* studies were (apparently) very well suited to the study of simple societies which were (apparently) *of a type*, and possessed no reliable historical records. I say *apparently* because contemporary anthropologists have found it necessary to question these assumptions. It is also clear that this distinction fitted very well into the schema of Durkheim (which Radcliffe-Brown adopted), and seemed to make plain the necessity of *both* a *historical and* a *functional*

* *A Natural Science of Society*, p. 89.

735

account in any full explanation of social facts. Even here one would like to take issue with Radcliffe-Brown, because he asserted—quite without supporting reason—that the process of history was *'always accident'*. These are large claims to drop without justification. Still . . . it would take us too far from our course to deal with every detail.

The point is that one can well see why the distinction had its appeal and its use to Radcliffe-Brown, and perhaps it had its justification, though there are grave doubts as to this. What is certain, however, is that—coupled with the distinction between 'statics' and 'dynamics'—this gave rise to a peculiarly different conception from that which had been intended. *Now*, it came to be thought that 'Functionalism' provided a *static analysis* of a society at one point of time; indeed that the 'structural-functional' method was appropriate for achieving such a static, functional analysis; and that 'theories of social change' were quite distinct and had to employ additional dimensions of analysis. This was an utter misconception, a complete error, and one which was to have far-reaching consequences—but one can see how it came about.

(VIII) THE UNCRITICAL ACCEPTANCE OF DURKHEIM

To say that Radcliffe-Brown was uncritical of Durkheim is not wholly true. He criticized Durkheim for his 'reification' of social facts, and, as we shall see, he critically amended some of his specific theories. Still, he fell into Durkheim's basic errors, so it is probably better to say he was not critical enough.

The extent of this *adoption* of Durkheim's sociology can most plainly be seen in the appendix of *A Natural Science of Society*—which consists of the notes which Radcliffe-Brown circulated for his seminar. These, it is only fair to say, were notes for *directing discussion* to significant points, but, in all the ensuing treatment, his commitment to them was perfectly clear. Here, we need only note those aspects of this commitment which substantiate the criticisms we have made.

We have seen that his rejection of the actuality of *purpose* in human activities and institutions, and his acceptance of scientific conceptions and methods which took 'purpose' to be of no account (i.e. his lack of awareness that *different* concepts and methods were required in human science), led him into a very limited conception of 'function' and of the 'social system' as an articulated set of institutional parts. The *functions* of *elements of structure* were solely the contribution they made to the articulated operation of the whole. The *system*, its *parts*, the *functions* of all its parts within the whole, and the functional *consistency* and *unity* of the whole, could be satisfactorily analysed without resort to *purposeful action* (though one had to employ the 'logical fictions' of 'interests'). We have seen furthermore that his treatment of the distinctions between 'statics and dynamics' and 'synchronic and diachronic' studies laid the basis (though not intending it) of the 'fallacy of the stationary'. The study of social systems in *static* (unchanging) conditions was distinguished from the study of social systems in conditions of *change*.

In his notes on Durkheim all these positions and emphases in his work were substantially reinforced; that is to say—his commitment to them was made even more plain. He claimed quite dogmatically, for example, that: 'Function must be rigidly distinguished from "purpose" and from "usefulness" . . .' and that: 'A social system is not purposive.' He seemed to think, too, that the objections to this were dispelled by pointing out that it was the social system which provided human beings not only with means, but also 'ends' (with 'instrumentalities' and 'evaluations'), and also with 'ostensible purposes'. But the 'ostensible purposes' of a social usage only *exceptionally* corresponded to its function. But he went further than this and asserted that:

'What are final ends for the individual (e.g. the pursuit of truth, beauty, and goodness) are, within the social system, means of *adaptation* and *integration*.'*

Now quite apart from the fact that *some* final ends which individuals have held have been *mal*-adaptive and *disruptive* within social systems (such ends do not need to be final ones either!) we can see here—very plainly stated—some other assumptions which Radcliffe-Brown built into his conception of articulated social systems: namely that the *functions* of institutions were essentially related to the *adaptation* and *integration* of entire systems. If 'functions' were to be rigidly distinguished from 'purposes' or 'usefulness'—what *were* they? Radcliffe-Brown was very clear.

'The function of any social usage,' he wrote, '(or of any belief, idea, or sentiment, that is part of a social system) consists of the contribution which it makes to the "proper" or "essential" activity of the social system of which it is a part . . .†

The proper or essential activity of a social system is (*a*) to provide a certain *adaptation* to a particular environment and (*b*) to provide a certain *integration*, i.e. a uniting of individuals into an orderly arrangement. The

* *A Natural Science of Society*, p. 155. † *Ibid.*, p. 154.

function of any social usage (or belief) in a given social system is the totality of the effects it has in relation to adaptation and integration.'

Now—with all the qualifications that can properly be made on behalf of Radcliffe-Brown, in that the influences which stemmed from his conceptions were not always those which he intended—it is still surely the case that this kind of statement supplemented and reinforced solidly any tendency there was in his notions to suggest the 'functionalist' analysis of social systems in terms of 'functional consistency, unity, adaptation, and integration'. If people fell into error here, perhaps they could not be entirely blamed.

The fact is that this was a spilling over of the error of Durkheim into the re-formulated anthropology. Malinowski and Radcliffe-Brown together imported sociology into anthropology, but Radcliffe-Brown imported especially *Durkheimian* sociology—and this, it seems to me, was the largest single root of the 'Error of Functionalism and of Social Anthropology'. It is at least abundantly clear that Malinowski was free of all those conceptual insufficiencies which plagued Radcliffe-Brown's work with ambiguity and error.

Positive Contributions of Radcliffe-Brown's own 'system'

Having been adversely critical to a very considerable extent, and having made these necessary qualifications, we can now come back briefly to a more positive estimation of Radcliffe-Brown's contribution. Despite being open to all these grounds of criticism, it remains the case that, like Malinowski, he produced studies of the simpler societies of great influence and importance. It is not necessary to outline his own 'structural-functional' system in its entirety (as we did with Malinowski) because the nature of it is already plain,* and, in any case, it did not possess the kind of detailed analysis of 'institutions' which Malinowski presented. Two things can be selected for special emphasis.

(I) THE SCIENTIFIC CORRECTION OF THEORIES

The first contribution of real worth that stemmed directly from the application of the 'generalizing', 'comparative', and 'testing' approach of his conceptual system was that he subjected certain theories to test, and was able clearly to amend and advance them. Radcliffe-

* The clearest statement of it is to be found in three sections of *Structure and Function in Primitive Society:* (1) The *Introduction* (2) Ch. IX. *On the Concept of Function in Social Science,* and (3) Ch. X. *On Social Structure.*

Brown did not simply advocate the production of descriptive 'monographs' of isolated primitive societies. He systematically *compared* the knowledge of such societies to test specific theories about them. Here, we will briefly take three examples, and it may be said that in these studies of particular topics Radcliffe-Brown's work was infinitely more careful and exacting than our adverse criticisms of his conceptual apparatus would suggest, and also, that in each of them there was a cumulative reinforcement of a particular theoretical position which—after all—brought him into the closest agreement with the other sociological theorists, and on most important grounds. This we shall be able to bring together clearly as our statement of his second major contribution.

In 1929, Radcliffe-Brown produced a paper on *The Sociological Theory of Totemism.** In this, he accepted Durkheim's theory (as presented in 'The Elementary Forms of the Religious Life') as an important and permanent—but not a *complete*—theory of totemism. Durkheim had held that the totem (animal or plant) was 'sacred' to the group of which it was the totem, and that it symbolized the *social order* itself. It was the solidarity of society which was being symbolized, served, and worshipped in 'totemism' as the earliest form of religion. Radcliffe-Brown summarized Durkheim's position in the following way:

'A social group such as a clan can only possess solidarity and permanence if it is the object of sentiments of attachment in the minds of its members. For such sentiments to be maintained in existence they must be given occasional collective expression . . . all regular collective expressions of social sentiments tend to take on a ritual form. And in ritual . . . some more or less concrete object is required which can act as the representative of the group. So that it is a normal procedure that the sentiment of attachment to a group shall be expressed in some formalized collective behaviour having reference to an object that represents the group itself.
 . . . the theory is that the totem is "sacred" as Durkheim says, or is an object of ritual attitude, as I prefer to say, because it is the concrete representative or emblem of a social group. And the function of the ritual attitude towards the totem is to express and so to maintain in existence the solidarity of the social group.'†

This is an excellently clear statement—and we might note in it, again, the central emphasis upon *sentiments* and their perpetuation and reinforcement by *collective ritual expression*. Radcliffe-Brown agreed with this theory, but did not think it complete. Durkheim had held that the choice of totemic symbols—particular animals or

* Re-printed as Ch. VI in *Structure and Function in Primitive Society*.
† *Structure and Function in Primitive Society*, pp. 124–5.

plants—lay in the fact that they could be used in the graphic designing of totemic emblems. By comparative studies, however, Radcliffe-Brown showed that this could not be so: because in many tribes (and sections of tribes, and clans), no designs of the totems were made at all; and, in any case, he felt that this was too 'accidental' a basis of explanation of such a widely founded institution. But also, he demonstrated the existence of many cases in which animals or plants were objects of ritual—but where there was no practice of totemism. And even in totemic societies *some* of the animals or plants forming the objects of ritual were *not* of totemic significance. A satisfactory theory of totemism had therefore to be broader than that which Durkheim offered.

On the basis of the same comparative studies Radcliffe-Brown proposed an *amended* theory; not a complete rejection of Durkheim's ideas (with whose central emphasis he agreed), but an *amendment* of them to take into account these additional facts. His theory had two strands. First, he showed that particular animals, plants, or objects of nature on which men were dependent (and to which they were therefore intimately related) tended to become personified in myth and ritual as ancestors or heroes. This ritual attitude towards them was a *ritual relation between man and nature*. In the simplest case, a whole society would be related to the one single natural object (or to several such important objects). The second strand in the theory was that as a *segmentation of groups* took place within the total society, each group came to be distinguished by *one* object within the entire '*sacra*' of the society. Totemism, in short was a *ritual specialization* which coupled together (*a*) the ritual relations of men to nature, and (*b*) their ritual relations to each other in the process of group differentiation. It was a pattern of ritual which bound groups of men together in society, and the whole of the social order together with the order of nature.

All the totemic objects were of importance to the society as a whole, but each of them now had a special significance for a special group within the whole. Radcliffe-Brown believed that this process of totemic 'ritual specialization' was a very important principle in social development as a whole, and he gave other illustrations of it.

'. . . to take only one example . . . in the Roman Church the saints are sacred to all members of the church as a whole. But the church is segmented into local congregations and a congregation is often placed in a special relation to one particular saint to whom its chapel is dedicated. This is, I think, parallel to clan or group totemism.'*

* *Structure and Function in Primitive Society*, p. 127.

His theory therefore involved the two propositions:

(1) 'Any object or event which has important effects upon the well-being (material or spiritual) of a society, or any thing which stands for or represents any such object or event, tends to become an object of the ritual attitude.'*

And—given social differentiation or segmentation—

(2) '. . . that natural species are selected as representatives of social groups, such as clans, because they are already objects of the ritual attitude on quite another basis, by virtue of the general law of the ritual expression of social values stated above.'*

Again, let us notice that this was a ritual expression of social *values*. Concerning the link between *social organization* and men's relations to elements in their *natural* environment, Radcliffe-Brown wrote:

'Although there is always a danger in short formulas I think it does not misrepresent Australian totemism to describe it as a mechanism by which a system of social solidarities is established between man and nature.'†

And this introduced a very important element into his theory: namely, the suggestion that the commonplace distinction between the *social* order and the order of *nature* had to be considered very carefully if it was not to be misleading. For (by ritual and myth) the order of nature was made *a part* of the social order. In a sense the social order *included* the order of nature for the members of that society. A particular 'cosmology' was literally a part of their 'social structure'.

Radcliffe-Brown thus amended and extended Durkheim's theory of totemism not only in such ways as to correct it, but also to open up the entire theory of the nature and functions of religion in society in very important and promising ways. Having shown that 'totemism' was part of a larger pattern and process (a larger 'whole') of ritualization and organizational specialization, he then suggested that:

'. . . one important way in which we can characterize this whole is that it provides a representation of the universe as a moral or social order. Durkheim's . . . conception seems to have been that the process by which this takes place is by a projection of society into external nature. On the contrary, I hold that the process is one by which, in the fashioning of

* *Structure and Function in Primitive Society*, p. 129.   † *Ibid.*, p. 131.

741

culture, external nature, so called, comes to be incorporated in the social order as an essential part of it.

Now the conception of the universe as a moral order is not confined to primitive peoples, but is an essential part of every system of religion. It is, I think, a universal element in human culture.'*

This, clearly, was an important and intriguing step forward—which Radcliffe-Brown was himself to develop later; but here it is enough to see how, by employing his generalizing, comparative approach, he was able to test, and to improve upon specific theories. As with all the theorists of this period—the desire to move from theory to theories was a marked characteristic of his work. The clarification of his 'structural-functional' method had been for the better production of *new knowledge* and *testable theories*, and it was in producing the latter rather than in his conceptual analysis as such that his chief contribution lay.

Our consideration of the two other examples—on the subjects of 'Taboo' and 'Religion'—can be very brief because (in this place) they are only referred to as illustrations of the same point; but I want, even so, to stress certain aspects of them for reasons that will soon be very clear.

Radcliffe-Brown's discussion of *Taboo* was given in *The Frazer Lecture* in 1939 and was a similar kind of amending comment on Frazer's own conceptions. But also, it was a study which further emphasized the *first* proposition in his theory of totemism: namely that natural objects of importance in the life of men became objects of ritualization. Here, I wish only to note the emphases of Radcliffe-Brown's treatment (*a*) to show how they were the outcome of a consistent application of his conceptual system, and (*b*) to show that, again, their emphasis was upon the primary importance of *sentiments* and *values* in the institutions and rituals of society.

First, let us see the clear statement of his premises:

'A society consists of a number of individuals bound together in a network of social relations. A social relation exists between two or more persons when there is some harmonization of their individual interests, by some convergence of interest and by limitation or adjustment of divergent interests . . . the first necessary condition of the existence of a society is that the individual members shall agree in some measure in the values that they recognize . . .

Social relations . . . require the existence of common interests and of social values.'†

The *primacy* of values for the very existence of social relations

* *Structure and Function in Primitive Society*, p. 131.   † *Ibid.*, p. 140.

could not be stated more strongly; and following this, Radcliffe-Brown then addressed himself specifically to this question: what is the particular relation of ritual values to social values and to the essential constitution of human society?

He was, of course, especially referring to 'taboos', and his answer to the above question can be seen in the clearest possible form in his conclusion about the taboos surrounding childbirth among the Andaman Islanders. These taboos, he wrote:

'. . . are the obligatory recognition in a standardized symbolic form of the significance and importance of the event to the parents and to the community at large. They thus serve to fix the social value of occasions of this kind.'

And—more generally:

'For every rule that *ought* to be observed there must be some sort of sanction or reason. For acts that patently affect other persons the moral and legal sanctions provide a generally sufficient controlling force upon the individual. For ritual obligations conformity and rationalisation are provided by the ritual sanctions . . .

The primary basis of ritual . . . is the attribution of ritual value to objects and occasions which are either themselves objects of important common interests linking together the persons of a community or are symbolically representative of such objects . . .

. . . the negative and positive rites of savages exist and persist because they are part of the mechanism by which an orderly society maintains itself in existence, serving as they do to establish certain fundamental social values. The beliefs by which the rites themselves are justified and given some sort of consistency are the rationalizations of symbolic actions and of the sentiments associated with them.'*

Again, then, Radcliffe-Brown was able, by generalization and careful comparative study, to amend in a clear and useful way the earlier theory of Frazer. But before leaving this, let us note two things: (a) the emphasis again upon *sentiments* and *values*, at the very core of institutions, rituals, and beliefs, and (b) his theoretical *consistency*.

'The theory,' he wrote, 'is not concerned with the historical origin of ritual, nor is it another attempt to explain ritual in terms of human psychology; it is a hypothesis as to the relation of ritual and ritual values to the essential constitution of human society, i.e. to those invariant general characters which belong to all human societies, past, present and

* *Structure and Function in Primitive Society*, pp. 150, 151, 153.

future. It rests on the recognition of the fact that while in animal societies social coaptation depends on instinct, in human societies it depends upon the efficacy of symbols of many different kinds.'*

The same continuity of theoretical concern, and the same consistency, marked the third example we might note—Radcliffe-Brown's 'Henry Myers Lecture' (in 1945) on 'Religion and Society'. Here, again, I would like to draw attention to the central emphases. From our earlier comments on his theory of totemism, it can be seen that Radcliffe-Brown thought that religion united the natural and social order for men in expressing a *sense of dependence* on a spiritual or moral power outside themselves; but he began his consideration of religion by, again, stating certain basic premises.

'. . . an orderly social life amongst human beings depends upon the presence in the minds of the members of a society of certain sentiments, which control the behaviour of the individual in his relation to others. Rites can be seen to be the regulated symbolic expressions of certain sentiments. Rites can therefore be shown to have a specific social function when, and to the extent that, they have for their effect to regulate, maintain and transmit from one generation to another sentiments on which the constitution of the society depends.'†

Following this, Radcliffe-Brown then went on to stress the functions of the *ritual* elements of religion, especially in perpetuating and reinforcing particular sentiments. Of the many rituals of Confucianism, for example, he wrote:

'The rites gave regulated expression to certain human feelings and sentiments and so kept these sentiments alive and active.'‡

And—when discussing 'ancestor worship' in particular, and in relation to the large *lineages* of the clans in a society like that of traditional China—he emphasized again the central function of sustaining and strengthening the *sentiments* and *values* on which social relations rested.

'In such a society, what gives stability to the social structure is the solidarity and continuity of the lineage, and of the clan composed of related lineages. For the individual, his primary duties are those to his lineage. These include duties to the members now living, but also to those who have died and to those who are not yet born. In the carrying out of these duties he is controlled and inspired by the complex system of sentiments of which we may say that the object on which they are centred

* *Structure and Function in Primitive Society*, p. 150.
† *Ibid.*, p. 157.   ‡ *Ibid.*, p. 160.

is the lineage itself, past, present and future. It is primarily this system of sentiments that is expressed in the rites of the cult of the ancestors. The social function of the rites is obvious: by giving solemn and collective expression to them the rites reaffirm, renew and strengthen those sentiments on which the social solidarity depends.'*

Now in all this,, Radcliffe-Brown was seeking not to *deny* Durkheim's theory (that the function of religion—putting it much too simply—was to sustain the solidarity of society) because he largely agreed with it. He was seeking only to broaden and deepen this theory by adding to it this other dimension that the *distinctive* sentiments and values underlying religion were aspects of this *sense of dependence on a larger power.* We are not concerned with this theory as such here, but we might note that—besides recognizing these aspects of religious and moral sentiments in the rituals and institutions of society, Radcliffe-Brown also thought of them as important factors entering into the process of *socialization of the individual.*

'. . . what makes and keeps a man a social animal,' he wrote, 'is not some herd instinct, but the sense of dependence in the innumerable forms that it takes. The process of socialization begins on the first day of an infant's life and it has to learn that it both *can* and *must* depend on its parents. From them it has comfort and succour; but it must submit also to their control. . . the sense of dependence always has these two sides. We can face life and its chances and difficulties with confidence when we know that there are powers, forces and events on which we can rely, but we must submit to the control of our conduct by rules which are imposed.'†

In these directions of study, then, Radcliffe-Brown did demonstrate how generalizations and theories about the nature and processes of society could be tested, amended, and advanced by the careful use of the comparative method; and these three examples are sufficient to show the great interest of the new hypotheses which he put forward. It is also a point substantially in favour of Radcliffe-Brown that, in putting forward these new, amended theories, he deliberately limited his theoretical statements to the scope of his studies and made it plain that they were still vulnerable to further, and better, tests. They were not final. After having stated his theory of religion, this was his comment:

'Like any other scientific theory it is provisional, subject to revision and modification in the light of future research. It is offered as providing what seems likely to be a profitable method of investigation. What is needed to

* *Structure and Function in Primitive Society*, p. 164. † *Ibid.*, p. 176.

745

test and further elaborate the theory is a number of systematic studies of various types of religion in relation to social systems in which they occur.'*

From theory to theor*ies* . . . The emphasis was plain.

(II) THE FULLEST AGREEMENT WITH EARLIER AND CONTEMPORARY SOCIOLOGISTS

In these several examples of the testing of theories which Radcliffe-Brown undertook, I quoted some of his own statements for a definite purpose. They show, without any doubt whatever, the most substantial agreement with one of the basic positions adopted by all the sociologists of the early twentieth century from Tönnies onwards. It is clear that a large number of his studies were devoted to several interrelated aspects of one central persuasion—that the establishment of social usages and institutions rested fundamentally upon *values*, and that these took the form of *sentiments* which were upheld and sustained by *ritual* and *regular, institutional procedures*. Over and over again, one finds in his work the statement that a system of *morality* was *essential* to the existence and continuity of a system of social relationships; that *justice* was the one universal structural principle of which he was most sure; and we have seen that his pre-occupations with 'taboo', 'totemism', 'ritual values and social values', and 'religion' were all part of this preoccupation with the establishment and maintenance of the *moral* order which was the essential basis of society. I believe that this has already been clearly substantiated in the examples we have given, but two other aspects of this agreement are worth pressing further—in order to show exactly how extensive and deeply founded this agreement was.

The first is simply that—like all the other theorists, Radcliffe-Brown thought of the *sentiments* and the *evaluations* they embraced as emerging from the operation of *instinct* in the constraining context of *social facts*. He did not distinguish animal from human social behaviour in that the former *only* rested upon instinct and the latter did not include instinct *at all*—but only on *culture*. He thought that *instinct and culture* were the dominant and significant grounds for distinguishing the kinds of regulation of behaviour between the two; but he was quite clear that human society involved culture *and* instinct. He wrote this:

'The moment we compare animal with human societies we come upon an important distinction. In animal societies social coaptation is by instinct. In human societies, on the contrary, it is by instinct *plus* culture . . . I am

* *Structure and Function in Primitive Society*, p. 176.

not at all certain whether weaver birds do not to some extent *learn* how to make their nests. There is a certain continuity in their colonies; it has been maintained that they build their nests on tradition, in which case there is here an instance of culture . . . instances of such behaviour may exist, but it does not seem to be very significant or very important, because the amount of such behaviour becomes minimal in comparison with the part played by instinct . . . The characteristic is a constant within a single species; therefore, however the continuity is explained, the particular instinct is part of a genetic system, acquired by offspring from parents through physical inheritanc. The word "culture" . . . is not characteristic of a species but of a particular society or group of societies and therefore is characteristic, not of a genetic system, but of a social system.'*

We do not need to make more of this point here. Radcliffe-Brown recognized that knowledge of 'instinct' was still limited at the time when he was writing; but he certainly did not discount it, and would have been ready to entertain new knowledge of it. His only (and correct) point was to distinguish *culture* from it as a distinctively human addition to the ways of ordering and regulating experience and behaviour. But our only point is to see the complete agreement between Radcliffe-Brown and other writers on this *sequence* of instinct, activity, social constraints, sentiments and values, and institutionalization. The agreement on this was widespread almost to the point of unanimity.

The second further consideration is simply a reinforcement of this. For we find that in certain other articles Radcliffe-Brown's position was indistinguishable—on all these points and others besides—from that of Westermarck. The best examples are the two articles which he wrote for the Encyclopaedia of the Social Sciences in 1933—one on *Social Sanctions*, the other on *Primitive Law*.

In the article on *Social Sanctions*, Radcliffe-Brown not only agreed completely about the central importance of the 'sentiments' (exactly as Westermarck)† but also on the related importance of the 'sanctions' which were the public expression of the intensity with which they were held, and even upon the basic importance of the emotions of 'approval and disapproval'. The extent of this agreement is at least indicated in this statement.

'The application of any sanction is a direct affirmation of social sentiments by the community and thereby constitutes an important, possibly essential, mechanism for maintaining these sentiments. Organized negative sanctions in particular, and to a great extent the secondary sanctions, are expressions of a condition of social dysphoria brought about by some deed. The function of the sanction is to restore the social euphoria by giving definite

* *A Natural Science of Society*, pp. 91–2.   † And, of course, Durkheim.

collective expression to the sentiments which have been affected by the deed, as in the primary sanctions and to some extent in the secondary sanctions, or by removing a conflict within the community itself. The sanctions are thus of primary significance to sociology in that they are reactions on the part of a community to events affecting its integration.'*

In exactly the same way, in the article on *Primitive Law*, he concluded that:

'A full understanding of the beginnings of law in simpler societies can . . . be reached only by a comparative study of whole systems of social sanctions.'†

In the final outcome, then, the central tenets of Radcliffe-Brown's sociology; the central body of theory which came from his comparative studies; were such as to be in the closest agreement with the ideas we have so fully discussed in the systems of others. His 'development' of sociology coincided with theirs, despite the limited nature of his conceptual statements.

Conclusion

After the to-ing and fro-ing of these negative and positive appraisals of Radcliffe-Brown's contribution, the dimensions of the dilemma of assessing his work with meticulous accuracy and fairness must have become clear. But having seen them clearly . . . that is enough. His own outline of the nature of sociological analysis was limited and insufficient in ways we have seen, and certainly contained philosophical assertions and faults from which Malinowski was free. At the same time, he was clearly as influential as Malinowski in re-shaping anthropology by the introduction of sociology, and in providing a simplified outline of sociological analysis which was suitable for field-research and which made possible fruitful empirical studies. And he himself undertook such studies in ways which not only *demonstrated* how theories could be tested and improved, but which also actually *did* test, improve, and advance certain theories of much interest and importance. And in all this, his work bore out the validity of the basic ideas which were being clarified in all the other 'developments' of sociology at this time.

Radcliffe-Brown was also very realistic in his estimation of the possibilities ahead for the satisfactory development of the science of society. Quite apart from the intrinsic difficulties in the nature of the subject itself—for example, the wide grasp of comparative

* *Structure and Function in Primitive Society*, p. 211.   † *Ibid.*, p. 219.

and historical knowledge about societies which the student required, and which could not be quickly and easily gained; and quite apart from the perennial 'illusions' which the subject had to try and dispel —for example, the illusion that all explanation was a matter of chronological history, or that social facts could be explained by individual psychology since society was composed of individuals; there were two graver obstacles he foresaw. One was the tyranny of practice, or immediate practical advantage, over theory in research.

'We are faced,' he wrote, 'with a situation in which the demands for *practical* results are so insistent that it is unlikely any considerable amount of attention will be devoted, in our times, to the purely theoretical science of human society.'*

Many would think that this particular tide has turned nowadays, but this is a threat to which we shall return at the very end of our study. Radcliffe-Brown was unquestionably right. And finally, he saw clearly what we ourselves called earlier the danger of 'professionalization'. One of the greatest obstacles, he thought, to the full clarification of an intellectually satisfactory science of society lay in the vested interests of social science departments. It was the social scientists who were most likely to make sociology impossible. Here again, his insight and foresight was devastatingly true. And to this again we must come back at the end of our work. The tyranny (and ignorance) of the 'practitioners', and the tyranny and vested interests (and ignorance) of the 'professionals' these are the most intractable—and possibly insurmountable—obstacles, still, to the satisfactory making of sociology.

* *A Natural Science of Society*, p. 148.

Summary

Our summary conclusions concerning the supposed development of 'Functionalism' can be very brief and very clear.

(1) 'Functionalism' as a distinctive theoretical position in sociology never existed.

(2) 'Social Anthropology' as a social science distinct from sociology never existed.

(3) Both Malinowski and Radcliffe-Brown said so.

(4) Malinowski and Radcliffe-Brown (with varying degrees of sufficiency) accepted *the full 'conspectus' of sociology*, and their aim and achievement was that of re-shaping anthropology, and of re-orientating and re-directing the field-investigation of existing primitive societies in accordance with it.

(5) For them 'social' anthropology was simply that branch of sociology which concerned itself especially with the study of the primitive societies.

(6) Their contribution to the making of sociology was not, therefore, one of *theoretical advance*. They made no distinctive advance in the apparatus of conceptual analysis and theory as such (though perhaps a claim could be made that the *simplification* of what went into a 'structural-functional analysis'—e.g. Malinowski's analysis of the components of 'institutions'—was an advance in itself). Their contribution lay rather in the direction of *clarifying sociological analysis* for *use* in their own field of study and interest. Both scholars produced (with varying degrees of sufficiency) a simplified outline of sociological analysis suitable for their purposes. Structural-Functional analysis was a central component—but not by any means the only component—of this; and we need not list again the mistaken interpretations that accumulated about this point. We will list such errors of judgment clearly later.

(7) They both produced admirable and influential empirical studies which proved the value of their re-shaping of anthropology; which demonstrated how theories could be stated, tested, amended, and advanced; and which did, in fact, offer, test, and advance particular theories of importance.

(8) The making of sociology was therefore considerably advanced in that the subject was now effectively extended to the study of a particular range of societies in ways which had never been accomplished before. A wide range of fresh knowledge was made available which had, and has continued to have, many and profound effects

750

upon 'theories' of human society at all levels (i.e. going far beyond the 'primitive' societies alone.)

(9) At the same time the theoretical orientations and the empirical studies produced were also such as to buttress in the most fundamental way the basic ideas of the other sociologists and social-psychologists of the period. The picture of instinct, action, co-operation and conflict, communication (through cumulative cultural symbols), and the emergence of *sentiments* and *values* at the heart of the rules and procedures of *institutions*, and at the heart of the process of socialization of individuals . . . all this was essentially the same in Malinowski and Radcliffe-Brown as it was in the other writers from Tönnies, Westermarck, and Durkheim to Cooley, Mead, Freud and Pareto. The making of sociology was also advanced then in this additional but basic sense of having this growing *consensus* still further demonstrated and reinforced. It will be a surprise to many to see Malinowski and Radcliffe-Brown linked with 'evolutionists' like Westermarck (and other supposedly 'large-scale' theorists), but the *consensus* is there beyond any doubt. The supposed sharp differences are misconceptions.

(10) The entire emphasis of this 'development' was upon *theory for research*. The clear outline of analysis was *not* for its own sake, but for the sake of being able to undertake effective investigations, to state specific theories, and to test them. From theor*y* to theor*ies*: this—for both Malinowski and Radcliffe-Brown—was the core of their teaching and research.

The 'Error of Functionalism'; the 'Error of Social Anthropology' . . . these were not, therefore, of the making of these two 'Fathers'. They were not 'Fathers' of anything. They were—if any designation is required other than 'sociologists'—simply the sociological saviours of anthropology. The 'Errors' were certainly not of their own intention. However, some of their emphases, and the subsequent interpretations of them, were such as to give rise to it. What Radcliffe-Brown called the 'dense fog' certainly descended; and it was to darken in the post-war years, as we shall see.

These conclusions are simple and clear enough, and—I hope—have been fully demonstrated.

751

(5)
Early Twentieth Century Developments: A Summary Statement

Summary and Conclusions

We have now completed the task we set ourselves, and have critically appraised the five major areas of work in which significant developments were made during the first forty years of the present century:

(1) the theories of social evolution and 'typological' interpretations of social change,

(2) the objective study of the phenomenal aspects of social facts,*

(3) the subjective understanding of meaningfully orientated social action,*

(4) the study of the psychological aspects of society, and

(5) the supposed development of 'functionalism' and its application to the study of one particular range of societies.

It has become increasingly clear throughout our discussion, that these five directions of work were all developments of particular 'components' of the nineteenth century conspectus as we outlined it earlier, and all such as to supplement each other in moving towards a full system of sociological analysis. Each component was more deeply explored and clarified in itself, but all were seen more satisfactorily in their interrelationships within a fuller and more reliable set of concepts for the study of the nature and diversities of human societies.

Our division of these studies into five 'fields' has, of course, itself only been a convenient arrangement in accordance with the predominant emphasis, interest, and theoretical concern of the writers concerned—so that we could see and estimate their contributions in the clearest possible way. But even this division, as we have seen, must be regarded with caution. It has become quite plain that in concentrating on *one* aspect of the subject, most of these men were quite conscious of the importance of *other* approaches. Though each was developing his ideas with the use of slightly different concepts of his own, elements of fundamental agreement pervaded them all. All these writers—in their various ways, and to varying degrees—were interested in *all* the components of the subject. Their treatment overlapped the boundaries we have drawn. They were all concerned with the making of *a satisfactory science of man and society* in all its respects, though each focused his attention upon those dimensions which seemed most important to him.

We can now draw all these apparently different threads together.

* Though we thought it worthwhile to think of (2) and (3) in relation to each other in one section.

755

Clearly, we cannot reiterate all the many details established, or do justice, within a summary statement, to all the points of importance which have been made. In any case, during our argument many of the connections and similarities between these writers have been quite firmly established, and do not really need reinforcing statement, and we have already, to some extent, summarized their contributions at the end of each section. Nonetheless, it is a worthwhile effort, now, to try to see them in clear relationship with each other, even if in a summary way: to see their rootedness in the nineteenth century foundations; and to see the ways in which—critically appreciating these roots, and growing deliberately from them—they accomplished a clear and substantial advance.

Again, I hope I shall be forgiven a certain tenacity in this. I want to make these links, continuities, and developments clear beyond the slightest doubt. Later, after our critical assessment of post-war controversies (chiefly American), we shall then be able to draw all these components together in a statement of that system of sociological analysis to which—taken together—they lead; but here we will stop a little short of that task. At this stage our concern is only to *see* these developments clearly, and to see *equally* clearly the many errors of judgment which have been formed about them. These can then be put—decidedly and confidently—into the waste-paper basket where they belong, and we shall be able to come to our final study of the post-war work with a clear and prepared mind.

Agreements with the Nineteenth Century Foundations

On these first points, happily, our tenacity need not be exercised too much. It is enough simply to look back to our earlier statement of 'The Foundations of Sociology' (of the nineteenth century agreements) with all our recent discussions in mind.*

The point—of the very greatest interest—that becomes immediately and perfectly clear, is that not one single element of the conspectus then established was abandoned or even basically altered in these developments of the early twentieth century. Every single component continued intact, as did the same over-all framework of analysis. There was a quite basic agreement about these 'Foundations' among all the authors we have considered. Despite the criticism and the critical developments which certainly took place, not one element was rejected. All these authors *accepted* this conspectus and worked *within* it. The foundations were, and remained, unquestionably firm.

Exercising just a little tenacity here—but without going into anything approaching elaborate detail—let us, first of all, simply see how extensive this general agreement on the basic elements of the 'conspectus' was. This will serve as a simple 'reminding statement' of those foundations which were now not only established, but *consolidated*. We can then go on to stress points of special interest within this over-all agreement, and see in what ways clear and useful advances had been made.

It is worthwhile to remind ourselves that the entire range of work which we have reviewed in this book—under the heading of 'Developments'—was accomplished more or less simultaneously within a period of forty to fifty years, and that it brought us up to the time of the second world war. The making of sociology had developed quickly from the turn of the century. All its dimensions had been scrutinized and developed simultaneously. This critical consolidation and improvement of its foundations really amounted to the making of the subject for our own time. These points of 'reminding clarification' are therefore, of immediate use and relevance for ourselves. They bring us very close to a clear understanding of the nature of sociology *now*.

* *The Making of Sociology*, Volume I, p. 601.

A *SCIENCE AND KNOWLEDGE*

There was, first of all, complete agreement on the nineteenth century insistence that the methods of science alone were productive of *testable knowledge* as distinct from *conjectural opinion*. All the twentieth century writers agreed that science was *accurate* directly in relation to its *prescribed limitations*. Science *as such* was carefully limited in that it confined itself to those propositions about the world of our *experience* that could be *tested*. Each *particular* science was further limited in that it dealt appropriately with a *distinctive range* or *level* of subject-matter within our experience. They agreed that the crucial distinguishing feature of scientific method was that it subjected its propositions to clearly specified conditions of test, and abandoned any concern for propositions about 'ultimates' which could not be submitted to test.* They agreed that theory *guided* empirical research, but also that it should always be checked in relation to it. They agreed that science was rooted in reflection upon common sense, but also went beyond it; discovering 'laws' (connections between phenomena) which lay beyond common perception. They agreed that the sciences could be clearly classified in accordance with their distinctive subject-matter (and problems), and that each science was concerned to clarify the nature of its specific 'level' of subject-matter (the 'static' analysis of its 'distinctive consensus') and, in the light of this, to conduct empirical studies of the actual instances of its subject-matter which existed in the world ('dynamics'). They saw, too, the intimate connection between prediction, action, and control: that *explanation* and *effective control* were closely connected, and that *prediction* was their common feature. They nonetheless agreed that scientific knowledge was never *final*, but, though *relative*, was never *arbitrary* either. They were sensible enough to realize that science was limited in its efforts to understand the world, and that elements of evaluation and critical judgment going beyond science frequently entered into its *application*. Even so, they were in agreement that such degrees of exact knowledge as *could* be established about any aspect of the world, could *only* be established by pursuing scientific methods as exactly as was possible in each field of study.

On all these basic questions regarding the nature, limitations, and promise of science there was therefore very wide agreement and the same was true of wider and equally fundamental assumptions.

* i.e. the scientist *as scientist* abandoned such concern. As a *person*, he might well remain concerned about them.

758

THE SCIENCES AND THE STUDY OF NATURE, MAN AND SOCIETY: PERSPECTIVES OF KNOWLEDGE

The early twentieth century scholars also completely accepted the nineteenth century position concerning the wider *context* and *perspectives* of ideas within which their conception and practice of science were couched. They accepted the view that distinctive *forms* and *kinds of order* in the world were aspects of *process*, and that no specific *form* in nature could be understood excepting within the context of its environmental conditions. They accepted the concept of 'Evolution' in the same basic way that Herbert Spencer did—as a basis for understanding the emergence, maintenance, change, development, and dissolution of the distinctive 'forms' in nature. They agreed that insight into the 'normal' processes of forms could sometimes be gained by a study of pathological conditions (i.e. of *mal*-functioning). They were quite clear that each science was defined in terms of its appropriateness for the study of one distinctive 'level' of such forms, and that though there was a clear notion of scientific method in general, there was not likely to be a uniformity of concepts, techniques and procedures among *all* the sciences, since the methods of each science were worked out in accordance with its specific subject-matter: material, organic, social processes, etc.* And in all this they were also agreed about the changed perspective on 'man's place in nature' which the new knowledge of the sciences had brought about, and that—among the sciences—the most crucial conceptual distinctions were those involved in the correct recognition of man and his societies as constituting a legitimate 'subject-matter' for scientific enquiry.

On the several aspects of this latter question they were also in complete agreement. They saw the material and biological roots of man in nature: that man, like all else, could only be satisfactorily known within the context of material and biological processes. At the same time, they all agreed that explanation at these levels alone was not sufficient. They recognized *associational processes—social systems—* as a new, distinctive 'level' of phenomena, and, indeed, that man the *person* was so much a product of *social* influences that it was necessary to understand the processes of society in order fully to understand the

* Even Durkheim and Radcliffe-Brown who were least satisfactory on these distinctions were nonetheless agreed about the error of *reducing* the explanations of one 'level' of subject-matter (e.g. the social) to the elements of another (e.g. the biological or psychological).

759

nature of individual personalities. (This was true even of Freud who was so strongly persuaded of the importance of organically rooted elements of experience.) They were also all agreed that man was distinctively a *cultural* being: that he had had to win his social and cultural conditions (i.e. to *make* his cultural environment) by working upon the material resources of nature; and that the elements of this cumulative, historical, *material* activity would always form an important part of any explanation of his social and personal life. And in this, they all recognized that man differed from everything else in nature in that he was capable of the perception of *ends*, the calculation of means, and of deliberation, choice, conscious purpose, and self-directed *action*.* Man, therefore, was not only involved in *adapting* himself to nature, but also in *transforming* nature by his purposive activities. Man was *not* only a *phenomenon* who could be *observed* through the *senses*, but also a *purposeful actor* whose *conduct* required to be *understood* by the *imputation of meaning*.

Science, properly formulated, could produce *such testable knowledge as was possible* about this whole range of 'forms' in nature, including man and his societies. The sciences, properly classified, could therefore provide a conspectus of knowledge in all these fields, and sociology itself (since the development of the sciences was part of its subject-matter) could be of help in accomplishing such a systematic arrangement.

In all these wider perspectives, then, all the basic nineteenth century orientations were accepted.

* Again, though they denied and excluded the relevance of this for methods of sociological explanation, Durkheim and Radcliffe-Brown did at least accept it as a *fact;* even if, as Radcliffe-Brown held, it had to be dealt with by means of a 'logical fiction'.

c SOCIOLOGY: THE SCIENCE OF SOCIETY

The same was true about all the basic conceptions of the nature and scope of sociology itself. There was complete agreement that sociology was necessary as a science because of the existence of *social systems—of associational processes—*which were creative, causative processes going beyond those of a material and bio-psychological nature, and which therefore required a new level of concepts, methods of study, and kinds of explanation. *Social Systems* were thus the distinctive subject-matter of sociology.

In this field of study, as in all others, it was agreed that testable knowledge was only possible by the employment of the methods of science—*to such a degree of exactitude as proved possible.* Here, too, 'metaphysical' speculation was abandoned. At the same time, there was no facile assumption of a 'necessitarian determinism'. Only Durkheim and Radcliffe-Brown came close to such an extreme. Most of these more recent authors agreed with most of the earlier authors that man's 'teleological' qualities and capacities required *some degree* of explanation in terms of *meaning* and *will.* There was also a clear and ready agreement that though the entire conspectus of sociology could be, and *was,* clearly defined, it was obviously beyond the capacity of any single scholar to be master of it all. Indeed all the twentieth century scholars favoured *specialization* within sociology— not at all in the sense of falsely dividing either society, or the study of it, into separate 'bits'—but in the sense of focusing upon that *area* within the entire conspectus which most interested them, and, above all, in moving from *theory* to theor*ies:* in enriching the theoretical apparatus of the subject by trying to produce *definitive* empirical studies, which would thus demonstrate its correctness and worth. There was complete agreement that sociology was a *generalizing* and therefore essentially a *theoretical* and *comparative* subject, and that its empirical investigations should be theoretically guided. *Sociography* was clearly seen, however, to have its place as a way of collecting facts required.* And in all this there was also a general agreement concerning the nineteenth century division of the subject into 'Statics' and 'Dynamics', and about the elements of analysis held to be important under each head.

(I) SOCIAL STATICS

As to 'Social Statics'—the analysis of the distinctive *nature* of social

---

* See Appendix, p. 832.

761

systems (the kind of 'consensus' they were)—all the important nine-teenth century positions were agreed upon.

The basic importance of studying the *population* of a society within its *environmental·conditions* (the importance of *ecological* studies) was generally and clearly seen. There was the same persuasion that quantitative and qualitative *distributions* of a population within a territory, or of traits within a population,* bore important relations to aspects of *institutionalization*: for example—the 'dynamic density' of population and its relation to the division of labour and collective socio-psychological conditions (Durkheim), and the distribution of certain qualities, and their relation to the changing nature of élites (Pareto.)

There was complete agreement that the institutions of a total society comprised a 'consensus' (a distinctive kind of interconnection and interdependence) of associational forms, and that *structural-functional analysis* was required for the study of it. And there was agreement on many aspects of this.

It was agreed that '*functional requisites*' or '*functional imperatives*' could be clarified, and that certain associational forms could be shown to be appropriate to them. There was therefore an acceptance of the same outline of the basic and universal institutions of society as had been proposed by the nineteenth century writers: domestic institutions (and kinship organization), economic institutions (the division of labour, property, etc), regulatory institutions (custom, law, morality, government, religion), institutions for education and training, and the ranks, grades and classes attendant upon the status-distinctions in the hierarchical organization of tasks. The systematic analysis of institutions in relation to distinguishable 'functional requisites' was therefore a common element of sociology—plain to be seen—from the work of Comte and John Stuart Mill right through to that of Malinowski.

It was also agreed that there was a 'functional interconnection' *among* the associational forms of a society; that these 'forms' were interdependent in their operation; and that structural-functional analysis could also uncover and clarify this. The functions of institutions were therefore (*a*) the ways in which they met certain requisites (needs and purposes of various kinds), (*b*) the part they played in the interconnected operation of other institutions, and (*c*) the unfore-seen consequences that changes in them had upon their own struc-ture and membership, or upon those of other institutions.

It was clearly agreed, too, that social growth and development were accompanied by an increasing *differentiation* of structure and function. Out of a relatively simple context of regulated custom

* i.e. in general—the *composition* of a population.

762

there came to be a proliferation of interests and purposes and a more complex set of related organizations; a 'specialization' of institutions. Some of these specialized 'associations' were extremely complicated in the organization of the 'roles' of their members—but, even so, structural-functional analysis remained clearly applicable, and could clarify both the entire structure of the organization, and the specific tasks and relationships of individuals.

There was also no 'fallacy of the stationary' in all this. All these authors were in complete agreement that social systems were *essentially historical* processes; that *persisting order* as well as *changing form* was a historical continuity, and, indeed, properly understood, a process of *change*.* And they all accepted the corollary of this assumption—that the study of the very *nature* of social systems entailed a study of temporal persistence, change, development, evolution: in short, of their historical processes.

There was widespread agreement too on other attendant points: that the institutional order of society was the outcome of *conflict* as well as *co-operation*; that the 'functional interconnection of institutions by no means implied functional *'unity'* or *'integration'*;† that patterns of adaptation to change could be studied in *'equilibrium-disequilibrium'* terms; and that here—as in other sciences—the study of *pathological* conditions of social facts (social systems in disarray, disruption and conditions of *mal*-functioning) might well be able to throw light upon their *normal* functioning in societies of particular types.

It was also agreed, however, that structural-functional analysis was not in itself *sufficient* for explanation. Elements of social structure were not *entities* involved in cause-and-effect relations among themselves, independent of men's *activities*. Institutions were ordered arrangements of *activities*, and all the elements of these activities (collective psychological conditions, motives, interests, ends, theories, resources, calculations, etc.) had also to enter into any satisfactory explanation.

There was also full agreement about the several aspects of the nineteenth century position concerning the psychological aspects of society. It was agreed that biology and general psychology could provide knowledge of the bio-psychological endowment of human nature, and that an understanding of human society required a knowledge of man's primary instinctive dispositions and needs. At the same time it was also fully agreed that many distinctive attributes

---

* This was what Radcliffe-Brown was seeking to make clear in his distinction between *synchronic* and *diachronic* studies. *Both* were studies of *change*.

† Though, again, we must note Durkheim's and Radcliffe-Brown's ambiguities here.

763

of human nature—of human *persons*—were essentially rooted in
association. The understanding of the 'self' could not be achieved
without an understanding of 'society'. There was therefore complete
agreement about the necessity of the *associational context* for a
satisfactory human psychology. All the nineteenth century doubts
about the validity of a human psychology excepting within this context were fully and strongly upheld. There were further points of
agreement as to the worthwhileness of studying the psychological
aspects of 'roles' within organizations, and the psychological processes
of distinctive kinds of groups—such as 'In-Groups' and 'Out-
Groups', and (now) 'Primary Groups' and 'Secondary Groups';*
and of exploring apparent connections between 'types' of social
structure, and 'types' of individual personality (or particular constellations of character-traits).

It was perfectly clear that these authors still saw no *cleavage* whatever between psychology and sociology; indeed, that they saw the
two subjects as being necessarily interrelated. Most of them built
societal and psychological elements into their systems of analysis
with no difficulty at all—not just loosely, or arbitrarily, but carefully
and deliberately, with no conceptual vagueness or ambiguity. We
have seen that even men especially concerned with the founding of
psychology proper—McDougall and Freud—also couched their
ideas within a social context; whilst the sociologists who were offering the most large-scale systems for the analysis of societies—
Hobhouse, Durkheim, Pareto and others—nonetheless also emphasized the psychological aspects of both the 'self' and the process
of 'institutionalization'. And they were able to do this without in
any sense falling into the error of psychological 'reductionism'—
something to which they were all opposed.

There was widespread agreement too (though this was not unani-
mous†) that neither structural-functional analysis, nor a knowledge
of the psychological aspects of society, were enough for sociological
explanation. They were *necessary* components, but *insufficient* without the *additional* element of the explanation of social *action* in terms
of *meaning*. Here there was wide support for the insistence of most of
the nineteenth century writers upon the recognition of the 'teleological' characteristics of man. This recognition of deliberate
purposive *action* was not only of crucial importance in distinguishing

* Perhaps we should note that Cooley himself did not use the term *'secondary group'* as a specific concept—his emphasis was centrally upon the importance of *'primary groups'*; but his entire treatment *contrasted* primary groups with the larger groups and organizations of society, so that the conceptual distinction was clearly and substantially there.
† Here, Durkheim and Radcliffe-Brown positively disagreed.

the subject-matter of sociology as being of a category quite different from mere *events*, but also in clearly pointing to the need for concepts and methods quite different from those of the natural sciences. There was agreement here, too, with the new methods which the nineteenth century writers had proposed—the construction of 'types' or 'models' of social action which made possible the interpretation of action by the imputation of meaning. Even the same 'types' (e.g. the 'impulsive, traditional, rational') were substantially agreed upon and developed.

There was also, however, a final point of agreement (under the head of 'Statics'), namely: that—no matter how purposive man might be—the complexities of social processes always involved *more* than human purposes, and that therefore a satisfactory analysis of society always required a study of the *unintended consequences* of social action and social change.

The nineteenth century claim that all these components taken together were necessary to provide a satisfactory analysis of the *nature* of social systems was completely upheld by the twentieth century writers.

(II) SOCIAL DYNAMICS

Exactly the same can be said of the proposals for 'Social Dynamics': the application of the above analysis to the study of actual societies.

It was agreed completely that since sociology was a theoretical and generalizing science—*comparative study* was essential, and that this necessarily entailed the *classification* of *types* of society. It was even agreed that two kinds of classification seemed warranted: one resting on 'degrees of social composition' which made a large-scale arrangement of descriptive knowledge possible, and one resting on a more sharply constructed 'typology' which embodied an explicit 'theory'. The comparative method, too, could legitimately be of these two kinds—one consisting of systematic description and arrangement,* and one constituting the most exact alternative to controlled experiment (for the posing and testing of specific theories).

There was agreement too on many aspects of the construction of 'types' and 'models'. The theoretical types actually constructed (e.g. by Tönnies, Durkheim, Weber) did in fact all include structural-functional components, socio-psychological components, and elements of purposeful action interpreted in terms of meaning. There

---

* Though it was readily agreed that even this would have its 'theoretical' presuppositions (e.g. that even the 'degree of composition' of societies was, somehow, taken to be an attribute of general theoretical significance).

was also, in them, a marked concern for the understanding of that particular pattern of social *change* which had been thought to be of crucial importance throughout the nineteenth century: that is—the rapid transition from relatively simple traditional communities to highly complex industrialized societies and the many-sided 'malaise' which accompanied this. They showed, too, a marked concern for discovering ways of over-coming it. Here, as we have seen, Durkheim (despite his epistemological dogmas) was just as rational, ethical, and purposeful as anyone else. But in all these writers—Tönnies, Hobhouse, Weber, Cooley, Freud, Malinowski (as well as Durkheim) —the same central preoccupation was clear. And there was also firm agreement on quite specific elements in all this.

First—again—that society was *essentially* historical, and that the conceptions of change, growth, evolution, development, and progress, were inescapably involved in any satisfactory study of it. And second —that there was an over-all and undeniable *perspective* of social change and social evolution which pointed to a highly significant point of arrival and departure in modern times. A long process of genetic development within which knowledge had been gradually accumulated, clarified, advanced, and applied; and during which man's control over nature and society had been extended; had culminated in the contemporary situation in which man was faced with the task of assuming a conscious and deliberate responsibility for the making of his own society and for the direction of his own future. Knowledge, rationality, ethical clarity, deliberate legislation and administration . . . these had come increasingly into the fore-ground of the *actual development of institutions*. There was, then, a further agreement concerning an apparently inescapable *commitment* —intellectual, moral, political—in this study of society. The making of sociology was still at the heart of the making of society—and seemed to involve an ideological commitment which was part and parcel of its very scientific perspectives! But this we must come back to. It is enough here to see that the nineteenth century commitments —as well as the proposals for a new science—were not lost, not changed, but continued and reinforced.

(III) METHODS

It remains only to say that there were also substantial agreements concerning the methods which were held to be distinctive of socio-logy. It was agreed that all the methods of the other sciences—careful observation, description, classification, the submitting of hypotheses to conditions of test, etc.—should be employed and pressed as far as they possibly could. But it was also agreed that *additional* methods were made necessary by sociology's distinctive subject-matter. The *historical* method was necessary—since social systems were cumulative, cultural, historical kinds of facts. The *comparative* method was necessary—since it was the only conceivable alternative to experiment as a way of *testing theories*. And also all the methods attendant upon the recognition of man's distinctive '*teleological*' attributes (the construction of 'types' in terms of meaning) were also necessary, and quite different from those employed in the sciences concerned with the study of *phenomenal events* only.

Similarly, and finally, there were agreements about the *limitation* of the claims—but, nonetheless, the *firm* claims—of the new science. These developments in the making of sociology, like all the work which had gone into its foundation, were not advanced in arrogance in standing opposed to casual and ill-founded 'theories' about human nature and human society, or theories which stood on metaphysical or theological dogma. They explicitly stated the *limitations* of what was possible in a science of man and society. They explicitly renounced any claim to *finality* of the theories and knowledge which the subject might produce. They agreed that human knowledge was indisputably *relative* to certain conditions. Even so, they showed also that such knowledge as the newly defined methods and procedures could produce was not *arbitrary*, but rested upon carefully delineated concepts and carefully assembled evidence. With all its explicit limitations, then—indeed exactly *because* of them—sociology was the only reliable way of establishing knowledge about man and society. Only the methods it proposed could provide the knowledge which could form a reliable basis for prediction and action. The sociological perspective was the only reliable perspective for the study of man and society; for understanding the significant changes of society at any time; and for providing that body of knowledge within which the soundest possible judgments might be made for the formulation of social and political action. It must be repeated: these claims were not made in arrogance. They were made after the most rigorous and critical efforts to arrive at the concepts and methods which were the most accurate possible, whilst taking every care not to under-estimate the subtleties and profundities of the subject-matter.

On all these elements of the nineteenth century 'Foundations'— each of them deserving of a much more basic and important emphasis than a summary statement like this can possibly give—the early twentieth century scholars were in substantial agreement. A scrupulous consideration of our earlier statement of the nineteenth century 'Foundations' and of our discussion of the developments dealt with in this book will demonstrate the continuity of these agreements beyond any possible measure of doubt.* There was no lack of clarity whatever in all this.

These, however, were only *minimal general agreements*.

I have deliberately *not* stopped at each point to indicate the relevant substantive points made by each of the writers we have dealt with (from Tönnies to Radcliffe-Brown): hoping on the one hand that I have had no need to do so—that, after our discussion, all these points would be clear; but also fearing, on the other, that if I tried *too* tenaciously to load my treatment *too* much, I would make it too burdensome and tedious. I have therefore simply stated these agreements in the plainest possible way.

Now, however, I would like to unleash enthusiasm a little, and emphasize those points arising in this statement which are of the very greatest interest for our purpose of clarifying the firm consolidations and the clear, continuous, achievements which attended the ongoing making of the subject. Some of these, however, are simply points of special emphasis which I do not want us to lose sight of; and these can be outlined very quickly, before we concentrate on making clear the advances upon these basic agreements which the early twentieth century authors achieved.

* Vol. I, pp. 601–42. The full appreciation of this continuity is much more important than it seems, and the necessity of establishing it firmly cannot be too much emphasized, for we shall see in our study of post-war developments that quite false perspectives have been foisted on to the subject by an insufficient awareness of it.

POINTS OF SPECIAL EMPHASIS

(1) NO BREAK IN CONTINUITY

The first point that arises most clearly from our critical survey of all these contributions is the very satisfactory one that there was a perfectly consistent continuity in the making of the subject. There was no intellectual impeding of it. There were no great clashes of disagreement whereby the early foundations were found to be gravely in error. There was no slowing of the pace or intensity of application of intellectual effort to the clarification and advancement of the subject. On the contrary, it moved forward clearly, consistently, and substantially from the achieved basis of the nineteenth century foundations. Every 'component' of the 'conspectus' was explored more fully; every direction of analysis was considered more deeply; every 'building block' of the new science was shaped more fittingly with regard to its place within the envisaged entirety of the structure. From the exploratory deliberations of the meetings of the British Sociological Society in 1903 which so clearly denoted the international awareness of the significant juncture at which the subject had arrived, to the publication of Malinowski's and Radcliffe-Brown's essays at roughly the time of the second world war, the dimensions of sociology had been successively developed in a rich variety of ways, and ways which—under their apparent disconnectedness and diversity—showed a remarkable consistency of concepts and agreements, and supplemented each other within the same continuing framework of ideas. There was no break, no discontinuity, but a considerable advancement of ideas within an over-all conspectus of agreement.

(2) NO DIVISION INTO 'SCHOOLS'

The second point which was clearly noticeable in all this, is that no one of these authors was at all concerned deliberately to put forward a sharply separate 'school'. Hobhouse and Westermarck did not subscribe to an 'Evolutionary' school—they fully embraced all the other components of the subject within their own theories. McDougall did not found an 'Instinct' school. Mead did not found a school of 'Social Behaviourism'. Weber did not suggest a 'Verstehen' school. Malinowski and Radcliffe-Brown did not found a school of 'Functionalism'. It does not matter to which development of theory we turn—we invariably find the same thing: that the author was focusing his attention upon that special component (or those few related aspects) of the subject which (*a*) were of greatest interest to him, (*b*)

769

seemed to him of special theoretical significance, (c) seemed to him to be insufficiently explored and clarified, (d) seemed to promise the illumination of certain dimensions of human social and personal actuality which had not yet been seen with sufficient clarity and (e) seemed of particular use for the specific kinds of study he wished to carry out. But this was *never* a focus of attention which claimed exclusive truth for itself and which denied the validity and utility of all other approaches to the subject. Thus Durkheim, in concentrating upon rules for the 'objective study of social facts' did not *deny* the *evolutionary* perspective in sociology, did not *deny* the importance of the *psychological* aspects of society; on the contrary, he wished to move towards what he saw as a better appreciation of what was involved in the study of them. He focused all his energies upon persuading people to see the *psychological creativity of association*; not because he thought it was *everything*, but because he thought that there was a great intellectual *blindness* about it, and that the furtherance of sociology depended upon a recognition of it. The same will readily be seen in the work of every single theorist we have considered.

In all these 'developments', then, there was a clear, considerable, and consistent *continuity*: not a springing up of a fragmented and disconnected set of special and opposed 'schools', but simply a continuity in the making of *sociology* as an entire science of society.

(3) THE INTRICACY OF THE CROSS-CURRENTS OF INFLUENCE
    IN THIS CONTINUITY. THE GROWTH OF INTERNATIONAL
    AWARENESS IN THE SCHOLARSHIP OF SOCIOLOGY

On the same point, it is also worthwhile to draw attention to the great depth, intricacy, and extent of the continued influence of the nineteenth century ideas upon those of the early twentieth century writers. This need not be laboured—but it is important to see that the ideas of the nineteenth century were far from being some kind of dust-covered objects in a Victorian lumber-room, whose use had been discarded by more modern men. On the contrary, they were *living* ideas which new thinkers were striving critically to assess and develop. I will mention only a few examples.

The ideas of Comte and Mill, coupled with those of Spencer were right at the heart of the work of Hobhouse and Westermarck. And it must be remembered that at the turn of the century Comte's ideas were still in process of being translated, interpreted, and promulgated by a number of scholars in England. For a man like Gilbert Murray, for example, Comte's ideas were a matter of *current* interest. Indeed, it was true in general that this period of forty years was one in which all the works of the scholars we have mentioned—of Tönnies and

Durkheim (Weber was not translated and known to any great extent even yet) as well as earlier writers like Comte—were being gradually made more available. The complexity of the connections of influence were only gradually becoming apparent. But Comte, Mill, Spencer were also intimately at the heart of Durkheim's considerations—and in all fields: in his discussions of the definition of sociology, the 'associational' context for psychology, the division of labour, the nature of the comparative method, the classification of societies, and many other things besides. And we have seen that the ideas of Comte were of significant influence in Mead, and in Radcliffe-Brown. The influences of Comte were still widespread throughout America and Europe.

Spencer, too, was no dried-up Victorian antique—despite the volume of 'aphorisms' drawn from his works. His ideas were *living* ideas, though not, of course, accepted without criticism. But they were at the centre of Durkheim's considerations, and—with equal force—influenced Pareto and Radcliffe-Brown. Radcliffe-Brown's notions of social evolution were, as he acknowledged, drawn directly from Spencer.

Karl Marx was also a long time dying. In sociology, he was a powerful influence in the ideas of Tönnies and Weber especially—though, again, by way of critical digestion. The early Americans—Ward, Sumner, and Giddings—also exercised a continuing influence among the twentieth century scholars. Hobhouse was much influenced by them. They were part of the immediate American influence upon the direction of work of Cooley and Mead. But Sumner too must have had considerable influence among anthropologists: his analysis of institutions was well-nigh identical with that later offered by Malinowski, and Malinowski certainly knew his work.* We saw, too, how the 'types of social action' developed by Weber had already been stated with considerable clarity by Giddings in particular. And of course the influences among the early twentieth century scholars themselves—between Tönnies and Durkheim; Tönnies and Weber; Hobhouse, Westermarck, Malinowski and Radcliffe-Brown; Durkheim and Radcliffe-Brown; Freud and Malinowski . . . (the interconnections have almost endless ramifications!) were continuous, and continuously growing.

We saw that Hobhouse, Westermarck, McDougall, Tönnies, Durkheim actually participated—by attendance or by correspondence —in the early proceedings of the British Sociological Society; and all these men were leading figures in the substantial developments which were to take place over the next few decades. The present century began with a definite international awareness of the body of ideas

* See *The Making of Sociology*, Vol I, p. 529, and Vol. II, pp. 697–8, 708.

which comprised the 'Foundations of Sociology'. They were living ideas which gave rise to the developments we have outlined; and by the time of the second world war the scope and range of international scholarship in the subject had extended considerably. Books were translated and commonly read. The awareness of the literature of the subject was growing, and the interconnected part played by all these contributions to the making of the subject were becoming clear.

My major point here, however, is that there was no distinction whatever between 'ancient and modern' in the literature and ideas of the subject during this period. It was rather a period during which the whole range of available ideas in the subject was becoming known, and when all the various approaches were being mulled over, critically assessed, and developed in specific directions. All the ideas were living ideas. And it is the close *immediacy* to our own time of this complex consideration of the entire fund of ideas which had gone in to the founding and developing of sociology that I want to emphasize.

The ideas of Spencer were hot in Pareto's mind when Mussolini was harnessing Italy in preparation for the second world war. The ideas of Comte, Mill, Spencer, Darwin, Ward, were at work in the minds of Hobhouse and Westermarck when they felt the gloom and threat of a new totalitarianism in the nineteen-thirties. Malinowski was formulating his outline of sociological analysis for the study of the simpler societies—with his references to Frazer, Sumner, Westermarck, Durkheim—actually during the second world war. And Radcliffe-Brown was upholding the ideas of Montesquieu, Comte, and Spencer, as well as those of Durkheim, in introducing his outline of 'structural-functional analysis' just *after* the war. All these ideas were living ideas in the consolidation of the foundations of the subject and in the significant developments within it, right up to our own door-step in time. They are living ideas still.

Other connections of influence, and other agreements on quite fundamental ideas, were also of great importance but these are better considered as part of the specific developments in the clarification of the subject which these early twentieth century writers achieved.

Critical Developments of the Nineteenth Century Foundations: A Clear Statement of the Elements of Sociological Analysis

In this statement I think it most useful to consider these agreements and advances *not* in the order in which they emerged during the course of our discussion, but in one which allows us to see them as critical developments of the necessary parts of a whole system of sociological analysis.

Bearing in mind, then, all the basic agreements already set out as to the distinctive subject-matter of sociology, and its nature and elements as a science, the following are the more important developments which the early twentieth century writers made. Their clarification of these several elements was really the definitive formulation of the elements of modern sociological analysis.

(1) THE STUDY OF SOCIAL SYSTEMS: THE OBJECTIVE STUDY OF THE PHENOMENAL ASPECTS OF SOCIAL FACTS

It was generally agreed that *associational processes*, and the interconnection of them in entire *social systems*, constituted a *level of actuality* distinguishable from material, biological, and individual psychological processes. This was an acceptance and reinforcement of the basic idea which continued from the nineteenth century conspectus. Now, however, certain developments were accomplished.

(i) A clear statement had been achieved of the *psychological creativity of human association.*

(ii) A clear statement had been achieved of the *incorrectness* of the long-standing assumption that the collective facts produced by association could be explained in terms of elements of *individual* psychology at the *pre-associational* level (or at any level *independent* of association).

(iii) A clear statement had been achieved of the persuasion that *associational facts* possessed determinate and observable attributes going beyond the individuals who behaved within the context of them. These associational facts possessed definite, observable forms of social organization—a definite *structure*; definite, distinguishable attributes of a *collective psychological* nature; and emerged in relation

773

to some social *function*. Furthermore, they were *functionally inter-connected* in that they were to some extent involved in each other in their operation within society as a whole. They were also, however, essentially cumulative, *historical* facts.

(iv) A clear statement had been achieved of those *objective characteristics* in terms of which these associational facts could be recognized and studied *as if* they were things. They were *external* to individuals, *constraining* upon them, and *general* within the group which shared the same collective conditions.

(v) A *clear set of rules* had been provided for the observation, description, classification, and comparative study of associational facts whereby *explanations* of them could be achieved. Such explanations were inclusive of *quantitative* statements, but were essentially *correlative* statements. Whether qualitative, quantitative, or both, they were statements of *concomitant variations*. These rules also provided for the illumination (within carefully classified 'types' of society) of the *normal* functioning of associational facts by a study of their *mal*-functioning in abnormal (pathological) conditions. They also provided for the *testing* of explanations. In short, a clear set of rules* had been provided for the *objective study of the phenomenal aspects of social facts*, and for the undertaking of *definitive studies of them*.

(vi) Clear examples of carefully delimited (definitive) studies of specific social facts had been successfully undertaken which demonstrated the effective application of these rules.

(vii) A clear statement had been achieved, as part of these rules, of a mode of analysing any *total society* in terms of all its elements of *social structure*, their *functions* (in meeting certain 'requisites' or 'imperatives'), their *functional interconnections* (in operating in relation to each other in the total system), and their *unforseen consequences*. An extremely clear 'structural-functional' analysis had been formulated. This could be systematically employed in empirical investigation, and—with carefully formulated comparative studies— could provide both descriptive and analytical knowledge, and explanatory theories, which could be tested.

(viii) A clear statement had been achieved whereby each element of social structure (each 'institution') could be analysed in detail— and, in particular, whereby its entire structure could be analysed into the 'roles' which constituted the clear behavioural requirements demanded of its individual members. This made possible the analysis of all forms of organization, and—within and among them (i.e. in their interconnections as well as within themselves)—the ordered,

* It would be too lengthy and is unnecessary to repeat these rules. They were, of course, those of Durkheim, pp. 332–56, Malinowski, pp. 697–9, etc.

regulated acts of individuals. This knowledge, too, was testable.

(ix) It was also completely and clearly agreed that social facts were essentially *historical* processes—that *persisting order* and *change* alike were dynamic, temporal processes—and that structural-functional analysis had *essentially* to include historical dimensions. Putting this the other way round, historical analysis itself had, in part, to be of a structural-functional nature if it was to ensure systematic and satisfactory study. The essential point of agreement was that *both* structural-functional *and* historical dimensions *combined* were necessary for the satisfactory study of social facts. There was no conflict, no 'static'-'dynamic' separation, between them. Both were parts of that systematic method of study which the distinctive nature of social facts made necessary.

All these points amounted to the fact that the propositions of this kind made by the nineteenth century writers were not only *agreed* upon, but a meticulously clear set of concepts and rules had also been provided whereby a trained investigator could assemble objective knowledge about his subject-matter (social systems) and produce definitive studies and theories which could be *tested* as exactly as the subject-matter would permit. A great stride had therefore been taken towards the proven establishment of a *science*.

We have clearly seen that *all* the writers we have studied held that associational facts constituted a distinctive level of actuality, that 'structural-functional' analysis was a necessary part of sociology for the study of them, that an objective knowledge of the phenomenal aspects and interconnections of these facts was possible and desirable, and that *definitive* studies were to be aimed at. Even so, it was obviously the special contribution of Durkheim to insist upon all this and make it emphatically clear, though Malinowski and Radcliffe-Brown (in working out a simple outline for their own purposes) also made further contributions in clarifying 'structural-functional' analysis for use in empirical investigation.

Durkheim had provided studies of the Division of Labour in Society, Religion, and Suicide, and both Malinowski and Radcliffe-Brown had produced detailed monographs and comparative tests of theories proving the usefulness of these concepts, rules and methods.

It was clear, however, that Durkheim's zeal in insisting on the *objectivity* of social facts (and Radcliffe-Brown's acceptance of his position) had gone to the unwarranted extreme of denying the *purposive action* of men as a category distinct from mere phenomenal events, and, as such, requiring different and additional methods of explanation.

There was a philosophical error here which could not be accepted. Nonetheless, it is important to see one point very clearly.

Associational facts *did possess* the phenomenal attributes which Durkheim insisted upon even though they *also* possessed *other dimensions* which he did not recognize and incorporate. The objective study of social facts by the employment of these rules could still therefore be correctly pressed as far as possible despite this theoretical qualification, and could be productive of the kind of testable knowledge which its methods claimed, *even though something else was also required.* *

The provision of these rules for the objective study of the phenomenal aspects of social facts was therefore a clear and decided advance: a definitive contribution of permanent worth to the making of a satisfactory system of sociological analysis. It was a contribution which remained, and still remains, firm.

(2) THE STUDY OF SOCIAL SYSTEMS: THE SUBJECTIVE UNDERSTANDING OF MEANINGFULLY ORIENTATED SOCIAL ACTION

It was (with the exception of Durkheim) also widely agreed that the crucial characteristics which distinguished human social and personal behaviour from all other kinds of behaviour (of material objects and processes, or animals) was that it was *purposive.* Man *directed* many of his activities. Being aware of *ends*, he sought and employed *means* in ways *calculated* to *attain* those ends. He established *knowledge* in his *pragmatic* activities, and he formulated *evaluations* and *standards of judgment*, in regulating his practical social conduct. He did not simply *adapt* himself to his environmental circumstances, but creatively *transformed* those circumstances in the pursuit of his *interests*, for the more satisfactory attainment of his ends.

It was agreed, in short, that human social systems entailed *action* which was a category of actuality quite distinct from *phenomenal events*, and that no satisfactory explanation of action could be accomplished by a study of its phenomenal aspects alone—no matter how exhaustively these were investigated. It required *in addition* a subjective *understanding* in terms of *meaning*. And *meaning* was of a conceptual level quite distinct from 'structural-functional' *organizational* facts and collective *psychological* facts alike.

This again was a reinforcement of the entire insistence on the recognition of elements of choice, will, and the 'teleological' attributes

* We may remind ourselves that Durkheim's definition of a social fact—which emphasized its externality, constraining power, and generality throughout the group—was, nonetheless, framed in terms of '*a way of acting . . .*'. A link was therefore possible with Mead's 'Social Behaviourism' and Weber's meaningful *interpretation* of action.

776

of the human mind, and of elements of *character* as well as those of *personality*, that had been made right through the nineteenth century—from the limited and incomplete statements of Comte and Mill to the quite clear and elaborate statements of Ward, Sumner, and Giddings. Now, however, certain developments were accomplished.

(i) A clear statement had been achieved of the distinctive level of the category of *meaning* in *action*, making an explanation *other* than those in terms of the phenomenal facts of social organization and collective psychology necessary.

(ii) Clear definitions had been provided distinguishing *action* from *social action:* clearly delimiting the theoretical concern of sociology to *social action* alone; and setting out *types* of social action for use in the *imputation* of meaning.

(iii) A *clear set of rules* had been provided for the construction of '*ideal-types*' of social action whereby a *causal explanation* of specific concrete sequences of social action could be accomplished in terms of the imputation of meaning. These rules also provided an account of a particular use of the comparative method whereby such a causal explanation could be *tested*. The rules therefore provided for the undertaking of *definitive* studies of concrete sequences of social action *to such a degree of exactitude as was possible*.

(iv) A clear statement had been accomplished of all those categories of social relationships and social groups which were necessary for the construction of ideal-types.

(v) Clear and detailed examples of such typological explanations of historically significant sequences of social action had been provided. Substantive *theories* about specific, concrete sequences of social change had been produced—by Tönnies and Weber especially —which proved the effectiveness of this theoretical approach.

(vi) A clear statement had been accomplished liberating sociological investigation from the imposition of any supposedly entire 'scheme of knowledge' or 'system of categories' in terms of which explanations could, in some sense, be 'deduced'. Any such entire 'compendium of knowledge' or entire 'system of categories' was rejected as being beyond the bounds of possibility, and a positive obstacle to the formulation, study, and testing of particular causal theories. Such schemes were rejected as unnecessary burdens.

Again, the nineteenth century propositions about the distinctive 'teleological' attributes of man were not only agreed upon and reinforced, but an advancement had been achieved in that a clear set of concepts and rules had been provided for *use*: whereby any trained investigator could undertake definitive studies to such degree of accuracy as seemed possible. The same kind of stride towards the establishment of a satisfactory *science* had been made with regard to this dimension of the subjective understanding of action as had been made in the objective study of social facts. Both, of course, sought *testable statements possessing objective truth*: one in terms of *observable phenomena*, the other in terms of *imputed meaning*.

It will readily be seen that almost all the writers we have studied agreed with this recognition of the distinctive attributes of *social action* and what it implied for distinctive methods. Hobhouse, Westermarck, McDougall, Cooley, Mead, Pareto, Simmel, Freud, Malinowski, all included conscious reason and purpose in their systems. All the earlier writers too—in their construction of 'types' (Comte, Spencer, Giddings, etc.)—had incorporated this kind of analysis of action. The emphasis upon the purposive capacities of man in his practical activities had been made from the beginning. Even so, it was obviously the distinctive contribution of Max Weber to make this particular dimension of sociological analysis clear, and he had also demonstrated the utility of his 'apparatus' of analysis by providing substantive studies (examples) which made use of it. Tönnies too, however, had provided a 'typological' explanation of this kind that was equally impressive in its interpretation of modern social change.

Again, then, a new set of concepts, rules and methods had been provided which was necessary for the effective study of a distinctive dimension of human social actuality.

The same point must be made here, however, that we made with regard to Durkheim—though, in this case, it is not made necessary by any 'blindness' on Weber's (or Tönnies') part. It is simply that the fact that sequences of social action require understanding in terms of meaning does *not* mean that the institutions, collective psychological conditions, and social situations within which they are carried out do *not* possess observable *phenomenal* attributes *in addition*. They *do*. And Weber was quite clear that a knowledge of these phenomenal characteristics should be provided *as well as* a causal explanation in terms of meaning.

It had been made quite clear, then, that the *objective study of the phenomenal aspects of social facts* and the *subjective understanding of meaningfully-orientated social action* were not at odds with each other, but supplemented each other, and therefore contributed to a more complete knowledge of the dimensions of social actuality than either could provide of itself.

There is the final and very important point that the provision of *both* these components of analysis was *liberative* in the making of sociology. Both Durkheim and Weber emphasized conceptual and theoretical clarity for *use*. Both emphasized the move from theor*y* to theor*ies*. Both actually provided (as, in their way, the structural-functional anthropologists provided) *sets of rules* for clear guidance and use in investigation: in the statement, study, and testing of specific theories. Both stressed the need—in the quest for scientific advance— to aim at the production of *definitive* studies.

A clear advance had therefore been made in these two areas.

Neither Durkheim nor Weber, however, though both acknowledging the importance of associational—or collective—*psychological processes* in society, had directed much attention to the analysis of them. This was the third distinctive area in which clear developments were made.

(3) THE STUDY OF SOCIAL SYSTEMS: THE PSYCHOLOGICAL ASPECTS OF SOCIETY

It was generally agreed that many of the attributes distinguishing human nature from the nature of other animal species were *not* purely rooted in biological differences (though these certainly existed) but were also, and to a very important degree, the product (in some way) of *association*, and the cumulative creation of tradition, culture, and the elaborate fabric of social institutions which developed from it. Human *association* was *psychologically creative*—both collectively (in the making of 'institutions') and individually (in the ordering of experience within the 'self'). The many and complex products of association—the collective and privately experienced psychological elements in institutionalized conduct (sentiments, ideals, values, rules, attitudes: all known and expressed in terms of commonly held symbols, including language)—could not be explained in terms of previously existing individual 'selves' (entire and intact entities before association had taken place.) On the contrary, these collective psychological experiences and the ordering of the experience and behaviour of individual 'selves' were created *in the processes of association*. A knowledge of conditions and processes of association was therefore necessary to understand and explain the emergence and maintenance of *both* the *institutional order and* of *individual 'selves'* alike. Association was a causative, creative, socio-psychological level of human actuality quite distinctive from all other 'interconnections of phenomena' in nature. These collective psychological actualities (sentiments, values, attitudes, etc.) were held to be vitally important *both* for the *objective study of social facts*—since they lay at the heart of all elements of social structure (they constituted the core of institutions); *and* for the *subjective understanding of social action*—since they lay at the heart of individual 'selves' (the ends men sought, the

779

principles they adopted, the motives which drove them in their social action, were rooted in them). It was generally agreed, then, that an *associational context* was necessary for a satisfactory human psychology; and that the study of the psychological aspects of society was necessary to provide 'middle principles' of explanation—between biology and general psychology on the one hand, and generalizations about the patterns of experience and behaviour in 'society' on the other.

This general position was, of course, a reinforcement of the ideas strongly and clearly maintained in the nineteenth century conspectus by Comte and Mill—right through to Ward, Sumner, and Giddings (who had achieved an excellent statement of analysis in relation to it), and also by Marx who denied the validity of any science of human psychology which did not recognize the human creativity of sociohistorical processes. Now, however, certain clear developments had been accomplished.

(i) A clear statement had been achieved of the interrelated nature of the 'Self' and 'Society' which gave full conceptual clarity (and degrees of autonomy) for each whilst also making clear their essential interdependence.

(ii) This clear statement avoided any facile 'determinism'. *Judgment, evaluation, reason* was involved throughout—and this meant that the *closest ties* were possible between the studies of the psychological aspects of associational processes *and* the subjective understanding of social action in terms of meaning.

(iii) This clear statement provided a set of concepts for analysing the processes of 'socialization': (*a*) the ways in which an individual came to act in accordance with all the requirements of the institutional order (coaptation as Radcliffe-Brown called it), and (*b*) the way in which the individual 'self' assumed a certain order of experience and conduct as a social 'person'. Again, this analysis did not assume any necessary postulate of 'harmony' or 'integration' or 'determinism'.

(iv) A clear statement had been achieved of the several important elements in this emergence of the 'self' within the processes of association. These elements especially included: (*a*) *communications* as the very heart, the very actuality of human association, (*b*) the interrelated *'reflection'* of judgments between any 'self' and 'others' in communication, and the consequent *ordering* of experience, (*c*) the importance of *symbols, gestures, acts*, and *pre-verbal* elements in communications as well as the related and supremely important element of *language*, (*d*) the importance of *primary groups* in such communications, and (*e*) the importance of *primary (group) ideals*. A clear analysis of the psychological aspects of association in terms of *groups, group-processes*, and *communications* was thus provided.

(v) A clear statement had been achieved of the interconnected nature of (*a*) the process of *institutionalization*, and (*b*) the *emergence of 'selfhood'*. In this statement, the supreme importance of the *sentiments* was clearly emphasized, and this had certain important aspects which were articulated with great clarity. A *process*, a *sequence*, of the psychological aspects of association was made clear in the emergence of order in both *institutionalization* and the '*self*'. *Instinct* and connected *mental mechanisms* were active within *primary groups* and primary group *communications*. In this context—in relation to *symbols* (of various kinds), and with the growing experience of the responses and *judgments* of others—the formation of *sentiments* took place. These sentiments entailed the focusing of emotion upon a symbol, but were also the psychological carriers (so to speak) of *constellations of values*, and had reference to the *regulation* of experience and *action*. They were, therefore, the effective constellations for the ordering of experience and action *within individual 'selves'*, and *within institutions*. 'Selves' took shape with the establishment of sentiments. And institutions *were* the regulated social order resting upon sentiments. The establishment of sentiments was the core of the psychological creativity of human association. And this was essentially the ordering of human impulse, emotion, judgment and reason about certain *values*. The establishment of *values* and the *attachment* to values was the central actuality in the creation of society: and *social*-order and *self*-order were interconnected parts of this *associational* creativity.

This was a formulation of the very greatest importance, and it can be seen at once to *link* all the other components of sociological analysis together in the most intimate way. The sentiments, the constellations of values and attachment to them, were at the heart of the psychological aspects of society, but they were also the core of 'objective social facts', and were inescapably at work in the social actions which men pursued. In this conception—the very central nucleus of human society was laid bare—about which all the components of sociological analysis could find their clear arrangement. But this ground for the 'unification' of sociological analysis was clarified even further.

(vi) A clear statement had been achieved of a satisfactory 'Social Behaviourism' which gave this socio-psychological analysis a clear *observational* ground. This new formulation of 'behaviourism' (not at all of the Watsonian 'conditioned reflex' kind) linked the analysis of the *experience* of *selves* in *communication* and *association* (sentiments, values, principles, ideals, etc.) with the *institutional structuring of relationships* by focusing upon *the act*. And it was such as to link with excellent efficacy *both* the insistence upon recognizing the distinctive 'teleological' attributes of man *and* the objective (phenomenally observable) facts of his institutionalized social life. For *acts* were *observable facts*; they were parts of the *institutional framework of society*; they did include a clear ordering of psychological experience; but they could not even be *phenomenally distinguished excepting* by the *imputation* of *meaning*. The study of the psychological aspects of society was therefore given a firm observational basis, but in such a way as to link, with superb clarity, the other dimensions of sociological analysis. We may recall, again, that Durkheim defined 'social facts' as 'ways of *acting*', and, of course, Weber's focus upon social 'action' needs no additional mention.

An extremely important basis for the unification of the various 'components' of sociological analysis had therefore not only been seen to be possible, but had been accomplished.

(vii) Clear statements (though by no means definitive) had also been achieved of many of the *mental mechanisms* which characterized the operation of the human mind in experiencing these many constraints and creativities of association. These statements, again, were not 'deterministic' in any facile sense (though the cynicism* and ambiguity† of some statements sometimes gave this impression). The clear operation of conscious reason, logical inference, and impartial judgment in human mentality were recognized, but, at the same time, the great power of impulse, emotion, appetite, and sentiment in swaying conscious reason through the operation of these various 'mechanisms', was made clear. The massive power of the 'non-rational' and the 'irrational' in human society—even in the manipulation of 'reason' itself—was laid bare as never before; and these new concepts furthered the possibility of a deeper and more reliable analysis of these important dimensions.

(viii) Clear statements had also been accomplished about certain other areas of the 'psychological aspects' of society which linked the study of social systems, specific institutions, and individuals, together in useful and perhaps even more definite ways. Each of these was extremely important in its own right, but must be mentioned here only briefly.

Role Analysis. It was now clearly seen to be possible to study the roles within the structures of institutions (and within groups—including primary groups) in terms of a specific regulation of behaviour, and the experiences, attitudes, and expectations involved: so that 'structural-functional analysis' and socio-psychological analysis could be linked with each other in the most intimate way. There was a completely clear link between the analysis of social organization on

---

* Pareto.   † Freud.

the one hand, and the behaviour and experience of individuals on the other—and yet as parts of the same entire process of association. This development clearly extended social psychology beyond the study of the processes of 'socialization' alone, and linked it with every field of social action and organization.

The Analysis of Groups and Group Relations. The grounds for a wider and more systematic analysis of groups had also been clarified. It was clearly seen that within the structure of social institutions, the analysis of differing kinds of relationships in groups of different types, was possible; and this was furthered by the addition of Cooley's distinction between 'primary and secondary' groups to Sumner's earlier distinction between 'In-Groups and Out-Groups'.

Communications. In close connection with role and group analysis, the central importance of *communications* in society had been made clear. Indeed, the very concept of communications had been deepened considerably—as though, almost, it was the very stuff of human association, within the context of which human 'selves' and social 'institutions' took shape; and it was taken far beyond the normal considerations of language into every dimension of psychological, behavioural, and cultural symbolism. The great utility and significance for a knowledge of society of the analysis of every level of communications—from 'primary-group', through 'secondary-group', to 'mass-communications'—had been not only indicated, but (chiefly by Cooley and Mead) to a considerable extent carried out and proved.

Socio-Psychological 'Forms'. An analysis had also been clearly provided of certain socio-psychological 'forms' of human relationships ('authority-submission', etc) which were *universal* in the sense of being found in *all* areas of institutionalized behaviour (whether 'economic', 'religious', 'familial', etc.). This, like Weber's subjective understanding of social action in terms of 'meaning', promised a mode of explanation which went beyond, and showed the insufficiency of, any simple mode of explanation which proceeded by a 'weighting' of descriptive institutional categories. This was the contribution of Simmel, but it is interesting to note that Radcliffe-Brown introduced the notion of 'structural principles' in a very similar way: as universal principles in the organization of human relationships which cut right across all 'institutional' boundaries. These ideas were little more than suggestions: but they obviously promised much.

Élites. An analysis had also been suggested for the study of the psychological aspects of the many élites in society, and of the *circulation* of these élites with special reference to those who *governed* and those who did not. This, too, suggested very forcibly the importance of social psychology, even its indispensability, for any satisfactory study of even the largest-scale aspects of social institutions and processes of social change.

In all these many ways, then, this third 'component' of sociological analysis had been developed very considerably indeed. At the turn of the century, only the major insistence of the nineteenth century founders—coupled, it is true, with the systematic statements of the early Americans, and of Giddings in particular—had existed. Within the space of only forty years or so, the study of the psychological aspects of society had been pushed forward with very considerable achievement on all these fronts. But perhaps the most interesting and important thing for us to notice at this stage is the way in which this 'third dimension' was not only making advancements in its own right, but was inter-linking, in the most significant way, the 'objective study of social facts' as outlined chiefly by Durkheim and the 'subjective understanding of social action' as outlined by Weber. This entire development of the 'psychological aspects of society' fell completely within Durkheim's over-all conception of 'the psychological creativity of society'. The many aspects of this development were really a detailed filling in of all the dimensions of this conception; a detailed elaboration of it. And yet they went beyond Durkheim and beyond the errors of his conceptual limitation, by incorporating, too, all the further dimensions of choice, will, deliberation, purposive action on which Weber's 'subjective understanding' insisted—and which, as we know, had been an insistence in sociology from the very beginning. The study of the 'psychological aspects of society' was not simply, then, a 'third component' *alone*. It was not a separate component. It was a third aspect of those other developments which were reciprocally adding richer dimensions to each other, even though they had been clarified independently, and were in certain ways conceptually distinct; and it linked them together in much more detailed and satisfactory ways.

It is plain that the three 'components' we have clarified so far were not only *developed* during this period, they were also developed in such ways as to be seen to be *growing into each other*. They were developing *interdependently*. Each exploring conceptually distinct areas of study, they were nonetheless coming to be seen as different dimensions of the same complex subject-matter; as different, but necessary, elements of one entire system of analysis. The development was towards *sociological analysis as a whole*.

But other agreements and developments which were especially significant in emphasizing this clarification of sociological analysis as a whole emerged very strongly during this period. Each of them deserves clear and separate statement.

(4) SIGNIFICANT AGREEMENT AMONG ALL THEORISTS: THE
BIOLOGICAL BASIS OF SOCIOLOGY

We have seen that certain basic points agreed upon by the
'psychologically' oriented theorists (McDougall, Cooley, Mead,
Freud, etc.) were not *only* shared by them, but were in fact agreed
upon—with a striking degree of unanimity—by *all* the theorists we
have studied. Strictly speaking, there was no boundary between them.
All the theorists embraced the same socio-psychological components
within their systems of analysis. We shall come back to the significance
of this. For the moment two basic agreements must be noted as being
of importance.

First: all these twentieth century writers were completely agreed
on consolidating the recognition of the biological basis for the study
of man and society. They were agreed that whatever might be said
in psychological and sociological terms about the nature of man,
human beings and their societies had definite biological roots. The
changed perspective on man's place in nature brought about by
the 'Biological Revolution'* of the nineteenth century had completely won the day. The new orientation was now firmly accepted
and adopted as a foundation. This point—now so much taken for
granted—has importance for our summary in two ways.

We may remind ourselves, first of all, that this recognition of the
biological basis of human nature was still playing a fundamental
part not only in the development of all the 'components' of sociology,
but also, simultaneously, in the making of other human sciences.
In sociology we have seen plainly enough that the biological theory
of evolution gave the grounding of knowledge from which many
dimensions of the analysis of social institutions stemmed. This
was true in Tönnies, Westermarck, Hobhouse, Durkeim, Weber,
Pareto—indeed, in all the theorists in one way or another. The
nature of functional 'requisites' or 'imperatives'; the *sequence* of
'instinct, habit, sentiment-formation, custom, reason, etc.', in
institutionalization; these and other elements of analysis all
rested upon the knowledge of the anatomical, physiological, and
behavioural aspects of human nature provided by biology. But also,
we have seen that the struggles of men like McDougall and Freud
in their making of *psychology* were in large part efforts to establish
the subject on an improved biological and physiological basis, in
place of an earlier, and insufficient, philosophical one. Similarly,
the making of anthropology had rested centrally on biology; and
even in the new development of *social* anthropology, we have seen
how great was Malinowski's emphasis upon the biological aspects

* And the *Geological Revolution*.

785

of man's nature, and his physiologically given needs. Biology was clearly seen to be the necessary basis of psychology, anthropology and sociology alike. Indeed, the new biological perspective embraced all these subjects in a clearly seen unity—and without in any sense involving *reductionist* assumptions.

The 'Biological Revolution'—then much more basic and fundamental than we now think—was still working its way through the whole fabric of human thought, reformulating all the human sciences (indeed, all subjects) in accordance with its new perspectives.

The second point is no more than a corollary of this same basic perspective—but of sigificance nonetheless. It is that in all the work we have studied there was a considerable growth and development in *the comparative study of animal behaviour* in relation to the study of man. Growth—in that there was more of it, and its place and relevance was increasingly recognized. Development—in that such studies were becoming much more sophisticated. We have seen that Weber recognized the relevance of animal studies for appreciating the distinctiveness of the human mind and the action and social action of which it was capable. Westermarck was insistent that comparative studies of social behaviour should not be arbitrarily confined to man, and that animal societies should also be included. Hobhouse actually undertook such comparative and experimental studies himself (and was continuously aware of the comparative psychology developed by Lloyd Morgan and others). Freud was always seeking to link his theories concerning the human mind with those he took to be established about other animals. And, of course, comparative psychology was an essential part of McDougall's efforts to establish experimental psychology on a firm and reliable footing.

Underlying all these developments, there was the clearly accepted assumption that though distinctive from other animal species in quite important respects, man nonetheless shared certain features of anatomy, physiology, behaviour and experience, with them. The comparative studies of sociology needed therefore to be extended *beyond man*, to incorporate comparative studies of the social behaviour of other animals if the fullest accuracy and sufficiency of knowledge was to be achieved.

The importance of a biological basis for the human sciences was therefore firmly established; and the importance of comparative studies of animal behaviour was also established.* This recognized

* This is of particular interest in that—from about the mid-'thirties—the comparative study of animal behaviour itself developed in a conspicuous fashion, with the new title of Comparative Ethology: almost to the point of becoming regarded as a distinctive 'school'—which, of course, it is not.

intimacy of connection between biology, psychology and sociology was, however, the basis for an agreement of far greater importance: perhaps the most significant agreement of all.

(5) SIGNIFICANT AGREEMENT AMONG ALL THEORISTS: THE PROCESS OF INSTITUTIONALIZATION

Earlier, when summarizing the conceptual achievements of those who chiefly studied the 'psychological aspects of society', we noted the remarkable agreement in all their accounts of the close relationship between 'self' and 'society'. They were all agreed that the growth of the human 'self' was dependent upon *association*. Association was essentially a process of *communication*, and the 'consciousness of self' took shape within the context of the actions, values, and judgments of others. The regulated *order* assumed by the social-mental complex was *both* a social *and* an individual order. The *social pattern of regulated actions* and the *patterned experience and behaviour of individual 'selves'* were two aspects of the same socio-psychological process. And a certain *sequence* in this process was clarified. *Activities* were initially prompted by *instinctual* appetites or needs, and pursued the *interests* rooted in them. The co-operation and conflict with others, the acts and judgments of others, were encountered in such activities—and by *all* those who were involved. The associational activities had to be *regulated*; they assumed a *form*; and this regulated form of reciprocal *acts* was correlated with the order of experience and conduct established within the individual persons. *Both* rested upon established *habit* and established *sentiments*. And *sentiments* were, in fact, the constellations of *values* established during the course of these associational processes. They were *collective* psychological facts, but they were the core of psychological order and regulation in *individuals*. It was the sentiments which were the established constellations of feeling, value, attachment, obligation, in terms of which judgment, approval and disapproval, took place. *These* were the *norms* at the heart of institutions, and they were (as Durkheim put it) 'strongly engraven in all consciences'. The sentiments were the bedrock of social and individual order.

Now what has become clear with such striking forcefulness throughout all our studies, is that this was not only a matter of agreement among the 'psychologically oriented' theorists, but, quite literally, among *all* the theorists we have considered. This is a point worth dwelling on.

No matter how different these theorists may have appeared—

whether in the scale and range of their analysis, the apparent dissimilarity of their concepts, the apparent focus of their interests—they were all astonishingly exact in their agreement about this fundamental process of institutionalization, and the elements (and the *sequence* of these elements) which went into it. William McDougall seems a far cry from Emile Durkheim; Durkheim seems a far cry from Edward Westermarck; Cooley and Mead seem a far cry from Pareto; Freud seems a far cry from them all—but the emphasis must, as we have seen, be upon the word *seems*. Under the *apparently* most varied conceptual approaches there was the *fullest and most solid agreement* about *the process of institutionalization*. And the process of institutionalization, of course, was at the very heart of what sociology and social psychology were seeking to explain. *The process of institutionalization and the correlated growth of the 'self' was, in fact, the distinctive psychological creativity of human association.* This was the distinctive *level* of *society* which it had been the concern of every sociologist to emphasize—from Comte's initial statement onwards.

Now—the analysis of this central process had received a clear, articulate, agreed statement. The fundamental process of institutionalization—the emergence of a regulated order of social behaviour and personal experience out of the creative complexities of human association—was *understood*. This was an agreement of the utmost importance. There were many dimensions in it. We must take care to note them all.

(i) *The striking extent of this agreement*

First, let us note as precisely and fully as a summary statement will allow, this straightforward and impressive fact of an agreement very close to unanimity.

Tönnies, it will be remembered, gave an account of the growth of 'natural will' among persons within a shared community; the growth of an order of personal character within an order of traditional institutions. What were the elements involved? What was the sequence of them? *Natural instinct* was an awakening of impulses and appetites, and a pleasure in, and liking for, the objects, which satisfied them. Dispositions of behaviour were then patterned by '*habit*' in relation to social and practical experience, but this took place within the context of *learning* and the laying down of *memory*. Crucially, *sentiments* were established. These were the constellations of cognition, feeling, experience, thinking and *evaluation* which constituted the core and content of conscience and the basis of *judgment*. And they were also the values which lay at the heart of the *social order* of groups and institutions in the community.

Westermarck's analysis of 'institutions' was exactly the same. Institutions were the *'sanctioned'* relationships in society. What elements lay in the emergence and sustained force of these sanctions? And what was the sequence of them? *Natural instinct* prompted human beings to undertake activities and form relationships. Dispositions of *habit* were established, and—in close connection—*sentiments*. The sentiments were constellations of feeling built about centrally held *values*, and they especially included the emotions of *approval* and *disapproval*. But these sentiments and their values emerged in the context of social co-operation and conflict, and with the activation of the generalizing tendency of *sympathy*, and they thus assumed the *general* form of *custom*: the usages which were *sanctioned* in society. The development of the moral ideas was thus the growth of *sanctions*, and these were the basic reality, the binding force, of social institutions.

Hobhouse, too, postulated the instinctive basis of much human impulse, emotion, and action, but argued, like the others, that the distinctive qualities of human individuality emerged within the process of association. The 'self' and its order of values were a *social* product. In his analysis, the same sequence of instinct, communication, habit, and sentiment-formation was put forward in describing the emergence of institutions and values. The ordering of the personal 'will' was closely correlated with the order of the 'social tradition'. Hobhouse was exactly in agreement with Tönnies and Westermarck, and with Westermarck's dictum: 'Society is the birth-place of the moral consciousness.'

Durkheim's analysis of 'social facts' (the 'collective conscience') also turned out to be—quite plainly—an analysis of the *sentiments*, and his account was completely in agreement with that of Tönnies, Westermarck and Hobhouse. For him too, the elements which formed the core of social institutions were the *sentiments*—which were 'strongly engraven in all consciences'. Beginning (in his case) with the *externally observable* characteristics of social institutions—such as the framework of the *law* and the scale of *sanctions* which regulated and constrained behaviour in society—he then, nonetheless, concluded that it was the sentiments (with their beliefs, values, judgments, and the strength of their feelings of approval and disapproval) which were the collective psychological reality on which they rested. The formation of sentiments in the processes of association was the creation of an *order* of individuality and institutions alike. *Institutionalization was the creative socio-psychological process of society: and at its heart was the establishment of sentiments.*

Bearing all this in mind, it can be seen that Durkheim's definition of sociology: *'the science of institutions, of their genesis and of their*

functioning' was exactly the same conception as Westermarck's
'*origin and development of the moral ideas*' in his study of *sanctioned*
relationships—completely different though they seem at first glance,
and have often been assumed to be. There was an important core
of agreement here—not difference.

Among all those who studied the 'psychological aspects of society',
the same agreement was clear. McDougall saw the sentiments as
the basis of social institutions and morality in society, but also as
the basis of the growth of the 'self'. He also saw the growth of the
'self' as essentially a *social* process, though rooted in initial instinctual
dispositions, Cooley held exactly the same position. Human nature
had its instinctual basis, but the 'self' grew essentially in the context
of association. The *order* of experience and behaviour in individual,
group and community alike, rested upon the gradual establishment
of 'social sentiments and attitudes'—which were constellations of
feeling organized about the *ideals* and *values* experienced during
the process of communication in primary groups. Mead's analysis
was essentially the same, but, as we have seen, linked all this to a
clear emphasis upon the *act* which emerged in this socio-psychological order. The *acts* of the behavioural order (the observable *units*
of institutions) were themselves not simply phenomenal events, but
possessed (indeed, were defined by) all the symbolic significance of
the sentiments and their values. The link which the sentiments
formed between the *experiential order* within individuals and the
organizational order of social institutions was thus given a clear
basis of *observable action*; and this, as we have seen, linked Durkheim, Weber, and the 'social-psychologists' alike.

Freud, too, had exactly the same analysis. Human nature possessed
powerful instinctive dispositions, and the 'self' took shape as—
through the varied operation of the mental mechanisms—the values
and idealized objects of the outer social world came to be internalized
as elements of the 'super-ego' (establishing criteria for both inhibition and aspiration.) This was clearly another conceptual analysis
of 'sentiment' formation: the establishment of values which regulated
behaviour in accordance with institutional norms. In Pareto's
analysis, too—on the face of it so different—we saw the same
striking agreement on this central matter. For him too, the basic
ground of the 'residues' and 'derivations', which were the most
powerful forces of society (making for equilibrium or disequilibrium),
were the *sentiments*; and these, too, were rooted in man's instinctual
dispositions.

Finally—and it is most interesting to note this—exactly the same
agreement was found in the analysis offered by Malinowski and
Radcliffe-Brown. Here too there was a clear recognition of the

instinctual basis of human nature, but, on the basis of this, an analysis of the distinctively human order of 'self' and 'society' in terms of association and the establishment of sentiments and norms was developed. In both of these authors (despite their disagreements on other points), the process of institutionalization was held to be the same. It is interesting to note that—like Westermarck and Durkheim—Radcliffe-Brown actually *defined* institutions as *norms*, and thought of them essentially as established sentiments, values, and sanctions. 'An institution,' he wrote, 'is an established norm of conduct recognized as such by a distinguishable social group . . .' Indeed, the more one examines his various essays on 'Taboo', 'Religion', 'Law', 'Sanctions', and the like, the more (as with Durkheim) one comes to think of his whole work as being an exploration of *the process of institutionalization*; and essentially in terms of the formation of sentiments.

For the sake of completeness, I must note that we have not mentioned Weber and Simmel here. This is entirely because, in their preoccupation with 'social action' and 'forms' of social interaction, they deliberately stood aside from some of these socio-psychological questions. Even so, we have seen that Weber, for example, recognized the same sequence—from instinct, through sentiment and tradition, to reason—as did the others. The agreement can therefore be said to be well-nigh complete, though these theorists devoted themselves to other tasks.

Now this statement of agreement on this quite basic matter has been of a very summary nature—of necessity here. But it is worth-while to note that all these theorists were not only agreed about the centrality of the sentiments in the process of institutionalization; they also emphasized their *power*. 'Sentiment,' wrote Cooley, 'is the *chief motive-power of life* . . .' Pareto, Freud, Durkheim . . . all would have agreed with this forceful emphasis. Though, then, we can dwell on this no longer here, I would like to urge as full an appreciation as possible of this point. It is well worth while to look again at the statement of each theorist to see how extremely close this agreement was;* and this point has the further importance that when we come to consider strictly contemporary (post-war) theories —especially that of Talcott Parsons—we shall see that this question of the process of institutionalization plays a quite central part.

For now, however, we must briefly note one or two other points of importance which were connected with this agreement.

* See Tönnies p. 47, 70, Westermarck p. 89, 103, Hobhouse, p. 148–52, 215, 234–5, Durkheim, p. 264–9, McDougall, p. 479–80, Cooley, p. 485–501, Mead, p. 518–34, Freud, p. 560–74, 654–63, Malinowski, p. 695–99, Radcliffe-Brown, p. 715, 720, 742.

(ii) *The inter-linking of dimensions of theory which this agreement achieved*

A mere indication of the *extent* of this agreement is not sufficient to do justice to the accomplishments it represents. It is worthwhile to note, by means of a simple statement, the elements of theory which it satisfactorily drew together.

This account of institutionalization:

(*a*) Satisfactorily incorporated such knowledge of human nature as biology and psychology could provide (about instinct, emotion, maturation, etc.), without in any sense *reducing* explanation to these terms.

(*b*) It took full and satisfactory account of the fact that human activities were distinctively *purposive* and *evaluative*. The behaviour of men was not to be explained as a set of *phenomenal events*, necessarily determined by material and social factors, and mental mechanisms. Rooted in instinctual dispositions, couched in specific social conditions, human experience and behaviour involved *judgment*: the awareness of ends, the evaluation of qualities, the calculation of means. The *regulated order* of individual and social life was thus one which rested essentially upon values.

(*c*) It accomplished, on this basis, a detailed and agreed analysis of all the components (and their sequence) which went into the emergence of an institutional order. Instinct, interest, habit, learning, memory, conflict and co-operation, evaluation and judgment, regulation, sentiment-formation, custom, institutions, reason, morality, the purposeful re-making of institutions . . . all these were connected in a careful analysis, and this included practical, determinate, psychological and social factors *in close inter-connection* with elements of choice, deliberation, reason, and purpose. It was made clear how all these could be satisfactorily combined.

(*d*) It gave detailed substantiation to the view we have encountered in all the sociologists from Comte onwards that *values were at the heart of social institutions*. The process of institutionalization was essentially one of regulation resting upon values. Not necessarily harmonious values. The regulations came into being as an outcome of conflict as well as co-operation. But, nonetheless, a network of values which regulated human behaviour in relation to some fulfilment of interests. Society was essentially a network of values. Man was essentially a moral being.

(*e*) It gave a clear analysis of the *psychological creativity of society* which was the distinctive associational *level* insisted upon by all those who were convinced of the necessity of a science of sociology. The analysis of the emergence of an *institutional order* and of a related order of *individual personality* was linked by the understanding of the *sentiments* as collectively engendered constellations of values.

(*f*) It linked all this *both* with Durkheim's insistence upon observational exactitude (i.e. in terms of some *external* characteristics or indices) *and* Weber's insistence upon the understanding of action in terms of meaning, by clearly seeing the significance of the *act* as the phenomenal and meaningful embodiment of the sentiments. Psychological factors, material factors, collective social conditions, organizational factors, collectively engendered values together with their cultural symbols, behavioural factors, and the interpretation of *action* in terms of *meaning*, could all now be dealt with together within a clearly conceived 'Social Behaviourism'.

This again, is a brief summary statement only, but is enough, I hope, to show how many dimensions of earlier and apparently different approaches were successfully brought together and resolved in this new statement. Much more was accomplished here than can possibly be understood by a rapid acquaintance with these authors. A profound accomplishment was embodied in this agreement which emerged from their work.

(iii) *Morality at the heart of Institutions*
We have already mentioned this point—but it is worthwhile to note it separately again and give it special emphasis. In this agreed analysis of the process of institutionalization, and in their focus upon the importance of the sentiments as constellations of values, all these authors—like all the nineteenth century authors—voiced the perennial conviction that *morality lay at the heart of social institutions*. Institutionalization in all men's practical activities, and even in the simplest traditional order, was an establishment of values. *Nothing was more basic than this.* No 'material basis', no 'psychological necessities', no 'idealities' external to society were more '*primary*' than this. The *essential* nature of institutionalization was the establishment of values. It is important simply to see that there was as solid an agreement on this point among the twentieth century theorists as there had been among those of the nineteenth, and we shall see other important aspects of this agreement in a moment.

The upshot of these last few points is this. The contributions of the twentieth century theorists were not only such as to have clarified and provided a total system of sociological analysis, they were also such as to demonstrate a clear and substantial core of agreement about the basic subject-matter of sociology. The objective study of the phenomenal aspects of social facts, the subjective understanding of social action in terms of meaning, and the many dimensions of the psychological aspects of society, provided an interrelated set of concepts whereby testable knowledge could be achieved of all the aspects of any social system. In addition to this, however, the distinctive *level* of associational facts had now been clarified beyond any kind of vagueness or doubt, and, centrally, the process of *institutionalization* (the associational process creative of both social and personal order) had received a clear, articulate, agreed analysis. It was understood. All these elements, as we saw earlier, were rooted in the nineteenth century foundations, and even clearly declared there, but now they had received a much deeper examination, and clear rules for the satisfactory study of them had been established. This was therefore a very substantial development indeed: or rather, as we have so clearly seen, the interconnected outcome of several developments, each of which, for the particular theorist who undertook and accomplished it, had its own rationale.

(6) THE STUDY OF SOCIAL SYSTEMS: EVOLUTION

We have already pointed out—and it is of basic importance—that the major elements of sociological analysis incorporated in the objective study of social facts, the subjective understanding of social action, and the study of the psychological study of society—themselves insisted that associational facts were essentially of a historical nature. There was simply no problem of *separately* providing concepts for the study of social change. All these concepts were themselves couched within the context of a historical and evolutionary perspective. But extremely important achievements had been made in developing the concept of evolution itself and its application in sociological studies, and these, too, must be carefully noted. These, too, were definitive achievements, of perennial worth, but—a little later—were to be lost sight of and ignored.

(i) *Complete agreement about the Evolutionary perspective*
It is important to note very emphatically, first of all, that every single author who contributed to the making of sociology during the first half of the present century accepted the truth and importance of the evolutionary perspective and built his conceptual scheme within the context of it. Not one author denied it. It was as strongly present in Malinowski and Radcliffe-Brown, in Durkheim and Weber, in McDougall, Cooley, Mead, Freud, Pareto, as it was in Tönnies, Westermarck and Hobhouse; and as it had been in all the major theorists from Comte onwards. Evolution was never absent from sociological theory—excepting for those whose own

794

eyes were blind to it. But, as we shall see in Volume 3, even they had to learn that their field of vision was incomplete.

(ii) *Distinctive Usages of the concept of evolution*

The second point we must note is that in all the conceptual developments we have examined, distinct usages of the concept of evolution were made clear. All of them were valuable and appropriate in their own direction of enquiry, but they were not to be confused.

First of all there was the straightforward acceptance and use of the theory of *biological evolution* to account for those given and universal elements of human nature which were the springs of certain fundamental interests and actions, and with which social systems universally had to deal. There were basic elements of the bio-psychological endowment of man that underlay specific 'functional requisites' and 'imperatives' in society; which were basically involved in the process of institutionalization; and which remained active in all the mental mechanisms operative in complex social behaviour. Westermarck, Pareto, Malinowski, were good examples of this particular acceptance of biological evolution proper (though *all* theorists in fact accepted it) and it is perhaps necessary to note that this was not simply a matter of negative acceptance: it formed a positive basis for their analysis and wide comparative study of social institutions.

Secondly, closely following upon this conception, we have seen that in Durkheim and Westermarck especially (and in both of them alike) a complete clarity was achieved of the way in which evolutionary studies could illuminate the *origins* of institutions. In both cases it was made perfectly plain that the use of evolution was *not* that of seeking to uncover the first, chronological, historical events in which institutions had their birth; it was *not* a seeking for *origins* in this sense at all; but that of seeking to uncover the basic bio-psychological and associational elements which were (always and everywhere) the *primary causes* involved in *institutionalization*. When Westermarck sought the *origins* of moral ideas or sanctioned relationships; when Durkheim sought the *origins* of institutions; it was the uncovering of the most primary causative elements which they were seeking; and they believed the evolutionary perspective was essential for this.

Thirdly, there was the acceptance of the more basic form of the evolutionary conception (really Spencerian) that the nature of any 'form' of actuality (material, organic, social) was what it was essentially in relation to its environmental conditions. This was clearly applicable to the study of social systems—and all theorists adopted it. The emergence, maintenance, patterns of change, and dissolution, of institutions and societies were significantly related to their surrounding 'life conditions', and the framework of analysis should always be such as to take this into account.

Fourthly, there was the acceptance of the fact that human societies had 'evolved' in terms of certain observable, significant levels of aggregation and kinds of organization. Tribal societies resting chiefly upon bonds of kinship, and with a non-literate culture could be distinguished from civic nations (City States) or from large 'despotic' agrarian civilizations which did possess literacy, and a new complex hierarchy of social organization and authority; and the growth of both these 'types' could be traced in terms of certain kinds of aggregations of tribes. Empires, the feudal systems which replaced their disruption, modern Nation States and federations of states . . . all these could be distinguished. Without at all assuming *unlinear* or *inevitable* sequences, it was possible to classify societies and clarify the kinds of 'institutional consensus' which characterized each type. Now many enquiries were possible within such a vast field of study, but some things were perfectly clear. These 'kinds' of society should be *classified* as carefully as possible. A satisfactory *comparative study* of social institutions was impossible without such a classification. And certain *directions* of social evolution could be clarified: centrally—that of an increasing growth in the size and complexity of societies and an increasing *differentiation* of structure and function, an increasing *specialization*, within the field of institutions. All we need note here, of course, is, again, that *all* the theorists we have mentioned accepted this: Radcliffe-Brown and Durkheim as much as Hobhouse. Really, this was simply Spencer continued, but it was the merit of Hobhouse especially to have carried out a classificatory and comparative study on this basis which was of the richest detail. A superb contribution in terms of the clear, substantial assemblage of comparative *knowledge* about human societies had been made.

Fifthly, it had also been made clear—in the work of Tönnies and Weber especially—that the *'typological'* explanation of specific, concrete configurations of change could be accomplished within the context of universal elements of social evolution. Thus the elements of 'natural will' and 'rational' will were *universally* operative in human association and systems of institutions, but Tönnies demonstrated how richly *specific sequences* of social transformation could be illuminated by the sharp dichotomy of *'types'*. Weber's work, as we know, also emphasized and demonstrated the worth of this same method.

There was, however, a sixth development in applying the concept of evolution to the study of human society which was of the very greatest importance, and which many have completely failed to see. This, too, was strongly rooted in the basic persuasions of the nineteenth century 'conspectus', and almost all the twentieth century theorists accepted it, but it was undoubtedly Hobhouse who stated it with the greatest and most compelling clarity. It stemmed directly from his demonstration that the growth of *mind* was the central feature of evolution, and that this was greatly and significantly extended by the cumulative growth of knowledge in the development of human society, and it was rooted with complete clarity in the initial conception of Comte and Mill. It was simply this.

In the origin and development (to use Darwin's words) of all species prior to man, evolution could well be explained in terms of genetic change and the operation of natural selection. The form and nature and survival of any species could be explained in terms of *adaptation*. To some extent, and especially with reference to the earliest and most culturally primitive human communities, the same could be said of the human species. *But*—with the cumulative extension of systematic knowledge and the *control* that this brought with it—the evolution of human society, of man as a species, and, indeed, of the entire process of life on the earth, became increasingly one of man's deliberate *transformation* of his life conditions. Increasingly conscious, deliberate, effective control took the place of submission to natural forces; *creative purpose* took the place of negative adaptation; the *responsible direction* of life took the place of powerless dependence.

Now the only absolutely essential point which we must be clear about here is that *this was a distinctive addition to the Darwinian apparatus of evolutionary explanation, a new emphasis within it, and henceforth the explanation of the changes of human societies in terms of adaptation only were insufficient and false.* Social systems were *not*—like mechanical or organic systems—systems of parts in *adaptation* to environmental conditions. Certainly environmental conditions had to be taken into account, but social systems were institutionalized patterns of *purposeful human activities*. There was deliberate purpose in terms of ends, priorities of choice, values, which *directed* the process of transformation.

This, clearly, was a point powerfully at the heart of Comte, Mill, Marx, Ward, Giddings—that men in the light of their ideals and purposes could not only understand but *change* the world—but now it was given a meticulously clear formulation, and supported by a wide range of comparative knowledge. It must also be seen in this that the major sociologists who contributed to the founding and development of the subject—though they used 'organic' analogies and spoke in terms of 'equilibrium and dis-equilibrium' adjustments in a way sometimes reminiscent of 'mechanical systems'—were, nonetheless, completely clear in *distinguishing* social systems from organic and mechanical systems. Social systems possessed these *additional* and quite *distinctive* characteristics of *purposive* activity based upon *knowledge, predictive foresight, and values.*

This, then, was a major development—distinctively *changing* the conception of evolutionary explanation and taking it *beyond* that of Darwin—and moving sociological theory, again, decisively towards Weber's insistence that sociological explanation required *understanding* in terms of *purpose* and *meaning*, if it was to be satisfactorily *explained.*

The concept of evolution was therefore clarified in quite distinctive ways by these theorists, and these were developments of the most vital importance.

(7) THE STUDY OF SOCIAL SYSTEMS: AGREEMENT ON EVOLU-
TIONARY PERSPECTIVES: THE 'NET' RESULT OF SOCIAL
EVOLUTION AND THE MODERN 'MALAISE'

One important point follows immediately upon this consideration of 'evolution' but deserves separate statement. We have seen that all the twentieth century theorists—though having their various approaches and emphases in the study of the evolutionary aspects of society—were solidly agreed about what Hobhouse called the 'Net' outcome of social evolution in the contemporary world. They all agreed in their characterization of the actual juncture at which human societies (whatever the historical courses by which they had travelled) had now arrived. All their generalizations were similar to each other, similar to those of the nineteenth century theorists, and showed the same concerns. Fundamentally, they all clarified, in one way or another, the great transformation of the modern world—from traditional community to highly complex industrial society—and they all characterized this as a two-sided malaise: as possessing great promise, but also grave threat.

We saw that throughout the nineteenth century the making of sociology was for the critical task of social reconstruction: the making of a new society. The *ancien régime* had gone—but no satisfactory institutions had taken their place. Knowledge, effort, and purposive political reconstruction was required. Among the twentieth century theorists the perspective was the same, and each of them illuminated it additionally in his own way.

Tönnies portrayed the significant transformation as that from 'Community' to 'Society', bringing the promise of technical advance and material wealth, but also a threatened dehumanization of relationships limited to calculated contracts alone. Rationality could ride with smart efficiency over other dimensions of the human spirit. Westermarck saw *reason* as promising 'enlightenment' in its reflection upon custom, but, remembering the emphasis he placed upon the sentiments, he too saw that social disintegration could come. It is well known that he believed that the family, as a unit, was strong enough to survive the vicissitudes of modern social change; but it is not so well known that, as we have seen, he *only* thought this because of the strength of certain sentiments* '. . . if there will be a time when conjugal and parental sentiments have vanished, I think that nothing in the world can save marriage and the family from destruction.' Hobhouse (like Comte), saw the modern transformation as one of critical and experiential reconstruction of an 'empirical order' genetically established, and characterized it as a period of 'realistic humanitarianism'. He saw the great promise which this reconstruction of institutions could achieve in terms of human freedom, happiness, and fulfilment, but also the grave threat of a new totalitarian power which the new degrees of knowledge and power made possible. Durkheim described the transformation as that from 'mechanical' to 'organic' solidarity, and saw the progress in individual freedom and social justice that this made possible. But he also saw (like Comte) the *anomie* which attended it: the lack of coherence in the thought, feeling, action of men with the lack of moral rules to guide them. Weber described the transition as being that from a traditional type of authority and social solidarity to one based upon a rational-legal system of the rule of law which could be supremely efficient and just. But he was also fearful of the great power possessed by such new bureaucracies, and feared their dominion over individuals. Cooley saw the transformation as one from a relatively simple community of predominantly primary groups—in which primary values were clearly relevant throughout the whole social order, to that of a complex 'mass' society which gave rise to 'formalism' and 'disorganization'. He saw the promise of human welfare in these changes, but was fearful of the loss of primary ideals under the domination of 'mass-communications'. Freud, aware of the possibility of mature rational knowledge and self-control, was also aware of the massive emotional needs at the heart of human anxiety, and viewed the human situation essentially as a tragedy. Pareto was, as we have seen, a kind of thinker very different from all the others: and yet, even in his cynicism, he had to describe the modern transformation as one in which great struggles were taking place for humanitarian ideals, for a reconstitution of states in the direction of democracy, and by a growing

* i.e. in *The Future of Marriage in Western Civilization*, p. 265.

dominance of science and its application in human affairs. But for him, this was just one more 'danse macabre' of the residues and the derivations.

The picture was essentially the same: of a gigantic flux of institutional change—from traditional solidarity to rational insecurity—which promised and threatened much, but which was, above all, a distinctive modern malaise requiring responsible reconstruction for its solution. The distinctively modern dilemma—conspicuously born at the time of the French Revolution, and at the heart of all the nineteenth century theories—was still the central issue, the central concern, the central theoretical orientation, in twentieth century sociology.

It is almost as simple as this: that all these theorists were struggling with the problem of how to create a humane society out of the human promise and the inhuman threat of industrial capitalism. This, as Weber would have put it, was the problem 'of cultural significance' in our time.

(8) THE STUDY OF SOCIAL SYSTEMS: FACT AND VALUE

This, however, was not by any means the end of the matter. One other great achievement of this period was that the entire matter of the distinction between the philosophical clarification of ethical criteria and the scientific clarification of procedures for the study of facts was made completely clear, as were many of the relations between them in substantive sociological studies. Not all difficulties in this difficult area of thinking were eliminated, but the basic issues were clarified, and in such a way as to have a highly significant bearing on the nature of sociological studies. Let us move point by point.

(*a*) It was made completely clear by Hobhouse especially, but also by Weber, that the scientific study of phenomenal facts could never possibly, in itself, provide the *criteria of ethical evaluation* in the light of which the rightness or wrongness, the progress or retrogression, of such facts could be judged.

(*b*) It was also made clear that it was only by philosophical enquiry independent of science that the *presuppositions* of human moral judgments could be made explicitly clear and thus stated as *criteria (standards) of judgment*.

(*c*) It was also made clear that neither in the statements of scientific hypotheses about facts nor in the statements of philosophical clarification of ethical criteria could anything of the nature of *absolute* truth be claimed. This, in any case, was not necessary. The necessary things were (i) that the clearest reasoning should be brought to bear upon each kind of question, and that these questions should remain *open* to such scrutiny, and (ii) that the correctness of the separateness of the two enquiries should be plainly recognized and observed. Given the acceptance of this method then questions of 'progress' (or any other such question pertaining to justice) were perfectly legitimate questions. They could always be challenged. But in all cases the *grounds of reason* for preferring one rather than another position were essentially required. Otherwise (as has happened) such questions would fall into the realm of sheer, careless, irresponsible assertion; in short into both scientific and philosophical naivety.

There were, however, difficult complications in the study of man and society, but these too were clearly resolved.

(*d*) Any satisfactory scientific study of 'objective' facts in human society had necessarily to be as well informed as possible in moral philosophy, for the simple reason that the actual judgments men made in their social activities had reference to ethical principles and ideals—and these could only be 'known' by subjective understanding; by the imputation of meaning. Social facts were not 'phenomena' as we have seen, and could not be satisfactorily known whilst conceived as such. The simple truth was that moral and social philosophy and social science could not be separated at all in the actuality of their work, unless a worthless naivety was to result. Their conceptual (and logical) levels were distinct (as above), but in the actuality of their work they could not leave each other. This, again, was stated with particular clarity by Hobhouse.

(*e*) It would seem that this 'inseparability' of these logical disciplines would be bound to lead to confusion in sociological studies, but this was not so, and here it was the achievement of Weber to make matters clear. Weber's argument in simple terms was this. (1) The social scientist's selection of a problem—which he wished to explain—necessarily rested upon some *evaluation*; it would be a problem he judged to be 'of cultural significance'. (2) The social scientist was certainly bound to employ all the subtlety of imagination and intellectual acuteness he possessed—including his philosophical clarification of ethical ideals—in *imputing meaning* to the participants in the *social configuration* he desired to explain. (3) All the criteria he employed could be made plain as far as he was capable. (4) The elements of evaluation, however, now made plain, need not remain *subjective assessments of an ethical nature*. They could be conceptually incorporated in defining the '*object of knowledge*' which he was seeking to understand. The '*ideal type*' he constructed would be such as particularly to point to the comparisons with actuality by which the logical validity of his interpretations might be tested. In these ways the study of actuality (including moral judgments) could include the interpretations and evaluations of the investigator (including his ethical criteria), but in such a way as to be open to logical criticism and empirical test. And Weber was insistent that once the 'object of knowledge' *had* been defined, then accuracy of logical criticism and empirical test (i.e. the rigours of scientific method) were supreme; and any *insufficiencies* of an ideal-type interpretation could then be revealed.

(*f*) This amounts to the fact, then, that two kinds of situation were clarified: one in which one was deliberately exercising an ethical judgment about certain social facts, e.g. as to whether they shared 'progress' or 'retrogression' compared with others; and a second in which ethical interpretations were actually forming a part of the imputation of meaning in an empirical study. In both cases a clear statement had been achieved.

(9) THE STUDY OF SOCIAL SYSTEMS: RATIONALITY, PURPOSE, AND ETHICAL PRINCIPLE INCREASINGLY IN THE ACTUALITY OF SOCIAL INSTITUTIONS

Many of these earlier points can now be drawn together in a further agreement of the twentieth century theorists which was of the very greatest importance. We have seen their insistence that the process of institutionalization was essentially an establishment of values (the actuality of which was the *sentiments*). We have seen that this was a reinforcement of the perennial conception that *morality* lay at the heart of social institutions. We have seen their view that the significant transformation of the modern world was one in which *traditional institutions* (with their *traditional values*) were giving way to a new rationality of contractual relationships which possessed both promise and threat. We have seen that they had clarified—to a very considerable extent—the relations between ethics and social science, and also that, in various ways, they all saw a science of society as a necessary basis for social reconstruction.

The extremely interesting point which we can now clearly see, is that in their agreement about the evolutionary perspectives of society, about the 'net' result of this, about the significant transformation of the modern world, and about the efforts towards re-construction that should be made, all these theorists were also agreed that *rationality, deliberate purpose, and ethical principle* were increasingly a part of the *actuality* of *institutional change*. In short the *actual nature of social institutions* in the radically changing modern situation could not possibly be explained excepting in terms (and to an increasing extent) of *rational calculation, ethical principle*, and *deliberate purpose*. Now this contains very important elements.

First, let us note clearly how true it is that this was a substantial agreement among almost all these men. For Tönnies, in his analysis of 'Gesellschaft', the matter is obvious. Hobhouse, too, directly claimed all this. Weber's method was specifically oriented towards it. But also we have seen how astonishingly true it was of Durkheim —and in ways which completely belied his rejection of 'teleology'. Durkeim not only insisted on the purposive attempt to reconstruct 'industrial corporations' and to build a fabric of 'intercalary' institutions between State and family for the resuscitation of 'community', but especially insisted upon the conspicuous growth of *rationality* and *justice* in institutions. Quite radically, he not only pointed to the *prevalence* of the pressure towards *justice* in modern institutions (i.e. as a social *fact*) but also *ethically* urged that it was essential that we *ought* to see that they were just. The fact is that Durkheim not only saw quite clearly that modern institutional change could only be understood in terms of growing rationality and ethical principle, but also—every bit as passionately and directly as Hobhouse—insisted upon the working out of a rational ethic in relation to a scientific understanding of society, and the application of this in the task of social reconstruction. For Cooley also, the same could be said. And it is interesting to note that Malinowski was just as zealous on these matters as Hobhouse or Durkheim. His attack on totalitarianism, his attack on racialism, were as ethically committed as any position could be.

Second, however, it is important to see that this position was not just negatively assumed by these thinkers. On the contrary, they forthrightly adopted a positive ethical position of their own which was exactly like that of Comte—with which sociology began. It was entirely, as Weber expressed it, an 'ethic of responsibility' as against an 'ethic of inspiration'. In the new, rational, complex, contractual order, it was no longer enough to admire an ideal and abide by it. Men were responsible for complex decisions, resting on knowledge and judgment in complex, changing situations. There had to be a recognition of human responsibility for the making of society, and a continuous alertness, energy, acuteness and diligence of mind and character in the continuous implementation of it. It was, as Hobhouse expressed it, an ethic of 'realistic humanitarianism'. But the important thing to note is that all these men were committed to such a position—even Durkheim the 'determinist'.

The third element is, of course, that this decidedly clear perspective on the significant social transformation of modern times coupled with this ethical clarification and commitment, was such as to provide a clear basis for statesmanship. The making of sociology was for the making of society in the most tangible way. As Comte had it, the science of society was the necessary basis for the realistic art of politics. The theorists of the early decades of the twentieth century, far from moving away from such a conception, had richly developed it.

The central, important points were very clear.

The urgency of the nineteenth century view that man must recognize his own responsibility for the re-making of his own society and his own destiny, was strongly reinforced. The perspective of social science—in analysing the actuality of the modern transformation; the perspective of ethical principle—in urging the responsible reconstruction of institutions; were the same now as then. Ethics and sociology—clearly distinct at their logical levels—were inseparable in this task. The making of sociology was for the making of society—and, a thing we asserted at the outset of this study, and which is now thoroughly clear—in displacing other doctrines about the nature of society, sociology was itself morally committed in very decided ways. Sociology inescapably carried an ideology of a distinctive kind.

Before leaving this point, which seems to me of the most crucial importance, let us take Durkheim as an excellent illustration of two things: (a) that even those who did not explicitly clarify the ethical principles they employed, nonetheless employed them, and (b) that they did so with the emphatic conviction that scientifically, ethically, and in terms of practical political policy, the *actuality* of modern institutions could not be understood without them. Durkheim wrote quite directly:

'For the obligatory force of a contract to be complete . . . it is necessary for it to be *just*, and it is not just by virtue of mere verbal consent . . . It is not enough that there be rules; they must be *just* . . .'
The task of the most advanced societies is, then, a work of justice. That they, in fact, feel the necessity of orienting themselves in this direction is what we have shown and what everyday experience proves to us . . . our ideal is to make social relations always more equitable, so as to assure the free development of all our socially useful forces.'

Now Durkheim did not make it plain what the nature of this 'justice' was. Hobhouse did. But the essential point that I want to leave clear without a trace of doubt comes clearly through this statement of Durkheim and is this: that the detailed pursuit of the clarification and realization of social justice was seen to be an empirical actuality in the nature of modern social institutions; it was the distinctive *actuality* at the heart of the modern transformation of society; and therefore a philosophical clarification of *what justice was* was an essential ingredient of scientific sociological understanding. This was a fundamental persuasion of most of those who devoted themselves to the development of sociology during this period, and not to see this is to lose sight of the most profound and essential dimensions of the subject.

(10) THE STUDY OF SOCIAL SYSTEMS: LIBERATION AND PROFESSIONALIZATION

These same dimensions must be borne in mind in noting one other development and accomplishment of these early decades of the twentieth century. This was the *liberation* of the practising sociologist to work according to his own predilections and choice of problem within the over-all 'conspectus' of the subject, and it was the direct outcome of certain theoretical positions which had been made clear. In this, Durkheim and Weber were undoubtedly the men of greatest influence.

In the first place, there was the emphasis upon the movement from theor*y* to theor*ies*. Weber was especially clear in rejecting the possibility and the validity of either a 'compendium of knowledge' or a 'total system of categories' which could be satisfactory for all problems and all time. Our conception of the scientific activity of sociology, he argued, should not be of that kind. Scientific problems were always the specific problems selected by the investigator, in accordance with what was of significance to him. He should be free to select and study these problems. The scientific aim should be to produce a definitive study which was exposed to testability; and the task of sociology was to provide rules, procedures, concepts, methods, as *tools* for the most accurate accomplishment of this end. Sociology was not a blanket-like 'conspectus' which fell like a burden on all alike, but—within the clearly defined nature and scope of the subject—a continual *activity*, using the clarified 'tools' of method in the accurate study of whatever problems investigators took to be of interest and importance. The emphasis of Durkheim, too, was entirely in this direction of liberating the science by advocating the production of definitive theor*ies*, and the further important development was that both he and Weber produced clearly stated sets of *rules* whereby such studies could be carried out.

The science of sociology therefore advanced not only in terms of a clearer and richer conceptual definition of the several dimensions of analysis, but also in terms of becoming a multiplicity of scientific activities rather than an attempt to clarify an over-all 'conspectus' alone. The movement from theor*y* to theor*ies* is perhaps the best way to describe it. We may note—but need not elaborate this—that many advancements had been made in actual *methods* as such. The methods of classification; the construction of 'types' or 'models' and their use and application in empirical studies; the several conceptions of the comparative method; these and other methods had all been outlined in much clearer terms—and for *use*. But all this we have seen sufficiently.

This liberation *within* the agreed conspectus of sociology, can also, however, be expressed in terms of *specialization* and *professionalization*: both highly significant in many ways. The movement from *theory* to definitive *theories* was itself an emphasis upon specialization, but it is also worth noting that the movement towards specialization was thought to be a significant development in society as a whole. Durkheim almost made an *ethic* of specialization—and Cooley, too, had much the same emphasis. This specialization *of* the subject and *within* the subject was, then, part of a more general process of *professionalization*, and this was further emphasized by Weber's (and Mead's) insistence that sociology, as a science, was a research-oriented discipline.

Now all this was unquestionably a clear development, an advancement in the making of the subject, and does not need, as such, any adverse criticism. However, certain qualifications may simply be aired in this place, and some qualifications about the positions of these theorists made. They are very important matters to which we must come especially in Volume 3, but here we will only note them.

The first point is this. Tönnies in particular had pointed, in a telling and arresting way, to the grave threat that attended specialization and professionalization. When human relationships and undertakings rested essentially upon a contractual basis of rationally calculated interest, it was an easy matter for all commitments to larger values and ideals to be lost. The prevailing ethic was only that of keeping contracts made, and then only whilst they continued to serve the specific interest for which they were entered into. Convention and politeness could come to veil a recognized actuality of shrewd and ruthless negotiation for limited contractual interest alone. Now science itself was a supremely rational activity: analytical, precise in its defined limitations, lending itself to specific application and pragmatic use. Science itself could therefore become part of these limiting, calculating, manipulating characteristics of 'Gesellschaft'.

The grave threat which arose with this *liberation* and *professionalization* within sociology was therefore that which attended *all* contractual specialization—and, indeed, all those inhumane characteristics of industrial society which Durkheim, Weber, Hobhouse,

Tönnies, passionately attacked. Why should expert practitioners of sociology remain committed to the ethical principles which the founders of the subject had thought so important? Why should they not undertake *any* specific research for *any* client? For the Nazi party, the Communist Party, the Church of England, or a large industrial enterprise? Why should they remain concerned about the evolutionary perspectives of human society?—about an 'ethic of responsibility' or a 'realistic humanitarianism'? Why, indeed, should they continue to take seriously scientific *truth* itself— beyond the expedient requirements of the research they were selling? Why should they bother about the close relationship between ethics and social science? Like all other specialists in society, why should they not concern themselves with their own well-being, their own promotion, their own career?

This was a grave threat indeed. In liberating scientific activities within their subject were sociologists producing one more body of professionals, experts in society, who would themselves pursue their own limited interests like any other specialist group? Were they producing an expertise which would increase and make more effective the manipulation of man by man? Could sociology itself become one more weapon in the de-humanization of modern society? If the very science that could establish knowledge about man and society could itself be deployed in these self-interested and manipulatory ways—here was a danger of the utmost gravity.

We will let the note of this danger remain. The promise and threat of the transformation of modern society was paralleled by the promise and threat within the subject which had arisen to serve it. The modern 'malaise' could well become deeply written into the very nature of sociology itself.

What we must do here, however, is to note quite clearly the positions on these matters of the twentieth century theorists themselves. We have seen some things without any doubt whatever.

Firstly, though doing their utmost to liberate scientific activity within sociology, and to establish a firm professionalization within the subject, Durkheim and Weber did not seek this *for the sake of the professionals themselves.* They remained committed in the fullest sense to the larger ethical and political perspective that sociology was to be the most accurate basis of knowledge for the responsible re-making of society; and they remained powerful advocates of commitment to an 'ethic of responsibility'. And secondly, though advocating the pursuit of *definitive studies* of specific problems, and thus supporting *specialization* in this sense, there was, nonetheless, nothing of narrowness or fragmentation in their point of view. They still retained a clear view of sociology as an entire discipline, of

807

society as an entire network of institutions, and the definitive studies they proposed, undertook, and advocated, were all of issues quite central to the nature and problems of modern society, and—as Weber put it—of 'cultural significance'. And even in Durkheim's view of *specialization* in the division of labour in society, he was emphatic that this could only be satisfactory within a coherent, cohesive, and meaningful view of the whole; and all his efforts were towards the achievement of such a whole view which might make possible the re-establishment of community within the complexity of society.

There was no doubt, then, where the theorists themselves stood. All of them (with the exception of Pareto) shared the same large perspective of analysis concerning the significant transformation of modern society; the same ethical commitment to a humane resolution of it; and the same political concern to provide a basis for statesmanship and purposive social reconstruction.

Liberation, specialization, professionalization had also their promise and their threat, but there was no doubt where these scholars stood.

(11) SOME FINAL POINTS

These attempts to draw together the more important developments of the early part of the century, to see the emphases of the several authors in relation to each other, and to state them clearly, have, of course, been made in summary fashion, but I hope that they have not been too sparse to fail to carry with them the full substantiation of them which was elaborated in our earlier studies. It is a large task to try to see the whole development of the subject with an over-all clarity, whilst giving proper attention to all the details which have gone into it; and it is necessarily a *labour* of criticism and synthesis. I hope, however, that we have been both thorough and clear and that we end this study having appreciated the detail of the specific contributions but also seeing clearly the common strands and inter-connections of them, and, particularly, the clear shape and direction of the subject as a whole which remained. The many developments were not fragmentations, but *all seams* and *galleries* as it were, of the one entire exploratory system, and I hope our picture of the detailed entirety remains intact.

What is sure is that this sustained critical assessment of the developments of the subject is necessary for a full comprehension of all the important dimensions of the subject, and, especially, if we are to be able to assess, clearly and satisfactorily, the extraordinarily diverse *explosion* of post-war sociology. This we can at least approach in a moment.

Here, however, a few final points are worth mention.

We have systematically traced the developments in the making of sociology from the 'Point of Arrival and Departure' which was so clearly evidenced in the meetings of the British Sociological Society round about 1903. We have seen how that juncture itself, and all the developments we have studied, were rooted in the 'conspectus' that had been clearly accomplished by the end of the nineteenth century. We have seen too, the strong, persistent, and clearly demonstrable continuity in the making of the subject from the common sense assumptions* and the early social theories† from which it sprang, through its basic nineteenth century foundations, to this culmination at the time of the second world war. The long established unity of conception of the subject has been made perfectly clear, and we can see even more clearly now the superficiality and the absurdity of those who have claimed that sociology is a science *newer* than other social sciences, that it has been a 'rag-bag' of disconnected contributions that bear no relation to each other, that it has shown no cumulative and consistent development, that it does not constitute a clearly defined discipline, and the like. If such views do not rest on ignorance of the literature, they can only rest on incapacity of comprehension. The body of work is there to belie them. We have also noticed that at least two points of continuity stemmed *from* the end of the period we have considered here into the post-war period. These were: firstly, the attempt of Talcott Parsons—in *The Structure of Social Action*—to trace a theoretical consensus among some of these theorists, and secondly, the statement of a supposed 'Functionalism' which served as a ground for anthropological field studies. These will form our starting point in Volume 3. The sequence and pattern of our argument remains clear.

There are two particular points I would like to touch on again slightly in concluding this section of developments. I made much of what I called the 'Error of Psychology' and the 'Error of Social Anthropology', and the points I made need not be reiterated here. I would simply like to press these matters a little further. I argued that it had not only been demonstrated that the *associational context* was essential for a satisfactory *human psychology*, and that no psychological science of man could possibly be adequate without it, but also that the conceptual apparatus for analysing such an *associational psychology* had been (by McDougall, Cooley, Mead, Freud, especially) successfully provided. We also saw that McDougall

* *The Making of Sociology*, Volume I, p. 33, 70. † *Ibid.*, p. 76.

and Freud in their own attempts towards a satisfactory making of *psychology*, drew into their conceptual systems, as necessary components, the processes of *association*. What I now want to suggest is that—far from it being the case that '*social psychology*' is a 'poor relation' hovering on the boundaries of psychology and sociology alike—*social psychology* is the only context for a satisfactory human psychology, and, furthermore, *the making of sociology was the making of such a satisfactory psychology*. Cooley and Mead were sociologists, and it was their work especially (inclusive as it was of a 'Weberian-kind' imputation of *meaning* into the *act* and its *symbols*) which provided the conceptual apparatus necessary for a satisfactory understanding of the relationship between 'self' and 'society'. Similarly, the work of Malinowski and Radcliffe-Brown was a re-vitalizing of anthropology by the application of *sociology*. *The making of sociology was the making of social anthropology*. When this is thought about a little further, however, it can be put rather differently like this. The new formulation of *psychology*, and the new formulation of *social anthropolgy*, were two direct examples of the *developing influence of sociology*. The making of sociology had now become of telling significance. Scholars in other fields saw its relevance, and their new formulations were a direct incorporation of it. Sociology was beginning to show its worth in all fields of the human sciences.

This point could be stated more strongly. Sociology—from Comte on, but especially now in the work of these outstanding scholars of the early twentieth century—was clarifying with an ever-increasing forcefulness, the *creativity of human association*. Despite his ambiguities, it is probably in Durkheim's work that this received its most powerful statement. In earlier ages, men attributed so much—of their mental and spiritual and social nature—to forces beyond them: in nature itself, or in a realm of the spiritual, indeed of the divine. Increasingly, the socio-psychological creativity of *society* was coming to be uncovered, clarified, understood. And—more and more—the explanations stemming from this source were gaining credence. This cannot be elaborated here, but it can be put simply like this. Whereas, in the nineteenth century, there had taken place a *Biological Revolution* which had disturbed all human thought and brought about a reformulation of the human sciences; in the twentieth century, there was taking place a *Sociological Revolution* which brought new and equally disturbing perspectives, and which was gradually making necessary a reformulation of all departments of human thought. Comte had seen that sociology was not only a new and separate science, but a science which brought with it a reformulation of all branches of thought within which all the

810

sciences would have their place. It is in this sense, too, that in displacing earlier 'doctrines' and 'theories' about the nature of man and his beliefs and morality, sociology could not remain ethically and ideologically neutral—and we have seen the several inescapable dimensions of this.

Sociology then, far from failing to qualify as an intellectual 'discipline' was a discipline of such power that it was forcing a re-orientation upon others. Scholars who saw its worth welcomed it, but it is in this, perhaps, that the antagonism of many other critics lay. In such a position, sociology can easily seem the usurper.

A few points about concepts and methods must be made. First, the two crucially distinguishing features of sociology—the *distinctive level of the associational,* and the *teleological qualities and capacities of the human mind in social action*—had been clearly defined by Durkheim and Weber especially, and appropriate methods had been clearly devised. The chief thing to say here is that it was undoubtedly the explanation of social configurations by the *imputation of meaning,* and the construction of *types* for this purpose, which was the feature of sociological theory *most* distinguishing it from the procedures of other sciences, and though this (resting on the persuasion of the 'teleological' qualities of human action) had long been recognized, it was the work of Tönnies and Weber which most richly and powerfully demonstrated it. This aside, however, *all* the components of the nineteenth century conspectus could now be seen in more satisfactory relation to each other; all could be satisfactorily arranged, for example, in the kind of schema outlined as a framework by John Stuart Mill. We must also note that significant developments had been achieved in particular aspects of method: in the classification of societies, in the construction of 'types' and their application in empirical studies, in various formulations of the 'comparative method', etc. But these have all been sufficiently discussed earlier. The one particular point which deserves a final emphasis is this. We noted when discussing Pareto that he chose a 'mechanical system' as his model for analysing the 'equilibrium conditions of social systems'. Radcliffe-Brown on the other hand rejected this, and argued that the 'organic' model was more appropriate. Others, as we have seen, clearly distinguished social systems from both. However, this is a point to remember. We shall see that in much contemporary sociology, the 'organic' analogy is greatly criticized, but, almost unwittingly, another analogy creeps in: the analogy of the *machine.* We shall later argue that this is a great mistake, and, indeed, a *retrogression* in sociological theory.

Perhaps finally, we should return to this central theme of the movement from *theory* to *theories*; from the nineteenth century

811

conspectus to *specialization* within it; but only to emphasize one major point: that—though devoting themselves to the furtherance of scientific accuracy by these means—all the theorists we have studied were still committed to the classical nineteenth century conception of sociology, and still committed to the large task of the re-making of society which it hoped to serve.

With all his insistence upon specialization and the carrying of the 'sociological perspective' into other disciplines, Durkheim was not *abandoning* the initial conception of Comte, but, on the contrary, claiming that with these developments:

'. . . the Comtist conception will cease to be a vision of the mind, and will become a reality.'

Moreover, he argued, once the human sciences have been penetrated and re-formulated by the sociological perspective, they will form:

'. . . the subject-matter of a renewed and rejuvenated social philosophy that is positive and progressive, like those very sciences whose crown it will be.'

In May 1822, at the very foundation of the subject, Comte had written:

'A social system in its decline, a new system arrived at maturity and approaching its completion—such is the fundamental character which the general progress of civilization has assigned to the present epoch. In conformity with this state of things, two movements, differing in their nature, agitate society; one a movement of disorganization, the other of reorganization. By the former, considered apart, society is hurried towards a profound moral and political anarchy which appears to menace it with a near and inevitable dissolution. By the latter it is guided to the definitive social condition of the human race, that best suited to its nature, and in which all progressive movements should receive their completest development and most direct application. In the co-existence of these two opposed tendencies consists the grand crisis now experienced by the most civilized nations; and this can only be understood when viewed under both aspects.

The only way of ending this stormy situation, of staying the anarchy which day by day invades society . . . consists in inducing the civilized nations to . . . turn all their efforts towards the formation of the New Social System as the definitive object of the crisis and that for the attainment of which everything hitherto accomplished is only a preparation.'

The two-sided malaise, the dilemma, the promise and threat, of the modern transformation had remained the central issue throughout the development of sociology. All the efforts of the twentieth century theorists were still focused upon it, and committed to the resolution of it. As we have seen earlier, in the nineteen-thirties, Morris Ginsberg wrote:

'The history of humanity is the story of an increasing conflict between the rational and irrational elements in human nature. Factors making for unity and co-operation are blended with others making for rivalry and exclusiveness, fears and jealousies. As the scale of operation expands, the conflict is embittered by the growing complexity of life, and the multiplication of opportunities for discord. The notion that this vast process can, and ought, to be consciously controlled or directed, has emerged in theory. But the conception of a self-directed humanity is new, and as yet vague in the extreme. To work out its full theoretical implications, and, with the aid of other sciences, to inquire into the possibilities of its realization, may be said to be the ultimate object of sociology.'

This, at one time, might have been taken to be a typically English statement, but we have seen that Tönnies, Durkheim, Weber, Cooley, Malinowski, and many others were all committed to the conception and perspective which it portrayed.

The making of sociology was—after all these developments—still for the making of society, and in the most committed way.

Some Fallacies and Errors of Assessment

I said at the end of Volume 1 that after our study of these early twentieth century developments, we would be able to clarify and throw into the wastepaper-basket—decidedly and confidently—a score of fallacies which were ruining the contemporary perspectives of the subject and breeding misunderstandings. We are now, happily, in that position—the only slight difference being that if we were quite literally to treat each error separately, they would number far more than a score! For convenience, however, we will group them here and there. Some of these errors are more serious than others, but all are of quite basic importance. Here we will do no more than *list* them—in as simple a statement as is possible. It will be seen, however, that they have been fully established by all our studies so far, and that, in this form, they will provide a clear and firm basis for our critical assessment, in Volume 3, of those contributions to the making of the subject which have been made between the second world war and the present day, and which have been claimed as advancements.

Some of this contemporary work is undoubtedly of positive worth, but I shall argue that much of it is a hectically coloured cloud of professionalization (really a concomitant of the institutionalized superficiality of the modern educational scene), a coloured dust not only in the eyes of beholders (I mean some educationalists, social workers and administrators, some window-dressing Vice-Chancellors, and the like, who have their own dust of professionalization in their eyes and who are really only after the dust which gives the brightest glitter), but also in the eyes of many sociologists who think that Scientific Sociology is something which sailed across the Atlantic in distinctive American regalia after the war, with Talcott Parsons like some moving figure-head in the prow—declaiming his 'General Theory' in passages, as Noel Annan once put it, 'of *rare* lucidity'. In Volume 3 we shall examine this star-spangled banner—to which so many disciples have flocked—and try to make clear, and assess, the actuality which is holding it up.

Meanwhile, however, and in preparation for these engagements to come: the list of errors.

Error 1: That sociology lacked clear definition until the post-war years
It is an error to think that the definition of sociology—of its

814

subject-matter, its nature, methods and scope—was vague or unclear until the post-war period. For those who would *read*, it had been clearly defined from its foundation onwards, and developed consistently within this definition.

Error 2: That it was a new post-war clarification to define sociology in terms of 'social systems'

It is an error to think that the clear definition of sociology waited upon certain post-war efforts especially attendant upon a new illumination that the central and distinctive concern of the subject was *the analysis of social systems*. This had always been plainly understood, explicitly stated, and had never varied. In all the work of the nineteenth century founders, and in that of all those who developed the subject during the early part of the present century, the definition of sociology was perfectly clear. *Sociology was the scientific study of social systems*. This it was in Comte's earliest formulation. This it remained throughout.

Error 3: That the making of sociology up to the second world war was a creation of separate, distinct and divergent 'schools'

It is an error to think that those who contributed to the foundation and development of sociology up to the second world war set up distinctive 'schools' which were separate and 'divergent'. There never did exist an 'Evolutionary' school, a 'Functionalist' school, a 'Verstehen' school, a 'Sociologistic' school, a 'Psychologistic' school, an 'Instinctivist' school, and the like. *All* the sociologists we have studied were evolutionists. All of them accepted structural-functional analysis. All of them (though with Durkheim inconsistently) accepted the understanding of action in terms of meaning as well as the objective study of phenomenal events. All of them recognized the distinctive level of 'associational facts'. None of them were psychological 'reductionists'. All of them accepted the place of instinct in human nature and in the process of institutionalization. Furthermore, none of these elements were *separated* from the others in their systems of ideas. They were all seen, in their interconnection, as parts of *sociology as a whole. Schools* of sociology are the *inventions of teachers or text-book writers*. They are *false* and distorting divisions.

Error 4: That the progress of sociology lay in the 'convergence' of these 'schools'

It is an error to think that the progress towards the clarification of sociology *as a whole* took the form of a latter-day coming together of

815

separate 'schools'. This is a false and harmful perspective. There had always been a clear and comprehensive definition of *sociological analysis as a whole*, and the developments we have studied were all of important *dimensions* within it, and were not such as to deny the importance of *other* dimensions. The correct perspective, as we have seen, is that a 'conspectus' of the nature of sociology had been clarified by the end of the nineteenth century, and that the efforts of the few following decades were a *deepening* of each dimension within it, a clarification of the concepts and methodological issues appropriate to each dimension, but *always* within the context of the whole. The perspective was one of a deepening and enriching of all the components of an agreed conspectus, *not* a latter-day coming together of disconnected bits. Certainly *agreements* became more richly evident—as, for example, *on the nature of the process of institutionalization*; and certainly the connections and interrelationships *between* the dimensions were made more clear—as, for example, in Mead's linking of the elements of psychology, meaning, observable 'act', and structured institutions; but these were illuminations of the same agreed subject-matter resulting from the exploration of its several dimensions. It was sociological analysis *as a whole, as a unity*, and *in all its dimensions*, which was being substantially developed within its own defined nature—not a latter-day dragging together of disparate 'schools' in terms of an awareness of their connections not previously seen.

The harmfulness of the *false* perspective is that it can lead to the *ignoring* of many aspects of supposed 'schools' (the 'evolutionary', 'functionalist', 'instinctivist' schools, etc.) which are not thought to be relevant to the supposed 'convergence'; and this can lead to an impoverishing of the subject if all these supposed 'schools' were really developments of essential elements of the whole. It can lead, in short, to a 'selective perception' of the most narrowing kind, and—worse—the setting up of a *doctrine* rather than the careful, indeed jealous, maintenance of a rich many-faceted subject within which all dimensions can be freely studied.

Error 5: That 'Positivism' was a 'school' limiting sociology to the concepts and methods of the 'natural sciences'

It is an error to think that 'Positivism' was a school or even an approach to sociology clearly distinguishable from others by its insistence that its *subject-matter* was completely like that of the natural sciences (i.e. consisting of *phenomenal events*) and that the methods it should pursue and the 'laws' it could establish—to be truly scientific—must be confined to those of the natural sciences. *All* the sociologists we have studied were *positivists* in the straightforward (and only valid) sense that they recognized and observed the requirements of positive science for the production of testable knowledge: but this had *never* stipulated only the methods of the natural sciences. Even at the outset, Comte's statement of 'positive science' was such as *especially to emphasize* that each science studied a *distinctive level of subject-matter* which required *distinctive methods* and established 'laws' (statements of regular interconnection) *at a distinctive level*. His statement also especially emphasized those aspects of both subject-matter and method which *distinguished sociology from the other sciences*, and Comte's own 'types' of society, constructing his 'rational fiction', were quite explicitly orders of *'Feeling, Thinking, and Acting'*. The identification of 'Positivism' with a narrow 'natural-science' orientation to the study of social facts as if they were only 'phenomena', is therefore a false and distorting caricature, and to set it up as a 'school' *opposed* to, or in *conflict* with, Max Weber's kind of subjective understanding of social *action*, and as denying the concepts and methods appropriate to such interpretation, is obvious nonsense.

Error 6: That 'Organicism', similarly, was a distinguishable school of sociology
It is a similar error to think that there was some separable school of sociology especially insisting that society was an organism indistinguishable from a biological organism, and to be observed only in terms of 'phenomenal events' and not at all in terms of social *action*. *All* the sociologists we have studied were completely clear that they were studying *social* systems, and though occasional thinkers—like Pareto—used the analogy with *mechanical systems* for specific purposes, they *all* (including him) used the *organic analogy* to indicate what they meant by the 'consensus' of social institutions. But *no* theorist equated society with a *biological organism*.

It is true that Durkheim in many ways came close to conceptual extremes of this kind (i.e. of both 'positivism' and 'organicism' as falsely conceived), and that Radcliffe-Brown followed him in this. But even Durkheim was clearly insistent that *social systems* were a level of actuality quite distinct from *organic systems*, and defined 'social facts' as *'ways of acting'*. And we have seen that his emphasis resulted really from his efforts to find *observable indices* for the inner facts of sentiments and values, and to make clear the *associational level of human psychology*. He was guilty of ambiguity, but not an intransigent 'organicism' when all his ideas are laid bare.*

* Even if Durkheim and Radcliffe-Brown were themselves prone to narrowness, it is obviously an error to use terms with connotations only appropriate to them. 'Positivism', as a statement of the nature of science, is far older and wider than one limited conception of it.

To link 'positivism' falsely conceived with 'organicism' falsely conceived and to set them up as a separate conceptual position (e.g. 'positivistic organicism') which ignored other dimensions of the subject—such as the subjective understanding of *action*—is therefore not only a nonsensical thing to do, it is an outright misconception and misrepresentation of what was, in fact, the case in the founding and development of sociology.

Error 7: That 'Functionalism' or 'Structural-Functional Analysis' was ever a separate school or theoretical position in sociology

It is also an error to think that 'Functionalism' ever existed as a separate or even special position in sociology (or in social anthropology) before the time of the second world war. It is even an error to think that Social Anthropology was founded upon it as a basis. It is an error to think that 'structural-functional analysis' was ever a mode of studying social systems separated or disconnected from all the other dimensions of sociological analysis. It is also an error to think that 'structural-functional analysis' is, or ever was, to be *identified* with sociological analysis as a whole. Sociological analysis always *contained* this and much more besides.

Error 8: That 'Structural-Functional Analysis' assumed a functional harmony and integration of social institutions and did not take account of conflict in society

It is an error to think that 'structural-functional analysis' ever postulated or assumed something to be called a close 'harmony' or 'integration' among social institutions. Social 'forms' clearly existed and were inter-connected in their origins, operations, changes and developments, in society, and it was certainly supposed that there were 'strains to consistency' and 'strains to harmony' among them. Structural-functional analysis was considered necessary for investigating this interconnected network of institutions—this distinctive kind of 'consensus'—but it was *always* recognized that the activities of men in society were characterized by *conflict* as well as *co-operation*, and that institutions and their values took shape to deal with, and to *regulate*, both. It is an error, therefore, to think that 'functional theory' ever assumed only co-operation and harmonious adjustment, and that a separate kind of theory—'conflict theory'—was necessary to introduce greater realism into its appreciation of social actuality. 'Functional theory' and 'Conflict theory' are not opposites. This is a confusion. It is true that Simmel showed that even conflict contributed to associational bonds, but this did not in any sense deny or suggest a diminished conception of the power of tendencies either to conflict or co-operation in society, and we have seen that the emphasis upon *both* conflict *and* co-operation was a common strand running throughout the work of all theorists from the very beginning of the subject.

Error 9: That 'Structural-Functional Analysis' was a 'static' theory of society, and not applicable to studies of social change

It is an error to juxtapose 'functional analysis' and 'theories of social change' as though they had nothing to do with each other, and were mutually incompatible. Structural-Functional analysis was *never* conceived as a mode of analysing a society in a *static* condition, or in a condition of harmony or integration, within which no causes of social change could arise. Neither were systematic studies of social change ever undertaken without structural-functional analysis. It is false to think that some *other* element of theory—'conflict theory' or some other 'dynamic' theory of change—was ever required to render structural-functional analysis *capable* of examining social change. *All* those who accepted structural-functional analysis also *insisted* that societies were *essentially* historical, changing processes, *always* experiencing conflict as well as co-operation. Indeed, all the major theories of social change and social evolution were in fact produced by theorists who insisted on the employment of the structural-functional method (as well as other methods) of sociological analysis. Comte, Spencer, Marx, Ward, Sumner, Giddings, Tönnies, Hobhouse, Durkheim, Weber, Cooley, Pareto, Malinowski, Radcliffe-Brown . . . it is an impressive list. The problem is, really, to find a theory of social change which did *not* utilize structural-functional analysis; and a structural-functional analysis of society which *denied* that society was a process of change. It is perhaps worthwhile especially to emphasize that Malinowski and Radcliffe-Brown—often thought of as 'Functionalists'—were explicitly clear about this, and were like everybody else. They made it perfectly plain that a 'functional' analysis of society was in no way in conflict with theories of evolution or change.

Error 10: That Social Statics *studied a* stationary *condition of society, and that Social* Dynamics *studied society in a condition of change*

It is an error to think that the terms 'statics' and 'dynamics' referred in any sense to a *stationary* or *mobile* condition of society. To think of structural-functional analysis as a major element of 'social statics' in *this* sense is what Ward had called 'the Fallacy of the Stationary'. *No sociological theorist ever maintained that society was ever stationary and that structural-functional analysis was particularly appropriate to the study of such a social condition.* Structural-functional analysis was certainly held, and properly, to be an important element of '*Social Statics*'—but this was that part of sociological method concerned with the analysis of the distinctive nature of its subject-matter: i.e. *social systems*: and social systems were held to be (among other things) essentially of a historical nature; essentially *processes* of *change*. Similarly, 'dynamics' was *not* the study of the *static* social system now in *movement*. '*Dynamics*' was that detailed study of the variety of societies actually existing in the world of history, which utilized the analysis of the distinctive nature of social systems which '*Statics*' had provided.

This error is therefore simply a confusion about the meaning of terms.

We may note that even Radcliffe-Brown, who tried to be more meticulous than most in this, and extended his conception to distinguish (additionally) between 'Synchronic' and 'Diachronic' studies, was nonetheless insistent that these were *both* studies of *change*: one—of the processes whereby the activities of a social system *sustained its form* (though experiencing continuous changes within it), and one—whereby the activities of a social system led to a *change in its form* (so that it became a different type of society).

This matter was therefore perfectly clear. To identify structural-functional analysis with the *static* study of a society and to think it inapplicable in explanations of social change, is a mistake. Structural-functional analysis was always one important element in the entire conspectus of sociological analysis which studied social systems as being (among other things) *essentially* processes of change.

Error 11: That 'Structural-Functional analysis' was separate from, and in conflict with 'Evolutionary Theory'

It is an error to think that structural-functional analysis was ever thought of as being opposed to (or incompatible with) historical studies and explanations, and, more specifically, to theories of social evolution. *All* the theorists who *explicitly* put forward theories of social evolution—Spencer, Hobhouse, Durkheim, Weber, and others—*explicitly* used structural-functional analysis. Also, those who especially wished to use structural-functional analysis as a basis for clearly formulated empirical studies—Malinowski and Radcliffe-Brown—took pains to make it *explicitly* clear that they *accepted* evolutionary theory, and that their concentration upon the use of the one did not deny their acceptance of the other. There was never any separation or conflict here.

Error 12: That there was a distinguishable school of 'Evolutionary Sociology' from which specific elements of theory had to win their freedom

It is an error to think that 'evolutionary sociology' ever existed as a particular kind of sociology, well-defined in separation from other elements of theory. *All* sociology was *evolutionary*, in the sense that it studied social systems within the wider context of the evolutionary perspective, and in the sense that concepts of social evolution formed an essential part of its analysis. Every theorist we have considered accepted, included, and made use of, 'evolutionary' concepts. However, we have seen it to be a vast over-simplification to think that there ever was *one* such thing as 'evolutionary theory' in sociology. Many things were studied under this heading: the implications of biological evolution for the clarification of 'functional requisites' and for the study of the process of institutionalization; the study of 'origins' in the sense of basic, universal 'causes'; the study of patterns of institutional change—of the differentiation and specialization of structure and function, etc., the study of mind and knowledge, their growing powers of control, and their influences upon directions of institutional change; these and many other questions were involved.

Furthermore, structural-functional analysis, the understanding of social action, the construction of 'types', the explicit use of certain psychological assumptions were all involved in these many kinds of 'evolutionary theory'. To think of these elements as winning their freedom from 'evolutionary sociology' is therefore a wrong perspective.

The correct perspective, again, is really that of *sociological analysis as such* having been given a clear initial statement which incorporated *all* these components in interrelationship with each other—being deepened as each element became more richly developed, and as their implications of method became more elaborately worked out. In fact, as we have seen, *none* of the distinguishable components of sociological analysis *did* free themselves from 'evolutionary theory', nor did they want to. They still accepted it and worked within its context and with its assumptions. Evolutionary theory was never abandoned in sociology.

Error 13: That evolutionary theories were monocausal

It is an error to think that any of the major theories of social evolution were 'monocausal'. Spencer, Westermarck, Hobhouse, Durkheim, Weber, and others all introduced many causal factors into their theories. To think otherwise is simply not to know their work.

821

Hobhouse, for example, stressed a central *feature* of evolution—the growing power of mind to control the natural environment, society, and the conditions for its own action—but a multiplicity of factors were considered in relation to this. The same is true of 'typological' accounts of specific (though large-scale) configurations of change. Tönnies, for example, emphasized the *one* dichotomy between 'natural' and 'rational' will—but, of course, a wide range of factors was drawn into this deliberately sharpened *interpretive scheme.*

Error 14: That the evolutionary theories traced historical 'origins'

It is an error to think that evolutionary theories traced 'origins' in the sense of seeking to uncover original historical events, and then hoping to explain subsequent social developments in these terms. They were seeking *basic elements of causation.* But though it was thought that these could account for the *common existence* and the *persistence* of certain social requisites and patterns of institutionalization, it was certainly never thought that they could explain all the historical complexities of social change. The essential thing, however, is that this was one approach to the clarification of the elements of causation underlying social institutions, it was not a business of historical chronology.

Error 15: That the evolutionary theories were 'unilinear' and 'historicist'

It is an error to think that any of the major evolutionary theories we have discussed were *unilinear* in the sense of specifying one single line of social development through which all societies, necessarily, had to pass. Sometimes Spencer wrote in ways that seemed to suggest this—but a full study of his work shows quite clearly that he explicitly guarded against it. He clarified 'types' of society and sequences of change from one to another, but his propositions were always of an 'If ... then ...' nature. *If* conditions constraining a society towards militancy increased, *then* the social structure would change to approximate to a certain 'type'. But Hobhouse and others guarded themselves so explicitly against this error as to make the criticism a mere absurdity. No *inevitability* of sequence from type to type of society was claimed and no 'historicist' *prediction* of inevitable future states of society was indulged in. All these theorists sought to clarify these processes of patterned change to provide a basis for *judgment* and *action*; and all emphasized *human responsibility* for the future making of society.

Error 16: That 'Action Theory' as developed by Weber was a new orientation in sociology

It is an error to think that Weber's distinction between *social action* (which could only be explained by the imputation of meaning) and *phenomenal events* was new. Throughout the founding and development of sociology, the distinctive *teleological* attributes of the human mind in all its practical and social activities had been recognized, and explanations had included elements of choice, deliberation, character, ends sought and means calculated, values and purposes employed, in *social action*. We saw, too, that towards the end of the nineteenth century, in the work of Giddings especially, these matters were stated quite explicitly even to the point of clarifying 'types' of social action almost identical with those developed by Weber. However, the point of this observation is not at all a matter of establishing who said what first.

The essential point is this. It is a great error to suppose that sociology was 'positivistic', 'organicist', 'evolutionary', or whatever other word one might wish to employ to suggest that it was such as completely to ignore (or fail to recognize) this dimension of *action* before it was introduced as a new and distinctive orientation by Weber. This is a false and harmful perspective.

Sociology *always* included these considerations as to the qualitatively distinctive nature of men in society—as a subject-matter for science—and the problems for appropriate and satisfactory methods which this recognition posed. To set an 'organism-environment' kind of sociology and an 'actor-situation' kind of sociology *against* each other, as two distinct and opposed orientations to sociology, is therefore to pose a dichotomy which never existed, and to belie the whole course of the making of sociology. Sociology *always* included *both* these in an entire scheme of analysis which—whilst making proper logical distinctions—had never found it necessary to separate the two.

None of this—it will be readily understood—is at all to deny or to belittle the great worth of Weber's development of this dimension of analysis. It is only to deny the false perspective.

Error 17: That 'Action Theory' was opposed to 'Positivism'

It is an error to suppose that Weber's methods for the subjective understanding of social action were at sharp odds with 'Positivism' as a statement of the nature of science. Positivism had always clearly maintained that each science had to develop its own methods to deal satisfactorily with its own distinctive *level* of subject-matter. Weber elaborated a method of explanation by the disciplined imputation of meaning *exactly to accord with the demands of positive science for a testable causal explanation*. There was no conflict here.

Error 18: That 'Action Theory' was isolated from, opposed to, or failed to see the relevance of 'Structural-Functional Analysis'

It is an error to think that 'Action Theory' was put forward by Weber in isolation from all the other elements of sociological analysis. Weber was an evolutionist. He thought that 'collective psychological configurations' were of importance. He thought that structural-functional analysis was *indispensable* as a preliminary basis for the formulation of 'types' of social action as he envisaged them. He accepted the necessity and validity of all the other dimensions of sociology. He simply *concentrated* (as a matter of choice for his own work) upon the subjective interpretation of social action. His rejection of a 'scheme of categories' from which explanations might be deduced was *not* because he failed to see the relevance of structural-functional analysis but because he did not think it a feasible business of science to try to set up 'schemes of categories' sufficient for the statement of all kinds of problems. Sociological concepts and methods were *tools* for getting the investigator closer to grips with the actuality of the concrete configuration of action which he was seeking to understand and explain. And the scientist should be free to pose such problems as he felt to be of cultural significance—not be tied to, and burdened by, a 'categoreal scheme'. A sociologist needed a bag of good tools, not an all-embracing doctrine of postulates and deductive procedures—a kind of casuistry of inference. The skill required in sociology was not primarily that of logic but that of the accurate, incisive imputation of *meaning* at work in concrete configurations of action, together with the ability of marshalling knowledge in such a way as rigorously to test such interpretive explanations. It was *research-oriented*. Theory was a servant to the accurate explanation of empirical fact.

Weber aside—we have also seen that all the other sociologists (again with Durkheim and Radcliffe-Brown as the exceptions) combined the study (and meaningful interpretation) of human activities with structural-functional analysis with no difficulty whatever, and with no sense of any lack of fit.

Error 19: That Sociology was opposed to Psychology and ignored or excluded it

It is an error to think that in the founding and development of sociology there was anything but the closest relationship between psychology and sociology. We saw earlier that all the nineteenth century founders of sociology sought a correct relationship between the two subjects. Comte and Mill had clear statements about it at the outset—and very well considered ones; and Ward and Giddings had very clear and elaborate statements about it at the turn of the century. We have now seen also, however, that all those who developed sociology in the early part of the present century were not only persuaded about the importance of the place of psychology in sociology but were as psychological as the psychologists. Indeed, we have seen that a great contribution was made *within sociology* to *the satisfactory making of psychology*. A detailed way of analysing the associational context which was essential for a satisfactory human psychology was actually established. Durkheim's apparent attack on psychology was, as we have seen, a correct attack on an insufficiently conceived *individual* psychology, and on an incorrect assumption that this could explain *associational facts*. When Durkheim is understood, however, far from demolishing psychology negatively, it could be claimed that he was one of the greatest contributors to the *making* of the subject. What is certain is that there were not only the closest relationships between the two subjects, but that these were now clearly seen to be even closer still. Indeed, the subjects were seen—in important ways—to be *part of each other*.

Error 20: That the psychological emphases in sociology were 'reductionist' or 'psychologistic'

It is an error to think that the considerable pre-occupation with the psychological aspects of institutionalization on the part of some theorists was *ever* of a *reductionist* nature. *No* theorist we have considered (not even McDougall or Freud) thought that associational processes could be explained by some more basic 'individual psychology'. On the contrary *all* of them thought that the distinctively human qualities of the individual 'self' were the outcome of association, and inseparable from the establishment of social 'sentiments', values, ideals, etc. We saw earlier that Mill was not guilty of the supposed error of 'psychologism', as contrasted with other theories such as that of Marx. Now we have seen that all the twentieth century theorists were even more plainly free from this error. The striking truth is that these men, in the making of sociology, established the only satisfactory basis for a human psychology. Or perhaps it might be better to say that the making of sociology and a satisfactory psychology of man were all of a piece.

To think that any of these men—Westermarck, for example—was a 'psychological reductionist' as against others—say Durkheim—who was not, is, as we have plainly seen, a simple error. The positions of these men were far more in agreement than disagreement, and both of them, indeed *all* the theorists we have studied, took their stand on their conviction concerning the *psychological creativity of association*. They were all solidly agreed on what we can make our final statement on this: that it is an error to think that a satisfactory human psychology is *possible* independent of the context of association and communication.

Perhaps it is worth a note, too, that there was no such group as a group of 'psychological sociologists' distinguishable from the rest. Our studies have clearly demonstrated that *all* the sociologists of the early twentieth century included the *same* psychological elements. They *all* emphasized the importance of them and incorporated them in a wider scheme of analysis. Sociological analysis was *a whole*, and *included* psychological elements among the other essential elements in its entirety.

Error 21: That sociology 'in the grand manner' was not 'empirical'

It is an error to think that the large-scale theoretical work of those who founded and developed sociology, including their large-scale theories of social evolution and social change, were not empirically oriented or empirically based. On the contrary, we have seen that *all* these theoretical developments were efforts to *engage* with the *distinctive actuality* of human society in ways which were as scientifically accurate as possible and such as to do full justice to the intricate nature of the subject-matter. There are some who think of *facts* in society only in terms of numbers of heads, numbers of houses, numbers of water-closets in houses, the scales of wealth and poverty existing among the population, the state of the roads. They think of *empirical* sociology as a process of *getting to know these facts*—by way of social surveys, door-to-door interviews, the collection of statistics, and the like. They thus think that Booth, Rowntree, Le Play, Branford and Geddes, were *empirical*, and the *grand theories* of Westermarck, Hobhouse, Durkheim, Weber, were not.

Now this is a simple error, and it is clear that people who advance this point of view have simply not begun to understand sociology at all. No one—certainly none of the 'grand theorists'—would wish to deny the great importance of discovering how many houses in society lacked piped water, or what the sizes of school classes were. They saw clearly the important place of *sociography*. Indeed Tönnies and Weber gave their attention to quite specific investigations of this kind, and Hobhouse was much concerned with social conditions, wages negotiations, and the like. Furthermore, we have seen that Booth, Rowntree, Geddes, Beatrice Webb, William Beveridge mingled quite happily with men like Graham Wallas, Westermarck and Hobhouse in the early meetings of the British Sociological Society, and listened there to papers from Durkheim and correspondence from Tönnies. There was no problem; no lack of understanding here. But, as we have seen, the theorists who devoted themselves to the development of sociology were concerned with much more profound issues than these; and with conceptual problems of quite a different level. They were concerned to understand the very nature of human nature in society itself: the nature of institutionalization, the creativity of human association, the nature and change of social 'forms', the entire development of human societies and the juncture which all these processes appeared to have reached in the significant modern transformation.

But in all this their *entire emphasis* was *empirical*. Their entire effort was towards the production of testable explanations of all the distinctive dimensions of social actuality. And, as we have seen, their entire effort was a movement from *theory* to *theories, from a conspectus of analysis to* the production of *definitive theories* in defined areas of study, in order to develop the accuracy and sufficiency of the subject. Furthermore, their books were full of a rich array of systematic comparative knowledge, drawn from the best sources they could find, and certainly more wide-ranging and exhaustive *in their factual content* than anything else that had previously been produced. The criticism that their work was not empirical really makes one gasp.

The only conclusion one can reach here is that there are some critics who have not only not studied the literature of sociology, but simply do not have a philosophical grasp of the problems with which it is concerned.

Error 22: That sociology was not of Use.

A further serious error follows from this misconception. It is an error to think that sociology was not of *use* in society, or did not aim at being of use, simply because it did not produce a schedule of facts about the bric-à-brac of the social apparatus (e.g. buildings, road and rail services, school milk-services, and the like). This again is an error of *levels*. Sociology as a science was *not* (whatever people might think) simply a way of collecting facts of this kind. It did not aim to be *useful* at this level; though sociographic studies certainly could be. However, at another level, we have seen that nothing was of greater power in the minds of those who devoted themselves to the making of sociology than that the subject should be of use in the vast task of the re-making of institutions in the global transformation of societies in the modern period. All these theorists (Pareto still the one exception) had a humane concern at the heart of their scientific efforts. All of them emphasized the centrality of values and morality in society, the importance of an 'ethic of responsibility' in the approach to social reconstruction, and all of them saw the production of reliable knowledge as a necessary basis for wise judgment and effective action. The fact is that—as from the earliest statement of Comte—all these theorists saw sociology as that basic science on which the great *political task* of the modern world should rest. Sociology was a necessary (though not the only) basis for the *art* of politics.

It is in this same sense that it is an error to think of sociology as a training for social work or social administration in any simple or limited sense. Social work and social administration are *arts* in society with specific tasks in view. Certainly they could benefit from resting upon an education which included sociology and its perspectives. But to think of sociology as part of a professional training for these tasks is simply misguided. Again, it is a question of the philosophical grasp of what is involved. There are educationalists, social workers and others, who think that sociology (they think the same about psychology and moral philosophy) is something which can be provided for their trainees in courses of a few months duration. This is what I meant earlier by the institutionalized superficiality of the modern educational scene. This sort of thing simply cannot be done. It rests upon misconceptions and sheer impossibilities.

Sociology was certainly made for use, and was demonstrably *of* use, but in a much broader and deeper way than such misconceptions could suppose.

Error 23: That sociology was of more recent development than the other social sciences, and either a 'collection' or a 'residuary legatee' of them

It is an error, as we have now seen with overwhelming evidence, to think that sociology was a relatively late 'newcomer' to the social sciences. From the early nineteenth century to the time of the second world war—almost the mid-twentieth century—the foundation and the development of sociology had been firm, continuous, consistent and clear. The idea that economics, political science, or any other 'special' social science existed before it is simply not true. The men who were supposedly 'economists'—Adam Smith, John Stuart Mill, Marx, Pareto—were in fact participants in the making of an entire science of society within which economic systems of production and exchange formed only a part. It is high time that the myth of the earlier development of the special social sciences was exploded: for myth it is. Similarly, we have seen that it is an error to think that sociology was ever thought of as an over-all 'collection', or 'bringing together' of already existing and clearly defined special social sciences. Another myth ripe for explosion! As is also the idea that sociology was the 'residuary legatee' of the other social sciences: that political science studied the political aspects of society, economics the economic aspects of society (and so on . . .), and that sociology was then necessary to study the *social*—the subject-matter left behind. Really! When you consider the views of this kind which have been seriously advanced by professors of social science, you begin to believe that 'Academia' is a home for the mentally retarded!

At any rate, we have seen that the nature and scope of sociology was clearly defined and established during the nineteenth century, extensively developed in all its dimensions during the earlier part of the twentieth, and that by the time of the second world war its nature and range of application was very well founded. Indeed, we have seen that, far from *deriving* from other human sciences, its nature was very powerfully influencing the growth and formulation of others. The improved formulation of psychology and anthropology, for example, owed as much to the influence of sociology as they did to that of biology.

The truth is that sociology *was not conspicuous in the universities*, and it has been thought to be a newcomer among the social sciences simply because, after the second world war, it *did* become a subject in the universities. But this was *not* a measure of the existence of a subject, but of the conservatism and intransigence of the universities—as well, no doubt, as of a mere lack of endowment. Universities are places in which the defence of entrenched interests is only moderated by the provision of attractive endowments. A subject which brings money is respectable. This is why the dust that gives the brightest glitter matters. Institutionalized education has not had much to do with the making of new subjects; much more with the stereo-typing of them. Creative thought is put into the hands of teachers and administrators, for whom the organization of it becomes a career.

One important and forceful aspect of this point about these conceptions of the relations between the social sciences lies in this fact that such supposed divisions are not only intellectual considerations, but grounds for the distribution of resources in the universities. They are grounds for academic intrigue and war. And never has this war been waged with more virulence than now. All the comments which Professor Wenley made in 1906 to the British Sociological Society about the problems of establishing sociology as a university subject could be made in the present academic scene—and with far deeper truth than he could then have realized.

Error 24: That social anthropology exists as a subject distinct from sociology

One matter of the supposed relationship between social sciences deserves special mention—though this can be brief. It is an error to think that Social Anthropology is, or ever was created as a subject distinct from Sociology. What came to be called Social Anthropology was quite straightforwardly the application of Sociology in Anthropology. It was the use of sociology in the study of the social systems of primitive (non-literate) peoples. There are not two subjects, but one.

Error 25: That the scientific and professional development of the subject meant that sociology became 'value-free'

It is an error to think that the achievement of a clear distinction between philosophical ethics and the scientific study of social fact, led to any change whatever in the moral and ideological commitment of sociology, and a situation in which sociology was 'value-free'. We have seen that there were many important elements in this complex issue, and they cannot be reiterated here. It was clear, however, that the extent to which *social fact* could be *scientifically known* by an accurate and sufficient *imputation of meaning* without an explicit philosophical clarification of *ethical criteria* (such as 'justice'), was shown to be highly dubious. It was clearly agreed that ethical criteria were increasingly important in the *actual nature* of social facts, and in the deliberately brought about changes of them; and that an understanding of moral purpose entered necessarily into any explanation of them. It was clearly agreed that the selection of scientific problems and (in Weber's sense) the construction of the 'object of knowledge' could not be value-free (and, indeed, that such an ethical neutrality was not demanded by science). And it was also agreed that the scientific rigour of study independent of the values involved in selecting a problem, was itself a commitment to the impartial pursuit of truth—itself an important value. In all this activity of the most searching kind for accuracy of criteria in seeking reliable knowledge and judgment, it was also clear that sociology had necessarily to take issue with all other theories which ignored such standards of criticism and test. Sociology therefore inescapably carried an ideology of its own in engaging with other ideologies.

All this aside, we have seen that almost all the theorists we have studied—whether prone to ambiguities or not—rejected any simple-minded notion of ethical 'relativism'. They advocated and adopted a position of moral responsibility. Their position was that which, from the beginning, had been rooted in Comte and upheld by all the thinkers of the nineteenth century. They believed that a great transformation of human society was afoot; that it promised much for human dignity and welfare, but carried grave threats of de-humanization. They believed that a satisfactory resolution of its many aspects required responsible judgment and deliberate action; that—for this—the most exact knowledge was required as a basis, and that no reliance upon traditional beliefs and values, on an 'ethic of inspiration', was any longer sufficient. An ethic of 'responsibility'* of 'realistic

* Weber.

humanitarianism'* no longer worked out in the arm-chair in the study, but in the thick of the study of complex social facts,† was required—indeed, was necessary. And such an ethic they tried both to provide and to uphold.

Whether philosophically correct or not—but we have seen that substantial grounds were given for it—what is certain is that in accomplishing a professional liberalization of sociology and a firm basis of freedom for research-oriented work, the men responsible for these developments did not at all envisage, or advocate, or themselves adopt, any change in the ethical commitments of the subject. The professionalization of the subject was not for the sake of the professionals themselves—but for the accurate and sufficient explanation of problems of cultural significance. And these explanations provided knowledge for judgment and action: for the avoidance of inhuman evils in modern industrial society—narrow, ruthless, contractual expediency; the disorganization of institutions and the disorientation of persons; the self-interested manipulation of masses by élites; the dangerous power of efficient bureaucracy; and for the creation of more humane conditions—the achievement of a new and appropriate community in society, of a satisfactory specialization within a meaningful whole, of justice in the whole fabric of institutions, etc. It was not only Marx, but also the great majority of these theorists, who saw the malaise of modern industrial capitalism, and who wanted not only to *understand* society, but also to *change* it; who saw the long perspectives of human struggle in the historical making of societies, and who now saw the possibility of the making of a new, more dignified, more humane society in which the achievements of civilization could at last be made available to all, and in which the dignity of the individual human person, as such, could at last be realized. They all saw the modern juncture as one in which man was responsible for making himself.

The making of sociology was still for the making of society. All its dimensions as a science had been richly developed. Its ethical commitments too remained unchanged. Its moral purposes were undiminished.

* Hobhouse.   † Durkheim.

Appendix
The Sociographers

At the end of Book I (Appendix III) we noted the contribution to the making of sociology of Frederic Le Play, and briefly outlined his 'ecological' approach to the study of communities. At the beginning of our present study of the early twentieth century developments of the subject we saw that Victor Branford was one of the prime movers in the foundation of the British Sociological Society in 1903; that Patrick Geddes—who was his elder colleague and teacher—contributed papers on 'Civics' to these early meetings; and that both these men adopted, and sought to continue and develop, Le Play's conceptions of community and his methods of study. We have also noted that certain theorists—Tönnies especially—saw and defined a clear place for *sociographical* studies, and, from time to time, we have seen that *sociography* has tended to be sharply contrasted with other developments in sociology—as being devoid of theory and much more empirical; indeed, as being essentially a matter of *descriptive fact-finding*.

Now in all this, and in the very fact that I have chosen to deal with these aspects of sociology *in appendices*, it is difficult to avoid giving the impression that (at least as an implication of my own selectivity) these sociologists have been of only minor worth in the making of the subject. It is therefore necessary to say a few things about them— both to acknowledge and appraise their work and its influence (for it has, in fact, been very considerable), and, more especially, to try to throw a new perspective over the relationship between their ideas and those of the other theorists we have discussed. The fact is that there is not the striking gap between them that is commonly supposed.

Let me begin with the direct point that the reason why I have not included their work as a major section is simply that I do not think that they contributed distinctively to sociological *theory*, or to the clear definition of the nature, scope, concepts and methods of the subject. And when I say they did not contribute in these directions, I do *not* mean two things. I do *not* mean that they *lacked* such general theoretical notions, only that they did not *contribute* them. In fact, they *used* and *brought together* the concepts, theories and methods of *others*: especially of Comte and Le Play. And I do *not* mean that they made no contribution of worth to the establishment of the subject. They *did*—but it was *not in these directions*. Their contribution lay in

832

the direction of organizing large-scale survey-type studies of communities (of a fact-finding nature) and linking these to issues of constructive community-planning and social administration. In these studies they also improved certain *techniques* of collecting and collating information and of *measuring* degrees or scales of social conditions (such as 'poverty').

I want to emphasize above all that this estimation of the *direction* of their contribution is not a *derogatory* one; not by any means. It is simply a matter of selectivity with regard to what, in this study, we want essentially to make clear. That is all. And I want now briefly to indicate that the supposed gulf which separates this large body of work from that of the other theorists is an illusion—though it is an illusion which has tended to be raised to the level of a hard fact by stark contemporary allegiances.

Some facts can come first. Just as other elements of theory established during the nineteenth century 'straddled' the two centuries in the work of some men—Tönnies, Durkheim, Hobhouse, etc.; so the ecological approach of Le Play was not lost, or even diminished in its influence, but continued in full force in the efforts and ideas of other men. Of central importance in this was Patrick Geddes* (for whom, we might note, the first Chair in Sociology in The University of London was intended). Like Le Play himself, Geddes was rooted in the natural and biological sciences, and his 'ecological' studies were especially rooted in botany; but also like Le Play, he saw human communities as part of nature, as groups within 'natural environments' in the broadest sense—and in a sense which necessitated bringing all the sciences into relationship with each other in the study of all aspects of the human situation. It is enough to say that—having the closest tie with thought and public affairs in France—he founded the Outlook Tower in Edinburgh, and devoted himself to the study of *cities* (of Edinburgh in particular) as a part of *civics*—the positive task of community-making. Closely associated with him was Victor Branford,† a financier, who was indefatigable in founding and organizing these studies, but also in helping to found the Sociological Society and *The Sociological Review*.

The few points essential for our purposes, are these. First—the systematic regional and community studies promoted and undertaken by these men were based completely on Le Play's 'formula' of the close tie between '*place, work*, and *family*' in the making of social systems and communities. Their empirical investigations were exactly of the kind proposed and and carried out by Le Play. Secondly, however—and this seems nowadays not to be at all emphasized—their conception of *civics* was couched deliberately and entirely within the

* 1854–1932.   † 1864–1930.

theoretical perspective of Comte. Their perspective was entirely that shared by all the theorists we have mentioned earlier—namely that the rapid transition from traditional community to industrial society, though bearing much promise for human betterment, had brought disorganization in its train, and that an effort of responsible social reconstruction was required. They were *not* mere *fact-finders*. They were men committed to the same perspective as were the other theorists, and committed to the same constructive effort to create a more humane society. For them, as for Comte, knowledge was a basis for judgment and action. Far from being any simple continuity of a 'Le Play School' therefore, this development of Geddes and Branford and the Sociological Society was a deliberate bringing together of Le Play's sociographic methods with Comte's perspective of theory. And, furthermore, it was a deliberate fusing of intellectual and practical purpose. It was at one and the same time an academic and administrative undertaking.

Two other points follow from this orientation towards both fact-finding and creative social action within an accepted theoretical perspective. One is that the influence of the work then undertaken, and the methods then used and established (of ecological 'mapping', etc.) has had a far greater influence than is commonly known. In the city-development reports of men like Sir Patrick Abercrombie, the 'Land-Utilization Survey' in England, and similar regional surveys, the work of Geddes and Branford has had a very great impact upon the ways of establishing knowledge for community-planning and administrative decision. And secondly, it seems almost certain that it was their influence which, taken to Chicago*, stimulated the growth of what has since come to be called the 'Chicago School' of ecological studies in sociology.

Before coming to this, however, we must note another root of sociographic studies: the great social surveys of Charles Booth (in particular) and Seebohm Rowntree. Without any doubt whatever, these were 'fact-finding' studies. They did not have the same conceptual framework or theoretical perspective of the Geddes-Branford community studies, but they employed similar methods and were certainly powerfully motivated by the possibility of social reconstruction and the effort to achieve a more humane society. For them, too, knowledge was for social action. Booth 'mapped out' the areas of poverty in his survey of the 'Life and Labour of the People in London',† and perhaps the greatest contribution was the introduction of a defined way of *measuring* the conditions of poverty in society: the well-known 'poverty-line'. Rowntree, in his study of poverty in

---

* By Charles Zueblin, in the eighteen-nineties.　　　　† 17 volumes, 1903.

York* introduced the further distinction between 'primary' and 'secondary' poverty, and, through the subsequent studies of Bowley, Burnett-Hurst, Hogg, and others, there has been a clear line of development of ever more sensitive methods of measurement, up to the present conception of 'relative deprivation'. The 'relativity' of such measurements have long been clear. Silverman, for example, writing in 1928, put the matter quite clearly.

'There is no unanimity on the definition of poverty, since it is essentially a relative term. What constitutes "poverty" varies from one person to another according to upbringing, environment and needs. An income that means "poverty" to a skilled artisan might mean a large degree of comfort to an agricultural labourer. The interpretation also varies with time, for, with the advance in civilization, what is considered sufficient for a person's requirements in one period may be found inadequate in the next.'

Again, then, it is plain that these studies contributed to the development of *techniques* of investigation rather than to any new *theoretical* orientations. It is worth emphasis again, however, that they were not concentrations upon purely *material* matters of fact, and were not studies of facts *for the sake of the knowledge itself*. They were measured studies of facts which were thought to carry *human degradation*, and they were motivated by a desire to *demonstrate* the *need* for social reconstruction and the *directions* it should most properly take. Beatrice Webb argued this very forcefully:

'It is a special feature of destitution in modern urban communities that it means not merely a lack of food, clothing and shelter, but also a condition of mental degradation. Destitution in the desert may have been consistent with a high level of spiritual refinement. But destitution is a densely crowded modern city means, as all experiences shows, not only oncoming disease and premature death from continued privation, but also, in the great majority of cases, the degradation of the soul.'†

It is worthwhile to recall again, at this stage, the fact that in the meetings of the British Sociological Society at the beginning of the century *all these people discussed these matters together*. Geddes and Branford met with Booth and Rowntree; all of them met with Beatrice Webb, with William Beveridge; and—what seems more telling nowadays—all of them met with supposed 'theorists' such as Westermarck and Hobhouse, and listened to papers from Durkheim and letters from Tönnies. All of them considered the ideas of Comte and Spencer, and the 'conspectus' which had been established during the nineteenth century, and—what is important—it was Branford

---

* *Poverty, A Study of Town Life*, 1901.
† Sidney and Beatrice Webb. *The Prevention of Destitution.*

835

(the upholder of Le Play-type regional surveys) who introduced the continuity of these ideas to them. No division existed among them as to how 'empirical' they were, or what ethical perspectives they held. They *shared* their scientific and ethical perspectives. All were concerned with accuracy of knowledge, and all wanted knowledge for action. But Geddes and Branford were as committed to the theories of 'social evolution' as were Westermarck and Hobhouse. Durkheim was as much concerned—ethically and practically—with understanding and changing the division of labour in society, as were Beatrice Webb, Beveridge, and Hobhouse. The sharp distinctions simply *were not there.*

In the making of sociology in Britain, then, it is a mistake to think of the sociographers as constituting a 'school' quite separate and distinct from other developments and theories in the subject. A word might also be said about the 'Chicago School'—for now everybody talks about the 'Chicago School', but nobody about Le Play, Geddes, Branford, and Booth. We have already pointed to the influence between Geddes and scholars in Chicago, and it is no derogatory comment on the Chicago sociologists whatever to say, further, that their ecological studies were straightforward developments of what had initially been laid down by Le Play.

Some—even here—would claim originality and the setting up of a distinct 'ecological school' in Chicago, as though the very idea of such studies had not occurred until then. Thus Nicholas Timasheff writes*:

'The idea of applying the ecological approach and these concepts to human relations first appeared in the early twentieth century in the work of Charles Galpin, *Social Anatomy of an Agrarian Community* (1915). Galpin, who did not use the term ecology, collected data about families living in an agrarian county in Wisconsin pertaining to such questions as where they bought their supplies, where they banked, what church they attended, and what school their children attended. The findings were plotted on a map—the cartographic technique was to become quite common in ecology. Although the various areas of activity studied by Galpin did not exactly coincide spatially, nevertheless his evidence justified the claim that determinable ("natural areas") exist in human society.'

Now this, of course, was Le Play, Geddes, Branford all over again. Timasheff then goes on to describe the work of Robert Park† and Ernest Burgess on the ecology of cities (which was beginning to appear about the same time) as the formation of a distinctive ecological 'school', but, although these studies certainly contributed new

* *Sociological Theory: its Nature and Growth*, p. 211.   † 1864–1944.

knowledge on the growth and development of cities, they were not in any sense distinguishable from the earlier European and British conceptions. Sorokin has had the great merit of always seeing such developments in a proper historical context. However, my emphasis here is not to denigrate the Chicago ecologists, but only (*a*) to point to them as an important group of sociographers, and (*b*) also, especially, to show that in this field, as in all others we have mentioned, there was a clear continuity and development during the early decades of the twentieth century of positions firmly founded towards the end of the nineteenth.

I would like, finally, simply to give some little evidence of what I claimed earlier.

The fact that Geddes and Branford accepted Comte's theoretical perspectives (i.e. as a theoretical analysis of society and as a ground for positive social re-construction) is perhaps best seen not in their surveys as such, but in books which they produced as a series on '*The Making of the Future*'. In '*Our Social Inheritance*'* for example (of which they were joint authors), they wrote:

'In our *Coming Polity* we have already pointed out that the needed outline of a modern organization of knowledge has been clearly initiated, not by German philosophers, nor yet by our own, but by Auguste Comte . . .

Comte's fertile impulse has ranged far beyond his immediate followers, the professed Positivists in France or Britain; for as expressing this wide influence every continental historian reckons not simply those who, like John Stuart Mill, acknowledged him, but scarcely less fully Spencer and Huxley, who alike fiercely criticized him; for their sharpest dissents are now seen as magnified personal equations, and as but of minor difference within substantial agreement. And similarly for Darwin himself, and substantially for our other scientific leaders, little or nothing though they may have read of Comte's writings. For his view and system was essentially the rebound of the scientific mind from all preceding metaphysical systems: in fact to what are now current conceptions, as notably (1) that the sciences have to be systematized and unified within and among themselves; (2) that they are thus no longer limited to mathematics, physics and chemistry as so many think, plus biology, or at most with their respective applications; but that they must also be related to all "the Humanities", and these to them, in terms of a further science—Sociology.'

And their entire acceptance of the perspective shared by Comte with all the other scholars who contributed to the foundation and development of sociology—of the disorganizing and dehumanizing dangers of industrialization and the need for a responsible re-making of institutions—can be plainly seen in statements such as the following:

* Le Play House Press, 1919.

'Since the Industrial Revolution, there has gone on an organized sacrifice of men to things, a large-scale subordination of life to machinery . . . a growing tendency to value personal worth in terms of wealth. To the millionaire has, in effect, passed the royal inheritance of "right divine".

Things have been in the saddle and ridden mankind. The cult of force in statecraft has been brought to logical perfection in Prussian "frightfulness". The cult of "profiteering" in business has had a similar goal in the striving for monopoly by ruthless elimination of rivals. Prussianism and profiteering are thus twin evils. Historically they have risen together. Is it not possible they are destined to fall together before the rising tide of a new vitalism?

The reversal of all these tendencies, mechanistic and venal, would be the preoccupation of a more vital era than that from which we are escaping. Its educational aim would be to think out and prepare the needed transition from a machine and a money economy, towards one of Life, Personality and Citizenship.'

This, it will be seen, was not only in accord with Comte, but also with Mill, Marx, Tönnies, Hobhouse, Durkheim, Weber, and almost every major theorist we have considered. And within this context, 'Civics' was not at all thought of (as the two authors put it) in terms of its '. . . too aldermanic associations . . .', but as the creative task of social reconstruction, of community-making, which should employ the social sciences and moral philosophy in a synthesis for purposeful action. (Comte again!)

'For Reconstruction, economics and ethics are no longer distinct, like the "Business" and "Philanthropy" of our past paleotechnic century which in separation became the first sordid and the second mostly futile. Their future is as Ethico-economics, that is Civics: it is in proportion as this social renewal becomes manifest to all concerned, that individual lives will best and most speedily return to vigour and health, and that arts and industries will advance together . . .

'Awakening to their deprivation, the Peoples are everywhere demanding their birthright in the Social Inheritance. To make good the inheritance of the People should in the nature of things be constructive of the social order, not disruptive. But with the present demand for restitution goes a grave indictment of State and Church, of Education and Business, as they are and have long been. The Chiefs, Emotionals and Intellectuals of the existing social order are accused by the People whom they should serve, of betraying their Trust. A court has been opened by the Peoples of Europe for the Grand Assize of Western Civilization. But indictment is one thing and restitution another. And beyond both is the vision of a new world, which, could it unite all men of goodwill, all parties of constructive aim, might be realized by an architectonic handling of the materials available. For this let Chiefs plan and organize; Emotionals dream and energize; Intellectuals think and scheme. In the measure of their attainment will be restored to the People that birthright in the Great Estate of Man, from which they have so long been disinherited.

'. . . the imperative call of our times is for a mobilizing of the resources available for rebuilding. And that, as we see it, means the preparation of definite Surveys, Reports, Plans, for Regional and Civic Eutopias; and all the time their concurrent application by experiment, steady, judicious, bold, to this, that and the other, village, town, city, countryside. Surely it is through this vibrant impulse of the eutopian vision that a community awakening into an age of science humanized, must act, if it is to obey the inspired injunction that bids us seek first the kingdom of the ideal.'

This language may now seem rather quaint—especially the blend of a high idealism on the one hand and the mundane mention of 'surveys, reports, plans, etc.' on the other. *But this is exactly the point.* No passage could more clearly demonstrate the acceptance of Comte's largest ideas about the contemporary human situation, but, at the same time, show also that the undertaking of factual surveys and reports was seen within this context. The sociographers were no less committed to these large perspectives of explanation and ethical aspiration than were the 'grand theorists'. The 'grand theorists' were no less committed to empirical accuracy than were the sociographers. The distinctions—beyond a proper delineation of differing *kinds of study*—were absurd. Men followed the kinds of study, the levels of theory, the dimensions of analysis which they themselves thought most important and which they themselves felt most fitted to undertake. But all shared the same perspectives and objectives—intellectual, ethical and political alike.

I have left the sociographers to appendices, then, *only out of selectivity.* For the theoretical definition of the nature and scope of the subject, their contribution was *secondary*: they accepted the conceptual orientations of others. It must now be clear, however, that this does not entail any idea that their contribution was of little worth. Their contribution lay in a different direction—that of establishing techniques of investigation, and producing accurate descriptive knowledge of the contemporary conditions of society, which, in addition to other knowledge, could provide a vitally necessary basis for judgment, decision, and action. For them too, no less than for the other theorists, the making of sociology was for the making of society. It was simply that their contribution to this same end was of a different kind.

Bibliography
(For reference and further reading)

Authors dealt with in Volume 1 have, obviously, been frequently mentioned in the text, but books from the bibliography of Volume 1 have not been repeated here except when they contain material which is specially relevant to the subject-matter of the present volume, or when it has seemed particularly useful to have a reference immediately available.

ANTONI, C. (1962), *From History to Sociology*, Merlin Press (Ch. 4 on Max Weber)

ARON, RAYMOND (1967), *Main Currents of Sociological Thought*, Vol. 11 (On Pareto, Durkheim, and Weber), Basic Books, Weidenfeld and Nicolson, 1968.

ARON, RAYMOND (1962), *German Sociology* (For much on Simmel and Tönnies and an excellent chapter on Max Weber), Free Press paperback.

BARNES, H. E. (1958), *L. T. Hobhouse: Evolutionary Philosophy in the Service of Democracy and Social Reform* (See Ch. XXXII, 'An Introduction to the History of Sociology'), University of Chicago Press.

BECKER, ERNEST (1968), *The Structure of Evil*, George Braziller, N.Y.

BENDIX, R. (1966), *Max Weber: An Intellectual Portrait*, Methuen (University Paperbacks).

BEVERIDGE, W. H. (1906), 'The Problem of the Unemployed' (*Sociological Papers*, Vol. III), Macmillan.

BOOTH, CHARLES (1903), *Life and Labour of the People in London* (17 Vols.), Macmillan.

BORKENAU, F. (1936), *Pareto*, New York and London.

BRANFORD, VICTOR (1904), 'On the Origin and Use of the Word Sociology, with a Note on the History of Sociology' (*Sociological Papers*, Vol. 1), Macmillan.

BRANFORD, VICTOR (1919), *Our Social Inheritance* (with Geddes), Le Play House Press.

BRITISH SOCIOLOGICAL SOCIETY (1904), *Sociological Papers*, Vol. I; Vol. III, 1906, Macmillan.

COBB, ROBERT, P. (1955), *Society Versus Solitude: Studies of Emerson, Thoreau, Hawthorn and Whitman* (Unpublished dissertation), University of Michigan.

COHEN, PERCY (1968), *Modern Social Theory*, Heinemann.

COOLEY, C. H. (1918), *Social Process*.

COOLEY, C. H. (1964), *Human Nature and the Social Order*, Schocken Books (paperback).

COOLEY, C. H. (1962), *Social Organization*, Schocken Books (paperback).

CHILDE, V. GORDON (1942), *What Happened in History*, Penguin Books.

CHILDE, V. GORDON (1951), *Social Evolution*, Watts.

CHILDE, V. GORDON (1956), *Man Makes Himself* (3rd edition), London.

841

THE MAKING OF SOCIOLOGY

CRAWLEY, A. E. (1906), 'The Origin and Function of Religion' (*Sociological Papers*, Vol. III), Macmillan.
DEWEY, R. (1958), *Charles Horton Cooley: Pioneer in Psychosociology* (Ch. XLIII: 'An Introduction to the History of Sociology', Ed. H. E. Barnes), University of Chicago Press.
DURKHEIM, E. (1904), 'On the Relations of Sociology to the Social Sciences and to Philosophy'; and (with M. E. Fauconnet) 'Sociology and the Social Sciences' (*Sociological Papers*, Vol. I), Macmillan.
DURKHEIM, E. (1960), *The Division of Labour in Society* (Tr. G. Simpson), Free Press.
DURKHEIM, E. (1962), *The Rules of Sociological Method* (Ed. G. E. C. Catlin), Free Press.
DURKHEIM, E. (1952), *Suicide: A Study in Sociology* (Ed. G. Simpson), Routledge and Kegan Paul.
DURKHEIM, E. (1915), *The Elementary Forms of the Religious Life*, Allen & Unwin.
DURKHEIM, E. (1963), *Primitive Classification* (with M. Mauss. Tr. by R. Needham), Cohen & West.
DURKHEIM, E. (1960), *Montesquieu and Rousseau: Forerunners of Sociology*, University of Michigan Press.
DURKHEIM, E. (1953), *Sociology and Philosophy* (Tr. by D. F. Pocock. Introduced by J. G. Peristiany), Cohen & West.
FINER, S. E. (1966), *Vilfredo Pareto: Sociological Writings*, Pall Mall Press.
FLETCHER, R. (1966), *Instinct in Man*, Schocken Books. 1968, Allen & Unwin.
FLETCHER, R. (1971), *The Making of Sociology*, Vol. I, '*Beginnings and Foundations*', Michael Joseph.
FLETCHER, R. (1965), *Human Needs and Social Order*, Michael Joseph.
FREUD, S. (1949), *Group Psychology and the Analysis of the Ego*, Hogarth Press.
FREUD, S. (1927), *An Autobiographical Study*.
FREUD, S. (1950), *Beyond the Pleasure Principle*, Hogarth Press.
FREUD, S. (1949), *New Introductory Lectures*, Hogarth Press.
FREUD, S. (1940), *An Outline of Psycho-Analysis*, Hogarth Press.
FREUD, S. (1927), *The Ego and the Id*, Hogarth Press.
FREUD, S. (1927), *The Future of an Illusion*.
FREUD, S. (1951), *Civilization and its Discontents*.
(See also *Collected Papers*), Hogarth Press.
GALTON, F. (1904), 'Eugenics: Its Definition, Scope and Aims' (*Sociological Papers*, Vol. I), Macmillan.
GALTON, F. (1907), *Inquiries into Human Faculty and its Development*, Everyman's Edition.
GEDDES, P. (1904), 'Civics as Applied Sociology' (*Sociological Papers*, Vol. I), Macmillan.
GEDDES, P. (1906), 'A Suggested Plan for a Civic Museum and its Associated Studies' (*Sociological Papers*, Vol. III), Macmillan.
GEDDES, P. (1919), *Our Social Inheritance* (with Branford), Le Play House Press.

GIDDENS, A. (July 1970), *Durkleim as Review Critic* (Sociological Review.)

GINSBERG, M. (1937), *Sociology*, Home University Press.

GINSBERG, M. (1947), *Reason and Unreason in Society* (See: Ch. III. 'The Life and Work of Edward Westermarck'; Ch. I. 'The Problems and Methods of Sociology'; Ch. IV. 'The Sociology of Pareto'; Ch. II. 'The Contribution of L. T. Hobhouse to Philosophy and Sociology'), Longmans Green.

GINSBERG, M. (1921), *The Psychology of Society*, Methuen.

GINSBERG, M. (1962), *On the Diversity of Morals*, Heinemann: Mercury Books.

GISSING, G. (1903), *The Private Papers of Henry Ryecroft*, Constable.

GREEN, T. H. (1883), *Prolegomena to Ethics*, Oxford University Press.

HINKLE, R. C., and HINKLE, G. J. (1954), *The Development of Modern Sociology*, Random House.

HOBBES, THOMAS, *Leviathan*, Everyman's Edition.

HOBHOUSE, L. T. (1921), *The Rational Good*, London.

HOBHOUSE, L. T. (1922), *The Elements of Social Justice*, Allen & Unwin.

HOBHOUSE, L. T. (1893), *The Labour Movement*, Fisher Unwin.

HOBHOUSE, L. T. (1915), *The Material Culture and Social Institutions of the Simpler Peoples* (with G. C. Wheeler and M. Ginsberg), London.

HOBHOUSE, L. T. *Liberalism*, Williams and Norgate.

HOBHOUSE, L. T. (1913), *Development and Purpose*, Macmillan.

HOBHOUSE, L. T. (1896), *The Theory of Knowledge*, Methuen.

HOBHOUSE, L. T. (1951), *Morals in Evolution*, Chapman and Hall.

HOBHOUSE, L. T. (1915), *Mind in Evolution*, Macmillan.

HOBHOUSE, L. T. (1924), *Social Development*, Allen & Unwin.

HOBHOUSE, L. T. (1915), *The World in Conflict*, Fisher Unwin.

HOBHOUSE, L. T. (1966), *Sociology and Philosophy: A Centenary Collection of Essays* (Introduction by M. Ginsberg), L. S. E. and G. Bell & Sons.

HUGHES, H. S. (1959), *Consciousness and Society. The Re-orientation of European Social Thought*, London.

KARDINER, A., and PREBLE, E. (1961), *They Studied Man* (Includes essays on Durkheim, Freud, Malinowski—as well as on Spencer, Tylor, Frazer, etc.), Secker and Warburg.

MAINE, SIR HENRY (1913), *Ancient Law*, Routledge.

MAIRET, P. (1957), *Pioneer of Sociology: the Life and Letters of Patrick Geddes*, Lund Humphries.

MALINOWSKI, B. (1944), *A Scientific Theory of Culture*, University of North Carolina Press.

MARRETT, R. R. (1936), *Custom is King* (Essays presented to Marrett, Ed. L. H. Dudley Buxton. Contains interesting papers by Seligman, Fortes, Firth, Evans-Pritchard, and others), Hutchinson.

MEAD, G. H. (1965), *George Herbert Mead on Social Psychology* (Ed. A. Strauss), University of Chicago Press.

MEAD, G. H. (1934), *Mind, Self and Society* (Ed. C. W. Morris), University of Chicago Press.

MEISEL, J. H. (Ed.) (1965), *Pareto and Mosca* (Contains several good essays on Pareto), Prentice-Hall.

MILL, J. S. (1884), *A System of Logic* (Book VI), People's Edition, Longmans Green.

MOORE, M. H. (Ed.) (1936), *Movements of Thought in the Nineteenth Century*, University of Chicago Press.

MORRIS, C. W. (Ed.) (1938), *The Philosophy of the Act*, University of Chicago Press.

MORRIS, C. W. (Ed.), *Mind, Self and Society* (See Mead above).

MUMFORD, LEWIS (1958), *Patrick Geddes, Victor Branford, and Applied Sociology in Britain: The Social Survey, Regionalism, and Urban Planning.* (Ch. XXXV, 'An Introduction to the History of Sociology'. Ed. H. E. Barnes), University of Chicago Press.

MURPHY, A. E. (1932), *The Philosophy of the Present*, Open Court Publishing Co.

MCDOUGALL, W. (1948), *An Introduction to Social Psychology*, Methuen (1908) 29th Edn.

PARETO, VILFREDO (1966), *Vilfredo Pareto: Sociological Writings* (Selected and introduced by S. E. Finer), Pall Mall Press.

PARETO, VILFREDO (1935), *The Mind and Society* (English translation of the *Treatise of General Sociology*, by A. Livingston and A. Bongiorno. 4 Vols.), New York and London.

PARSONS, TALCOTT (1968), *The Structure of Social Action* (2 vols.), Free Press (paperback).

RADCLIFFE-BROWN, A. R. (1964), *A Natural Science of Society*, Free Press.

RADCLIFFE-BROWN, A. R. (1952), *Structure and Function in Primitive Society*, Cohen & West.

RAISON, T. (Ed.) (1969), *The Founding Fathers of Social Science*, Penguin Books.

ROWNTREE, S. (1901), *Poverty, A Study of Town Life.*

SHAND, A. F. (1914), *Foundations of Character*, London.

SILVERMAN, H. A. (1928), *The Economics of Social Problems*, University Tutorial Press.

SIMMEL, G. (1950), *The Sociology of Georg Simmel* (Tr. and introduction by K. H. Wolff), Free Press (paperback).

SIMMEL, G. (1955), *Conflict and the Web of Group-Affiliations* (Tr. K. H. Wolff and R. Bendix), Free Press (paperback).

SOROKIN, P. (1928), *Contemporary Sociological Theories*, Harper.

SUMNER, W. G., *Folkways* (Paperbacks), Dover Edn., 1959, Mentor Books, 1960

TIMASHEFF, N. S. (1955), *Sociological Theory: Its Nature and Growth*, Doubleday.

TÖNNIES, F. (1955), *Community and Association* (Tr. C. P. Loomis), Routledge & Kegan Paul.

TÖNNIES, F. (1961), *Custom* (An Essay on Social Codes: Tr. A. F. Borenstein), Free Press.

TÖNNIES, F. (1904), 'Note on the British Sociological Society' (*Sociological Papers*, Vol. I), Macmillan.

TROTTER, W. (1921), *Instincts of the Herd in Peace and War*, Fisher Unwin (Enlarged Edition).

WALLAS, GRAHAM (1917), *The Great Society*, Macmillan.

WARD, LESTER (1907), *Pure Sociology*, Macmillan, N.Y. (2nd Edn.).

WEBB, MRS. SIDNEY (1906), 'Methods of Investigation' (*Sociological Papers*, Vol. III), Macmillan.

WEBER, MAX (1930), *The Protestant Ethic and the Spirit of Capitalism*, Allen & Unwin.

WEBER, MAX (1966), *The Sociology of Religion* (Tr. E. Fischoff. Introduced by Talcott Parsons), Social Science Paperbacks.

WEBER, MAX (1949), *The Methodology of the Social Sciences* (Introduced by E. Shils), Free Press.

WEBER, MAX (1947), *Theory of Social and Economic Organization* (Introduced by Talcott Parsons), Free Press.

WEBER, MAX (1961), *General Economic History*, Collier Books (paperback).

WEBER, MAX (1948), *From Max Weber: Essays in Sociology* (Ed. H. H. Gerth & C. Wright Mills), Routledge and Kegan Paul.

WELLS, H. G. (1906), 'The So-Called Science of Society' (*Sociological Papers*, Vol. III), Macmillan.

WENLEY, R. M. (1906), 'Sociology as an Academic Subject' (*Sociological Papers*), Macmillan.

WESTERMARCK, E. A. (1904), 'On the Position of Women in Early Civilization' (*Sociological Papers*, Vol. I), Macmillan.

WESTERMARCK, A. E. (1936), *The History of Human Marriage*, Macmillan.

WESTERMARCK, E. A. (1912), *The Origin and Development of the Moral Ideas* (2 vols.), Macmillan.

WESTERMARCK, E. A. (1936), *The Future of Marriage in Western Civilization*, Macmillan.

WESTERMARCK, E. A. (1933), *Pagan Survivals in Mohammedan Civilization*, Macmillan.

WESTERMARCK, E. A. (1932), *Early Beliefs and their Social Influences*, Macmillan.

WESTERMARCK, E. A. (1926), *The Goodness of the Gods*, Watts.

WHITEHEAD, A. N. (1928), *Symbolism: Its Meaning and Effect*, Cambridge University Press.

WRIGHT MILLS, C. (1958), *Edward Alexander Westermarck and the Application of Ethnographic Methods to Marriage and Morals* (Ch. XXXIII, 'An Introduction to the History of Sociology'. Ed. H. E. Barnes), University of Chicago Press.

WRIGHT MILLS, C. (1959), *The Sociological Imagination*, Oxford University Press, New York.

Subject Index

Author (and Name) Index